CROSSWORD

PROPER NAME

FINDER

CROSSWORD
PROPER NAME FINDER

John C. Plankinton

First Edition

CREATIVE ARTS BOOK COMPANY

BERKELEY, CALIFORNIA

2000

For information contact:
Creative Arts Book Company
833 Bancroft Way
Berkeley, California 94710
(800) 848-7789

ISBN 088739-318-7
Library of Congress Catalog Number 99-[Pending]

Printed in the United States of America

PREFACE

Compiling this book began as a hobby, but soon became an obsession. The writer has for years worked one or two crossword puzzles daily. We were vexed at the number of proper names used by the puzzle creators, and started a hand written list of names to hopefully help with future puzzles. The list soon became unwieldy in its handwritten form with no alphabetical order. At that point we turned to the computer and printed our list, now in alphabetical order--a simple task for the computer.

Somewhere along the line the idea evolved to try to list enough selected names to anticipate future puzzles. Finally this book evolved. It has several sections. Section I, The Main Dictionary, is an alphabetical listing of Proper Names including Movie and TV Actors, Writers, Musicians, Dancers, Artists, Statesmen, Sports Figures, Nobel, Pulitzer, some Grammy Award Winners, and many others. This main list has 51,000+ entries; many are double entered, so there are not that many individuals.

Section II --in two parts-- with Part A. alphabetically listing Individuals in its first column, then a Vehicle Column (Film, Title, Pen Name, Play, Etc.); and finally a Product Column(Movie Name, TV Show Name, Book Title, Etc.) with which the Named Individual is associated. Part B. is a reverse listing of the information in the Part A., now alphabetically listing the Products and then the Persons involved in its second column. The Vehicle column appears only in Part A.

There are currently 6,400 entries in Part A. Considering that more than 45,000 movies have been made and God knows how many books written, it would require a library to hold a complete listing.

Section III, The AWARD Section, chronologically lists all Nobel Prize winners, many Pulitzer Prize winners, Principal Oscar winners, winners of Annual Awards in Major Sports, some Grammy Award and Olympic Gold Medal winners.

All the individuals named in the AWARD Section are also in the Main Dictionary with a Designation Code key to their awards.

The final Section IV, we term your BONUS Section. It deals in depth with Rivers, including Geographical Locations, Tributaries, and Bodies of Water into which many of the listed Rivers flow.

Each section has "Operating Instructions" preceding it.

To conclude this preface, we must acknowledge the accurate Proof Reading performed endlessly by the author's wife, Mary. Without her excellent efforts, this book would be a collection of typos, because the author can read right over an obvious mistake apparently without seeing it.

Have fun and find those Proper Names.

John C. Plankintoin

TABLE OF CONTENTS

CROSSWORD PROPER
NAME FINDER

SECTION I
MAIN DICTIONARY

Before using the Main Dictionary, become
acquainted with the Operating Instructions
and the accompanying Name Designation
Codes, which immediately follow this page.

OPERATING INSTRUCTIONS FOR
THE MAIN DICTIONARY

The Main Dictionary contains names of persons(and some fictional characters) which are likely to be requested by clues in cross word puzzles. Many names are double entered to accommodate puzzle clues citing a first name, and requesting the surname. Here are both halves of a double entry:

   Alda,   ALAN d,tv+ Last Name first, followed by a comma - then FIRST NAME in CAPS

   Alan   ALDA d,tv+ First Name first with no comma - then SURNAME in CAPS.

The "d, tv+" following Alan Alda's name is a designation code, in this case meaning he is a director(the d), tv actor(the tv) and movie actor(the +). All codes are explained in the NAME DESIGNATION CODE immediately following these instructions.

Movie actors represent the most numerous designation in this book. If a person is purely a movie actor, he or she will have NO CODE LETTER after the name. Further the "+" code after another code means that person is also a movie actor. Actors who have won OSCAR Awards, have these awards listed following their Surname, FIRST NAME listing as, for example:

      Pickford, MARY o-a'29

Television Actors are numerous with the "tv" code following the name. Many tv actors are also movie actors, as Alan Alda above, and will carry the "tv+" code.

Writers - "w", and related poets - "po", historians - "h" , biographers - "bio", journalists - "j" and critics - "ct" are the next most numerous entries. Writers' names were selected from puzzle clues, plus authors of the world's great literature, and writers who have made the national or regional weekly best sellers list for the past few years. There are 3,500+ writers in this dictionary. A new national chain super bookstore, recently opened in our area, advertises 82,000 writers in stock; so by comparison, our collection seems paltry.

Instructions for the Main Dictionary(cont.)

There are also many musicians "m" , singers "s", composers "c". and conductors "cn". In many cases a specific instrument or singing voice, or singing category is identified. Many of the musicians are further classified as to their type of music as "mj" for jazz musicians.

All award winners are in the main dictionary as well as in Section III, the chronological award section. In the main dictionary, their awards are listed by code following the Surname, FIRST NAME listing as shown for Mary Pickford earlier.

This may seem overwhelming with so many codes to consider. Relax and memorize the following popular codes and look up others if necessary.

> No code, an Oscar Code, or code followed by a
> "+" sign   means Movie Actor
> tv means Television
> w means Writer
> po means Poet
> s   means Singer

To help, at the start of each new letter in the Main Dictionary, the Designation Codes beginning with that letter are presented.

Nationality codes are indicated for many of the categories but NOT for movie or tv actors, or team sports figures.

MAIN DICTIONARY DESIGNATION CODES

no code	MOVIE ACTOR		furn	FURNITURE
+	ALSO MOVIE ACTOR		g	GOLFER
ac	ARCHITECT		geog	GEOGRAPHER
an	ANTHROPOLOGIST		geol	GEOLOGIST
ar	ARMY		gg	BASEBALL GLD GLVE AWRD
arc	ARCHEOLOGIST		gos	GOSPEL
as	ASTRONAUT		guit	GUITAR
astr	ASTRONOMER		gy	GYMNAST
at	ARTIST(not p or su)		h	HISTORIAN
b	BASEBALL		hf	HALL OF FAME MEMBER
ba	BALLET or DANCE		ho	HOCKEY
bari	BARITONE		hr	BABEBALL HOMERUN LEAD
bat	BASEBALL BATTING CHAMP		i	INVENTOR
bb	BASKETBALL		id	INDUSTRIALIST
bbc	BASKETBALL COACH,OWNER		illus	ILLUSTRATOR
bmg	BASEBALL MANAGER,OWNER		j	JOURNALIST
bbr	BASKETBALL REFEREE		kbds	KEYBOARDS
bu	BASEBALL UMPIRE		l	LAWYER OR JURIST
bio	BIOGRAPHER		la	LEGITIMATE ACTOR
bus	BUSINEESSMAN		m	MUSICIAN
c	COMPOSER		math	MATHEMATICIAN
cm	COMIC		md	MEDICINE FIGURE
cn	CONDUCTOR		me	MEDIA FIGURE
cnt	COUNTRY		mer	MERCHANT
cr	CARTOONIST		mj	MUSICIAN - JAZZ
ct	CRITIC		mo	MODEL
d	DIRECTOR		mr	MUSICIAN - ROCK
decor	DECORATOR		m-rap	MUSICIAN - RAP
drm	DRUMS		nav	NAVY
ds	DESIGNER		p	PAINTER
e	EDUCATOR		pb	PUBLISHER
ec	ECONOMIST		ph	PHILOSOPHER
ed	EDITOR		po	POET
eng	ENGINEER		pr	PRODUCER
engr	ENGRAVER		ps	PSYCHIATRIST, PSYCHOANALYST
etch	ETCHER			
f	FINANCIER, PHILANTHROPIST		pupp	PUPPETS
			r	RELIGIONIST
fb	FOOTBALL		rbi	BASEBALL RUNS-BATTD-IN
fbc	FOOTBALL COACH, OWNER		re	REVOLUTIONARY
fc	FICTIONAL CHARACTER		ref	REFORMER
fe	FEMINIST		r&b	RYTHYM & BLUES MUSIC
fly	FLYER		ru	RUNNER
fo	PHOTOGRAPHER		s	SINGER

		supr		
sc	SCIENTIST	ct	SUPREME COURT
sk	SKATER	sw	SWIMMER
ski	SKIER	t	TENNIS PLAYER
soc	SOCIOLOGIST	tv	TELEVISION ACTOR
sopr	SOPRANO	viol	VIOLIN
sp	SPORTS FIGURE	w	WRITER
st	STATESMAN,GOVT.FIGURE	ws	SONG WRITER
su	SCULPTOR	x	EXPLORER

NATIONALITY CODES

Am	AMERICAN	Lith	LITHUANIAN
Arg	ARGENTINIAN	Mex	MEXICAN
Aus	AUSTRIAN	N.Zea	NEW ZEALANDER
Austr	AUSTRALIAN	Nica	NICARAGUAN
Belg	BELGIAN	Nor	NORWEGIAN
Bol	BOLIVIAN	P.Rico	PUERTO RICAN
Br	BRITISH	Parag	PARAGUAYAN
Braz	BRAZILIAN	Phil	PHILLIPPINO
Bulg	BULGARIAN	Pol	POLISH
Can	CANADIAN	Port	PORTUGESE
Colom	COLOMBIAN	Ro	ROMAN
CostaR	COSTA RICAN	Rom	ROMANIAN
Croat	CROATIAN	Rus	RUSSIAN
Czech	CZECHOSLOVAKIAN	S.Afr	SOUTH AFRICAN
Dan	DANISH	S.Leon	SIERRA LEONEAN
Dut	DUTCH	Salv	SALVADOREAN
Ecu	ECUADOREAN	Scot	SCOTTISH
Finn	FINNISH	Sp	SPANISH
Fr	FRENCH	Swe	SWEDISH
Ger	GERMAN	Swi	SWISS
Gr	GREEK	Transyl	TRANSYLVANIAN
Hung	HUNGARIAN	Turk	TURKISH
Ir	IRISH	Urug	URUGUAYAN
Isr	ISRAELI	Venz	VENEZUELIAN
It	ITALIAN	W.Ind	WEST INDIAN
Jap	JAPANESE	Yugo	YUGOSLAVIAN
Lat	LATVIAN		

DESIGNATION CODES FOR AWARDS

NOBEL PRIZES

n-c	Nobel Prize Chemistry	n-m	Nobel Prize Medicine,
n-e	Nobel Prize Economics		Bio-chem, Physiology
n-l	Nobel Prize Literature	n-p	Nobel Prize Physics
		n-x	Nobel Prize Peace

PULITZER PRIZES

p-b	Pulitzer Prize Biography	p-m	Pulitzer Prize Music
p-c	Pulitzer Prize Criticism	p-n	Pulitzer Prize NonFiction
p-d	Pulitzer Prize Drama	p-p	Pulitzer Prize Photography
p-e	Pulitzer Prize Editorial	p-q	Pulitzer Prize Poetry
p-f	Pulitzer Prize Fiction	p-r	Pulitzer Prize Reporting
p-h	Pulitzer Prize History	p-x	Pulitzer Prize Cartooning

OSCAR AWARDS

o-a	Oscar-Best Actor(Actress)
o-d	Oscar-Best Director
o-s	Oscar-Best Supporting Actor(Actress)
o-p	Oscar-Best Picture

GRAMMY AWARD

g-r	Grammy Award

POET LAUREATE--GR. BRITAIN

pol	Poet Laureate

SPORTS AWARDS

o-g	Olympic Gold Medal
hf	Sports Hall of Fame

HOCKEY AWARDS

ho-m	HO Most Valuable Player

BASEBALL AWARDS

b-mv	B Most Valuable Player
b-cy	B Cy Young Award-Pitching

BASKETBALL AWARDS

bb-m	BB Most Valuable Player

FOOTBALL AWARDS

fb-d	FB Most Valuable Player--Defense
fb-m	FB Most Valuable Player--Offense

Remember:

All pol's are British. All Pulitzer Winners are American. No Nationalities are indicated for Oscar Winners, or for Winners of Awards in Professional Sports.

CROSSWORD

PROPER NAME

FINDER

"A" NAME DESIGNATION CODES

```
no code MOVIE ACTOR
+       (after another code)=
        MOVIE ACTOR
ac      ARCHITECT
an      ANTHROPOLOGIST
ar      ARMY
arc     ARCHEOLOGIST
as      ASTRONAUT
at      ARTIST-not p, scu
```

"A" NATIONALITY CODES

```
Am -AMERICAN  Aus- AUSTRIAN
    Arg - ARGENTINEAN
    Aust - AUSTRALIAN
```

TEN MOST NUMEROUS PROFESSIONS AND THEIR DESIGNATION CODES

```
MOVIE ACTORS-- no code,
  a "+" sign following
  another code, or Oscar
  eg: o-a'YR, o-s'YR
TELEVISION ACTORS -- tv
WRITERS       --     w
POETS         --     po
SINGERS       --     s
ROCK MUSICIANS --    mr
STATESMEN     --     st
EDUCATORS     --     e
JAZZ MUSICIANS --    mj
PAINTERS      --     p
```

"A"

```
A.A.      MILNE w,po Br
A.B.      GUTHRIE Jr w Am
A.C.      BENSON w Br
A.C.      BRADLEY e,ct Br
A.D.      HOPE po Aust
A.E.      HOUSMAN po,e Br
A.E.W.    MASON w Br
A.J.      AYER(Sir) ph
A.J.      CRONIN w,md Br
A.J.      FOYT racecars Am
A.J.      LANGER tv
A.J.M.    SMITH po,ct Can
A.J.P.    TAYLOR h,e Br
A.L.      ROWSE ct,po Br
A.M.      KLEIN po Can
A.P.      CARTER m,s Am
A.R.      AMMONS po Am
A.S.      BYATT w Br
A(lfred). ALVAREZ ct,po Br
A. Thomas SMITH
Aage      BOHR sc Dan
Aagesen,  SVEND h Dan
Aagje     DEKEN po,w Dut
Aaida,    MARIANN tv
Aaker,    LEE tv+
```

```
Aakjaer,  JEPPE w,po Dan
Aalto,    ALVAR ac Finn
Aames,    ANGELA tv+
Aames,    WILLIE tv+
Aanrud,   HANS w Nor
Aariana   KNOWLES tv
Aaron     BURR st Am
Aaron     COPLAND c Am
Aaron     ECKHART
Aaron     ELKINS w Am
Aaron     FRENCH i Am
Aaron     KERNIS c Am
Aaron     KLUG sc S.Afr
Aaron     METCHIK tv
Aaron     NEVILLE s-pop Am
Aaron     NORRIS d
Aaron     OGDEN l,st Am
Aaron     TEICH
Aaron Montgomery WARD mer Am
Aaron,    BETSY tv
Aaron,    HANK b-mv'57,hf
Aaron,    PAUL d
Aart van der NEER p Dut
Aasen,    IVAR w, Nor
Aasmund   VINJE po,j,ref Nor
Abagail   ADAMS w Am
Abauzit,  FIRMIN r,ph Fr
Abba      EBAN st Isr
Abbas al- AQQAD j,po Egypt
Abbate,   NICCOLO dell' p It
Abbe      LANE s,tv+ Am
Abbe      PREVOST w Fr
Abbe,     CLEVELAND weath Am
Abbe,     ERNST sc,id Ger
Abbey     LINCOLN mj-s+ Am
Abbey,    EDWIN p,illus Am
Abbie     HOFFMAN w,re Am
Abbot,    CHARLES astr,w Am
Abbot,    EZRA r Am
Abbot,    FRANCIS r,ph Am
Abbot,    HENRY eng,ar Am
Abbott,   BERENICE fo Am
Abbott,   BRUCE
Abbott,   BUD cm+ Am
Abbott,   CHARLES l Br
Abbott,   DIAHNNE
Abbott,   GEORGE d,p-d'60
Abbott,   GRACE fe,w,e Am
Abbott,   JOHN
Abbott,   JOHN(Sir) st,e Can
Abbott,   LYMAN w,r,ed Am
Abbott,   PHILLIP tv+
Abby      DALTON tv+
Abd       MENOU ar Fr
Abdul     FAKIR mr-s Am
Abdul     KASSEM ar,st Iraq
Abdul Razak, TUN st Malay
Abdul,    PAULA mr,ba,s Am
Abdul-Jabbar K.bb-m'71'2'6 &
Abdul-Jabbar KAREEM bb-m'77 &
Abdul-Jabbar KAREEM bb-m'80
```

Abdus	SALAM sc Pakistan		Abse,	DANNIE po,w Welsh
Abe	BEAME st Am		Abt,	FRANZ c Ger
Abe	BURROWS w Am		Abu	MANSUR st Muslim
Abe	FORTAS l Am		Abu	RAZI md,ph Persia
Abe	VIGODA tv+		Abu Madi,	ILIYA po,j Arab
Abegg,	RICHARD sc Ger		Abu al-	KAFUR st Egypt
Abel	BONNARD W Fr		Abulafia,	MEIR e, w Sp
Abel	BUELL id,i Am		Aby	WARBURG h-art Ger
Abel	FERRERA d		Abzug,	BELLA fe Am
Abel	GANCE d Fr		Acala Zamora,NICETO st Sp
Abel	SALAZAR		Acavone,	JAY tv
Abel	TASMAN x Dut		Ace	FREHLEY mr-guit,s Am
Abel,	ELIE j,st Am		Ace	GRUENIG bb hf
Abel,	FREDERICK(Sir)sc		Ace	KEFFORD mr-bass Br
Abel,	JOHN sc,e Am		Ace	PARKER fb hf
Abel,	KARL c Ger		Ace,	GOODMAN j-humor Am
Abel,	NIELS math Nor		Achard,	FRANZ sc Ger
Abel,	RUDOLF spy Rus		Achebe,	CHINUA w Nigeria
Abel,	SID ho-m'49		Acheson,	DEAN st,p-h'70
Abel,	WALTER tv+		Achille	FOULD st Fr
Abell,	ARUNAH j,pb,ed Am		Achim von ARNIM po,w Ger
Abell,	KJELD w,ct Dan		Acker,	SHARON tv+
Abell,	WESTCOTT(Sir)ac		Ackerman,	CHANTAL d
Aber,	JOHN w Am		Ackerman,	DIANE w Am
Abercrombie, IAN			Ackerman,	LESLIE
Abetz,	HEINRICH st Ger		Ackerman,KONRAD la Ger
Abigail	VAN BUREN j Am &		Ackermann,LOUISE po Fr
Abigail	VAN BUREN(Ask Abby)		Ackland,	JOSS
Abington, FANNY la Br			Ackroyd,	DAVID tv+
Abioseh	NICOL w S.Leone		Acosta Garcia,JULIO st CostaR
Abney,	WM.deWIVELESLIE e		Acosta,	JOAQUIN ar,h Colom
Abott,	FRANCIS r,ph Am		Acosta,	JOSE de r Sp
Abou	BEN ADHEM fc		Acton,	JOHN h Br
About,	EDMOND.j,w Fr		Acton,	JOHN(Sir)navy
Abraham	BENRUBI tv		Acuff,	ROY s-cntry,tv Am
Abraham	BOSSE p,ac Fr		Acuna,	CRISTOBAL de r Sp
Abraham	CAHAN j,w Am		Acuna,	HERNANDO de po,ar,st Sp
Abraham	COWLEY po Br		Acuna,	WANDA tv
Abraham	DARBY id-iron Br		Ad	REINHARDT p Am
Abraham	ELZEVIR pb Dut		Ad-Rock,	KING m-rap Am
Abraham	KOOK r-rabbi Palest		Ada	INCE
Abraham	KUYPER e,st Dut		Ada	MARIS tv
Abraham	MAPU w Lith		Ada	NEGRI po,w It
Abraham	MIGNON p Dut		Ada	REHAN la+ Am
Abraham	RYDBERG w Swe		Ada Ellen BAYLY w Br
Abraham	SOFAER		Adah	MENKEN la Am
Abraham	STOKER(Bram)w Ir		Adair,	DEBORAH tv+
Abraham,	F. MURRAY o-a'84		Adair,	JOHN maps Scot
Abraham,	KARL ps Ger		Adair,	RED oil fires Am
Abraham,	KEN		Adalbert	FALK st Ger
Abrahams, ISRAEL w Br			Adalbert	STIFTER w Aus
Abrahams, JIM d			Adam	ANT mr,s+ Br
Abrahams, MICK mr-guit Br			Adam	ARKIN tv+
Abram	CHASINS piano		Adam	ASNYK po,w Pol
Abram	HEWITT id,st		Adam	BALDWIN
Abramovitz, RAFAEL tv			Adam	CARL tv
Abrams,	CREIGHTON ar Am		Adam	CLAYTON mr-bass Ir
Abrell,	SARAH tv		Adam	GORDON po Aust
Abreu,	JOAO h,e Braz		Adam	KENNEDY tv
Abril,	VICTORIA		Adam	La VORGNA tv
Absalon	BEYER e,w Nor			

Adam	MOLTKE st Dan	Adamson,	AL d
Adam	OESER p Ger	Adamson,	JOY sc,w Br
Adam	RICH tv	Adamson,	STUART mr-guit,s Br
Adam	ROARKE	Addams,	CHARLES, cr Am
Adam	SANDLER cm,tv Am	Addams,	DAWN
Adam	SILBAR tv	Addams,	JANE fe,w,n-x'31
Adam	SMITH ec,e Scot	Adderly,	HERB fb hf
Adam	STORKE	Adderly,	JULIAN mj Am &
Adam	TRESE	Adderly,	JUL.= CANNONBALL
Adam	WADE tv	Addie	JOSS b hf
Adam	WELCH r,w Scot	Addison	MIZNER ac Am
Adam	WEST tv+	Addison	VERRILL sc,e Am
Adam Clayton POWELL r,st Am		Addison,	BERNARD mj-guit Am
Adam van der MEULEN p Belg		Addison,	JOSEPH po,ct Br
Adam,	ADOLPHE c Fr	Addy,	WESLEY tv+
Adam,	JULIETTE w Fr	Ade,	GEORGE w-humor Am
Adam,	PAUL w Fr	Adela	ST. JOHNS j Am
Adam,	ROBERT ac Scot	Adelaide	HALL mj-s Am
Adamic,	LOUIS w Am	Adelaide	RISTORI la It
Adams,	ABIGAIL w Am	Adele	ASTAIRE ba Am
Adams,	ALICE w Am	Adele	JERGENS tv+
Adams,	ALVIN bus Am	Adele	MARA tv+
Adams,	ANDY cowboy,w Am	Adele	SIMPSON ds Am
Adams,	ANSEL fo Am	Adelina	PATTI sopr Am
Adams,	BEVERLY	Adeline	GENEE(Dame)ba Dan
Adams,	BROOKE	Adelung,	JOHANN w,e Ger
Adams,	BROOKS h Am	Aden	YOUNG
Adams,	BRYAN mr,s,ws	Adenauer,	KONRAD st Ger &
Adams,	CASEY	Adenauer,	KONRAD=Der Alte
Adams,	CECIL w	Ader,	CLEMENT eng,i Fr
Adams,	CHARLES po Am	Adhemar da SILVA o-g'52'56	
Adams,	CHARLES rrs,h Am	Adjani,	ISABELLE
Adams,	CHARLES.Jr h Am	Adlai Ewing STEVENSON st,w Am	
Adams,	CINDY j,tv	Adler,	ALFRED ps Aus
Adams,	DON tv+	Adler,	CYRUS e Am
Adams,	DOUGLAS w Br	Adler,	DANKMAR ac Am
Adams,	EDIE s,tv+ Am	Adler,	FELIX e Am
Adams,	ERNIE	Adler,	JAY
Adams,	FRANK geol Can	Adler,	LUTHER tv+
Adams,	FRANKLIN PIERCE j	Adler,	MATT
Adams,	HANNAH h Am	Adler,	MORTIMER e,ph Am
Adams,	HENRY h,bio,e Am	Adler,	NATHAN r Br
Adams,	HERBERT h Am	Adler,	RICHARD c Am
Adams,	HERBERT su Am	Adler,	STELLA la,e Am,
Adams,	JAMES TRU. p-h'22	Adler,	VICTOR st Aus
Adams,	JANE	Adlersparre, GEORG ed,w Swe	
Adams,	JOHN 2nd Prs. w	Adlon,	PERCY d
Adams,	JOHN Q.6th Prs.w	Adlum,	JOHN sc Am
Adams,	JOHN astr,e Br	Adna	CHAFFEE ar Am
Adams,	JOSEPH e Am	Adolf	BERLE l,st Am
Adams,	JULIE(Julia) tv+	Adolf	ENGLER sc,e Ger
Adams,	MASON tv+	Adolf	FICK sc,e Ger
Adams,	MAUDE la,tv+ Am	Adolf	FREY po,h,e Swi
Adams,	NICK tv+	Adolf	HITLER st Nazi Ger
Adams,	OLETA s-soul,w	Adolf	KLAUBER pr-stage Am
Adams,	ROGER sc,e Am	Adolf	MEYER ps,e Am
Adams,	SAMUEL w,j Am	Adolf	WINDAUS sc,e Ger
Adams,	SARAH po,hymns Br	Adolf von BAEYER sc,e Ger	
Adams,	TED	Adolf von KNIGGE w Ger	
Adams,	WALTER astr Am	Adolfo	CELI
Adams,	WILLIAM w,ed Am	Adolfo	DIAZ st Nica

Adolfo	HUERTA st Mex	Afer,	DOMITIUS st Ro
Adolfo	VENTURI h-art It	Affonso	REIDY ac Braz
Adolph	CAESAR	Affre,	DENIS r Fr
Adolph	GREEN	Afonso	PENA st Braz
Adolph	KNOPF geol,e Am	Afrika	BAMBAATAA m-rap
Adolph	LOOS ac Aus	Agar,	HERBERT j,w Am
Adolph	MENZEL p,illus Ger	Agar,	JOHN
Adolph	OCHS pb Am	Agassi,	ANDRE t Am
Adolph	RUPP bbc hf	Agassiz,	ALEXANDER sc Am
Adolph	SCHAYES bb hf	Agassiz,	JEAN e,w Am
Adolph	SUTRO eng-mines Am	Agate,	JAMES ct Br
Adolph	ZUKOR pr-films Am	Agatha	CHRISTIE(Dame)w Br
Adolphe	ADAM c Fr	Agathon	FAIN h Fr
Adolphe	APPIA ds Swi	Agbayani,	TETCHIE
Adolphe	MARTENS w Belg	Agee,	JAMES p-f'58
Adolphe	MAX st Belg	Agee,	TOMMIE b,gg'70
Adolphe	MENJOU tv+	Ager,	MILTON ws Am
Adolphe	MOURON at,ds Fr	Agnes	ARBER sc,w Br
Adolphe	PEGOUD fly Fr	Agnes	BOOTH la Am
Adolphe	YVON p Fr	Agnes	De MILLE ba Am
Adolphe,	ADAM c Fr	Agnes	SORAL
Adolphson,	EDVIN	Agnes	VARDA d
Adolphus	BUSCH id-beer,f Am	Agnesi,	MARIA math,e It
Adolphus	GREELY ar,x Am	Agnew,	CHARLIE mj,cn, Am
Ador,	GUSTAVE st Swi	Agnew,	DAVID md,e Am
Adoree,	RENEE	Agnew,	PETE mr-bass,s
Adorf,	MARIO	Agnew,	SPIRO st Am
Adorno,	THEODOR ph,ct Ger	Agnieszka	HOLLAND d
Adret,	SOLOMON r Sp	Agnon,	SAMUEL n-l'66 Isr
Adriaan	VLACQ math Dut	Agostino	NIFO ph,e It
Adriadne	WELTER	Agoult,	MARIE w Fr
Adriaen van OSTADE p Dut		Agren,	JANET
Adriaen van der WERFF p Dut		Agrippa,	MARCUS ar,st Ro
Adrian	BOULT(Sir)cn	Agronsky,	MARTIN tv
Adrian	DUNBAR	Aguado,	ALEJANDRO f Sp
Adrian	HOVEN	Aguilar,	ANTONIO
Adrian	LYNE d	Aguilar,	GRACE w Br
Adrian	PASDAR	Aguilar,	LUIS
Adrian	PAUL tv+	Aguinaldo,	EMILIO st, Phil
Adrian	ROLLINI mj-sax Am	Aguirre,	LOPE de x Sp
Adrian	SMITH mr-guit Br	Agustin	DURAN ct,po Sp
Adrian	ZMED tv+	Agustin	EDWARDS f,st Chile
Adrian,	EDGAR n-m'32 Br	Agustin	YANEZ w Mex
Adrian,	IRIS	Agustus	THOMAS w Am
Adriano	BALBI geog It	Agustus	PUGIN ac Fr
Adrien	DUPORT st Fr	Agutter,	JENNY
Adrienne	BARBEAU tv+	Ahamad al-JAZZAR st Turk	
Adrienne	CORRI	Aharon	IPALE
Adrienne	La RUSSA tv	Aherne,	BRIAN
Adrienne	RICH po Am	Ahlmann,	HANS sc,e Swe
Adrienne	SHELLY	Ahmad	RAISULI brigand
Ady	ROSNER mj,cn Pol	Ahmad	RASHAD fb,tv Am
Ady,	ENDRE po Hung	Ahmad	SHAWQI w Egypt
Aelius	DONATUS e,w Ro	Ahmed	NEDIM po Turk
Aernout	DROST w Dut	Ahn,	PHILIP
Aert	GELDER p Dut	Aicard,	JEAN po,w Fr
Aeryk	EGAN	Aichinger,	ILSE w Ger
Aesop	--- w(fables)Gr	Aida	TURTURRO
Aetius,	FLAVIUS ar Ro	Aidan	QUINN
Afanasy	FET po Rus	Aidman,	CHARLES
Afansay	NIKITIN w Rus	Aiello,	DANNY

Aiken,	CONRAD w,p-q'31	Al	FREEMAN Jr tv+
Aiken,	GEORGE la,w Am	Al	GREEN w,s-r&b Am
Aiken,	HOWARD math,i Am	Al	HERMAN d
Aikman,	TROY fb	Al	HODGE tv
Aileen	PRINGLE	Al	JARREAU mj-s Am
Ailey,	ALVIN ba Am	Al	JOLSON s+ Am
Ailly,	PIERRE d' r,e Fr	Al	KALINE b hf
Aime	ARGAND sc,i Swi	Al	KATZ mj,cn Am
Aime	CESAIRE po,w Mart.	Al	LEONG
Aime	HERVE j Fr	Al	LEWIS tv+
Aime,	VALCOUR agric Am	Al	LOPEZ b hf
Aimee	ECCLES	Al	MARKIM tv
Aimee	GRAHAM	Al	MORGAN s,piano,tv
Aimee,	ANOUK	Al	MUNDY(Big)mj,c,cn
Ainmiller,	MAX p Ger	Al	McGUIRE bbc hf
Aino	KALLAS w Finn	Al	NICHOL mr-guit,s
Ainslie,	HEW po Am	Al	OERTER discus Am
Ainsworth,	WILLIAM w Br	Al	OLIVER b
Aird,	JOHN(Sir)eng	Al	PACINO
Aird,	THOMAS po Scot	Al	PURDY po Can
Airy,	GEORGE(Sir)astr	Al	RAMSEY mr-guit Am
Aitamov,	CHINGIZ w Rus	Al	ROKER tv-host
Aitken,	JOHN sc Scot	Al	ROLLINS ho
Aitken,	ROBERT astr Am	Al	ROSEN b
Aitken,	ROBERT su Am	Al	SHEAN cm,la+ Am
Aitken,	WILLIAM st,pb Br	Al	SHEAR
Aiton,	WILLIAM sc Scot	Al	SIMMONS b hf
Ajalbert,	JEAN l,w Fr	Al	SMITH st Am
Ajay	NAIDU	Al	ST. JOHN(Fuzzy)
Ajaye,	FRANKLIN	Al	STEWART w,s Scot
Ajita	WILSON	Al	UNSER racecars Am
Akeley,	CARL su,x Am	Al	WAXMAN tv+
Akeley,	MARY sc,w Am	Al	WILSON mr-guit,s
Akenside,	MARK po,md Br	Al B.	SURE! tv
Akers,	KAREN s-cabaret	Alabama	--- mr-s Am
Akhmadulina,	BELLA po Rus	Alagna,	ROBERTO tenor Fr
Akhmatova,	ANNA po Rus	Alaimo,	MARC
Aki	ALEONG	Alain	CUNY
Akins,	CLAUDE tv+	Alain	DELON
Akins,	ZOE p-d'35	Alain	LESAGE w Fr
Akira	KUBO	Alain	LOCKE e,ct Am
Akira	TERAO	Alain	RESNAIS d
Akiro	ENDO cn	Alaina	REED-HALL tv
Akosua	BUSIA	Alaman,	LUCAS h, st Mex
Aksakov,	SERGEI po Rus	Alan	ALDA d,tv+
Akselrod,	PAVEL st Rus	Alan	ARKIN tv+
Akst,	HARRY mj-piano &	Alan	BADEL
Akst,	HARRY cn,c Am	Alan	BATES
Al	ADAMSON d	Alan	BAXTER
Al	ALBERTS s Am	Alan	BERGMAN tv
Al	BARLICK b hf	Alan	BLAKLEY mr-guit Br
Al	BOWLLY mj-s Br	Alan	BRIDGE
Al	CAPONE gangster	Alan	BURSKY tv
Al	CAPP cr Am	Alan	CADDY mr-guit Br
Al	CERVI bb hf	Alan	CLARK mr-kbds Am
Al	CLIVER	Alan	COLLINS
Al	COHN mj-sax Am	Alan	CURTIS
Al	CORLEY tv	Alan	DALE mj-s,tv Am
Al	DUBIN lyrics Am	Alan	DUGAN po Am
Al	EBEN tv	Alan	DeWITT tv
Al	FANN	Alan	FREED

Alan	GIBSON d		Alben	BARKLEY st-VP Am
Alan	GORRIE mr-bass,s		Albeniz,	ISAAC piano,c Sp
Alan	GRATZER mr-drum		Alberdi,	JUAN st,l,ph Arg
Alan	HALE Jr tv+		Alberghetti,	ANNA MARIA
Alan	HALE Sr		Alberni,	LUIS
Alan	HODGKIN(Sir)md		Albers,	HANS
Alan	HOWARD mr-bass Br		Albers,	JOSEF p Am
Alan	JONES barit sax		Albert	AUSTIN
Alan	KING cm+ Am		Albert	BALLIN id Ger
Alan	KING pr-tv Am		Albert	BAND d
Alan	KIRK navy Am		Albert	BELLE b,rbi'93'5'6
Alan	LADD		Albert	BESNARD p Fr
Alan	LERNER lyrics Am		Albert	BONI pb Am
Alan	LEVI d		Albert	BROOKS cm,ws,tv+
Alan	MARSHAL		Albert	CAMUS w Fr
Alan	MARX		Albert	CLAUDE sc Belg
Alan	MENKEN c Am		Albert	CUYP p Dut
Alan	MILNE(A.A.)w,po Br		Albert	DAUZAT e,w Fr
Alan	MOWBRAY tv+		Albert	DEKKER
Alan	NAPIER tv+		Albert	DICEY l,e Br
Alan	NORTH tv+		Albert	FALL st Am
Alan	OSMOND s,tv Am		Albert	FINK eng,i Am
Alan	PAGE fb hf		Albert	FINNEY
Alan	PAKULA d		Albert	GORE Jr st-vp Am
Alan	PARKER d		Albert	HACKETT w Am
Alan	PATON w S.Afr		Albert	HAGUE tv
Alan	PRICE mr-kbds Am		Albert	HALL
Alan	RACHINS tv+		Albert	HART h Am
Alan	REED Jr. tv+		Albert	HAUCK r,e Ger
Alan	RICKMAN		Albert	HEIM geol Swi
Alan	ROBERTS d		Albert	KING mj-guitar Am
Alan	ROTH m,cn,tv Am		Albert	LASKER ads,f Am
Alan	RUCK tv+		Albert	LEBRUN st,eng Fr
Alan	RUDOLPH d		Albert	LIEVEN
Alan	SCARFE tv+		Albert	LIZZIO cn
Alan	SCOTT tv		Albert	LUTULI ref S.Afr
Alan	SEEGER po Am		Albert	MARQUET p Fr
Alan	SEYMOUR w Aust		Albert	MOCKEL po,ct Belg
Alan	SHEPARD as Am		Albert	MUNSELL p Am
Alan	SMITHEE d		Albert	MYER ar Am
Alan	STEEL		Albert	NOCK w Am
Alan	SUES cm,tv Am		Albert	OPPEL geol,e Ger
Alan	THICKE tv+		Albert	PAINE w,ed Am
Alan	VINT		Albert	POPE id Am
Alan	WATTS ph,r,w Am		Albert	POPWELL tv
Alan	WEBB		Albert	PREJEAN
Alan	WELLMAN mj-trump,cn		Albert	PYUN d
Alan	YOUNG tv+		Albert	READ navy Am
Alannah	CURRIE sax,s N.Zea		Albert	REED tv
Alarcon,	PEDRO de w Sp		Albert	REMY
Alarik	HOLMGREN md,e Swe		Albert	ROUSSEL c Fr
Alas,	LEOPOLDO w,ct Sp		Albert	RYDER p Am
Alastair	REID d		Albert	SABIN md,e Am
Alastair	SIM		Albert	SALMI tv+
Albaleg,	ISAAC ph Sp		Albert	SAMAIN po Fr
Alban	BERG c Aus		Albert	SANDLER mj-viol,cn
Albanese,	LICIA s It		Albert	SARRAUT st Fr
Albani,	EMMA(Dame) s Can		Albert	SAUVEUR sc,e Am
Albani,	FRANCESCO p It		Albert	SHAW ed Am
Albee,	EDWARD p-d'67 &		Albert	SIKLOS cello,c
Albee,	EDWARD p-d'75'94		Albert	SPEER,ac,Nazi,st

Albert	STEFFEN w Swi		Alden,	PRISCILLA pilgrim
Albert	STEVENS fo-air Am		Alder,	KURT n-c'50
Albert	TERHUNE w,ed Am		Aldine	KING tv
Albert	VERWEY po,ct Dut		Aldington,RICHARD w,po Br
Albert de MUN st,w Fr			Aldiss,	BRIAN w Br
Albert von TILZER c Am			Aldo	LEOPOLD trees Am
Albert,	EDDIE tv+		Aldo	MORO st,e It
Albert,	EDWARD tv+		Aldo	PUGLISI
Albert,	HEINRICH c,organ Ger	Aldo	RAY m+ Am
Albert,	JOSEPH fo Ger		Aldo	SAMBREL
Albert,	STEPHEN p-m'85		Aldon,	MARI
Alberta	GRANT tv		Aldous	HUXLEY w Br
Alberta	HUNTER mj-viol Am		Aldredge,	TOM
Alberta	VAUGHN		Aldrich,	BESS w Am
Alberta	WATSON tv+		Aldrich,	GARY w Am
Alberti,	LEON w,ac,p It		Aldrich,	NELSON st Am
Alberti,	RAFAEL po,w Sp		Aldrich,	ROBERT d
Albertina RASCH ba Am			Aldrich,	THOMAS po,w,j Am
Albertini,LUIGI j,st It			Aldridge,	IRA la Am
Alberto	ASCARI racecar It		Aldrin,	EDWARD Jr as Am
Alberto	LUPO		Aldrin,	EDWARD Jr = Buzz
Alberto	MORAVIA w It		Aldrovandi, ULISSE sc,md It
Alberto	MORIN tv		Aldus	MANUTIUS print It
Alberto	SALAZAR ru Cuba		Aleandro, NORMA
Alberto	SORDI		Alec	BALDWIN
Alberts,	AL s(Four Aces)Am		Alec	FRANCIS
Albertson,FRANK			Alec	GUINESS(Sir)
Albertson,JACK o-s'68,tv+			Alec	McCOWEN
Albertson,MABEL tv			Alec	WAUGH w Br
Albin	ZOLLINGER w,po Swi		Alec	WILDER mj,cn,c Am
Albinoni, TOMASO c It			Alecsandri,VASILE po Rom
Albion	SMALL soc, e Am		Alegria,	CIRO w Peru
Albion	TOURGEE w Am		Aleichem,	SHALOM w Rus-Am
Albo,	JOSEPH ph Sp		Aleister	CROWLEY po,w Br
Albornoz, GIL ar,r Sp			Aleixandre, VICENTE po &
Albrecht	DURER p,engr Ger		Aleixandre, VICENTE n-l'77
Albrecht	KOSSEL sc,e Ger		Alejandro AGUADO f Sp
Albrecht	PENCK geog,e Ger		Alejandro PENA b
Albrecht	ROON ar,st Prussia		Alejandro REY tv+
Albrecht, BERNIE mr-guit Br			Alejo	CARPENTIER Cuba
Albright,	HARDIE		Aleksander FREDRO w Pol
Albright,	IVAN p Am		Aleksander, GRANT tv
Albright,	JACOB r Am		Aleksandr BLOK po Rus
Albright,	LOLA tv+		Aleksandr BORODIN c Rus
Albright,	WILLIAM arc		Aleksandr GRIN w Rus
Alciati,	ANDREA l It		Aleksandr HERZEN j,w Rus
Alcide	De GASPERI st It		Aleksandr KUPRIN w Rus
Alcindor, LEW bb-m'71			Aleksandr POPOV sc,eng Rus
Alcock,	JOHN r Br		Aleksandr PUSHKIN po,w Rus
Alcock,	JOHN(Sir)fly		Aleksandr SEROV c Rus
Alcott,	AMOS e,po Am		Aleksandr YASHIN po,w Rus
Alcott,	AMY g Am		Aleksandrov, TODOR re Rus
Alcott,	BRONSON e,w Am		Aleksandur TSANKOV st Bulg
Alcott,	LOUISA MAY w Am		Aleksey	KALEDIN ar Rus
Alda,	ALAN d,tv+		Aleksey	KOLTSOV po Rus
Alda,	FRANCES sopr		Aleksey	KOSYGIN st Rus
Alda,	ROBERT tv+		Aleksey	LVOV c,cn Rus
Alda,	RUTANYA		Aleksey	PESHKOV w Rus
Alden	NOWLAN po,w Can		Aleksey	REMIZOV w Rus
Alden,	JOHN pilgrim Am		Aleksey	RYKOV st Rus
Alden,	NORMAN tv+		Aleksey	SUVORIN j,pb Rus

Aleksey	TOLSTOY w Rus	Alexander	HAIG st Am
Aleksis	KIVI w,po Finn	Alexander	HALL d
Alem,	LEANDRO st Arg	Alexander	JOHNSON tv
Aleman,	JULIO	Alexander	KING tv
Aleman,	MATEO w Sp	Alexander	KIPNIS basso Am
Alembert,	JEAN math,sc,ph Fr	Alexander	KNOX
Alencar,	JOSE de w Braz	Alexander	KOHUT r-rabbi Am
Aleni,	GIULIO r It	Alexander	KORDA(Sir)pr-films
Aleong,	AKI	Alexander	LAING x Scot
Aler,	PAUL r,e Belg	Alexander	LOU
Aleshkovsky,	YUZ w Rus	Alexander	MOISSI la It
Alessandro ALLORI p It		Alexander	NASMYTH p Scot
Alessandro GUIDI po It		Alexander	PARKES sc,i Br
Alessandro MANZONI w,po It		Alexander	PATCH ar-Gen. Am
Alessandro POERIO po It		Alexander	POPE po,w Br
Alessandro TASSONI po,w It		Alexander	ROSLIN p Swe
Alessandro VOLTA sc It		Alexander	SELKIRK mariner
Alessi,	GALEAZZO ac It	Alexander	SHANA w,tv
Aletter,	FRANK tv	Alexander	SUPAN ed,e Ger
Alex	CHILTON mr-guit,s	Alexander	TODD(Sir)sc
Alex	COMFORT w Br	Alexander	WALTERS tv
Alex	CORD tv+	Alexander	WILDER c Am
Alex	DESERT tv	Alexander	WINTON id,cars Am
Alex	GARLAND w Br	Alexander	WYANT p Am
Alex	HALEY w Am	Alexander Graham BELL id Am	
Alex	JOHNSON b	Alexander,BEN tv+	
Alex	KARRAS fb,tv+	Alexander,BROOKE tv	
Alex	KUBIK	Alexander,DENISE tv	
Alex	LIFESON mr-guit	Alexander,FRANZ md,ps Am	
Alex	La GUMA w S.Afr	Alexander,GARY guit,s Am	
Alex	MANGO tv	Alexander,GROVER CLEV. b hf	
Alex	MUNTHE md,w Swe	Alexander,HAROLD ar Br	
Alex	McARTHUR	Alexander,JACE	
Alex	NICOL	Alexander,JANE	
Alex	NORTH c Am	Alexander,JASON tv+	
Alex	NORTON	Alexander,JEFF s+ Am	
Alex	OLMEDO t Am	Alexander,JEROME sc,w Am	
Alex	RAYMOND cr Am	Alexander,JOHN	
Alex	ROCCO tv+	Alexander,JOHN p Am	
Alex	SCOTT	Alexander,KHANDI	
Alex	TREBEK tv-host Am	Alexander,RICHARD	
Alex	Van HALEN mr Dut	Alexander,SAMUEL ph,e Br	
Alex	WINTER	Alexandra BASTEDO	
Alexa	KENIN	Alexandra PAUL	
Alexander AGASSIZ sc Am		Alexandra PIGG	
Alexander BACHE sc,e Am		Alexandra POWERS	
Alexander BAIN ph,ps Scot.		Alexandra STEWART	
Alexander BROWN sc,e Scot		Alexandra WILSON tv	
Alexander CALDER p,su Am		Alexandre BIZET c Fr	
Alexander COZENS p Br		Alexandre DUMAS w Fr	
Alexander D'ARCY		Alexandre EIFFEL eng Fr	
Alexander DALLAS l,st Am		Alexandre HARDY w,po Fr	
Alexander DAVIS ac Am		Alexandre LAMETH ar,st Fr	
Alexander DOYLE su Am		Alexandre LECOCQ c Fr	
Alexander DRAKE illus,ct Am		Alexandre PETION ar,st Haiti	
Alexander ELLIS math Br		Alexandre YERSIN sc Swi	
Alexander FLEMING(Sir)sc,e		Alexandria SIMMONS tv	
Alexander GAUGE tv		Alexandros SOUTSOS po Gr	
Alexander GODUNOV		Alexandros ZAIMIS st Gr	
Alexander GRANACH		Alexei	BATALOV d+
Alexander GRANT ba Br		Alexei	SAYLE

Alexi	SEMENOV mj,cn Rus	Alfred	KAZIN w,ct Am
Alexie,	SHERMAN w Native Am	Alfred	KIDDER arc Am
Alexis	CARREL md,sc,e Fr	Alfred	KINSEY sc,w-sex Am
Alexis	KANNER	Alfred	KROEBER an,e Am
Alexis	LEGER po,st Fr	Alfred	LANDON(Alf)st Am
Alexis	PARIS e,ed Fr	Alfred	LANE geol,e Am
Alexis	PETIT sc Fr	Alfred	LOISY w,ph,r Fr
Alexis	PIRON po,w Fr	Alfred	LUNT la+ Am
Alexis	SMITH tv+	Alfred	MAHAN navy,h,e Am
Alf	LANDON st Am	Alfred	METRAUX an,w Swi
Alfalfa	SWITZER	Alfred	MILNER st Br
Alfaro,	ELOY ar,st Ecu	Alfred	MOLINA
Alfaro,	RICARDO st Panama	Alfred	NOBEL i,id,f Swe
Alfie	WISE tv	Alfred	NOYES po Br
Alfieri,	VITTORIO po It	Alfred	ORAGE ed Br
Alfons De	RIDDER w Dut	Alfred	PAGET
Alfonse	CAPONE mafia Am &	Alfred	RETHEL p Ger
Alfonse	CAPONE=Scarface	Alfred	ROMER sc,e Am
Alfonse	D'AMATO st Am	Alfred	SAKER r Br
Alfonse	DAUDET w Fr	Alfred	SCHOLZ c
Alfonsina	STORNI po Arg	Alfred	SCHULZE p Fr
Alfonso	ARAU	Alfred	SHARPE(Sir)st
Alfonso	MEJIAS	Alfred	SISLEY p Fr
Alfonso	PENA st Braz	Alfred	SLOAN id-GM Am
Alfonso	REYES w,po Mex	Alfred	SMITH(Al)st Am
Alfonso	RIBEIRO tv+	Alfred	TOZZER an,e,w Am
Alfonso	SASTRE ph,w Sp	Alfred	UHRY w Am
Alfonso	X(The Sage)w,po Ro	Alfred	VAIL id-telegr Am
Alfonso	ZAYAS	Alfred	VOHRER d
Alfonso,	KRISTIAN tv	Alfred	WALLACE sc,w Br
Alford,	HENRY r Br	Alfred	WERNER sc,e Swi
Alfre	WOODARD tv+	Alfred de	MUSSET w Fr
Alfred	ADLER ps Aus	Alfred de	VIGNY w,po Fr
Alfred	ARNETH h Aus	Alfredo	CASELLA piano,c It
Alfred	AUSTIN pol,ed Br	Alfredo	CODONA trapeze Mex
Alfred	AYER(Sir) ph,e	Alfredo	MAYO
Alfred	BEIT f&f Br	Alfredo	ORIANI w It
Alfred	BESTER w-scifi Am	Alfredo	TAUNAY w,h Braz
Alfred	BINET ps Fr	Alfven,	HANNES n-p'70
Alfred	BREHM sc Ger	Alfven,	HUGO c,e Swe
Alfred	BROOKS geol Am	Alger	HISS spy Am
Alfred	BURKE	Alger	RUSSELL st Am
Alfred	CAPUS j,w Fr	Alger,	CYRUS id,i Am
Alfred	COPPARD w Br	Alger,	HORATIO Jr w Am
Alfred	CORTOT piano,cn Fr	Algernon	SIDNEY martyr Br
Alfred	DOBLIN md,w Ger	Algren,	NELSON w Am
Alfred	DOMETT po Br	Ali	MUBARAK st Egypt
Alfred	De CELLES j Can	Ali	MacGRAW tv+
Alfred	EAST(Sir)p	Ali	NEVA'I po Turk
Alfred	ESCHER st Swi	Ali,	MUHAMMAD boxer+ Am
Alfred	EWING(Sir)eng Scot	Alice	ADAMS w Am
Alfred	FRIED peace Aus	Alice	BARDEN tv
Alfred	GILBERT bus,sp Am	Alice	BARRETT tv
Alfred	GILBERT(Sir)su	Alice	BORDEN tv
Alfred	GREEN d	Alice	BRADY
Alfred	HADDON an,e Br	Alice	BROWN w Am
Alfred	HERSHEY md Am	Alice	CARY po Am
Alfred	HETTNER geog,x Ger	Alice	COOPER
Alfred	JARRY w Fr	Alice	COOPER s,ws Am
Alfred	JODL ar-Nazi Ger.	Alice	EARLE w Am
Alfred	KASTLER sc,e Fr	Alice	FAYE

Alice	FRENCH w Am	Allan	NEVINS h,w,e Am
Alice	FROST tv	Allan	RAMSAY po Scot
Alice	GREEN h Ir	Allan	ROYAL tv
Alice	HIRSON tv+	Allan	SHERMAN cm,ws Am
Alice	HOBART w Am	Allan	WALKER tv
Alice	HOFFMAN w Am	Allan,	DAVID p Scot
Alice	KAPLAN w Am	Allan,	ELIZABETH
Alice	KRIGE	Allan,	HUGH(Sir)f Can
Alice	LISLE st Br	Allbritton, LOUISE	
Alice	MARBLE t Am	Allee,	WARDER sc,e Am
Alice	MEYNELL po,w Br	Allegret, MARC d	
Alice	MILLER w Am	Allegret, YVES ds,d Am	
Alice	MUNRO w Can	Alleine,	JOSEPH r Br
Alice	NUNN tv	Allen	CASE tv
Alice	PAUL fe Am	Allen	COLLINS mr-guit
Alice	PEARCE tv	Allen	CURNOW po,ed N.Zea
Alice	RICE w Am	Allen	DRURY w.j Am
Alice	WALKER po,w Am	Allen	Du MONT id,i Am
Alice	WHITE	Allen	FAWCETT tv
Alice,	MARY	Allen	FUNT tv
Alicia	ALONSO ba Cuban	Allen	JENKINS tv+
Alicia	JOHNSON tv	Allen	LANE(Sir)pb
Alicia	MORO	Allen	LUDDEN tv
Alicia,	ANA tv+	Allen	PLONE d
Alida	RAUFFE	Allen	PRICE tv
Alida	VALLI	Allen	TATE po,bio,ct Am
Alighieri,DANTE po It		Allen,	ARLO(Woody's son)
Alimi	BALLARD tv	Allen,	BOB mj-s,cn Am
Aline	CENAL tv	Allen,	BYRON tv
Aline	MacMAHON	Allen,	CARL h Dan
Aline	TOWNE	Allen,	CHAD tv+
Alinsky,	SAUL ref Am	Allen,	COREY d
Alisan	PORTER tv	Allen,	DEBBIE ba+
Alison	DOODY	Allen,	DENNIS tv
Alison	KRAUSS s-cnt Am	Allen,	DICK b-mv'72 &
Alison	LURIE w Am	Allen,	DICK hr'72'4
Alison	La PLACA tv	Allen,	DUANE s-cnt Am
Alison	MOYET mr-s Br	Allen,	EDGAR md,e Am
Alison	SWEENEY tv	Allen,	ELISHA st Am
Alison,	ARCHIBALD r Scot	Allen,	ELIZABETH po Am
Alistair	COOKE tv	Allen,	ELIZABETH tv
Alix	ELIAS tv*	Allen,	ETHAN ar,w Am
Alix	TALTON tv	Allen,	FRED cm,tv+ Am
Alizia	GUR	Allen,	FREDERICK ed,w Am
Alla	NAZIMOVA	Allen,	GARY tv
Allais,	MAURICE n-e'88	Allen,	GINGER
Allan	ARBUS tv+	Allen,	GRACIE cm,tv+ Am
Allan	ARKUSH d	Allen,	HENRY ar Am
Allan	CLARKE mr-s Br	Allen,	HERVEY w,po Am
Allan	CORMACK md Am	Allen,	HORATIO eng,id Am
Allan	DAFOE md Can	Allen,	HUGH(Sir)cn,c
Allan	DWAN d	Allen,	IRA st Am
Allan	EDWALL	Allen,	IRWIN d
Allan	FRANK tv	Allen,	JAMES w,e Am
Allan	HUNT tv	Allen,	JAMES(Sir)st N.Zea
Allan	JONES	Allen,	JOAN
Allan	KAYSER tv	Allen,	JOHN dentist Am
Allan	LANE(Rocky)	Allen,	JONELLE tv+
Allan	MELVIN tv	Allen,	JUDITH
Allan	MILLER tv+	Allen,	KAREN
Allan	MOYLE d	Allen,	LEWIS d

Allen,	MEL tv+		Almon,	JOHN w Br
Allen,	NANCY		Almond,	MARC mr,s Br
Allen,	PAPA DEE mr-kbds,s		Almond,	PAUL d
Allen,	PATRICK		Almonte,	JUAN ar,st Mex
Allen,	PAUL po Am		Almqvist,	CARL w Swe
Allen,	PHILLIP tv		Almroth	WRIGHT(Sir)md,sc
Allen,	RALPH f Br		Alois	HABA c,e Cz
Allen,	RAYMOND tv		Alois	JIRASEK w,e Cz
Allen,	REX		Alois	RASIN st Cz
Allen,	RICK mr-drm Br &		Alois	RIEHL ph,e Ger
Allen,	R.=1-armed drummer		Aloisius	MUENCH r Am
Allen,	ROBERT		Alomar,	ROBERTO b,6x-gg's
Allen,	ROD mr-bass,s Br		Alomar,	SANDY b
Allen,	SHEILA		Alonso	CANO p,su Sp
Allen,	STEVE tv+		Alonso de	OJEDA x Sp
Allen,	TIM tv		Alonso,	ALICIA ba Cuba
Allen,	TODD		Alonso,	AMADO e,ed Sp
Allen,	VERDEN mr-kbds Br		Alonso,	CHELO
Allen,	VIOLA la Am		Alonso,	MARIA
Allen,	WOODY o-d'77+		Alonso,	MATEO su Arg
Allen,	ZACHARIAH i Am		Alou,	FELIPE b
Allende,	FERNANDO tv+		Alou,	JESUS b
Allende,	ISABEL w Chile		Alou,	MATTIE b
Allesandro	VOLTA sc It		Alou,	MOISES b
Allessandra	FERN ba Br		Aloys	REDING st Swi
Alley	MILLS tv+		Alp,	ARSLAN st Tur
Alley,	ALVIN ba Am		Alpert,	HERB mj,c,g-r'65 Am
Alley,	KIRSTIE tv+		Alphen,	CORINNE
Alleyne,	EDWARD la,e Br		Alpheus	HYATT sc,e Am
Allgood,	SARA		Alpheus	VERRILL x Am
Allison	BALSON tv		Alphonse	DAUDET w Fr
Allison	HAYES		Alphonse	JUIN ar Fr
Allison	MILLS tv		Alphonse	KARR j,w Fr
Allison	McKAY tv		Alphonse	LEGROS p,etch Br
Allison	SMITH tv		Alphonse	MUCHA p,illus Cz
Allison,	DOROTHY w Am		Alphonse	PICOU mj,cn Am
Allison,	FRAN tv+		Alphonse	RENARD geol Belg
Allison,	JERRY mr-drm Am		Alsberg,	CARL sc Am
Allman,	ELVIA tv		Alsop,	JOSEPH(Wright)j,w
Allman,	GREGG mr-kbds,s		Alsop,	MARY w Am
Allon,	HENRY r Br		Alsop,	STEWART(J.O.)j,w Am
Allori,	ALESSANDRO p It		Alsop,	VINCENT r Br
Allott,	ROBERT po,ed Br		Alston,	BARBARA s Am
Allport,	CHRISTOPHER		Alston,	EMMETT d
Allston,	WASHINGTON p,w Am		Alston,	SHIRLEY s Am
Allsup,	MIKE mr-guit Am		Alston,	WALT bmg hf
Allwyn,	ASTRID		Alstyne,	EGBERT van c Am
Ally	SHEEDY		Alt,	CAROL mo+ Am
Ally	WALKER		Altea,	ROSEMARY w Am
Allyce	BEASLEY tv+		Alten,	KARL ar Ger
Allyn	JOSLYN tv+		Alter,	DAVID sc,md Am
Allyn	McLERIE tv+		Alterio,	HECTOR
Allyson,	JUNE tv+		Althea	GIBSON t Am
Alma	GLUCK sopr Am		Alther,	LISA w Am
Alma	RUBENS		Althouse,	PAUL tenor Am
Alma	WHITE r Am		Altman,	ARTHUR c Am
Almada,	MARIO		Altman,	BENJAMIN mer Am
Almagor,	GILA		Altman,	JEFF tv+
Almedovar,	PEDRO d		Altman,	ROBERT d
Almeida,	BRITES de heroine		Altman,	SIDNEY n-c'89 Am
Almeida,	MANUEL de w Braz		Aluko,	TIMOTHY w Nigeria

Alun	LEWIS po Welsh		Amasa	WALKER ec,e,st Am
Alva	BELMONT fe Am		Amati,	ANDREA violins It
Alva	MYRDAL st Scot		Amati,	ANTONIO violins It
Alva,	LUIGI tenor It		Amati,	GIROLAMO viols It
Alvan	CLARK astr Am		Amati,	NICCOLO violins It
Alvar	AALTO ac Finn		Amato,	PASQUALE bari It
Alvar	CABEZA de VACA x Sp		Ambler,	ERIC w Br
Alvarado, CROX			Ambrogio di SPINOLA ar It
Alvarado, PEDRO de ar Sp			Ambroise	PARE md Fr
Alvarado, TRINI			Ambroise	THOMAS c Fr
Alvarez,	A(lfred). po,w Br		Ambroise	VOLLARD mer,pb Fr
Alvarez,	JUAN st Mex		Ambros,	AUGUST c,e Cz
Alvarez,	JULIA w Am		Ambrose	BIERCE w,j Am
Alvarez,	LUIS n-p'68		Ambrose	HILL ar Am
Alvaro	OBREGON ar,st Mex		Ambrose	PHILIPS po,w Br
Alvaro de BAZAN navy Sp			Ameche,	DON o-s'85
Alvaro de LUNA st Sp			Amelia	BARR w Am
Alvear,	CARLOS re Arg		Amelia	BLOOMER fe Am
Alvear,	MAXIMO st Arg		Amelia	EARHART fly Am
Alvin	ADAMS bus Am		Amelia	EDWARDS w Br
Alvin	AILEY ba Am		Amelia	OPIE w Br
Alvin	CARTER m-folk Am &		Ameling,	ELLY sopr Br
Alvin	CARTER=A.P.Carter		Amenta,	PINA d
Alvin	COBURN fo Br		Amery,	LEOPOLD j,st Br
Alvin	HANSEN ec,e,w Am		Ames Brothers,THE s Am
Alvin	JULIAN bbc hf		Ames,	ED s,tv Am
Alvin	KELLY stunts Am &		Ames,	FISHER st Am
Alvin	KELLY = Shipwreck		Ames,	JOSEPH bibliog Br
Alvin	RAKOFF d		Ames,	JOSEPH sc,e Am
Alvin	SAMPLES(Junior)tv		Ames,	LEON tv+
Alvin	YORK ar,hero Am		Ames,	NANCY tv
Alvino	REY m,cn,tv Am		Ames,	OAKES id,f,st Am
Alvis	OWENS s-ctry,tv &		Ames,	OAKES sc,e Am
Alvis	OWENS = Buck		Ames,	WINTHROP pr Am
Alvise	CA'DA MOSTO x It		Ami	BOUE geol,w Aus
Alvy	MOORE tv+		Ami	DOLENZ
Alvy	WEST mj,cn Am		Ami	FOSTER tv
Alworth,	LANCE fb hf		Ami	PERRIN st Swi
Alwyn	KURTS		Amichai,	YEHUDA po,w Isr
Alyce	KING S,tv Am		Amici,	GIOVANNI astr It
Alyssa	MILANO tv+		Amick,	MADCHEN
Alzado,	LYLE fb,tv+		Amiel,	HENRI po,ph Swi
Alzon,	EMMANUEL r Fr		Amilcar	CABRAL st Guinea
Amadeo	NAZZARI		Amin al-	HUSAYNI st Arab
Amadeo	VIVES c Sp		Amin,	IDI st Uganda
Amadeus	GRABAU sc,e Am		Amiot,	JEAN r Fr
Amadi,	ELECHI w Nigeria		Amir	WILLIAMS tv
Amado	ALONSO e,w Sp		Amir Ali, SAYYID l,w India
Amado de NERVO po,st Mex			Amis,	KINGSLEY w Br
Amado,	JORGE w Braz		Amis,	MARTIN w Br
Amalrik,	ANDREI w Rus		Amis,	SUZY
Amanda	BEARSE tv+		Amman,	JOST p Swi
Amanda	BLAKE tv+		Ammelrooy,WILLEKE van
Amanda	DONOHOE tv+		Ammons,	A(rchie). po Am
Amanda	McKERROW ba Am		Amory,	THOMAS w Br
Amanda	PAYS tv+		Amos	ALCOTT po,e Am
Amanda	PLUMMER		Amos	EATON sc,w,e Am
Amanda	ROOT		Amos	ELON j,w Isr
Amanda	WYSS		Amos	KENDALL ed,st Am
Amanz	GRESSLY geol Swi		Amos	KOLLEK d+
Amara,	LUCINE sopr		Amos	OTIS b

Amos OZ w Israel	Anderson, BILL s-cnt Am
Amos RUSIE b hf	Anderson, BRAD cr Am
Amos TUTUOLA w Nigeria	Anderson, BRIDGETTE
Amos Alonzo STAGG fbc	Anderson, CARL DAVID n-p'36
Amos, JOHN tv+	Anderson, CARL THOMAS cr Am
Amos, TORI mr-s Am	Anderson, ED(Rochester)tv+
Amos, WALLYid-choc cooky	Anderson, GILLIAN tv
Ampere, ANDRE-MARIE sc Fr	Anderson, HAROLD bbc hf
Ampere, JEAN h,ph Fr	Anderson, HARRY tv+
Amritraj, VIJAY t,tv+ India	Anderson, IAN mr-flute,s
Amsterdam,MOREY cm,tv+ Am	Anderson, JACK j Am
Amundsen, ROALD x Nor	Anderson, JOHAN geol Swe
Amy ALCOTT g Am	Anderson, JOHN tv+
Amy CARLSON tv	Anderson, JON mr-drm,s Br
Amy FARRELL tv	Anderson, JUDITH(Dame)la,tv+
Amy GRANT s-gospel Am	Anderson, KEN fb-m'81
Amy IRVING	Anderson, KEVIN
Amy JOHNSON fly Br	Anderson, LAURIE s Am
Amy LINKER tv	Anderson, LEROY c,cn Am
Amy LOCANE	Anderson, LINDSAY d+
Amy LOWELL po,ct Am	Anderson, LONI tv+
Amy LYNNE tv	Anderson, LYNN s-cnt Am
Amy MADIGAN	Anderson, MARIAN contralto
Amy STEEL tv+	Anderson, MARY la Am
Amy STOCK tv	Anderson, MAXWELL p-d'33
Amy TAN w Am	Anderson, MELISSA SUE tv+
Amy WRIGHT	Anderson, MELODY tv+
Amy YASBECK	Anderson, MICHAEL Jr tv+
Amyot, JACQUES r,e Fr	Anderson, MICHAEL Sr d
Amyraut, MOISE r,e Fr	Anderson, PHILIP n-p'77
Amzie STRICKLAND tv	Anderson, RASMUS w,ed,e,st
An WANG eng,id Am	Anderson, RICHARD tv+
Ana ALICIA tv+	Anderson, RICHARD DEAN tv
Ana MARTIN	Anderson, RICK mr-bass Am
Ana TORRENT	Anderson, ROBERT w Am
Ana Louisa PELUFFO	Anderson, SHERWOOD w Am
Ana Maria MATUTE w Sp	Anderson, SPARKY bmg
Anais NIN w Am	Anderson, TOM ho-m'42
Ananiashvili,NINA ba Rus	Anderson, WARNER tv+
Anastas MIKOYAN st Rus	Anderssen,ADOLF chess Ger
Anastasio SOMOZA st-ar Nica	Andersson,BENNY mr-kbds,s Swe
Anatole FRANCE w Fr	Andersson,BIBI
Anatole Le BRAZ w Fr	Andersson,HARRIET
Anatole de MONZIE st,pb Fr	Andersson,KARELL x Swe
Anatoli, JACOB md,ph Fr	Andes, KEITH tv+
Anatoly KARPOV chess Rus	Andie MacDOWELL
Anatoly LYADOV c Rus	Andoche JUNOT ar Fr
Anderman, MAUREEN tv	Andra MILLIAN tv+
Anders CELSIUS astron Swe	Andra WILLIS s,tv Am
Anders PALM d	Andrade, MARIO de po,w
Anders RANDOLF	Andrade, OSWALD de po,w
Anders RETZIUS an,md Swe	Andras BALINT
Anders VEDEL h Dan	Andras FAY w Hung
Anders ZORN p,su,etch Swe	Andrassy, GYULA st Hung
Anders, LUANA	Andre AGASSI t Am
Anders, MERRY tv+	Andre AMPERE sc,e Fr
Anders, WLADYSLAW ar Pol	Andre ANTOINE la Fr
Andersen, HANS CHRISTIAN w	Andre BARUCH tv
Andersen, TRYGGVE w Nor	Andre BEAUFRE ar Fr
Anderson, ALFA s Am	Andre BRETON w,po,ct Fr
Anderson, BARBARA tv	Andre CAMPRA c Fr

Andre	CHARLOT pr-stg Br	Andrei	AMALRIK w Rus
Andre	CITROEN id-cars Fr	Andrei	BELY po,w Rus
Andre	DANJON astr Fr	Andrei	BITOV w Rus
Andre	DAWSON b	Andrej	HLINKA r Slovak
Andre	DERAIN p Fr	Andres	BELLO po Venz
Andre	DUPIN l,st Fr	Andres	SEGOVIA guit Sp
Andre	FAVORY p Fr	Andres	SOLER
Andre	GIDE w,ed Fr	Andress,	URSULA
Andre	GOWER tv+	Andretti,	MARIO racecars Am
Andre	GREGORY	Andrew	BRADLEY e,ct Br &
Andre	GRETRY c Fr	Andrew	BRADLEY = A.C.
Andre	HASSELT po Belg	Andrew	CASSESE tv
Andre	JACOBS	Andrew	CLAY tv
Andre	KERTESZ fo Am	Andrew	DAVIS d
Andre	LENOTRE ac-land Fr	Andrew	DIVOFF
Andre	LHOTE p,w Fr	Andrew	DUGGAN tv+
Andre	LWOFF md Fr	Andrew	DUNCAN(Sir)st
Andre	MALRAUX w,ct Fr	Andrew	FARRISS mr-kbds Aust
Andre	MASSON ar,p Fr	Andrew	FOSTER b hf
Andre	MAUROIS w,bio Fr	Andrew	HUXLEY md Br
Andre	MORELL	Andrew	KEIR
Andre	PREVIN cn Am	Andrew	KIM r Korea
Andre	RIGAUD ar,re Haiti	Andrew	LANG w Scot
Andre	ROUSSIN w Fr	Andrew	LAUER tv
Andre	TAYRI ba,tv Am	Andrew	LAWSON geol,e Am
Andre	WATTS piano Ger	Andrew	LOWERY
Andre	WILMS	Andrew	MARVELL po Br
Andre de	CHENIER po Fr	Andrew	MELLON id,f Am
Andre de	TOTH d	Andrew	McCARTHY
Andre,	GABY	Andrew	McLAGLEN d
Andre,	JOHN ar Br	Andrew	PHILPOT tv
Andre,	LONA	Andrew	PRINE tv+
Andrea	ALCIATI l It	Andrew	RAY
Andrea	AMATI violins It	Andrew	SHUE tv
Andrea	BARBER tv	Andrew	STEVENS tv+
Andrea	BOCELLI tenor It	Andrew	STILL md Am
Andrea	DORIA navy,ss It	Andrew	STONE d
Andrea	ELSON tv	Andrew	WEIL w Am
Andrea	FERREOL	Andrew	WHITE e,st Am
Andrea	KING	Andrew	WYETH p Am
Andrea	LEEDS	Andrew Dice CLAY	
Andrea	LOWELL tv	Andrew Lloyd WEBBER c,pr Br	
Andrea	MARTIN tv+	Andrew,	JOHN st Am
Andrea	MOAR tv	Andrew,	SIMON
Andrea	MOEN tv	Andrews Sisters THE s+	
Andrea	ORCAGNA p,su,ac It	Andrews,	ANTHONY
Andrea	RAU	Andrews,	BARRY mr-kbds Br
Andrea	RICCIO su It	Andrews,	CHARLES h,e Am
Andrea	SACCHI p It	Andrews,	DANA
Andrea	SACINO tv	Andrews,	DAVID
Andrea dal POZZO r,ac,p It		Andrews,	EDWARD tv+
Andrea del SARTO p It		Andrews,	FRANK ar Am
Andrea di CIONE p,su,ac It		Andrews,	HARRY
Andrea,	JAKOB r,w Ger	Andrews,	JULIE o-a'64,s,tv
Andreas	HADIK ar Aus	Andrews,	ROY CHAPMAN sc,x,w
Andreas	HEUSLER e Ger	Andrews,	STANLEY tv+
Andreas	KALVOS po Gr	Andrews,	THOMAS sc,e Ir
Andreas	LIBAU md,sc,e Ger	Andrews,	TIGE tv
Andree,	KARL geog Ger	Andrey	BELY w,po Rus
Andree,	SALOMON eng,x Swe	Andrey	GROMYKO st Rus
Andreeff,	STARR	Andrey	KURBSKI ar Rus

Andrey	MARKOV math,e Rus	Angelo	D'ALEO mr-s Am
Andrey	RUBLYOV p Rus	Angelo	DUNDEE mgr-boxing
Andrey	ZHDANOV st Rus	Angelo	MUSCAT tv
Andreyev,	LEONID w Rus	Angelo,	GIORGIO SANT' ds
Andric,	IVO n-l'61	Angelou,	MAYA w,po,s,ba+
Andropov,	YURI Rus	Angharad	REES
Andros,	EDMUND(Sir)st	Angiallieri,	CECCO po It
Andrzej	WAJDA d,pr-films	Angie	DICKINSON tv+
Andy	ADAMS cowboy,w Am	Angie	EVERHART mo+ Am
Andy	BELL mr,s Br	Angiolini,	GASPARO ba,c It
Andy	CLYDE tv+	Anglin,	MARGARET la Am
Andy	COX mr-guit Br	Ango,	JEAN ships Fr
Andy	DEVINE tv+	Angstrom,	ANDERS astr,sc
Andy	FRASER mr-bass Br	Angus	SCRIMM
Andy	GARCIA	Angus	WILSON(Sir)bio,w
Andy	GIBB tv	Angus	YOUNG mr-guit Scot
Andy	KAUFMAN tv+	Anholt,	TONY tv
Andy	KIM s Am	Ani	DiFRANCO s-punk,
Andy	KIRK mj-sax cn Am	Anibal	PINTO st Chile
Andy	MacKAY reeds Br	Anikita	REPNIN ar Rus
Andy	PHILLIP bb hf	Anissa	JONES tv
Andy	RAZAF lyrics Am	Anita	BAKER s-r&b Am
Andy	ROBERTS tv	Anita	BARONE tv
Andy	ROMANO tv+	Anita	BRYANT s,tv Am
Andy	ROONEY tv-j Am	Anita	COLBY tv
Andy	SCOTT mr-guit	Anita	DESAI w Br
Andy	SIDARIS d	Anita	EKBERG
Andy	SUMMERS mr-guit,s	Anita	GORDON tv
Andy	TAYLOR mr-guit	Anita	HILL l,e Am
Andy	TIPALDI mj,cn Am	Anita	KERR s,cn,tv Am
Andy	WARHOL p,pr-film	Anita	LOOS w Am
Anerio,	FELICE c It	Anita	LOUISE tv+
Anethan,	JULES st,r Belg	Anita	MANN ba,tv Am
Aneurin,	BEVAN st Br	Anita	MORRIS
Anfinsen,	CHRISTIAN n-c'72	Anita	O'DAY mj-s Am
Ang	LEE d	Anita	PAGE
Angas,	GEORGE ships Br	Anita	POINTER s Am
Angel	CORDERO jockey Am	Anita	WARD s Am
Angel	GANIVET w Sp	Anita Kerr Singers,THE s Am	
Angel	RIVAS po,w Sp	Anitra	FORD
Angel,	HEATHER	Anjanette COMER	
Angel,	VANESSA mo+ Am	Anka,	PAUL s+ Can
Angela	AAMES tv+	Ankers,	EVELYN
Angela	BASSET	Ankrum,	MORRIS
Angela	DAVIS re Am	Ann	BARNES tv
Angela	LEE tv+	Ann	BEATTIE w Am
Angela	MAO	Ann	BLYTH
Angela	MOLINA	Ann	BURR tv
Angela	McGREGOR	Ann	CLEEVES w Br
Angela	PATON tv	Ann	COMPTON j Am
Angela	POWELL tv	Ann	CREED w Am
Angela	WATSON tv	Ann	DAVIS tv+
Angela	WINKLER	Ann	DORAN tv+
Angeli,	PIER	Ann	DVORAK
Angelica	HUSTON	Ann	ELDER tv
Angelico,	FRA p It	Ann	HARDING
Angelika	HAUFF	Ann	HEARN tv+
Angell,	JAMES e,ps Am	Ann	JILLIAN tv+
Angell,	NORMAN(Sir)w &	Ann	KELSEY tv
Angell,	NORMAN n-x'33	Ann	LANDERS j Am

Ann	LEE r-Shakers &	Anne	BOELYN wf of &
Ann	LEE = Mother LEE	Anne	BOELYN Hnry8th Br
Ann	MEYERS bb hf	Anne	BRONTE w Br
Ann	MILLER ba+ Am	Anne	DONOVAN bb hf
Ann	MORRISS tv	Anne	DeSALVO
Ann	McCREA tv	Anne	EDGREN w Swe
Ann	NELSON tv+	Anne	FALKNER tv
Ann	NESBY s-soul Am	Anne	FRANCIS tv+
Ann	RANDALL tv	Anne	FRANK w Ger
Ann	RYERSON tv	Anne	GILLIS
Ann	SAVAGE	Anne	GWYNNE
Ann	SORG tv	Anne	HECHE tv+
Ann	SOTHERN tv+	Anne	HEYWOOD
Ann	TODD tv+	Anne	JACKSON
Ann	TURKEL	Anne	KLEIN ds Am
Ann	TYRRELL tv	Anne	LAMOTT w Am
Ann	WARREN tv	Anne	MACY e,w Am
Ann	WELDON tv	Anne	MEARA cm,tv+ Am
Ann	WILSON mr-s Am	Anne	MURRAY s Can
Ann-Margret---		Anne	NAGEL
Anna	CAPRI	Anne	NICHOLS w Am
Anna	CARROLL w,ct Am	Anne	PARRISH w Am
Anna	GAEL	Anne	PERRY w Br
Anna	GALIENA	Anne	PUTNAM witch
Anna	GORENKO po Rus	Anne	RAMSAY tv
Anna	GREEN w Am	Anne	RAMSEY
Anna	HELD la Am	Anne	REVERE
Anna	KARINA	Anne	RICE w Am
Anna	LEE tv+	Anne	ROYALL w,j Am
Anna	LEVINE tv	Anne	SAVARY ar st Fr
Anna	LISA tv	Anne	SEXTON po Am
Anna	MAGNANI	Anne	SEYMOUR tv+
Anna	MASSEY	Anne	SHIRLEY
Anna	MERRITT p Am	Anne	TWOMEY
Anna	MOFFO sopr Am	Anne	TYLER w Am
Anna	MOSES(Grandma)p Am	Anne	WHITNEY su Am
Anna	MOWATT w.la Am	Anne	WYNDHAM tv
Anna	NEAGLE	Anne de	STAEL w Fr
Anna	NILSSON	Anne-Marie	JOHNSON tv+
Anna	PAQUIN	Anne-Marie	MARTIN tv
Anna	PAVLOVA ba Rus	Anne-Robt.	TURGOT ec,st Fr
Anna	QUAYLE	Annette	BENING
Anna	SEGHERS w Ger	Annette	O'TOOLE
Anna	SEWARD po,w Br	Annibale	CARO po It
Anna	SEWELL w Br	Annie	BESANT w Br
Anna	SHAW r,md,fe Am	Annie	DILLARD w Am
Anna	SLOTKY tv	Annie	FARGE tv
Anna	STEN	Annie	GOLDEN
Anna	SUI ds Am	Annie	LENNOX s,ws Scot
Anna May	WONG	Annie	MEYER e,w Am
Annabella	---	Annie	McENROE
Annabella	LWIN mr-s Burma	Annie	OAKLEY markswoman
Annabella	SCIORRA	Annie	PECK mtn climber
Annabeth	GISH	Annie	POTTS tv+
Annakin,	KEN d	Annie	ROSS
Annaud,	JEAN w,d Fr	Annie Jump	CANNON astr Am
Anne	ARCHER tv+	Anning,	MARY sc Br
Anne	ASKEW r Br	Annis,	FRANCESCA
Anne	AYRES r Am	Anny	DUPEREY
Anne	BAXTER tv+	Anny	ONDRA
Anne	BLOOM tv+	Anona	WINN mj-s Br.

Anouilh,	JEAN w Fr		Anthony,	LYSETTE
Anouk	AIMEE		Anthony,	MICHAEL mr-bass Am
Ansara,	MICHAEL tv+		Anthony,	PIERS w-scifi Br
Ansel	ADAMS fo Am		Anthony,	RAY mj,cn,tv Am
Anselme	PAYEN sc Fr		Anthony,	SUSAN B. fe Am
Ansermet,	ERNEST cn Swi		Antin,	DAVID po Am
Anson	WEEKS mj,cn,c Am		Antin,	MARY w Am
Anson,	CAP(Pop) b,bmg hf		Antin,	STEVE
Anson,	GEORGE navy Br		Antoine	BALARD sc,e Fr
Anspach,	SUSAN tv+		Antoine	BARYE su Fr
Anstey,	CHRISTOPHER po Br		Antoine	BAUME sc Fr
Ant,	ADAM mr,s+ Br		Antoine	BRUMEL c Fr
Antal	DORATI cn,c Am		Antoine	BRUNI x FR
Antanas	MERKYS st,ar Lith		Antoine	BUSSY sc,e Fr
Antanas	SMETONA st Lith		Antoine	CARON p Fr
Ante	PAVELIC st Croat		Antoine	DANTAN su Fr
Ante	TRUMBIC st Croat		Antoine	DROZ p Fr
Antero de	QUENTAL po Port		Antoine	ETEX su,p,ac Fr
Anthony	ANDREWS		Antoine	GARNIER(Tony)ac Fr
Anthony	ASQUITH d		Antoine	GROS p Fr
Anthony	BEK r Br		Antoine	La MOTHE ar Fr
Anthony	BLUNT h,spy Br		Antoine	Le NAIN p Fr
Anthony	BURGESS w,e Br		Antoine	PESNE p Fr
Anthony	BUSHELL		Antoine	PEVSNER su,p Fr
Anthony	CARUSO		Antoine	SAX id-music Belg
Anthony	DAWSON tv+		Antoine	WALKER bb
Anthony	DENISON tv+		Antoine	WATTEAU p Fr
Anthony	EDEN(Sir)st		Antoine,	ANDRE la Fr
Anthony	EDWARDS tv+		Antoinette	PERRY la Am
Anthony	EISLEY tv+		Antoinette	SIBLEY ba Br
Anthony	FOKKER id-planes		Anton	ARENSKY c Rus
Anthony	GEARY		Anton	CARLSON me,e Am
Anthony	GEORGE tv		Anton	CERMAK st Am
Anthony	HALL tv+		Anton	CHEKHOV w Rus
Anthony	HAWKINS(Sir)w		Anton	DOHRN sc Ger
Anthony	HEALD		Anton	DOLIN ba Br
Anthony	HECHT po Am		Anton	DONI w,ed It
Anthony	HICKOX d		Anton	KLIEGL bus Am
Anthony	HIGGINS		Anton	KOROSEC r,st Slav
Anthony	HOPKINS		Anton	MAUVE p Dut
Anthony	JAMES		Anton	MENGS p Ger
Anthony	KIEDIS mr-s Am		Anton	MUSSERT eng,st Dut
Anthony	LaPAGLIA		Anton	REICHA c Cz
Anthony	MORE(Sir)p Dut		Anton	SAILER ski Aus
Anthony	MUNDAY po,w Br		Anton	TITL c Ger
Anthony	NEWLEY c+ Br		Anton von	WEBERN c Aus
Anthony	PAGE d		Anton,	SUSAN s+ Am
Anthony	PERKINS		Antonelli,	LAURA
Anthony	POWELL w Br		Antonescu,	ION ar Rom
Anthony	QUAYLE(Sir)d,la+		Antoni	LANGE po,ct Pol
Anthony	QUINN		Antonia	FRASER(Lady)w Br
Anthony	RAPP		Antonia	MERCE ba Arg
Anthony	STEEL		Antonia	WHITE w,j Br
Anthony	STEFFEN		Antonin	ARTAUD la,w po Fr
Anthony	TOPHAM mr-guit Br		Antonin	DVORAK c Cz
Anthony	VanDYCK(Sir)p Belg		Antonin	LAUZUN ar Fr
Anthony	WAYNE(Mad)ar-re Am		Antonin	MERCIE su Fr
Anthony	WEST w,ct Br		Antonin	NOVOTNY st Cz
Anthony	WICKERT tv		Antonin	SOVA w Cz
Anthony	ZERBE tv+		Antonio	AGUILAR
Anthony John	DENISON			

Antonio	AMATI viloins It	Applegate,EDDIE tv
Antonio	CAMPI p It	Applegate,JESSE pioneer Am
Antonio	CANOVA su It	Appleton, EDWARD(Sir)n-p'47
Antonio	CESTI c It	Appling, LUKE b hf
Antonio	FARGAS tv+	Aprea, JOHN tv+
Antonio	GAUDI ac Sp	April CLOUGH tv
Antonio	GOMES c Braz	April LERMAN tv
Antonio	JOBIM c Braz	Apted, MICHAEL d
Antonio	LEAL po Port	Aqqad, ABBAS al-j,po Eg
Antonio	LISBOA su,ac Braz	Aquinas, THOMAS(Saint)ph
Antonio	LOTTI c It	Aquino, CORAZON st
Antonio	MACHADO po Sp	Arafat, YASIR st,n-x'94 &
Antonio	MONIZ md Port	Arafat, YASIR Palest
Antonio	MORENO	Arago, FRANCOIS sc,e Fr
Antonio	NETO st,po Angola	Aragon, LOUIS, w,po Fr
Antonio	NOBRE po Port	Aram AVAKIAN d
Antonio	PASTOR la Am	Aram, EUGENE e,murder Br
Antonio	PEREDA p Sp	Arana, TOMAS
Antonio	SABATO	Aranha, OSWALDO l,st Braz
Antonio	SABATO Jr tv	Arany, JANOS po Hung
Antonio	SALIERI c It	Aranyi, JELLY EVA d' &
Antonio	SCARPA md It	Aranyi, JELLY E. viol Hung
Antonio	SOLARI p It	Arason, JON r,po Iceland
Antonio	SOLER c Sp	Aratama, MICHIYO
Antonio	VERRIO p It	Arau, ALFONSO
Antonio	VIEIRA r,w Port	Arber, AGNES sc,w Br
Antonio	VIVALDI viol,c It	Arber, EDWARD e,ed Br
Antonio da PONTE ac It		Arber, WERNER n-m'78
Antonio da SILVA w Port		Arbuckle, FATTY(Roscoe)
Antonio de OQUENDO x Sp		Arbus, ALLAN tv+
Antonio de SUCRE ar,re Venz		Arbus, DIANE fo Am
Antonio de ZAMORA w,po Sp		Arcangelo CORELLI viol,c It
Antonio, LOU d		Arcaro, EDDIE jockey Am
Antonutti,OMERO		Arce, MANUEL ar,st Salv
Antony	CARBONE tv+	Arcel, RAY mgr-boxing Am
Antony	HEWISH sc Br	Arch HALL Jr.
Antony	TUDOR ba Br	Arch JOHNSON tv
Antony,	MARK st Ro	Arch WHITING tv
Antschel, PAUL po Ger		Arch, JOSEPH st Br
Antun	SAADA agitator Syr	Archainbaud, GEORGE d
Anwar	SADAT st Egypt	Archdale JONES
Anwar,	GABRIELLE	Archer MARTIN sc Br
Anya	SETON w Am	Archer, ANNE tv+
Anza,	JUAN de x Sp	Archer, BEVERLY tv
Anzilotti,PERRY tv		Archer, FREDERICK fo,su
Aoki,	ROCKY	Archer, FREDERICK jockey
Apafi,	MICHAEL st Transyl	Archer, JEFFREY w Br
Aparicio, LUIS b hf		Archer, JOHN
Aparna	SEN	Archer, THOMAS ac Br
Apeles	--- p Gr	Archer, WILLIAM ct,w Scot
Apgar,	VIRGINIA md,e Am	Archibald ALISON r Scot
Aphra	BEHN(Mrs.)w Br	Archibald BARR eng,i Scot
Apirana	NGATA(Sir)st N.Zea	Archibald GEIKIE(Sir)geol Sc
Apolinario MABINI re Phil		Archibald HILL md Br
Apollonia	---	Archibald MacLEISH po,w Am
Apollonia KOTERA(Patricia)tv		Archibald WAVELL ar Br
Appert,	NICOLAS chef,i Fr	Archibald WILLARD p Am
Appia,	ADOLPHE ds Swi	Archibald,NATE bb hf
Appice,	CARMINE mr-drm	Archie BLEYER tv
Appleby,	JOHN i Am	Archie DUNCAN tv
Applegate,CHRISTINA tv+		Archie HAHN tv+

Archie	MOORE boxer+ Am		Arlene	FRANCIS tv+
Archie	SMITH tv		Arlene	GOLONKA tv+
Archimedes	--- i,math Gr		Arlene	HOWELL tv
Arcon,	JEAN ar,eng,i Fr		Arlene	McQUADE tv
Ardant,	FANNY		Arletty	---
Arden,	ELIZABETH id Am		Arline	JUDGE
Arden,	EVE tv+		Arliss	HOWARD
Arden,	JOHN w Br		Arliss,	GEORGE la+,o-a'30
Arden,	VICTOR mj,cn Am		Arlo	ALLEN(Woody's son)
Ardigo,	ROBERTO ph,e It		Arlo	GUTHRIE s-folk+ Am
Ardolino,	EMILE d		Arlo	HULTS organ,tv Am
Ardrey,	ROBERT w Am		Armad	RASHAD fb,tv
Arenas,	ROSITA		Armand	ASSANTE
Arendt,	HANNAH e,ed Am		Armand	HAMMER id,f Am
Arene,	PAUL w,po Fr		Armand	PLESSIS ar,st Fr
Arensky,	ANTON e Rus		Armand	QUICK sc-md,e Am
Arent,	EDDI		Armand	RANCE r Fr
Aretha	FRANKLIN s-r&b Am		Armando	CALVO
Aretino,	PIETRO w It		Armando	DIAZ ar It
Argall,	SAMUEL(Sir)x		Armando	ORTEGA tv
Argand,	AIME sc,i Swi		Armani,	GIORGIO ds It
Argand,	EMILE geol,e Swi		Armas	LONNBOHM po Finn
Argand,	JEAN math Swi		Armas,	TONY b,hr'81'84
Argent,	ROD mr-kbds Br		Armatrading, JOAN s,ws	
Argenta,	DARIO d		Armendariz, PEDRO Jr. tv+	
Argento,	DOMINICK p-m'75		Armendariz, PEDRO Sr.	
Argenziano, CARMEN tv+			Armetta,	HENRY
Arget,	EUGENE fo Fr		Armfelt,	GUSTAF ar,st Swe
Argo,	VICTOR		Armi	RATIA ds-textileFinn
Argue,	DAVID		Armida	---
Arguedas,	ALCIDES st,w Bol		Armour,	PHILIP id-meat,f
Arguedas,	JOSE MARIA w,po		Arms,	RUSSELL s,tv+
Arguello,	LUIS st Mex-Calif		Armstead, HENRY su Br	
Ari	MEYERS tv+		Armstrong,ALUN	
Ari	ONASSIS f-ships Gr		Armstrong,BESS tv+	
Ariadne	WELTER		Armstrong,BILLIE JOE s,ws Am	
Arias,	HARMODIO st Panama		Armstrong,CURTIS tv+	
Aribau,	BUENAVENTURA w Sp		Armstrong,EDWIN eng,e,i Am	
Arie	LUYENDYK racecar Am		Armstrong,GILLIAN d	
Ariosto,	LUDOVICO po It		Armstrong,HAMILTON FISH j Am	
Arista,	MARIANO ar,st Mex		Armstrong,HENRY boxer Am	
Aristide	BRIAND st Fr		Armstrong,HENRY(Harry)c Am	
Aristide	MAILLOL p,su Fr		Armstrong,JACK	
Aristotle	--- ph Gr		Armstrong,LEE tv	
Aristotle	ONASSIS f-ships Gr		Armstrong,LOUIS mj,s,tv+ Am	
Arizin,	PAUL bb hf		Armstrong,NEIL ALDEN as Am	
Arkell,	WILLIAM sc,e Br		Armstrong,PAUL w Am	
Arkhipava,IRINA sopr			Armstrong,R.G. tv+	
Arkin,	ADAM tv+		Armstrong,ROBERT	
Arkin,	ALAN d,w,tv+ Am		Armstrong-Jones,ANTONY C. fo	
Arkush,	ALLAN d		Arnaud,	HENRI ar,r Fr
Arky	VAUGHN b hf		Arnaz,	DESI Jr m,tv+
Arledge,	ROONE tv-exec Am		Arnaz,	DESI Sr m,cn,tv+
Arleen	SORKIN tv+		Arnaz,	LUCIE tv+
Arleen	WHELAN		Arnd(t),	JOHANN r Ger
Arlen	SNYDER		Arndt,	ERNST st,w Ger
Arlen	SPECTOR st Am		Arne	CARLSON st Am
Arlen,	HAROLD c Am		Arne	GARBORG w,po Nor
Arlen,	MICHAEL w Br		Arne	OLDBERG c Am
Arlen,	RICHARD		Arne,	PETER
Arlene	DAHL tv+		Arne,	THOMAS c Br

Arness,	JAMES tv+	Arrigo	BOITO c,po,w It
Arneth,	ALFRED h Aus	Arrivi,	FRANCESCO w P.Rico
Arnetia	WALKER tv+	Arrol,	WILLIAM(Sir)eng
Arnie	PALMER g Am	Arrow,	KENNETH n-e'72
Arnim,	ACHIM von po,w	Arrowsmith,	AARON geog Br
Arnim,	BETTINA von w Ger	Arsenio	HALL tv+
Arnim,	HARRY st Ger	Arshile	GORKY p Am
Arnim,	KARL st Ger	Arslan	ALP st Turk
Arnim,	LUDWIG von w,po	Art	BAKER tv+
Arnim,	LUDWIG w,po Ger	Art	CARNEY tv+
Arno	HOLZ po,w,ct Ger	Art	DAVIS
Arno	PENZIAS sc Am	Art	DONOVAN fb hf
Arno,	PETER cr Am	Art	EVANS tv+
Arno,	SIEGFRIED	Art	FLEMING tv
Arnold	BENNETT w,j Br	Art	GILMORE tv
Arnold	DALY la,pr Am	Art	HINDLE tv+
Arnold	GESELL ps,md,e Am	Art	KASSEL mj,cn Am
Arnold	GUYOT geog,geol Am	Art	LANDRY mj,cn Am
Arnold	HEEREN h,e Ger	Art	LUND tv+
Arnold	HERBER fb hf	Art	LaFLEUR
Arnold	KEPPEL ar Dut	Art	MALIK
Arnold	LUNN(Sir)ski,w	Art	METRANO tv+
Arnold	MOSS	Art	MIX
Arnold	PALMER(Arnie)g Am	Art	MONK fb
Arnold	RUGE w Ger	Art	NEVILLE mr,kbds,s
Arnold	STANG cm,tv+ Am	Art	PEPPER mj,sax Am
Arnold	TOYNBEE h Br	Art	ROONEY fb hf
Arnold	VOSLOO	Art	SANSOM cr Am
Arnold	WESKER w Br	Art	SHELL fb hf
Arnold	ZWEIG w Ger	Art	SMITH
Arnold,	BENEDICT traitor Am	Art	TATUM mj-piano,c Am
Arnold,	EDDY s-cnt,tv+ Am	Art	TAYLOR mj-drm,cn Am
Arnold,	EDWARD	Art	YOUNG cr,ref Am
Arnold,	EDWIN(Sir)po,j	Artaud,	ANTONIN la,pr,po Fr
Arnold,	HARRYmj-reeds,cn	Arte	JOHNSON cm,tv+
Arnold,	HENRY(Hap)ar Am	Artedi,	PETER sc Swe
Arnold,	JACK d	Artemas	WARD ar-re Am
Arnold,	MATTHEW po,ct Br	Artemus	WARD w-humor,ed Am
Arnold,	ROSEANNE(Barr)tv+	Arthur	ALTMAN c Am
Arnold,	SAMUEL organ,c Br	Arthur	ASHE t Am
Arnold,	THOMAS e Br	Arthur	AUWERS astr Ger
Arnold,	TOM tv+	Arthur	BAER(Bugs)j Am
Arnoldson,	KLAS w,st,n-x'08	Arthur	BLISS(Sir)c
Arnon	ZADOK	Arthur	BOWLEY(Sir)ec,e
Arnoul	GREBAN po Fr	Arthur	CASSELL tv
Arnstein,	KARL ds-airships	Arthur	CAYLEY math,e Br
Arnt,	CHARLES	Arthur	CLARKE w-scifi Can
Aron	KINCAID	Arthur	CLOUGH po Br
Aron	NIMZOWITSCH chess Rus	Arthur	COMPTON sc Am
Aron,	RAYMOND ph Fr	Arthur	DAVIES p Am
Aronson,	JUDIE tv+	Arthur	DAY sc Am
Arp,	JEAN(Hans)at,po Fr	Arthur	DIGNAM
Arquette,	LEWIS tv+	Arthur	DOVE p Am
Arquette,	PATRICIA	Arthur	DREWS ph Ger
Arquette,	ROSANNA	Arthur	EVANS(Sir)arc
Arrabal,	FERNANDO w Sp	Arthur	FADDEN(Sir)st Aust
Arrau,	CLAUDIO piano Am	Arthur	FARWELL c,ct Am
Arrest,	HEINRICH d' astr	Arthur	FLEMING(Sir)eng,id
Arrhenius,	SVANTE A.n-c'03	Arthur	FRANZ
Arriaga,	JUAN c Sp	Arthur	FROST illus Am
Arriaga,	MANUEL de st Port	Arthur	GIRY h Fr

Arthur	GODFREY tv+	Arthur,	KAREN d
Arthur	GROSSER tv	Arthur,	ROBERT
Arthur	HAILEY w Can	Arthur,	TIMOTHY w Am
Arthur	HALLAM po,w Br	Artie	MALVIN tv
Arthur	HARDEN(Sir)sc,e	Artie	SHAW mj,cn Am
Arthur	HAYS l Am	Artin,	EMIL math,e Aus
Arthur	HILL tv+	Artur	RODZINSKI cn
Arthur	HILLER d	Arturo	RAWSON ar,Arg
Arthur	HOLMES geol,e Br	Artusi,	GIOVANNI c It
Arthur	JUDSON viol,cn Am	Arunah	ABELL j,pb,ed Am
Arthur	KEITH(Sir)an Scot	Arundhati	ROY w India
Arthur	KENNEDY	Arye	GROSS
Arthur	KOBER w Am	Arzhak,	NICOLAY w Rus
Arthur	KOPIT w Am	Asa	CANDLER id Am
Arthur	KORN sc Ger	Asa	FITCH sc Am
Arthur	LAKE tv+	Asa	GRAY sc Am
Arthur	LEE mr-guit,s Am	Asa	WHITNEY i,id Am
Arthur	LEWIS(Sir)ec,e	Asachi,	GHEORGHE w Rom
Arthur	LITTLE id-pulp Am	Asaph	HALL astron Am
Arthur	LOFT	Asawa,	RUTH su Am
Arthur	LOWE	Asbury,	FRANCIS r Am
Arthur	LUBIN d	Asbury,	HERBERT j,w Am
Arthur	MACHEN w Welsh	Ascari,	ALBERTO racecar It
Arthur	MALET tv+	Asch,	SHOLEM w Pol-Am
Arthur	MEE j,ed,w Br	Ascham,	ROGER e,w Br
Arthur	MEIGHEN st Can	Aschoff,	KARL md,e Ger
Arthur	MILLER w Am	Ascoli,	GRAZIADIO e It
Arthur	MURPHY la,w Ir	Aselli,	GASPARO md It
Arthur	NIELSEN pools Am	Asger	HAMERIK c Dan
Arthur	NIKISCH m,cn Hung	Asger	JORN p Dan
Arthur	NOYES sc,e Am	Ash,	LESLIE
Arthur	PENN d	Ashbee,	CHARLES ac Br
Arthur	PHAYRE st,ar Br	Ashbel	SMITH md,st Am
Arthur	PIGOU ec,e Br	Ashbery,	JOHN p-q'76
Arthur	PINERO(Sir)la,w	Ashbrook,	DANA tv+
Arthur	PORTER tv	Ashbrook,	DAPHNE tv+
Arthur	RACKHAM illus Br	Ashburn,	RICHIE b hf
Arthur	RANKIN	Ashby,	HAL d
Arthur	RANSOME w Br	Ashcroft,	PEGGY(Dame)la+ &
Arthur	RIMBAUD po Fr	Ashcroft,	PEGGY(Dame)o-s'84
Arthur	ROBERTS	Ashe,	ARTHUR t Am
Arthur	SAVAGE id-arms Am	Ashe,	JOHN re,ar Am
Arthur	SHIELDS	Ashenafi,	KEESHA tv
Arthur	SPACE tv+	Asher	BRAUNER
Arthur	SYMONS po,ct Br	Asher	DURAND p,engr Am
Arthur	TALBOT eng,e Am	Asher,	JANE
Arthur	TAPPAN anti-slave	Asher,	PETER s Br
Arthur	TAXIER tv	Ashford,	BAILEY md Am
Arthur	UPFIELD w Aust	Ashford,	DAISY w Br
Arthur	WALEY h-orient Br	Ashford,	MARGARET w Br &
Arthur	WONG tv	Ashford,	MARGARET=Daisy
Arthur	WONTNER	Ashford,	MATTHEW tv
Arthur Conan DOYLE(Sir)w		Ashford,	NICKOLAS s Am
Arthur,	BEATRICE(Bea)tv+	Ashford,	ROSALIND mr,s Am
Arthur,	CHESTER ALAN &	Ashlee	LEVITCH tv
Arthur,	CHESTER 21st Pres.	Ashley	DUKES ct,w Br
Arthur,	GEORGE(Sir)ar,st	Ashley	JOHNSON tv
Arthur,	JEAN tv+	Ashley	JUDD
Arthur,	JOHNNY	Ashley	OLSEN tv
Arthur,	JOSEPH sc,e Am	Ashley	TUTTLE ba Am
Arthur,	JULIA la Am	Ashley,	ELIZABETH tv+

Ashley,	JENNIFER
Ashley,	JOHN tv+
Ashley,	MAURICE h, bio Br
Ashley,	WILLIAM x,furs Am
Ashley,	WILLIAM(Sir)ec,e
Ashman,	HOWARD lyrics Am
Ashmole,	ELIAS h Br
Ashmun,	JEHUDI r,st Am
Ashton,	FREDERICK(Sir)ba
Ashton,	JOHN tv+
Ashton,	WINIFRED w Br
Ashton-Warner,SYLVIA w N.Zea
Ashwell,	LENA la Br
Asia	VIEIRA
Asimov,	ISAAC w,sc,e Am
Askegard,	CHARLES ba Am
Askew,	ANNE r Br
Askew,	LUKE
Asner,	ED(Edward) tv+
Asnyk,	ADAM po,w Pol
Aspar,	FLAVIUS ar Ro
Aspdin,	JOSEPH i Br
Aspin,	LES st Am
Asplund,	ERIK ac Swe
Asquith	ANTHONY d
Assad,	HAFEZ-al st Syria
Assaf	DAYAN
Assante,	ARMAND
Asser,	TOBIAS n-x'11
Assumpta	SERNA tv+
Asta	NIELSEN
Astaire,	ADELE ba Am
Astaire,	FRED ba,tv+
Astbury,	IAN mr,s Br
Astell,	MARY w Br
Asther,	NILS
Astin,	JOHN tv+
Astin,	SEAN
Astle,	THOMAS h Br
Astley	KEY(Sir)navy
Astley,	JACOB(Sir)ar
Astley,	PHILIP horses,ar Br
Astley,	RICK s,ws Br
Aston	BARRETT mr Jamaica
Aston	WEBB(Sir)ac
Aston,	FRANCIS n-c'22
Aston,	JAY mr,s Br
Aston,	JOHN mr,s Br
Astor,	BROOKE j,w Am
Astor,	GERTRUDE
Astor,	JOHN JACOB f, Am
Astor,	MARY o-s'41
Astor,	WILLIAM f,j Br
Astrid	ALLWYN
Astrid	VARNAY s-opera
Astruc,	JEAN md,w Fr
Asturias,	MIGUEL po,n-l'67
Ataturk,	KEMAL st Turk
Atchley,	HOOPER
Ate	De JONG d
Ates,	ROSCOE
Atget,	EUGENE fo Fr
Athena	LORDE tv
Athene	SEYLER
Atherton,	WILLIAM tv+
Athol	FUGARD w,d+ S.Afr
Athole	STEWART
Atkins,	CHET m-cnt,tv+
Atkins,	CHRISTOPHER tv+
Atkins,	DOUG fb hf
Atkins,	EILEEN
Atkins,	TOM tv+
Atkinson,	PAUL mr-guitar Br
Atkinson,	ROWAN
Atkinson,	THOMAS po Am
Atlas	KING
Atlas,	CHARLES phys.cult
Atom	EGOYAN d
Attar,	FARID od-DIN po
Attenborough,RICHARD o-d'82+
Atterbury,	MALCOLM tv+
Attila	JOZSEF po Hung
Attilla	--- Huns King
Attlee,	CLEMENT st Br
Atwater,	EDITH tv+
Atwill,	LIONEL
Atwood,	GEORGE math Br
Atwood,	MARGARET w,po Can
Atwood,	WALLACE geol Am
Aub,	MAX w Sp
Auber,	DANIEL c Fr
Auber,	ESPRIT c Fr
Auberjonois, RENE
Auberon	WAUGH w,j Br
Aubert,	JACQUES viol,c Fr
Aubert,	LENORE
Aubree	MILLER
Aubrey	De VERE po Ir
Aubrey	MATHER
Aubrey	MENEN w Br
Aubrey,	JAMES
Aubrey,	JOHN h,w Br
Auchincloss, LOUIS w Am
Auclair,	MICHEL
Auden,	WYSTAN p-q'48
Audie	MURPHY
Audley,	JAMES(Sir)knight
Audley,	THOMAS st Br
Audra	LINDLEY tv+
Audran,	EDMOND c Fr
Audran,	STEPHANE
Audrey	DALTON
Audrey	HEPBURN
Audrey	LANDERS tv+
Audrey	MEADOWS tv
Audrey	TOTTER tv+
Audrie J. NEENAN tv
Audubon,	JOHN at-birds Am
Auel,	JEAN w Am
Auer,	CARL sc,i Am
Auer,	LEOPOLD viol Hung
Auer,	MISCHA

Auerbach, ERICH e Ger	Auriol, VINCENT st Fr
Auerbach, RED bbc hf	Aurobindo, SRI po,st India
Auermann, NADJA mo Ger	Aurore CLEMENT
Auersperg, ANTON von po Aus	Ausias MARCH po Sp
Auger, CLAUDINE	Austen LAYARD(Sir)sc,w
Augie MEYERS mr-kbds Am	Austen, JANE w Br
Augier, EMILE po,w Fr	Austin CLARK po Irish
August AMBROS c,e Ger	Austin DOBSON po Br
August BEBEL st,w Ger	Austin FLINT Jr md Am
August BELMONT f Am	Austin FLINT Sr md Am
August BOCKH e Ger	Austin O'BRIEN
August DERLETH w,po Am	Austin PALMER handwrite
August EICHLER sc,e Ger	Austin PECK tv
August FICK e Ger	Austin STOKER
August FOLLEN po,st Ger	Austin, ALBERT
August IFFLAND la,d Ger	Austin, ALFRED pol'1896+
August KISS su Ger	Austin, FREDERIC s, c Br
August KOPISCH p,po Ger	Austin, HERBERT id-cars Br
August KROGH sc-md,e Dan	Austin, JOHN l,e,w Br
August KUNDT sc,e Ger	Austin, KAREN tv+
August MACKE p Ger	Austin, MARY w Am
August MOBIUS astro,w Ger	Austin, RAY d
August PAULY ed Ger	Austin, STEPHEN st Am-TX
August POTT e,w Ger	Austin, TERI tv
August SENOA w Croat	Austin, TERRI
August WILSON w Am	Auteuil, DANIEL
August von HOFMANN sc Ger	Auth, TONY p-x'76
August von PLATEN po,w Ger	Autran, JOSEPH po,w Fr
August, BILLIE d	Autry, GENE s,tv+ Am
Augusta DABNEY	Auwers, ARTHUR astr Ger
Augusta HOLMES c Fr	Ava BARBER tv
Auguste COMTE ph Fr	Ava FABIAN
Auguste FOREL ps,sc Swi	Ava GARDNER tv+
Auguste La RIVE sc Swi	Avakian, ARAM d
Auguste MAQUET w Fr	Avalon, FRANKIE m,tv+ Am
Auguste PAVIE st,x Fr	Avalos, FERNANDO ar Sp
Auguste PERRET ac Fr	Avalos, LUIS tv+
Auguste PICOT ar Fr	Avati, PUPI d
Auguste RENOIR p Fr	Avedis, HOWARD(Hikmet)d
Auguste RODIN su Fr	Avedon, RICHARD fo Am
Augustin CAUCHY math,e Fr	Avenel, GEORGES d' ec,h Fr
Augustin DALY w Am	Avenol, JOSEPH st Fr
Augustin FRESNEL sc Fr	Averback, HY d
Augustin PAJOU su Fr	Averill, EARL b hf
Augustin SCRIBE w Fr	Avery BROOKS
Augustine BIRRELL w,st Br	Avery HOPWOOD w Am
Augusto RIGHI sc,e It	Avery, JAMES tv+
Augusto SANDINO re Nica	Avery, MARGARET
Augustus EGG p Br	Avery, MILTON p Am
Augustus PUGIN ac,arc Fr	Avery, OSWALD sc, md Am
Augustus SIEBE i Ger	Avery, PHYLLIS tv
Aukrust, OLAV po Nor	Avery, SAMUEL at,engr Am
Aulard, FRANCOIS h Fr	Avery, TEX cr Am
Auletta, KEN j,w Am	Avery, VAL
Aulus GELLIUS w Ro	Avid SIQUEIROS p Mex
Aumont, JEAN-PIERRE	Avila, ROBERTO(Bobby)b
Aumont, MICHEL	Avildsen, JOHN G. d
Aumont, TINA	Aviles, RICK
Aung San Suu Kyi --- n-x'91	Avison, CHARLES organ,c Br
Aurel JOLIAT ho	Avogadro, AMEDEO sc,e It
Aurel STEIN(Sir)archeol	Avon LONG tv

Avory,	MICK mr-drums Br
Axel	BROSTROM ships Swe
Axel	MUNTHE md,w Swe
Axel	STORDAHL m,cn,tv Am
Axel	THUE math,e Nor
Axelrod,	JULIUS n-m'70
Axl	ROSE mr,s Am
Axman,	HANNE
Axton,	HOYT s,tv+ Am
Ayala,	EUSEBIO st Parag
Ayala,	JUAN de x(SFBay)Sp
Aybak,	IZZ od-BIN st Egypt
Ayckbourn,	ALAN w Br
Aydelotte,	FRANK e Am
Ayer,	A, J.(Sir)ph
Ayer,	ALFRED(Sir) ph,e
Ayer,	FRANCIS ads Am
Aykroyd,	DAN cm,tv+ Am
Aylesworth,	REIKO tv
Ayllon,	LUCAS x Sp
Aylmer,	FELIX
Aylmer,	JOHN r Br
Ayme,	MARCEL w Fr
Ayn	RAND w Am
Ayrer,	JAKOB w Ger
Ayres,	ANNE r Am
Ayres,	LEW tv+
Ayres,	MITCHELL mj,cn,tv
Ayrton,	WILLIAM eng,i Br
Ayscue,	GEORGE(Sir)navy
Ayton,	ROBERT(Sir)po Scot
Aytoun,	WILLIAM po Scot
Azais,	PIERRE ph,w Fr
Azaria,	HANK tv
Aznavour,	CHARLESs,ws+ Fr
Azuela,	MARIANO md,w Mex
Azuma Tokuho --- ba Japan	
Azzara,	CANDICE tv+

"B" NAME DESIGNATION CODES

b	BASEBALL	
ba	BALLET, DANCE,	
	CHOREOGRAPHER	
bat	BASEBALL BATTING CHAMP	
bb	BASKETBALL	
bbc	BASKETBALL COACH, OWNER	
bmg	BASEBALL MANAGER,OWNER	
bbr	BASKETBALL REFEREE	
bu	BASEBALL UMPIRE	
bio	BIOGRAPHER	
bus	BUSINESSMAN	
b-cy	BASEBALL CY YOUNG AWARD	
b-mv	BASEBALL MOST VALUABLE	
	PLAYER	
bb-m	BASKETBALL MOST VALUABLE	
	PLAYER	

"B" NATIONALITY CODES

Belg	-	BELGIAN
Bol	-	BOLIVIAN
Br	-	BRITISH
Braz	-	BRAZILIAN
Bulg	-	BULGARIAN

"B's"

B.	TRAVEN w Ger
B. Reeves EASON d	
B.B.	KING mj-blues Am
B.D.	WONG
B.F.	SKINNER ps,e.w Am
B.G.	NORMAN tv
B.J.	THOMAS s-pop Am
Baade,	WALTER astr Ger
Baader,	FRANZ r,ph,e Ger
Babatunde,	OBBA
Babbit,	HARRY s Am
Babbitt,	ISAAC i Am
Babcock,	BARBARA tv+
Babe	KANE
Babe	PRATT ho
Babe	RUTH b,HR king hf
Babe	SIEBERT ho
Babe Didrikson ZAHARIAS g+	
Babel,	ISAAC w Rus
Babell,	WILLIAM organ,c Br
Babenco,	HECTOR d
Babes,	VICTOR md,sc Rom
Babette	DEUTSCH po,ct Am
Babeuf,	FRANCOIS re,j Fr
Babic,	LJUBOMIR po Yugo
Babilonia,	TAI sk Am
Babineau,	BABS mj-s Can
Babits,	MIHALY w Hung
Babo,	JOSEPH von w Ger
Babson,	THOMAS tv
Baburen,	DIRCK van p Dut
Baby	DODDS mj-drums Am
Bacall,	LAUREN tv+

Baccala,	DONNA tv	Bai(j),	TOMMASO tenor,c It
Baccelli,	GUIDO md,st It	Baif,	JEAN de po Fr
Bach,	BARBARA	Baikie,	WILLIAM sc,md
Bach,	CARL PHIL. c Ger	Bailey	ASHFORD md,ar Am
Bach,	CATHERINE tv+	Bailey	WHITE w Am
Bach,	JOHANN CHRIS.m,c	Bailey	WILLIS geol,e Am
Bach,	JOHANN SEBASTIAN c	Bailey,	BILL tv+
Bach,	JOHN	Bailey,	DAVID tv
Bach,	WILHELM m,c Ger	Bailey,	F. LEE l,tv
Bacharach,	BURT c Am	Bailey,	G.W. tv+
Bache,	ALEXANDER sc,e Am	Bailey,	HENRY w Br
Bachelard,	GASTON ph,w Fr	Bailey,	JACK tv
Bachman,	RANDYmr-guit,s Can	Bailey,	JAMES circus Am
Bachman,	RICHARD w Am	Bailey,	LIBERTY HYDE sc
Bachman,	ROBBIE mr-drm Can	Bailey,	MILDRED s-blues Am
Back,	GEORGE(Sir)x	Bailey,	NATHAN w-dicts Br
Backus,	HENNY tv	Bailey,	PEARL s,tv+ Am
Backus,	ISAAC r Am	Bailey,	PHILIP mr,s Am
Backus,	JIM tv+	Bailey,	RAYMOND tv+
Bacon,	DELIA w Am	Bailey,	SOLON astr Am
Bacon,	FRANCIS ph,w Br	Bailey,	TOM mr-kbds,s Br
Bacon,	HENRY ac Am	Baillie,	GRIZEL(Lady)po Scot
Bacon,	IRVING	Baillie,	JOANNA w,po Scot
Bacon,	KEVIN	Bailly,	JEAN astr,st Fr
Bacon,	LEONARD p-q'41	Baily,	EDWARD su Br
Bacon,	LLOYD d	Bain,	ALEXANDER ph,ps
Bacon,	ROGER sc,ph,w Br	Bain,	BARBARA tv+
Baddeley,	HERMIONE tv+	Bain,	CONRAD tv+
Bade,	JOSSE id,e Belg	Bain,	CYNTHIA
Badel,	ALAN	Bainbridge,	BERYL w Br
Baden-Powell,	ROBERT BSA Br	Baini,	GIUSEPPE c It
Badeni,	KASIMIR st Aus	Bainter,	FAY o-s'38
Badgro,	MORRIS(Red)fb hf	Baio,	JIMMY tv+
Badham,	JOHN d	Baio,	SCOTT tv+
Badin,	STEPHEN r Am	Baird,	BIL pupp Am
Badiyi,	REZA d	Baird,	CORA pupp Am
Badja	DJOLA	Baird,	JOHN i-tv Scot
Badler,	JANE tv+	Bairnsfather,	BRUCE cr,ar Br
Baeck,	LEO r Ger	Bajer,	FREDRIK n-x'08 Dan
Baedeker,	KARL pb Ger	Bajza,	JOZSEF j, po Hung
Baer,	ARTHUR j-spts Am	Bakalayan,	RICHARD
Baer,	ARTHUR=Bugs	Bakalyan,	DICK tv
Baer,	BUDDY boxer+Am	Baker	KAI
Baer,	HARRY	Baker,	ANITA s-r&b Am
Baer,	MAX boxer Am	Baker,	ART tv+
Baer,	PARLEY tv+	Baker,	BLANCHE
Baeyer,	ADOLF von n-c'05	Baker,	BOB
Baez,	JOAN s-folk,ws+ Am	Baker,	CARROLL
Baffin,	WILLIAM x Br	Baker,	CHERYL mr-s Br
Bagdikian,	BEN w Am	Baker,	CHET mj-trump Am
Bagehot,	WALTER ec,ct,j Br	Baker,	DIANE
Baggetta,	VINCENT tv	Baker,	DON tv
Bagley,	WILLIAM e Am	Baker,	DUSTY b, bmg
Bagnold,	ENID w Br	Baker,	DYLAN
Bagot,	CHARLES(Sir)st	Baker,	GEORGE cr Am
Bagration,	PYOTR ar Rus	Baker,	GEORGE e-drama Am
Bagwell,	JEFF b-mv'94	Baker,	GINGER mr-drm Br
Bahar,	MOHAMMAD po Iran	Baker,	HOME RUN b hf
Bahner,	BLAKE	Baker,	JAMES ADDISON st
Bahr,	HERMANN j,w Aus	Baker,	JIM tv
Bahrdt,	CARL r,e Ger	Baker,	JOBY tv

Baker,　　JOE tv
Baker,　　JOE DON tv+
Baker,　　KATHY
Baker,　　KENNY
Baker,　　LENNIE tv
Baker,　　MICKEY s Am
Baker,　　RAY p-b'40
Baker,　　RAY tv+
Baker,　　ROY d
Baker,　　STANLEY
Baker,　　TOM
Baker,　　VIN bb
Baker-Finch, IAN g Br
Bakewell, WILLIAM(Billy)
Bakke,　　BRENDA
Bakker,　　JIM r, tv
Bakker,　　TAMMY FAYE r,tv Am
Bakshi,　　RALPH d,w,animator
Bakst,　　LEON p Rus
Bakula,　　SCOTT
Bal　　　TILAK ed,e,ref Ind
Bal,　　　JEANNE tv
Balaban,　BOB
Balanchine, GEORGE ba Rus-Am
Balard,　　ANTOINE sc,e Fr
Balbi,　　ADRIANO geog It
Balbo,　　CESARE st,w It
Balbo,　　ITALO fly It
Balboa,　　VASCO N.de x Sp
Balbus,　　LUCIUS st Ro
Balch,　　EMILY n-x'46
Balchin,　NIGEL w Br
Balcom,　　WILLIAM c Am
Balcon,　　MICHAEL(Sir)pr
Baldacci, DAVID w Am
Baldavin, BARBARA tv
Balding,　REBECCA tv
Baldwin,　ADAM
Baldwin,　ALEC
Baldwin,　CURTIS tv
Baldwin,　DANIEL
Baldwin,　JAMES w Am
Baldwin,　LOAMMI eng Am
Baldwin,　ROGER ref Am
Baldwin,　STEPHEN tv+
Baldwin,　WILLIAM
Bale,　　CHRISTIAN
Balen,　　HENDRICK van p Belg
Balenda,　CARLA tv
Balfe,　　MICHAEL s,c Ir
Balfour,　MICHAEL tv+
Balgobin, JENNIFER
Balin,　　INA
Balin,　　MARTY mr,s Am
Balint,　　ANDRAS
Balk,　　FAIRUZA
Ball,　　DAVID mr-kbds Br
Ball,　　ERNEST c Am
Ball,　　FRANK
Ball,　　HUGO la,w Ger
Ball,　　LUCILLE cm,tv+ Am

Ball,　　ROGER m-sax Scot
Ball,　　THOMAS su Am
Ball,　　VINCENT
Balla,　　GIACOMO p It
Ballantine, CARL tv+
Ballantine, IAN pb Am
Ballard,　ALIMI tv
Ballard,　HANK s,ws Am
Ballard,　KAYE cm,tv+ Am
Ballesteros, SEVE g Sp
Ballew,　　SMITH mj-s,cn+ Am
Ballin,　　ALBERT ships Ger
Ballou,　　HOSEA r,ed,w Am
Balmer,　　JOHANN math,sc Swi
Balmes,　　JAMIE ph,r,e Sp
Balodis,　JANIS ar,st Lat
Balon,　　JEAN ba Fr
Balsam,　　MARTIN o-s'65 tv+
Balsam,　　TALIA
Balsley,　PHILIP s Am
Balson,　　ALLISON tv
Balta,　　JOSE ar Peru
Baltasar　BRUM l,st Urug
Baltasar　GRACIAN w Sp
Balthazar GETTY
Balthazar VORSTER st S.Afr
Baltimore,DAVID n-m'75
Balue,　　JEAN r,st Fr
Baluze,　　ETEINNE h,e Fr
Balzac,　　HONORE de w Fr
Bambaataa,AFRIKA m-rap Am
Bambi　　LINN tv
Bamman,　GERRY
Ban　　　JOHNSON bmg hf
Banach,　STEFAN math,e Pol
Banas,　　BOB ba, tv
Bancroft, ANNE o-a'62
Bancroft, DAVE b hf
Bancroft, GEORGE
Bancroft, HUBERT h Am
Bancroft, KELLY po Am
Band,　　ALBERT d
Band,　　CHARLES d
Bandeira, MANUEL po,w Braz
Bandel,　ERNST von su Ger
Bandello, MATTEO r,ar,w It
Banderas, ANTONIO
Bando,　　SAL b
Bandula,　MAHA ar Burma
Baner,　　JOHAN ar Swe
Banerjee, CHITRA w India
Banerjee, VICTOR
Banes,　　LISA tv+
Banfield, BEVER-LEIGH tv
Bangert,　JOHNNY tv
Bangs,　　JOHN w-humor,ed Am
Banim,　　JOHN po,w Ir
Bank,　　FRANK tv
Bankes,　JOHN(Sir)l
Bankhead, TALLULAH la,tv+ Am
Bankole,　ISAACH de

Banks,	ERNIE b-mv'58'59 hf	Barbara	JEFFORD
Banks,	ISABELLA w Br	Barbara	KENT
Banks,	JOAN tv	Barbara	LEAMING bio,w Am
Banks,	JONATHAN tv+	Barbara	LEE mr-s Am
Banks,	LESLIE	Barbara	LEIGH
Banks,	RUSSELL w Am	Barbara	LODEN d,tv+
Banks,	TONY mr-kbds Br	Barbara	LUNA
Banks,	TYLER tv	Barbara	MacLEAN tv
Banks,	TYRA mo+ Am	Barbara	McNAIR tv+
Bannen,	IAN	Barbara	MEEK tv
Banner,	JOHN tv+	Barbara	MINKUS tv
Bannister,	REGGIE	Barbara	MOORE tv
Bannister,	ROGER miler Br	Barbara	MURRAY
Bannon,	JACK tv+	Barbara	NICHOLS tv+
Banting,	FREDERICK(Sir)n-m'23	Barbara	O'NEIL
Bantock,	GRANVILLE(Sir)c	Barbara	PARKINS tv+
Banvard,	JOHN p,w Am	Barbara	PAYTON
Banzie,	BRENDA de	Barbara	PEPPER tv+
Baptie,	NORVAL sk Am	Barbara	PERRY tv
Bar,	FRANCOIS de h Fr	Barbara	PYM w Br
Bara,	NINA tv+	Barbara	RHOADES tv+
Bara,	THEDA	Barbara	ROBBINS tv
Baraka,	IMAMU po,w Am	Barbara	RUICK tv+
Baranski,	CHRISTINE tv+	Barbara	RUSH tv+
Barany,	ROBERT n-m'14	Barbara	SHARMA tv
Barasch,	MARC w Am	Barbara	SHELLEY
Barash,	OLIVIA tv+	Barbara	SIGEL tv
Barat,	MADELEINE r Fr	Barbara	STEELE
Barbara	ALSTON s Am	Barbara	STOCK tv+
Barbara	BABCOCK tv+	Barbara	STUART tv
Barbara	BACH	Barbara	SUKOWA
Barbara	BAIN rv+	Barbara	TUCHMAN h Am
Barbara	BARRIE tv+	Barbara	WALTERS tv-j Am
Barbara	BATES tv+	Barbara	WARD ec,w Am
Barbara	BAXLEY	Barbara	WERLE tv
Barbara	BEDFORD	Barbara	WHITING tv
Barbara	BENSON tv	Barbara	WOODS
Barbara	BOSSON tv+	Barbara,	JOSEPH tv
Barbara	BOSTOK tv	Barbari,	JACOPO de p It
Barbara	BOUCHET	Barbata,	JOHN mr-drm Am
Barbara	BOXER st Am	Barbeau,	ADRIENNE tv+
Barbara	BRITTON tv+	Barbee,	VICTOR ba Am
Barbara	BROWN	Barber,	ANDREA tv
Barbara	BRYNE tv	Barber,	AVA tv
Barbara	CARNEY tv	Barber,	DONN ac Am
Barbara	CARRERA mo,tv+ Nica	Barber,	FRANCES
Barbara	CASON tv	Barber,	RED j-sp,tv Am
Barbara	COOK soprano Am	Barber,	SAMUEL p-m'58,'63
Barbara	EDELMAN tv	Barbera,	JOSEPH tv
Barbara	EDEN tv+	Barberini,	URBANO
Barbara	EVEREST	Barbi	BENTON tv+
Barbara	FELDON tv+	Barbie,	KLAUS st Nazi Ger
Barbara	FERRIS tv+	Barbier,	GEORGE
Barbara	GARRICK	Barbieri,	FEDORA mezzo It
Barbara	HALE tv+	Barbon,	PRAISE-GOD r Br
Barbara	HAMBLY w-scifi Am	Barboura	MORRIS
Barbara	HARRIS	Barbusse,	HENRI w,ed Fr
Barbara	HECK r Am	Barclay,	DON
Barbara	HELLER tv	Barclay,	FLORENCE w Br
Barbara	HERSHEY tv+	Barclay,	JOAN
Barbara	HOWARD tv	Barclay,	ROBERT r,w Scot

Barcroft,	ROY	Barnum,	PHINEAS circus Am
Bard,	JOHN md Am	Baroja,	PIO w Sp
Bardeen,	JOHN n-p'56,'72	Baron,	BRUCE
Barden,	ALICE tv	Baron,	JEFFREY tv
Bardette,	TREVOR tv+	Baron,	SANDY
Bardi,	GIOVANNI m,w It	Barone,	ANITA tv
Bardolph,	DANA tv	Barr,	AMELIA w Am
Bardolph,	PAIGE tv	Barr,	ARCHIBALD eng,i Scot
Bardot,	BRIGITTE	Barr,	DOUGLAS tv
Barenboim,	DANIEL cn Ger	Barr,	JULIA tv
Barents,	WILLEM x Dut	Barr,	PATRICK
Barfield,	JESSE b,hr'86	Barr,	RAY tv
Bargeron,	DAVE mr-tromb Am	Barr,	ROSEANNE (Arnold) tv+
Bargy,	ROY piano,cn,tv Am	Barr,	STRINGFELLOW e Am
Bari,	LENNY tv	Barr,	Wm. (Gen.) l,st Am
Bari,	LYNN tv+	Barra,	FRANCISCO st Mex
Baring,	MAURICE w,po Br	Barras,	PAUL re,ar Fr
Barker,	BOB tv-host Am	Barratt,	ROBERT
Barker,	CLIVE w Br	Barrault,	JEAN-LOUIS
Barker,	LEX	Barrault,	MARIE-CHRISTINE
Barker,	RONNIE	Barrere,	PAUL mr-guit Am
Barker.	GEORGE po Br	Barres	MAURICE w,j,st Fr
Barkin,	ELLEN	Barret	OLIVER
Barkla,	CHARLES n-p'17 Br	Barreto,	BRUNO d
Barkley,	ALBEN st-vp Am	Barrett	WENDELL e Am
Barkley,	CHARLES bb-m'93	Barrett,	ALICE tv
Barkly,	HENRY(Sir) st	Barrett,	ASTON mr-bass Jam
Barlach,	ERNST su,po,w Ger	Barrett,	MAJEL tv
Barlick,	AL b hf	Barrett,	MARCIA mr-s Jama
Barlow,	HOWARD cn,tv Am	Barrett,	RAY
Barlow,	JOEL po,st Am	Barrett,	RONA j,tv Am
Barlow,	THOMAS bb hf	Barrett,	SYD mr-guit,s Br
Barnabe	GOOGE po Br	Barri	MURPHY
Barnabe	RICH ar,w Br	Barrie,	BARBARA tv+
Barnack,	OSKAR eng Ger	Barrie,	JAMES(Sir)w Scot
Barnard	BEE ar Am	Barrie,	MONA
Barnard	HUGHES tv+	Barrie,	WENDY tv+
Barnard,	CHRISTIAAN md SAfr	Barrier,	EDGAR
Barnard,	GEORGE su Am	Barrios,	EDUARDO w Chile
Barnes,	ANN tv	Barrios,	JUSTO ar,st Guat
Barnes,	BINNIE	Barris,	CHUCK tv-pr
Barnes,	CHRISTOPHER tv	Barron,	CLARENCE ed,pb Am
Barnes,	DJUNA w,p Am	Barron,	ROBERT
Barnes,	GEORGENE tv	Barron,	ZELDA d
Barnes,	JOANNA tv+	Barros,	JOAO de h,st Port
Barnes,	MARGARET p-f'32	Barrot,	ODILON st Fr
Barnes,	PRISCILLA tv+	Barrow,	EDWARD b hf
Barnes,	WALTER mj,cn Am	Barrow,	ISAAC math, e Br
Barnes,	WILLIAM po Br	Barry	ANDREWS mr-kbds Br
Barnet,	CHARLIE mj-sax,cn	Barry	BONDS b
Barnett	NEWMAN p Am	Barry	BROWN
Barnett,	STEVE d	Barry	BYRNE ac Am
Barnett,	VINCE	Barry	COE tv+
Barney	BIGARD mj-clarin Am	Barry	CORBIN tv+
Barney	KESSEL mj-guit Am	Barry	COWSILL mr-bass,s
Barney	LEM fb hf	Barry	CUTLER tv
Barney	MARTIN tv	Barry	EVANS tv
Barney	RAPP mj,cn Am	Barry	FOSTER
Barney	SEDRAN bb hf	Barry	GIBB mr-guit,s Br
Barney	SUMNER mr-guit,s Br	Barry	GORDON tv+
Barnouw,	ERIK tv	Barry	JENNER tv

Barry	JONES	Bartholomew,	FREDDIE
Barry	KELLEY tv+	Bartlett,	BONNIE tv+
Barry	LARKIN b	Bartlett,	DEBORAH tv
Barry	LAWS tv	Bartlett,	DIANA tv
Barry	MANILOW mj-s Am	Bartlett,	JOHN pb,w Am
Barry	MANN c Am	Bartlett,	ROBIN
Barry	MILLER tv+	Bartok,	BELA piano,c Hung
Barry	MORSE tv+	Bartok,	EVA
Barry	MacKAY t,tv+ Am	Bartold,	NORMAN tv
Barry	NELSON tv+	Bartold,	VASILY an Rus
Barry	NEWMAN tv+	Bartoli,	CECILIA s It
Barry	NOLAN tv	Bartolome	BERMEJO p Sp
Barry	PEARL tv	Bartolome	MITRE ar,st,w Arg
Barry	PRIMUS tv+	Bartolome	MURRILO p
Barry	SANDERS fb	Bartolome	deLasCASAS h,r Sp
Barry	SEARS w Am	Bartolomeu	DIAS x Port
Barry	SOBEL tv+	Bartolommeo,	FRA p It
Barry	ST. LEGER ar Br	Barton	HEYMAN
Barry	TUBB	Barton	MacLANE tv+
Barry	Van DYKE tv	Barton	STONE r Am
Barry	WHITE s-r&b,ws Am	Barton,	BRUCE bio,wst Am
Barry	WILSON mr-drums Br	Barton,	BUZZ
Barry	WOOD mj-s Am	Barton,	CHARLES d
Barry,	DAVE w Am	Barton,	CLARA founds ARC
Barry,	DONALD(Don"Red")tv+	Barton,	DEREK(Sir)n-c'69
Barry,	GENE tv+	Barton,	EILEEN tv
Barry,	IVOR tv	Barton,	ENOS id-G.E. Am
Barry,	J.J. tv	Barton,	JAMES
Barry,	JACK tv	Barton,	PETER tv+
Barry,	MARION st-mayor Am	Barton,	TOD tv
Barry,	PATRICIA	Bartram,	WILLIAM sc,x,w Am
Barry,	PHILIP w Am	Bartsch,	KARL ct,e Ger
Barry,	RAYMOND	Bartsch,	RUDOLF w Aus
Barry,	RICK bb hf	Barty,	BILLY tv+
Barry,	SAM bbc hf	Baruch	SPINOZA ph Dut
Barry,	SPRANGER la Ir	Baruch,	ANDRE tv
Barry,	TONY	Baruch,	BERNARD f,st,w Am
Barrymore,DREW		Barye,	ANTOINE su Fr
Barrymore,ETHEL o-s'44		Baryshnikov,	MIKHAIL ba+ Lat
Barrymore,JOHN		Barzun,	JACQUES e,w Am
Barrymore,JOHN BLYTHE Jr. tv+		Basch,	HARRY tv
Barrymore,LIONEL o-a'31		Basehart,	RICHARD tv+
Barson,	MIKE mr-kbds Br	Basie,	COUNT mj,cn,tv Am
Barstow,	STAN w Br	Basil	BROOKE st Ir
Bart	BURNS tv	Basil	BUNTING po Br
Bart	PATTEN tv	Basil	DEARDON d
Bart	SIMPSON fc	Basil	HOFFMAN tv+
Bart	STARR fb,fbc hf	Basil	RADFORD
Bartel,	PAUL d+	Basil	SPENCE(Sir)ac
Barth	LECK p Dut	Basil	SYDNEY
Barth,	EDDIE tv+	Basil	WALLACE
Barth,	HEINRICH x Ger	Basil,	TONI s+ Am
Barth,	JOHN w Am	Basinger,	KIM o-s'98,tv+
Barth,	KARL r,e Ger	Baskin,	ELYA
Barth,	PAUL e,w Ger	Basquette,LENA	
Barthelme,DONALD w Am		Bass	OTIS p Am
Barthes,	ROLAND ct,w Fr	Bass,	EMORY tv
Barthlemess,	RICHARD	Bass,	JULES d
Barthol,	BRUCE mr-bass Am	Bass,	SAM outlaw Am
Bartholdi,FREDERIC su Fr		Bassani,	GEORGIO po,w It
Bartholomeus v d HELST p Dut		Basserman,ALBERT	

Bassett,	ANGELA
Bassett,	LESLIE p-m'66
Bassi,	UGO r It
Basso,	HAMILTON w Am
Bastedo,	ALEXANDRA
Bat'a	TOMAS id Czech
Bat-Adam,	MICHAL
Bataille,	GEORGES w Fr
Batalov,	ALEXEI d+
Bate,	WALTER p-b'64'78
Bateman,	HESTER id-silver Br
Bateman,	JASON tv+
Bateman,	JUSTINE tv+
Bates,	ALAN
Bates,	BARBARA tv+
Bates,	BLANCHE la Am
Bates,	FLORENCE
Bates,	H.E. w Br
Bates,	JEANNE tv+
Bates,	JIM tv
Bates,	JIMMY tv
Bates,	KATHARINE e,po Am
Bates,	KATHY o-a'90
Bates,	MARSTON sc,e Am
Bates,	PERCY(Sir)ships
Bates,	RALPH
Bateson,	F.W. ct,w Br
Bathgate,	ANDY ho-m'59
Batinkoff,	RANDALL
Battista	FRANCO p It
Battiste,	HAROLD tv
Battisti,	CESARE j It
Battle,	KATHLEEN sopr Am
Battles,	CLIFF fb hf
Baty,	GASTON w,pr Fr
Batz,	JEAN de st Fr
Bauchau,	PATRICK
Baudelaire,	CHARLES po Fr
Baudry,	PAUL p Fr
Bauer,	BELINDA
Bauer,	EVGENII d
Bauer,	HANK b
Bauer,	JAIME LYN tv
Bauer,	LOUIS(Dr.)tv
Bauer,	MICHELLE
Bauer,	STEVEN tv+
Baugh,	SAMMY fb hf
Baum,	L. FRANK j,w Am
Baum,	VICKI w Am
Bauman,	JON(Bowzer)tv
Baume,	ANTOINE sc Fr
Baumer,	GERTRUD w,ref Ger
Baumgartner,	STEVE w+ Am
Baur,	ELIZABETH tv
Baur,	HARRY
Bausch,	JOHN id-optics Am
Bava,	LANBERTO d
Bava,	MARIO d
Bavier,	FRANCIS tv+
Bax,	ERNEST w Br
Baxley,	BARBARA

Baxley,	CRAIG d
Baxter,	ALAN
Baxter,	ANNE o-s'46, tv+
Baxter,	JEFF mr-guit Am &
Baxter,	JEFF = SKUNK
Baxter,	RICHARD w,r Br
Baxter,	WARNER o-a'29
Baxter-Birney,	MEREDITH tv+
Bay,	FRANCIS
Bay,	PETER cn Am
Bayard	RUSTIN civil rts Am
Bayard	TAYLOR w Am
Baye,	NATHALIE
Bayer,	FRIEDRICH id Ger
Bayer,	GARY tv+
Bayes,	NORA la,s Am
Bayeu,	FRANCISCO p Sp
Bayh,	EVAN st Am
Bayle,	PIERRE ph,ct Fr
Baylor,	DON b-mv'79,rbi'79
Baylor,	ELGIN bb hf
Baylor,	HAL tv
Bayly,	ADA ELLEN w Br
Bazan,	ALVARO de navy Sp
Bazille,	JEAN p Fr
Bazin,	HENRI eng Fr
Bazna,	ELYESA spy Albania
Bazzi,	GIOVANNI p It
Bea	ARTHUR tv+
Bea	PONS tv
Beach Boys,	THE mr,tv
Beach,	MICHAEL tv+
Beach,	MOSES j,i Am
Beach,	REX w Am
Beacham,	STEPHANIE tv+
Beacom,	GARY sk Can
Beadle,	ERASTUS pb Am
Beadle,	GEORGE n-m'58
Beaird,	BETTY tv
Beaird,	DAVID d
Beaird,	PAMELA tv
Beaky	--- m-guitar Br
Beal,	GIFFORD p Am
Beal,	JOHN
Beals,	JENNIFER
Beame,	ABE st Am
Bean,	ORSON tv+
Bean,	SEAN
Bear	BRYANT(Paul)fbc Am
Beard,	CHARLES A. h Am
Beard,	DANIEL p,e,BSA Am
Beard,	FRANK mr-drums Am
Beard,	JAMES chef,w-ckbks
Beard,	MATTHEW(Stymie)
Beardsley,	AUBREY illus Br
Bearse,	AMANDA tv+
Beart,	EMMANNUELLE
Beasley,	ALLYCE tv+
Beatie	EDNEY
Beatles,	THE mr,c,g-r'67 Br
Beaton,	CECIL(Sir)fo,ds

Beatrice	ARTHUR(Bea) tv+
Beatrice	COLEN tv
Beatrice	HINKLE ps Am
Beatrice	KAY tv
Beatrice	LILLIE(Bea)
Beatrice	ROMAND
Beatrice	VARLEY tv+
Beatrice	WEBB h,e Br
Beatrix	POTTER w Br
Beattie,	ANN w Am
Beattie,	JAMES po,w Scot
Beattle,	ANN w Am
Beatty,	CLYDE circus Am
Beatty,	NED tv+
Beatty,	ROBERT
Beatty,	WARREN tv+
Beaty,	FRANK tv
Beau	BRIDGES tv+
Beauchamp,	RICHARD tv
Beauchemin,	NEREE po Fr Can
Beaudine,	WILLIAM d
Beaufre,	ANDRE ar Fr
Beaumont & Fletcher ---w's Br	
Beaumont,	ELIE de geol,e Fr
Beaumont,	FRANCIS w Br
Beaumont,	HARRY d
Beaumont,	HUGH tv+
Beauvoir,	SIMONE de w Fr
Beavers,	LOUISE tv+
Bebe	DANIELS
Bebe	KELLY tv
Bebel,	AUGUST st,w Ger
Bechet,	SIDNEY mj sax Am
Beck	--- s,ws Am
Beck,	JACKSON,
Beck,	JEFF mr-guit Br
Beck,	JOHN tv+
Beck,	JULIAN
Beck,	KIMBERLY tv+
Beck,	MICHAEL tv+
Beckel,	GRAHAM
Becker,	BORIS t Ger
Becker,	ERNEST p-n'74
Becker,	GARY n-e'92
Becker,	HAROLD d
Becker,	TONY tv
Becker,	WALTER mr-bass Am
Beckett,	SAMUEL n-l'69
Beckett,	SCOTTY
Beckford,	WILLIAM w Br
Beckley,	JAKE b hf
Beckley,	JERRY guit,s Am
Beckley,	WILLIAM tv
Beckman,	HENRY tv
Beckman,	JOHN bb hf
Beckx,	PIERRE r Belg
Becky	SHARP fc
Becky	THATCHER fc
Becque,	HENRY w Fr
Bedaux,	CHARLES efficiency
Beddoe,	DON

Beddoes,	THOMAS w,po Br
Bede,	THE VENERABLE h Br
Bedel,	MAURICE w Fr
Bedelia,	BONNIE
Bedford,	BARBARA
Bedford,	MARK mr-guitar Br
Bedi,	KABIR
Bedier,	JOSEPH w,e Fr
Bedil,	MIZRA po India
Bednarik,	CHUCK, fb hf
Bednorz,	J. GEORG n-p'87
Bednyi,	DEMYAN po Rus
Bedrich	HROZNY arch,h,e Cz
Bedrich	SMETANA c Czech
Bedrosian,	STEVE b-cy'87
Bee,	BARNARD j,w Am
Beeb	BIRTLES m-guitar Dut
Beebe,	CHARLES sc,x Am
Beebe,	DON fb
Beebe,	FORD d
Beebe,	LUCIUS j,w Am
Beecham,	THOMAS(Sir)cn
Beecher,	HENRY r,pb,w Am
Beecher,	LYMAN r,w Am
Beechey,	WILLIAM(Sir)p
Beefheart,	CAPTAIN mr,s Am
Beene,	GEOFFREY ds Am
Beer,	GEORGE h Am
Beer,	JACQUELINE tv
Beer,	MICHAEL w Ger
Beer,	THOMAS w Am
Beerbohm,	MAX(Sir)cr,w
Beernaert,	AUGUSTE n-x'09
Beers,	CLIFFORD ref Am
Beers,	ETHEL po Am
Beery,	NOAH Jr. tv+
Beery,	NOAH Sr.
Beery,	WALLACE
Beesly,	EDWARD h,e Br
Beeson	CARROLL tv
Beethoven,	LUDWIG van c Ger
Beets,	NICOLAAS r,w,e Dut
Bega,	LESLIE tv
Begas,	KARL p Ger
Begin,	LOUIS r,e Can
Begin,	MENACHEM n-x'78
Begley,	ED Jr. tv+
Begley,	ED Sr.o-s'62,tv+
Behaine,	RENE w Fr
Beham,	HANS p Ger
Behan,	BRENDAN w Irish
Behm,	ERNST geog Ger
Behn,	APHRA(Mrs.)w Br
Behn,	SOSTHENES id Am
Behrens,	PETER ac Ger
Behrens,	SAM tv+
Behring,	EMIL von n-m'01
Behrman,	S(amuel).N. w Am
Beiderbecke,	BIX mj-cornet Am
Beilby,	GEO.(Sir)sc,id Scot
Beilstein,	FRIEDRICH sc,w Ger

Beit,	ALFRED f&f Br		Belladonna,	JOEY mr,s Am
Beith,	JOHN w Br		Bellamy,	DIANA tv
Bejart,	MAURICE ba Fr		Bellamy,	EARL d
Bek,	ANTHONY r Br		Bellamy,	EDWARD w Am
Beke,	CHARLES geog,x Br		Bellamy,	GEORGE mr-guit Br
Bekesy,	GEORG von n-m'61		Bellamy,	MADGE
Bel	KAUFMAN w Am		Bellamy,	RALPH tv+
Bel Geddes,	BARBARA tv+		Bellamy,	TONY mr-guit,s Am
Bel Geddes,	NORMAN ds-furn.Am		Bellamy,	WALT bb hf
Bel,	MATYAS h,j Hung		Bellaver,	HARRY tv
Bela	BARTOK piano,e Hung		Bellay,	JOACHIM du po Fr
Bela	IMREDY st Hung		Belle	STARR outlaw Am
Bela	KUN st,re Hung		Belle,	ALBERT b,rbi'93'5'6
Bela	LUGOSI la+ Am		Beller,	KATHLEEN tv+
Bela	SCHICK md,e Am		Beller,	MARY LINN tv
Bela,	DEJAS mj,cn Rom-Ger		Belli,	CARLOS po Peru
Belafonte,	GINA tv		Belli,	GIUSEPPE po It
Belafonte,	HARRY		Belli,	MELVIN l,tv Am
Belafonte,	HENRY s Am		Belli,	PIERINO ar,l It
Belafonte-Harper,	SHARI s,tv		Bellini,	GENTILE p It
Belasco,	DAVID pr,w Am		Bellini,	GIOVANNI p It
Belasco,	LEON		Bellini,	JACOPO p It
Belford,	CHRISTINE tv+		Bellini,	VINCENZO c It
Belgard,	MADELINE tv		Bello,	ANDRES po Venz
Belin,	EDOUARD eng,i Fr		Belloc,	HILAIRE po,w Br
Belinda	BAUER		Belloc,	MARIE w Br
Belinda	CARLISLE s,w-songs		Bellow,	SAUL n-l'76,p-f'76
Belisario	PORRAS st Panama		Bellows,	GEORGE p,etch Am
Belita	MORENO tv		Bellwood,	PAMELA tv+
Beliveau,	JEAN ho-m'56'64		Belmando,	JEAN-PAUL
Bell,	ALEXANDER GRAHAM i		Belmont,	ALVA fe Am
Bell,	ANDY mr-s Br		Belmont,	AUGUST f Am
Bell,	BERT fb hf		Belmont,	ELEANOR la,f Am
Bell,	BOBBY fb hf		Beloch,	KARL h,e Ger
Bell,	CLIVE ct,w Br		Belon,	PIERRE sc Fr
Bell,	COOL PAPA b hf		Belov,	SERGEL bb hf
Bell,	DARRYL tv		Below,	FRITZ von ar Ger
Bell,	FELICIA tv		Beltran,	ROBERT
Bell,	GEORGE b-mv'87 &		Belushi,	JAMES tv+
Bell,	GEORGE rbi'87		Belushi,	JOHN cm,tv+
Bell,	GERTRUDE x,an,w Br		Belva	LOCKWOOD l Am
Bell,	HANK		Belva	PLAIN w Am
Bell,	HENRY eng,ds Scot		Bely,	ANDREI po,w Rus
Bell,	ISAAC(Sir)sc,id Scot		Belzer,	RICHARD tv+
Bell,	JAMES		Bem,	JOZEF ar Pol
Bell,	JEANNE		Bembo,	PIETRO r,h It
Bell,	JOHN j,w Scot		Bemelmans,	LUDWIG w,p Am
Bell,	JOHN su Br		Bemis,	CLIFF tv
Bell,	LAWRENCE ds-air Am		Bemis,	SAMUEL h,e Am
Bell,	MARSHALL		Bemont,	CHARLES h Fr
Bell,	NANCY tv		Ben	BERNIE mj,cn Am
Bell,	REX		Ben	BLUE tv+
Bell,	RICKY mr,s Am		Ben	BRADLEE w Am
Bell,	ROBERT mr-bass Am		Ben	CROSS
Bell,	RONALD m-sax Am		Ben	GAZZARA tv+
Bell,	TITA tv		Ben	GRAUER tv
Bell,	TOM tv+		Ben	GREET(Sir)la
Bella	ABZUG fe Am		Ben	HAMMER
Bella	KOVACS tv		Ben	HECHT j,w Am
Bella,	GIANO della st It		Ben	HEPNER tenor Can
Bella,	STEFANO della ds,It		Ben	HOGAN g Am

Ben	HUR spts		Benford,	TOMMY mj-drm Am
Ben	JOHNSON tv+		Bengel,	JOHANN r,w Ger
Ben	JONES tv+		Bengt	LIDNER po Swe
Ben	JONSON w,po Br		Bengt	SAMUELSSON md
Ben	KING mr-s Am		Beniamino	GIGLI tenor It
Ben	LESSY tv+		Benicio	Del TORO
Ben	LYON		Benigni,	ROBERTO d+,o-s'99
Ben	MASTERS tv+		Bening,	ANNETTE
Ben	MOREELL navy Am		Benioff,	HUGO sc,e Am
Ben	MURPHY tv+		Benita	HUME tv+
Ben	OGLIVIE b		Benito	JUAREZ re,st Mex
Ben	PIAZZA tv+		Benito	LYNCH w Arg
Ben	POLLACK mj-drm,cn		Benjamin	ALTMAN mer Am
Ben	POWERS tv		Benjamin	BRITTEN c Br
Ben	SAVAGE tv+		Benjamin	CARDOZA l Am
Ben	SHAHN p,fo Am		Benjamin	CAUNT boxer Br
Ben	STILLER		Benjamin	CHURCH md,spy Am
Ben	TURPIN		Benjamin	CLARK(Bob)d
Ben	VEREEN tv+		Benjamin	DUKE id-tobacco Am
Ben	WEBSTER mj-sax Am		Benjamin	GOULD astr Am
Ben Adhem	ABOU fc		Benjamin	LATROBE ac,eng Am
Ben-Gurion,	DAVID st Isr		Benjamin	LUM tv
Ben-Zvi,	ITZHAK st Isr		Benjamin	LUNDY abolition Am
Benacerraf,	BARUJ n-m'80		Benjamin	ORR mr-bass,s Am
Benaderet,	BEA tv		Benjamin	SPOCK md,w Am
Benaert van	ORLEY p Belg		Benjamin	TOMPSON e,po Am
Benard,	MAURICE tv		Benjamin	TUCKER j,anarchy Am
Benatar,	PAT mr,s Am		Benjamin	VAUTIER p,illus Swi
Benavente,	JACINTO n-l'22		Benjamin	WEST p Am
Benben,	BRIAN		Benjamin	WHORF linguist Am
Benbow,	JOHN navy Br		Benjamin,	ARTHUR piano,c Br
Bench,	JOHNNY b-mv'70'2 hf		Benjamin,	ASHER ac Am
Benchley,	PETER w Am		Benjamin,	JULIA tv
Benchley,	ROBERT w-humor+ Am		Benjamin,	PAUL
Benda,	JULIEN ph,w Fr		Benjamin,	RICHARD d+
Bender,	CHIEF b hf		Benjamin,	WALTER ph,ct Ger
Bender,	JOEL d		Benji	GREGORY tv
Bender,	RUSS		Benmont	TENCH mr-kbds Am
Bender,	SUE w Am		Benn,	ERNEST(Sir)pb,w
Benders,	STAN mj-pia,cn Belg		Benn,	WILLIAM st Br
Bendix,	VINCENT id,i Am		Bennent,	HEINZ
Bendix,	WILLIAM tv+		Bennet,	SPENCER d
Bendl,	KAREL c Cz		Bennett	CERF pb,ed,w Am
Benedek,	LASLO d		Bennett,	ARNOLD w,ct Br
Benedetto	CROCE ct,h It		Bennett,	BRIAN mr-drm Br
Benedetto	VARCHI h It		Bennett,	BRUCE
Benedict	ARNOLD ar,traitor		Bennett,	CONSTANCE
Benedict	KIELY w,ct Ir		Bennett,	DONN tv
Benedict	TAYLOR		Bennett,	ESTELLE s Am
Benedict,	BILLY		Bennett,	FLOYD fly Am
Benedict,	DIRK tv+		Bennett,	HYWEL
Benedict,	GREG tv		Bennett,	JAMES j,ed Am
Benedict,	PAUL tv+		Bennett,	JILL
Benedict,	RUTH an, e Am		Bennett,	JOAN tv+
Benegal	RAU(Sir)l,st India		Bennett,	MICHAEL ba,p-d'76
Beneke,	TEX mj,cn Am		Bennett,	MICHELLE tv
Benelli,	SEM w It		Bennett,	PATRICIA s Am
Benes,	EDVARD st Cz		Bennett,	PETER tv
Benet,	STEPHEN V.p-q'29'44		Bennett,	RAY
Benet,	WILLIAM p-q'42		Bennett,	RICHARD la,pr Am
Benfey,	THEODOR e Ger		Bennett,	ROBERT c,cn Am

Bennett,	SUE tv	Berceo,	GONZALO de po Sp
Bennett,	TONY s,tv+,g-r'62	Bercovici,	KONRAD w Am
Bennett,	WM.S.(Sir)piano,c	Bercovici,	LUCA
Bennie	BORGMAN bb hf	Berdis,	BERT tv
Bennie	MOTEN mj,piano,c Am	Berdyayev,	NIKOLAI ph,w Rus
Bennigsen,	LEONTY ar Rus	Berendt,	JOHN w
Benny	CARTER mj-reeds Am	Berenger,	TOM
Benny	DAVIS ws Am	Berenice	ABBOTT fo Am
Benny	GOODMAN mj,cn Am	Berenson,	BERNARD ct-art Am
Benny	HILL cm,tv+ Br	Berenson,	MARISA
Benny	LEONARD boxer Am	Berent,	WACLAW w Pol
Benny	RUBIN tv+	Beresford,	BRUCE d
Benny	STRONG mj-drm,cn Am	Beresford,	JOHN w Br
Benny,	JACK cm,tv+ Am	Berg,	ALBAN c Aus
Benoit	REGENT	Berg,	ELIZABETH w Am
Benoit,	PATRICIA tv	Berg,	GERTRUDE tv
Benoit,	PIERRE c Belg	Berg,	MATRACA s-cnt Am
Benoit,	PIERRE w Fr	Berg,	MAX ac Ger
Benozzo di	LESE p It	Berg,	MOE b
Benrubi,	ABRAHAM tv	Berg,	PATTY g Am
Benso,	CAMILLO st It	Berg,	PAUL n-c'80
Benson	FONG	Berg,	PETER
Benson,	A.C. w Br	Bergbom,	KAARLO w Finn
Benson,	BARBARA tv	Bergen	EVANS tv
Benson,	EDWARD w Br	Bergen,	CANDICE tv+
Benson,	FRANK p Am	Bergen,	EDGAR pupp,tv+
Benson,	FRANK(Sir)la,bio,e	Bergen,	FRANCES tv+
Benson,	GEORGE g-r'76 Am &	Bergen,	NICOLE
Benson,	GEORGE m-guit,s Am	Bergen,	POLLY tv+
Benson,	IRVING tv	Berger,	ERNA sopr Ger
Benson,	LUCILLE	Berger,	HELMUT tv+
Benson,	MARTIN	Berger,	MICHAEL tv
Benson,	RED tv	Berger,	SENTA
Benson,	RENALDO s Am	Berger,	THOMAS w Am
Benson,	ROBBY	Berger,	VICTOR ed,st Am
Benson,	WILLIAM navy Am	Berger,	WILLIAM
Bensten,	LLOYD st Am	Bergere,	LEE tv
Bent,	CHARLES pioneer Am	Bergey,	DAVID sc,e Am
Bent,	JAMES archeol,x Br	Bergh,	HENRY ref Am
Bentham,	JEREMY l,ph Br	Bergin,	PATRICK
Bentley	MITCHUM	Bergius,	FRIEDRICH n-c'31
Bentley,	BEVERLY tv	Bergman,	ALAN tv
Bentley,	E.C. w Br	Bergman,	BO HJALMAR po Swe
Bentley,	JOHN	Bergman,	HENRY
Bentley,	MAX ho-m'46	Bergman,	HJALMAR w Swe
Bentley,	RICHARD r,ct Br	Bergman,	INGMAR d,pr,w Swe
Bentley,	ROY po Am	Bergman,	INGRID o-a'44'56 &
Benton,	BARBI tv+	Bergman,	INGRID o-s'74,tv+
Benton,	LEE tv	Bergman,	MARILYN tv
Benton,	ROBERT o-d'79	Bergman,	PETER tv
Benton,	THOMAS p Am	Bergman,	RICHARD tv
Benvenuto	CELLINI su It	Bergman,	SANDAHL
Benvenuto	TISI p It	Bergman,	TORBERN sc Swe
Benz,	CARL eng,id Ger	Bergmeier,	JANE tv
Beolco,	ANGELO la,w It	Bergner,	ELISABETH
Beradino,	JOHN b,tv	Bergonzi,	CARLO tenor It
Beradino,	LEE	Bergson,	HENRI e,ph,n-l'27
Berain,	JEAN at,ds Fr	Bergstrom,	SUNE n-m'82
Beran,	JOSEF r Cz	Beria,	LAVRENTY st Rus
Beranger,	PIERRE de po Fr	Berigan,	BUNNY mj-trump Am
Beraud,	HENRI w Fr	Bering,	VITUS JON.x Dan

Berke, WILLIAM d	Bernard, TRISTAN w Fr
Berkeley, BUSBY d+	Bernardes, ARTUR st Braz
Berkeley, GEORGE r,ph,w Ir	Bernardi, HERSCHEL tv+
Berkeley, LENNOX(Sir)c	Bernardo BUIL r,x Sp
Berkley, XANDER	Bernardo HOUSSAY ps,e Arg
Berkner, LLOYD sc,eng Am	Bernardo STROZZI p,engr It
Berkoff, STEVEN	Bernat METGE po Sp
Berkowitz,DAVID serial killer	Bernd ZIMMERMANN c Ger
Berlage, HENDRIK ac Dut	Bernds, EDWARD d
Berl, JACQUES ws Fr	Bernhard DUHM r Ger
Berle, ADOLF l,st Am	Bernhard FERNOW forester Am
Berle, MILTON cm,tv+ Am	Bernhard KLEIN c Ger
Berlin, IRVING ws Am	Bernhard VAREN geog Ger
Berlin, ISAIAH(Sir)ph,w	Bernhard WEISS r,e Ger
Berlin, JEANNIE	Bernhard von BULOW st Ger
Berlinda TOLBERT tv	Bernhard, SANDRA
Berliner, EMILE i Am	Bernhardt,CURTIS d
Berlinger,WARREN tv+	Bernhardt,SARAH la Fr
Berlioz, HECTOR c,cn Fr	Berni, FRANCESCO po It
Berman, SHELLEY tv+	Berni, MARA
Bermejo, BARTOLOME p Sp	Bernice STEGERS
BernNadette STANIS tv	Bernie CALVERT mr-bass Br
Bernadette BIRKETT tv	Bernie CASEY
Bernadette La FONT	Bernie GOZIER tv
Bernadette PETERS tv+	Bernie GREEN m,cn,tv Am
Bernadette WITHERS tv	Bernie KOPELL tv+
Bernal, JOHN sc,e Br	Bernie LEADON mr-guit,s Am
Bernanos, GEORGES w Fr	Bernie LOWE tv
Bernard ADDISON mj-guit,cn	Bernie TAUPIN lyrics Br
Bernard BARUCH f,st,w Am	Bernie WHITE
Bernard BLIER	Bernie, BEN mj,cn Am
Bernard DUDLEY tv	Bernini, GIAN su,ac,p It
Bernard De VOTO w,ed Am	Bernini, LORENZO su,ac It
Bernard EDWARDS mr-bass Am	Bernini, PIETRO su It
Bernard FOX tv+	Bernis, FRANCOIS r,st Fr
Bernard FRESSON	Bernsen, CORBIN
Bernard GORCEY	Bernstein,LEONARD c,cn Am
Bernard GUI r Fr	Berr, HENRI h,ph,e Fr
Bernard HEPTON	Berra, YOGI b-mv'51'4'5 hf
Bernard HILL	Berri, CLAUDE d,pr+ Fr
Bernard KATZ(Sir)md	Berridge, ELIZABETH
Bernard LAMY r,e,w Fr	Berry KROEGER
Bernard LEACH id-pottery Br	Berry OAKLEY mr-bass Am
Bernard LEE	Berry, BILL mr-drm Am
Bernard LODER l Dut	Berry, CHU mj-sax Am
Bernard LOVELL(Sir)astr	Berry, CHUCK mr-guit,s,tv
Bernard LYOT astron,i Fr	Berry, EDWARD sc,e Am
Bernard MALAMUD w Am	Berry, FRED tv
Bernard MILES	Berry, GLEN
Bernard O'DOWD po Aust	Berry, HALLE
Bernard RANDS c Am	Berry, JAN s Am
Bernard VORHAUS d	Berry, JOHN d
Bernard WHITE tv	Berry, KEN tv+
Bernard, CRYSTAL tv	Berry, RAYMOND fb hf
Bernard, DOROTHY tv	Berry, RICHARD
Bernard, ED tv+	Berryman, DOROTHEE tv+
Bernard, EMILE p Fr	Berryman, JOHN p-q'65
Bernard, JASON tv	Berryman, MICHAEL
Bernard, JEAN w Fr	Bert BELL fb hf
Bernard, MAURICE tv	Bert BERDIS tv
Bernard, TOMMY tv	Bert CONVY tv+

Bert	FREED		Bestia,	LUCIUS st Ro
Bert	GORDON d		Beswick,	MARTINE
Bert	JONES fb		Beth	GRANT
Bert	LAHR la,cm+ Am		Beth	HENLEY w Am
Bert	LYTELL tv		Beth	HOWLAND tv
Bert	PARKS tv+		Beth	JACOBS tv
Bert	REMSEN tv+		Beth	LORDAN w Am
Bert	ROACH		Beth	MARION
Bert	ROSARIO tv		Beth	RUYAK tv
Bert	SAKMANN md Ger		Bethe,	HANS n-p'67
Bert	TAYLOR(B.L.T.)j Am		Bethel	LESLIE tv
Bert	WHEELER tv+		Bethlen,	GABOR king Hung
Bert,	PAUL md,e,st Fr		Bethlen,	ISTVAN st Hung
Bertha	SKRAM w Nor		Bethune,	IVY tv
Bertha	TEAGUE bbc hf		Bethune,	MARY e Am
Bertha vonSUTTNER w Aus			Bethune,	ZINA tv
Berthe	MORISOT p Fr		Beti,	MONGO w Cameroon
Berthrong,DEIRDRE tv			Betjeman,	JOHN(Sir)po,pol'72
Berti,	DEHL tv+		Betsy	AARON tv
Bertie	FORBES pb Am		Betsy	PALMER tv+
Bertil	OHLIN ec,st Swe		Betsy	ROSS (US Flag)
Bertin,	LOUIS j,pb Fr		Betsy	RUSSELL
Bertin,	ROLAND		Betta	St. JOHN
Bertinelli, VALERIE tv+			Bette	CHAPEL tv
Bertold	HALLER r Swi		Bette	DAVIS tv+
Bertolt	BRECHT w,po Ger		Bette	MIDLER s+ Am
Bertolucci, BERNARDO d			Bettelheim, BRUNO ps,e,w Am	
Berton	CHURCHILL		Bettger,	LYLE tv+
Berton,	PIERRE m,cn Fr		Betti,	ENRICO math,e It
Bertram	GOODHUE ac Am		Betti,	LAURA
Bertram	MILLS circus Br		Betti,	UGO w,po It
Bertrand	BLIER d		Bettina	BRENNA tv+
Bertrand	DAWSON royal md Br		Bettina von ARNIM w Ger	
Bertrand	RUSSELL ph,ref,w Br		Bettis,	JOHN tv
Berwald,	FRANZ c,e Swe		Betts,	DICKEY guit,s Am
Berwick,	BRAD tv		Betty	BEAIRD tv
Berwick,	RAY tv		Betty	BLYTHE
Beryl	GREY ba Br		Betty	BREWER tv
Beryl	MERCER		Betty	BRONSON
Beryl	REID		Betty	BUCKLEY
Beryl	WALLACE		Betty	COMDEN lyrics Am
Berzelius,JONS sc,e,p Swe			Betty	COMPSON
Besant,	ANNIE w Br		Betty	CONNER tv
Besant,	WALTER(Sir)w		Betty	FARIA
Besch,	BIBI		Betty	FIELD
Besnard,	ALBERT p Fr		Betty	FRIEDAN fe Am
Bess	ALDRICH w Am		Betty	FURNESS tv+
Bess	MYERSON tv		Betty	GARDE tv
Bessel,	FRIEDRICH astr Ger		Bet+v	GARRETT tv+
Bessell,	TED tv+		Betty	GRABLE
Bessemer,	HENRY(Sir)id,i		Betty	HARFORD tv
Besser,	JOE tv+		Betty	HUTTON tv+
Besserer, EUGENIE			Betty	KARLAN tv
Bessey,	CHARLES sc,e Am		Betty	LUSTER tv
Bessie	LOVE		Betty	LYNN
Bessie	SMITH s-blues Am		Betty	MACK
Besson,	LUC d		Betty	MILES
Best,	CHARLES md,e Can		Betty	McDOWALL
Best,	JAMES tv+		Betty	McGUIRE tv
Best,	WILLIE tv+		Betty	THOMAS tv+
Bester,	ALFRED w-scifi Am		Betty	WHITE tv

Betty Ann	CARR tv	Biff	MANARD tv+
Betty Lou	KEIM tv	Biff	McGUIRE
Betty Lou	WALTERS tv	Big Al	MUNDY mj,c
Betz,	CARL tv	Big Bill	BROONZY s-blues Am
Betz,	MATTHEW	Big Bill	TILDEN t Am
Betz,	PAULINE t Am	Big Daddy	KANE m-rap,ws Am
Beulah	BONDI	Big Joe	TURNER s-r&b Am
Beulah	QUO	Bigagli,	CLAUDIO
Beust,	FRIEDRICH st Ger	Bigard,	BARNEY mj clarin Am
Beuys,	JOSEPH su Ger	Bigelow,	JOHN w,st Am
Bevan,	ANUERIN(Nye)st Br	Bigelow,	KATHRYN d
Bevan,	BILLY	Biggers,	DAN tv
Bevans,	CLEM	Biggers,	EARL DERR w Am
Beverly	ADAMS	Biggio,	CRAIG b-gg'97
Beverly	ARCHER tv	Biggs,	ROXANN
Beverly	BENTLEY tv	Bikel,	THEODORE
Beverly	CLEARY w Am	Bil	BAIRD pupp Am
Beverly	D'ANGELO	Bil	KEANE cr Am
Beverly	DENNIS tv	Bilbo,	THEODORE st Am
Beverly	FAVERTY tv	Biletnikoff, FRED fb, hf	
Beverly	GARLAND tv+	Bill	BAILEY tv+
Beverly	JOHNSON mo Am	Bill	BERRY mr-drm Am
Beverly	SANDERS tv	Bill	BIXBY d,tv+
Beverly	SILLS sopr Am	Bill	BLASS ds Am
Beverly	TODD tv+	Bill	BOGGS tv
Beverly	TYLER tv	Bill	BRADLEY bb hf
Beverly	YOUNGER tv	Bill	BRANDT fo Br
Beverly,	HELEN	Bill	BROONZY s-blues Am
Beverly,	ROBERT h Am	Bill	BRUFORD mr-drm Br
Bevin,	ERNEST labor,st Br	Bill	BRYSON w Am
Bewick,	THOMAS illus Br	Bill	BURRUD tv
Bexley,	DON tv	Bill	CALVERT tv+
Bey,	TURHAN	Bill	COBBS
Beyer,	ABSALON e,w Nor	Bill	CODY
Beyer,	TROY tv+	Bill	COSBY tv+
Beyers,	CHRISTIAAN st SAfr	Bill	COWLEY ho
Beyle,	MARIE w Fr	Bill	COWSILL mr-guit,s
Beymer,	RICHARD tv+	Bill	CULLEN tv
Beze,	THEODORE de l,po Fr	Bill	DAILY tv+
Bhutto,	ZULFIKAR st Pakis	Bill	DANA tv+
Bialik,	HAYYIM po Jewish	Bill	DICKEY b hf
Bialik,	MAYIM tv	Bill	DUDLEY fb hf
Bianca	DeGARR tv	Bill	DUKE d,tv+
Bianchi,	DANIELA	Bill	EVANS mj-piano Am
Biber,	HEINRICH viol,c Ger	Bill	FANNING tv
Biberman,	ABNER	Bill	FAWCETT
Bibi	BESCH	Bill	FIORE tv
Bibi	OSTERWALD	Bill	FISHER tv
Bichat,	MARIE md,w Fr	Bill	FRANCIS mr-kbds,s
Bichette,	DANTE b rbi'95	Bill	FRASER
Bickford,	CHARLES tv+	Bill	GEORGE fb hf
Biddle,	FRANCIS l,w Am	Bill	GERBER tv
Biddle,	NICHOLAS f Am	Bill	GOODWIN tv+
Biden,	JOSEPH st Am	Bill	GWINN tv
Bidwell,	CHARLES fb hf	Bill	HALEY mj-mr Am
Biehn,	MICHAEL	Bill	HARRIS tv
Biel,	GABRIEL ph,r,e Ger	Bill	HART tv
Bielski,	MARCIN h,po Pol	Bill	HARTY mj-drm Am
Bierce,	AMBROSE w,j Am	Bill	HAYES tv
Bieri,	RAMON tv+	Bill	HENRY tv
Bierstadt,	ALBERT p Am	Bill	HEWITT fb hf

Bill	HOLMAN cr Am	Billie Jean KING t Am	
Bill	HUNTER	Billings, JOSH w-humor Am	
Bill	IRWIN	Billings, WILLIAM c Am	
Bill	KERR	Billingsley, BARBARA tv+	
Bill	KLEM bu hf	Billingsley, JENNIFER	
Bill	LAZARUS tv	Billingsley, KELLY tv	
Bill	LEYDEN tv	Billingsley, PETER tv+	
Bill	LONG m-cnt,cn tv Am	Billingsley, RAY cr Am	
Bill	LUXTON tv	Billingsley, SHERMAN tv	
Bill	MACATEE tv	Billy	BARTY tv+
Bill	MACY tv+	Billy	BEVAN
Bill	MADLOCK b	Billy	BLANKS
Bill	MAHER tv+	Billy	BRAGG s-r&b,punk
Bill	MEDLEY s Am	Billy	CASPAR g Am
Bill	MELTON b	Billy	COHEN tv
Bill	MONROE tv-j Am	Billy	CONN boxer Am
Bill	MOREY tv	Billy	CORGAN mr-guit,s Am
Bill	MOSELEY	Billy	COTTON mj-drm,cn
Bill	MOYERS w,tv-j Am	Billy	CRYSTAL tv+
Bill	MURRAY tv+	Billy	CURRIE mr-kbds Br
Bill	McGOWAN b hf	Billy	DAVIS Jr mr-s Am
Bill	McINTYRE tv	Billy	DRAGO
Bill	McKINNEY	Billy	DeBECK cr Am
Bill	McMAIN m-cnt,tv	Billy	DeWOLFE tv+
Bill	NUNN	Billy	EVANS b
Bill	O'REILLY tv	Billy	FRANEY
Bill	OWEN	Billy	GIBBONS mr-guit,s
Bill	PAXTON	Billy	GILBERT
Bill	PAYNE mr-kbds Am	Billy	GOULD mr-bass Am
Bill	PINKNEY mr-bass Am	Billy	GRAHAM r,tv Am
Bill	PULLMAN	Billy	GRAY tv+
Bill	QUINN tv+	Billy	GUY s-bari Am
Bill	RAISCH tv	Billy	HALOP tv+
Bill	RAYMOND	Billy	HATTON mr-bass Br
Bill	RUSSELL bb	Billy	HERMAN b hf
Bill	SCOTT tv	Billy	HOUSE
Bill	SHADEL tv	Billy	HUFSEY tv+
Bill	SHARMAN bb hf	Billy	IDOL s,ws Br
Bill	SLATER tv	Billy	JACOBY tv+
Bill	SNARY tv	Billy	JAYNE tv
Bill	STERN tv	Billy	JOEL c Am
Bill	TERRY b hf	Billy	JOEL mr Am
Bill	THALL tv	Billy	KRAMER mr-s Br
Bill	THURMAN	Billy	MAY tv
Bill	TRAVERS d+	Billy	MUMY tv+
Bill	VEECK bmg hf	Billy	MUNN mj-piano Br
Bill	VINT	Billy	OCEAN s-folk,mr
Bill	WALKER m-cnt,cn,tv	Billy	POWELL mr-kbds Am
Bill	WALSH fbc hf	Billy	PRESTON
Bill	WALTON bb hf	Billy	ROSE pr Am
Bill	WARD mr-drm Br	Billy	SANDS tv
Bill	WENDELL tv	Billy	SMITH ho
Bill	WHITE b,tv	Billy	SQUIER mr-s Am
Bill	WILLIS fb hf	Billy	SUNDAY r Am
Bill	WITHERS s-pop,guit	Billy	TAYLOR mj,cn Am
Bill	WYMAN mr-bass Br	Billy	VAN tv
Bill,	TONY	Billy	VERA m,cn,tv+ Am
Billie	AUGUST d	Billy	Van ZANDT tv
Billie	BIRD	Billy	WALKER tv
Billie	BURKE la+ Am	Billy	WARLOCK tv+
Billie	HOLIDAY mj,s-blues	Billy	WILDER d

Billy	WIRTH
Billy	ZANE
Billy Green BUSH	
Billy Ray CYRUS s-cnt,pop	
Binchy,	MAEVE w Am
Binet,	ALFRED ps Fr
Bing	CROSBY s,tv+ Am
Bing	RUSSELL
Bing,	DAVE bb hf
Bing,	HERMAN
Bing,	RUDOLF opera-mgr
Binger,	LOUIS x Fr
Bingham,	GEORGE p Am
Bingham,	HIRAM r,x Am
Bink	SHAPIRO tv
Binkis,	KAZYS po Lith
Binkley,	GREG tv
Binkley,	LANE tv
Binnie	BARNES
Binnie	HALE
Binnig,	GERD n-p'86
Binns,	EDWARD tv+
Binoche,	JULIETTE o-s'96
Binyon,	LAWRENCE po,h Br
Bion	--- po Gr
Biondi,	MATT sw,5x o-g'88
Biondo,	FLAVIO h It
Biot,	JEAN math,sc,e Fr
Bipin	PAL j India
Biran,	MARIE st,ph,w Fr
Birch,	PAUL tv+
Birch,	THORA
Bird	PARKER mj-sax,c Am
Bird,	BILLIE
Bird,	LARRY bb-m'84'5'6 &
Bird,	LARRY bbc hf
Bird,	VICKI tv
Birdseye,	CLARENCE i,id Am
Birger	SJOBERG po Swe
Birger,	JARL nobleman Swe
Birgit	NILSSON sopr Swe
Birk,	RAYE tv
Birkett,	BERNADETTE tv
Birkin,	JANE
Birman,	LEN
Birney,	DAVID tv+
Birney,	EARLE po,w Can
Biron,	ERNST st Ger
Birrell,	AUGUSTINE w,st Br
Birrell,	PETE mr-bass Br
Birtles,	BEEB m-guit Dut
Bischof,	WERNER fo Swi
Bishara al- KHURI st Lebanon
Bishop,	ED
Bishop,	ELIZABETH p-q'56
Bishop,	HENRY(Sir)cn,c
Bishop,	J.MICHAEL n-m'89
Bishop,	JENNIFER tv+
Bishop,	JOEY tv+
Bishop,	JOHN tv

Bishop,	JOHN w Am
Bishop,	JULIE tv+
Bishop,	WILLIAM fly Can
Bisley,	STEVE
Bismark,	OTTO st Ger
Bisoglio,	VAL tv
Bissel,	WHIT tv+
Bissell,	RICHARD w Am
Bisset,	JACQUELINE
Bissett,	JOSIE tv+
Bitov,	ANDREI w Rus
Bitzer,	GEORGE cameraman Am
Biviano,	JOSEPH tv
Bixby,	BILL d,tv+
Bixio,	NINO ar,st It
Bizet,	ALEXANDRE c Fr
Bjorkman,	JONAS t Swe
Bjorling,	JUSSI tenor Swe
Bjorn	BORG t Swe
Bjorn	GRANATH
Bjorn	ULVAEUS mr-guit,s
Bjornson,	BJORNSTERNE n-l'03
Bjornsson,	SVEINN st Iceland
Bjornstrand,	GUNNAR
Black,	CILLA s,tv Br
Black,	CLINT s-cnt,ws Am
Black,	GERRY tv
Black,	HUGO l-supr ct,st
Black,	JAMES(Sir)n-m'88
Black,	JET mr-drm Br
Black,	KAREN tv+
Black,	MARIANNE tv
Black,	NOEL d
Black,	SHAWN ba Am
Blackburn,	DOROTHY tv
Blackburn,	PAUL po Am
Blackburn,	THOMAS po,ct Br
Blackett,	PATRICK n-p'48 Br
Blackie	KING
Blackman,	HONOR
Blackman,	JOAN tv+
Blackmer,	SIDNEY
Blackmon,	LARRY m-drm,s Br
Blackmore,	RICHARD w Br
Blackmore,	RITCHIE mr-guit Br
Blackmore,	STEPHANIE tv
Blackmur,	R.P. ct,po Am
Blackstone,	WILLIAM(Sir)l,w
Blackton,	JAMES d,pr Am
Blackton,	JAY tv
Blackwelder,	ELIOT geol,e Am
Blackwell,	ED mj-drm Am
Blackwood,	ALGERNON w Br
Blackwood,	CAROLINE w
Blackwood,	NINA tv
Blacque,	TAUREAN tv+
Bladd,	STEPHEN mr-drm,s Am
Blades,	RUBEN
Blaeu,	WILLEM math Dut
Blaga,	LUCIAN po Rom
Blaich,	HANS w Ger

Blain, GERARD	Bland, JOHN tv
Blaine, JAMES st Am	Blanda, GEORGE fb hf
Blaine, JIMMY s,tv	Blandick, CLARA
Blaine, VIVIAN tv+	Blane, GILBERT(Sir)md Scot
Blair BROWN tv+	Blane, SALLY
Blair MOODY tv	Blankfield, MARK tv+
Blair TEFKIN tv+	Blanks, BILLY
Blair, BONNIE sk-speed Am	Blanton, JIMMY mj,bass Am
Blair, DAVID ba Br	Blasco Ibanez, VICENTE w Sp
Blair, ERIC w Br	Blasis, CARLO ba,e It
Blair, FRANK tv	Blass, BILL ds Am
Blair, JANET mj-s,tv+ Am	Blatch, HARRIOT fe Am
Blair, JOHN l Am	Blazejowski, CAROL bb hf
Blair, JUNE tv	Blease, COLEMAN st Am
Blair, KEVIN tv+	Blech, HANS-CHRISTIAN
Blair, LINDA	Bledsoe, TEMPESTT tv
Blair, PATRICIA tv	Blee, DEBRA
Blais, MARIE w,po Can	Blegen, CARL arc,sc,e Am
Blaisdell,BRAD tv	Bleriot, LOUIS fly Fr
Blaise PASCAL ph,sc,w Fr	Blessed, BRIAN
Blake BAHNER	Blessing, JACK tv
Blake CLARK	Blest Gana, ALBERTO w Chile
Blake EDWARDS d,w Am	Bleuler, EUGEN ps,e Swi
Blake, AMANDA tv+	Bleyer, ARCHIE tv
Blake, EUBIE mj,piano,c Am	Blier, BERNARD
Blake, GEORGE j,w Scot	Blier, BERTRAND d
Blake, JAMES piano,c Am &	Blige, MARY s-pop,soul Am
Blake, JAMES=Eubie	Bligh, WILLIAM navy Br
Blake, JON	Blind Owl WILSON mr-guit,s Am
Blake, JOSH tv	Blish, JAMES w-scifi Am
Blake, JULIA	Bliss CARMAN po Can
Blake, MADGE tv	Bliss PERRY e,ct Am
Blake, NOAH tv	Bliss, ARTHUR(Sir)c
Blake, OLIVER tv	Bliss, TASKER ar Am
Blake, PAMELA	Bloch, ERNEST c Swi-Am
Blake, ROBERT(Bobby)tv+	Bloch, ERNST ph,e Ger
Blake, TOE ho-m'39	Bloch, FELIX n-p'52
Blake, WHITNEY tv	Bloch, KONRAD E. n-m'64
Blake, WILLIAM po,p Br	Bloch, RAY mj,cn,tv Am
Blakelock,RALPH p Am	Block, HAL tv
Blakely, COLIN	Block, HERBERT p-x'42'54'79
Blakely, SUSAN tv+	Block, HUNT tv+
Blakeney, OLIVE tv+	Block, MARTIN tv
Blakeslee,SANDRA w Am	Blocker, DAN tv+
Blakley, ALAN mr-guit Br	Blocker, DIRK tv
Blakley, RONEE	Blodgett, KATHERINE sc Am
Blanc, ERIKA	Bloembergen, NICOLAAS n-p'81
Blanc, LOUIS j,st,w Fr	Bloemen, PIETER van p Belg
Blanc, MEL tv+	Blois, FRANCOIS r,w Belg
Blanc, MICHEL	Blok, ALEKSANDR po Rus
Blanca GUERRA	Blom, FRANS sc Dan
Blanca SANCHEZ	Blomstedt,HERBERT cn
Blanchard,RACHEL tv	Blondel, MAURICE ph Fr
Blanche BAKER	Blondell, GLORIA tv
Blanche BATES la Am	Blondell, JOAN tv+
Blanche BRUCE st Am	Blood McNALLY fb hf
Blanche SWEET	Blood & Guts PATTON ar Am
Blanche YURKA	Blood, ERNEST bbc hf
Blanchot, MAURICE ct,w Fr	Bloom, ANNE tv+
Bland, BOBBY s Am	Bloom, CLAIRE
Bland, JAMES ws Am	Bloom, ERIC mr-guit Am

Bloom,	JEFFREY d	Bob	BRAUN tv
Bloom,	JOHN tv+	Bob	BROWN tv
Bloom,	LINDSAY tv+	Bob	CARROLL tv
Bloom,	SCOTT tv	Bob	CLARK(Benjamin)d
Bloom,	VERNA	Bob	COOK tv
Bloomer,	AMELIA fe Am	Bob	COSTAS tv
Bloomingdale,	BETSY w Am	Bob	COUSY bb,hf
Bloor,	ELLA communist,w	Bob	COWSILL mr-guit,s
Blore,	ERIC	Bob	CRANE tv+
Blossom,	ROBERTS	Bob	CROSBY m,cn,tv Am
Blouet,	PAUL w Fr	Bob	CURTIS tv
Blount,	LISA	Bob	DAVIES b hf
Blount,	MEL fb hf	Bob	DENVER tv+
Blount,	THOMAS h,w Br	Bob	DISHY tv+
Blow,	JOHN organ,c Br	Bob	DIXON tv
Blow,	KURTIS m-rap Am	Bob	DRURY tv
Bloy,	LEON w,at Fr	Bob	DUGGAN tv
Blucher,	VASILY ar Rus	Bob	DYLAN s,ws+
Blue	WEAVER mr-org Welsh	Bob	EBERLE mj,s,tv+Am
Blue,	BEN tv+	Bob	ELLIOTT b
Blue,	MONTY	Bob	ELLIOTT tv+
Blue,	VIDAb-mv'71,b-cy'71	Bob	EMERY tv
Bluechel,	TED Jr mr-drums,s	Bob	EUBANKS tv
Bluhm,	BRANDON tv	Bob	FELLER b hf
Blum,	LEON st Fr	Bob	FORTIER tv
Blum,	MARK	Bob	FOSSE ba,d+ Am
Blumberg,	BARUCH n-m'76	Bob	GAUDIO organ,s Am
Blume,	JUDY w Am	Bob	GIBSON b hf
Blumenfeld,	ALAN	Bob	GOEN tv
Blundell,	GRAEME	Bob	GRIESE fb hf
Blunden,	EDMUND po,ct Br	Bob	GUNTON(Robt.)tv+
Blunstone,	OLIN mr,s Br	Bob	HARCUM tv
Blunt,	ANTHONY h,spy Br	Bob	HARRIS tv
Blunt,	WILFRID po,w,x Br	Bob	HOGAN tv
Bly,	ROBERT po,ed Am	Bob	HOLT tv
Blyden,	LARRY tv	Bob	HOPE cm,tv+ Am
Blye,	MARGARET	Bob	HOSKINS
Blyth,	ANN	Bob	HOWARD pr-tv Am
Blyth,	EDWARD sc,w Br	Bob	KEESHAN tv
Blythe	DANNER tv+	Bob	KNIGHT bbc hf
Blythe,	BETTY	Bob	KORTMAN
Blyton,	ENID w-children	Bob	KURLAND bb hf
Bo	DEREK	Bob	LANG mr-bass Br
Bo	DIDDLEY mj-blu,guit+	Bob	LANIER bb hf
Bo	HOPKINS tv+	Bob	LEMON b hf
Bo	JACKSON fb,b	Bob	LIDO violin,tv Am
Bo	LINKS w Am	Bob	LILLY fb hf
Bo	SABATO	Bob	LURIE bmg
Bo	SVENSON tv+	Bob	MARLEY mr-guit,s
Bo Hjalmar	BERGMAN po Swe	Bob	MATHIAS decath.,tv &
Bo Osten	UNDEN st,e Swe	Bob	MATHIAS o-g'48'52
Boardman,	ERIC tv	Bob	MAY tv
Boardman,	NAN tv	Bob	MAZA
Boas,	FRANZ an,w.e Am	Bob	MERRILL lyrics Am
Boatman,	MICHAEL tv	Bob	MINOS
Bob	ALLEN mj-s,cn Am	Bob	MORTON tv
Bob	BAKER	Bob	MOSLEY mr-bass Am
Bob	BALABAN	Bob	McADOO bb hf
Bob	BANAS ba, tv	Bob	McCLURG tv
Bob	BARKER tv-host Am	Bob	NELSON
Bob	BOGLE mr-guit,bass	Bob	NEWHART tv+

Bob	NOLAN	Bobby	HACKETT mj-corn,cn
Bob	OKAZAKI tv	Bobby	HELMS s
Bob	PECK	Bobby	HULL ho
Bob	PERLOW tv	Bobby	HYATT tv
Bob	PETTIT bb hf	Bobby	JACOBY tv+
Bob	PRINCE tv	Bobby	JONES g Am
Bob	RALSTON pian,org,tv	Bobby	JORDAN
Bob	RANDALL tv	Bobby	KIMBALL mr-s Am
Bob	RANDOM tv	Bobby	LAUHER tv
Bob	ROZARIO tv	Bobby	LAYNE fb hf
Bob	RUSSELL tv	Bobby	LORD tv
Bob	SAGET tv	Bobby	McFERRIN s Am
Bob	SEAGREN tv	Bobby	McGUIRE tv
Bob	SEGER s,ws Am	Bobby	MORROW o-g'56
Bob	SHEPARD tv	Bobby	NELSON
Bob	SHERRY tv	Bobby	ORR hockey
Bob	SHREEVE tv	Bobby	RIGGS t Am
Bob	SIROTT tv	Bobby	RIHA tv
Bob	SLOANE tv	Bobby	ROTH d
Bob	SMITH tv	Bobby	RYDELL tv
Bob	ST. CLAIR fb hf	Bobby	SANDLER tv
Bob	STANTON tv	Bobby	SEALE blk panther
Bob	STEELE tv+	Bobby	SHANTZ b
Bob	STRONG mj-sax,cn Am	Bobby	SHERMAN tv
Bob	SWEENEY tv+	Bobby	TROUP tv
Bob	TERRY	Bobby	UNSER racecar Am
Bob	TODD tv	Bobby	VAN
Bob	TURLEY b	Bobby	VEE s,ws Am
Bob	UECKER b,tv+ Am	Bobby	VINTON tv+
Bob	WARREN tv	Bobby	WANZER bb hf
Bob	WEIR mr-guit Am	Bobby	WATSON
Bob	WELCH b	Bobby	WOMACK s-r&b,gosp
Bob	WIELAND tv	Bobby G	--- mr,s Br
Bob	WILLS mj,cn,s-cnt	Bocage,	MANUEL navy,po Port
Bob	WILSON tv	Boccherini,	LUIGI c It
Bob	ZURKE mj-piano,cn	Bocelli,	ANDREA tenor It
Bobatoon,	STAR-SHEMAH tv	Bochco,	STEVEN pr-tv,w Am
Bobbi	JORDAN tv	Bochner,	HART
Bobbie	BRESEE	Bochner,	LLOYD tv+
Bobbie	ENNIS mj-s Am	Bock,	FEDOR von ar Ger
Bobbie	SMITH mr-s Am	Bock,	JERRY p-d'60
Bobby	AVILA b	Bockh,	AUGUST e,w Ger
Bobby	BELL fb hf	Bocskay,	ISTVAN st Hung
Bobby	BLAKE tv+	Bode,	JOHANN astr Ger
Bobby	BLAND s Am	Bodel,	JEHAN w Fr
Bobby	BREEN s+ Am	Bodenheim,	MAXWELL po,w Am
Bobby	BROWN s-r&b,ba Am	Bodin,	JEAN l,ph,w Fr
Bobby	BURGESS tv	Bodley,	THOMAS (Sir) st,e
Bobby	BYRNE mj-tromb,tv	Bodmer,	JOHANN i,id Swi
Bobby	CLARKE ho	Boe,	JACQUES po Fr
Bobby	COLOMBY mr-drm,s	Boehm,	JOSEPH (Sir) su
Bobby	DARIN s+ Am	Boehm,	KARL-HEINZ
Bobby	DIAMOND tv	Boeing,	WILLIAM id-planes
Bobby	DOERR b hf	Boen,	EARL tv
Bobby	DiCICCO	Boesky,	IVAN investmts Am
Bobby	ELLIOTT mr-drm Br	Boetticher,	BUDD d
Bobby	ELLIS tv	Bogan,	LOUISE po,ct Am
Bobby	FARRELL mr-s W.Ind	Bogarde,	DIRK
Bobby	FITE tv	Bogardus,	JAMES i Am
Bobby	FREEMAN s,ws Am	Bogardus,	STEPHEN tv
Bobby	GRICH b	Bogart,	HUMPHREY o-a'51,tv+

Bogart,	PAUL d		Bonacelli,PAOLO	
Bogdan	HASDEU h Rom		Bonaduce,	DANNY tv+
Bogdanovich,	PETER d		Bonald,	LOUIS ph,st Fr
Bogert,	TIM mr-bass Am		Bonamy	DOBREE ed,w Br
Bogert,	WILLIAM tv		Bonar	LAW st Br
Boggs,	BILL tv		Bonar,	HORATIUS r Scot
Boggs,	GAIL tv		Bonar,	IVAN tv+
Boggs,	WADE b,bat'82'5' &		Bonard,	LOUIS navy Fr
Boggs,	WADE bat'86'7'8		Bonaventura ELZEVIR pb Dut	
Bogle,	BOB mr-guit,bass Am		Bond	GIDEON tv+
Bogosian,	ERIC w+ Am		Bond,	CARRIE ws Am
Bohay,	HEIDI tv		Bond,	CYNTHIA
Bohlau,	HELENE w Ger		Bond,	DEREK
Bohlen,	CHARLES st Am		Bond,	EDWARD w Br
Bohm,	GEORG organ, c Ger		Bond,	FORD tv
Bohm,	KARL cn Aus		Bond,	J. BLASINGAME tv
Bohm,	THEOBALDflute,c Ger		Bond,	JAMES(007) fc
Bohme,	JAKOB mystic,w Ger		Bond,	MICHAEL w Br
Bohmer,	JOHANN h Ger		Bond,	RALEIGH tv
Bohn,	HENRY pb Br		Bond,	RONNIE mr-drm Br
Bohr,	AAGE n-p'75		Bond,	STEVE
Bohr,	HARALD math,e Dan		Bond,	SUDIE tv+
Bohr,	NIELS n-p'22 Dan		Bond,	WARD tv+
Bohringer,RICHARD			Bondarev,	YURY w Rus
Boiardo,	MATTEO po It		Bonde,	GUSTAF st Swe
Boie,	HEINRICH w Ger		Bondi,	BEULAH
Boies	PENROSE st Am		Bonds,	BARRY b-mv'90'2'3
Boileau,	NICOLAS po,ct It		Bonds,	GARY(U.S.)mr,s Am
Boilly,	LOUIS p Fr		Bone,	HENRY p Br
Bois,	CURT		Boner,	ULRICH r,w Swi
Boisset,	YVES d		Bonerz,	PETER tv+
Boitano,	BRIAN sk Am		Bonet,	LISA tv+
Boito,	ARRIGO po,c,w It		Bonet,	NAI
Bojer,	JOHAN w Nor		Bonfils,	FREDERICK pb Am
Bok,	EDWARD ed,p-b'21		Bong,	RICHARD ar,fly Am
Bolam,	JAMES		Bonghi,	RUGGIERO w, st It
Bolan,	MARC mr-guit,s Br		Bonham Carter, HELENA	
Boland,	MARY		Bonheur,	ROSA p Fr
Bolden,	CHAS.(Buddy)mj,c Am		Boni,	ALBERT pb Am
Boldini,	GIOVANNI p It		Bonin,	EDUARD von ar Ger
Boles,	JOHN		Bonita	GRANVILLE
Boleyn,	ANNE wf Henry VIII		Bonnaire,	SANDRINE
Bolger,	RAY ba,s,tv+ Am		Bonnard,	ABEL w Fr
Bolivar,	SIMON st Venz		Bonnard,	PIERRE p Fr
Bolkan,	FLORINDA		Bonnat,	LEON p Fr
Boll,	HEINRICH n-l'72		Bonnefoy,	YVES po,ct Fr
Bolling,	TIFFANY		Bonner,	FRANK tv+
Bolo	YEUNG		Bonner,	ROBERT pb Am
Bologna,	JOSEPH tv+		Bonner,	TONY
Bolognini,MAURO d			Bonner,	YELENA st Rus
Bolt,	ROBERT w Br		Bonnet,	CHARLES ph,sc,w Swi
Bolton,	CHRISTOPHER tv		Bonney,	WILLIAM outlaw Am
Bolton,	GUY R. w Br		Bonnie	BEDELIA
Bolton,	HERBERT h,e Am		Bonnie	BLAIR sk-speed Am
Bolton,	MICHAEL s-pop Am		Bonnie	HELLMAN tv
Bolyai,	FARKAS math,e Hung		Bonnie	HUNT tv+
Bombal,	MARIA w Chile		Bonnie	POINTER s Am
Bombeck,	ERMA tv pr Am		Bonnie	RAITT s Am
Bon	SCOTT mr-s Scot		Bonnie	SCOTT tv
Bon Jovi,	JON s-mr,pop,ws Am		Bonnie	TYLER s Welsh
Bon de	MONCEY ar Fr		Bonnie Lou EWINS tv	

Bono	--- mr,s,ws Ir	Boris	KARLOFF tv+
Bono,	CHASTITY tv	Boris	KURAKIN st Rus
Bono,	SONNY s,st,tv+ Am	Boris	PILNYAK w Rus
Bonomi,	IVANOE st It	Boris	SAGAL d
Bonsall,	BRIAN tv+	Boris	STURMER st Rus
Bonsall,	JOE s-cnt Am	Boris	VIAN w Fr
Bontemps,	ARNA w Am	Boris	VOGAU w Rus
Boog	POWELL b	Boris	YELTSIN st Rus
Booke,	SORRELL tv+	Borla,	JANICE mj-s Am
Booker T.	JONES mr-kbds Am	Borlaug,	NORMAN n-x'70
Boole,	GEORGE math,e Br	Borman,	FRANK as Am
Boom Boom	MANCINI	Born,	DAVID tv
Boomer	ESIASON fb	Born,	IGNAZ von sc Aus
Boomer,	LINWOOD tv	Born,	MAX n-p'54
Boomie	RICHMAN mj-sax Am	Born,	ROSCOE tv+
Boone,	BRENDON tv	Born,	STEVEN tv
Boone,	DANIEL pioneer Am	Borne,	LUDWIG w Ger
Boone,	DEBBY s Am	Borno,	LOUIS st Haiti
Boone,	LESLEY tv	Borodin,	ALEKSANDR c Rus
Boone,	PAT s,tv+ Am	Boros,	JULIUS g Am
Boone,	RANDY tv	Borque,	RAY ho
Boone,	RICHARD tv+	Borrego,	JESSE tv+
Boone,	STEVE mr-bass,s Am	Borron,	ROBERT de po Fr
Boorman,	CHARLEY	Borrow,	GEORGE w Br
Boos,	MARTIN r Ger	Borsche,	DIETER
Booth	SAVAGE tv	Borsos,	PHILLIP d
Booth,	AGNES la Am	Boryers,	LUCY tv
Booth,	CONNIE	Borzage,	FRANK o-d'28+
Booth,	EDWIN la Am	Boscan Almogaver, JUAN po Sp	
Booth,	FELIX(Sir)id	Bosch,	CARL sc,id Ger
Booth,	JAMES	Bosch,	HIERONYMUS p Dut
Booth,	JOHN WILKES la Am	Bosch,	KARL n-c'31
Booth,	JUNIUS BRUTAS la Am	Bosch,	ROBERT eng,id Ger
Booth,	SHIRLEY o-a'52,tv+	Bosco	HOGAN
Booth,	WILLIAM salv.army Br	Bosco,	GIOVANNI r It
Boothe,	POWERS	Bosco,	HENRI w Fr
Boots	MALLORY	Bosco,	PHILLIP
Boots	RANDOLPH m-sax Am	Bose,	JAGADIS(Sir)sc Ind
Bopp,	FRANZ w,e Ger	Bose,	LUCIA
Bora,	KATHARINA von r Ger	Bose,	SUBHAS st India
Borah,	WILLIAM st Am	Bosio,	FRANCOIS su Fr
Borda,	JEAN math,astr Fr	Bosley,	TOM tv+
Borden,	ALICE tv	Boss	CROKER(Richard)st
Borden,	GAIL i-cond milk Am	Boss	TWEED(Wm.) st Am
Borden,	LIZZIE suspect Am	Boss,	LEWIS astr Am
Borden,	LYNN tv+	Bosse,	ABRAHAM p,ac,e Fr
Bordet,	JULES n-m'19 Belg	Bosson,	BARBARA tv+
Borel,	EMILE math,e Fr	Bossy,	MIKE ho
Borg,	BJORN t Swe	Bostic,	EARL mr Am
Borg,	VEDA ANN	Bostock,	BARBARA tv
Borge,	VICTOR cm,tv+ Dan	Bostwick,	BARRY tv+
Borges,	JORGE w,po Arg	Boswell,	JAMES l,bio,w Scot
Borgese,	GIUSEPPE e,ct,w It	Bosworth,	HOBART
Borglum,	GUTZON su Am	Boteler,	WADE
Borgman ,	BENNIE bb hf	Botev,	KHRISTO po Bulg
Borgnine,	ERNEST o-s'55,tv+	Both,	JAN p Dut
Bori,	LUCREZIA sopr It	Botha,	LOUIS st S.Afr
Boring,	EDWIN ps,e Am	Botha,	PIETER WIL.st SAfr
Boris	BECKER t Ger	Bothe,	WALTHER n-p'54
Boris	BUGAEV po,w Rus	Botsford,	SARA
Boris	GODUNOV st-tsar Rus	Botta,	CARLO md,h It

Botticelli,	SANDRO p It	Bowery Boys THE s	
Bottome,	PHYLLIS w Br	Bowes,	MAJOR EDWARD tv
Bottomley,	GORDON po,w Br	Bowie,	DAVID mr, tv+
Bottomley,	JIM b hf	Bowie,	JAMES ar,pioneer Am
Bottoms,	JOSEPH	Bowker,	JUDI
Bottoms,	SAM	Bowker,	RICHARD ed,w Am
Bottoms,	TIMOTHY	Bowles,	CHESTER ec,st Am
Bottum,	RODDY mr-kbds Am	Bowles,	JANE w Am
Botwinick,	AMY tv	Bowles,	PAUL w
Bou-Sliman,	NOELLE tv	Bowles,	PETER
Bouchard,	JOE mr-bass,s Am	Bowley,	ARTHUR(Sir)ec,e
Boucher,	FRANCOIS p Fr	Bowlly,	AL mj-s Br-Am
Boucher,	SHERRY tv	Bowman,	ISAIAH geog,e Am
Bouchet,	BARBARA	Bowman,	LEE tv+
Bouchor,	MAURICE po,w Fr	Bowra,	CECIL(Sir)e,w
Boucicault,	DION la,w Am	Box,	MICK ws Br
Boudin,	EUGENE p Fr	Boxer,	BARBARA st Am
Boudleaux	BRYANT s-cnt Am	Boxleitner,	BRUCE tv+
Boudreau,	LOU b-mv'48 hf	Boy George	--- mr-s Br
Boue,	AMI geol,w Aus	Boyce,	WILLIAM organ,c Br
Boughton,	RUTLAND c Br	Boyd	GAINES tv+
Bouise,	JEAN	Boyd	MATSON tv
Boulanger,	NADIA e-music Fr	Boyd	RAEBURN mj,cn Am
Boule,	MARCELLIN sc,e Fr	Boyd Orr,	JOHN sc,n-x'49
Boulez,	PIERRE c Fr	Boyd,	GUY tv+
Boult,	ADRIAN(Sir)cn	Boyd,	JAMES w Am
Bouquet,	CAROL	Boyd,	JIMMY tv
Bouquet,	MICHEL	Boyd,	LINN st Am
Bourgeois,	LEON n-x'20	Boyd,	MARTIN BECKETTw Swi
Bourget,	PAUL po,w,ct Fr	Boyd,	STEPHEN
Bourjaily,	VANCE w Am	Boyd,	WILLIAM tv+
Bourke,	RICHARD(Sir)ar	Boyden,	SETH i,id Am
Bourke-White,	MARGARET fo Am	Boye,	KARIN po Swe
Bourne,	HAL mj,cn,tv Am	Boyen,	HERMANN von ar Ger
Bourne,	RANDOLPH ct,w Am	Boyer,	CHARLES tv+
Bournonville,	AUGUST ba Dan	Boyer,	CLETE b
Boursault,	EDME w Fr	Boyer,	KEN b-mv'64
Bourvil	---	Boyer,	MIRIAM
Bousono,	CARLOS po Sp	Boyer,	PAUL sc,e,n-c'97
Bousova,	SVELTANA ba Lith-Br	Boyer,	SULLY
Boutens,	PIETER po Dut	Boyett,	WILLIAM tv
Bouton,	JIM b	Boylan,	JOHN tv
Bouton,	NOEL ar Fr	Boyle,	KAY w,po Am
Bouts,	DIRCK p Dut	Boyle,	LARA FLYNN
Boutsikaris,	DENNIS tv+	Boyle,	PETER tv+
Bovasso,	JULIE	Boyle,	ROBERT sc Br
Boveri,	THEODOR sc,e Ger	Boys,	CHARLES(Sir)sc,i
Bovet,	DANIELE n-m'57	Boz	BURRELL mr-bass Br
Bow,	CLARA	Boz	SCAGGS mr-guit,s Am
Bowe,	RIDDICK boxer Am	Braak,	MENNO ter ct Dut
Bowell,	MACKENZIE(Sir)stCan	Braaten,	OSKAR w Nor
Bowen,	ELIZABETH w Ir	Bracco,	LORRAINE
Bowen,	IRA astr Am	Bracco,	ROBERTO w It
Bowen,	MICHAEL	Bracken,	EDDIE tv+
Bowen,	NORMAN sc,e Am	Brackenridge,	HUGH w,po Am
Bowen,	ROGER tv+	Brad	BERWICK tv
Bowens	MALICK tv+	Brad	DAVIS tv+
Bower,	FREDERICK sc,e Br	Brad	DELP guit,s Am
Bower,	TOM tv+	Brad	DEXTER
Bowering,	GEORGE po,w Can	Brad	DOURIF
Bowers,	CLAUDE j,h Am	Brad	HALL tv+

Brad	HARRIS	Bramante,	DONATO ac It
Brad	JOHNSON tv+	Bramlett,	BONNIE s Am
Brad	LOGAN tv	Bramlett,	3DELANY guit,s Am
Brad	MAULE tv	Bramley,	RAYMOND tv
Brad	MOSSEN tv	Bramwell	FLETCHER
Brad	MOXLEY mj-piano Can	Brana,	FRANCISCO(Frank)
Brad	PITT	Branagh,	KENNETH
Brad	RENFRO	Brancato,	LILLO
Brad	RIJN	Branch	RICKEY bbm hf
Brad	SAVAGE tv	Brand,	HENNIG sc Ger
Brad	ZUTAUT	Brand,	NEVILLE tv+
Bradbrook,MURIEL e,ct,w Br		Brand,	QUINTIN(Sir)fly
Bradbury, MALCOLM w,ct Br		Brandauer,KLAUS MARIA	
Bradbury, RAY w-scifi Am		Brande,	WILLIAM sc,w Br
Bradbury, ROBERT NORTH d		Brandeis,	LOUIS l,w Am
Braddock, JAMES boxer Am		Brandes,	GEORG ct Dan
Braddock, MICKEY tv		Brandham,	JoALLEN w Am
Bradford DILLMAN tv+		Brandis	KEMP tv+
Bradford, ANDREW pb Am		Brandis,	JONATHAN
Bradford, KRISTA tv		Brando,	JOCELYN
Bradford, LANE		Brando,	MARLON o-a'54,tv+
Bradford, RICHARD		Brandon	BLUHM tv
Bradford, ROARK w Am		Brandon	CALL tv+
Bradford, WILLIAM id Am		Brandon	CRANE tv
Bradlee,	BEN w Am	Brandon	CRUZ tv
Bradley	FISKE navy,i Am	Brandon	De WILDE tv
Bradley	TOMLIN p Am	Brandon	DOUGLAS tv
Bradley,	ANDREW(A.C.)e,ct	Brandon	HURST
Bradley,	BILL bb, hf	Brandon	LEE
Bradley,	DAVID	Brandon	MAGGART tv+
Bradley,	ED tv	Brandon,	CLARK tv+
Bradley,	F.H. ph,w Br	Brandon,	HENRY
Bradley,	JESSE mj,tv Am	Brandon,	MICHAEL
Bradley,	OMAR ar Am	Brands,	X. tv
Bradley,	TRUMAN tv	Brandt,	BILL fo Br
Bradshaw, TERRY fb hf, tv		Brandt,	CAROLYN
Bradstreet, ANNE po Am		Brandt,	HANK tv
Brady,	ALICE o-s'37	Brandt,	WILLY n-x'71
Brady,	JAMES(Diam.Jim)f Am	Brandy,	J.C. tv
Brady,	MATHEW fo(Linc,)Am	Branicki,	KSAWERY ar Pol
Brady,	PAT s,tv+ Am	Branly,	EDOUARD sc,i Fr
Brady,	SCOTT tv+	Branner,	HANS CHRISTIAN w
Braeden,	ERIC tv+	Brannon,	FRED d
Braga,	SONIA	Brant,	JOSEPH chief Am Ind
Braga,	TEOFILO w,e Port	Brant,	SEBASTIAN po Ger
Bragg,	BILLY s-r&b,punk Br	Branting,	KARL n-x'21
Bragg,	BRAXTON ar Am	Brantley,	BETSY
Bragg,	MELVYN w Br	Braque,	GEORGES p Fr
Bragg,	WM.H.(Sir)n-p'15	Brasch,	CHARLES po,ed N.Zea
Bragg,	WM.L.(Sir)n-p'15	Brasfield,AUNT SAP tv	
Brahe,	PER ar,st Swe	Brasfield,ROD tv	
Brahe,	TYCHO astr Dan	Brasfield,UNCLE CYP tv	
Brahm,	JOHN d	Brasseur,	CLAUDE
Brahm,	OTTO ct,d Ger	Brasseur,	PIERRE
Braid,	JAMES g Br	Brathwaite, EDWARD w Barba	
Braid,	LES mr-bass Br	Brathwaite, RICHARD po Br	
Braille,	LOUIS e-blind Fr	Brattain,	WALTER n-p'56
Braine,	JOHN w Br	Bratton,	CREED mr-guit Am
Bram	MARTIN mj,cn Br	Braudel,	FERNAND h Fr
Bram	STOKER w Ir	Braugher,	ANDRE tv+
Bramah,	JOSEPH eng,i Br	Braulio	CARRILLO st CostaR

Braun,	BOB tv	Brent	STAIT
Braun,	EVA Hitler's wf	Brent,	EVELYN
Braun,	KARL n-p'09	Brent,	GEORGE
Braun,	LILLIAN JACKSON w	Brent,	ROMNEY
Braun,	LILY fe,w Ger	Brent,	TIMOTHY
Braun,	OTTO st Ger	Brentano,	CLEMENS po Ger
Braun,	WEHRNER von rockts	Brentano,	LUJO ec,w,e Ger
Brauner,	ASHER	Brenz,	JOHANNES ref Ger
Braunn,	ERIK mr-guit,s Am	Breon,	EDMUND
Brautigan,	RICHARD w,po Am	Bresdin,	RODOLPHE etch Fr
Braverman,	BART tv+	Bresee,	BOBBIE
Bravo,	DANNY tv	Breslin,	PAT tv
Braxton	BRAGG ar Ar	Bresnahan,	ROGER b hf
Braxton,	TONI s-r&b Am	Bressart,	FELIX
Bray,	ROBERT tv	Bresson,	ROBERT d,w Fr
Bray,	THOM tv	Brest,	MARTIN d
Brazen,	RANDI tv	Brestoff,	RICHARD tv
Brazza,	PIERRE x Fr	Bret	HARTE w Am
Brazzi,	ROSSANO tv+	Bretherton,	HOWARD d
Breathed,	BERKE cr,p-x'87	Breton,	ANDRE po,w,ct Fr
Breaute,	FALKES de ar Br	Brett	BUTLER cm,tv Am
Brecht,	BERTOLT po,w Ger	Brett	CULLEN
Breck,	PETER tv+	Brett	HALSEY tv+
Breckinridge,	JOHN st-vp Am	Brett	HAVRE fb
Breen,	BOBBY s+ Am	Brett	HULL ho
Breen,	PATRICK tv+	Brett	SOMERS tv
Bregman,	BUDDY m,cn,tv-host	Brett,	GEORGE b-mv'80 &
Brehm,	ALFRED sc Ger	Brett,	GEORGE bat'80'90 hf
Brel	JACQUES	Brett,	JEREMY tv+
Bremer,	FREDRIKA w Swe	Brett,	KEN b
Bremer,	LUCILLE	Brett,	REGINALD st Br
Bremner,	SCOTT tv	Breuer,	MARCEL ac,e Am
Brenda	BAKKE	Breugel,Breughel see Brueghel	
Brenda	BRUCE	Breuil,	HENRI arc,e Fr
Brenda	DOUMANI tv	Brew,	KWESI po Ghana
Brenda	FRICKER	Brewer,	BETTY tv
Brenda	LEE mr,s Am	Brewer,	DAVID l Am
Brenda	SCOTT tv+	Brewer,	DONALD mr-drm Am
Brenda	VACCARO	Brewer,	TERESA s,tv Am
Brenda de BANZIE		Brewster,	DIANE tv
Brendan	BEHAN w Ir	Brewster,	WILLIAM pilgrim Am
Brendan	FRASER	Brewton,	MAIA tv+
Brendan	GILL j,w Am	Brezhnev,	LEONID ILYICH st
Brendel,	EL	Brialy,	JEAN-CLAUDE
Brendon	BOONE tv	Brian	AHERNE
Brendon	DILLON tv	Brian	ALDISS w Br
Brenna,	BETTINA tv	Brian	BENBEN
Brennan,	CHRISTOPHER po	Brian	BENNETT mr-drm Br
Brennan,	EILEEN tv+	Brian	BLESSED
Brennan,	JOSEPH bb hf	Brian	BOITANO sk Am
Brennan,	WALTER o-s'36'38 &	Brian	BONSALL tv+
Brennan,	WALTER o-s'40,tv+	Brian	COLE mr-bass,s Am
Brenneman,	AMY tv	Brian	COUSINS
Brenner,	DAVID cm,tv-host Am	Brian	COX
Brenner,	DORI tv+	Brian	DEACON
Brenno	TORI tv	Brian	DENNEHY
Brent	BRISCOE tv	Brian	DONLEVY tv+
Brent	HUFF	Brian	DOWNEY mr-drm Ir
Brent	JASMER tv	Brian	DOYLE-MURRAY tv+
Brent	MASON m-cnt,guit Am	Brian	ENO mr-synth,pr Br
Brent	SPINER tv+	Brian	FONG tv

Brian	FORSTER tv	Bright,	PATRICIA cm,tv Am
Brian	GIBSON d	Bright,	RICHARD
Brian	GLOVER	Bright,	SUSIE w Am
Brian	GRANT tv	Brigid	BROPHY ct,w Br-Ir
Brian	GREEN tv+	Brigid	WALSH tv
Brian	HOLLAND c Am	Brigitte	BARDOT
Brian	KEENAN mr-drm Am	Brigitte	FOSSEY
Brian	KEITH tv+	Brigitte	MIRA
Brian	KELLY tv+	Brigitte	NIELSEN
Brian	KERWIN tv+	Brigitta	VALBERG
Brian	KRAUSE	Bril(l),	PAUL(us)p Belg
Brian	LANDO tv	Brill,	CHARLIE cm,tv+ Am
Brian	MAY mr-guit Br	Brill,	MARTY tv
Brian	MOORE w Can	Brimley,	WILFORD tv+
Brian	McNAMARA tv+	Brin,	DAVID w-scifi Am
Brian	NASH mr-guit,tv Br	Brinckerhoff, BURT d	
Brian	O'HARA mr-guit,s Br	Brind,	BRIONY ba Br
Brian	O'NOLAN w Ir	Brinegar,	PAUL tv+
Brian	ORSER sk Can	Brinke	STEVENS
Brian	POOLE mr-s Br	Brinkley,	CHRISTIE mo Am
Brian	SABEAN bmg	Brinkley,	DAVID tv-j Am
Brian	SMIAR tv	Brinkley,	RITCH tv
Brian	TOCHI tv+	Brinon,	FERNAND de j,st Fr
Brian	TRAVERS mr-sax Br	Brion,	JAMES
Brian	WILSON mr-bass,s Am	Brion,	LUIS navy Colom
Brian	WIMMER tv+	Briony	BRIND ba Br
Brian de	PALMA d	Briot,	NICOLAS engr Fr
Brian,	DAVID tv+	Briquette,PETE mr-bass,s Ir	
Brian,	HAVERGAL c Br	Briscoe,	BRENT tv
Brian,	MARY	Brisebois,DANIELLE tv+	
Briand,	ARISTIDE n-x'26	Brissette,TIFFANY tv	
Brianne	LEARY tv	Brit	HELFER
Briant,	SHANE	Brites de ALMEIDA heroinePort	
Brice,	FANNY s+ Am	Britt	EKLAND
Brice,	PIERRE	Britt	HUME tv
Brickell,	BETH tv+	Britt	LEACH
Brickell,	EDIE s,ws Am	Britt	LOMOND tv
Bridel,	PHILIPPE r,w Swi	Britt	NICHOLS
Bridge,	ALAN	Britt	WOOD
Bridge,	FRANK c,cn Br	Britt,	ELTON s-cnt Am
Bridge,	LOIS tv	Brittain,	VERA w Br
Bridges,	BEAU tv+	Brittany	CRAVEN tv
Bridges,	JEFF	Brittany	MURPHY tv
Bridges,	LLOYD tv+	Brittany	MORGAN tv+
Bridges,	ROBERT pol'13	Britten,	BENJAMIN c Br
Bridges,	STYLES st Am	Britton,	BARBARA tv+
Bridges,	TODD tv+	Britton,	CHRIS mr-guit Br
Bridget	FONDA	Britton,	PAMELA tv+
Bridget	GLESS tv	Britton,	TONY
Bridget	HALL mo Am	Broad,	C.D.(Charlie)ph,w
Bridget	HANLEY tv	Broadbent,JIM	
Bridget	MICHELE tv	Broca,	PAUL md,an Fr
Bridgman,	PERCY n-p'46	Broch,	HERMANN w Aus
Brier,	ROYCE p-r'34	Brock	PETERS
Briers,	RICHARD	Brock,	LOU b hf, tv
Brieux,	EUGENE w Fr	Brock,	STAN tv+
Brigati,	EDDIE mr-drm,s Am	Brock,	THOMAS(Sir)su
Briggs,	BUNNY mj-s Am	Brocksmith, ROY	
Briggs,	CLARE cr Am	Brod,	MAX w,bio Aus
Briggs,	DAVID m-guit Am	Broderick,HELEN	
Brigham	YOUNG r Am	Broderick,JAMES	

Broderick,	MATTHEW		Brooks,	FOSTER tv+
Broderick,	RICHARD po Am		Brooks,	GARTH s-cnt,ws
Brodie	GREER tv		Brooks,	GERALDINE tv+
Brodie,	JEAN fc		Brooks,	GWENDOLYN p-q'50
Brodie,	JOHN fb-m'70+		Brooks,	JAMES o-d'83
Brodie,	STEVE tv+		Brooks,	JASON tv
Brodsky,	JOSEPHpo,ct,n-l'87		Brooks,	JEAN
Broekman,	DAVID tv		Brooks,	JOE tv
Brogan,	DENIS(Sir)e		Brooks,	JOEL tv+
Brogan,	ROD tv		Brooks,	KIX s-cnt Am
Brogger,	WALDEMAR geol Nor		Brooks,	LALA s Am
Broglie,	LOUIS de n-p'29		Brooks,	LESLIE
Brokaw,	TOM tv-j,anchor+		Brooks,	LOUISE
Brokenshire, NORMAN tv			Brooks,	MARTIN tv
Brolin,	JAMES tv+		Brooks,	MATTHEW tv
Brolin,	JOSH tv+		Brooks,	MEL d,tv+
Brombeck,	ERMA j Am		Brooks,	NED tv
Bromberg,	J. EDWARD		Brooks,	PETER tv
Brome,	RICHARD w Br		Brooks,	PHYLLIS
Bromfield, JOHN tv+			Brooks,	RAND
Bromfield, LOUIS p-f'27			Brooks,	RANDI
Bromfield, VALRI			Brooks,	RAY
Bromley,	SHEILA tv+		Brooks,	RICHARD d,tv+
Bron,	ELEANOR		Brooks,	ROXANNE tv
Bronck,	JONAS pioneer Dan		Brooks,	STEPHEN tv
Bronk,	DETLEV md,e Am		Brooks,	VAN WYCK p-h'37
Bronn,	HEINRICH sc,w Ger		Broom,	ROBERT sc S.Afr
Bronowski, JACOB sc,po,w Br			Broome,	WILLIAM po Br
Bronson	ALCOTT e,w Am		Broonzy,	BILL(Big)s-blues
Bronson	PINCHOT tv+		Brophy,	BRIGID ct,w Br-Ir
Bronson,	BETTY		Brophy,	EDWARD
Bronson,	CHARLES tv+		Brophy,	KEVIN tv+
Bronson,	LILLIAN tv+		Brophy,	SALLIE tv
Bronson,	PO w Am		Brosio,	MANLIO st It
Bronte,	ANNE w Br		Brosnan,	PIERCE tv+
Bronte,	CHARLOTTE w Br		Brosse,	SALOMON de ac Fr
Bronte,	EMILY w Br		Brostrom,	AXEL ships Swe
Brook,	CLAUDIO		Brothers,	JOYCE(Dr.)ps,tv+
Brook,	CLIVE		Broughton, RHODA w Br
Brooke	ADAMS		Broun,	HEYWOOD j,w Am
Brooke	ASTOR j,w Am		Brouthers, DAN b hf
Brooke	BUNDY		Broux,	LEE de tv
Brooke	SHIELDS		Brower,	OTTO d
Brooke	THEISS tv		Brown,	ALICE w Am
Brooke,	BASIL st Ir		Brown,	BARBARA
Brooke,	FRANCES w Can		Brown,	BARRY
Brooke,	HILLARY tv+		Brown,	BLAIR tv+
Brooke,	RUPERT po Br		Brown,	BOB tv
Brooke,	SANDY		Brown,	BOBBY s-r&b,ba Am
Brooke,	WALTER tv		Brown,	BRYAN
Brooker,	GARY mr-kbds,s Br		Brown,	CHARLES B.w,ed Am
Brookes,	JACQUELINE tv+		Brown,	CHARLES D.
Brookes,	NORMAN(Sir)t Aust		Brown,	CHARLES F.w-humor
Brookner,	ANITA w Br		Brown,	CHARNELE tv
Brooks	ADAMS h Am		Brown,	CHELSEA tv
Brooks	WEST tv		Brown,	CHRISTOPHER tv
Brooks,	ALBERT cm,ws,tv+		Brown,	CLANCY
Brooks,	ALFRED geol Am		Brown,	CLARENCE d
Brooks,	AVERY		Brown,	CLAUDE w Am
Brooks,	CLAUDE tv		Brown,	CRUM sc,e Scot
Brooks,	CLEANTH e,ct,w Am		Brown,	DAVID mr-bass Am

Brown,	DORIS tv	Brown,	WALLY tv+
Brown,	EARL s,cn,tv Am	Brown,	WAYNE cn
Brown,	ERIC tv+	Brown,	WILLIAM w,po Am
Brown,	ERROL mr-s Jamaica	Brown,	WILLIE fb hf
Brown,	EVANGELINE w Am	Brown,	WOODY tv+
Brown,	FORD MADOX p Br	Browne	CORAL
Brown,	GARRETT tv	Browne,	DIK cr Am
Brown,	GEORG tv+	Browne,	HABLOT illus Br
Brown,	GEORGE mr-drm Am	Browne,	ISAAC po Br
Brown,	GEORGIA	Browne,	JACKSON mr,s,ws Am
Brown,	HAROLD mr-drm Am	Browne,	LUCILLE
Brown,	HELEN GURLEY w,j,ed	Browne,	ROBERT tv
Brown,	HENRY su Am	Browne,	ROSCOE LEE tv+
Brown,	HERBERT n-c'79	Browne,	THOMAS(Sir)md,w
Brown,	IAN mr-s Br	Brownell,	WILLIAM j,ct Am
Brown,	JAMES mj-blues Am	Browning,	ELIZ. BARRETT po Br
Brown,	JAMES mr+ Am	Browning,	ROBERT po Br
Brown,	JAMES tv	Browning,	SUSAN tv
Brown,	JIM ED tv	Browning,	TOD d
Brown,	JIMfb-m'58'63'5 hf+	Browns	THE s Am
Brown,	JIMMY mr-drm Br	Broz,	JOSIP--TITO st Yugo
Brown,	JOE E.(Evan) cm.tv+	Brubaker,	ROBERT tv
Brown,	JOHN st-abolit.Am	Brubeck,	DAVE mj-piano,c Am
Brown,	JOHN tv	Bruce	ABBOTT
Brown,	JOHN MASON tv	Bruce	BARON
Brown,	JOHNNY MACK	Bruce	BARTHOL mr-bass Am
Brown,	JOHNNY tv	Bruce	BENNETT
Brown,	JULIE	Bruce	CABOT
Brown,	LARRY fb-m'72	Bruce	CATTON w,ed Am
Brown,	LEROY s	Bruce	COLIN tv+
Brown,	LES Jr. tv	Bruce	COWLING
Brown,	LES mj,cn,tv	Bruce	DAVISON tv+
Brown,	LISA tv	Bruce	DERN tv+
Brown,	MICHAEL S.n-m'85	Bruce	DRAKE bbc hf
Brown,	MICHAEL mr-kbds Am	Bruce	EDWARDS
Brown,	MORDECAI b hf &	Bruce	FOOTE tv
Brown,	MORDECAI 3 fingered	Bruce	FOXTON mr-guit Br
Brown,	NACIO c Am	Bruce	GARY mr-drm Am
Brown,	OLIVIA tv	Bruce	GLOVER tv+
Brown,	PAMELA	Bruce	GORDON tv
Brown,	PAUL fbc hf	Bruce	HALL mr-bass Am
Brown,	PETER tv+	Bruce	HORNSBY mr-kbds,s
Brown,	PHIL	Bruce	JENNER sp+ Am
Brown,	PHILIP tv+	Bruce	KIMBALL tv
Brown,	RALPH	Bruce	KIRBY tv+
Brown,	RAY mj-bass Am	Bruce	LEE tv+
Brown,	REB	Bruce	LESTER
Brown,	RITA MAE w Am	Bruce	LI
Brown,	RITZA	Bruce	MAHLER tv+
Brown,	ROBERT tv+	Bruce	MacVITTIE tv
Brown,	ROOSEVELT fb hf	Bruce	McGILL tv+
Brown,	ROSELLEN w Am	Bruce	McLAREN carrace NZ
Brown,	RUTH tv	Bruce	PAYNE
Brown,	SANDRA ba Am	Bruce	PENHALL tv+
Brown,	SANDRA w Am	Bruce	ROGERS ds-books,pb
Brown,	TED tv	Bruce	SMITH fb
Brown,	THOMAS tv	Bruce	SOLOMON tv
Brown,	TIMOTHY tv+	Bruce	SPENCE
Brown,	TINA ed Am	Bruce	SUTTER b
Brown,	TOM tv+	Bruce	THOMAS tv
Brown,	VANESSA tv+	Bruce	WAGNER tv

Bruce	WATSON mr-guit Can	Bruns,	MONA tv
Bruce	WEITZ tv+	Bruns,	PHIL tv
Bruce	WELCH mr-guit Br	Bruns,	PHILIP
Bruce	WILLIS tv+	Brush,	CHARLES i,id Am
Bruce	YARNELL tv	Brush,	GEORGE p Am
Bruce,	BLANCHE st Am	Bruskotter, ERIC tv
Bruce,	BRENDA	Bruson,	RENATO bari Braz
Bruce,	CAROL tv	Brutus,	DENNIS po S.Afr
Bruce,	DAVID tv+	Brutus,	MARCUS JUNIUS st Ro
Bruce,	DAVID(Sir) md	Bry,	ELLEN tv
Bruce,	ED tv	Bryan	ADAMS s,ws Am
Bruce,	EVEREND geol Can	Bryan	BROWN
Bruce,	JACK mr-bass,s Scot	Bryan	DATTILO tv
Bruce,	LENNY cm+ Am	Bryan	DONKIN eng,i BrAm
Bruce,	MICHAEL po,e Scot	Bryan	FERRY s,ws Br
Bruce,	NIGEL	Bryan	FORBES d+
Bruce,	ROBERT king Scot	Bryan	GENESSE tv+
Bruce,	VIRGINIA	Bryan	MacLEAN mr-guit,s
Bruce,	WM. SPIERS x Scot	Bryan	O'DELL tv
Bruch,	MAX c Ger	Bryan	PROCTER po Br
Bruck,	KARL von st Aus	Bryan	RENFRO tv
Brucke,	ERNST md,e Ger	Bryan,	DAVID mr,pop-kbds
Brucker,	JANE tv	Bryan,	DORA
Bruckner,	ANTON organ,c Aus	Bryan,	JANE
Bruegel,	JAN p Belg	Bryan,	WILLIAM JENNINGS st
Bruegel,	PIETER p Belg	Bryan,	ZACHERY tv
Bruegel,	PIETER(Younger)p	Bryant	GUMBEL tv-news,spts
Brueghal,	see BRUEGEL	Bryant,	ANITA s,tv Am
Brueys,	DAVID de w Fr	Bryant,	BOUDLEAUX s-cnt Am
Bruford,	BILL mr-drm Br	Bryant,	KOBE bb
Bruggen,	JOCHEM van w SAfr	Bryant,	LEE tv
Brugnon,	JACQUES(Toto)t Fr	Bryant,	MARDI tv
Bruhanski,ALEX tv	Bryant,	MEL tv
Bruhl,	HEINRICH von st	Bryant,	NANA tv+
Bruhn,	ERIK ba Dan	Bryant,	PAUL(Bear)fbc Am
Bruiser	KINARD fb hf	Bryant,	WILLIAM tv+
Brule,	ETIENNE x Fr	Bryant,	WM.CULLEN ct,po,ed
Brulier,	NIGEL de	Bryar,	CLAUDIA tv
Brum,	BALTASAR l,st Urug	Bryce,	EDWARD tv
Brumel,	ANTOINE c Fr	Bryce,	JAMES l,h,st Br
Brummell,	GEORGE(Beau)dandyBr	Bryn	TERFEL bari Welsh
Brun,	RUDOLF st Swi	Bryne,	BARBARA tv
Brundage,	AVERY bus,sp Am	Brynn	THAYER
Brune,	GUILLAUME ar Fr	Brynner,	YUL o-a'56,tv+
Brunel,	MARC(Sir)eng,i	Byron	DENNIS mr-drm Welsh
Brunelleschi, FILIPPO ac It	Bryson,	BILL w Am
Brunet,	JEAN po Fr	Bryson,	LYMAN tv
Brunetto LATINI w It	Bryson,	PEABO s-pop Am
Bruni,	ANTOINE x Fr	Bryton	McCLURE tv
Bruning,	HEINRICH st Ger	Bryusov,	VALERY po,w Rus
Brunner,	EDDIE mj,cn Swi	Brzezicki,MARK m-drm Br
Brunner,	EMIL e,w Swi	Buade,	LOUIS ar Fr
Bruno	BARRETO d	Bubba	SMITH fb+
Bruno	CREMER	Bubber	MILEY mj-trump Am
Bruno	GANZ	Buber,	MARTIN ph,w Isr
Bruno	KIRBY	Bubka,	SERGEI o-g'88
Bruno	REY	Bucer,	MARTIN r Ger
Bruno	ROSSI sc Am	Buch,	LEOPOLD von geol
Bruno	VeSOTA	Buchan,	JOHN(Sir) w Scot
Bruno	WALTER cn Am	Buchanan, BUCK fb hf
Bruno	ZAMIN	Buchanan, EDGAR

Buchanan, EDNA w Am	Buddy HOLLY mr Am
Buchanan, IAN tv+	Buddy JOHNSON mj,r&b,cn
Buchanan, JAMES 15th pres	Buddy KNOX s-cnt,rk Am
Buchanan, JAMES M. n-e'86	Buddy LESTER tv+
Buchanan, JOHN tv	Buddy MERRILL m-guit,tv
Buchanan, LARRY d	Buddy MORENO mj-guit,s
Buchanan, PAUL s Scot	Buddy O'CONNOR ho
Bucher, WALTER geol Am	Buddy RICH mj,drm,cn Am
Buchholz, HORST	Buddy RYAN fb
Buchner, EDUARD n-c'07	Buddy WEED tv
Buchner, GEORG w Ger	Buddy WELCOME mj-sax Am
Buchwald, ART j,w,tv Am	Buddy WISE mj-sax Am
Buck CLAYTON mj-trump Am	Bude, GUILLAUME w,e Fr
Buck EWING b	Budes, JEAN ar Fr
Buck HENRY tv+	Budge, DON t Am
Buck JONES	Budge, WALLIS(Sir)arc
Buck LEONARD b hf	Buelah QUO
Buck OWENS s-cnt,tv	Buell, ABEL id,i Am
Buck TAYLOR tv+	Buell, MARJORIE cr Am
Buck TRENT tv	Buenaventura ARIBAU ec,w Sp
Buck, FRANK hunter Am	Buenaventura BAEZ st Domin
Buck, PEARL n-l'38,p-f'32	Bueno, MARIA t Am
Buck, PETER mr-guit Am	Bufano, VINCENT tv
Buckingham, LINDSEY mr-guit,s	Buff COBB tv
Buckley, BETTY	Buff ESTES mj-sax Am
Buckley, WILLIAM w,ed Am	Buffalo JONES hunter Am
Buckman, PHIL tv	Buffalo Bill CODY
Buckman, TARA tv	Buffalo Bill Jr. ---
Buckminster FULLER eng,i Am	Buffano, JULES mj,piano,tv
Buckner, SUSAN tv	Buffer, MICHAEL tv
Bucksey, COLIN d	Buffett, JIMMY s,ws+ Am
Bucky DENT b	Buffon, GEORGES de sc,w Fr
Bucky HARRIS b hf	Buford, ELEANOR w Br
Bucky WALTERS b	Buga, KAZIMIERAS linguist
Bud ABBOTT cm+ Am	Bugaev, BORIS po,w Rus
Bud CHASE tv	Bugden, SUE tv
Bud COLLYER tv	Bugge, SOPHUS w,e Nor
Bud CORT	Bugs BAER(Arthur)j-spts
Bud FISHER cr Am	Buhl, VILHELM st Dan
Bud FOSTER bb hf	Buhner, JAY b,gg'96
Bud GEARY	Buick, DAVID id-cars Am
Bud HARRIS(Percy)tv	Buil, BERNARDO r Sp
Bud ISAAC m-cnt Am	Buisson, FERDINAND n-x'27
Bud OSBORNE	Bujold, GENEVIEVE
Bud PALMER tv	Bukeley, MORGAN b hf
Bud POWELL mj cn Am	Buktenica,RAYMOND
Bud SELIG bmg commiss	Bulat OKUDZHAVA po,w Rus
Bud SPENCER	Bulfinch, CHARLES ac Am
Bud YORKIN d	Bulgakov, MIKHAIL A. w Rus
Budd BUSTER	Bulgakov, SERGEY ec,e Rus
Budd SCHULBERG w Am	Bulifant, JOYCE tv
Budd, WILLIAM md Br	Bull, JOHN organ,c Br
Buddy BAER boxer Am	Bull, OLAF JACOB po Nor
Buddy BREGMAN m,cn,tv-hst	Bull, OLE B.viol Nor
Buddy De FRANCO mj-clari	Bull, PETER
Buddy De SYLVA lyrics Am	Bull, RICHARD tv+
Buddy EBSEN tv+	Bullard, EDWARD(Sir)sc
Buddy FOSTER tv	Bullaty, SONJA fo Am
Buddy GRECO s,piano,tv Am	Bulldog TURNER fb hf
Buddy GUY m-blues guit Am	Bulle OGIER
Buddy HACKETT cm,tv+	Buller, REDVERS(Sir)ar

Bullett,   GERALD w Br
Bullfinch, HOMAS e,w Am
Bullins,   ED w,po Am
Bullitt,   WILLIAM st,w Am
Bullock,   JM J. tv
Bullock,   SANDRA tv+
Bullock,   TREVOR tv
Bulnes,   MANUEL ar,st Chile
Bulos,   YUSEF tv
Bulot,   CHUCK tv
Bulow,   BERNHARD von st
Bulow,   HANS von piano,cn
Buloz,   FRANCOIS j,ed Fr
Bulwer-Lytton EDWARD w Br
Bumet,   F.MacFARL(Sir)&
Bumet,   F.MacFARL n-m'60
Bun   CARLOS mr-drm Am
Bunche,   RALPH J. n-x'50
Bundy,   BROOKE
Bunin,   HOPE pupp tv
Bunin,   IVAN po,n-l'33
Bunin,   MOREY pupp tv
Bunk   JOHNSON mj-cornet
Bunker,   CLIVE mr-drm Br
Bunker,   ELLSWORTH st,id Am
Bunnag,   CHUANG st Siam
Bunnell,   DEWEY guit,s Br
Bunner,   HENRY w,ed Am
Bunny   BERIGAN mj-trump Am
Bunny   BRIGGS mj-s Am
Bunny   WAILER mr-drm,s
Bunsen,   ROBERT W. sc Ger
Bunshaft,   GORDON ac Am
Bunting,   BASIL po Br
Buntline,   NED w Am
Buntrock,   BOBBY tv
Bunuel,   LUIS d Sp
Bunyan,   JOHN r,w Br
Buono,   CARA
Buono,   VICTOR
Bupp,   SONNY
Burbage,   JAMES la Br
Burbage,   RICHARD la Br
Burch,   YVONNE tv
Burchfield, CHARLES p Am
Burchill,   CHARLIE mr-guit
Burckhardt, JAKOB h Swi
Burdon,   ERIC s-pop Br
Burger,   WARREN l Am
Burgess   MEREDITH tv+
Burgess,   ANTHONY w Br
Burgess,   BOBBY tv
Burgess,   GELETT illus,w Am
Burgess,   HUGH i Am
Burgess,   THORNTON w Am
Burgh,   HUBERT de st Br
Burghoff,   GARY tv+
Burgi,   JOOST math Swi
Burgos,   JOSE r,st Phil
Burgoyne,   JOHN ar,w Br
Burkard   WALDIS po,w,r Ger

Burkat   SHUDi id-harpsi Br
Burke   BYRNES tv
Burke,   ALFRED
Burke,   BILLIE la+ Am
Burke,   CHRISTOPHER tv
Burke,   DELTA tv+
Burke,   EDMUND st,w Br
Burke,   JAMES
Burke,   JAMES LEE w Am
Burke,   JOHNNY lyrics Am
Burke,   KENNETH ph,w Am
Burke,   PAUL tv+
Burke,   ROBERT
Burke,   SOLOMON s-cnt,r&b
Burke,   THOMAS w Br
Burkett,   JESSE b hf
Burkley,   DENNIS tv+
Burl   IVES m+ Am
Burleigh   GRIMES b hf
Burlinson, TOM
Burmester, LEO tv+
Burne   HOGARTH cr Am
Burne-Jones, EDWARD(Sir)p
Burnel,   JEAN mr-bass Br
Burnet,   MACFARLANE(Sir)md,e
Burnett,   CAROL cm,tv+
Burnett,   DON tv
Burnett,   FRANCES w Am
Burnett,   RAMONA tv
Burnett,   WHIT j,ed Am
Burnette,   OLIVIA tv
Burnette,   SMILEY tv+
Burney,   FANNY w Br
Burns,   BART tv
Burns,   DAVID tv
Burns,   EDWARD
Burns,   GEORGE cm,o-s'75 &
Burns,   GEORGE tv+
Burns,   JACK tv
Burns,   JERE tv+
Burns,   MARILYN
Burns,   MARK
Burns,   MICHAEL tv+
Burns,   ROBERT
Burns,   ROBERT po Scot
Burns,   RONNIE tv
Burns,   STEPHAN tv
Burns,   TOMMY boxer Can
Burns,   WM. JOHN detective
Burnside,   AMBROSE ar Am
Burpee,   WASH. ATLEE seeds
Burr   McINTOSH
Burr   TILLSTROM tv
Burr,   AARON st 2nd vp
Burr,   ANN tv
Burr,   RAYMOND tv+
Burrell,   BOZ mr-Bass Br
Burrell,   MARYEDITH tv
Burritt,   ELIHU pacifist Am
Burroughs, EDGAR RICE w Am
Burroughs, JACKIE

Burroughs,	JEFF b-mv'74	Bushell,	ANTHONY
Burroughs,	JOHN sc,w,po Am	Bushman,	FRANCIS X. la+ Am
Burroughs,	WILLIAM S. w Am	Bushy,	RONALD mr-drm Am
Burroughs,	WILLIAM i Am	Busia,	AKOSUA
Burrows,	ABE p-d'62	Busoni,	FERRUCCIO m,c It
Burrows,	DARREN E. tv	Bussy,	ANTOINE sc,e Fr
Burrud,	BILL tv	Bustani,	BUTRUS al- w Arab
Burrus,	SEXTUS ar Ro	Buster	CRABBE sw+ Am
Bursky,	ALAN tv	Buster	DOUGLAS boxer Am
Burstyn,	ELLEN o-a'74,tv+	Buster	KEATON d+
Burt	KENNEDY d	Buster,	BUDD
Burt	KWOUK	Butades,	SICYON su Gr
Burt	MUSTIN tv	Butch	JENKINS
Burt	WARD tv+	Butch	PATRICK tv
Burt	WILDER sc,e Am	Butenandt,	ADOLF n-c'39
Burt	YOUNG	Butkus,	DICK fb-d'67'70 &
Burt,	CYRIL(Sir)ps,e	Butkus,	DICK hf, tv+
Burt,	HEINZ mr-bass Ger	Butler,	BRETT cm,tv Am
Burt,	STRUTHERS w Am	Butler,	DAVID d+
Burt,	WILLIAM i Am	Butler,	DAWS tv
Burton	GILLIAM tv	Butler,	DEAN tv+
Burton	GILLIS mj-sax Br	Butler,	ELLIS w-humor Am
Burton	LANE c Am	Butler,	GEEZER mr-bass Br
Burton	RICHTER sc Am	Butler,	JERRY s Am
Burton	WHEELER st Am	Butler,	JOE mr-drm,s Am
Burton,	HAROLD l,st Am	Butler,	JOHNNY tv
Burton,	LAURIE tv	Butler,	LOIS tv+
Burton,	LeVAR tv+	Butler,	MARTHA ba Am
Burton,	NORMAN tv+	Butler,	NICHOLAS n-x'31
Burton,	RICHARD	Butler,	PAUL tv+
Burton,	RICHARD F.(Sir)x,w	Butler,	RICHARD mr-s,ws Br
Burton,	ROBERT	Butler,	ROBERT d
Burton,	ROBERT r,w Br	Butler,	ROBERT p-f'93
Burton,	SHELLEY tv	Butler,	ROBERT p-n'76
Burton,	SKIP tv	Butler,	SAMUEL po(d 1680)Br
Burton,	STEVE tv	Butler,	SAMUEL w(d 1902)Br
Burton,	TIM d	Butler,	SMEDLEY ar Am
Burton,	TONY	Butler,	TOM
Burton,	VIRGINIA w Am	Butler,	TONY mr-bass Br
Burton,	WENDELL tv+	Butor,	MICHEL w Fr
Burton,	WILLIAM sc,id Am	Butrick,	MERRITT tv+
Buruma,	IAN w	Butrus al- BUSTANI w Arab	
Bury,	JOHN h Br	Butt,	CLARA ELLEN(Dame)s
Busby,	RICHARD r,e Br	Butt,	ISAAC l,st Ir
Buscaglia,	LEO w Am	Butterfield, BILLY mj,cn Am	
Buscemi,	STEVE	Butterfield, HERB tv	
Busch,	ADOLPHUS id-beer,f	Butterfly McQUEEN tv+	
Busch,	MAE	Butterick, EBENEZER i-pattern	
Busch,	WILHELM po Ger	Butterworth, CHARLES	
Busey,	GARY	Butterworth, SHANE tv	
Busfield,	TIMOTHY tv+	Button,	DICK sk,o-g'48'52
Bush,	BILLY GREEN	Buttons,	RED cm,o-s'57,tv+
Bush,	GEORGE HERBERT &	Buttram,	PAT tv+
Bush,	GEORGE H.41st Pres	Butts,	K.C. tv
Bush,	GRAND	Butz,	EARL st Am
Bush,	JAMES	Bux,	KUDA tv
Bush,	KATE s,ws Br	Buxtehude, DIETRICH m,c Dan	
Bush,	OWEN tv	Buxton,	THOMAS(Sir)f,id Br
Bush,	TOMMY tv	Buys,	PAULUS st Dut
Bush,	VANNEVAR eng Am	Buysse,	CYRIEL sc,e Dut
Bush-Brown, HENRY su Am		Buz	SAWYER fc

Buzatti,	DINO j,w It			
Buzz	ALDRIN Jr as Am			
Buzz	BARTON			
Buzz	COOPER tv			
Buzz	KULIK d			
Buzzi,	RUTH cm,tv+			
Buzzy	HENRY			
Byas,	DON mj-sax Am			
Byatt,	A.S. w Br			
Byington,	SPRING tv+			
Bykov,	VASILY w Rus			
Byner,	JOHN cm,tv+ Am			
Byng,	JULIAN ar Br			
Byrd,	DAVID tv			
Byrd,	DICK tv			
Byrd,	RALPH tv+			
Byrd,	RICHARD x Am			
Byrd,	TOM tv			
Byrd,	WILLIAM organ,c Br			
Byrne,	BARRY ac Am			
Byrne,	BOBBY mj-tromb,tv			
Byrne,	DAVID s,ws,d Am			
Byrne,	GABRIEL			
Byrne,	JOSH tv			
Byrne,	MARTHA tv+			
Byrnes,	BURKE tv			
Byrnes,	EDD(Kookie)tv+			
Byrnes,	JAMES l,st Am			
Byrnes,	JIM tv			
Byrns,	JOSEPH st Am			
Byrom,	JOHN po Br			
Byron	ALLEN tv			
Byron	CHERRY tv			
Byron	CHUNG tv			
Byron	FOULGER tv+			
Byron	GILLIAM tv			
Byron	HASKIN d			
Byron	JOHNSON(Ban)bmg hf			
Byron	KEITH tv			
Byron	MABE			
Byron	MINNS tv			
Byron	MORROW tv			
Byron	NELSON g Am			
Byron	STEWART tv+			
Byron	WHITE fb,l-supr ct			
Byron,	CAROL tv			
Byron,	DAVID mr-s Br			
Byron,	DENNIS mr-drums			
Byron,	GEORGE(Lord) po Br			
Byron,	JEAN tv			
Byron,	KATHLEEN			
Byron,	WALTER			
Byrum	SAAM tv			

"C" NAME DESIGNATION CODES

c	COMPOSER
cm	COMIC
cn	CONDUCTOR
cr	CARTOONIST
ct	CRITIC

"C" NATIONALITY CODES

Can	-	CANADIAN
Colom	-	COLOMBIAN
CostaR	-	COSTA RICAN
Croat	-	CROATIAN
Cz	-	CZECHOSLOVAKIAN

"C's"

C. Aubrey	SMITH(Sir)
C. Henry	GORDON
C. Pete	MUNRO tv
C. Thomas	HOWELL tv+
C.D.	BROAD(Charlie)ph Br
C.E.M.	JOAD ph,st Br
C.F.	TURNER m-bass,s Can
C.K.	OGDEN ps,w Br
C.P.	SNOW w,sc,st Br
C.P. Henrik	DAM md Dan
C.S.	LEWIS w,e Br
Caan,	JAMES tv+
Cab	CALLOWAY mj,cn Am
Cabal,	ROBERT tv
Caballe,	MONSTERRAT s
Cabanne,	CHRISTY d
Cabell,	ENOS b
Cabell,	JAMES B. w Am
Cabeza de Vaca,	ALVAR x Sp
Cable,	GEO. WASHING.w Am
Cabot,	BRUCE
Cabot,	GEORGE id Am
Cabot,	JOHN x It
Cabot,	SEBASTIAN tv+
Cabot,	SEBASTIAN x It
Cabot,	SUSAN
Cabral,	AMILCAR st Guinea
Cabral,	PEDRO x Port
Cabrilho,	JOAO R. x Port
Cabrol,	FERNAND r Fr
Caccialanza,	LORENZO tv
Caccini,	GIUILO s,c It
Cada Mosto,	ALVISE x It
Cadbury,	GEORGE id Br
Caddy,	ALAN mr-guit Br
Cadell,	FRANCIS x Scot
Cadieux,	JASON
Cadman,	CHARLES c Am
Cadore,	LEON b
Cadorette,	MARY tv
Cady	McCLAIN tv
Cady,	FRANK tv
Caen,	HERB j,p-r'96
Caesar	RODNEY re,st Am

Caesar,	ADOLPH		Callan,	MICHAEL tv+
Caesar,	SID mj-sax,tv+		Callas,	CHARLIE cm,tv Am
Caeser,	JULIUS st Ro		Callas,	MARIA s+ Am
Caeser,	UXOR(Julius'wife)		Callaway,	CHERYL tv
Caffaro,	CHERI		Callaway,	THOMAS tv
Caffey,	CHARLOTTE mr-s Am		Callcott,	AUGUSTUS(Sir)p
Caffrey,	STEPHEN tv+		Calleia,	JOSEPH
Cage,	JOHN c Am		Calles,	PLUTARCO ar,st Mex
Cage,	NICOLAS o-a'95		Callot,	JACQUES p Fr
Cagney,	JAMES o-a'42,tv+		Callow,	SIMON
Cagney,	JEANNE		Calloway,	CAB mj,cn,tv+
Cagnolatti,	DAMIAN tv		Calve,	EMMA sopr Fr
Cahan,	ABRAHAM j,w Am		Calvert	VAUX ac-landscape
Cahill,	CATHY tv		Calvert,	BERNIE mr-bass Br
Cahill,	THADDEUS i Am		Calvert,	BILL tv+
Cahill,	THOMAS w Am		Calvert,	PHYLLIS
Cahn,	EDWARD d		Calvet,	CORRINE
Cahn,	SAMMY lyrics Am		Calvin	JUNG
Cain,	DEAN tv+		Calvin	KLEIN ds Am
Cain,	JAMES j,w Am		Calvin	LEVELS
Cain,	JEFF tv		Calvin	MURPHY bb hf
Cain,	JONATHAN mr-kbds		Calvin	PEETE g Am
Cain,	MADELYN tv		Calvin	THOMAS tv
Caine,	HALL(Sir)w		Calvin,	HENRY tv+
Caine,	HOWARD tv+		Calvin,	JOHN r, Fr
Caine,	MICHAEL o-s'86		Calvin,	JOHN tv+
Caitlin	DULANY		Calvin,	MELVIN n-c'61
Caius	CIBBER su Dan		Calvino,	ITALO w It
Cajori,	FLORIAN math,e Am		Calvo,	ARMANDO
Cakmak,	FEVZI ar,st Turk		Calvo,	CARLOS st Arg
Cal	HAYNES		Camacho,	CORINNE tv
Cal	HOWARD tv		Camara	LAYE w Guinea
Cal	HUBBARD b hf		Camarata,	TUTTI m,cn,c tv
Cal	HUBBARD fb hf		Cambert,	ROBERT c Fr
Cal	RIPKIN Jr b		Cambini,	GIUSEPPE viol,c It
Calabro,	THOMAS tv		Cambridge,	GODFREY
Calder,	ALEXANDER p,su Am		Cameron	DYE
Calder,	KING tv		Cameron	SMITH tv
Calderisi,	DAVID tv		Cameron,	CANDACE tv
Calderon de la Barca, PEDRO w			Cameron,	DEAN
Calderon,	ERMA w		Cameron,	JAMES o-d'98
Caldwell,	ERSKINE w Am		Cameron,	JULIA fo Br
Caldwell,	SARAH cn Am		Cameron,	KIRK tv+
Caldwell,	TAYLOR w Am		Cameron,	ROD tv+
Caldwell,	ZOE		Cameron,	VERNEY x Br
Cale,	JOHN mr-kbds,s		Camilla	CARR
Caleb	CARR w Am		Camilla	COLLETT fe Nor
Caleb	CUSHING l,st Am		Camille	CODURI
Calfa,	DON		Camille	RATEAU eng,i Fr
Calhern,	LOUIS		Camilli,	DOLPH b-mv'41
Calhoun,	JOHN st(vp)		Camillo	BENSO st It
Calhoun,	LEE o-g'60		Camillo	GOLGI md,e It
Calhoun,	RORY tv+		Camillo	RATEAU arc Fr
Cali,	JOSEPH tv+		Camillo	SITTE ac Aus
California,	RANDY mr-guit,s		Camilo Jose CELA po,w Sp	
Caliri,	JON tv		Caminiti,	KEN b-gg'95'6'7
Calkins,	MARY ph,ps Am		Camoes,	LUIZ VAZ de po Port
Call,	BRANDON tv+		Camp,	COLLEEN
Callaghan,	MORLEY w Can		Camp,	HAMILTON tv+
Callahan,	JAMES tv+		Camp,	JOHN w Am
Callahan,	JOHN tv			

Camp,	WALTER fb,fbc Am	Candace	SAVALAS tv
Campanella,	JOSEPH tv+	Candice	AZZARA tv+
Campanella,	ROYb-mv'51'3'5,hf	Candice	BERGEN tv+
Campbell	SCOTT	Candice	RIALSON
Campbell,	ALAN tv	Candido,	CANDY mj-bass Am
Campbell,	ALI mr-guit,s Br	Candler,	ASA id Am
Campbell,	ARCHIE tv	Candrix,	FUD mj-sax,cn Belg
Campbell,	BILL	Candy	CANDIDO mj-bass Am
Campbell,	BRUCE	Candy	CLARK
Campbell,	CHERYL	Candy	JOHNSON
Campbell,	DOUGLAS H. sc,e Am	Candy	MOORE tv+
Campbell,	DUANE R. tv	Candy	RAYMOND
Campbell,	EARL fb-m'78'9'80hf	Candy,	JOHN tv+
Campbell,	ERIC	Canetti,	ELIAS n-l'81
Campbell,	FLORA tv	Canfield,	MARY GRACE tv
Campbell,	GLEN s,g-r-68,tv+	Canin,	ETHAN w Am
Campbell,	JUDY	Canitz,	FRIEDRICH von st,po
Campbell,	JULIA	Cankar,	IVAN w Czech
Campbell,	KEN HUDSON tv	Cann,	HOWARD bbc hf
Campbell,	LOUISE	Cann,	WARREN mr-drm Can
Campbell,	MALCOM(Sir)racer Br	Canning,	LISA tv
Campbell,	MARK tv	Cannon Ball ADDERLY mj Am
Campbell,	MIKE mr-guit Am	Cannon,	ANNIE JUMP as Am
Campbell,	Mrs. PATRICK la Br	Cannon,	DYAN
Campbell,	NAOMI mo Br	Cannon,	GLENN tv
Campbell,	NEVE	Cannon,	J.D. tv+
Campbell,	NICHOLAS tv+	Cannon,	JIMMY tv
Campbell,	PHIL tv	Cannon,	JOSEPH(UncleJoe)st
Campbell,	ROBIN mr-guit,s	Cannon,	KATHERINE tv+
Campbell,	ROY po Br	Cannon,	KATHY d
Campbell,	THOMAS po Br	Cannon,	MAUREEN tv
Campbell,	TISHA tv+	Cannon,	MICHAEL tv
Campbell,	WILLIAM ED. w Am	Cannon,	WANDA tv
Campbell,	WILLIAM tv+	Cannon,	WILLIAM tv
Campbell,	WILLIAM W.ast Am	Cano,	ALONSO p,su,ac Sp
Campbell,	WILLIAM WIL.po Can	Canova,	ANTONIO su It
Campe,	JOACHIM e Ger	Canova,	DIANA tv+
Camper,	PIETER md,e Dut	Canrobert,CERTAIN ar Fr
Campero,	NARCISO ar,st Bol	Canseco,	JOSE b-mv'88
Campi,	ANTONIO p,ac It	Cansler	LARRY m,cn,tv
Campi,	GALEAZZO p It	Canth,	ULRIKA fe,w Finn
Campi,	GIULIO p It	Cantor,	CHARLIE tv
Campi,	VINCENZO p It	Cantor,	EDDIE s,tv+
Campin,	ROBERT p Belg	Cantor,	IDA(Eddie's wife)
Campion,	JANE d	Cantrell,	LANA s+
Campion,	THOMAS po, c Br	Cantu,	CARLOS tv
Campo,	PUPI mj,cn,tv Am	Canutt,	YAKIMA
Campo,	WALLY	Canvass	WHITE eng Am
Campos,	RAFAEL tv+	Cao,	DIOGO x Port
Campos,	VICTOR tv	Cap	ANSON(Pop)b.bmg hf
Campra,	ANDRE c Fr	Capa,	ROBERT fo Am
Camus,	ALBERT n-l'57	Capaldi,	JIM mr-drm,s Br
Canada	LEE	Capaldi,	PETER
Canadeo,	TONY fb hf	Cape,	JONATHAN pb Br
Canal,	GIOVANNI p It	Capek,	KAREL w,j Cz
Canale,	GIANA	Capelen,	GODERT st Dut
Canaletto,ANTONIO p It	Capelja,	JAD
Canary,	DAVID tv+	Caper,	DOM fbc
Canby,	HENRY w,ed Am	Capers,	VIRGINIA tv+
Candace	CAMERON tv	Capone,	AL gangster Am &
Candace	HUTSON tv	Capone,	AL=Scarface

Caposella,FRED tv	Carey, RON tv+
Capote, TRUMAN w Am	Carey, THOMAS(Mutt)mj,cn
Capp, Al cr,tv Am	Carey, TIMOTHY
Capps, EDWARD e Am	Cargill, OSCAR ct,e Am
Capps, LISA tv	Carhart, GEORGIANA tv
Cappuccilli PIERO bari	Carhart, TIMOTHY
Capra, FRANK o-d'34'38	Cari SHAYNE tv
Capra, JORDANA tv+	Caridi, CARMINE tv
Capri, ANNA	Carillo, JULIAN viol,c Mex
Capriati, JENNIFER t Am	Cariou, LEN
Capshaw, KATE	Carl AKELEY su,sc,x Am
Capt.FrederickMARRYATnavy,wBr	Carl ALLEN h Dan
Captain COOK(James)x Br	Carl ALSBERG sc,e Am
Captain KIDD pirate Br	Carl AUER sc,i Am
Capuana, LUIGI w,ct,j It	Carl BAHRDT r Ger
Capucine ---	Carl BENZ id-cars Ger
Capus, ALFRED j,w Fr	Carl BETZ tv
Cara BUONO	Carl BLEGEN arc,e Am
Cara, IRENE s,tv+	Carl BOSCH sc Ger
Carafa, MICHELE c It	Carl CARUS md,ph Ger
Carafotes,PAUL tv+	Carl CORI md Am
Caravaggio, MICHELANGELO p It	Carl CROW tv
Caraway, HATTIE st Am	Carl DREYER d Dan
Caray, HARRY b-announce Am	Carl ELLER fb
Carbone, ANTONY tv+	Carl FRANK tv
Carbone, JOEY m,cn,tv Am	Carl GARDNER mr-s Am
Carcaterra, LORENZO w Am	Carl GAUSS astr,e Ger
Card, KATHRYN tv	Carl GORDON tv
Card, ORSON SCOTT w Am	Carl HAMBRO st Nor
Cardenas, ELSA	Carl HEID tv
Cardi, PAT tv	Carl HIAASEN w Am
Cardin, PIERRE ds Fr	Carl HOFF m,cn,tv Am
Cardinal, TANTOO	Carl HOVLAND ps,e Am
Cardinale,CLAUDIA	Carl HUBBELL b hf
Cardone, J.S. d	Carl JACOBI math,e Ger
Cardozo, BENJAMIN l Am	Carl JUNG ps Swi
Carducci, GIOSUE po,ct,n-l'06	Carl KOLLER md-eyes Am
Cardwell, JAMES B.	Carl LARSSON p,etch Swe
Caren KAYE tv+	Carl LAVAL eng,id Swe
Carew, JAN w Guyana	Carl LEE
Carew, RICHARD po Br	Carl LEWIS sp-track Am
Carew, ROD b-mv'77 hf &	Carl LINDE eng,id-02 Ger
Carew, ROD 7xbat'70-'78	Carl LUMBLY tv+
Carew, THOMAS po Br	Carl MILLES su Am
Carey LOFTIN tv	Carl MOHNER
Carey LOWELL	Carl MUCK cn Ger
Carey ORR cr Am	Carl NIELSEN c,cn Dan
Carey, CLARE tv	Carl NORDEN i Dut
Carey, DREW cm,tv	Carl ORFF c Ger
Carey, HARRY Jr.	Carl PALMER mr-drm Br
Carey, HARRY Sr.	Carl PAYNE II tv
Carey, HENRY po,c Br	Carl PERKINS s,tv+ Am
Carey, JOYCE	Carl PETERS x Ger
Carey, JULIUS III tv	Carl PITTI
Carey, MacDONALD tv+	Carl RAKOSI po Am
Carey, MARIAH s-pop Am	Carl RAVAZZA mj,cn Am
Carey, MATHEW pb Am	Carl REID tv+
Carey, MAX b hf	Carl REINER d,tv+
Carey, MICHELE tv+	Carl RIECKE sc,e Ger
Carey, OLIVE tv	Carl RITTER geog Ger
Carey, PHILIP(Phil)tv+	Carl ROGERS ps,e Am

Carl	ROSSBY weather,e Am	Carlo	GOZZI w It
Carl	RUGGLES c Am	Carlo	LEVI md,p,w It
Carl	SAGAN astron Am	Carlo	PIAGGIA x It
Carl	SAUER geog,e Am	Carlo	PONTI pr It
Carl	SCHEELE sc Swe	Carlo	PORTA po It
Carl	SCHULTZ d	Carlo	RUBBIA sc It
Carl	SCHURZ ar,st,ref Am	Carlo	SIGONIO h It
Carl	SMITH tv	Carlo	VANZINA d
Carl	SPAATZ fly Am	Carlo	ZENO navy It
Carl	STEVEN tv	Carlo,	JOHANN tv
Carl	STUMPF ph,ps,e Ger	Carlos	ALVEAR re Arg
Carl	SWITZER(Alfalfa)	Carlos	BELLI po Peru
Carl	Van DOREN ed,ct,bio Am	Carlos	BOUSONO po Sp
Carl	VINSON st Am	Carlos	CALVO l,st Arg
Carl	WAYNE mr-s Br	Carlos	CANTU tv
Carl	WEBER c Ger	Carlos	CHAVEZ c,cn Mex
Carl	WILHELM cn,c Ger	Carlos	DAVILA j,st Chile
Carl	WILSON mr-guit,s Am	Carlos	FINLAY md,sc Cuba
Carl	ZAHLE st Dan	Carlos	FUENTES w Mex
Carl	ZEISS id-optics Ger	Carlos	GARCIA st Phil
Carl	ZELLER c Aus	Carlos	IBANEZ ar,st Chile
Carl	ZELTER c,cn Ger	Carlos	La CAMARA tv
Carl	ZOLLNER c Ger	Carlos	LOPEZ st Para
Carl Philipp BACH c Ger		Carlos	MONTOYA m-flamenco
Carl von	LINNE sc,md,w Swe	Carlos	REYLES w Urug
Carl von	MENGER ec,e Aus	Carlos	RIVAS
Carl von	SIEBOLD sc,e Ger	Carlos	ROMERO tv
Carl von	VOIT ps,e Ger	Carlos	ROMULO ar,st,j Phil
Carl von	WEBER c Ger	Carlos	SANTANA mr-guit,s
Carl,	ADAM tv	Carlos	SAURA d
Carla	BALENDA tv	Carlos,	BUN mr-drmsAm
Carla	FRACCI ba+ It	Carlos,	DON(Span.Prince)
Carla	GRAVINA	Carlotta	GRISI ba It
Carla	GUGINO tv+	Carlson,	AMY tv
Carla	LEHMANN	Carlson,	ANTON md,e Am
Carla	MARLIER	Carlson,	ARNE st Am
Carle,	FRANKIE mj-piano,c	Carlson,	CHESTER i Am
Carlene	WATKINS tv	Carlson,	H.C.(Dr.)bbc hf
Carleton	COON an,e Am	Carlson,	KAREN tv+
Carleton	YOUNG tv+	Carlson,	LINDA tv
Carleton,	CLAIRE tv+	Carlson,	RICHARD tv+
Carleton,	WILL po Am	Carlton	COON an,e Am
Carleton,	WILLIAM w Ir	Carlton,	EFFIE la,w Am
Carli,	GIAN ec,h,e It	Carlton,	HOPE
Carlile,	RICHARD pb,ref Br	Carlton,	STEVE b-cy'72'7 &
Carlin	GLYNN tv+	Carlton,	STEVE b-cy'80'2 hf
Carlin,	GEORGE tv+	Carly	SIMON s,ws,w Am
Carlin,	LYNN tv+	Carlyle,	RICHARD tv
Carlisle Hart, KITTY tv+		Carlyle,	THOMAS w,e Scot
Carlisle,	BELINDA s,ws Am	Carman,	BLISS po,w Can
Carlisle,	JOHN st Am	Carmel	MYERS
Carlisle,	MARY	Carmel	QUINN tv
Carlo	BLASIS ba,e It	Carmel,	ROGER tv+
Carlo	BOTTA md,h It	Carmelita	POPE tv
Carlo	CARRA p It	Carmen	MASTREN tv
Carlo	CASSOLA w It	Carmen	MAURA
Carlo	CIGNANI p It	Carmen	McRAE mj,s Am
Carlo	DATI w It	Carmen	MIRANDA s+
Carlo	DOLCI p It	Carmen,	ERIC mr-s Am
Carlo	GADDA w It	Carmen,	JULIE tv+
Carlo	GOLDONI w It		

Carmet, JEAN	Carole GOLDMAN tv
Carmichael, HOAGY mj,c,tv Am	Carole KING mr,s,c Am
Carmichael, IAN	Carole LANDIS
Carmichael, LEONARD ps,e Am	Carole LAURE
Carmichael, RALPH tv	Carole LOMBARD
Carmine APPICE mr-drm Am	Carole MATHEWS tv
Carmine CARIDI tv	Carole WELLS tv+
Carnap, RUDOLF ph Am	Carole Ita WHITE t
Carne, JUDY tv+	Carolina NAIRNE ws Scot
Carne, MARCEL d	Caroline CARTER la Am
Carnegie, ANDREW f,id Am	Caroline GOODALL
Carnegie, DALE w,e,speaker Am	Caroline GORDON w Am
Carnera, PRIMO boxer Am	Caroline KAVA
Carnesecca, LOU bbc hf	Caroline LAMB(Lady) w Br
Carnevale,BEN bbc hf	Caroline MILLER w Am
Carney, ART o-a'74,tv+	Caroline MUNRO
Carney, BARBARA tv	Caroline NORTON w Br
Carney, GRACE tv	Caroline SCHLITT tv
Carney, HARRY mj-sax Am	Carolsue WALKER tv
Carney, ROBERT navy Am	Carolyn BRANDT
Carnie WILSON s Am	Carolyn CONWAY tv
Carnot LAZARE ar.st Fr	Carolyn DANIELS tv
Carnot, SADI st Fr	Carolyn DUNN tv+
Carnovsky,MORRIS	Carolyn GILBERT tv
Caro, ANNIBALE po It	Carolyn JONES tv+
Caro, MIGUEL st Colom	Carolyn KEENE w Am
Caro, ROBERT bio(LBJ)Am	Carolyn KIZER po Am
Carol ALT mo+ Am	Carolyn SEYMOR
Carol BOUQUET	Carolyn SILAS tv
Carol BRUCE tv	Carolyn WELLS w Am
Carol BURNETT cm,tv+ Am	Caron, ANTOINE p Fr
Carol BYRON tv	Caron, LESLIE
Carol COLEMAN tv	Carossa, HANS po,w,md Ger
Carol FAYLEN tv	Carothers,WALLACE sc Am
Carol HANEY tv	Caroto, GIAN p It
Carol HENNING tv	Carpaccio,VITTORE p It
Carol HENRY ba,tv Am	Carpeaux, JEAN su Fr
Carol HUGHES	Carpenter,EDWARD w Br
Carol HUSTON tv	Carpenter,JOHN c,id Am
Carol JENKINS tv	Carpenter,KEN tv
Carol KANE tv+	Carpenter,MARY CHAPIN s,ws Am
Carol LYNLEY tv+	Carpenter,PAUL
Carol MARSH	Carpentier, ALEJO Cuba
Carol MARTIN tv	Carpentier, GEORGES boxer Fr
Carol OHMART	Carper, JEAN w Am
Carol POTTER tv	Carpi, UGO da at It
Carol REED(Sir)d	Carr, BETTY ANN tv
Carol SALINE j,w Am	Carr, CALEB w Am
Carol SHELLY tv	Carr, CAMILLA
Carol SHIELDS w Am	Carr, CLARK tv
Carol SPEED	Carr, DARLEEN tv
Carol STONE tv	Carr, DAVID mr-kbds Br
Carol WAYNE	Carr, DIDI tv
Carol WHITE	Carr, EMILY p,w Can
Carol Ann SUSI tv	Carr, GERALDINE tv
Carol Higgins CLARK w Am	Carr, JANE tv
Carol, JEAN tv	Carr, JOE fb hf
Carol, LILY ANN mj-s Am	Carr, MARY
Carol, MARTINE	Carr, NANCY tv
Carol-Ann PLANTE tv	Carr, PAUL tv+
Carole DAVIS	Carr, PHILIPPA w Br

Carr,	THOMAS d+	Carson,	JACK tv+
Carr,	VIKKI	Carson,	JEAN tv
Carra,	CARLO p It	Carson,	JEANNIE tv+
Carrack,	PAUL mr-s,ws Br	Carson,	JOHN
Carradine,DAVID tv+		Carson,	JOHN DAVID tv+
Carradine,JOHN tv+		Carson,	JOHNNY tv-host Am
Carradine,KEITH		Carson,	KEN tv
Carradine,ROBERT		Carson,	KIT frontier Am
Carraher, HARLEN tv		Carson,	MINDY tv
Carre	OTIS mo+ Am	Carson,	RACHEL w,sc Am
Carreiro, TONY tv		Carson,	SUNSET
Carrel,	ALEXIS n-m'12	Carsten,	PETER
Carrera Andrade, JORGE po,w		Carstens, ASMUS p Ger	
Carrera, BARBARA mo,tv+		Carstensen, MARGIT	
Carrere,	JOHN ac Am	Cartan,	ELIE math,e Fr
Carrere	TIA	Carte,	RICHARD m Br
Carrey,	JIM cm+ Am	Carter	GLASS st Am
Carricart,ROBERT tv		Carter	WONG
Carrie	BOND ws Am	Carter	WOODSON h,e Am
Carrie	CATT fe Am	Carter,	ALVIN(A.P.)m,s Am
Carrie	FISHER	Carter,	BENNY mj-reeds Am
Carrie	MOSS tv	Carter,	CAROLINE a
Carrie Chapman CATT fe Am		Carter,	CAROLINE=Mrs.Leslie
Carrier, WILLIS eng,i Am		Carter,	CONLAN tv
Carriera, ROSALBA p It		Carter,	DEANA s-cnt Am
Carriere, EUGENE p Fr		Carter,	DIXIE tv
Carriere, MATTHIEU		Carter,	ELIZABETH po Br
Carrillo, BRAULIO st CostaR		Carter,	ELLIOTT p-m'60'73
Carrillo, ELPIDIA		Carter,	FINN
Carrillo, JULIAN viol,c Mex		Carter,	HELEN tv
Carrillo, LEO tv+		Carter,	HELENA
Carrol,	REGINA	Carter,	HODDING j,w Am
Carroll	BAKER	Carter,	HOWARD arc Br
Carroll	GIBBONS mj-piano,cn	Carter,	JACK tv+
Carroll	O'CONNOR tv+	Carter,	JANIS
Carroll	PETRIE st@UN Am	Carter,	JIM
Carroll,	ANNA w,ct Am	Carter,	JIMMY 39th pr &
Carroll,	BEESON tv	Carter,	JIMMY(James Earl)
Carroll,	BOB tv	Carter,	JOE b,rbi'86
Carroll,	CHARLES st Am	Carter,	JOHN tv
Carroll,	DIAHANN tv+	Carter,	JUNE tv
Carroll,	EARL pr-stage Am	Carter,	LYNDA tv+
Carroll,	EDDIE tv	Carter,	MICHAEL tv
Carroll,	JANET tv+	Carter,	MOTHER MAYBELLE tv
Carroll,	JEANNE mj-s Am	Carter,	NELL s,tv+ Am
Carroll,	JIM w Am	Carter,	NICK fc-sleuth
Carroll,	JIMMY piano,s,tv	Carter,	PERRY
Carroll,	JOHN	Carter,	RALPH tv
Carroll,	LEO tv+	Carter,	RAY tv
Carroll,	LEWIS w,math Br	Carter,	RON mj-bass Am
Carroll,	MADELEINE	Carter,	T.K. tv+
Carroll,	NANCY tv+	Carter,	TERRY tv+
Carroll,	PAT tv+	Carter,	THOMAS tv+
Carroll,	ROBERT tv	Carteris, GABRIELLE tv+	
Carroll,	ROCKY tv	Cartier,	JACQUES x Fr
Carroll,	VICTORIA tv	Cartier-Bresson, HENRI fo Fr	
Carry	NATION fe(wctu)Am	Cartlidge,KATRIN	
Carson	McCullers w Am	Cartwright, ALEXANDER. bmg hf	
Carson,	CHARLES	Cartwright, ANGELA tv+	
Carson,	CHRISTOPHER(Kit)st	Cartwright, NANCY tv	
Carson,	HUNTER	Cartwright, VERONICA tv+	

Cartwright,	WILLIAM w Br		Casimir	PULASKI ar Pol-Am
Carty,	JOHN eng Am		Caskey	SWAIM tv
Carty,	RICO b,bat'70		Casnoff,	PHILIP tv+
Carus,	CARL md,ph Ger		Cason,	BARBARA tv
Carus,	MARCUS AURELIUSstRo		Cason,	JOHN
Carus,	PAUL ed,ph Am		Caspar	WESSEL math Nor
Caruso,	ANTHONY		Caspar	WISTAR id-glass &
Caruso,	DAVID tv+		Caspar	WISTAR 1st in Am
Caruso,	ENRICO tenor It		Caspar,	BILLY g Am
Carver,	GEO. WASHINGTON sc		Caspin,	SAM mj-trump Am
Carver,	JOHN pilgrim Br		Cass	GILBERT ac Am
Carver,	JONATHAN x Am		Cass	HAGAN mj,cn Am
Carver,	LYNNE		Cass,	LEWIS st Am
Carver,	MARY tv		Cass,	PEGGY tv+
Carver,	RANDALL tv		Cassandra	WILSON mj-s Am
Carver,	ROBERT c Scot		Cassatt,	MARY p Am
Carver,	ZEBE tv		Cassavetes,	JOHN d,tv+
Carvey,	DANA cm,tv+ Am		Cassavetes,	NICK
Cary	ELWES		Cassel,	ERNEST(Sir)f,f Br
Cary	GRANT		Cassel,	GUSTAV ec,e Swe
Cary	WEIS cm,tv Am		Cassel,	JEAN-PIERRE
Cary,	ALICE po Am		Cassel,	SEYMOUR tv+
Cary,	CHRISTOPHER tv		Cassell,	ARTHUR tv
Cary,	JOYCE w Ir		Cassell,	MALCOLM tv
Cary,	PHOEBE po Am		Cassese,	ANDREW tv
Cary-Hiroyuki TAGAWA			Cassey,	CHUCK tv
Caryn	RICHMAN tv		Cassidy,	DAVID tv+
Casadesus, ALBERT tv			Cassidy,	ED mr-drm Am
Casady,	JACK mr-bass,guit		Cassidy,	EDWARD
Casal,	JULIAN del po Cuba		Cassidy,	JACK tv+
Casals,	PABLO cello,c,cn,tv		Cassidy,	JOANNA tv+
Casanova,	FERNANDO		Cassidy,	PATRICK
Casanova,	GIACOMO w It		Cassidy,	SHAUN tv+
Casanova,	GIOVANNI lover It		Cassidy,	TED tv+
Casares	MARIA		Cassie	COLE tv
Case,	ALLEN tv		Cassie	STUART
Case,	EVERETT bbc hf		Cassie	YATES tv+
Case,	NELSON tv		Cassin,	RENE n-x'68
Case,	RUSS tv		Cassinelli,	CLAUDIO
Case,	SHARON tv		Cassini,	OLEG ds Fr
Case,	SHIRLEY w,e Am		Cassirer,	ERNST ph,e Ger
Casella,	ALFREDO piano,c It		Cassisi,	JOHN tv+
Casella,	MAX tv		Cassity,	KRAIG tv
Casey	ADAMS		Cassola,	CARLO w It
Casey	ELLISON tv		Cast,	TRICIA tv
Casey	JONES rr eng Am		Castel,	LOU
Casey	KASEM		Castellaneta, DAN tv+	
Casey	STENGEL b,bmg hf		Castellano, RICHARD	
Casey,	BERNIE		Castellari, ENZO G. d	
Casey,	HARRY mr-kbds,s Am		Castelli, IGNAZ j,w Aus	
Casey,	RICHARD st Aust		Castenada, MOVITA tv	
Casey,	ROBERT tv		Casti,	GIOVANNI po,w It
Cash	FLAGG		Castile,	CHRISTOPHER tv+
Cash,	JOHNNY s-cnt,tv+		Castilho,	ANTONIO po Port
Cash,	JUNE tv+		Castle,	IRENE ba Am
Cash,	NORM tv		Castle,	JO ANN mj,pian,tv
Cash,	ROSALIND		Castle,	JOHN
Cash,	ROSANNE s-cnt Am		Castle,	NICK ba,d,tv Am
Cashin,	MICHAEL(Sir)st Can		Castle,	PEGGY tv+
Casimir	FUNK sc,e Am		Castle,	VERNON ba,fly Br
Casimir	PERIER st Fr		Castle,	WILLIAM md,e Am

Castlemon,	HARRY w Am	Catulle	MENDES w Fr
Castro,	CIPRIANO st Venz	Catusi,	JIM tv
Castro,	EUGENIO de po Port	Catya	SASOON (Cat)
Castro,	FIDEL (Ruz) st Cuba	Caubere,	PHILIPPE
Castro,	INES de noble Sp	Cauchy,	AUGUSTIN math Fr
Castro,	RON tv	Caufield,	JOAN tv+
Castro,	ROSALIA de w Sp	Caufield,	MAXWELL tv+
Castulo	GUERRA tv	Caunt,	BENJAMIN boxer Br
Cat	SASSOON	Cavalcanti,	GUIDO po It
Cat	STEVENS s,ws Br	Cavaliere,	FELIX mr-kbds,s Am
Cat	THOMPSON bb hf	Cavallero,	UGO ar It
Cat,	CHRISTOPHER pubs Br	Cavanagh,	PAUL
Catalani,	ALFREDO c It	Cavanaugh,	HOBART
Catarina	CELLINO tv	Cavanaugh,	MICHAEL tv
Catena,	VINCENZO di p It	Cavani,	LILIANA d
Cates,	GEORGE m,c,cn,tv Am	Cavanna,	ELISE
Cates,	PHOEBE	Cavarretta,	PHIL b-mv'45
Catesby,	MARK sc Br	Cave,	EDWARD j Br
Catfish	HUNTER b hf	Cavell,	EDITH md Br
Cather,	WILLA p-f'23	Cavell,	MARC tv
Catherall,	JOANNE mr-s Br	Cavendish,	HENRY sc Br
Catherine	BACH tv+	Cavett,	DICK tv-host+ Am
Catherine	COULSON tv	Cawthorn,	JOSEPH
Catherine	DENEUVE	Caxton,	WILLIAM id,mer Br
Catherine	DISHER tv	Cayley,	ARTHUR math,e Br
Catherine	DONAHUE tv	Cazale,	JOHN
Catherine	FERRAR tv	Cazenove,	CHRISTOPHER tv+
Catherine	HICKS tv+	Cazin,	JEAN p Fr
Catherine	KEENER tv+	CCH	POUNDER tv+
Catherine	McKINLEY w Am	Cease,	JEFF guit Am
Catherine	O'HARA tv+	Cec	LINDER
Catherine	PARR wf-HenryVIII	Cec	VERRELL
Catherine	ROUVEL	Ceccaldi	DANIEL
Catherine	SCHELL tv+	Cecchetti,	ENRICO ba It
Catherine	SPAAK	Cece	PENISTON s-soul,rk
Catherine	STEWART	Cecelia	BARTOLI s It
Catherine	TRAILL w Can	Cech,	SVATOPLUK po,w Cz
Cathleen	NESBITT tv+	Cech,	THOMAS n-c'89
Cathleen	SCHINE w Am	Cecil	BEATON (Sir) fo,ds
Cathryn	DAMON tv	Cecil	BOWRA (Sir) e,w
Cathy	CAHILL tv	Cecil	COOPER b
Cathy	COOPER tv	Cecil	FIELDER b &
Cathy	DOWNS	Cecil	FIELDER rbi'90'1'2
Cathy	HORYN j Am	Cecil	MERCER w Br
Cathy	LEWIS tv	Cecil	PARKER
Cathy	RIGBY gy Am	Cecil	POWELL sc,e Br
Cathy	SILVERS tv	Cecil	RHODES st S.Afr
Cathy	TYSON	Cecil	SHARP m,e Br
Cathy Lee	CROSBY tv+	Cecil	TAYLOR mj-piano,cn
Cativiela,	JEAN-PAUL w Am	Cecil B.	DeMILLE d
Catlett,	MARY tv	Cecil of Chelwood	--- n-x'37
Catlett,	SIDNEY mj,drm Am	Cecil,	DAVID (Lord) w,ct Br
Catlett,	WALTER	Cecilia	BARTOLI s It
Catlin,	GEORGE p,w Am	Cecilia	JAMISON w,p Am
Catlin,	VICTORIA tv+	Cecilia	PARKER
Cato,	MARCUS (Elder) st Ro	Cecilia	PECK
Cats,	JAKOB po Dut	Cedric	SMITH
Catt,	CARRIE fe Am	Cela,	CAMILO JOSE n-l'89
Cattell,	JAMES ps,e Am	Cele,	HENRY
Catton,	BRUCE j,p-h'54	Celeste	HOLM tv+
Cattrall,	KIM	Celeste	YARNALL

Celestin	JONNART st Fr		Chad	STUART mr-guit,s Br
Celi,	ADOLFO		Chadwick,	GEORGE cn,c Am
Celia	JOHNSON		Chadwick,	HENRY b hf
Celia	WESTON tv+		Chadwick,	JAMES(Sir)n-p'35
Celicia	JOHNSON tv+		Chadwick,	JUNE tv+
Celine	DION s Fr-Can		Chadwick,	LES mr-bass Br
Celine,	LOUIS-FERDINAND w		Chafee,	ZECHARIAH l,e Am
Cella,	LEN tv		Chaffee,	ADNA ar Am
Cellier,	FRANK		Chaffee,	ROGER as Am
Cellier,	PETER		Chaffee,	SUZY ski Am
Cellini,	BENVENUTO su It		Chaffey,	DON d
Cellini,	KAREN tv		Chagall,	MARC p Fr
Cellino,	CATARINA tv		Chagas,	CARLOS md,sc Braz
Celsius,	ANDERS astr Swe		Chaim	POTOK w Am
Cenal,	ALINE tv		Chaim	SOUTINE p Fr
Cendrars,	BLAISE po,w Fr		Chaim	TOPOL
Centolella,	THOMAS po Am		Chaim	WEIZMANN sc,st Rus
Cepeda,	ORLANDO b-mv'67 hf		Chain,	ERNST(Sir)n-m'45
Ceran	ST.VRAIN fur trade		Chaka	KHAN mr-s Am
Cerezo,	MATEO p Sp		Chakiris,	GEORGE o-s'61
Cerf,	BENNETT w,pb,ed Am		Chaliapin,	FEODOR basso Rus
Cerf,	PHYLLIS tv		Challe,	MAURICE airforce Fr
Cermak,	ANTON st Am		Chalmers,	ALEXANDER w,ed Scot
Cervantes,	DON tv		Chamberlain,	AUSTEN(Sir) &
Cervantes,	MIGUEL de w,po Sp		Chamberlain,	AUSTEN n-x'25
Cervi,	AL bb hf		Chamberlain,	GEORGE w Am
Cervi,	GINO		Chamberlain,	LEE tv
Ces	LINDER		Chamberlain,	NEVILLE st-PM Br
Cesaire,	AIME po,w Martin		Chamberlain,	OWEN n-p'59
Cesana,	RENZO tv+		Chamberlain,	WILT bb-m'60'6 &
Cesar	CHAVEZ labor Am		Chamberlain,	WILT 67'8 hf+
Cesar	CUI c Rus		Chamberlin,	BETH tv
Cesar	FRANCK organ,c Fr		Chamberlin,	GUY fb hf
Cesar	MORO po Peru		Chamberlin,	RICHARD tv+
Cesar	RITZ hotels Swi		Chamberlin,	THOMAS geol,e Am
Cesar	ROMERO tv+		Chambers,	EDDIE mj-sax Am
Cesar	VALLEJO po Peru		Chambers,	GEORGE m-bass,s Am
Cesar	VICHARD h Fr		Chambers,	HENNEN tv
Cesare	BALBO st,w It		Chambers,	JOE m-guit,s Am
Cesare	DANOVA tv+		Chambers,	LESTER m-harm,s Am
Cesare	PAVESE w,po It		Chambers,	MARILYN
Cesare	SIEPI basso It		Chambers,	MARTIN mr-drm Br
Cesario	VERDE po Port		Chambers,	PHIL tv
Cespedes,	CARLOS de re Cuba		Chambers,	ROBERT pb,ed Scot
Cespedes,	PABLO de p,w Sp		Chambers,	TERRY mr-drm Br
Cesti,	ANTONIO c It		Chambers,	WHITTAKER l,w Am
Cetera,	PETER s Am		Chambers,	WILLIE m-guit,s Am
Ceulen,	LUDOLPH van math,e		Chamblis,	WOODY tv
Ceva,	GIOVANNI math,e It		Chamisso,	ADALBERT von w,sc
Ceveris,	MICHAEL tv+		Champ	CLARK st Am
Cey,	RON b		Champion,	GOWER ba+
Cezanne,	PAUL p Fr		Champion,	MARGE ba+
Chabrol,	CLAUDE d		Champion,	MICHAEL
Chacon,	LAZARO ar,st Guat		Champlain,	SAMUEL de x Fr
Chad	ALLEN tv+		Champlin,	IRENE tv+
Chad	EVERETT tv+		Chan	WAI
Chad	HAYWARD		Chan,	CHARLIE fc-sleuth
Chad	LOWE		Chan,	JACKIE
Chad	McQUEEN		Chan,	MICHAEL
Chad	REDDING tv		Chance,	DEAN b-cy'64
Chad	SHEETS		Chance,	FRANK b hf

Chance,	NAOMI	Charbonneau,	JEAN po Fr-Can
Chancellor,	JOHN tv-j Am	Charbonneau,	PATRICIA tv+
Chanda	ROMERO	Chardin,	JEAN p Fr
Chandler,	CHAS mr-bass Br	Charisse,	CYD ba+ Am
Chandler,	CHICK tv+	Charlaine	WOODARD
Chandler,	GENE s,ws Am	Charlene	SALERNO tv
Chandler,	GEORGE tv+	Charlene	TILTON tv
Chandler,	HAPPY(Commish)b hf	Charles	ABBOT astr
Chandler,	HELEN	Charles	ABBOTT l Br
Chandler,	JEFF	Charles	ADAMS Jr h Am
Chandler,	KYLE tv	Charles	ADAMS po Am
Chandler,	LANE	Charles	ADAMS rrs,h Am
Chandler,	LORETTA tv	Charles	ADDAMS cr Am
Chandler,	RAYMOND w Am	Charles	AIDMAN
Chandler,	SPURGEON b-mv'43	Charles	ANDREWS h,e Am
Chandra,	VIKRAM w India	Charles	ARNT
Chanel,	COCO ds Fr &	Charles	ASHBEE ac Br
Chanel,	COCO=Gabrielle	Charles	ATLAS physical cult
Chaney,	LON Jr. tv+	Charles	AVISON organ,c Pol
Chaney,	LON Sr.	Charles	BAGOT(Sir)st
Chang	YI	Charles	BAND d
Chanin	HALE tv	Charles	BARKLA sc Br
Channing,	CAROL s,tv Am	Charles	BARKLEY bb
Channing,	STOCKARD	Charles	BARTON d
Chantal	AKERMAN d	Charles	BEARD h Am
Chanute,	OCTAVE eng-aero Am	Charles	BEDAUX eng-effici.
Chao,	ROSALIND tv+	Charles	BEEBE sc,x Am
Chapais,	THOMAS(Sir)l,st Can	Charles	BEKE geog,x Br
Chapel,	BETTE tv	Charles	BEMONT h Fr
Chapel,	LOYITA tv	Charles	BENT pioneer Am
Chapelle	JAFFE	Charles	BESSEY sc,e Am
Chapin	HARRIS dentist Am	Charles	BEST md Can
Chapin,	LAUREN tv	Charles	BIDWELL fb hf
Chapin,	MILES	Charles	BOHLEN st Am
Chapin,	ROY id Am	Charles	BOLDEN mj,cn Am
Chaplin,	CHARLIE(Sir)d+	Charles	BONNET sc,ph Swi
Chaplin,	GERALDINE	Charles	BOYER tv+
Chaplin,	JOSEPHINE	Charles	BOYS(Sir)sc,i
Chaplin,	OONA(Ch's wife)	Charles	BRASCH po,ed N.Zea
Chaplin,	SYDNEY	Charles	BRONSON tv+
Chapman,	EDWARD	Charles	BROWN
Chapman,	FRANK birds Am	Charles	BROWNE w-humor Am
Chapman,	GARY s,c Am	Charles	BRUSH i Am
Chapman,	GEORGE po,w Br	Charles	CADMAN c Am
Chapman,	GRAHAM	Charles	CARROLL st Am
Chapman,	JOHN p,etch Am	Charles	CARSON
Chapman,	JOHN(J.Appleseed)	Charles	CHILD sc,e Am
Chapman,	JOSEPH tv	Charles	CIOFFI tv+
Chapman,	LONI	Charles	COBURN
Chapman,	MARGEURITE	Charles	COCHRAN(Sir)pr Br
Chapman,	MARK tv	Charles	COLLE w Fr
Chapman,	ROBERT tv	Charles	COOPER bb hf
Chapman,	ROGER s Br	Charles	COOPER tv
Chapman,	TRACY s-folk,ws Am	Charles	COPE p Br
Chapone,	HESTER w Br	Charles	CORRELL tv
Chappell,	CRYSTAL tv	Charles	COTTET p Br
Chappell,	JOHN tv	Charles	COTTON po Br
Chapu,	HENRI su Fr	Charles	COULOMB sc Fr
Chapygin,	ALEKSEY w Rus	Charles	CRANE id,st Am
Chaquico,	CRAIG mr-guit,s Am	Charles	CURTIS st 31st vp
Char,	RENE po Fr	Charles	DANA j,ed Am

Charles	DANCE	Charles	HIRES root beer Am
Charles	DARWIN sc Br	Charles	HORN s,c Br
Charles	DAWES l,f,st-vp Am	Charles	HUGGINS md Am
Charles	DAZEY w Am	Charles	HYNE w Br
Charles	DEMUTH p Am	Charles	INGLIS r Can
Charles	DENNER	Charles	IVES c Am
Charles	DESPIAU su Fr	Charles	JARROTT d
Charles	DIBDIN w,la,c Br	Charles	JERVAS p Ir
Charles	DICKENS w Br	Charles	JOHNSON b
Charles	DIERKOP tv+	Charles	JONES hunter for &
Charles	DILKE ct,h Br	Charles	JONES Buffalo Am
Charles	DINGLE	Charles	JUDD ps,e,w Am
Charles	DODGSON math,w Br	Charles	KECK su Am
Charles	DOUAY ar Fr	Charles	KEMPER
Charles	DOUGHTY w Br	Charles	KICKHAM w Ir
Charles	DOW j-finance Am	Charles	KING(Blackie)
Charles	DRAKE tv+	Charles	KLEIN b hf
Charles	DRAPER eng-aero Am	Charles	KOFOID sc Am
Charles	Du FAY st Fr	Charles	KURALT w,tv-j Am
Charles	DUFFY(Sir)j,ref Ir	Charles	LAMB w,ct Br
Charles	DULLIN la,pr Fr	Charles	LAMONT d
Charles	DURNING tv+	Charles	LAMPKIN tv
Charles	DURYEA i,id autos	Charles	LANE tv+
Charles	DUTTON	Charles	LANMAN h,e Am
Charles	EAMES ds-furnit Am	Charles	LAVERAN md Fr
Charles	ELIOT e Am	Charles	Le BRUN p Fr
Charles	ELIOT(Sir)st,w	Charles	LEITH geol Am
Charles	ELLET eng Am	Charles	LELAND po Am
Charles	EPEE r,e Fr	Charles	LEVER w Irish
Charles	EVANS(Chick)g Am	Charles	LEVIN tv
Charles	FABRY sc,e Fr	Charles	LIGNE ar Belg
Charles	FARRELL	Charles	LISTON boxer Am &
Charles	FAVART w,d Fr	Charles	LISTON=Sonny
Charles	FELLOWS(Sir)arc	Charles	LUMMIS w,ed Am
Charles	FOSDICK w Am	Charles	LYELL(Sir)geol
Charles	FOX st Br	Charles	MACKLIN w,la Br
Charles	FRANK tv+	Charles	MAJOR w Am
Charles	FRAZIER d	Charles	MANSON murderer &
Charles	FREER art coll,id	Charles	MANSON cult Am
Charles	FRENCH	Charles	MASON astr Br
Charles	FULLER w Am	Charles	MATURIN w Ir
Charles	FURSE p Br	Charles	MAURRAS w,pb Fr
Charles	GIBSON illus Am	Charles	McGRAW tv+
Charles	GILPIN la Am	Charles	McKIM ac Am
Charles	GLIDDEN id-phone Am	Charles	MERRIAM id,pb Am
Charles	GOBAT st,f Swi	Charles	MESSIER astr Fr
Charles	GORDON r,w Can	Charles	MILLER mr-reeds Am
Charles	GORDONE w Am	Charles	MINGUS mj,bass,c Am
Charles	GOREN bridge Am	Charles	MORGAN w,ct Br
Charles	GOUNOD c,cn Fr	Charles	MORICE w Fr
Charles	GRAY tv+	Charles	MUNCH cn Fr
Charles	GREY st Br	Charles	MURRAY po,eng Scot
Charles	GRODIN	Charles	.NAPIER
Charles	HAID tv+	Charles	NEVILLE mr-sax Am
Charles	HALL sc,i,id Am	Charles	NIEHAUS su Am
Charles	HALL x Am	Charles	NORRIS w Am
Charles	HALTON	Charles	NORTON w,e Am
Charles	HARPUR po Aust	Charles	NUNEZ tv
Charles	HAVAS j Fr	Charles	OGDEN(C.K.)ps,w Br
Charles	HAWTREY	Charles	OLSON po.e Am
Charles	HAWTREY(Sir)la	Charles	OMAN(Sir)h

Charles	ONIONS ed-dictionBr	Charles	VOUGHT eng,ds-aero
Charles	OSGOOD tv-anchor Am	Charles	VOYSEY ac,ds Br
Charles	PARNELL ref Irish	Charles	WALTERS d
Charles	PARRY(Sir)c,h,e	Charles	WARNER ed,w Am
Charles	PASLEY(Sir)ar,eng	Charles	WEIDMAN ba Am
Charles	PATHE pr-films Fr	Charles	WESLEY r,hymns Br
Charles	PEACH geol Br	Charles	WHITMAN sc,e Am
Charles	PEALE p Am	Charles	WIDOR organ,c Fr
Charles	PEGUY po,w Fr	Charles	WILKES navy,x Am
Charles	PEIRCE sc,math Am	Charles	WILSON sc Scot
Charles	PERCIER ac Fr	Charles	WOLFE po,w Ir
Charles	PERRON w,ct Dut	Charles	WRIGHT po Am
Charles	PICARD math,e Fr	Charles	WURTZ sc,e Fr
Charles	POOR astr Am	Charles	YERKES f Am
Charles	PORTAL fly,st Br	Charles A.BEARD w,h Am
Charles	POST id-foods Am	Charles B.BROWN w,ed Am
Charles	QUIGLEY	Charles Buddy ROGERS
Charles	RAMUZ w Swi	Charles de GAULLE st Fr
Charles	RAY	Charles de KOCK w Fr
Charles	READE w Br	Charles de LAFOSSE p Fr
Charles	REILLY tv	Charles de VALOIS ar Fr
Charles	REMUE mj,cn Belg	Charles Evans HUGHES l, &
Charles	RICHET sc-md,e Fr	Charles E.H.1st Supr Ct Just
Charles	RICHTER sc-quakes	Charles, EZZARD boxer Am
Charles	ROBB st Am	Charles, JOSH
Charles	ROBERTS(Sir)po,w	Charles, NICK fc-sleuth
Charles	ROCKET tv+	Charles, RAY piano,s,tv+
Charles	ROGIER st Br	Charleson,IAN
Charles	ROHLFS ds-furni	Charleson,LESLIE tv
Charles	ROLLS flyer,id-cars	Charleston,SCAR b hf
Charles	ROMINE tv	Charley BOORMAN
Charles	SANFORD m,cn,tv Am	Charley CHASE
Charles	SANSON execution Fr	Charley CONERLY fb
Charles	SCHULZ cr Am	Charley PRIDE s-cnt Am
Charles	SCHWAB bus-broker	Charley RICH s-cnt,ws Am
Charles	SCHWAB id-steel Am	Charlie AGNEW mj,cn,ws Am
Charles	SEEL tv	Charlie BARNET mj-sax,cn
Charles	SELLON	Charlie BRILL cm,tv+
Charles	SHEELER p,fo Am	Charlie BROAD(C.D.)ph Br
Charles	SHELDON r,w Am	Charlie CALLAS cm,tv
Charles	SIEBERT tv	Charlie CANTOR tv
Charles	SIEMANS(Sir)i,id	Charlie CHAN fc-sleuth
Charles	SIGSBEE navy Am	Charlie CHAPLIN(Sir)cm+
Charles	SIMIC po Am	Charlie CHASE tv
Charles	SMITH	Charlie DELL tv
Charles	STARK tv	Charlie DOBSON tv
Charles	STINE sc Am	Charlie ELGAR mj-viol,cn
Charles	STROUSE c Am	Charlie FARRELL tv+
Charles	STURT x Br	Charlie JOHNSON mj,cn Am
Charles	SUMNER st Am	Charlie JOINER fb
Charles	TAINTER i Am	Charlie JONES tv
Charles	TIFFANY jeweler Am	Charlie KORSMO
Charles	TORREY h,e Am	Charlie McCARTHY pupp
Charles	TOWNES sc Am	Charlie McCOY m-cnt,cn,tv
Charles	TUPPER(Sir)st Can	Charlie PARKER(Bird)sax,c
Charles	TYNER tv+	Charlie RUGGLES tv+
Charles	Van EMAN tv	Charlie SHEEN
Charles	Van HISE geol,e Am	Charlie SPIVAK mj,cn Am
Charles	VANEL	Charlie TAYLOR fb hf
Charles	VIDOR d	Charlie TRIPPI fb hf
Charles	VOGEL c Fr	Charlie WATTS mr-drm Br

Charlie	WHITNEY mr-guit Br	Chaykin,	MAURY
Charlot,	ANDRE pr-theater Br	Chazz	PALMINTERI
Charlotte	BRONTE w Br	Che	GUEVARA re Arg &
Charlotte	CAFFEY mr-s Am	Che	GUEVARA=Ernesto
Charlotte	GILMAN fe,w Am	Checker,	CHUBBY mr Am
Charlotte	HENRY	Cheech	MARIN(Richard)
Charlotte	LEWIS	Cheek,	MOLLY tv
Charlotte	MEW po Br	Cheever,	JOHN p-f'79
Charlotte	RAE tv+	Chekhov,	ANTON w Rus
Charlotte	STEWART tv+	Chelcie	ROSS
Charlotte	WYNTERS	Chelo	ALONSO
Charlotte	YONGE w,ed Br	Chelsea	BROWN tv
Charlton	HESTON tv+	Chelsea	FIELD
Charmoli,	TONY ba,tv Am	Chelsea	NOBLE tv
Charnele	BROWN tv	Chen	KAIGE d
Charney,	JORDAN tv	Chen	SHING
Charo	--- tv+	Chen	SING
Charpak,	GEORGES n-p'92	Chen Ning Yang	--- n-p'57
Charpentier,	GUSTAVE c Fr	Chen,	JOAN tv+
Charpentier,	MARC organ,c Fr	Chenault,	RENEE tv
Charpin	---	Cheney,	SHELDON ct,ed Am
Charters,	SPENCER	Chenier,	ANDRE de po Fr
Chartier,	ALAIN w,st Fr	Chennault,	CLAIRE ar,flyer Am
Chartier,	EMILE ph,w Fr	Cheong,	GEORGE tv
Chartoff,	MELANIE tv+	Cher	--- o-a'87,tv+
Chase,	BUD tv	Cherenkov,	PAVEL n-p'58
Chase,	CHARLEY	Cheret,	JULES p Fr
Chase,	CHARLIE tv	Cheri	CAFFARO
Chase,	CHEVY tv+	Cheri	OTERI tv
Chase,	ERIC tv	Cherie	CURRIE
Chase,	ILKA tv+	Cherie	JOHNSON tv
Chase,	JENNIFER	Cherie	LUNGHI
Chase,	LUCIA ba Am	Cherkassov,	NIKOLAI
Chase,	MARY ELLEN w,e Am	Chernov,	VIKTOR j,st Rus
Chase,	MARY p-d'45	Chernyshevsky,	NIKOLAY ct,ed
Chase,	SALMON st,l Am	Cherrie	CURRIE s Am
Chase,	STEVE	Cherry,	BYRON tv
Chase,	SYLVIA tv	Cherry,	DON tv
Chase,	WILLIAM p Am	Cherry,	HUGH tv
Chasins,	ABRAM piano Am	Cherry,	NENEH s-pop,rap Swe
Chastain,	DON tv	Cherubini,	LUIGI c It
Chastity	BONO tv	Cheryl	BAKER mr,s Br
Chatterjee,	BANKIM w India	Cheryl	LADD tv+
Chatterjee,	SOUMITRA	Cheryl	MILLER bb hf
Chatterton,	RUTH	Cheryl	MILLER tv+
Chatterton,	THOMAS po Br	Cheryl	POLLAK
Chau-Li	CHI tv	Cheryl	SMITH(Rainbeaux)
Chaucer,	GEOFFREY po Br	Cheryl	TIEGS mo,w Am
Chaudet,	DENIS su,p Fr	Cheryl	WATERS
Chauncey	DEPEW l,id,st Am	Cheryl"Rainbeaux"---	
Chauncey	OLCOTT la,s,c Am	Cherylene	LEE tv
Chausson,	ERNEST c Fr	Chesbro,	JOHN b hf
Chautemps,	CAMILLE st Fr	Cheseboro,	GEORGE
Chauvel,	JEAN st Fr	Chesis,	EILEEN tv
Chaves,	RICHARD tv+	Chesney,	DIANA tv
Chavez,	CARLOS c,cn Mex	Chesnutt,	CHARLES w,e,l Am
Chavez,	CESAR labor Am	Chester	BOWLES ec,st Am
Chavez,	ROBERT tv+	Chester	CARLSON i Am
Chay	LENTIN tv	Chester	COLEY tv
Chayefsky,	PADDY w Am	Chester	CONKLIN
Chayefsky,	SIDNEY(Paddy)w Am	Chester	GOULD cr Am

Chester	HIMES w Am	Chinh,	KIEU
Chester	MORRIS	Chino	WILLIAMS tv
Chester	NIMITZ navy Am	Chinua	ACHEBE w Nigeria
Chester Alan ARTHUR 21st pres		Chip	FRYE tv
Chester,	COLBY tv	Chip	LUCIO
Chester,	GEORGE w Am	Chip	MAYER
Chesterton, G.K. j,w,po Br		Chip	ZIEN tv
Chet	ATKINS s-cnt Am	Chippendale,THOMAS furnit	
Chet	BAKER mj-trump Am	Chirico,	GEORGIO De p It
Chet	HUNTLEY tv-j Am	Chishu	RYU
Chet	ROBLE tv	Chisum,	JOHN cattleman Am
Chettle,	HENRY w Br	Chita	RIVERA s,tv+ Am
Cheung,	LESLIE	Chitta	DAS st India
Chevalier de LAMARCK sc,w Fr		Chloe	FRANKS
Chevalier,ALBERT la Br		Chloe	WEBB tv+
Chevalier,MAURICE		Cho,	MARGARET cm+
Chevalier,ULYSSE r,e Fr		Choate,	JOSEPH l,st Am
Cheves,	LANGDON f,st Am	Choate,	RUFUS l,st Am
Chevrolet,LOUIS id-cars Am		Choate,	TIM
Chevy	CHASE tv+	Chocano,	JOSE po Peru
Cheyney,	PETER w Br	Chomsky,	MARVIN tv-pr,d
Chez	LISTER tv	Chomsky,	NOAM linguist Am
Chi,	CHAU-LI tv	Chong,	JUN
Chia	KAI	Chong,	RAE DAWN
Chia	LING	Chong,	THOMAS(Tommy)
Chiaki,	MINORU	Chopin,	FREDERIC c Pol
Chiang Kaishek---ar,st China		Chopin,	KATE w Am
Chiang,	DAVID	Chopra,	DEEPAK w India
Chiba,	SONNY	Choquette,ROBERT po,w Can	
Chic	JOHNSON	Chou Enlai --- st China	
Chic	SALE	Choudray,	SARITA
Chic	YOUNG cr Am	Chris	BRITTON mr-guit Br
Chichester,FRANCIS(Sir)fly		Chris	COLUMBUS d
Chick	COREA mj,piano,c	Chris	COOPER
Chick	EVANS(Chas)g Am	Chris	CORNELLmr-drm,s,w
Chick	HAFEY b hf	Chris	CROSS mr-bass Br
Chick	HEARN tv	Chris	CURTIS mr-drm,s
Chick	VENNERA	Chris	De BURGH s,ws Arg
Chick	WEBB mj-dum,cn Am	Chris	DIFFORD mr-guit,s
Chicken	HIRSCH mr-drm Br	Chris	DREJA mr-guit Br
Chico	MARX la,cm+ Am	Chris	ELLIOTT cm,w,tv+
Chief	BENDER b hf	Chris	EMERY tv
Chief Dan GEORGE		Chris	EVERT t,tv Am
Chieko	NANIWA	Chris	FARLEY tv+
Chiklis,	MICHAEL tv	Chris	FOREMAN mr-guit Br
Child,	CHARLES sc,e Am	Chris	FRANTZ drm Am
Child,	FRANCIS w Am	Chris	GRATTON fb
Child,	JULIA chef,w,tv	Chris	HAYES mr-guit Am
Child,	LYDIA fe,w Am	Chris	HAYWOOD
Childe	HASSAM p Am	Chris	HEBERT tv
Childe,	VERE sc Aust	Chris	HILLMAN mr-bass,s
Childress,ALVIN tv		Chris	HUTSON tv
Childs,	SUZANNE tv	Chris	ISAAK s+ Am
Chiles,	LINDEN tv+	Chris	LEMMON
Chiles,	LOIS tv+	Chris	LOWE mr-kbds Br
Chill	WILLS tv+	Chris	MAZZA w Am
Chilton,	ALEX mr-guit,s Am	Chris	MITCHUM
Chilvers,	SIMON	Chris	MULKEY tv+
Chin,	TSAI	Chris	NOEL tv
Ching,	WILLIAM	Chris	REA s,ws Br
Chingiz	AITAMOV w Rus	Chris	ROCK tv+

Chris SQUIRE mr-bass Br	Christina PICKLES tv
Chris STACY tv	Christina RAINES tv+
Chris STANLEY tv	Christina RICCI
Chris STEIN mr-guit Am	Christina STEAD w Aust
Chris TUCKER	Christine BELFORD tv+
Chris WALKER tv	Christine ELISE tv+
Chris WALLACE tv	Christine KAUFMAN
Chris WHITE mr-bass Br	Christine LAHTI
Chris WIGGINS tv+	Christine LAKIN tv
Chris YOUNG tv+	Christine McGUIRE tv
Chrisholm,HUGH j,ed Br	Christine McINTYRE
Chrissie HYNDE mr-s Am	Christine McVIE mr-kbds,s Br
Christa DENTON	Christine NELSON tv
Christensen, TODD tv	Christine PASCAL
Christiaan BEYERS ar,st S.Af	Christine TACHIK w Am
Christiaan EIJKMAN md,sc Dut	Christine TUCCI tv
Christiaan HUYGENS math,sc	Christine WHITE tv
Christiaan de WETar,st S.Af	Christine,VIRGINIA tv+
Christian BALE	Christipher JOY tv
Christian COUSINS tv	Christmas,ERIC tv+
Christian DIOR ds Fr	Christof PERICK cn Ger
Christian DOPPLER sc,e Aus	Christoff,BORIS basso Bulg
Christian DUGUAY d	Christoph GLUCK c Aus
Christian FALSEN st Nor	Christophe, FRANCOISE
Christian GRABBE w Ger	Christophe, HENRI king-Haiti
Christian HERTER st Am	Christopher ALLPORT
Christian JACOBS tv	Christopher ANSTEY po Br
Christian KROGH p Nor	Christopher ATKINS tv+
Christian KUPPER p Dut	Christopher BARNES tv
Christian LANGE st,peace Nor	Christopher BOLTON tv
Christian Le BLANC tv	Christopher BRENNAN po Aust
Christian NEEFE c Ger	Christopher BROWN tv
Christian OSMOND tv	Christopher BURKE tv
Christian ROHLFS p Ger	Christopher CARSON=Kit &
Christian SLATER	Christopher C. Indian Scout
Christian VULPIUS w Ger	Christopher CARY tv
Christian WOLFF ph,math Ger	Christopher CASTILE tv+
Christian de DUVE md Belg	Christopher CAT tavern Br
Christian,CHARLIE mj,guit Am.	Christopher COLLET
Christian,CLAUDIA	Christopher CROSS guit,s Am
Christian FLETCHER mutiny Br	Christopher DOUGLAS tv
Christian,GARRY s Br	Christopher DURANG
Christian,JOHN	Christopher FRY w Br
Christian,LINDA	Christopher FULLER tv
Christian,MICHAEL tv+	Christopher GABLE ba+ Br
Christian,ROGER s Br	Christopher GEORGE tv+
Christian,RUSSELL s Br	Christopher GIST frontier Am
Christian,SHAWN tv	Christopher GRIEVE po Scot
Christian,WILLIAM tv	Christopher GUEST tv+
Christiansen,JACK fb,hf	Christopher HEWETT tv
Christiansen,ROSEANNA tv	Christopher JONES tv+
Christie CLARK tv	Christopher KNIGHT tv+
Christie, AGATHA(Dame)w	Christopher LAMBERT
Christie, AUDREY tv+	Christopher LASCH h,e Am
Christie, DINAH tv	Christopher LEE
Christie, JULIE o-a'65	Christopher LLOYD tv+
Christie, LOU s,ws Am	Christopher MARLOWE w Br
Christina FERRARE tv+	Christopher MARTIN
Christina HAAG tv	Christopher MAYER tv
Christina NIGRA tv	Christopher McDONALD
	Christopher MORLEY w,ed Am

Christopher MURNEY	Chukovskaya, LIDIA w Rus
Christopher NEAME	Chung, BYRON tv
Christopher NORRIS tv	Chung, CONNIE tv-j Am
Christopher NOTH tv+	Church, BENJAMIN md,spy Am
Christopher OKIGBO po Nigeria	Church, FRANK st Am
Christopher PENN	Church, FREDERIC p Am
Christopher PETTIET tv	Church, RICHARD po,w,ct Br
Christopher PLUMMER	Church, THOMAS HADEN tv
Christopher REEVE	Church, WILLIAM i Am
Christopher REID	Churchill,BERTON
Christopher RICH tv+	Churchill,CHARLES r,po Br
Christopher ROUSE c Am	Churchill,RANDOLPH w,j Br
Christopher RYDELL	Churchill,SARAH po+ Br
Christopher SHOLES i Am &	Churchill,WINSTON w Am
Christopher SH. typewriter	Churchill,WINSTON(Sir)n-l'53
Christopher SMART po,j Br	Chus LAMPREAVE
Christopher SOWER pb Am	Ciampa, JO
Christopher STEARNS tv	Ciampi, VINCENZO c It
Christopher STONE tv+	Ciannelli,EDUARDO tv+
Christopher TYE c Br	Ciano, GALEAZZO st It
Christopher WALKEN	Ciaran MADDEN
Christopher WIELAND po,w Ger	Ciardi, JOHN po.e,ct Am
Christopher WREN(Sir)ac	Cibber, CAIUS su Dan
Christopher, DENNIS	Cibber, COLLEY w,po,la Br
Christopher, GERARD tv	Cibrian, EDDIE tv
Christopher, WILLIAM tv+	Ciccolella, JUDE
Christus, PETRUS p Belg	Cicely TYSON tv+
Christy CABANNE d	Cicero, MARCUS st,ph Ro
Christy, DOROTHY	Cid, EL ar,hero Sp
Christy, EDWIN la, s Am	Cierva, JUAN de la i,eng Sp
Christy, HOWARD illus,p Am	Cignani, CARLO p It
Christy, JUNE mj-s Am	Cigoli, LODOVICO da p,ac It
Christy, KEN tv	Cilea, FRANCESCO c It
Christy, MICHAEL tv	Cilento, DIANE
Chrysler, WALTER id-cars Am	Cilla BLACK s,tv Br
Chu BERRY mj-sax Am	Cima, GIOVANNI p It
Chu Hsi --- r,w China	Ciment, JILL w Am
Chu, STEVEN n-p'97	Cimino, MICHAEL o-d'78
Chuang BUNNAG st Siam	Cindi LAUPER s+ Am
Chubb, THOMAS r,w Br	Cindy ADAMS j,tv
Chubby CHECKER mr Am	Cindy MORGAN tv
Chubby Chuck ROE cm, tv	Cindy PICKETT tv+
Chuck BARRIS tv-pr	Cindy ROBBINS tv
Chuck BERRY mr,tv Am	Cindy WILSON mr-guit,s
Chuck BULOT tv	Cinna, GAIUS HELVIUSpo Ro
Chuck CASSEY tv	Cinnamon IDLES
Chuck CONNORS tv+	Cioffi, CHARLES tv+
Chuck DALY bbc hf	Cione, ANDREA di p,su,ac
Chuck HENRY tv	Cipollina, JOHN mr-guit Am
Chuck HYATT bb hf	Cipriano CASTRO st Venz
Chuck McCANN	Cipriano de RORE c Belg
Chuck NEGRON mr-s Am	Cirillo, JOE tv
Chuck NOLL fb hf	Ciro ALERRIA w Peru
Chuck NORRIS tv+	Ciro FERRI p It
Chuck PANOZZO mr-bass Am	Cis RUNDLE tv
Chuck PORTZ mr-bass Am	Cisar, GEORGE tv
Chuck RAYNER ho	Cisneros, SANDRA w Sp
Chuck SHAMATA	Citino, DAVID w Am
Chuck TRANUM tv	Citroen, ANDRE id-cars Fr
Chuck VINCENT d	Citti, FRANCO
Chuck YEAGER test fly Am	Cladel, LEON w Fr

Claiborne,LIZ ds,mer Am

Clair,   JANY

Clair,   RENE w,d+ Fr+

Clair,   RICHARD tv

Claire   BLOOM

Claire   DANES tv+

Claire   KELLY

Claire   MAURIER

Claire   McDOWELL

Claire   TREVOR

Claire   YARLETT tv

Claire,   DOROTHY tv

Claire,   INA

Clancy   BROWN

Clancy,   TOM w Am

Clanny,   WILLIAM md,i Br

Clapp,   GORDON tv+

Clapperton, HUGH x Scot

Clapton, ERIC mr Br &

Clapton, ERIC 2 g-r's'92

Clara   BARTON ARC am

Clara   BOW

Clara   BUTT(Dame)contralto

Clara   DAVIES s,e Br

Clara   MORRIS la Am

Clara   REEVE w Br

Clara   VIEBIG w Ger

Clara   YOUNG

Clara   ZETKIN fe,st Ger

Clare   BRIGGS cr Am

Clare   CAREY tv

Clare   HIGGINS

Clare   WREN tv+

Clare Boothe LUCE pb Am

Clare,   JOHN po Br

Clare,   MARY

Clarence BARRON ed,pb Am

Clarence BROWN d

Clarence DARROW l Am

Clarence DAY Jr w Am

Clarence EDDY organ,c Am

Clarence FELDER tv+

Clarence GAINES bbc hf

Clarence GILYARD Jr. tv+

Clarence HENRY s Am

Clarence HOUSER o-g'24'28

Clarence KOLB tv+

Clarence McCLUNG sc,e Am

Clarence MULFORD w Am

Clarence MUSE tv+

Clarence PARKER(Ace)fb hf

Clarence SMITH mj-s Am &

Clarence SMITH=Pinetop

Clarendon,EDWARD w,st Br

Clari,   GIOVANNI c It

Clarice   TAYLOR tv

Clarimond,AIME

Clark   BRANDON tv+

Clark   CARR tv

Clark   GABLE

Clark   HOWAT tv

Clark   JOHNSON tv+

Clark   KENT fc

Clark   MILLS su Am

Clark   WISSLER an Am

Clark   YOCUM mj-s Am

Clark,   ALAN mr-kbds Am

Clark,   ALVAN astr,id Am

Clark,   BLAKE

Clark,   BOB(Benjamin)d

Clark,   CANDY

Clark,   CAROL HIGGINS w Am

Clark,   CHAMP st Am

Clark,   CHRISTIE tv

Clark,   DANE tv+

Clark,   DAVE mr-drm Br

Clark,   DICK tv+

Clark,   DUTCH fb hf

Clark,   ERNEST tv

Clark,   EUGENE tv

Clark,   FRED tv+

Clark,   GAGE tv

Clark,   GEORGE re,ar Am

Clark,   GRAEME mr-bass

Clark,   GREYDON d

Clark,   HARRY tv

Clark,   JACK tv

Clark,   JAMES racecar Br

Clark,   JOHN ec,e Am

Clark,   JOHN l-supr ct Am

Clark,   KENNETH h-art Br

Clark,   LIDDY

Clark,   MARK ar Am

Clark,   MARLENE tv+

Clark,   MARY HIGGINS w Am

Clark,   MATT

Clark,   OLIVER tv+

Clark,   PETULA s-pop+

Clark,   PHILIP tv

Clark,   ROY s-cnt,tv Am

Clark,   STEVE

Clark,   STEVE mr-guit Br

Clark,   SUSAN tv+

Clark,   TOM st Am

Clark,   WALTER van w Am

Clark,   WILFRID(Sir)md,an

Clark,   WILL b,rbi'88

Clark,   WILLIAM ar,x Am

Clarke   HINKLE fb hf

Clarke,   ALLAN mr-s Br

Clarke,   ARTHUR w-scifi Can

Clarke,   AUSTIN po Ir

Clarke,   BOBBY ho-m'73'5'6

Clarke,   FRANK sc,e Am

Clarke,   FRED b hf

Clarke,   GARY tv+

Clarke,   HELEN ed,w Am

Clarke,   JEREMIAH organ,c Br

Clarke,   JOHN tv

Clarke,   KENNY mj,drm Am

Clarke,   LENNY tv

Clarke,   MAE

Clarke,	MICHAEL mr-drm Am
Clarke,	MINDY
Clarke,	ROBERT
Clarke,	ROBERT w Am
Clarke,	VAN NESSA tv
Clarke,	VINCE mr-kbds Br
Clarke,	WARREN
Clarkson,	JOHN b hf
Clarkson,	LANA
Clarkson,	PATRICIA
Clarkson,	PATTI tv
Claro	RECTO st Phil
Clary,	ROBERT tv+
Clash,	KEVIN tv
Claude	AKINS tv+
Claude	BERRI d,pr-films+ Fr
Claude	BOWERS j,h Am
Claude	BROOKS tv
Claude	BROWN w Am
Claude	CHABROL d
Claude	DAUPHIN
Claude	DEBUSSY c Fr
Claude	GELLEE p Fr
Claude	GILLOT p Fr
Claude	JARMAN Jr.
Claude	JOHNSON tv
Claude	JONES tv+
Claude	LEDOUX ac Fr
Claude	LELOUCH d
Claude	LORRAIN p Fr
Claude	MAURIAC w Fr
Claude	McKAY po,w Am
Claude	MICHEL su Fr
Claude	MONET p Fr
Claude	PAJOL ar Fr
Claude	PEPPER st Am
Claude	PHELPS(Jackie)tv
Claude	RAINS
Claude	RICH
Claude	SAUTET d
Claude	SIMON w Fr
Claude	VILLARS st,ar Fr
Claude de	FORBIN navy Fr
Claude de	ROUVROY ref Fr
Claude Lorrain--- p Fr	
Claude,	ALBERT n-m'74
Claude,	GEORGES sc Fr
Claudel,	PAUL w,po,st Fr
Claudette	COLBERT
Claudette	NEVINS tv+
Claudette	WELLS tv
Claudia	BRYAR tv
Claudia	DELL
Claudia	DRAKE
Claudia	LAMB tv
Claudia	LONOW tv
Claudia	OHANA
Claudine	AUGER
Claudio	ARRAU piano Am
Claudio	BIGAGLI
Claudio	BROOK

Claudio	COELLO p Sp
Claudio	MERULO organ,c It
Claudio da	COSTA po Braz
Claudius	DORNIER id-aero Ger
Claus	SLUTER su Dut
Claussen,	SOPHUS po Dan
Clavell,	JAMES w Am
Clawson,	CONNIE tv
Clay	HART s,tv Am
Clay,	ANDREW DICE
Clay,	ANDREW tv
Clay,	HENRY st Am
Clay,	NICHOLAS
Clayburgh,	JILL
Claydes	SMITH mr-guit Am
Clayton	MOORE tv+
Clayton	PRINCE tv
Clayton	ROHNER
Clayton,	ADAM mr-bass Ir
Clayton,	BUCK mj-trump Am
Clayton,	HENRY st Am
Clayton,	JAN tv
Clayton,	JOHN st Am
Clayton,	MERRY tv
Clayton-Thomas,	DAVID mr-s
Clea	LEWIS tv+
Cleanth	BROOKS e,ct,w Am
Cleary,	BEVERLY w Am
Cleavon	LITTLE tv+
Cleese,	JOHN
Cleeves,	ANN w Br
Clegg,	TOM d
Cleghorne,	ELLEN tv
Cleland,	JOHN w Br
Clem	BEVANS
Clem	McCARTHY horseraces
Clemence	DANE w Br
Clemenceau,	GEORGES st,w Fr
Clemens	WINKLER sc,e Ger
Clemens,	JACOBUS c Belg
Clemens,	MARK w Am
Clemens,	PAUL
Clemens,	ROGER b-mv'86 &
Clemens,	ROG.b-cy'86'7,'91'7
Clemens,	SAMUEL w Am
Clement	ADER eng,i Fr
Clement	ATLEE st Br
Clement	MAROT po Fr
Clement	MOORE po,e Am
Clement	WEBB ph,e,w Br
Clement	WOOD w Am
Clement,	AURORE
Clement,	RENE d
Clemente,	ROBERTO b-mv'86 &
Clemente,	ROBERTO gg's hf
Clementi,	MUZIO piano,c It
Clementi,	PIERRE
Clements,	JOHN
Clennon,	DAVID tv+
Cleo	LAINE mj-s Am
Cleon	JONES b

Clerk,	DUGALD(Sir)eng,i		Clive	CUSSLER w Am
Clery,	CORINNE		Clive	DONNER d
Clete	BOYER b		Clive	IRVING j,w Am
Cleve,	JOOS van p Belg		Clive	LEWIS w,e Br
Cleve,	PER TEODOR sc Swi		Clive	MORTON
Cleveland ABBE weather Am			Clive	REVILL
Cleveland,GEORGE tv+			Clive	TAYLOR mr-bass
Cleveland,GROVER 22nd &			Clive	WOOD
Cleveland,GROVER 24th Pres			Clive,	COLIN
Cleveland,JAMES s-gospel Am			Clive,	E.E.
Cleveland,JOHN po Br			Clive,	KITTY la Br
Cleveland,ODESSA tv			Clive,	ROBERT st Br
Cliburn,	VAN piano Am		Cliver,	AL
Cliff	BATTLES fb hf		Cloete,	STUART w S.Afr
Cliff	BEMIS tv		Clohessy,	ROBERT tv
Cliff	DeYOUNG tv+		Clooney,	GEORGE tv+
Cliff	EDWARDS m-uke,tv+		Clooney,	ROSEMARY s,tv+ Am
Cliff	GORMAN		Cloos,	HANS geol, e Ger
Cliff	HAGAN bb hf		Clopton	HAVERS md Br
Cliff	HALL tv		Close,	DEL
Cliff	NAZARRO		Close,	ERIC tv
Cliff	NORTON cm,tv Am		Close,	GLENN
Cliff	OSMOND		Closterman, JOHN p Br	
Cliff	POTTER tv		Clouet,	FRANCOIS p Fr
Cliff	POTTS tv+		Clouet,	JEAN p Belg
Cliff	RICHARD mr-drm,s		Clough,	APRIL tv
Cliff,	JIMMY s,ws Jamaica		Clough,	ARTHUR po Br
Clifford	BEERS ref Am		Clouse,	ROBERT d
Clifford	EVANS		Clower,	JERRY tv
Clifford	ODETS w Am		Clu	GULAGER tv+
Clifford	SALES tv		Cluett,	SANFORD eng,i,id Am
Clifford	STOLL w Am		Clurman,	HAROLD pr,d,ct Am
Clifford, DOUG m-folk,drm Am			Clute,	SIDNEY tv
Clifford, GRAEME d			Cluzet,	FRANCOIS
Clifford, JACK			Clyde	BEATTY circus Am
Clifford, NATHAN l,st Am			Clyde	FITCH w Am
Clift,	MONTGOMERY		Clyde	KUSATSU tv+
Clifton	DAVIS tv+		Clyde	McCOY mj,cn Am
Clifton	FADIMAN w,ed,tv Am		Clyde	TURNER fb hf &
Clifton	JAMES tv+		Clyde	TURNER=Bulldog
Clifton	JONES tv		Clyde,	ANDY tv+
Clifton	WEBB		Clyde,	JEREMY mr-guit,s
Clifton, ELMER d			Clyde,	JUNE
Cline,	EDDIE d		Clyfford	STILL p Am
Cline,	PATSY s Am		Clynes,	JOHN unions,st Br
Clint	BLACK s-cnt,ws		Coase,	RONALD n-e'91
Clint	HOLMES tv		Coates,	FLORENCE po Am
Clint	HOWARD tv+		Coates,	KIM tv+
Clint	WALKER tv+		Coates,	PHYLLIS tv+
Clint	WARWICK mr-bass Br		Cobb,	BUFF tv
Clinton	FISK ar,f,e Am		Cobb,	EDMOND
Clinton, BILL 42nd pres			Cobb,	HENRY ac Am
Clinton, CHELSEA b's daugh			Cobb,	HOWELL st Am
Clinton, DeWITT st Am			Cobb,	IRVIN w-humor,j Am
Clinton, GEORGE s-funk Am			Cobb,	JOE
Clinton, HILLARY RODHAM &			Cobb,	JOHN racecar Scot
Clinton, HILLARY R.1st Lady			Cobb,	JULIE tv
Clive	BARKER w Br		Cobb,	KEITH tv
Clive	BELL ct,w Br		Cobb,	LEE J.
Clive	BROOK		Cobb,	RANDALL(TEX)
Clive	BUNKER mr-drm Br		Cobb,	TY(Geo.Peach)b hf

Cobb,	TYRUS see Ty	Cohen,	J.J.
Cobbe,	FRANCES f,w Br	Cohen,	JILL tv
Cobbett,	WILLIAM w,j Br	Cohen,	LARRY d
Cobbs,	BILL	Cohen,	LEONARD s,po,ws Can
Cobden,	RICHARD st,ec Br	Cohen,	MARTY tv
Cobina	WRIGHT Jr.	Cohen,	MOE mj-sax Am
Cobler,	JAN tv	Cohen,	MYRON cm Am
Coburn,	ALVIN fo Br	Cohen,	OCTAVUS w Am
Coburn,	CHARLES o-s'43, tv+	Cohen,	STANLEY n-m'86
Coburn,	DONALD p-d'78	Cohen-Tannoudji, CLAUDE &
Coburn,	JAMES o-s'99	Cohen-Tannoudji, CL. n-p'97
Coca,	IMOGENE tv+	Cohn,	AL mj-sax Am
Cochise	--- Apache chief	Cohn,	EDWIN sc,e Am
Cochran,	CHARLES(Sir)pr	Cohn,	FERDINAND sc.e Ger
Cochran,	EDDIE mr Am	Cohn,	MINDY tv
Cochran,	JACQUELINE fly Am	Cohn,	ROY l Am
Cochran,	ROBERT	Cohoon,	PATTI tv
Cochran,	RON tv	Coin	HARVEY ec Am
Cochran,	STEVE	Coke,	EDWARD(Sir)l,st
Cochran,	THAD st Am	Cokie	ROBERTS tv-news Am
Cochrane	MICKEY b-mv'34 hf	Cola di	RIENZO re It
Cochrane,	ROBERT tv	Colasanto,NICHOLAS tv
Cockburn,	ALICIA po Scot	Colbert,	CLAUDETTE o-a'34
Cockcroft,JOHN(Sir)n-p'51	Colbert,	PAT tv
Cocker,	JOE mr Am	Colbert,	ROBERT tv
Coco	CHANEL ds Fr	Colbin,	ROD tv
Coco,	JAMES	Colburn,	IRVING i,id Am
Cocteau,	JEAN po,w,d Fr	Colby	CHESTER tv
Codona,	ALFREDO trapeze Mex	Colby,	ANITA tv
Codrescu,	ANDREI w Am	Colby,	FRANK ed,e Am
Coduri,	CAMILLE	Colby,	MARION tv
Cody,	BILL	Cole	PORTER c,lyrics Am
Cody,	IRON EYES	Cole	YOUNGER desparado
Cody,	WILLIAM(Buff.Bill)Am	Cole,	BRIAN mr-bass,s Am
Coe,	BARRY tv+	Cole,	CASSIE tv
Coe,	FRED pr-tv	Cole,	COZY mj drums Am
Coe,	GEORGE	Cole,	DENNIS tv+
Coe,	ROGER miler Br	Cole,	FAY-COOPER an,e Am
Coe,	SEBASTIAN o-g'80'84	Cole,	GARY tv+
Coehlo Neto, ENRIQUE w Braz	Cole,	GEORGE
Coelho,	PAULO w Braz	Cole,	GEORGE ec,e Br
Coello,	CLAUDIO p Sp	Cole,	HARRY tv
Coen,	ETHAN w Am	Cole,	LLOYD mr-guit,s Br
Coen,	JOEL w,d Am	Cole,	MICHAEL tv+
Coffey,	SCOTT	Cole,	NAT KING s,tv+ Am &
Coffield,	KELLY tv	Cole,	NAT KING 2g-r's'91
Coffin,	FREDERICK	Cole,	NATALIE s,tv+ Am &
Coffin,	HOWARD eng-cars Am	Cole,	NATALIE 2g-r's'91
Coffin,	ROBERT w,p-q'36	Cole,	OLIVIA tv+
Coffin,	TRISTRAM(Tris)	Cole,	ROCKY tv
Cogan,	SHAYE tv	Cole,	THOMAS p Am
Coghill,	NIKKI	Cole,	TINA tv
Coghlan,	FRANK"JUNIOR"	Coleby,	ROBERT
Coghlan,	JOHN mr-drm Br	Coleen	GRAY tv+
Coghlan,	ROSE la Am	Coleen	MOORE
Cohan,	GEORGE M.la,w,pr	Coleman	BLEASE st Am
Cohen,	BILLY tv	Coleman	HAWKINS mj-sax Am
Cohen,	DAVID mr-kbds Am	Coleman,	CAROLE tv
Cohen,	ELLEN tv	Coleman,	CY m,cn,tv Am
Cohen,	ERNST sc Dut	Coleman,	DABNEY tv+
Cohen,	EVAN tv	Coleman,	EMIL m,cn,tv Am

Coleman, GARY tv+
Coleman, JACK tv+
Coleman, JAMES tv
Coleman, ORNETTE mj,sax Am
Coleman, SIGNY tv
Colen, BEATRICE tv
Coleridge,SAMUEL po,ct Br
Coles, KIM tv
Coles, ROBERT p-n'73
Colette, SIDONIE w Fr
Coley, DORIS mr-s Am
Colgate, WILLIAM id Am
Colgrass, MICHAEL p-m'78
Colicos, JOHN tv+
Colihan, PATRICE tv
Colin BLAKELY
Colin BRUCE tv+
Colin BUCKSEY d
Colin CLIVE
Colin DAVIS(Sir)c,cn
Colin DEXTER w Br
Colin FIRTH
Colin FRIELS
Colin GORDON
Colin HAY s Scot
Colin MALE tv
Colin POWELL ar,w Am
Colin TAPLEY tv
Colin WILSON w,ct Br
Colin, MARGARET tv+
Colla, JOHNNY mr-sax,guit
Colla, RICHARD d
Colle, CHARLES w Fr
Colle, RAFFAELLO dal p It
Colleen CAMP
Collen, PHIL mr-guit Br
Colles, HENRY ct,w Br
Collet, CHRISTOPHER
Collett, CAMILLA fe,w Nor
Colley CIBBER w,po,la Br
Colley, DON PEDRO tv
Colley, KENNETH
Collier, CONSTANCE la+ Br
Collier, DICK tv
Collier, DON tv
Collier, JOHN ct Br
Collier, JOHN w Am
Collier, LOIS tv
Collier, MARIAN tv
Collier, RICHARD tv
Collingwood, CHARLES tv
Collingwood, ROBIN h,e,w Br
Collins, ALAN
Collins, ALLEN mr-guit Am
Collins, DOROTHY tv
Collins, EDDIE b,bmg hf
Collins, GARY tv
Collins, JACK tv
Collins, JACKIE w Am
Collins, JAMES b hf
Collins, JOAN tv+

Collins, JOHNNIE III tv
Collins, JUDYmr,folk,guit Am
Collins, LEWIS
Collins, MICHAEL as Am
Collins, PAT tv
Collins, PHIL mr-s,g-r'90+
Collins, RAY tv+
Collins, ROBERTA
Collins, RUSSELL
Collins, RUTH
Collins, SHAD mj-trump Am
Collins, STEPHEN tv+
Collins, TED tv
Collins, WILKIE w Br
Collins, WILLIAM po Br
Collinson,PETER d
Collison, WILSON w Am
Collyer, BUD tv
Collyer, JUNE tv+
Colm FEORE
Colm MEANEY tv+
Colman, GEORGE w Br &
Colman, GEORGE=The Elder
Colman, RONALD o-a'47,tv+
Colman, SAMUEL p Am
Colmar von der GOLTZ ar Ger
Colombe, MICHEL su Fr
Colombo, REALDO md It
Colomby, BOBBY mr-drm,s Am
Colomby, SCOTT
Colonel HOUSE(Edw.)st Am
Colonel SANDERS mer-KFC Am
Colonel John D. CRAIG tv
Colonna, FRANCESCO w,r It
Colonna, JERRY
Colonna, VITTORIA po It
Colorado, HORTENSIA tv
Colt, JOHNNY mr-bass Am
Colt, MACKENZIE tv
Colt, MARSHALL tv+
Colt, SAMUEL i,id-guns Am
Colter, JOHN x Am
Coltrane, JOHN mj-sax Am
Coltrane, ROBBIE
Colum, PADRAIC po,w Ir
Columbo, RUSS mj,c Am
Columbus, CHRIS d
Colvin, JACK tv+
Colvin, SIDNEY(Sir)ct,e
Comaneci, NADIA gy,3x o-g'76
Comar, RICHARD tv
Combe, WILLIAM w Br
Combes, EMILE st Fr
Combs, EARLE b hf
Combs, JEFFREY
Combs, RAY tv
Comden, BETTY lyrics Am
Comegys, KATHLEEN tv
Comer, ANJANETTE
Comfort, ALEX w Br
Comi, PAUL tv

Comiskey,	CHARLES bmg hf	Connie	CLAWSON tv
Commager,	HENRY h Am	Connie	FRANCIS s,tv Am
Commoner,	BARRY e,sc Am	Connie	HAWKINS bb hf
Como,	PERRY s,tv+ Am	Connie	HINES tv
Compere,	LOYSET c Fr	Connie	IZAY tv
Compson,	BETTY	Connie	MACK b,bmg hf
Compton,	ANN j	Connie	NEEDHAM tv
Compton,	ARTHUR n-p'27	Connie	RAY tv
Compton,	GAIL tv	Connie	RUSSELL tv
Compton,	GAY tv	Connie	SELLECA tv+
Compton,	JOYCE	Connie	SMITH
Compton,	KARL sc,e Am	Connie	STEVENS tv+
Compton,	RICHARD d	Connolly,	BILLY cm,tv+ Scot
Compton,	WALTER tv	Connolly,	BRIAN s Scot
Compton-Burnett,	IVY(Dame)w	Connolly,	CYRIL w,ct Br
Comstock,	HENRY id-mines Am	Connolly,	MAUREEN t Am &
Comstock,	JOHN sc,e,w Am	Connolly,	MAUREEN=Little Mo
Comte de	La PEROUSE x Fr	Connolly,	THOMAS H. b hf
Comte,	AUGUSTE ph Fr	Connolly,	WALTER
Conan	LEE	Connor,	GEORGE fb hf
Conan	O'BRIEN tv	Connor,	KENNETH
Conant,	JAMES e,sc Am	Connor,	KEVIN d
Conaway,	CRISTI	Connor,	ROGER b hf
Conaway,	JEFF tv+	Connor,	WHITFIELD tv
Conca,	SEBASTIANO p It	Connors,	CHUCK tv+
Concetta	TOMEI tv+	Connors,	JIMMY t Am
Conchata	FERRELL tv+	Connors,	MIKE tv+
Concini,	CONCINO roue Fr	Conny	Van DYKE
Conde	NAST pb Am	Conor	O'BRIEN h,ct,st Ir
Conde	PALLEN ed Am	Conquest,	ROBERT po,w Br
Condon,	EDDIE mj-guit,tv+	Conrad	AIKEN po,ct,w Am
Condon,	EDWARD sc,e,id Am	Conrad	BAIN tv+
Condra,	JULIE tv	Conrad	DOBER ws Am
Cone,	DAVID b-cy'94	Conrad	GESNER md,ps Swi
Conerly,	CHARLEY fb-m'59	Conrad	HILTON hotels Am
Congreve,	WILLIAM w Br	Conrad	JANIS tv+
Conklin,	CHESTER	Conrad	MEYER po,w Swi
Conklin,	HAROLD(Hal)tv	Conrad	NAGEL
Conkling,	ROSCOE st Am	Conrad	RICHTER w Am
Conlan	CARTER tv	Conrad	VEIDT
Conlan,	JOCKO b hf	Conrad	WEISER Indian agent
Conlee,	JOHN s Am	Conrad,	FRANK eng,i,id Am
Conley,	CORINNE tv	Conrad,	JOSEPH w Br
Conley,	DARLENE tv	Conrad,	MICHAEL tv+
Conley,	JOE tv	Conrad,	NANCY tv
Conn,	BILLY boxer Am	Conrad,	ROBERT tv+
Conn,	DIDI tv+	Conrad,	WILLIAM tv+
Connell,	EVAN w Am	Conried,	HANS tv+
Connell,	JIM tv	Conroy,	FRANCES
Connellan,	LEO po Am	Conroy,	FRANK
Connelly,	CHRISTOPHER tv+	Conroy,	KEVIN tv
Connelly,	JENNIFER	Conroy,	PAT w Am
Connelly,	MARC p-d'30	Conscience,	HENDRIK w Belg
Connelly,	PEGGY tv	Conseco,	JOSE b,hr'88'91
Conner,	BETTY tv	Considine,	BOB tv
Conner,	MICHAEL w Am	Considine,	JOHN
Connery,	JASON	Considine,	TIM tv+
Connery,	SEAN o-s'87	Constable,	HENRY po Br
Connick,	HARRY Jr.mj,s Am	Constable,	JOHN p Br
Connie	BOOTH	Constance	BENNETT
Connie	CHUNG tv-j Am	Constance	COLLIER la+ Br

Constance FORD		Cook,	PETER tv+
Constance HARPER tv		Cook,	ROBIN w Am
Constance McCASHIN tv+		Cook,	RODERICK tv+
Constance MOORE tv+		Cook,	STU m-folk,drm Am
Constance ROURKE h Am		Cook,	THOMAS tourists Br
Constance SKINNER w Am		Cook,	WILL m,c Am
Constance TOWERS		Cooke,	ALISTAIR tv
Constance WOOLSON w Am		Cooke,	HENRY c,cn Br
Constance WORTH		Cooke,	JENNIFER tv+
Constant LAMBERT c Br		Cooke,	JOHN w Am
Constant, PAUL d'E.de n-x'09		Cooke,	ROSE w Am
Constantin GUYS illus Fr		Cooke,	SAM s-gospel,r&b
Constantine, EDDIE		Cooke,	THOMAS po,j Br
Constantine, MICHAEL tv+		Cooksey,	DANNY tv
Consuelos,MARK tv		Cool Papa BELL b
Contardo, JOHNNY tv		Cool,	HARRY mj-s Am
Conte, JOHN tv+		Coolbrith,INA po Am
Conte, NICOLAS sc Fr		Coolidge, CALVIN 30th Pres
Conte, RICHARD		Coolidge, CHARLES ac Am
Conti, TOM		Coolidge, MARTHA d
Conti, VINCE tv		Coolidge, PHILIP tv
Contner, JAMES A. d		Coolidge, RITA s-cnt Am
Contreras,ROBERTO tv		Coolidge, WILLIAM sc,id Am
Converse, CHARLES c Am		Coon, CARLETON an,e Am
Converse, FRANK tv+		Coonce, RICKY drm Am
Converse-Roberts,WILLIAM tv+		Cooney, JOAN GANZ pr-tv Am
Convy, BERT tv+		Cooper HUCKABEE
Conway TEARLE		Cooper, ALICE
Conway TWITTY s-cnt+		Cooper, ALICE mr-s,ws Am
Conway, CAROLYN tv		Cooper, BUZZ tv
Conway, GARY tv+		Cooper, CATHY tv
Conway, JACK d		Cooper, CECIL b,rbi'80'83
Conway, JILL w Am		Cooper, CHARLES bb hf
Conway, KEVIN		Cooper, CHARLES tv
Conway, MORGAN		Cooper, CHRIS
Conway, PAT(female) tv		Cooper, GARY o-a'41,'52
Conway, PAT(male) tv+		Cooper, GEORGE
Conway, RUSS tv		Cooper, GILES w Br
Conway, SHIRL tv		Cooper, GLADYS tv+
Conway, TIM tv+		Cooper, INEZ
Conway, TOM tv+		Cooper, JACKIE d,tv+
Conwy MORGAN sc,ps,e,w		Cooper, JAMES FENIMORE w
Conzelman,JIM fb hf		Cooper, JEANNE tv+
Cooder, RY m-flk,blues &		Cooper, JEFF tv+
Cooder, RY guit,c Am		Cooper, LEON n-p'72
Coogan, JACKIE tv+		Cooper, MAGGIE tv+
Coogan, KEITH		Cooper, MARILYN tv
Coogan, RICHARD tv		Cooper, MELVILLE
Cook, BARBARA sopr Am		Cooper, MERIAN w,pr Am
Cook, BOB tv		Cooper, MORT b-mv'42
Cook, DONALD		Cooper, PAT
Cook, ELISHA Jr. tv+		Cooper, PETER id,f Am
Cook, FIELDER pr,d,tv		Cooper, SAMUEL p Br
Cook, FREDERICK md,x Am		Coote, EYRE(Sir)ar
Cook, GEORGE w,po Am		Coote, ROBERT tv+
Cook, JAMES(Cpt.)x Br		Copage, MARC tv
Cook, JEFF kbds,strngs,s		Cope, CHARLES p Br
Cook, JOSEPH(Sir)st Aust		Cope, EDWARD sc,e Am
Cook, NATHAN tv		Cope, JULIAN mr-bass,s
Cook, NORMAN mr-s Br		Copeau, JACQUES la,d Fr
Cook, PAUL mr-drm Br		Copeland, ALAN m,cn,tv Am

Copeland, CRAIG tv
Copland, AARON p-m'45
Copley, JOHN p Am
Copley, TERI
Coppard, ALFRED w Br
Coppee, FRANCIS w Fr
Copperfield, DAVID magic,tv
Coppola, FRANCIS FORD o-d'74
Coppola, SOFIA
Cora BAIRD puppets Am
Cora MIAO
Cora SANDEL w Nor
Coral BROWNE
Corbett MONICA tv
Corbett, GLENN tv+
Corbett, GRETCHEN tv+
Corbett, HARRY
Corbett, JAMES boxer Am &
Corbett, JAMES=Gentleman Jim
Corbett, JOHN tv
Corbin BERNSEN
Corbin, BARRY tv+
Corbucci, SERGIO d
Corbusier,LE ac,p,su Swi
Corby, ELLEN tv+
Corcoran, KELLY tv
Corcoran, KEVIN
Corcoran, NOREEN tv
Cord, ALEX tv+
Cord, ERRETT id-cars Am
Corday, JO tv
Corday, MARA
Corday, RITA
Cordell HULL st Am
Cordero, ANGEL jockey Am
Cordero, JOAQUIN
Cordoba, PEDRO de
Corea, CHICK mj-piano,c Am
Corelli, ARCANGELO viol,c It
Corelli, FRANCO s-opera It
Corelli, MARIE w Br
Corello, CLAUDIO p Sp
Coretta KING w Am
Corey ALLEN d Am
Corey FELDMAN tv+
Corey HAIM
Corey PARKER
Corey, ELIAS n-c'90
Corey, IRWIN tv
Corey, JEFF
Corey, JILL tv
Corey, JOE tv
Corey, WENDELL tv+
Corgan, BILLY mr-guit,s Am
Cori, CARL n-m'47
Cori, GERTY n-m'47
Cori, LISA tv
Corin NEMEC(Corky) tv+
Corin REDGRAVE
Corinne ALPHEN
Corinne CALVET

Corinne CAMACHO tv
Corinne CLERY
Corinne CONLEY tv
Corinth, LOVIS p Ger
Cork HUBBERT tv+
Corky NEMEC tv+
Corky PIGEON tv
Corley, AL tv
Corley, MARJORIE tv
Corley, PAT tv+
Corliss, GEORGE i,id Am
Cormack McCARTHY w Am
Cormack, ALLAN n-m'79
Corman, MADDIE tv+
Corman, ROGER d+
Corneille HEYMANS md,e Belg
Corneille, PIERRE w Fr
Corneille, THOMAS w Fr
Cornejo, MARIANO st,l Peru
Cornel WILDE
Cornelia SHARPE
Cornelia Otis SKINNER la,w
Cornelis CORT p Dut
Cornelis DONGEN p Dut &
Cornelis DONGEN=Kees van
Cornelis FLORIS ac,su Belg
Cornelis TIELE r,e Dut
Cornelis de HOUTMAN x Dut
Cornelis de VOS p Belg
Cornelius KEEFE
Cornelius TACITUS h Ro
Cornelius,HELEN m-cntry Am
Cornelius,PETER von p Ger
Cornell, CHRIS mr s Am
Cornell, DON tv
Cornell, EZRA f&f Am
Cornell, JOSEPH su Am
Cornell, KATHARINE la Am
Cornell, LYDIA tv
Cornford, FRANCES po Br
Cornforth,JOHN W. n-c'75
Cornick, GLENN mr-bass Br
Corning, ERASTUS id-rrs Am
Cornish, GENE mr-guitar Can
Cornu, PAUL eng Fr
Cornwell, DEAN illus,p Am
Cornwell, HUGH mr-guitar,s Br
Cornwell, PATRICIA w Am
Corot, JEAN p Fr
Corraface,GEORGES
Correggio,ANTONIO de p It
Correll, CHARLES tv
Correll, RICHARD tv
Correns, KARL sc,e Ger
Corri, ADRIENNE
Corri, NICK
Corrigan, LLOYD tv+
Corrigan, MAIREAD n-x'76
Corrigan, RAY
Corry, MONTAGU st,f Br
Corseaut, ANETA tv+

Corsia,	TED de tv+		Cotton,	CHARLES po Br
Corso	DONATI st It		Cotton,	JOHN r,w Br
Corso,	GREGORY po Am		Cotton,	ROBT.(Sir)collector
Cort,	BUD		Coty,	FRANCOIS id Fr
Cort,	CORNELIS p Dut		Coty,	RENE st Fr
Cort,	HENRY i Br		Couder,	LOUIS p Fr
Cortazar,	JULIO w Arg		Coue,	EMILE ps Fr
Corte-Real,	GASPAR x Port		Coues,	ELLIOT birds,w Am
Cortes,	HERNAN ar Sp		Coufos,	PAUL
Cortes,	MAPITA		Cougar,	JOHN s Am
Cortese,	JOE		Coughlan,	DICK tv
Cortese,	VALENTINA		Coughlin,	FRANCIS tv
Cortez,	HERNANDO st Sp		Coughlin,	KEVIN tv
Cortez,	RICARDO		Coulier,	DAVID tv
Corti,	LUIGI st It		Coulomb,	CHARLES sc Fr
Cortot,	ALFRED piano,cn Fr		Coulouris,	GEORGE
Cory	TYLER tv		Coulson,	CATHERINE tv
Cory	WELLS mr-s Am		Coulton,	JIM tv
Cory,	WILLIAM po,e Br		Count	BASIE mj,cn,c Am
Coryell,	JOHN w Am		Countee	CULLEN po Am
Cosa,	FRANCESCO Del p It		Countess	VAUGHN tv
Cosa,	JUAN de la x Sp		Country Joe McDONALD mr &
Cosby,	BILL tv+		Country Joe McDONALD guit,s
Cosell,	HOWARD sp tv+ Am		Couperus,	LOUIS w Dut
Cosenz,	ENRICO ar It		Coupland,	DOUGLAS w Can
Cosmatos,	GEORGE d		Courbet,	JEAN p Fr
Cosme	TURA p It		Couric,	KATIE tv
Cosmo	INNES antiq,e Scot		Cournand,	ANDRE F. n-m'56
Coss,	STEWART tv		Court,	HAZEL tv+
Cossa,	FRANCESCO del p It		Court,	MARGARET SMITH t
Cossa,	PIETRO w It		Courteney	COX tv+
Cossart,	ERNEST		Courteney,	TOM
Costa,	CLAUDIO da po Braz		Courtland,	JEROME
Costa,	ISAAC da po Dut		Courtney	GAINS
Costa,	LORENZO p It		Courtney	LOVE mr-s Am
Costa,	MARY tv		Courtney	PELDON tv
Costa,	MICHAEL(Sir)cn,c Br		Courtney	VANCE
Costa,	PETER tv		Courtney,	ALEX tv+
Costa,	URIEL da r,w Port		Courtney,	CHARLES coach,e Am
Costain,	THOMAS w Can		Courtney,	INEZ
Costanzo	FESTA s,c It		Courtney,	WILLIAM ph,j Br
Costanzo	VAROLIO md,e It		Courtois,	JACQUES p Fr
Costanzo,	ROBERT		Cousin	JODY tv
Costas,	BOB tv		Cousin,	JEAN Jr p Fr
Costell,	DAVID mr-bass Am		Cousin,	VICTOR ph Fr
Costello,	ELVIS mr,s Am		Cousins,	BRIAN
Costello,	LOU cm, tv+		Cousins,	CHRISTIAN tv
Costello,	MARICLARE tv+		Cousins,	JOSEPH tv
Costello,	PAT pr-tv		Cousins,	NORMAN j,ed Am
Coster,	NICHOLAS tv+		Cousteau,	JACQUES x,tv Fr
Costin,	MIRON po Moldavia		Coustou,	GUILLAUME su Fr
Costner,	KEVIN		Coustou,	NICHOLAS su Fr
Cosway,	RICHARD p Br		Cousy,	BOB bb-m'57 hf
Cotler,	KAMI tv+		Couzens,	JAMES id,st Am
Cotman,	JOHN p Br		Covan,	DeFOREST tv
Coto,	MANNY d		Covarrubias,	MIGUEL p Mex
Cotten,	JOSEPH tv+		Coveleski,	STAN b hf
Cotter	SMITH tv+		Coventry	PATMORE po Br
Cottet,	CHARLES p Fr		Cover,	FRANKLIN tv
Cotton	MATHER r,w Am		Coverdale,	DAVID mr-s Br
Cotton,	BILLY mj-drm,cn		Covilha,	PERO da x Port

Cowan,	JEROME tv+	Craig,	DON tv
Coward,	NOEL(Sir)c,w,la	Craig,	EDWARD la,pr Br
Cowell,	HENRY c Am	Craig,	HELEN tv+
Cowen,	FREDERIC(Sir)c,cn	Craig,	JAMES
Cowen,	JOSHUA i,id Am	Craig,	JOHN(Colonel)tv
Cowens,	DAVE bb-m'73 hf	Craig,	MALIN ar Am
Cowgil,	DAVID tv	Craig,	MICHAEL
Cowl,	JANE la Am	Craig,	MIKEY mr-bass Br
Cowley,	ABRAHAM po,w Br	Craig,	ROGER fb-m'88
Cowley,	BILL ho-m'41'3	Craig,	YVONNE tv+
Cowley,	HANNAH w Br	Craigie,	PEARL w Br
Cowley,	MALCOLM ct,w Am	Craik,	DINAH w Br
Cowling,	BRUCE	Crain,	JEANNE
Cowling,	SAM tv	Cram,	DONALD n-c'87
Cowper,	NICOLA	Cram,	RALPH w,e,ac Am
Cowper,	WILLIAM po Br	Cramer,	FLOYD mj-piano Am
Cowsill,	BARRY mr-bass,s Am	Cramer,	JOHANN piano,c Br
Cowsill,	BILL mr-guit,s Am	Cramer,	RICHARD
Cowsill,	BOB mr-guit,s Am	Cramp,	WILLIAM id-ships
Cowsill,	JOHN mr-drm Am	Crampton,	BARBARA tv+
Cowsill,	PAUL mr-kbds,s Am	Crampton,	CYDNEY tv
Cowsill,	SUE mr-s Am	Crampton,	THOMAS i,id Br
Cox,	ANDY mr-guit Br	Cranach,	LUCAS(Elder)p Ger
Cox,	BRIAN	Crane,	BOB tv+
Cox,	COURTENEY tv+	Crane,	BRANDON tv
Cox,	DAVID p Br	Crane,	CHARLES id,st Am
Cox,	GEORGE w Br	Crane,	HART po Am
Cox,	JAMES pb,st Am	Crane,	ICHABOD fc
Cox,	KENYON p,w Am	Crane,	LES tv
Cox,	PALMER illus,w Am	Crane,	NORMA tv+
Cox,	RICHARD	Crane,	RICHARD
Cox,	RONNY tv+	Crane,	STEPHEN w,po Am
Cox,	RUTH tv+	Crane,	WALTER p Br
Cox,	WALLY tv+	Cranham,	KENNETH
Cox,	WENDY tv	Cranko,	JOHN ba S.Afr
Cox,	WILLIAM w Irish	Cranshaw,	PAT tv
Coxey,	JACOB bus,st Am	Crashaw,	RICHARD po Br
Coxie,	MICHIEL van p Belg	Cratchit,	BOB fc
Coy,	WALTER tv	Cratchit,	TINY TIM fc
Coyote,	PETER	Craufurd,	QUINTIN w Scot
Cozens,	ALEXANDER p Br	Crauk,	GUSTAVE su Fr
Cozy	COLE mj-drm Am	Craven,	BRITTANY tv
Cozzens,	JAMES G. p-f'49	Craven,	FRANK la,w+ Am
Crabbe,	BUSTER sw+ Am	Craven,	JAMES
Crabbe,	GEORGE po Br	Craven,	LACEY tv
Crabtree,	LOTTA la,cm Am	Craven,	MATT
Cracker,	JOE mr Am	Craven,	WES d
Crafts,	JAMES sc,e Am	Crawford,	BOBBY Jr. tv
Craig	BAXLEY d	Crawford,	BRODERICKo-a'49,tv+
Craig	BIGGIO b-gg'97	Crawford,	CHRISTINA w Am
Craig	FROST mr-kbds Am	Crawford,	CINDY mo Am
Craig	GARDNER tv	Crawford,	EDWARD tv
Craig	GINI tv	Crawford,	FRANCIS w Am
Craig	HILL tv+	Crawford,	JOAN o-s'45
Craig	LUCAS w Am	Crawford,	JOHN tv+
Craig	NELSON tv+	Crawford,	JOHNNY tv+
Craig	RIVERA tv	Crawford,	MICHAEL s+
Craig	SHEFFER	Crawford,	PERCY tv
Craig	STEVENS tv+	Crawford,	RACHAEL tv
Craig	WASSON rv+	Crawford,	RANDY mr,r&b-s,ws
Craig,	DIANE	Crawford,	ROBERT tv

Crawford,	SAM b hf		Crockett,	SAMUEL w Scot
Crawford,	THOMAS su Am		Croft,	MARY JANE tv
Crawford,	WAYNE		Croft,	WILLIAM organ,c Br
Cray,	ROBERT m-r&b,s,ws		Crofts,	DASH mr-guit Am
Craze,	GALAXY w+		Crofts,	FREEMAN eng,w Ir
Crazy Legs	HIRSCH fb hf		Croisset,	FRANCIS de w Fr
Credi,	LORENZO di p It		Croker,	JOHN w,ed Br
Cree	SUMMER tv		Croker,	RICHARD(Boss)st Am
Creed	BRATTON mr-guit Am		Croly,	HERBERT ed,w Am
Creed,	ANN w Am		Crombie,	JONATHAN
Creel,	GEORGE j,ed Am		Crome,	JOHN(Old Crome)p Br
Creeley,	ROBERT po,w Am		Crompton,	SAMUEL i Br
Cregar,	LAIRD		Crompton,	WILLIAM i,id Am
Crehan,	JOSEPH		Cromwell,	JAMES tv+
Creighton	ABRAMS ar Am		Cromwell,	JOHN d
Creighton	HALE		Cromwell,	OLIVER ar,st Br
Creme,	LOL mr-guit,s Br		Cromwell,	RICHARD
Cremer,	BRUNO		Cronenberg,	DAVID d
Cremer,	JACOBUS w Dut		Cronin,	A.J. w,md Br
Cremer,	WILLIAM(Sir)n-x'03		Cronin,	JAMES n-p'80
Crenna,	RICHARD tv+		Cronin,	JOE b hf
Crespi,	GIOVANNI p It		Cronin,	KEVIN mr-s Am
Crespi,	GIUSEPPE p It		Cronin,	PATRICK tv
Crespi,	JUAN x Sp		Cronje,	PIET re S.Afr
Crespi,	TODD tv		Cronkite,	WALTER tv-j Am
Creston,	PAUL c Am		Cronyn,	HUME
Cret,	PAUL ac Am		Crook,	LORIANNE tv
Crevecoeur,	MICHEL de w Am		Crookes,	WILLIAM(Sir)sc
Crews,	HARRY w,j Am		Crooks,	RICHARD tenor Am
Crews,	LAURA la Am		Cropper,	STEVE mr-guit Am
Crewsdon,	ROY mr-guit Br		Crosby,	BING s,tv+,o-a'84
Crewson,	WENDY tv+		Crosby,	BOB m,cn,tv Am
Cribb,	TOM boxer Br		Crosby,	CATHY LEE tv+
Crichton,	DON ba,tv Am		Crosby,	DAVID m-guit,s Am
Crichton,	MICHAEL w,d,pr Am		Crosby,	DENISE tv+
Crick,	FRANCIS n-m'62		Crosby,	FRANCES w-hymns &
Crile,	GEO. WASH. md,e Am		Crosby,	FRANCES=Fanny
Crippen,	HAWLEY murderer Am		Crosby,	GARY tv+
Crisp,	DONALD o-s'41		Crosby,	MARY tv+
Crisp,	SAMUEL w Br		Crosby,	NORM cm Am
Crispin	GLOVER		Crosby,	ROBERT w Am
Criss,	PETER mr-drm,s Am		Crosley,	POWEL id-radio Am
Crissy	WILZAK tv		Cross,	AMANDA w Am
Cristal,	LINDA		Cross,	BEN
Cristal,	PERLA		Cross,	CHRIS mr-bass Br
Cristea,	MIRON r Rom		Cross,	CHRISTOPHER guit,s
Cristi	CONAWAY		Cross,	DENNIS tv+
Cristina	RAINES tv+		Cross,	HARDY eng,e Am
Cristobal	de ACUNA r Sp		Cross,	HARLEY tv+
Cristobal	de OLID ar Sp		Cross,	WILBUR e,st Am
Cristobal	de VIRUES po Sp		Crosse,	RUPERT tv
Cristofer,MICHAEL p-d'77			Crossley,	SYD
Cristopher CARSON(Kit)scout			Crotch,	WILLIAM c Br
Crittenden,	JAMES tv		Crothers,	SCATMAN
Crittenden,	JOHN st Am		Crouch,	FREDERICK c Br
Crittenton,	CHARLES id,f Am		Crough,	SUZANNE tv
Croce,	BENEDETTO ct,h It		Crouse,	LINDSAY
Croce,	GIOVANNI c It		Crouse,	RUSSEL p-d'46
Crocker,	FRANCIS eng,id Am		Crow,	CARL tv
Crockett,	DAVID(Davy)frontier		Crow,	EMILIA
Crockett,	JAN tv		Crow,	SHERYL s-pop,ws Am

Crowden,	GRAHAM
Crowder,	ENOCH ar Am
Crowder,	RANDY tv
Crowe,	EYRE(Sir)st
Crowe,	RUSSELL
Crowe,	TONYA tv
Crowell,	LUTHER i Am
Crowley,	ALEISTER po,w Br
Crowley,	GENE mj-s Br
Crowley,	KATHLEEN tv+
Crowley,	PAT
Crowley,	PATRICIA tv
Crowne,	JOHN w Br
Crox	ALVARADO
Cruce,	EMERIC w Fr
Crue,	MOTLEY mr Am
Cruikshank,	GEORGE caric. &
Cruikshank,	GEORGE illus Br
Cruikshank,	RUFUS tv
Cruise,	TOM
Crum	BROWN sc,e Scot
Crum,	DENNY bbc hf
Crumb,	GEORGE p-m'68
Crutchley,	ROSALIE
Crutzen,	PAUL n-c'95
Cruz,	BRANDON tv
Cruz,	RAMON de la w Sp
Cruz,	SOR JUANA de la po
Cruze,	JAMES d
Cryer,	JON
Crystal	BERNARD tv
Crystal	FOX tv
Crystal	GAYLE s-cnt Am
Crystal	KEYMAH tv
Crystal	WATERS s-soul Am
Crystal,	BILLY tv+
Cserhalmi,	GYORGY
Cua,	PAULUS w Vietnam
Cuba	GOODING Jr
Cubberley,	GARY tv
Cudahy,	MICHAEL id-meat Am
Cuellar,	MIKE b-cy'69
Cuervo,	RUFINO w Colom
Cuff,	SIMON tv
Cugat,	XAVIER mj,cn,c+
Cui,	CESAR c Rus
Cukor,	GEORGE o-d'64+
Culbertson,	ELY bridge Am
Culea,	MELINDA tv
Culkin,	KIERAN
Culkin,	MACAULAY
Cullen,	BILL tv
Cullen,	BRETT
Cullen,	COUNTEE po Am
Cullen,	PETER tv
Cullen,	WILLIAM tv
Cullimore,	STAN mr-bass Br
Cullum,	JOHN tv+
Cully,	ZARA tv
Culp,	CURLY fb-d'75
Culp,	ROBERT tv+

Culver,	HOWARD tv+
Culver,	MICHAEL
Culver,	ROLAND
Cumbuka,	JI-TU tv
Cummings,	BOB tv
Cummings,	BURTON mr-kbds,s
Cummings,	CANDY b hf
Cummings,	CONSTANCE
Cummings,	E.E. po,p Am
Cummings,	GEORGE mr-guit Am
Cummings,	IRVING d
Cummings,	QUINN tv+
Cummings,	RICHARD Jr. tv+
Cummings,	ROBERT
Cummins,	JULIETTE
Cummins,	PEGGY
Cunard,	SAMUEL(Sir)ships
Cundill,	LIAM
Cunha,	TRISTAO da x Port
Cunningham,	ALLAN po,w Scot
Cunningham,	BILL bass,piano
Cunningham,	BILLY bb hf
Cunningham,	DENNIS tv
Cunningham,	IMOGEN fo Am
Cunningham,	J.V. po,ct Am
Cunningham,	MARION w,j Am
Cunningham,	MERCE ba Am
Cunningham,	MICHAEL w Am
Cunningham,	SARAH tv
Cunningham,	TOM mr-drm Scot
Cunningham,	ZAMAH tv
Cunninghame Graham, ROBERT w	
Cuny,	ALAIN
Cuomo,	MARIO st,mayor Am
Cuppy,	WILL ct,humor Am
Curb,	MIKE tv
Curie,	IRENE n-c'35
Curie,	MARIE n-c'11 &
Curie,	MARIE n-p'03
Curie,	PIERRE n-p'03 &
Curie,	PIERRE n-c'35
Curley,	JAMES st Am
Curly	CULP fb
Curly	DRESDEN
Curly	GIBBS s Am
Curly	HOWARD
Curly	LAMBEAU f,fbc
Curnow,	ALLEN po,ct,ed N.Z.
Curreri,	LEE tv
Currie,	ALANNAH sax,drm,S
Currie,	BILLY mr-kbds Br
Currie,	CHERIE
Currie,	CHERRIE s Am
Currie,	FINLAY
Currie,	LOUISE
Currie,	SONDRA
Currier,	NATHANIEL lithos Am
Curry,	JABEZ e Am
Curry,	JOHN p Am
Curry,	TIM
Curt	BOIS

Curt	DAWKINS w Am	Cy	YOUNG b hf
Curt	GOWDY tv-spts Am	Cyd	HAYMAN
Curt	JURGENS	Cyndi	LAUPER s+ Am
Curt	LOWENS	Cyndi	PASS
Curt	SACHS musicology,e	Cyndy	GARVEY tv
Curt	SMITH mr-bass,s Br	Cynewulf	--- po
Curtin,	JANE cm,tv+ Am	Cynthia	BAIN
Curtin,	VALERIE	Cynthia	GEARY tv
Curtis	BALDWIN tv	Cynthia	GIBB tv+
Curtis	LeMAY flyer Am &	Cynthia	HARRIS tv+
Curtis	LeMAY =Iron Pants	Cynthia	HOWARD tv
Curtis	PETERS cr Am	Cynthia	LYNN tv
Curtis	SLIWA Guard,Angels	Cynthia	NIXON
Curtis,	ALAN	Cynthia	OZICK w Am
Curtis,	BOB tv	Cynthia	PEPPER tv
Curtis,	CHARLES st,31st vp	Cynthia	RHODES
Curtis,	CHRIS mr-drm,s Br	Cynthia	ROWLEY ds Am
Curtis,	CYRUS pb Am	Cynthia	SIKES tv+
Curtis,	DAN d	Cynthia	WATROS tv
Curtis,	DICK cm,tv+ Am	Cynthia	WELL c Am
Curtis,	DONALD	Cyon,	ELIE de ps,e Rus
Curtis,	EDWARD fo Am	Cypher,	JON tv+
Curtis,	G.W. w,ed Am	Cyprian	EKWENSI w Nigeria
Curtis,	GEORGE l,w Am	Cyprian	NORWID w Pol
Curtis,	HELEN tv	Cyrano de Bergerac,SAVIN. po	
Curtis,	HELENE hair care	Cyriel	BUYSSE w Belg
Curtis,	JAMIE LEE tv+	Cyril	BURT(Sir)ps
Curtis,	JANET tv	Cyril	CUSACK
Curtis,	KEENE tv+	Cyril	NEVILLE mr-drm,s Am
Curtis,	KEN tv+	Cyril	O'REILLY
Curtis,	LIANE	Cyril	RAYMOND
Curtis,	SONNY mr-guit Am	Cyril	RITCHARD
Curtis,	TONY tv+	Cyril	SCOTT piano,c Br
Curtis,	VIRGINIA tv	Cyril	SMITH tv
Curtis-Hall, VONDIE		Cyrus	ADLER e Am
Curtiss,	GLENN i,id,fly Am	Cyrus	ALGER id i Am
Curtius,	JULIUS st Ger	Cyrus	CURTIS pb Am
Curtiz,	MICHAEL o-d'43	Cyrus	DALLIN su Am
Curvey,	TROY Jr. tv	Cyrus	EATON id Am
Curwood,	JAMES OLIVER w Am	Cyrus	FIELD f Am
Cusack,	CYRIL	Cyrus	HAMLIN r Am
Cusack,	JOAN	Cyrus,	BILLY RAY s-cnt Am
Cusack,	JOHN	Czerny,	KARL piano,c Aus
Cusack,	SINEAD	Czeslaw	MILOSZ po,w Lith
Cushing,	CALEB l,st Am	Czonka,	LARRY fb hf,tv
Cushing,	PETER		
Cussler,	CLIVE w Am		
Cust,	EDWARD(Sir)h Br		
Custer,	GEORGE ar Am		
Cuthbert, BETTY o-g'56'64			
Cuthbertson, IAIN			
Cutler,	BARRY tv		
Cutler,	WENDY tv		
Cutrona,	HANNAH tv		
Cutter,	LISE tv+		
Cutts,	PATRICIA tv		
Cuyler,	KIKI b hf		
Cuyp(Cuijp), ALBERT p Dut			
Cuypers,	PETRUS ac Dut		
Cy	COLEMAN m,cn,tv Am		
Cy	KENDALL		

"D" NAME DESIGNATION CODES

d	-	DIRECTOR
decor	-	DECORATOR
ds	-	DESIGNER

"D" NATIONALITY CODES

Dan - DANISH   Dut - DUTCH

"D's"

D'Abo,	MARYAM
D'Abo,	OLIVIA tv+
D'Albert,	EUGEN pian,c Ger
D'Aleo,	ANGELO mr-s Am
D'Amato,	ALFONSE st(sen,NY)
D'Ambrosio,	VITO tv
D'Andrea,	TOM tv+
D'Angelo,	BEVERLY
D'Annunzio,	GABRIELE po,w It
D'Arbanville,	PATTI tv+
D'Arby,	TERENCE s-r&b,ws Am
D'Arc,	JEANNE see Joan of Arc
D'Arcy,	ALEXANDER
D'Arcy	THOMPSON(Sir) sc
D'Ewes,	SIMONDS(Sir)h
D'Onofrio,	VINCENT
D'Orsay,	FIFI
D'Orso,	WISA tv
D'Souza,	DINESH w India
D'Urfey,	THOMAS c,w Br
D'Urville	MARTIN
D. Franki	HORNER tv
D.B.	SWEENEY
D.B. Wyndham	LEWIS w,bio Br
D.G.	JONES po,ct Can
D.M.	THOMAS po,w Welsh
D.S.	SULAITIS w Am
D.W.	MOFFETT
Da Ponte,	LORENZO po It
da Silva,	HOWARD
Dabbs	GREER tv+
Dabney	COLEMAN tv
Dabney,	AUGUSTA
Dabrowska,	MARIA w,ct Pol
Dach,	SIMON po Ger
Dache,	LILLY ds-hats Am
Dachlan,	KIJAI reform Indon
Dack	RAMBO tv+
Dael	ORLANDERSMITH w Am
Dafoe,	ALLAN md Can
Dafoe,	JOHN j Can
Dafoe,	WILLEM
Daft,	LEO eng Am
Dagerman,	STIG w Swe
Dagly,	GERHARD p Belg
Dagmar	--- tv+
Dagmar	LASSANDER
Dagobert von	WURMSER ar Aus
Dagover,	LIL
Daguerre,	LOUIS. p,i Fr
Dahl,	ARLENE tv+
Dahl,	JOHAN p Nor
Dahl,	MICHAEL p Swe
Dahl,	ROALD w Br
Dahlbeck,	EVA
Dahlberg,	EDWARD ct,w,po Am
Dahlstierna,	GUNNO po Swe
Dahn,	FELIX h,po Ger
Daiches,	DAVID ct,w Scot
Dailey,	DAN tv+
Dailey,	FRANK tv
Dailley,	JANET w Am
Daily,	BILL tv+
Daily,	ELIZABETH
Daimler,	GOTTLEIB id-cars Ger
Daisy	ASHFORD w Br
Dakin	MATTHEWS tv+
Dakin,	HENRY sc Br
Dakota,	TONY tv
Dal	McKENNON tv
Dalai	LAMA r Tibet
Dale	EVANS s+ Am
Dale	MIDKIFF
Dale	MURPHY b
Dale,	ALAN mj-s,tv Am
Dale,	DICK s,sax,tv Am
Dale,	ESTHER
Dale,	GLEN mr-guitar,s Br
Dale,	HENRY(Sir)n-m'36
Dale,	JENNIFER
Dale,	JIM
Dale,	JIMMY m,cn,tv Am
Dalen,	NILS i,n-p'12
Daley	THOMPSON o-g
Daley,	RICHARD J. st Am
Daley,	ROSIE chef,w-ckbks Am
Dalhart,	VERNON s-cntry Am
Dali,	SALVADOR p Sp
Daliah	LAVI
Dalin,	OLOF von po,h Swe
Dalio,	MARCEL tv+
Dall,	JOHN
Dallas,	ALEXANDER l,st Am
Dallas,	GEORGE st,US-vp
Dallesandro,	JOE
Dallimore,	MAURICE tv
Dallin,	CYRUS su Am
Dallin,	SARAH mr-s Br
Dalou,	JULES su Fr
Dalton	TRUMBO w Am
Dalton,	ABBY tv+
Dalton,	AUDREY
Dalton,	HUGH st Br
Dalton,	JOHN sc Br
Dalton,	ROBERT outlaw Am
Dalton,	TIMOTHY tv+
Daltrey,	ROGER
Daltrey,	ROGER mr-s Br
Daly,	ARNOLD la,pr Am
Daly,	AUGUSTIN w Am
Daly,	CHUCK bbc hf
Daly,	GARY mr-s Br
Daly,	JAMES tv+

Daly,	JONATHON tv		Dana	DELANY tv+
Daly,	MARCUS id-mines Am		Dana	ELCAR tv+
Daly,	RAD tv		Dana	HILL
Daly,	TIMOTHY tv+		Dana	IVEY tv+
Daly,	TYNE tv+		Dana	PLATO
Dalziel,	JAMES ph Br		Dana	SPARKS tv
Dam,	C.P.HENRIK n-m'43		Dana	WYNTER
Dam,	JOSE van barit Belg		Dana	YOUNG tv
Damad	FERID PASA st Turk		Dana,	BILL tv+
Damas,	LEON w,ct,st Guiana		Dana,	CHARLES j,ed Am
Dameron,	TADD mj-piano,c Am		Dana,	JAMES geol Am
Damian	O'FLYNN tv+		Dana,	JUSTIN tv
Damien	THOMAS		Dana,	LEORA
Damita	FREEMAN tv		Dana,	RICHARD H.l,w Am
Damon	EVANS tv		Danby,	FRANCIS p Irish
Damon	RASKIN tv		Dance,	CHARLES
Damon	RUNYON j,w Am		Dance,	GEORGE ac Br
Damon	WAYANS cm,tv+ Am		Dancourt,	FLORENT la,w Fr
Damon,	CATHRYN tv		Dando,	EVAN s-pop Am
Damon,	GABRIEL tv+		Dandridge,	DOROTHY
Damon,	JERRY tv		Dandridge,	RAY b hf
Damon,	MARK		Dandridge,	RUBY tv
Damon,	MATT		Dane	CLARK tv+
Damone,	VIC s,tv+ Am		Dane,	CLEMENCE w Br
Damrosch,	LEOPOLD cn Am		Dane,	LAWRENCE
Damrosch,	WALTER cn Am		Dane,	NATHAN l,w Am
Damski,	MEL d		Dane,	PATRICIA
Damu	KING		Danelli,	DINO mr-drm Am
Dan	AYKROYD		Danes,	CLAIRE tv+
Dan	BIGGERS tv		Danev,	STOYAN st Bulg
Dan	BLOCKER tv+		Dangen,	CORNELIS p Dut
Dan	CURTIS d		Dangerfield,	RODNEY cm,tv+ Am
Dan	DAILEY tv+		Danica	McKELLAR tv+
Dan	DURYEA		Daniel	AUBER c Fr
Dan	ENRIGHT tv		Daniel	AUTEUIL
Dan	FERRO tv		Daniel	BALDWIN
Dan	FOUTS fb hf,tv-spts		Daniel	BEARD p,e,BSA Am
Dan	FRAZER tv		Daniel	BOONE pioneer Am
Dan	HEDAYA		Daniel	DEFOE j,w Br
Dan	ISSEL bb hf		Daniel	EMMETT s,ws Am
Dan	JENKINS j,w Am		Daniel	FAGUNWA w Nigeria
Dan	LAURIA tv+		Daniel	FRENCH su Am
Dan	LENO cm,ba,s Br		Daniel	GELIN
Dan	LUNDEN tv		Daniel	GERROLL
Dan	MARINO fb		Daniel	GILMAN e Am
Dan	MILLER tv		Daniel	GOOCH(Sir)eng-rrs
Dan	PEEK m-guitar,s Am		Daniel	GOOKIN colonist Br
Dan	QUAYLE st,ex-vp Am		Daniel	GREENE tv+
Dan	RATHER tv-anchor Am		Daniel	HAYS w Am
Dan	REEVES fb hf		Daniel	KUHLAU c Dan
Dan	RESIN tv+		Daniel	LAMBERT fat man Br
Dan	RICE clown Am		Daniel	MACLISE p Irish
Dan	ROWAN cm,tv Am,		Daniel	MALAN st S.Afr
Dan	SEYMOUR tv+		Daniel	MANNIX r Austra
Dan	SHOR tv+		Daniel	MASSEY
Dan	SORKIN tv		Daniel	MENDOZA boxer Br
Dan	TOBIN tv+		Daniel	NATHANS md Am
Dan	VADIS		Daniel	OWEN po,w Welsh
Dan	ZISKIE		Daniel	PALMER chiroprac Am
Dana	ANDREWS		Daniel	PETRIE d
Dana	CARVEY cm,tv+ Am		Daniel	PILON

Daniel	QUARE id-clocks Br	Danny	De La PAZ
Daniel	ROEBUCK	Danny	DeVITO d,tv+
Daniel	ROSEN tv	Danny	GANS tv
Daniel	SCHORR tv-j Am	Danny	GELLIS tv
Daniel	SHAYS ar-re Am	Danny	GERARD tv+
Daniel	SICKLES ar,st Am	Danny	GILMORE
Daniel	SILVER tv	Danny	GLOVER
Daniel	STERN	Danny	GOLDMAN tv
Daniel	TODD tv	Danny	HUTTON mr-s Irish
Daniel	TSUI sc,e,n-p'98	Danny	KAYE tv+
Daniel	WEBSTER st,orat Am	Danny	KLEIN mr-bass Am
Daniel	WESSON i,id-guns Am	Danny	McMURPHY tv
Daniel	WHEDON r,e Am	Danny	MUMMERT
Daniel	WOLFF w Am	Danny	NUCCI tv+
Daniel	YERGIN w Am	Danny	NUNEZ tv
Daniel C.	BEARDw,illus,BSA Am	Danny	PONCE tv
Daniel,	JEFFREY mr-s Am	Danny	RAPP mr-s Am
Daniel,	JOE mj-drums,cn Br	Danny	SHORE tv
Daniel,	ROD d	Danny	THOMAS tv+
Daniel,	SAMUEL po,w Br	Danny	WELLS tv
Daniel,	YULY w Rus	Danny	WOOD mr-s Am
Daniela	BIANCHI	Dano,	LINDA tv
Daniele	BOVET md,sc It	Dano,	ROYAL
Daniele	VARE st,w It	Danone	SIMPSON tv
Daniell,	HENRY	Danova,	CESARE tv+
Danielle	HARRIS	Danson,	TED tv+
Danielle	MARDI tv	Dantan,	ANTOINE su Fr.
Danielle	SPENCER tv	Dante	ALIGHIERI po It
Danielle	STEEL w Am	Dante	BICHETTE b,rbi'95
Danielle von ZERNECK		Dante	LAVELLI fb hf
Daniels,	BEBE	Dante,	JOE d
Daniels,	CAROLYN tv	Dante,	MICHAEL
Daniels,	FRANK cm Am	Dante,	NICHOLAS p-d'76
Daniels,	J.D. tv	Dantine,	HELMUT tv+
Daniels,	JEFF	Danton	STONE
Daniels,	JOHN	Danton,	GEORGES l,re Fr
Daniels,	JONATHAN j,w Am	Danton,	RAY tv+
Daniels,	JOSEPHUS j,st Am	Dany	SAVAL
Daniels,	MICKEY	Danza,	TONY tv+
Daniels,	PHIL	Danziger,	CORY tv
Daniels,	WILLIAM tv+	Danzinger,MAIA	
Daniely,	LISA tv	Daphna	KASTNER
Daniil	GRANIN w Ger	Daphne	ASHBROOK
Danitra	VANCE tv+	Daphne	MERKIN w,j Am
Danitza	KINGSLEY	Daphne	REID tv
Danjon,	ANDRE astr Fr	Daphne	ZUNIGA
Dankl,	VIKTOR ar Aus	DaPron,	LOUIS ba,tv
Dankmar	ADLER ac Am	Daquin,	LOUIS organ,c Fr
Danko,	RICK mr-bass,s Can	Dar	ROBINSON
Danks,	HART PEASE c-hymn	Daranyi,	KALMAN von st Hung
Dann	FLOREK tv	Darbo,	PATRIKA tv+
Dannay,	FREDERIC w,ed Am	Darby	HINTON
Danner,	BLYTHE tv+	Darby	JONES
Dannie	ABSE po,w Welsh	Darby,	ABRAHAM id-iron Br
Danning,	SYBIL	Darby,	KIM tv+
Danny	AIELLO	Darc,	MIREILLE
Danny	BRAVO tv	Darcel,	DENISE
Danny	COOKSEY tv	Darcy	DEMOSS
Danny	CRUM bbc hf	Darcy,	GEORGINE tv
Danny	DAVIS s Am	Darden,	SEVERN
Danny	DAYTON tv	Dare,	VIRGINIA#1 Am child

Daria	NICOLODI	Datta,	MICHAEL po Gengal
Darieck	SCOTT w Am	Dattilo,	BRYAN tv
Darin,	BOBBY s,g-r'59,tv+ Am	Daubigny.	CHARLES p Fr
Dario	ARGENTA d	Daubler,	THEODOR po Ger
Dario	FO w It	Daud Khan,	SARDAR st Afgan
Dario	MICHAELIS	Daudet,	ALPHONSE w Fr
Dario,	RUBEN po,w Nicar	Daudet,	LEON j,w Fr
Darius	McCRARY tv	Dauer,	JOHN tv
Darius	MILHAUD c Fr	Daughton,	JAMES
Dark,	JOHNNY tv+	Daulton,	DARREN b,rbi'92
Darkie	WICKENS mj-drms,cn Can	Daumier,	HONORE p,at Fr
Darla	HOOD	Dauphin,	CLAUDE
Darla	SLAVENS	Dausset,	JEAN n-m'80
Darlan,	JEAN navy,st Fr	Dauzat,	ALBERT e,w Fr
Darlanne	FLUEGEL tv+	Davalos,	ELYSSA
Darleen	CARR tv	Davalos,	RICHARD
Darlene	CONLEY tv	Dave	BARRY w Am
Darley,	FELIX illus Am	Dave	BING bb hf
Darley,	GEORGE po Irish	Dave	BRUBECK mj-pia,cn Am
Darling,	JAY(Ding)cr Am	Dave	CLARK mr-drm Br
Darling,	JENNIFER tv	Dave	COWENS bb hf
Darling,	JOAN tv+	Dave	DAVIES mr-guit,s Br
Darling,	RON b,gg'89	Dave	DAVIS tv
Darnell,	LINDA	Dave	DEE mr-s Br
Darr,	LISA tv	Dave	GAHAN mr-s Br
Darrel	MAURY tv	Dave	GOELZ puppets,tv Am
Darrell	EVANS b	Dave	HILL mr-guit Br
Darrell	LARSON tv+	Dave	KETCHUM tv
Darrell	ROODT d	Dave	KINGMAN b
Darren	DAULTON b,rbi'92	Dave	KNIGHTS mr-bass Br
Darren	McGAVIN tv+	Dave	MACON mj,s Am
Darren,	JAMES tv+	Dave	MADDEN tv
Darrieux,	DANIELLE	Dave	MARASH tv
Darro,	FRANKIE	Dave	MASON mr-guit,s Br
Darrow	IGUS tv	Dave	MOUNT mr-drm,s Br
Darrow,	CLARENCE l Am	Dave	MURRAY mr-guit Br
Darrow,	HENRY	Dave	O'BRIEN
Darrow,	JOHN	Dave	PARKER b
Darryl	BELL tv	Dave	PIRNER mr-s Am
Darryl	HICKMAN tv	Dave	RYAN(Chico)tv
Darryl	RICHARD tv	Dave	SHARP mr-guit Br
Darryl	ZANUCK pr-films Am	Dave	STEWART mr-guit Br
Daru,	PIERRE ar,h Fr	Dave	STIEB b
Darvas,	LILI	Dave	STREET tv
Darwell,	JANE o-s'40	Dave	THOMAS tv+
Darwin,	CHARLES sc,w Br	Dave	TOUGH mj-drm Am
Darwin,	ERASMUS md,sc,po Br	Dave	WHITE mr-s Am
Daryl	DRAGON m-pop,kbds Am	Dave	WILLOCK tv
Daryl	DUKE d	Davenant,	WILLIAM(Sir)w,po
Daryl	HALL mr-guit,s Am	Davenport,	BASIL tv
Daryl	HANEY	Davenport,	EDWARD la Am
Daryl	HANNAH	Davenport,	HARRY
Das,	CHITTA st India	Davenport,	NIGEL
Dasent,	GEORGE(Sir)e,ed	Davenport,	THOMAS i Am
Dash	CROFTS mr-guit,mand	Daves,	DELMER d
Dashiell	HAMMETT w Am	Davey,	JOHN tree md Am
Dass,	PETTER r,po Nor	Davi,	ROBERT
Dassin,	JULES d	David	ACKROYD tv+
Daste,	JEAN	David	AGNEW md,e Am
Daszynski,	IGNACY st Pol	David	ALLAN p Scot
Dati,	CARLO w It	David	ALTER sc,md Am

David	ANDREWS	David	FAYE cm Am
David	ANTIN po Am	David	FERRIER(Sir)md Scot
David	ARGUE	David	FROMAN tv
David	BAILEY tv	David	FROST tv
David	BALL mr-keybds Br	David	GALE
David	BEAIRD d	David	GARNETT w Br
David	BELASCO w,pr Am	David	GARRICK la,pr Br
David	BERGEY sc,e Am	David	GATES mr-kbds,s Am
David	BIRNEY tv+	David	GEFFEN pr-recrds Am
David	BLAIR ba Br	David	GIBBS tv
David	BORN tv	David	GORCEY
David	BOWIE mr, tv+	David	GOSS
David	BRADLEY	David	GRAF
David	BRENNER cm,tv-hostAm	David	GRANT
David	BREWER l Am	David	GREENE d
David	BRIAN tv+	David	GRIER tv+
David	BRIGGS m-guit Aust	David	GROH tv+
David	BRIN w-scifi Am	David	GUION ws Am
David	BROWN mr-bass Am	David	HARE w Br
David	BRUCE	David	HARPER tv+
David	BRUCE(Sir)md,sc	David	HART tv
David	BRUEYS	David	HARTMAN tv
David	BRYAN mr,pop-kbds Am	David	HAYMANN
David	BUICK id-cars Am	David	HAYS w
David	BURNS tv	David	HAYWARD tv+
David	BUTLER d+	David	HEDISON tv+
David	BYRD tv	David	HEMBLEN
David	BYRNE s,d Scot	David	HESS
David	BYRON mr-s Br	David	HEWLETT
David	CANARY tv+	David	HILBERT math,e Ger
David	CARR mr-kbds Br	David	HOCKNEY p Br
David	CARUSO tv+	David	HUBBARD tv
David	CASSIDY tv+	David	HUBEL md Am
David	CECIL(Lord) w,ct	David	HUFFMAN
David	CHIANG	David	HUME ph,h Scot
David	CITINO w Am	David	IGATOW po,ed Am
David	CLENNON tv+	David	IRELAND w Aust
David	COHEN mr-kbds Am	David	JANNSEN tv+
David	CONE b	David	JONES p,w Br
David	COSTELL mr-bass Am	David	JONES tv
David	COULIER tv	David	JORDAN sc,e,w Am
David	COWGIL tv	David	JORIS r Dut
David	COX p Br	David	KASDAY tv
David	CROSBY m-guit,s Am	David	KEITH tv+
David	DAICHES ct,w Scot	David	KELLY tv+
David	DAVIS l,st Am	David	KNELL tv
David	De Vries colony Dut	David	LADD
David	DeCOTEAU d	David	LANDAU
David	DERGEY sc,e Am	David	LANDER
David	DEVANT magic Br	David	LEAN(Sir)d
David	DIOP po Senegal	David	LEISURE tv
David	DOREMUS tv	David	LEVITAN tv
David	DOYLE tv+	David	LINDSAY(Sir)po,w Scot
David	DRIMMER tv	David	LOCHARY
David	DUKE st,racist Am	David	LODGE
David	DUKES tv+	David	LOW(Sir)cr
David	DUNDAS(Sir)ar	David	LUBIN mer,agric Am
David	EDDINGS w Am	David	MACKLIN tv
David	ESSEX	David	MALLET po Scot
David	EVANS w Welsh	David	MAMET d,w Am
David	FARRAR	David	MANNERS

David	MANNES viol,cn,e Am	David	WALSH bbr hf
David	MASSON ed,e,w Scot	David	WARBECK
David	McCALLUM tv+	David	WARD d
David	MILLER d	David	WARNER
David	MOFFAT id,f Am	David	WAYNE tv+
David	MOIR md,po,w Scot	David	WELL ba Br
David	MORSE tv+	David	WHITE tv+
David	MUZZEY h,e Am	David	WHYTE w Br
David	N'KENA	David	WILKIE(Sir)p Scot
David	NELSON tv+	David	WILSON tv+
David	NERMAN tv	David	WINTERS d
David	NEVIN w Am	David	WOHL tv+
David	NEWSOM tv	David	WOOSTER ar-re Am
David	NIVEN tv+	David	ZINMAN cn
David	OLIVER tv	David	ZUCKER d
David	OTWELL tv	David d'Angers,PIERRE su Fr
David	PACKARD id,w Am	David de BRUEYS w Fr
David	PACKER	David, ELEANOR
David	PAICH mr-kbds,s Am	David, GERARD p Dut
David	PAUL	David, HAL lyrics Am
David	PAYMER tv+	David, JACQUES-LOUIS p Fr
David	PINSKI w AM	David KEITH
David	PRESTON tv	David, THAYER
David	PRIOR d	Davidovich, LOLITA
David	PROVAL	Davidovsky, MARIO p-m'71
David	PROWSE	Davidson, BOAZ d
David	RABE w Am	Davidson, EILEEN tv
David	RASCHE tv+	Davidson, JAMES tv
David	REMNICK w Am	Davidson, JAYE mo+ Am
David	RICARDO ec,st Br	Davidson, JO su Am
David	RICH d	Davidson, JOHN tv-host+ Am
David	RIZZIO m It	Davidson, LENNY mr-guitar Br
David	ROSE cn,songs,tv Am	Davidson, MARTIN d
David	ROTH mr-s Am	Davidson, SARA w Am
David	RUDKIN w Br	Davidson, TOMMY cm, tv
David	RUFFIN mr-s Am	Davidson, TROY tv
David	SANBORN tv	Davidtz, EMBETH
David	SARNOFF id-RCA Am	Davie, DONALD po,ct Br
David	SCHRAMM tv	Davies, ARTHUR p Am
David	SELBY tv+	Davies, BOB bb hf
David	SEYMOUR fo-j Am	Davies, CLARA s,e Br
David	SHARPE	Davies, DAVE mr-guit,s Br
David	SHEINER tv	Davies, EMILY fe,e Br
David	SHIPLER w Am	Davies, GEOFFREY tv
David	SMITH c,e Am	Davies, GERAINT s
David	SMITH su Am	Davies, HENRY(Sir)organ,c Br
David	SOUL tv+	Davies, HUBERT w Br
David	SOUTER l-Supr Ct Am	Davies, IVA mr-guit,s Aust
David	SPADE tv	Davies, JOHN(Sir)l,po
David	SPARKS tv	Davies, JOSEPH l,st Am
David	STEELE mr-kbds, Br	Davies, PETER w Am
David	STIERS tv+	Davies, RHYS w Welsh
David	STOREY w Br	Davies, RICHARD mr-kbds,s Br
David	STRAUSS ph,r Ger	Davies, ROBERTSON w Can
David	SUCHET	Davies, RUDI
David	SYLVIAN mr-guit,s Br	Davies, RUPERT
David	TENIERS(Elder)p Belg	Davies, WILLIAM(W.H.)po Welsh
David	TOBEY bbr hf	Davila, CARLOS j,st Chile
David	TRIMBLE st, n-x'98	Davis ROBERTS tv
David	WALKER mr-kbds Am	Davis Sis MARY FRAN.PENNICK s
David	WALLACE	Davis Sister BETTY JACK s Am

Davis,	AL fbc hf	Davis,	THOMAS po Irish
Davis,	ALEXANDER ac Am	Davis,	VIVEKA
Davis,	ANDREW d	Davis,	WARWICK
Davis,	ANGELA re Am	Davis,	WENDY tv
Davis,	ANN B. tv+	Davis,	WILLIAM geol,e Am
Davis,	ART	Davis,	WILLIE fb hf
Davis,	BENNY ws Am	Davis-Voss,	SAMMI tv+
Davis,	BETTE o-a'35'38,tv+	Davison,	BRUCE tv+
Davis,	BILLY Jr mr-s Am	Davison,	WILD BILL cornet,c Am
Davis,	BRAD tv+	Davisson,	CLINTON n-p'37
Davis,	CAROLE	Davoli,	NINETTO
Davis,	CLIFTON tv+	Davy	JONES mr-s+ Br
Davis,	COLIN(Sir)c,cn	Davy,	HUMPHRY(Sir)sc
Davis,	DANNY s Am	Dawan	SCOTT tv
Davis,	DAVE tv	Dawber,	PAM tv+
Davis,	DAVID B. p-n'67	Dawes,	CHARLES n-x'25 vp
Davis,	DAVID l,st Am	Dawes,	EDMUND(Skipper) tv
Davis,	DON tv	Dawidoff,	NICHOLAS w Am
Davis,	DONALD tv	Dawkins,	CURT w Am
Davis,	DUANE	Dawn	ADDAMS
Davis,	DWIGHT st,t Am	Dawn	DUNLAP
Davis,	EDDIE(Lockjaw)sax Am	Dawn	LYN tv
Davis,	ELMER j,radio Am	Dawn	POWELL w Am
Davis,	GAIL tv+	Dawn	UPSHAW soprano Am
Davis,	GEENA o-s'88,tv+	Dawn	WELLS tv+
Davis,	GLENN o-g'56'60	Dawn,	DOLLY mj-s Am
Davis,	HAROLD p-f'36	Dawn,	SUGAR
Davis,	HERBERT e,ed Br	Dawnn	LEWIS tv
Davis,	JANETTE tv	Daws	BUTLER tv
Davis,	JEFFERSON presid. CSA	Dawson,	ANDRE b-mv'87,hr'87
Davis,	JENNIFER tv	Dawson,	ANTHONY d+
Davis,	JIM cr Am	Dawson,	BERTRAND royal md Br
Davis,	JIM tv+	Dawson,	GREG tv
Davis,	JIMMY st Am	Dawson,	HENRY p Br
Davis,	JO tv	Dawson,	JANET w Austra
Davis,	JOAN tv+	Dawson,	JOHN(Sir)geol Can
Davis,	JOE billiards Br	Dawson,	LEN fb hf
Davis,	JOHN x Br	Dawson,	RICHARD tv+
Davis,	JOSIE tv	Day George,	LINDA tv+
Davis,	JUDY	Day,	ARTHUR sc Am
Davis,	KENNY tv	Day,	CLARENCE Jr.at,w Am
Davis,	MAC tv+	Day,	DENNIS s,tv Am
Davis,	MARK b-cy'89	Day,	DIANNE tv
Davis	MARTHA mr-s Am	Day,	DORIS s,tv+ Am
Davis,	MILES mj-trump,c Am	Day,	DOROTHY j,ref Am
Davis,	NANCY	Day,	EDMUND ec,e Am
Davis,	OSSIE tv+	Day,	HOLMAN w Am
Davis,	OWEN p-d'23	Day,	JOHN w Br
Davis,	PATTI tv	Day,	JOSETTE
Davis,	PAUL mr-kbds Br	Day,	LARAINE tv+
Davis,	PHILIP	Day,	LEON b, hf
Davis,	PHYLLIS tv	Day,	MARCELINE
Davis,	REBECCA w Am	Day,	MARILYN tv
Davis,	RICHARD j,w Am	Day,	MARK mr-guit Br
Davis,	ROB mr-s Br	Day,	PAT jockey Am
Davis,	ROGER tv+	Day,	ROBERT d
Davis,	RUFE tv	Day,	THOMAS w Br
Davis,	SAMMY Jr s,tv+	Day-Lewis,	CECIL po,w Br
Davis,	SONNY	Day-Lewis,	DANIEL o-a'89
Davis,	SPENCER guit Welsh	Dayan,	ASSAF
Davis,	STUART p Am	Dayan,	MOSHE ar,st Isr

Dayle	HADDON		De Vries,	DAVID colonizer Dut
Dayna	WINSTON tv		De Vries,	PETER w Am
Dayne,	TAYLOR s-pop,soul Am		De Wilde,	BRANDON tv
Dayton	LUMMIS tv		De Wint,	PETER p Br
Dayton,	DANNY tv		De Wolfe,	ELLA la,decor Am
Dayton,	ELIAS ar,st Am		De Young,	MICHEL j,pb Am
Dayton,	JUNE tv		Deacon	JONES fb hf
Daza,	HILARION ar,st Bol		Deacon,	BRIAN
Dazey,	CHARLES w Am		Deacon,	JOHN mr-bass Br
Dazzy	VANCE b hf		Deacon,	RICHARD tv+
DDE	IKE st		Deak,	FERENC st Hung
De Bernardi, FORREST bb hf			Deakins,	LUCY
De Bono,	EMILIO ar st It		Dean	BUTLER tv+
De Burgh,	CHRIS s,w-songs Arg		Dean	CAIN tv+
De Busschere, DAVE bb hf			Dean	CAMERON
De Carlo,	YVONNE tv+		Dean	CHANCE b
De Celles,ALFRED j Can			Dean	ING w-scifi Am
De Chair,	DUDLEY(Sir)navy		Dean	JAGGER tv+
De Costa,	TONY tv		Dean	JONES
De Forest,JOHN w Am			Dean	KOONTZ w Am
De Forest,LEE i Am			Dean	MARTIN s,cm,tv+
De Franco,BUDDY mj-clarinet Am			Dean	MILLER tv
De Gasperi, ALCIDE st It			Dean	RUSK st Am
De Golyer,EVERETTE sc-oil Am			Dean	SMITH bbc hf
De Gore,	JANET tv		Dean,	DIZZY b hf
De Haven,	GLORIA		Dean,	EDDIE
De Havilland,GEOFFREY(Sir)planes			Dean,	EVERETT bbc hf
De Jong,	ATE d		Dean,	IVOR tv
De Kova,	FRANK tv+		Dean,	JAMES tv+
De Koven,	REGINALD c Am		Dean,	JAY HANNA(Dizzy)b
De La Hoya, OSCAR boxer Am			Dean,	JIMMY tv+
De La Paz,DANNY			Dean,	LARRY s,tv Am
De La Renta, OSCAR ds Am			Dean,	LOREN
De la Rey,JACOBUS ar S.Afr			Dean,	MAN MOUNTAIN wrestler
De la Roche, MAZO w Can			Dean,	MARGIA
De la Rue,WARREN astron,i Br			Dean,	RICK
De Laurentis, DINO pr It			Dean,	RON tv+
De Lint,	DEREK		Deana	CARTER s-cnt Am
De Lisser,HERBERT w Jamaica			Deana	JURGENS
De Luca,	GIUSEPPE bariton It		Deane,	LESLIE
De Mar,	JAKI tv		Deane,	SILAS l,st Am
De Medeiros, MARIA			Deanna	DURBIN s+
De Morgan,WILLIAM p,w Br			Deanna	LUND tv+
De Niro,	ROBERT o-s'74 o-a'80		Deardon,	BASIL d
De Palma,	RALPH racer-cars Am		Deat,	MARCEL st Fr
De Quincey, THOMAS w,ct Br			Debarge,	EL m,s,pr-recrds Am
De Reszke,EDOUARD basso Pol			Debbi	MORGAN
De Reszke,JEAN tenor Pol			Debbi	PETERSON mr-drm,s Am
De Sales,	FRANCIS tv		Debbie	ALLEN ba+ Am
De Santis,JOE tv+			Debbie	GIBSON s,ws Am
De Santis,STANLEY tv			Debbie	REYNOLDS s+ Am
De Selle,	LORRAINE		Debbie	SLEDGE mr-s Am
De Sica,	VITTORIO d+		Debbie	WATSON tv
De Smet,	PIERRE r Am		Debby	BOONE s Am
De Soto,	ROSANA		Debby	HARRIS tv
De Spirito, ROMOLO tv			DeBeck,	BILLY cr Am
De Sylva,	BUDDY lyrics Am		DeBell,	KRISTINE
De Valera,EAMON st Irish			DeBello,	JOHN d
De Vere,	AUBREY po Irish		Debi	MAZAR
De Voreaux WHITE tv			Debi	THIBEAULT
De Voto,	BERNARD w,p-h'48		Debi	THOMAS sk Am

Debierne,	ANDRE sc Fr	Dees,	RICK tv
Deborah	ADAIR tv+	Deezen,	EDDIE
Deborah	FOREMAN	Def	LEPPARD mr
Deborah	GROVER tv+	Defauw,	DESIRE viol,cn Belg
Deborah	HARMON tv+	Defoe,	DANIEL w,j Br
Deborah	HARRY	DeFore,	DON tv+
Deborah	HARRY mr-s Am	DeForest	COVAN tv
Deborah	KERR	DeForest	KELLEY tv+
Deborah	MAY tv+	Deforest,	CALVERT tv+
Deborah	PRATT tv	DeForest,	JOHN w Am
Deborah	RAFFIN	DeFreitas,	DICK tv
Deborah	RENNARD tv+	DeFreitas,	SCOTT tv
Deborah	RICHTER	DeGarr,	BIANCA tv
Deborah	SHELTON tv+	Degas,	EDGAR p Fr
Deborah	TAYLOR tv	DeGeneres,	ELLEN cm,tv
Deborah	TUCKER tv	Degermark,	PIA
Deborah	UNGER	Dehl	BERTI tv+
Deborah	WALLEY tv+	Dehmel,	RICHARD po Ger
Deborah	WATLING tv	Dehmelt,	HANS n-p'89
Deborah	WINTERS	Dehner,	JOHN tv+
Debra	BLEE	Dehnert,	DUTCH bb hf
Debra	FEUER	Dehon,	LEON r Fr
Debra	JOHNSON tv	Deidre	HALL tv
Debra	LAMB	Deidre	O'CONNELL
Debra	MOONEY tv	Deighton,	LEN w Am
Debra	PAGET	Deirdre	BERTHONG tv
Debra	RUSH tv	Deisenhofer,	JOHANN n-c'88
Debra	WINGER	Dejas	BELA mj,cn Ger
Debrah	FARENTINO tv+	Dejazet,	PAULINE la Fr
Debralee	SCOTT tv+	Deke	SLAYTON as Am
Debrett,	JOHN pb,w Br	Deken,	AAGJE po,w Dut
Debreu,	GERARD n-e'82	Dekker,	ALBERT
Debs,	EUGENE labor Am	Dekker,	DESMOND s,ws Jam
Debussy,	CLAUDE c Fr	Dekker,	THOMAS w Br
Debye,	PETER n-c'36	Del	CLOSE
DeCamp,	ROSEMARY tv+	Del	MONROE tv
Decazes,	ELIE st Fr	Del	MOORE tv
Deck,	JOSEPH ceramics Fr	Del	REEVES s Am
Decker,	DIANA tv	Del	RUSSEL tv
DeCoteau,	DAVID d	Del	SHANNON mr Am
Dedee	PFEIFFER	Del	ZAMORA
Dee	MORAN	Del Monaco,	MARIO tenor It
Dee Dee	KENNIBREW s Am	Del Prete,	DUILIO
Dee Dee	RAMONE mr-bass Am	Del Rio,	DELORES
Dee Wallace	STONE tv+	Del Ruth,	ROY d
Dee,	DAVE mr-s Br	Del Sol,	LAURA
Dee,	FRANCES	Del Toro,	BENICIO
Dee,	JOEY mr-s Am	Del Tredici,	DAVID p-m'80
Dee,	JOHN math,astrol Br	Delacroix,	EUGENE p Fr
Dee,	KIKI s-pop Br	Delafield,	E.M. w Br
Dee,	RUBY tv+	Delage,	YVES sc,e Fr
Dee,	SANDRA tv+	Delahanty,	ED b hf
Deedy	PETERS tv	DeLaHubbard,	RON
Deems	TAYLOR c,ct,tv Am	Delair,	SUZY
Deems,	MICKEY tv	Delamare,	LISE
Deena	FREEMAN tv	Deland,	MARGARET w Am
Deepak	CHOPRA w India	DeLane	MATTHEWS tv
Deeping,	WARWICK w Br	Delaney,	KIM tv+
Deere,	JOHN i,id-plows Am	Delaney,	STEVE tv
Deering,	WILLIAM id Am	Delano,	JANE md-nurse Am
Dees,	JULIE tv	Delano,	MICHAEL tv+

Delany,	DANA tv+	DeLuise,	PETER tv+
Delany,	PAT tv	Delvaux,	LAURENT su Belg
Delany,	PATRICK eng,i Am	DeLyon,	LEO tv
Delany,	SHELAGH w Br	DeMain,	GORDON
Delaroche,	PAUL p Fr	Demarest,	WILLIAM tv+
DeLarrocha,	ALICIA piano Sp	DeMarney,	DERRICK
Delaunay,	JULES-ELIE p Fr	DeMarney,	TERENCE tv
Delaunay,	ROBERT p Fr	DeMartino,	ALBERTO d
Delaunay,	SONIA p Fr	DeMauro,	GINO tv+
Delavigne,	JEAN w,po Fr	DeMauro,	NICK tv
Delbert	MANN d	DeMave,	JACK tv
Delbert	McCLINTON ws Am	DeMay,	JANET tv
Delbos,	YVON st Fr	Demazis,	ORANE
Delbruck,	HANS h,e Ger	Demi	MOORE
Delbruck,	MAX n-m'69	Demian	SLADE tv
Deledda,	GRAZIA n-l'26	Demidova,	ALLA
Delevanti,	CYRIL tv	DeMille,	AGNES ba Am
Delgado,	EMILIO tv	DeMille,	CECIL B. d
Delgado,	LUIS tv	DeMille,	HENRY w Am
Delia	BACON w Am	DeMille,	KATHERINE
Delia	SHEPPARD	Demme,	JONATHAN o-d'91,pr,w
Delibes,	LEO c Fr	Demond	WILSON tv
Delibes,	MIGUEL w Sp	Demongeot,	MYLENE
DeLillo,	DON w Am	DeMornay,	REBECCA
Delius,	FREDERICK c Br	Demoss,	DARCY
Dell'Abate,	GARY tv	Dempsey,	JACK boxer
Dell,	CHARLIE tv	Dempsey,	PATRICK
Dell,	CLAUDIA	Dempster,	CAROL
Dell,	ETHEL w Br	DeMunn,	JEFFREY
Dell,	FLOYD j,w Am	Demuth,	CHARLES p Am
Dell,	GABRIEL tv+	Demyan	BEDNYI po Rus
Dell,	MYRNA tv+	Dena	DIETRICH tv
Della	REESE s,tv+ Am	Denby,	EDWIN st Am
Della	STREET fc	Dench,	JUDI o-s'99
Della Casa,	GIOVANNI r,w It	Deneuve,	CATHERINE
Della Robbia,	LUCA su It	Deney	TERRIO tv
Delmar	KAPLAN mj-bass Am	Deng	XIAOPING st China
Delmer	DAVES d	Denham,	DIXON x Br
Delmonico,	LORENZO restaur Am	Denham,	JOHN(Sir)po
Delmont,	EDOUARD	Denham,	MAURICE
Delmore	SCHWARTZ po,w,ct Am	Denhardt,	CLEMENS x Ger
Delo,	KEN s Am	Denhardt,	GUSTAV x Ger
Delon,	ALAIN	Denholm	ELLIOTT
Delon,	NATHALIE	Denice	DUFF
Delora,	JENNIFER	Denice	KUMAGAI tv
DeLorenzo,	MICHAEL tv	Deniece	PEARSON mr-s Br
Delores	Del RIO	Deniece	WILLIAMSs-pop,gosp Am
Delores	HART	Denier,	LYDIE tv+
Delores	WELLS	Denis	AFFRE r Fr
Delorme,	PHILIBERT ac Fr	Denis	BROGAN(Sir)e
Deloy,	GEORGE tv	Denis	CHAUDET su,p Fr
Delp,	BRAD guit,s Am	Denis	DIDEROTw,ph,po,ct Fr
Delphi	LAWRENCE	Denis	FOREST tv
Delphine	SEYRIG	Denis	GLOVER po,ed N.Zea
Delpy,	JULIE	Denis	KAUFMAN d Rus
Delroy	LINDO	Denis	LAWSON
Delroy	PEARSON mr-s Br	Denis	LEARY
Delta	BURKE tv+	Denis	O'DEA
Delugg,	MILTON tv	Denis	PAPIN sc Fr
DeLuise,	DOM tv+	Denis	PAYTON m-sax Br
DeLuise,	MICHAEL tv	Denis	PETAU r Fr

Des Barres, MICHAEL tv+	DeWaart, EDO cn Dut
Desai, ANITA w Br	Dewaere, PATRICK
DeSalvo, ANNE	Dewar, JAMES(Sir) sc
Descartes,RENE math, ph Fr	DeWeldon, FELIX su Am
Descaves, LUCIEN w Fr	Dewey MARTIN
Deschamps,EMILE po Fr	Dewey MARTIN mr-drms,s Can
Deschanel,MARY JO tv+	Dewey REDMAN mj-sax Am
Descher, SANDY tv+	Dewey, GEORGE navy Am
Desert Fox ROMMEL ar Ger	Dewey, JOHN e,ph Am
Desert, ALEX tv	Dewey, MELVIL e,library Am
Desi ARNAZ Jr.mj,tv+	Dewey, THOMAS l,st Am
Desi ARNAZ Sr.mj,tv+	Dewhurst, COLLEEN tv+
Desiderio,ROBERT tv+	DeWilde, FREDERIC(Fritz) tv
Desiderius ERASMUS ph Dut	Dewing, THOMAS p Am
DeSimone, TONY m,tv	DeWitt CLINTON st Am
Desire DEFAUW viol,cn Belg	DeWitt JENNINGS
Desire MERCIER r,ph Belg	DeWitt LEE
Desire NISARD j,ct Fr	DeWitt WALLACE ed,pb Am
Desmond DEKKERs,ws Jama	DeWitt, ALAN tv
Desmond MacCARTHY(Sir)j,ct	DeWitt, GEORGE tv
Desmond O'GRADY po Irish	DeWitt, JOYCE tv
Desmond TUTU r,st S.Afr	DeWolf HOPPER la Am
Desmond, JOHNNY tv	DeWolfe, BILLY tv+
Desmond, PAUL mj-sax Am	Dexter FLETCHER
Desmond, WILLIAM	Dexter GORDON mj-sax Am
Desnos, ROBERT po Fr	Dexter, BRAD
Desny, IVAN	Dexter, COLIN w Br
Desoir, LUDWIG la Ger	Dexter, GORDON mj,sax Am
Despiau, CHARLES su Fr	Dexter, PETE w Am
Despotovich, NADA	Dexter, TIMOTHY mer,f Am
Destinn, EMMY soprano Czech	Dey YOUNG
Destouches, LOUIS md,w Fr	Dey, SUSAN tv+
Detaille, EDOUARD p Fr	DeYoung, CLIFF tv+
Detective Larry GROSS tv	Deyoung, DENNIS mr-kbds,s Am
Detlev BRONK md,e Am	Dezhnyov, SEMYON x Rus
Detlev von LILIENCRON po Ger	Dezso MAGYAR d
Detmers, MARUSCHKA	Dhionisios SOLOMOS po Gr
Dett, ROBERT N. cn,c Am	Di Leo, FERNANDO d
Deuel, PETER tv	Diaghilev,SERGEY ba Rus
Deus Ramos, JOAO de po Port	Diahann CARROLL tv+
Deutch, HOWARD d	Diahnne ABBOTT
Deutsch, BABETTE po,ct Am	Diamond Jim BRADY(James)f Am
Devane, WILLIAM tv+	Diamond, BOBBY tv
Devant, DAVID magic Br	Diamond, DON tv
DeVarona, DONNA tv	Diamond, NEIL mj-s,ws+
Devay, MATYAS r Hung	Diamond, JARED p-n'98
Deveraux, JUDE w	Diamond, REED
Devers, GAIL runner o-g'92,6	Diamond, SELMA tv+
Devers, JACOB ar Am	Dian FOSSEY an Br
Devey, GEORGE ac Br	Diana BELLAMY tv
Devin RATTRAY	Diana CANOVA tv+
Devine, ANDY tv+	Diana CHESNEY tv
Devine, LORETTA tv+	Diana DECKER tv
DeVito, DANNY d,tv+	Diana DORS tv+
Devito, TOMMY mr-guit,s Am	Diana DOUGLAS tv
DeVol, FRANK m,cn,tv Am	Diana GOODMAN tv
Devon ODESSA tv	Diana HYLAND tv+
Devon SCOTT tv	Diana LEWIS
Devon, LAURA tv	Diana LORYS
DeVries, JON	Diana LYNN
DeVries, PETER w Am	Diana MULDAUR tv+

Diana	QUICK	Dick	GAUTIER tv+
Diana	RIGG tv+	Dick	GROAT b
Diana	ROSS s+ Am	Dick	HAYMES s+ Am
Diana	SANDS	Dick	JONES tv
Diana	SCARWID	Dick	JURGENS mj-trum,cn Am
Diana	SCOTT tv	Dick	KALLMAN tv
Diana	TRASK tv	Dick	LANE(NightTran)fb hf
Diane	ARBUS fo Am	Dick	LOWRY d
Diane	BAKER	Dick	MARTIN tv+
Diane	CILENTO	Dick	McGUIRE bb hf
Diane	CRAIG	Dick	MILLER tv+
Diane	JERGENS tv	Dick	MOORES cr Am
Diane	JOHNSON w Am	Dick	O'NEILL tv+
Diane	KEATON	Dick	ORKIN tv
Diane	LADD tv+	Dick	PEABODY tv
Diane	LANDER tv	Dick	POWELL tv+
Diane	LANE	Dick	PURCELL
Diane	MARKOFF tv	Dick	SARGENT tv+
Diane	McBAIN	Dick	SHAWN
Diane	ROBIN tv	Dick	SMOTHERS cm,tv+ Am
Diane	ROTER tv	Dick	STABILE mj-sax,cn Am
Diane	SAWYER tv-j,host Am	Dick	TAYLOR mr-guit Br
Diane	SHERRY tv	Dick	THOMAS tv
Diane	VARSI	Dick	TUFELD tv
Diane	VENORA	Dick	Van DYKE tv+
Dianik	ZURAKOWSKA	Dick	Van PATTEN tv+
Dianne	DAY tv	Dick	WESSON tv+
Dianne	FOSTER	Dick	WICKMAN mj,cm Am
Dianne	HULL	Dick	WILSON tv
Dianne	KAY tv+	Dick	YORK tv+
Dianne	LENNON s,tv Am	Dick,	DOUGLAS tv+
Dianne	WIEST	Dick,	GEORGE md,e Am
Dias,	BARTHOLOMEU x Port	Dick-Read,	GRANTLY md,w Br
Dias,	DINIS x Port	Dickens,	CHARLES w Br
Diaz del Castillo,BERNAL ar,w Sp		Dickenson VIC mj-tromb Am	
Diaz,	ADOLFO st Nicarag	Dickerson,B.B. mr-bass,s Am	
Diaz,	ARMANDO ar It	Dickerson,ERIC fb	
Diaz,	JUNOT w Am	Dickerson,GEORGE	
Diaz,	PORFIRIO ar,st Mex	Dickerson,NAT s,tv Am	
Diaz,	VIC	Dickey	BETTS guit,s Am
Dibdin,	CHARLES w,la,c Br	Dickey,	BILL b hf
Dibdin,	THOMAS h Br	Dickey,	JAMES po,w Am
DiCaprio	LEONARDO tv+	Dickie	HARRISON tv
DiCenzo,	GEORGE tv+	Dickie	MOORE
Dicey,	ALBERT l,e Br	Dickin	RICHARDS Jr md Am
DiCicco,	BOBBY	Dickinson,ANGIE tv+	
Dick	ALLEN b	Dickinson,BRUCE mr-s Br	
Dick	BUTKAS fb,tv+	Dickinson,EMILY po Am	
Dick	BUTTON sk,tv Am	Dickinson,THOROLD d	
Dick	BYRD tv	Dicksee,	FRANCIS(Sir)p
Dick	CAVETT tv-host+ Am	Dicopoulos, FRANK tv	
Dick	CLARK tv+	Diddle,	EDGAR bbc hf
Dick	COLLIER tv	Diddley,	BO mj-blue,guit,s+
Dick	CURTIS cm,tv+ Am	Diderot,	DENIS w,ph,po,ct Fr
Dick	DALES s,sax,tv Am	Didi	CARR tv
Dick	DUDLEY tv	Didi	CONN tv+
Dick	ENBERG tv spts	Didier	PAIN
Dick	FORAN	Didion,	JOAN w Am
Dick	FOSBURY hijump Am	Didot,	FIRMIN pb Fr
Dick	FRANCIS w Br	Didot,	LEGER i Fr
Dick	GARTON tv	Diedre	HALL tv

Diego	CAO x Port	Dingle,	HERBERT sc Br
Diego	RIVERA p Mex	Dingo,	ERNIE
Diehl,	JOHN tv+	Dinis	DIAS x Port
Diels,	OTTO n-c'50	Dinning Sisters, THE s Am
Diener,	JOAN tv	Dinnyes,	LAJOS st Hung
Dierdorf,	DAN fb,tv	Dino	BUZATTI j,w It
Dierkop,	CHARLES tv+	Dino	DANELLI mr-drm Am
Dierx,	LEON po Fr	Dino	De LAURENTIS pr It
Dies,	MARTIN st Am	Dino	MARTIN(Dean)s,cm,tv+
Diesel	RUDOLF i Ger *ViN*	Dinsmore,	ELSIE fc
Dieter	BORSCHE	Dinu	LIPATTI piano,c
Dieter	LASER	Dio,	RONNIE mr-s Am
Dieterle,	WILLIAM d	Diogo	CAO x Port
Dietrich	WINKEL i Ger	Diogo	FEIJO r,st Braz
Dietrich,	DENA tv	Diogo	GOMES x Port
Dietrich,	MARLENE	Dion	BOUCICAULT la,w Am
Dietz,	HOWARD lyrics Am	Dion	DIMUCCI mr-s Am
Difford,	CHRIS mr-guit,s Br	Dion,	CELINE s Can-Fr
Diffring,	ANTON tv+	Dionne	WARWICK s-pop,gos Am
DiFranco,	ANI s-punk-folk Am	Dionne Quint ANNETE Can
Digby,	KENELM(Sir)navy,w	Dionne Quint CECILE Can
Digges,	DUDLEY	Dionne Quint EMELIE Can
Dignam,	ARTHUR	Dionne Quint MARIA Can
DiHigo,	MARTIN b hf	Dionne Quint YVONNE Can
Dik	BROWNE cr Am	Dionne Quints Moth ELZIRE Can
Dikembe	MUTOMBO bb	Dionne Quints Papa OLIVA Can
Dilke,	CHARLES ct,h Br	Diop,	DAVID po Senegal
Dill,	JOHN(Sir)ar	Dior,	CHRISTIAN ds Fr
Dillard,	ANNIE p-n'75	Dirac,	PAUL n-p'33
Dillard,	MIMI tv	Dirck	BOUTS p Dut
Diller,	PHYLLIS cm,tv+ Am	Dirck van BABUREN p Dut
Dillinger,JOHN outlaw Am	Dirk	BLOCKER tv
Dillman,	BRADFORD tv+	Dirk	BOGARDE
Dillon,	BRENDON tv	Dirk	LONDON tv
Dillon,	DENNY tv	Dirk Jan de GEER st Dut
Dillon,	EMILE j Br	Dirks,	RUDOLPH cr Am
Dillon,	GEORGE p-q'32	Dirty Dan McBRIDE tv
Dillon,	KEVIN	Disher,	CATHERINE tv
Dillon,	MATT	Dishy,	BOB tv+
Dillon,	MELINDA	Disney,	ANTHEA ed,pub Br-Am
DiMaggio,	JOE b-mv'39'41'7 hf	Disney,	WALTER ELIAS pr,tv
Dimitri	LOGOTHETIS d	Disraeli,	BENJAMIN w,st Br
Dimitri	TIOMKIN piano,c Am	DiStefano,JAMES tv
Dimitriev,RADKO ar Bulg	Dita	PARLO
Dimitrov,	GEORGI st Bulg	Ditka,	MIKE fb,fbc hf,tv
Dimucci,	DION mr-s Am	Ditko,	STEVE cr Am
Dina	MERRILL	Ditlev	MONRAD r,st Dan
Dina	OUSLEY tv	Ditmars,	RAYMOND sc Am
Dinah	CRAIK w Br	Ditzen,	RUDOLF w Ger
Dinah	CRAIK w Br	Divine	---
Dinah	MANOFF tv+	Divini,	EUSTACHIO id-clocks It
Dinah	SHERIDAN	Divoff,	ANDREW
Dinah	SHORE s+ Am	Dix,	DOROTHEA ref,f Am
Dinehart,	ALAN	Dix,	DOROTHY j,w Am
Dinehart,	MASON III tv	Dix,	JOHN ar,st Am
Dines,	WILLIAM weather Br	Dix,	OTTO p Ger
Dinesen,	ISAK w Dan	Dix,	RICHARD
Dinesen,	KAREN w Dan	Dix,	ROBERT
Dinesh	D'SOUZA w India	Dixie	CARTER tv
Ding	DARLING cr Am	Dixie	WHATLEY
Dingle,	CHARLES	Dixon	DENHAM x Br

Dixon,	BOB tv		Dody	GOODMAN tv+
Dixon,	DONNA tv+		Doe,	JOHN
Dixon,	GEORGE boxer Am		Doerr,	BOBBY b hf
Dixon,	GEORGE x Br		Does,	JOHAN van der st Dut
Dixon,	IVAN		Doggett,	THOMAS la Irish
Dixon,	JEANE astrolog,w Am		Doherty,	DENNY s Can
Dixon,	JEREMIAH survey Br		Doherty,	HUGH L. t Br
Dixon,	JOSEPH id,i Am		Doherty,	REGINALD t Br
Dixon,	KENT po Am		Doherty,	SHANNEN tv+
Dixon,	PAMELA		Dohm,	ERNST w,ed Ger
Dixon,	PAUL tv		Dohnanyi,	CHRISTOPH von cn
Dixon,	RICHARD po Br		Dohnanyi,	ERNO piano,c Hung
Dixon,	ROLAND an,e Am		Dohring,	KELSEY tv
Dixon,	WILLY ws Am		Dohring,	KRISTEN tv
Dixy	RAY sc,st Am		Dohrn,	ANTON sc Ger
Diz	WHITE		Doig,	IVAN w Am
Dizon,	JESSE tv		Doisy,	EDWARD n-m'43
Dizzy	DEAN b hf		Dolan,	ELLEN tv
Django	REINHARDT mj-guit Fr		Dolce,	LODOVICO w It
Djola,	BADJA		Dolci,	CARLO p It
Djuna	BARNES w,p Am		Dole,	SANFORD l,st Am
Dlugosz,	JAN h Pol		Dolenz,	AMI
Dmitry	MENDELEYEV sc,e Rus		Dolenz,	MICKEY mr-drm,s,tv
Dmitry	PISAREV w,j Rus		Dolin,	ANTON ba Br
Dmitry	SHOSTAKOVICH c Rus		Dollar,	LYNN tv
Dmowski,	ROMAN st Pol		Dollar,	ROBERT ships Am
Dmytryk,	EDWARD d		Dolley	MADISON wf-James
Doak	WALKER fb hf		Dolly	DAWN mj-s Am
Dobb,	GILLIAN tv		Dolly	PARTON s-cnt,tv+
Dobell,	SYDNEY po,ct Br		Dolores	GRAY tv+
Dober,	CONRAD w-songs Am		Dolph	CAMILLI b
Dobereiner,	JOHANN sc Ger		Dolph	LUNDGREN
Dobie,	JAMES w-folklore Am		Dolph	SCHAYES bb hf
Doblin,	ALFRED md,w Ger		Dolph	SWEET tv+
Dobree,	BONAMY ed,w Br		Dolphy,	ERIC mj-alto sax Am
Dobrowolska,	GOSIA		Dom	CAPER fbc
Dobson,	AUSTIN po,w Br		Dom	DeLUISE tv+
Dobson,	CHARLIE tv		Dom	MORAES po,j India
Dobson,	FRANK su Br		Domagk,	GERHARD n-m'39
Dobson,	KEVIN d,tv+		Domat,	JEAN l,w Fr
Dobson,	TAMARA		Dombrovsky,	YURI w Rus
Dobson,	WILLIAM p Br		Domenichino,	--- p It
Dobtcheff,	VERNON		Domenico	FETTI p It
Dobyns,	LLOYD tv		Domenico	GNOLI po It
Doc	PAMUS c Am		Domergue,	FAITH
Doc	SEVERINSEN cn,tv Am		Domett,	ALFRED po Br
Doc	SMITH(E.E.)w-scif Am		Domingo,	PLACIDO tenor+ It
Doctorow,	E.L. w Am		Dominic	GUARD
Dodd,	LEE w Am		Dominic	HOFFMAN tv
Dodd,	WILLIAM h,e Am		Dominick	ARGENTO c Am
Dodds,	JOHNNY mj-clarint Am		Dominique	PARODI po,w Fr
Dodds,	WARREN(Baby)mj-drums		Dominique	SANDA
Dodge,	HENRY ar,st Am		Domino,	FATS mj,pian Am
Dodge,	MARY w Am		Domitius	AFER st Roman
Dodge,	RAYMOND ps,e Am		Dommartin	SOLVEIG
Dodgson,	CHARLES math,w Br		Domonico	MODUGNO s It
Dodie	MARSHALL		Don	ADAMS tv+
Dodo	MARMAROSA mj-pian Am		Don	AMECHE tv+
Dodoens,	JUNIUS sc Dut		Don	BAKER tv
Dodsley,	ROBERT w,po Br		Don	BARCLAY
Dodson,	JACK tv+		Don	BAYLOR b

Don	BEDDOE	Don	REDMAN mj-reed,cn Am
Don	BEEBE fb	Don	REID s-cnt,pop Am
Don	BEXLEY tv	Don	RICH tv
Don	BUDGE t Am	Don	RICKLES tv+
Don	BURNETT tv	Don	RUSSELL tv
Don	BYAS mj-sax Am	Don	SHANKS tv+
Don	CALFA	Don	SHARP d
Don	CARLOS prince Sp	Don	SHULA fbc
Don	CHAFFEY d	Don	SIEGEL d+
Don	CHERRY tv	Don	SPARKS tv
Don	COLLIER tv	Don	STARR tv
Don	CORNELL tv	Don	STROUD tv+
Don	CRAIG tv	Don	SWAYZE
Don	DAVIS tv	Don	TAYLOR
Don	DeFORE tv+	Don	TAYLOR d
Don	DeLILLO w Am	Don	WILSON mr-guit Am
Don	DIAMOND tv	Don	WILSON(TheDragon) tv+
Don	DOUGLAS	Don	YESSO tv
Don	DUBBINS	Don Pedro	COLLEY tv
Don	DUNPHY tv	Don Red	BARRY
Don	DURANT tv	Dona	DRAKE
Don	ELLIS mj-trump,cn Am	Dona	SPEIR
Don	EVERLY s-cnt Am	Donahoe,	TERRY tv
Don	FRANCKS	Donahue,	CATHERINE tv
Don	GIBSON s-cnt Am	Donahue,	ELINOR tv+
Don	GODDARD tv	Donahue,	MARY tv
Don	GORDON tv+	Donahue,	MICHAEL tv
Don	GRADY tv	Donahue,	MIKE tv
Don	HARRON tv	Donahue,	PATRICIA tv
Don	HARVEY	Donahue,	PHIL tv-host Am
Don	HAYDEN tv	Donahue,	TROY tv+
Don	HENLEY s-pop Am	Donal	DONNELLY
Don	HERBERT tv	Donal	McCANN
Don	HO s Am	Donald	BARRY(Don"Red")
Don	HUTSON fb hf	Donald	BREWER mr-drm Am
Don	JOHNSON tv+	Donald	COBURN w Am
Don	KEEFER tv	Donald	COOK
Don	KING pr-boxing Am	Donald	CRAM sc Am
Don	KNIGHT tv	Donald	CRISP
Don	KNOTTS tv+	Donald	CURTIS
Don	LARGE s,cn,tv Am	Donald	DAVIE po,ct Br
Don	LARSEN b pitcher	Donald	DAVIS tv
Don	LEIFERT	Donald	DUNN mr-bass Am
Don	MARQUIS j,w-humor Am	Donald	FAGEN mr-kbds,s Am
Don	MAYNARD fb hf	Donald	FEHR b-union Am
Don	McBRIDE tv	Donald	FOSTER tv
Don	McGUIRE	Donald	GLASER sc Am
Don	McLEAN mr-s,ws Am	Donald	GRAY tv+
Don	MEGOWAM	Donald	HALL po,ed Am
Don	MESSICK tv	Donald	HOUSTON
Don	MURRAY tv+	Donald	JUSTICE po Am
Don	NELSON bb,bbc	Donald	KEELER tv
Don	NEWCOMB b	Donald	KEITH
Don	NOVELLO tv+	Donald	MacBRIDE
Don	OPPER	Donald	MANN(Sir)rr's Can
Don	PARDO tv	Donald	MARTINO c Am
Don	PAUL	Donald	MAY tv+
Don	PENNY tv	Donald	MEEK
Don	PORTER tv+	Donald	MOFFATT
Don	PULLEN mj,piano Am	Donald	O'CONNOR tv+
Don	QUINE tv	Donald	PEATTIE nature Am

Donald	PETRIE d	Donnelly,	JACQUELINE tv
Donald	REGAN st Am	Donnelly,	RUTH
Donald	SINDEN	Donnelly,	TIM tv+
Donald	TOVEY(Sir)c,w	Donner,	CLIVE d
Donald	TRUMP f Am	Donner,	GEORG su Aus
Donald	WOLFIT	Donner,	RICHARD d
Donald	WOODS tv+	Donner,	ROBERT tv+
Donald	YORK(Donny)tv	Donnie	OSMOND s,tv+ Am
Donald,	JAMES	Donnie	VanZANDT mr-guit,sAm
Donald,	PETER tv	Donny	MOST tv
Donaldson,ROGER d		Donny	YORK(Donald)tv
Donaldson,SAM tv-j,anchor Am		Donohoe,	AMANDA tv+
Donat,	PETER tv+	Donoso,	JOSE w Chile
Donat,	ROBERT o-a'39	Donovan	LEITCH
Donatello	--- su It	Donovan,	ANNE bb hf
Donati,	CORSO st It	Donovan,	ART fb hf
Donatien	SADE(Marq.de)ar,w Fr	Donovan,	KING tv+
Donato	BRAMANTE ac It	Donovan,	MARTIN
Donatus,	AELIUS e,w Roman	Donovan,	TATE
Donders,	FRANS md,e Dut	Donovan,	WM.(Wld Bill)l,st Am
Donegan,	LONNIE m-r&b,s Scot	Doodles	WEAVER
Donen,	STANLEY d	Doody,	ALISON
Dongen,	KEES van p Dut	Doohan,	JAMES tv+
DonHowe,	GWYDA tv	Dooley	WILSON piano,tv+ Am
Doni,	ANTON w.ed It	Dooley,	PAUL tv+
Donitz,	KARL navy Ger	Doolittle,HILDA po Am	
Donizetti,GAETANO c It		Doolittle,JAMES H.aviat Am	
Donkin,	BRYAN eng,i Br	Doppler,	CHRISTIAN sc Aus
Donlan,	YOLANDE	DoQui,	ROBERT tv+
Donleavy, J.P. w Irish		Dor,	KARIN
Donlevy,	BRIAN tv+	Dora	BRYAN
Donn	BARBER ac Am	Doran,	ANN tv+
Donn	BENNETT tv	Doran,	GEORGE pb Am
Donn	PIATT j,ed Am	Doran,	MARY
Donna	BACCALA tv	Dorati,	ANTAL cn,c Am
Donna	DENTON tv+	Dore	SCHARY pr-films Am
Donna	DeVARONA tv	Dore,	GUSTAVE illus,at Fr
Donna	DIXON tv+	Doreen	WILSON tv
Donna	DOUGLAS tv+	Doremus,	DAVID tv
Donna	FARGO s Am	Dorff,	STEPHEN
Donna	JEPSON tv	Dorgan,	THOMAS cr,j Am
Donna	KARAN ds Am	Dorgeles,	ROLAND w Fr
Donna	KING s tv	Dori	BRENNER tv+
Donna	La BRIE tv	Doria,	ANDREA navy It
Donna	LOREN tv+	Dorian	HAREWOOD tv+
Donna	MARTELL	Dorian	LOPINTO tv
Donna	MILLS tv+	Doris	BROWN tv
Donna	PESCOW tv+	Doris	COLEY mr-s Am
Donna	READING tv	Doris	DAY s,tv+ Am
Donna	REED tv+	Doris	DOWLING tv+
Donna	SUMMER s Am	Doris	GOODWIN w Am
Donna	TARTT w Am	Doris	LESSING w Br
Donna	WILKES tv+	Doris	LLOYD
Donna	WOOD s Am	Doris	PACKER tv
Donna Wood HER DON JUANS s Am		Doris	PEARSON mr-s Br
Donnadieu,MARGUERITE w, pr Fr		Doris	ROBERTS tv+
Donnay,	MAURICE w Fr	Dorleac,	FRANCOISE
Donne,	JOHN po Br	Dorman	EATON l,ref Am
Donnell,	JEFF	Dorman,	LEE mr-bass Am
Donnelly	RHODES	Dorn,	ED po,w Am
Donnelly,	DONAL	Dorn,	HEINRICH c Ger

Dorn,	MICHAEL tv+		Dots	JOHNSON
Dorn,	PHILIP		Dottie	WEST s+ Am
Dorne,	SANDRA		Dotty	MACK tv
Dorner,	ISAAK r,e Ger		Dou,	GERRIT p Dut
Dornier,	CLAUDIUS id-planes Ger		Douay,	CHARLES ar Fr
Doro	MERANDE tv+		Doubleday,	ABNER pb,bmg Am
Dorothea	DIX ref,f Am		Doucet,	CHARLES w Fr
Dorothea	JORDAN la Irish		Doucette,	JEFF tv
Dorothea	LANGE fo Am		Doucette,	JOHN tv+
Dorothee	BERRYMAN tv+		Douffet,	GERARD p Dut
Dorothy	ALLISON w Am		Doug	ATKINS fb hf
Dorothy	BERNARD tv		Doug	DRABEK b
Dorothy	CHRISTY		Doug	FIEGER mr-guit,s Am
Dorothy	CLAIRE tv		Doug	FLYNN b
Dorothy	COLLINS tv		Doug	HENNING magic,tv Can
Dorothy	DAY j,ref Am		Doug	INGLE mr-kbds,s Am
Dorothy	DIX j,w Am		Doug	McCLURE tv+
Dorothy	DWAN		Doug	McKEON tv+
Dorothy	EUSTIS f Am		Doug	MOSSMAN tv
Dorothy	FIELDS ws Am		Doug	SAHM mr-guit,s Am
Dorothy	FISHER w Am		Doug	SAVANT tv+
Dorothy	GILMAN w		Doug E.	DOUG
Dorothy	GISH la+ Am		Doug,	DOUG E.
Dorothy	GRANGER		Doughty,	CHARLES w Br
Dorothy	GREEN tv		Doughty,	NEAL mr-keybds Am
Dorothy	GREENER tv		Doughty,	SUSAN ceramics Br
Dorothy	HAMILL sk Am		Dougie	THOMSON mr-bass Scot
Dorothy	HART tv		Douglas	ADAMS w Br
Dorothy	HODGKIN sc Br		Douglas	BARR tv
Dorothy	JARNAC tv		Douglas	DICK tv+
Dorothy	KIRSTEN soprano Am		Douglas	EDWARDS tv
Dorothy	LAMOUR		Douglas	EMERSON tv
Dorothy	LEE		Douglas	EVANS
Dorothy	LOUDON mj,s Am		Douglas	FOWLEY tv+
Dorothy	LOVETT		Douglas	FREEMAN ed,w Am
Dorothy	LUCEY tv		Douglas	HAIG ar Br
Dorothy	LYMAN tv+		Douglas	HOGG st Br
Dorothy	MALONE tv+		Douglas	HYDE po,w,st Irish
Dorothy	McGUIRE tv+		Douglas	KENNEDY
Dorothy	NEUMAN tv		Douglas	KIKER w,tv Am
Dorothy	PARKE tv		Douglas	LOWE o-g'24'28
Dorothy	PARKER w,po,ct Am		Douglas	MAWSON(Sir)x,geolAust
Dorothy	PROVINE tv+		Douglas	MOORE c Am
Dorothy	REVIER		Douglas	SEALE tv+
Dorothy	SAYERS w Br		Douglas	SHEEHAN tv
Dorothy	SHORT		Douglas	SIRK d
Dorothy	TUTIN		Douglas	STEWART po,w Austra
Dorothy	WILSON		Douglas	WALTON
Dorothy's	dog TOTO		Douglas	WILMER
Dorr	FELT i Am		Douglas,	BRANDON tv
Dorr,	JULIA w,po Am		Douglas,	BUSTER boxer Am
Dorrie	THOMSON tv		Douglas,	CHRISTOPHER tv
Dorris,	MICHAEL w Am		Douglas,	DIANA tv
Dors,	DIANA tv+		Douglas,	DON
Dorset,	MARION sc Am		Douglas,	DONNA tv
Dorsett,	TONY fb hf		Douglas,	GAWIN po,r Scot
Dorsey,	JIMMY mj,cn,tv+ Am		Douglas,	ILLEANA
Dorsey,	TOMMY mj,cn,tv+ Am		Douglas,	JACK D. tv
Dos Passos,	JOHN w Am		Douglas,	JACK tv-host Am
Dostoyevsky,	FYODOR w Rus		Douglas,	JAMES tv
Dotrice,	ROY tv+		Douglas,	KIRK

Douglas,	LORD ALFRED po Br
Douglas,	MELVYN o-s'63'79,tv+
Douglas,	MICHAEL o-a'87,tv+
Douglas,	MIKE tv
Douglas,	NORMAN w,st Br
Douglas,	PAUL tv+
Douglas,	ROBERT
Douglas,	RONALDA tv
Douglas,	SARAH tv+
Douglas,	STEPHEN st Am
Douglas,	SUZANNE tv
Douglas,	WILLIAM l,w Am
Douglass	NORTH ec Am
Douglass,	ROBYN tv+
Douhet,	GIULIO ar It
Doumani,	BRENDA tv
Doumer,	PAUL st Fr
Doumic,	RENE w,ct Fr
Dourif,	BRAD
Dove,	ARTHUR p Am
Dove,	HEINRICH sc,e Ger
Dove,	RITA p-q'87
Dover	WILSON e,ed Br
Doveton	STURDEE(Sir)navy
Dow,	CHARLES j-finance Am
Dow,	HAROLD tv
Dow,	HERBERT id,i Am
Dow,	NEAL temperance Am
Dow,	TONY tv+
Dowdell,	ROBERT tv
Dowland,	JOHN c,m Am
Dowling,	DORIS tv+
Down,	LESLEY-ANNE tv+
Downes,	OLIN ct-music Am
Downey,	BRIAN mr-drm Irish
Downey,	MORTON Jr tv-host+Am
Downey,	MORTON tv
Downey,	ROBERT d
Downey,	ROBERT Jr. tv+
Downey,	ROMA
Downing,	WILFRID tv
Downs,	CATHY
Downs,	HUGH tv-host+ Am
Downs,	JOHNNY
Dowson,	ERNEST po Br
Doyen,	GABRIEL p Fr
Doyle,	ALEXANDER su Am
Doyle,	ARTHUR CONAN(Sir)w
Doyle,	DAVID tv+
Doyle,	FRANCIS(Sir)po,e
Doyle,	JOHN p,cr Br
Doyle,	RICHARD cr,p Br
Doyle,	RODDY w Br
Doyle-Murray,BRIAN tv+
Dozsa,	GYORGY rebel Hng
Dozy,	REINHART h,e Dut
Dr.	DRE m-rap Am
Dr.	JOHN s-r&b,rk Am
Dr.	JOHNSON l,e,po Br
Dr.	SEUSS w,illus Am
Drabble,	MARGARET w Br

Drabek,	DOUG b-cy'90
Drabowsky,MOE b
Drache,	HEINZ
Drachmann,HOLGER w Dan
Drago,	BILLY
Dragon	LEE
Dragon,	DARYL m-pop,kbds Am
Drake	HOGESTYN tv
Drake,	ALEXANDER illus,ct Am
Drake,	BRUCE bbc, hf
Drake,	CHARLES tv+
Drake,	CLAUDIA
Drake,	DONA
Drake,	EDWIN id-oil Am
Drake,	ELLEN tv
Drake,	FRANCES
Drake,	FRANCIS(Sir)x
Drake,	GABE m,bass,tv Am
Drake,	GEORGIA tv
Drake,	JOSEPH po Am
Drake,	LARRY tv+
Drake,	STAN cr Am
Drake,	TOM
Draper,	CHARLES eng-aero Am
Draper,	JOHN sc,w Am
Draper,	LYMAN h Am
Draper,	POLLY tv+
Dravic,	MILENA
Drayton,	MICHAEL po Br
Dre,	DR. m-rap Am
Dred	SCOTT slave Am
Dreiser,	THEODORE w Am
Dreja,	CHRIS mr-guit Br
Drescher,	FRAN tv+
Dresden,	CURLY
Dresser,	LOUISE
Dressler,	MARIE cm,la+,o-a'31
Drew	CAREY cm,tv Am
Drew	McVETY tv
Drew	PEARSON w,j Am
Drew	SNYDER
Drew,	ELLEN
Drew,	JOHN Jr. la Am
Drew,	JOHN la Am
Drew,	PAULA tv
Drews,	ARTHUR ph Ger
Dreyer,	CARL d
Dreyer,	MAX j,w Ger
Dreyfuss,	LORIN
Dreyfuss,	RANDY tv
Dreyfuss,	RICHARD o-a'77,tv+
Drier,	MOOSIE tv+
Driesch,	HANS sc,ph Ger
Drimmer,	DAVID tv
Drinkwater,	JOHN po,w Br
Driscoll,	BOBBY
Driscoll,	PADDY fb hf
Driscoll,	PATRICIA tv
Driver,	MINNIE
Drobisch,	MORITZ math,ph Ger
Dropsie,	MOSES l Am

Drost,	AERNOUT w Dut	Ducommun,	ELIE j,n-x'02
Droz,	ANTOINE p Fr	Ducommun,	RICK tv+
Droz,	JULES su Fr	Dud	DUDLEY ironmastr Br
Droz,	NUMA j,st Swi	Dudikoff,	MICHAEL
Dru,	JOANNE tv+	Dudley	De CHAIR(Sir)navy
Druckman,	JACOB p-m'72	Dudley	DIGGES
Drude,	PAUL KARL sc,e Ger	Dudley	MOORE
Drummond,	HENRY r,w Scot	Dudley	POUND(Sir)navy
Drummond,	WILLIAM po Can	Dudley	SUTTON
Druon,	MAURICE w Fr	Dudley,	BERNARD tv
Drury,	ALLEN p-f'60	Dudley,	BILL fb hf
Drury,	BOB tv	Dudley,	DICK tv
Drury,	JAMES tv+	Dudley,	DUD ironmaster Br
Drusky,	ROY s-cnt Am	Dudok,	WILLEM ac Dut
Dryden,	JOHN po Br	Duell,	WILLIAM tv+
Dryden,	MACK tv	Duer,	WILLIAM re,st Am
Dryden,	SPENCER mr-drm Am	Dufay,	GUILLAUME c Fr
Dryer,	FRED	Duff	GREEN j,st Am
Drysdale,	DON b-cy'62,hf,tv	Duff Rose McKAGAN mr-bass Am	
Drzic,	MARIN w Croatia	Duff,	DENICE
Du Bois,	GUY p,ct Am	Duff,	HOWARD tv+
Du Bois,	W.E.B.civil rts,w Am	Duff-Gordon, LUCIE(Lady)w Br	
Du Buat,	PIERRE eng Fr	Duffy,	CHARLESj,ref Irish
Du Camp,	MAXIME j Fr	Duffy,	EDMUND cr Am
Du Chaillu,	PAUL x Am	Duffy,	HUGH b hf
Du Fay,	CHARLES st Fr	Duffy,	JACK tv
Du Maurier,	GEORGE w,illus.Br	Duffy,	JULIA tv+
Du Mont,	ALLEN id,i Am	Duffy,	PATRICK tv+
Duane	ALLEN s-cnt Am	Dufy,	RAOUL p Fr
Duane	DAVIS	Dugald	CLERK(Sir)eng,i Scot
Duane	EDDY mr-guit Am	Dugald	STEWART ph,e Scot
Duane	JONES	Dugan,	ALAN p-q'62
Duane,	WILLIAM sc,e Am	Dugan,	DENNIS tv+
Duarte,	JOSE st Salv	Dugan,	TOM
Dub	TAYLOR tv+	Duggan,	ANDREW tv+
Duban,	FELIX ac Fr	Duggan,	BOB tv
DuBarry,	DENISE tv	Dughet,	GASPARD p Fr
Dubbins,	DON	Duguay,	CHRISTIAN d
Dube,	JOHN j,e S.Afr	Duhamel,	GEORGES w,po Fr
Dubin,	AL lyrics Am	Duhem,	PIERRE sc,ph Fr
Dubin,	GARY tv	Duhm,	BERNHARD r Ger
Dubnow,	SIMON h Rus-Jew	Duigan,	JOHN d
Dubois,	EUGENE md,sc Dut	Duilio	Del PRETE
DuBois,	JA'NET	Dujardin,	EDOUARD w,po,ed Fr
DuBois,	MARIE	Dukakis,	OLYMPIA o-s'87
DuBois,	MARTA tv+	Dukas,	PAUL c Fr
Dubois,	PAUL su Fr	Duke	ELLINGTON c,cn,tv+Am
Dubois,	THEODORE c Fr	Duke	FARLEY tv
Dubos,	RENE p-n'69	Duke	SNIDER b hf
DuBose	HEYWARD w.po Am	Duke,	BENJAMIN id-tobac Am
Dubost,	PAULETTE	Duke,	BILL d,tv+
Dubov,	PAUL	Duke,	DARYL d
Dubs,	JAKOB st Swi	Duke,	DAVID st,racist Am
Dubuc,	NICOLE tv	Duke,	PATTY o-s'62,tv+
Dubuffet,	JEAN p Fr	Duke,	ROBIN tv+
Ducasse,	ISIDORE po Fr	Duke,	VERNON c Am
Duchamp,	GASTON p,etch Fr	Dukes,	ASHLEY c,w Br
Duchamp,	MARCEL p Fr	Dukes,	DAVID tv+
Duchaussoy,	MICHAEL	Dulac,	EDMUND illus,ds Br
Duchovny,	DAVID	Dulany,	CAITLIN
Ducis,	JEAN w Fr	Dulbecco,	RENATO n-m'75

Dulcie	GRAY		Dunn,	EDDIE
Dullea,	KEIR		Dunn,	EMMA
Dulles,	JOHN FOSTER l,st Am		Dunn,	GEORGE tv
Dullin,	CHARLES la,pr Fr		Dunn,	JAMES o-s'45,tv+
Dulo,	JANE tv		Dunn,	KEVIN tv+
Dumas	MALONE bio,e Am		Dunn,	LARRY mr-kbds Am
Dumas,	ALEXANDRE(fils)w Fr		Dunn,	MICHAEL
Dumas,	ALEXANDRE(pere)w Fr		Dunn,	NORA cm,tv+ Am
DuMaurier,DAPHNE w Fr			Dunn,	PETE tv
Dumbrille,DOUGLASS tv+			Dunne,	FINLEY j,w-humor Am
Dumbrys,	SUSAN w Am		Dunne,	GRIFFIN
Dumitru	IONESCU(Take) st Rom		Dunne,	IRENE tv+
Dumont,	EDME su Fr		Dunne,	JOHN GREGORY w
Dumont,	FRANCOIS su Fr		Dunne,	JOHN W.id,ph Br
Dumont,	MARGARET tv+		Dunne,	STEVE tv+
Dumont,	PIERRE su Fr		Dunnham,	STEPHANIE tv
Dun,	DENNIS tv+		Dunninger,JOSEPH tv
Dun,	ROBERT mer,f Am		Dunnock,	MILDRED
Dun,	TAN c,cn Am		Dunphy,	DON tv
Duna,	STEFFI		Dunsany,	LORD w,po Irish
Dunant,	JEAN HENRI n-x'01		Dunsmore,	ROSEMARY
Dunaway,	DENNIS m-bass Am		Dunstable,JOHN c Br
Dunaway,	FAYE o-a'76		Duparc,	HENRI c Fr
Dunbar,	ADRIAN		Duperey,	ANNY
Dunbar,	OLIVE tv		Dupin,	ANDRE l,st Fr
Dunbar,	PAUL po,w Am		DuPois,	STARLETTA
Dunbar,	WILLIAM po Scot		Duport,	ADRIEN st Fr
Duncan	GRANT p Scot		Dupre,	GIOVANNI su It
Duncan	HINES ct-food,w Am		Dupre,	GUILLAUME su Fr
Duncan	PHYFE id-cabinets Am		Dupre,	JULES p Fr
Duncan	REGEHR tv+		Dupre,	MARCEL organ, c Fr
Duncan	RENALDO tv+		Duprez,	JUNE
Duncan	ROSS tv		Duran	ROBERTO boxer Am
Duncan	SCOTT po Can		Duran,	AGUSTIN ct,po Sp
Duncan,	ANDREW(Sir)st		Duran,	PROFIAT r Fr-Jew
Duncan,	ARCHIE tv		Duran,	SIMEON r sp-Jew
Duncan,	GARY mr-guit Am		Durand,	ASHER p,engrav Am
Duncan,	ISADORA ba Am		Durang,	CHRISTOPHER
Duncan,	KENNE		Durant,	ARIEL p-n'68
Duncan,	LINDSAY		Durant,	DON tv
Duncan,	PATRICK(Sir)st S.Afr		Durant,	HENRY r,e Am
Duncan,	RACHEL tv		Durant,	THOMAS id-rrs Am
Duncan,	ROBERT po Am		Durant,	WILL e,ph,p-n'68
Duncan,	SANDY tv+		Durant,	WILLIAM id-autos Am
Duncan,	THOMAS p Scot		Durante,	JIMMY cm,tv+ Am
Dundas,	DAVID(Sir)ar Br		Durao,	JOSE de r,po Braz
Dundas,	JENNIE		Duras,	MARGUERITE w,pr Fr
Dundee,	ANGELO mgr-boxing		Durbin,	DEANNA s+ Am
Duner,	NILS astron Swe		Durer,	ALBRECHT p,engr Ger
Dunhill,	THOMAS c,e Br		Durey,	LOUIS c Fr
Duni,	EGIDIO c It		Durfee,	MINTA
Dunlap,	DAWN		Durning,	CHARLES tv+
Dunlap,	RICHARD tv pr		Duroc,	GERAUD ar,st Fr
Dunlap,	WILLIAM p,w,h Am		Durocher,	LEO(TheLip)bmg hf,tv
Dunleavy,	STEVE tv		Durrell,	GERALD sc,w Br
Dunlop,	JOHN i,id-tires Scot		Durrell,	LAWRENCE w,po Br
Dunlop,	STEVE tv		Durrenmatt, FRIEDRICH w Swi
Dunlop,	VICTOR(Vic)tv+		Durston,	GIGI tv
Dunmont,	ULISES		Duruy,	VICTOR h,e Fr
Dunn,	CAROLYN tv+		Durward	KIRBY tv
Dunn,	DONALD mr-bass Am		Dury,	IAN mr-s+

Duryea,	CHARLES i,id-cars Am	Dye,	JOHN tv+
Duryea,	DAN tv+	Dyer,	ELIPHALET l Am
Dusan	SIMOVIC ar,st Yugo	Dyer,	JOHN po Br
Dusay,	MARJ tv+	Dyk,	VIKTOR w Czech
Duse,	ELEONORA la It	Dykers,	THOMAS M. tv
Dusenberry, ANN		Dykes,	JOHN r,c Br
Dushku,	ELIZA	Dykstra,	LEN(Lenny)b
Dussault, NANCY tv		Dylan	BAKER
Dussek,	JAN piano,c Ger	Dylan	NEAL tv
Dussollier, ANDRE		Dylan	WALSH tv
Dustin	HOFFMAN	Dylan,	BOB mr,s+
Dustin	NGUYEN tv+	Dyneley,	PETER
Duston,	HANNAH heroine Am	Dysart,	RICHARD tv+
Dusty	BAKER b,bmg	Dyson,	FRANK(Sir)astr
Dusty	SPRINGFIELD s-folk Br	Dyson,	WILLIAM etch,cr Br
Dutch	CLARK fb hf	Dzundza,	GEORGE tv+
Dutch	DEHNERT bb hf		
Dutch	LONBORG bbc hf		
Dutourd,	JEAN w Fr	**"E" NAME DESIGNATION CODES**		
Dutra,	EURICO ar,st Braz	e	-	EDUCATOR
Dutronc,	JACQUES	ec	-	ECONOMIST
Dutton,	CHARLES S.	ed	-	EDITOR
Dutton,	EDWARD pb Am	eng	-	ENGINEER
Duun,	OLAV w Nor	engr	-	ENGRAVER
Duval,	JOSEY	etch	-	ETCHER
Duval,	PAUL w Fr		
Duvalier,	FRANCOIS(Doc)st Hait	**"E" NATIONALITY CODE**		
Duvall,	ROBERT o-a'83	Ecu	-	ECUADORIAN
Duvall,	SHELLEY		
Duvall,	SUSAN tv	**"E's"**		
Duve,	CHRISTIAN de n-m'74	E. Allen	WARREN
Duveneck,	FRANK p,su,e Am	E. Annie	PROULX w Am
Duvet,	JEAN engr Fr	E. Donnall THOMAS md Am	
Duvivier,	JULIEN d	E. Katherine KERR	
Duyse,	PRUDENS van w Belg	E.B.	PUSEY r,e,w Br
Dvorak,	ANN	E.B.	WHITE w-humor Am
Dvorak,	ANTONIN c Ger	E.C.	BENTLEY l,ph Br
Dwan,	SMITH tv	E.E.	CLIVE
Dwan,	ALLAN d	E.E.	SMITH(Doc) w-scifi Am
Dwan,	DOROTHY	E.J.	PEAKER tv
Dwayne	HICKMAN tv+	E.J.	PRATT po Can
Dweezil	ZAPPA mr-guit+ Am	E.M.	FORSTER w Br
Dwight	DAVIS st,t Am	E.T.A.	HOFFMAN c,w Ger
Dwight	EVANS b	E.V.	LUCAS w Br
Dwight	FRYE	E.W.	HOWE(Ed)j,ed,w Am
Dwight	GOODEN b	E.Y.	HARBERG(Yip)lyrics Am
Dwight	LITTLE d	E.Z.C.	JUDSON w Am
Dwight	MOODY r Am	Eadie,	JOHN r Scot
Dwight	MORROW l,banks,st Am	Eads,	JAMES eng,i Am
Dwight	SCHULTZ tv+	Eaglen,	JANE soprano Br
Dwight	WEIST tv	Eaker,	IRA C. ar Am
Dwight	YOAKAM c-cntry Am	Eakins,	THOMAS p Am
Dwight,	TIMOTHY po,e Am	Eames,	CHARLES ds-furn Am
Dwight-Smith, MICHAEL tv		Eames,	EMMA soprano Am
Dwire,	EARL	Eamon	De VALERA st Irish
Dwyer,	HILARY	Eanes,	GIL x Port
Dyall,	VALENTINE	Eareckson,JONI	
Dyan	CANNON	Earhart,	AMELIA flyer Am
Dyanne	THORNE	Earl	AVERILL b hf
Dyce,	WILLIAM p Scot	Earl	BOEN tv
Dye,	CAMERON	Earl	BOSTIC mr Am

Earl	BROWN s,cn,tv Am	Ebe	STIGNANI mezzo
Earl	BUTZ st Am	Ebel,	JOHANN r Ger
Earl	CARROLL pr-stage Am	Eben,	AL tv
Earl	DWIRE	Ebenezer	BUTTERICK i-pattern Am
Earl	HAMMOND tv	Ebenezer	ELLIOTT po Br
Earl	HINDMAN tv+	Ebenezer	JONES po Br
Earl	HINES(Fatha) mj Am	Ebenezer	PROUT c Br
Earl	HYMAN tv	Ebenezer	ZANE pioneer Am
Earl	LAMBEAU(Curly)f,fbc	Eber,	PAUL r,e Ger
Earl	MORRELL fb	Eberhardt,THOM d
Earl	OWENSBY	Eberhart, RICHARD p-q'66
Earl	REDDING tv	Eberle,	BOB mj,s,tv+ Am
Earl	ROSS tv	Eberle,	RAY mj-s,cn Am
Earl	SCRUGGS m-bluegrss Am	Ebers,	GEORG M. w Ger
Earl	STROM bbr hf	Ebersole, CHRISTINE tv+
Earl	Van DORN ar Am	Ebert,	ROGER ct-films,tv Am
Earl	WARREN st,ch just Am	Ebonie	SMITH tv
Earl	WEAVER b,tv	Eboue,	FELIX st Fr
Earl	WILD cm,tv Am	Ebsen,	BUDDY tv+
Earl	WILSON tv+	Eburne,	MAUDE
Earl Derr BIGGERS w Am	Eccard,	JOHANNES c Ger
Earle	BIRNEY po,w Can	Eccles,	AIMEE
Earle	COMBS b hf	Eccles,	JOHN(Sir)n-m'63
Earle	HODGINS tv+	Eccles,	MARRINER ec Am
Earle	PAGE(Sir)st Aust	Eccleston,CHRISTOPHER
Earle G.	WHEELER ar(gen)	Echegaray,JOSE n-1'04
Earle,	ALICE w Am	Echevarria, ROCKY tv
Earle,	MERIE tv	Echeverria, ESTEBAN po Arg
Earle,	RALPH p Am	Echols,	JOHN mr-guitar Am
Earle,	STEVE s-cnt,ws Am	Eck,	JOHANN r Ger
Early	WYNN b hf	Eckener,	HUGO aeronaut Ger
Early,	JUBAL ar(CSA)Am	Eckermann,JOHANN w Ger
Early,	STEPHEN j,st Am	Eckersley,DENNISb-cy'82,b-mv'92
Earnest	HOOTON an Am	Eckhart,	AARON
Earnhardt,DALE racer-cars Am	Eckhel,	JOSEPH coins,e Aus
Earp,	WYATT lawman Am	Eckhouse, JAMES tv+
Eartha	KITT s+ Am	Eckstein, BILLY mj-s,cn+
Easen,	TONY fb	Eckstein, ERNST humor Ger
Eason,	B. REEVES d	Eco,	UMBERTO w It
East,	ALFRED(Sir) p Br	Ed	AMES s,tv Am
East,	JEFF	Ed	ASNER tv+
Easterbrook, LESLIE tv+	Ed	BEGLEY Jr. tv+
Eastham,	RICHARD tv	Ed	BEGLEY Sr. tv+
Eastman	JOHNSON p Am	Ed	BERNARD tv+
Eastman,	GEORGE	Ed	BISHOP
Eastman,	GEORGE i,id-photo Am	Ed	BRADLEY tv
Eastman,	MAX w,ed Am	Ed	BRUCE tv
Easton,	ELLIOT mr-guit Am	Ed	BULLINS w,po Am
Easton,	SHEENA s,tv+ Scot	Ed	CASSIDY mr-drums Am
Eastwood, CLINT o-d'92, tv+	Ed	DORN po,w Am
Eastwood, JAYNE	Ed	GARRETT tv
Eaton,	AMOS sc,w Am	Ed	GRADY tv
Eaton,	CYRUS id Am	Ed	HALL tv
Eaton,	DORMAN l,ref Am	Ed	HARRIS
Eaton,	SHIRLEY	Ed	HEALEY fb hf
Eaton,	WYATT p Am	Ed	HERLIHY tv
Eb	LOTTIMER	Ed	HINTON tv
Eban,	ABBA st Israel	Ed	HOLMES tv
Ebb,	FRED lyrics Am	Ed	HOWE(E.W.)j,ed,w Am
Ebbe	RODE	Ed	KEMMER tv
Ebbie	GOODFELLOW ho	Ed	KOCH st Am

Ed	LAUTER tv+		Eddings,	LEIGH w Am
Ed	McBAIN w Am		Eddra	GALE
Ed	McMAHON tv-host+ Am		Eddy	ARNOLD s,tv+ Am
Ed	NELSON tv+		Eddy	GRANT s,songs Guyana
Ed	O'NEILL tv+		Eddy,	CLARENCE organ,c Am
Ed	O'ROSS		Eddy,	DUANE mr-guitar Am
Ed	PLANK b hf		Eddy,	HELEN JEROME
Ed	REIMERS tv		Eddy,	MARY BAKER r Am
Ed	WALSH b hf		Eddy,	NELSON s+ Am
Ed	WYNN cm,tv+ Am		Edel,	LEON p-b'63
Eda	LeSHAN w,j Am		Edel,	ULI d
Edberg,	STEFAN t Swe		Edelhagen,KURT mj-piano,cn Ger
Edd	BYRNES(Kookie)tv+		Edelman,	BARBARA tv
Edd	ROUSH b hf		Edelman,	GERALD n-m'72
Eddi	ARENT		Edelman,	HERB tv+
Eddie	ALBERT tv+		Edelman,	HOPE w Am
Eddie	ARCARO jockey Am		Eden	PHILLPOTTS w Br
Eddie	BARTH tv+		Eden,	ANTHONY(Sir)st
Eddie	BRACKEN tv+		Eden,	BARBARA tv+
Eddie	BRIGATI mr-drm,s Am		Eden,	NILS st,h Swe
Eddie	BRUNNER mj,cn Swi		Eder,	RICHARD ct-books Am
Eddie	CANTOR s+ Am		Ederle,	GERTRUDE sw
Eddie	CARROLL tv		Edgar	ADRIAN md, e Br
Eddie	CIBRIAN tv		Edgar	ALLEN md, e Am
Eddie	CLINE d		Edgar	BARRIER
Eddie	COCHRAN mr Am		Edgar	BERGEN, pupperts, tv+
Eddie	COLLINS b,bmg hf		Edgar	DEGAS p Fr
Eddie	CONDON mj,cn,tv+ Am		Edgar	DIDDLE bbc hf
Eddie	DAVIS(Lockjaw)sax Am		Edgar	GUEST j,po Am
Eddie	DEAN		Edgar	HICKEY bbc hf
Eddie	DEEZAN		Edgar	JONES Jr tv
Eddie	DUNN		Edgar	KENNEDY
Eddie	EGAN tv+		Edgar	MASTERS po,w Am
Eddie	ELKINS mj,cn Am		Edgar	MORTARA r It
Eddie	FISHER s,tv+ Am		Edgar	NYE w-humor Am
Eddie	FLOYD s-r&b,ws Am		Edgar	QUINET w,st Fr
Eddie	FOY Jr. tv+		Edgar	SALTUS w Am
Eddie	FOY la,cm Am		Edgar	SNOW j,w Am
Eddie	HODGES		Edgar	TINEL piano,c Belg
Eddie	JACKSON tv		Edgar	ULMER d
Eddie	JONES bb		Edgar	WALLACE w Br
Eddie	JONES tv+		Edgar	WINTERmr-blue,keyb Am
Eddie	LEVERT mr-s Am		Edgar Allan POE w Am
Eddie	LITTLE SKY		Edgard	VARESE c Am
Eddie	LOPAT(Steady) b		Edge,	GRAEME mr-drm Br
Eddie	MARR tv+		Edge,	THE mr-guitar Welsh
Eddie	MEKKA tv		Edge,	WALTER pb,st Am
Eddie	MONEY s Am		Edgeworth,MARIA w Br
Eddie	MURPHY cm,tv+ Am		Edgren,	ANNE w Swe
Eddie	MURRAY b		Edie	ADAMS s,tv+ Am
Eddie	NUGENT		Edie	BRICKELL s,ws Am
Eddie	QUILLAN tv+		Edie	FALCO
Eddie	RABBIT s,ws Am		Edie	LEHMANN tv
Eddie	RITTEN mj-tromb Am		Edie	MAGNUS tv-j Am
Eddie	RYDER tv		Edie	McCLURG tv+
Eddie	SHORE ho		Edie	SEDGWICK
Eddie	STROUD mj,cn Can		Edillo,	OFFICER MARETE tv
Eddie	Van HALEN mr,s Dut		Edison,	THOMAS ALVA i Am
Eddie	VEDDER mr,s Am		Edita	GRUBEROVA sopr Slovak
Eddie	VELEZ tv+		Edith	ATWATER tv+
Eddings,	DAVID w Am		Edith	CAVELL md Br

Edith	EVANS (Dame) la+ Br	Edouard	BELIN eng,i Fr
Edith	HEAD ds-costumes Am	Edouard	BRANLY sc,i Fr
Edith	MASSEY	Edouard	De RESZKE basso Pol
Edith	NESBIT w,po Br	Edouard	DELMONT
Edith	PIAF s Fr	Edouard	LALO c Fr
Edith	RICKERT e,w Am	Edouard	LARTET archeol Fr
Edith	ROGERS st Am	Edouard	MANET p Fr
Edith	SCOB	Edouard	MARTEL sc-caves Fr
Edith	SITWELL (Dame) po,w,ct	Edouard	NAVILLE an-egypt Swi
Edith	STEIN r,ph Ger	Edouard	ROD w Swi
Edith	WHARTON w Am	Edsel	FORD id-cars Am
Edman,	IRWIN ph,e Am	Edson	PELE soccer Braz
Edme	BOURSAULT w Fr	Edson	STROLL tv
Edme	DUMONT su Fr	Edson,	RICHARD tv+
Edmond	ABOUT j,w Fr	Eduard	BUCHNER sc Ger
Edmond	AUDRAN c Fr	Eduard	FRANZ tv+
Edmond	FISHER md Am	Eduard	HITZIG ps,e Ger
Edmond	FREMY sc,e Fr	Eduard	LASSEN c,cn Belg
Edmond	HALLEY astron Br	Eduard	MEYER h,e Ger
Edmond	HOYLE w-games Br	Eduard	MORIKE po,w Ger
Edmond	JALOUX w,ct Fr	Eduard	MULLER st Swi
Edmond	LEBOEUF ar,st Fr	Eduard	SCHMID w Ger
Edmond	NOCARD vet,sc Fr	Eduard	STUDY math,e Ger
Edmond	O'BRIEN tv+	Eduard	SUESS geol,e,w Aus
Edmond	PICARD l,w Belg	Eduard	TAAFFE st Aus
Edmond	ROSTAND w Fr	Eduard von BONIN ar Ger
Edmonds,	JIM b-gg'97	Eduardo	BARRIOS w Chile
Edmonds,	KENNETH (Babyface) s Am	Eduardo	FREI st Chile
Edmonds,	WALTER w Am	Eduardo	MALLEA w Arg
Edmonton,	JERRY mr-drums Can	Eduardo	SANTOS st,pb Colom
Edmund	ANDROS (Sir) st	Eduoard	ROD w Swi
Edmund	BLUNDEN po,ct Br	Edvard	BENES st Czech
Edmund	BREON	Edvard	GREIG c Nor
Edmund	BURKE st Br	Edvard	MUNCH p Nor
Edmund	COBB	Edwall,	ALLAN
Edmund	DAWES tv	Edward	ALBEE w Am
Edmund	DAY ec,e Am	Edward	ALBERT tv+
Edmund	DUFFY cr Am	Edward	ALDRIN Jr as Am
Edmund	DULAC illus,ds Br	Edward	ALLEYNE la,e Br
Edmund	GILBERT tv	Edward	ANDREWS tv+
Edmund	GOSSE (Sir) po,ct	Edward	ARBER e Br
Edmund	GWENN	Edward	ARNOLD
Edmund	HILLARY (Sir) x	Edward	ASNER (Ed) tv+
Edmund	HUSSERL ph Ger	Edward	BAILY su Br
Edmund	KEAN la Br	Edward	BARROW b hf
Edmund	LOWE tv+	Edward	BEESLEY h,e Br
Edmund	LUDLOW st Br	Edward	BELLAMY w Am
Edmund	MALONE ct,w Irish	Edward	BENSON w Br
Edmund	PURDOM	Edward	BERNDS d
Edmund	RUFFIN agricult Am	Edward	BERRY sc Am
Edmund	SPENSER po Br	Edward	BINNS tv+
Edmund	STEDMAN po,ct,bus Am	Edward	BLYTH sc,w Br
Edmund	WALLER po Br	Edward	BOK bio,ed Am
Edmund	WILSON ct,w,po Am	Edward	BOND w Br
Edna	FERBER w Am	Edward	BROPHY
Edna	O'BRIEN w Irish	Edward	BRYCE tv
Edna	SKINNER tv	Edward	BULLARD (Sir) sc
Edna May	OLIVER	Edward	BURNS
Edna St.Vincent MILLAY po Am	Edward	CAHN d Am
Edney,	BEATIE	Edward	CAPPS e Am
Edo	DeWAART cn Dut	Edward	CASSIDY

Edward	CAVE j Br	Edward	SHELDON w Am
Edward	CHAPMAN	Edward	SHIPPEN st Am
Edward	COKE(Sir)l,st Br	Edward	SIMMONS p Am
Edward	CONDON sc,e Am	Edward	SORIN r,e Am
Edward	COPE sc e Am	Edward	SOTHERN la Am
Edward	CRAIG la,pr Br	Edward	SQUIBB md,id-drugs Am
Edward	CURTIS fo Am	Edward	STONE ac Am
Edward	CUST(Sir)ar,h Br	Edward	TATUM n-m'58
Edward	DMYTRYK d	Edward	TATUM sc-md,e Am
Edward	DOISY sc,e Am	Edward	TAYLOR r,po Am
Edward	DUTTON pb Am	Edward	TEACH(Blkbrd)pirateBr
Edward	ELGAR(Sir)c	Edward	TELLER sc Am
Edward	ELLIS	Edward	THOMAS po,ct Br
Edward	EYRE x Br	Edward	THRING e Br
Edward	FILENE mer Am	Edward	TYLOR(Sir)an,e,w
Edward	FLEGEL x Ger	Edward	Van SLOAN
Edward	FOX,	Edward	VERNON(OldGrog)navyBr
Edward	FURLONG	Edward	VICKERS id-steel Br
Edward	GARNETT w Br	Edward	WACHTER bb hf
Edward	GERMAN(Sir)c	Edward	WARING math,e Br
Edward	GIBBON w,h Br	Edward	WESTON fo Am
Edward	GIFFORD an,e Am	Edward	WESTON walker Am
Edward	GROVER tv	Edward	WHITE as Am
Edward	HALE r,w Am	Edward	WHYMPER engr,mtns Br
Edward	HEATH st Br	Edward	WILSON w Am
Edward	HERBERT st,ph Br	Edward	WINSLOW st-Plymouth
Edward	HICKS p Am	Edward	WINTER tv
Edward	HOPPER p Am	Edward	WOOD st Br
Edward	HOUSE(Col.)st Am	Edward	YOUNG po,w Br
Edward	HULTON(Sir)newspaper	Edward	YOUNG x Br
Edward	JUDD	Edward	ZWICK d
Edward	JUDSON w,pb Am	Edward Everett HORTON tv+	
Edward	KENDALL sc-md,e Am	Edward R. MURROW j,tv-j Am	
Edward	KLEBAN w Am	Edward von STEINLE p Aus	
Edward	LARSON h Am	Edwards,	AGUSTIN f,st Chile
Edward	LEAR p,po Br	Edwards,	AMELIA w Br
Edward	LEWIS md Am	Edwards,	ANTHONY tv+
Edward	LYTTON w,st Br	Edwards,	BERNARD mr-bass Am
Edward	MALBONE p Am	Edwards,	BLAKE d,w Am
Edward	MARTIN ed,w Am	Edwards,	BRUCE
Edward	MARTYN w Irish	Edwards,	CLIFF m-uke,tv+ Am
Edward	McCOOK ar,st Am	Edwards,	DOUGLAS tv
Edward	MEYER h,e Ger	Edwards,	GAIL tv+
Edward	MIALL r,j Br	Edwards,	GEOFF tv
Edward	MILNE astr,e Br	Edwards,	GERALD tv
Edward	MORGAN tv	Edwards,	GUS c Am
Edward	MULHARE tv+	Edwards,	JAMES
Edward	NEALE ref Br	Edwards,	JENNIFER
Edward	NICHOLS sc,e Am	Edwards,	JONATHAN r,ph Am
Edward	NORRIS	Edwards,	LUKE tv+
Edward	O'BRIEN w,ed Am	Edwards,	NOKIE mr-guit Am
Edward	OLMOS tv+	Edwards,	OWEN(Sir)w Welsh
Edward	PATTEN s-pop Am	Edwards,	PENNY
Edward	PLATT tv+	Edwards,	RALPH tv
Edward	POTTER su Am	Edwards,	RONNIE tv+
Edward	POYNTER(Sir)p	Edwards,	SHERMAN c Am
Edward	PRIOR ac,e Br	Edwards,	SNITZ
Edward	PURCELL sc Am	Edwards,	STEPHANIE tv
Edward	ROUTH math,e Br	Edwards,	STEVE tv
Edward	SAPIR an,e Am	Edwards,	TURK fb hf
Edward	SAVAGE p,engr Am	Edwards,	VINCE tv+

Edwige	FENECH	Eggleston,COLIN d	
Edwige	FRENCH	Eggleston,EDWARD w Am	
Edwin	ABBEY p,illus Am	Eggleston,GEORGE w	
Edwin	ARNOLD(Sir)po,j	Egi,	STAN
Edwin	BOOTH la Am	Egidio	DUNI c It
Edwin	BORING ps,e,w Am	Egleson,	JAN d
Edwin	CHRISTY la,s Am	Eglevsky,	ANDRE ba Am
Edwin	COHN sc,e Am	Egloff,	GUSTAV sc,id Am
Edwin	DENBY st Am	Egly,	HENRY r Am
Edwin	DRAKE id-oil Am	Ego,	SANDRA tv
Edwin	FORREST la Am	Egon	SCHIELE p Aus
Edwin	FROST astron Am	Egoyan,	ATOM d
Edwin	GINN pb Am	Eguren,	JOSE po Peru
Edwin	GODKIN ed,w Am	Ehrenburg,ILYA w Rus	
Edwin	GOLDMAN c,cn Am	Ehricke,	KRAFFT eng-aero,sc Am
Edwin	HALL sc,e Am	Ehrlich,	PAUL n-m'08
Edwin	HART tv	Ehrling,	THOREmj-trmp,cn,c Swe
Edwin	HOLT ps,ph Am	Eichendorff, JOSEPH von po Ger	
Edwin	HUBBLE astr Am	Eichhorn, LISA	
Edwin	KLEBS sc,md,e Ger	Eichler,	AUGUST sc,e Ger
Edwin	KREBS md Am	Eichwald, HFKAN von mj,cn Swe	
Edwin	LAND sc,i,id Am	Eiding,	PAUL tv
Edwin	LINK i,id-flying Am	Eielsen,	ELLING r Am
Edwin	MARKHAM po Am	Eiermann,	EGON ac Ger
Edwin	MAXWELL	Eiffel,	ALEXANDRE eng Fr
Edwin	MONTAGU st Br	Eigen,	MANFRED n-c'67
Edwin	MUIR po,ct Scot	Eiji	FUNAKOSHI
Edwin	NEHER md Ger	Eiji	OKADA
Edwin	NEWMAN tv-host Am	Eijiro	TONO
Edwin	PORTER d,cameraman Am	Eijkman,	CHRISTIAAN n-m'29
Edwin	ROE(Sir)id-planes	Eikenberry, JILL tv+	
Edwin	SANDYS r Br	Eilbacher,CINDY tv	
Edwin	TEALE fo,w Am	Eilbacher,LISA tv+	
Edwin L.	MARIN d	Eilber,	JANET tv
Edy	WILLIAMS	Eileen	ATKINS
Eeden,	FREDERIK van w,md Dut	Eileen	BARTON tv
Eekhoud,	GEORGES w,po Belg	Eileen	BRENNAN
Eero	SAARINEN ac Am	Eileen	CHESIS tv
Effen,	JUSTUS van w Dut	Eileen	FARRELL s-opera,mj Am
Effergee	WARE mj-guitar Am	Eileen	FORD mo-agency Am
Effie	CARLTON la,w Am	Eileen	FULTON tv
Efimova,	NINA puppets Rus	Eileen	HECKART tv+
Efrain	FIGUERROA tv	Eileen	O'NEILL tv
Efrem	ZIMBALIST Jr.tv+	Eileen	PERCY
Egan,	AERYK	Eileen	WILSON s,tv Am
Egan,	EDDIE tv+	Eilers,	SALLY
Egan,	JENNIFER w Am	Eimen,	JOHNNY tv
Egan,	JENNY tv	Einar	KVARAN j,ed,w Iceland
Egan,	PETER	Einstein, ALBERT n-p'21	
Egan,	PIERCE j,w Br	Einstein, BOB tv	
Egan,	RICHARD	Einthoven,WILLEM n-m'24	
Egan,	WALTER mr-s Am	Eisaku	SATO st Jap
Egana,	JUAN st,w Chile	Eiseley,	LOREN an,w,e Am
Egas Moniz, ANTONIO md,st Port		Eisenberg, ARON	
Egbert	Van ALSTYNE c Am	Eisenhower, DWIGHT D.34th Pres	
Ege,	JULIE	Eisenstaedt, ALFRED fo Am	
Egede,	HANS r Nor	Eisenstein, SERGEI d	
Egg,	AUGUSTUS p Br	Eisley,	ANTHONY tv+
Eggar,	SAMANTHA	Eisner,	KURT j,st Ger
Egge,	PETER w Nor	Eisner,	MICHAEL tv
Eggert,	NICOLE tv+	Eitner,	ROBERT h-music Ger

Ekberg,	ANITA	Elers,	JOHN ceramics Br
Ekelof,	GUNNAR po Swe	Elg,	TAINA d+
Ekhof,	KONRAD la,d Ger	Elgar,	CHARLIE mj-viol,cn Am
Ekland,	BRITT	Elgar,	EDWARD(Sir)c
Ekman,	GOSTA	Elgart,	LARRY mj-sax Am
Ekman,	VAGN sc-oceans Swe	Elgart,	LES mj-trump,cn Am
Ekwensi,	CYPRIAN w Nigeria	Elgin	BAYLOR bb hf
El	BRENDEL	Eli	MANDEL po,ed,ct Can
El	CID ar,hero Sp	Eli	MINTZ tv
El	DEBARGEm,s,pr-recdsAm	Eli	RICH
El	GRECO p Sp	Eli	WALLACH
El Gallo	GOMEZ matador Sp	Eli	WHITNEY i Am
Elaine	GIFTOS tv+	Elia	KAZAN la,d,w+
Elaine	JOYCE tv+	Eliade,	MIRCEA ph,w Rom
Elaine	KAGAN tv	Elias	ASHMOLE h,ar Br
Elaine	MAY tv+	Elias	CANETTI w Bulg-Br
Elaine	MILES tv	Elias	COREY sc Am
Elaine	PAGELS w Am	Elias	DAYTON ar,st Am
Elaine	RILEY	Elias	ELLER r Ger
Elaine	SHORE tv	Elias	FRIES sc,e Swe
Elaine	STRITCH s,tv+ Am	Elias	HOLL ac Ger
Elaine	ZAYAK sk Am	Elias	HOWE i Am
Elam,	JACK tv+	Elias	KOTEAS
Elayne	HEILVEIL	Elias	LONNROTw-folklre Finn
Elbert	GARY l,id Am	Elias,	ALIX tv+
Elbert	HUBBARD w,ed,pb Am	Elie	ABEL j,st Am
Elcano,	JUAN de x Basque	Elie	CARTAN math,e Fr
Elcar,	DANA tv+	Elie	DECAZES st Fr
Elder,	ANN tv	Elie	DUCOMMUN j,ed Swi
Elder,	JOHN eng-ships Scot	Elie	FAURE h-art Fr
Elder,	LEE g Am	Elie	FOREY ar Fr
Eldredge,	JOHN tv	Elie	FRERON j,ed Fr
Eldridge,	FLORENCE	Elie	LESCOT st Haiti
Eldridge,	GEORGE	Elie	METCHNIKOFF md-sc Fr
Eldridge,	ROY mj-trumpet,s Am	Elie	NADELMANN su Fr
Eleanor	BELMONT la,f Am	Elie	SIEGMEISTER c Am
Eleanor	BRON	Elie	WIESEL w Am
Eleanor	BUFORD w Br	Elie de	BEAUMONT geol,e Fr
Eleanor	DAVID	Elie de	CYON ps,e Rus
Eleanor	ESTES w Am	Elie,	MARIO bb
Eleanor	FARJEON w Br	Eliel	SAARINEN ac Fimm
Eleanor	HIBBERT w Br	Elihu	BURRITT pacifist Am
Eleanor	PARKER tv+	Elihu	ROOT l,st Am
Eleanor	PORTER w Am	Elihu	THOMSON eng-elct,i Am
Eleanor	POWELL	Elihu	VEDDER p,illus Am
Eleanor	SMEAL fe-NOW Am	Elihu	YALE st Br
Eleanor	STEBER soprano Am	Elijah	FENTON po,ed Br
Eleanor	STERNIG w Am	Elijah	IMPEY(Sir)l
Eleanor	STEWART	Elijah	LEVITA w Jewish
Eleanor	WARNER tv	Elijah	LOVEJOYr,abolition Am
Eleanora	DUSE la It	Elijah	WHITE md,pioneer Am
Eleazar	KALIR po Hebrew	Elijah	WOOD
Eleazar	WHEELOCK r,e Am	Elikann,	LARRY d
Eleazar	WILLIAMS r Am	Elin	WAGNER w,j Swe
Elechi	AMADI w Nigeria	Elinor	DONAHUE tv+
Elem	KLIMOV d	Elinor	FAIR
Elena	OBRAZTSOVA mezzo Rus	Elinor	GLYN w Br
Elena	SAHAGUN	Elinor	WYLIE po,w Am
Elena	VERDUGO tv+	Elio	VITTORINI w,ct It
Eleniak,	ERIKA tv+	Elio,	FRANCISCO ar Sp
Elenora	GIORGI	Elion,	GERTRUDE n-m'88

Eliot	PORTER fo Am	Elizabeth	STANTON fe Am
Eliot,	CHARLES e Am	Elizabeth	TAYLOR tv+
Eliot,	CHARLES(Sir)st,w	Elizabeth	TAYLOR w Br
Eliot,	GEORGE w Br	Elizabeth	WALKER(Tippy)tv
Eliot,	T.S. po,n-l'48	Elizabeth	WILSON tv+
Eliott,	JESSE navy Am	Elizabeth	WURTZEL w Am
Eliphalet	DYER l Am	Elizondo,	HECTOR tv+
Elisa	HEINSOHN tv	Elizur	WRIGHT reform,e Am
Elisabet	NEY su Am	Elkanah	SETTLE w Br
Elisabeth	BERGNER	Elkanah	WATSON bus-cattle Am
Elisabeth	FRASER tv+	Elke	SOMMER
Elisabeth	RISDON	Elkin,	STANLEY w Am
Elisabeth	SHUE	Elkins,	AARON w Am
Elise	CAVANNA	Elkins,	EDDIE mj,cn Am
Elise,	CHRISTINE tv+	Ella	BLOOR communist,w Am
Elisha	ALLEN st Am	Ella	De WOLFE la,decor Am
Elisha	COOK Jr tv+	Ella	GRASSO st Am
Elisha	GRAY i Am	Ella	JOYCE tv
Elisha	KANE x,w Am	Ella	RAINES tv+
Elisha	OTIS i,id Am	Ella	WILCOX j,po Am
Elissa	LANDI	Ella	YOUNG e Am
Eliza	DUSHKU	Elle	MACPHERSONmo,tv+Austr
Eliza	HAYWOOD w Br	Ellen	BARKIN
Elizabeth	ALLAN	Ellen	BRY tv
Elizabeth	ALLEN po Am	Ellen	BURSTYN tv+
Elizabeth	ALLEN tv	Ellen	COHEN tv
Elizabeth	ARDEN id-beauty Am	Ellen	CORBY tv+
Elizabeth	ASHLEY tv+	Ellen	DOLAN tv
Elizabeth	BAUR tv	Ellen	DRAKE tv
Elizabeth	BERG w Am	Ellen	DREW
Elizabeth	BISHOP po Am	Ellen	FENWICK tv
Elizabeth	BOWEN w Irish	Ellen	FOLEY tv+
Elizabeth	CARTER po Br	Ellen	GEER tv+
Elizabeth	DAILY	Ellen	GLASGOW w Am
Elizabeth	FARREN la Br	Ellen	GOODMAN j,w Am
Elizabeth	FRY f Br	Ellen	GREENE
Elizabeth	GASKELL w Br	Ellen	HOLLY
Elizabeth	GEORGE w Am	Ellen	HOOPER po Am
Elizabeth	GILMER j Am	Ellen	KEY fe,w Swi
Elizabeth	GOUDGE w Br	Ellen	MAXTED tv
Elizabeth	HANNA tv	Ellen	McRAE tv
Elizabeth	HARTMAN	Ellen	PARKER tv
Elizabeth	HOFFMAN tv	Ellen	REGAN tv
Elizabeth	HUDDLE tv	Ellen	SCRIPPS ed,pb,f Am
Elizabeth	HURLEY mo+ Br	Ellen	STARR fe Am
Elizabeth	JORDAN w Am	Ellen	TERRY(Dame)la Br
Elizabeth	KAITAN	Ellen	WESTON tv
Elizabeth	KENNY nurse Aust	Eller,	CARL fb-d'71
Elizabeth	KERR tv	Eller,	ELIAS r Ger
Elizabeth	KREUZER	Ellerbee,	LINDA tv-news Am
Elizabeth	LESLIE tv	Ellery	QUEEN w Am
Elizabeth	MacRAE tv	Ellet,	CHARLES eng Am
Elizabeth	McGOVERN	Ellie	MacLURE
Elizabeth	PENA tv+	Ellie May	EWING fc
Elizabeth	PERKINS	Elling	EIELSEN r Am
Elizabeth	REDDIN tv	Ellington,	DUKE mj,c,cn,tv+Am
Elizabeth	ROBERTS w Am	Elliot	COUES birds,e Am
Elizabeth	RUSSELL	Elliot	EASTON mr-guit Am
Elizabeth	RYAN t Am	Elliot	PAUL w Am
Elizabeth	SEAMAN j Am	Elliot	SPRINGS flyer,id,w Am
Elizabeth	SELLARS	Elliot,	JANE tv

Elliot,	WIN tv	Elmo	ROPER j,polls Am
Elliott	CARTER c Am	Elmo	ZUMWALT navy Am
Elliott	GOULD tv+	Elmore	LEONARD w Am
Elliott	REID tv+	Elmore,	FRANCIS i,sc Br
Elliott,	BOB b-mv'47	Elmore,	GREG mr-drums Am
Elliott,	BOB tv+	Elna	HUBBELL tv
Elliott,	BOBBY mr-drm Br	Eloise	HARDT tv
Elliott,	CHRIS cm,w,tv+ Am	Eloise	McELHONE tv
Elliott,	DENHOLM	Elon,	AMOS j,w Israel
Elliott,	DENNIS mr-drm Br	Eloy	ALFARO ar,st Ecuad
Elliott,	EBENEZER po Br	Elphick,	MICHAEL
Elliott,	EVAN tv	Elpidia	CARRILLO
Elliott,	GEORGE P, w Am	Elpidio	QUIRINO st Phil
Elliott,	JOE mr-s Br	Elroy	HIRSCH fb hf
Elliott,	JOHN	Els,	ERNIE g S.Afr
Elliott,	MAXINE la Am	Elsa	CARDENAS
Elliott,	ROBERT	Elsa	KLENSCH w Am
Elliott,	SAM tv+	Elsa	LANCHESTER tv+
Elliott,	SARAH B. w Am	Elsa	MARTINELLI
Elliott,	SHAWN	Elsa	MAXWELL j,hostess Am
Elliott,	STEPHEN tv+	Elsa	MORANTE w It
Elliott,	WILD BILL	Elsa	RAVEN tv
Elliott,	WILLIAM tv	Elsa	SCHIAPARELLI ds Fr
Ellis	BUTLER w-humor Am	Elsa	TRIOLET w Fr
Ellis	WYNNE w Welsh	Elsie	FOGERTY e-voice Br
Ellis,	ALEXANDER math,e Br	Elsie	JANIS la Am
Ellis,	BOBBY tv	Elsie	PARSONS an,w Am
Ellis,	DON mj-trump,cn Am	Elsie	VENNER fc
Ellis,	EDWARD	Elskamp,	MAX po Belg
Ellis,	GEORGE w Br	Elsom,	ISOBEL
Ellis,	HARVEY ac Am	Elson,	ANDREA tv
Ellis,	HAVELOCK md,w Br	Elssler,	FANNY ba Aus
Ellis,	HERB tv	Elster,	JULIUS sc Ger
Ellis,	KATHALEEN tv	Elston	HOWARD b
Ellis,	LARRY tv	Elswit,	RIK mr-guit,s Am
Ellis,	PATRICIA	Eltinge,	JULIAN entertain Am
Ellis,	PERRY ds-perfumes Am	Elton	BRITT s-cntry Am
Ellis,	RALPH mr-guit,s Br	Elton	JOHN mr-s+ Br
Ellis,	ROBERT	Elton,	OLIVER h,e Br
Ellis,	SEGERmj-piano,s,cn Am	Eluard,	PAUL po Fr
Ellis,	SHIRLEY s-soul Am	Elvia	ALLMAN tv
Ellison,	CASEY tv	Elvin	HAYES bb hf
Ellison,	JAMES	Elvin	JONES mj-drm Am
Ellison,	RALPH w Am	Elvin,	VIOLETTA ba Br
Ellmann,	RICHARD p-b'89	Elvis	STOJKO sk Can
Ellroy,	JAMES w Am	Elvis Aaron PRESLEY s,tv+ Am	
Ellsworth BUNKER st,id Am		Elwell	OTIS ar Am
Ellsworth KELLY p,su Am		Elwes,	CARY
Ellsworth STATLER hotels Am		Elwin	ROE(Preacher)b
Ellsworth VINES t Am		Elwood	HAYNES i,sc Am
Ellsworth,LINCOLN x Am		Elwyn	WHITE w Am
Elly	AMELING soprano Br	Ely	CULBERTSON bridge Am
Elman,	MISCHA violin Am	Ely	POUGET
Elmen,	GUSTAV eng Am	Ely,	RICHARD ec,e Am
Elmer	CLIFTON d	Ely,	RON tv+
Elmer	DAVIS w, radio Am	Elya	BASKIN
Elmer	FLICK b hf	Elyesa	BAZNA spy Albania
Elmer	LACH ho	Elyot,	THOMAS(Sir)st,w
Elmer	RICE w Am	Elyse	KNOX
Elmer	SPERRY eng,id,i Am	Elyse,	SALLEE
Elmo	LINCOLN	Elyssa	DAVALOS

Elytis,	ODYSSEUS po,n-l'79	Emile	COUE ps Fr
Elzevir,	ABRAHAM pb Dut	Emile	DILLON j Br
Elzevir,	BONAVENTURA pb Dut	Emile	FABRE w Fr
Elzevir,	ISAAC pb Dut	Emile	FAGUET ct,e Fr
Elzie	SEGAR cr Am	Emile	GALLE id-glass Fr
Elzire	DIONNE quints' Mother	Emile	GENTIL st Fr
Emants,	MARCELLUS po,w Dut	Emile	HAUG geol,e Br
Emanuel	HIEL po Belg	Emile	HERZOG w Fr
Emanuel	LASKER chess Ger	Emile	LOUBET st Fr
Emanuel	LEUTZE p Am	Emile	MATHIEU c,e Belg
Emanuel de WITTE p Dut		Emile	PATHE pr-films Fr
Emanuele	RINCON c It	Emile	ZOLA w Fr
Embden,	GUSTAV sc,e Ger	Emilia	CROW
Embeth	DAVIDTZ	Emiliano	ZAPATA re Mex
Embrey,	JOAN tv	Emilio	De BONO ar.st It
Embury,	PHILIP r Am	Emilio	ESTEVEZ
Emden,	JACOB r Ger	Emilio	MOLA ar Sp
Emer	McCOURT	Emilio	PRAGA po It
Emeric	CRUCE w Fr	Emilio	PUCCI ds It
Emeric	PRESSBURGER	Emilio	SEGRE sc Am
Emerson	HOUGH w Am	Emily	BALCH ec,w Am
Emerson	TRACY	Emily	BRONTE w Br
Emerson,	DOUGLAS tv	Emily	CARR p,w Can
Emerson,	FAYE tv	Emily	DAVIES fe,e Br
Emerson,	HOPE tv+	Emily	FITZROY
Emerson,	JOHN d	Emily	LAWLESS w Irish
Emerson,	KEITH mr-kbds Br	Emily	LLOYD
Emerson,	PETER fo Br	Emily	MEIER w Am
Emerson,	RALPH WALDO po Am	Emily	POST w,j Am
Emery	WALKER(Sir)engr	Emily Ann LLOYD tv	
Emery,	BOB tv	Emlen	TUNNELL fb hf
Emery,	CHRIS tv	Emlyn	WILLIAMS w,la+ Welsh
Emery,	GILBERT	Emlyn,	THOMAS r Br
Emery,	JOHN	Emma	ALBANI(Dame)s Can
Emery,	PAT tv	Emma	CALVE s Fr
Emery,	RALPH tv	Emma	DUNN
Emil	ARTIN math,e Aus	Emma	EAMES soprano Am
Emil	BRUNNER e,w Swi	Emma	GOLDMAN anarchist Am
Emil	FISCHER sc Ger	Emma	LAZARUS po,w Am
Emil	FRIDA w Czech	Emma	SAMMS
Emil	GILELS piano Rus	Emma	WILLARD e Am
Emil	HACHA l,st Czech	Emmaline	HENRY tv
Emil	HOLUB x Ger	Emmanuel	ALZON r Fr
Emil	KIRDORF id Ger	Emmanuel	POIRE illus Fr
Emil	KOCHER md Swi	Emmanuel	SIEYES re Fr
Emil	LUDWIG w,bio Ger	Emmanuelle BEART	
Emil	NOLDE p Ger	Emmerich von STENDL ac Hung	
Emil	ORLIK p,etch Ger	Emmerich von VATTEL l Swi	
Emil	POST math,e Am	Emmet,	ROBERT st Irish
Emil	SIEG e,Ger	Emmet,	THOMAS l,st Irish
Emil	WELTI st Swi	Emmett	ALSTON d
Emil	ZATOPEK runner Czech	Emmett	KELLY clown Am
Emil von BEHRING sc Ger		Emmett	LYNN
Emil von SKODA id,eng Czech		Emmett,	DANIEL s,w-songs Am
Emil,	MICHAEL	Emmitt	SMITH fb
Emile	ARGAND geol Swi	Emmuska	ORCZY w Br
Emile	AUGIER po,w Fr	Emmy	DESTINN soprano Czech
Emile	BERNARD p Fr	Emo	PHILLIPS cm Am
Emile	BOREL math,e Fr	Emory	BASS tv
Emile	CHARTIER ph,w Fr	Emory	PARNELL tv+
Emile	COMBES st Fr		

Emory	UPTON ar,w Am	Enya	--- s,c Irish
Empson,	WILLIAM(Sir)po,ct	Enzo	CASTELLARI d
Emre,	YUNUS po Turk	Enzo	FERRARI id-cars It
En-lai,	CHOU st China	Eoin	O'DUFFY ar-IRA Irish
Ena	HARTMAN tv	Eotves,	LORANT sc Hung
Enberg,	DICK tv-spts	Eotvos,	JOZSEF st,w Hung
Encina,	JUAN del w,c Sp	Epee,	CHARLES r,e Fr
Encke,	JOHANN astron Ger	Ephraim	McDOWELL md Am
Endacott,	PAUL bb hf	Ephraim	SHAY i-rrs Am
Ender,	OTTO st Aus	Ephraim	SQUIER arc,st Am
Enders,	JOHN n-m'54	Ephraim	WILLIAMS ar Am
Enders,	RUTH tv	Ephron,	NORA d,w Am
Endicott	PEABODY e Am	Epitacio da	PESSOA st,l Braz
Endo,	AKIRO cn	Eplin,	TOM tv
Endo,	HARRY tv	Epp,	FRANZ von ar Ger
Endo,	SHUSAKU w Jap	Eppa	RIXEY b hf
Endre	ADY po Hung	Epps,	OMAR
Enescu,	GHEORGHE c Rom	Epstein,	JACOB(Sir)su
Engel,	GEORGIA tv+	Equiano,	OLAUDAH w Africa
Engel,	JOHANN w Ger	Erard,	SEBASTIEN id Fr
Engel,	SCOTT mr-s Am	Erasmus	DARWIN md,sc,po Br
Engelbert	KAMPFER md Ger	Erasmus,	DESIDERIUS ph Dut
Engels,	FRIEDRICH re,w Ger	Erastus	BEADLE pb Am
Engels,	WERA	Erastus	CORNING id-rrs Am
Engle,	ROY tv	Erastus	FIELD p Am
Engler,	ADOLF sc,e Ger	Erastus	PALMER su Am
English,	JOHN d	Erben,	KAREL po,w Cz
English,	THOMAS md,l,w Am	Ercker,	LAZARUS sc Ger
Englund,	PAT tv	Erckmann.	EMILE w Fr
Englund,	ROBERT tv+	Erdelyi,	JANOS w,pb Hung
Enid	BAGNOLD w Br	Erdman,	NIKOLAY w Rus
Enid	BLYTON w-children	Erdman,	RICHARD tv+
Enid	KENT tv	Erdrich,	LOUISE w Am
Enid	MARKEY tv+	Erenburg,	ILYA w,po,j Rus
Enke,	KARIN sk,o-g'80'4'4	Erhard	MILCH flyer Ger
Ennis,	BOBBIE mj-s Am	Erhard	RATDOLT id-print Ger
Ennis,	RAY mr-guit,s Br	Erhard,	LUDWIG ec,st Ger
Ennis,	SKINNAY mj-drm,cn Am	Eric	AMBLER w Br
Ennius,	QUINTUS po Ro	Eric	BARNOUW tv
Eno,	BRIAN mr-synthes,pr Br	Eric	BLAIR w Br
Enoch	CROWDER ar Am	Eric	BLOOM mr-guit Am
Enos	BARTON id-GE Am	Eric	BLORE
Enos	CABELL b	Eric	BRAEDEN tv+
Enos	SLAUGHTER b hf	Eric	BROWN tv+
Enric	MADRIGUERA mj,cn,c Am	Eric	BURDON s-pop Br
Enrico	BETTI math, e It	Eric	CARMEN mr-s Am
Enrico	CARUSO tenor It	Eric	CHASE tv
Enrico	COSENZ ar It	Eric	CLAPTON mr+ Br
Enrico	FERMI sc Am	Eric	CLOSE tv
Enright,	DAN tv	Eric	DOLPHY m-alto sax Am
Enright,	JAMES bbr hf	Eric	ERIKSON ps,w Am
Enright,	RAY d	Eric	FLEMING tv+
Enrique	LARRETA w Arg	Eric	GILL su Br
Enrique	LIHN po,w Chile	Eric	GURRY
Enrique	LUCERO	Eric	HAYDOCK mr-bass Br
Enrique	RAMBAL	Eric	HEIDEN sk-speed Am
Enrique de	VILLENA w Sp	Eric	HOFFER ph Am
Enriquez,	RENE tv+	Eric	IDLE
Ensign,	MICHAEL tv+	Eric	KARSON d
Entner,	WARREN mr-guitar,s Am	Eric	LEE
Entwistle.	JOHN mr-bass Br	Eric	LINDEN

Eric	LINDROS ho	Erma	BOMBECK tv-pr
Eric	OLSON tv	Erma	BROMBECK j Am
Eric	OSMOND tv	Erma	CALDERON w
Eric	PORTER	Erman,	JOHANN h-Egypt Ger
Eric	PORTMAN	Ermey,	R. LEE
Eric	ROBERTS	Erna	BERGER soprano Ger
Eric	ROHMER d,w Fr	Ernest	BALL lyrics Am
Eric	SCHWEIG	Ernest	BAX w Br
Eric	SCOTT tv+	Ernest	BECKER w Am
Eric	SERVER tv	Ernest	BENN(Sir)pb,w
Eric	STEWART mr-guit,s Br	Ernest	BEVIN st Br
Eric	STOLTZ,	Ernest	BLOCH c Swi-Am
Eric	THAL	Ernest	BLOOD bbc hf
Eric	TILL d	Ernest	BORGNINE tv+
Eric Allen	KRAMER tv+	Ernest	CASSEL(Sir)f&f Br
Eric The Red	--- x Nor	Ernest	CLARK tv
Erica	BLANC	Ernest	COSSART
Erica	GIMPEL tv	Ernest	DOWSON po Br
Erica	JONG w,po Am	Ernest	FLAGG ac Am
Erica	MARIN violin	Ernest	FLATT ba,tv Am
Erica	YOHN tv+	Ernest	GAINES w Am
Erich	FROMM ps Am	Ernest	GRAHAM ac Am
Erich	HECKEL p Ger	Ernest	HARDEN Jr tv
Erich	KLEIBER cn Aus	Ernest	HELLO w Fr
Erich	RAEDER navy,Nazi Ger	Ernest	HORNUNG w Br
Erich	SALOMON fo Ger	Ernest	LAVISSE h,e Fr
Erich	SEGAL w Am	Ernest	MOERAN c Br
Erickson,	LEIF tv+	Ernest	NEWMAN ct-music Br
Erico	VERISSIMO w Braz	Ernest	POOLE w Am
Ericson,	JOHN tv+	Ernest	PYLE j Am
Ericson,	LEIF x Nor	Ernest	QUIGLEY bbr hf
Ericsson,	JOHN eng,i Am	Ernest	RENAN ct,w Fr
Erik	ASPLUND ac Swe	Ernest	RENSHAW t Br
Erik	BARNOUW tv	Ernest	RHYS ed,w Br
Erik	BRAUNN mr-guitar,s Am	Ernest	RUSKA sc Ger
Erik	BRUHN ba Dan	Ernest	SCHMIDT bb hf
Erik	ESTRADA tv+	Ernest	SHEPARD illus,cr Br
Erik	GEIJER h,e,c,po Swe	Ernest	SMITH w Br
Erik	RHODES	Ernest	SOLVAY sc,i,id,f Belg
Erik	SATIE c Fr	Ernest	THOMAS tv
Erik	SJOBERG po Swe	Ernest	TOCH(Ernst)c,e Am
Erik	TUXEN mj,cn Pol	Ernest	TRUEX tv+
Erika	BLANC	Ernest	TUBB s-cntry Am
Erika	ELENIAK tv+	Ernest	VESTINE sc,e Am
Erika	MORINI violin	Ernest	WALTON sc Irish
Eriksen,	KAJ-ERIK tv	Ernest Thompson SETON sc,w,p Am	
Erikson,	ERIC ps,p-n'70	Ernest von KOERBER st Aus	
Eriksson,	LEIF x Nor	Ernestine WADE tv	
Erin	GRAY tv+	Ernesto	GUEVARA(Che)re Arg
Erin	MORAN tv+	Ernesto	MESTRE w Am
Erin	MORIARITY tv	Ernesto	MONETA j,pacifist It
Erin	OZKER puppets,tv	Ernesto	SABATO w Arg
Erin	TORPEY tv	Ernie	ADAMS
Eriq	La SALLE	Ernie	BANKS b
Erkel,	FRANZ cn,c Hung	Ernie	DINGO
Erland	JOSEPHSON	Ernie	ELS g S.Afr
Erlanger,	JOSEPH n-m'44	Ernie	FIELDS mj-tromb,cn Am
Erle	KENTON d	Ernie	HATRAK piano,tv
Erle Stanley GARDNER w Am,		Ernie	HUDSON
Erlenborn,RAY tv		Ernie	KOVACS tv+
Erlenmeyer, RICHARD sc Ger		Ernie	NEVERS b,fb hf

Ernie	PINTOFF d	Esai	MORALES
Ernie	PYLE j Am	Esaias	TEGNER po,e,r Swe
Ernie	REYES Jr tv	Esaias van de VELDE p Dut
Ernie	SABELLA tv	Esaki,	LEO n-p'73
Erno	DOHNANYI piano,c Hung	Esbjorn,	LARS r,e Am
Erno	RUBIK i-cube Hung	Esch,	JOHN st Am
Ernst	ABBE sc,id Ger	Escher	GODEL w Am
Ernst	ARNDT st,w Ger	Escher,	ALFRED st Swi
Ernst	BARLACH su,po,w Ger	Escher,	MAURITS at Dut
Ernst	BEHM geogr Ger	Escoffier,AUGUSTE chef,w Fr
Ernst	BIRON st Ger	Esek	HOPKINS navy Am
Ernst	BLOCH ph,e Ger	Esenin,	SERGEI po Rus
Ernst	BRUCKE md,e Ger	Eshkol,	LEVI st Israel
Ernst	CHAIN(Sir)sc,e	Esiason,	BOOMER fb,tv
Ernst	COHEN sc,e Dut	Eskew,	JACK tv
Ernst	DOHM w,ed Ger	Eskola,	PENTTI geol Finn
Ernst	FISCHER sc,w Ger	Eslava,	MIGUEL c Sp
Ernst	HAECKEL sc,e Ger	Esme	PERCY
Ernst	HARDT po,w Ger	Esmond	KNIGHT
Ernst	HASSE st,e Ger	Esmond,	JILL
Ernst	JUNGER w,ph Ger	Ensor,	JAMES(Baron)p Belg
Ernst	MACH sc,ph,e Aus	Esper	LARSEN sc-rocks Am
Ernst	RAUPACH w Ger	Espinoza, MARK DAMON tv
Ernst	REUTER st Ger	Esposito, GIANCARLO
Ernst	ROHM ar Ger	Esposito, GIANNI
Ernst	TOCH c,e Am	Esposito, PHIL ho-m'69'74
Ernst	TOLLER w,po Ger	Esprit	AUBER c Fr
Ernst	UDET flyer,ar Ger	Espronceda y Delgado, JOSE po Sp
Ernst	WEBER sc,e Ger	Espy,	JAMES weather Am
Ernst	ZAHN w Swi	Espy,	MIKE st Am
Ernst von BANDEL su Ger	Esquivel, ADOLFO su,n-x'80
Ernst von SIEMANS id Ger	Esquivel, LAURA w
Ernst,	MAX p,su Ger	Essen,	HANS von ar Swe
Ernst,	PAUL w Ger	Essex,	DAVID s+ Br
Ernst,	RICHARD n-c'91	Essy	PERSSON
Eron	TABOR	Esteban	ECHEVERRIA po Arg
Errett	CORD id-cars Am	Estebanez Calderon, SERAFIN w Sp
Errickson,KRISTA tv+	Estefan,	GLORIA s-pop Cuba
Errico,	GREG mr-drm Am	Estelle	BENNETT s Am
Errol	BROWN mr-s Jamaica	Estelle	GETTY tv+
Errol	FLYNN	Estelle	LORING s,tv Am
Errol	GARNER mj-piano,c Am	Estelle	PARSONS
Errol	MORRIS d	Estelle	SLOANE tv
Errol,	LEON	Estelle	TAYLOR
Erskine	HOLLAND(Sir)l,e	Estelle	WINWOOD
Erskine	SANFORD	Ester	MINCIOTTI
Erskine,	JOHN e,w Am	Estes,	BUFF mj-sax Am
Erskine,	MARILYN tv	Estes,	ELEANOR w Am
Erte	--- ds,su,at Fr-Am	Estes,	ROB tv
Ertha	KITT s+ Am	Estes,	SIMON s,baritone Am
Ervin,	SAM st Am	Estevez,	EMILIO
Ervine,	ST. JOHN w Irish	Estevez,	JOE
Erving,	JULIUS bb-m'81 hf+	Estevez,	RENEE
Erwin	MUELLER sc,e Am	Esther	DALE
Erwin	PANOFSKY h-art Am	Esther	RALSTON
Erwin	PISCATOR pr,d Ger	Esther	ROLLE tv+
Erwin	ROMMEL ar Ger &	Esther	WILLIAMS sw+ Am
Erwin	ROMMEL=Desert Fox	Estrada,	ERIK tv+
Erwin,	STUART(Stu) tv+	Estrup,	JACOB st Dan
Esa	TIKKANEN ho	Etex,	ANTOINE su,p,ac Fr
Esa-Pekka SALONEN cn	Ethan	ALLEN ar-re Am

Ethan	CANIN w Am	Eugene	O'CURRY antiq Irish
Ethan	COEN w Am	Eugene	O'NEILL w Am
Ethan	HAWKE d+	Eugene	ORMANDY cn Am
Ethan	RANDALL	Eugene	POTTIER w-songs,st Fr
Ethan	WAYNE tv	Eugene	PREVOST w Fr
Ethel	BEERS po Am	Eugene	ROCHE tv+
Ethel	DELL w Br	Eugene	ROUHER st Fr
Ethel	MERMAN la,s+ Am	Eugene	SANDOW strongman Am
Ethel	SMYTH(Dame)c,w,fe	Eugene	SEERS w,ct Can
Ethel	VANCE tv	Eugene	SUE w Fr
Ethel	WALES	Eugene	VOGUE w,st Fr
Ethel	WATERS s,tv+ Am	Eugene	WIGNER sc Am
Ethel	WILSON tv	Eugene	YSAYE viol,cn,c Belg
Ethel	WILSON w Can	Eugenia	PAUL tv
Ethelbert	NEVIN c Am	Eugenie	BESSERER
Etherege,	GEORGE(Sir)w	Eugenio	FLORIT po,ct Cuba
Etheridge,	MELISSA mr-s Am	Eugenio	MONTALE po,ct It
Etienne	BALUZE h,e Fr	Eugenio de CASTRO po,e Port	
Etienne	BRULE x Fr	Eugenio de HOSTOS w,l PuRico	
Etienne	GILSON ph,e Fr	Eugenio de OCHOA w.ed Sp	
Etienne	HALLET ac Am	Euler,	LEONHARD math Swi
Etienne	LENOIR i Fr	Euler-Chelp., HANS von n-c'29	
Etienne	MALUS eng,sc Fr	Eure,	WESLEY
Etienne	MAREY sc,e Fr	Eurico	DUTRA ar,st Braz
Etienne	MEHUL c Fr	Eusden,	LAURENCE pol'1718 Br
Etienne	TACHE(Sir)st,md Can	Eusebio	AYALA st Parag
Etta	JAMES s-r&b,mr+ Am	Eusebio	KINO r Sp
Etta	KETT fc	Eustache	Le SUEUR p Fr
Etta	LEE	Eustachio DIVINI id-clocks It	
Ettore	MANNI	Eustis,	DOROTHY f Am
Ettore	PAIS h,e It	Eva	BARTOK
Ettore	SCHMITZ w It	Eva	BRAUN Hitler's wf
Ettore	SCOLA d	Eva	GABOR tv+
Etty,	WILLIAM p Br	Eva	LaRUE
Eubank,	SHARI	Eva	MATTES
Eubank,	WEEB fb	Eva	PERON st Arg
Eubanks,	BOB tv	Eva	RAS
Eubie	BLAKE(Jms)mj-piano Am	Eva	RENZI
Eucken,	RUDOLF ph,n-l'08	Eva Marie SAINT	
Euclid	--- math Gr	Evalina	FERNANDEZ tv
Eudes,	JEAN(Saint)r Fr	Evan	BAYH st Am
Eudora	WELTY w Am	Evan	COHEN tv
Eugen	BLEULER ps Swi	Evan	CONNELL w Am
Eugen	D'ALBERT piano,c Ger	Evan	DANDO s-pop Am
Eugen	HUBER l,e Swi	Evan	ELLIOTT tv
Eugen	JOCHUM cn Ger	Evan	EVANS po Welsh
Eugen	LANGEN eng Ger	Evan	GREEN w Am
Eugen	SANGER eng-rocket Aus	Evan	HUNTER w Am
Eugene	ARAM e,murderer Br	Evan	PICONE ds
Eugene	ATGET fo Fr	Evan	RICHARDS
Eugene	BOUDIN p Fr	Evan	SHELBY ar-militia Am
Eugene	BRIEUX w Fr	Evangeline BROWN w Am	
Eugene	CLARK tv	Evangelista, LINDA mo Can	
Eugene	DEBS labor Am	Evangii	BAUER d
Eugene	DUBOIS md,sc Dut	Evanovich,JANET w Am	
Eugene	FIELD po,j Am	Evans,	ART tv+
Eugene	GRINDEL po Fr	Evans,	ARTHUR(Sir)arc
Eugene	IONESCO w Fr	Evans,	BARRY tv
Eugene	LABICHE w Fr	Evans,	BERGEN tv
Eugene	LEVY tv+	Evans,	BILL mj-piano Am
Eugene	MARTIN tv	Evans,	BILLY b hf

Evans,	CHARLES(Chick)g Am	Everett	SHINN p Am
Evans,	CLIFFORD	Everett	SLOANE
Evans,	DALE s+ Am	Everett,	CHAD tv+
Evans,	DAMON tv	Everett,	RUPERT
Evans,	DARRELL b,hr'85	Everette	De GOLYER sc-oil Am
Evans,	DAVID w Welsh	Everhard,	NANCY tv+
Evans,	DOUGLAS	Everhart,	ANGIE mo+
Evans,	DWIGHT b,hr'81	Everly,	DON s-cnt,tv Am
Evans,	EDITH(Dame)la+ Br	Everly,	PHIL s-cnt,tv Am
Evans,	EVAN po Welsh	Evers,	JASON
Evans,	FREDERICK fo Br	Evers,	JOHN b hf
Evans,	GENE tv+	Evers,	MEDGAR e,civ rts Am
Evans,	GIL mj-piano,c Am	Evert,	CHRIS t,tv Am
Evans,	HARRY ed,st Am	Evegnii	BAUER d
Evans,	HERBERT sc-md,e Am	Evigan,	GREG tv+
Evans,	JANET sw,o-g'88'92	Evinrude,	OLE i-outboards Am
Evans,	JOHN(Sir)arc	Ewald	HERING md,ps,e Ger
Evans,	JOSH	Ewald	KLEIST po,ar Ger
Evans,	LINDA tv+	Ewald,	JOHANNES po,w Dan
Evans,	MADGE	Ewan	McGREGOR
Evans,	MARK mr-bass Aust	Ewans,	KAI mj-reeds,cn Dan
Evans,	MARY BETH tv	Ewart,	JOHN
Evans,	MARY(Geo.Eliot)w Br	Ewart,	WILLIAM st Br
Evans,	MAURICE la,tv+ Am	Ewbank,	WEEB fb hf
Evans,	MIKE tv	Ewell,	RICHARD ar Am
Evans,	MONICA tv	Ewell,	TOM tv+
Evans,	MURIEL	Ewing,	ALFRED(Sir)sc,engScot
Evans,	NANCY tv	Ewing,	BUCK b hf
Evans,	NICHOLAS w Br	Ewing,	ELLIE MAY fc
Evans,	OLIVER i Am	Ewing,	GEOFFREY tv
Evans,	PETER tv	Ewing,	JAMES md,e Am
Evans,	RICHARD PAUL w Am	Ewing,	MAURICE geol,e Am
Evans,	RICHARD tv	Ewing,	OSCAR tv
Evans,	ROBLEY(FightgBob)navy	Ewing,	PATRICK bb
Evans,	RUDULPH su Am	Ewing,	ROGER tv
Evans,	TROY tv+	Ewins,	BONNIE LOU tv
Evans,	WALKER fo am	Ewry,	RAY 8 x o-g'00'04'08
Evans,	WILBUR tv	Exner,	JUDITH mistress-JFK Am
Evarts,	WILLIAM l, st Am	Export,	VALIE d
Evatt,	HERBERT l,st Aust	Eyck,	HUBERT van p Belg
Eve	ARDEN tv+	Eyck,	JAN van p Belg
Eve	MILLER	Eydie	GORME s Am
Eve	PLUMB tv+	Eyer,	RICHARD tv+
Eve	QUELER cn Am	Eyre	COOTE(Sir)ar Br
Eve	YOUNG tv	Eyre	CROWE(Sir)st
Evel	KNIEVEL stunts Am	Eyre,	EDWARD x Br
Evelyn	ANKERS	Eyre,	PETER
Evelyn	BRENT	Eyth,	MAXMILIAN von eng,iGer
Evelyn	KEYES	Eythe,	WILLIAM
Evelyn	KNAPP	Eyvind	JOHNSON w Swe
Evelyn	SCOTT tv	Ezekiel	LANDAU r-rabbi Pol
Evelyn	STEWART	Ezekiel	MPHAHLELE w,ct S.Afr
Evelyn	VENABLE	Ezekiel,	MOSES su Am
Evelyn	WAUGH w Br	Ezio	PINZA s+ It
Evelyn,	JOHN w Br	Ezra	ABBOT r Am
Everend	BRUCE geol Can	Ezra	CORNELL f&f Am
Everest,	BARBARA	Ezra	POUND po Am
Everett	CASE bbc hf	Ezra	STILES r Am
Everett	DEAN bbc hf	Ezzard,	CHARLES boxer Am
Everett	McGILL tv+		
Everett	SHELTON bbc hf		

"F" NAME DESIGNATION CODES

f	-FINANCIER OR PHILANTHROPIST
fb	FOOTBALL
fbc	FOOTBALL COACH, OWNER
fc	FICTIONAL CHARACTER
fe	FEMINIST
fly	FLYER
fo	PHOTOGRAPHER
furn	FURNITURE
fb-d	FOOTBALL MVP-DEFENSE
fb-m	FOOTBALL MVP OFFENSE

"F" NATIONALITY CODES

Finn - FINNISH   Fr - FRENCH

"F's"

F. Lee   BAILEY l,tv
F. MacFarl BUMET(Sir)md
F. Murray ABRAHAM
F. William PARKER tv
F.E.   MILLER
F.H.   BRADLEY ph,w Br
F.J.   O'NEILL tv
F.R.   LEAVIS ct,ed.w Br
F.R.   SCOTT po,l Can
F.W.   BATESON ct,w Br
F.W.   MURNAU d Ger
Fabares,   SHELLEY tv+
Faber,   GEOFFREY(Sir)pb,w
Faber,   JOHANN id Ger
Faber,   URBAN b hf
Faberge,   PETER jeweler Rus
Fabian   --- s+ Am
Fabian,   AVA
Fabian,   FRANCOISE
Fabiana   UDENIO
Fabiani,   JOEL tv+
Fabio   TESTI
Fabio   URENA
Fabray,   NANETTE tv+
Fabre,   EMILE w Fr
Fabre,   JEAN sc Fr
Fabritius,CAREL p Dut
Fabrizi,   FRANCO
Fabrizio   RUFFO r,ar It
Fabry,   CHARLES sc,e Fr
Facta,   LUIGI st It
Fadden,   ARTHUR(Sir)st Aust
Fadden,   TOM tv
Fadiman,   CLIFTON w,ed,tv Am
Fafara,   STANLEY tv
Fagen,   DONALD mr-kbds,s Am
Fagerbakke, BILL tv
Faguet,   EMILE ct,e Fr
Fagunwa,   DANIEL w Nigeria
Fahey,   JEFF
Fahey,   MYRNA tv
Fahrenheit, DANIEL sc Ger
Failly,   PIERRE ar Fr
Fain,   AGATHON h Fr

Fain,   SAMMY c Am
Fair,   ELINOR
Fairbanks,DOUGLAS Jr. tv+
Fairbanks,DOUGLAS Sr.
Fairchild,DAVID sc Am
Fairchild,MORGAN tv+
Fairfax,   JIMMY tv
Fairfield OSBORN w-conserv Am
Fairman,   MICHAEL tv
Fairuza   BALK
Fairweather-Low,ANDY mr,s Welsh
Faison,   FRANKIE tv+
Faison,   SANDY tv
Faith   DOMERGUE
Faith   FORD tv+
Faith   HILL s-cnt Am
Faith   POPCORN consultant Am
Faith   PRINCE
Faith,   PERCYmj,cn,g-r'60 Am
Faithfull,MARIANNE s-folk,rk Br
Fajans,   KASIMIR sc,e Am
Fakir,   ABDUL mr-s Am
Falana,   LOLA s+ Am
Falco   --- s,ws Aus
Falco,   EDIE
Falcon,   JUAN ar,st Venz
Falconer,   EARL mr-bass Br
Faldo,   NICK g Br
Falk,   ADALBERT st Ger
Falk,   HARRY d
Falk,   JOHANNES w Ger
Falk,   PETER tv+
Falkberget, JOHAN w Nor
Falkenburg, JINX tv
Falkes de BREAUTE ar Br
Falkner,   ANNE tv
Fall,   ALBERT st Am
Fall,   LEOPOLD c Aus
Falla,   MANUEL de c Sp
Fallaci,   ORIANA j,w It
Falsen,   CHRISTIAN st Nor
Faltskog,   AGNETHA mr-s Swe
Fambrough,HENRY mr-s Am
Fame,   GEORGIE mr-kbds,s Br
Famke   JANSSEN
Fanaka,   JAMAA d
Fane,   JOHN ar,st Br
Fangen,   RONALD w,ct Nor
Fangio,   JUAN racer-cars Am
Fann,   AL
Fannie   FARMER w-ck bk Am
Fannie   FLAGG tv+
Fannie   HURST w Am
Fanning,   BILL tv
Fanny   ARDANT
Fanny   BRICE s+ Am
Fanny   BURNEY w Br
Fanny   CROSBY w-hyms Am
Fanny   ELSSLER ba Aus
Fanny   LEWALD w Ger
Fanny   WRIGHT ref Am

Fano	SUPILO st Croat
Fanon,	FRANTZ ph W.Ind
Fanti,	MANFREDO ar It
Fantoni,	SERGIO
Faracy,	STEPHANIE tv+
Faraday,	MICHAEL sc Br
Fard,	WALLACE r Am
Farentino,	DEBRAH tv+
Farentino,	JAMES tv+
Fargas,	ANTONIO tv+
Farge,	ANNIE tv
Fargo,	DONNA s Am
Fargo,	JAMES d
Fargo,	WILLIAM f,bus Am
Faria,	BETTY
Farid od-Din ATTAR po Persia	
Farigoule,	LOUIS w Fr
Farina	HOSKINS
Farina,	DENNIS tv+
Farina,	SALVATORE w It
Farini,	LUIGI md,h,st It
Farjeon,	ELEANOR w Br
Farkas	BOLYAI math,e Hung
Farley	GRANGER
Farley	MOWAT w Can
Farley,	CHRIS tv+
Farley,	DUKE tv
Farley,	JAMES st, id Am
Farlow,	WILLIAM sc,e Am
Farman,	HENRI id-planes Fr
Farman,	MAURICE id-planes Fr
Farmer,	FANNY w-cook bk Am
Farmer,	FRANCES
Farmer,	JOHN c Br
Farmer,	LILLIAN tv
Farmer,	MIMSY
Farmer,	MOSES i Am
Farnaby,	GILES c Br
Farner,	MARK mr-guit,s Am
Farnham,	ELIZA ref,w Am
Farnsworth,	PHILO eng Am
Farnsworth,	RICHARD
Farnum,	FRANKLIN
Farnum,	WILLIAM
Faron	YOUNG s+ Am
Farquhar,	GEORGE w Br
Farr,	FELICIA
Farr,	JAMIE tv+
Farr,	LEE tv
Farragut,	DAVID navy Am
Farrah	FAWCETT tv+
Farrakhan,	LOUIS r-muslim Am
Farrar,	DAVID
Farrar,	FREDERIC r,w Br
Farrar,	GERALDINE soprano Am
Farrar,	JOHN pb,w Am
Farrell,	AMY tv
Farrell,	BOBBY mr-s W.Indies
Farrell,	CHARLES(Charlie)tv+
Farrell,	EILEEN s-opera,mj Am
Farrell,	GLENDA

Farrell,	GWEN tv
Farrell,	JAMES w Am
Farrell,	JUDY tv
Farrell,	MIKE d,w+ Am
Farrell,	SHARON
Farrell,	SHEA tv
Farrell,	TERRY
Farrell,	TIM tv
Farrell,	TIMOTHY
Farrell,	TOMMY tv+
Farren,	ELIZABETH la Br
Farrer,	WILLIAM sc Br
Farriss,	ANDREW mr-kbds Aust
Farriss,	JON mr-drm,s Aust
Farrow,	JOHN d
Farrow,	MIA tv+
Farrow,	TISA
Farwell,	ARTHUR c,ct Am
Fasch,	JOHANN c Ger
Fassbinder,	RAINER WERNER d
Fassler,	RON tv
Fast,	HOWARD w Am
Fates,	GIL tv
Fath,	JACQUES ds Fr
Fatha	HINES mj-piano,c Am
Fats	DOMINO mj,mr,piano Am
Fats	NAVARRO mj Am
Fats	WALLER mj-pian,s,c Am
Fats,	MINNESOTA pool Am
Fatso	MARCO tv
Fatty	ARBUCKLE(Roscoe)
Faulk,	JOHN tv
Faulkner,	ANNE tv
Faulkner,	ERIC mr-guitar Scot
Faulkner,	JAMES
Faulkner,	WM.n-l'49,p-f'55'63
Faure,	ELIE h-art Fr
Faure,	GABRIEL c Fr
Faust,	FREDERICK w Am
Faust,	JOHANN magic Ger
Faustin	JEANJEAN mj-tromb Fr
Faustino,	DAVID tv+
Fausto	GUERZONI
Fausto	TOZZI
Favart,	CHARLES w,d Fr
Faverty,	BEVERLY tv
Favory,	ANDRE p Fr
Favre,	JULES l,st Fr
Fawcett,	ALLEN tv
Fawcett,	BILL
Fawcett,	FARRAH tv+
Fawcett,	GEORGE
Fawcett,	WILLIAM
Fawkes,	GUY conspirator Br
Fawn	HALL secy-Ol.North Am
Fawn	SILVER
Fax,	JESSLYN tv
Fay	BAINTER
Fay	HAUSER
Fay	HOLDEN
Fay	McKENZIE

Fay	SPAIN
Fay	WRAY tv+
Fay,	ANDRAS w Hung
Fay,	MEAGAN tv
Fay,	SIDNEY h,e Am
Fay-Cooper COLE an,e Am	
Faye	DUNAWAY
Faye	EMERSON tv
Faye	GRANT tv+
Faye,	ALICE
Faye,	DAVID cm Am
Faye,	HERBIE tv
Faye,	HERVE astr Fr
Faye,	JOEY tv
Faylen,	CAROL tv
Faylen,	FRANK tv+
Fayrfax,	ROBERT c Br
Fazenda,	LOUISE
Fazil	ISKANDER w,po Rus
Fazio,	RON
Fazy,	JEAN st,j,w Swi
FDR's dog FALA	
Feargal	SHARKEY mr-s Irish
Feargus	O'CONNOR st Irish
Fearing,	KENNETH w Am
Fears,	TOM fb hf
Fechner,	GUSTAV sc,e Ger
Feddis,	SHELBY
Feder,	GOTTFRIED ec,st Ger
Federico	GAMBOA w Mex
Federigo	TOZZI w It
Federov,	SERGEI ho-m'94
Fedin,	KONSTANTIN w Rus
Fedor von BOCK ar Ger	
Fedora	BARBIERI mezzo It
Fee	WAYBILL mr-s Am
Feeney,	JOE s,w,tv Am
Fehr,	DONALD b-union Am
Fei,	LUNG
Fei,	MENG
Feiffer,	JULES cr,w Am
Feijo,	DIOGO r,st Braz
Feininger,LYONEL p Am	
Feinstein,ALAN tv+	
Feinstein,JOHN	
Feith,	RHIJNVIS w Dut
Fejer,	LIPOT math,e Hung
Feke,	ROBERT p Am
Feld,	FRITZ
Felder,	CLARENCE tv+
Feldkampf,ELMER mj-s Am	
Feldman,	COREY tv+
Feldman,	MARTY tv+
Feldon,	BARBARA tv+
Feldshuh,	TOVAH
Felice	ANERIO c It
Felice	ORSINI re It
Felice	SCHACTER tv
Felicia	BELL tv
Felicia	FARR
Felicia	HEMANS po Br

Feliciano,JOSE mr-guit,s P.Rico	
Felicien	ROPS p Belg
Felicity	KENDAL
Felicity	LOTT soprano Br
Felipe	ALOU b
Felipe	PEDRELL c Sp
Felipe	TRIGO w Sp
Felix	ADLER e Am
Felix	AYLMER
Felix	BLOCH sc Am
Felix	BOOTH(Sir)id-gin
Felix	DAHN h,po Ger
Felix	DARLEY illus Am
Felix	DeWELDON su Am
Felix	DUBAN ac Fr
Felix	EBOUE st Fr
Felix	GRAS w Fr
Felix	MASSE c Fr
Felix	MELINE st Fr
Felix	MOTTL c,cn Aus
Felix	POUCHET e,nature Fr
Felix	PYAT w,st Fr
Felix	SALTEN w Hung
Felix	SAVART md,sc,e Fr
Felix	WANKEL rotary engsGer
Felix d'	HERELLE sc Can
Felix,	MARIA
Fell,	JOHN r Br
Fell,	NORMAN tv+
Feller,	BOB b hf
Fellini,	FEDERICO d+
Fellows,	CHARLES(Sir)arc
Felltham,	OWEN w Br
Felmy,	HANSJORG
Felt,	DORR i Am
Felton	PERRY tv+
Felton,	NORMAN tv-pr Am
Felton,	REBECCA st,w Am
Felton,	VERNA tv+
Femia,	JOHN tv
Femina,	MICHAEL
Fender,	FENDER m-cnt,s
Fenech,	EDWIGE
Fenella	FIELDING
Fenelon,	FRANCOIS de r,w Fr
Feng,	KU
Fenmore,	TANYA tv+
Fenn,	SHERILYN tv+
Fennelly,	PARKER tv
Fenneman,	GEORGE tv+
Fenno,	JOHN ed Am
Fenton	HORT r Br
Fenton,	ELIJAH po Br
Fenton,	FRANK
Fenton.	LAVINIA la Br
Fenton,	LESLIE
Fenton,	ROGER fo Br
Fenwick,	ELLEN tv
Fenwick,	MILLICENT tv
Feodor	LYNEN sc Ger
Feore,	COLM

Ferber,	EDNA p-f'2
Ferd	SEBASTIAN d
Ferde	GROFE c,cn Am
Ferdin,	PAMELYN tv
Ferdinand	BUISSON e,st Fr
Ferdinand	COHN sc,e Ger
Ferdinand	FOCH ar,st Fr
Ferdinand	HEBRA md Aus
Ferdinand	LOT h,e Fr
Ferdinand	MARCOS st Phili
Ferdinand	MAYNE(Ferdy)
Ferdinand	POISE c Fr
Ferdinand	RAIMUND w Aus
Ferdinand	SOMMER e,w Ger
Ferdinand	WRANGEL x Rus
Ferdinand	ZIRKEL minerals,e Ger
Ferdinand	de LESSEPS st Fr
Ferdinando	PAER c It
Ferdy	MAYNE
Fere,	TAWNY
Ferenc	DEAK st Hung
Ferenc	HERCZEG w Hung
Ferenc	KOLCSEY po,ct Hung
Ferenc	MOLNAR w Hung
Ferenc,	JUHASZ po Hung
Ferenczi,	SANDOR ps Hung
Fergus	HUME w Br
Ferguson	JENKINS b
Ferguson,	AL
Ferguson,	ALLYN m,cn,tv Am
Ferguson,	FRANK tv
Ferguson,	HARRY id-planes Irish
Ferguson,	JAY mr-s Am
Ferguson,	JAY R. tv
Ferguson,	MAYNARDmj-trump,cn Am
Ferid	MURAD md,e,n-m'98
Ferid Pasa	DAMAD st Turk
Ferlin	HUSKY s-cnt+ Am
Fermat,	PIERRE de math,st Fr
Fermi,	ENRICO n-p'38
Fern	FITZGERALD tv
Fern,	ALLESSANDRA ba Br
Fernald,	MERRITT sc Am
Fernamdez	de Lizardi,JOSE w Mex
Fernand	BRAUDEL h Fr
Fernand	CABROL r Fr
Fernand	GREGH po Fr
Fernand	LABORI l Fr
Fernand	LEDOUX
Fernand	LEGER p,at Fr
Fernand	SEVERIN po Belg
Fernand	WIDAL md,e Fr
Fernand	de BRINON j,st Fr
Fernandel	---
Fernandes,	ALVARO x Port
Fernandes,	JOAO x Port
Fernandes,	MIGUEL tv
Fernandez,	ABEL tv
Fernandez,	EVALINA tv
Fernandez,	JAMIE

Fernandez,	JUAN
Fernandez,	JUAN x(b 1536)Sp
Fernandez,	PETER JAY tv
Fernandez,	SID b
Fernando	ALLENDE tv+
Fernando	ARRABAL w Sp
Fernando	AVALOS ar Sp
Fernando	Di LEO d
Fernando	GOMEZ
Fernando	LAMAS
Fernando	PESSOA po Port
Fernando	REY
Fernando	SOLER
Fernando	SOR guitar,c Sp
Fernando	SOTO
Fernando	de HERRERA po Sp
Fernando	de ROJAS w Sp
Fernao	LOPES h Port
Fernao	PINTO w Port
Fernel,	JEAN md,astron Fr
Fernow,	BERNHARD forester Am
Ferraday,	LISA tv
Ferrar,	CATHERINE tv
Ferrar,	NICHOLAS r Br
Ferrare,	CHRISTINA tv+
Ferrari,	ENZO id-cars It
Ferrari,	GAUDENZIO p It
Ferraro,	GERALDINE st Am
Ferratti,	REBECCA
Ferre,	GIANFRANCO ds It
Ferreau,	JON
Ferrel,	WILLIAM weather Am
Ferrell,	CONCHATA tv+
Ferrell,	RAY tv
Ferrell,	RICK b hf
Ferrell,	TODD tv
Ferrell,	TYRA tv+
Ferreol,	ANDREA
Ferrer,	JOSE la,d+ o-a'50
Ferrer,	LUPITA
Ferrer	MEL
Ferrer,	MIGUEL tv+
Ferrera,	ABEL d
Ferrero,	MARTIN tv+
Ferri,	CIRO p It
Ferrier,	DAVID(Sir)md Scot
Ferrier,	KATHLEEN contralto Br
Ferrigno,	LOU
Ferris,	BARBARA tv+
Ferris,	GEORGE eng Am
Ferris,	IRENA tv
Ferro,	DAN tv
Ferruccio	BUSONI piano,c It
Ferruccio	PARRI st It
Ferrugia,	JOHN tv
Ferry,	BRYAN s,ws Br
Ferry,	JULES st Fr
Fersen,	FREDRIK st,ar Swe
Ferzetti,	GABRIEL
Fesca,	FRIEDRICH viol,c Ger
Fesch,	JOSEPH r Fr

Fess	PARKER tv+
Festa,	COSTANZO s,c It
Festus,	SEXTUS w Roman
Fet,	AFANASY po Rus
Fetchit,	STEPIN
Fetis,	FRANCOIS c,w Belg
Fetti,	DOMENICO p It
Feuchtwanger,	LION w Ger
Feuer,	DEBRA
Feuerbach,	LUDWIG ph Ger
Feuillet,	OCTAVE w Fr
Feury,	PEGGY
Feval,	PAUL w Fr
Fevzi	CAKMAK ar,st Turk
Fewkes,	JESSE sc Am
Feydeau,	GEORGES w F
Feyder,	JACQUES d Fr
Feynman,	RICHARD n-p'65
Fialin,	JEAN st Fr
Fibber	McGEE & Molly cms Am
Fibich,	ZDENEK c Czech
Fibiger,	JOHANNES n-m'26
Fichard	POHL w Ger
Fichte,	JOHANN ph Ger
Ficino,	MARSILIO ph It
Fick,	ADOLF sc,e Ger
Fick,	AUGUST e Ger
Ficker,	JULIUS von l,h Ger
Fidel	CASTRO(Ruz)st Cuba
Fidler,	JIMMY tv
Fiedler,	ARTHUR cn,tv Am
Fiedler,	JOHN tv+
Fiedler,	LESLIE w,ct Am
Fieger,	DOUG mr-guitar,s Am
Field,	BETTY
Field,	CHELSEA
Field,	CYRUS f Am
Field,	ERASTUS p Am
Field,	EUGENE po,j Am
Field,	HENRY an,e Am.
Field,	MARSHALL mer Am
Field,	NATHAN la,w Br
Field,	SALLY o-a'79'84,tv+
Field,	SHIRLEY
Field,	SYLVIA tv
Field,	TODD
Field,	VIRGINIA
Fielder	COOK pr,d,tv
Fielder,	CECIL b,rbi'90'1'2
Fielder,	JIM mr-bass Am
Fielding	YOST(Hurry Up)fbc
Fielding,	FENELLA
Fielding,	HENRY w Br
Fielding,	JERRY m,cn,tv Am
Fields,	DOROTHY w-songs Am
Fields,	ERNIE mj-tromb,cn Am
Fields,	GRACIE cm Am
Fields,	KIM tv
Fields,	SHEP mj-sax,cn Am
Fields,	TOTIE cm,la Am
Fields,	W.C. cm+ Am

Fiennes,	RALPH
Fierstein,	HARVEY
Fifi	D'ORSAY
Fifth(5th)	Dimension g-r'67'69
Figg,	JAMES boxer Br
Fighting Bob	EVANS navy Am
Figl,	LEOPOLD st Aus
Figner,	VERA re,w Rus
Figuerroa,	EFRAIN tv
Filene,	EDWARD mer Am
Filipovic	ZLATA w Bosnia
Filippino	LIPPI p It
Filippo	JUVARRA ac It
Fillion,	NATHAN tv
Fillmore,	MILLARD 13th pres
Filmer,	ROBERT(Sir)w
Filson,	JOHN frontier,w Am
Fimple,	DENNIS tv+
Fina,	JACK mj-piano,cn Am
Finch,	JON
Finch,	PETER o-a'76
Finch,	RICHARD mr-bass Am
Finck,	HEINRICH c Ger
Fine,	LARRY
Fine,	ORONCE math Fr
Fine,	TRAVIS tv
Finefrock,	CHRIS tv
Finer,	JEM banjo Irish
Fingers,	JOHNNIEmr-kbds,s Ir
Fingers,	ROLLIEb-cy'81-mv'81 hf
Fink,	ALBERT eng,i Am
Fink,	MIKE frontier Am
Finkel,	NATHAN e Israel
Finks,	JIM fb hf
Finlay	CURRIE
Finlay,	CARLOS md,sc Cuba
Finlay,	FRANK
Finlayson,	JAMES
Finley	DUNNE j,w-humor Am
Finley,	MARTHA w Am
Finley,	PAT tv
Finley,	STEVE b,gg'95'6
Finn	CARTER
Finn	RONNE x Am
Finn,	JOHN
Finn,	PAT tv
Finn,	TIM mr-kbds,s N.Zea
Finnegan,	BOB tv
Finneran,	MIKE tv
Finnerty,	WARREN
Finney,	ALBERT
Finney,	JACK w Am
Finnur	JONSSON r,h Iceland
Finola	HUGHES tv+
Finsen,	NIELS n-m'03
Fio Rito,	TED mj-kbds,cn Am
Fiona	LEWIS
Fiona	REID
Fiona	RICHMOND
Fiona	SHAW
Fionnula	FLANAGAN tv+

Fiore, BILL tv	Fithian, JOE tv
Fiore, PASQUALE l,w It	Fittig, RUDOLF sc Ger
Fiorentino, LINDA	Fitts, RICK tv+
Fiorillo, TIBERIO la It	Fitz HALLECK po Am
Firbank, RONALD w Br	Fitzgerald, BARRY o-s '44
Firestone,HARVEY id Am	FitzGerald, EDWARD po Br
Firman, SIDNEY mj,cn Br	Fitzgerald, ELLA mj,s,tv+ Am
Firmin ABAUZIT r, ph Fr	Fitzgerald, F. SCOTT KEY w Am
Firmin DIDOT pb Fr	Fitzgerald, FERN tv
Firmin GEMIER la Fr	FitzGerald, GEORGE sc Irish
Firoz NOON(Sir)st Pakistan	Fitzgerald, GERALDINE
Firpo, LUIS boxer Am	Fitzgerald, NUALA tv
Firstenberg, SAM d	Fitzgerald, WALTER
Firth, COLIN	Fitzgerald, WILBUR tv
Firth, PETER	Fitzpatrick, JAMES(Jim) tv
Fischer, EMIL n-c'02	Fitzroy, EMILY
Fischer, ERNST n-c'73	Fitzsimmons, ROBERT(Bob)boxer Am
Fischer, HANS n-c'30	Fitzsimmons, TOM tv
Fischer, KAI	Fix, PAUL tv+
Fischer, KUNO ph Ger	Flach, JACQUES l,h Fr
Fischer, LOUIS w,j Am	Flack, ROBERTA g-r'73
Fischer, VERA	Flagg, CASH
Fish, . HAMILTON st Am	Flagg, ERNEST ac Am
Fish, NANCY	Flagg, FANNIE tv+
Fishbein, MORRIS md,ed Am	Flagg, JAMES p,illus Am
Fishburne,LAURENCE(Larry)	Flagstad, KIRSTEN soprano Nor
Fisher AMES st Am	Flaherty. JOE tv+
Fisher STEVENS	Flaherty, RAY fb hf
Fisher, BILL tv	Flaherty, ROBERT pr-film Am
Fisher, BUD(Harry)cr Am	Flambard, RANULF r,st Br
Fisher, CARRIE	Flammarion, CAMILLE sc,w Fr
Fisher, DOROTHY w Am	Flanagan, FIONNULA tv+
Fisher, EDDIE s,tv+ Am	Flanagan, JOHN o-g'00'04'08
Fisher, EDMOND H. n-m'92	Flanagan, KELLIE tv
Fisher, FRANCES	Flanagan, MIKE b-cy'79
Fisher, FRED c Am	Flanagan, PAT tv
Fisher, GAIL tv	Flanagan, RALPH mj-piano,cn Am
Fisher, GEORGE(Shug)tv+	Flanders, ED tv+
Fisher, IRVING ec,w Am	Flandin, GASTON st Fr
Fisher, MARY w Am	Flanery, SEAN
Fisher, MATTHEW mr-kbds Br	Flann O'BRIEN w Irish
Fisher, NELLIE ba,tv Am	Flannagan,JOHN su Am
Fisher, NORMAN(Sir)st	Flanner, JANET j,w Am
Fisher, ROGER mr-guit Am	Flannery O'CONNOR w Am
Fisher, SHUG	Flannery SUSAN tv+
Fisher, TERENCE d	Flannigan,BILL s Irish
Fisher, TRICIA	Flash JENKINS tv
Fishman, MICHAEL tv	Flatt, ERNEST ba,tv Am
Fisk, CLINTON ar,f,e Am	Flatt, LESTER s-cnt Am
Fisk, JACK d	Flaubert, GUSTAVE w Fr
Fisk, SCHUYLER	Flaus, JOHN
Fiske, BRADLEY navy,i Am	Flavin, JAMES tv+
Fiske, HALEY bus Am	Flavin, MARTIN p-f'44
Fiske, MINNIE la Am	Flavio BIONDO h It
Fitch, ASA sc Am	Flavius AETIUS ar Roman
Fitch, CLYDE w Am	Flavius ASPAR ar Roman
Fitch, JOHN i Am	Flavius JOSEPHUS Jewish
Fitch, LOUISE tv	Flaxman, JOHN su Br
Fitch, VAL n-p'80	Flea --- s+
Fite, BOBBY tv	Fleay, FREDERICK h Br
Fithian, JEFF tv	Fleck, JOHN

Flecker,   JAMES po,w Br
Fleetwood,MICK mr-drums Br
Fleetwood,SUSAN
Flegel,   EDWARD x Ger
Fleischer,CHARLES tv+
Fleischer,RICHARD d
Fleischmann, ALBERT c
Fleischmann, STEPHANIE w Am
Fleming,   ALEXANDER(Sir)n-m'45
Fleming,   ART tv
Fleming,   ARTHUR(Sir)eng,id
Fleming,   ERIC tv+
Fleming,   IAN w+ Br
Fleming,   JOHN(Sir)eng
Fleming,   LONE
Fleming,   PEGGY sk,o-g'68
Fleming,   RENEE s,opera Am
Fleming,   RHONDA
Fleming,   VICTOR o-d'39
Flemyng,   JASON
Flemyng,   ROBERT
Fletcher, AARON tv
Fletcher, ALICE sc,w Am
Fletcher, ANDY mr-kbds Br
Fletcher, BRAMWELL
Fletcher, DEXTER
Fletcher, GILES(Younger)po Br
Fletcher, HARVEY sc,e,id Am
Fletcher, JOHN ct,p-q'39
Fletcher, LOUISE o-a'75
Fletcher, PHINEAS po Br
Flettner, ANTON eng,i Ger
Flexner,   SIMON md,e Am
Flick,   ELMER b hf
Flinck,   GOVAERT p Dut
Flinders   PETRIE(Sir)archeol
Flint,   AUSTIN Jr. md Am
Flint,   AUSTIN Sr. md Am
Flint,   FRANK po Br
Flint,   RICHARD glaciers Am
Flint,   SAM
Flip   MARK tv
Flip   WILSON cm,tv+ Am
Flippen,   JAY tv+
Flippin,   LUCY tv
Flo   JOYNER track Am
Flo   SOLDER tv
Flor   SILVESTRE
Flora   CAMPBELL tv
Flora   NWAPA w Nigeria
Flora   ROBSON
Florek,   DANN tv
Floren,   MYRON accordian,tv Am
Florence   BARCLAY w Br
Florence   BATES
Florence   COATES po Am
Florence   HALOP tv
Florence   KELLEY fe Am
Florence   LAKE
Florence   LARUE,mr-s Am
Florence   MARLY

Florence   RICE
Florence   RINARD tv
Florence   SMITH w Br
Florence   STANLEY tv+
Florence   VIDOR
Florent   DANCOURT la,w Fr
Florent   SCHMITT c Fr
Florenz   ZIEGFELD pr-follies Am
Florey,   HOWARD n-m'45
Floria,   HOLLY
Florian   CAJORI math,e Am
Florian   OCAMPO h Sp
Florian   ZABACH tv
Florida   FRIEBUS tv
Florinda   BOLKAN
Floris,   CORNELIS ac,su Belg
Florit,   EUGENIO po,ct Cuba
Flory,   PAUL n-c'74
Flotow,   FRIEDRICH c Ger
Flower,   GEORGE
Floyd   BENNETT flyer Am
Floyd   CRAMER piano Am
Floyd   DELL j,w Am
Floyd   SNEED mr-drm Can
Floyd,   EDDIE s-r&b,ws Am
Flue,   NIKLAUS l,hero Swi
Fluegel,   DARLANNE tv+
Fluellen, JOEL
Flynn,   DOUG b,gg'80
Flynn,   ERROL
Flynn,   JOE tv+
Flynn,   MIRIAM tv
Flynn,   SALLI s,tv Am
Fo,   DARIO n-l'97 It
Focas,   SPIROS
Foch,   FERDINAND ar,st Fr
Foch,   NINA tv+
Focke,   HEINRICH ds-planesGer
Fogazzaro,ANTONIO w,po It
Fogel,   JERRY tv
Fogel,   LEE tv
Fogel,   ROBERT n-e'93
Fogel,   VLADIMAR
Fogelberg,DAN mr-guit,s,ws Am
Fogerty,   ELSIE e-voice Br
Fogerty,   JOHN m-folk,guit,s Am
Fokine,   MICHEL ba Am
Fokker,   ANTHONY id-planes Am
Folco   LULLI
Folengo,   TEOFILO po,r It
Foley,   ELLEN tv+
Foley,   JOSEPH tv
Foley,   MACKA
Foley,   RED s-cnt Am
Folger,   HENRY id-oil Am
Follen,   AUGUST po,st Ger
Follet,   KEN w Am
Follows,   MEGAN tv+
Folmer,   WILLIAM i,id Am
Folz,   HANS s,ws Ger
Fomich   NIJINSKY ba Rus

Fonck,	PAUL flyer Fr
Fonda	LYNN
Fonda,	BRIDGET
Fonda,	HENRY o-a'81,tv+
Fonda,	JANE o-a'71
Fonda,	PETER
Fong,	BENSON
Fong,	BRIAN tv
Fong,	HAROLD tv
Fong,	KAM tv
Fong,	LEO
Fontaine	FOX cr Am
Fontaine,	EDDIE tv
Fontaine,	FRANK cm,tv Am
Fontaine,	JOAN o-a'41
Fontana,	WAYNE mr-s Br
Fontanne,	LYNN la Am
Fontenelle,	BERNARD de w Fr
Fonteyn,	MARGOT(Dame)ba Br
Fonvizin,	DENIS w Rus
Foote,	BRUCE tv
Foote,	HALLIE
Foote,	HORTON Jr.
Foote,	HORTON p-d'95
Foote,	SAMUEL la,w Br
Foppa,	VINCENZO p It
Forain,	JEAN p,illus Fr
Foran,	DICK
Foray,	JUNE tv
Forbes,	BERTIE pb Am
Forbes,	BRYAN d+
Forbes,	MARY
Forbes,	RALPH
Forbes,	SCOTT tv
Forbin,	CLAUDE de navy Fr
Force,	PETER h,id Am
Ford	BEEBE d
Ford	BOND tv
Ford	FRICK b hf
Ford	RAINEY tv+
Ford Madox BROWN p Br	
Ford Madox FORD w,ed Br	
Ford,	ANITRA
Ford,	CONSTANCE
Ford,	EDSEL id-cars Am
Ford,	EILEEN mo-agency Am
Ford,	FAITH tv+
Ford,	FORD MADOX w,ed Br
Ford,	FRANCIS
Ford,	FRANKIE s Am
Ford,	GERALD 38th pres
Ford,	GLENN tv+
Ford,	HARRISON
Ford,	HENRY id-cars Am
Ford,	JANIE tv
Ford,	JOHN o-d'35'40'41
Ford,	JOHN w Br
Ford,	LEN fb hf
Ford,	LITA mr-guitar Br
Ford,	MARIA
Ford,	MARY mj-s Am

Ford,	MICK
Ford,	PAUL tv+
Ford,	PETER tv
Ford,	RICHARD p-f'96
Ford,	ROSS tv
Ford,	TENNESSEE ERNIE s,tv+
Ford,	WALLACE tv+
Ford,	WHITEY b-cy'61 hf
Foree,	KEN
Forel,	AUGUSTE ps,sc Swi
Foreman,	CHRIS mr-guit Br
Foreman,	DEBORAH
Foreman,	GEORGE boxer Am
Forest	MOULTON astron,e Am
Forest	WHITAKER
Forest,	DENIS tv
Forest,	FREDERIC tv
Forest,	MARK
Forest,	MICHAEL
Forester,	C.S. w Br
Forey,	ELIE ar Fr
Forman,	JOEY tv
Forman,	MILOS o-d'75'84, d+
Forner,	JUAN w Sp
Foronjy,	RICHARD
Forrest	GREGG fb hf
Forrest	LEWIS tv+
Forrest	REID w,ct Irish
Forrest	TAYLOR tv+
Forrest	TUCKER tv+
Forrest,	EDWIN la Am
Forrest,	FREDERIC
Forrest,	HELEN s Am
Forrest,	RAY tv
Forrest,	SALLY
Forrest,	STEVE tv+
Forsh,	OLGA w Rus
Forslund,	CONSTANCE
Forssi,	KEN mr-Bass Am
Forssmann,	WERNER n-m'56
Forster,	BRIAN tv
Forster,	E.M. w Br
Forster,	MAX e,pb Ger
Forster,	ROBERT
Forsyth,	ROSEMARY
Forsythe,	BROOKE tv
Forsythe,	DREW
Forsythe,	HENDERSON
Forsythe,	JOHN tv+
Forsythe,	PAGE tv
Forsythe,	WILLIAM
Fort,	PAUL po Fr
Fortas,	ABE l Am
Forte,	IKE fb
Forten,	JAMES ref,bus Am
Fortier,	BOB tv
Fortmann,	DANIEL(Dr.)fb hf
Fortune,	JIMMY m-r&b,cnt Am
Fortune,	NICK mr-bass Am
Fosbury,	DICK hijump o-g'88
Foscolo,	UGO w,po It

Fosdick,	CHARLES w Am	Fox,	LUKE x Br
Fosdick,	HARRY r Am	Fox,	MICHAEL J. tv+
Foss,	SAM ed,po-humor Am	Fox,	NANCY tv
Fosse,	BOB o-d'72,d+	Fox,	NELLIE b-mv'59, hf
Fossey,	BRIGITTE	Fox,	PAULA w Am
Fossey,	DIAN an Br	Fox,	PETER tv+
Foster	BROOKS tv+	Fox,	RICHARD pb Am
Foster,	AMI tv	Fox,	ROY mj-cornet,cn Br
Foster,	ANDREW b hf	Fox,	SAMANTHA s-pop Br
Foster,	BARRY	Fox,	SONNY tv
Foster,	BUD bb hf	Fox,	STEVE tv
Foster,	BUDDY tv	Fox,	VIRGIL organ Am
Foster,	DIANNE	Fox,	VIVICA
Foster,	DONALD tv	Fox,	WALLACE d
Foster,	GEORGE b-mv'77,hr77'8	Foxe,	JOHN w Br
Foster,	GILES d	Foxton,	BRUCE mr-guitar Br
Foster,	GLORIA	Foxworth,	JAIMEE tv
Foster,	HAL cr Am	Foxworth,	ROBERT tv+
Foster,	HELEN	Foxx,	JAMIE tv
Foster,	JODIE o-a'88,'91	Foxx,	JIMMIE b-mv'32'3'8 hf
Foster,	JOHN st Am	Foxx,	REDD cm,tv+ Am
Foster,	JULIA	Foy,	EDDIE Jr. tv+
Foster,	KIMBERLY tv+	Foy,	EDDIE la,cm Am
Foster,	LINDA tv	Foy,	FRED tv
Foster,	MEG tv+	Foyt,	A.J. racer-cars Am
Foster,	PHIL tv+	Foyt,	VICTORIA
Foster,	PRESTON tv+	Fra	ANGELICO p It
Foster,	STAN tv	Fra	BARTOLOMMEO p It
Foster,	STEPHEN w-songs Am	Fra Filippo LIPPI p It
Foster,	WILLIAM labor Am	Fracci,	CARLA ba+ It
Foucault, JEAN sc Fr	Frakes,	JONATHAN tv+
Foucault, MICHEL w,ph Fr	Frame,	RODDY mr-guit,s Scot
Fould,	ACHILLE st Fr	Frampton, PETER guit,s,songs Br
Foulger,	BYRON tv+	Fran	ALLISON tv+
Foulis,	ROBERT mer-books Scot	Fran	DRESCHER tv+
Foulk,	ROBERT tv	Fran	ROBINSON tv
Fountain, PETE mj-clarinet Am	Fran	RYAN tv+
Fouque,	FRIEDRICH w Ger	Fran	SHEEHAN mr-bass Am
Fouquet,	JEAN p Fr	Franc	LUZ
Four Aces THE s/AL ALBERTS Am	Franc	RODDAM d
Fourdrinier, HENRY & SEALY i's Br	France	NUYEN tv+
Fournier, HENRI w Fr	France,	ANATOLE n-1'21
Fouts,	DANfb-m'82 hf,tv-spts	Francen,	VICTOR
Fouts,	TOM(Stubby)tv	Frances	ALDA soprano N.Zea
Fowler,	FRANCIS lexicog Am	Frances	BARBER
Fowler,	HENRY lexicog Br	Frances	BERGEN tv+
Fowler,	JIM tv	Frances	BROOKE w Can
Fowler,	JOHN(Sir)eng Br	Frances	BURNETT w Am
Fowler,	WILLIAM n-p'83	Frances	COBBE f,w Br
Fowles,	JOHN w Br	Frances	CONROY
Fowley,	DOUGLAS tv+	Frances	CROSBY w-hyms Am
Fox	HARRIS	Frances	DEE
Fox,	BERNARD tv+	Frances	DRAKE
Fox,	CHARLES st Br	Frances	FARMER
Fox,	CRYSTAL tv	Frances	FISHER
Fox,	EDWARD	Frances	GIFFORD
Fox,	FONTAINE cr Am	Frances	KEMBLE(Fanny)la,w Br
Fox,	GEORGE r-Quakers Br	Frances	KEYES w Am
Fox,	HUCKLEBERRY	Frances	LANGFORD
Fox,	JACKIE mr-bass Am	Frances	LEAR ed Am
Fox,	JAMES	Frances	McCAIN

Frances	MERCER tv	Francis	PARKMAN h Am
Frances	OSGOOD po Am	Francis	PEASE astron Am
Frances	PERKINS st-labor Am	Francis	PICABIA p Fr
Frances	REID tv	Francis	PRATT i,id Am
Frances	TOMELTY	Francis	QUARLES po Br
Francesc	MACIA st Sp	Francis	ROSSI mr-guitar,s Br
Francesca ANNIS		Francis	ROUS sc-md Am
Francesca ROBERTS tv+		Francis	SHEED pb Br
Francesco ALBANI p It		Francis	SMITH(Sir)i-propeller
Francesco ARRIVI w Puerto Rico		Francis	STANLEY i-steamcar Am
Francesco BERNI po It		Francis	THOME c Fr
Francesco CILEA c It		Francis	VEBER d
Francesco COLONNA w,r It		Francis	VERE(Sir)ar
Francesco COSSA p It		Francis	YOUNG w Br
Francesco GUARDI p It		Francis Ford COPPOLA d	
Francesco MOLZA po It		Francis Scott KEY l,po Am	
Francesco NITTI ec,st,w It		Francis X. BUSHMAN la+ Am	
Francesco QUINN		Francis, ALEC	
Francesco RABAL		Francis, ANNE tv+	
Francesco REDI md,po It		Francis, ARLENE tv+	
Francesco SELMI md-sc It		Francis, BILL mr-kbds,s Am	
Francesco del COSA p It		Francis, CONNIE s,tv Am	
Franchot TONE tv+		Francis, DICK w Br	
Francine TACKER tv		Francis, FREDDIE d	
Francine YORK tv+		Francis, GENIE tv+	
Francine, ANNE tv		Francis, IVOR	
Franciosa,ANTHONY(Tony) tv+		Francis, KAY	
Francis	ABBOT r,ph Am	Francis, MISSY tv	
Francis	ASBURY r Am	Francis, NOEL	
Francis	ASTON sc Br	Francis, PANAMA mj-drm,cn Am	
Francis	AYER advertising Am	Francis, RYAN tv	
Francis	BACON ph,w Br	Francisco BARRA st Mex	
Francis	BAVIER tv+	Francisco BAYEU p Sp	
Francis	BAY	Francisco BRANA(Frank)	
Francis	BIDDLE l,w Am	Francisco ELIO ar Sp	
Francis	CADELL x Scot	Francisco MELO ar,h,po Port	
Francis	CHILD w,e Am	Francisco PALOU r Sp	
Francis	COPPEE w Fr	Francisco RIBALTA p Sp	
Francis	CRICK md Br	Francisco SILVELA st Sp	
Francis	CROCKER eng,id Am	Francisco VILLA bandit,re Mex	
Francis	DANBY p Irish	Francisco de GOYA p Sp	
Francis	De SALES tv	Francisco de HERRERA p Sp	
Francis	DICKSEE(Sir)p	Francisco de QUEVEDO po,w Sp	
Francis	DOYLE(Sir)po	Francisco de RIOJA po Sp	
Francis	DRAKE(Sir)x	Franciscus, JAMES tv+	
Francis	ELMORE sc,i Br	Franck, CESAR organ,c Fr	
Francis	FORD	Franck, JAMES n-p'25	
Francis	FOWLER lexicogr Br	Franck, MELCHIOR c Ger	
Francis	GALTON(Sir)sc	Francke, KUNO h,e Am	
Francis	GUINAN tv	Francken, JEROM p Belg	
Francis	HADEN(Sir)etch	Francks, DON	
Francis	HINCKS(Sir)j,st Can	Franco CITTI	
Francis	HORNER ct Br	Franco CORELLI as-opera It	
Francis	ILES w Br	Franco FABRIZI	
Francis	JAMMES po,w Fr	Franco HARRIS fb hf	
Francis	JEFFREY ct,l Scot	Franco LEONI c It	
Francis	LAI c Fr	Franco NERO	
Francis	LEDERER	Franco RAMON tv+	
Francis	LIEBER sc-politics Am	Franco, BATTISTA p It	
Francis	MARION(SwampFox)ar Am	Franco, JESS(Jesus) d	
Francis	McDONALD	Franco, JULIO b,bat'91	

Franco,	RAMON tv+	Frank	BRIDGE c,cn Br
Francois	ARAGO sc,e Fr	Frank	BUCK hunter,x Am,
Francois	AULARD h,e Fr	Frank	CADY tv
Francois	BABEUF re,j Fr	Frank	CAPRA d
Francois	BERNIS r,st Fr	Frank	CELLIER
Francois	BLOIS r,w Belg	Frank	CHANCE b
Francois	BOSIO su Fr	Frank	CHAPMAN birds Am
Francois	BOUCHER p Fr	Frank	CHURCH st Am
Francois	BULOZ j,ed Fr	Frank	CLARKE sc,e Am
Francois	CLOUET p Belg	Frank	CLARKE sc,e Am
Francois	CLUZET	Frank	COGHLAN(Junior)
Francois	COTY id-perfume Fr	Frank	COLBY ed,e Am
Francois	DUMONT su,p Fr	Frank	CONRAD eng,i,id Am
Francois	FENELON r,st Fr	Frank	CONROY
Francois	FETIS c,w,e Belg	Frank	CRAVEN
Francois	GARNEAU h,po Can	Frank	DAILEY tv
Francois	GENY l,e Fr	Frank	DANIELS cm Am
Francois	GOSSEC c Fr	Frank	De KOVA tv+
Francois	GUIZOT h,e,st Fr	Frank	DeVOL m,cn,tv
Francois	HAXO eng-ar Fr	Frank	DOBSON su Br
Francois	HOTMAN l,e Fr	Frank	DYSON(Sir)astron
Francois	JACOB md Fr	Frank	FAYLEN tv+
Francois	LACROIX sc,e Fr	Frank	FENTON
Francois	Le MOYNE p Fr	Frank	FINLAY
Francois	LEMOT su Fr	Frank	FLINT po Br
Francois	MATTHES geol Am	Frank	FURNESS ac Am
Francois	MAURIAC w Fr	Frank	GALLOP tv
Francois	NAVEZ p Belg	Frank	GATSKY fb hf
Francois	PERIER	Frank	GERSTLE
Francois	QUESNAY md,e Fr	Frank	GIFFORD fb,tv hf
Francois	RAOULT sc,e Fr	Frank	GILROY w Am
Francois	RUDE su Fr	Frank	GOODNOW e Am
Francois	TOURTE violin bows Fr	Frank	GORSHIN
Francois	VIDOCQ police Fr	Frank	GOTCH wrestler Am
Francois	VIETE math,l Fr	Frank	HAGUE st Am
Francois	VILLON po Fr	Frank	HARRIS j,w Am
Francois de BAR h Fr		Frank	HERBERT w-scifi Am
Francois de FENELON r,w Fr		Frank	HUBBARD(Kin)w-humorAm
Francois de La NOUE ar Fr		Frank	JENKS tv+
Francois du JON r,ed Dut		Frank	KEANEY bbc hf
Francois, JACQUES		Frank	KELLOGG l,st Am
Francoise DORLEAC		Frank	KERMODE ct,h Br
Francoise FABIAN		Frank	KINARD fb hf
Francoise ROSAY		Frank	KING cr Am
Francoise SAGAN w Fr		Frank	KNOX pb Am
Franey,	BILLY	Frank	LaRUE
Frank	ADAMS geol,e Can	Frank	LATEUR w Belg
Frank	ALETTER tv	Frank	LAWTON
Frank	ANDREWS ar Am	Frank	LESLIE pb Am
Frank	BALL	Frank	LILLIE sc,e Am
Frank	BANK tv	Frank	LLOYD d
Frank	BEARD mr-drm Am	Frank	LOESSER c,lyrics Am
Frank	BEATY tv	Frank	LOVEJOY tv+
Frank	BENSON p Am	Frank	LUCAS w,ct,po Br
Frank	BENSON(Sir)la,bio,e	Frank	MAXWELL tv+
Frank	BLAIR tv	Frank	MAYO
Frank	BONNER tv+	Frank	McCLURE tv
Frank	BORMAN as Am	Frank	McCOURT w Am
Frank	BORZARGE d+	Frank	McDONALD d
Frank	BRANA	Frank	McGEE tv
		Frank	McGRATH tv

Frank	McGUIRE bbc hf	Frankie	AVALON s,tv+ Am
Frank	McHUGH	Frankie	CARLE mj-piano Am
Frank	McRAE	Frankie	DARRO
Frank	MORGAN	Frankie	FAISON tv+
Frank	MOTT e,j,w Am	Frankie	FORD s Am
Frank	MUNSEY pb Am	Frankie	FRISCH b hf
Frank	NELSON tv	Frankie	HOWERD
Frank	NORRIS w Am	Frankie	LAINE s Am
Frank	O'CONNOR w Irish	Frankie	LYMON mr,tv Am
Frank	O'HARA po,ct-art,w Am	Frankie	THOMAS tv
Frank	ORTH tv	Frankie	THORN
Frank	OVERTON tv+	Frankie	VALLI s+ Am
Frank	OZ puppets,d,tv+ Br	Frankl,	PAUL ct-art,h Ger
Frank	PARKER tv	Franklin	ADAMS j-humor Am
Frank	PERRY d	Franklin	AJAYE
Frank	PIERSON d	Franklin	COVER tv
Frank	PUGLIA	Franklin	FARNUM
Frank	RAMSEY bb hf	Franklin,	ARETHA s-r&b Am
Frank	RICE	Franklin,	BENJAMIN st,w,i,sc Am
Frank	SCOTT piano,tv Am	Franklin,	BONNIE tv+
Frank	SILVERA tv+	Franklin,	CARL tv
Frank	SINATRA Jr.	Franklin,	CASS tv
Frank	SINATRA s,tv+ Am	Franklin,	DIANE
Frank	SMEDLEY w Br	Franklin,	DON tv
Frank	SPRAGUE eng-elec,i Am	Franklin,	JOHN(Sir)x
Frank	STEWART	Franklin,	MILES w Austr
Frank	STRAYER d	Franklin,	NANCY tv
Frank	SUTTON tv	Franklin,	PAMELA
Frank	TASHLIN d	Franklyn	SEALES tv+
Frank	THOMAS b	Franko,	IVAN w,j Ukraine
Frank	THOMAS tv	Franks,	CHLOE
Frank	VINCENT	Frann,	MARY
Frank	VIOLA b	Franny	MICHEL tv
Frank	WELKER tv	Frans	BLOM archeol Dan
Frank	WHALEY	Frans	DONDERS md,e Dut
Frank	WILCOX tv+	Frans	FRANZEN po Swe
Frank	WILLARD cr Am	Frans	HALS p Dut
Frank	WILMOT po Aust	Frans	SNYDERS p Dut
Frank	WILSON	Frantisek	KUPKA p,illus Cz
Frank	WISBAR tv	Frantisek	LANGER w,md Cz
Frank	WOLFF	Frantisek	RIEGER st Cz
Frank	YERBY w Am	Frantisek	SALDA ct,po,w Czech
Frank	ZAPPA mr+ Am	Frantisek	UDRZAL st Czech
Frank Lloyd WRIGHT ac Am		Frantz	FANON ph W.Ind
Frank,	ALLAN tv	Frantz,	CHRIS drm Am
Frank,	ANNE w Ger	Franz	ABT c Ger
Frank,	CARL tv	Franz	ACHARD sc, e Ger
Frank,	CHARLES tv+	Franz	BERWALD c Swe
Frank,	GARY tv+	Franz	BOAS an Am
Frank,	GLENN e,ed Am	Franz	BOPP w,e Ger
Frank,	HORST	Franz	EPP ar Ger
Frank,	ILYA n-p'58	Franz	ERKEL cn,c Hung
Frank,	JOANNA tv+	Franz	GALL md Ger
Frank,	LEONHARD w Ger	Franz	GEIBEL po Ger
Frank,	MELVIN d	Franz	GRUBER organ,c Aus
Frank,	RICHARD tv	Franz	HABERL r,m Ger
Frank,	WALDO w Am	Franz	HALDER ar Ger
Franken,	STEVE tv+	Franz	KAFKA w Aus
Frankenheimer, JOHN d		Franz	KLENZE ac Ger
Frankeur, PAUL		Franz	KLINE p Am
Frankfurter, FELIX e,l Am		Franz	KUGLER h-art Ger

Franz	LEHAR c Hung		Fred	FOY tv
Franz	LEYDIG sc Ger		Fred	GRAHAM
Franz	LISZT piano,c Hung		Fred	GRANDY tv
Franz	MARC p Ger		Fred	GWYNNE tv+
Franz	MESMER md Ger		Fred	HOYLE(Sir)sc,e,w-sifi
Franz	PFORR p Ger		Fred	KAREMAN tv
Franz	RICHTER c Ger		Fred	KOHLER Jr.
Franz	SIGEL ar,ed,pb Am		Fred	LYNN b
Franz	WERFEL po,w Ger		Fred	MacMURRAY tv+
Franz	WULLNER cn,c Ger		Fred	McGriff b
Franz	ZACH astron Ger		Fred	MILANO tenor Am
Franz von BAADER r,ph,w Ger			Fred	NIBLO d
Franz von EPP ar Ger			Fred	NOONAN flyer Am
Franz von HAUER geol Aus			Fred	NORRIS tv
Franz von MERCY ar Aus			Fred	RAY d
Franz von PAPEN st,ar Ger			Fred	ROBBINS tv
Franz von POCCI at,m,po Ger			Fred	ROSE w-cnt,s Am
Franz von STUCK p,su Ger			Fred	SAVAGE tv+
Franz,	ARTHUR		Fred	SCHEPISI d
Franz,	DENNIS tv+		Fred	SCOTT tv+
Franz,	EDUARD tv+		Fred	SHERMAN tv
Franz,	ROBERT organ,c Ger		Fred	SHIELDS tv
Franzen,	FRANS po Swe		Fred	STEIN tv
Franzen,	JONATHAN w Am		Fred	TAYLOR bbc hf
Fraser,	ANDY mr-bass Br		Fred	Van de VENTER tv
Fraser,	ANTONIA(Lady)w		Fred	WALTON d
Fraser,	BILL		Fred	WARD
Fraser,	BRENDAN		Fred	WARING mj,cn,tv Am
Fraser,	ELISABETH tv+		Fred	WILLARD tv+
Fraser,	G.S. po,ct Scot		Fred	ZIERER mj-violin Am
Fraser,	HARRY d		Freda	JACKSON
Fraser,	JAMES su Am		Freda	PAYNE s-r&b Am
Fraser,	LIZ		Freda,	RICARDO d
Fraser,	NEALE t Austra		Freddie	FRANCIS d
Fraser,	SALLY		Freddie	GARRITY mr-s Br
Fratkin,	STUART tv+		Freddie	JACKSON s-r&b,ws Am
Fraunhofer, JOSEPH von sc Ger			Freddie	JONES
Frawley,	WILLIAM tv+		Freddie	KEPPARD mj-trump,cn Am
Frayn,	MICHAEL j,w Br		Freddie	LEISTON tv
Frazee,	JANE tv+		Freddie	MARSDEN mr-drm Br
Frazer,	DAN tv		Freddie	PRINZE tv
Frazer,	JAMES(Sir)an,e Scot		Freddie	STONE mr-guit Am
Frazer,	JAYNE tv		Freddy	FENDER m-cnt,s
Frazer,	ROBERT		Freddy	MARTIN mj,cn Am
Frazier,	CHARLES w Am		Frederic	AUSTIN s,c Br
Frazier,	JOE boxer Am		Frederic	CHOPIN c Pol
Frazier,	SHEILA		Frederic	CHURCH p Am
Frazier,	WALT bb hf		Frederic	COWEN(Sir)c,cn
Frears,	STEPHEN d		Frederic	DANNAY w,ed Am
Freberg,	STAN cm,tv Am		Frederic	DeWILDE(Fritz)tv
Frechette, LOUIS j,po Can			Frederic	FARRAR r,w Br
Fred	ALLEN cm,tv+ Am		Frederic	FOREST tv
Fred	ASTAIRE ba+ Am		Frederic	GOUDY id-print Am
Fred	BERRY tv		Frederic	IVES i Am
Fred	BRANNON d		Frederic	La HARPE st Swi
Fred	CLARK tv+		Frederic	Le PLAY eng-mines Fr
Fred	CLARKE b hf		Frederic	LENNE tv+
Fred	COE tv-pr		Frederic	MANNING w Aust
Fred	DRYER tv+		Frederic	MISTRAL po Fr
Fred	EBB lyrics Am		Frederic	PASSY ec,st Fr
Fred	FISHER c Am		Frederic	SAUSER w Swi

Frederic   SEEBOHM h-ec Br
Frederick ABEL(Sir) sc
Frederick ALLEN ed,w Am
Frederick ARCHER fo,su Br
Frederick ARCHER jockey Br
Frederick ASHTON(Sir)ba
Frederick BANTING(Sir)md Can
Frederick BONFILS pb Am
Frederick BOWER sc,e Br
Frederick CHURCH p Am
Frederick COFFIN
Frederick COOK md,x Am
Frederick CROUCH m,c Br
Frederick DELIUS c Br
Frederick EVANS fo Br
Frederick FAUST w Am
Frederick FLEAY h Br
Frederick GENTH sc,e Am
Frederick GREENE tv
Frederick GROVE w Can
Frederick HOPKINS(Sir)sc,e
Frederick JANE w Br
Frederick KIESLER ac,su Am
Frederick KOEHLER tv
Frederick LENZ(Rama)w,cults Am
Frederick LOEWE piano,c Am
Frederick NIVEN w Scot
Frederick NOVY sc Am
Frederick O'NEAL tv
Frederick OLMSTED ac-land Am
Frederick OPPER illus,cr Am
Frederick PASSY st Fr
Frederick PIPER
Frederick PURSH sc,w Am
Frederick ROBBINS md Am
Frederick ROLFE w Br
Frederick SANGER sc Br
Frederick SEARLE j,w Br
Frederick SELOUS hunter,x Br
Frederick SIEVERS su Am
Frederick SODDY sc,e Br
Frederick STANG l,st Nor
Frederick STOKES(Sir)i,eng
Frederick TURNER h,e Am
Frederick VALK
Frederick VINSON l,ch just Am
Frederick WARNE pb Br
Frederick ZEUNER geol,e Br
Frederick,HAL tv
Frederick,LYNNE
Fredericks, DEAN tv
Frederico GAMBOA w Mex
Frederico PENA st
Frederik   POHL w Am
Frederik de KLERK ac Dut
Frederik van EEDEN w,md Dut
Fredric   LEHNE tv+
Fredric   MARCH la+ Am
Fredrick   PIPER
Fredrik   BAJER st,w Dan

Fredrik   FERSEN st,ar Swe
Fredrik   PACIUS violin,c Finn
Fredrik   STORMER math,sc,e Nor
Fredrika   BREMER w Swe
Fredriksson, MARIE mr-s Swe
Fredro,   ALEKSANDER w Pol
Freed,   ALAN
Freed,   BERT
Freed,   PAULIE mj-piano Am
Freed,   SAM tv
Freedley, VINTON tv
Freedman, WINIFRED tv
Freeling, NICOLAS w Br
Freeman   CROFTS eng,w Irish
Freeman   GOSDEN tv
Freeman   KING tv
Freeman,   AL Jr. tv+
Freeman,   BOBBY s,ws Am
Freeman,   DAMITA JO tv
Freeman,   DEENA tv
Freeman,   DOUGLAS ed,p-b'35'58
Freeman,   HOWARD
Freeman,   J. PAUL tv
Freeman,   J.E.
Freeman,   JOAN
Freeman,   KATHLEEN tv+
Freeman,   MARY w Am
Freeman,   MICKEY tv
Freeman,   MONA
Freeman,   MORGAN d+
Freeman,   PAM tv
Freeman,   PAUL
Freeman,   RALPH(Sir)eng
Freeman,   RICHARD md,w Br
Freeman,   TICKER piano,tv Am
Freemont   RIDER ed,pb Am
Freer,   CHARLESart collect Am
Frees,   PAUL tv+
Frege,   GOTTLOB math,ph,e Ger
Frehley,   ACE mr-guit,s Am
Frei,   EDUARDO st Chile
Freiberg, DAVID mr-bass Am
Freire,   RAMON ar,st Chile
Fremont,   JOHN x,ar,st Am
Fremstad, OLIVE soprano Am
Fremy,   EDMOND sc,e Fr
French,   AARON i Am
French,   ALICE w Am
French,   CHARLES
French,   DANIEL su Am
French,   EDWIGE
French,   LEIGH cm, tv
French,   MARILYN w Am
French,   VICTOR tv+
Freneau,   PHILIP po Am
Freni,   MIRELLA s-opera It
Frere,   JOHN antiquary Br
Freron,   ELIE j,ed Fr
Fresnay,   PIERRE la+ Fr
Fresnel,   AUGUSTIN sc Fr
Fresson,   BERNAARD

Freud,	LUCIAN p Br
Freud,	SIGMUND md,ps Aus
Frewer,	MATT tv+
Frey,	ADOLF po,h Swi
Frey,	GLENN ws,s Am
Frey,	LEONARD
Frey,	SAMI
Freya	STARK(Dame)w Br
Freyre,	GILBERTO an,h Braz
Freytag,	GUSTAV w Ger
Frick,	FORD b hf
Frick,	HENRY id Am
Fricker,	BRENDA o-s'89
Frid,	JONATHAN
Frida	LYNGSTAD mr-s Swe
Frida,	EMIL w Czech
Fridtjof	NANSEN x,sc,st Nor
Friebus,	FLORIDA tv
Fried,	ALFRED n-x'11
Fried,	IAN tv
Fried,	OSKAR c,cn Ger
Frieda	HEMPEL soprano Ger
Frieda	INESCORT tv+
Friedan,	BETTY fe Am
Friederike	NEUBER la Ger
Friedkin,	WILLIAM o-d'71
Friedlieb	RUNGE sc Ger
Friedman,	BRUCE w Am
Friedman,	JEROME I. n-p'90
Friedman,	MAX bb hf
Friedman,	MILTON n-e'76
Friedman,	PETER tv+
Friedrich	BAYER id Ger
Friedrich	BESSEL astron,e Ger
Friedrich	BEUST st Ger
Friedrich	ENGELS re,w Ger
Friedrich	FESCA violin,c Ger
Friedrich	FLOTOW c Ger
Friedrich	FOUQUE w Ger
Friedrich	GOLTZ md.e Ger
Friedrich	HEBBEL po,w Ger
Friedrich	JACOBI ph,w,e Ger
Friedrich	KAPP st Ger
Friedrich	KLINGER w Ger
Friedrich	KONIG i,id-print Ger
Friedrich	KRUPP id-iron Ger
Friedrich	LOFFLER sc Ger
Friedrich	MOHS minerals,e Ger
Friedrich	MURNAU d ger
Friedrich	PANETH sc,e Aus
Friedrich	PLUMPE d Ger
Friedrich	RATZEL geog,e Ger
Friedrich	RITSCHL w Ger
Friedrich	ROEMER geol,e Ger
Friedrich	RUCKERT po Ger
Friedrich	SCHUR math,e Ger
Friedrich	VISCHER po,ct,e Ger
Friedrich	WENT sc,e Dut
Friedrich	WITT cello,c Ger
Friedrich	WOHLER sc,e Ger
Friedrich	ZACHOW organ,c,e Ger

Friedrich von CANITZ st,po Ger	
Friedrich von HAYEK ec Aus	
Friedrich von HUGEL r Br	
Friedrich,CASPER p Ger	
Friedrich,JOHN	
Friels,	COLIN
Friendly,	FRED e,tv-exec Am
Fries,	ELIAS sc,e Swe
Friesz,	OTHON p Fr
Frigyes	RIESZ math,e Hung
Friis,	JOHANN st Dan
Friml,	RUDOLF piano,c Am
Frings,	KETTI p-d'58
Friniwyd	JESSE w Br
Fripp,	ROBERT mr-guit Br
Frisch,	FRANKIE b-mv'31 hf
Frisch,	KARL von n-m'73
Frisch,	MAX w Swi
Frisch,	RAGNER n-e'69
Frischman,DAN tv	
Frisi,	PAOLO sc,astr,e It
Frith,	REBECCA la+ Aust
Frith,	WILLIAM p Br
Frits	ZERNIKE sc,e Dut
Fritsch,	WILLY
Fritts,	STAN m,cn,tv Am
Fritz	DeWILDE tv
Fritz	FELD
Fritz	HABER sc Ger
Fritz	KIERSCH d
Fritz	KORTNER
Fritz	LANG d,pr Am
Fritz	LIPMANN md Am
Fritz	LONDON sc,e Ger
Fritz	MONDALE(Walter)st Am
Fritz	PREGL sc Aus
Fritz	RASP
Fritz	REINER cn Am
Fritz	TODT eng-ar Ger
Fritz	WEAVER
Fritz	ZWICKY astro,sc,e Swi
Fritz von BELOW ar Ger	
Fritz von OPEL id-cars Ger	
Fritz von UHDE p Ger	
Fritz von UNRUH w,po Ger	
Frizzel,	LOU tv
Frizzell,	LEFTY s-cntry Am
Frobe,	GERT
Frobisher,MARTIN(Sir)x	
Froding,	GUSTAF po Swe
Froissart,JEAN po Fr	
Froler,	SAMUEL
Froman,	DAVID tv
Frome,	MILTON tv+
Fromental	HALEVY c,e Fr
Fromm,	ERICH ps,w Am
Frost,	ALICE tv
Frost,	ARTHUR illus Am
Frost,	CRAIG mr-kbds Am
Frost,	DAVID tv
Frost,	EDWIN astr Am

Frost,	LINDSAY tv+
Frost,	RBRT. p-q'24'31'37'43
Frost,	SADIE
Frost,	TERRY
Frost,	WARREN tv+
Fry,	CHRISTOPHER w Br
Fry,	ELIZABETH f Br
Fry,	MARTIN mr-s Br
Fry,	ROGER ct,p Br
Fry,	STEPHEN w Br
Fry,	TAYLOR tv+
Fry,	WILLIAM c,ct Am
Fryderyk	SKARBEK w,ec Pol
Frye,	CHIP tv
Frye,	DWIGHT
Frye,	NORTHROP ct,w Can
Frye,	SOLEIL MOON tv
Frye,	VIRGIL
Fuad Pasa,	MEHMED st Turk
Fuccello,	TOM tv
Fuchs,	GABY
Fuchs,	IMMANUEL math,e Ger
Fuchs,	KLAUS sc,spy Ger
Fuchs,	LEO
Fuchsberger,	JOACHIM
Fucini,	RENATO po,w It
Fud	CANDRIX mj-sax,cn Belg
Fuentes,	CARLOS w Mex
Fuertes,	LOUIS illus Am
Fuest,	ROBERT d
Fugard,	ATHOL w,d+ S.Afr
Fujimori,	ALBERTO st Peru
Fujioka,	JOHN tv+
Fukada,	JUN d
Fukui,	KENICHI n-c'81
Fukuyama,	FRANCIS w
Fulci,	LUCIO d
Fulger,	HOLLY tv
Fulke	GREVILLEpo,courtierBr
Fulks,	JOE bb hf
Fuller,	BUCKMINSTER eng,i Am
Fuller,	CHARLES p-d'82
Fuller,	CHRISTOPHER tv
Fuller,	GEORGE p Am
Fuller,	HENRY w Am
Fuller,	KURT
Fuller,	LANCE
Fuller,	LOIE ba Am
Fuller,	MARGARET fe,ct,e Am
Fuller,	PENNY
Fuller,	R.BUCKMINSTER ac Am
Fuller,	ROBERT tv+
Fuller,	ROY po,w Br
Fuller,	SAMUEL d+
Fuller,	THOMAS r,w Br
Fullerton,	MELANIE tv
Fulmer,	RAY tv
Fulton	MacKAY
Fulton	OURSLER j,w Am
Fulton	SHEEN Cath. Bishop
Fulton,	EILEEN tv

Fulton,	ROBERT eng,i Am
Fulton,	WENDY tv
Funakoshi,	EIJI
Funicello,	ANNETTE tv+
Funk,	CASIMIR sc Am
Funk,	ISAAC pb,ed Am
Funt,	ALLEN tv
Funt,	PETER tv
Furay,	RICHIE mr-guitar,s Am
Furchgott,	ROBERT n-m'98
Furey,	JOHN
Furie,	SIDNEY d
Furlong,	EDWARD
Furlong,	KIRBY tv
Furman,	LAURA w Am
Furneaux,	YVONNE
Furness,	BETTY tv+
Furness,	FRANK ac Am
Furnifold	SIMMONS st Am
Furniss,	HARRY illus Br
Furphy,	JOSEPH w Austr
Furrer,	JONAS st Swi
Furse,	CHARLES p Br
Furst,	JOSEPH
Furst,	STEPHEN tv+
Furth,	GEORGE tv+
Furuholmen,	MAGS mr-kbds,s Nor
Fusco,	PAUL tv
Fuseli,	HENRY p Br
Futabatei	Shimei ---w Jap
Fux,	JOHANN c Aus
Fuzzy	KNIGHT
Fuzzy	St. JOHN
Fuzzy	VANDIVIER bb hf
Fyffe,	WILL la+ Scot
Fyodor	GLADKOV w Rus
Fyodor	LITKE x,geog Rus
Fyodor	SOLOGUB w,po Rus
Fyodor	TREPOV st-police Rus
Fyodor	VOLKOV la Rus

"G" NAME DESIGNATION CODES

g	-	GOLFER
geog	-	GEOGRAPHER
geol	-	GEOLOGIST
gg	-	BASEBALL GOLD GLOVER
gy	-	GYMNAST
g-r	-	GRAMMY AWARD

"G" NATIONALITY CODES

Ger - GERMAN   Gr - GREEK

"G's"

G. Gordon	LIDDY st,tv+ Am
G. Wilson	KNIGHT ct,w Br
G.E.	MOORE ph,e Br
G.E.	SMITH m,cn,tv Am
G.S.	FRASER po,ct Scot
G.W.	BAILEY tv+

G.W.	CURTIS w,ed Am	Gaby	HOFFMAN
Gabai,	RICHARD	Gadda,	CARLO w It
Gabaldon,	DIANA w	Gaddi,	TADDEO p It
Gabb,	PETER tv	Gaddis,	WILLIAM w Am
Gabby	HARTNETT b	Gade,	NIELS c Dan
Gabby	HAYES	Gael	GREENE ct-food Am
Gabe	DRAKE m-bass,tv Am	Gael,	ANNA
Gabe	GALINAS mj-sax Am	Gaetano	DONIZETTI c It
Gabe	KAPLAN cm,tv+ Am	Gaetano	MOSCA sc-politic,e It
Gabe	KOTTER fc	Gaffin,	MELANIE tv
Gabe	WITCHER tv	Gagarin,	YURY 1st Russ as
Gabel,	SCILLA	Gage	CLARK tv
Gabin,	JEAN la+ Fr	Gage,	NICHOLAS w Am
Gable,	CHRISTOPHER ba+ Br	Gagern,	HANS st Ger
Gable,	CLARK o-a'34	Gagnier,	HOLLY tv
Gable,	JUNE tv	Gagnier,	JASMINE tv
Gabo,	NAUM su Am	Gago,	JENNY tv+
Gabor	BETHLEN king Hung	Gahan	WILSON cr Am
Gabor,	DENNIS n-p'71	Gahan,	DAVE mr-s Br
Gabor,	EVA tv+	Gahn,	JOHAN sc Swe
Gabor,	MAGDA	Gaia	GERMANI
Gabor,	ZSA ZSA	Gail	BOGGS tv
Gaboriau,	EMILE w Fr	Gail	BORDEN i Am
Gabriel	BIEL ph,e Ger	Gail	COMPTON tv
Gabriel	BYRNE	Gail	DAVIS tv+
Gabriel	DAMON tv+	Gail	DEVERS runner Am
Gabriel	DELL tv+	Gail	EDWARDS tv+
Gabriel	DOYEN p Fr	Gail	FISHER tv
Gabriel	FAURE c Fr	Gail	GODWIN w Am
Gabriel	GARCIA w Col	Gail	JOHNSON tv
Gabriel	HEATTER j,radio Am	Gail	KOBE tv
Gabriel	LAME math,eng,e Fr	Gail	KUBIK c Am
Gabriel	MABLY ph,h Fr	Gail	O'GRADY
Gabriel	MARCEL ph,w,ct Fr	Gail	PATRICK
Gabriel	MARQUEZ w	Gail	RUSSELL
Gabriel	MELGAR tv	Gail	SHEEHY w Am
Gabriel	METSU p Dut	Gail	YOUNGS
Gabriel	MIRO w Sp	Gail,	MAX
Gabriel	NAUDE md,h Fr	Gail,	MAXWELL tv
Gabriel	OKARA po,w Nigeria	Gailard	SARTAIN tv+
Gabriel	OUVARD bus,f Am	Gaile,	JERI tv
Gabriel	PIERNE cn,c Fr	Gaillard,	DAVID ar,eng Am
Gabriel	TERRA l,st Uruguay	Gaines,	BOYD tv+
Gabriel	VOISIN id-planes Fr	Gaines,	CLARENCE bbc hf
Gabriel de VALDES po Cuba		Gaines,	ERNEST w Am
Gabriel,	PETER s Br	Gaines,	JIM tv+
Gabriel,	ROMAN fb-m'69	Gains,	COURTNEY
Gabriela	MISTRAL po Chile	Gainsborough, THOMAS p Br	
Gabriela	SABATINI t Arg	Gainsbourg, SERGE	
Gabriele	TINTI	Gaitan,	JORGE st Colum
Gabrieli,	ANDREA organ,c It	Gaitskill,MARY w Am	
Gabriella PALLOTTI		Gaius Helvius CINNA po Ro	
Gabrielle ANWAR		Gaj,	LJUDEVIT w Croat
Gabrielle CARTERIS tv+		Gajdusek, CARLETON n-m'76	
Gabrielle CHANEL(Coco)ds Fr		Galabru,	MICHEL
Gabrielle LONG w Br		Galarraga,ANDRES b rbi'96 &	
Gabrielle ROSE		Galarraga,ANDRES bat'93	
Gabrielle ROY w Can		Galaup,	JEAN de x Fr
Gabrielle, MONIQUE		Galaxy	CRAZE w+
Gaby	ANDRE	Galba,	SERVIUS st Ro
Gaby	FUCHS	Galbraith,JOHN ec,w Am	

Gale	GORDON tv+
Gale	HANSEN
Gale	ROBBINS
Gale	SAYERS fb hf
Gale	STORM tv+
Gale,	DAVID
Gale,	EDDRA
Gale,	JUNE
Gale,	LAUREN bb hf
Gale,	ZONA p-d'21
Galeazzo	ALESI ac It
Galeazzo	CAMPI p It
Galeazzo	CIANO st It
Galen	--- md,ph Gr
Gales,	JOSEPH j,pb Am
Galiena,	ANNA
Galik,	DENISE tv
Galilei,	GALILEO sc,ph It
Galina,	STACY tv
Galinas,	GABE mj-sax Am
Gall(Pizi)	---Indian Chief Am
Gall,	FRANZ md Ger
Gallagher,	MEGAN tv+
Gallagher,	PETER
Gallagher,	RICHARD(Skeets)
Gallant,	MAVIS w Can
Gallatin,	HARRY bb hf
Gallaudet,	THOMAS e-deaf Am
Galle,	EMILE id-glass Fr
Galle,	JOHANN astron Ger
Gallego,	GINA tv+
Gallego,	JUAN po Sp
Gallegos,	ROMULO w,e,st It
Galli-Curci,	AMELITA soprano Am
Gallichio,	JOSEPH m,cn,tv Am
Gallico,	PAUL j,w Am
Galligan,	ZACH
Gallimard,	GASTON pb Fr
Gallio,	JUNIUS st Ro
Gallison,	JOE tv
Gallivan,	MEGAN tv
Gallo,	LEW tv
Gallo,	MARIO tv
Gallo,	WILLIAM tv
Gallop,	FRANK tv
Galloway,	DON tv+
Galloway,	MICHAEL tv
Gallup,	GEORGE polls Am
Galsworthy,	JOHN n-l'32
Galt,	JOHN w Scot
Galton,	FRANCIS(Sir)sc
Galusha	GROW st Am
Galvani,	LUIGI md,sc It
Galvez,	JOSE
Galvez,	MANUEL w Arg
Galvin,	PUD b hf
Galway	KINNELL w,po Am
Galway,	JAMES m-flute Ir
Galyn	GORG
Gam,	RITA
Gama,	JOSE po Braz

Gama,	VASCO Da x Port
Gamal	NASSER st Egypt
Gamboa,	FEDERICO w Mex
Gambon,	MICHAEL
Gammell,	ROBIN
Gammon,	JAMES
Gamow,	GEORGE sc,e Am
Gampu,	KEN
Gance,	ABEL d Fr
Gandhi,	INDIRA st India
Gandhi,	MAHATMA st India
Gandhi,	RAJIV flyer,st India
Gandolf,	RAY tv
Gandolfini,	AMES
Ganios,	TONY
Ganivet,	ANGEL w Sp
Ganjiro	NAKAMURA
Ganku	--- p Jap
Gannett,	HENRY geog Am
Gans,	DANNY tv
Gans,	JOE boxer Am
Ganus,	PAUL
Ganz,	BRUNO
Ganz,	RUDOLPH c,cn Am
Ganzel,	TERESA tv
Gaon,	YEHORAM
Gar	MOORE
Garagiola,	JOE b,tv
Garand,	JOHN i Am
Garas,	KAZ
Garasanin,	ILIJA st Serbia
Garber,	JOSEPH w Am
Garber,	TERRI tv
Garbo(u)rg,	ARNE w,po Nor
Garbo,	GRETA
Garborg,	ARNE w,po Nor
Garces,	MAURICIO
Garcia	ROBLES st Mex
Garcia,	ANDY
Garcia,	CARLOS st Phil
Garcia,	GABRIEL w Col
Garcia,	NICOLE
Gard,	ROGER du n-l'37
Garde,	BETTY tv
Garden,	MARY soprano Am
Gardener,	HELEN fe Am
Gardenia,	VINCENT tv+
Gardiner,	HERB ho-m'27
Gardiner,	REGINALD tv+
Gardiner,	SAMUEL h Br
Gardner	REA cr Am
Gardner,	AVA tv+
Gardner,	CARL mr-s Am
Gardner,	CRAIG tv
Gardner,	ERLE STANLEY w Am
Gardner,	HY tv
Gardner,	JACK bbc, hf
Gardner,	JOAN
Gardner,	JOHN w,h Am
Gardner,	PERCY arc,e Br
Gardner,	TERRI tv

Gareth	HUNT	Garrick,	DAVID la,pr Br
Garette	RATLIFFE tv	Garrick,	JOHN
Garewood	VAN mj,cn Am	Garrigue,	JEAN po,w Am
Garfat,	JANCE mr-bass,s Am	Garrison	KEILLOR w Am
Garfield	OXNAM r,e,w Am	Garrison,	DAVID tv+
Garfield	WOOD id-boats,racr	Garrison,	WILLIAM j,pb Am
Garfield,	ALLEN(Gooritz)	Garrity,	FREDDIE mr-s Br
Garfield,	JAMES ABRAM 20thPres	Garros,	PEY de po Fr
Garfield,	JOHN	Garros,	ROLAND flyer Fr
Garfield,	JOHN DAVID	Garroway,	DAVID(Dave)tv-hostAm
Garfolo,	JANEANE	Garry	GOODROW
Garfunkel,	ART s+ Am	Garry	MARSH
Gargan,	WILLIAM tv+	Garry	MOORE tv
Gari	MELCHERS p Am	Garry	TRUDEAU cr Am
Garis,	HOWARD w Am	Garry	WALBERG tv
Garko,	GIANNO	Garry	WILLS w Am
Garko,	JOHN	Garry	WILLS w Am
Garland,	ALEX w Br	Garshin,	VSEVOLOD w Rus
Garland,	BEVERLY tv+	Garson	KANIN d
Garland,	HAMLIN p-b'22	Garson,	GREER o-a'42
Garland,	JUDY g-r'61,tv+	Garth	BROOKS s-cntry Am
Garland,	MARGARET tv	Garth	HUDSON organ Br
Garland,	RED mj-piano Am	Garth,	JENNIE tv
Garlington,	LEE	Garton,	DICK tv
Garn	STEPHENS tv	Gartside,	GREEN mr-s Welsh
Garneau,	FRANCOIS h,po Can	Garver,	KATHY tv
Garner,	ERROL mj-piano,c Am	Garvey,	CYNDY tv
Garner,	JACK tv	Garvey,	STEVE b-mv'74,tv
Garner,	JAMES tv+	Garwood,	JULIE w Am
Garner,	JAMES FINN(J.F.)w Am	Gary	ALDRICH w Am
Garner,	JOHN NANCE st Am	Gary	ALLEN tv
Garner,	MOUSIE tv	Gary	BAYER tv+
Garner,	PEGGY	Gary	BEACOM sk Can
Garnett,	DAVID w Br	Gary	BECKER ec Am
Garnett,	EDWARD ct,w Br	Gary	BONDS(U.S.)mr,s Am
Garnett,	KEVIN bb	Gary	BROOKER mr-kbds,s Br
Garnett,	TAY d	Gary	BUSEY
Garnier,	ANTOINE(Tony)ac Fr	Gary	CHAPMAN s,c Am
Garnier,	ROBERT w Fr	Gary	CLARKE tv+
Garofalo,	JANEANE cm,tv+	Gary	COLE tv+
Garr,	RALPH b.bat'74	Gary	COLEMAN tv+
Garr,	TERI tv+	Gary	COLLINS tv
Garralaga,	MARTIN	Gary	CONWAY tv+
Garrani,	IVO	Gary	COOPER
Garrett	BROWN tv	Gary	CROSBY tv+
Garrett	MORRIS tv+	Gary	DALY mr-s Br
Garrett	TAYLOR tv	Gary	DUBIN tv
Garrett,	BETTY tv+	Gary	DUNCAN mr-guit Am
Garrett,	ED tv	Gary	FRANK tv+
Garrett,	GEORGE po,w Am	Gary	GLITTER s,ws Br
Garrett,	HANK tv+	Gary	GRAHAM tv+
Garrett,	JIMMY tv	Gary	GRAVER d
Garrett,	JOAO w,st Port	Gary	GRAY
Garrett,	KATHLEEN tv	Gary	GRIMES
Garrett,	KELLY tv	Gary	HART st Am,
Garrett,	LEIF	Gary	HIRSCH(Chicken)mr Br
Garrett,	PATSY tv+	Gary	HUDSON
Garrett,	SUSIE tv	Gary	KEMP mr-guit Br
Garrick	UTLEY tv-j,anchor Am	Gary	KROEGER tv+
Garrick,	BARBARA	Gary	LAKE p,at Am
		Gary	LAKES tenor Am

Gary	LARSON cr Am	Gatti,	JENNIFER
Gary	LEEDS m-drm Am	Gatty,	HAROLD flyer Austr
Gary	LEWIS mr-drm,s Am	Gaudenzio	FERRARI p It
Gary	MERRILL tv+	Gaudi,	ANTONIO ac Sp
Gary	MORRIS s-cnt,tv Am	Gaudio,	BOB organ,s Am
Gary	NELSON d	Gauge,	ALEXANDER tv
Gary	NUMAN mr-s Br	Gauguin,	PAUL p Fr
Gary	OLDMAN	Gaulle,	CHARLES de ar,st Fr
Gary	OWENS tv+	Gaurini,	GIAMBATTISTA po It
Gary	PAGETT tv	Gauss,	CARL astr,e Ger
Gary	PAYTON bb	Gauthier,	DAN tv+
Gary	RAYMOND tv+	Gautier,	DICK tv+
Gary	SANDY tv	Gautier,	THEOPHILE /po,w Fr
Gary	SHERMAN d	Gavan	O'HERLIHY tv+
Gary	SINISE	Gavin	GORDON
Gary	SNYDER po,w Am	Gavin	MacLEOD tv+
Gary	SWANSON	Gavin	MAXWELL w,bio Scot
Gary	SWEET	Gavin	MILLAR d
Gary	TALLEY mr-guit Am	Gavin	MUIR tv+
Gary	THORNE tv	Gavin,	JAMES ar Am
Gary	VINSON tv	Gavin,	JOHN
Gary,	BRUCE mr-drm Am	Gavrilo	PRINCIPassassin Serb
Gary,	ELBERT l,id Am	Gawin	DOUGLAS po,r Scot
Gary,	LORRAINE	Gay	COMPTON tv
Gary,	ROMAIN w Fr	Gay	HAGEN tv
Gascoigne,	GEORGE po Br	Gay	TALESE w Am
Gaskell,	ELIZABETH w Br	Gay,	JOHN po,w Br
Gaspar	CORTE-REAL x Port	Gay-Lussac,	JOSEPH sc,e Fr
Gaspar de	PORTOLA ar Sp	Gaye,	LISA tv+
Gaspara	STAMPA po It	Gaye,	MARVIN mr,s Am
Gaspard	DUGHET p Fr	Gaye,	PAT tv
Gaspard	MOLLIEN x,st Fr	Gayle	HUNNICUTT tv+
Gaspard	MONGE math,sc,e Fr	Gayle,	CRYSTAL s-cntry Am
Gaspard	RICHE math,eng Fr	Gayle,	JACKIE
Gasparo	ASELLI md It	Gayle,	TINA tv
Gasparo	GOZZI w It	Gayley,	JAMES sc,i Am
Gaspe,	PHILIPPE de w Can	Gaylor,	RUTH mj-s Am
Gass,	WILLIAM w,ph Am	Gaylord	PERRY b hf
Gasser,	HERBERT n-m'44	Gaylord,	MITCH gy Am
Gassman,	VITTORIO	Gaynes,	GEORGE tv+
Gaster,	MOSES r,e Br	Gaynor,	JANET o-a'28
Gastineau,	MARK fb-d'82	Gaynor,	JOCK tv
Gaston	BATY w,pr Fr	Gaynor,	MITZI
Gaston	DUCHAMP p,etch Fr	Gazelle,	WENDY
Gaston	FLANDIN ph,st Fr	Gazzara,	BEN tv+
Gaston	LEROUX w Fr	Gazzo,	MICHAEL
Gaston	MEANS swindler Am	Geary,	ANTHONY
Gaston	MODOT	Geary,	BUD
Gaston	RAMON sc Fr	Geary	CYNTHIA tv
Gastoni,	LISA	Geary,	PAUL tv
Gates	McFADDEN tv+	Ged,	WILLIAM at-gold Scot
Gates,	DAVID mr-keybds,s Am	Gedda,	NICOLAI tenor Swe
Gates,	LARRY	Gedde	WATANABE
Gates,	NANCY	Geddes,	NORMAN BEL ds,ac Am
Gates,	POP bb hf	Geddes,	PATRICK(Sir)sc,eScot
Gates,	RUTH tv	Geddy	LEE mr-bass,s Can
Gateson,	MARJORIE tv+	Gedrick,	JASON
Gatlin Bros.:	RUDIE,STEVE s Am	Geena	DAVIS tv+
Gatlin,	RUDY s Am	Geer,	DIRK JAN de st Dut
Gatsby,	JILL	Geer,	ELLEN tv+
Gatsky,	FRANK fb hf	Geer,	WILL tv+

Geeson,	JUDY	Gene	WILDER
Geeson,	SALLY	Genee,	ADELINE (Dame) ba Dan
Geezer	BUTLER mr-bass Br	Genesse,	BRYAN tv+
Geffen,	DAVID pr-records Am	Genet,	JEAN w Fr
Gehman,	MARTHA	Genet,	MICHAEL tv
Gehrig,	LOU b-mv'36 hf	Genevieve BUJOLD	
Gehring,	TED tv	Genevieve PAGE	
Gehringer,	CHARLEY b-mv'37 hf	Genghis Kahn	--- st Mongol
Gehringer,	LINDA tv	Genie	FRANCIS tv+
Geibel,	FRANZ po Ger	Genn,	LEO
Geiger,	JOHANNES sc Ger	Gennaro,	PETER tv
Geijer,	ERIK h,e,c,po Swe	Gennes,	PIERRE de n-p'91
Geikie,	ARCHIBALD (Sir) geoScot	Gennie	JAMES
Geils,	J. mr-guit Am	Geno	SILVA
Geisel,	THEODOR SEUSS w Am	Genovese,	MIKE tv
Gelber,	JACK w Am	Genth,	FREDERICK sc,e Am
Gelbwaks,	JEREMY tv+	Gentil,	EMILE st Fr
Gelder,	AERT p Dut	Gentile	BELLINI p It
Geldof,	BOB mr-s+ Ir	Gentile da Fabriano	--- p It
Gelett	BURGESS illus,w Am	Gentileschi, ORAZIO p It	
Gelin,	DANIEL	Gentleman JACKSON boxer Br	
Gell-Mann,	MURRAY n-p'69	Gentleman Jim CORBETT boxer Am	
Gellee.	CLAUDE p Fr	Gentry,	MINNIE
Geller,	HARRY tv	Geny,	FRANCOIS l,e Fr
Geller,	URI magic Aus	Geoff	EDWARDS tv
Gellis,	DANNY tv	Geoffrey	BEENE ds Am
Gellius,	AULUS w Roman	Geoffrey	CHAUCER po Br
Gelman,	KIMIKO tv	Geoffrey	DAVIES tv
Gelman,	LARRY tv+	Geoffrey	DENNIS w Br
Gemier,	FIRMIN la FR	Geoffrey	EWING tv
Gemignani,	RHODA tv	Geoffrey	FABER (Sir) pb,w
Gemma	JONES	Geoffrey	HOLDER
Gemma,	GIULIANO	Geoffrey	HORNBY (Sir) navy
Gemser,	LAURA	Geoffrey	KEEN
Gena	ROWLANDS tv+	Geoffrey	LEWIS tv+
Gene	AUTRY s,tv+	Geoffrey	LOWER tv
Gene	BARRY	Geoffrey	NAUFFTS tv
Gene	CORNISH mr-guit Can	Geoffrey	NORMAN w Am
Gene	EVANS tv+	Geoffrey	O'HARA c,ws Am
Gene	HACKMAN	Geoffrey	OWENS tv
Gene	KARDOS mj,cn Am	Geoffrey	RUSH
Gene	KELLY tv+	Geoffrey	SCOTT tv+
Gene	KRUPA mj-drm tv+	Geoffrey	THORNE tv
Gene	LYONS tv	Geoffrey	TORY p Fr
Gene	NELSON s+ Am	Geoffrey	WOLFF w Am
Gene	PITNEY s,ws Am	Geoffreys, STEPHEN	
Gene	PORTER w Am	Geoffrion, BERNIE ho-m'29	
Gene	RAY tv	Georg	BOHM organ,c Ger
Gene	RAYBURN tv	Georg	BRANDES ct Dan
Gene	RAYMOND tv+	Georg	BUCHNER w Ger
Gene	ROSS	Georg	DONNER su Aus
Gene	SAKS d+	Georg	EBERS w Ger
Gene	SARAZEN g Am	Georg	GORTZ st Ger
Gene	SHALIT ct-films,tv Am	Georg	HARING j,w Ger
Gene	SHELDON tv+	Georg	HEGEL ph,e Ger
Gene	SIMMONS	Georg	HERMES r,ph,e Ger
Gene	SIMMONS mr-s Israel	Georg	HERWEGH po Ger
Gene	SISKEL ct-films,tv	Georg	HEYM po Ger
Gene	TIERNEY	Georg	KAISER w Ger
Gene	TUNNEY boxer Am	Georg	LIST ec,w Am
Gene	UPSHAW fb hf	Georg	MOLLER ac Ger

Georg	MUFFAT c Ger	George	CHESTER w Am
Georg	MULLER ps,e Ger	George	CISAR tv
Georg	OHM sc,e Ger	George	CLARK re,ar Am
Georg	PENCZ p,engr Ger	George	CLINTON s-funk Am
Georg	PERTZ h Ger	George	CLOONEY tv+
Georg	QUINCKE sc,e Ger	George	COE
Georg	RIEMANN math,e Ger	George	COLE
Georg	RUMPF sc Ger	George	COLE ec,e Br
Georg	SIMMEL ph,e Ger	George	COLMAN(Elder)w Br
Georg	SOLTI cn Hung	George	CONNOR fb hf
Georg	STELLER sc,x Ger	George	COOK w,po Am
Georg	TRAKL po Aus	George	COOPER
Georg	VOGLER organ,c,w Ger	George	CORLISS i,id Am
Georg	WAITZ h Ger	George	COX w Br
Georg	WISSOWA w Ger	George	CRABBE po Br
Georg	WITTIG sc,e Ger	George	CREEL j,ed Am
Georg Stanford BROWN tv+		George	CRUMB c Am
Georg von BEKESY ps Am		George	CUKOR d+
Georg von HEVESY sc,e Hung		George	CURTIS l,w Am
Georgann JOHNSON tv		George	CUSTER ar Am
George	ABBOTT d,w Am	George	DALLAS st-vp Am
George	ADE w-humor Am	George	DANCE ac Br
George	AIKEN la,w Am	George	DARLEY po Irish
George	AIRY(Sir)astr	George	DASENT(Sir)e,ed
George	ANGAS mer,ships Br	George	DELOY tv
George	ANSON navy Br	George	DERN id-mines,st Am
George	ARLISS la+ Br	George	DEVEY ac Br
George	ARTHUR(Sir)ar,st	George	DEWEY navy Am
George	ATWOOD math Br	George	DeWITT tv
George	AYSCUE(Sir)navy Br	George	DiCENZO tv+
George	BACK(Sir)x	George	DICK md e Am
George	BAKER cr Am	George	DILLON po Am
George	BAKER e-drama Am	George	DIXON boxer Am
George	BARBIER	George	DIXON x Br
George	BARKER po Br	George	DORAN pb Am
George	BARNARD su Am	George	DUNN tv
George	BEADLE sc,e Am	George	DZUNDZA tv+
George	BEER h Am	George	EASTMAN
George	BEILBY(Sir)sc,idScot	George	EASTMAN i,id-photo Am
George	BELL	George	ELIOT w Br
George	BELLAMY mr-guit Br	George	ELLIS w Br
George	BELLOWS p,etch Am	George	FAWCETT
George	BENSON m-guit,s Am	George	FERRIS eng Am
George	BINGHAM p Am	George	FISHER(Shug)tv+
George	BITZER cameraman Am	George	FLOWER
George	BLAKE j,w Scot	George	FOREMAN boxer Am
George	BLANDA fb hf	George	FOSTER b
George	BOOLE math,e Br	George	FOX r-Quakers Br
George	BORROW w Br	George	FULLER p Am
George	BRENT	George	FURTH tv+
George	BRETT b	George	GALLUP polls Am
George	BROWN mr-drm Am	George	GAMOW sc,e Am
George	BRUSH p Am	George	GARRETT po,w Am
George	BURNS cm,tv+ Am	George	GAYNES tv+
George	BYRON(Lord) po Br	George	GERVIN bb
George	CABOT id Am	George	GISSING w Br
George	CADBURY id Br	George	GIVOT
George	CARLIN tv+	George	GOBEL(Lonesome)cm,tv+
George	CATES m,cn,c,tv Am	George	GOOCH h,st Br
George	CATLIN p,w Am	George	GOSCHEN st Br
George	CHEONG tv	George	GRANT ph,e Can

George	GROSZ p Ger-Am	George	MIFFLIN pb Am
George	GROVE(Sir)ed,ct-m&art	George	MIKAN bb hf
George	HALAS fbc hf	George	MILLER d
George	HALE astr,e Am	George	MINOT md Am
George	HALL mj-violin,cn Am	George	MOORE w,po,ct Irish
George	HANDEL c Ger-Br	George	MORLAND p,engr Br
George	HARVEY j,ed,pb Am	George	MORRIS j,po Am
George	HAYES(Gabby)	George	MURDOCK tv+
George	HEARN	George	MURPHY tv+
George	HEARST id-mines Am	George	NADER tv+
George	HENTY w Br	George	NARES(Sir)navy
George	HEPBURN bbc hf	George	NATHAN ed,ct Am
George	HERBERT po Br	George	NEISE tv
George	HILL d	George	NEWBERN
George	HILTON	George	NEWNES(Sir)pb
George	HOUSTON	George	NICHOLS
George	HOYT bbc hf	George	NORRIS st Am
George	INNESS Jr p Am	George	O'BRIEN
George	INNESS p Am	George	O'HANLON Jr. tv+
George	IRVING	George	O'HANLON tv
George	IVES tv	George	OPPEN po Am
George	JESSEL cm,tv+ Am	George	ORWELL w,ct Br
George	JOLLY la Br	George	OSBORNE piano,c Ir
George	KARL bbc	George	PABST d-films Ger
George	KAUFMAN w Am	George	PALADE md Am
George	KELL b hf	George	PALERMO tv
George	KELLY b hf	George	PATTON(Bld&Guts)ar Am
George	KELLY la,w Am	George	PAXTON mj-sax,cn Am
George	KELLY(MchinGun)gangs.	George	PEABODY mer,f Am
George	KENNEDY tv+	George	PEELE w,po Br
George	KEOGAN bbc hf	George	PEPPARD tv+
George	KRAPP e,w Am	George	PERLE c Am
George	LADD ps,ph Am	George	PERLEY(Sir)bus,st Can
George	LAMMING w Barbados	George	PETRIE tv
George	LAYTON tv	George	PETTIE w Br
George	LAZENBY tv+	George	PIGOT mer,st Br
George	LEWES ph,ct Br	George	PORTER(Sir) sc
George	LEWIS tv	George	PULLMAN i-rr cars Am
George	LILLO w Br	George	PUTNAM tv
George	LINDSEY tv	George	RAFT tv+
George	LINK i,id-flying Am	George	RAPP r Am
George	LOONEY w Am	George	REEVES tv+
George	LORIMER ed Am	George	REID(Sir)st Aust
George	LUCAS d	George	REISNER arc Am
George	LUKS p,cr Am	George	RHODES tv
George	MacBeth po,w Scot	George	RIPLEYr,ct,ref Am
George	MAHARIS tv+	George	RITCHEY astr Am
George	MARION Sr.	George	RIVERO
George	MARTIN	George	ROBEY(Sir)cm,la
George	MASON re-st,agric Am	George	ROMERO d
George	MATHEWS tv	George	ROMNEY p Br
George	MAYO ps,e,w Am	George	ROOKE(Sir)navy
George	McAFEE fb hf	George	ROOT c,e Am
George	McDANIEL tv	George	ROSE
George	McMANUS cr Am	George	RUSSELL mj-piano,c Am
George	MEAD ph,ps,e Am	George	RUSSELL w Ir
George	MEANY labor Am	George	SALA w Br
George	MEEKER	George	SAND w Fr
George	MEMMOLI tv	George	SANDERS
George	MERRIAMid-print,pb Am	George	SARTON h-science,e Am
George	MICHAEL s,tv Br	George	SAVALAS tv

George	SCHICK tv	George M.	COHAN la,w,pr Am
George	SCOTT b	George P.	ELLIOTT w Am
George	SCOTT(Sir) ac	George Wash.	CABLE w Am
George	SCROPE geol Br	George Wash.	CARVER sc Am
George	SEATON d	George Wash.	CRILE md,w Am
George	SEGAL p,su Am	George Wash.	PIERCE sc,e Am
George	SEITZ d	George,	ANTHONY tv
George	SELDEN l,i Am	George,	BILL fb hf
George	SELTI c	George,	CHIEF DAN
George	SELWYN r Br	George,	CHRISTOPHER tv+
George	SHELTON tv	George,	ELIZABETH w Am
George	SHERMAN d	George,	GLADYS
George	SHIRAS l,supr ct Am	George,	JOHN tv
George	SHOUP mer,st Am.	George,	LYNDA DAY tv+
George	SHULL sc,e Am	George,	PHYLLIS tv
George	SIDNEY d	George,	STEFAN po Ger
George	SIMPSON(Sir)x Can	George,	SUSAN tv+
George	SIMS j,w Br	Georgene	BARNES tv
George	SISLER b hf	Georges	BRAQUE p Fr
George	SITWELL(Sir)w	Georges	CHARPAK sc Pol-Fr
George	SNELL md Am	Georges	CLAUDE sc Fr
George	SOMERS(Sir)navigator	Georges	CORRAFACE
George	SPELL	Georges	DANTON l,re Fr
George	STEINER w,ct Am	Georges	DUHAMEL w,po Fr
George	STEVENS d	Georges	EEKHOUD w,po Belg
George	STIGLER ec,e Am	Georges	FEYDEAU w Fr
George	STONE	Georges	KOEHLER md Ger
George	STONEY sc,e Ir	Georges	MELIES d Fr
George	STRAIT s-cnt Am	Georges	MOINAUX w-humor Fr
George	STREET ac Br	Georges	ONSLOW c Fr
George	STUBBS p Br	Georges	PERROT arc Fr
George	SZELL cn Am	Georges	PIRE r,e Belg
George	TAKEI tv+	Georges	PRETRE cn Fr
George	THOMSON(Sir)sc,e	Georges	RAYET astr Fr
George	TICKNOR e,h Am	Georges	ROUAULT p Fr
George	TOBIAS tv+	Georges	SEURAT p Fr
George	TRAFTON fb hf	Georges	SIMENON w Fr
George	Van EPS mj-guit Am	Georges	SOREL ref,w Fr
George	VIERECK w Am	Georges	THILL tenor Br
George	WAGGNER d	Georges d'AVENEL ec,h Fr	
George	WALD sc Am	Georges de BUFFON sc,w Fr	
George	WALKER c Am	Georges de La TOUR p Fr	
George	WALLACE	Georges-Picot, OLGA	
George	WALSH	Georgette HEYER w Br	
George	WATTS p,su Br	Georgi	DIMITROV st Bulg
George	WEISS b hf	Georgia	BROWN
George	WENDT tv+	Georgia	DRAKE tv
George	WHIPPLE sc-md,e Am	Georgia	ENGEL tv+
George	WILKENS(Sr)x,fly Aust	Georgia	IRWIN la,s Am
George	WITHER po,w Br	Georgia	O'KEEFFE p Am
George	WRIGHT b hf	Georgiade,NICK tv	
George	WYLE m,cn,tv Am	Georgiana CARHART tv	
George	WYNER tv+	Georgie	FAME mr-keybds,s Br
George	WYTHE l,st Am	Georgina	HALE
George	YOUNG mr-guit Scot	Georgine	DARCY tv
George	ZUCCO	Georgio	BASSANI po,w It
George Bernard SHAW w Br		Georgios	GRIVAS st Gr
George C. SCOTT d,tv+		Georgy	LVOV st Rus
George Dawes GREEN w Am		Georgy	VLADIMOV w Rus
George de la PENA		Georgy	ZHUKOV ar,st Rus
George Herman RUTH(Babe)b hf		Geraghty,	CARMELITA

Geraint	DAVIES tv		Gerolamo	ROVETTA w It
Gerald	BULLETT w Br		Gerome,	JEAN p Fr
Gerald	DURRELL sc,w Br		Gerrit	DOU p Dut
Gerald	EDELMAN md Am		Gerrit	GRAHAM
Gerald	EDWARDS tv		Gerrit	JENSEN id-furn Br
Gerald	GRIFFIN w Ir		Gerrit	RIETVELD ac,ds Dut
Gerald	JANN tv		Gerrit	VOS philology,e Dut
Gerald	MASSEY po Br		Gerritsen,LISA tv	
Gerald	McRANEY tv+		Gerroll,	DANIEL
Gerald	MOHR tv+		Gerry	BAMMAN
Gerald	THOMAS d		Gerry	BLACK tv
Gerald	WILSON mj-trump,cn Am		Gerry	GOFFIN lyrics Am
Geraldine	BROOKS tv+		Gerry	JOHNSON tv
Geraldine	CARR tv		Gersak,	SAVINA
Geraldine	CHAPLIN		Gershom	SCHOLEM h,w Israel
Geraldine	FARRAR soprano Am		Gershon,	GINA
Geraldine	FERRARO st Am		Gershwin,	GEORGE c Am
Geraldine	FITZGERALD		Gershwin,	IRA lyrics,p-d'32
Geraldine	PAGE la+ Am		Gerstle,	FRANK
Geraldo	--- mj-piano,cn Br		Gert	FROBE
Geraldo	RIVERA tv-host Am		Gert,	VALESKA
Gerard	BLAIN		Gertrud von Le FORT w Ger	
Gerard	DAVID p Dut		Gertrude	ASTOR
Gerard	DEBREU ec Fr-Am		Gertrude	BELL arch,x,w Br
Gerard	DOUFFET p Dut		Gertrude	BERG tv
Gerard	HOPKINS po,r Br		Gertrude	EDERLE sw Am
Gerard	OURY		Gertrude	ELION md Am
Gerard	PHILIPPE		Gertrude	HOFFMAN tv
Gerard	SCHWARZ cn Am		Gertrude	JEKYLL ac-land Br
Gerard	SWOPE eng,id-GE Am		Gertrude	MICHAEL
Gerard	TER BORCH p Dut		Gertrude	OLMSTED
Gerard	TICHY		Gertrude	RAINEY(Ma)s-blues Am
Gerard,	DANNY tv+		Gertrude	STEIN w Am
Gerard,	GIL tv+		Gerty	CORI sc,e Am
Gerard,	PENNY tv		Gertz,	JAMI tv+
Gerardo	MURILLO p,w Mex		Gerun,	TOMMY mj,cn Am
Gerardus	MERCATOR geog Belg		Gervin,	GEORGE bb
Gerardus van der LEEUW ref,e Dut			Gesell,	ARNOLD ps,md,e Am
Geraud	DUROC ar,st Fr		Gesner,	CONRAD md,sc Swi
Geray,	STEVE		Gessi,	ROMOLO ar,x It
Gerber,	BILL tv		Gessler,	OTTO st Ger
Gerd	BINNIG sc Ger		Gessner,	SALOMON po Swi
Gere,	RICHARD		Geter,	LEO tv
Gerhard	DAGLY p Belg		Getty,	BALTHAZAR
Gerhard	DOMAGK sc,e Ger		Getty,	ESTELLE tv+
Gerhard	MUNTHE p,illus Nor		Getty,	JEAN id,f Am
Geri	JEWELL tv		Getulio	VARGAS st Braz
Gering,	RICHARD tv		Getz,	JOHN tv+
Gering,	ULRICH pb Swi		Getz,	STAN mj-sax Am
Gerlach,	HELLMUT j,st Ger		Getzoff,	JIMMY tv
Germain	PILON su Fr		Geyl,	PIETER h,e Dut
Germaine	GREER fe,w Br		Geza	ROHEIM ps Hung
German	HOUDE		Gezelle,	GUIDO po,r,e Belg
German	ROBLES		Ghalib,	MIRZA po India
German,	EDWARD(Sir)c		Ghelderode MICHEL de w Belg	
German,	MARTHA		Gheorge	ENESCU c Rom
Germani,	GAIA		Gheorghe	ASACHI w Rom
Germer,	LESTER sc Am		Gheorghe	ENESCU viol,c Rom
Gernreich,RUDI ds			Ghiberti,	LORENZO su It
Gernsback,HUGO pb,i Am			Ghil,	RENE po Fr
			Ghita	NORBY

Ghostley, ALICE tv+	Gibson, BRIAN d
Gia SCALA	Gibson, CHARLES p,illus Am
Giaches WERT c Belg	Gibson, DEBBIE s,ws Am
Giacometti, ALBERTO p,su Swi	Gibson, DON s-cnt Am
Giacomo BALLA p It	Gibson, HENRY cm,tv+ Am
Giacomo JOCHMUS mercenary Ger	Gibson, HOOT
Giacomo PUCCINI c It	Gibson, JOHN tv
Giacomo da VIGNOLA ac It	Gibson, JOSH b hf
Giacosa, GIUSEPPE w It	Gibson, KIRK b-mv'88
Giaever, IVAR n-p'73	Gibson, MEL o-d'95
Giambalvo,LOUIS tv+	Gibson, MIMI
Giambattista GAURINI po It	Gibson, THOMAS
Giambattista MARINO po It	Gibson, VIRGINIA tv+
Giambattista VICO ph,e It	Gibson, WILLIAM illus Am
Giammarese, CARL mr-guit Am	Gide, ANDRE n-l'47
Gian BERNINI su,ac,p It	Gideon MANTELL geol Br
Gian CARLI ec,h,e It	Gideon WELLES st,ed Am
Gian CAROTO p It	Gideon von LAUDON ar Aus
Gian Marie VOLANTE	Gideon, BOND tv+
Gian, JOSEPH tv+	Gidley, PAMELA
Gian-Carlo MENOTTI c Am	Gielgud, JOHN(Sir) o-s'81
Giana CANALE	Gierke, OTTO l,e Ger
Gianasi, RICK	Gieseking,WALTER piano Ger
Gianfranco FERRE ds It	Gifford BEAL p Am
Gianni ESPOSITO	Gifford PINCHOT forests,st Am
Gianni RIZZO	Gifford, EDWARD an,e Am
Gianni VERSACE ds It	Gifford, FRANCES
Giannini, AMADEO banker Am	Gifford, FRANK fb-m'56 hf,tv
Giannini, GIANCARLO	Gifford, KATHY LEE w, tv
Gianno GARKO	Gift, ROLAND mr-s Br
Giano della BELLA st It	Giftos, ELAINE tv+
Giauque, WILLIAM n-c'49	Gig YOUNG tv+
Gibb McLAUGHLIN	Gigi DURSTON tv
Gibb, ANDY tv	Gigi PERREAU tv+
Gibb, BARRY mr-guit,s Br	Gigi RICE tv
Gibb, CYNTHIA tv+	Gigi VORGAN tv
Gibb, MAURICE mr-bass,s Br	Gigli, BENIAMINO tenor It
Gibb, ROBIN mr-s Br	Giglio, SANDRO
Gibbes, ROBYN	Giguere, ROLAND po,p Can
Gibbins, MIKE mr-drm Welsh	Giguere, RUSS mr-guit,s Am
Gibbon, EDWARD w,h Br	Gijsbert VOET r,e Dut
Gibbons, BILLY mr-guit,s Am	Gil EANES x Port
Gibbons, CARROLL mj-pia,cn Br	Gil EVANS mj,c Am
Gibbons, KAYE w Am	Gil FATES tv
Gibbons, LEEZA tv	Gil GERARD tv+
Gibbons, ORLANDO organ,c Br	Gil HODGES b
Gibbons, REGINALD po Am	Gil LAMB
Gibbs, CURLY s Am	Gil SMITH tv
Gibbs, DAVID tv	Gil VICENTE w Port
Gibbs, JAMES ac Br	Gil de SILOE su Sp
Gibbs, JOSIAH sc,e Am	Gila ALMAGOR
Gibbs, MARLA tv+	Gila GOLAN
Gibbs, OLIVER sc Am	Gilbert BLANE(Sir)md Scot
Gibbs, TERRI s-cnt Am	Gilbert EMERY
Gibbs, TIMOTHY tv+	Gilbert MURRAY w,h,e Br
Gibran, KAHLIL w,po Syria-Am	Gilbert PARKER(Sir)w,ed Can
Gibson GOWLAND	Gilbert PATTEN w Am
Gibson, ALAN d	Gilbert PIERCE st,w Am
Gibson, ALTHEA t Am	Gilbert ROBERTS(Sir)eng
Gibson, BOB b-cy'68'70 and	Gilbert ROLAND
Gibson, BOB b-mv'68 hf, tv	Gilbert RYLE ph,w Br

Gilbert	SELDES j,w Am	Gillian	DOBB tv
Gilbert	STUART p Am	Gillian	GILBERT mr-kbds Br
Gilbert,	ALFRED bus,o-g'08 Am	Gillian	HILLS
Gilbert,	ALFRED(Sir)su	Gilliland,RICHARD tv+
Gilbert,	BILLY	Gillin,	HUGH tv
Gilbert,	CAROLYN tv	Gilling,	JOHN d
Gilbert,	CASS ac Am	Gillis,	ANNE
Gilbert,	EDMUND tv	Gillis,	BURTON mj-sax Br
Gilbert,	GILLIAN mr-kbds Br	Gillis,	JAMES
Gilbert,	GROVE geol Am	Gillman,	SID fb hf
Gilbert,	HELEN	Gillot,	CLAUDE p Fr
Gilbert,	HENRY c Am	Gilman,	CHARLOTTE fe,w Am
Gilbert,	HUMPHREY(Sir)x	Gilman,	DANIEL e Am
Gilbert,	JANICE tv	Gilman,	DOROTHY w
Gilbert,	JOHN	Gilman,	KENNETH DAVID tv
Gilbert,	JONATHON tv	Gilman,	KENNETH tv+
Gilbert,	LEWIS d	Gilman,	TONI tv
Gilbert,	MELISSA tv+	Gilmer,	ELIZABETH j Am
Gilbert,	MICHAEL w Br	Gilmore,	ART tv
Gilbert,	RUFUS md,i Am	Gilmore,	DANNY
Gilbert,	SARA tv+	Gilmore,	JIMMIE s-cnt Am
Gilbert,	WALTER n-c'80	Gilmore,	LOWELL
Gilbert,	WILLIAM md,sc Br	Gilpin,	CHARLES la Am
Gilbert,	WILLIAM(Sir)w	Gilpin,	JACK
Gilberto	FREYRE an,h Braz	Gilpin,	JOHN ba Br
Gilberto,	STRUD 2g-r's'64 Braz	Gilpin,	PERI tv
Gilchrist,CONNIE	Gilroy,	FRANK p-d'65
Gilchrist,ELLEN w Am	Gilson,	ETIENNE ph,e Fr
Gilda	RADNER tv+	Gilyard,	CLARENCE Jr. tv+
Gilels,	EMIL piano Rus	Gimbel,	ISAAC mer Am
Giles	COOPER w Br	Gimpel,	ERICA tv
Giles	FARNABY c Br	Gimpera,	TERESA
Giles	FOSTER d	Gina	GALLEGO tv+
Giles	WALKER d	Gina	GERSHON
Giles,	MIKE mr-drm Br	Gina	GILLESPIE tv
Giles,	WARREN b hf	Gina	HECHT tv
Gilford,	JACK tv+	Gina	NEMO tv
Gilg	TSCHUDI h Swi	Gina	RAVERA
Gilkin,	IWAN w Belg	Ginastera,ALBERTO c Arg
Gill,	BRENDAN j,w Am	Gines	PEREZ de HITA w,ar Sp
Gill,	ERIC su Br	Ginette	LeCLERC
Gill,	IRVING ac Am	Ging,	JACK tv+
Gill,	PETER mr-drums Br	Ginger	ALLEN
Gill,	RUSTY tv	Ginger	BAKER mr-drm Br
Gill,	SLATS bbc, hf	Ginger	JONES tv
Gill,	VINCE s-cnt Am	Ginger	ORSI tv
Gillan,	IAN mr-s Br	Ginger	ROGERS
Gilles	MENAGE l,w Fr	Gingold,	HERMIONE tv+
Gilles de RAIS ar Fr	Gingrich,	NEWT st,w Am
Gilles de RETZ ar st Fr	Gini,	CRAIG tv
Gillespie,DIZZY mj-trump,cn Am	Ginkel,	GODARD van ar Gr
Gillespie,GINA tv	Ginn,	EDWIN pb Am
Gillette,	ANITA tv+	Ginny	SIMMS
Gillette,	HELEN tv	Gino	CERVI
Gillette,	KING CAMP i,id Am	Gino	DeMAURO tv+
Gillette,	WILLIAM la Am	Gino	MARCHETTI fb hf
Gilliam,	BURTON tv	Gino	VANNELLI s,ws Can
Gilliam,	BYRON tv	Ginsberg,	ALLEN po Am
Gilliam,	STU tv	Ginsburg,	ROBIN tv
Gilliam,	TERRY d,w+ Am	Ginsburg,	RUTH justice Am
Gillian	ARMSTRONG d	Ginty,	ROBERT tv+

Ginzburg,	NATALIA w It	Giry,	ARTHUR h Fr
Gio	PETRE	Gisela	HAHN
Gioacchino ROSSINI c It		Gisela	UHLEN
Giono,	JEAN w Fr	Gish	JEN w Am
Giordano	BRUNO ph It	Gish,	ANNABETH
Giordano,	LUCA p It	Gish,	DOROTHY la+ Am
Giorgi,	ELENORA	Gish,	LILLIAN la+ Am
Giorgio	NORANDI p It	Gish,	SHEILA
Giorgio	VASARI p,ac,h-art It	Gissing,	GEORGE w,ct Br
Giorgio de CHIRICO p It		Gist,	CHRIST'ER frontier Am
Giorgio Sant'ANGELO ds		Gist,	ROBERT tv+
Giorgio,	ARMANI ds It	Gist,	ROD tv
Giorgione	--- p It	Giuditta	PASTA soprano It
Gioseffo	ZARLINO c It	Giulia	GRISI s It
Giovanni	AMICI astron It	Giulia	RUBINI
Giovanni	ARTUSI c It	Giuliana	SANTINI tv
Giovanni	BARDI m,w,st It	Giuliano	GEMMA
Giovanni	BAZZI p It	Giulietta MASINA	
Giovanni	BELLINI p It	Giulio	ALENI r It
Giovanni	BOSCO r It	Giulio	CACCINI s,e It
Giovanni	CANAL p It	Giulio	CAMPI p It
Giovanni	CASTI po It	Giulio	NATTA n-c'63
Giovanni	CEVA math, e It	Giulio Romano --- p,ac It	
Giovanni	CIMA p It	Giuseppe	BAINI c It
Giovanni	CLARI c It	Giuseppe	BELLI po It
Giovanni	CRESPI p It	Giuseppe	BORGESE e,ct,w It
Giovanni	CROCE c It	Giuseppe	CAMBINI viol,c It
Giovanni	DELLA CASA r,w It	Giuseppe	CRESPI p It
Giovanni	DUPRE su It	Giuseppe	De LUCA bari It
Giovanni	LANCISI md,sc It	Giuseppe	GIACOSA w It
Giovanni	MELI md,po It	Giuseppe	GIUSTI po It
Giovanni	MORONI p It	Giuseppe	MOTTA st Swi
Giovanni	PACINI c It	Giuseppe	PARINI po It
Giovanni	PANNINI p It	Giuseppe	PEANO math,e It
Giovanni	PASCOLI e,po It	Giuseppe	PITONI c It
Giovanni	PISANO su It	Giuseppe	SARTI c It
Giovanni	PONTANO po,st It	Giuseppe	VERDI c It
Giovanni	RISSO sc It	Giuseppe A.BORGESE e,ct,w It	
Giovanni	ROSSI arc It	Giuseppe de NITTIS p It	
Giovanni	ROSSO p It	Giusti,	GIUSEPPE po It
Giovanni	SACCHIS p It	Giusti,	PAUL
Giovanni	TIEPOLO p It	Givens,	ROBIN tv+
Giovanni	VERGA w It	Givot,	GEORGE
Giovanni	VIOTTI viol,cn It	Gjellerup,	KARL A. n-l'17
Giovanni	VITALI c It	Gladkov,	FYODOR w Rus
Giovanni,	NIKKI po Am	Gladstone,	WILLIAM st Br
Giovio,	PAOLO bio,h It	Gladys	COOPER tv+
Girard,	HENRY tv	Gladys	GEORGE
Girard,	JOSEPH	Gladys	KNIGHT mr-s Am
Girard,	STEPHEN bus,f Am	Glaser,	DONALD n-p'60
Girard,	WENDY tv	Glaser,	PAUL tv+
Girardin,	RAY tv	Glasgow,	ELLEN p-f'42
Girardot,	ANNIE	Glashow,	SHELDON n-p'79
Girardot,	HIPPOLYTE	Glaspell,	SUSAN w Am
Girolamo	AMATI violins It	Glass,	CARTER st Am
Girolamo	VIDA po It	Glass,	HUGH frontier Am
Girolamo	ZANCHI r It	Glass,	NED tv+
Gironella, JOSE w Sp		Glass,	PHILIP c Am
Girotti,	MASSIMO	Glass,	RON tv+
Girtin,	THOMAS p Br	Glassco,	JOHN w,po Can
Girty,	SIMON ar,re Am	Glaum,	LOUISE

Glavin,	TOM b-cy'91	Gloria	McMILLAN tv
Gleason,	JACKIE cm,tv+ Am	Gloria	SHEA
Gleason,	JAMES tv+	Gloria	STEINEM fe Am
Gleason,	JOANNA tv+	Gloria	STROOCK tv
Gleason,	PAT	Gloria	STUART
Gleason,	PAUL	Gloria	SWANSON
Gleason,	RUSSELL	Gloria	TALBOTT
Gleb	USPENSKY w Rus	Gloria	VAN tv
Gleim,	JOHANN po Ger	Gloria	WINTERS tv
Glen	BERRY	Gloux,	OLIVIER w Fr
Glen	DALE mr-guit,s Br	Glover,	BRIAN
Glen	GRAY mj,cn Am	Glover,	BRUCE tv+
Glen	RICE bb	Glover,	CRISPIN
Glen,	IAIN	Glover,	DANNY
Glenda	FARRELL	Glover,	DENIS po,ed N.Zea
Glenda	JACKSON	Glover,	JOHN
Glenn	CANNON tv	Glover,	JULIA la Ir
Glenn	CLOSE	Glover,	JULIAN
Glenn	CORBETT tv+	Glover,	KARA
Glenn	CORNICK mr-bass Br	Glover,	ROGER mr-bass Welsh
Glenn	CURTISS i,id,fly Am	Gluck,	ALMA sopr Am
Glenn	DAVIS o-g'56'60	Gluck,	CHRISTOPH c Aus
Glenn	FORD tv+	Gluck,	LOUISE p-q'63
Glenn	FRANK e,ed Am	Glueck,	SHELDON e-crimes Am
Glenn	FREY ws,s Am	Gluskin,	LUD m,cn,tv Am
Glenn	GORDON tv+	Gluyas	WILLIAMS cr Am
Glenn	GOULD piano Can	Glyn	HOUSTON
Glenn	GREGORY mr-s Br	Glyn,	ELINOR w br
Glenn	HUBBARD b	Glynis	JOHNS s,tv+ S.Afr-Am
Glenn	JEPSEN sc,e Am	Glynn	TURMAN tv+
Glenn	JORDAN d	Glynn,	CARLIN tv+
Glenn	LANGAN	Glynnis	O'CONNER
Glenn	MARTIN id-planes Am	Gmelin,	JOHANN sc Ger
Glenn	MILLER mj,cn+ Am	Gnaeus	SCIPIO ar Roman
Glenn	OSSER m,cn,tv Am	Gnagy,	JON tv
Glenn	PLUMMER	Gneist,	RUDOLF von l,st Ger
Glenn	ROBARDS tv	Gnoli,	DOMENICO po It
Glenn	SEABORG sc Am	Goaz,	HARRY tv
Glenn	SHADIX	Gobaldon,	DIANA w
Glenn	STRANGE tv+	Gobat,	CHARLES n-x'02
Glenn	TIPTON mr-guit Br	Gobbi,	TITO bari It
Glenn	WARNER(Pop)fbc Am	Gobel,	GEORGE(Lonesme)cm,tv+
Glenn,	JOHN HERSCHE as,st Am	Goble,	GRAHAM guit Aust
Glenn,	SCOTT	Goblet,	RENE st Fr
Glenne	HEADLY	Godard van GINKEL ar Br	
Glenway	WESCOTT w,po Am	Godard,	JEAN-LUC d
Gless,	BRIDGET tv	Goddard,	DON tv
Gless,	SHARON tv+	Goddard,	MARK tv+
Glickman,	MARTY tv	Goddard,	PAULETTE
Glidden,	CHARLES id-teleph Am	Goddard,	RAYNER l Br
Glinka,	MIKHAIL c Rus	Goddard,	ROBERT sc Am
Glitter,	GARY s,ws Br	Godden,	RUMER w Br
Gloria	De HAVEN	Godel,	ESCHER w Am
Gloria	ESTEFAN s-pop Cuba	Godel,	KURT math,e Am
Gloria	FOSTER	Godert	CAPELEN st Dut
Gloria	GORDON tv	Godey,	LOUIS pb Am
Gloria	GRAHAME tv+	Godfrey	CAMBRIDGE
Gloria	HENDRY	Godfrey	HO d
Gloria	HOLDEN	Godfrey	KNELLER(Sir)p
Gloria	LAMBERT tv	Godfrey,	ARTHUR tv+
Gloria	Le ROY tv	Godfrey,	THOMAS po Am

Godfrey,   THOMAS Sr math,i Am
Godin,   JACQUES
Godkin,   EDWIN w,ed Am
Godley,   KEVIN mr-drm,s Br
Godunov,   ALEXANDER
Godunov,   BORIS st-tsar Rus
Godwin,   GAIL w Am
Godwin,   WILLIAM w Br
Godwin-Austen,HENRY x,geol Br
Goebbels, JOSEPH st Nazi Ger
Goeje,   JAN de e Dut
Goelz,   DAVE puppets,tv Am
Goen,   BOB tv
Goeppert-Mayer, MARIA n-p'63
Goes,   HUGO van der p Belg
Goethe,   JOHANN von po,w Ger
Goetz,   PETER tv+
Goff,   JOHN
Goffin,   GERRY lyrics Am
Goga,   OCTAVIAN w,st Rom
Gogarty,   OLIVER md,w Ir
Gogh,   VINCENT van p Dut
Gogi   GRANT mj-s Am
Gogol,   NIKOLAY w Rus
Goins,   JESSE D. tv
Gokhale,   GOPAL e,st India
Gola,   TOM bb hf
Golan,   GILA
Golan,   MENAHEM d
Gold,   HERBERT w Am
Gold,   JACK d
Gold,   LOUISE pupp,tv Am
Gold,   MISSY tv
Gold,   TRACEY tv
Golda   MEIR st Isr
Goldberg, BERNARD tv
Goldberg, JASON tv
Goldberg, RUBE cr Am
Goldberg, WHOOPI tv+
Goldblum, JEFF
Golden,   ANNIE
Golden,   HARRY ed,w Am
Golden,   WILLIAM s-cnt Am
Goldie   HAWN tv+
Goldie   HILL tv
Goldin,   RICKY PAULL
Golding,   LOUIS w,po Br
Golding,   LYNVAL mr-guit Br
Golding,   META tv
Golding,   WILLIAM n-l'83
Goldkettle, JEAN mj-piano,cn Am
Goldman,   CAROLE tv
Goldman,   DANNY tv
Goldman,   EDWIN c,cn Am
Goldman,   EMMA anarchist Am
Goldman,   ROY tv
Goldman,   WILLIAM w Am
Goldmark, KARL c Hung
Goldmark, PETER eng Am
Goldoni,   CARLO w It

Goldoni,   LELIA
Goldsboro,BOBBY s,tv Am
Goldschmidt, HANS sc Ger
Goldschmidt, MEIR w,st Dan
Goldsmith,CLIO
Goldsmith,JONATHAN tv
Goldsmith,OLIVER po,w Br
Goldstein,JOSEPH n-m'85
Goldstone,JAMES d
Goldthwaite, BOB(Bobcat)
Goldwyn,   SAMUEL pr-films Am
Goldwyn,   TONY
Golgi,   CAMILLO n-m'06
Golino,   VALERIA
Golm,   LIZA
Golonka,   ARLENE tv+
Goltz,   COLMAR von der ar Ger
Goltz,   FRIEDRICH md-sc Ger
Goltz,   RUDIGER von der ar Ger
Goltzius,   HENDRIK engr,p Dut
Gombell,   MINNA
Gomberg,   MOSES sc Am
Gombert,   NICOLAS c Belg
Gombos,   GYULA ar,st Hung
Gombrich,   E.H.(Sir)h
Gombrowicz, WITOLD w Pol
Gomelsky,   ALEXANDR bbc hf
Gomer   PYLE fc
Gomes   ZURARA h Port
Gomes,   ANTONIO c Braz
Gomes,   DIOGO x Port
Gomes,   MARK tv
Gomez de la Serna, RAMON w Sp
Gomez,   FERNANDO
Gomez,   JOSE(ElGallo)matad Sp
Gomez,   LEFTY b hf
Gomez,   THOMAS
Gompers,   SAMUEL labor Am
Goncalves Dias, ANTONIO po Braz
Goncharov,IVAN w Rus
Goncourt,   EDMOND de w Fr
Goncourt,   JULES de w Fr
Gong   LI
Gongora,   LUIS de po Sp
Gonne,   MAUDE la,st Ir
Gonska,   MASCHA
Gonzales Prada, Manuel w,po Peru
Gonzalez,   JOSE p,at Sp
Gonzalez,   JULIO su,p Sp
Gonzalo de BERECO po Sp
Gooch,   DANIEL(Sir)eng-rrs
Gooch,   GEORGE h,st Br
Goodall,   CAROLINE
Goodall,   JANE an,w Am
Gooden,   DWIGHT b-cy'85
Gooden,   SAM mr-s Am
Goodeve,   GRANT tv+
Goodfellow, EBBIE ho-m'28
Goodfriend, LINDA tv
Goodhue,   BERTRAM ac Am
Gooding,   CUBA Jr o-s'96

Goodliffe,MICHAEL		Gordon,	BERT d
Goodman	ACE j-humor Am	Gordon,	BRUCE tv
Goodman,	BENNY mj,cn Am	Gordon,	C. HENRY
Goodman,	DIANA tv	Gordon,	CARL tv
Goodman,	DODY tv+	Gordon,	CAROLINE w Am
Goodman,	ELLEN j,w Am	Gordon,	CHARLES r,w Can
Goodman,	JOHN tv+	Gordon,	COLIN
Goodman,	PAUL w,po,ct,ph Am	Gordon,	DEXTER mj-sax Am
Goodnight,CHARLES cattleman Am		Gordon,	DON tv+
Goodnow,	FRANK e Am	Gordon,	GALE tv+
Goodpasture,	ERNEST md,e Am	Gordon,	GAVIN
Goodrich,	BENJAMIN id-tires Am	Gordon,	GLEN tv+
Goodrich,	FRANCES p-d,95	Gordon,	GLORIA tv
Goodrich,	SAMUEL w Am	Gordon,	JOE b-mv'42
Goodrow,	GARRY	Gordon,	JUDAH w Lith
Goodrow,	MICHAEL tv	Gordon,	KEITH
Goodspeed,EDGAR e Am		Gordon,	LEO
Goodwin,	BILL tv+	Gordon,	MACK lyrics Pol-Am
Goodwin,	DORIS p-h'95	Gordon,	MARK tv
Goodwin,	HAROLD	Gordon,	MARY
Goodwin,	JOSHUA tv	Gordon,	MARY w Am
Goodwin,	KIA tv	Gordon,	NOAH w Am
Goodwin,	MICHAEL tv+	Gordon,	PHIL tv
Goodyear,	CHARLES sc,i Am	Gordon,	RUTH o-s'68,w
Googe,	BARNABE po Br	Gordon,	VIRGINIA tv
Googie	WITHERS	Gordon,	WILLIAM tv
Googy	GRESS	Gordone,	CHARLES p-d'70
Gookin,	DANIEL colonist Br	Gordy	HOWE ho
Goorian,	LEN tv	Gordy	TAPP tv
Gooritz	GARFIELD	Gore	VIDAL w Am
Goose	GOSLIN b hf	Gore,	ALBERT Jr st-vp
Goose	GOSSAGE b	Gore,	LESLEY s Am
Goossens,	EUGENE c,cn Br	Gore,	MARTIN mr-kbds Br
Gopal	GOKHALE e,st India	Goren,	CHARLES bridge Am
Goranson,	LECY tv	Gorenko,	ANNA po Rus
Gorbechev,MIKHAIL n-x'90		Gorg,	GALYN
Gorbechev,RAISA M's wife		Gorgas,	WILLIAM ar,md Am
Gorcey,	BERNARD	Gorgeous George WAGNER wrestler A	
Gorcey,	DAVID	Gorham,	JABEZ silversmith Am
Gorcey,	LEO	Gorham,	NATHANIEL st Am
Gordie	TAPP tv	Gorham,	SCOTT mr-guitar Am
Gordimer,	NADINE n-l'91	Gorham,	STEVE mr-drums Am
Gordin,	JACOB w Am	Goring,	HERMANN st Nazi Ger
Gordon	CLAPP tv+	Goring,	MARIUS
Gordon	DeMAIN	Gorky,	ARSHILE p Am
Gordon	HARKER	Gorky,	MAKSIM w Rus
Gordon	HESSLER d	Gorman	THOMAS b
Gordon	HEWART l,st Br	Gorman,	CLIFF
Gordon	JACKSON	Gorman,	JAMES w Am
Gordon	JENKINS b	Gorman,	MARI tv
Gordon	JONES tv+	Gorman,	ROBERT tv+
Gordon	JUMP tv+	Gorme,	EYDIE s-pop Am
Gordon	MacRAE s,tv+	Gormley,	JIM tv
Gordon	OLIVER	Goronwy	OWEN r,po Welsh
Gordon	PINSENT	Gorrie,	ALAN mr-bass,s Scot
Gordon	SCOTT	Gorrie,	JOHN i Am
Gordon	THOMSON tv	Gorshin,	FRANK
Gordon	WALLER s Scot	Gorski,	VIRGINIA tv
Gordon,	ADAM po Aust	Gorst,	JOHN(Sir)st
Gordon,	ANITA tv	Gorter,	HERMAN po Dut
Gordon,	BARRY tv+	Gortner,	MARJOE tv+

Gortz,	GEORG st Ger	Gower	CHAMPION ba+
Goschen,	GEORGE bus,st Br	Gower,	ANDRE tv+
Gosden	FREEMAN tv+	Gower,	JOHN po Br
Gosfield,	MAURICE tv	Gowin	KNIGHT sc Br
Goslin,	GOOSE b hf	Gowland,	GIBSON
Goss,	DAVID	Goya,	FRANCISCO de p Sp
Gossage,	GOOSE b	Goyen,	JAN van p Dut
Gosse,	EDMUND(Sir)po,ct	Goytisolo,	JUAN w Sp
Gosse,	PHILIP sc-marine Br	Goz,	HARRY tv+
Gossec,	FRANCOIS c Fr	Gozier,	BERNIE tv
Gossett,	LOUIS Jr o-s'82,tv+	Gozzi,	CARLO w It
Gosta	EKMAN	Gozzi,	GASPARO w It
Got,	ROLAND	Gqoba,	WILLIAM w Bantu
Gotch,	FRANK wrestler Am	Graaff,	SIMON de st Dut
Gotell,	WALTER	Grabau,	AMADEUS sc,e Am
Gothard,	MICHAEL	Grabbe,	CHRISTIAN w
Gothie,	ROBERT tv	Grable,	BETTY
Gottfried	BENN md,po,w Ger	Grabowski,	NORM tv
Gottfried	FEDER ec,st Ger	Grace	ABBOTT fe,w Am
Gottfried	JOHN	Grace	AGUILAR w Br
Gottfried	KELLER w,po Swi	Grace	CARNEY tv
Gottfried	KINKEL po,h,e Ger	Grace	JONES s+ Am
Gottfried	SEMPER ac Ger	Grace	KELLY tv+
Gottfried,	GILBERT tv+	Grace	MOORE s-opera+ Am
Gotthold	LESSING w,ct Ger	Grace	PALEY w Am
Gotti,	JOHN reptd mafia Am	Grace	SLICK mr-s Am
Gottlieb	DAIMLER id-cars Ger	Grace	WHITNEY tv
Gottlob	FREGE math,ph,e Ger	Grace,	MARY tv
Gottlob	SCHULZE ph,e Ger	Grace,	NICKOLAS
Gottschalk,	LOUIS piano,c Am	Grace,	WILLIAM mer,ships Am
Gotz,	HERMANN c Ger	Gracian,	BALTASAR r,w Sp
Goudal,	JETTA	Gracie	ALLEN cm,tv+ Am
Goudge,	ELIZABETH w Br	Gracie	FIELDS cm
Goudreau,	BARRY mr-guit Am	Graciliano	RAMOS w Braz
Goudy,	FREDERIC printer Am	Gradisher,	RANDY fb-d'78
Gough,	LLOYD tv	Grady	NUTT(Rev.) tv
Gough,	MICHAEL	Grady	SUTTON tv+
Gouin,	LOMER(Sir)st Can	Grady,	DON tv
Goujon,	JEAN su Fr	Grady,	ED tv
Gould,	BENJAMIN astr Am	Graeme	CLARK mr-bass Scot
Gould,	BILLY mr-bass Am	Graeme	EDGE mr-drm Br
Gould,	CHESTER cr Am	Graeme	KELLING mr-guit Scot
Gould,	ELLIOTT tv+	Graetz,	HEINRICH h Ger
Gould,	GLENN piano Can	Graetz,	PAUL
Gould,	HAROLD tv+	Graf	SPEE navy Ger
Gould,	JAY mer,f Am	Graf,	DAVID
Gould,	JOHN birds Br	Graf,	STEFFI t Ger
Gould,	MARTIN p-m'95	Graf,	URS at,engr Swi
Gould,	SANDRA tv	Graff,	ILENE tv
Gould,	WILLIAM	Graff,	JERRY tv
Goulding,	EDMUND d	Graff,	RANDY tv
Goulding,	RAY tv	Graff,	TODD
Gouldman,	GRAHAM mr-s Br	Grafton,	SAMUEL tv
Goulet,	ROBERT s+ Am	Grafton,	SUE w Am
Gounod,	CHARLES c Fr	Graham	BECKEL
Gourmont,	REMY de w Fr	Graham	CHAPMAN
Gouverneur	KEMBLE id-arms,st Am	Graham	CROWDEN
Govaert	FLINK p Dut	Graham	GOBLE guit Austra
Gove,	PHILIP dictionary Am	Graham	GREENE
Gow,	NIEL viol,c Scot	Graham	GREENE w Br
Gowdy	CURT tv-sports Am	Graham	JARVIS tv+

Graham	JONES mr-guit Br	Grant,	AMY s-gos Am
Graham	KERR chef,tv,w Am	Grant,	BETH
Graham	NASH mr-guit Br	Grant,	BRIAN tv
Graham	PARKER mr-s Br	Grant,	CARY
Graham	RUSSELL mr-s Br	Grant,	DAVID
Graham	WALLAS sc-politics Br	Grant,	DUNCAN p Scot
Graham,	AIMEE	Grant,	EDDY s,ws Guyana
Graham,	BILLY r,tv Am	Grant,	FAYE tv+
Graham,	ERNEST ac Am	Grant,	GEORGE ph,e Can
Graham,	FRED	Grant,	GOGI mj-s Am
Graham,	GARY tv+	Grant,	HEBER r-Morman Am
Graham,	GERRIT	Grant,	HORACE bb
Graham,	HEATHER tv+	Grant,	HUGH
Graham,	HUGH pb Can	Grant,	KIRBY tv+
Graham,	JORIE p-q'96	Grant,	LAWRENCE
Graham,	JUNE ba, tv	Grant,	LEE o-s'75,tv+
Graham,	KATHARINE p-b'98	Grant,	RICHARD
Graham,	LARRY mr-guit Am	Grant,	RODNEY
Graham,	MARTHA ba Am	Grant,	TED m-cnt,viol,tv
Graham,	OTTO fb hf	Grant,	ULYSSES HIRAM 18th Pr
Graham,	RONNY tv+	Grantham,	GEORGE mr-drm,s Am
Graham,	SONNY tv	Grantland	RICE j-sports Am
Graham,	THOMAS sc,e Scot	Grantly	DICK-READ md,w Br
Graham,	VIRGINIA tv	Granville	BANTOCK(Sir)c
Graham,	W.S. po Scot	Granville	HALL ps,e Am
Graham,	WILLIAM d	Granville	HICKS w,ct Am
Grahame,	GLORIA o-s'52, tv+	Granville	VanDUSEN
Grahame,	KENNETH w Br	Granville,	BONITA
Grahame,	MARGOT	Granville-Barker,HARLEY w,d,,la B:
Grahn,	LUCILE ba Dan	Grapewin,	CHARLEY
Grainger,	PERCY piano,c Am	Gras,	FELIX w Fr
Gram,	HANS md,e Dan	Grass,	GUNTER w,po,n-l'99 Ger
Gramm,	LOU mr-s Am	Grassle,	KAREN tv+
Gramme,	ZENOBE eng,i Belg	Grasso,	ELLA st Am
Grammer,	KELSEY tv	Gratton,	CHRIS fb
Granach,	ALEXANDER	Gratzer,	ALAN mr-drums Am
Granados,	ENRIQUE piano,c Sp	Grau,	JACINTO w Sp
Granath,	BJORN	Grau,	MAURICE pr,d-opera Am
Grand	BUSH	Grau,	SHIRLEY p-f'65
Grandbois,ALAIN po Can		Grauer,	BEN tv
Grandi,	GUIDO math,e It	Grauman,	WALTER d
Grandin,	ISABEL tv	Graun,	KARL c Ger
Grandma	MOSES p Am	Graver,	GARY d
Grandpa	JONES tv	Graves,	PETER tv+
Grandy,	FRED tv	Graves,	RALPH
Grange,	RED fb hf	Graves,	ROBERT po,w,ct Br
Granger,	DOROTHY	Graves,	RUPERT
Granger,	FARLEY	Graves,	TERESA tv
Granger,	STEWART tv+	Gravina,	CARLA
Granik,	THEODORE tv	Gravitte,	BEAU tv
Granin,	DANIIL w Rus	Gray,	ASA sc Am
Granit,	RAGNAR n-m'67	Gray,	BILLY tv+
Granlund,	NILS T.	Gray,	CHARLES tv+
Grant	GOODEVE tv+	Gray,	COLEEN tv+
Grant	HILL bb	Gray,	DOLORES tv+
Grant	SHAUD tv+	Gray,	DONALD tv+
Grant	SHOW tv	Gray,	DULCIE
Grant	WITHERS	Gray,	ELISHA i Am
Grant	WOOD p Am	Gray,	ERIN tv+
Grant,	ALBERTA tv	Gray,	GARY
Grant,	ALEXANDER ba Br		

Gray,	GLEN mj,cn Am	Greene,	ELLEN
Gray,	HAROLD cr Am	Greene,	FREDERICK(Dennis)tv
Gray,	JAMES(Sir)sc,e	Greene,	GAEL ct-food Am
Gray,	JOHN w Am	Greene,	GRAHAM
Gray,	LES mr-s Br	Greene,	GRAHAM w Br
Gray,	LINDA tv+	Greene,	JACK s-cnt Am
Gray,	ROBERT tv	Greene,	JAMES tv+
Gray,	ROBERT x Am	Greene,	JOE(Mean)fb-d'72'4hf+
Gray,	SALLY	Greene,	KIM tv
Gray,	SIMON w Br	Greene,	LORNE tv+
Gray,	SPALDING	Greene,	LYNNIE tv
Gray,	THOMAS po Br	Greene,	MARGE tv
Grayco,	HELEN tv	Greene,	MICHAEL
Grayson	HALL	Greene,	MICHELLE tv+
Grayson	McCOUCH tv	Greene,	MORT tv
Grayson,	KATHRYN	Greene,	PETER
Grazia	DELADDA w It	Greene,	RICHARD tv+
Graziadio	ASCOLI e It	Greene,	ROBERT po,w Br
Graziano,	ROCKY boxer,tv Am	Greene,	SHECKY tv+
Greasy	NEALE fb hf	Greener,	DOROTHY tv
Greaves,	R.B. m-r&b Am	Greenlee,	DAVID tv
Greaza,	WALTER tv	Greenough,	HORATIO su Am
Greb,	HARRY boxer Am	Greenspan,	ALAN ec,st Am
Greban,	ARNOUL po Fr	Greenspoon,	JIMMY organ Am
Grebb,	MARTY mr-kbds Am	Greenstreet,	SYDNEY
Greco,	BUDDY s,piano,tv Am	Greenwood,	ALAN mr-keybds Am
Greco,	EL p Sp	Greenwood,	BRUCE tv+
Greco,	JOSE ba Sp	Greenwood,	CHARLOTTE
Greeley,	HORACE j,ref,pb Am	Greenwood,	JOAN
Greely,	ADOLPHUS ar,x Am	Greenwood,	LEE s-cnt Am
Green,	ADOLPH	Greer	GARSON
Green,	AL s-r&b,ws Am	Greer	ROBSON
Green,	ALFRED d	Greer,	BRODIE tv
Green,	ALICE h Irish	Greer,	DABBS tv+
Green,	ANNA w Am	Greer,	GERMAINE fe,w Br
Green,	BERNIE m,cn,tv Am	Greer,	HAL bb, hf
Green,	BRIAN tv+	Greer,	JANE
Green,	DOROTHY tv	Greer,	ROBIN tv
Green,	DUFF j,st Am	Greet,	BEN(Sir)la
Green,	EVAN w Am	Greg	BINKLEY tv
Green,	GEORGE DAWES w Am	Greg	DAWSON tv
Green,	GUY d	Greg	ELMORE mr-drm Am
Green,	HENRY w Br	Greg	ERRICO mr-drm Am
Green,	JOHN tv	Greg	EVIGAN tv+
Green,	JULIEN w Fr	Greg	HAM m-sax,kbds Aust
Green,	KARL mr-bass Br	Greg	HENRY
Green,	KERRI	Greg	KINNEAR tv
Green,	LYNDA tv	Greg	LAKE mr-bass,s Br
Green,	MARIKA	Greg	MADDUX b
Green,	MITZIE	Greg	MORRIS tv
Green,	NIGEL	Greg	MORTON tv
Green,	PAUL p-d'27	Greg	NETTLES b
Green,	SETH	Greg	NORMAN g Aust
Green,	WILLIAM labor Am	Greg	ROMAN tv
Greenaway,	PETER d,w Welsh	Greg	WEBB tv+
Greenberg,	HANK b-mv'40 hf	Greg,	W.W.(Sir)w
Greenberg,	STANLEY w Am	Gregg	ALLMAN mr-kbds,s Am
Greenbush,	LINDSAY tv	Gregg	FORREST tv
Greenbush,	SIDNEY tv	Gregg,	FORREST fb hf
Greene,	DANIEL tv+	Gregg,	JOHN i-shorthnd,pb Am
Greene,	DAVID d	Gregg,	JOSIAH frontier Am

Gregg,	VIRGINIA tv+	Gries,	JONATHAN
Gregh,	FERNAND po Fr	Gries,	TOM d
Gregor	MENDEL sc Aus	Griese,	BOB fb-m'71 hf
Gregorio,	ROSE	Grieve,	CHRISTOPHER po Scot
Gregory	CORSO po Am.	Grifasi,	JOE
Gregory	HINES ba+ Am	Griffeth,	SIMONE tv+
Gregory	La CAVA d	Griffey,	KEN Jr b-hr'94,gg'97 &
Gregory	PECK	Griffey,	KEN Jr gg'97,b-mv'97
Gregory	RATOFF d+	Griffin	DUNNE
Gregory	SALATA tv	Griffin	O'NEAL
Gregory	SIERRA tv+	Griffin,	GERALD w Ir
Gregory	WALCOTT tv+	Griffin,	MERV tv
Gregory,	ANDRE	Griffin,	WALTER ac Am
Gregory,	BENJI tv	Griffith	JONES
Gregory,	GLENN mr-s Br	Griffith,	ANDY tv+
Gregory	HORACE po,ct Am	Griffith,	ARTHUR j,st Irish
Gregory,	ISABELLA(Lady)w Ir	Griffith,	CLARK b hf
Gregory,	JAMES tv+	Griffith,	D.W. d,pr
Gregory,	MARK	Griffith,	EMILE boxer
Gregory,	MARY tv+	Griffith,	HUGH o-s'59
Gregory,	SYLVER tv	Griffith,	JAMES tv+
Gregory,	THEA	Griffith,	KENNETH
Gregson,	JACK tv	Griffith,	KEVIN w Am
Gregson,	JOHN	Griffith,	MELANIE tv+
Grein,	JACOB(Jack)ct Br	Griffith,	NANCI s-folk
Greist,	KIM	Griffith,	RAYMOND
Grenfell,	JOYCE	Griffith,	THOMAS
Grenier,	ZACH tv	Griffith,	TRACY
Gresham,	THOMAS(Sir)f	Griffiths,	RICHARD
Gress,	GOOGY	Griggs,	JEFF
Gressly,	AMANZ geol Swi	Griggs,	JOHN st,l Am
Greta	GARBO	Griggs,	JOHN tv
Greta	GYNT	Grignard,	VICTOR n-c'12
Greta	SCACCHI	Grigorovich,	DMITRY w Rus
Gretchen	CORBETT tv+	Grijalba,	JUAN de x Sp
Gretchen	WYLER tv+	Grika,	JOHANNA
Gretry,	ANDRE c Fr	Grill,	ROB mr-bass,s Am
Gretzky,	WAYNEho-m'80'1'2'3'4 &	Grillparzer,	FRANZ w Aus
Gretzky,	WAYNE ho-m'85'6'7'9	Grimes,	BURLEIGH b hf
Greuze,	JEAN p Fr	Grimes,	GARY
Greville,	FULKE po,courtier Br	Grimes,	JACK tv
Grevy,	JULES st Fr	Grimes,	JACKIE tv
Grew,	JOSEPH st Am	Grimes,	MARTHA w Am
Grey,	BERYL ba Br	Grimes,	SCOTT
Grey,	CHARLES st Br	Grimes,	TAMMY
Grey,	JANE(Lady)st Br	Grimes,	TINY mj Am
Grey,	JENNIFER	Grimke,	SARAH fe Am
Grey,	JOEL	Grimm,	HANS w Ger
Grey,	NAN	Grimm,	JACOB w Ger
Grey,	SHIRLEY	Grimm,	TIM tv
Grey,	VIRGINIA	Grimm,	WILHELM w Ger
Grey,	ZANE w Am	Grin,	ALEKSANDR w Rus
Greydon	CLARK d	Grinan,	JOSE tv
Gribbon,	HARRY	Grindel,	EUGENE po Fr
Grieco,	RICHARD tv+	Grinius,	KAZYS st Lith
Grieg,	EDVARD c Nor	Grinnage,	JACK tv
Grieg,	JOHAN po,w Nor	Gris,	JUAN p Sp
Griem,	HELMUT	Grisham,	JOHN w Am
Grier,	DAVID tv+	Grisi,	CARLOTTA ba It
Grier,	PAM	Grisi,	GIULIA s It
Grier,	ROOSEVELT fb,tv+	Grissom,	GUS as Am

Grissom,	MARQUIS b	Guard,	DOMINIC
Grist,	RERI s-opera,ba Am	Guard,	KIT
Grivas,	GEORGIOS st Gr	Guardi,	FRANCESCO p It
Grizel	BAILLIE(Lady)po Scot	Guardia,	TOMAS st CostaR
Grizzard,	GEORGE	Guardino,	HARRY tv+
Groat,	DICK b-mv'60	Guardino,	JEROME tv
Grodin,	CHARLES	Guare,	JOHN w Am
Grody,	KATHRYN	Guarnieri,	JOHNNY tv
Groener,	HARRY tv	Guas,	JUAN ac Sp
Groening,	MATT cr Am	Gubanova,	IRINA
Grofe,	FERDE c,cn Am	Guccione,	BOB pb Am
Groh,	DAVID tv+	Gudegast,	HANS tv
Gromyko,	ANDREY st Rus	Gudmundur	KAMBAN w Iceland
Gronberg,	AKE	Guedalla,	PHILIP w
Groom,	SAM tv+	Guerin,	JULES p Am
Groom,	WINSTON w Am	Guerra,	BLANCA
Groot,	HUIGH e,st Dut	Guerra,	CASTULO tv
Gropius,	WALTER ac Am	Guerrero,	EVELYN tv+
Gropper,	WILLIAM p Am	Guerrero,	FRANCO
Gros,	ANTOINE p Fr	Guerrero,	PEDRO b
Grosbard,	ULU d	Guerzoni,	FAUSTO
Gross,	ARYE	Guesde,	JULES ref Fr
Gross,	DET. LARRY tv	Guest,	CHRISTOPHER tv+
Gross,	MARY tv+	Guest,	EDGAR j,po Am
Gross,	MASON tv	Guest,	LANCE tv+
Gross,	MICHAEL tv+	Guest,	NICHOLAS
Gross,	MILT cr Am	Guest,	WILLIAM s-pop Am
Gross,	PAUL	Guevara,	CHE(Ernesto)re Arg
Grosser,	ARTHUR tv	Gueye,	LAMINE st Sengal
Grossman,	DAVID w Am	Guggisberg,	PAUL mj-drm Swi
Grossman,	VASILY w,j Rus	Gugino,	CARLA tv+
Grosvenor,	GILBERT geog,ed Am	Guglielmo	MARCONI sc,i It
Grosz,	GEORGE p Ger-Am	Gui,	BERNARD r Fr
Groth,	KLAUS w,po,e Ger	Guich	KOOCK tv+
Groucho	MARX la,cm,tv+	Guidi,	ALESSANDRO po It
Groulx,	LIONEL h,e Can	Guido	GEZELLE po,r,e Belg
Grove	GILBERT geolAm	Guido	MAZZONI su It
Grove,	FREDERICK w Can	Guido	RENI p It
Grove,	GEORGE(Sir) ed, ct	Guido di Pietro	--- p It
Grove,	LEFTY b-mv'31 hf	Guido,	GRANDI math,e It
Grover	LOENING id-planes Am	Guidry,	RON b-cy'78
Grover,	DEBORAH tv+	Guilbert,	ANN tv
Grover,	EDWARD tv	Guilbert,	YVETTE s Fr
Grover,	STANLEY tv	Guild,	NANCY tv+
Groves,	REGINA tv	Guilfoyle,	PAUL
Grow,	GALUSHA st Am	Guillame	DUFAY c Fr
Groza,	LOU fb hf	Guillaume	BRUNE ar Fr
Gruber,	FRANZ organ,c Aus	Guillaume	BUDE e,w Fr
Gruber,	MAX von sc,e Aus	Guillaume	COUSTOU su Fr
Gruberova,	EDITA sopr Slovak	Guillaume	DUFAY c Fr
Gruelle,	JOHN cr Am	Guillaume	DUPRE su Fr
Gruen,	VICTOR ac Am	Guillaume,	CHARLES n-p'20
Gruenig,	ACE bb hf	Guillaume,	ROBERT tv+
Grumman,	LEROY id-planes Am	Guillemin,	ROGER n-m'77
Grundtvig,	NICOLAI po,w Dan	Guillen,	JORGE po Sp
Grundy,	HUGH mr-drums Br	Guillen,	NICOLAS po Cuba
Grundy,	REUBEN tv	Guillermin,	JOHN d
Grunewald,	MATHIAS p Ger	Guillman,	OFELIA
Gruson,	HERMANN id Ger	Guinan,	FRANCIS tv
Gryphius,	ANDREAS po,w Ger	Guinan,	MARY(Texas)la+ Am
Gua(st),	PIERRE colonizer Fr		

Guinee,	TIM	Gustav	HUSAK st Czech
Guiney,	LOUISE po,w Am	Gustav	KAUPERT su Ger
Guinn	WILLIAMS tv+	Gustav	KLEMM an Ger
Guinness,	ALEC(Sir) o-a'57	Gustav	KLIMT p Aus
Guion,	DAVID ws Am	Gustav	MAHLER cn,c Aus
Guiraldes,	RICARDO w,po Arg	Gustav	MEYRINK w Ger
Guisan,	HENRI ar Swi	Gustav	NOSKE st Ger
Guisewite,	CATHY cr Am	Gustav	STRUBE cn,c Am
Guitry,	LUCIEN la Fr	Gustav	VINTAS
Guitry,	SACHA w,la Fr	Gustav	WIED w Dan
Guizar,	TITO	Gustav	ZEUNER sc,eng Ger
Guizot,	FRANCOIS h,e,st Fr	Gustav von	KAHR st Ger
Gulager,	CLU tv+	Gustav von	MOSER w Ger
Gulick,	LUTHER e Am	Gustave	ADOR st Sw
Gulliver,	DOROTHY	Gustave	CRAUK su Fr
Gullstrand,	ALLVAR n-m'11	Gustave	DORE illus Fr
Gully,	JOHN boxer,st Br	Gustave	HIRN sc Fr
Gulpilil,	DAVID	Gustave	KAHN po,w Fr
Gumbel,	BRYANTtv-news,spts Am	Gustave	Le BON soc Fr
Gumilyov,	NIKOLAY po Rus	Gustave	MOREAU p Fr
Gummo	MARX vaudville,mer Am	Gustave	SARZEC arc,st Fr
Gungl,	JOSEPH c,cn Hung	Gustave	ZEDE eng-naval Fr
Gunilla	HUTTON tv	Gustavo	ROJO
Gunkel,	HERMANN e Ger	Gustavus	SWIFT f,id-meat Am
Gunn,	MOSES tv+	Gutenberg,	BENO sc Am
Gunn,	NEIL w Scot	Gutenberg,	JOHANNES i-print Ger
Gunn,	THOM po Br	Guthrie	McCLINTOCK tc
Gunnar	BJORNSTRAND	Guthrie,	A.B. Jr. p-f'50
Gunnar	EKELOF po,w Swe	Guthrie,	ARLO s-folk,ws+
Gunnar	HEIBERG w Nor	Guthrie,	TANI PHELPS
Gunnar	KNUDSEN id,st Nor	Guthrie,	WOODY s-folk,c Am
Gunnar	MYRDAL ec,e,st Swe	Gutierrez	Najera,MANUEL po,w Mex
Gunnarsson,	GUNNAR w,po Iceland	Guttenberg,	STEVE tv+
Gunne	SAX ds Am	Gutteridge,	LUCY
Gunter	GRASS w,po Ger	Guttuso,	RENATO p It
Gunther,	IGNAZ su Ger	Gutzkow,	KARL w Ger
Gunther,	JOHANN po Ger	Gutzon	BORGLUM su Am
Gunther,	JOHN w,j,tv Am	Guy	BOLTON w Br
Gunton,	BOB(Robert)tv+	Guy	BOYD tv+
Gur,	ALIZIA	Guy	DUBOIS p Am
Gurie,	SIGRID	Guy	FAWKES conspirator Br
Gurko,	IOSIF ar Rus	Guy	GREEN d
Gurley,	RALPH f Am	Guy	HOVIS tv
Gurry,	ERIC	Guy	KEY mj-trump Am
Gus	EDWARDS c Am	Guy	KIBBEE
Gus	GRISSOM as Am	Guy	LAFLEUR ho
Gus	KAHN lyrics Am	Guy	MADISON tv+
Guss,	LOUIS	Guy	MARKS tv
Gustaaf	IMHOFF colonist Dut	Guy	MOLLET st Fr
Gustaf	ARMFELT ar,st Swe	Guy	RAYMOND tv
Gustaf	BONDE st Swe	Guy	ROLFE
Gustaf	FRODING po,w Swe	Guy,	BILLY s-bari Am
Gustafson,	RALPH po Can	Guy,	BUDDY m-blues,guit Am
Gustav	CASSEL ec Swe	Guy,	JASMINE tv+
Gustav	EGGLOFF sc-oil Am	Guylaine	ST. ONGE tv
Gustav	ELMEN eng Am	Guyon,	JOE fb hf
Gustav	EMBDEN sc Ger	Guyon,	RICHARD mercenary Br
Gustav	FECHNER sc,e Ger	Guyot,	ARNOLD geog,geol Am
Gustav	FREYTAG w Ger	Guys,	CONSTANTIN illus Fr
Gustav	HERTZ sc,e Ger	Guzman,	LUIS
Gustav	HOLST c,e Br	Guzman,	MARTIN w Mex

Gwen	FARRELL tv		Haba,	ALOIS c,e Czech
Gwen	KENYON		Haber,	FRITZ n-c'18
Gwen	VERDON ba+ Am		Haberl,	FRANZ r,m Ger
Gwen	WATFORD		Haberlin,	PAUL ph,e Swi
Gwen	WELLES		Habich,	MATTHIAS
Gwendolyn	BROOKS po,w Am		Hablot	BROWNE illus Br
Gwendolyn	MacEWEN po,w Can		Hacha,	EMIL l,st Czech
Gwenn,	EDMUND o-s'47		Hack	WILSON b hf
Gwinn,	BILL tv		Hack,	SHELLEY tv+
Gwinn,	WILLIAM tv		Hacker,	JOSEPH tv+
Gwyda	DonHOWE tv		Hackert,	JACOB p Ger
Gwyn,	NELL la Br		Hackett,	ALBERT p-d'56
Gwyneth	PALTROW		Hackett,	BOBBY mj-cornet,cn Am
Gwynn,	STEPHEN w,po,j Ir		Hackett,	BUDDY cm,tv+ Am
Gwynn,	TONY b-7x bat champ		Hackett,	JOAN tv+
Gwynne,	ANNE		Hackett,	KARL
Gwynne,	FRED tv+		Hackman,	GENE o-a'71,o-s'92
Gwynne,	MICHAEL		Haddock,	JULIE tv
Gwynyth	WALSH		Haddon,	ALFRED an,e Br
Gylian	ROLAND		Haddon,	DAYLE
Gyngell,	KIM		Haddon,	LAURENCE tv
Gynt,	GRETA		Haddon,	RAYMOND tv
Gyorgy	CSERHALMI		Haden,	FRANCIS(Sir)etch
Gyorgy	DOZSA rebel Hung		Haden,	SARA
Gyorgy	KLAPKA ar,st Hung		Hadfield,	ROBERT(Sir)sc
Gyorgy	LUKACS ph,ct Hung		Hadik,	ANDREAS ar Aus
Gypsy Rose	LEE stripper+ Am		Hadji	SALIM st,r Indonesia
Gyula	ANDRASSY st Hung		Hadley,	HENRY c Am
Gyula	GOMBOS ar,st Hung		Hadley,	NANCY tv
			Hadley,	REED tv+
			Hadley,	TONY mr-s Br

"H" NAME DESIGNATION CODES

h	HISTORIAN	Hadow,	WILLIAM(Sir)w
hf	SPORTS HALL-OF-FAMER	Haeckel,	ERNST sc,e Ger
ho	HOCKEY PLAYER	Hafey,	CHICK b hf
hr	BASEBALL HOMERUN LEADER	Hafez-al	ASSAD st Syria
ho-m	HOCKEY MOST VALUABLE	Hafiz	--- po Persia
	PLAYER	Hafstein	HANNES st,po Icelnd
		Hagan,	CASS mj,cn Am
		Hagan,	CLIFF bb hf

"H" NATIONALITY CODE

Hung - HUNGARIAN	Hagan,	MOLLY tv+
	Hagar,	SAMMY mr-guit,s Am
	Hagen,	GAY tv

"H's"

		Hagen,	JEAN tv+
		Hagen,	JOHANN ast Aus
H. Allen	SMITH w-humor Am	Hagen,	KEVIN tv
H. Ellsworth	VINES t Am	Hagen,	ROSS tv+
H.B.	WARNER	Hagen,	UTA
H.C.	CARLSON(Dr.)bbc hf	Hagen,	WALTER g Am
H.C.	POTTER d	Hager,	JIM tv
H.E.	BATES w Br	Hager,	JON tv
H.F.	SAINT w-scifi Br	Hagerthy,	RON tv
H.G.	WELLS w-scifi,j Br	Hagerty,	JULIE
H.L.	MENCKEN j,ed,ct Am	Haggard,	HENRY(Sir)w
H.V.	KALTENBORN j-tv Am	Haggard,	MERLE s-cntry Am
Haag,	CHRISTINA tv	Haggerty,	DAN tv+
Haas,	HUGO	Haggerty,	DON tv
Haas,	JOSEPH c,e Ger	Haggin,	JAMES bus,l Am
Haas,	LUKAS	Hagler,	MARVIN boxer
Haase,	HUGO st Ger	Hagman,	HEIDI tv
Haast,	JOHN(Sir)geol,x	Hagman,	LARRY tv+
Haavelmo,	TRYGVE n-e'89	Hagstrom,	ROBERT w Am

Hague,	ALBERT tv	Hale,	BARBARA tv+
Hague,	FRANK st Am	Hale,	BINNIE
Hague,	STEVEN tv	Hale,	CHANIN tv
Hahn,	ARCHIE tv+	Hale,	CREIGHTON
Hahn,	GISELA	Hale,	EDWARD r,w Am
Hahn,	HERMANN su Ger	Hale,	GEORGE ast,e Am
Hahn,	JESS	Hale,	GEORGINA
Hahn,	JESSICA mo+	Hale,	JONATHAN
Hahn,	OTTO n-c'44	Hale,	LOUISE
Hahn,	REYNALDO c Venz	Hale,	LUCRETIA w Am
Hahn,	SUSAN po Am	Hale,	MONTE
Hahn-Hahn,	IDA von w Ger	Hale,	NANCY tv
Hahnemann,	SAMUEL md Ger	Hale,	NATHAN st,hero Am
Hai,	MANG	Hale,	SARAH w,ed Am
Haid,	CHARLES tv+	Haleloke	--- tv
Haiduc,	ION	Halevy,	FROMENTAL c Fr
Haig,	ALEXANDER st Am	Halevy,	LUDOVIC w Fr
Haig,	DOUGLAS ar Br	Haley	FISKE bus Am
Haig,	SID	Haley,	ALEX w Am
Haile Selassie --- st Ethiopia		Haley,	BILL mj-mr Am
Hailey,	ARTHUR w Can	Haley,	JACK
Haim,	COREY	Haley,	JACKIE EARLE
Haines,	JESSE b hf	Haley,	JACKIE tv
Haines,	RANDA d	Halfdan	KJERULF c Nor
Haines,	WILLIAM	Halford,	ROB mr-s Br
Haing S. NGOR		Haliburton,	THOMAS l,w Can
Haining,	MARK tv	Halid	USAKHGIL w Turk
Hairston,	JESTER tv	Hall	CAINE(Sir)w
Haje,	KHRYSTYNE tv	Hall	JOHNSON s,cn Am
Hakan	WESTERGREN	Hall,	ADELAIDE mj-s Am
Hakeem	OLAJUWON bb	Hall,	ALBERT
Hakim,	TAWFIQ al- w Egypt	Hall,	ALEXANDER d
Hal	ASHBY d	Hall,	ANTHONY tv+
Hal	BAYLOR tv	Hall,	ARCH Jr.
Hal	BLOCK tv	Hall,	ARSENIO tv+
Hal	BOURNE mj,cn,tv	Hall,	ASAPH astron Am
Hal	CONKLIN tv	Hall,	BRAD tv+
Hal	DAVID lyrics Am	Hall,	BRIDGET mo Am
Hal	FOSTER cr Am	Hall,	BRUCE mr-bass Am
Hal	GREER bb hf	Hall,	CHARLES sc,i,id Am
Hal	KEMP mj.cn Am	Hall,	CHARLES x Am
Hal	LINDEN tv+	Hall,	CLIFF tv
Hal	LINDES mr-guit Am	Hall,	DARYL mr-guit,s Am
Hal	LOMAN tv	Hall,	DEIDRE tv
Hal	MARCH tv-host Am	Hall,	DONALD po,ed Am
Hal	McRAE b	Hall,	ED tv
Hal	NEEDHAM d	Hall,	EDWIN sc,e Am
Hal	PEARY	Hall,	FAWN secy-Ol.North Am
Hal	PORTER w Austra	Hall,	GEORGE mj-viol,cn Am
Hal	PRICE	Hall,	GRANVILLE ps,e Am
Hal	ROACH d	Hall,	GRAYSON
Hal	SMITH tv	Hall,	HENRY
Hal	WALLIS pr-films Am	Hall,	HENRY mj,cn,c Br
Halaire	BELLOC w Br	Hall,	HUNTZ
Halas,	GEORGE fbc hf	Hall,	JAMES w Am
Halbe,	MAX w Ger	Hall,	JERRY mo Am
Haldane,	JOHN sc Scot	Hall,	JON tv+
Haldeman,	HARRY st,w Am	Hall,	KEVIN
Halder,	FRANZ ar Ger	Hall,	MICHAEL tv
Hale,	ALAN Jr tv+	Hall,	MONTY tv
Hale,	ALAN Sr	Hall,	PHILIP tv+

Hall,	PORTER		Hamilton	FISH st Am
Hall,	RADCLYFFE w Br		Hamilton	HARTY(Sir)c,cn
Hall,	RICH tv+		Hamilton	JORDAN st Am
Hall,	RUTH		Hamilton	SMITH md Am
Hall,	SEAN tv		Hamilton,	ALEXANDER st,w Am
Hall,	TERRY mr-s Br		Hamilton,	ALICE sc-md Am
Hall,	THURSTON tv+		Hamilton,	ANTONY tv+
Hall,	TOM s Am		Hamilton,	BERNIE tv+
Hall,	ZOOEY		Hamilton,	BILL b hf
Hallahan,	CHARLES tv+		Hamilton,	CARRIE tv+
Hallam,	ARTHUR po,w Br		Hamilton,	EDITH e,w Am
Hallam,	HENRY h Br		Hamilton,	GEORGE tv+
Hallam,	JOHN		Hamilton,	GUY d
Hallam,	LEWIS la Br		Hamilton,	HENRY tv
Hallaren,	JANE		Hamilton,	JANE actress
Halldor	LAXNESS po Iceland		Hamilton,	JANE w Am
Halle	BERRY		Hamilton,	JOHN tv+
Halleck,	FITZ po Am		Hamilton,	LINDA tv+
Haller,	BERTOLD r Swi		Hamilton,	MARGARET tv+
Haller,	MELONIE tv		Hamilton,	MURRAY tv+
Hallet,	ETIENNE ac Am		Hamilton,	NEIL tv+
Hallett,	MAL mj,cn Am		Hamilton,	RICHARD tv+
Halley,	EDMOND ast Br		Hamilton,	SCOTT sk,o-g'84 Am
Halley,	RUDOLPH tv		Hamilton,	SUZANNA
Hallick,	TOM tv+		Hamilton,	TOM mr-bass Am
Hallie	FOOTE		Hamish	STUART mr-guit,s Scot
Hallie	TODD tv		Hamlin	GARLAND bio,w Am
Hallier,	LORI		Hamlin,	CYRUS r Am
Halliwell	HOBBES		Hamlin,	HARRY tv+
Hallman,	VICTORIA tv		Hamlisch,	MARVIN p-d'76
Hallstrom,	LASSE ds,d		Hamlisch,	MARVIN piano,c Am
Halop,	BILLY tv+		Hammarskjold,	DAG n-x'61
Halop,	FLORENCE tv		Hammer	--- m-rap Am
Halper	LEIVICK po,w Am		Hammer,	ARMAND id,f Am
Halpin,	LUKE tv+		Hammer,	BEN
Halpin,	MILES tv		Hammer,	JAY tv
Hals,	FRANS p Dut		Hammer,	W.C. mr
Halsey	WILSON pb Am		Hammerstein,	OSCAR pr, p-d'50
Halsey,	BRETT tv+		Hammett,	DASHIELL w Am
Halsey,	BULL ar Am		Hammond,	EARL tv
Halsman,	PHILIPPE fo Am		Hammond,	JOHN eng-mines Am
Halstead,	HENRY mj,cn Am		Hammond,	JOHN Jr eng,i Am
Halton,	CHARLES		Hammond,	LAURENS i Am
Halvor	HOEL st Nor		Hammond,	NANCI tv
Halyalkar,	JONATHAN tv		Hammond,	NICHOLAS
Ham	LARSEN		Hammond,	PETER tv
Ham,	GREG m-sax,kbds Aust		Hamo	THORNYCROFT(Sir)su
Ham,	JACK fb hf		Hamp,	JOHNNY mj,cn Am
Ham,	PETE mr-guit,s Welsh		Hampden,	WALTER la+ Am
Hama,	MIE		Hampshire,	SUSAN
Hamann,	JOHANN ph,st Ger		Hampton,	JAMES tv+
Hambly,	BARBARA w-scifi Am		Hampton,	LIONEL mj-vibes,cn+Am
Hambro,	CARL st Nor		Hampton,	PAUL
Hamel,	VERONICA tv+		Hampton,	SLIDE mj Am
Hamer,	RUSTY tv		Hampton,	WADE st,ar-CSA Am
Hamerik,	ASGER c Dan		Hamsun,	KNUT n-l'20
Hamil,	JAYNE		Han	SOLO fc starwars
Hamill,	DOROTHY sk,o-g'76		Han Yu	--- w,po,ph China
Hamill,	MARK tv+		Han,	ULRICH print Aus
Hamilton	BASSO w Am		Hana	MANDLIKOVA t Czech
Hamilton	CAMP tv+		Hancock,	HERBIE mj-piano,c Am

Hancock,	JOHN st Am	Hans	ARP p,po Fr
Hancock,	KATE w Am	Hans	BEHAM p Ger
Hancock,	LYNN tv	Hans	BETHE sc Am
Hancock,	PRENTIS tv	Hans	BLAICH w Ger
Hand,	LEARNED l,w Am	Hans	CAROSSA po,w,md Ger
Handel,	GEORGE c Br	Hans	CLOOS geol,e Ger
Handke,	PETER w,po Aus	Hans	CONRIED tv+
Handl,	IRENE	Hans	DEHMELT sc Ger-Am
Handl,	JAKOB c Slov	Hans	DRIESCH sc,ph Ger
Handleman,	STANLEY tv	Hans	EGEDE r Nor
Handy,	JAMES	Hans	FISCHER sc,e Ger
Handy,	WILLIAM mj,c Am	Hans	FOLZ s,ws Ger
Haney,	CAROL tv	Hans	GAGERN st Ger
Haney,	DARYL	Hans	GRAM md,e Dan
Hank	AARON b-mv'57 hf	Hans	GRIMM w Ger
Hank	AZARIA tv	Hans	HARTUNG p Fr
Hank	BALLARD s,ws Am	Hans	HASSLER organ,c Ger
Hank	BAUER b	Hans	HEDTOFT st Dan
Hank	BELL	Hans	HOLBEIN(Elder)p Ger
Hank	BRANDT tv	Hans	HOLBEIN(Younger)p Ger
Hank	GARRETT tv+	Hans	HOLT
Hank	IBA bbc hf	Hans	HOPF tenor
Hank	KANUI tv	Hans	HOTTER bari Ger
Hank	KETCHAM cr Am	Hans	HUBER c,e Swi
Hank	LOCKLIN s-cntry Am	Hans	JAEGER w Nor
Hank	MANN	Hans	JANSSON st Swe
Hank	MARVIN mr-guit Br	Hans	JARTA st Swe
Hank	MEDRESS mr-s tenor	Hans	JENSEN sc,e Ger
Hank	SAUER b	Hans	KAALUND po Dan
Hank	SNOW s-cnt,tv Am	Hans	KINCK w Nor
Hankel,	WILHELM sc,e Ger	Hans	KREBS(Sir)sc Br
Hankey,	MAURICE ar,st Br	Hans	LUFFT p Ger
Hanks,	TOM o-a'93'94,tv+	Hans	MAKART p Aus
Hanley,	BRIDGET tv	Hans	MEMLING p Belg
Hanley,	JAMES w Br	Hans	ORSTED sc Dan
Hanley,	JIMMY	Hans	POELZIG ac Ger
Hanley,	PETER tv	Hans	RICHTER cn Ger
Hanley,	ROBERT tv	Hans	RICHTER p,pr-films Am
Hann,	JULIUS weather,e Aus	Hans	SACHS po,w,s Ger
Hanna	SCHYGULLA	Hans	SLOANE(Sir)sc,md
Hanna,	ELIZABETH tv	Hans	SPEMANN md-sc,e Ger
Hanna,	MARCUS mer,st Am	Hans	SUSS p Ger
Hannah	ADAMS w Am	Hans	THOMA p Ger
Hannah	ARENDT e Am	Hans	ZIETEN ar Prussia
Hannah	COWLEY w Br	Hans	ZINSSER sc-md e Am
Hannah	CUTRONA tv	Hans Christian	BRANNER w Dan
Hannah	DUSTON heroine Am	Hans von	BULOW piano,cn Ger
Hannah	MORE w,r Br	Hans von	ESSEN ar Swe
Hannah,	DARYL	Hans von	MAREES p Ger
Hannah,	JOHN fb hf	Hans von	SEECKT ar,w Ger
Hannah,	PAGE	Hans-Christian BLECH	
Hannay,	JAMES r,w Ir	Hans-Jurgen WALTHER cn Ger	
Hanne	AXMAN	Hansard,	LUKE print Br
Hannes	ALFVEN sc Swe	Hansard,	PAUL tv
Hannes	HAFSTEIN st,po Icelnd	Hansberry,	LORRAINE w Am
Hanns	OERTEL e,w Ger	Hansen,	ALVIN ec,e,w Am
Hanns	ZISCHLER	Hansen,	GALE
Hanold,	MARILYN tv	Hansen,	JANIS tv
Hans	AANRUD w Nor	Hansen,	JENS j,st Dan
Hans	AHLMANN sc Swe	Hansen,	JOACHIM
Hans	ALBERS	Hansen,	JUDITH tv

Hansen,	LIANE radio-host Am	Harford,	BETTY tv
Hansen,	PATTI	Hargitay,	MARISKA tv+
Hansen,	PETER tv	Hargreaves,	JAMES i Br
Hansen,	RON w	Hargreaves,	JOHN
Hansjorg	FELMY	Hari	RHODES tv+
Hanson,	CURTIS d	Hari Krishen --- guru India	
Hanson,	HOWARD p-m'44	Hari,	MATA ba,spy Dut
Hanson,	LARS	Harimoto,	DALE tv
Hanson,	PETER tv	Haring,	GEORG j,w Ger
Hanson,	VICTOR bb hf	Harington,	JOHN(Sir)w
Hansson,	OLA w Swe	Hariri,	al- po Arab
Hansson,	PER st Swe	Harker,	GORDON
Hanya	HOLM ba Am	Harket,	MORTEN mr-s Nor
Hap	ARNOLD ar,fly Am	Harkins,	JOHN tv+
Hapgood,	NORMAN ed,w Am	Harkness,	RICHARD tv
Happy	CHANDLER b-commish hf	Harlan	LEONARD mj-sax,cn Am
Har	KHORANA md Am	Harlan	STONE l-chief just Am
Hara,	SETSUKO	Harlan,	KENNETH
Harada,	MEIKO	Harlan,	OTIS
Harald	BOHR math,e Dan	Harland	SANDERS(Col.)KFC Am
Harald	KIDDE w Dan	Harland,	MICHAEL tv
Harald	LANDER ba Dan	Harland,	ROBERT tv
Harald	LEIPNITZ	Harlen	CARRAHER tv
Harald	REINL d	Harley	CROSS tv+
Harareet,	HAYA	Harley	KOZAK
Harbach,	OTTO w, Am	Harley	WOOD
Harbison,	JOHN p-m'87	Harley,	STEVE mr-s Br
Harburg,	E.Y.(Yip)lyrics Am	Harlin,	RENNY d
Harcum,	BOB tv	Harlon	HILL fb
Hardaway,	ANFERNEE bb	Harlow	SHAPLEY ast,e Am
Hardaway,	TIM bb	Harlow,	JEAN
Harden,	ARTHUR(Sir)n-c'29	Harmer,	SHIRLEY tv
Harden,	ERNEST Jr. tv	Harmodio	ARIAS st Panama
Harden,	MARCIA	Harmon,	DEBORAH tv+
Harden,	MAXIMILIAN j,w Ger	Harmon,	KRISTIN tv
Hardie,	KEIR labor,st Br	Harmon,	MARK tv+
Hardin,	JERRY tv+	Harmon,	MILLARD ar,flyer Am
Hardin,	MELORA	Harmon,	STEVE tv
Hardin,	TY tv+	Harnick,	SHELDON p-d'60
Harding	WARREN G.29th pres	Haro,	LUIS de st Sp
Harding,	ANN	Harold	ARLEN c Am
Harding,	HARVEY tv	Harold	BECKER d
Harding,	JUNE tv	Harold	BROWN mr-drm Am
Harding,	LYN	Harold	BURTON l,st Am
Harding,	TANYA sk Am	Harold	CLURMAN pr,d,ct Am
Hardison,	KADEEM tv+	Harold	CONKLIN tv
Hardt,	ELOISE tv	Harold	DAVIS w Am
Hardt,	ERNST po,w Ger	Harold	DOW tv
Hardwicke,	CEDRIC	Harold	FONG tv
Hardy	CROSS eng,e Am	Harold	GATTY fly Aust
Hardy	KRUEGER	Harold	GOODWIN
Hardy,	ALEXANDRE w Fr	Harold	GOULD tv+
Hardy,	OLIVER cm+ Am	Harold	GRAY cr Am
Hardy,	ROBERT	Harold	HOPKINS
Hardy,	SAM	Harold	HUBER
Hardy,	THOMAS w,po Br	Harold	ICKES st Am
Hare,	DAVID w Br	Harold	LASKI w,e,ec Br
Hare,	JAMES fo Am	Harold	LLOYD cm,d+ Am
Hare,	JOHN(Sir)la	Harold	LLOYD Jr.
Hare,	LUMSDEN	Harold	MELVIN m-soul
Harewood,	DORIAN tv+	Harold	MONRO po,ed r Br

Harold	PEARY	Harris,	DEBBY tv
Harold	PINTER w Br	Harris,	ED
Harold	PRINCE d	Harris,	FOX
Harold	RAMIS d,w,tv+ Am	Harris,	FRANCO fb hf
Harold	REID m-pop,cnt Am	Harris,	FRANK j,w Am
Harold	ROBBINS w Am	Harris,	HOWARD(Stony) tv
Harold	ROME c Am	Harris,	HOWEL r Welsh
Harold	ROSS ed Am	Harris,	JACK mj-viol,cn Am-Br
Harold	RUGG e,ed Am	Harris,	JO ANN tv+
Harold	RUSSELL	Harris,	JOEL j,w Am
Harold	SAKATA	Harris,	JOHN w-scifi Br
Harold	STARK navy Am	Harris,	JONATHAN tv
Harold	STASSEN st Am	Harris,	JOSHUA tv
Harold	STERN mj,cn Am	Harris,	JULIE tv+
Harold	STONE tv+	Harris,	JULIUS
Harold	TEEN fc	Harris,	LARA
Harold	UREY sc,e Am	Harris,	LEE tv
Harold	VARMUS md-sc Am	Harris,	LUISA bb hf
Harold	WADE(Steep)mj,cn Can	Harris,	MEL tv+
Harold	WRIGHT w Am	Harris,	NEIL PATRICK tv+
Harolde,	RALF	Harris,	PERCY(Bud) tv
Harper	LEE w Am	Harris,	PHIL mj-s,cn,cm+ Am
Harper,	CONSTANCE tv	Harris,	RICHARD
Harper,	DAVID W. tv+	Harris,	ROBERT tv
Harper,	JESSE fbc Am	Harris,	ROBIN
Harper,	JESSICA tv+	Harris,	ROSEMARY tv+
Harper,	JOHN tv	Harris,	ROY c Am
Harper,	ROBERT tv+	Harris,	STACY tv
Harper,	RON tv	Harris,	TIM fb-d'89
Harper,	TESS	Harris,	WILLIAM e,ph Am
Harper,	VALERIE tv+	Harrison	FORD
Harpo	MARX la,cm+ Am	Harrison	LIU
Harpur,	CHARLES po Aust	Harrison	MULLER
Harrell,	JACK tv	Harrison	OTIS ar,j Am
Harrelson,BUD b,gg'71		Harrison	PAGE tv+
Harrelson,WOODY tv+		Harrison,	BENJAMIN 23rd pres
Harridge, WILL b hf		Harrison,	BILLY mr-guit Ir
Harriet	HAWES sc,e Am	Harrison,	CATHRYN
Harriet	MILLER birds,w Am	Harrison,	DICKIE tv
Harriet	MONROE po,ed Am	Harrison,	GEORGE mr-guit Br
Harriet	NELSON tv	Harrison,	GREGORY tv+
Harriet	TUBMAN abolition Am	Harrison,	JENILEE tv+
Harriet	Van HORNE tv	Harrison,	JERRY mr-kbds Am
Harriet Beecher STOWE w Am		Harrison,	KATHLEEN
Harriman, WILLIAM st Am		Harrison,	KATHRYN w Can
Harrington, AL tv		Harrison,	LINDA tv+
Harrington, LAURA		Harrison,	LISA tv
Harrington, MICHAEL w Am		Harrison,	NOEL s,tv Am
Harrington, PAT Jr. tv		Harrison,	REX(Sir)o-a'64
Harriot	BLATCH fe Am	Harrison,	RICHARD
Harris	KAL tv	Harrison,	ROSS sc,e Am
Harris	SCOTT w Am	Harrison,	WILLIAM HNRY 9th Pres
Harris	YULIN	Harrold,	KATHRYN tv+
Harris,	BARBARA	Harron,	DON tv
Harris,	BILL tv	Harron,	JOHN
Harris,	BOB tv	Harron,	ROBERT
Harris,	BRAD	Harrow,	LISA
Harris,	BUCKY b hf	Harry	AKST mj-piano,cn,c Am
Harris,	CHAPIN dentist Am	Harry	ANDREWS
Harris,	CYNTHIA tv+	Harry	ARNIM st Ger
Harris,	DANIELLE	Harry	ARNOLD mj-reeds,cn Swe

Harry	BABBIT s Am	Harry	SHANNON
Harry	BAER	Harry	SHEARER tv+
Harry	BASCH tv	Harry	SIMEONE m,cn,tv Am
Harry	BAUR	Harry	SOSNIK m,cn,tv Am
Harry	CARAY b-announcer Am	Harry	STANTON
Harry	CAREY Jr.	Harry	STRANG
Harry	CAREY Sr.	Harry	STUTZ id-cars Am
Harry	CARNEY mj,sax Am	Harry	TOBIAS c Am
Harry	CASEY mr-kbds,s Am	Harry	VANDA mr-guitar Dut
Harry	CLARK tv	Harry	VARDON g Br
Harry	COLE tv	Harry	WARNER exec-films Am
Harry	CONNICK Jr mj,s Am	Harry	WARREN ws,c Am
Harry	COOL mj-s Am	Harry	WEXLER weather Am
Harry	CORBETT	Harry	WILSON w Am
Harry	CREWS w,j Am	Harry	WOODS
Harry	ENDO tv	Harry	WRIGHT b hf
Harry	EVANS ed,st Am	Harry von	TILZER c Am
Harry	FALK d	Harry von	ZELL radio,tv+ Am
Harry	FISHER(Bud)cr Am	Harry,	DEBORAH mr-s Am
Harry	FOSDICK r Am	Harry,	JACKEE tv
Harry	FRASER d	Harshman,	MARV bbc hf
Harry	FURNISS illus Br	Hart	BOCHNER
Harry	GELLER tv	Hart	CRANE po Am
Harry	GOAZ tv	Hart Pease	DANKS c-hymns Am
Harry	GOLDEN ed,w Am	Hart,	ALBERT h Am
Harry	GOZ tv+	Hart,	BILL tv
Harry	GREB boxer Am	Hart,	CLAY s,tv Am
Harry	GRIBBON	Hart,	DAVID tv
Harry	GROENER tv	Hart,	DELORES
Harry	HAMLIN tv+	Hart,	DOROTHY tv
Harry	HARVEY	Hart,	EDWIN tv
Harry	HARVEY Sr tv	Hart,	GARY st Am
Harry	HESS sc Am	Hart,	HARVEY d
Harry	HICKOX tv	Hart,	IAN
Harry	HOOPER b hf	Hart,	JOHN j,tv
Harry	HOPKINS st Am	Hart,	JOHNNY cr Am
Harry	HOPMAN t Aust	Hart,	JOSEPHINE w Am
Harry	HOUDINI magic,w Am	Hart,	LORENZ lyrics Am
Harry	JAMES mj-trump,cn+ Am	Hart,	MARVIN boxer Am
Harry	KELLAR magician Am	Hart,	MARY tv-hostess Am
Harry	LANDERS	Hart,	MICKYmr-drm,ws Am
Harry	LANGDON	Hart,	MOSS p-d'37
Harry	LAUDER(Sir)s Scot	Hart,	RALPH tv
Harry	LAUTER tv+	Hart,	ROXANNE
Harry	LEE(LghtHorse)ar,stAm	Hart,	SUSAN
Harry	LIME fc	Hart,	WILLIAM la+Am
Harry	LITWACK bbc hf	Harte,	BRET w,po Am
Harry	MILLIS ec,e Am	Hartford,	JOHN tv
Harry	MORGAN tv+	Hartley,	L.P. w Br
Harry	MURPHY tv	Hartley,	MARIETTE tv+
Harry	MYERS	Hartley,	MARSDEN p Am
Harry	NORTHUP tv	Hartlib,	SAMUEL ref Br
Harry	O'REILLY tv	Hartline,	HALDAN n-m'67
Harry	PARTCH c Am	Hartman,	DAVID tv
Harry	PHILBY x Br	Hartman,	ELIZABETH
Harry	PRIME mj-s Am	Hartman,	JOHN m-drm Am
Harry	REEMS porn actor Am	Hartman,	KAREN tv
Harry	REID geol,e Am	Hartman,	LISA tv+
Harry	RUBY c Am	Hartman,	PAUL tv
Harry	SALTER m,cn,tv Am	Hartman,	PHIL tv+
		Hartmann,	ENA tv

Hartmann, MORITZ w Ger	Hastings ISMAY ar Br
Hartmut MICHEL sc Ger	Hastings, BOB tv+
Hartnell, WILLIAM	Hastings, DON tv
Hartnett, GABBY b-mv'35 hf	Hastings, WARREN st Br
Hartung, HANS p Fr	Hatch, ORRIN st Am
Harty, BILL mj-drm Am	Hatch, RICHARD tv+
Harty, HAMILTON(Sir)c,cn	Hatcher HUGHES w Am
Harty, PATRICIA tv	Hatcher, TERI tv+
Hartzenbusch, JUAN w Sp	Hatfield, BOBBY mr-s Am
Haruko SUGIMURA	Hatfield, HURD
Harvard, JOHN r,f(HU) Am	Hathaway, AMY tv
Harve PRESNELL	Hathaway, ANNE wf-Wm Shaks
Harvey ELLIS ac Am	Hathaway, HENRY d
Harvey HARDING tv	Hathaway, NOAH tv+
Harvey HART d	Hatlo, JIMMY cr Am
Harvey HINSLEY mr-guit Br	Hatrak, ERNIE piano, tv
Harvey JASON tv+	Hattie CARAWAY st Am
Harvey KEITEL	Hattie JACQUES
Harvey KORMAN tv+	Hattie McDANIEL
Harvey LEMBECK tv+	Hattie WINSTON tv
Harvey MARTIN fb	Hatton, BILLY mr-bass Br
Harvey VERNON tv	Hatton, RAYMOND
Harvey WILEY sc,ref,st Am	Hatton, RONDO
Harvey, DON	Hauch, JOHANNES po,w Dan
Harvey, GEORGE j,ed,pb Am	Hauck, ALBERT r,e Ger
Harvey, HARRY	Hauer, FRANZ von geol Aus
Harvey, HARRY Sr. tv	Hauer, RUTGER
Harvey, HAYWARD i,id-steel Am	Hauff, ANGELIKA
Harvey, JOHN tv	Hauff, WILHELM w,po Ger
Harvey, JOHN(Sir)pr,la	Haufrect, ALAN tv
Harvey, LAURENCE	Haug, EMILE geol,e Fr
Harvey, MICHAEL tv	Hauk, MINNIE sopr Am
Harvey, NED m,cn,tv Am	Haupt, HERMAN eng Am
Harvey, PAUL tv+	Haupt, ULLRICH
Harvey, RODNEY	Hauptman, HERBERT n-c'85
Harvey, WILLIAM md,sc Br	Hauptmann,GERHART n-l'12
Harvey, WILLIAM(Coin)ec Am	Hauser, FAY
Hasan, MOULAY st Morocco	Hauser, KASPAR foundling Ger
Hasan, SAYYID r Somali	Hauser, WINGS
Hasdeu, BOGDAN h Rom	Hausmann, RAOUL p,fo Aus
Hasegawa, KAZUO	Hausner, JERRY tv
Hasek, JAROSLAV j,w Cz	Hauy, RENE sc,e Fr
Hasel, JOE tv	Hava LAMBERTO d
Haskell, JACK tv	Havas, CHARLES j Fr
Haskell, PETER tv+	Havel, VACLAV w,po Cz
Haskell, SUSAN tv	Havelock ELLIS md,w Br
Haskin, BYRON d	Haven, STEPHEN w Am
Haskins, LOLA w Am	Havens, RICHIE s-folk+ Am
Haslam, LU ANN tv	Haver, JUNE m,tv+
Hasner, LEOPOLD ec,st,e Aus	Havergal BRIAN c Br
Hassam, CHILDE p Am	Havers, CLOPTON md Br
Hassan, NORMAN mr-drums Br	Havers, NIGEL
Hasse, ERNST st,e Ger	Haviland MORRIS
Hasse, O.E.	Havilland,OLIVIA de o-a'46'49
Hassel, ODD n-c'69	Havlicek, JOHN bb hf
Hasselhoff, DAVID tv+	Havoc, JUNE
Hasselt, ANDRE po Belg	Havre, BRETT fb
Hassett, MARILYN	Hawes, HARRIET sc,e Am
Hassler, HANS organ,c Ger	Hawke, ETHAN d+
Hasso, SIGNE	Hawkes, JACQUETTA sc,w Br
Hastie, WILLIAM l,e,st Am	Hawkes, JOHN w Am

Hawking,	STEPHEN w Br	Hayes,	RON tv
Hawkins,	ANTHONY(Sir)w	Hayes,	RUTHERFORD 19th pres
Hawkins,	COLEMAN mj-sax Am	Hayes,	WOODY fbc Am
Hawkins,	CONNIE bb hf	Hayley	MILLS
Hawkins,	HAWKSHAW s-cnt, Am	Haym	SALOMON mer,f Am
Hawkins,	JACK	Haym,	RUDOLF ph,h,e Ger
Hawkins,	JIMMY tv	Hayman,	CYD
Hawkins,	JOHN(Sir)l,w	Hayman,	DAVID
Hawkins,	RICHARD(Sir)navy,x	Haymer,	JOHNNY tv
Hawkins,	VIRGINIA tv	Haymes,	DICK s+
Hawks,	HOWARD d	Haynau,	JULIUS ar Aus
Hawkshaw	HAWKINS s-cntry Am	Hayne,	PAUL po Am
Hawley	CRIPPEN murderer Am	Haynes,	CAL
Hawley,	MONTE	Haynes,	ELWOOD i,sc Am
Hawley,	WILLIS st Am	Haynes,	LLOYD tv
Hawn,	GOLDIE o-s'69,tv+	Haynes,	MIKE fb-d'84
Haworth,	JILL	Haynes,	ROBERTA
Haworth,	WALTER(Sir)n-c'37	Haynes,	ROY mj-drm Am
Hawthorne,	NATHANIEL w Am	Haynie,	JIM
Hawthorne,	NIGEL	Hays,	ARTHUR l Am
Hawtrey,	CHARLES	Hays,	DANIEL w Am
Hawtrey,	CHARLES(Sir)la	Hays,	DAVID w
Haxo,	FRANCOIS eng-ar Fr	Hays,	KATHRYN tv
Hay	PETRIE	Hays,	ROBERT tv+
Hay,	COLIN s Scot	Hays,	WILL l,st Am
Hay,	JOHN st,w,po Am	Haysbert,	DENNIS
Hay,	ROY mr-guit,kbds Br	Hayter,	JAMES
Haya	HARAREET	Hayward	HARVEY i,id-steel Am
Hayakawa,	SESSUE	Hayward,	CHAD
Hayashi,	MARC	Hayward,	DAVID tv+
Hayden	RORKE tv+	Hayward,	JUSTIN s-r&b,ws Br
Hayden,	DON tv	Hayward,	LOUIS tv+
Hayden,	JAN van der p Dut	Hayward,	SUSAN o-a'58
Hayden,	LINDA	Haywood	NELSON tv
Hayden,	ROBERT po Am	Haywood,	CHRIS
Hayden,	RUSSELL	Haywood,	ELIZA w Br
Hayden,	STERLING	Hayworth,	RITA
Haydn,	JOSEPH c Aus	Hayworth,	VINTON tv
Haydn,	RICHARD	Hayyim	BIALIK po Jewish
Haydock,	ERIC mr-bass Br	Hayyim	VITAL r Palestine
Hayek,	FRIEDRICH von n-e'74	Haze,	JONATHAN
Hayers,	SIDNEY d	Hazel	COURT tv+
Hayes,	ALLISON	Hazel	WIGHTMAN t Am
Hayes,	BILL tv	Hazelhurst,	NONI
Hayes,	CHRIS mr-guit Am	Hazen,	WILLIAM ar Am
Hayes,	ELVIN bb hf	Hazlitt,	WILLIAM w,ct Br
Hayes,	GABBY	Head,	EDITH ds-costumes Am
Hayes,	GEORGE(Gabby)	Headly,	GLENNE
Hayes,	HELEN o-a'32 &	Headon,	NICKY mr-drm Br
Hayes,	HELEN o-s'70,tv+	Heald,	ANTHONY
Hayes,	ISAAC mr,r&b,s,tv+ Am	Healey,	ED fb hf
Hayes,	ISAAC x Am	Healey,	JAMES tv
Hayes,	JOHN d	Healey,	JEFF guit,s,ws Can
Hayes,	KENDALL ws-cnt Am	Healey,	MYRON
Hayes,	LESTER fb-d'80	Healy,	JEREMIAH w Am
Hayes,	LINDA	Healy,	MARY tv
Hayes,	MARGARET tv+	Healy,	TED
Hayes,	PATRICIA	Heaney,	SEAMUS po,w Ir
Hayes,	PETER tv+	Heard,	JOHN
Hayes,	RICHARD tv	Hearn,	ANN tv+
Hayes,	ROLAND tenor Am	Hearn,	CHICK tv

Hearn,	GEORGE		Heeren,	ARNOLD h,e Ger
Hearn,	LAFCADIO j,w Am		Hefele,	KARL r,h,e Ger
Hearne,	SAMUEL x Br		Heflin,	VAN o-s'42, tv+
Hearns,	THOMAS boxer Am		Hefner,	HUGH pb Am
Hearon,	SHELBY w Am		Hegel,	GEORG w,ph,e Ger
Hearst,	GEORGE id-mines Am		Heggie,	O.P.
Hearst,	WILLIAM RNDLPH pb Am		Hegi,	URSULA w Am
Heasley,	MARIA tv		Hegyes,	ROBERT tv+
Heat-Moon,	JAMES LEAST w		Hehir,	PETER
Heath,	EDWARD st Br		Heiberg,	GUNNAR w Nor
Heath,	TED mj-tromb Br		Heid,	CARL tv
Heather	ANGEL		Heidegger,	MARTIN ph Ger
Heather	GRAHAM tv+		Heideman,	KATHLEEN po Am
Heather	McADAM tv		Heiden,	ERIC sk 5 x o-g'80
Heather	MENZIES		Heiden,	JANICE tv
Heather	O'ROURKE tv+		Heidenstam,	VERNER von n-l'16
Heather	RATTRAY		Heidi	BOHAY tv
Heather	SMITH tv		Heidi	HAGMAN tv
Heather	THOMAS tv+		Heidi	KLING
Heather	YOUNG tv		Heidi	PAINE
Heatherton,	JOEY tv+		Heidi	VAUGHN
Heaton,	PAUL mr-guit,s Br		Heidi	ZEIGLER tv
Heatter,	GABRIEL j,radio Am		Heidt,	HORACE mj,cn,tv+ Am
Heavener,	DAVID d+		Heifetz,	JASCHA viol Am
Heaviside,	OLIVER sc Br		Heike	KAMERLINGH sc Dut
Hebbel,	FRIEDRICH po,w Ger		Heilbroner,	ROBERT ec,w Am
Hebel,	JOHANN po Ger		Heilmann,	HARRY b hf
Heber	GRANT r-Morman Am		Heilveil,	ELAYNE
Hebert,	CHRIS tv		Heim,	ALBERT geol Swi
Hebra,	FERDINAND md Aus		Hein,	MEL fb hf
Heche,	ANNE tv+		Hein,	PIET navy Dut
Hecht,	ANTHONY p-q'68		Heine,	HEINRICH po,w,j Ger
Hecht,	BEN j,w Am		Heinlein,	ROBERT w scifi Am
Hecht,	GINA tv		Heinrich	ABETZ st Ger
Hecht,	PAUL tv+		Heinrich	ALBERT c,po,organ Ger
Heck,	BARBARA r Am		Heinrich	ARREST ast,e Ger
Heckart,	EILEEN o-s'72,tv+		Heinrich	BARTH x Ger
Heckel,	ERICH p Ger		Heinrich	BIBER viol,c Ger
Heckerling,	AMY d		Heinrich	BOIE w Ger
Hector	ALTERIO		Heinrich	BOLL w Ger
Hector	BABENCO d		Heinrich	BRONN sc,w Ger
Hector	BERLIOZ c,cn Fr		Heinrich	BRUNING st Ger
Hector	LEFUEL ac Fr		Heinrich	DORN c Ger
Hector	MUNRO w Scot		Heinrich	DOVE sc,e Ger
Hector	SUAREZ		Heinrich	FINCK c Ger
Heda,	WILLEM p Dut		Heinrich	FOCKE ds-planes Ger
Hedaya,	DAN		Heinrich	GRAETZ h Ger
Hedda	HOPPER j,ct+ Am		Heinrich	HEINE po,w,j Ger
Hedin,	SERENE		Heinrich	HERTZ sc,e Ger
Hedin,	SVEN geog,x Swe		Heinrich	HIMMLER st Nazi Ger
Hedison,	DAVID tv+		Heinrich	KAYSER sc,e Ger
Hedley	MATTINGLY tv		Heinrich	KLUCK ar Ger
Hedren,	TIPPI		Heinrich	LAUBE w.d Ger
Hedrick,	JOHN p-b'95		Heinrich	LORIS po Swi
Hedtoft,	HANS st Dan		Heinrich	LUBKE st Ger
Hedwig,	JOHANN sc.e Ger		Heinrich	MANN w Ger
Hedy	LAMARR		Heinrich	OLBERS md,ast Ger
Heem,	JAN de p Dut		Heinrich	ROHRER sc Swi
Heenan,	JOHN boxer Am		Heinrich	SCHUTZ c Ger
Heep,	URIAH fc		Heinrich	SUSE mystic Ger
Heer,	OSWALD sc,w Swi		Heinrich	WIELAND sc,e Ger

Heinrich	WUTTKE h,st Ger
Heinrich	ZOLLNER c,cn,w Ger
Heinrich von BRUHL st Ger	
Heinrich von KLEIST w Ger	
Heinrich von SYBEL h Ger	
Heinse,	JOHANN w Ger
Heinsohn,	ELISA tv
Heinsohn,	TOM bb hf
Heinz	BENNENT
Heinz	BURT mr-bass Ger
Heinz	DRACHE
Heinz	WEHNER mj,cn Ger
Heinz,	HENRY id-foods Am
Heisenberg,	WERNER n-p'32
Heisler,	STUART d
Heisman,	JOHN fbc Am
Heitor	VILLA-LOBOS c Braz
Helaine	LEMBECK tv
Held,	ANNA la Am
Held,	JOHN Jr cr Am
Held,	KARL tv
Helen	BEVERLY
Helen	CARTER tv
Helen	CLARKE ed,w Am
Helen	CRAIG tv+
Helen	CURTIS tv
Helen	FORREST s Am
Helen	FOSTER
Helen	GILBERT
Helen	GRAYCO tv
Helen	HAYES la,tv+ Am
Helen	HUGHES
Helen	HUNT tv+
Helen	JACKSON po,w Am
Helen	KELLER(blind)w Am
Helen	KLEEB tv
Helen	MACK
Helen	MARTIN
Helen	MIRREN
Helen	MORGAN
Helen	MORSE
Helen	PALMER w Am
Helen	PARRISH
Helen	REDDY s,tv+ Aust
Helen	SHAVER
Helen	SLATER
Helen	TAMIRIS ba Am
Helen	TAUSSIG md,sc,e Am
Helen	THOMAS j Am
Helen	TRAUBEL sopr+
Helen	VINSON
Helen	WADDELL w Br
Helen	WALKER
Helen	WESTLY
Helen	WILLS MOODY t Am
Helen	WOOD tv
Helen Gurley BROWN w,j,ed Am	
Helen Jerome EDDY	
Helena	BONHAM CARTER
Helena	CARTER
Helena	RUBINSTEIN cosmetic Am

Helene	BOHLAU w Ger
Helene	CURTIS hair care Am
Helfer,	BRIT
Helga	LINE
Helga	SOMMERFELD
Helge	RODE po,w,ct Dan
Helge	ROSVAENGE tenor
Helgenberger, MARG tv+	
Helius	HESSUS po Ger
Hell,	RICHARD mr-bass Am
Hellbron, OLIE d	
Hellekant,CHARLOTTE mezzo Am	
Hellenga, ROBERT w	
Heller,	BARBARA tv
Heller,	JOSEPH w Am
Heller,	LINDA w Am
Heller,	RANDEE tv+
Heller,	YOM r-rabbi Ger
Helliwell,JOHN m-sax Br	
Hellman,	BONNIE tv
Hellman,	LILLIAN w Am
Hellmut	GERLACH j,st Ger
Hello,	ERNEST w Fr
Helm,	LEVON mr-drums,s+ Am
Helmholtz,HERMANN von sc,md Ger	
Helmond,	KATHERINE tv+
Helmore,	TOM
Helms,	BOBBY s
Helmsley,	LEONA busin Am
Helmut	BERGER tv+
Helmut	DANTINE tv+
Helmut	GRIEM
Helmuth von MOLTKE ar Ger	
Helper,	HINTON w Am
Helpmann,	ROBERT ba+ Br
Helprin,	MARK w Am
Helst,	BARTHOLO.van der p Dut
Helton,	PERCY tv
Helvetius,CLAUDE ph,w Fr	
Helwys,	THOMAS r Br
Hemans,	FELICIA po Br
Hemblen,	DAVID
Hemingway,ERNEST n-l'54,p-f'53	
Hemingway,MARGAUX	
Hemingway,MARIEL tv+	
Hemmings,	DAVID
Hemon,	LOUIS w Fr
Hempel,	FRIEDA sopr Ger
Hemphill, SHIRLEY tv	
Hemsley,	SHERMAN tv+
Hench,	PHILIP n-m'50
Hencke,	KARL ast Ger
Henderson,ALAN mr-bass Ir	
Henderson,ALBERT tv	
Henderson,ARTHUR st,n-x'34	
Henderson,BILL	
Henderson,BILLY mr-s Am	
Henderson,CHUCK tv	
Henderson,FLETCHER mj,cn Am	
Henderson,FLORENCE tv+	
Henderson,KELO tv	

Henderson,LUTHER Jr.m,cn,tv Am	Henri	TROYAT w,bio Fr
Henderson,MARCIA tv+	Henri	VIDAL
Henderson,RAY c Am	Henri	WALLON h,st,e Fr
Henderson,RICKEY b-mv'90	Henri de	JOMINI ar,w Swi
Henderson,SKITCH mj,cn,tv+ Am	Henri de	REGNIER po,ct,w Fr
Hendler, LAURI tv	Henri van der NOOT st Belg
Hendren, RON tv	Henri, ROBERT p Am
Hendrick van BALEN p Belg	Henri-Emile BAZIN eng Fr
Hendrickson, AL mj-guitar,w Am	Henrietta LEAVITT astron Am
Hendrickson, BENJAMIN tv	Henrietta SZOLD r,pb Am
Hendrik BERLAGE ac Dut	Henrik IBSEN po,w Nor
Hendrik LORENTZ sc,e Dut	Henrik MOHN weather Nor
Hendrik MARSMAN po,w,ct Dut	Henrik PORTHAN e Finn
Hendrik MESDAG p Dut	Henriksen,LANCE
Hendrik TOLLENS po Dut	Henry ABBOT eng Am
Hendrik Van LOON h,w Am	Henry ADAMS h,e Am
Hendrik de KEYSER ac,su Dut	Henry ALFORD r,e Br
Hendriks, JIM tv	Henry ALLEN ar Am
Hendriks, TED fb hf	Henry ALLON r Br
Hendrix, JIMI mr+ Am	Henry ARMETTA
Hendrix, NONA s Am	Henry ARNOLD(Hap)ar,flyr Am
Hendry, GLORIA	Henry BACON ac Am
Hendry, IAN	Henry BAILEY w Br
Henie, SONJA o-g'28'32'6,	Henry BARKLY(Sir)st
Henley, BETH p-d'81	Henry BECKMAN tv
Henley, DON s-pop Am	Henry BECQUE w Fr
Henley, WILLIAM po,w,ed Br	Henry BEECHER r,pb.w Am
Hennepin, LOUIS r,x Fr	Henry BELL i,ds Scot
Henner, JEAN p Fr	Henry BERGH reform Am
Henner, MARILU tv+	Henry BERGMAN
Hennig BRAND sc Ger	Henry BISHOP(Sir)cn,c
Henning, CAROL tv	Henry BOHN pb Br
Henning, DOUG magic,tv Can	Henry BONE p Br
Henny BACKUS tv	Henry BRANDON
Henny YOUNGMAN cm,tv+ Br	Henry BROWN su Am
Henreid, PAUL	Henry BUNNER w,ed Am
Henri AMIEL po,ph Swi	Henry CALVIN tv+
Henri ARNAUD r,ar Fr	Henry CANBY w,ed Am
Henri BAZIN eng Fr	Henry CAREY po,c Br
Henri BERAUD w Fr	Henry CELE
Henri BERGSON e,ph,w Fr	Henry CHETTLE w Br
Henri BERR h,ph Fr	Henry CLAY st Am
Henri BOSCO w Fr	Henry CLAYTON st Am
Henri BREUIL sc,e,r Fr	Henry COBB ac Am
Henri CHAPU su Fr	Henry COLLES ct,w Br
Henri DUPARC c Fr	Henry COOKE c,cn Br
Henri FARMAN id-planes Fr	Henry CORT i Br
Henri GUISAN ar Swi	Henry COWELL c Am
Henri HERZ piano,c,e Aus	Henry DAKIN sc Br
Henri JASPAR st Belg	Henry DALE(Sir)md
Henri JUNOD r,an,w Swi	Henry DANIELL
Henri LANDRU murderer Fr	Henry DARROW
Henri LEKAIN la Fr	Henry DAVIES(Sir)organ,c
Henri MATISSE p,su Fr	Henry DAWSON p Br
Henri MICHAUX po,p Fr	Henry DeMILLE w Am
Henri MOISSAN sc,e Fr	Henry DODGE ar,st Am
Henri MOUHOT x Fr	Henry DURANT r,e Am
Henri MURGER w Fr	Henry EGLY r Am
Henri NESTLE chocolate Swi	Henry FOLGER id-oil Am
Henri PITOT eng Fr	Henry FONDA tv+
Henri RABAUD c,cn Fr	

Henry	FORD id-cars Am	Henry	OSCAR
Henry	FOWLER lexicogr Br	Henry	POLIC II tv
Henry	FRICK id Am	Henry	POOR ec,w Am
Henry	FULLER w Am	Henry	PURCELL c Br
Henry	FUSELI p Br	Henry	PYE po Br
Henry	GANNETT geog Am	Henry	RAEBURN(Sir)p Scot
Henry	GIBSON cm,tv+ Am	Henry	RAINEY st Am
Henry	GILBERT c Am	Henry	RAMER
Henry	GIRARD tv	Henry	RIDLEY sc Br
Henry	GREEN w Br	Henry	ROGERS id-oil,f Am
Henry	HADLEY c Am	Henry	ROTH w Am
Henry	HAGGARD(Sir)w	Henry	ROWLAND sc,e Am
Henry	HALL	Henry	ROYCE(Sir)eng,id-cars
Henry	HALL mj,cn,c Br	Henry	SAVILE(Sir)e
Henry	HALLAM h Br	Henry	SCOGAN po Br
Henry	HEINZ id-foods Am	Henry	SHAW w-humor Am
Henry	HOLT pb,w Am	Henry	SHREVE mariner Am
Henry	HOWARD ar,po Br	Henry	SHUTE w-humor Am
Henry	HUDSON x Br	Henry	SIBLEY pioneer,st Am
Henry	HULL	Henry	SILVA
Henry	INMAN p Am	Henry	SLATE tv
Henry	IRETON ar,st Br	Henry	SLOCUM ar Am
Henry	IRVING(Sir)la	Henry	SMYTH sc Am
Henry	JACKSON st Am	Henry	SORBY geol Br
Henry	JAGLOM	Henry	ST. JOHN st,w Br
Henry	JAMES Jr w Am	Henry	STANLEY(Sir)x
Henry	JAMES ph,w Am	Henry	STIMSON st Am
Henry	JONES tv+	Henry	SURREY po Br
Henry	JONES(Sir)w	Henry	TANNER p Am
Henry	JORDAN fb hf	Henry	TATE(Sir)id-sugar,f
Henry	KAISER id,f Am	Henry	TAUBE sc Can
Henry	KENDALL	Henry	TAYLOR po Am
Henry	KENDALL sc Am	Henry	TAYLOR(Sir)po
Henry	KING d	Henry	THOMAS
Henry	KING r,po Br	Henry	THOREAU w,po Am
Henry	KOLKER	Henry	TIMKIN i,id Am
Henry	KOPLIK md Am	Henry	TIMROD po,j Am
Henry	KULKY tv	Henry	TRAVERS
Henry	LAURENS st Am	Henry	TREECE w,po Br
Henry	LAWES c Br	Henry	Van Dyke r,w Am
Henry	LAWSON w.po Aust	Henry	VANE(Sir)st
Henry	LEE(LtHrseHarry)ar,st	Henry	VAUGHAN po Br
Henry	LELAND id-cars Am	Henry	VELDE ac Belg
Henry	LEVIN d	Henry	VESTINE mr-guit Am
Henry	LEVINE(HotLips)mj,cn	Henry	VILLARD j,bus-rrs Am
Henry	LOMB id-optics Am	Henry	WALLACK la Am
Henry	MANCE(Sir)eng	Henry	WICKHAM(Sir)x
Henry	MANCINI m,cn,tv Am	Henry	WINKLER tv+
Henry	MANUSH b hf	Henry	WOOD(Sir)cn,c
Henry	MAYHEW j Br	Henry	WORK w-songs Am
Henry	McGEE tv	Henry	WOTTON(Sir)st,po
Henry	MEIGGS bus,st Am	Henry	WRIGHT ac Am
Henry	MILLER la,d Am	Henry	WRIGHT bmg Am
Henry	MILLER w Am	Henry	WYLD w,lexicog,e Br
Henry	MILMAN r,po,e,h Br	Henry	YORKE w Br
Henry	MOORE su Br	Henry Agard WALLACE st-vp Am	
Henry	MORE ph,po Br	Henry Cabot LODGE st,w Am	
Henry	MORGAN tv+	Henry R. LUCE ed,pb Am	
Henry	MORGAN(Sir)buccaneer	Henry Ross PEROT f Am	
Henry	NEWBOLT(Sir)po Br	Henry(Hap) ARNOLD ar,fly Am	
Henry	OSBORN sc Am	Henry, BILL tv	

Henry,	BUCK tv+	Herbert	GASSER md Am
Henry,	CAROL ba,tv Am	Herbert	GOLD w Am
Henry,	CHARLOTTE	Herbert	HERR eng,id Am
Henry,	CHUCK tv	Herbert	HEYES
Henry,	CLARENCE s Am	Herbert	HOOVER st Am
Henry,	EMMALINE tv	Herbert	LOM
Henry,	GREG	Herbert	MARCUSE ph,e Am
Henry,	JOSEPH sc Am	Herbert	PLUMER ar Br
Henry,	JUSTIN	Herbert	READ(Sir)po,ct
Henry,	LENNY	Herbert	RISLEY(Sir)an,st
Henry,	MIKE	Herbert	ROSS d
Henry,	O. w Am	Herbert	RUDLEY tv+
Henry,	PATRICK st,orator Am	Herbert	SAMUEL(Sir)st
Henry,	PETE fb hf	Herbert	SIMON ec Am
Henry,	ROBERT(Buzzy)	Herbert	SPENCER ph,ed,w Br
Henry,	WILLIAM	Herbert	SPINDEN an Am
Henryk	RZEWUSKI w Pol	Herbert	STEIN e,w
Henryk	SZERYNG viol Mex	Herbert	STROCK d
Hensen,	VIKTOR md-sc,e Ger	Herbert	TREE(Sir)la
Hensley,	KEN mr-kbds,guit,s Br	Herbert	WELLS(H.G.)w-sdifi Br
Hensley,	PAMELA tv+	Herbert	WILCOX d
Henson,	JIM(mupp) tv+	Herbert	WISE d
Henteloff,ALEX tv		Herbert L.BLOCK cr Am	
Hentgen,	PAT b-cy'96	Herbert von KARAJAN cn Aus	
Henty,	GEORGE w Br	Herbert,	DON tv
Henzi,	SAMUEL re Swi	Herbert,	EDWARD ph,st Br
Hepburn,	AUDREY o-a'53	Herbert,	FRANK w scifi Am
Hepburn,	GEORGE bbc, hf	Herbert,	GEORGE po Br
Hepburn,	KATHARINE o-a'33'67 &	Herbert,	HOLMES
Hepburn,	KATHARINE o-s'68'71	Herbert,	HUGH
Hepner,	BEN tenor Can	Herbert,	PERCY tv+
Hepplewhite, GEORGE ds-furnitur		Herbert,	VICTOR c,cn Am
Hepton,	BERNARD	Herbert,	XAVIER w Aust
Hepworth, BARBARA(Dame)su Br		Herbert,	ZBIGNIEW po Pol
Heracleitus --- ph Gr		Herbie	FAYE tv
Herb	ADDERLY fb hf	Herbie	HANCOCK mj-piano,c Am
Herb	ALPERT mj,cn Am	Herbie	MANN mj-flute Am
Herb	CAEN j Am	Herczeg,	FERENC w Hung
Herb	EDELMAN tv+	Herd,	RICHARD tv+
Herb	ELLIS tv	Herder,	JOHANN ph,ct Ger
Herb	PENNOCK b hf	Heredia,	JOSE de po Cuba
Herb	POLESIE tv	Herek,	STEPHEN d
Herb	SHRINER w,radio,tv Am	Herelle,	FELIX d' sc Can
Herb	VOLAND tv	Herford,	OLIVER w,illus Am
Herb	WIEDOFT mj,cn Am	Hergesheimer, JOSEPH w Am	
Herbart,	JOHANN ph Ger	Hering,	EWALD md,ps,e Ger
Herber,	ARNOLD fb hf	Herlihy,	ED tv
Herbert	ADAMS h,e Am	Herlihy,	WALTER tv
Herbert	ADAMS su Am	Herman	BING
Herbert	AGAR j,w Am	Herman	GORTER po Dut
Herbert	ASBURY j,w Am	Herman	HAUPT eng Am
Herbert	AUSTIN id-cars Br	Herman	HICKMAN tv
Herbert	BOLTON h,e Am	Herman	McCOY s,cn,tv Am
Herbert	BROWN sc Am	Herman	McNEILE w Br
Herbert	CROLY ed,w Am	Herman	PORTAAS po Nor
Herbert	DAVIS e,ed Br	Herman	SNELLEN md-eyes Dut
Herbert	De LISSER w Jamaica	Herman	WOUK w Am
Herbert	DINGLE sc Br	Herman von SODEN r,e Ger	
Herbert	DOW id Am	Herman,	AL d
Herbert	EVANS sc-md,e Am	Herman,	BILLY b hf
Herbert	EVATT l,st Austr		

Herman,	JERRY c Am
Herman,	WOODY mj-clari,cn Am
Hermann	BAHR j,w Aus
Hermann	BROCH w Aus
Hermann	GORING st Nazi Ger
Hermann	GOTZ c Ger
Hermann	GRUSON id Ger
Hermann	GUNKEL e Ger
Hermann	HAHN su Ger
Hermann	HESSE w,po Ger
Hermann	KOLBE sc,e Ger
Hermann	KOPP sc,e Ger
Hermann	KURZ w Ger
Hermann	ONCKEN h,e Ger
Hermann	PREY bari
Hermann	WEYL math,e,w Ger
Hermann	ZILCHER c Ger
Hermann J. MULLER md Am
Hermann von BOYEN ar Ger
Hermann,	IRM
Hermann,	MARIANNE w Am
Hermes,	GEORG r,ph,e Ger
Hermione	BADDELEY tv+
Hermione	GINGOLD tv+
Hernan	CORTES st,ar,x Sp
Hernandez,	JOSE po Arg
Hernandez,JUANO
Hernandez,KEITH b-mv'79,bat'79
Hernandez MIGUEL de po,w Sp
Hernandez,WILLIE b-cy,-mv'84
Hernando CORTEZ st,ar,x Sp
Hernando SILES st Bol
Hernando de ACUNA po,st,ar Sp
Hernando de SOTO x Sp
Herne,	JAMES w Am
Hero or Heron --- sc Gr
Herold,	LOUIS c Fr
Heron,	JOAN mj,pop-s Br
Heron,	KAY mj,pop-s Br
Heron,	WENDY mj,pop-s Br
Herr,	HERBERT eng,id Am
Herrera y Reissig,JULIO po Urug
Herrera,	FERNANDO de po Po
Herrera,	FRANCISCO de p Sp
Herrick,	MYRON st Am
Herrick,	ROBERT po(d 1674)Am
Herrick,	ROBERT w(d 1938)Br
Herrier,	MARK
Herriman,	GEORGE cr Am
Herring,	LYNN tv
Herrington, ROWDY d
Herriot,	JAMES vet,w Br
Herrmann, EDWARD
Herschbach, DUDLEY n-c'86
Herschel BERNARDI tv+
Herschell LEWIS d
Herschel,	JOHN(Sir)ast
Herschel,	WILLIAM(Sir)ast
Hersey,	JOHN j,p-f'45
Hersha	PARADY tv
Hershberger, GARY tv

Hershey,	ALFRED n-m'69
Hershey,	BARBARA tv+
Hershey,	MILTON id-candy Am
Hershiser,OREL b-cy'88
Hersholt,	JEAN la+ Am
Herta	WARE
Herter,	CHRISTIAN st Am
Hertford,	CHELSEA tv
Hertwig,	OSKAR sc-md,e Ger
Hertz,	GUSTAV n-p'25
Hertz,	HEINRICH sc,e Ger
Hertzog,	JAMES ar,st S.Afr
Herve	FAYE astrom Fr
Herve	VILLECHAIZE tv+
Herve,	AIME j Fr
Hervey	ALLEN w,po,bio Am
Hervey,	IRENE tv+
Hervey,	JASON tv+
Hervey,	JOHN st,w Br
Herwegh,	GEORG po Ger
Herz,	HENRI piano,c,e Aus
Herz,	MARCUS md,ph Ger
Herz,	MICHAEL d
Herzberg,	GERHARD n-c'71
Herzen,	ALEKSANDR j,w Rus
Herzfeld,	JOHN d
Herzl,	THEODOR r,j Hung
Herzog,	EMILE w Fr
Herzog,	ISAAC r-rabbi Pol
Herzog,	WERNER d+
Hess,	DAVID
Hess,	HARRY sc Am
Hess,	JON d
Hess,	MYRA(Dame)piano Br
Hess,	RUDULF st,Nazi Ger
Hess,	VICTOR n-p'36
Hess,	WALTER n-m'49
Hesse,	HERMANN po,n-l'46
Hesseman,	HOWARD tv+
Hessler,	GORDON d
Hessus,	HELIUS po Ger
Hester	BATEMAN id-silver Br
Hester	CHAPONE w Br
Hester	PIOZZI w Br
Hester	THRALE confidante Br
Heston,	CHARLTON o-a'59,tv+
Hetrick,	JENNIFER tv
Hettner,	ALFRED geog,x Ger
Hetzel,	PIERRE pb Fr
Heusler,	ANDREAS e Ger
Heuss,	THEODOR st,j,w Ger
Hevesy,	GEORG de n-c'43
Hew	AINSLIE po Am
Hewart,	GORDON l,st Br
Hewett,	CHRISTOPHER tv
Hewett,	HOWARD s Am
Hewish,	ANTONY n-p'74
Hewitt,	ABRAM id,st Am
Hewitt,	BILL fb hf
Hewitt,	MARTIN
Hewitt,	VIRGINIA tv

Hewlett, DAVID	Hilaire BELLOC w Br
Hexum, JON tv	Hilarion DAZA ar,st Bol
Heyburn, WELDON	Hilary DWYER
Heydar, SHEYKH r Persia	Hilary MASON
Heydt, LOUIS	Hilary Van DYKE tv
Heyer, GEORGETTE w Br	Hilbert, DAVID math,e Ger
Heyerdahl,THOR x,w Nor	Hilboldt, LISE
Heyes, HERBERT	Hilda DOOLITTLE po Am
Heym, GEORG po Ger	Hildegarde NEFF
Heyman, BARTON	Hildy PARKS tv
Heymans, CORNEILLE n-m'38	Hill, AMBROSE ar Am
Heyrovsky,JAROSLAV n-c'59	Hill, ANITA l,e Am
Heyse, PAUL w Ger	Hill, ARCHIBALD n-m'22
Heyward, DuBOSE w,po Am	Hill, ARTHUR tv+
Heyward, NICK mr-guit,s Br	Hill, BENNY cm,tv+ Br
Heywood, BROUN j,w Am	Hill, BERNARD
Heywood, ANNE	Hill, CRAIG tv+
Heywood, JOHN w,po Br	Hill, DANA tv+
Heywood, THOMAS w Br	Hill, DAVE mr-guit Br
Hezekiah NILES ed Am	Hill, FAITH s-cnt Am
Hfkam von EICHWALD mj,cn Swe	Hill, GEORGE ROY d
Hiaasen, CARL w Am	Hill, GOLDIE tv
Hibbert, ELEANOR w Br	Hill, GRANT bb
Hichens, ROBERT w Br	Hill, HARLON fb-m'55
Hickey, EDGAR bbc hf	Hill, JACK d+
Hickey, WILLIAM tv+	Hill, JAMES d
Hickland, CATHERINE tv+	Hill, JAMES f Am
Hickman, DARRYL tv+	Hill, JOE ws,labor Am
Hickman, DWAYNE tv+	Hill, JOHNNY tv
Hickman, HERMAN tv	Hill, LAURYN
Hickok, WILD BILL ar,hero Am	Hill, MARIANNA
Hickox, ANTHONY d	Hill, OCTAVIA ref Br
Hickox, HARRY tv	Hill, PATTY e Am
Hicks, CATHERINE tv+	Hill, RICHARD tv+
Hicks, EDWARD p Am	Hill, ROBERT ba Am
Hicks, GRANVILLE w,ct Am	Hill, ROBERT d
Hicks, HILLY tv	Hill, ROWLAND r Br
Hicks, JOHN(Sir)n-e'72	Hill, STEVEN tv+
Hicks, RUSSELL	Hill, TERENCE
Hicks, TONY mr-guitar Br	Hill, THOMAS tv
Hicks, WILLIAM	Hill, WALTER d
Hickson, JOAN	Hillaire, MARCEL tv
Hidari, SACHIKO	Hillary BROOKE tv+
Hideki Yukawa --- n-p'49	Hillary SMITH tv
Hideko TAKAMINE	Hillary WAUGH w Am
Hideyo NOGUCHI sc,e Am	Hillary, EDMUND(Sir)x
Hiel, EMANUEL po Belg	Hillebrand, RED tv
Hielm, JONAS st Nor	Hiller, ARTHUR d
Hieronymus BOSCH p Dut	Hiller, WENDY o-s'58
Hierta, LARS j,st Swe	Hillerman, JOHN tv+
Higden, RANULF r Br	Hillerman, TONY w Am
Higginbotham,JAY(J.C.)mj-tromb A	Hilliard, NICHOLAS p Br
Higgins, ANTHONY	Hillie, VERNA
Higgins, CLARE	Hillman, CHRIS mr-bass,s Am
Higgins, JACK w Irish-Br	Hills, GILLIAN
Higgins, JOE tv+	Hilly HICKS tv
Higgins, JOEL tv	Hillyer, LAMBERT d
Higgins, MICHAEL tv+	Hillyer, ROBERT p-q'34
Higginson,THOMAS r,ar,w Am	Hilton, CONRAD hotels Am
Hijuelos, OSCAR p-f'90	Hilton, GEORGE
Hikmet, NAZIM po,j Turk	Hilton, JAMES w Br

Hilton-Jacobs, LAWRENCE		Hjalmar	BERGMAN w Swe
Himes,	CHESTER w Am	Hjalmar	JONSSON po Iceland
Himmler,	HEINRICH st,Nazi Ger	Hjalmar	SCHACHT f-banker Ger
Hincks,	FRANCIS(Sir)j,st Can	Hjort,	JOHAN sc,e Nor
Hindemith,PAUL viol,c Ger-Am		Hlinka,	ANDREJ r Slovak
Hindle	ART tv+	Ho Chi Minh --- st VietN
Hindman,	EARL tv+	Ho,	DON s Am
Hinds,	SAMUEL	Ho,	GODFREY d
Hine,	LEWIS fo Am	Hoag,	JUDITH tv+
Hines,	CONNIE tv	Hoag,	MITZI tv
Hines,	DUNCAN ct-food,w Am	Hoagland, EDWARD w,j Am
Hines,	EARL(Fatha)pian,c Am	Hoagy	CARMICHAEL mj,c+ Am
Hines,	GREGORY ba+ Am	Hoar,	SAMUEL l,st Am
Hines,	JANEAR tv	Hoban,	JAMES ac Am
Hingis,	MARTINA t Swi	Hobart	BOSWORTH
Hingle,	PAT	Hobart	CAVANAUGH
Hinkle,	BEATRICE ps Am	Hobart,	ALICE w Am
Hinkle,	CLARKE fb hf	Hobart,	ROSE
Hinnant,	SKIP tv	Hobbema,	MEINDERT p Dut
Hinshelwood, CYRIL n-c'56		Hobbes,	HALLIWELL
Hinsley,	HARVEY mr-guitar Br	Hobbes,	THOMAS ph Br
Hinton	HELPER w Am	Hobbs,	JACK(Sir)sp-cricket
Hinton,	DARBY tv+	Hobel,	MARA
Hinton,	ED tv	Hobson,	HOWARD bbc hf
Hinton,	MILT mj-bass Am	Hobson,	VALERIE
Hinton,	S.E. w Am	Hoby,	THOMAS(Sir)st
Hintze,	PAUL von navy,st Ger	Hoccleve, THOMAS po Br
Hippel,	THEODOR w Ger	Hochhuth,	ROLF w Ger
Hippocrates --- md(H.Oath) Gr	Hochwalder, FRITZ w Aus
Hippolyte GIRARDOT		Hocking,	SILAS r,w Br
Hippolyte TAINE ph,h,ct Fr	Hocking,	WILLIAM ph,e Am
Hiram	BINGHAM r,x Am	Hockney,	DAVID p Br
Hiram	JOHNSON st Am	Hodding	CARTER j,w Am
Hiram	KELLER	Hodge,	AL tv
Hiram	MAXIM(Sir)i,id	Hodge,	KATE
Hiram	POWERS su Am	Hodge,	PATRICIA
Hiram	SIBLEY bus-telegr Am	Hodge,	STEPHANIE tv
Hiram Ulysses GRANT 18th pres	Hodges,	EDDIE
Hird,	THORA	Hodges,	GIL b
Hires,	CHARLES id-rt beer Am	Hodges,	JOHNNY mj-sax Am
Hirn,	GUSTAVE sc Fr	Hodges,	RUSS b,tv
Hirohito --- emperor Japan	Hodges,	TOM tv+
Hirsch,	ELROY(CrazyLegs)fb hf	Hodges,	WILLIAM w Am
Hirsch,	GARY(Chicken)mr-drm	Hodgins,	EARLE tv+
Hirsch,	JUDD tv+	Hodgkin,	ALAN(Sir)n-m'63
Hirsch,	MORITZ von bus,f Ger	Hodgkin,	DOROTHY n-c'64
Hirsch,	STEVEN tv	Hodgson,	RALPH po Br
Hirschfeld, GEORG w Ger	Hodgson,	ROGER mr-guit Br
Hirschfield, ROBERT tv	Hodiak,	JOHN
Hirson,	ALICE tv+	Hodson,	JIM tv
His,	WILHELM md,e Ger	Hodza,	MILAN st Cz
Hiss,	ALGER spy Am	Hoe,	RICHARD i,id Am
Hitchcock,ALFRED(Sir)d, tv+	Hoe,	ROBERT id Am
Hitchcock,EDWARD geol Am	Hoeg,	PETER w Dan
Hitchcock,RUSSELL mr-s Aust	Hoel,	HALVOR st Nor
Hitchings,GEORGE n-m'88	Hoel,	SIGURD w Nor
Hite,	SHERE w Am	Hoevell,	WOLTER st Dut
Hitler,	ADOLF st,w Nazi Ger	Hoey,	DENNIS
Hitti,	PHILIP h,e Am	Hofer,	KARL p,e Ger
Hittorf,	JOHANN sc Ger	Hoff,	CARL m,cn,tv Am
Hitzig,	EDUARD ps,e Ger	Hoffa,	JAMES(Jimmy)labor Am

Hoffer, ERIC ph Am	Holden, WILLIAM o-a'53
Hoffman, ABBIE w,re Am	Holder, GEOFFREY
Hoffman, ALICE w Am	Holder, NODDY mr-guitar,s Br
Hoffman, BASIL tv+	Hole, JONATHAN tv
Hoffman, DOMINIC tv	Holger PEDERSEN w Dan
Hoffman, DUSTIN o-a'79,'88	Holiday, BILLIE mj,s-blues Am
Hoffman, ELIZABETH tv	Holinshed,RAPHAEL w,h Br
Hoffman, GABY	Holl, ELIAS ac Ger
Hoffman, GERTRUDE tv	Holland SMITH mariner Am
Hoffman, JANE	Holland TAYLOR tv+
Hoffman, MALVINA su Am	Holland, AGNIESZKA d
Hoffman, PHILIP	Holland, BRIAN c Am
Hoffmann, AUGUST po,h Aus	Holland, ERSKINE(Sir)l,e
Hoffmann, CECIL tv	Holland, JOHN
Hoffmann, ERNST(E.T.A.)c,w Ger	Holland, JOHN i,id Am
Hoffmann, ROALD n-c'81	Holland, KRISTINA tv
Hoffs, SUSANNA mr-guit,s Am	Holland, VYVYAN w Br
Hofmann, AUGUST von sc Ger	Hollander,DAVID tv
Hofmann, HANS p Am	Hollar, WENZEL engr Cz
Hofmann, ISABELLA tv	Holldobler, DALE p-n'91
Hofmann, JOSEF piano Am	Hollerhagen, ERNEST mj-clari Ger
Hofmannsthal, HUGO von w,po Aus	Holles, DENZIL st Br
Hofstadter,DONALD p-n'80	Holley, ROBERT n-m'68
Hofstadter,RICHARD p-n'64p-h'56	Holliday, ART tv
Hofstadter,ROBERT n-p'61	Holliday, FRED tv
Hogan, BEN g Am	Holliday, JUDY o-a'50
Hogan, BOB tv	Holliday, KENE tv
Hogan, BOSCO	Holliday, POLLY tv+
Hogan, HULK wrestler+ Am	Holliman, EARL tv+
Hogan, JACK tv	Hollis IRVING tv
Hogan, MICHAEL	Hollis, JEFF tv
Hogan, PAT	Hollis, MARKmr-kbds,guit,s Br
Hogan, PAUL	Holloway, STANLEY
Hogan, ROBERT tv+	Holloway, STERLING tv+
Hogan, SUSAN tv+	Hollowell,TODD tv
Hogarth, BURNE cr Am	Holly FLORIA
Hogarth, WILLIAM p Br	Holly FULGER tv
Hogben, LANCELOT sc,r,w Br	Holly GAGNIER tv
Hoge, JOHN tv	Holly HUNTER
Hogestyn, DRAKE tv	Holly JOHNSON mr-s Sudan
Hogg, DOUGLAS st Br	Holly PALANCE tv+
Hogg, IMA f Am	Holly, BUDDY mr Am
Hogg, JAMES po Scot	Holly, ELLEN
Hogg, QUINTIN reform,f Br	Holly, LAUREN
Hoke HOWELL tv+	Holm, CELESTE o-s'47,tv+
Hoke SMITH st Am	Holm, HANYA ba Am
Holabird WILLIAM ac Am	Holm, IAN
Holbach, PAUL pb Fr	Holman DAY w Am
Holbein, HANS(elder)p Ger	Holman HUNT p Br
Holbein, HANS(younger)p Ger	Holman, BILL cr Am
Holberg, LUDVIG w Nor	Holman, NAT bb hf
Holbrook, DAVID po,w,e Br	Holmes HERBERT
Holbrook, HAL tv+	Holmes, ARTHUR geol,e Br
Holcomb, KATHRYN tv+	Holmes, AUGUSTA c Fr
Holcomb, ROD d	Holmes, CLINT tv
Holcombe, WENDY tv	Holmes, DENNIS tv
Holden, FAY	Holmes, ED tv
Holden, GLORIA	Holmes, IAN
Holden, ISAAC(Sir)i	Holmes, JANET po Am
Holden, MARJEAN	Holmes, JENNIFER tv
Holden, REBECCA tv+	Holmes, LARRY boxer Am

Holmes,	LeROY m,cn,tv Am	Hooch,	PIETER de p Dut
Holmes,	LUREE	Hood,	DARLA
Holmes,	MARY w Am	Hood,	THOMAS po,ed Br
Holmes,	OLIVER WENDELL Jr lAm	Hooft,	PIETER h,po,w Dut
Holmes,	OLIVER WENDELL md,e	Hook,	JAMES organ,c Br
Holmes,	PHILLIPS	Hook,	PETER mr-bass Br
Holmes,	SHERLOCK fc-sleuth	Hook,	SIDNEY ph,e Am
Holmes,	TAYLOR	Hooke,	ROBERT sc Br
Holmgren,	ALARIK md,e Swe	Hooker,	JOHN mj-blues Am
Holphers,	ARNE mj,cn Swe	Hooker,	JOSEPH ar Am
Holst,	GUSTAV c,e Br	Hooker,	RICHARD tv
Holste,	LUC scholar Ger	Hooks,	JAN tv+
Holt	McCALLANY	Hooks,	KEVIN tv+
Holt,	BOB tv	Hooks,	ROBERT tv+
Holt,	EDWIN ps,ph Am	Hooper	ATCHLEY
Holt,	HANS	Hooper,	ELLEN po Am
Holt,	HENRY pb,w Am	Hooper,	HARRY b hf
Holt,	JACK	Hooper,	LARRY s,piano,tv
Holt,	JENNIFER	Hooper,	TOBE d
Holt,	LUTHER md Am	Hoot	GIBSON
Holt,	PATRICK	Hooten,	PETER
Holt,	TIM	Hooton,	EARNEST an,e Am
Holt,	ULA	Hoover,	HERBERT 31st pres
Holt,	VICTORIA w Br	Hoover,	JOHN EDGAR fbi Am
Holtby,	WINIFRED w Br	Hope	BUNIN pupp,tv Am
Holtei,	KARL von la,w Ger	Hope	CARLTON
Holty,	LUDWIG po Ger	Hope	EDELMAN w Am
Holtz,	LOU fbc	Hope	EMERSON tv+
Holub,	EMIL x Ger	Hope	LANGE tv+
Holyfield,	EVANDER boxer Am	Hope	SUMMERS tv
Holz,	ARNO po,w,ct Ger	Hope,	A.D. po Aust
Holzman,	RED bbc hf	Hope,	BOB cm,tv+ Am
Homans,	ROBERT	Hope,	LESLIE tv+
Home Run	BAKER b	Hope,	RICHARD
Home,	WILLIAM w Br	Hope,	VIDA
Homeier,	SKIP tv+	Hopf,	HANS tenor
Homer	--- po Gr	Hopkin,	MARY mr-s Welsh
Homer	LEA ar,w Am	Hopkins,	ANTHONY o-a'91
Homer	MARTIN p Am	Hopkins,	BO tv+
Homer	SWIFT md Am	Hopkins,	ESEK navy Am
Homer,	LOUISE contralto Am	Hopkins,	FREDERICK(Sir)n-m'29
Homer,	WINSLOW p Am	Hopkins,	GERARD po,r Br
Homolka,	OSCAR	Hopkins,	HAROLD
Honda Inoshiro --- d		Hopkins,	HARRY st Am
Hondt,	JOOST de engr Belg	Hopkins,	JOHNS mer,f Am
Hone	TUWHARE po N.Zea	Hopkins,	MARK e Am
Hone,	PHILIP bus,w Am	Hopkins,	MIRIAM
Honegger,	ARTHUR c Fr	Hopkins,	SAM(Lightnin)mj,s Am
Honey	RUSSELL bb hf	Hopkins,	STEPHEN d
Hong,	JAMES tv+	Hopkins,	TELMA mr-s,tv+ Am
Hongo,	KOJIRO	Hopman,	HARRY t Austra
Honor	BLACKMAN	Hoppe,	ROLF
Honor	TRACY w Br	Hoppe,	WILLIAM billards Am
Honore	DAUMIER p,at Fr	Hopper,	DENNIS d+
Honore	MERCIER st Can	Hopper,	DeWOLF la Am
Honore	REILLE ar Fr	Hopper,	EDWARD p Am
Honore	RIQUETI st Fr	Hopper,	HEDDA j,ct+ Am
Honore d'	URFE w Fr	Hopper,	SEAN mr-kbds Am
Honore de	BALZAC w Fr	Hopper,	WILLIAM tv+
Honthorst,	GERRIT van p Dut	Hopton,	RUSSELL
Honus	WAGNER b hf	Hopwood,	AVERY w Am

Hopwood,	KEITH mr-guit Br	Horton,	EDWARD EVERETT tv+
Horace	--- po Roman	Horton,	MICHAEL tv
Horace	GRANT bb	Horton,	PETER tv+
Horace	GREELEY j,ref,pb Am	Horton,	ROBERT tv+
Horace	GREGORY po,ct Am	Horup,	VIGGO j,st Dan
Horace	HEIDT mj,cn,tv+ Am	Horvath,	MIHALY r,st Hung
Horace	LAMB(Sir)math,sc,e	Horvath,	ODON von w Ger
Horace	LURTON l,ar-CSA Am	Horyn,	CATHY j Am
Horace	MANN e,st Am	Hosea	BALLOU r,ed,w Am
Horace	McCOY w Am	Hoskins,	BOB
Horace	McMAHON tv+	Hoskins,	FARINA
Horace	MURPHY	Hosni	MUBURAK st Egypt
Horace	PIPPIN p Am	Hostetter,	JOHN tv
Horace	SILVER mj-piano,cn Am	Hostos,	EUGENIO de e,w P.Rico
Horace	VACHELL w Br	Hot Lips	LEVINE mj,cn Am
Horace	WALPOLE w,h Br	Hot Lips	PAGE(Oran)mj,cn Am
Horace	WELLS dentist Am	Hot Lips	SWIT tv+
Horacio	QUIROGA w Urug	Hotchkis,	JOAN tv
Horatio	ALGER r,w Am	Hotman,	FRANCOIS l,e Fr
Horatio	ALLEN eng-rrs Am	Hotter,	HANS baritone Ger
Horatio	LAY st Br	Houbregs,	BOB bb hf
Horatio	NELSON navy Br	Houde,	GERMAN
Horatio	PALMER c,e Am	Houdini,	HARRY magic,w Am
Horatio	PARKER c,e Am	Houdon,	JEAN su Fr
Horatio	WRIGHT ar Am	Hough	LOVE sc,e Br
Horatius	BONAR r Scot	Hough,	EMERSON w Am
Hordern,	MICHAEL	Hough,	JOHN d
Horgan,	PATRICK tv	Houghton,	AMORY id-glass Am
Horgan,	PAUL w Am	Houghton,	JAMES tv
Hormuzd	RASSAM arc Turk	Houle,	LISA tv
Horn,	CHARLES s,c Br	Houlihin,	KERI tv
Hornaday,	WILLIAM sc Am	Hounsfield,	GODFREY n-m'79
Hornby,	GEOFFREY(Sir)navy	Housay,	BERNARDO md,e Arg
Horne,	LENA s+ Am	House	JAMESON tv
Horne,	MARILYN mezzo Am	House	PETERS
Horner,	D. FRANKI tv	House,	BILLY
Horner,	FRANCIS ct Br	House,	EDWARD(Colonel)st Am
Horney,	KAREN ps,e,w Am	House,	ROYAL i Am
Hornsby,	BRUCE mr-kbds,s Am	Houseman,	JOHN o-s'73,tv+
Hornsby,	ROGERS b hf	Houser,	CLARENCE o-g'24'28
Hornung,	ERNEST w Br	Houser,	JERRY
Hornung,	PAUL fb hf	Housman,	A.E. po,e Br
Horovitz,	ISRAEL w Am	Housman,	LAURENCE w,illus Br
Horowitz,	VLADIMIR piano Am	Houssay,	BERNARDO ps,e Arg
Horrocks,	JANE	Houston,	DONALD
Horse,	MICHAEL tv+	Houston,	GEORGE
Horsford,	ANNA MARIA tv+	Houston,	GLYN
Horsley,	LEE tv	Houston,	JOFF
Horst	BUCHHOLZ	Houston,	KEN fb hf
Horst	FRANK	Houston,	RENEE
Horst	JANSON	Houston,	SAMUEL(SAM)ar,st Am
Horst	STORMER sc,e,n-p'98	Houston,	WHITNEmr,s,g-r'93 Am
Horst	WESSEL ws Nazi Ger	Hout,	JAN van h,po Dut
Horst,	JASON tv	Houtman,	CORNELIS de x Dut
Horst,	LOUIS piano,c,ba Am	Hoven,	ADRIAN
Hort,	FENTON r Br	Hoven,	LOUISE tv
Horta,	VICTOR ac Belg	Hovey,	RICHARD po Am
Hortense	CALISHER w Am	Hovhaness,	ALAN c Am
Hortensia	COLORADO tv	Hoving,	THOMAS tv
Horton	FOOTE Jr.	Hovis,	GUY tv
Horton	FOOTE w Am	Hovis,	LARRY tv

Hovis,	RALNA tv	Howard,	BOB pr-tv Am
Hovland,	CARL ps,e Am	Howard,	CAL tv
Howard	AIKEN math,i Am	Howard,	CLINT tv+
Howard	ASHMAN lyrics Am	Howard,	CURLY
Howard	AVEDIS d	Howard,	CYNTHIA tv
Howard	BARLOW cn,tv Am	Howard,	DENNIS tv
Howard	CAINE tv+	Howard,	ELSTON b-mv'63
Howard	CANN fbc hf	Howard,	HENRY ar,po Br
Howard	CARTER arc Br	Howard,	JAN s-cnt Am
Howard	CHRISTY illus,p Am	Howard,	JOHN tv+
Howard	COFFIN eng-cars Am	Howard,	JUWAN bb
Howard	COSELL sp tv+ Am	Howard,	KEN tv+
Howard	CULVER tv	Howard,	LESLIE la+ Br
Howard	da SILVA	Howard,	MARY
Howard	DEUTCH d	Howard,	MOE
Howard	DIETZ lyrics Am	Howard,	PHILIP l,w Am
Howard	DUFF tv+	Howard,	RANCE tv
Howard	FAST w Am	Howard,	RICHARD p-q'70
Howard	FLOREY md Br	Howard,	RON d,tv+
Howard	FREEMAN	Howard,	RONALD tv+
Howard	GARIS w Am	Howard,	ROY j Am
Howard	HANSON c,e Am	Howard,	SHEMP
Howard	HARRIS tv	Howard,	SHERMAN tv
Howard	HAWKS d	Howard,	SIDNEY p-d'25
Howard	HEWETT s Am	Howard,	SUSAN tv+
Howard	HOBSON bbc hf	Howard,	TOM tv
Howard	HUGHES id,fly Am	Howard,	TREVOR
Howard	JOHNSON b	Howard,	VINCE tv
Howard	JOHNSON mer-foods Am	Howarth,	ROGER tv
Howard	JONES e,w Am	Howat,	CLARK tv
Howard	JONES s,ws Br	Howe,	ED(E.W.)j,ed,w Am
Howard	KAYLAN sax,x Am	Howe,	ELIAS i Am
Howard	KEEL tv+	Howe,	GORDY ho-m'52'3'7 &
Howard	KELLY md,i,e Am	Howe,	GORDY ho-m'58'60'63
Howard	LEESE mr-kbds,guit Am	Howe,	IRVING ct,h Am
Howard	LINDSAY w,pr,la Am	Howe,	JULIA w,fe Am
Howard	McNEAR tv+	Howe,	QUINCY tv
Howard	MORRIS tv+	Howe,	SAMUEL md,e,ref Am
Howard	MORTON tv	Howe,	STEVE mr-guit,s Br
Howard	MYLES tv	Howel	HARRIS r Welsh
Howard	NEMEROV po,w Am	Howell	COBB st Am
Howard	NORMAN w Am	Howell,	ARLENE tv
Howard	ODUM sociol,e Am	Howell,	C. THOMAS tv+
Howard	PLATT tv	Howell,	HOKE tv+
Howard	PYLE illus,w Am	Howells,	URSULA
Howard	RICE tv	Howells,	WILLIAM w,ct,po Am
Howard	ROLLINS Jr. tv+	Howerd,	FRANKIE
Howard	SACKLER w Am	Howes,	REED
Howard	SCOTT guit.s Am	Howes,	SALLY ANN
Howard	SPRING w Br	Howie	JOHNSON mr-drm Am
Howard	ST. JOHN tv+	Howie	LONG fb
Howard	STERN w,tv Am	Howie	MANDEL cm,tv+ Can
Howard	TEMIN md,e Am	Howie	MORENZ ho
Howard	THOMAS tv	Howland,	BETH tv
Howard	VERNON	Howland,	JOBYNA
Howard	VICKERY navy Am	Howland,	OLIN
Howard	ZIEFF d	Howlin,	OLIN tv
Howard K.	SMITH tv-j,anchor Am	Hoxby,	SCOTT tv
Howard,	ALAN mr-bass Br	Hoxie	JACK
Howard,	ARLISS	Hoxie,	VINNIE su Am
Howard,	BARBARA tv	Hoy,	BOB tv

Hoy,	LINDA tv		Hudson,	MARK tv
Hoy,	ROBERT tv		Hudson,	ROCHELLE tv+
Hoyle,	EDMOND w-cards Br		Hudson,	ROCK tv+
Hoyle,	FRED(Sir)sc,e,w-scifi		Hudson,	TONI
Hoyt	AXTON s,tv+ Am		Hudson,	WILLIAM sc,w Br
Hoyt	WILHELM b hf		Hudson,	WILLIAM tv+
Hoyt,	GEORGE bbc hf		Huerta,	ADOLFO de la st Mex
Hoyt,	JOHN tv+		Hues,	MATTHIAS
Hoyt,	LaMAR b-cy'83		Huet	PAUL p Fr
Hoyt,	WAITE b hf		Huey	LEWIS mr-s Am
Hrbek,	KENT b		Huey	LONG(Kingfish)st Am
Hrdlicka,	ALES an,ed Am		Huff,	BRENT
Hrozny,	BEDRICH arch,h,e Czch		Huff,	SAM fb hf
Hua	KUO-FENG st China		Huffman,	DAVID
Huascar	--- ruler Incas		Huffman,	ROSANNA tv
Hubbard,	CAL b hf		Hufsey,	BILLY tv+
Hubbard,	CAL fb hf		Hugel,	FRIEDRICH von r Br
Hubbard,	DAVID tv		Hugel,	KARL von x,sc Aus
Hubbard,	ELBERT w,ed,pb Am		Hugg,	MIKE mr-drm Br
Hubbard,	GLENN b,gg'86		Huggins,	CHARLES n-m'66
Hubbard,	JOHN		Huggins,	MILLER b, hf
Hubbard,	L. RON w Am		Huggins,	WILLIAM(Sir)ast
Hubbard,	LUCINDA tv		Hugh	ALLAN(Sir)ships,f Can
Hubbell,	CARL b-mv'33'36,hf		Hugh	ALLEN(Sir)organ,cn
Hubbell,	ELNA tv		Hugh	BURGESS i Am
Hubbert,	CORK tv+		Hugh	CHERRY tv
Hubble,	EDWIN astron Am		Hugh	DALTON st Br
Hubel,	DAVID n-m'81		Hugh	DOHERTY t Br
Huber,	EUGEN l,e Swi		Hugh	DOWNS tv-host+ Am
Huber,	HANS c,e Swi		Hugh	DUFFY b hf
Huber,	HAROLD		Hugh	GILLIN tv
Huber,	MAX l,e Swi		Hugh	GLASS frontier Am
Huber,	ROBERT n-c'88		Hugh	GRAHAM pb Can
Huber,	WOLF p Ger		Hugh	GRANT
Hubert	DAVIES w Br		Hugh	GRUNDY mr-drm Br
Hubert	LANGUET st,w Fr		Hugh	HEFNER pb Am
Hubert	NEWTON ast,e Am		Hugh	HERBERT
Hubert	POOT po Dut		Hugh	KENNER w,ct Can
Hubert	SELBY Jr w Am		Hugh	LANE(Sir)mer-art Ir
Hubert van EYCK p Belg			Hugh	LATIMER r,ref Br
Hubert-Whitten, JANET tv			Hugh	LEGARE l,ed Am
Hubley,	SEASON		Hugh	LOFTING w,illus Br
Huc,	REGIS r Fr		Hugh	MARLOWE
Huch,	RICARDA w,po Ger		Hugh	McCRAE po Aust
Huckabee,	COOPER		Hugh	MILLgeog,weather Scot
Huckleberry FOX			Hugh	O'BRIAN tv+
Hucknall, MICK(Red)mr-s Br			Hugh	O'CONNOR tv
Hucko,	PEANUTS tv		Hugh	RAY(Shorty)fb hf
Hudde,	JOHAN van math Dut		Hugh	REILLY tv+
Huddie	LEDBETTER mj,s-bluesAm		Hugh	THOMAS w,h Br
Huddle,	ELIZABETH tv		Hugh	WALPOLE(Sir)w
Huddleston, DAVID tv+			Hugh	WOLFF cn Am
Hudlin,	REGINALD d, pr		Hugh-Kelly, DANIEL tv+	
Hudlin,	WARRINGTON d, pr		Hughes,	BARNARD tv+
Hudson	LOWE(Sir)ar		Hughes,	CAROL
Hudson,	ERNIE		Hughes,	CHAS.EVANS l,ch just
Hudson,	GARTH organ Br		Hughes,	FINOLA tv+
Hudson,	GARY		Hughes,	HATCHER p-d'24
Hudson,	HENRY x Br		Hughes,	HELEN
Hudson,	JEFFREY(Sr)dwarf,arBr		Hughes,	HOWARD id,fly Am
Hudson,	MANLEY l,e,st Am		Hughes,	JOHN d

Hughes,	KAY	Humes,	MARY tv
Hughes,	KEN d	Humfrey,	PELHAM md,c Br
Hughes,	LANGSTON po,w Am	Hummel,	JOHANN piano,c Ger
Hughes,	LLOYD	Humperdinck,	ENGELBERT c Ger
Hughes,	MARY BETH	Humperdinck,	ENGELBERT s-pop Am
Hughes,	MICHAEL tv	Humphrey	BOGART tv+
Hughes,	MIKO	Humphrey	DAVY(Sir)sc
Hughes,	RICHARD w,po Br	Humphrey	GILBERT(Sir)x
Hughes,	ROBIN tv	Humphrey	REPTON ac-land Br
Hughes,	TED pol-1984+ Br	Humphrey	WARD(Mrs.)w Br
Hughes,	TERRY d	Humphrey,	DORIS ba Am
Hughes,	THOMAS l,reform,w Br	Humphrey,	HUBERT st-vp Am
Hughes,	WENDY	Humphreys,	PAUL mr-keybds Br
Hugo	ALFVEN c,e Swe	Humphries,	BILL tv
Hugo	BALL la,w Ger	Humphries,	TESSA
Hugo	BENIOFF sc,e Am	Humphry	DAVY(Sir)sc,w
Hugo	BLACK l-supr ct,st Am	Huneker,	JAMES ct-m+art Am
Hugo	ECKENER id-aero Ger	Hung,	SAMO
Hugo	HAAS	Hunley,	LEANN tv
Hugo	HAASE st Ger	Hunnicutt,	ARTHUR
Hugo	JUNKERS eng-planes Ger	Hunnicutt,	GAYLE tv+
Hugo	KAUN c Ger	Hunt	BLOCK tv+
Hugo	PREUSS l,st Ger	Hunt,	ALLAN tv
Hugo	RIEMANN h-music Ger	Hunt,	BONNIE tv+
Hugo	SOTO	Hunt,	GARETH
Hugo	STINNES id Ger	Hunt,	HELEN o-a'98,tv
Hugo	WEAVING	Hunt,	HOLMAN p Br
Hugo	WOLF c Aus	Hunt,	LAMAR fb hf
Hugo de	VRIES sc,e Dut	Hunt,	LEIGH j,w,po Br
Hugo van der	GOES p Belg	Hunt,	LINDA o-s'83
Hugo von	MOHL sc,e Ger	Hunt,	MARSHA tv+
Hugo,	VICTOR po,w Fr	Hunt,	MARTITA
Hugues	MARET st Fr	Hunt,	PETER d
Huguet,	JAIME p Sp	Hunt,	RICHARD tv
Huie,	WILLIAM tv	Hunt,	SUSAN tv
Huigh	GROOT e,st Dut	Hunt,	SUZANNE tv
Hulbert,	WILLIAM b hf	Hunt,	VIOLET bio,w Br
Hulce,	TOM	Hunt,	WARD l,supr ct Am
Hulin,	PIERRE ar Fr	Hunt,	WILL tv
Hulk	HOGAN wrestler+ Am	Hunter	CARSON
Hull,	BOBBY ho-m'65'6	Hunter	TYLO tv
Hull,	BRETT ho-m'91	Hunter	Von LEER tv
Hull,	CORDELL n-x'45	Hunter,	ALBERTA mj-violin Am
Hull,	DIANNE	Hunter,	BILL
Hull,	HENRY	Hunter,	CATFISH b-cy'74 hf
Hull,	JOSEPHINE o-s'50	Hunter,	EVAN w Am
Hull,	WARREN tv+	Hunter,	HOLLY
Hullah,	JOHN organ,c Br	Hunter,	IAN mr-guitar,s Br
Hulls,	JONATHAN i Br	Hunter,	IAN tv+
Hulme,	THOMAS ct,ph,po Br	Hunter,	JEFFREY tv+
Hulse,	RUSSELL n-p'93	Hunter,	JIM(Catfish)b-cy'74
Hulton,	EDWARD(Sir)newspaper	Hunter,	KAKI
Hults,	ARLO organ,tv Am	Hunter,	KIM o-s'51
Humberstone,	H. BRUCE d	Hunter,	TAB tv+
Humbert	WOLFE po Br	Hunter,	TIM d
Hume	CRONYN	Huntington,	COLLIS id-rrs Am
Hume,	BENITA tv+	Huntington,	ELLSWORTH geog,x Am
Hume,	BRITT tv	Huntington,	NICOLE tv
Hume,	DAVID ph,h Scot	Huntley,	CHET tv-j Am
Hume,	FERGUS w Br	Huntley,	RAYMOND
Hume,	JOHN st, n-x'98	Huntz	HALL

Hunyadi,	JANOS ar,hero Hung
Huppert,	ISABELLE
Hur,	BEN sp
Hurban,	JOZEF w Slovak
Hurd	HATFIELD
Hurd,	PETER p Am
Hurley,	ELIZABETH mo+ Br
Hurley,	PATRICK st Am
Hurok,	SOL impress Am
Hurricane	SMITH mj,cn Br
Hurry Up	YOST fbc
Hurst,	BRANDON
Hurst,	FANNIE w Am
Hurst,	PAUL
Hurst,	RICK tv
Hurst,	VERONICA
Hurston,	ZORA NEALE w Am
Hurt,	JO tv
Hurt,	JOHN
Hurt,	MARY BETH
Hurt,	WILLIAM o-a'85
Hus,	JAN r Czech
Husa,	KAREL p-m'69
Husain,	JORY tv
Husain,	ZAKIR st India
Husak,	GUSTAV st Czech
Husayni,	AMIN al- st Arab
Husband	KIMMEL navy-Adm Am
Husky,	FERLIN s-cntry+ Am
Huss,	JOHN r,reform Czech
Hussein,	SADDAM st Iraq
Hussein,	WARIS d
Husserl,	EDMUND ph Ger
Hussey,	OBED i Am
Hussey,	OLIVIA
Hussey,	RUTH
Hussey,	WAYNE mr-guitar,s Br
Husson,	JULES w Fr
Huston,	ANJELICA o-s'85
Huston,	CAROL tv
Huston,	JOHN d,w+ Am
Huston,	PATRICIA tv
Huston,	VIRGINIA
Huston,	WALTER la+,o-s'48
Huszar,	KAROLY j,st Hung
Hutchence,	MICHAEL mr-s Austra
Hutchins,	ROBERT e,w Am
Hutchins,	WHEEZER
Hutchins,	WILL tv+
Hutchinson,	JIVER mj,cn WInd
Hutchinson,	JOSEPHINE
Hutson,	CANDACE tv
Hutson,	CHRIS tv
Hutson,	DON fb hf
Hutten,	ULRICH von noble Ger
Hutter,	MARK tv
Hutter,	RALF mr-kbds,drms,s Ger
Hutton,	BETTY tv+
Hutton,	DANNY mr-s Irish
Hutton,	GUNILLA tv
Hutton,	INA RAY s Am

Hutton,	JIM tv+
Hutton,	LAUREN
Hutton,	MARION mj-s Am
Hutton,	RIF tv
Hutton,	ROBERT
Hutton,	TIMOTHY o-s'80
Huub	STAPEL
Huxley,	ALDOUS w Br
Huxley,	ANDREW n-m'63
Huxley,	JULIAN sc,w Br
Huxley,	RICK mr-guitar Br
Huxley,	THOMAS sc,e Br
Huxtable,	ADA ct Am
Huygens,	CHRISTIAAN math Dut
Huysmans,	JORIS w Fr
Hwang Jang	LEE
Hy	AVERBACK d
Hy	GARDNER tv
Hyacinthe	RIGAUD p Fr
Hyams,	LEILA
Hyams,	PETER d
Hyatt,	ALPHEUS sc,e Am
Hyatt,	BOBBY tv
Hyatt,	CHUCK bb hf
Hyatt,	JOHN i Am
Hyde	PARKER(Sir)navy
Hyde,	DOUGLAS po,w,st Irish
Hyde-White,	ALEX
Hyde-White,	WILFRID
Hyer,	MARTHA
Hyerdahl,	THOR w Nor
Hyland,	DIANA tv+
Hylands,	SCOTT tv+
Hylton,	JACK mj,cn Br
Hylton,	JANE tv+
Hyman	RICKOVER navy-Adm Am
Hyman,	EARL tv
Hyman,	LIBBIE sc,e,w Am
Hymans,	PAUL st Belg
Hymer,	WARREN
Hymie,	RED mj-trump Am
Hynde,	CHRISSIE mr-s Am
Hyne,	CHARLES w Br
Hypatia	--- ph Gr
Hyrtl,	JOSEPH md,e Aus
Hyser,	JOYCE tv+
Hywel	BENNETT

"I" NAME DESIGNATION CODES

i	INVENTOR
id	INDUSTRIALIST
illus	ILLUSTRATOR

"I" NATIONALITY CODE

Ir	- IRISH	Isr	- ISRAEL
		It	- ITALIAN

"I's"

I. Stanford	JOLLEY
I.F.	STONE j,w Am
I.M.	PEI ac Am

I.S.	JOHAR
Iacocca,	LEE id-cars,bio Am
Iain	CUTHBERTSON
Iain	GLEN
Ian	ASTBURY mr,s Br
Ian	BAKER-FINCH g Br
Ian	BANNEN
Ian	BROWN mr-s Br
Ian	BURUMA w
Ian	DURY mr-s Br
Ian	FLEMING w+ Br
Ian	FRIED tv
Ian	GILLAN mr-s Br
Ian	HART
Ian	HENDRY
Ian	HOLM
Ian	HOLMES
Ian	HUNTER mr-guit,s Br
Ian	HUNTER tv+
Ian	KEITH
Ian	MARSH mr-kbds Br
Ian	McDONALD mr-sax Br
Ian	McKELLAN la+ Br
Ian	McLAGAN mr-kbds Br
Ian	McNEICE
Ian	McSHANE tv+
Ian	MUNE
Ian	OGILVY
Ian	PAICE mr-drm Br
Ian	SHARP d
Ian	TRACEY
Ian	WATKIN
Ian	WOLFE
Ian	WOOSNAM g Br
Ian	YULE
Ian	ZIERING tv
Ian,	JANIS s-folk,rk Am
Iba,	HANK bbc hf
Ibanez,	CARLOS ar,st Chile
Ibarra,	MIRTHA
Ibert,	JACQUES c Fr
Ibrahim	SINASI w,j Turk
Ibsen,	HENRIK w,po Nor
Ice Cube	--- m-rap Am
Ice T.	--- mr,tv Am
Ice,	VANILLA m-rap Am
Ichabod	CRANE fc
Ichaso,	LEON d
Ichino,	LAURIE tv
Ichiro	SUGAI
Ickes,	HAROLD st Am
Ictinus	--- ac Gr
Ida	CANTOR(Eddie's wife)
Ida	JAMES
Ida	LUPINO tv+
Ida	MOORE tv
Ida	TARBELL w,ed Am
Ida	WYLIE w Br
Ida Bell	WELLS j,ed,ref Am
Iddings,	JOSEPH geol,e Am
Idi	AMIN st Uganda

Idle,	ERIC
Idles,	CINNAMON
Idol,	BILLY s,ws Br
Ieoh Ming	PEI(I.M.)ac Am
Iffland,	AUGUST la,d Ger
Iggy	POP s,ws Am
Iglesias,	JULIO s-pop,ws Sp
Ignacio	TARSO
Ignacio	ZULOAGA p Sp
Ignarro,	LOUIS n-m'98
Ignatow,	DAVID po,ed Am
Ignaz	GUNTHER su Ger
Ignaz	PLEYEL c,id-pianos Aus
Ignaz	SEIPEL r,st Aus
Ignaz von	BORN sc Aus
Ignazio	SILONE w It
Ignico,	ROBIN tv
Igor	TAMM sc,e Rus
Igus,	DARROW tv
Ihimaera,	WITI w N.Zea
Ike	FORTE fb
Ike	ISAACA mj-bass Am
Ike	PAPPAS
Ike	TURNER s,ws Am
Ikebe,	RYO
Ilan	MITCHELL-SMITH
Ilene	GRAFF tv
Iles,	FRANCIS w Br
Ilgowski,	LOFKA mj,cn Pol
Ilie	NASTASE t Rom
Iliya	ABU MADI po,j Arab
Ilka	CHASE tv+
Ille Pooh,	WINNIE fc
Illeana	DOUGLAS
Illing,	PETER
Illinois	JACQUET mj-sax Am
Illsley,	JOHN mr-bass Br
Ilona	MASSEY
Ilse	Von GLATZ tv
Ilya	FRANK sc Rus
Ilya	KULIK sk
Ilya	REPIN p,e Rus
Ima	HOGG f Am
Imamu	BARAKA po,w Am
Iman	--- mo Somalia
Imber,	NAPHTALI po Isr
Imel,	JACK ba,tv Am
Imelda	MARCOS wife-F. Phill
Imhoff,	GUSTAAF colonist Dut
Immanuel	FUCHS math,e Ger
Immanuel	KANT ph,e Ger
Immelmann,	MAX fly Ger
Immermann,	KARL po,w Ger
Imogen	STUBBS
Imogene	COCA tv+
Imperato,	CARLO tv
Impert,	MARGARET tv
Impey,	ELIJAH(Sir)l
Imre	MADACH po Hung
Imre	NAGY st Hung
Imredy,	BELA st Hung

Ina	BALIN	Iosif	GURKO ar Rus
Ina	CLAIRE	Ipale,	AHARON
Ina Ray	HUTTON s Am	Ipatieff,	VLADIMIR sc Am
Ince,	ADA	Ippolito	NIEVO w,po It
Ince,	THOMAS d,pr Am	Iqbal,	MUHAMMAD(Sir)po,phInd
Inclan,	RAFAEL	Ira	ALLEN st Am
Increase	MATHER r,e,w Am	Ira	BOWEN ast Am
Indiana	JONES fc	Ira	EAKER ar Am
Indira	GANDHI st India	Ira	LEVIN w Am
Indy,	VINCENT d' c Fr	Ira	REMSEN sc,e Am
Ines de	CASTRO noblewoman Sp	Ira	SANKEY r,w-hyms Am
Inescort,	FRIEDA tv+	Ira	WOLFERT w Am
Inez	COOPER	Iredell,	JAMES l,st Am
Infante,	PEDRO	Ireland,	DAVID w Aust
Infeld,	LEOPOLD sc,e Pol	Ireland,	JILL
Ing,	DEAN w-scifi Am	Ireland,	JOHN
Inga	SWENSON tv+	Ireland,	JOHN organ,c Br
Ingamells,	REX po Aust	Ireland,	KATHY mo+ Am
Inge,	WILLIAM p-d'53	Ireland,	PATRICIA fe Am
Ingels,	MARTY	Irena	FERRIS tv
Ingemann,	BERNARD po,w Dan	Irene	CARA s,tv+
Inger	STEVENS tv+	Irene	CASTLE ba Am
Ingle,	DOUG mr-kbds Am	Irene	CURIE sc Fr
Ingle,	JOHN tv	Irene	DUNNE
Ingles,	RED mj-sax Am	Irene	HANDL
Inglis,	CHARLES r Can	Irene	HERVEY tv+
Inglis,	JOHN(Sir)ar	Irene	JACOB
Ingmar	BERGMAN d,pr,w Swe	Irene	MIRACLE
Ingraham,	LLOYD	Irene	PAPAS tv+
Ingram,	JACK	Irene	RICH
Ingram,	JAMES s-r&b,ws Am	Irene	RYAN tv
Ingram,	REX	Irene	TEDROW tv+
Ingres,	JEAN p Fr	Irene	TSU
Ingrid	BERGMAN tv+	Irene	VERNON tv
Ingrid	PITT	Irene	WARE
Ingrid	THULIN tv+	Irene	WORTH
Inigo	JONES ac Br	Ireton,	HENRY ar,st Br
Inigo	MENDOZA po Sp	Iriarte,	TOMAS de po Sp
Ink Spots,	THE s Am	Iris	ADRIAN
Inkster,	JULI g Am	Iris	MURDOCH(Dame)w,ph Br
Inman,	HENRY p Am	Irish	McCALLA
Innes,	COSMO antiquar,e Scot	Irm	HERMANN
Innes,	MICHAEL w Br	Irma	ROMBAUER w-cookbk Am
Innes,	NEIL mr-kbds,s Br	Irma	SEIGEL tv
Inness,	GEORGE Jr p Am	Iron Eyes	CODY
Inness,	GEORGE p Am	Iron Pants	Le MAY airforce Am
Innis,	ROYcivil rghts Vir.Is.	Irons,	JEREMY o-a'90
Inonu,	ISMET ar,st Turk	Ironside,	MICHAEL
Insana,	TINO	Irvin	COBB w,j Am
Inshiro	HONDA d	Irvin	McDOWELL ar Am
Inskip,	THOMAS st,l Br	Irvin	REA illus Am
Insull,	SAMUEL id-elec Am	Irvin	YALOM ps,w Am
Ioannis	METAXAS ar,st Ger	Irvin,	MONTE b hf
Iommi,	TONY mr-guitar Br	Irving	BACON
Ion	HAIDUC	Irving	BENSON tv
Ion	MIHALACHE st Rom	Irving	BERLIN c,ws Am
Ion	OTESCU c Rom	Irving	COLBURN i,id Am
Ione	SKYE	Irving	FISHER ec,w Am
Ionesco,	EUGENE w Fr	Irving	GILL ac Am
Ionescu,	DUMITRU(Take) st Rom	Irving	HOWE ct,h Am
Iorga,	NICOLAE h,e,st Rom	Irving	LAYTON po Can

Irving	PICHEL	Isaak,	CHRIS s+ Am
Irving	RAPPER d	Isabel	ALLENDE w Chile
Irving	STONE w,bio Am	Isabel	GRANDIN tv
Irving R.	LEVINE tv-j Am	Isabel	JEANS
Irving,	AMY	Isabel	JEWELL
Irving,	CLIVE j,w Am	Isabel	LORCA
Irving,	GEORGE	Isabel	SANFORD tv+
Irving,	HENRY(Sir)la	Isabella	BANKS w Br
Irving,	HOLLIS tv	Isabella	GREGORY(Lady)w Irish
Irving,	JOHN w Am	Isabella	HOFMANN tv
Irving,	MARGARET tv	Isabella	ROSSELLINI
Irving,	WASHINGTON w Am	Isabelle	ADJANI
Irwin	ALLEN d	Isabelle	HUPPERT
Irwin	COREY tv	Isabelle	LEIGHTON tv
Irwin	EDMAN ph,e Am	Isabelle	MEJIAS
Irwin	SHAW w Am	Isabey,	JEAN p Fr
Irwin,	BILL	Isacksen,	PETER tv
Irwin,	GEORGIA la,s Am	Isadora	DUNCAN ba Am
Irwin,	MAY la,s Am	Isaiah	BERLIN(Sir)ph,w
Irwin,	WALLACE w,bio,h Am	Isaiah	BOWMAN geol,e Am
Irwin,	WILL j,w Am	Isaiah	SELLERS river pilot Am
Irwin,	WYNN tv	Isaiah	THOMAS bb
Isa	MIRANDA	Isak	DINESEN w Dan
Isaac	ALBENIZ piano,c Sp	Isamu	NOGUCHI su Am
Isaac	ASIMOV w-films,sc,e Am	Isao	KIMURA
Isaac	BABBITT i Am	Isela	VEGA
Isaac	BABEL w Rus	Isenberg,	BARBARA tv
Isaac	BACKUS r Am	Ish	KABBIBLE mj,s,tv Am
Isaac	BARROW math,e Br	Isham	JONES mj,cn,c Am
Isaac	BELL(Sir)sc,id Scot	Ishmael	REED w,po Am
Isaac	BROWNE po Br	Isidor	RABI sc,e Am
Isaac	BUTT l,st Irish	Isidor	STRAUS mer Am
Isaac	ELZEVIR pb Dut	Isidor	TRAUBE sc,e Ger
Isaac	FUNK pb,ed Am	Isidore	DUCASSE po Fr
Isaac	GIMBEL mer Am	Iskander,	FAZIL w,po Rus
Isaac	HAYES mr,r&b,s,tv+ Am	Isla y Rojo,	JOSE de r,w Sp
Isaac	HAYES x Am	Isla,	JOSE de w,e Sp
Isaac	HERZOG r-rabbi Pol	Isley,	O'KELLY s Am
Isaac	HOLDEN(Sir)i	Islip,	SIMON r Br
Isaac	JOGUES(Saint)r Fr	Ismael	MONTES st Boliv
Isaac	LEESER r-rabbi Am	Ismay,	HASTINGS ar Br
Isaac	MAZRAHI	Ismet	INONU ar,st Turk
Isaac	MURPHY jockey Am	Isobel	ELSOM
Isaac	NEWTON(Sir)sc,math,e	Isola	JONES mezzo soprano
Isaac	PERETZ w Pol	Isouard,	NICOLAS c Fr
Isaac	PITMAN(Sir)e,i	Israel	JUARBE tv
Isaac	REED ed Br	Israel	LIPKIN r-rabbi Lith
Isaac	RUIZ tv	Israel	QUERIDO w Dut
Isaac	STERN viol+ Rus-Am	Israel	SINGER w,j Am
Isaac	STORY po Am	Israel	ZEVIN j,w Am
Isaac	WATTS r,w-hymns Br	Israels,	JOZEF p Dut
Isaac B.	SINGER w Am	Issel,	DAN bb hf
Isaac da	COSTA po Dut	Istvan	BETHLEN st Hung
Isaac M.	SINGER i,id Am	Istvan	BOCSKAY st Hung
Isaac Newton LEWIS ar,i Am		Istvan	SZABO d
Isaac van de PUTTE st Dut		Isuzu	YAMADA
Isaac,	BUD m-cnt Am	Ital	REDING st Swi
Isaach	de BANKOLE	Italo	BALBO fly It
Isaacs,	IKE mj-bass Am	Italo	CALVINO w It
Isaak	DORNER r,e Ger	Italo	SVEVO w It
Isaak	JOST h Ger	Itami,	JUZO d+

Itard,	JEAN md-ar Fr		**"J" NAME DESIGNATION CODE**
Ithiel	TOWN ac Am		j - JOURNALIST
Ito,	LANCE l(OJ trial)Am		
Ito,	MIDORI sk Japan		**"J" NATIONALITY CODE**
Ito,	ROBERT tv+		Jap - JAPANESE
Iturbi,	JOSE piano,cn Sp		
Itzhak	BEN-ZVI st Isr		**"J's"**
Itzhak	PERLMAN viol Isr		
Iuliu	MANIU st Rom	J.	GEILS mr-guit Am
Iva	DAVIES mr-guit,s Aust	J. Anthony	LUKAS w Am
Ivan	BOESKY investmts Am	J. Carrol	NAISH tv+
Ivan	BONAR tv+	J. Dallas	SHIRLEY bbr hf
Ivan	BUNIN po,w Rus	J. Eddie	PECK tv+
Ivan	CANKAR w Slav	J. Edward	BROMBERG
Ivan	DESNY	J. Farrell	MacDONALD
Ivan	DIXON	J. Georg	BEDNORZ s Ger
Ivan	DOIG w Am	J. Lee	THOMPSON d
Ivan	FRANKO w,j Ukraine	J. Michael	BISHOP md Am
Ivan	KONEV ar Rus	J. Pat	O'MALLEY tv+
Ivan	KRYLOV w Rus	J. Patrick	McNAMARA tv
Ivan	NAGY ba,d+ Am	J. Paul	FREEMAN tv
Ivan	NECHUV w Ukraine	J. Pierpoint	MORGAN f,f Am
Ivan	NIKITIN po Rus	J.A.	JANCE w Am
Ivan	PASSER d	J.A.	PRESTON tv+
Ivan	PAVLOV sc,md Rus	J.C.	BRANDY tv
Ivan	REITMAN d,pr Cz	J.C.	POWYS w,po Br
Ivan	ROGERS	J.C.	QUINN
Ivan	SUBASIC st Yugo	J.C.	SQUIRE(Sir)po,ed
Ivan	VAZOV po,w,st Bulg	J.D.	CANNON tv+
Ivan	ZAJC c Croat	J.D.	DANIELS tv
Ivana	TRUMP(Donald's ex)Am	J.E.	FREEMAN
Ivanek,	ZELJKO	J.Eddie	PECK tv+
Ivanoe	BONOMI st It	J.F.	GARNER w Am
Ivanov,	LEV ba Rus	J.H.	PLUMB h Br
Ivar	AASEN w Nor	J.I.M.	STEWART w,ct Br
Ivar	KANTS	J.J.	BARRY tv
Ivar,	STAN tv	J.J.	COHEN
Ivens,	JORIS d Dut	J.J.	JOHNSON mj-trom Am
Ivens,	TERRI tv	J.P.	McGOWAN d+
Ives,	BURL s+,o-s'58 Am	J.R.R.	TOLKIEN w Br
Ives,	CHARLES p-m'47	J.S.	CARDONE d
Ives,	FREDERIC i Am	J.S.	Le FANU w Ir
Ives,	GEORGE tv	J.T.	SNOW b
Ivey,	DANA tv+	J.T.	WALSH
Ivey,	JUDITH tv+	Ja'net	DuBOIS
Ivo	ANDRIC w Serb	Jabez	CURRY e Am
Ivo	GARRANI	Jabez	GORHAM id-silver Am
Ivo,	TOMMY tv	Jace	ALEXANDER
Ivor	BARRY tv	Jacinto	GRAU w Sp
Ivor	DEAN tv	Jacinto	PICON w,ct-art Sp
Ivor	FRANCIS	Jack	ARNOLD d
Ivor	NOVELLO la,w,c Br	Jack	BAILEY tv
Ivory,	JAMES d,pr	Jack	BANNON tv+
Ivy	BETHUNE tv	Jack	BARRY tv
Ivy	LEE public relat Am	Jack	BENNY cm,tv+ Am
Iwan	GILKIN w Belg	Jack	BRUCE mr-bass,s Scot
Iwashita,	SHIMA	Jack	BURNS tv
Iyer,	PICO w Br	Jack	CARSON tv+
Izaak	WALTONbio,w-angler Br	Jack	CARTER tv+
Izard,	RALPH re Am	Jack	CASADY mr-bass Am
Izay,	CONNIE tv	Jack	CASSIDY tv+

Jack	CLARK tv	Jack	MacGOWRAN
Jack	COLEMAN tv+	Jack	MANNING tv
Jack	COLLINS tv	Jack	McCOY tv
Jack	COLVIN tv+	Jack	McDOWELL b
Jack	CONWAY d	Jack	MILES w
Jack	DeMAVE tv	Jack	MINER nature Can
Jack	DEMPSEY boxer Am	Jack	MITCHUM tv
Jack	DODSON tv+	Jack	MULHALL
Jack	DOUGLAS tv-host Am	Jack	MURDOCK tv
Jack	DUFFY tv	Jack	NANCE tv+
Jack	ELAM tv+	Jack	NARZ tv
Jack	ESKEW tv	Jack	OAKIE
Jack	FINA mj-piano,cn Am	Jack	ORRISON tv
Jack	FINNEY w Am	Jack	PAAR tv-host+ Am
Jack	FISK d	Jack	PALANCE tv+
Jack	GARDNER bbc hf	Jack	PARNELL tv
Jack	GARNER tv	Jack	PAYNE mj,cn Br
Jack	GELBER w Am	Jack	PERKINS tv
Jack	GILFORD tv+	Jack	PERRIN
Jack	GILPIN	Jack	PLANT mj-s Br
Jack	GING tv+	Jack	PRINCE s,tv Am
Jack	GOLD d	Jack	RAMSAY bbc hf
Jack	GREENE s-cnt Am	Jack	RANDALL
Jack	GREGSON tv	Jack	REGAS tv
Jack	GREIN ct-drama Br	Jack	RILEY tv+
Jack	GRIMES tv	Jack	ROTH tv
Jack	HALEY	Jack	SCALIA tv+
Jack	HAM fb hf	Jack	SHELDON tv
Jack	HARRELL tv	Jack	SHOLDER d
Jack	HARRIS mj-viol,cn Br	Jack	SMIGHT d
Jack	HASKELL tv	Jack	SMITH tv
Jack	HAWKINS	Jack	SOO tv+
Jack	HIGGINS w Ir-Br	Jack	STANTON tv
Jack	HILL d+	Jack	TAYLOR
Jack	HOBBS(Sir) sp-cricket	Jack	TWORKOV p Am
Jack	HOGAN tv	Jack	TWYMAN bb hf
Jack	HOLT	Jack	WAGNER tv+
Jack	HOXIE	Jack	WALLACE tv+
Jack	HYLTON mj,cn Br	Jack	WARDEN tv+
Jack	IMEL ba,tv Am	Jack	WARNER
Jack	INGRAM	Jack	WATSON
Jack	JOHNSON boxer Am	Jack	WEBB tv+
Jack	JOHNSON mj,cn Br	Jack	WESTON tv+
Jack	JUDGE vaudville,c Br	Jack	WILD
Jack	KEHOE	Jack	WYRTZEN tv
Jack	KELLY tv+	Jack	YALLEN lyrics Am
Jack	KEROUAC(Jack) w Am	Jack D.	DOUGLAS tv
Jack	KETCH hangman Br	Jackee	---
Jack	KILTY	Jackee	HARRY tv
Jack	KLUGMAN tv+	Jacki	WEAVER
Jack	KNIGHT tv	Jackie	CHAN
Jack	LAMBERT fb hf	Jackie	COLLINS w Am
Jack	LAMBERT tv+	Jackie	COOGAN tv+
Jack	LANG st Aus	Jackie	COOPER d,tv+
Jack	LARSON tv+	Jackie	FOX mr-bass Am
Jack	LaRUE tv+	Jackie	GAYLE
Jack	LEMMON tv+	Jackie	GLEASON cm,tv+ Am
Jack	LINDINE tv	Jackie	GRIMES tv
Jack	LINDSAY po Aust	Jackie	HALEY tv
Jack	LONDON w Am	Jackie	JACKSON mr,s Am
Jack	LORD tv+	Jackie	JENKINS(Butch)

Jackie	JENSEN b	Jackson,	SHIRLEY w Am
Jackie	JOSEPH tv	Jackson,	STONEY tv+
Jackie	KELK tv	Jackson,	THOMAS(Stonewall)ar
Jackie	MASON cm Am	Jackson,	TITO mr-s Am
Jackie	McCAULEY mr-kbds Ir	Jackson,	TONY mr-bass,s Br
Jackie	MORAN	Jackson,	TRAVIS b hf
Jackie	PHELPS tv	Jackson,	VICTORIA
Jackie	SEARL	Jackson,	WANDA tv
Jackie	SMITH fb hf	Jaclyn	SMITH tv+
Jackie	STEWARTautoracer Scot	Jacob	ANATOLI md,ph Fr
Jackie	SWANSON tv	Jacob	ASTLEY(Sir)ar
Jackie	VAN s,tv Am	Jacob	COXEY bus,st Am
Jackie	VINSON tv	Jacob	DEVERS ar Am
Jackie	WADDELL tv	Jacob	EMDEN r Ger
Jackie	WILSON mr Am	Jacob	EPSTEIN(Sir)su
Jackie	WRIGHT tv	Jacob	ESTRUP st Dan
Jackie Earle HALEY		Jacob	GORDIN w Am
Jackling, DANIEL eng-mine Am		Jacob	GREIN(Jack)ct Br
Jacks,	LAWRENCE r,ph,w Br	Jacob	GRIMM w Ger
Jackson	BROWNE s-mr,ws Am	Jacob	HACKERT p Ger
Jackson	POLLOCK p Am	Jacob	JAVITS st Am
Jackson,	ANDREW 7th pres	Jacob	PARKER tv
Jackson,	ANNE	Jacob	PERKINS i Am
Jackson,	BO b,fb	Jacob	RIIS j,w,ref Am
Jackson,	EDDIE tv	Jacob	RUPPERT id,bmg Am
Jackson,	FREDA	Jacob	SCHIFF banker,f Am
Jackson,	FREDDIEs-r&b,ws Am	Jacob van LENNEP po,w Dut	
Jackson	GLENDA o-a'73	Jacob,	FRANCOIS n-m'65
Jackson,	GORDON	Jacob,	IRENE
Jackson,	HELEN po,w Am	Jacob,	MAX w,po Fr
Jackson,	HENRY(Scoop) st Am	Jacob,	VIOLET w,po Scot
Jackson,	JACKIE mr-s Am	Jacobi,	CARL math,e Ger
Jackson,	JANET s,tv+ Am	Jacobi,	DEREK
Jackson,	JEREMY tv	Jacobi,	FRIEDRICH w,ph Ger
Jackson,	JERMAINE mr-s Am	Jacobi,	LOU tv+
Jackson,	JERRY s,cn,tv Am	Jacobs,	ANDRE
Jackson,	JESSE civil rts Am	Jacobs,	BETH tv
Jackson,	JOE s,ws Br	Jacobs,	CHRISTIAN tv
Jackson,	JOHN	Jacobs,	LAWRENCE-HILTON tv
Jackson,	JOHN boxer Br	Jacobs,	MANNY
Jackson,	KATE tv+	Jacobs,	MARILYN tv
Jackson,	KEITH tv	Jacobs,	PARKER tv
Jackson,	LaTOYA strip,porn	Jacobs,	RACHAEL tv
Jackson,	LAURA w,po,ct Am	Jacobs,	WILLIAM w Br
Jackson,	MAHALIA s Am	Jacobsen,	ARNE ac Dan
Jackson,	MARJORIE 2x o-gs'52	Jacobsen,	JENS po,w Dan
Jackson,	MARLON mr-s Am	Jacobson,	DAN w S.Afr
Jackson,	MARY ANN	Jacobson,	JILL tv
Jackson,	MARY tv+	Jacobsson,ULLA	
Jackson,	MICHAEL mr,s,tv+ Am	Jacobus	CLEMENS c Belg
Jackson,	MILT mj-vibes,guit	Jacobus	CREMER w Dut
Jackson,	PAUL tv	Jacobus	De la REY ar S.Afr
Jackson,	PERVIS mr-s Am	Jacobus	KAPTEYN astron Dut
Jackson,	PETER boxer W.Indi	Jacobus	OUD ac Dut
Jackson,	REGGIE b-mv'73 &	Jacobus	REVIUS w Dut
Jackson,	REGGIE rbi'73 hf	Jacobus van LOOY p Dut	
Jackson,	ROSEMARIE tv	Jacobus van't HOFF sc Dut	
Jackson,	SAMMY tv+	Jacoby,	BILLY tv+
Jackson,	SAMUEL	Jacoby,	BOBBY tv+
Jackson,	SELMER tv+	Jacoby,	SCOTT
Jackson,	SHERRY tv+	Jacopo	BELLINI p It

Jacopo	PALMA p It	Jaffe,	CHAPELLE
Jacopo	PERI c It	Jaffe,	RONA ct,w,tv Am
Jacopo	RICCATI math It	Jaffe,	SAM tv+
Jacopo	ROBUSTI p It	Jaffe,	SETH
Jacopo de	BARBARI p It	Jaffe,	SUSAN ba Am
Jacotot,	JEAN e Fr	Jaffe,	TALIESIN tv
Jacquard	JOSEPH i Fr	Jaffrey,	MADHUR
Jacqueline	BEER tv	Jaffrey,	SAEED
Jacqueline	BISSET	Jag	MUNDHRA d
Jacqueline	BROOKES tv+	Jagadis	BOSE(Sir)sc,e India
Jacqueline	COCHRAN fly Am	Jagger,	DEAN o-s'49,tv+
Jacqueline	JAMES s,tv Am	Jagger,	MICK mr+ Br
Jacqueline	SCOTT tv	Jaglom,	HENRY
Jacqueline	WELLS	Jahn,	OTTO sc,w,ct Ger
Jacqueline	WHITE	Jai	UTTAL m,cn India
Jacques	AMYOT r,e Fr	Jaime	BALMES ph,r,e Sp
Jacques	AUBERT viol,c Fr	Jaime	BAUER tv
Jacques	BARZUN e,w Am	Jaime	NUNO cn,c Sp
Jacques	BERL ws Fr	Jaime	ROGERS ba,tv Am
Jacques	BOE po Fr	Jaime	SANCHEZ
Jacques	BRUGNON(Toto)t Fr	Jaimee	FOXWORTH tv
Jacques	CALLOT p Fr	Jake	BECKLEY b hf
Jacques	CARTIER x Fr	Jake	JUNDEF tv
Jacques	COPEAU la,d Fr	Jake	LaMOTTA boxer Am
Jacques	DAVID p Fr	Jakes,	JOHN w Am
Jacques	DUTRONC	Jaki	De MAR tv
Jacques	FATH ds Fr	Jakob	ANDREA r,w Ger
Jacques	FEYDER d Fr	Jakob	AYRER w Ger
Jacques	FLACH j,h,e Fr	Jakob	BOHME mystic,w Ger
Jacques	GODIN	Jakob	CATS po Dut
Jacques	IBERT c Fr	Jakob	DUBS st Swi
Jacques	LARAMIE trapper Am	Jakob	GRIMM w Ger
Jacques	LOEB sc,e Am	Jakob	HANDL c Slov
Jacques	MAZAS viol,c Fr	Jakob	JUD e,w Swi
Jacques	MIGNE r,ed Fr	Jakob	Le BLON p,engr Ger
Jacques	MONOD md-sc Fr	Jakob	Le MAIRE x Dut
Jacques	NECKER f,st,w Fr	Jakob	LENZ po,w Ger
Jacques	OGE re Haiti	Jakob	STAINER viols Aus
Jacques	PERRIN	Jakob van	OOST p Belg
Jacques	PLANTE ho	Jakobson,	ROMAN e Am
Jacques	PREVERT po,w Fr	Jakov	SKOMOROVSKY mj,cn
Jacques	ROUMAIN w,st Haiti	Jakub,	LISA
Jacques	SCOTT tv	Jalal	MERHI
Jacques	SERNAS	Jalbert,	PIERRE tv
Jacques	STURM math,e Fr	Jaleel	WHITE tv
Jacques	TATI d+	Jaloux,	EDMOND w,ct Fr
Jacques	VILLON p Fr	Jam,	JIMMIE m-r&b,pr Am
Jacques,	BREL	Jamaa	FANAKA d
Jacques,	HATTIE	Jamaica	KINCAID w W.Indies
Jacques,	JULES ar,x Belg	Jamal	SHAH
Jacques-Louis	DAVID po Fr	James	AGATE ct Br
Jacquet,	ILLINOIS mj-sax Am	James	AGEE w Am
Jacquet,	JEFFREY tv	James	ALLEN w,e Am
Jacquetta	HAWKES arc,w Br	James	ALLEN(Sir)st N.Zea
Jad	CAPELJA	James	ANGELL e,ps Am
Jada	PINKETT tv+	James	ARNESS tv+
Jadrien	STEELE	James	AUBREY
Jadunath	SARKAR(Sir)h,e Ind	James	AUDLEY(Sir)knight
Jaeckel,	RICHARD tv+	James	AVERY tv+
Jaeckin,	JUST d	James	BAILEY circus Am
Jaeger,	HANS w Nor		

James	BAKER st Am	James	DANA geol,e Am
James	BALDWIN w Am	James	DARREN tv+
James	BARRIE(Sir)w Scot	James	DEAN tv+
James	BARTON	James	DePAIVA tv
James	BEARD p,chef,w Am	James	DEWAR(Sir)sc Scot
James	BEATTIE po,w Scot	James	DICKEY po,w Am
James	BELL	James	DOBIE folklore,w Am
James	BELUSHI tv+	James	DONALD
James	BENNETT j,ed Am	James	DOOHAN tv+
James	BENT arc,x Br	James	DOUGLAS tv
James	BEST tv+	James	DRURY tv+
James	BLACK(Sir)md	James	DUNN
James	BLAINE st Am	James	EADS eng,i Am
James	BLAKE piano,c Am &	James	EDWARDS
James	BLAKE = Eubie	James	ELLISON
James	BLAND ws Am	James	ELLROY w Am
James	BLISH w-scifi Am	James	ENRIGHT bbr hf
James	BOLAM	James	ENSOR(Baron)p Belg
James	BOND(007) fc	James	ESPY weather Am
James	BOOTH	James	EWING md,e Am
James	BOSWELL bio,w Scot	James	FARGO d
James	BOWIE ar,pioneer Am	James	FARLEY st,id Am
James	BOYD w Am	James	FARRELL w Am
James	BRADY f Am &	James	FAULKNER
James	BRADY=Diamond Jim	James	FIGG boxer Br
James	BRAID g Br	James	FLAGG p,illus Am
James	BROLIN tv+	James	FLAVIN tv+
James	BROOKS d	James	FLECKER po,w Br
James	BROWN mj-blues Am	James	FORTEN ref,id Am
James	BROWN mr+ Am	James	FOX
James	BROWN tv	James	FRANCK sc,e Ger-Am
James	BRYCE l,h,st Br	James	FRASER su Am
James	BURBAGE la Br	James	FRAZER(Sir)an,e Scot
James	BURKE	James	GALWAY flute Ir
James	BUSH	James	GAMMON
James	BYRNES l,st Am	James	GARNER tv+
James	CAAN tv+	James	GAVIN ar Am
James	CABELL w Am	James	GAYLEY sc,i Am
James	CAGNEY	James	GIBBS ac Br
James	CAIN j,w Am	James	GILLIS
James	CATTELL ps,e Am	James	GLEASON tv+
James	CLARK auto-racer Br	James	GORMAN w Am
James	CLAVELL w Am	James	GRAY(Sir)sc,e
James	COBURN	James	GREENE tv+
James	COCO	James	GREGORY tv+
James	COLEMAN tv	James	HAGGIN bus,l Am
James	COLLINS b hf	James	HALL w Am
James	CONANT e,sc Am	James	HAMPTON tv+
James	COOK(Capt.)x Br	James	HANDY
James	CORBETT boxer Am	James	HANLEY w Br
James	COUZENS id,st Am	James	HANNAY r,w Irish
James	COX pb,st Am	James	HARE fo Am
James	COZZENS w Am	James	HAYTER
James	CRAFTS sc,e Am	James	HEALEY tv
James	CRAIG	James	HERNE w Am
James	CRAVEN	James	HERRIOT vet,w Br
James	CRONIN sc Am	James	HERTZOG ar,st S.Afr
James	CRUZE d	James	HILL d
James	CURLEY st Am	James	HILTON w Br
James	DALY tv+	James	HOBAN ac Am
James	DALZIEL ph Br		

James	HOFFA labor Am	James	PACKARD eng-cars,i
James	HOGG po Scot	James	PAGET (Sir) md,sc
James	HONG tv+	James	PANKOW m-tromb Am
James	HOOK organ,c Br	James	PARTON w Am
James	HUNEKER ct-m+art Am	James	PATTIE frontier Am
James	INGRAM s-r&b,ws Am	James	PAYN w Br
James	IREDELL l,st Am	James	PENNEY mer Am
James	IVORY d,pr	James	PETIGRU l,st Am
James	JEANS (Sir) sc,e,w Br	James	PICKENS Jr tv
James	JOHNSON l,e,po Am	James	POND mgr-lectures
James	JOHNSON mj,c Am	James	PRIME mr-kbds Scot
James	JONES w Am	James	PURDY w Am
James	JOULE sc Br	James	QUIN la Ir
James	JOY id-rrs f Am	James	RANDALL j,ws Am
James	JOYCE w,po Ir	James	READ
James	JUSTICE	James	REBHORN
James	KAREN tv+	James	REDPATH j,abolit Am
James	KEACH	James	RELLY r Br
James	KEANE tv	James	REMAR
James	KIBERD tv	James	RENWICK ac Am
James	KILLIAN e Am	James	RESTON j,w Am
James	KIRKUP w,po Br	James	ROSS (Sir) x Scot
James	KOK mj,cn Rom-Ger	James	RUMSEY i Am
James	KOMACK tv	James	RUSSO
James	LAPINE w Am	James	RYAN
James	LEE tv	James	SANBORN bus-spices
James	LeGROS	James	SCRIPPS pb Am
James	LEUBA ps,e Am	James	SCULLIN st Aust
James	LICK f,f Am	James	SEAY
James	LOEB f,m,f Am	James	SHERMAN st Am
James	LOEWEN w Am	James	SHIGETA
James	LOWELL po,w Am	James	SHIRLEY w Br
James	LUISI tv+	James	SHORT id-optics Sct
James	MACE (Jem) boxer Br	James	SIKKING tv+
James	MacKAYE la,pr,w Am	James	SLOYAN
James	MANN st Am	James	SPADER
James	MARCUS	James	STACY
James	MASON tv+	James	STALEY tv+
James	MAXTON st Br	James	STARKEY po,ed Ir
James	McAULEYpo,e,ct Aust	James	STARLEY i Br
James	McCLAIN tv	James	STEVENS w Am
James	McCLURE w Br	James	STEWART tv+
James	McEACHIN tv+	James	SUMNER sc,e Am
James	McGILL furs,f Can	James	TATE po Am,
James	McINTYRE r Am	James	TAYLOR s-folk Am
James	MEADE ec Br	James	THOMSON po Br
James	MELTON tv	James	THURBER w,cr Am
James	MERRILL po,w Am	James	TISSOT p,engr Fr
James	MILL ec,ph,h Scot	James	TOBIN ec Am
James	MORIER st Br	James	TODD tv+
James	MURDOCH la Am	James	TOLKAN
James	MURDOCK tv	James	TUCKEY x Br
James	MURRAY	James	USSHER r,e,w Ir
James	NEILSON d	James	VALLELY tv
James	NEWILL	James	Van ALLEN sc Am
James	NGUGI w Kenya	James	Van PATTEN tv+
James	NOBLE tv+	James	VARNUM l,ar-re Am
James	NOLAN tv	James	VICK sc,bus,pb Am
James	O'ROURKE b hf	James	VILLERS
James	OLSON	James	WARWICK
James	OTIS l-colonial Am	James	WATSON Jr tv

James	WATSON md Am	Jamie	ROSE tv+
James	WATT i,eng Scot	Jamie	UYS d
James	WEDDELL x Br	Jamie	WALTERS tv
James	WHALE d	Jamie	FOXX tv
James	WIDDOES tv	Jamie Lee	CURTIS tv+
James	WILBY	Jamie Lyn	BAUER tv
James	WILDER tv+	Jamison,	CECILIA w,p Am
James	WOLFE ar-Gen Br	Jamison,	MIKKI tv
James	WOODS	Jammes,	FRANCIS po,w Fr
James	WRIGHT po Am	Jamsetji	TATA id India
James	YOUNG mr-guit Am	Jan	BERRY s Am
James A.	CONTNER d	Jan	BOTH p Dut
James Earl	JONES tv+	Jan	BRUEGEL p Belg &
James Earl	RAY killed MLK Am	Jan	BRUEGEL = Velvet
James Fenimore	COOPER w Am	Jan	CAREW w Guyana
James Finn	GARNER(J.F.)w Am	Jan	CLAYTON tv
James Lee	BURKE w Am	Jan	COBLER tv
James Oliver	CURWOOD w Am	Jan	DUSSEK piano,c Ger
James Truslow	ADAMS h Am	Jan	EGLESON d
James Whitcomb	RILEY po,j Am	Jan	HOOKS tv+
James,	ANTHONY	Jan	HOWARD s-cnt Am
James,	BRION	Jan	HUS r Cz
James,	CLIFTON tv+	Jan	JORDAN tv
James,	DENNIS tv	Jan	KADAR d
James,	ETTA s-r&b,mr+ Am	Jan	KARON w Am
James,	GENNIE	Jan	KOLLAR po,r Slovak
James,	HARRY mj-trump,cn+	Jan	LASKI r,st Pol
James,	HENRY Jr w Am	Jan	LUYKEN po Dut
James,	HENRY p-b'31	Jan	MASARYK s Czech
James,	IDA	Jan	MERLIN tv+
James,	JACQUELINE s,tv	Jan	MINER tv+
James,	JERI LOU tv	Jan	MORRIS j,w Br
James,	JESSE outlaw Am	Jan	MURRAY tv
James,	JOHN tv+	Jan	NERUDApo,w,j,ct Cz
James,	KEN tv+	Jan	NIKLAS
James,	MARQUIS p-b'30	Jan	PASEK ar Pol
James,	OLGA tv	Jan	PEERCE tenor Am
James,	P.D. w Br	Jan	RUBES
James,	RICK s-funk,ws Am	Jan	SIMA mj,cn Cz
James,	SHEILA tv	Jan	SMUTS st S.Afr
James,	SIDNEY	Jan	STEEN p Dut
James,	SONNY s-cnt+ Am	Jan	STURSA su Cz
James,	STEPHANIE tv	Jan	TROELL d
James,	STEVE	Jan	VERMEER p Dut
James,	TOMMY mr-s Am	Jan	WEENIX p Dut
James,	WALTER	Jan	WILEY
James,	WILLIAM ph,ps,e Am	Jan	WILLEMS po,ed Belg
Jameson	PARKER tv+	Jan	ZELEZNY o-g'92'96
Jameson	SAMPLEY tv	Jan	ZIZKA ar Ger
Jameson	THOMAS	Jan de	GOEJE e,w Dut
Jameson,	HOUSE tv	Jan de	HEEM p Dut
Jameson,	JERRY d	Jan de	WINTER navy Dut
Jameson,	JOYCE	Jan Josephzoon van GOYENp Dut	
Jamet,	MARIE r Fr	Jan van	EYCK p Belg
Jamey	SHERIDAN tv+	Jan van	GOYEN p Dut
Jami	--- po Persia	Jan van	HOUT h,po Dut
Jami	GERTZ tv+	Jan van	KRIMPEN ds-type Dut
Jamie	FARR tv+	Jan van	NIJLEN po Belg
Jamie	FOXX tv	Jan van der HEYDEN p Dut	
Jamie	HUGUET p Sp	Jan van der MEER p Dut	
Jamie	LUNER tv	Jan van der NOOT po Dut	

Jan-Michael	VINCENT tv+	Janet	De GORE tv
Jana	NOVATNA t Cz	Janet	DeMAY tv
Janacek,	LEOS c Cz	Janet	DeMAY tv
Jance	GARFATmr-bass,s Am	Janet	EVANS sw Am
Jance,	J.A. w Am	Janet	FLANNER j,w Am
Janda,	KRYSTYNA	Janet	GAYNOR
Jane	ADAMS	Janet	HOLMES po Am
Jane	ADDAMS fe,w Am	Janet	JACKSON s,tv+ Am
Jane	ASHER	Janet	JOHNSON tv
Jane	AUSTEN w Br	Janet	JONES
Jane	BADLER tv+	Janet	JONES ba,tv Am
Jane	BIRKIN	Janet	JULIAN tv+
Jane	BOWLES w Am	Janet	LAKE tv
Jane	BRUCKER tv	Janet	LANGARD tv
Jane	BRYAN	Janet	LEIGH
Jane	CAMPION d	Janet	LENNON s,tv Am
Jane	CARR tv	Janet	MUNRO
Jane	COWL la Am	Janet	RENO st Am
Jane	CURTIN cm,tv+ Am	Janet	SUZMAN
Jane	DARWELL	Janet	WALDO tv
Jane	DELANO md-nurse Am	Janet	WOOD
Jane	DULO tv	Janet	ZAPPALA
Jane	EAGLEN sopr Br	Janet,	PIERRE ps,md Fr
Jane	ELLIOT tv	Janette	DAVIS tv
Jane	FONDA	Janice	BORLA mj-s Am
Jane	FRAZEE tv+	Janice	GILBERT tv
Jane	GOODALL an,w Am	Janice	HEIDEN TV
Jane	GREER	Janice	RULE
Jane	GREY(Lady)st Br	Janice	ST. JOHN tv
Jane	HOFFMAN	Janice	WOLFE tv
Jane	HYLTON tv+	Janie	FORD tv
Jane	KEAN tv	Janin,	JULES w Fr
Jane	LEEVES tv	Janine	TURNER tv+
Jane	MANDER w N.Zea	Janis	BALODIS ar,st Latv
Jane	MERROW	Janis	CARTER
Jane	MORGAN tv	Janis	HANSEN tv
Jane	NIGH tv+	Janis	JOPLIN s-mr,blues
Jane	PAULEY tv-j Am	Janis	PAIGE tv+
Jane	PORTER w Br	Janis,	CONRAD tv+
Jane	POWELL tv+	Janis,	ELSIE la Am
Jane	ROSE tv	Janis,	IANs-folk,mr,ws Am
Jane	RUSSELL	Janko	KRAL po Slovak
Jane	SEYMOUR	Janko,	PAULvon piano,i Hu
Jane	SEYMOUR('50's)tv	Jann,	GERALD tv
Jane	SIBBETT tv	Janna	MICHAELS tv
Jane	SMILEY w Am	Janney,	LEON tv+
Jane	WILSON tv	Jannings,	EMIL la+,o-a'28
Jane	WITHERS	Jannis,	VIVI tv
Jane	WYATT tv+	Janos	ARANY po Hung
Jane	WYMAN tv+	Janos	ERDELYI w.pb Hung
Jane,	FREDERICK w Br	Janos	GARAY po,w Hung
Jane,	PAULA tv	Janos	HUNYADI ar,hero Hun
Janeane	GAROFALO cm,tv+ Am	Janos	KADAR st Hung
Janear	HINES tv	Janos	PROHASKA tv
Janee	MICHELLE	Janos	RICHTER cn Ger
Janet	AGREN	Jansky,	KARL eng Am
Janet	BLAIR mj-s,tv+ Am	Janson,	HORST
Janet	CARROLL tv+	Janson,	KRISTOFER w Nor
Janet	CURTIS tv	Janssen,	DAVID tv+
Janet	DAILLEY w Am	Janssen,	FAMKE
Janet	DAWSON w Aust	Jansson,	HANS st Swe

January,	LOIS
Janwillem van de WETERING w	
Jany	CLAIR
Jaques--Dalcroze, EMIL c Swi	
Jaquetta	HAWKES sc,w Br
Jardine,	AL mr-guit,s Am
Jared	DIAMOND w Am
Jared	MARTIN tv+
Jared	RUSHTON
Jared	SPARKS h,ed,e Am
Jarir,	--- po Iraq
Jarl	BIRGER nobleman Swe
Jarl	KULLE
Jarman,	CLAUDE Jr.
Jarman,	DEREK d
Jarmusch,	JIM d
Jarnac,	DOROTHY tv
Jaroslav	HASEK j,w Cz
Jaroslav	SEIFERT po,j Cz
Jarratt,	JOHN
Jarreau,	AL mj-s Am
Jarrell,	RANDALL po,w,ct Am
Jarrett,	KEITH mj-piano Am
Jarrott,	CHARLES d
Jarry,	ALFRED w Fr
Jarta,	HANS st Swe
Jarvi,	NEEME cn
Jarvis,	GRAHAM tv+
Jarvis,	JOHN p Am
Jascha	HEIFETZ viol Am
Jasmer,	BRENT tv
Jasmine	GAGNIER tv
Jasmine	GUY tv+
Jason	BATEMAN tv+
Jason	BERNARD tv
Jason	BROOKS tv
Jason	CADIEUX
Jason	CONNERY
Jason	EVERS
Jason	FLEMYNG
Jason	GEDRICK
Jason	HERVEY tv+
Jason	HORST tv
Jason	KIDD bb
Jason	LEE
Jason	LIVELY
Jason	LONDON
Jason	MARSDEN tv
Jason	MILLER w+ Am
Jason	PATRIC
Jason	PRESSON
Jason	RICHTER
Jason	ROBARDS Jr.
Jason	ROBARDS Sr.
Jason	WARREN tv
Jason	WILES tv
Jason,	HARVEY tv+
Jason,	PETER
Jason,	RICK tv+
Jason,	SYBIL
Jaspar,	HENRI st Belg

Jasper	JOHNS p,su Am
Jasper	MAYNE w,r Br
Jasper,	STAR
Jaspers,	KARL ps,ph Ger
Jastrow,	MORRIS e,w Am
Jatho,	KARL flyer,id Ger
Jaures,	JEAN pb,h,st Fr
Javier	SOLIS
Javits,	JACOB st Am
Jawaharlal NEHRU st Ind	
Jawlensky,	ALEXEY von p Rus
Jaworski,	LEON l Am
Jay	ACAVONE tv
Jay	ADLER
Jay	ASTON mr,s Br
Jay	BUHNER b
Jay	DARLING cr Am
Jay	FLIPPEN tv+
Jay	GOULD mer,f Am
Jay	HAMMER tv
Jay	JOHNSON tv
Jay	KIRBY
Jay	LANIN tv
Jay	LENO cm,tv-host+ Am
Jay	NORTH tv+
Jay	NOVELLO tv+
Jay	OSMOND s,tv Am
Jay	OWEN tv
Jay	PARINI w Am
Jay	SANDERS tv+
Jay	SIEGEL barit Am
Jay	STEWART tv
Jay	TARSES tv
Jay	THOMAS tv+
Jay	VARELA tv
Jay	WILBUR mj,cn Br
Jay Hanna DEAN(Dizzy)b hf	
Jay,	JOHN l,st Am
Jaya	NARAYAN st India
Jaye P.	MORGAN s,tv+ Am
Jayne	FRAZER tv
Jayne	HAMIL
Jayne	KENNEDY
Jayne	MEADOWS tv+
Jayne	WHITNEY mj-s Am
Jayne,	BILLY tv
Jayston,	MICHAEL
Jazzar,	AHMAD al- st Turk
Jazzie B.	--- m-rap Br
Jean	AGASSIZ c,w Am
Jean	AICARD po,w Fr
Jean	AMIOT r,w Fr
Jean	AMPERE h,ph,e Fr
Jean	ANGO(T) ships Fr
Jean	ANNAUD w,d Fr
Jean	ANOUILH w Fr
Jean	ARCON ar,eng,i Fr
Jean	ARGAND math Swi
Jean	ARP p,po Fr
Jean	ARTHUR tv+
Jean	ASTRUC md,w Fr

Jean	AUEL w Am	Jean	KEROUAC(Jack)w,po
Jean	BAILLY astr,st Fr	Jean	KERR w,tv Am
Jean	BALON ba Fr	Jean	LABAT r Fr
Jean	BALUE r,st Fr	Jean	LAFIT(T)E pirate Fr
Jean	BAZILLE p Fr	Jean	LECLAIR viol,c Fr
Jean	BERAIN at,ds Fr	Jean	LINDET st Fr
Jean	BERNARD w Fr	Jean	LIOTARD p Swi
Jean	BIOT math,sc,e Fr	Jean	LULLY c Fr
Jean	BODIN ph Fr	Jean	LURCAT p,ds Fr
Jean	BORDA math,astr Fr	Jean	MARAIS
Jean	BOUISE	Jean	MARAT md,st,re Fr
Jean	BRODIE fc	Jean	MAROT ac Fr
Jean	BROOKS	Jean	MARSH tv+
Jean	BRUNET po Fr	Jean	MARTIN
Jean	BURNEL mr-bass Br	Jean	MICHE r Fr
Jean	BYRON tv	Jean	MILLET p Fr
Jean	CARMET	Jean	MONNET ec,st,id Fr
Jean	CAROL tv	Jean	NATTIER p Fr
Jean	CARPER w Am	Jean	NICOLET x Fr
Jean	CARSON tv	Jean	NOLLET sc,e Fr
Jean	CAZIN p Fr	Jean	NOVERRE ba Fr
Jean	CHARDIN p Fr	Jean	OEBEN id-furniture Fr
Jean	CHAUVEL st Fr	Jean	OLIER r Fr
Jean	CLOUET p Belg	Jean	OMER mj,cn Belg
Jean	COCTEAU po,w,d Fr	Jean	ORRY ec Fr
Jean	COROT p Fr	Jean	OUDRY p,illus Fr
Jean	COURBET p Fr	Jean	PARKER
Jean	COUSIN p Fr	Jean	PATER p Fr
Jean	DARLAN navy,st Fr	Jean	PERRIN sc,e Fr
Jean	DASTE	Jean	PETERS
Jean	DAUSSET md Fr	Jean	PIAGET ps Swi
Jean	De RESZKE tenor Pol	Jean	PIAT
Jean	DOMAT l,w Fr	Jean	PICARD astr Fr
Jean	DOUTARD w Fr	Jean	PLAIDY w Br
Jean	DUCIS w Fr	Jean	PONS astr Fr
Jean	DUVET engraver Fr	Jean	PUCELLE p Fr
Jean	EUDES(Saint)r Fr	Jean	PYL tv
Jean	FABRE sc,e Fr	Jean	RACINE w Fr
Jean	FAZY st,j,w Swi	Jean	RAMEAU c Fr
Jean	FERNEL md,astr Fr	Jean	RASEY tv
Jean	FIALIN st Fr	Jean	RECLUS geog,w Fr
Jean	FORAIN p,illus Fr	Jean	REGNARD w Fr
Jean	FOUQUET p Fr	Jean	RENOIR d Fr
Jean	GABIN la+ Fr	Jean	RHYS w Br
Jean	GENET w Fr	Jean	RIBAULT navy Fr
Jean	GEROME p Fr	Jean	RICHER astr Fr
Jean	GETTY id,f Am	Jean	RICHTER w Ger
Jean	GIONO w Fr	Jean	ROGERS
Jean	GOUJON su Fr	Jean	SABLE pioneer Am
Jean	GREUZE p Fr	Jean	SAGAL tv
Jean	HAGEN tv+	Jean	SARASIN po Fr
Jean	HARLOW	Jean	SARTRE ph,e,w Fr
Jean	HENNER p Fr	Jean	SAY ec,ed Fr
Jean	HOUDON su Fr	Jean	SCOTT tv
Jean	INGRES p Fr	Jean	SEBERG
Jean	ISABEY p Fr	Jean	SEGRAIS po Fr
Jean	ITARD md-ar Fr	Jean	SERVAIS
Jean	JACOTOT e Fr	Jean	SIMMONS
Jean	JAURES pb,h,st Fr	Jean	SMART
Jean	KENT	Jean	STAS sc,e Belg
		Jean	STEEL tv

Jean	TOOMER w Am	Jeff	BAXTER mr-guit Am
Jean	VADE po,w Fr	Jeff	BECK mr-guit Br
Jean	Van der PYL tv	Jeff	BRIDGES
Jean	VAUCHER sc,r,e Swi	Jeff	CAIN tv
Jean	VIANNEY r Fr	Jeff	CEASE guit Am
Jean	VILAR la,d Fr	Jeff	CONAWAY
Jean	VONCK st Belg	Jeff	COOK kbds,s Am
Jean	WALLACE	Jeff	COOPER tv+
Jean	WALTZ cr,w Fr	Jeff	COREY
Jean	WEBSTER w Am	Jeff	DANIELS
Jean	YANNE	Jeff	DONNELL
Jean de	BAIF po Fr	Jeff	EAST
Jean de	BATZ st Fr	Jeff	FAHEY
Jean de	GALAUP x Fr	Jeff	FITHIAN tv
Jean de	LABADIE r,ref Fr	Jeff	GRIGGS
Jean de	LAMARCK sc,w Fr	Jeff	HEALEYguit,s,ws Can
Jean de	ROTROU w Fr	Jeff	HOLLIS tv
Jean,	NORMA tv	Jeff	KOBER tv+
Jean-Claude BRIALY		Jeff	LYNNE mr-guit,s Br
Jean-Claude Van DAMME		Jeff	MacKAY tv
Jean-Luc GODARD d		Jeff	MacNELLY cr Am
Jean-Marie LEHN sc Fr		Jeff	MARCUS tv
Jean-Pierre AUMONT		Jeff	MAXWELL tv
Jean-Pierre CASSEL		Jeff	MORROW tv+
Jean-Pierre LEAUD		Jeff	NOON w,m,p Br
Jeana	TOMASINA	Jeff	PUSTIL tv
Jeanane	GARFOLO	Jeff	SHAARA w Am
Jeane	DIXON astrologer,w	Jeff	SILVER tv
Jeanette	LOFF	Jeff	SMITH tv-chef Am
Jeanette	MacDONALD s+ Am	Jeff	TRACHTA tv
Jeanette	NOLAN tv+	Jeff	WINCOTT tv+
Jeanjean, FAUSTIN mj-trump		Jeff	YAGHER
Jeanmaire, RENEE ba Fr		Jeff	YORK tv+
Jeanna	MICHAELS tv	Jeffers,	ROBINSON po Am
Jeanne	BAL tv	Jefferson DAVIS pres CSA	
Jeanne	BATES tv+	Jefferson Airplane --- mr Am	
Jeanne	BELL	Jefferson, BLIND LEMON mj,s	
Jeanne	CAGNEY	Jefferson, HERBERT Jr tv+	
Jeanne	CARROLL mj-s Am	Jefferson, JOSEPH la Am	
Jeanne	COOPER tv+	Jefferson, THOMAS 3rd Pres	
Jeanne	CRAIN	Jefford, BARBARA	
Jeanne	d'ARCsee Joan of A	Jeffrey	ARCHER w Br
Jeanne	MOREAU	Jeffrey	BARON tv
Jeannette RANKIN(1st congr w)		Jeffrey	BLOOM d
Jeannette, BUDDY bb hf		Jeffrey	COMBS
Jeannie	BERLIN	Jeffrey	DANIEL mr-s Am
Jeannie	CARSON tv+	Jeffrey	DeMUNN
Jeannie	KENDALL s Am	Jeffrey	HUDSON(Sir)dwarf,ar
Jeannie	RUSSELL tv	Jeffrey	HUNTER tv+
Jeannie	WILSON tv	Jeffrey	JACQUET tv
Jeannine	RILEY	Jeffrey	JONES
Jeannot	SZWARC d	Jeffrey	LYNN tv+
Jeans,	ISABEL	Jeffrey	OSBORNE mr-s,w Am
Jeans,	JAMES(Sir)sc,e,w	Jeffrey	RICHMAN tv
Jeans,	URSULA	Jeffrey	SAMS
Jebavy,	VACLAV po Cz	Jeffrey	TAMBOR tv+
Jebb,	RICHARD(Sir)w Scot	Jeffrey	TATE cn Br
Jed	PROUTY	Jeffrey	WRIGHT
Jedediah	SMITH fur trade,x	Jeffrey,	FRANCIS ct,l Scot
Jeff	ALTMAN tv+	Jeffrey,	PETER
Jeff	BAGWELL b	Jeffreys, ANNE tv+	

Jeffreys,	CHUCK	Jennifer	RUNYON tv+
Jeffries	WYMAN md,sc,e Am	Jennifer	SALT tv+
Jeffries,	ADAM tv	Jennifer	SAVIDGE tv
Jeffries,	HERBERT	Jennifer	TILLY
Jeffries,	LANG tv+	Jennifer	Van DYCK tv
Jeffries,	LIONEL	Jennifer	WARNES s-pop,tv Am
Jehan	BODEL w Fr	Jennifer	WARREN tv+
Jehudi	ASHMUN r,st Am	Jennifer-Jason LEIGH	
Jekyll,	GERTRUDE ac-land Br	Jennings,	CLAUDIA
Jelacic,	JOSIP ar,st Croat	Jennings,	DeWITT
Jellicoe	ANN w,d Br	Jennings,	HUGH b hf
Jelly Eva d' ARANYI viol Hung		Jennings,	PETER tv-j Am
Jelly Roll MORTON mj,piano,c Am		Jennings,	WAYLON s-cnt+ Am
Jem	FINER banjo Ir	Jenny	AGUTTER
Jem	MACE boxer Br	Jenny	EGAN tv
Jemma	REDGRAVE	Jenny	GAGO tv+
Jen,	GISH w Am	Jenny	JONES tv
Jenco,	SAL tv	Jenny	LEWIS tv+
Jenilee	HARRISON tv+	Jenny	LIND soprano Swe
Jenkins,	ALLEN tv+	Jenny	LUMET
Jenkins,	CAROL tv	Jenny	NEUMANN
Jenkins,	DAN j,w Am	Jenny	O'HARA tv+
Jenkins,	FERGUSON b-cy'71,hf	Jenny	RUNACRE
Jenkins,	GORDON mj,cn Am	Jenny	WRIGHT
Jenkins,	JACKIE(Butch)	Jens	HANSEN j,st Dan
Jenkins,	KEN tv	Jens	JACOBSEN po,w Dan
Jenkins,	LARRY(Flash)tv	Jens	JENSEN ac-land Am
Jenkins,	LOUIS po Am	Jens	JUEL p Dan
Jenkins,	MEGS	Jens	SKOU sc,e,n-c'97
Jenkins,	REBECCA	Jens,	SALOME tv+
Jenkins,	RICHARD	Jensen,	GERRIT furniture Br
Jenks,	FRANK tv+	Jensen,	HANS n-p'63
Jenks,	SI	Jensen,	JACKIE b-mv'58
Jenn	THOMPSON tv	Jensen,	JENS ac-land Am
Jenna	Von OY tv	Jensen,	JOHANNES n-l'44
Jenner,	BARRY tv	Jensen,	KAREN tv+
Jenner,	BRUCE o-g'76+	Jensen,	MAREN tv
Jenney,	LUCINDA	Jensen,	SANDI tv
Jenney,	WILLIAM ac Am	Jensen,	SANFORD tv
Jennie	DUNDAS	Jensen,	SASHA
Jennie	GARTH tv	Jenson,	ROY tv+
Jennifer	ASHLEY	Jeppe	AAKJAER w,po Dan
Jennifer	BEALS	Jepsen,	GLENN sc,e Am
Jennifer	BISHOP tv+	Jepson,	DONNA tv
Jennifer	CHASE	Jere	BURNS tv+
Jennifer	COOKE tv+	Jeremiah	CLARKE organ,c Br
Jennifer	DALE	Jeremiah	DIXON surveyor Br
Jennifer	DARLING tv	Jeremiah	HEALY w Am
Jennifer	DAVIS tv	Jeremiah	SIMPSON st Am
Jennifer	DELORA	Jeremy	BENTHAM l,ph Br
Jennifer	EDWARDS	Jeremy	BRETT tv+
Jennifer	EGAN w Am	Jeremy	CLYDE mr-guit,s Br
Jennifer	GATTI	Jeremy	IRONS
Jennifer	GREY	Jeremy	JACKSON tv
Jennifer	HETRICK tv	Jeremy	KEMP
Jennifer	HOLMES tv	Jeremy	LICHT tv+
Jennifer	HOLT	Jeremy	LLOYD tv
Jennifer	JONES	Jeremy	LONDON tv
Jennifer	LOPEZ	Jeremy	MILLER tv+
Jennifer	O'NEILL tv+	Jeremy	PIVEN tv+
Jennifer	RUBIN	Jeremy	RIFKIM w Am

Jeremy	SLATE tv+	Jerry	THORPE d
Jeremy	TAYLOR r,w Br	Jerry	VALE s-pop Am
Jergens,	ADELE tv+	Jerry	Van DYKE tv+
Jergens,	DIANE tv	Jerry	WALD mj,cn Am
Jeri	GAILE tv	Jerry	WARREN d
Jeri Lou	JAMES tv	Jerry	WEST bb,bbc hf
Jeritza,	MARIA sopr Cz	Jerry Lee	LEWIS mr,s,ws Am
Jermain	JOHNSON tv	Jervas,	CHARLES p Ir
Jermaine	JACKSON mr-s Am	Jerzy	SKOLIMOWSKI d
Jerne,	NIELS n-m'84	Jerzy	STUHR
Jeroen	KRABBE	Jespersen,	OTTO e,w Dan
Jerom	FRANCKEN p Belg	Jess	FRANCO d
Jerome	COWAN tv+	Jess	HAHN
Jerome	KARLE sc Am	Jess	WILLARD boxer Am
Jerome	KERN c Am	Jesse	BORREGO tv+
Jerome	PAMUS(Doc)c Am	Jesse	BRADLEY mj,tv Am
Jerome	ROBBINS d,ba Am	Jesse	BURKETT b hf
Jerome	SMITH mr-guit Am	Jesse	DIZON tv
Jerome	THOR tv	Jesse	FEWKES sc Am
Jerome	TRAVERS g Am	Jesse	HAINES b hf
Jerome	WEIDMAN w Am	Jesse	HARPER fbc Am
Jerome,	JEROME K. w Br	Jesse	JACKSON civ rights Am
Jerome,	JERRY m,cn,tv	Jesse	JAMES outlaw Am
Jerry	ALLISON mr-drm Am	Jesse	LASKY pr-films Am
Jerry	BECKLEY guit,s Am	Jesse	LAZEAR md Am
Jerry	BOCK w Am	Jesse	OWENS runner Am
Jerry	BUTLER s Am	Jesse	RAMSDEN id-astr Br
Jerry	CLOWER tv	Jesse	RENO ar Am
Jerry	COLONNA	Jesse	STOCK tv
Jerry	DAMON tv	Jesse	STRANG r Am
Jerry	FOGEL	Jesse	STUART po,w Am
Jerry	GRAFF tv	Jesse	TENDLER tv
Jerry	HALL mo Am	Jesse	UNRUH st-Calif Am
Jerry	HARDIN tv+	Jesse	VENTURA
Jerry	HAUSNER tv	Jesse	VINT
Jerry	HERMAN c Am	Jesse	WELLES tv
Jerry	HOUSER	Jesse	WHITE tv+
Jerry	JACKSON s,cn,tv Am	Jesse	YOUNG mr-guit,s Am
Jerry	JAMESON d	Jesse D.	GOINS tv
Jerry	JEROME m,cn,tv Am	Jesse,	FRINIWYD w Br
Jerry	KAPLAN w Am	Jessel,	GEORGE cm,tv+ Am
Jerry	LEIBER c Am	Jessica	HAHN mo+
Jerry	LESTER cm,tv Am	Jessica	HARPER tv+
Jerry	LEVINE tv+	Jessica	LANGE
Jerry	LEWIS cm,tv+ Am	Jessica	LUNDY tv+
Jerry	LUCAS bb hf	Jessica	MITFORD w Am
Jerry	MARTINI m-sax Am	Jessica	NELSON tv
Jerry	MATHERS tv+	Jessica	PLAYER tv
Jerry	MILLER mr-guit Am	Jessica	PRUNELL tv
Jerry	NELSON tv	Jessica	SALEM tv
Jerry	ORBACH	Jessica	SAVITCH tv-anch Am
Jerry	PACKER tv	Jessica	STEEN tv+
Jerry	PARIS d, tv	Jessica	TANDY
Jerry	POTTER tv	Jessica	WALTER tv+
Jerry	REED s+ Am	Jessie	LANDIS
Jerry	RICE fb	Jessie	MATTHEWS
Jerry	ROSS tv	Jessie	RALPH
Jerry	SHERK fb	Jesslyn	FAX tv
Jerry	SIEGEL cr Am	Jessner,	LEOPOLD d,pr Ger
Jerry	STILLER tv+	Jessup,	PAUL tv
Jerry	SUPRIAN tv	Jessup,	RYAN tv

Jesup,	MORRIS mer,f Am	Jim	HODSON tv
Jesus	ALOU b	Jim	HUNTER(Catfish)b
Jesus	FRANCO d	Jim	HUTTON tv+
Jesus	LOPEZ-COBOS cn	Jim	KAAT b
Jet	BLACK mr-drums Br	Jim	KELLY
Jeter,	MICHAEL tv+	Jim	KERR mr-s Am
Jethro	TULL farms,i Br	Jim	LAMPLEY tv
Jett,	JOAN m-guit,sr+ Am	Jim	LANGE tv
Jetta	GOUDAL	Jim	LANGER fb hf
Jevons,	WILLIAM ec,e Br	Jim	LEHER tv
Jewel	SHEPARD	Jim	LONBORG b
Jewell,	GERI tv	Jim	MARTIN mr-guit Am
Jewell,	ISABEL	Jim	McCARTY mr-drm Br
Jewett,	SARAH ORNE w Am	Jim	McMULLAN tv
Jewison,	NORMAN d	Jim	MESSINA mr-guit,s
Jhabvala,	RUTH w Br	Jim	METZLER
Ji-Tu	CUMBUKA tv	Jim	MITCHUM
Jill	BENNETT	Jim	NABORS s,tv+ Am
Jill	CIMENT w Am	Jim	OTTO fb hf
Jill	COHEN tv	Jim	PALMER b hf
Jill	CONWAY w Am	Jim	PARKER fb hf
Jill	COREY tv	Jim	PAYMAR tv
Jill	ESMOND	Jim	PERRY b
Jill	GATSBY	Jim	POLLARD bb hf
Jill	HAWORTH	Jim	REEVES s-cnt Am
Jill	IRELAND	Jim	REID mr-guit,s Scot
Jill	LARSAN tv	Jim	RICE b
Jill	PHELPS tv-pr	Jim	RINGO fb hf
Jill	St.JOHN	Jim	ROBERTS tv
Jill	TRACY tv	Jim	RUHL tv
Jill	WHELAN tv	Jim	SASSER st(Sen TN)
Jill	WHITLOW	Jim	SEALS mr-guit,s Am
Jillian,	ANN tv+	Jim	SHANE tv
Jillson,	JOYCE tv+	Jim	SIMPSON tv
Jilot,	YOLANDA	Jim	STAAHL tv
Jim	BACKUS	Jim	TAYLOR fb hf
Jim	BAKER tv	Jim	THORPE fb hf+
Jim	BAKKER r,tv Am	Jim	TRUE
Jim	BATES tv	Jim	TUCKER mr-guit Am
Jim	BOUTON b	Jim	TULLY w Am
Jim	BROWN fb+	Jim	TURNER tv+
Jim	BYRNES tv	Jim	VARNEY tv+
Jim	CAPALDI mr-drm,s Br	Jim	WATKINS tv
Jim	CARREY cm	Jim	WILSON tv
Jim	CARROLL w Am	Jim	YESTER mr-guit,s Am
Jim	CARTER	Jim	YOUNGS
Jim	CATUSI tv	Jim Ed	BROWN tv
Jim	CONNELL tv	Jimenez,	JUAN po,n-l'56
Jim	COULTON tv	Jimi	HENDRIX mr+ Am
Jim	DALE	Jimmie	FOXX b hf
Jim	DAVIS cr Am	Jimmie	GILMORE s-cntry Am
Jim	DAVIS tv+	Jimmie	RODGERS s-cnt,c Am
Jim	EDMONDS b	Jimmie	WALKER tv+
Jim	FIELDER mr-bass Am	Jimmie F.	SKAGGS
Jim	FINKS fb hf	Jimmy	BAIO tv+
Jim	FOWLER tv	Jimmy	BATES tv
Jim	GAINES tv+	Jimmy	BLAINE s,tv Am
Jim	GORMLEY tv	Jimmy	BLANTON mj-bass Am
Jim	HAGER tv	Jimmy	BOYD tv
Jim	HAYNIE	Jimmy	BROWN mr-drm Br
Jim	HENSEN muppets,tv+	Jimmy	BUFFETT s,ws+ Am

Jimmy	CANNON tv	Jo Anne	WORLEY tv	
Jimmy	CARROLL piano,s,tv	Jo de	WINTER tv	
Jimmy	CARTER(James Earl)	Joachim	CAMPE e Ger	
Jimmy	CLIFF s,ws Jama.	Joachim	HANSEN	
Jimmy	CONNORS t Am	Joachim	JUNGE ph,sc,e Ger	
Jimmy	DALE m.cn,tv Am	Joachim	MURAT ar Fr	
Jimmy	DAVIS st Am	Joachim	WACH r,e Am	
Jimmy	DEAN tv+	Joachim du BELLAY po Fr		
Jimmy	DORSEY mj,tv+ Am	Joachim von WATT po Swi		
Jimmy	DURANTE cm,tv+ Am	Joachim,	JOSEPH viol,c Hung	
Jimmy	FAIRFAX tv	Joad,	C.E.M. ph,st Br	
Jimmy	FIDLER tv	Joan	ALLEN	
Jimmy	FORTUNE m-flk,r&b	Joan	BAEZ s-folk,ws+ Am	
Jimmy	GARRETT tv	Joan	BANKS tv	
Jimmy	GETZOFF tv	Joan	BARCLAY	
Jimmy	HANLEY	Joan	BENNETT tv+	
Jimmy	HATLO cr Am	Joan	CHEN tv+	
Jimmy	HAWKINS tv	Joan	COLLINS tv+	
Jimmy	HOFFA labor Am	Joan	CUSACK	
Jimmy	JAM s-soul,r&b,pr	Joan	DARLING tv+	
Jimmy	JOHNSON fb hf	Joan	DAVIS tv+	
Jimmy	JOY mj-clari,cn Am	Joan	DIDION w Am	
Jimmy	JOYCE s,cn,tv Am	Joan	DIENER tv	
Jimmy	LEA mr-bass,viol Br	Joan	EMBREY tv	
Jimmy	LITTLE tv	Joan	FREEMAN	
Jimmy	LLOYD	Joan	GARDNER	
Jimmy	LYDON	Joan	HACKETT tv+	
Jimmy	MATHERS tv	Joan	HERON mj,pop-s Br	
Jimmy	McHUGH c Am	Joan	HICKSON	
Jimmy	McNICHOL	Joan	JETT mr-guit,s+ Am	
Jimmy	NELSON tv	Joan	KJAR tv	
Jimmy	NOONE mj-reeds Am	Joan	LESLIE	
Jimmy	O'NEILL tv	Joan	MARSH	
Jimmy	OSMOND s,tv Am	Joan	MAUDE	
Jimmy	PAGE mr-guit Br	Joan	MIRO p Sp	
Jimmy	POWERS tv	Joan	O'BRIEN	
Jimmy	RIDDLE tv	Joan	PATRICK tv	
Jimmy	ROGERS	Joan	PRINGLE tv	
Jimmy	RUSHING mj,s Am	Joan	RIVERS tv-host+	
Jimmy	SMITS tv+	Joan	RYAN j,w Am	
Jimmy	SOMMERS tv	Joan	SHAWLEE tv+	
Jimmy	Van HEUSEN c Am	Joan	SILVER d	
Jimmy	WAKELY	Joan	SIMS	
Jimmy	WALKER st Am	Joan	STALEY tv	
Jimmy	WEBB c Am	Joan	TAYLOR tv+	
Jimmy	WINSTON mr-organ Br	Joan	Van ARK tv+	
Jimmy	YANCEY mj-piano Am	Joan	VOHS tv+	
Jirasek,	ALOIS w Cz	Joan Ganz COONEY pr-tv Am		
Jiro	TAMIYA	Joan of Arc(Jeanne d'Arc)Ste		
Jiver	HUTCHINSON mj,cn	Joanie	SOMMERS s Am	
JM J.	BULLOCK tv	Joann	THOMPSON tv	
Jo	CIAMPA	JoAnn	WILLETTE tv	
Jo	CORDAY tv	Joanna	BAILLIE w,po Scot	
Jo	DAVIS tv	Joanna	BARNES tv+	
Jo	HURT tv	Joanna	CASSIDY tv+	
Jo	JONES mj-drm Am	Joanna	FRANK tv+	
Jo	VanFLEET	Joanna	GLEASON tv+	
Jo Ann	CASTLE mj-piano,tv	Joanna	KERNS tv+	
Jo Ann	HARRIS tv+	Joanna	LEE	
Jo Ann	MIYA tv	Joanna	LUMLEY	
Jo Ann	PFLUG tv+	Joanna	MILES	

Joanna	MOORE	Joe	ELLIOTT mr-s Br
Joanna	PACULA	Joe	ESTEVEZ
Joanna	PETTET	Joe	FEENY s,w,tv Am
Joanne	DRU tv+	Joe	FITHIAN tv
Joanne	SAMUEL	Joe	FLYNN tv+
Joanou,	PHIL d	Joe	FRAZIER boxer Am
Joao	ABREU h,e Braz	Joe	FULKS bb hf
Joao	GARRETT w,st Port	Joe	GANS boxer Am
Joao	ZARCO x Port	Joe	GORDON b
Joao de	BARROS h,st Port	Joe	GREENE(Mean Joe)fb+
Joaquim	NABUCO st,w Braz	Joe	GRIFASI
Joaquin	ACOSTA ar,h Colum	Joe	GUYON fb hf
Joaquin	CORDERO	Joe	HASEL tv
Joaquin	MILLER po,w Am	Joe	HIGGINS tv+
Joaquin	MURIETA outlaw Mex	Joe	HILL ws,labor Am
Joaquin	TURINA c Sp	Joe	JACKSON s,ws Br
Jobert,	MARLENE	Joe	KELLEY b hf
JoBeth	WILLIAMS	Joe	KELLY tv
Jobim,	ANTONIO c Braz	Joe	KEYES tv
Jobs,	STEVE id Am	Joe	KING
Joby	BAKER tv	Joe	KLECKO fb
Jobyna	HOWLAND	Joe	LAMBIE tv
Jobyna	RALSTON	Joe	LEEWAY mr-drm Br
Jocelyn	BRANDO	Joe	LISI
Jocelyne	ZUCCO tv	Joe	LIVOTI viol,tv Am
Jochem van	BRUGGEN w S.Afr	Joe	LOSS mj,pop,cn Br
Jochmus,	GIACOMO mercenary	Joe	LOUIS boxer Am
Jochum,	EUGEN cn Ger	Joe	MALONE tv
Jock	GAYNOR tv	Joe	MANTELL tv
Jock	MAHONEY tv+	Joe	MAROSS tv
Jocko	CONLAN b	Joe	McINTYRE mr-s Am
Jodhi	MAY	Joe	MEDWICK b hf
Jodi	LONG	Joe	MONTANA fb,tv
Jodi	O'KEEFE tv	Joe	MORGAN b hf,tv
Jodi	THELEN tv	Joe	MORTON tv+
Jodie	FOSTER	Joe	MUSSO fb hf
Jodie	SWEETIN tv	Joe	NAMATH fb hf+
Jodl,	ALFRED ar-Nazi Ger	Joe	NANTON mj-tromb Am
Jody	KAY	Joe	NASH tv
Jody	McCREA tv+	Joe	ORTON w,ct Br
Jody	WATLEY s Am	Joe	PASS mj-guit Am
Jody,	COUSIN tv	Joe	PATERNO fbc
Joe	BAKER tv	Joe	PENNY tv+
Joe	BESSER tv+	Joe	PERRY fb hf
Joe	BONSALL s-cnt Am	Joe	PERRY mr-guit Am
Joe	BROOKS tv	Joe	PESCI
Joe	BUTLER mr-drm,s Am	Joe	PHELAN
Joe	CARR fb hf	Joe	PISCOPO tv+
Joe	CARTER b	Joe	QUEENAN w Am
Joe	CIRILLO tv	Joe	RIPLEY tv
Joe	COBB	Joe	ROSARIO tv
Joe	COCKER mr Am	Joe	ROSS tv
Joe	CONLEY tv	Joe	ROTH d
Joe	COREY tv	Joe	SAKIC ho
Joe	CORTESE	Joe	SANTOS tv+
Joe	CRACKER mr Am	Joe	SAWYER tv
Joe	CRONIN b hf	Joe	SCHMIDT fb hf
Joe	DANIEL mj-drm,cn Br	Joe	SCOTT tv
Joe	DANTE d	Joe	SENECA
Joe	DAVIS billiards Br	Joe	SEWELL b hf
Joe	De SANTIS	Joe	SHEA tv

Joe	SILVER tv+	Johan van	HUDDE math Dut
Joe	SPANO tv+	Johan van der	DOES st,w Dut
Joe	SPINELL	Johann	ADELUNG w,e Ger
Joe	TATA(Joey)tv	Johann	ARND(T) r Ger
Joe	TINKER b hf	Johann	BALMER math,sc Swi
Joe	TORRE b	Johann	BENGEL r,w Ger
Joe	TURKEL	Johann	BODE astr Ger
Joe	TURNER mj,s-blues	Johann	BODMER i,id Swi
Joe	VENUTI mj,viol Am	Johann	BOHMER h Ger
Joe	WALSH mr-guit,s Am	Johann	CARLO tv
Joe	WARREN tv	Johann	CRAMER piano,c Br
Joe	WEBER cm,pr Am	Johann	EBEL r Ger
Joe	WILSON tv &	Johann	ECK r Ger
Joe	WILSON=Whispering	Johann	ENCKE astr Ger
Joe	YULE	Johann	ENGEL w Ger
Joe Don	BAKER tv+	Johann	ERMAN h-Egypt Ger
Joe E.(Evan)	BROWN cm,tv+ Am	Johann	FABER id Ger
Joeal	NICASSIO tv	Johann	FASCH c Ger
Joel	BARLOW po,st Am	Johann	FAUST magic Ger
Joel	BENDER d	Johann	FICHTE ph Ger
Joel	BROOKS tv+	Johann	FUX c Aus
Joel	COEN w,d Am	Johann	GALLE astr Ger
Joel	FABIANI tv+	Johann	GLEIM po Ger
Joel	GREY	Johann	GMELIN sc,x Ger
Joel	HARRIS j,w Am	Johann	GOETHE po,w Ger
Joel	HIGGINS tv	Johann	GUNTHER po Ger
Joel	McCREA tv+	Johann	HAGEN astr Aus
Joel	MURRAY tv+	Johann	HAMANN ph,st Ger
Joel	SILBERG d	Johann	HEBEL po Ger
Joel,	BILLY mr Am	Johann	HEDWIG sc,e Ger
Joel,	DENNIS tv	Johann	HERBART ph,e Ger
Joest	LIPS ph,e Belg	Johann	HERDER ph,ct Ger
Joey	BISHOP tv+	Johann	HITTORF sc,e Ger
Joey	CARBONE m,cn,tv Am	Johann	HUMMEL piano,c Ger
Joey	DEE ms-s Am	Johann	JUNG w Ger
Joey	FAYE tv	Johann	KALB ar Ger
Joey	FORMAN tv	Johann	KANDLER su Ger
Joey	KRAMER mr-drm Am	Johann	KASTNER c Ger
Joey	MOLLAND mr-kbds,s	Johann	KERLL organ,c Ger
Joey	RAMONE mr-s Am	Johann	KINAU w Ger
Joey	TATA tv	Johann	KUHNAU organ,c Ger
Joey	WALSH tv	Johann	KUSSER c,cn Hung
Joff	HOUSTON	Johann	LAVATER po,w Swi
Joffe,	MARK d	Johann	LOEWE c Ger
Joffe,	ROLAND d	Johann	MAYR c Ger
Joffrey,	ROBERT ba Am	Johann	MERCK w,ct Ger
Jogues,	ISAAC(Saint)r Fr	Johann	MULLER astr Ger
Johan	BANER ar Swe	Johann	MUSAUS w Ger
Johan	BOJER w Nor	Johann	NAHL su Ger
Johan	DAHL p Nor	Johann	NEANDER h,r Ger
Johan	GAHN sc Swe	Johann	PALISA astron Aus
Johan	GRIEG po,w Nor	Johann	PALM mer-books,pb
Johan	HEINSE w Ger	Johann	PFAFF math,e Ger
Johan	HJORT sc,e Nor	Johann	QUANTZ flute,c Ger
Johan	KJELLEN poli-sc Swe	Johann	REIL md Ger
Johan	LEYSEN	Johann	REINKEN organ,c Ger
Johan	RANTZAU ar Ger	Johann	REIS sc Ger
Johan	ROMAN viol,c Swe	Johann	RIST po Ger
Johan	SCHUCK h-lit,e Swe	Johann	SCHADOW su Ger
Johan	VOGT geol,e Nor	Johann	SCHAPER ceramics
Johan	WALLIN r,hymns Swe	Johann	SCHEIN c Ger

Johann	SCHOBER st Aus	John	ALDEN pilgrim Am
Johann	SCHULTE e Ger	John	ALLEN dentist Am
Johann	SEGNER sc,e Ger	John	ALMON w-polit Br
Johann	SEIDL j,po Aus	John	AMOS tv+
Johann	SEMLER r,e Ger	John	ANDRE ar Br
Johann	STAMITZ viol,c Ger	John	ANDREW st Am
Johann	STEIN id-pianos Ger	John	APPLEBY i Am
Johann	STRAUSS c Aus	John	APREA tv+
Johann	TIETZ astr,e Ger	John	ARCHER
Johann	UZ po Ger	John	ARDEN w Br
Johann	VOGL po Aus	John	ASHE re,ar Am
Johann	WALTHER organ,c Ger	John	ASHLEY tv+
Johann	WASER st Swi	John	ASHTON tv+
Johann	WYSS w,ph,e Swi	John	ASTIN tv+
Johann	ZEUSS h,philology	John	ASTON mr,s Br
Johann	ZINN sc Ger	John	AUBREY h,w Br
Johann	ZUMPE piano Ger	John	AUDUBON at-birds Am
Johann Christian	BACH m,c Ger	John	AUSTIN l,e,w Br
Johann Sebastian	BACH c Ger	John	AYLMER r Br
Johann von	GOETHE po Ger	John	BACH
Johann von	LAMONT astr Ger	John	BADHAM d
Johann von	WERTH ar Ger	John	BAIRD i-tv Scot
Johanna	GRIKA	John	BANGS w-humor Am
Johanna	MATZ	John	BANIM po,w Ir
Johanna	SPYRI w Swi	John	BANKES(Sir)l
Johannes	BRAHMS c Ger	John	BANNER tv+
Johannes	BRENZ ref Ger	John	BANVARD p,w Am
Johannes	ECCARD c Ger	John	BARBATA mr-drm Am
Johannes	EWALD po,w Dan	John	BARD md Am
Johannes	FALK w Ger	John	BARDEEN sc Am
Johannes	FIBIGER sc-md,e Dan	John	BARENDT w
Johannes	GEIGER sc Ger	John	BARTH w Am
Johannes	HAUCH po,w Dan	John	BAUSCH id-optics Am
Johannes	JENSEN po,w Dan	John	BEAL
Johannes	KEPLER astr Ger	John	BECK tv+
Johannes	SCHLAF w Ger	John	BECKMAN bb hf
Johannes	SCHONERast,geog Ger	John	BEITH w Br
Johannes	STARK sc,e Ger	John	BELL j,w Scot
Johannes	WARMING sc,e Dan	John	BELL su Br
Johannes	WIDMAN math Ger	John	BELUSHI
Johannes van der	WAALS sc Dut	John	BENBOW navy Br
Johannes von	MIQUEL st Ger	John	BENTLEY
Johansen, DAVID		John	BERNAL sc Br
Johansson,PAUL tv+		John	BERRY d
Johar,	I.S.	John	BETTIS tv
John	ABBOTT	John	BIGELOW w,st Am
John	ABBOTT(Sir)st,e Can	John	BISHOP tv
John	ABEL sc,e Am	John	BISHOP w Am
John	ABER w Am	John	BLAIR l Am
John	ACTON h Br	John	BLAND tv
John	ACTON(Sir)navy	John	BLOOM tv+
John	ADAIR geog Scot	John	BLOW c Br
John	ADAMS 2nd Pres	John	BOLES
John	ADAMS astr,e Br	John	BOYD ORR sc,e Scot
John	ADLUM sc Am	John	BOYLAN tv
John	AGAR	John	BRAHM d
John	AIRD(Sir)eng	John	BRAINE w Br
John	AITKEN sc Scot	John	BRODIE fb+
John	ALCOCK r,st,e Br	John	BROWN st-abolit Am
John	ALCOCK(Sir)fly	John	BROWN tv

John	BUCHAN(Sir)w Scot	John	CUSACK
John	BULL organ,c Br	John	DAFOE j Can
John	BUNYAN r,w Br	John	DALL
John	BURY h,e Br	John	DALTON sc,e Br
John	BYNER cm,tv+ Am	John	DANIELS
John	BYROM po Br	John	DARROW
John	BYRON po Br	John	DAUER tv
John	CABOT x It	John	DAVEY tree-md Am
John	CAGE c Am	John	DAVIES(Sir)l,po
John	CALE mr-kbds,s Wel	John	DAVIS x Br
John	CALHOUN st Am	John	DAWSON(Sir)geol Can
John	CALVIN r,w Fr	John	DAY w Br
John	CALVIN tv+	John	DEACON mr-bass Br
John	CAMP w Am	John	DeBELLO d
John	CANDY tv+	John	DEBRETT pb,w Br
John	CARRERE ac Am	John	DEE math,astrol Br
John	CARROLL	John	DEERE id-plows,etc
John	CARSON	John	DeFOREST w Am
John	CARTER tv	John	DEHNER tv+
John	CARTY eng Am	John	DENHAM(Sir)po
John	CARVER colonist Am	John	DENNY b
John	CASON	John	DENVER s+
John	CASSISI tv+	John	DEREK d,tv+
John	CASTLE	John	DEWEY ph,e Am
John	CAZALE	John	DIEHL tv+
John	CHAPMAN p,etch Am &	John	DIX ar,st Am
John	CHAPMAN=Appleseed	John	DOE
John	CHEEVER w Am	John	DONNE po Br
John	CHESBRO b hf	John	DOWLAND c,m Br
John	CHISUM cattleman Am	John	DOYLE p,cr Br
John	CIARDI po,ct Am	John	DRAPER sc,w Am
John	CLARE po Br	John	DREW la Am
John	CLARK ec,e Am	John	DRYDEN po Br
John	CLARKE l,supr ct Am	John	DUBE j,e S.Afr
John	CLARKE tv	John	DUIGAN d
John	CLAYTON st Am	John	DUNLOP i-tires Scot
John	CLEESE	John	DUNNE ds-planes,ph
John	CLELAND w Br	John	DUNNE w Am
John	CLYNES labor,st Br	John	DYE tv+
John	COBB racecars Scot	John	DYER po Br
John	COGHLAN mr-drm Br	John	DYKES r,c Br
John	COLICOS tv+	John	EADIE r Scot
John	COLLIER j,ct Br	John	ECCLES(Sir)md
John	COLLIER w Am	John	ECHOLS mr-guit Am
John	COLTER x Am	John	ELDER eng-ships Scot
John	CONLEE s	John	ELERS ceramics Br
John	CONTE tv+	John	ELLIOTT
John	COOKE w Am	John	EMERSON
John	COPLEY p Am	John	EMERY
John	CORBETT tv	John	ENDERS sc Am
John	CORYELL w Am	John	ENGLISH d
John	COTMAN p Br	John	ERICSON tv+
John	COUGAR s Am	John	ERSKINE e,w Am
John	COWSILL mr-drm Am	John	ESCH st Am
John	CRANKO ba S.Afr	John	EVANS(Sir)arc
John	CROKER w,ct Br	John	EVELYN w Br
John	CROME p Br &	John	EVERS b
John	CROME=Old Crome	John	EWART
John	CROWNE w Br	John	FANE ar,st Br
John	CULLUM tv+	John	FARMER c Br
John	CURRY p Am	John	FARRAR pb,w Am

John	FARROW d Am	John	HALLAM
John	FAULK tv	John	HAMMOND eng-mine Am
John	FELL r Br	John	HAMMOND Jr eng,i Am
John	FEMIA tv	John	HANCOCK st Am
John	FENNO ed Am	John	HANNAH fb hf
John	FIEDLER tv+	John	HARE (Sir) la
John	FILSON frontier,w Am	John	HARKINS tv+
John	FINN	John	HARPER tv
John	FITCH i Am	John	HARRIS w-scifi Br
John	FLAUS	John	HARRON
John	FLAXMAN su Br	John	HART j,tv Am
John	FLECK	John	HARTMAN m-drm Am
John	FLEMING (Sir) eng,e	John	HARVARD r,f Am
John	FOGERTYm-flk,guit,s	John	HARVEY tv
John	FORD d	John	HARVEY (Sir) la,pr
John	FORD w Br	John	HAWKES w Am
John	FOSTER st Am	John	HAWKINS (Sir) l,w
John	FOWLER (Sir) eng	John	HAY st,w,po Am
John	FOWLES w Br	John	HAYES d
John	FOXE w Br	John	HEARD
John	FREMONT x,ar,st Am	John	HEDRICK w Am
John	FRERE antiquary Br	John	HEENAN boxer Am
John	FUJIOKA tv+	John	HEISMAN fbc Am
John	FUREY	John	HELD Jr cr Am
John	GALT w Scot	John	HERSEY w,j Am
John	GARAND i Am	John	HERVEY st,w Br
John	GARDNER w,h Am	John	HEYWOOD w,po Br
John	GARKO	John	HICKS (Sir) ec
John	GARRICK	John	HODIAK
John	GAVIN	John	HOGE tv
John	GAY po,w Br	John	HOLLAND
John	GEORGE tv	John	HOOKER mj-blues Am
John	GETZ tv+	John	HOUGH d
John	GIBSON tv	John	HOWARD tv+
John	GIELGUD (Sir)	John	HOYT tv+
John	GILBERT	John	HUBBARD tv+
John	GILLING d	John	HUGHES d
John	GILPIN ba Br	John	HULLAH organ,c Br
John	GLASSCO w,po Can	John	HUME st, n-x'98
John	GLENN as,st Am	John	HURT
John	GLOVER	John	HUSS r.ref Cz
John	GOFF	John	HUSTON d,w+ Am
John	GOODMAN tv+	John	HYATT i Am
John	GORRIE i Am	John	ILLSLEY mr-bass Br
John	GORST (Sir) st	John	INGLE tv
John	GOTTI mafia Am	John	INGLIS (Sir) ar
John	GOULD sc-birds Br	John	IRELAND
John	GOWER po Br	John	IRELAND organ,c Br
John	GRAY w Am	John	IRVING w Am
John	GREEN tv	John	JACKSON
John	GREGG i,pb Am	John	JACKSON boxer Br
John	GREGSON	John	JAKES w Am
John	GRIGGS st,l Am	John	JAMES tv+
John	GRIGGS tv	John	JARRATT
John	GRISHAM w Am	John	JARVIS p Am
John	GRUELLE cr Am	John	JAY l,st Am
John	GUARE w Am	John	JOHNSON fb hf
John	GULLY boxer,st Br	John	JOLY sc,e Ir
John	GUNTHER j,w,tv Am	John	JONES tv
John	HAAST (Sir) geol,x	John	JONES (Casey) rr eng
John	HALDANE sc Scot	John	KANDER c Am

John	KANE p Am	John	LOMAX w-folklore Am
John	KANI	John	LONE
John	KAPELOS	John	LONG w Am
John	KARLEN tv+	John	LONGDEN tv+
John	KASSIR tv	John	LOWES e,w Am
John	KAY mr-guit,s Ger	John	LUBBOCK(Sir)ast,mth
John	KEATS po Br	John	LUND
John	KEBLE r,po,e Br	John	LUPTON tv+
John	KEELY fraud Am	John	LURIE
John	KELLOGG md,e,id Am	John	LYDGATE r,po Br
John	KELLOGG tv+	John	LYDON mr-s Br
John	KEMBLE la Br	John	LYLY w Br
John	KEMENY math,e,i Am	John	LYNCH
John	KENDREW(Sir)sc	John	LYNCH l,st,ar,slve Am
John	KENSETT p Am	John	MACHEN r,e,w Am
John	KENYON e,w Am	John	MACHIN math Br
John	KERR tv+	John	MacKAY
John	KERR(Sir)sc,e	John	MACKEY fb hf
John	KETCH hangman Br &	John	MacVANE tv
John	KETCH = Jack	John	MADDEN fbc,tv Am
John	KIERAN j-sports,tv Am	John	MAHONEY
John	KIERAN Jr tv	John	MANLY w,e Am
John	KING tv	John	MARIN p Am
John	KING(Dusty)	John	MARLEY
John	KNOWLES w Am	John	MARSH c Br
John	KNOX r,w Scot	John	MARSTON w Br
John	KORTY d	John	MARTIN
John	KUNDLA bbc hf	John	MASTERS w Br
John	LaFARGE r,w Am	John	MAUCHLY sc,eng.i Am
John	LAMBTON st Br	John	MAUS s Am
John	LAMOTTA tv+	John	MAXWELL tv+
John	LANDEN math Br	John	MAYALL mr-kbds Br
John	LANDIS d	John	McCLOY st Am
John	LANE pb Br	John	McCRAE md,po Can
John	LANG(Jack)st Aust	John	McENERY
John	LARCH tv+	John	McENROE t,tv-spts
John	LARKIN tv	John	McEWEN(Sir)c
John	LATHAM birds,w Br	John	McGIVER tv+
John	LAUNER tv	John	McGRAW b,bmg hf
John	LAURIE	John	McINTIRE tv+
John	LAVERY(Sir) p	John	McLIAM tv+
John	LAW f Scot	John	McMARTIN tv+
John	LAWLOR tv	John	McMASTER h Am
John	le CARRE w Br	John	McNALLY mr-guit,s Br
John	LEDYARD x Am	John	McNALLY(Blood)fb hf
John	LEECH cr Br	John	McPHEE w,e Am
John	LEHMANN ed,po Br	John	McQUADE tv
John	LEJEUNE marines Am	John	McVie mr-bass Br
John	LENNON mr+,c Br	John	MEILLON
John	LEWIS mj-piano,c Am	John	MERTON
John	LINDLEY sc Br	John	MILFORD tv
John	LITEL tv+	John	MILL ph,ec Br
John	LITHGOW tv+	John	MILLAIS(Sir)p
John	LIU	John	MILLER geol,e Am
John	LLOYD	John	MILLS
John	LOCKE mr-kbds Am	John	MILTON po,w Br
John	LOCKE ph,w Br	John	MINER nature Can
John	LODER	John	MITCHUM
John	LODGE	John	MONASH(Sir)eng Aust
John	LODGE mr-bass Br	John	MOODY analyst-f,w
John	LOGAN po,ed,ct Am	John	MORLEY st,w Br

John	MOSBY ar,st,w Am.	John	REITH(Sir)eng-BBC
John	MOTLEY h Am	John	RENNIE eng Scot
John	MOTT r,YMCA Am	John	RICH la,mgr Br
John	MOXEY d	John	RIDGELY
John	MUIR natur,w Am	John	RIGGINS fb hf
John	MUNONYE w Nigeria	John	RITTER tv+
John	MURPHY p Am	John	ROARKE tv
John	MURRAY ed,ct Br	John	ROCK md,e Am
John	MURRY w,ct,ed Br	John	ROEBUCK md,i Br
John	NAVIN Jr. tv	John	ROOSMA bb hf
John	NEAGLE p Am	John	RUSKIN w,ct-art Br
John	NEF sc,e Am	John	RUSSELL tv+
John	NELSON tv	John	SANDYS(Sir)h,e
John	NESBITT tv	John	SANKEY l,st Br
John	NEVILLE tv+	John	SARGENT p Am
John	NEWBERY pb Br	John	SARIS mer,marin Br
John	NEWLAND tv	John	SARTAIN engr Am
John	NEWLOVE po Can	John	SAVAGE
John	NEWMAN r,w Br	John	SAXON tv+
John	NEWTON tv+	John	SAYLES d+
John	NICOLAY bio Am	John	SCHUCK tv+
John	NIMS po Am	John	SCOPES e Am
John	NOYES reform,w Am	John	SEELEY(Sir)h
John	NUGENT la,w Am	John	SEITZ
John	O'HARA w Am	John	SELDEN l,w Br
John	O'REILLY po,ed Am	John	SEVIER ar,st Am
John	OATES mr-guit,s Am	John	SHEA
John	OLERUD b,bat 93	John	SHEARIN tv
John	ORCHARD tv	John	SHERMAN st Amm
John	ORR(Lord)st Br	John	SHORT tv
John	OSBORNE w Br	John	SIMCOE ar st Br
John	PAINE organ,e,c Am	John	SIMON(Sir)l,st
John	PANKOW tv+	John	SKELTON po Br
John	PANOZZO mr-drm Am	John	SLOAN p Am
John	PATRICK w Am	John	SLOAT navy Am
John	PAYNE la,w,pr Am	John	SMEATON eng Br
John	PAYNE tv+	John	SMIBERT p Am
John	PELL math,e Br	John	SMITH colonist,x Am
John	PENRY w,pb Welsh	John	SMITH tv
John	PERRY tv	John	SMOLTZ b
John	PETO p Am	John	SNYDER tv
John	PHILBIN	John	SOANE(Sir)ac
John	PIATT j,po Am	John	SOTHEBY auctions Br
John	PINETTE tv	John	SPEKE x Br
John	POLANYI sc Can	John	SPENCER tv+
John	POOLE w Am	John	SPOONER l,st Am
John	POPE ac Am	John	SPRIGG(Sir)st S.Afr
John	POPLE sc,e,n-c'98	John	SQUIRE mr-guit Br
John	POWELL geol,x Am	John	ST. POLIS
John	POWELL(Boog)b	John	STAINER(Sir)organ,c
John	POWER d	John	STAMOS tv+
John	PURDUE mer,f Am	John	STANTON
John	PYM st Br	John	STAX mr-bass Br
John	QUADE	John	STEEL mr-drm Br
John	QUALEN	John	STEINER
John	QUIDOR p Am	John	STETSON id-hats Am
John	RAE x Scot	John	STEVENS i Am
John	RAGIN tv	John	STOSSEL tv
John	RANSOM po,ct Am	John	STOW h Br
John	REED j,po,radical	John	STRUTT sc,e Br
John	REILLY tv+	John	STUART

John	STURGES d	John	ZAREMBA TV
John	SUTTER pioneer Am	John	ZEE tv
John	SUTTON	John	ZENGER j Am
John	SWANTON an Am	John A.	MILLER w Am
John	SYMONDS po,w,h Br	John Allen	NELSON tv+
John	SYNGE w Ir	John C.	McGINLEY
John	TAYLOR mr-bass Br	John Cameron	SWAYZE tv-news
John	TAYLOR w,po Br	John D.	LeMAY tv+
John	TENNIEL(Sir)cr	John David	CARSON tv+
John	TERRY	John de	LANCIE tv+
John	TESH tv	John Edgar	HOOVER fbi Am
John	THAW	John Foster	DULLES 1.st Am
John	TOLAND w Am	John Henry	TAYLOR g Br
John	TOOLE w Am	John Jacob	ASTOR f,furs Am
John	TYNDALL sc,e Ir	John L	LEWIS labor Am
John	UPDIKE w Am	John Maynard	KEYNES ec,w Br
John	UPDIKE w,po Am	John Nance	GARNER st Am
John	Van EYSSEN	John Paul	JONES mr-bass Br
John	Van VLECK sc Am	John Paul	JONES navy Am
John	VANE md Br	John Phillip	LAW
John	VARLEY p Br	John Phillip	SOUSA m,c,cn Am
John	VENN e,w Br	John Quincy	ADAMS 6th Pres
John	VERNON	John Scott	TROTTER mj,cn,tv
John	VIVYAN tv	John von	NEUMANN math Am
John	WAIN w,po,ct Br	John Wesley	SHIPP tv+
John	WAITE s,ws Br	John Wilkes	BOOTH la Am
John	WALKER sc,e,n-c'97	John,	DR.s-r&b,blues,rk
John	WALSH tv	John,	ELTON mr-s+ Br
John	WARD b hf	John,	GOTTFRIED
John	WATERS	Johnnie	COLLINS III tv
John	WATERS d	Johnnie	FINGERSmr-kbds,s Ir
John	WATSON ps,e Am	Johnnie	McPHEE tv
John	WATSON r,w Scot	Johnnie	RAY s Am
John	WAYNE tv+	Johnny	ARTHUR
John	WEAVER ba Br	Johnny	BANGERT tv
John	WEBSTER w Br	Johnny	BENCH b hf
John	WEIDER mr-bass Br	Johnny	BROWN tv
John	WELSH tv	Johnny	BURKE lyrics Am
John	WESLEY r,w Br	Johnny	BUTLER tv
John	WEST mr-guit Am	Johnny	CARSON tv-host Am
John	WETTON mr-bass,s Br	Johnny	CASH s-cnt,tv+ Am
John	WHITE tv	Johnny	COLLA mr-sax,guit
John	WHITING w Br	Johnny	COLT mr-bass Am
John	WHITLEY st Br	Johnny	DARK tv+
John	WIDEMAN w Am	Johnny	DEPP tv+
John	WIGMORE l,e Am	Johnny	DESMOND tv
John	WILBYE c Br	Johnny	DODDS mj-clari Am
John	WILDMAN	Johnny	DOWNS
John	WILKES j,w,ref Br	Johnny	EIMEN tv
John	WILLYS id-cars,st	Johnny	HAMP mj,cn Am
John	WILSON w Am	Johnny	HART cr Am
John	WISE baloons Am	Johnny	HAYMER tv
John	WOO d	Johnny	HILL tv
John	WOOD	Johnny	HODGES mj-sax Am
John	WOODEN bb,bbc hf	Johnny	KIDD mr-s Br
John	WOOL ar Am	Johnny	LEE mr-s Am
John	WORDEN navy Am	Johnny	MANN m,cn,tv Am
John	WRIGHT tv	Johnny	MARKS c Am
John	WYCLIF r,ref Br	Johnny	MARR mr-guit Br
John	WYNDHAM w-scifi Br	Johnny	MATHIS s-pop Am
John	YORK tv	Johnny	McAFEE mj-s,tv Am

Johnny	MERCER s,c Am	Johnson,	JACK mj-tromb,cn Br
Johnny	MINCE mj-clari Am	Johnson,	JAMES l,e,po Am
Johnny	MIZE b hf	Johnson,	JAMES mj,c Am
Johnny	NASH mr	Johnson,	JANET tv
Johnny	OLSEN tv	Johnson,	JAY tv
Johnny	OTIS m-r&b,drm,w Am	Johnson,	JERMAIN tv
Johnny	RAMONE mr-guit Am	Johnson,	JIMMY fb hf
Johnny	RIVERS mr,s Am	Johnson,	JOHN fb hf
Johnny	SAIN b	Johnson,	JOSEPHINE p-f'35
Johnny	SEVEN tv	Johnson,	JUDY tv
Johnny	STEARNS tv	Johnson,	KEG mj-trombone Am
Johnny	UNITAS fb hf	Johnson,	KEN mj,cn Br
Johnny	WINTER m-r&b,guit	Johnson,	LAMONT d
Johnny Mack BROWN		Johnson,	LAURA tv+
Johns	HOPKINS mer,f Am	Johnson,	LIONEL po,ct Br
Johns,	GLYNIS s,tv+ S.Afr	Johnson,	LYNDON B.36th pres
Johns,	JASPER p,su Am	Johnson,	LYNN-HOLLY
Johns,	MERVYN	Johnson,	MAE
Johns,	STRATFORD	Johnson,	MAGIC bb-m'87'9'90
Johns,	TRACY tv	Johnson,	MICHELLE
Johnson,	ALEX b,bat'70	Johnson,	NOBLE
Johnson,	ALEXANDER tv	Johnson,	OSA x Am
Johnson,	ALICIA tv	Johnson,	PAMELA w,ct Br
Johnson,	AMY fly Br	Johnson,	PAULINE po Can
Johnson,	ANDREW 17th pres	Johnson,	PENNY tv
Johnson,	ANNE-MARIE tv+	Johnson,	PHILIP ac Am
Johnson,	ARCH tv	Johnson,	RANDY b-cy'95
Johnson,	ARTE cm,tv+ Am	Johnson,	REVERDY st Am
Johnson,	ASHLEY tv	Johnson,	RICHARD
Johnson,	BEN o-s'71, tv+	Johnson,	RITA
Johnson,	BEVERLY mo Am	Johnson,	ROBERT s-blues Am
Johnson,	BRAD tv+	Johnson,	RUSSELL tv+
Johnson,	BUDDYmj-pia,r&b,cn	Johnson,	SAMUEL ph,e Am
Johnson,	BUNK mj-cornet Am	Johnson,	SAMUEL(Dr.)w,po Br
Johnson,	BYRON(Ban)bmg hf	Johnson,	SUNNY
Johnson,	CANDY	Johnson,	TAJ tv
Johnson,	CELIA	Johnson,	TONY tv+
Johnson,	CELICIA tv+	Johnson,	TOR
Johnson,	CHARLERS b,gg'96'7	Johnson,	UWE w Ger
Johnson,	CHARLIE mj,cn Am	Johnson,	VAN tv+
Johnson,	CHERIE tv	Johnson,	WALTER b hf
Johnson,	CHIC	Johnson,	WILLIAM bb hf
Johnson,	CLARK tv+	Johnson,	WILLIAM(Judy)b, hf
Johnson,	CLAUDE tv	Johnston	ANNIE w Am
Johnson,	DEBRA tv	Johnston,	GEORGE j,w Austra
Johnson,	IANE w Am	Johnston,	JOHN DENNIS
Johnson,	DON tv+	Johnston,	JOHNNY tv
Johnson,	DOTS	Johnston,	KRISTEN tv
Johnson,	EASTMAN p Am	Johnston,	LYNN cr Am
Johnson,	EYVIND n-1'74	Johnston,	NEIL bb hf
Johnson,	GAIL tv	Joi	LANSING tv+
Johnson,	GEORGANN tv	Joie	LEE
Johnson,	GERRY tv	Joiner,	CHARLIE fb
Johnson,	HALL s,cn Am	Joinville,	JEAN de h Fr
Johnson,	HIRAM l,st Am	Joio,	NORMAN p-m'57
Johnson,	HOLLY mr-s Sudan	Jokai,	MOR w Hung
Johnson,	HOWARD b,hr'91	Jokl,	NORBERT e,w Czech
Johnson,	HOWARD mer-foods Am	Joleen	LUTZ tv
Johnson,	HOWIE mr-drm Am	Joliat,	AUREL ho-m'34
Johnson,	J.J. mj-tromb,cn Am	Joliot-Curie,FREDERIC n-c'35	
Johnson,	JACK boxer Am	Joliot-Curie,IRENE n-c'35	

Jolivet,	ANDRE c Fr	Jonathan	FRID
Jolley,	I. STANFORD	Jonathan	GILBERT tv
Jolley,	NORMAN tv	Jonathan	GRIES
Jolliet,	LOUIS x Fr	Jonathan	HALE
Jolliffe,	DAVID tv	Jonathan	HARRIS tv
Jolly,	GEORGE la Br	Jonatnan	HAZE
Jolson,	AL s+ Am	Jonathan	HOLE tv
Joly,	JOHN sc,e Irish	Jonathan	HULLS i Br
Jolyot,	PROSPER po Fr	Jonathan	KAPLAN d
Jomini,	HENRI de ar,w Swi	Jonathan	KNIGHT mr-s Am
Jon	ARASON r,po Iceland	Jonathan	LARSON w Am
Jon	BAUMAN(Bowzer) tv	Jonathan	LYNN tv
Jon	BLAKE	Jonathan	ODELL ar,w Am
Jon	BON JOVI s-pop,mr Am	Jonathan	PRINCE tv+
Jon	CALIRI tv	Jonathan	PRYCE
Jon	CRYER	Jonathan	RICHMAN s Am
Jon	CYPHER tv+	Jonathan	SCHMOCK tv
Jon	DeVRIES	Jonathan	SWIFT r,po,w Br
Jon	FARRISSmr-drm,sAust	Jonathan	WARD tv+
Jon	FERREAU	Jonathan	WEINER w Am
Jon	FINCH	Jonathan	WELCH tv
Jon	GNAGY tv	Jonathan	WILD thief Br
Jon	HAGER tv	Jonathan	WINTERS cm,tv+
Jon	HALL tv+	Jonathan Ke QUAN tv+	
Jon	HESS d	Jonelle	ALLEN
Jon	HEXUM tv	Jones	VERY po,w Am
Jon	JOST d	Jones,	ALAN m-sax Welsh
Jon	KEEBLE mr-drm Br	Jones,	ALLAN
Jon	KORKES	Jones,	ANISSA tv
Jon	LORD mr-kbds Br	Jones,	ARCHDALE tv
Jon	LORMER tv	Jones,	BARRY
Jon	LOVITZ tv+	Jones,	BEN tv+
Jon	MOSS mr-drm Br	Jones,	BERT fb-m'76
Jon	PENNELL tv	Jones,	BOOKER T. mr-kbds
Jon	POLITO tv+	Jones,	BUCK
Jon	PROVOST tv+	Jones,	CAROLYN tv+
Jon	SECADA	Jones,	CHARLES(Bufflo)hunt
Jon	SEDA	Jones,	CHARLIE tv
Jon	TENNEY tv+	Jones,	CHRISTOPHER tv+
Jon	THOR	Jones,	CLAUDE tv+
Jon	VIDALIN r Iceland	Jones,	CLEON b
Jon	VOIGHT	Jones,	CLIFTON tv
Jon,	FRANCOIS du r,ed	Jones,	D.G. po,ct Can
Jonas	BRONCK pioneer Dan	Jones,	DARBY
Jonas	FURRER st Swi	Jones,	DAVID p,w Br
Jonas	HIELM st Nor	Jones,	DAVID tv
Jonas	LIE w,po Nor	Jones,	DAVY mr-s+ Br
Jonas	SALK md Am	Jones,	DEACON fb-d'67'8 hf
Jonas,	JUSTUS ref Ger	Jones,	DEAN
Jonathan	BANKS tv+	Jones,	DICK tv
Jonathan	BRANDIS	Jones,	DUANE
Jonathan	CAIN mr-kbds Am	Jones,	EBENEZER po Br
Jonathan	CAPE pb Br	Jones,	EDDIE bb
Jonathan	CARVER x Am	Jones,	EDDIE tv+
Jonathan	CROMBIE	Jones,	EDGAR Jr tv
Jonathan	DALY tv	Jones,	ELVIN mj-drm Am
Jonathan	DANIELS j,w Am	Jones,	FREDDIE
Jonathan	DEMME d,pr,w Am	Jones,	GEMMA
Jonathan	EDWARDS r,ph Am	Jones,	GINGER tv
Jonathan	FRAKES tv+	Jones,	GORDON tv+
Jonathan	FRANZEN w Am	Jones,	GRACE s+ Jamaica

Jones,	GRAHAM mr-guit Br	Jones,	TOM s-pop Welsh
Jones,	GRIFFITH	Jones,	TOMMY LEE
Jones,	HENRY tv+	Jones,	WARNER tv
Jones,	HENRY(Sir)w,ct	Jong,	ERICA po,w Am
Jones,	HOWARD p-n'65	Jongen,	JOSEPH c,e Belg
Jones,	HOWARD s,ws Br	Jongkind,	JOHAN p Dut
Jones,	INDIANA fc	Joni	MITCHELL mr,s Can
Jones,	INIGO ac Br	Joni	SLEDGE mr-s Am
Jones,	ISHAM mj,cn,c Am	Jonni	MYYRA o-g'20'24
Jones,	ISOLA mezzo-sopr	Jonson,	BEN w,po Br
Jones,	JAMES EARL tv+	Jonsson,	FINNUR r,h Iceland
Jones,	JAMES w Am	Jonsson,	HJALMAR po Iceland
Jones,	JANET	Joon	KIM
Jones,	JANET ba,tv	Joos van	CLEVE p Belg
Jones,	JEFFREY	Jooss,	KURT ba Ger
Jones,	JENNIFER o-a'43	Joost	BURGI math Swi
Jones,	JENNY tv	Joost de	HONDT engr Belg
Jones,	JO mj-drm Am	Joost van	den VONDEL p,w Dut
Jones,	JOHN PAUL mr-bass	Joplin,	JANIS s-mr,blues Am
Jones,	JOHN PAUL navy Am	Joplin,	SCOTT mj-piano,c Am
Jones,	JOHN tv	Jordaens,	JACOB p Belg
Jones,	JOHN(Casey)rr eng	Jordan	CHARNEY tv
Jones,	K.C. bb hf	Jordan	KNIGHT mr-s Am
Jones,	KENNY mr-drm,s Br	Jordan,	BOBBI tv
Jones,	L.Q. tv+	Jordan,	BOBBY
Jones,	LeROI po Am	Jordan,	DAVID sc,e,w Am
Jones,	LIHANN tv	Jordan,	DOROTHEA la Ir
Jones,	LOUIS(Grandpa)tv	Jordan,	ELIZABETH w Am
Jones,	MARCIA	Jordan,	GLENN d
Jones,	MARY(Mother)labor	Jordan,	HAMILTON st Am
Jones,	MICK mr-guit,s Br	Jordan,	HENRY fb hf
Jones,	MICKEY drm,tv Am	Jordan,	JAN tv
Jones,	MORGAN tv	Jordan,	JUDY tv
Jones,	NEIL mr-guit Welsh	Jordan,	LONNIE mr-kbds,s Am
Jones,	OWEN ac Br	Jordan,	LOUIS mj,r&b,cn Am
Jones,	PAMELA tv	Jordan,	MARSHA
Jones,	PAUL m-harmon,s Br	Jordan,	MICHAEL bb-m'91'2 &
Jones,	PHIL tv	Jordan,	MICHAEL bb-m'88
Jones,	PHILLY JOE mj-drm Am	Jordan,	MICHAEL ="Air"
Jones,	QUINCY mj,pr Am	Jordan,	RICHARD
Jones,	RANDY b-cy'76	Jordan,	ROBERT tv
Jones,	RAY mr-bass Br	Jordan,	S. MARC tv
Jones,	RENEE tv	Jordan,	TED tv
Jones,	RICKIE mj-s,ws Am	Jordan,	WILLIAM tv+
Jones,	ROBERT(Bobby) g Am	Jordana	SHAPIRO(Bink)tv
Jones,	RODNEY po Am	Jordanna	CAPRA tv+
Jones,	RUFUS e,r Am	Jorge	AMADO w Braz
Jones,	SAM	Jorge	BORGES w,po Arg
Jones,	SAM bb hf	Jorge	GAITAN st Colom
Jones,	SAM tv	Jorge	GUILLEN po Sp
Jones,	SHIRLEY o-s'60,tv+	Jorge	LUKE
Jones,	SIMON tv+	Jorge	MISTRAL
Jones,	SPIKE mj,cn,tv+ Am	Jorge	PORCEL
Jones,	STAN fb hf	Jorge	RIGAUD
Jones,	STAN tv	Jorge	RIVERO
Jones,	STEVE mr-guit Br	Jorge	RUSSEK
Jones,	STEVEN tv	Jorge	SANZ
Jones,	TERRY	Jorgen	MOE po,folklore Nor
Jones,	THAD mj-trump Am	Jorgensen,	BEN tv
Jones,	THOMAS su Am	Jorie	GRAHAM po Am
Jones,	TIM tv	Joris	IVENS d Dut

Joris,	DAVID r Dut	Josef	RESSEL i Aus
Jorn	SUNDQUIST	Josef	SOMMER
Jorn,	ASGER p Dan	Josef	STEFAN sc,e Aus
Jory	HUSAIN tv	Josef	STRAUSS c Aus
Jory,	VICTOR tv+	Josef	SUK viol,c Cz
Jose	BALTA ar Peru	Josef	TISO r,st Slovak
Jose	BURGOS r,st Phil	Josef	ZITEK ac Cz
Jose	CANSECO b	Joseph	ADAMS e,ed Am
Jose	CHOCANO po Peru	Joseph	ADDISON po, ct Br
Jose	DONOSO w Chile	Joseph	ALBERT fo Ger
Jose	DUARTE st Salv	Joseph	ALBO ph Sp
Jose	EGUREN po Peru	Joseph	ALLEINE r Br
Jose	FERRER la,d+ Am	Joseph	ALSOP j,w Am
Jose	GALVEZ	Joseph	AMES bibliog Br
Jose	GAMA po Braz	Joseph	AMES sc,e Am
Jose	GOMEZ matador Sp	Joseph	ARCH st Br
Jose	GRECO ba Sp	Joseph	ARTHUR sc,e,ed Am
Jose	GRINAN tv	Joseph	ASPDIN i Br
Jose	ITURBI piano,cn Sp	Joseph	AUTRAN po,w Fr
Jose	LEWGOY	Joseph	AVENOL st Fr
Jose	LIMON ba Am	Joseph	BARBERA tv
Jose	LINARES st Bol	Joseph	BEDIER w,e Fr
Jose	MARMOL w Arg	Joseph	BEUYS su Ger
Jose	MARTI st,w,po Cuba	Joseph	BIDEN st Am
Jose	MEDINA h,pb Chile	Joseph	BIVIANO tv
Jose	MELIS m,cn,tv Am	Joseph	BOEHM(Sir)su
Jose	MUTIS md Sp	Joseph	BOLOGNA
Jose	OBANDO st Colom	Joseph	BOTTOMS
Jose	OLMEDO st Ecu	Joseph	BRAMAH eng,i Br
Jose	OROZCO p Mex	Joseph	BRANT chief Am Ind
Jose	PAEZ ar,st Venz	Joseph	BRENNAN b
Jose	PANDO ar,st Bol	Joseph	BRODSKY po,ct Rus
Jose	PEREZ st Chile	Joseph	BYRNS st Am
Jose	PEREZ tv+	Joseph	CALI tv+
Jose	POSADA at Mex	Joseph	CALLEIA
Jose	RIVERA w,po Colom	Joseph	CANNON st Am
Jose	RIZAL st,w Phil	Joseph	CHAPMAN tv
Jose	RODO ph,w Urug	Joseph	CHOATE l,st Am
Jose	SERRATO st Urug	Joseph	CONRAD w Br
Jose	SILVA po Colom	Joseph	COOK(Sir)st Aust
Jose	SUAREZ	Joseph	CORNELL su Am
Jose	TORVAY	Joseph	COTTEN tv+
Jose	VALENTE po Sp	Joseph	COUSINS tv
Jose	Van DAM barit Belg	Joseph	CREHAN
Jose	WILKER	Joseph	DAVIES l,st Am
Jose	ZELAYA st Nica	Joseph	DECK ceramics Fr
Jose de	ACOSTA r Sp	Joseph	DENT pb Br
Jose de	ALENCAR w Braz	Joseph	DIXON id,i Am
Jose de	DURAO r,po Braz	Joseph	DRAKE po Am
Jose de	HERIDIA po Cuba	Joseph	ECKHEL coins,e Aus
Jose de	ISLA w,e Sp	Joseph	FESCH r Fr
Jose de	MACEDO w Port	Joseph	FOLEY tv
Jose de	MARINS	Joseph	FURPHY w Aust
Jose de	PEREDA w Sp	Joseph	FURST
Jose de	RIBERA p Sp	Joseph	GALES j,pb Am
Jose van	DAM barit Belg	Joseph	GARBER w Am
Josef	ALBERS p Am	Joseph	GIAN tv+
Josef	BERAN r Cz	Joseph	GIRARD
Josef	HOFMANN piano Am	Joseph	GREW st Am
Josef	KOHLER l,w Ger	Joseph	GUNGL c,cn Hung
Josef	MACHAR po Cz	Joseph	HAAS c,e Ger

Joseph	HACKER tv+	Joseph	ROPARTZ c Fr
Joseph	HAYDN c Aus	Joseph	ROY ct Can
Joseph	HELLER w Am	Joseph	RUBEN d
Joseph	HENRY sc Am	Joseph	RUSKIN
Joseph	HOOKER ar Am	Joseph	SARGENT d
Joseph	HYRTL md,e Aus	Joseph	SAWYER
Joseph	IDDINGS geol,e Am	Joseph	SAXTON i Am
Joseph	JOACHIM viol,c Hung	Joseph	SCOTT tv
Joseph	JONGEN c,e Belg	Joseph	SEVERN p Br
Joseph	JOUBERT w-morals Fr	Joseph	SIMMONS m-rap Am
Joseph	JUKES geol Br	Joseph	SIROLA tv
Joseph	KANE d	Joseph	SMITH r-Mormon Am
Joseph	KEARNS tv	Joseph	STALIN st Ris
Joseph	KEIFER l,ar,st Am	Joseph	STELLA p Am
Joseph	KENNEDY bus,st Am	Joseph	STIELER p Ger
Joseph	KEPPLER cr Am	Joseph	STURGE ref,f Br
Joseph	KESSEL j,w Fr	Joseph	SWAN(Sir)sc
Joseph	KRAMM w Am	Joseph	TAYLOR la Br
Joseph	KRUTCH ct,w,e Am	Joseph	TAYLOR sc Am
Joseph	LAFITAU r Fr	Joseph	TODD tv
Joseph	LAI d	Joseph	TURNER p Br
Joseph	LAKANAL e,st Fr	Joseph	VILLELE st Fr
Joseph	LAMAR l Am	Joseph	WARTON ct,e Br
Joseph	LANNER ba Aus	Joseph	WEIGL c Aus
Joseph	LARMOR(Sir)math,e	Joseph	WHARTON id Am
Joseph	LASH bio Am	Joseph	WHIPP tv
Joseph	Le BEL sc Fr	Joseph	WIDMANN w Swi
Joseph	LISTER md,e Br	Joseph	WIRTH st Ger
Joseph	LOCKYER(Sir)astr,e	Joseph	WISEMAN tv+
Joseph	LOSEY d	Joseph	WRIGHT p Br
Joseph	LYONS st Austra	Joseph	ZEDLITZ po,w Aus
Joseph	MAHER	Joseph	ZITO d
Joseph	MARCELL tv	Joseph de	LALANDE astron Fr
Joseph	MASCOLO tv	Joseph von	BABO w Ger
Joseph	MAZELLO	Joseph von	MERING md,e Ger
Joseph	McCARTHY bmg hf	Joseph,	JACKIE tv
Joseph	McCARTHY st Am	Joseph,	RONALD tv
Joseph	McCOY cattleman Am	Josephine	CHAPLIN
Joseph	McKENNA l,st Am	Josephine	HART w Am
Joseph	MEDILL j Am	Josephine	HULL
Joseph	MERHI d	Josephine	JOHNSON w Am
Joseph	MEYER c Am	Josephine	MILES po,w Am
Joseph	MOHR r,po Aus	Josephine	TEY w Scot
Joseph	MONIER i Fr	Josephson,RIAN n-p'73	
Joseph	MURRAY md Am	Josephson,ERLAND	
Joseph	NASI st,f Port	Josephus	DANIELS j,st Am
Joseph	NIEPCE sc Fr	Josephus,	FLAVIUS h Jewish
Joseph	PARRY c Welsh	Josette	DAY
Joseph	PAXTON(Sir)ac	Josey	DUVAL
Joseph	PENNELL etch Am	Josh	BLAKE tv
Joseph	PERRY tv	Josh	BROLIN tv+
Joseph	PEVNEY d	Josh	BYRNE tv
Joseph	PEYRE w Fr	Josh	CHARLES
Joseph	PICKETT p Am	Josh	EVANS
Joseph	QUERARD w Fr	Josh	GIBSON b hf
Joseph	RAFF c Ger	Josh	KOENIG tv
Joseph	RANK id,pr-film Br	Josh	MOSTEL
Joseph	REDLICH l,st Aus	Josh	SAVIANO tv
Joseph	RENAN ph,ct,w Fr	Josh	TAYLOR tv
Joseph	RHINE ps,e Am	Joshua	COWEN i,id Am
Joseph	ROMAN tv	Joshua	GOODWIN tv

Joshua	HARRIS tv	Joyce	SMIGHT tv
Joshua	LOGAN d,w Am	Joyce	Van PATTEN tv+
Joshua	MAURER tv+	Joyce	WILSON mr-s Am
Joshua	MILLER	Joyce	WILSON tv
Joshua	MORROW tv	Joyce Carol OATES w,po,ct Am	
Joshua	REDMAN mj-sax Am	Joyce,	BRENDA
Joshua	SHELLEY tv	Joyce,	ELAINE tv+
Joshua,	LARRY	Joyce,	ELLA tv
Josiah	GIBBS sc,e Am	Joyce,	JAMES w,po Irish
Josiah	GREGG frontier Am	Joyce,	JIMMY s,cn,tv Am
Josiah	MEIGS l,e Am	Joyce,	MIKE mr-dr Br
Josiah	QUINCY l,st Am	Joyce,	YOOTLA
Josiah	ROYCE ph,e,w Am	Joyeux,	ODETTE
Josiah	SPODE id pottery Br	Joyner,	FLO 2 - o-g's'88
Josiah	SPURR geol Am	Jozef	BEM ar Pol
Josiah	WARREN ref Am	Jozef	HURBAN w Slovak
Josiah	WHITNEY geol,e,w Am	Jozef	ISRAELS p Dut
Josias de SOULAS la Fr		Jozef	SCHMIDT o-g'60'64
Josie	BISSET tv+	Jozef	ZALESKI po Pol
Josie	DAVIS tv	Jozsef	BAJZA j,po Hung
Josif	GURKO ar Rus	Jozsef	EOTVOS st,w Hung
Josika,	MIKLOS w Hung	Jozsef	KATONA l,w Hung
Josip	JELACIC ar,st Croat	Jozsef,	ATTILA po Hung
Josip..Tito BROZ st Yugo		Juan	ALBERDI st,l,ph Arg
Joslyn,	ALLYN tv+	Juan	ALMONTE ar,st Mex
Joss	ACKLAND	Juan	ALVAREZ st Mex
Joss,	ADDIE b, hf	Juan	ARRIAGA c Sp
Josse	BADE id,e Belg	Juan	CRESPI x Sp
Joselyn,	RANDY tv	Juan	EGANA st,w Chile
Jost	AMMAN p Swi	Juan	ELCANO x Basque
Jost,	ISAAK h Ger	Juan	FALCON ar,st Venz
Jost,	JON d	Juan	FANGIO carrace Am
Joubert,	JOSEPH w-morals Fr	Juan	FORNER w Sp
Joubert,	PETRUS ar,st S.Afr&	Juan	GALLEGO po Sp
Joubert,	PETRUS = Piet	Juan	GRIS p Sp
Jouhaux,	LEON n-x'51	Juan	GUAS ac Sp
Joule,	JAMES sc Br	Juan	MANUEL st,w Sp
Jourdan,	LOUIS	Juan	MASIP p Sp
Jouve,	PIERRE po,w,ct Fr	Juan	NEGRIN st,e Sp
Jouvet,	LOUIS la,d+ Fr	Juan	O'GORMAN ac Mex
Jovan	RISTIC st Serb	Juan	ONETTI w Urug
Jovellanos, GASPAR st,w Sp		Juan	PERON st-dict. Arg
Jovovich, MILLA		Juan	RUIZ po Sp
Joy	ADAMSON sc,w Br	Juan	RULFO w Mex
Joy	MORTON id-salt,mer Am	Juan	SACASA st Nica
Joy,	CHRISTIPHER	Juan de	ANZA x Sp
Joy,	JAMES id-rrs f Am	Juan de	AYALA x(SF Bay)Sp
Joy,	JIMMY mj-clari,cn Am	Juan de	ELCANO x Sp
Joy,	LEATRICE	Juan de	MENA po Sp
Joy,	ROBERT	Juan de	ONATE x Sp
Joyce	CAREY	Juan de	PAREJA p Sp
Joyce	CARY w Br	Juan de	ROSAS dictator Arg
Joyce	COMPTON	Juan de la CIERVA i,eng Sp	
Joyce	DeWITT tv	Juan de la COSA x Sp	
Joyce	HYSER tv+	Juan del	ENCINA w,c Sp
Joyce	JAMESON	Juan del	MAZO p Sp
Joyce	JILLSON tv+	Juanita	MOORE
Joyce	KILMER po Am	Juano	HERNANDEZ
Joyce	MAYNARD w Am	Juarbe,	ISRAEL tv
Joyce	MEADOWS	Juarez,	BENITO re,st Mex
Joyce	MENGES tv	Jubal	EARLY ar CSA

Jud	STRUNK tv		Judy	NUGENT tv
Jud	TAYLOR tv		Judy	PACE tv+
Jud,	JAKOB e,w Swi		Judy	PARFITT
Judah	GORDON w,po Lith		Judy	PARRISH tv
Judah	MAGNES r,e Am		Juel,	JENS p Dan
Judah	SOMMO w It		Juel,	NIELS navy Dan
Judd	HIRSCH tv+		Juergen	PROCHNOW
Judd	NELSON		Juhasz,	FERENC po Hung
Judd	OMEN		Juice	NEWTON s-cntry Am
Judd	ROSE tv		Juin,	ALPHONSE ar Fr
Judd	TAYLOR d		Jukes,	JOSEPH geol Br
Judd,	ASHLEY		Jule	STYNE c Am
Judd,	CHARLES ps,e,w Am		Jules	ANETHAN st,r Belg
Judd,	EDWARD		Jules	BASS d
Judd,	NAOMI s-cntry Am		Jules	BORDET sc Belg
Jude	CICCOLELLA		Jules	BUFFANO mj-pian,tv
Jude	DEVERAUX w		Jules	CHERET p Fr
Judge	REINHOLD		Jules	DALOU su Fr
Judge,	ARLINE		Jules	DASSIN d
Judge,	JACK vaudville,c Br		Jules	DROZ su Fr
Judi	BOWKER		Jules	DUPRE p Fr
Judi	DENCH		Jules	FAVRE l,st Fr
Judi	LUCIANO tv		Jules	FEIFFER cr,w Am
Judi	MEREDITH tv		Jules	FERRY st Fr
Judie	ARONSON		Jules	GREVY st Fr
Judith	ALLEN		Jules	GUERIN p Am
Judith	EXNER mistress-JFK		Jules	GUESDE reform Fr
Judith	HANSEN tv		Jules	HUSSON w Fr
Judith	HOAG tv+		Jules	JACQUES ar,x Belg
Judith	IVEY tv+		Jules	JANIN w Fr
Judith	KATZ w Am		Jules	OPPERT h-orient Fr
Judith	KRANTZ w Am		Jules	PASCIN p Fr
Judith	LIGHT tv		Jules	PEAN md Fr
Judith	LOWRY tv		Jules	RENARD w Fr
Judith	MALINA		Jules	ROMAINS w.po Fr
Judith	ROSSNER w Am		Jules	SIMON ph,st,e Fr
Judith	WARNER w Am		Jules	VALLES j Fr
Judith	WRIGHT po,ct Aust		Jules	VERNE w Fr
Judson	LAIRE tv		Jules	VIOLLE sc,e Fr
Judson	SCOTT tv		Jules de	GONCOURT w Fr
Judson,	ARTHUR viol,cn Am		Jules-Elie	DELAUNAY p Fr
Judson,	E.Z.C. w Am		Juli	INKSTER g Am
Judson,	EDWARD w,pb Am.		Juli	REDING
Judy	ARONSON tv+		Julia	ADAMS tv+
Judy	BLUME w Am		Julia	ALVAREZ w Am
Judy	CARNE tv+		Julia	ARTHUR la Am
Judy	COLLINS mr,guit,s		Julia	BARR tv
Judy	DAVIS		Julia	BENJAMIN tv
Judy	FARRELL tv		Julia	BLAKE
Judy	GARLAND tv+		Julia	CAMERON fo Br
Judy	GEESON		Julia	CAMPBELL
Judy	JOHNSON tv		Julia	DORR w,po Am
Judy	JORDAN tv		Julia	DUFFY tv+
Judy	KAHAN tv		Julia	FOSTER
Judy	LANDERS tv+		Julia	GLOVER la Irish
Judy	LEDFORD tv		Julia	HOWE w,fe Am
Judy	LEWIS tv		Julia	MARLOWE la Am
Judy	LOPATIN w Am		Julia	MOORE po Am
Judy	LYNN tv		Julia	NEILSON la Br
Judy	MORRIS		Julia	NIXON-SOUL
Judy	NORTON-TAYLOR tv+		Julia	ORMOND tv+

Julia	ROBERTS	Juliette	LOW founder GSA Am
Julia	STIMSON nurse Am	Julio	ALEMAN
Julia	SWEENEY tv+	Julio	FRANCO b,bat'91
Julia,	RAUL	Julio	PENA
Julian	ADDERLY mj Am	Julio	ROCA ar,st Arg
Julian	BECK	Julissa	---
Julian	BYNG ar Br	Julius	AXELROD md Am
Julian	CARRILLO viol,c Mex	Julius	BOROS g Am
Julian	COPE mr-bass,s Wel	Julius	CAESAR st Ro
Julian	GLOVER	Julius	CAREY III tv
Julian	HUXLEY sc,w Br	Julius	CURTIUS st Ger
Julian	KLACZKO ct,w Pol	Julius	ELSTER sc Ger
Julian	LENNON mr-s,ws3 Br	Julius	ERVING bb+ hf
Julian	MARIAS PH,W sP	Julius	HANN weather,e Aus
Julian	RIVERO	Julius	HARRIS
Julian	SANDS	Julius	HAYNAU ar Aus
Julian	STEWARD an,e,w Am	Julius	La ROSA mj-s Am
Julian	SYMONS po,ct Br	Julius	MOSEN po,w Ger
Julian del CASAL po Cuban		Julius	NEPOS st-emp Ro
Julian,	ALVIN bbc hf	Julius	PLUCKER math,sc,e Ger
Julian,	JANET tv+	Julius	RAAB st Aus
Julian,	PERCY sc,e,id Am	Julius	RIETZ c,cn Ger
Julianne	MOORE	Julius	SPITTA e-music Ger
Julianne	MORRIS tv	Julius	VOGEL(Sir)st n.Zea
Julianne	PHILLIPS tv+	Julius von FICKER l,h,e Ger	
Julie	ADAMS(Julia)tv+	Julius von PAYER x,p Aus	
Julie	ANDREWS s,tv+ Br	Julius von SACHS sc,e Ger	
Julie	BISHOP tv+	Juliusz	SLOWACKI po,w Pol
Julie	BOVASSO	Julliard, AUGUSTUS e-music Am	
Julie	BROWN	Jump,	GORDON tv+
Julie	CARMEN tv+	Jun	CHONG
Julie	COBB tv	Jun	FUKADA d
Julie	CONDRA tv	Junayd,	SHAYKH r Persia
Julie	DEES tv	Junco,	TITO
Julie	DELPY	Jundef,	JAKE tv
Julie	EGE	June	ALLYSON tv+
Julie	GARWOOD w Am	June	BLAIR tv
Julie	HADDOCK tv	June	CARTER tv
Julie	HAGERTY	June	CASH tv+
Julie	HARRIS tv+	June	CLYDE
Julie	KAVNER tv+	June	COLLYER tv+
Julie	KRONE jockey Am	June	CRISTY s
Julie	LONDON s,tv+ Am	June	DAYTON tv
Julie	NEWMAR tv+	June	DUPREZ
Julie	PARRISH tv+	June	FORAY tv
Julie	SALAMON w Czech-Am	June	GABLE tv
Julie	SOMMARS tv+	June	GALE
Julie	STEVENS tv	June	GRAHAM ba,tv
Julie	STRAIN	June	HARDING tv
Julie	WALTERS	June	HAVER m,tv+
Julie	WARNER	June	HAVOC
Julien	BENDA ph,w Fr	June	MARLOWE
Julien	GREEN w Fr	June	POINTER s Am
Julien	TEMPLE d	June	TAYLOR ba,tv Am
Julien,	PIERRE su Fr	June	TRAVIS
Juliet	MILLS tv+	June	VALLI tv
Julieta	SERRANO	June	VINCENT
Juliette	ADAM w Fr	Juneau,	SOLOMON st Am
Juliette	BINOCHE	Jung,	CALVIN
Juliette	CUMMINS	Jung,	CARL ps Swi
Juliette	LEWIS tv+	Jung,	JOHANN w Ger

Junge,	JOACHIM ph,sc,e Ger	"K" NAME DESIGNATION CODES	
Junger	ERNST w,ph Ger	kbds - KEYBOARDS	
Junie	KEEGAN tv		
Junior	SAMPLES tv		
Junior	SEAU fb	"K's"	
Junior	WALKER mr-sax,s Am	K. Alex	MULLER sc Swi
Junior	ZIELINSKI tv	K.C.	BUTTS tv
Junipero	SERRA missionary Sp	K.C.	JONES bb hf
Junius	DODOENS sc Dut	K.C.	MARTEL tv
Junius	GALLIO st Roman	K.D.	LANG s-cnt Can
Junius	MORGAN banker,f Am	K.T.	OSLIN s+ Am
Junius Brutus BOOTH la Am		K.T.	STEVENS
Junker,	WILHELM x Ger	Kaalund,	HANS po Dan
Junkers,	HUGO id planes Ger	Kaare	KLINT ds-furnit Dan
Junod,	HENRI r,an,w Swi	Kaarlo	BERGBOM w Finn
Junot	DIAZ w Am	Kaat,	JIM b
Junot,	ANDOCHE ar Fr	Kabat-zinn, JON w Am	
Jurado,	KATY	Kabbible,	ISH mj,s,tv Am
Jurasik,	PETER tv+	Kabir	BEDI
Jurgen	OVENS p Dan	Kaczmarek, JANE tv+	
Jurgens,	CURT	Kadar,	JAN d
Jurgens,	DEANA	Kadar,	JANOS st Hung
Jurgens,	DICK mj-trump,cn Am	Kadeem	HARDISON tv+
Jurgenson, SONNY fb hf		Kael,	PAULINE ct-movies Am
Jussi	BJORLING tenor Swe	Kafka,	FRANZ w Aus
Just	JAECKIN d	Kafur,	ABU al- st Egypt
Justice,	DONALD p-q'80	Kagan,	ELAINE tv
Justice,	JAMES	Kagawa,	KYOKO
Justice,	KATHERINE	Kahan,	JUDY tv
Justin	DANA tv	Kahan,	STEVE tv+
Justin	HAYWARD s-blues Br	Kahane,	MEIR st,r Isr
Justin	HENRY	Kahlil	GIBRAN w,po Syria-Am
Justin	LOUIS tv+	Kahn,	CHAKA mr-s Am
Justin	M'CARTHy w,st Irish	Kahn,	GUS lyrics Am
Justin	PERKINS r Am	Kahn,	GUSTAVE po,w Fr
Justin	SCOTT w Am	Kahn,	LOUIS ac Am
Justin	TARR tv	Kahn,	MADELINE tv+
Justin	WHALIN tv+	Kahn,	OTTO banker,f Am
Justin	WINSOR h Am	Kahn,	SAMMY lyrics Am
Justine	BATEMAN tv+	Kahr,	GUSTAV von st Ger
Justinus	KERNER po,md Ger	Kai	BAKER
Justman,	SETH mr-keybds,s Am	Kai	EWANS mj-reeds,cn Dan
Justo	BARRIOS ar, st Guat	Kai	FISCHER
Justus	JONAS reform Ger	Kai	WINDING mj-tromb,c Am
Justus	MOSER h,l Ger	Kai	WULFF
Justus van EFFEN w Dut		Kai Manne SIEGBAHN sc Swe	
Justus von LIEBIG sc,e Ger		Kai,	CHIA
Juvarra,	FILIPPO ac It	Kai,	LANI tv
Juvenal	--- po Roman	Kaige,	CHEN d
Juwan	HOWARD bb	Kaiser,	GEORG w Ger
Juxon,	WILLIAM r,e Br	Kaiser,	HENRY id,f Am
Juzo	ITAMI d+	Kaitan,	ELIZABETH
		Kaj	MUNK w,r Dan
REMEMBER:		Kaj-Erik	ERIKSEN tv
		Kajanus,	ROBERT c Finn
All Pulitzer Prize Winners		Kaki	HUNTER
are Americans		Kal,	HARRIS tv
		Kalb,	JOHANN ar Ger
All Poets Laureate		Kaledin,	ALEKSEY ar Rus
in this book are British		Kaleena	KIFF tv
		Kalem,	TONI

Kalember,	PATRICIA tv+		Kaplan,	ALICE w Am
Kalff,	WILLEM p Dut		Kaplan,	DELMAR mj-bass Am
Kalidasa	--- w, po India		Kaplan,	GABE cm,tv+ Am
Kaline,	AL b hf		Kaplan,	JERRY w Am
Kalinin,	MIKHAIL st Rus		Kaplan,	JONATHAN d
Kalir,	ELEAZAR po Hebrew		Kaplan,	MARVIN tv+
Kallas,	AINO w Finn		Kaplan,	VIKTOR i Aus
Kallay,	MIKLOS st Hung		Kapoor,	SHASHI
Kallen,	KITTY s Am		Kapp,	FRIEDRICH st Ger
Kallio,	KYOSTI st Finn		Kaprisky,	VALERIE
Kallman,	DICK tv		Kapteyn,	JACOBUS astr Dut
Kalm,	PEHR sc Swe		Kapture,	MITZI tv+
Kalman	TISZA st Hung		Kara	GLOVER
Kalman von DARANYI st Hung			Karabatsos, RON tv+	
Kaltenborn, H.V. j-tv Am			Karajan,	HERBERT von cn Aus
Kalvos,	ANDREAS po Gr		Karamzin, NIKOLAY h Rus	
Kalwitz,	SETH c Ger		Karan,	DONNA ds Am
Kam	FONG tv		Kardos,	GENE mj,cn Am
Kam	KONG		Karel	BENDL c Cz
Kam	TONG tv		Karel	CAPEK w Cz
Kamala	LOPEZ		Karel	ERBEN po,w Cz
Kamar	REYES		Karel	HUSA c Am
Kamban,	GUDMUNDUR w Iceland		Karel	KRAMAR st Cz
Kamen,	MILT cm,tv		Karel	MACHA po,w Cz
Kamenev,	LEV st Rus		Karel	ZEMAN d
Kamerlingh, HEIKE n-p'13			Karel van MANDER p,w Dut	
Kami	COTLER tv+		Kareman,	FRED tv
Kamil,	MUSTAFA st Egypt		Karen	AKERS s-cabaret Am
Kaminski, DANA tv			Karen	ALLEN
Kamm,	KRIS tv		Karen	ARTHUR d
Kampfer.	ENGELBERT md Ger		Karen	AUSTIN tv+
Kampmann, STEVEN tv			Karen	BLACK tv+
Kanaly,	STEVE tv+		Karen	BLIXEN w Dan
Kanan,	SEAN tv+		Karen	CARLSON tv+
Kanarades,MELINA tv			Karen	CELLINI tv
Kandinsky,WASSILY p Rus			Karen	DINESEN w Dan
Kandler,	JOHANN su Ger		Karen	GRASSEL tv+
Kane	KOSUGI		Karen	HARTMAN tv
Kane	RICHMOND		Karen	HORNEY ps,e,w Am
Kane,	BABE		Karen	JENSEN tv+
Kane,	BIG DADDY m-rap,ws Am		Karen	KELLY tv
Kane,	CAROL tv+		Karen	KOPINS tv+
Kane,	ELISHA x,w Am		Karen	MACHON tv
Kane,	JOHN p Am		Karen	MISTAL tv+
Kane,	JOSEPH d		Karen	MORLEY
Kane,	PAUL p Can		Karen	MORROW tv
Kaneko,	NOBUO		Karen	PHILLIP tv
Kani,	JOHN		Karen	PURCILL tv
Kanin,	GARSON d		Karen	RUSSELL
Kankrin,	YEGOR st Ger		Karen	SHARPE tv
Kanner,	ALEXIS		Karen	STEELE
Kant,	IMMANUEL ph,e Ger		Karen	VERNE
Kantemir	ANTIOKH po Rus		Karen	WITTER
Kantner,	PAUL mr-guitar Am		Karen	YOUNG
Kantor,	MacKINLAY p-f'56		Karen,	JAMES tv+
Kantor,	RICHARD tv		Kari	LIZER tv+
Kantorovich, LEONID n-e'75			Kari	WHITMAN
Kants,	IVAR		Kari	WUHRER
Kanui,	HANK tv		Karin	BOYE po Swe
Kapelos	JOHN		Karin	DOR
Kapitsa,	PYOTR n-p'78		Karin	ENKE sk E.Ger

Karin	MANI	Karl	SWENSON tv
Karin	SCHUBERT	Karl	VERNER philology Dan
Karin,	RITA	Karl	WREDE ar Ger
Karina,	ANNA	Karl	ZIEGLER sc,e Ger
Kario	SALEM tv+	Karl	ZUMPT w Ger
Karis,	VASSILLI	Karl von	FRISCH sc Aus
Karl	ABEL c Ger	Karl von	HOLTEI la,w Ger
Karl	ALTEN ar Ger	Karl von	HUGEL x,sc Aus
Karl	ANDREE geog Ger	Karl von	MILTIZ r Ger
Karl	ARNIM st Ger	Karl von	PERFALL c Ger
Karl	ASCHOFF md,e Ger	Karl von	PILOTY p Ger
Karl	BARTH r,e Swi	Karl von	STURGKH st Aus
Karl	BARTSCH ct,e Ger	Karl von	WEBER c Ger
Karl	BEGAS p Ger	Karl von	ZITTEL geol e Ger
Karl	BELOCH h,e Ger	Karl,	GEORGE bbc
Karl	BOHM cn Aus	Karl-Heinz	BOEHM
Karl	BOSCH sc Ger	Karla	MONTANA
Karl	BRAUN sc,e Ger	Karle,	JEROME n-c'85
Karl	COMPTON sc,e Am	Karlen,	BETTY tv
Karl	CORRENS sc,e Ger	Karlen,	JOHN tv+
Karl	CZERNY piano,c Aus	Karlfeldt,	ERIK po,n-l'31
Karl	DONITZ(Adm)navy Ger	Karloff,	BORIS tv+
Karl	GRAUN c Ger	Karlson,	PHIL d
Karl	GREEN mr-bass Br	Karman,	THEODOR von sc,eng
Karl	GUTZKOW w Ger	Karn,	RICHARD tv
Karl	HACKETT	Karnes,	ROBERT tv
Karl	HEFELE r,h,e Ger	Karns,	ROSCOE tv+
Karl	HELD tv	Karns,	TODD tv
Karl	HENCKE astr Ger	Karoline	PICHLER w Aus
Karl	HOFER p Ger	Karoly	HUSZAR j,st Hung
Karl	JANSKY eng Am	Karoly	MAKK d
Karl	JASPERS ps,ph Ger	Karoly,	KERENYI w,ph Hung
Karl	JATHO fly,id Ger	Karolyi,	MIHALY st Hung
Karl	KAUTSKY marxist,w Ger	Karon,	JAN w Am
Karl	KLICat,print-roto Ger	Karpov,	ANATOLY chess Rus
Karl	KNEBEL po Ger	Karr,	ALPHONSE j,w Fr
Karl	KORNER po,w Ger	Karr,	MARY w Am
Karl	KORTUM md,w Ger	Karras,	ALEX fb,tv+
Karl	KRAUS w,ct,po Ger	Karrer,	PAUL n-c'37
Karl	LASHLEY ps,e Am	Karron,	RICHARD tv
Karl	LUEGER st Aus	Karsavina,	TAMARA ba Br
Karl	MALDEN tv+	Karson,	ERIC d
Karl	MALONE bb	Kartini,	RADEN fe Java
Karl	MARX w,re,ph Ger	Karvelas,	ROBERT tv
Karl	MAUCH x Ger	Kary	MULLIS sc Am
Karl	MAY w Ger	Karyn	PARSONS tv
Karl	MEIXNER	Karyo,	TCHEKY
Karl	NAGELI sc,e Swi	Kasday,	DAVID tv
Karl	NAUMANN geol Ger	Kasem,	CASEY
Karl	PEARSON math,e Br	Kasey	ROGERS tv
Karl	POPPER ph,e Br	Kasi	LEMMONS
Karl	RADEK st Rus	Kasimir	BADENI st Aus
Karl	RAHNER r,e Ger	Kasimir	FAJANS sc,e Am
Karl	RAMLER po Ger	Kaspar	HAUSER foundling Ger
Karl	RENNER st Aus	Kasparov,	GARRY chess Rus
Karl	SEITZ st Aus	Kassak,	LAJOS w,po Hung
Karl	SHAPIRO po,ct,e Am	Kassebaum,	NANCY st Am
Karl	SIMROCK w,e Ger	Kassel,	ART mj,cn Am
Karl	STAUDT math,e Ger	Kassem,	ABDUL ar,st Iraq
Karl	STUDENT ar Nazi Ger	Kassie	WESLEY tv

Kassir,	JOHN tv	Kathleen	NOONE tv
Kastler,	ALFRED n-p'66	Kathleen	NORRIS w Am
Kastner,	DAPHNA	Kathleen	QUINLAN
Kastner,	JOHANN c Ger	Kathleen	RAINE po Br
Kastner,	PETER	Kathleen	TURNER
Kasznar,	KURT tv+	Kathleen	WIDDOES
Katarina	WITT sk Ger	Kathleen	YORK tv+
Katayev,	VALENTIN w Rus	Kathrin	LAUTNER
Katayev,	YEVGENY w Rus	Kathryn	BIGELOW d
Katch,	KURT	Kathryn	CARD tv
Kate	BUSH s,ws Br	Kathryn	GRAYSON
Kate	CAPSHAW	Kathryn	GRODY
Kate	CHOPIN w Am	Kathryn	HARROLD tv+
Kate	HANCOCK w Am	Kathryn	HAYS tv
Kate	HODGE	Kathryn	HOLCOMB tv+
Kate	JACKSON tv+	Kathryn	KINLEY tv
Kate	LYNCH	Kathryn	LAYNG tv
Kate	MILLETT fe Am	Kathryn	LUBRAN tv
Kate	MOSS mo Br	Kathryn	MULLER pupp,tv Am
Kate	MULGREW tv+	Kathryn	SCOTT
Kate	NcNEIL tv	Kathryn	WALKER
Kate	O'MARA tv+	Kathy	BAKER
Kate	PIERSON mr-organ,s Am	Kathy	BATES
Kate	REID tv+	Kathy	CANNON
Kate	SMITH s+ Am	Kathy	GARVER tv
Kate	SWEET tv	Kathy	IRELAND mo+ Am
Kate	VERNON tv+	Kathy	KINNEY tv
Kate	WIGGIN w,e Am	Kathy	LENNON s,tv Am
Kate	WINSLET	Kathy	McCULLEN tv
Katerndahl,	LUCETTE ba Am	Kathy	NAJIMY
Katey	SAGAL tv+	Kathy	NOLAN tv
Kath,	TERRY mr-guit Am	Kathy	SHOWER
Kathaleen	ELLIS tv	Kathy	LEDGE mr-s Am
Katharina	KLAFSKY sopr Hung	Kathy Lee	GIFFORD w,tv Am
Katharina	von BORA r Ger	Katie	COURIC tv
Katharine	BATES e,po Am	Katie	RICH tv
Katharine	CORNELL la Am	Katie	SWEET tv
Katharine	GRAHAM w Am	Katina	PAXINOU
Katharine	HEPBURN	Katkov,	MIKHAIL j,ed Rus
Katharine	ROSS tv+	Katon,	ROSANNE
Katharine	TYNAN po,w Irish	Katona,	JOZSEF l.w Hung
Katherine	CANNON tv+	Katsuhiko	SUSAKI
Katherine	DeMILLE	Katsulas,	ANDREAS
Katherine	HELMOND tv+	Katt Shea	RUBEN d+
Katherine	JUSTICE	Katt,	NICKY tv
Katherine	LANG tv	Katt,	WILLIAM tv+
Katherine	PORTER w Am	Katy	JURARDO
Katherine	STONE w Am	Katya	WYETH
Katherine	VICTOR	Katz,	AL mj,cn Am
Kathleen	BATTLE sopr Am	Katz,	BERNARD(Sir)n-m'70
Kathleen	BELLER tv+	Katz,	JUDITH w Am
Kathleen	BYRON	Katz,	OMRI tv+
Kathleen	COMEGYS tv	Katz,	STEVE mr-guit,s Am
Kathleen	CROWLEY tv+	Katzur,	YFTACH
Kathleen	FERRIER contralto Br	Kauffman,	JANET w Am
Kathleen	FREEMAN tv+	Kaufman,	ANDY tv+
Kathleen	GARRETT tv	Kaufman,	BEL w Am
Kathleen	KELLY	Kaufman,	CHRISTINE
Kathleen	KINMONT	Kaufman,	DENIS d Rus
Kathleen	LASKEY tv+	Kaufman,	GEORGE p-d'32'37,tv
Kathleen	LLOYD tv+	Kaukonen,	JORMA mr-guit Am

Kaun,	HUGO c Ger		Keanan,	STACI tv
Kaunitz,	WENZEL st Aus		Keane,	BIL cr Am
Kaupert,	GUSTAV su Ger		Keane,	JAMES tv
Kaurismaki,	AKI d		Keane,	KERRIE tv+
Kautsky,	KARL w-marxism Ger		Keane,	ROBERT
Kava,	CAROLINE		Keaney,	FRANK bbc hf
Kavafian,	ANI viol		Keanu	REEVES
Kaverin,	VENYAMIN w Rus		Kearns,	JOSEPH tv
Kavi	RAZ tv		Kearns,	SANDRA tv
Kavner,	JULIE tv+		Keating,	LARRY tv+
Kawabata,	YASUNARI n-l'68		Keaton,	BUSTER d+
Kawasaki,	GUY w Am		Keaton,	DIANE o-a'77
Kay	BOYLE w,po Am		Keaton,	MICHAEL
Kay	FRANCIS		Keats,	JOHN po Br
Kay	HERON mj,pop-s Br		Keats,	STEVEN
Kay	HUGHES		Keble,	JOHN r,po,e Br
Kay	KENDALL		Keck,	CHARLES su Am
Kay	KUTER tv		Kedrova,	LILA o-s'64
Kay	KYSER mj,tv+ Am		Keeble,	JON mr-drm Br
Kay	LENZ s, tv+		Keefe,	CORNELIUS
Kay	LEVIN w Am		Keefe,	TIMOTHY b hf
Kay	MEDFORD tv+		Keefer,	DON tv
Kay	SAGER		Keegan,	JUNIE tv
Kay	STARR mj-s Am		Keel,	HOWARD tv+
Kay	WALSH		Keeler,	DONALD tv
Kay,	DIANNE tv+		Keeler,	RUBY
Kay,	JODY		Keeler,	WM.(Wee Willie) b hf
Kay,	JOHN mr-guit,s Ger		Keely	SMITH s-pop Am
Kay,	MARY ELLEN		Keely,	JOHN fraud Am
Kayama,	YUZO		Keen,	GEOFFREY
Kaye	BALLARD cm,tv+ Am		Keen,	MALCOLM tv
Kaye	GIBBONS w Am		Keen,	NOAH tv
Kaye,	CAREN tv+		Keena	NOMKEENA tv
Kaye,	DANNY tv+		Keenan	WYNN tv+
Kaye,	LILA		Keenan Ivory WAYANS tv+	
Kaye,	NORA ba		Keenan,	BRIAN mr-drums Am
Kaye,	NORMAN		Keene	CURTIS tv+
Kaye,	SAMMY mj-clari,cn,tv		Keene,	CAROLYN w Am
Kaye,	STUBBY tv+		Keene,	LAURA la Am
Kaye-Smith,	EMILY w Br		Keene,	TOM
Kaylan,	HOWARD sax,s Am		Keenen,	MARY tv
Kayser,	ALLAN tv		Keener,	CATHERINE tv+
Kayser,	HEINRICH sc,e Ger		Keens,	MICHAEL tv
Kaz	GARAS		Keep,	STEPHEN tv
Kazakov,	YURY w Rus		Kees van	DONGEN p Dut
Kazan,	ELIA o-d'47'54,w+		Keeshan,	BOB tv
Kazan,	LAINIE tv+		Kefauver,	ESTES st Am
Kazankina,	TATYANA o-g'76'80		Kefford,	ACE mr-bass Br
Kazantzakis,	NIKOS w,po Gr		Keg	JOHNSON mj-tromb Am
Kazimieras BUGA linguist Lith			Kegan	PAUL pb,w Br
Kazimierz PULASKI noble Pol			Kehoe,	JACK
Kazin,	ALFRED w,ct Am		Kei	SATO
Kazuo	HASEGAWA		Keifer,	JOSEPH l,ar,st Am
Kazurinsky,	TIM tv+		Keiji	SADA
Kazys	BINKIS po Lith		Keiko	KISHI
Kazys	GRINIUS st Lith		Keillor,	GARRISON w Am
Keach,	JAMES		Keim,	BETTY LOU tv
Keach,	STACY tv+		Keir	DULLEA
Kean,	EDMUND la Br		Keir	HARDIE labor,st Br
Kean,	JANE tv		Keir,	ANDREW
Kean,	MARIE		Keiser,	REINHARD c Ger

Keita,	MODIBO st Mali	Kellogg,	FRANK B.n-x'29
Keitel,	HARVEY	Kellogg,	JOHN md,e,id Am
Keitel,	WILHELM ar-Nazi Ger	Kellogg,	JOHN tv+
Keith	ANDES tv+	Kellogg,	RAY tv
Keith	CARRADINE	Kellogg,	WILL id-cornflakes Am
Keith	COBB tv	Kelly	GARRETT tv
Keith	COOGAN	Kelly	Le BROCK
Keith	EMERSON mr-kbds Br	Kelly	LYNCH
Keith	GORDON	Kelly	McGILLIS
Keith	HOPWOOD mr-guit Br	Kelly	MINTER
Keith	JACKSON tv	Kelly	NEAL tv
Keith	JARRETT mj-piano Am	Kelly	PETERS tv
Keith	KNUDSEN mr-drm,s Am	Kelly	PRESTON
Keith	LARSEN tv+	Kelly	RENO
Keith	MICHELL	Kelly	WOLF
Keith	MOON	Kelly	WOOD tv
Keith	ROBERTS ba Am	Kelly,	ALVIN(Shpwrck)stnt Am
Keith	TAYLOR tv	Kelly,	BEBE tv
Keith	VITALI	Kelly,	BRIAN tv+
Keith,	ARTHUR(Sir)an,w Scot	Kelly,	CLAIRE
Keith,	BRIAN tv+	Kelly,	DAVID tv+
Keith,	BYRON tv	Kelly,	ELLSWORTH p,su Am
Keith,	DAVID tv+	Kelly,	EMMETT clown Am
Keith,	DONALD	Kelly,	GENE d, tv+
Keith,	IAN	Kelly,	GEO.(MchineGun)gangs
Keith,	LARRY tv	Kelly,	GEORGE b hf
Keith,	PENELOPE tv+	Kelly,	GEORGE p-d'26
Keith,	RICHARD tv	Kelly,	GRACE o-a'54,tv+
Keith,	ROBERT	Kelly,	HOWARD md,i,e Am
Keith,	RONALD tv	Kelly,	JACK tv+
Keith,	SHEILA	Kelly,	JIM
Keith,	WILLIAM p Am	Kelly,	JOE tv
Kelk,	JACKIE tv	Kelly,	KAREN tv
Kelker-Kelly, ROBERT tv		Kelly,	KATHLEEN
Kell,	GEORGE b hf	Kelly,	KEVIN w
Kellar,	HARRY magician Am	Kelly,	KING b hf
Kellaway	CECIL	Kelly,	LEROY fb hf
Kellen	WINSLOW fb hf	Kelly,	LEW
Keller,	GOTTFRIED w,po Swi	Kelly,	MARK mr-kbds Ir
Keller,	HELEN(blind)w Am	Kelly,	MOIRA
Keller,	HIRAM	Kelly,	NANCY
Keller,	MARTHE	Kelly,	NED outlaw Austra
Keller,	MARY tv+	Kelly,	PATSY
Keller,	NORA OKJA w Am	Kelly,	PAUL
Kellerman,FAYE w Am		Kelly,	PAULA s Am
Kellerman,JOHN w,fo Am		Kelly,	PAULA tv+
Kellerman,JONATHAN w Am		Kelly,	ROBERT po,ed Am
Kellerman,SALLY tv+		Kelly,	ROZ
Kelley,	BARRY tv+	Kelly,	WALT cr Am
Kelley,	DeFOREST tv+	Kelman,	RICKEY tv
Kelley,	FLORENCE fe Am	Kelsey	DOHRING tv
Kelley,	JOE b hf	Kelsey	GRAMMER tv
Kelley,	SHEILA tv+	Kelsey,	ANN tv
Kelley,	STEVE tv	Kelsey,	LINDA tv+
Kelli	MARONEY	Kelton,	PERT
Kelli	TAYLOR tv	Kemal	ATATURK st Turk
Kelli	WILLIAMS	Kemal,	NAMIK j,w Turk
Kellie	FLANAGAN tv	Kemble,	FRANCES(Fanny)la,w Br
Kellie	MARTIN tv+	Kemble,	GOUVERNEURid-arms,stAm
Kellin,	MIKE	Kemble,	JOHN la,mgr Br
Kelling,	GRAEME mr-guit Scot	Kemeny,	JOHN math,e,i Am

Kemmer,	ED tv	Kendal,	MADGE(Dame)la Br
Kemmerling,	WARREN	Kendall	HAYES w-cntry Am
Kemp	NALONE dictionary Am	Kendall,	AMOS ed,st Am
Kemp,	BRANDIS tv+	Kendall,	CY
Kemp,	GARY mr-guit Br	Kendall,	EDWARD n-m'50
Kemp,	HAL mj,cn Am	Kendall,	HENRY
Kemp,	JEREMY	Kendall,	HENRY n-p'90
Kemp,	MARTIN	Kendall,	KAY
Kemp,	MARTIN mr-bass Br	Kendall,	SUZY
Kemp,	MATTY	Kendall,	TONY
Kemp,	SHAWN bb	Kendalls,	The JEANNIE s(daugh)
Kemp,	WILLIAM cm,ba,la Br	Kendalls,	The ROYCE s(father)
Kempe,	MARGERY mystic Br	Kendis,	SONNY piano,tv
Kemper,	CHARLES	Kendrew,	JOHN(Sir)n-c'62
Kempson,	RACHEL	Kendricks,	EDDIE mr-s Br
Ken	ABRAHAM	Keneally,	THOMAS w Aust
Ken	ANNAKIN d	Kenelm	DIGBY(Sir)w,navy
Ken	AULETTA j,w Am	KenesawMountainLANDIS	b-comm hf
Ken	BERRY tv+	Kenichi	FUKUI sc Japan
Ken	BOYER b	Kenin,	ALEXA
Ken	BRETT b	Kenji	MISUMI d
Ken	CARSON tv	Kenji	SAHARA
Ken	CHRISTY tv	Kenne	DUNCAN
Ken	CURTIS tv+	Kennedy,	ADAM tv
Ken	DELO s Am	Kennedy,	ARTHUR
Ken	FOLLET w Am	Kennedy,	BURT d
Ken	FOREE	Kennedy,	DOUGLAS
Ken	FORSSI mr-guit Am	Kennedy,	EDGAR
Ken	GAMPU	Kennedy,	GEORGE o-s'67, tv+
Ken	GRIFFEY Jr b	Kennedy,	JAYNE
Ken	HENSLEY mr-kbds,s Br	Kennedy,	JOHN F. p-b'57 &
Ken	HOUSTON fb hf	Kennedy,	JOHN F.35th pres
Ken	HOWARD tv+	Kennedy,	JOHN F.Jr. ed Am
Ken	HUGHES d	Kennedy,	JOSEPH f,st Am
Ken	JAMES tv+	Kennedy,	LEON
Ken	JENKINS tv	Kennedy,	LINDSAY tv
Ken	JOHNSON mj,cn Br	Kennedy,	MARGARET w Br
Ken	KESEY w Am	Kennedy,	MATTHEW bbr hf
Ken	KWAPIS d	Kennedy,	MERNA
Ken	La RON tv	Kennedy,	MIMI tv
Ken	LANE tv	Kennedy,	ROBERT st Am
Ken	LERNER	Kennedy,	SARAH tv
Ken	LETNER tv	Kennedy,	TED ho-m'55
Ken	MAYER tv	Kennedy,	TED st Am
Ken	MAYNARD	Kennedy,	TOM
Ken	MURRAY tv+	Kennedy,	WILLIAM p-f'84
Ken	NORTON boxer,tv+ Am	Kennelly,	ARTHUR eng-elect,e Am
Ken	OGATA	Kenner,	HUGH w,ct Can
Ken	OLIN tv+	Kenneth	ARROW ec Am
Ken	ORLANDT tv	Kenneth	BRANAGH
Ken	OSMOND tv	Kenneth	BURKE ph,w Am
Ken	POGUE tv+	Kenneth	CLARK h-art Br
Ken	RUSSELL d	Kenneth	COLLEY
Ken	SAGOES tv+	Kenneth	CONNOR
Ken	STABLER fb	Kenneth	CRANHAM
Ken	STRONG fb hf	Kenneth	EDMONDS(Babyface)s Am
Ken	TOBEY tv	Kenneth	FEARING w Am
Ken	WAHL tv+	Kenneth	GILMAN tv+
Ken	WALSH	Kenneth	HARLAN
Ken,	THOMAS r,w-hymns Br	Kenneth	KIMMINS tv+
Kendal,	FELICITY		

Kenneth	KOCH po,w Am	Keren	WOODWARD mr-s Br
Kenneth	MARS tv+	Kerenyi,	KAROLY w,ph Hung
Kenneth	McMILLAN tv+	Keri	HOULIHIN tv
Kenneth	MORE	Kerll,	JOHANN organ,c Ger
Kenneth	NELSON tv	Kermit	MAYNARD
Kenneth	PATCHEN po,w Am	Kermode,	FRANK ct,h Br
Kenneth	ROBERTS w Am	Kern,	JEROME c Am
Kenneth	ROBESON w	Kerner,	JUSTINUS po,md Ger
Kenneth	SLESSOR po,j Austra	Kernis,	AARON JAY n-m'98
Kenneth	STARR l Am	Kerns,	JOANNA tv+
Kenneth	THOMSON	Kerns,	SANDRA tv
Kenneth	TOBEY	Kerouac,	JEAN(Jack)w,po Am
Kenneth	TYNAN ct-drama Br	Kerr,	ANITA s,cn,tv Am
Kenneth	WELSH	Kerr,	BILL
Kenneth	WHITE tv	Kerr,	DEBORAH
Kenneth	WILSON sc Am	Kerr,	E. KATHERINE
Kennibrew,	DEE DEE s Am	Kerr,	ELIZABETH tv
Kenny	BAKER	Kerr,	GRAHAM chef,tv,w Am
Kenny	CLARKE mj-drm Am	Kerr,	JEAN w,tv Am
Kenny	DAVIS tv	Kerr,	JIM mr-s Am
Kenny	JONES mr-drm Br	Kerr,	JOHN tv+
Kenny	LAO tv	Kerr,	JOHN(Sir)sc,e
Kenny	LOGGINS m-s.ws Am	Kerr,	MICHAEL l,st Am
Kenny	ROGERS s-cnt,tv+ Am	Kerr,	PHILLIP w
Kenny G.	--- mj-sax Am	Kerr,	WALTER w,ct-theatr Am
Kenny,	ELIZABETH nurse Aust	Kerri	GREEN
Kensett,	JOHN p Am	Kerridge	LINDA
Kensit,	PATSY	Kerrie	KEANE tv+
Kent	DIXON po Am	Kerrigan,	J.M.
Kent	HRBEK b	Kerrigan,	NANCY sk-figure Am
Kent	McCORD tv+	Kerry	LIVGREN mr-guit Am
Kent	PERKINS tv	Kerry	MACK
Kent	SMITH tv+	Kerry	MILLERICK tv
Kent	TAYLOR tv+	Kershaw,	WHITNEY tv
Kent	TEKULVE b	Kershner,	IRVIN d
Kent	WILLIAMS tv	Kertesz,	ANDRE fo Am
Kent,	BARBARA	Kerwin	MATHEWS
Kent,	CLARK fc	Kerwin,	BRIAN tv+
Kent,	ENID tv	Kerwin,	LANCE tv+
Kent,	JEAN	Kesey,	KEN w Am
Kent,	LILA tv	Keshia Knight	PULLIAM tv
Kent,	ROBERT	Kesner,	DICK viol, tv
Kent,	ROCKWELL p,illus Am	Kessel,	BARNEY mj-guit Am
Kent,	WILLLIAM p,ac Br	Kessel,	JOSEPH j,w Fr
Kenton,	ERLE d	Kessel,	MAURICE w Fr
Kenton,	SIMON ar-scout Am	Kessler,	QUIN
Kenton,	STAN mj,c,cn Am	Kessler,	RONALD w Am
Kenyatta,	JOMO st Kenya	Ketch,	JOHN(Jack)hangman Br
Kenyon,	COX p,w Am	Ketcham,	HANK cr Am
Kenyon,	GWEN	Ketchel,	STANLEY boxer Am
Kenyon,	JOHN phonetics,e Am	Ketchum,	DAVE tv
Kenyon,	SANDY tv	Kett,	ETTA fc
Kenzaburo	OE w Japan	Kettering,	CHARLES eng,i Am
Keogan,	GEORGE bbc hf	Ketti	FRINGS w Am
Keokuk	--- Am Indian Chief	Ketty	LESTER tv
Kepler,	JOHANNES astron Ger	Kevin	BACON
Keppard,	FREDDIE mj-trum,cn Am	Kevin	BLAIR tv+
Keppel,	ARNOLD ar Dut	Kevin	BROPHY tv+
Keppler,	JOSEPH cr Am	Kevin	CLASH tv
Ker,	WILLIAM e Br	Kevin	CONNOR d
Kercheval,	KEN tv+	Kevin	CONROY tv

Kevin	CONWAY	Kidde,	HARALD w Dan
Kevin	COSTNER	Kidder,	ALFRED arc,e Am
Kevin	CRONIN mr-s Am	Kidder,	MARGOT tv+
Kevin	DILLON	Kidder,	TRACY p-n'82
Kevin	DOBSON d,tv+	Kidman,	NICOLE
Kevin	DUNN tv+	Kidston,	ROBERT sc Br
Kevin	GARNETT bb	Kiedis,	ANTHONY mr-s,ws Am
Kevin	GODLEY mr-drm,s Br	Kiel	MARTIN tv+
Kevin	HAGEN tv	Kiel,	RICHARD
Kevin	HALL	Kielland,	ALEXANDER w Nor
Kevin	HOOKS tv+	Kiely,	BENEDICT w,ct Ir
Kevin	KELLY w	Kier,	UDO
Kevin	KLINE	Kieran	CULKIN
Kevin	McCARTHY tv+	Kieran,	JOHN j-sports Am
Kevin	MOONEY mr-bass Br	Kieran,	JOHN Jr. tv
Kevin	NEALON tv+	Kieran,	JOHN tv
Kevin	O'CONNOR	Kierkegaard,	SOREN ph Dan
Kevin	O'NEAL tv	Kiernan,	WALTER tv
Kevin	POLLAK tv+	Kieron	MOORE
Kevin	ROWLAND mr-guit,s Br	Kiersch,	FRITZ d
Kevin	SCHULTZ tv	Kiesler,	FREDERICK ac,su Am
Kevin	SPACEY tv+	Kiesling,	WALT fb hf
Kevin	TENNEY d	Kieu	CHINH
Kevin	TIGHE tv+	Kiff,	KALEENA tv
Key,	ASTLEY(Sir)navy	Kiger,	ROBBIE tv+
Key,	ELLEN fe,w Swe	Kiger,	SUSAN
Key,	FRANCIS SCOTT l,po Am	Kijai	DACHLAN ref Indo
Key,	GUY mj-trump Am	Kika	MARKHAM
Key,	VALDIMER politi-sc Am	Kiker,	DOUGLAS w,tv Am
Keye	LUKE tv+	Kiki	CUYLER b hf
Keyes,	EVELYN	Kiki	DEE s-pop Br
Keyes,	FRANCES w Am	Kiki	SHEPARD tv
Keyes,	JOE tv	Kilbourne,	WENDY tv
Keyloun,	MARK	Kilbride,	PERCY
Keymah,	T'KEYAH(Crystal)tv	Kilburn,	TERENCE
Keynes,	JOHN MAYNARD ec,w Br	Kiley,	RICHARD tv+
Keyser,	HENDRIK de ac,su Dut	Kilgallen,	DOROTHY tv
Keyserling,	HERMANN ph Estonia	Kilian,	VICTOR tv+
Khachaturian,	ARAM ILICH c Armenia	Killebrew,	HARMON b-mv'69 hf
Khambatta,	PERSIS	Killian,	JAMES e Am
Khan,	CHAKA mr-s Am	Kilmer,	JOYCE po Am
Khandi	ALEXANDER	Kilmer,	VAL
Khayyam,	OMAR astr,po Persia	Kilpatrick,	ERIC tv
Kheraskov,	MIKHAIL po Rus	Kilpatrick,	JAMES Jr. tv-j Am
Khlebnikov,	VELEMIR po Rus	Kilpatrick,	LINCOLN tv+
Khorana,	HAR n-m'68	Kilpatrick,	PATRICK
Khristo	BOTEV po Bulg	Kilpi,	VOLTER w Finn
Khrushchev,	NIKITA st Rus	Kilty,	JACK
Khrystyne	HAJE tv	Kim	CATRALL
Khuri,	BISHARA al- st Leban	Kim	COATES tv+
Khushwant	SINGH h,w India	Kim	COLES tv
Kia	GOODWIN tv	Kim	DARBY tv+
Kibbee,	GUY	Kim	DELANEY tv+
Kiberd,	JAMES tv	Kim	FIELDS tv
Kickham,	CHARLES w Ir	Kim	GREENE tv
Kid	NICHOLS b hf	Kim	GREIST
Kid	ORY mj-tromb Am	Kim	GYNGELL
Kid McCoy	SELBY boxer Am	Kim	HUNTER
Kidd,	JASON bb	Kim	MIYORI tv+
Kidd,	JOHNNY mr-s Br	Kim	NOVAK
Kidd,	WM.(Capt.)pirate Br	Kim	SLEDGE mr-s Am

Kim	STANLEY	King,	FRANK cr Am
Kim	THOMSON	King,	FREEMAN tv
Kim	TYLER tv	King,	HENRY d
Kim	WAYANS tv	King,	HENRY(d 1669)r,po Br
Kim	WILDE s,ws Br	King,	JOE
Kim	WINONA tv	King,	JOHN tv
Kim	ZIMMER tv	King,	JOHN"Dusty"
Kim,	ANDREW r Korea	King,	KIP tv
Kim,	ANDY s Am	King,	LARRY tv-host Am
Kim,	JOON	King,	LUISE s,tv Am
Kimball,	BOBBY mr-s Am	King,	MABEL tv+
Kimball,	BRUCE tv	King,	MARILYN s,tv Am
Kimberly	BECK tv+	King,	MARK mr-bass,s Br
Kimberly	FOSTER tv+	King,	MARTIN LU.Jr n-x'54 &
Kimberly	RUSSELL tv	King,	MARTIN LUTH.Jr r,w Am
Kimbrough,CHARLES tv+		King,	MAXINE s,tv Am
Kimiko	GELMAN tv	King,	PEE WEE s-cnt,c Am
Kimmel,	HUSBAND navy-Adm Am	King,	PEGGY tv
Kimmins,	KENNETH tv+	King,	PERRY tv+
Kimmy	ROBERTSON tv	King,	REGINA tv
Kimura,	ISAO	King,	REINA tv
Kin	HUBBARD w-humor Am	King,	RICHARD rancher AM-TX
Kin	SHRINER tv+	King,	RORI tv
Kin	VASSEY guit,tv Am	King,	RUFUS st Am
Kinard,	FRANK(Bruiser)fb hf	King,	SLIM m-cnt,cn,tv Am
Kinau,	JOHANN w Ger	King,	STEPHEN w Am
Kincaid,	ARON	King,	T.W. tv
Kincaid,	JAMAICA w W.Indies	King,	TONY tv+
Kincannon,KIT tv		King,	WALTER
Kinck,	HANS w Nor	King,	WAYNE tv
Kind,	RICHARD tv	King,	WILLIAM mr-trump Am
Kiner,	RALPH b hf	King,	WILLIAM st Can
King	AD-ROCK mrap Am	King,	WRIGHT tv+
King	CALDER tv	King,	YVONNE s,tv(King sis)
King	DONOVAN tv+	King,	ZALMAN d,tv+
King	KELLY b hf	Kingdom,	ROGER o-g'84'88
King	MOODY tv+	Kingfish	LONG(Huey)st Am
King	OLIVER mj-corn,cn Am	Kingi,	WIREMU chf.Maori,NZea
King	VIDOR d	Kingman,	DAVE b,hr'79'82
King Camp GILLETTE i,id Am		Kingo,	THOMAS po,r Dan
King Cole, NAT s Am		Kingsford,WALTER	
King Dick SEDDON st N.Zea		Kingsley	AMIS w Br
King Sisters,THE tv &		Kingsley	WOOD(Sir)st
King Sisters=ALYCE & YVONNE		Kingsley,	BEN o-a'82
King,	ALAN cm+ Am	Kingsley,	CHARLES(Rev.)r,w,poBr
King,	ALAN pr-tv Am	Kingsley,	DANITZA
King,	ALBERT mj-guit Am	Kingsley,	SIDNEY p-d'34
King,	ALDINE tv	Kingston Trio --- mj,s Am	
King,	ALEXANDER tv	Kingston,	MAXINE HONG w Am
King,	ALYCE s,tv(King sis)	Kingston,	NATALIE
King,	ANDREA	Kinkead,	MAEVE tv
King,	ATLAS	Kinkel,	GOTTFRIED po,h,e Ger
King,	B.B. mj-blues Am	Kinley,	KATHRYN tv
King,	BEN mr-s Am	Kinmont,	KATHLEEN
King,	BILLIE JEAN t,tv Am	Kinnear,	GREG tv
King,	CAROLE s Am	Kinnear,	ROY
King,	CHARLES(Blackie)	Kinnell,	GALWAY w,p-q'83
King,	CORETTA w Am	Kinney,	KATHY tv
King,	DAMU	Kinney,	TERRY
King,	DON pr-boxing Am	Kino,	EUSEBIO r Sp
King,	DONNA s,tv	Kinsella,	THOMAS po Irish

Kinsella,	WALTER tv		Kitt,	EARTHA s+ Am
Kinsey,	ALFRED sc,w-sex Am		Kittel,	RUDOLF e,h Ger
Kinskey,	LEONID tv+		Kittredge,	GEORGE e,w Am
Kinski,	KLAUS		Kitty	CLIVE la Br
Kinski,	NASSTASSIA		Kitty	HART tv+
Kinuyo	TANAKA		Kitty	KALLEN s Am
Kip	KING tv		Kitty	WELLS s-cnt Am
Kip	NIVEN		Kitty	WINN
Kipling,	RUDYARD w,po,n-l'07		Kitzmiller,	JOHN
Kipnis,	ALEXANDER basso Am		Kivi,	ALEKSIS w,po Finn
Kipp	MARCUS tv		Kix	BROOKS s-cnt Am
Kipphardt,	HEINAR md,w Ger		Kizer,	CAROLYN p-q'85
Kirby	FURLONG tv		Kjar,	JOAN tv
Kirby	GRANT tv+		Kjeld	ABELL w,ct Dan
Kirby	PUCKETT b		Kjellen,	JOHAN sc-politics Swe
Kirby,	BRUCE tv+		Kjerulf,	HALFDAN c Nor
Kirby,	BRUNO		Klabund	--- w,po Ger
Kirby,	DURWARD tv		Klaczko,	JULIAN ct,w Pol
Kirby,	JAY		Klafsky,	KATHARINA sopr Hung
Kirby,	MICHAEL		Klapka,	GYORGY ar,st Hung
Kirby,	RANDY tv		Klas	ARNOLDSON w,st Swe
Kirby,	ROLLIN cr Am		Klauber,	ADOLF pr-theater Am
Kirchenbauer,	BILL tv		Klaus	BARBIE st Nazi Ger
Kirchhoff,	GUSTAV sc Ger		Klaus	FUCHS sc,spy Ger
Kirchner,	ERNST p Ger		Klaus	GROTH w,po,e Ger
Kirchner,	LEON p-m'67		Klaus	KINSKI
Kirdorf,	EMIL id Ger		Klaus Maria	BRANDAUER
Kiri	PARAMORE		Klaus von	KLITZING sc W.Ger
Kiri	Te KENAWA(Dame)c NZea		Klaw,	MARC theater mgr Am
Kirk	CAMERON tv+		Kleban,	EDWARD p-d'76
Kirk	DOUGLAS		Klebs,	EDWIN sc,md,e Ger
Kirk	GIBSON b		Klecko,	JOE fb-d'81
Kirk	MORRIS		Klee,	PAUL p Swi
Kirk,	ALAN navy Am		Kleeb,	HELEN tv
Kirk,	ANDY mj-sax,cn Am		Kleiber,	ERICH cn Aus
Kirk,	NORMAN st N.Zea		Klein,	A.M. po Can
Kirk,	PHYLLIS tv+		Klein,	ANNE ds Am
Kirk,	TOMMY		Klein,	BERNHARD c Ger
Kirke,	SIMON mr-drm Welsh		Klein,	CALVIN ds Am
Kirkland,	SALLY		Klein,	CHARLES b-mv'32, hf
Kirkman,	TERRY mr-kbds,s Am		Klein,.	DANNY mr-bass Am
Kirkpatrick,	JEAN st Am		Klein,	LAWRENCE n-e'80
Kirkup,	JAMES w,po Br		Klein,	MELANIE ps,w Br
Kirkwood,	JAMES p-d'76		Klein,	ROBERT cm,tv+ Am
Kirov,	SERGEY st Rus		Klein-Rogge,	RUDOLF
Kirsopp	LAKE r,e,w Br		Kleinzahler,	AUGUST w Am
Kirsten	FLAGSTAD sopr Nor		Kleiser,	RANDAL d
Kirsten,	DOROTHY sopr Am		Kleist,	EWALD po,ar Ger
Kirstie	ALLEY tv+		Kleist,	HEINRICH von w Ger
Kirwan,	RICHARD sc Irish		Klem,	BILL bu hf
Kiser,	TERRY tv+		Klemm,	GUSTAV an Ger
Kishi,	KEIKO		Klemperer,	OTTO cn Ger
Kiss,	AUGUST su Ger		Klemperer,	WERNER tv
Kissinger,	CHARLES		Klenau,	PAUL c,cn Dan
Kissinger,	HENRY st,n-x'73		Klengel,	PAUL viol,c,e Ger
Kit	CARSONindian scout Am		Klensch,	ELSA w Am
Kit	GUARD		Klenze,	FRANZ ac Ger
Kit	TAYLOR		Klerk,	FREDERIK de n-x'93
Kitaen,	TAWNY tv+		Klerk,	MICHEL de ac Dut
Kitchell,	ALMA tv		Klic,	KARL at,print-rotoGer
Kitchen,	MICHAEL		Kliegl,	ANTON bus-lights Am

Klimov,	ELEM d		Knud	RASMUSSEN x Dan
Klimt,	GUSTAV p Aus		Knudsen,	GUNNAR id,st Nor
Kline,	FRANZ p Am		Knudsen,	KEITH mr-drm,s Am
Kline,	KEVIN o-s'88		Knudsen,	PEGGY
Kline,	RICHARD tv		Knudsen,	WILLIAM id-cars Am
Kling,	HEIDI		Knut	HAMSUN w Nor
Klinger,	FRIEDRICH w Ger		Knut	PEDERSON w Nor
Klinger,	MAX p,su Ger		Knut	WICKSELL ec,e Swe
Klint,	KAARE ds-furnit Dan		Knute	ROCKNE fbc
Klitzing,	KLAUS von n-p'85		Kobe	BRYANT bb
Kloos,	WILLEM po,ct Dut		Kobe,	GAIL tv
Klous,	PAT tv		Kober,	ARTHUR w Am
Kluck,	HEINRICH ar Ger		Kober,	JEFF tv+
Klug,	AARON n-c'82		Koch,	ED st Am
Klugman,	JACK tv+		Koch,	KENNETH po,w Am
Klyn,	VINCENT		Koch,	MARIANNE
Kmetko,	STEVE tv		Koch,	MARTIN w Swe
Knapp,	EVELYN		Koch,	ROBERT n-m'05
Knapp,	SEAMAN agriculture Am		Koch,	ROBERT tv
Knebel,	KARL po Ger		Kochanowski,	JAN po Pol
Knell,	DAVID tv		Kocher,	EMIL n-m'09
Kneller	GODFREY(Sir)p		Kock,	CHARLES de w Fr
Knepper,	ROB		Kodaly,	ZOLTAN c Hung
Knievel,	EVEL stunts Am		Koehler,	FREDERICK tv
Knigge,	ADOLF von w Ger		Koehler,	GEORGES n-m'84
Knight,	BOB bbc hf		Koelsch,	PATRICE
Knight,	CHRISTOPHER tv+		Koenig,	JOSH tv
Knight,	DON tv		Koenig,	WALTER tv+
Knight,	ESMOND		Koerber,	ERNEST von st Aus
Knight,	FUZZY		Koestler,	ARTHUR w Br
Knight,	G. WILSON ct,w Br		Koffka,	KURT ps Ger
Knight,	GLADYS mr-s Am		Kofoid,	CHARLES sc Am
Knight,	GOWIN sc Br		Kohler,	FRED Jr.
Knight,	JACK tv		Kohler,	JOSEF l,w Ger
Knight,	JONATHAN mr-s Am		Kohut,	ALEXANDER r-rabbi Am
Knight,	JORDAN mr-s Am		Kohn,	WALTER sc,e,n-c'98
Knight,	MERALD mr-s Am		Koji	YAKUSHO
Knight,	MICHAEL tv+		Kojima,	NAOYA ba Jap
Knight,	SANDRA		Kojiro	HONGO
Knight,	SARAH bus,w Am		Kok,	JAMES mj,cn Rom-Ger
Knight,	SHIRLEY		Kokoschka,	OSKAR p,w Aus
Knight,	TED tv+		Kolb,	CLARENCE tv+
Knight,	WYATT		Kolb,	MINA tv
Knights,	DAVE mr-bass Br		Kolbe,	HERMANN sc,e Ger
Knoblauch,	CHUCK b-gg'97		Kolcsey,	FERENC po,ct Hung
Knopf,	ADOLPH geol,e Am		Kold,	KRISTEN e Dan
Knopfler,	DAVID mr-guit Scot		Kolker,	HENRY
Knopfler,	MARK mr-guit,s Scot		Kollar,	JAN po,r Slovak
Knorr,	LUDWIG sc Ger		Kollek,	AMOS d+
Knotts,	DON tv+		Koller,	CARL md-eyes Am
Knowles,	AARIANA tv		Kollwitz,	KATHE at,su Ger
Knowles,	JOHN w Am		Koltsov,	ALEKSEY po Rus
Knowles,	PATRIC		Komack,	JAMES tv
Knox,	ALEXANDER		Komunyakaa,	YUSEF p-q'94
Knox,	BUDDY s-cnt,rk Am		Kondraty	RYLEYEV po,re Rus
Knox,	ELYSE		Konev,	IVAN ar Rus
Knox,	FRANK pb Am		Kong	PUN
Knox,	JOHN r,w Scot		Kong,	KAM
Knox,	PHILANDER l,st Am		Kong,	QUEEN
Knox,	TERENCE tv+		Konig,	FRIEDRICH i-print Ger
Knud	RAHBEK po,w,ct Dan		Konitz,	LEE mj-sax Am

Konopka, MAGDA	Kotter, GABE fc
Konrad BLOCH md Am	Kottke, LEO guit, m
Konrad EKHOF la,d Ger	Kotto, YAPHET
Konrad LORENZ sc,e,w Aus	Koufax, SANDY b-cy'63'5'6, &
Konrad WITZ p Ger	Koufax, SANDY b-mv'63 hf,tv
Konstantin FEDIN w Rus	Koussevitzky, SERGE cn Am
Konstantin PATS st Est	Kovacs, BELLA tv
Konstantin SIMINOV w,j,ed Rus	Kovacs, ERNIE tv+
Konstanty,JIM b-mv'50	Kovak, NANCY
Konwicki, TADEUSZ w,d Pol	Kove, MARTIN tv+
Koo STARK	Kozak, HARLEY
Koock, GUICH tv+	Kozeluh, LEOPOLD c Ger
Kook, ABRAHAM r-rabbi Pales	Kozlowski,LINDA
Kool Rock --- m-rap Am	Krabbe, JEROEN
Kooning, WILLEM de p Am	Krafft EHRICKE eng, sc Am
Koontz, DEAN w Am	Krafft-Ebing,RICHARD von md,ps
Koopmans, TJALLING n-e'75	Kraig CASSITY tv
Kopell, BERNIE tv+	Kral, JANKO po Slovak
Kopins, KAREN tv+	Kramar, KAREL st Cz
Kopisch, AUGUST p,po Ger	Kramer, BILLY mr-s Br
Kopit, ARTHUR w Am	Kramer, ERIC tv+
Koplik, HENRY md Am	Kramer, JOEY mr-drm Am
Kopp, HERMANN sc.e Ger	Kramer, STEPFANIE tv
Koppel, TED tv-j Am	Kramm, JOSEPH p-d'52
Koppen, WLADIMIR weather Ger	Krantz, JUDITH w Am
Koppers, WILHELM an,r,e Ger	Krapp, GEORGE e,w Am
Korbut, OLGA gy,3x o-g'72	Krasner, LEE p Am
Korda, ALEXANDER(Sir)pr	Krasny, PAUL d
Korda, ZOLTAN d	Kratochzil, TOM tv
Korf, MIA tv	Kraus, KARL w,po,j Aus
Korkes, JON	Krause, BRIAN
Korman, HARVEY tv+	Krause, MOOSE bb hf
Korn, ARTHUR sc Ger	Krause, PETER tv
Kornberg, ARTHUR n-m'59	Krauss, ALISON s-cnt Am
Kornbluth,CYRIL w-scifi Am	Krauss, WERNER
Korner, KARL po,w Ger	Kravits, LENNY s,ws Am
Korngold, ERICH m,c,cn Am	Krebs, EDWIN n-m'92
Kornilov, LAVR ar Rus	Krebs, HANS(Sir) n-m'53
Kornman, MARY	Kreisler, FRITZ viol,c Am
Korosec, ANTON r,st Slovak	Krenn, SHERRIE tv
Korsmo, CHARLIE	Kreppel, PAUL tv
Kortman, ROBERT(Bob)	Kreskin --- tv
Kortner FRITZ	Kress, SAMUEL mer Am
Kortum, KARL md,w Ger	Kretzer, MAX w Ger
Korty, JOHN d	Kreuger, IVARid,f,swindler Swe
Koscina, SYLVA	Kreutzmann, BILL Jr mr-drm Am
Kosinski, JERZY w Am	Kreuzer, ELIZABETH
Kosleck, MARTIN	Kreve, VINCAS w,po,e Lith
Koslo, PAUL tv+	Krieger, ROBBIE mr-guit Am
Kossel, ALBRECHT n-m'10	Krige, ALICE
Kossoff, PAUL mr-guit Br	Krimmer, WORTHAM tv
Kossuth, LAJOS st Hung	Krimpen, JAN van ds-type Dut
Kostelanetz, ANDRE cn Am	Kris KAMM tv
Kostis PALAMAS(Koster) po Gr	Krista MURPHY tv
Kosugi, KANE	Kristel, SYLVIA
Kosugi, SHO	Kristen DOHRING tv
Kosygin, ALEKSEY st Rus	Kristen KOLD e Dan
Kotcheff, TED d	Kristen, MARTA tv+
Koteas, ELIAS	Kristi SOMERS
Kotero, PATRICIA(Apollonia)tv	Kristian ALFONSO tv
Kotler, ODED	Kristin HARMON tv

Kristina	HOLLAND tv		Kunitz,	STANLEY ed,p-q'59
Kristine	DeBELL		Kuno	FISCHER ph Ger
Kristine	MILLER		Kuno	FRANCKE h Am
Kristofer	JANSON w Nor		Kuo-feng,	HUA(prs.China'76-80)
Kristofer	UPPDAL w Nor		Kupka,	FRANTISEKp,illus Cz
Kristoff	ST. JOHN tv		Kupper,	CHRISTIAN p Dut
Kristofferson, KRIS s-cnt+ Am			Kuprin,	ALEKSANDR w Rus
Kristy	McNICHOL tv+		Kura	SEDGWICK
Kristy	SWANSON tv+		Kurakin,	BORIS st Rus
Kroc,	RAY mer-hamburgers Am		Kuralt,	CHARLES w,tv-j Am
Kroeber,	ALFRED an,e,w Am		Kurbski,	ANDREY ar Rus
Kroeger,	BERRY		Kurland,	BOB bb hf
Kroeger,	GARY tv+		Kurosawa,	AKIRA d
Kroetsch, ROBERT w,po Can			Kurt	ALDER sc,e Ger
Krofft Puppets tv			Kurt	EISNER j,st Ger
Kroft,	STEVE tv		Kurt	FULLER
Krogh,	AUGUST sc-md Dan		Kurt	GODEL math,e Am
Krogh,	CHRISTIAN p Nor		Kurt	JOOSS ba Ger
Krogh,	SCHACK n-m'20		Kurt	KASZNAR tv+
Krone,	JULIE jockey Am		Kurt	KATCH
Kropotkin,PYOTR geog,x,ph Rus			Kurt	KOFFKA ps Ger
Krueger,	REGINA tv		Kurt	LEWIN ps,e Am
Kruger,	HARDY		Kurt	MASUR cn Ger-Am
Kruger,	OTTO tv+		Kurt	McKINNEY tv
Kruger,	PAUL(Oom)st S.Afr		Kurt	NEUMANN d
Kruif,	PAUL de sc,w Am		Kurt	PAUL tv
Krupa,	GENE mj-drm,c,tv+ Am		Kurt	RAAB
Krupa,	OLEK		Kurt	RUSSELL
Krupp,	FRIEDRICH id-iron Ger		Kurt	SUCKERT j,w It
Kruschen, JACK tv+			Kurt	WEILL c Am
Krutch,	JOSEPH ct,w,e Am		Kurth,	WALLY tv
Krylov,	IVAN w Rus		Kurtis	BLOW m-rap Am
Krystyna	JANDA		Kurts,	ALWYN
Ksawery	LUBECKI ar,st Rus		Kurtwood	SMITH tv+
Ku	FENG		Kurty,	LEE tv
Kubek,	TONY b,tv		Kurtz,	SWOOSIE tv+
Kubik,	ALEX		Kurtzman,	KATY tv+
Kubik,	GAIL p-m'52		Kurz,	HERMANN w Ger
Kublai Kahn --- Mongol emp			Kusakari,	TAMIYO
Kubo,	AKIRA		Kusatsu,	CLYDE tv+
Kubrick,	STANLEY d,pr,w Am		Kusch,	POLYKARP n-p'55
Kuda	BUX tv		Kushner,	TONY p-d'93
Kudrow,	LISA tv		Kusser,	JOHANN c,cn Hung
Kugler,	FRANZ h-art Ger		Kuter,	KAY tv
Kuhlau,	DANIEL c Dan		Kuyper,	ABRAHAM e,st Dur
Kuhlke,	NORMAN mr-drm Br		Kuznets,	SIMON n-e'71
Kuhn,	RICHARD n-c'38		Kuznetsov,ANATOLY w Rus	
Kuhn,	WALT p,illus Am		Kuzyk,	MIMI tv+
Kuhnau,	JOHANN organ,c Ger		Kvaran,	EINAR w,ed Iceland
Kulik,	BUZZ d		Kwan Hi	LIM tv
Kulik,	ILYA sk		Kwan,	NANCY
Kulky,	HENRY tv		Kwapis,	KEN d
Kulle,	JARL		Kwesi	BREW po Ghana
Kulp,	NANCY tv+		Kwouk,	BURT
Kulpe,	OSWALD ph,ps,w Ger		Kyd,	THOMAS w Br
Kumagai,	DENICE tv		Kyle	ROTE tv
Kumin,	MAXINE w,p-q'73		Kyle	SECOR
Kun,	BELA st,re Hung		Kylie	TENNANT w Austra
Kundera,	MILAN w Cz		Kyo,	MACHIKO
Kundla,	JOHN bbc hf		Kyoko	KAGAWA
Kundt,	AUGUST se,e Ger		Kyoko	MORI w Am

Kyosti	KALLIO st Finn		La Rue,	LASH
Kyra	SEDGWICK		La Rue,	PIERRE de c Belg
Kyser,	KAY mj,cn,tv+ Am		La Russa,	ADRIENNE tv
Kyte,	SYDNEY mj-viol,cn Br		La Salle,	ERIQ

La Salle, SIEUR(Rene-Rbt)de x Fr
La Torre, TONY tv

"L" NAME DESIGNATION CODE
1   LAWYER OR JURIST
la LEGITIMATE ACTOR, ACTRESS

La Tour du Pin,PATRICE de po Fr
La Tour,   GEORGES de p Fr
La Tour,   MAURICE de p Fr
La Verne   NOYES id,i Am

"L" NATIONALITY CODES
Lat   -   LATVIAN
Lith   -   LITHUANIAN

La Vorgna,ADAM tv
La Vryle   SPENCER w
La Wanda   PAGE tv+
Labadie,   JEAN de r,ref Fr

"L's"
L'Amour,   LOUIS w Am
L'Engle,   MADELEINE w-scifi Am
L'Hermite,FRANCOIS w Fr
L. Frank   BAUM j,w Am
L. Ron   HUBBARD w Am
L.L. Cool J --- m-rap Am
L.P.   HARTLEY w Br
L.Q.   JONES tv+
La Brie,   DONNA tv
La Bruyere, JEAN de w Fr
La Camara,CARLOS tv
La Cava,   GREGORY d
La Farge, JOHN r,w Am
La Farge, OLIVER p-f'30
La Fayette, MARIE de w Fr
La Flesche, SUSETTE reform Am
La Fleur, ART
La Follette, ROBERT Jr st Am
La Follette, ROBERT l,st Am
La Font,   BERNADETTE
La Fontaine, JEAN de po,w Fr
La Forge, LOUIS de ph Fr
La Grue,   TOM tv
La Guma,   ALEX w S.Afr
La Harpe, FREDERIC st Swi
La Hire,   LAURENT de p Fr
La Marche,MAURICE tv
La Mettrie, JULIEN de md,ph Fr
La Montaine, JOHN p-m'59
La Mothe, ANTOINEar,colonist Fr
La Motte, MARC adventurer Fr
La Noue,   FRANCOIS de ar Fr
La Paglia,ANTHONY
La Perouse, COMTE de x Fr
La Placa, ALISON tv
La Plante,LAURA
La Rive,   AUGUSTE sc Swi
La Roche, MARY tv+
La Roche, SOPHIE von w Ger
La Rocque,ROD
La Ron,   KEN tv
La Rosa,   JULIUS tv
La Rose,   SCOTT tv
La Rue,   EVA tv+
La Rue,   FRANK

Laban,   RUDOLF ba Hung
Labat,   JEAN r Fr
Labe,   LOUISE po Fr
LaBelle,   PATTI s-pop,soul+ Am
Labeo,   MARCUS l Ro
Labiche,   EUGENE w Fr
Labori,   FERNAND l Fr
Laborteaux, MATTHEW tv+
Laborteaux, PATRICK tv
Lacey   CRAVEN tv
Lacey,   RONALD
Lach,   ELMER ho-m'45
Lachaise, GASTON su Am
Lacher,   TAYLOR tv
Lack,   STEPHEN
Lackey,   MERCEDES w Am
Laclos,   PIERRE de w Fr
Lacombe,   LOUIS piano,c Fr
Lacoste,   RENE t
Lacroix,   FRANCOIS sc,e Fr
Lacy,   PETER ar Ir
Ladd,   ALAN
Ladd,   CHERYL tv+
Ladd,   DAVID
Ladd,   DIANE tv+
Ladd,   GEORGE ps,ph Am
Ladd,   MARGARET tv
Lady   REED
Lady Caroline LAMB w Br
Laer,   PIETER van p Dut
LaFaro,   SCOTT mj-bass Am
Lafayette,MARQUIS de st Fr
Lafcadio   HEARN j,w Am
Lafe   McKEE
Laffit   PINCAY Jr jockey Am
Lafitau,   JOSEPH r Fr
Lafit(t)e,JEAN pirate Fr
Lafleur,   GUY ho-m'77'8
Lafontaine, HENRI n-x'13
Laforgue, JULES po Fr
Lafosse,   CHARLES de p Fr
Lagerfeld,KARL ds
Lagerkvist, PAR n-l'51
Lagerlof, SELMA n-l'09
Lagrange, JOSEPH math,e,w Fr
Lagrange, VALERIE
LaGuma,   ALEX w S.Afr

Lahaye,	LOUIS de w,st Fr	Lambeau,	EARL(Curly)fbc Am
Lahr,	BERT la,cm+ Am	Lambert	HILLYER d
Lahti,	CHRISTINE	Lambert	SIMNEL imposter Br
Lai,	FRANCIS c Fr	Lambert	WILSON
Lai,	JOSEPH d	Lambert	WINKEL philology Dut
Laidlaw,	PATRICK(Sir)md	Lambert,	CHRISTOPHER
Laila	ROBINS tv+	Lambert,	CONSTANT c Br
Laine,	CLEO mj-s Am	Lambert,	DANIEL fat man Br
Laine,	DENNY mr-guit,s Br	Lambert,	GLORIA tv
Laine,	FRANKIE s,tv Am	Lambert,	JACK fb-d'83 hf
Laing,	ALEXANDER x Scot	Lambert,	JACK tv+
Laing,	R.D. ps,w Scot	Lambert,	WARD bbc hf
Lainie	KAZAN tv+	Lamberto	BAVA d
Laird	CREGAR	Lambie,	JOE tv
Laird,	MACGREGOR mer,x Scot	Lambton,	JOHN st Br
Laire,	JUDSON tv	Lame,	GABRIEL math,eng,e Fr
Lajoie,	NAPOLEON b hf	Lameth,	ALEXANDRE ar,st Fr
Lajos	DINNYES st Hung	Lamine	GUEYE st Sengal
Lajos	KASSAK w,po Hung	Lamm,	ROBERT mr-kbds,s Am
Lajos	KOSSUTH st Hung	Lamming,	GEORGE w Barbados
Lajos	LOCZY geol,e Hung	Lamont	JOHNSON d
Lajpat Rai,	LALA st,w Hindu	Lamont,	CHARLES d
Lakanal,	JOSEPH e,st Fr	Lamont,	JOHANN von astr Ger
Lake,	ARTHUR tv+	Lamonte	McLEMORE mr-s Am
Lake,	FLORENCE	Lamott,	ANNE w Am
Lake,	GARY p,at Am	LaMotta,	JAKE boxer
Lake,	GREG mr-bass,s Br	Lamotta,	JOHN tv+
Lake,	JANET tv	Lamour,	DOROTHY
Lake,	KIRSOPP r,e,w Br	Lampert,	ZOHRA tv+
Lake,	RICKI tv+	Lampkin,	CHARLES tv
Lake,	SIMON ac-naval Am	Lampley,	JIM tv
Lake,	VERONICA	Lampreave,	CHUS
Lakes,	GARY tenor Am	Lamy,	BERNARD r,e,w Fr
Lakin,	CHRISTINE tv	Lan,	TSE
Lal	SHASTRI st India	Lana	CANTRELL st Am
Lala	BROOKS s Am	Lana	CLARKSON
Lala	LAJPAT RAI st,w Hindu	Lana	TURNER tv+
Lalande,	JOSEPH de astron Fr	Lana	WOOD tv+
Lalique,	RENE id-crystal Fr	Lanbeau,	CURLY fb hf
Lally,	THOMAS de w Fr	Lancaster,	ALAN mr-bass Br
Lalo	SCHIFRIN mj Am	Lancaster,	BURT o-a'60,d,tv+
Lalo,	EDOUARD c Fr	Lancaster,	STUART
Lalor,	PETER eng,st Austra	Lance	ALWORTH fb hf
Lama,	DALAI n-x'89	Lance	FULLER
LaMar	HOYT b	Lance	GUEST tv+
Lamar	HUNT fb hf	Lance	ITO l(OJ trial)Am
Lamar,	JOSEPH l Am	Lance	KERWIN tv+
Lamar,	MIRABEAU st Am	Lance	LeGAULT tv+
Lamarck,	JEAN de sc,w Fr	Lancelot	HOGBEN sc,e,w Br
Lamarr,	HEDY	Lanchester,	ELSA tv+
Lamas,	FERNANDO	Lancie,	JOHN de tv+
Lamas,	LORENZO tv+	Lancisi,	GIOVANNI md,sc It
Lamb,	CAROLINE(Lady)w Br	Land,	EDWIN sc,i,id Am
Lamb,	CHARLES w Br	Landau,	DAVID
Lamb,	CLAUDIA tv	Landau,	EZEKIEL r-rabbi Pol
Lamb,	DEBRA	Landau,	LEV n-p'62
Lamb,	GIL	Landau,	MARK w Russ
Lamb,	HORACE(Sir)math,sc,e	Landau,	MARTIN o-s'94,tv+
Lamb,	WALLY w Am	Landen,	JOHN math Br
Lamb,	WILLIS n-p'55	Lander,	DAVID
Lambaud,	VALERY w Fr	Lander,	DIANE tv

Lander,	HARALD ba Dan	Lang,	k.d. s-cnt Can
Landers,	ANN j Am	Lang,	KATHERINE tv
Landers,	AUDREY tv+	Lang,	MATHESON la Br
Landers,	HARRY	Lang,	PERRY
Landers,	JUDY tv+	Lang,	RICHARD d
Landers,	LEW d	Lang,	SHIRLEY tv
Landesburg,	STEVE tv+	Lang,	STEPHEN tv+
Landham,	SONNY	Lang,	WALTER d
Landi,	ELISSA	Langan,	GLENN
Landi,	SAL	Langard,	JANET tv
Landis,	CAROLE	Langdon,	HARRY
Landis,	JESSIE	Langdon,	LILLIAN
Landis,	JOHN d	Langdon,	SUE ANE tv+
Landis,	KENESAW MTN. b comm hf	Lange,	ANTONI po,ct Pol
Lando,	BRIAN tv	Lange,	CHRISTIAN n-x'21
Landon,	ALFRED(Alf)st Am	Lange,	DOROTHEA fo Am
Landon,	LAURENE	Lange,	HOPE tv+
Landon,	LETITIA po,w Br	Lange,	JESSICA o-s'82,o-a'94
Landon,	MICHAEL tv+	Lange,	JIM tv
Landor,	WALTER po,ct,w Br	Lange,	TED tv+
Landowska,	WANDA harpsic Pol	Langedijk,	JACK tv+
Landru,	HENRI murderer Fr	Langella,	FRANK
Landry,	ART mj-clari,cn Am	Langen,	EUGEN eng Ger
Landry,	TOM fbc hf	Langenkamp,	HEATHER tv+
Landsberg,	DAVID tv+	Langer,	A.J. tv
Landsburg,	VALERIE tv	Langer,	FRANTISEK w,md Cz
Landseer,	EDWIN(Sir)p	Langer,	JIM fb hf
Landsteiner,	KARL n-m'30	Langer,	SUSANNE ph,e,w Am
Lane	BINKLEY tv	Langer,	WILLIAM h,e Am
Lane	SMITH tv+	Langford,	FRANCES
Lane Sisters	THE s Am	Langhorn	SCRUGGS tv
Lane,	ABBE s,tv+ Am	Langley,	SAMUEL astr,e Am
Lane,	ALFRED geol,e Am	Langlois,	LISA
Lane,	ALLAN(Rocky)	Langmuir,	IRVING n-c'32
Lane,	ALLEN(Sir)pb	Langrick,	MARGARET
Lane,	BURTON c Am	Langston	HUGHES w,po Am
Lane,	CHARLES tv+	Langston,	MURRAY tv+
Lane,	DIANE	Langton,	PAUL tv+
Lane,	DICK(NightTrain)fb hf	Langton,	STEPHEN r,st Br
Lane,	HUGH(Sir)art Ir	Langtry,	LILLIE la Br
Lane,	JOHN pb Br	Languet,	HUBERT st,w Fr
Lane,	KEN tv	Lani	KAI tv
Lane,	LOLA	Lani	O'GRADY tv
Lane,	LUPINO	Lanier,	BOB bb hf
Lane,	MIKE	Lanier,	MONIQUE tv
Lane,	NANCY tv	Lanier,	SIDNEY po,e Am
Lane,	NATHAN	Lanier,	SUSAN tv
Lane,	PRISCILLA mj-s+ Am	Lanier,	WILLIE fb hf
Lane,	RICHARD	Lanin,	JAY tv
Lane,	RONNIE mr-bass Br	Lankester,	EDWIN(Sir)sc,e
Lane,	ROSEMARY mj-s Am	Lankford,	KIM tv+
Lane,	SARA tv+	Lanman,	CHARLES h,e Am
Lane,	SCOTT tv	Lanner,	JOSEPH ba Aus
Lane-Block,	SHANA tv	Lannes,	JEAN ar Fr
Laneuville,	ERIC tv	Lannom,	LES tv
Lanfield,	SIDNEY d	Lanny	MOORE fb hf
Lanford	WILSON w Am	Lanny	REES tv
Lang,	ANDREW w Scot	Lanny	ROSS tv
Lang,	BOB mr-bass Br	Lanny	WADKINS g Am
Lang,	FRITZ d,pr Am	Lanoux,	VICTOR
Lang,	JOHN(Jack)st Aust	Lansbury,	ANGELA tv+

Lansel,	PEIDER po,w It	Larry	GATES
Lansford,	CARNEY b,bat'81	Larry	GELMAN tv+
Lansing,	JOI tv+	Larry	GRAHAM mr-guitar Am
Lansing,	ROBERT l,st Am	Larry	HAGMAN tv+
Lansing,	ROBERT tv+	Larry	HOLMES boxer Am
Lansing,	SHERRY bus-movies Am	Larry	HOOPER s,piano,tv Am
Lanson,	SNOOKY s,tv Am	Larry	HOVIS tv
Lanston	TOLBERT i Am	Larry	JENKINS(Flash)tv
Lantz,	WALTER cr Am	Larry	JOSHUA
Lanza,	MARIO s+ Am	Larry	KEATING tv+
Lanzi,	LUIGI arc It	Larry	KEITH tv
Lao She	--- w China	Larry	KING tv-host Am
Lao Tzu	--- ph China	Larry	LARSEN tv
Lao,	KENNY tv	Larry	Le SUEUR tv
Lapchick,	JOE bb,bbc hf	Larry	LITTLE fb hf
Lapine,	JAMES p-d'85	Larry	MacPHAIL b hf
Laplace,	PIERRE astr,st Fr	Larry	MANETTI tv+
Lapointe,	PAUL-MARIE po Can	Larry	MANN tv
Lapotaire,	JANE	Larry	MATHEWS tv
Lapread,	RONALD mr-bass Am	Larry	McMURTRY w Am
Lar	LUBOVITCH ba Am	Larry	McNEELEY tv
Lara	HARRIS	Larry	MILLER
Lara	MILLER tv	Larry	MULLEN Jr mr-drms Iris
Lara	PARKER	Larry	PARKS
Lara	PIPER tv	Larry	PEERCE d
Lara	WENDELL	Larry	PENNELL tv
Lara Flynn BOYLE		Larry	RAMOS Jr mr-guit,s Am
Laraine	DAY tv+	Larry	RIVERS p,su Am
Laraine	NEWMAN	Larry	SCOTT tv+
Laramie,	JACQUES Trapper Am	Larry	SIMMS
Larbaud,	VALERY w Fr	Larry	SMITH mr-drm Br
Larch,	JOHN tv+	Larry	STORCH tv+
Lardner,	RING w Am	Larry	TAYLOR mr-bass Am
Larenz	TATE tv+	Larry	WALKER b
Large,	DON s,cn,tv Am	Larry	WATSON w Am
Largent,	STEVE fb hf	Larry	WILCOX tv+
Largo	WOODRUFF	Larry	WILSON fb hf
Larivey,	PIERRE de w Fr	Lars	ESBJORN r, e Am
Lark	VOORHIES tv	Lars	HANSON
Larkin,	BARRY b-mv'95,gg'96	Lars	HIERTA j,st Swe
Larkin,	JOHN tv	Lars	ONSAGER sc Am
Larkin,	PHILIP po,w Br	Larsan,	JILL tv
Larkin,	SHEILA tv	Larsen,	DON b
Larmor,	JOSEPH(Sir)math,e	Larsen,	EDWARD J. p-h'98
Larosa,	JULIUS mj-s Am	Larsen,	ESPER sc-rocks Am
Larra,	MARIANO de j,w Sp	Larsen,	HAM
Larreta,	ENRIQUE w Arg	Larsen,	KEITH tv+
Larroquette, JOHN		Larsen,	LARRY tv
Larry	BIRD bb,bbc	Larsen,	WOLF tv
Larry	BLYDEN tv	Larson,	DARRELL tv+
Larry	BROWN fb	Larson,	DENNIS tv
Larry	CANSLER m,cn,tv	Larson,	GARY cr Am
Larry	COHEN d	Larson,	JACK tv+
Larry	CZONKA fb hf	Larson	JONATHAN p-d'96
Larry	DEAN s,tv Am	Larsson,	CARL p,etch Swe
Larry	DRAKE tv+	Lartet,	EDOUARD archeol Fr
Larry	DUNN mr-kbds Am	Larue,	FLORENCE mr-s Am
Larry	ELGART mj-sax Am	LaRue,	JACK tv+
Larry	ELIKANN d	Lary,	YALE fb hf
Larry	ELLIS tv	Las Casas,	BARTOLOME de h,r Sp
Larry	FINE	Lasch,	CHRISTOPHER h,e Am

Laser,	DIETER	Laura	GEMSER
Lash	La RUE	Laura	JACKSON po,ct,w Am
Lash,	JOSEPH p-b'72	Laura	JOHNSON tv+
Lashley	KARL ps,e Am	Laura	KEENE la Am
Lasker,	ALBERT ads,f Am	Laura	La PLANTE
Lasker,	EMANUEL chess Ger	Laura	LINNEY
Laskey,	KATHLEEN tv+	Laura	RIDING po,ct,w Am
Laski,	HAROLD w,ec,e Br	Laura	SADLER
Laski,	JAN r,st Pol	Laura	SISK
Lasky,	JESSE pr-films Am	Laura	SODE tv
Lasky,	ZANE tv	Laura	TATE
Laslo	BENEDEK d	Laura	WEBER tv
Laslo	PAPAS	Laura	WILDER w Am
Lasorda,	TOMMY bmg hf	Laura Hope CREWS la Am	
Lassander,DAGMAR		Laurance, MATTHEW tv+	
Lasse	HALLSTROM ds,d	Laure,	CAROLE
Lasse	VIREN 4x o-g'72'76	Laurel,	STAN cm+ Am
Lassell,	WILLIAM astron Br	Lauren	BACALL tv+
Lassen,	EDUARD c,cn Belg	Lauren	CHAPIN tv
Lasser,	LOUISE tv+	Lauren	GALE bb hf
Lassick,	SYDNEY	Lauren	HOLLY
Lasso,	ORLANDO di c Belg	Lauren	HUTTON
LaStarza,	ROLAND tv	Lauren	MALONEY tv
Lastman,	PIETER p Dut	Lauren	ROMAN tv
Laszlo	MOHOLY-HAGYp,ds,foHun	Lauren	TEWES tv+
Laszlo	SZABO	Lauren	TOM
Latelle,	LYLE	Lauren,	RALPH ds Am
Lateur,	FRANK w Belg	Lauren,	TAMMY tv
Latham,	JOHN birds,w Br	Laurence	BINYON po,h Br
Latham,	LOUISE	Laurence	EUSDEN po Br
Lathrop,	MARY r,w,po Am	Laurence	HADDON tv
Latifah,	QUEEN m-rap,tv Am	Laurence	HARVEY
Latimer,	HUGH r,ref Br	Laurence	HOUSMAN w,illus Br
Latini,	BRUNETTO w It	Laurence	OLIVIER(Sir)la+
Latorraca,NEY		Laurence	PAYNE
Latoya	JACKSON strip,porn Am	Laurence	STERNE w,r Br
Latrobe,	BENJAMIN ac,eng Am	Laurence	TISCH tv-exec Am
Lattanzi,	MATT	Laurence, ASHLEY	
Lattimore,RICHMOND po Am		Laurencin,MARIE p Fr	
Lattisaw,	STACY m-r&b Am	Laurene	LANDON
Lau,	WESLEY tv	Laurens	HAMMOND i Am
Laube,	HEINRICH w,d Ger	Laurens	Van der POST w S.Afr
Laud,	WILLIAM r Br	Laurens,	HENRY st Am
Lauder,	HARRY(Sir)s,ws Scot	Laurenson,JAMES	
Laudon,	GIDEON von ar Aus	Laurent	DELVAUX su Belg
Laue,	MAX von n-p'14	Laurent	MALET
Lauer,	ANDREW tv	Laurent	TERZIEFF tv+
Lauer,	MATT tv	Laurent de La HIRE p Fr	
Laughlin,	JOHN tv+	Laurent,	REMY
Laughlin,	ROBERT n-p'98	Laurent,	YVES SAINT ds Fr
Laughlin,	TOM	Laurette	LUEZ tv+
Laughton,	CHARLES la+,o-a'33	Laurette	SPANG tv
Lauher,	BOBBY tv	Lauri	HENDLER tv
Launer,	JOHN tv	Lauria,	DAN tv+
Lauper,	CYNDI s+ Am	Laurie	BURTON tv
Laura	BETTI	Laurie	ICHINO tv
Laura	CREWS la Am	Laurie	METCALF tv+
Laura	Del SOL	Laurie	ROSE
Laura	DERN	Laurie	SIBBALD tv
Laura	DEVON tv	Laurie	WALTERS tv+
Laura	FURMAN w Am	Laurie	WEEKS w Am

Laurie,	JOHN	Lawrence,	BRUNO
Laurie,	PIPER tv+	Lawrence,	CAROL e,w Am
Laurier,	WILFRID(Sir)st Can	Lawrence,	D.H. w,po Br
Lauryn	HILL	Lawrence,	DAVID j,pb Am
Lauter,	ED tv+	Lawrence,	DELPHI
Lauter,	HARRY tv+	Lawrence,	ELLIOT mj,cn,tv Am
Lautner,	KATHRIN	Lawrence,	ERNEST n-p'39
Lautrec,	ODET de ar Fr	Lawrence,	GERTRUDE la+ Br
Lautrec,	TOULOUSE p Fr	Lawrence,	GREG tv
Lauzun,	ANTONIN ar Fr	Lawrence,	JOEY tv+
Lavagetto,	COOKIE b	Lawrence,	MARC
Laval	NUGENT ar Irish	Lawrence,	MARTIN tv+
Laval,	CARL eng,id Swe	Lawrence,	MARY tv
Laval,	PIERRE st Fr	Lawrence,	MATTHEW tv
Lavan,	RENE tv	Lawrence,	PETER LEE
Lavater,	JOHANN po,w Swi	Lawrence,	ROSINA
Lavelli,	DANTE fb hf	Lawrence,	STEVE tv+
Laver,	ROD t Aust	Lawrence,	T.E.(of Arabia)sc,w Br
Laveran,	CHARLES n-m'07	Lawrence,	THOMAS(Sir) p
Lavern,	ROGER mr-kbds Br	Lawrence,	VICKI tv
Lavery,	JOHN(Sir)p	Lawrence-Hilton JACOBS tv
Lavi,	DALIAH	Laws,	BARRY tv
Lavin,	LINDA tv+	Laws,	SAM tv
Lavinia	FENTON la Br	Laws,	SAMUEL e Am
Lavisse,	ERNEST h,e Fr	Lawson,	ANDREW geol,e Am
Lavon,	PINHAS st Isr	Lawson,	DENIS
Lavr	KORNILOV ar Rus	Lawson,	HENRY w,po Aust
Lavrenty	BERIA st Rus	Lawson,	LEIGH
Lavrov,	PYOTR re,ed Rus	Lawson,	LEN fb
Law,	BONAR st, Br	Lawson,	LINDA tv
Law,	JOHN f Scot	Lawson,	RICHARD tv+
Law,	JOHN PHILLIP	Lawson,	VICTOR j,pb Am
Law,	PHYLLIDA	Lawson,	WILFRED
Law,	SALLIE nurse-CSA Am	Lawton,	FRANK
Law,	VERNON b-cy'60	Laxness,	HALLDOR po,n-l'55
Law,	WILLIAM w Br	Lay,	HORATIO st Br
Lawes,	HENRY c Br	Lay,	RODNEY tv
Lawes,	LEWIS prisons Am	Layamon	--- po Br
Lawford,	PETER tv+	Layard,	AUSTEN(Sir)sc,st
Lawler,	RAY w Aust	Laye,	CAMARA w Guinea
Lawless,	EMILY w Ir	Layne,	BOBBY fb hf
Lawless,	RICK tv	Layng,	KATHRYN tv
Lawlor,	JOHN tv	Layton,	GEORGE tv
Lawrence	BELL ds aircraft Am	Layton,	IRVING po Can
Lawrence	DANE	Lazare	CARNOT ar.st Fr
Lawrence	DURRELL w,po Br	Lazarendo,	NORMA
Lawrence	GRANT	Lazarev,	PYOTR md,sc Rus
Lawrence	JACKS r,ph,w Br	Lazaro	CHACON ar,st Guat
Lawrence	KLEIN ec Am	Lazarus	ERCKER sc Ger
Lawrence	MONOSON	Lazarus,	BILL tv
Lawrence	OATES x Br	Lazarus,	EMMA po,w Am
Lawrence	PAYTON mr-s Am	Lazear,	JESSE md Am
Lawrence	SANDERS w Am	Lazenby,	GEORGE tv+
Lawrence	SPIVAK tv-j Am	Lazzeri,	TONY b hf
Lawrence	TAYLOR fb	Le	CORBUSIER ac,p,su Swi
Lawrence	TIBBETT barit Am	Le	TARI tv
Lawrence	TIERNEY	Le Beauf,	SABRINA tv
Lawrence	WELK m,cn,tv Am	Le Bel,	JOSEPH sc Fr
Lawrence,	BARBARA	Le Blanc,	CHRISTIAN tv
Lawrence,	BERKE tv	Le Blon,	JAKOB p,engr Ger
Lawrence,	BILL tv	Le Bon,	GUSTAVE soc Fr

Le Braz, ANATOLE w Fr	Lebaudy, PAUL id Fr
Le Brock, KELLY	Lebedev, SERGEY sc,e Rus
Le Brun, CHARLES p Fr	Leblanc, MAURICE w Fr
Le Carre, JOHN w Br	Leboeuf, EDMOND ar,st Fr
Le Duc Tho --- n-x'73	Lebon, SIMON mr-s Br
Le Fanu, J.S. w Ir	Lebrun, ALBERT st,eng Fr
Le Fanu, SHERIDAN w Ir	Lecavele, ROLAND w Fr
Le Fort, GERTRUD von w Ger	Lech WALESA st Pol
Le Guin, URSULA w-scifi Am	Leck, BARTH p Dut
Le Maire, JAKOB x Dut	Lecky, WILLIAM h Ir
Le May, JOHN tv+	Leclair, JEAN violin,c Fr
Le Moyne, FRANCOIS p Fr	LeClerc, GINETTE
Le Nain, ANTOINE p Fr	Lecocq, ALEXANDRE c Fr
Le Pew, PEPE fc	Lecoste RENE t Am
Le Play, FREDERIC eng-mines Fr	Lecy GORANSON tv
Le Roy, GLORIA tv	Led Zeppelin --- mr Am
Le Sueur, EUSTACHE p Fr	Ledbetter,HUDDIE(L'dbelly)mj Am
Le Sueur, LARRY tv	Leder, PAUL d
Le Vau, LOUIS ac Fr	Lederberg,JOSHUA n-m'58
Lea MASSARI	Lederer, FRANCIS
Lea SALONGA s,tv+ Phil	Lederer, SUZANNE tv+
Lea, HOMER ar,w Am	Lederman, DAVID ROSS d
Lea, JIMMY mr-bass,viol Br	Lederman, LEON n-p'88
Lea, NICHOLAS tv	Ledford, JUDY tv
Leach, BERNARD id-pottery Br	Ledoux, CLAUDE ac Fr
Leach, BRITT	Ledoux, FERNAND
Leach, ROBIN tv	Leduc, VIOLETTE w Fr
Leach, ROSEMARY	Ledyard, JOHN x Am
Leachman, CLORIS o-s'71,tv+	Lee AAKER tv+
Leacock, PHILIP d	Lee BENTON tv
Leacock, STEPHENec,e,humor Can	Lee BERGERE tv
Leadbelly --- mj,s-blues Am	Lee BOWMAN tv+
Leadon, BERNIE mr-guitar,s Am	Lee BRYANT tv
Leah PINSENT	Lee CALHOUN o-g'60
Leah RABIN(Y,s wife)Isrel	Lee CURRERI tv
Leah RAY	Lee De FOREST i Am
Leahy, WILLIAM navy,st Am	Lee DODD w Am
Leake WILLIAM antiquar,ar Br	Lee DORMAN mr-bass Am
Leakey, LOUIS an,w Br	Lee ELDER g Am
Leal, ANTONIO po Port	Lee FARR tv
Leaming, BARBARA bio,w Am	Lee FOGEL tv
Lean, DAVID(Sir)o-d'57	Lee GRANT tv+
Leandro ALEM st Arg	Lee HARRIS tv
Leandro de MORATIN w Sp	Lee HORSLEY tv
Leann HUNLEY tv	Lee IACOCCA id-cars,bio Am
LeAnn RIMES s-cnt Am	Lee KONITZ mj-sax Am
Lear, EDWARD p,po Br	Lee KRASNER p Am
Lear, FRANCES ed Am	Lee KURTY tv
Lear, NORMAN pr Am	Lee MAJORS tv+
Lear, TOBIAS st Am	Lee MARVIN tv+
Lear, WILLIAM id-planes Am	Lee McCAIN tv
Learned HAND l,w Am	Lee MILLER tv
Learned, MICHAEL tv+	Lee NORRIS tv
Leary, BRIANNE tv	Lee OSKAR mr-harmon Den
Leary, DENIS	Lee PATRICK tv+
Lease, MARY fe,e Am	Lee PHILIPS d
Lease, REX	Lee POWELL
Leatrice JOY	Lee PURCELL
Leaud, JEAN-PIERRE	Lee REMICK
Leavis, F.R. ct,ed,w Br	Lee RUSSEK tv
Leavitt, HENRIETTA astr Am	Lee SAVOLD boxer Am

Lee	SMITH b	Lee,	RUTA tv+
Lee	SMITH w Am	Lee,	SHERYL tv+
Lee	TRACY tv+	Lee,	SIDNEY(Sir)j,ed,w
Lee	TREVINO g Am	Lee,	SPIKE d+
Lee	Van ATTA	Lee,	STAN w,pr Am
Lee	Van CLEEF	Lee,	STEPHEN
Lee	VING	Lee,	TSUNG-DAO n-p'57
Lee	WEAVER tv	Lee,	YUAN TSEH n-c'86
Lee	WILKOF tv	Leech,	JOHN cr Br
Lee de	BROUX tv	Leeds,	ANDREA
Lee Harvey	OSWALDassassin-JFK Am	Leeds,	GARY m-drm Am
Lee J.	COBB	Leeds,	PETER tv
Lee Roy	SELMON fb hf	Leeds,	PHIL tv+
Lee,	ANG d	Leek,	TIIU tv
Lee,	ANGELA tv	Leemans,	TUFFY fb hf
Lee,	ANN(Mother)r-Shakrs Am	Leese,	HOWARD mr-kbds,guit Am
Lee,	ANNA tv+	Leeser,	ISAAC r-rabbi Am
Lee,	ARTHUR mr-guit,s Am	Leeuw,	GERARDUS van der e Dut
Lee,	BARBARA mr-s Am	Leeuwenhoek,	ANTONI van sc Dut
Lee,	BERNARD	Leeves,	JANE tv
Lee,	BRANDON	Leeway,	JOE mr-drums Br
Lee,	BRENDA mr-s Am	Leeza	GIBBONS tv
Lee,	BRUCE tv+	Lefty	GOMEZ b hf
Lee,	CANADA	Lefty	GROVE b hf
Lee,	CARL	Lefty	O'DOUL b
Lee,	CHERYLENE tv	Lefuel	HECTOR ac Fr
Lee,	CHRISTOPHER	LeGallienne,	EVA pr,d+ Am
Lee,	CONAN	Legare,	HUGH l,ed Am
Lee,	DENNIS po,ed,ct Can	LeGault,	LANCE tv+
Lee,	DeWITT	Leger	DIDOT i Fr
Lee,	DOROTHY	Leger,	ALEXIS st,po Fr
Lee,	DRAGON	Leger,	FERNAND p,at Fr
Lee,	ERIC	Legere,	PHOEBE
Lee,	ETTA	Legros,	ALPHONSE p,etch Br
Lee,	GEDDY mr-bass,s Can	LeGros,	JAMES
Lee,	GYPSY ROSE stripper+	Leguizamo,	JOHN
Lee,	HARPER p-f'61	Lehar,	FRANZ c,cn Hung
Lee,	HARPER w Am	Leher,	JIM tv
Lee,	HENRY(LtHorseHarry)ar	Lehman,	LILLIAN tv
Lee,	HWANG JANG	Lehman,	TRENT tv
Lee,	IVY public relat Am	Lehmann,	CARLA
Lee,	JAMES tv	Lehmann,	EDIE tv
Lee,	JASON	Lehmann,	JOHN ed,po Br
Lee,	JOANNA	Lehmann,	LILLI sopr Ger
Lee,	JOHNNY mr-s Am	Lehmann,	LOTTE sopr Am
Lee,	JOIE	Lehmann,	MICHAEL d
Lee,	LILA	Lehmann,	ORLA st Dan
Lee,	LORETTA mj-s Am	Lehmann,	ROSAMOND w Br
Lee,	LUANN tv	Lehn,	JEAN-MARIE n-c'87
Lee,	MANFRED w Am	Lehne,	FREDRIC tv+
Lee,	MARGARET	Lehr,	LEW cm,tv Am
Lee,	MARY ANN ba Am	Lei,	LYDIA tv
Lee,	MICHELE tv+	Leiber,	JERRY c Am
Lee,	PAMELA tv	Leibl,	WILHELM p Ger
Lee,	PATSY tv	Leibman,	RON tv+
Lee,	PEGGY s,tv Am	Leibniz,	GOTTFRIED math
Lee,	PINKY	Leibovitz,	ANNIE fo Am
Lee,	RIC mr-drm Br	Leif	GARRETT
Lee,	ROBERT E.ar,e CSA	Leif Eriksson	--- x Nor
Lee,	ROBERTA tv	Leifert,	DON
Lee,	ROWLAND d	Leigh	EDDINGS w Am

Leigh	FRENCH cm,tv Am	Len	BIRMAN
Leigh	HUNT j,w,po Br	Len	CARIOU
Leigh	LAWSON	Len	CELLA tv
Leigh	ORSI tv	Len	DAWSON fb hf
Leigh,	BARBARA	Len	DYKSTRA b
Leigh,	JANET	Len	FORD fb hf
Leigh,	JENNIFER JASON	Len	GOORIAN tv
Leigh,	MIKE d	Len	LAWSON fb
Leigh,	MITCH c Am	Len	LESSER
Leigh,	NELSON tv+	Lena	ASHWELL la Br
Leigh,	SUZANNA	Lena	HORNE s+ Am
Leigh,	VIVIEN o-a'39'51	Lena	NYMAN
Leigh-Hunt, RONALD tv		Lena	OLIN
Leighton, BERNIE m,cn,tv		Lena	STOLZE
Leighton, ISABELLE tv		Lenard,	MARK tv+
Leighton, LAURA tv		Lenard,	PHILIPP n-p'05
Leighton, MARGARET		Lenau,	NIKOLAUS po Aus
Leila	HYAMS	Lenglen,	SUZANNE t Fr
Leila	MARTIN la Am	Leni	RIEFENSTAHL d
Leilani	SARELLE	Lenin,	NIKOLAY = Vladimir
Leinsdorf,ERICH cn		Lenin,	VLADIMIR ILYICHst Rus
Leipnitz, HARALD		Lennep,	JACOB van w,po Dut
Leiston,	FREDDIE tv	Lennie	BAKER tv
Leisure,	DAVID tv	Lennon Sisters, THE s Am	
Leitch,	DONOVAN	Lennon,	DIANNE s,tv Am
Leith,	CHARLES geol Am	Lennon,	JANET s,tv Am
Leith,	LLOYD bbr hf	Lennon,	JOHN mr,c+
Leitzel,	LILLIAN trapeze Am	Lennon,	JULIAN mr-s,ws Br
Leivick,	HALPER po,w Am	Lennon,	KATHY s,tv Am
Lejeune,	JOHN marines Am	Lennon,	PEGGY s,tv Am
Lekain,	HENRI la Fr	Lennox,	ANNIE s,ws Scot
Leland	SMITH tv	Lenny	BARI tv
Leland,	CHARLES po Am	Lenny	BRUCE cm+ Am
Leland,	HENRY id-cars Am	Lenny	CLARKE tv
Lelia	GOLDONI	Lenny	DYKSTRA b
Lelio	SOZZINI r It	Lenny	HENRY
Leloir,	LUIS n-c'70	Lenny	KRAVITS s,ws Am
Lelouch,	CLAUDE d	Lenny	VonDOHLEN
Lely,	PETER(Sir) p	Lenny	WILKINS bb,bbc hf
Lelyveld, JOSEPH p-n'86		Lenny	WOLPE tv
Lem,	STANISLAW w-scifi Pol	Leno,	DAN cm,ba,s Br
Lema,	TONY g Am	Leno,	JAY cm,tv-host+ Am
Lemaitre, GEORGES sc,e Belg		Lenoir,	ETIENNE i Fr
Lemaitre, JULES w Fr		LeNoire,	ROSETTA tv
LeMat,	PAUL	Lenore	AUBERT
LeMay,	CURTIS(IrnPnts)fly Am	Lenore	ULRIC
Lemay,	LEON po,w Can	Lenore	ZANN
Lembeck,	HARVEY tv+	Lenormand,HENRI w Fr	
Lembeck,	HELAINE tv	Lenotre,	ANDRE ac-land Fr
Lembeck,	MICHAEL tv+	Lentin,	CHAY tv
Lemery,	NICOLAS sc,e,w Fr	Lenya,	LOTTE s,la+ Aus
LeMesurier, JOHN		Lenz,	FREDERICK(Rama)cult Am
Lemieux,	MARIO ho-m'88'93	Lenz,	JAKOB po,w Ger
Lemmon,	CHRIS tv+	Lenz,	KAY s,tv+
Lemmon,	JACK o-s'55o-a'73,tv+	Lenz,	PETER p,ac,su,r Ger
Lemmons,	KASI	Lenz,	RICHARD tv
Lemon,	BOB b hf	Lenz,	SIEGFRIED w Ger
Lemon,	MEADOWLARK bb	Lenzi,	UMBERTO d
Lemonnier,CAMILLE w Belg		Leo	BAECK r Ger
Lemot,	FRANCOIS su Fr	Leo	CARROLL tv+
Lemuel	SHAW l Am	Leo	DAFT eng Am

Leo	DELIBES c Fr	Leona	POWERS tv
Leo	DeLYON tv	Leonard	BACON po Am
Leo	ESAKI sc Japan	Leonard	COHEN s,po,ws Can
Leo	FONG	Leonard	FREY
Leo	FUCHS	Leonard	MALTIN ct-film Am
Leo	GENN	Leonard	MERRICK w Br
Leo	GETER tv	Leonard	NIMOY w,d,tv+ Am
Leo	GORCEY	Leonard	SACHS bbc hf
Leo	GORDON	Leonard	SANDEAU w Fr
Leo	KOTTKE guit Am	Leonard	SLATKIN cn Am
Leo	LYONS mr-bass Br	Leonard	SMITH tv
Leo	McCAREY d	Leonard	STONE tv
Leo	McKERN	Leonard	STRONG w,po Ir
Leo	PINSKER md Rus	Leonard	TROLAND ps,sc,i Am
Leo	ROBIN lyrics Am	Leonard	WARREN bari Am
Leo	ROSSI	Leonard	WOOD md,ar Am
Leo	ROSTEN w-humor Am	Leonard	WOOLF w Br
Leo	SAYER s,ws Br	Leonard	WOOLLEY(Sir)arc
Leo	SLEZAK tenor Cz	Leonard,	BENNY boxer Am
Leo	SOWERBY organ,e,c Am	Leonard,	BUCK b hf
Leo	SZILARD sc,e Am	Leonard,	ELMORE w Am
Leo	TOLSTOY w,ph Rus	Leonard,	HARLAN mj-sax,cn Am
Leo	WEINER c,e Hung	Leonard,	LU tv+
Leo	WIENER e Am	Leonard,	QUEENIE
Leo,	LEONARDO c It	Leonard,	RAY(Sugar)boxer Am
Leo,	MELISSA tv+	Leonard,	ROBERT
Leon	---	Leonard,	ROBERT d
Leon	ALBERTI w,ac,p It	Leonard,	SHELDON tv+
Leon	AMES tv+	Leonard,	WILLIAM po Am
Leon	BAKST p Rus	Leonardo	DiCAPRIO tv+
Leon	BAKST p Rus	Leonardo	LEO c It
Leon	BELASCO	Leonardo	VINCI c It
Leon	BLOY w,ct Fr	Leonardo da Vinci-p,su,ac,po It	
Leon	BLUM st Fr	Leone,	SERGIO d
Leon	BONNAT p Fr	Leonel	POWER c Br
Leon	CADORE b	Leonello	SPADA p It
Leon	CLADEL w Fr	Leonetti,	TOMMY tv
Leon	COOPER sc Am	Leong,	AL
Leon	DAMAS w.ct,st Guiana	Leonhard	EULER math Swi
Leon	DAUDET w Fr	Leonhard	FRANK w Ger
Leon	DAY b hf	Leoni,	FRANCO c It
Leon	DEHON r Fr	Leonid	KINSKEY tv+
Leon	DIERX po Fr	Leonid	LEONOV w Rus
Leon	EDEL bio Am	Leonid	UTESOV mj,cn Rus
Leon	ERROL	Leonid Ilyich BREZHNEV st Rus	
Leon	ICHASO d	Leonidas	POLK r,ar-CSA Am
Leon	JANNEY tv+	Leonide	MASSINE ba Rus
Leon	JOUHAUX labor,st Fr	Leonora	SPEYER po Am
Leon	LEMAY po,w Can	Leonov,	LEONID w Rus
Leon	LONTOC tv	Leontief,	WASSILY n-e'73
Leon	RIPPY	Leontyne	PRICE sopr Am
Leon	RUSSELL s-cnt,w Am	Leopardi,	GIACOMO po It
Leon	SANDERS fb	Leopold	AMERY j,st Br
Leon	SPINKS boxer Am	Leopold	AUER viol Hung
Leon	TROTSKY re,w Rus	Leopold	FALL c Aus
Leon	URIS w Am	Leopold	FIGL st Aus
Leon	WALRAS ed,e Fr	Leopold	HASNER ec,st,e Aus
Leon Isaac KENNEDY		Leopold	INFELD sc,e Pol
Leon,	LOLES	Leopold	JESSNER d,pr Ger
Leona	HELMSLEY f,id Am	Leopold	KOZELUH c Ger
Leona	MITCHELL soprano+	Leopold	MOZART viol,c Aus

Leopold	MYERS w Br	Leslie	CARON
Leopold	RUZICKA sc Swi	Leslie	CHEUNG
Leopold	SENGHOR po,st Senegal	Leslie	DEANE
Leopold	STAFF po,w Pol	Leslie	FENTON
Leopold	ZUNZ w Ger	Leslie	FIEDLER w,ct Am
Leopold von	BUCH geol Ger	Leslie	HOPE tv+
Leopold von	RANKE h,e Ger	Leslie	HOWARD la+ Br
Leopold,	ALDO forester Am	Leslie	McKEOWN mr-s Scot
Leopoldo	ALAS w,ct Sp	Leslie	MORRIS tv
Leopoldo	LUGONES po Arg	Leslie	NIELSON tv+
Leopoldo	TRIESTE	Leslie	PARRISH
Leora	DANA	Leslie	SPIER an,e Am
Leos	JANACEK c Czech	Leslie	STAHL tv-j Am
Leplat,	TED	Leslie	STEPHEN(Sir)w
Leppard,	DEF mr	Leslie	TOTH
Lerman,	APRIL tv	Leslie	UGGAMS s,tv+ Am
Lermontov,	MIKHAIL po,w Rus	Leslie	WHITE an,e,w Am
Lerner,	ALAN w,lyrics Am	Leslia	WINSTON tv
Lerner,	KEN	Leslie,	BETHEL tv
Lerner,	MICHAEL	Leslie,	ELIZABETH tv
LeRoi	JONES po Am	Leslie,	FRANK pb Am
Leroux,	GASTON w Fr	Leslie,	JOAN
Leroux,	XAVIER c Fr	Leslie,	NAN tv+
Leroy	GRUMMAN id-planes Am	Leslie,	WILLIAM tv
LeRoy	HOLMES m,cn,tv Am	Lesseos,	MIMI
Leroy	KELLY fb hf	Lesseps,	FERDINAND de st Fr
Leroy	MASON	Lesser,	LEN
Leroy	MAXIE mj-drm Am	Lessing,	DORIS w Br
Leroy	NEIMAN p Am	Lessing,	GOTTHOLD w,ct Ger
LeRoy,	MERVYN d	Lessy,	BEN tv+
LeRoy,	PHILLIPPE	Lester	FLATT s-cnt Am
Les	ASPIN st Am	Lester	GERMER sc Am
Les	BRAID mr-bass Br	Lester	HAYES fb
Les	BROWN Jr tv	Lester	PEARSON st Can
Les	BROWN mj,cn,tv+	Lester	PELTON i-turbine Am
Les	CRANE tv	Lester	YOUNG(Pres)mj,sax Am
Les	ELGART mj-trump,cn Am	Lester,	BRUCE
Les	GRAY mr-s Br	Lester,	BUDDY tv+
Les	LANNOM tv	Lester,	JERRY cm,tv Am
Les	MAGUIREmr-kbds,sax Br	Lester,	KETTY tv
Les	NEMES mr-bass Br	Lester,	MARK
Les	PAUL mj-guit Am	Lester,	RICHARD d
Lesage,	ALAIN w Fr	Lester,	TOM tv
Lescaze,	WILLIAM ac Am	Lethin,	LORI
Leschetizky,	THEODOR piano,c Pol	Leticia	ROMAN
Lescot,	ELIE st Haiti	Letitia	LANDON po,w Br
Lescoulie,	JACK tv	Letner,	KEN tv
Lese,	BENOZZO di p It	Letterman,	DAVID tv
Lesh,	PHIL mr-bass Am	Lettieri,	AL
LeShan,	EDA w,j Am	Leuba,	JAMES ps,e Am
Leskov,	NIKOLAY w Rus	Leung,	TONY
Lesley	BOONE tv	Leutze,	EMANUEL p Am
Lesley	GORE s Am	Lev	IVANOV ba Rus
Lesley	SELANDER d	Lev	KAMENEV st Rus
Lesley Ann	WARREN tv+	Lev	LANDAU sc Rus
Lesley-Anne	DOWN tv+	Lev	TOLSTOY w,pb Rus
Leslie	ASH	Levant,	OSCAR piano,c Am
Leslie	BANKS	LeVar	BURTON tv+
Leslie	BASSETT c Am	Levels,	CALVIN
Leslie	BEGA tv	Levene,	OSCAR tv
Leslie	BROOKS	Levene,	PHOEBUS sc Am

Levene,	SAM	Lewis	HINE fo Am
Levenson,	SAM tv	Lewis	LAWES prisons Am
Lever,	CHARLES w Ir	Lewis	Le VAU ac Fr
Leversee,	LORETTA tv	Lewis	MUMFORD ph,w Am
Levert,	EDDIE mr-s Am	Lewis	NAMIER(Sir)h,e
Levertov	DENISE po,w Am	Lewis	SAYRE md,e Am
Levesque,	RENE st Can	Lewis	SMITH
Levi	ESHKOL st Isr	Lewis	STADLEN tv
Levi	MORTON banker,st Am	Lewis	STONE
Levi	STRAUSS id-jeans Am	Lewis	TEAGUE d
Levi	STUBBS mr-s Am	Lewis	TERMAN ps,e,w Am
Levi,	ALAN d	Lewis	VanBERGEN
Levi,	CARLO md,p,w It	Lewis	WALLACE ar,w Am
Levi,	PRIMO w,po It	Lewis	WETZEL scout Am
Levi,	SYLVAIN h,e Fr	Lewis,	AL tv+
Levi,	YOEL cn Isr-Am	Lewis,	ALUN po Welsh
Levi-Montalcini, RITA n-m'86		Lewis,	ARTHUR(Sir)n-e'79
Levi-Strauss,CLAUDE an,w Fr		Lewis,	C.S. w,e Br
Levin,	CHARLES tv	Lewis,	CARL 3 o-g's'84'88
Levin,	HENRY d	Lewis,	CATHY tv
Levin,	IRA w Am	Lewis,	CHARLOTTE
Levin,	KAY w Am	Lewis,	CLEA tv+
Levin,	MEYER w,j Am	Lewis,	CLIVE w,e Br
Levine,	ANNA tv	Lewis,	D.B. WYNDHAM w,bio Br
Levine,	HENRY(HotLips)mj,cnAm	Lewis,	DAWNN tv
Levine,	IRVING R. tv-j Am	Lewis,	DIANA
Levine,	JERRY tv+	Lewis,	EDWARD n-m'95
Levine,	PHILLIP p-q'95	Lewis,	EMMANUEL tv
Levine,	ROBERT tv	Lewis,	FIONA
Levine,	TED tv+	Lewis,	FORREST tv+
Levinson,	BARRY o-d'88	Lewis,	GARY mr-drm,s Am
Levita,	ELIJAH w Jew	Lewis,	GEOFFREY tv+
Levitan,	DAVID tv	Lewis,	GEORGE tv
Levitch,	ASHLEE tv	Lewis,	HERSCHELL-GORDON d
Levni,	RESSAM p Turk	Lewis,	HUEY mr-s Am
Levon	HELM mr-drm,s+ Am	Lewis,	ISAAC ar,i Am
Levy,	EUGENE tv+	Lewis,	JENNY tv+
Levy,	MARV fbc	Lewis,	JERRY cm,d,tv+ Am
Levy,	URIAH navy Am	Lewis,	JERRY LEE mr,s,ws Am
Levy,	WEAVER tv	Lewis,	JOHN L. labor Am
Lew	AYRES tv+	Lewis,	JOHN mj-piano,c Am
Lew	GALLO tv	Lewis,	JUDY tv
Lew	KELLY	Lewis,	JULIETTE tv+
Lew	LANDERS d	Lewis,	LIGHTFIELD tv
Lew	LEHR cm,tv Am	Lewis,	MATTHEW w Br
Lew	MEEHAN	Lewis,	MEADE(Lux)mj-piano Am
Lew	PARKER tv	Lewis,	MEL mj-drm,c Am
Lew	STONE mj-piano,cn Br	Lewis,	MERIWETHER x Am
Lew	WALLACE ar,w Am	Lewis,	MINNABESS tv
Lewald,	FANNY w Ger	Lewis,	MITCHELL
Lewandowski, BOB tv		Lewis,	NANCY tv
Lewes,	GEORGE ph,ct Br	Lewis,	OSCAR an,w Am
Lewgoy,	JOSE	Lewis,	PHILL
Lewin,	KURT ps,e Am	Lewis,	RALPH
Lewis	ALLEN d	Lewis,	RAMSEY mj-piano
Lewis	BOSS astr Am	Lewis,	RICHARD tv+
Lewis	CARROLL w,math Br	Lewis,	ROBERT d
Lewis	CASS st Am	Lewis,	ROBERT tv-host Am
Lewis	COLLINS	Lewis,	RONALD
Lewis	GILBERT d	Lewis,	SAGAN tv
Lewis	HALLAM la Br	Lewis,	SHARI pupp Am

Lewis,	SINCLAIR n-l'30
Lewis,	SYLVIA tv
Lewis,	TED mj-clari,s,cn Am
Lewis,	TERRY pr-music Am
Lewis,	WANDA tv
Lewis,	WILLIAM tv
Lewis,	WYNDHAM w,p Br
Lex	BARKER
Ley,	ROBERT st-nazi Ger
Leyden,	BILL tv
Leydig,	FRANZ sc Ger
Leyner,	MARK w Am
Leysen,	JOHAN s+
Lezama Lima, JOSE po,w Cuba
Lhermitte,THIERRY
Lhote,	ANDRE p,w Fr
Li Ho	--- po China
Li Po	--- po China
Li Shang-yin --- po China
Li,	BRUCE
Li,	GONG
Lia	MATERA w Am
Liam	CUNDILL
Liam	NEESON
Liam	REDMOND
Liana	ORFEI
Liane	CURTIS
Liane	HANSEN radio-host Am
Libau,	ANDREAS md,sc,e Ger
Libbie	HYMAN sc,e,w Am
Libby,	WILLARD n-c'60
Libedinsky YURY w Rus
Liberace --- piano,c,tv Am
Liberace, WLADZUI-see Liberace
Libertini,RICHARD tv+
Liberty	BAILEY sc,e Am
Licht,	JEREMY tv+
Lichtenstein,ROY p Am
Licia	ALBANESE s It
Lick,	JAMES f,f Am
Liddy	CLARK
Liddy,	G. GORDON st,tv+ Am
Lidner,	BENGT po Swe
Lido,	BOB viol,tv Am
Lie,	JONAS w,po Nor
Lie,	SOPHUS math,e Nor
Lie,	TRYGVE st@UN Nor
Lieb,	ROBERT tv
Lieber,	FRANCIS politic-sc Am
Liebig,	JUSTUS von sc,e Ger
Lieh,	LO
Liem	WHATLEY
Lieven,	ALBERT
Lifar,	SERGE ba Fr
Lifeson,	ALEX mr-guitar Can
Lifford,	TINA tv+
Light Horse Harry LEE ar,st Am
Light,	JUDITH tv
Lightfield LEWIS tv
Lightfoot,GORDON s Am
Lightfoot,LEONARD tv

Lightman,	ALAN w Am
Lightnin HOPKINS mj-guit,s Am
Lightstone, MARILYN
Ligier	RICHIER su Fr
Ligne,	CHARLES ar Belg
Ligon	TOM
Ligorio,	PIRRO ac It
Lihann	JONES tv
Lihn,	ENRIQUE po,w Chile
Lil	DAGOVER
Lila	KAYE
Lila	KEDROVA
Lila	KENT tv
Lila	LEE
Lili	DARVAS
Lili	ST. CYR
Lili	TAYLOR
Lilia	PRADO
Lilia	SKALA
Liliana	CAVANI d
Liliencron, DETLEV von po Ger
Lilienthal, OTTO eng-aero Ger
Lilli	PALMER
Lillian	BRONSON tv+
Lillian	FARMER tv
Lillian	GISH la+ Am
Lillian	HELLMAN w Am
Lillian	LANGDON
Lillian	LEHMAN tv
Lillian	LEITZEL trapeze Am
Lillian	NORDICA soprano Am
Lillian	ROTH
Lillian	RUSSELL s,la Am
Lillian	SCHAAF tv
Lillian	SMITH w Am
Lillian	VERNON bus Am
Lillian	WALD nurse Am
Lillian Jackson BRAUN w Am
Lillie	LANGTRY la Br
Lillie,	BEATRICE(BEA)
Lillie,	FRANK sc,e Am
Lillo	BRANCATO
Lillo,	GEORGE w Br
Lilly	DACHE ds-hats Am
Lilly,	BOB fb hf
Lilo	PULVER(Liselotte)
Lily	BRAUN fe,j Ger
Lily	PONS sopr+ Am
Lily	TOMLIN tv+
Lily Ann	CAROL mj-s Am
Lilyan	TASHMAN
Lim,	KWAN HI tv
Limbaugh, RUSH radio Am
Lime,	HARRY fc
Lime,	YVONNE tv
Limon,	JOSE ba Am
Lin	McCARTHY tv+
Lin Yutang --- w China
Lin,	MAYA su Am
Lin,	TRACI
Lina	POLITO

Lina	RAYMOND	Lindsay	PRICE tv
Lina	WERTMULLER pr,d	Lindsay	WAGNER tv+
Lina	ROMAY	Lindsay,	DAVID(Sir)po,w Scot
Lina	SASTRI	Lindsay,	HOWARD p-d'46
Linares,	JOSE st Bol	Lindsay,	JACK po,w Aust
Lincoln	STEFFENS j Am	Lindsay,	MARGARET
Lincoln,	ABBEY mj-s+ Am	Lindsay,	MARK mr-sax,s Am
Lincoln,	ABRAHAM 16th pres	Lindsay,	NORMAN p,cr,w Aust
Lincoln,	ELMO	Lindsay,	VACHEL po Am
Lincoln,	MARY TODD wife-Abe	Lindsey,	GEORGE tv
Lind,	JENNY sopr Swe	Lindsey,	MORT m,cn,tv Am
Lind,	TRACI	Lindstrom,	FRED b hf
Linda	BLAIR	Lindstrom,	JON tv
Linda	CARLSON tv	Lindstrom,	PIA ct,tv
Linda	CRISTAL	Line,	HELGA
Linda	DANO tv	Ling,	CHIA
Linda	DARNELL	Ling,	MUNG tv
Linda	EVANS tv+	Ling-Feng,	SHANGKUAN
Linda	FOSTER tv	Link	LYMAN fb hf
Linda	GRAY tv+	Link,	EDWIN i,id-fly Am
Linda	HAYDEN	Link,	GEORGE i,id-fly Am
Linda	HAYES	Link,	MICHAEL tv
Linda	HELLER w Am	Linke,	PAUL tv
Linda	HOY tv	Linker,	AMY tv
Linda	HUNT	Linklater,	ERIC w Scot
Linda	KELSEY tv+	Linkletter,	ART tv+
Linda	LAVIN tv+	Links,	BO w Am
Linda	LAWSON tv	Linley,	THOMAS violin,c Br
Linda	MANZ	Linn	BOYD st Am
Linda	MARLOWE	Linn,	BAMBI tv
Linda	MILLER tv	Linn-Baker,	MARK tv+
Linda	PURL tv+	Linnaeus,	CAROLUS sc,w Swe
Linda	SCRUGGS tv	Linne,	CARL von sc,md,w Swe
Linda	THORSON tv	Linnea	QUIGLEY
Linda	WACHNER bus Am	Linney,	LAURA
Lindbergh,	ANNE MORROW. w,po Am	Lino	VENTURA
Lindbergh,	CHARLES A. p-b'54	Lins do Rego,	JOSE w Braz
Linde,	CARLeng,id-oxygen Ger	Linton,	RALPH an,e,w Am
Lindegren,	ERIK po Swe	Linus	PAULING sc Am
Linden	CHILES tv+	Linus	YALE i,id-locks Am
Linden,	ERIC	Linville,	LARRY tv+
Linden,	HAL tv+	Linwood	BOOMER
Linder,	CEC	Lion	SMITH mj-piano Am
Linder,	MAX	Lionel	ATWILL
Lindes,	HAL mr-guit Am	Lionel	GROULX h,e Can
Lindet,	JEAN st Fr	Lionel	HAMPTON mj,cn+ Am
Lindfors,	VIVECA	Lionel	JOHNSON po,ct Br
Lindgren,	ASTRID w Swe	Lionel	LUKIN id-coach Br
Lindine,	JACK tv	Lionel	RICHIE s,ws Am
Lindley	MURRAY l,mer,w Am	Lionel	ROYCE
Lindley,	AUDRA tv+	Lionel	STANDER tv+
Lindley,	JOHN sc,e Br	Lionel	WILSON tv
Lindo,	DELROY	Liotard,	JEAN p Swi
Lindo,	MARK w Dut	Liotard,	THERESE
Lindo,	OLGA	Liotta,	RAY
Lindros,	ERIC ho-m'95	Lipatti,	DINU piano,c
Lindsay	BLOOM tv+	Lipinski	EUGENE
Lindsay	CROUSE	Lipinski,	TARA sk,o-g'98
Lindsay	DUNCAN	Lipkin,	ISRAEL r-rabbi Lith
Lindsay	FROST tv+	Lipmann,	FRITZ n-m'53
Lindsay	KENNEDY tv	Lipot	FEJER math, e Hung

Lippi,	FILIPPINO p It		Lisle	WILSON tv
Lippi,	FILIPPO(Fra) p It		Lisle,	ALICE st Br
Lippi,	LORENZO po,p It		Lispector,	CLARICE w Braz
Lippmann,	GABRIEL n-p'08		List,	GEORG ec,w Am
Lippmann,	WALTER ed,w Am		List,	LULLY c Fr
Lipps,	THEODOR ph,e Ger		Lister,	CHEZ tv
Lips,	JOEST ph,e Belg		Lister,	JOSEPH md,e Br
Lipscomb,	DENNIS tv+		Lister,	TINY
Lipscomb,	WILLIAM Jr n-c'76		Liston,	CHARLES(Sonny)boxer Am
Lipsky,	LOUIS ed Am		Liszt,	FRANZ piano,c Hung
Lipton,	LYNN cm, tv		Lita	FORD mr-guit Br
Lipton,	MICHAEL tv		Lita	MILAN
Lipton,	PEGGY tv+		Litel,	JOHN tv+
Lipton,	ROBERT tv		Lithgow,	JOHN tv+
Lipton,	SIDNEY mj,cn Br		Litke,	FYODOR x,geog Rus
Lipton,	THOMAS(Sir)id,yachts		Little Eva --- s Am
Lisa	ALTHER w Am		Little Mo CONNOLLY t Am
Lisa	BANES tv+		Little Nell---
Lisa	BLOUNT		Little Richard --- mr Am
Lisa	BONET tv+		Little Sky, EDDIE
Lisa	BROWN tv		Little Stevie WRIGHT mr-s Br
Lisa	CANNING tv		Little Turtle --- Am Indian Chief
Lisa	CAPPS tv		Little Women-MEG,JO,BETH,AMY-fcs
Lisa	CORI tv		Little,	ARTHUR D.id,consultAm
Lisa	DANIELY tv		Little,	CLEAVON tv+
Lisa	DARR tv		Little,	DWIGHT d
Lisa	EICHHORN		Little,	JIMMY tv
Lisa	GASTONI		Little,	LARRY fb hf
Lisa	GAYE tv+		Little,	MICHELLE
Lisa	HARROW		Little,	RICH cm,tv+ Am
Lisa	HARTMAN tv+		Little,	TINY Jr piano,tv
Lisa	HOULE tv		Littlefield, LUCIEN tv+
Lisa	JAKUB		Litwack,	HARRY bbc, hf
Lisa	KUDROW tv		Liu,	HARRISON
Lisa	LONDON		Liu,	JOHN
Lisa	LORING tv		Liv	TYLER
Lisa	LU tv		Liv	ULLMANN
Lisa	NIEMI tv+		Lively,	JASON
Lisa	PELIKAN		Lively,	ROBIN tv+
Lisa	PELUSO tv		Livermore,MARY fe,ref Am
Lisa	PERSKY		Livesey,	ROGER
Lisa	RAGGIO tv		Livgren,	KERRY mr-guit Am
Lisa	RIEFFEL tv		Livingston, BARRY tv
Lisa	RINNA tv		Livingston, MICHELLE tv
Lisa	RYAN tv		Livingston, ROBERT(Bob)
Lisa	SEAGRAM tv		Livingston, STANLEY tv+
Lisa	SUTTON tv		Livingstone, DAVID r,x Scot
Lisa	TRUSEL tv		Livingstone, MARY tv
Lisa	VICE w Am		Livio	LORENZON
Lisa	WALTZ		Livoti,	JOE viol,tv Am
Lisa	ZANE		Livy	--- h Roman
Lisa,	ANNA tv		Liyong,	TABAN lO po,w,ct Ugan
Lisa,	MANUEL fur trade Am		Liz	FRASER
Lisboa,	ANTONIO su,ac Braz		Liz	PHAIR s-pop Am
Lise	CUTTER tv+		Liz	RENAY
Lise	DELAMARE		Liz	SAGAL tv
Lise	HILBOLDT		Liz	SMITH j-gossip+ Am
Lise	MEITNER sc,e Aus		Liz	TORRES tv+
Liselotte	PULVER		Liza	GOLM
Lisi,	JOE		Liza	MINNELLI
Lisi,	VIRNA		Liza	MORROW mj-s Am

Liza	PALMER tv	Locklear,	HEATHER tv+
Lizabeth	SCOTT	Locklin,	HANK s-cnt Am
Lizer,	KARI tv+	Locklyn,	LORYN
Lizette	REESE po Am	Lockwood,	BELVA l Am
Lizzie	BORDEN suspect Am	Lockwood,	GARY tv+
Lizzio,	ALBERT cn	Lockwood,	MARGARET
Ljubomir	BABIC po Yugo	Lockyer,	JOSEPH(Sir)astr,e
Ljudevit	GAJ w Croat	Locorriere,	DENNIS mr-s Am
Llewelyn,	DESMOND	Loczy,	LAJOS geol,e Hung
Llosa,	LUIS d	Loden,	BARBARA d,tv+
Lloyd	BACON d	Loder,	BERNARD l Dut
Lloyd	BENSTEN st Am	Loder,	JOHN
Lloyd	BERKNER sc eng Am	Lodge,	DAVID
Lloyd	BOCHNER tv+	Lodge,	HENRY CABOT st,w Am
Lloyd	BRIDGES tv+	Lodge,	JOHN
Lloyd	COLE mr-guit,s Br	Lodge,	JOHN mr-bass Br
Lloyd	DOBYNS tv	Lodge,	OLIVER(Sir)sc,e,w
Lloyd	GOUGH tv	Lodge,	THOMAS po,w Br
Lloyd	HAYNES tv	Lodovico	ARIOSTO po It
Lloyd	HUGHES	Lodovico	DOLCE w It
Lloyd	LEITH bbr hf	Lodovico da	CIGOLI p,ac It
Lloyd	NELSON	Loeb,	JACQUES sc,e Am
Lloyd	NOLAN tv+	Loeb,	JAMES f,m,f Am
Lloyd	PRICE mr,s Am	Loeb,	PHILIP tv
Lloyd	TEVIS bus,f Am	Loeffler,	KENNETH bbc hf
Lloyd	WANER b hf	Loening,	GROVER id-planes Am
Lloyd George,	DAVID st Br	Loerke,	OSKAR po Ger
Lloyd,	CHRISTOPHER tv+	Loesser,	FRANK p-d'62
Lloyd,	DORIS	Loew,	MARCUS pr-films Am
Lloyd,	EMILY	Loewe,	FREDERICK piano,c Am
Lloyd,	EMILY ANN tv	Loewe,	JOHANN c Ger
Lloyd,	FRANK o-d'33	Loewen,	JAMES w Am
Lloyd,	HAROLD cm,d+ Am	Loewi,	OTTO n-m'36
Lloyd,	HAROLD Jr.	Loewy,	RAYMOND id-design Am
Lloyd,	JEREMY tv	Loff,	JEANETTE
Lloyd,	JIMMY	Loffler,	FRIEDRICH sc,e Ger
Lloyd,	JOHN	Lofgren,	NILS m-guit,s,ws Am
Lloyd,	KATHLEEN tv+	Lofka	ILGOWSKI mj,cn Pol
Lloyd,	MARIE cm,s Br	Loft,	ARTHUR
Lloyd,	NORMAN	Loftin,	CAREY tv
Lloyd,	POP b hf	Lofting,	HUGH w,illus Br
Lloyd,	SUE	Logan	RAMSEY tv+
Llull,	RAMON po Sp	Logan,	BRAD tv
Llwyd,	MORGAN w Welsh	Logan,	JOHN po,ed,ct Am
Lo	LIEH	Logan,	JOSHUA p-d'50
Loammi	BALDWIN eng Am	Logan,	MARTHA tv
LoBianco,	TONY	Logan,	PHYLLIS
Loc,	TONE	Logan,	ROBERT F.
Locane,	AMY	Logan,	ROBERT tv
Lochary,	DAVID	Loggia,	ROBERT tv+
Locke,	ALAIN e,ct Am	Loggins,	KENNY m-s,ws Am
Locke,	JOHN mr-kbds Am	Logothetis,	DIMITRI d
Locke,	JOHN ph,w Br	Lohenstein,	DANIEL von w,po Ger
Locke,	RALPH tv	Lohr,	MARIE
Locke,	SONDRA	Loie	FULLER ba Am
Locke,	TAMMY tv	Lois	BRIDGE tv
Lockhart	ANNE tv+	Lois	BUTLER tv+
Lockhart	CALVIN	Lois	CHILES tv+
Lockhart,	GENE	Lois	COLLIER tv
Lockhart,	JUNE tv+	Lois	JANUARY
Lockjaw	DAVIS mj-sax Am	Lois	MAXWELL

Lois	MORAN tv		Long,	SHELLEY tv+
Lois	ROBERTS tv		Long,	STEPHEN ar,x Am
Lois	SMITH		Long,	WALTER
Lois	WILSON		Long,	WAYNE tv
Loisy,	ALFRED w,ph,r Fr		Longden,	JOHN tv+
Lol	CREME mr-guit,s Br		Longfellow, HENRY WADS. po,e Am
Lola	FALANA		Longhi,	PIETRO p It
Lola	HASKINS w Am		Longinus, CASSIUS ph Gr
Lola	LANE		Longley,	LUC bb
Lola	MONTEZ ba,w Am		Longmuir, DEREK mr-drm Scot
Loles	LEON		Longo,	TONY tv+
Lollobrigida,GINA tv+		Longstreth, EMILY
Lom,	HERBERT		Longworth, DAVID tv
Loman,	HAL tv		Loni	CHAPMAN
Loman,	WILLIE fc		Lonnbohm, ARMAS po Finn
Lomax,	JOHN w-folklore Am		Lonnen,	RAY
Lomax,	STAN tv		Lonnie	DONEGAN m-r&b,s Scot
Lomb,	HENRY id-optics Am		Lonnie	JORDAN mr-kbds,s Am
Lombard,	CAROLE		Lonnie	SCHORR tv
Lombard,	MICHAEL tv		Lonnie	TURNER mr-bass,s Am
Lombard,	PETER ph,w It		Lonnrot,	ELIAS w-folklore Finn
Lombardi,	ERNIE b-mv'38 hf		Lonow,	CLAUDIA tv
Lombardi,	VINCE fbc hf		Lonsdale, MICHAEL
Lombardo,	GUY mj,cn Am		Lontoc,	LEON tv
Lombroso,	CESARE md,ps,e It		Loo,	RICHARD
Lomer	GOUIN(Sir)st Can		Lookinland, MIKE tv
Lommel,	ULLI d+		Looney,	GEORGE w Am
Lomond,	BRITT tv		Looney,	PETER tv
Lon	CHANEY Jr. tv+		Loos,	ADOLPH ac Aus
Lon	CHANEY Sr.		Loos,	ANITA w
Lon	McCALLISTER		Looy,	JACOBUS van p Dut
Lon	NOL st Cambodia		Lopat,	EDDIE(Steady)b
Lona	ANDRE		Lopatin,	JUDY w Am
Lonborg,	DUTCH bbc hf		Lope de	AGUIRRE x Sp
Lonborg,	JIM b-cy'67		Lope de	RUEDA w Sp
London,	DIRK tv		Lope de	VEGA po,w Sp
London,	FRITZ sc,e Ger		Lopes,	FERNAO h Port
London,	JACK w Am		Lopez y Fuentes, GREGORIO w Mex
London,	JASON		Lopez,	AL b hf
London,	JEREMY tv		Lopez,	CARLOS st Para
London,	JULIE s,tv+ Am		Lopez,	JENNIFER
London,	LISA		Lopez,	KAMALA
London,	MEYER labor Am		Lopez,	LUIS po Colomb
London,	STEVE tv		Lopez,	MARCO tv
London,	TOM		Lopez,	MARGO
Lone	FLEMING		Lopez,	PERRY
Lone,	JOHN		Lopez,	SAL
Lonergan,	LEONORE tv		Lopez,	TRINI s+ Am
Lonergan,	LESTER Jr tv		Lopez,	VINCENT mj,cn.tv Am
Lonesome George GOBEL cm,tv+ Am		Lopez-Cobos, JESUS cn
Lonette	McKEE		Lopinto,	DORIAN tv
Long,	AVON tv		Loprieno,	JOHN tv
Long,	BILL m-cnt,cn,tv Am		Lor,	DENISE s,tv Am
Long,	GABRIELLE w Br		Lorado	TAFT su Am
Long,	HOWIE fb-d'85		Lorain,	SOPHIE tv
Long,	HUEY(Kingfish)st Am		Lorant	EOTVOS sc, e Hung
Long,	JODI		Lorca,	ISABEL
Long,	JOHN w Am		Lord	DUNSANY w,po Ir
Long,	LOTUS		Lord Alfred DOUGLAS po Br
Long,	NIA		Lord,	BOBBY tv
Long,	RICHARD tv+		Lord,	JACK tv+

Lord,	JON mr-kbds Br	Lorraine	MILLER
Lord,	MARJORIE tv+	Lorraine	PEARSON mr-s Br
Lordan,	BETH w Am	Lorre,	PETER
Lorde,	ATHENA tv	Lorrie	MOORE w Am
Lords,	TRACI	Lory	PATRICK tv
Lore	SEGAL po,w Am	Loryn	LOCKLYN
Lorea,	TONY	Lorys,	DIANA
Loren	DEAN	Losey,	JOSEPH d
Loren	EISELEY an,w,e Am	Loss,	JOE mj,pop,cn Br
Loren,	DONNA tv+	Lot,	FERDINAND h,e Fr
Loren,	SOPHIA o-a'61	Loti,	PIERRE w Fr
Loren,	TRAY	Lott,	FELICITY sopr Br
Lorena	VELASQUEZ	Lott,	RONNIE fb
Lorene	YARNELL tv	Lott,	TRENT st Am
Lorentz,	HENDRIK n-p'02	Lotte	LEHMANN sopr Am
Lorenz	HART lyrics Am	Lotte	LENYA s,la+ Aus
Lorenz	OKEN ph,natural Ger	Lotti,	ANTONIO c It
Lorenz,	KONRAD w,n-m'73	Lottimer,	EB
Lorenzo	BERNINI su,ac It	Lotto,	LORENZO p It
Lorenzo	COSTA p It	Lotus	LONG
Lorenzo	Da PONTE po It	Lotze,	RUDOLF ph,e Ger
Lorenzo	LAMAS tv+	Lou	ANTONIO d
Lorenzo	LIPPI po,p It	Lou	CASTEL
Lorenzo	LOTTO p It	Lou	CHRISTIE s,ws Am
Lorenzo	PEROSI r,c It	Lou	FRIZZEL tv
Lorenzo	SNOW r Am	Lou	GEHRIG b hf
Lorenzo	TONTI banker Fr	Lou	GOSSETT tv+
Lorenzo	VALLA w It	Lou	GRAMM mr-s Am
Lorenzo di CREDI p It		Lou	GROZA fb hf
Lorenzon, LIVIO		Lou	HOLTZ fbc
Loretta	DEVINE tv+	Lou	JACOBI tv+
Loretta	LEE mj-s Am	Lou	MYERS tv
Loretta	LYNN s-cnt Am	Lou	PHILLIPS
Loretta	SWIT(Hot Lips)tv+	Lou	PRANO mj-s Am
Loretta	YOUNG tv+	Lou	PROHUT tv
Lori	HALLIER	Lou	RAWLS s-r&b Am
Lori	LETHIN	Lou	REED mr,s,ws+ Am
Lori	MARTIN tv	Lou	WAGNER tv
Lori	NELSON	Lou	WILLS Jr tv
Lori	PETTY tv+	Lou,	ALEXANDER
Lori	SINGER tv+	Loubet,	EMILE st Fr
Lorianne	CROOK tv	Loudon,	DOROTHY mj,s Am
Lorimer,	GEORGE ed Am	Louella	PARSONS j-column Am
Lorin	DREYFUSS	Louganis,	GREG sw-diver Am
Lorin	MAAZEL cn Am	Loughlin,	LORI tv+
Loring,	ESTELLE s,tv Am	Loughnane,	LEE m-trump Am
Loring,	LISA tv	Louis	ADAMIC w Am
Loring,	LYNN tv+	Louis	ARAGON w Fr
Loring,	TEALA	Louis	BAUER(Dr.)tv
Lorinne	VOZOFF tv	Louis	BEGIN r,e Can
Loris,	HEINRICH po Swi	Louis	BERTIN j.ph Fr
Lormer,	JON tv	Louis	BINGER x Fr
Lorna	LUFT tv+	Louis	BLANC j,st,w Fr
Lorne	GREENE tv+	Louis	BLERIOT fly Fr
Lorne,	MARION tv+	Louis	BOILLY p Fr
Lorrain,	CLAUDE p Fr	Louis	BONALD ph,st Fr
Lorraine	BRACCO	Louis	BONARD navy Fr
Lorraine	De SELLE	Louis	BORNO l,st Haiti
Lorraine	GARY	Louis	BOTHA ar,st S.Afr
Lorraine	McINTOSH mr-s Scot	Louis	BRAILLE e-blind Fr
		Louis	BROGLIE sc Fr

Louis	BUADE ar Fr	Louis B.	MAYER pr-films Am
Louis	CALHERN	Louis de	La FORGE ph Fr
Louis	COUDER p Fr	Louis de	LAHAYE w,st Fr
Louis	DaPRON ba,tv	Louis,	JOE boxer Am
Louis	DAQUIN organ,c Fr	Louis,	JUSTIN tv+
Louis	DUREY c Fr	Louis,	MORRIS p Am
Louis	FISCHER w,j Am	Louis,	PIERRE po,w Fr
Louis	FUERTES illus Am	Louis-Dreyfus, JULIA tv+	
Louis	GODEY pb Am	Louis-Ferdinand CELINE w Fr	
Louis	GOLDING w,po Br	Louisa	MORITZ
Louis	GOSSETT(Lou)Jr. tv+	Louisa	NISBETT la Br
Louis	GUSS	Louisa May ALCOTT w Am	
Louis	HAYWARD tv+	Louise	BEAVERS tv+
Louis	HEMON w Fr	Louise	BOGAN po,ct Am
Louis	HEROLD c Fr	Louise	BROOKS
Louis	HEYDT	Louise	CURRIE
Louis	HORST piano,c,ba Am	Louise	DRESSER
Louis	IGNARRO md,e,n-m'98	Louise	ERDRICH w Am
Louis	JENKINS po Am	Louise	FAZENDA
Louis	JOLLIET x Fr	Louise	FITCH tv
Louis	JONES(Grandpa)tv	Louise	GLAUM
Louis	JORDAN mj,r&b,cn Am	Louise	GLUCK po Am
Louis	JOURDAN	Louise	GOLD pupp,tv Am
Louis	JOUVET la,d+ Fr	Louise	GUINEY po,w Am
Louis	KAHN ac Am	Louise	HALE
Louis	L'AMOUR w Am	Louise	HOMER contralto Am
Louis	LACOMBE piano,c Fr	Louise	HOVEN tv
Louis	Le VAU ac Fr	Louise	LABE po Fr
Louis	LEAKEY an,w Br	Louise	LASSER tv+
Louis	LIPSKY ed Am	Louise	LATHAM
Louis	LYAUTEY ar,st Fr	Louise	ROBEY tv
Louis	MALLE d	Louise	SOREL tv+
Louis	MALVY st, Fr	Louise	STANLEY
Louis	MOREAU p Fr	Louise,	ANITA tv+
Louis	NEEL sc Fr	Louise,	TINA tv+
Louis	NIZER l Am	Louw,	NICOLAAS po,w S.Afr
Louis	NYE cm, tv+	Louys,	PIERRE po,w Fr
Louis	PANICO mj-trump,cn Am	Love,	BESSIE
Louis	PASTEUR sc,e,md Fr	Love,	COURTNEY mr-s Am
Louis	PHAL boxer Senegal	Love,	HOUGH sc,e Br
Louis	PRIMA mj-trum,cn,c Am	Love,	LUCRETIA
Louis	QUINN tv+	Love,	MIKE mr-s Am
Louis	RANVIER md-sc Fr	Love,	MONTAGU
Louis	RENAULT id-cars Fr	Love,	SUZANNA
Louis	RENAULT l,e,st Fr	Love,	VICTOR
Louis	RIEL re Can	Lovecraft,H.P. w Am	
Louis	SEIGNER	Lovejoy,	ELIJAH r,abolition Am
Louis	SIMPSON po Am	Lovejoy,	FRANK tv+
Louis	SPOHR viol,c,cn Ger	Lovelace, RICHARD po Br	
Louis	SUCHET ar Fr	Lovelady, DAVE mr-drm Br	
Louis	THIERS st,h Fr	Loveless, PATTY s Am	
Louis	TIFFANY ds-jewelry Am	Lovell,	BERNARD(Sir)astr
Louis	TRIPP	Lovellette, CLYDE bb hf	
Louis	VANCE w Am	Lover,	SAMUEL w.ws Ir
Louis	VERJUS st Fr	Lovett,	DOROTHY
Louis	VIAUD navy,w Fr	Lovett,	LYLE s+ Am
Louis	VITET w,st Fr	Lovis	CORINTH p Ger
Louis	VIUTTON ds-luggage It	Lovitz,	JON tv+
Louis	WIRTH soc,e Am	Low,	DAVID(Sir)cr
Louis	WOLHEIM	Low,	JULIETTE found GSA Am
Louis	ZORICH tv+	Low,	SETH mer,st,e Am

Lowe,	ARTHUR	Lucan	--- po Roman
Lowe,	BERNIE tv	Lucas	ALAMAN h,st Mex
Lowe,	CHAD	Lucas	AYLLON x Sp
Lowe,	CHRIS mr-kbds Br	Lucas	CRANACH(Elder)p Ger
Lowe,	DOUGLAS o-g'24'28	Lucas,	CRAIG w Am
Lowe,	EDMUND tv+	Lucas,	E.V. w Br
Lowe,	FREDERICK c Am	Lucas,	FRANK w,ct,po Br
Lowe,	HUDSON(Sir)ar	Lucas,	GEORGE d
Lowe,	ROB	Lucas,	JERRY bb hf
Lowell	GILMORE	Lucas,	ROBERT Jr n-e'95
Lowell	SHERMAN d+	Lucas,	WILFRID
Lowell	THOMAS j,w Am	Lucchesi,	VINCENT tv
Lowell,	AMY p-q'26	Lucci,	SUSAN tv+
Lowell,	ANDREA tv	Luce,	CLARE BOOTHE w,ed Am
Lowell,	CAREY	Luce,	HENRY R. ed,pb Am
Lowell,	JAMES po,ct Am	Lucero,	ENRIQUE
Lowell,	PERCIVAL astron Am	Lucette	KATERNDAHL ba Am
Lowell,	ROBERT p-q'47	Lucey,	DOROTHY tv
Lowens,	CURT	Lucha	VILLA
Lowenstein, ROGER bio,w Am		Luchino	VISCONTI d
Lower,	GEOFFREY tv	Luchsinger, CHUCK tv	
Lowery,	ANDREW	Luchsinger, JACK tv	
Lowery,	ROBERT	Lucia	BOSE
Lowes,	JOHN e,w Am	Lucia	CHASE ba Am
Lowie,	ROBERT an,e Am	Lucia	VESTRIS la,s,pr Br
Lowry,	DICK d	Lucian	--- w Gr
Lowry,	JUDITH tv	Lucian	BLAGA po Rom
Lowry,	LYNN	Lucian	FREUD p Br
Lowry,	MALCOLM w Br	Lucianna	PALUZZI
Lowth,	ROBERT r,e Br	Luciano	PAVAROTTI tenor+ It
Loy,	MYRNA	Luciano,	JUDI tv
Loy,	TOMMIE trumpet	Lucie	ARNAZ tv+
Loyd,	SAMUEL puzzles Am	Lucien	GUITRY la Fr
Loyita	CHAPEL tv	Lucien	PRIVAL
Lu	LEONARD tv+	Lucien	SCOTT tv
Lu Ann	HASLAM tv	Lucile	GRAHN ba Dan
Lu Ann	SIMMS tv	Lucile	WATSON
Lu,	LISA tv	Lucille	BALL cm,tv+ Am
Luan	PETERS	Lucille	BENSON
Luana	ANDERS	Lucille	BREMER
Luana	WALTERS	Lucille	BROWNE
Luann	LEE tv	Lucille	REED s,tv Am
Luanna	PATTEN	Lucinda	HUBBARD tv
Lubbock,	JOHN(Sir)astr,math	Lucinda	JENNEY
Lubecki,	KSAWERY ar,st Rus	Lucine	AMARA sopr
Lubin,	ARTHUR d	Lucio	FULCI d
Lubin,	DAVID mer,agricult Am	Lucio,	CHIP
Lubitsch, ERNST d		Lucius	BALBUS st Ro
Lubke,	HEINRICH st Ger	Lucius	BEEBE j,w Am
Luboff,	NORMAN cn	Lucius	BESTIA st Ro
Lubovitch,LAR ba Am		Luckinbill, LAURENCE tv+	
Lubran,	KATHRYN tv	Lucking,	WILLIAM tv+
Lubran,	TIFFANY tv	Luckman,	SID fb hf
Luby,	S. ROY d	Lucretia	HALE w Am
Luc	BESSON d	Lucretia	LOVE
Luc	HOLSTE scholar Ger	Lucretia	MOTT fe Am
Luc	LONGLEY bb	Lucretius	--- po Ro
Luc	MERENDA	Lucrezia	BORI sopr It
Luca	MARENZIO c It	Lucy	BORYER tv
Luca	SAVELI st Roman	Lucy	DEAKINS
Luca della ROBBIA su It		Lucy	FLIPPIN tv

Lucy	STONE fe Am	Luis	LELOIR sc Arg
Lucy	WEBB tv	Luis	LLOSA d
Lud	GLUSKIN m,cn,tv Am	Luis	LOPEZ po Colomb
Lud(d),	NED rioter Br	Luis	MILAN m-vihuela,c Sp
Ludden,	ALLEN tv	Luis	PRENDES
Ludlow,	EDMUND st Br	Luis	PUENZO d
Ludlum,	ROBERT w Am	Luis	ROSALES po,ct Sp
Ludolph van CEULEN math,e Dut		Luis	TIANT b
Ludovic	HALEVY w Fr	Luis	TORRES x Sp
Ludovico	ZACCONI c It	Luis	VALDEZ d
Ludvig	HOLBERG w Nor	Luis de	GONGORA po Sp
Ludvik	SVOBODA ar,st Czech	Luis de	HARO st Sp
Ludwig	ARNIM w.po Ger	Luis de	MORALES p Sp
Ludwig	BORNE w Ger	Luis de	VARGAS p Sp
Ludwig	DESOIR la Ger	Luis de	VELASCO st Sp
Ludwig	ERHARD ec,st Ger	Luisa	HARRIS bb hf
Ludwig	HOLTY po Ger	Luisa	TETRAZZINI soprano It
Ludwig	KNORR sc Ger	Luise	KING s,tv Am
Ludwig	MOND sc,id Br	Luise	RAINER
Ludwig	PRANDTL sc-airflow Ger	Luisetti,	HANK bb hf
Ludwig	QUIDDE h,st Ger	Luisi,	JAMES tv+
Ludwig	SENFL c Swi	Luiz Vaz de CAMOES po Port	
Ludwig	STOSSEL tv+	Lukacs,	GYORGY ph,ct Hung
Ludwig	TIECK w Ger	Lukas	HAAS
Ludwig	UHLAND po Ger	Lukas,	J. ANTHONY p-n'86
Ludwig von ARNIM po,w Ger		Lukas,	PAUL o-a'43,la+ Am
Ludwig von MISES ec,e,w Am		Lukather,	STEVE mr-guitar Am
Ludwig von PASTOR h,e Ger		Luke	APPLING b
Ludwig von SIEGEN p,engr Ger		Luke	ASKEW
Ludwig,	EMIL w,bio Ger	Luke	EDWARDS tv+
Ludwig,	OTTO w Ger	Luke	FOX x Br
Ludwig,	PAMELA	Luke	HALPIN tv+
Lueger,	KARL st Aus	Luke	HANSARD print Br
Luez,	LAURETTE tv+	Luke	PERRY tv+
Lufft,	HANS p Ger	Luke	ROSSI tv
Luft,	LORNA tv+	Luke	WADDING r Ir
Lugene	SANDERS tv	Luke,	JORGE
Lugones,	LEOPOLDO po Arg	Luke,	KEYE tv+
Lugosi,	BELA la+ Am	Lukin,	LIONEL id-coach Br
Luhan,	MABEL w Am	Luks,	GEORGE p,cr Am
Luigi	ALVA tenor It	Lulli,	FOLCO
Luigi	CAPUANA w,ct,j It	Lully	LIST c Fr
Luigi	CORTI st It	Lully,	JEAN c Fr
Luigi	DENZA m,s,e,c It	Lulu	McCONNELL tv
Luigi	FACTA st It	Lulu	ROMAN tv
Luigi	FARINI md,h,st It	Lum,	BENJAMIN tv
Luigi	GALVANI md,sc It	Lumbly,	CARL tv+
Luigi	LANZI arc It	Lumet,	JENNY
Luigi	MONTINI	Lumet,	SIDNEY d,w Am
Luigi	PELLOUX ar,st It	Lumley,	JOANNA
Luigi	STURZO r,st It	Lummer,	OTTO sc,e Ger
Luigi Amedeo --- x It		Lummis,	CHARLES w,ed Am
Luis	AGUILAR	Lummis,	DAYTON tv
Luis	ALBERNI	Lumsden	HARE
Luis	ALVAREZ sc,e Am	Lun	RICH la,mgr Br
Luis	AVALOS tv+	Luna,	ALVARO de st Sp
Luis	BRION navy Colom	Luna,	BARBARA
Luis	BUNUEL d Sp	Lunceford, JIMMY mj-sax,cn,c Am	
Luis	DELGADO tv	Lund,	ART tv+
Luis	FIRPO boxer Am	Lund,	DEANNA tv+
Luis	GUZMAN	Lund,	JOHN

Lunden,	DAN tv	Lydon,	JIMMY
Lundgren,	DOLPH	Lydon,	JOHN mr-s Br
Lundigan,	WILLIAM tv+	Lye,	REG
Lundy,	BENJAMIN abolition Am	Lyell,	CHARLES(Sir)geol
Lundy,	JESSICA tv+	Lyle	ALZADO fb,tv+
Luner,	JAMIE tv	Lyle	BETTGER tv+
Lung	FEI	Lyle	LATELLE
Lung,	TI	Lyle	LOVETT s+ Am
Lunghi,	CHERIE	Lyle	TALBOT tv+
Lunn,	ARNOLD(Sir)ski,w	Lyle,	SPARKY b-cy'77
Lunt,	ALFRED la+ Am	Lyly,	JOHN w,po Br
Lupe	VELEZ	Lyman	ABBOTT r,w,ed Am
Lupi,	ROLDANO	Lyman	BAUM w,ed Am
Lupino	LANE	Lyman	BEECHER r,w Am
Lupino,	IDA tv+	Lyman	BRYSON tv
Lupita	TOVA	Lyman	DRAPER h Am
Lupita,	FERRER	Lyman	WARD
Lupo,	ALBERTO	Lyman,	DOROTHY tv+
LuPone,	PATTI s,tv+ Am	Lyman,	LINK fb hf
Lupton,	JOHN tv+	Lymon,	FRANKIE mr,tv Am
Lupus,	PETER tv+	Lyn	HARDING
Lurcat,	JEAN p,ds Fr	Lyn	OSBORN tv+
Luree	HOLMES	Lyn	STALMASTER tv
Lurene	TUTTLE tv+	Lyn,	DAWN tv
Luria,	SALVADOR n-m'69	Lynch,	BENITO w Arg
Lurie,	ALISON p-f'85	Lynch,	JOHN
Lurie,	JOHN	Lynch,	JOHN l,st,ar,slave Am
Lurie,	ROBERT(Bob) bmg	Lynch,	KATE
Lurton,	HORACE l,ar-CSA Am	Lynch,	KELLY
Lussy,	MELCHIOR ar,r Swi	Lynch,	PEG tv
Lustbader,ERIC w Am		Lynch,	RICHARD tv+
Luster,	BETTY tv	Lynch,	STAN mr-drm Am
Lustgarten, EDGAR tv		Lynd,	ROBERT soc,e Am
Lut(h)uli,ALBERT n-x'60		Lynd,	SARAH po Br
Luther	ADLER tv+	Lynda	CARTER tv+
Luther	CROWELL i Am	Lynda Day GEORGE tv+	
Luther	GULICK e Am	Lynda	GREEN tv
Luther	HOLT md Am	Lynda	WIESMEIER
Luther	WEIGLE r,e Am	Lynde,	PAUL tv+
Luther,	MARTIN r,w Ger	Lyne,	ADRIAN d
Luther,	SETH ref Am	Lynen,	FEODOR n-m'64
Lutz,	JOLEEN tv	Lynette	METTEY tv
Lux	LEWIS mj-piano Am	Lynette	WALDEN
Luxton,	BILL tv	Lynette	WINTER tv
Luyendyk,	ARIE racecars Am	Lyngstad,	FRIDA mr-s Swe
Luyken,	JAN po Dut	Lynley,	CAROL tv+
Luz,	FRANC	Lynn	BARI tv+
Luzinski,	GREG b,rbi'75	Lynn	BORDEN tv+
Lvov,	ALEKSEY c,cn Rus	Lynn	CARLIN tv+
Lvov,	GEORGY st Rus	Lynn	DOLLAR tv
Lwin,	ANNABELLA mr-s Burma	Lynn	HANCOCK tv
Lwoff,	ANDRE n-m'65	Lynn	HERRING tv
Lya de	PUTTI s Ger	Lynn	LIPTON cm,tv Am
Lyadov,	ANATOLY c Rus	Lynn	LORING tv+
Lyautey,	LOUIS ar,st Fr	Lynn	LOWRY
Lydgate,	JOHN r,po Br	Lynn	MARTA
Lydia	CHILD fe,w,ed Am	Lynn	MERRICK
Lydia	CORNELL tv	Lynn	POOLE tv
Lydia	LEI tv	Lynn	ROBERTS(Mary Hart)
Lydia	PINKHAM id-medicine Am	Lynn	SEYMOR ba Can
Lydie	DENIER tv+	Lynn	SHERR tv

Lynn	SWANN fb,tv
Lynn,	BETTY
Lynn,	CYNTHIA tv
Lynn,	DIANA
Lynn,	EMMETT
Lynn,	FONDA
Lynn,	FRED b-mv'75,bat'79
Lynn,	JEFFREY tv+
Lynn,	JONATHAN tv
Lynn,	JUDY tv
Lynn,	LORETTA s-cnt Am
Lynn,	MARA
Lynn,	VERA mj-s Br
Lynn-Holly JOHNSON	
Lynne	CARVER
Lynne	FREDERICK
Lynne	MOODY tv+
Lynne	OVERMAN
Lynne	THIGPEN tv+
Lynne,	AMY tv
Lynne,	JEFF mr-guit,s Br
Lynnie	GREENE tv
Lynott,	PHIL mr-bass,s Ir
Lynval	GOLDING mr-guit Br
Lyon,	BEN
Lyon,	MARY e Am
Lyon,	SUE
Lyonel	FEININGER p Am
Lyons,	GENE tv
Lyons,	JOSEPH st Aust
Lyons,	LEO mr-bass Br
Lyons,	ROBERT
Lyons,	TED b hf
Lyot,	BERNARD astron,i Fr
Lysenko,	TROFIM sc,e Rus
Lysette	ANTHONY
Lyte,	MC m-rap Am
Lytell,	BERT tv
Lytton,	EDWARD w,st Br

"M" NAME DESIGNATION CODES

m	MUSICIAN
math	MATHEMATICIAN
md	MEDICAL FIGURE
me	MEDIA FIGURE
mer	MERCHANT
mj	JAZZ MUSICIAN
mo	MODEL
mr	ROCK MUSICIAN
m-rap	RAP MUSICIAN

"M" NATIONALITY CODE

Mex - MEXICAN

"M's"

M'Carthy,	JUSTIN w,st Ir
M'Liss	McCLURE tv
M. Emmet	WALSH
Ma	RAINEY mj,s Am
Ma,	TZI
Ma,	YO-YO cello Fr
Maas,	PETER w Am

Maazel,	LORIN cn Am
Mabe,	BYRON
Mabel	KING tv+
Mabel	LUHAN w Am
Mabel	MERCER s Am
Mabel	NORMAND la+ Am
Mabini,	APOLINARIO re Phil
Mabley,	MOMS
Mably,	GABRIEL ph,h Fr
Mac	DAVIS tv+
Macal,	ZDENEK cn Am
Macarena	--- s,tv
MacArthur,	CHARLES j,w Am
MacArthur,	JAMES tv+
Macatee,	BILL tv
Macaulay	CULKIN
Macaulay,	ROSE (Dame) w Br
Macaulay,	THOMAS st,po,h,w Br
Macauley,	ED bb hf
MacBeth,	GEORGE po,w Scot
MacBride,	DONALD
MacBride,	SEAN n-x'74
MacCarthy,	DESMOND (Sir) j,ct
Macchio,	RALPH tv+
MacClelland,	ELIZABETH
MacCorkindale,	SIMON tv+
MacDiarmid,	HUGH po,ct Scot
MacDonald	CAREY tv+
Macdonald,	DWIGHT w,ct Am
Macdonald,	EDDIE mr-bass Welsh
MacDonald,	GEORGE w,po Scot
MacDonald,	J. FARRELL
MacDonald,	JAMES st Br
MacDonald,	JEANETTE s+ Am
MacDonald,	JOHN w Am
MacDonald,	LUCY MAUD w Can
Macdonald,	ROBIN mr-guit Scot
Macdonald,	ROSS w Am
MacDonald,	WALLACE
MacDonald,	WENDY
Macdonald-Wright,	STANTON p Am
MacDonnell,	KYLE tv
MacDowell,	ANDIE
MacDowell,	EDWARD c Am
MacDowell,	RODDY
Mace,	JAMES (Jem) boxer Br
Macedo,	JOSE de w Port
Macedo,	RITA
Macek,	VLADIMIR st Yugo
Macer,	STERLING Jr. tv
MacEwen,	GWENDOLYN po,w Can
Macfadden,	BERNARR pb,phys.cult
Macfarlane BURNET (Sir) md,e Aust	
MacGibbon,	HARRIET tv
MacGill,	MOYNA
MacGinnis,	NIALL
MacGowan,	SHANE mr-guit,s Br
MacGowan,	TARA
MacGowran,	JACK
MacGraw,	ALI tv+
Macgregor	LAIRD mer,x Scot

MacGregor, KATHERINE tv	MacLaine,	SHIRLEY o-a'83
Mach,	ERNST sc,ph,e Aus	MacLane,	BARTON tv+
Macha	MAGAL	MacLean,	BARBARA tv
Macha	MERIL	MacLean,	BRYAN mr-guitar,s Am
Macha,	KAREL po,w Cz	MacLeish,	ARCHIBALD p-d'59 &
Machado,	ANTONIO po Sp	MacLeish,	ARCHIBALD p-q'33'53
Machar,	JOSEF po Cz	MacLennan,HUGH w Can
Machen,	ARTHUR w Welsh	MacLeod,	GAVIN tv+
Machen,	JOHN r,e,w Am	Macleod,	JOHN n-m'23
Machiavelli, NICCOLO st,ph It	MacLeod,	MURRAY tv
Machiko	KYO	Maclise,	DANIEL p,illus Ir
Machin,	JOHN math Br	MacLure,	ELLIE
Machine GunKELLY(Geo)gangster	MacMahon,	ALINE
Machon,	KAREN tv	MacMichael,FLORENCE tv
Macht,	STEPHEN tv+	MacMillan,DONALD x Am
Macia,	FRANCESC st Sp	MacMurray,FRED tv+
MacInnes,	COLIN w Br	MacNaughton, ROBERT tv
MacInnes,	HELEN w Am	Macnee,	PATRICK
MacInnes,	THOMAS w Can	MacNeice,	LOUIS po,w Ir
MacIver,	ROBERT soc,e Am	MacNeil,	ROBERT tv j Am
Mack	DRYDEN tv	MacNelly,	JEFF cr Am
Mack	GORDON lyrics Am	MacNichol,PETER
Mack	SENNETT d+	Macon	McCALMAN tv+
Mack	SWAIN	Macon,	DAVE(Uncle)mj,s Am
Mack	WRIGHT d	MacPhail,	LARRY b hf
Mack,	BETTY	Macpherson, ELLE mo,tv+ Aust
Mack,	CONNIE b,bmg hf	Macpherson, JAMES po Scot
Mack,	DOTTY tv	MacPherson, JAY po Can
Mack,	HELEN	MacRae,	CARMEN mj,s Am
Mack,	KERRY	MacRae,	ELIZABETH tv
Mack,	TED tv-host Am	MacRae,	GORDON s,tv+ Am
Macka	FOLEY	MacRae,	MEREDITH tv+
Mackaill, DOROTHY	MacRae,	MICHAEL
MacKay,	ANDY m-sax,reeds Br	Macready,	GEORGE tv+
MacKay,	BARRY t,tv+ Am	Macready,	WILLIAM la Br
MacKay,	FULTON	MacVane,	JOHN tv
MacKay,	JEFF tv	MacVey	NAPIER l,ed Scot
MacKay,	JOHN	MacVittie,BRUCE tv
Mackay,	MARY w Br	Macy,	ANNE e,w Am
MacKaye,	JAMES la,pr,w Am	Macy,	BILL tv+
MacKaye,	PERCY po,w Am	Macy,	WILLIAM mer Am
Macke,	AUGUST p Ger	Mad Anthony WAYNE ar-re Am
Macken,	WALTER w,la,d Ir	Madach,	IMRE po Hung
Mackenzie BOWELL(Sir)st Can	Madchen	AMICK
Mackenzie COLT tv	Madden,	CIARAN
MacKenzie PHILLIPS	Madden,	DAVE tv
Mackenzie,COMPTON(Sir)w	Madden,	JOHN fbc,tv Am
Mackenzie,GEORGE chess Am	Maddern,	VICTOR tv
Mackenzie,GISELE s,tv+	Maddie	CORMAN tv+
Mackenzie,KENNETH w,po Aust	Maddux,	GREG b-cy'92'3'4'5 &
MacKenzie,PATCH	Maddux,	GREG many gg's
MacKenzie,PETER tv	Madeleine BARAT r Fr
MacKenzie,PHILIP CHARLES tv	Madeleine CARROLL
Mackenzie,RANALD ar Am	Madeleine L'ENGLE w-scifi Am
Mackenzie,WILL tv	Madeleine POTTER
Mackey,	JOHN fb. hf	Madeleine SMITH tv+
MacKinlay KANTOR w Am	Madeleine de SCUDERY w Fr
Macklin,	CHARLES w,la Br	Madeline BELGARD tv
Macklin,	DAVID tv	Madeline KAHN tv+
MacLachlan, JANET tv+	Madeline SMITH tv
MacLachlan, KYLE tv+	Madeline STOWE

Madelyn	CAIN tv
Madera,	YORLIN tv
Madge	BELLAMY
Madge	BLAKE tv
Madge	EVANS
Madge	KENDAL(Dame)la Br
Madhur	JAFFREY
Madigan,	AMY
Madison	MASON tv
Madison,	DOLLEY wf-James Am
Madison,	GUY tv+
Madison,	JAMES 4th pres
Madison,	NOEL
Madlock,	BILL bat'75'6'81,3
Madlyn	RHUE tv
Madolyn	SMITH
Madonna	--- s Am
Madriguera,ENRICmj-viol,cn,c	
Madsen,	MICHAEL
Madsen,	VIRGINIA
Mady	MAGUIRE tv
Mae	BUSCH
Mae	CLARKE
Mae	JOHNSON
Mae	MARSH
Mae	QUESTEL
Mae	WEST
Maen,	NORMAN ba,tv Am
Maerlant,	JACOB van po Belg
Maerten de VOS p Belg	
Maes(Mass), NICOLAES p Dut	
Maeterlinck,MAURICE po,n-l'11	
Maeve	BINCHY w Am
Maeve	KINKEAD tv
Maeztu	RAMIRO de w Sp
Maffeo	VEGIO r,w It
Magal,	MACHA
Magali	NOEL
Magda	GABOR
Magda	KONOPKA
Magee,	PATRICK
Magellan,	FERDINAND x Port
Maggart,	BRANDON tv+
Maggi	McNELLIS tv
Maggi	PARKER tv
Maggie	COOPER tv+
Maggie	PIERCE tv
Maggie	RENZI
Maggie	ROSWELL tv
Maggie	RUSH tv
Maggie	SMITH
Maggie	TEYTE sopr Br
Magic	JOHNSON bb hf
Maginot,	ANDRE st Fr
Maglie,	SAL b
Magnani,	ANNA o-a'55
Magnes,	JUDAH r,e Am
Magnus,	EDIE j,tv Am
Magnuson,	ANN tv+
Magritte,	RENE p Belg
Maguire,	LES mr-kbds,sax Br

Maguire,	MADY tv
Magyar,	DEZSO d
Maha	BANDULA ar Burma
Mahadev	RANADE l India
Mahaffey,	VALERIE
Mahalia	JACKSON mj-s Am
Mahan,	ALFRED navy,h,e Am
Maharidge,DALE p-n'90	
Maharis,	GEORGE tv+
Mahatma	GANDHI st India
Maher,	BILL tv+
Maher,	JOSEPH tv+
Mahfouz,	NAGUIB n-l'88
Mahler,	BRUCE tv+
Mahler,	GUSTAV cn,c Aus
Mahlon	PITNEY l,st Am
Mahoney,	JOCK tv+
Mahoney,	JOHN
Mahonri	YOUNG su,p,etch Am
Mahre,	PHIL ski,o-g'84
Mahre,	STEVE ski Am
Mai	ZETTERLING
Mai Tai	SING tv
Maia	BREWTON tv+
Maier,	TIM tv+
Mailer,	NORMAN p-f'80,p-n'69
Maillol,	ARISTIDE p,su Fr
Main,	MARJORIE
Maire	O'NEILL
Mairead	CORRIGAN st Ir
Maisie	WILLIAMS mr-s W.Indi
Maitland	WARD tv
Maitland,	MARNE
Maj	SJOWALL w Swe
Maj-Britt NILSSON	
Majel	BARRETT tv
Major Edward BOWES tv+	
Major,	CHARLES w Am
Majorino	TINA
Majors,	LEE tv+
Makarova,	ALICIA ba Br
Makart,	HANS p Aus
Makepeace,CHRIS	
Makk,	KAROLY d
Mako	---
Maksim	GORKY w Rus
Mal	HALLETT mj,cn Am
Mala	---
Mala	POWERS tv+
Malachi	THRONE tv
Malamud,	BERNARD p-f'67
Malan,	DANIEL st S.Afr
Malbone,	EDWARD p Am
Malcolm	CASSELL tv
Malcolm	COWLEY ct,w Am
Malcolm	KEEN tv+
Malcolm	LOWRY w Br
Malcolm	McDOWELL
Malcolm	YOUNG mr-guit Scot
Malcolm X	--- r,re,civl rts Am
Malcolm-Jamal WARNER tv	

Malden,	KARL o-s'51,tv+	Mander,	KAREL van p,w Dut
Male,	COLIN tv	Mander,	MILES
Malebranche, NICOLAS de ph Fr		Mandeville, BERNARD de ph Br	
Malenkov, GEORGY st Rus		Mandlikova, HANA t Czech	
Malet,	ARTHUR tv+	Mandrell,	BARBARA s-cntry,tv+
Malet,	LAURENT	Mandrell,	IRLENE tv
Malevich, KAZIMIR p Rus		Mandrell,	LOUISE tv
Malick	BOWENS tv+	Mandy	PATINKIN
Malik,	ART	Mandylor,	COSTAS
Malin	CRAIG ar Am	Manet,	EDOUARD p Fr
Malina,	JUDITH	Manetti,	LARRY tv+
Malkiel,	YAKOV sc,w Am	Manfred	EIGEN sc Ger
Malkovich,JOHN		Manfred	LEE w Am
Malle,	LOUIS d	Manfred	MANN mr-kbds S.Afr
Mallea,	EDUARDO w Arg	Manfredi,	NINO
Malleson, MILES		Manfredo	FANTI ar It
Mallet,	DAVID po Scot	Mang	HAI
Mallon,	MARY(Typhoid)carry Am	Mangano,	SILVANA
Mallory,	PATRICIA(Boots)	Mango,	ALEX tv
Malloy,	MATT	Mani,	KARIN
Malmsten, BIRGER		Manifold,	JOHN po,w Aust
Malneck,	MATTY mj-viol,cn,c Am	Manilow,	BARRY mj,s Am
Malone,	DOROTHY o-s'56,tv+	Maniu,	IULIU st Rom
Malone,	DUMAS bio,e Am	Mankiewicz, JOSEPH o-d'50	
Malone,	EDMUND ct,w Ir	Manley	HUDSON l,e,st Am
Malone,	JOE tv	Manley,	MARY de w Br
Malone,	KARL bb-m'97	Manlio	BROSIO st It
Malone,	KEMP dictionary Am	Manly,	JOHN w,e Am
Malone,	MARY tv	Mann,	ANITA ba,tv
Malone,	MOSES bb-m'79'82'3 hf	Mann,	BARRY c Am
Malone,	NANCY tv	Mann,	DELBERT o-d'55
Malone,	RAY tv	Mann,	DONALD(Sir)rr's Can
Maloney,	LAUREN tv	Mann,	HANK
Maloney,	PAIGE tv	Mann,	HEINRICH w Ger
Malory,	THOMAS(Sir)w	Mann,	HERBIE mj-flute Am
Malraux,	ANDRE w,ct Fr	Mann,	HORACE e,st Am
Malthus,	THOMAS ec,e,w Br	Mann,	JAMES st Am
Maltin,	LEONARD ct-film Am	Mann,	JOHNNY s,cn,tv Am
Malus,	ETIENNE eng,sc Fr	Mann,	LARRY tv
Malvin,	ARTIE tv	Mann,	MANFRED mr-kbds S.Afr
Malvina	HOFFMAN su Am	Mann,	TERRENCE
Malvy,	LOUIS st Fr	Mann,	THOMAS n-l'29
Mamet,	DAVID p-d'84,d	Mann,	TRACEY
Mamie	VAN DOREN	Manners,	DAVID
Mamoulian,ROUBEN d		Manners,	MICKEY tv
Man	RAY p,fo Am	Manners,	ZEKE mj-,ws Am
Man Mountain DEAN wrestle Am		Mannes,	DAVID viol,cn,e Am
Manard,	BIFF tv+	Mannes,	MARYA w,j Am
Manatovani --- mj,cn It-Br		Mannheim, LUCIE	
Mance,	HENRY(Sir)eng	Manni,	ETTORE
Mancini,	HENRYcn,g-r'58'61'3	Manning,	FREDERIC w Aust
Mancini,	OLYMPE mistress Fr	Manning,	JACK tv
Mancini,	RAY(Boom Boom)	Manning,	SEAN tv
Mancuso,	NICK tv+	Mannix,	DANIEL r Aust
Mandan,	ROBERT tv+	Manny	COTO d
Mandel,	DENNIS tv	Manny	JACOBS
Mandel,	ELI po,ed,ct Can	Mannyng,	ROBERT po Br
Mandel,	HOWIE cm,tv+	Manoff,	DINAH tv+
Mandela,	NELSON st,n-l'93	Manone,	WINGY mj-trump,cn Am
Mandelstan, OSIP po Rus		Manrique,	JORGE ar,po Sp
Mander,	JANE w N.Zea	Mansfield,IRVING tv	

Mansfield,JAYNE		Maravich,	PETE bb hf
Mansfield,SALLY tv		Marble,	ALICE t Am
Manson,	CHARLES murder,cults	Marc	ALAIMO
Manson,	PATRICK(Sir)sc.e	Marc	ALLEGRET d
Mansur,	ABU st Muslim	Marc	ALMOND mr,s Br
Mantan	MORELAND	Marc	BARASCH w Am
Mantee,	PAUL tv+	Marc	BOLAN mr-guit,s Br
Mantegna,	ANDREA p,engr It	Marc	BRUNEL(Sir)i,eng
Mantegna,	JOE	Marc	CAVELL tv
Mantell,	GIDEON geol Br	Marc	CHAGALL p-murals Fr
Mantell,	JOE tv	Marc	CLARK ar Am
Mantilla,	JOE d	Marc	COPAGE tv
Mantle,	MICKEYb-mv'56'7'62 hf	Marc	GOMES tv
Mantooth,	RANDOLPH tv	Marc	HAYASHI
Manuel	ARCE ar,st Salvad	Marc	KLAW theater mgr Am
Manuel	BOCAGE navy,po Port	Marc	La MOTTE adventure Fr
Manuel	BULNES ar,st Chile	Marc	McCLURE
Manuel	GALVEZ w Arg	Marc	MURET po,e Fr
Manuel	LISA fur trade Am	Marc	PRICE tv+
Manuel	MONTT st Chile	Marc	SEGUIN eng Fr
Manuel	ORIBE ar,st Urug	Marc	SINGER tv+
Manuel	PADILLA Jr tv	Marc	TAYLOR tv
Manuel	PARDO st Peru	Marc Scott TAYLOR tv	
Manuel	PONCE c Mex	Marc,	FRANZ p Ger
Manuel	PUIG w Arg	Marcantel,CHRISTOPHER tv	
Manuel	ROJAS w Chile	Marceau,	MARCEL mime+ Fr
Manuel	UGARTE w Arg	Marcel	AYME w Fr
Manuel de ALMEIDA w Braz		Marcel	BREUER ac Am
Manuel de ARRAIGA st Port		Marcel	CARNE d
Manuel de FALLA c Sp		Marcel	DALIO tv+
Manuel,	JUAN st,w Sp	Marcel	DEAT st Fr
Manuel,	NIKLAUS p,engr Swi	Marcel	DEPREZ eng Fr
Manuela	SAENZ mistress Ecu	Marcel	DUCHAMP p Fr
Manush,	HENRY b hf	Marcel	DUPRE organ,c Fr
Manutius,	ALDUS printer, It	Marcel	MARCEAU mime+ Fr
Manz,	LINDA	Marcel	MAUSS an,e,w Fr
Manza,	RALPH tv	Marcel	PAGNOL w,d Fr
Manzanera,PHIL m-guit Br		Marcel	PROUST w Fr
Manzarek,	RAY mr-keybds Am	Marcel	VALLEE
Manzoni,	ALESSANDRO w,po It	Marcel,	GABRIEL ph,w,ct Fr
Mao	ZEDONG st China	Marceline DAY	
Mao Tse-tung --- re,st China		Marcelino,MARIO tv	
Mao,	ANGELA	Marcell,	JOSEPH tv
Map,	WALTERw-satire,r Br	Marcellin BOULE sc,e Fr	
Mapita	CORTES	Marcellino, JOHN(Jocko)tv	
Mapu,	ABRAHAM w Lith	Marcellino, MUZZY mj,cn,tv Am	
Maquet,	AUGUSTE w Fr	Marcello MASTROIANNI	
Mara	BERNI	Marcellus EMANTS po,w Dut	
Mara	CORDAY	March,	AUSIAS po Sp
Mara	HOBEL	March,	FREDRIC la+,o-a'32'46
Mara	LYNN	March,	HAL tv-host Am
Mara,	ADELE tv+	Marchand,	GUY
Mara,	MARY	Marchand,	NANCY tv+
Mara,	TIM fb hf	Marchesi,	BLANCHE sopr Fr
Mara,	WELLINGTON fbc hf	Marchetti,GINO fb hf	
Marachuk,	STEVE	Marchini,	RON
Marais,	JEAN	Marcia	BARRETT mr,s Jamaica
Marakova,	ALICIA(Dame)ba Br	Marcia	HARDEN
Maran,	RENE w Fr	Marcia	MULLER w Am
Marash,	DAVE tv	Marcia	RODD tv+
Marat,	JEAN md,st,re Fr	Marcia	SOLOMON tv

Marcia	WALLACE tv+	Margaret	HAYES tv+
Marcia Mae JONES		Margaret	IMPERT tv
Marciano, ROCKY boxer Am		Margaret	IRVING tv
Marcil,	VANESSA tv	Margaret	KENNEDY w Am
Marcin	BIELSKI h,po Pol	Margaret	LADD tv
Marco	LOPEZ tv	Margaret	LEE
Marco	PIRRONI mr-guit Br	Margaret	LINDSAY
Marco	POLO x It	Margaret	MEAD an,w Am
Marco	SOTO st Honduras	Margaret	O'BRIEN
Marco	VIDA po,r It	Margaret	SANGER fe Am
Marco,	FATSO tv	Margaret	SEDDON
Marconi, GUGLIELMO n-p'09		Margaret	TRUMAN w Am
Marcos de NIZA r,x Fr		Margaret	UMBERS
Marcos,	FERDINAND st Phil	Margaret	WADE bbc hf
Marcos,	IMELDA wife-F.Phill	Margaret	WALKER po,w Am
Marcoux,	TED	Margaret	WEBSTER la,d Br
Marcovicci, ANDREA tv+		Margaret	WELSH tv+
Marcus	AGRIPPA ar,st Ro	Margaret	WHITING s,tv+ Am
Marcus	DALY id - mines Am	Margaret	WHITTON
Marcus	HANNA mer,st Am	Margaret	WILLOCK tv
Marcus	HERZ md,ph Ger	Margaret	WOODS w Br
Marcus	LABEO l Roman	Margaret Smith COURT t Am	
Marcus	LOEW pr-films Am	Margaretta SCOTT	
Marcus	WHITMAN pioneer,r	Margarita SIERRA tv	
Marcus Aurelius CARUS Ro emp		Marge	GREENE tv
Marcus Junius BRUTUS st Ro		Marge	PIERCY po,w Am
Marcus Porcius CATO st Ro		Marge	REDMOND tv
Marcus Tullius CICEROst,ph Ro		Margery	KEMPE mystic Br
Marcus,	JAMES	Margetts, MONTY tv	
Marcus,	JEFF tv	Margia	DEAN
Marcus,	KIPP tv	Margie	REGAN tv
Marcus,	RUDOLPH n-c'92	Margo	---
Marcus,	SPARKY tv	Margo	LOPEZ
Marcuse,	HERBERT ph-polit,e Am	Margo	WOODE
Marcy	WALKER tv	Margo,	MITCH s-tenor Am
Marcy,	WILLIAM l,st Am	Margo,	PHIL s-basso Am
Mardi	BRYANT tv	Margolin, JANET	
Mardi,	DANIELLE tv	Margolin, STUART tv+	
Mare	ROCCO d	Margolyes,MIRIAM	
Mare,	WALTER de la w,po Br	Margot	FONTEYN(Dame)la Br
Marees,	HANS von p Ger	Margot	GRAHAME
Maren	JENSEN tv	Margot	KIDDER tv+
Marenzio, LUCA c It		Margritte,RENE p	
Maret,	HUGUES st Fr	Marguerite CHAPMAN	
Marete	EDILLO(Officer)tv	Marguerite DURAS w,pr-films Fr	
Marete	Van KAMP tv+	Marguerite PEREY sc,e Fr	
Marey,	ETIENNE sc,e Fr	Marguerite PIAZZA tv	
Margai,	MILTON(Sir)st S.Leo	Marguerite RAY tv	
Margaret	ANGLIN la Am	Marguerite STEEN w Br	
Margaret	ASHFORD w Br	Margulies,DAVID	
Margaret	ATWOOD w,po Can	Margulies,STAN pr-tv Am	
Margaret	AVERY	Mari	ALDON
Margaret	BARNES w Am	Mari	GORMAN tv
Margaret	BLYE	Mari	MORROW tv
Margaret	CHO cm+	Mari	SANDOZ bio,h Am
Margaret	COLIN tv+	Mari	TOROCSIK
Margaret	DELAND w Am	Maria	AGNESI math,e It
Margaret	DRABBLE w Br	Maria	ALONSO
Margaret	DUMONT tv+	Maria	BOMBAL w Chile
Margaret	FULLER fe,ct Am	Maria	BUENO t Am
Margaret	GARLAND tv	Maria	CALLAS s Am

Maria	CASARES	Marie	TUSSAUD wax figs. Swi
Maria	FELIX	Marie	WILSON tv+
Maria	FORD	Marie	WINDSOR
Maria	HEASLEY tv	Marie de	SEVIGNE w Fr
Maria	JERITZA sopr Cz	Marie de la RAMEE w Br	
Maria	MAYER sc Am	Marie-Jose PAREC o-g'92	
Maria	MICHI	Marie,	ROSE tv
Maria	MONK imposter,w Fr	Marie,	TEENA mr s
Maria	MONTEZ	Marielle,	JEAN-PIERRE
Maria	PERSCHY	Marietta	DePRIMA tv
Maria	ROHM	Mariette	HARTLEY tv+
Maria	SCHELL	Marihugh,	TAMMY LEA tv
Maria	SHRIVER tv-j Am	Marika	GREEN
Maria	SOCAS	Marilia	PERA
Maria	TRAPP s Am	Marilu	HENNER tv+
Maria	TUCCI	Marilu	TOLO
Mariah	CAREY s-pop Am	Marilyn	BERGMAN tv
Marian	COLLIER tv	Marilyn	BURNS
Marian	MARSH	Marilyn	COOPER tv
Marian	MERCER tv	Marilyn	DAY tv
Mariangela MELATO		Marilyn	ERSKINE tv
Mariann	AAIDA tv	Marilyn	FRENCH w Am
Marianna	HILL	Marilyn	HANOLD tv
Marianne	BLACK tv	Marilyn	HASSETT
Marianne	HERMANN w Am	Marilyn	HORNE mezzo Am
Marianne	KOCH	Marilyn	JACOBS tv
Marianne	McISAAC tv	Marilyn	KING s,tv Am
Marianne	MOORE po Am	Marilyn	MAXWELL
Marianne	ROGERS tv	Marilyn	McCOO tv-host,mr-s+
Mariano	ARISTA ar,st Mex	Marilyn	MONROE
Mariano	AZUELA w,ar Mex	Marilyn	QUAYLE l.w,Dan's wf.
Mariano	CORNEJO st,l Peru	Marilyn	TOKUDA
Mariano	MORENO st Arg	Marin	DRZIC w Croatia
Mariano	PRADO ar,st Peru	Marin	SAIS
Mariano	VALLEJO ar,st Am	Marin,	EDWIN L. d
Mariano de LARRA j,w Sp		Marin,	JOHN p Am
Marias,	JULIAN ph,w Sp	Marin,	RICHARD(Cheech)
Mariategui, JOSE w Peru		Marin,	RIKKI
Maribel	VERDU	Marina	SIRTIS tv+
Marichal, JUAN b hf		Marina	VLADY
Mariclare COSTELLO tv+		Marinaro, ED tv+	
Marie	BELLOC w Br	Marini,	ERIKA viol
Marie	BEYLE w Fr	Marini,	MARINO su It
Marie	BICHAT me,w Fr	Marino	MARINI su It
Marie	BIRAN st,ph,w Fr	Marino	SANUDO h It
Marie	BLAIS w,po,ct Can	Marino,	DAN fb-m'84
Marie	CORELLI w Br	Marino,	GIAMBATTISTA po It
Marie	CURIE sc Pol	Marins,	JOSE de
Marie	DENN tv	Mario	ADORF
Marie	DuBOIS	Mario	ALMADA
Marie	JAMET r Fr	Mario	BAVA d
Marie	KEAN	Mario	CUOMO st Am
Marie	LLOYD cm,s Br	Mario	Del MONACO tenor It
Marie	LOHR	Mario	ELIE bb
Marie	McDONALD	Mario	GALLO tv
Marie	OSMOND s,tv+ Am	Mario	LANZA s+ Am
Marie	PISIER	Mario	LEMIEUX ho
Marie	PREVOST	Mario	MOLINO sc Mex-Am
Marie	RAMBERT(Dame)ba Br	Mario	PISU
Marie	SALLE ba Fr	Mario	PUZO w Am
Marie	STOPES sc,fe,w Br	Mario	YEDIDIA

Mario de	ANDRADE po,w Braz		Mark	EVANS mr-bass Aust
Marion	BARRY st-mayor Am		Mark	FARNER mr-guit,s Am
Marion	COLBY tv		Mark	FOREST
Marion	DORSET sc Am		Mark	GODDARD tv+
Marion	HUTTON mj-s Am		Mark	GORDON tv
Marion	LORNE tv+		Mark	GREGORY
Marion	MARLOWE tv		Mark	HAINING tv
Marion	MARTIN		Mark	HAMILL tv+
Marion	MORGAN s,tv Am		Mark	HARMON
Marion	MOTLEY fb hf		Mark	HELPRIN w Am
Marion	NIXON		Mark	HERRIER
Marion	ROSS tv+		Mark	HOLLIS mr-kbd,s Br
Marion	YUE tv		Mark	HOPKINS e Am
Marion,	BETH		Mark	HOWE ed,w Am
Marion,	FRANCIS(SwmpFox)ar Am		Mark	HUDSON tv
Marion,	GEORGE Sr.		Mark	HUTTER tv
Marion,	MARTIN b-mv'44		Mark	JOFFE d
Marion,	RICHARD tv		Mark	KELLY mr-kbds Irish
Maris	WRIXON		Mark	KEYLOUN
Maris,	ADA tv		Mark	KING mr-bass,s Br
Maris,	MONA		Mark	LANDAU w Rus
Maris,	ROGER b-mv'60'61		Mark	LENARD tv+
Marisa	MELL		Mark	LESTER
Marisa	PAVAN		Mark	LEYNER w Am
Marisa	PEREDES		Mark	LINDO w Dut
Marisa	REDANTY tv		Mark	LINDSAY mr-sax,s Am
Marisa	RYAN tv		Mark	McGUIRE b,hr'87,95 &
Marisa	SILVER d		Mark	McGUIRE hr'98(70)
Marisa	TOMEI tv+		Mark	MENDOZA mr-bass Am
Mariska	HARGITAY tv+		Mark	MESSIER ho
Maritain,	JACQUES ph,e Fr		Mark	METCALF
Maritza,	SARI		Mark	MILLER tv+
Marius	GORING		Mark	MOSES tv+
Marius	PETIPA ba Fr		Mark	O'TOOLE mr-bass Br
Marius	WEYERS		Mark	PIRRO d
Marius B.	WINTER mj,cn Br		Mark	PITTA tv
Marivaux,	PIERRE de w Fr		Mark	ROBSON d
Marj	DUSAY tv+		Mark	ROLSTON
Marjean	HOLDEN		Mark	ROTHKO p Am
Marjie	MILLAR tv		Mark	RUSSELL humor,tv Am
Marjoe	GORTNER tv+		Mark	RYDELL d
Marjorie	BUELL cr Am		Mark	SALSMAN w Am
Marjorie	CORLEY tv		Mark	SCHORER w,ct Am
Marjorie	GATESON tv+		Mark	SHERA tv
Marjorie	JACKSON 2x o-gs '52		Mark	SLADE tv
Marjorie	LORD tv+		Mark	SOBEL d
Marjorie	MAIN		Mark	SPITZ sw,7x o-g'72
Marjorie	RAMBEAU		Mark	STEIN mr-organ,s Am
Marjorie	RIORDAN		Mark	STEVENS tv+
Marjorie	TAYLOR		Mark	STRAND po,ed Am
Mark	ANTONY st Ro		Mark	SYKES(Sir) st,w
Mark	BEDFORD mr-guit Br		Mark	TOBEY p Am
Mark	BLUM		Mark	TWAIN w Am
Mark	BURNS		Mark	VALLEY tv
Mark	CATESBY sc,w Br		Mark	Van DOREN po,e,w Am
Mark	CHAPMAN tv		Mark	VOLMAN mr-sax,s Am
Mark	CLARK ar Am		Mark	WHITE mr-guit Br
Mark	CLEMENS w Am		Mark	WITHERS tv
Mark	DAMON		Mark,	FLIP tv
Mark	DAVIS b		Mark,	MARKY m-rap,mo Am
Mark	DAY mr-guit Br		Markevitch,	IGOR cn

Markey,	ENID tv+	Marquis	GRISSOM b
Markham,	EDWIN po Am	Marquis	JAMES j,w,bio Am
Markham,	KIKA	Marquis de	SADE ar,w Fr
Markham,	MONTE tv+	Marquis,	DON j,w-humor Am
Markham,	PIGMEAT tv	Marr,	EDDIE tv+
Markie	POST tv+	Marr,	JOHNNY mr-guit Br
Markim,	AL tv	Marr,	NIKOLAY arc Rus
Markland,	TED tv	Marriner	ECCLES banker Am
Marko	MARULIC po,ph Croat	Marriott,	STEVE mr-guit,s Br
Markoff,	DIANE tv	Marryat,	FREDERICK navy,w Br
Markov,	ANDREY math,e Rus	Mars,	KENNETH tv+
Markowitz,HARRY M. n-e'90		Mars,	MICK mr-guit Am
Marks,	GUY tv	Mars,	MLLE. la Fr
Marks,	JOHNNY c Am	Marsalis,	WYNTON mj-trump Am
Markus	REDMOND tv	Marsden	HARTLEY p Am
Markwell,	TERRY tv	Marsden,	FREDDIE mr-drm Br
Marky	MARK m-rap,mo Am	Marsden,	JASON tv
Marla	GIBBS tv+	Marsh,	CAROL
Marla	TRUMP(D's wife'94)Am	Marsh,	GARRY
Marlee	MATLIN tv+	Marsh,	IAN mr-kbds Br
Marlene	CLARK tv+	Marsh,	JEAN tv+
Marlene	DIETRICH	Marsh,	JOAN
Marlene	JOBERT	Marsh,	JOHN c Br
Marlene	WARFIELD tv	Marsh,	MAE
Marley,	BOB mr-guit,s Jamaica	Marsh,	MARIAN
Marley,	JOHN	Marsh,	NGAIO(Dame) w N.Zea
Marley,	ZIGGY s,ws Jamaica	Marsh,	OTHNIEL sc,e Am
Marlier,	CARLA	Marsh,	REGINALD p Am
Marlin	PERKINS zoos,tv Am	Marsha	HUNT tv+
Marlo	MORGAN w Am	Marsha	JORDAN
Marlo	THOMAS tv+	Marsha	MASON
Marlon	BRANDO tv+	Marsha	MOREAU tv
Marlon	JACKSON mr-s Am	Marsha	NORMAN w Am
Marlon	WAYANS	Marsha	SINETAR w Am
Marlowe,	CHRISTOPHER w,po Br	Marshal,	ALAN
Marlowe,	HUGH	Marshall	BELL
Marlowe,	JULIA la Am	Marshall	COLT tv+
Marlowe,	JUNE	Marshall	FIELD mer Am
Marlowe,	LINDA	Marshall	McLUHAN ct,w,ph Can
Marlowe,	MARION tv	Marshall	REED(1950's)tv
Marlowe,	NORA tv	Marshall	REED(1970's)tv
Marlowe,	NORMA tv	Marshall,	ANN tv
Marly,	FLORENCE	Marshall,	BILLIE mj-s Am
Marlyn	MASON tv	Marshall,	DODIE
Marmarosa,	DODO mj-piano Am	Marshall,	DON tv
Marmol,	JOSE w Arg	Marshall,	E.G. tv+
Marmont,	PERCY	Marshall,	GEORGE d
Marmontel,JEAN w Fr		Marshall,	GEORGE fb hf
Marne	MAITLAND	Marshall,	GEORGE n-x'53
Marner,	SILAS fc	Marshall,	GLORIA tv
Marni	NIXON mj-s Am	Marshall,	GREGORY tv
Maroney,	KELLI	Marshall,	HERBERT
Maross,	JOE tv	Marshall,	JAMES 1stGold in CA Am
Marot,	CLEMENT po Fr	Marshall,	JAMES tv+
Marot,	JEAN ac Fr	Marshall,	JOAN tv
Marquand,	JOHN(J.P.)p-f'38	Marshall,	JOHN l,ch just Am
Marquard,	RUBE b hf	Marshall,	JOHN(Sir)arc
Marquet,	ALBERT p Fr	Marshall,	KEN
Marquette,JACQUES r,x Fr		Marshall,	LINDA tv
Marquez,	GABRIEL n-l'82	Marshall,	MIKE b-cy'74
Marquina,	EDUARDO po Sp	Marshall,	MORT cm,tv Am

Marshall,	PAT tv	Martin	GUZMAN w Mex
Marshall,	PENNY d,tv+	Martin	HEWITT
Marshall,	PETER tv-host+ Am	Martin	KEMP
Marshall,	ROY K. tv	Martin	KEMP mr-bass Br
Marshall,	TRUDY	Martin	KOCH w Swe
Marshall,	TULLY	Martin	KOSLECK
Marshall,	WILLIAM	Martin	KOVE tv+
Marshall,	ZENA	Martin	LANDAU tv+
Marsilio	FICINO ph It	Martin	LUTHER r,w Ger
Marsman,	HENDRIK po,w,ct Dut	Martin	MARION b
Marston	BATES sc,e Am	Martin	MILLER
Marston,	JOHN w,po Br	Martin	MILNER tv+
Marta	DuBOIS tv+	Martin	MULL tv+
Marta	KRISTEN tv+	Martin	NEXO w Dan
Marta,	LYNN	Martin	NOTH r,e,w Ger
Martel,	EDOUARD sc-caves Fr	Martin	OPITZ po,ct Ger
Martel,	K.C. tv	Martin	PINZON x Sp
Martell,	DONNA	Martin	POTTER
Martell,	VINCE mr-guit Am	Martin	RATHKE md-sc Ger
Martens,	ADOLPHE w Belg	Martin	RITT d+
Marterie,	RALPH mj,cn Am	Martin	RYLE(Sir)astr
Martha	BUTLER ba AM	Martin	SHAW organ,c,ed Br
Martha	BYRNE tv+	Martin	SHAW tv+
Martha	DAVIS mr-s Am	Martin	SHEEN
Martha	FINLEY w Am	Martin	SHORT tv+
Martha	GEHMAN	Martin	SMITH w Am
Martha	GRAHAM ba Am	Martin	SOHR m,c Ger
Martha	GRIMES w Am	Martin	WALSER w Ger
Martha	HYER	Martin	YAN tv-chef Am
Martha	LOGAN tv	Martin	ZWEIG w-invests,tv Am
Martha	NIX tv	Martin a Beckett BOYD w SWI	
Martha	OSTENSO w Am	Martin du Gard, ROGER w Fr	
Martha	RAYE s,tv+ Am	Martin Luther KING Jr r,w Am	
Martha	REEVES mr-s Am	Martin,	ANA
Martha	SCOTT tv+	Martin,	ANDREA tv+
Martha	SMITH tv	Martin,	ANNE-MARIE tv
Martha	STEWART w,tv Am	Martin,	ARCHER n-c'52
Martha	THOMAS e Am	Martin,	BARNEY tv
Martha	TILTON s+ Am	Martin,	BRAM mj,cn Br
Martha	WRIGHT tv	Martin,	CAROL tv
Marthe	KELLER	Martin,	CHRISTOPHER
Marthinus	STEYN l,st S.Afr	Martin,	D'URVILLE
Marti	PELLOW mr-s Scot	Martin,	DEAN(Dino)s,cm,tv+ Am
Marti,	JOSE st,po,w Cuba	Martin,	DEWEY
Martin	AMIS w Br	Martin,	DEWEY mr-drm,s Can
Martin	BALSAM tv+	Martin,	DICK tv+
Martin	BENSON	Martin,	EDWARD ed,w Am
Martin	BLOCK tv	Martin,	EUGENE tv
Martin	BOOS r Ger	Martin,	FREDDY mj,cn Am
Martin	BREST d	Martin,	GEORGE
Martin	BROOKS tv	Martin,	GLENN id-planes Am
Martin	BUBER ph,w Aus-Isr	Martin,	HARVEY fb-d'77
Martin	BUCER r,ref Ger	Martin,	HELEN
Martin	DeHIGO b hf	Martin,	HOMER p Am
Martin	DIES st Am	Martin,	JARED tv+
Martin	DONOVAN	Martin,	JEAN
Martin	FERRERO	Martin,	JIM mr-guit Am
Martin	FLAVIN w Am	Martin,	JOHN
Martin	FRY mr-s Br	Martin,	KELLIE tv+
Martin	GORE mr-kbds Br	Martin,	KIEL tv+
Martin	GOULD c Am	Martin,	LEILA la Am

Martin,	LORI tv		Marvin	CHOMSKY tv-pr,d
Martin,	MARION		Marvin	GAYE mr,s Am
Martin,	MARY la,s,tv+ Am		Marvin	HAGLER boxer
Martin,	MELISSA tv		Marvin	HAMLISCH m-pia,c,w Am
Martin,	MERRY tv		Marvin	HART boxer Am
Martin,	MILLICENT tv+		Marvin	KAPLAN tv+
Martin,	NAN		Marvin	MILLER tv+
Martin,	PAMELA tv+		Marvin,	HANK mr-guit Br
Martin,	PETER ba		Marvin,	LEE tv+
Martin,	QUINN tv		Marvin,	TONY tv
Martin,	RICHARD		Marx Bros.,	THE cm,tv+ Am
Martin,	RICKY tv		Marx,	ALAN
Martin,	ROSS tv+		Marx,	CHICO la,cm+ Am
Martin,	SLATER bb hf		Marx,	GROUCHO la,cm,tv+ Am
Martin,	STEVE tv+		Marx,	GUMMO vaudvill,mer Am
Martin,	STROTHER tv+		Marx,	HARPO la,cm+ Am
Martin,	TONY tv+		Marx,	KARL w,re,ph Ger
Martin,	VIOLET w Ir		Marx,	RICHARD s,ws Am
Martin-Santos,	LUIS w Sp		Marx,	WILHELM st Ger
Martina	HINGIS t Swi		Marx,	ZEPPO la,cm+ Am
Martina	McBride s Am		Mary	AKELEY sc,w Am
Martina	NAVRATILOVA t Am		Mary	ALICE
Martindale,	WINK tv		Mary	ALSOP w Am
Martine	BESWICK		Mary	ANNING sc Br
Martine	CAROL		Mary	ANTIN w Am
Martineau,	HARRIET w Br		Mary	ASTELL w Br
Martineau,	JAMES r,e,ph Br		Mary	ASTOR
Martinelli,	ELSA		Mary	AUSTIN w Am
Martinez Ruiz,	JOSE w Sp		Mary	BETHUNE e Am
Martinez,	A. tv+		Mary	BLIGE s-pop,soul Am
Martinez,	EDGAR b,bat'95		Mary	BOLAND
Martinez,	JAMES tv		Mary	BRIAN
Martinez,	TINO b		Mary	CARR
Martinez	PEDRO b-cy'97		Mary	CARVER tv
Martinez,	TONY tv		Mary	CASSATT p Am
Martini,	JERRY m-sax Am		Mary	CHASE w Am
Martini,	SIMONE p It		Mary	CLARE
Martini,	STEVE w Am		Mary	COSTA tv
Martino,	DONALD p-m'74		Mary	CROSBY tv+
Martino,	SERGIO d		Mary	DODGE w Am
Martinson,	HARRY po,n-l'74		Mary	DONAHUE tv
Martinson,	MOA w Swe		Mary	DORAN
Martinus	NIJHOFF po Dut		Mary	EVANS(Geo.Eliot)w Br
Martita	HUNT		Mary	FISHER w Am
Martling,	JACKIE tv		Mary	FORBES
Marty	BALIN mr,s Am		Mary	FORD mj,s Am
Marty	BRILL tv		Mary	FRANN
Marty	COHEN tv		Mary	FREEMAN w Am
Marty	FELDMAN tv+		Mary	GARDEN sopr Am
Marty	GREBB mr-kbds Am		Mary	GORDON
Marty	INGELS		Mary	GORDON w Am
Marty	PAICH m,cn,tv Am		Mary	GRACE tv
Marty	ROBBINS m-cnt,tv+		Mary	GREGORY tv+
Marty	SCHIFF tv		Mary	GROSS tv+
Martyn	SANDERSON		Mary	GUINAN la+ Am
Martyn	WARE mr-synthesize Br		Mary	HART tv-hostess Am
Martyn,	EDWARD w Irish		Mary	HEALY tv
Marulic,	MARKO po,ph Croat		Mary	HOLMES w Am
Maruschka	DETMERS		Mary	HOPKIN mr-s Welsh
Marv	LEVY fbc Am		Mary	HOWARD
Marvell,	ANDREW po,st Br		Mary	HUMES tv

Mary	JACKSON tv+	Mary Beth HUGHES	
Mary	JONES(Mother)labor Am	Mary Beth HURT	
Mary	KARR w Am	Mary de MANLEY w Br	
Mary	KEENEN tv	Mary Ellen CHASE e,w Am	
Mary	KELLER tv+	Mary Ellen KAY	
Mary	41	Mary Grace CANFIELD tv	
Mary	La ROCHE tv+	Mary Higgins CLARK w Am	
Mary	LATHROP r,w,po Am	Mary Jane CROFT tv	
Mary	LEASE fe,e Am	Mary Jo CATLETT tv	
Mary	LYON e Am	Mary Linn BELLER tv	
Mary	MACKAY w Br	Mary Todd LINCOLN wife-Abe	
Mary	MALLON carrier Am	Mary Tyler MOORE cm,tv+ Am	
Mary	MALONE tv	Mary VandeKamp NOHL w Am	
Mary	MARA	Mary-Kate OLSEN tv	
Mary	MARTIN la,s,tv+ Am	Mary-Louise PARKER	
Mary	McCARTHY w Am	Marya MANNES w,j Am	
Mary	McCARTY tv	Marya ZATURENSKA po Am	
Mary	McGEEHAN tv	Maryam D'ABO	
Mary	MITFORD w Br	Maryedith BURRELL tv	
Mary	MOBLEY tv+	MaryVivian PEARCE	
Mary	MONTAGU(Lady)po,w Br	Masak, RON tv+	
Mary	MURFREE w Am	Masaryk, JAN s Cz	
Mary	MURPHY	Masaryk, TOMAS s Cz	
Mary	O'HARA w Am	Masaryk, TOMAS st,ph Cz	
Mary	OLIVER po Am	Masayuki MORI	
Mary	PEARCE	Mascagni, PIETRO c It	
Mary	PHILBIN	Mascaras, MIL	
Mary	PIPHER w Am	Mascha GONSKA	
Mary	PLACE tv+	Mascolo, JOSEPH tv	
Mary	QUANT ds(minis)Br	Masefield,JOHN po Br	
Mary	REGAN	Maserati, ERNESTO ds autos It	
Mary	RENAULT w S.Afr	Masina, GIULIETTA	
Mary	SHELLEY w Br	Masip, JUAN p Sp	
Mary	STEARNS tv	Mason ADAMS tv+	
Mary	STEWART(Lady)w,e Br	Mason GROSS tv	
Mary	TANNER tv	Mason WEEMS r,bio,w Am	
Mary	TAYLOR tv	Mason WILLIAMS tv	
Mary	TERRY tv	Mason, A.E.W. w Br	
Mary	THOMAS mr-s Am	Mason, BRENT m-cnt,guit Am	
Mary	TRAINOR	Mason, CHARLES astr Br	
Mary	TREEN tv+	Mason, DAVE mr-guit,s Br	
Mary	URE	Mason, GEORGE re-st,agric Am	
Mary	WALKER md,fe Am	Mason, HILARY	
Mary	WARD w Br	Mason, JACKIE cm+	
Mary	WEBB w Br	Mason, JAMES tv+	
Mary	WELLS m-pop,s Am	Mason, LEROY	
Mary	WELLS tv	Mason, MADISON tv	
Mary	WHITNEY astr,e Am	Mason, MARLYN tv	
Mary	WICKES tv+	Mason, MARSHA	
Mary	WIGMAN ba Ger	Mason, NICK mr-drm Br	
Mary	WILCOX tv	Mason, R.A.K po,ed,w N.Zea	
Mary	WILSON mr-s Am	Mason, TOM tv+	
Mary	WILSON tv+	Massari, LEA	
Mary	WOOLLEY e Am	Masse, FELIX c Fr	
Mary	WORONOV	Massen, OSA	
Mary Ann	EVANS((Geo.Eliot)w Br	Massenet, JULES c,e Fr	
Mary Ann	JACKSON	Massey, ANNA	
Mary Ann	LEE ba Am	Massey, DANIEL	
Mary Ann	McCALL mj-s Am	Massey, EDITH	
Mary Baker EDDY r Am		Massey, GERALD po Br	
Mary Beth EVANS tv		Massey, ILONA	

Massey,   RAYMOND tv+
Massi,   NICK mr-bass,s Am
Massimo   GIROTTI
Massimo   SERATO
Massine,   LEONIDE ba Rus
Massinger, PHILIP w Br
Massio,   NICCOLO di p It
Masson,   ANDRE ar,p Fr
Masson,   DAVID ed,e,w Scot
Massys,   QUENTIN p Belg
Master Mo MATZU ph China
Masters,   BEN tv+
Masters,   EDGAR po,w Am
Masters,   JOHN w Br
Masters-King, KENT tv
Masterson, CHASE
Masterson, FAY
Masterson, MARY STUART
Masterson, PETER d
Masterson, WILLIAM(Bat)lawman Am
Mastorakis, NICO d
Mastrangelo., CARLO mr-s Am
Mastrantonio, MARY ELIZABETH
Mastren,   CARMEN tv
Mastroianni, MARCELLO
Masur,   KURT cn Ger-Am
Masur,   RICHARD tv+
Mata Hari --- spy,ba Dut
Matchett, CHRISTINE tv
Mate,   RUDOLPH d
Mateo   ALEMAN w Sp
Mateo   ALONSO su Arg
Mateo   CEREZO p Sp
Matera,   LIA w Am
Mather,   AUBREY
Mather,   COTTON r,w Am
Mather,   INCREASE r,e,w Am
Mather,   STEPHEN id,conserv Am
Mathers,   JERRY tv+
Mathers,   JIMMY tv
Matheson LANG la Br
Matheson, DON tv
Matheson, MICHELE tv
Matheson, MURRAY tv
Matheson, TIM tv+
Mathew   BRADY fo(Lincoln)Am
Mathew   CAREY pb Am
Mathews,   CAROLE tv
Mathews,   CHARLES cm,la Br
Mathews,   EDDIE b hf
Mathews,   GEORGE tv
Mathews,   KERWIN
Mathews,   LARRY tv
Mathews,   THOM
Mathewson, CHRISTY b hf
Mathias,   BOB decath,o-g'48'52
Mathias,   BOB tv
Mathiesen, LEO mj-piano,cn Finn
Mathieu   MOLE l,st Fr
Mathieu,   EMILE c,e Belg
Mathilda MAY

Mathis,   JOHNNY s-pop Am
Mathis,   SAMANTHA
Matias   ROMERO ec,st Mex
Matija   VLACIC r,e Ger
Matilde   SERAO w,j It
Matisse,   HENRI p,su Fr
Matlin,   LEONARD ct-films,w Am
Matlin,   MARLEE o-a'86,tv+
Matraca   BERG s-cnt,ws Am
Matson,   BOYD tv
Matson,   OLLIE fb hf
Matt   ADLER
Matt   BIONDI sw Am
Matt   CLARK
Matt   CRAVEN
Matt   DAMON
Matt   DILLON
Matt   FREWER tv+
Matt   LAUER tv
Matt   MALLOY
Matt   McCOY
Matt   MOORE
Matt   MULHERN tv
Matt   SHAKMAN tv
Matt   WILLIS
Matta Echaurren, ROBERTO p Chile
Matteo   BOIARDO po It
Matteo   RICCI r It
Mattes,   EVA
Matthau,   WALTER o-s'66, tv+
Matthaus   SCHINER r Swi
Matthaus   ZELL r,ref Ger
Matthay,   TOBIAS piano,c,e Br
Matthes,   FRANCOIS geol Am
Matthew   ARNOLD po,ct Br
Matthew   ASHFORD tv
Matthew   BEARD(Stymie)
Matthew   BETZ
Matthew   BROOKS tv
Matthew   FISHER mr-kbds Br
Matthew   KENNEDY bbr hf
Matthew   LEWIS w Br
Matthew   MODINE
Matthew   NEWMARK tv
Matthew   PARIS h Br
Matthew   PERRY navy,st Am
Matthe   PERRY tv
Matthew   PRIOR po,st Br
Matthew   QUAY st Am
Matthew   RIDGWAY ar Am
Matthew   SIEGEL tv
Matthew   SLOWIK tv
Matthew   SWEET s,ws Am
Matthew   VASSAR id-beer,f Am
Matthew   WEBB sw Br
Matthew   WOLL labor Am
Matthews, BRANDER e,ct,w Am
Matthews, DAKIN tv+
Matthews, DeLANE tv
Matthews, FRANCIS
Matthews, IAN mr-guit,s Br

Matthews,	JESSIE	Maurice	BOUCHOR po,w Fr
Matthews,	LESTER tv+	Maurice	DENHAM
Matthias	HABICH	Maurice	DENIS p Fr
Matthias	HUES	Maurice	DONNAY w Fr
Matthiessen, F.O. e,ct Am		Maurice	DRUON w Fr
Matthiessen, PETER w Am		Maurice	EVANS la,tv+ Am
Matthieu	CARRIERE	Maurice	EWING geol,e Am
Matthieu	ORFILA sc Fr	Maurice	FARMAN id planes Fr
Matthijs de VRIES philology Dut		Maurice	GIBB mr-bass,s Br
Matthius,	GAIL tv	Maurice	GRAU pr,d-opera Am
Matti	PELLONPAA	Maurice	HANKEY ar,st Br
Mattia	PRETI p It	Maurice	KESSEL w Fr
Mattia	SBRAGIA	Maurice	La MARCHE tv
Mattie	ALOU b	Maurice	LEBLANC w Fr
Mattingly,DON b-mv'85,rbi'85		Maurice	MURPHY
Mattingly,HEDLEY tv		Maurice	PEARSON s,tv Am.
Mattson,	ROBIN	Maurice	PIALAT d
Matty	KEMP	Maurice	RAVEL c Fr
Matty	MELNECK mj-viol Am	Maurice	RICHARD ho
Mature,	VICTOR	Maurice	ROEVES
Maturin,	CHARLES w Ir	Maurice	RONET
Matuszak,	JOHN	Maurice	ROUVIER st Fr
Matute,	ANA MARIA w Sp	Maurice	SARRAIL ar Fr
Matyas	BEL h,j Hung	Maurice	SCEVE po Fr
Matyas	DEVAY r Hung	Maurice	SENDAK w,illus Am
Matyas	RAKOSI st Hung	Maurice	STERNE p,su Am
Matz,	JOHANNA	Maurice	THOREZ st Fr
Matz,	PETER m,cn,tv	Maurice	UTRILLO p Fr
Mauch,	KARL x Ger	Maurice	WILKINS md Am
Mauchly,	JOHN eng,i,sc,id Am	Maurice	WINNICK mj-viol,cn Br
Maud	ADAMS tv+	Maurice de La TOUR p Fr	
Maud	GONNE la,st Ir	Mauricio	GARCES
Maud	PARK reform,fe Am	Maurier,	CLAIRE
Maude	EBURNE	Maurits	ESCHER at Dut
Maude,	JOAN	Mauritz	STILLER d+ Swe
Maugham,	W. SOMERSET w Br	Mauro	BOLOGNINI d
Maui	POMARE(Sir)md,st Maori	Maurois,	ANDRE w, bio Fr
Maule,	BRAD tv	Maurras,	CHARLES w,pb Fr
Maunder,	WAYNE tv	Maury	CHAYKIN
Maupassant, GUY De w Fr		Maury	POVICH tv-host Am
Maura	TIERNEY	Maury	WILLS b,tv+
Maura	WEST tv	Maury,	DARREL tv
Maura,	CARMEN	Maus,	JOHN s Am
Maureen	CANNON tv	Mauser,	PETER i-guns Ger
Maureen	MUELLER tv	Mauser,	WILHELM i-guns Ger
Maureen	O'HARA	Mauss,	MARCEL an,e,w Fr
Maureen	TEEFY	Mauve,	ANTON p Dut
Maurel,	VICTOR barit Fr	Mavis	GALLANT w Can
Maurer,	JOSHUA tv+	Mavor,	OSBORNE md,w Scot
Maurey,	NICOLE	Mawson,	DOUGLAS(Sir)x,geol Aust
Mauriac,	CLAUDE ct,w Fr	Max	AUB w Sp
Mauriac,	FRANCOIS n-l'52	Max	BAER boxer Am
Mauriat,	PAUL mj,cn,c Br	Max	BAER Sr.
Maurice	ALLAIS ec Fr	Max	BENTLEY ho
Maurice	ASHLEY h,bio Br	Max	BERG ac Ger
Maurice	BARING w.po Br	Max	BORN sc Ger
Maurice	BARRES w,j,st Fr	Max	BROD w Aus
Maurice	BEDEL w Fr	Max	BRUCH c Ger
Maurice	BEJART ba Fr	Max	CAREY b hf
Maurice	BENARD tv	Max	CASELLA tv
Maurice	BLONDEL ph Fr	Max	DREYER j,w Ger

Max	EASTMAN ed,w Am	Maxwell,	ELSA j,hostess Am
Max	ELSKAMP po Belg	Maxwell,	FRANK tv+
Max	ERNST p,su Ger	Maxwell,	GAVIN w,bio Scot
Max	FORSTER e,w Ger	Maxwell,	JAMES sc,e Scot
Max	FRISCH w Swi	Maxwell,	JEFF tv
Max	GAIL	Maxwell,	JOHN tv+
Max	HALBE w Ger	Maxwell,	LOIS
Max	HUBER l,e Swi	Maxwell,	MARILYN
Max	JACOB w,po Fr	May	IRWIN la,s Am
Max	KLINGER p,su Ger	May	McAVOY
Max	KRETZER w Ger	May	ROBSON la+ Am
Max	LINDER	May	SARTON po,w Am
Max	MILLER w Am	May	SWENSON po Am
Max	OPHULS d	May	WHITTY
Max	PERLICH	May	WYNN tv+
Max	PERUTZ sc Br	May,	BILLY tv
Max	PHIPPS	May,	BOB tv
Max	PLANCK sc Ger	May,	BRIAN mr-guit Br
Max	REGER c,e Ger	May,	DEBORAH tv+
Max	ROACH mj-drm Am	May,	DONALD tv+
Max	SCHELER ph,e Ger	May,	ELAINE tv+
Max	SLEVOGT p Ger	May,	JODHI
Max	STEINER c Am	May,	KARL w Ger
Max	TERHUNE	May,	MATHILDA
Max	THAYER	May,	PHIL cr Br
Max	THEILER md,sc,e Am	May,	PHIL mr-s Br
Max	THOREK md,w Am	May,	ROLLO ps,w Am
Max	WALL	Maya	ANGELOU w,po,s,ba+ Am
Max	WALLER po Belg	Maya	LIN su Am
Max	WEBER h,e Ger	Mayall,	JOHN mr-kbds,harmo Br
Max	WEBER p Am	Mayall,	RIK
Max	WRIGHT tv+	Mayama,	MIKO tv
Max von	GRUBER sc,e Aus	Maybach,	WILHELM id-cars Ger
Max von	LAUE sc,e Ger	Mayberry,	RUSS d
Max von	SYDOW	Mayehoff,	EDDIE tv+
Max,	ADOLPHE st Belg	Mayer	CHIP
Maxey,	PAUL tv	Mayer,	CHRISTOPHER tv
Maxfield	PARRISH p,illus Am	Mayer,	KEN tv
Maxfield,	MIKE mr-guitar Br	Mayer,	LOUIS B. pr-films Am
Maxie,	LEROY mj-drm Am	Mayer,	MARIA sc Am
Maxim,	HIRAM(Sir)i,id	Mayf	NUTTER
Maxime	Du CAMP j Fr	Mayfield,	CURTIS s,ws,pr Am
Maxime	WEYGAND ar Fr	Mayhew,	HENRY j Br
Maximilian	HARDEN j,w Ger	Mayim	BIALIK
Maximo	ALVEAR st Arg	Mayle,	PETER w Am
Maximo	SANTOS st Urug	Maynard,	DON fb hf
Maxine	ELLIOTT la Am	Maynard,	JOYCE w Am
Maxine	KING s,tv Am	Maynard,	KEN
Maxine	KUMIN w,po Am	Maynard,	KERMIT
Maxine	MILLER tv	Maynard,	MIMI
Maxine	STUART tv+	Maynard,	PARRISH ba Am
Maxmilian	von EYTH eng,i Ger	Mayne	REID w Ir
Maxmillian	SCHELL tv+	Mayne,	FERDINAND(Ferdy)
Maxted,	ELLEN tv	Mayne,	JASPER w,r Br
Maxton,	JAMES st Br	Mayo	METHOT
Maxwell	GAIL tv	Mayo,	ALFREDO
Maxwell	PERKINS ed Am	Mayo,	FRANK
Maxwell	REED	Mayo,	GEORGE ps,e,w Am
Maxwell	SMART fc	Mayo,	VIRGINIA
Maxwell	TAYLOR ar,st Am	Mayo,	WHITMAN tv
Maxwell,	EDWIN	Mayo,	WILLIAM md Am

Mayr,   JOHANN c Ger
Mayron,   MELANIE tv+
Mays,   WILLIE b-mv'54'65 hf
Maza,   BOB
Mazar,   DEBI
Mazas,   JACQUES viol,c Fr
Mazes   MICHAEL tv
Mazo   De la ROCHE w Can
Mazo,   JUAN del p Sp
Mazrahi,   ISAAC
Mazurki,   MIKE tv+
Mazursky,   PAUL d+
Mazza,   CHRIS w Am
Mazzello,   JOSEPH
Mazzoni,   GUIDO su It
Mboya,   THOMAS(Tom) st Kenya
Mc   LYTLE m-rap Am
Mca   --- m-rap Am
McAdam,   HEATHER tv
McAdoo,   BOB bb-m'75 hf
McAdoo,   WILLIAM id-rr,st Am
McAfee,   GEORGE fb hf
McAfee,   JOHNNY mj-s,tv Am
McAleer,   DES
McAnally,   RAY
McArthur   ALEX
McAuley,   JAMES po,e.ct Aust
McAuliffe,   ANTHONY ar Am
McAvoy,   MAY
McBain,   DIANE
McBain,   ED w Am
McBride,   DIRTY DAN tv
McBride,   DON tv
McBride,   MARTINA s Am
McCaffery,   JOHN K.M. tv
McCain,   FRANCES
McCain,   LEE tv
McCall,   MARY ANN mj-s Am
McCall,   MITZI tv
McCall,   SHALANE tv
McCalla,   IRISH
McCallany,   HOLT
McCallion,   JAMES tv
McCallister, LON
McCallum,   DAVID tv+
McCallum,   NEIL tv
McCalman,   MACON tv+
McCambridge, MERCEDES o-s'49,tv+
McCann,   CHUCK
McCann,   DONAL
McCann,   SEAN tv+
McCarey,   LEO o-d'44
McCarthy,   ANDREW
McCarthy,   CHARLIE pupp
McCarthy,   CLEM horseraces,tv Am
McCarthy,   CORMACK w Am
McCarthy,   JOSEPH bmg hf
McCarthy,   JOSEPH st Am
McCarthy,   KEVIN tv+
McCarthy,   LIN tv+
McCarthy,   MARY w Am

McCarthy,   SHEILA
McCarthy,   THOMAS b hf
McCartney,   LINDA mr-pian,s,fo Am
McCartney,   PAUL mr,c+ Br
McCarty,   JIM mr-drm Br
McCarty,   MARY tv+
McCarty,   PATTI
McCarver,   TIM b,tv Am
McCary,   ROD tv+
McCashin,   CONSTANCE tv+
McCauley,   JACKIE mr-kbds Ir
McCauley,   PATRICK mr-drm Ir
McCay,   WINSOR cr Am
McClain,   CADY tv
McClain,   JAMES tv
McClanahan, ED w Am
McClanahan, RUE tv+
McClelland, DONALD tv
McClintick, DAVID w Am
McClintock, BARBARA n-m'83
McClintock, GUTHRIE tv
McClinton,   DELBERT s,ws Am
McClory,   SEAN tv+
McCloskey,   LEIGH tv+
McCloy,   JOHN st Am
McClung,   CLARENCE sc,e Am
McClure,   BRYTON tv
McClure,   DOUG tv+
McClure,   FRANK tv
McClure,   JAMES w Br
McClure,   M'LISS tv
McClure,   MARC
McClure,   MICHAEL po,w Am
McClure,   MOLLY
McClure,   PAULA tv
McClure,   S.S. j,ed Am
McClurg,   BOB tv
McClurg,   EDIE tv+
McCluskey,   ANDY mr-s Br
McConnell,   ED tv
McConnell,   JUDY tv
McConnell,   LULU tv
McCoo,   MARILYN tv-host,mr-s+
McCook,   EDWARD ar,st Am
McCord,   KENT tv+
McCormack,   JOHN tenor Am
McCormack,   MARY
McCormack,   MIKE fb hf
McCormack,   PATRICIA tv
McCormack,   PATTY
McCormick,   ANNE j Am
McCormick,   CAROLYN tv
McCormick,   CYRUS i,id Am
McCormick,   FRANK b-mv'40
McCormick,   MAUREEN tv+
McCormick,   MIKE b-cy'67
McCormick,   MYRON
McCormick,   PAT
McCormick,   ROBERT pb Am
McCouch,   GRAYSON tv
McCourt,   EMER

McCourt, FRANK w Am	McDuffie, GEORGE st Am
McCovey, WILLIE b-mv'69 hf	McEachin, JAMES tv+
McCowen, ALEC	McElhenny,HUGH fb hf
McCoy TYNER mj-piano,cn Am	McElhone, ELOISE tv
McCoy, CHARLIE m-cnt,cn,tv	McEnery, JOHN
McCoy, CLYDE mj-trump,cn Am	McEnery, PETER
McCoy, HERMAN s,cn,tv Am	McEnroe, ANNIE
McCoy, HORACE w Am	McEnroe, JOHN t,tv Am
McCoy, JACK tv	McEntire, REBA s-cnt+ Am
McCoy, JOSEPH cattleman Am	McEveety, VINCENT d
McCoy, MATT	McEwen, JOHN(Sir)c
McCoy, SID tv	McFadden, GATES tv+
McCoy, TIM	McFarland,GEORGE(SPANKY)
McCracken,BRANCH bb hf	McFeely, WILLIAM p-b'82
McCracken,JACK bb hf	McFerrin, BOBBY s Am
McCrae, HUGH po Aust	McGann, PAUL
McCrae, JOHN md,po Can	McGavin, DARREN tv+
McCrane, PAUL tv+	McGee, FIBBER & MOLLY cm Am
McCrary, DARIUS tv	McGee, FRANK tv
McCrary, TEX tv	McGee, HENRY tv
McCrea, ANN tv	McGee, THOMAS st,w Can
McCrea, JODY tv+	McGee, VONETTA
McCrea, JOEL tv+	McGee, WILLIE b-mv'85 &
McCullen, KATHY tv	McGee, WILLIE bat'85'90
McCullers,CARSON w Am	McGeehan, MARY tv
McCulloch,IAN mr-s Br	McGill, BRUCE tv+
McCullough, COLLEEN w Aust	McGill, EVERETT tv+
McCullough, DAVID p-b'93	McGill, JAMES furs,f Can
McCullough, JULIE tv+	McGillis, KELLY
McCullough, KIMBERLY	McGinley, JOHN
McCullough, PHILO	McGinley, PHYLLIS p-q'61
McCutchan,ARAD bbc hf	McGinley, TED tv+
McDaniel, GEORGE tv	McGinnis, SCOTT tv+
McDaniel, HATTIE o-s'39	McGinnity,JOE b hf
McDaniel, MEL s-cnt Am	McGiver, JOHN tv+
McDaniels,DARRYL D. m-rap Am	McGoohan, PATRICK tv+
McDermott,BOBBY bb hf	McGovern, ELIZABETH
McDermott,DYLAN	McGovern, TERRY tv
McDevitt, RUTH tv+	McGowan, BILL b hf
McDonald, CHRISTOPHER	McGowan, J.P. d+
McDonald, COUNTRY JOE mr-guit,s	McGrail, WALTER
McDonald, FRANCIS	McGrath, DEREK tv
McDonald, FRANK d	McGrath, FRANK tv
McDonald, IAN mr-sax Br	McGraw, CHARLES tv+
McDonald, MARIE	McGraw, JOHN b,bmg hf
McDonald, MICHAEL m-kbds,s,w Am	McGraw, TIM s-cnt Am
McDonald, MICHAEL tv	McGreevey,MIKE tv
McDonald, RYAN tv	McGregor, ANGELA
McDonald, SEVEN ANN tv	McGregor, EWAN
McDonnell,MARY tv+	McGriff, FRED b,hr'89'92
McDonough,MARY	McGuane, THOMAS w Am
McDonough,MARY ELIZABETH tv	McGuffey, WILLIAM e,w Am
McDormand,FRANCES o-a'96	McGuinn, ROGER(Jim)mr-guit,sAm
McDowall, BETTY	McGuinness, TOM mr-bass Br
McDowall, RODDY tv+	McGuire Sisters, THE s,tv Am
McDowell, CLAIRE	McGuire, AL bbc hf
McDowell, EPHRAIM md Am	McGuire, BETTY tv
McDowell, IRVIN ar Am	McGuire, BIFF
McDowell, JACK b-cy'93	McGuire, BOBBY tv
McDowell, MALCOLM	McGuire, CHRISTINE tv
McDowell, NELSON	McGuire, DICK bb hf

McGuire, DON	McLain, DENNY b-cy-mv'68'69
McGuire, DOROTHY tv+	McLaren, BRUCE race cars N.Zea
McGuire, FRANK bbc hf	McLarty, RON tv+
McGuire, MICHAEL	McLaughlin, ANDREA tv
McGuire, PHYLLIS tv	McLaughlin, GIBB
McGwire, MARK b,hr'87'95'98	McLean, DON mr-s,ws Am
McHattie, STEPHEN tv+	McLemore, LAMONTE mr-s Am
McHugh, FRANK	McLeod, NORMAN d
McHugh, JIMMY c Am	McLerie, ALLYN tv+
McIntire, JOHN tv+	McLiam, JOHN tv+
McIntire, TIM tv+	McLuhan, MARSHALL ct,w,ph Can
McIntosh, BURR	McMahon, ED tv-host+ Am
McIntosh, LORRAINE mr-s Scot	McMahon, HORACE tv+
McIntyre, BILL tv+	McMain, BILL m-cnt,tv Am
McIntyre, CHRISTINE	McManus, GEORGE cr Am
McIntyre, JAMES r Am	McManus, MICHAEL tv
McIntyre, JOE mr-s Am	McMartin, JOHN tv+
McIntyre, ONNIE mr-guit Scot	McMaster, JOHN h,e Am
McIntyre, OSCAR j,w Am	McMillan, EDWIN n-c'51
McIsaac, MARIANNE tv	McMillan, GLORIA tv
McK, MISHA tv	McMillan, KENNETH tv+
McKagan. DUFF ROSE mr-bass Am	McMillan, TERRY w Am
McKay, ALLISON tv	McMullan, JIM tv
McKay, CLAUDE po,w Am	McMurphy, DANNY tv
McKay, WANDA	McMurray, SAM tv
McKean, MICHAEL tv+	McMurtrey,JOAN tv
McKean, THOMAS st,l Am	McMurtry, LARRY p-f'86
McKechnie,BILL b hf	McNair, BARBARA tv+
McKee, LAFE	McNally, JOHN mr-guit,s Br
McKee, LONETTE	McNally, JOHN(Blood)fb hf
McKellan, IAN la+	McNally, STEPHEN tv+
McKellar, DANICA tv+	McNamara, BRIAN tv+
McKenna, JOSEPH l,st Am	McNamara, J. PATRICK tv
McKenna, REGINALD st Br	McNamara, ROBERT st,w,e Am
McKenna, SIOBHAN	McNamara, WILLIAM
McKenna, T.P.	McNaughton, HARRY tv
McKenna, TRAVIS tv	McNear, HOWARD tv+
McKenna, VIRGINIA	McNeeley, LARRY tv
McKenney, RUTH j,w Am	McNeice, IAN
McKennon, DAL tv	McNeil, KATE tv
McKenzie, FAY	McNeil, MICK mr-kbds Br
McKenzie, RICHARD tv	McNeile, HERMAN w Br
McKeon, DOUG tv+	McNellis, MAGGI tv
McKeon, NANCY tv+	McNichol, JIMMY
McKeon, PHILIP tv	McNichol, KRISTY tv+
McKeown, LESLIE mr-s Scot	McNulty, PAT tv
McKern, LEO	McPartland, JIMMY mj-trump Am
McKerrow, AMANDA ba Am	McPartland, MARIAN mj-piano Am
McKim, CHARLES ac Am	McPeak, SANDY
McKim, ROBERT	McPhatter,CLYDE s-pop,r&b Am
McKinley, CATHERINE w Am	McPhee, JOHN w,ed Am
McKinley, WILLIAM 25th pres	McPhee, JOHNNIE tv
McKinney, BILL	McPherson,AIMEE SEMPLE r Am
McKinney, KURT tv	McPherson,GRAHAM mr-s Br
McKinney, NINA MAE	McPherson,JAMES AL.p-f'78
McKinney, WILLIAM tv	McPherson,PATRICIA tv
McKinnon, PATRICIA tv	McQuade, ARLENE tv
McKuen, ROD po Am	McQuade, JOHN tv
McLagan, IAN mr-kbds Br	McQuarrie,MURDOCK
McLaglen, ANDREW W. d	McQueen, BUTTERFLY tv+
McLaglen, VICTOR o-a'35	McQueen, CHAD

McQueen,	STEVE tv+	Megan	GALLAGHER tv+
McQueeney,	ROBERT tv	Megan	GALLIVAN tv
McRae,	ELLEN tv	Megan	MULLALLY tv
McRae,	FRANK	Megan	WARD
McRae,	HAL b,rbi'82	Meghnad	SAHA astro,sc,e India
McRae,	MILTON pb Am	Megnot,	ROYA tv
McRaney,	GERALD tv+	Megowan,	DON
McReynolds, JAMES l Am		Megs	JENKINS
McShane,	IAN tv+	Mehmed	FAUD PASA st Turk
McTiernan, JOHN d		Mehmed	SOKOLLU st Turk
McVety,	DREW tv	Mehmed	TEVFIK po Turk
McVey,	PATRICK tv+	Mehmed	ZIYA w,e,st Turk
McVie,	CHRISTINE mr-kbds Br	Mehmet	SHEHU st Albania
McVie,	JOHN mr-bass Br	Mehta,	VED j,w India
McWilliams, CAROLINE tv+		Mehta,	ZUBIN cn India
Mead,	GEORGE ph,ps,e Am	Mehul,	ETIENNE c Fr
Mead,	MARGARET an,w Am	Meier,	EMILY w Am
Meade	LEWIS(Lux)mj-piano Am	Meier,	RANDY tv
Meade,	JAMES n-e'77 Br	Meiggs,	HENRY bus,st Am
Meader,	VAUGHN m,g-r'62	Meighan,	THOMAS
Meadowlark LEMON bb		Meighen,	ARTHUR st Can
Meadows,	AUDREY tv	Meigs,	JOSIAH l,e Am
Meadows,	JAYNE tv+	Meikle,	PAT tv
Meadows,	JOYCE	Meiklejohn, LINDA tv	
Meadows,	TIM tv	Meiko	HARADA
Meagan	FAY tv	Meillon,	JOHN
Mean Joe	GREENE fb	Meindert	HOBBEMA p Dut
Meaney,	COLM tv+	Meinong,	ALEXIUS ph,ps Aus
Means,	GASTON swindler Am	Meir	KAHANE st,r Isr
Meanwell, W.E.(Dr.)bbc hf		Meir,	GOLDA st Isr
Meany,	GEORGE labor Am	Meireles, CECILIA po Braz	
Meara,	ANNE cm,tv+ Am	Meisner,	RANDY mr-bass,s Am
Meat Loaf	--- mr,s Am	Meitner,	LISE sc Aus
Medak,	PETER d	Meixner,	KARL
Medardo	ROSSO su It	Mejias,	ALFONSO
Medawar,	PETER(Sir)n-m'60	Mejias,	ISABELLE
Medford,	KAY tv+	Mekhi	PHIFER
Medgar	EVERS e,civ rts Am	Mekka,	EDDIE tv
Medill,	JOSEPH j Am	Mel	ALLEN tv+
Medina,	JOSE h,pb Chile	Mel	BLANC tv+
Medina,	OFELIA	Mel	BLOUNT fb hf
Medina,	PATRICIA	Mel	BROOKS d, tv+
Medley,	BILL s Am	Mel	BRYANT tv
Medress,	HANK mr-s tenor,Am	Mel	DAMSKI d
Medtner,	NIKOLAY piano,c Rus	Mel	FERRER
Medwick,	JOE b-mv'37 hf	Mel	GIBSON
Medwin,	MICHAEL	Mel	HARRIS tv+
Mee,	ARTHUR j,ed,w Br	Mel	HEIN fb hf
Meehan,	LEW	Mel	LEWIS mj-drm,c Am
Meek,	BARBARA tv	Mel	McDANIEL s-cnt Am
Meek,	DONALD	Mel	OTT b hf
Meeker,	GEORGE	Mel	POWELL c Am
Meeker,	RALPH	Mel	SMITH
Meeno	PELUCE tv	Mel	STEWART tv
Meer,	JAN van der p Dut	Mel	STUART d
Meer,	SIMON van der n-p'84	Mel	TILLIS s,ws Am
Meg	FOSTER tv+	Mel	TORME s+ Am
Meg	RYAN	Mel	WELLES
Meg	TILLY	Melanie	GAFFIN tv
Meg	WYLLIE tv	Melanie	KLEIN ps,w Br
Megan	FOLLOWS tv+	Melanie	MAYRON tv+

Melanie	THON w Am	Menage,	GILLES l,w Fr
Melanie	WILSON tv	Menahem	GOLAN d
Melato,	MARIANGELA	Menander	--- w Gr
Melba	MOORE s-cnt+ Am	Menard,	MICHEL fur trade Am
Melba,	NELLIE(Dame)s Aust	Menchu,	RIGOBERTA n-x'92
Melchers,	GARI p Am	Mencken,	H.L. j,ed,ct Am
Melchior	FRANCK c Ger	Mendel,	GREGOR sc Aus
Melchior	LUSSY ar,r Swi	Mendel,	STEPHEN tv
Melchior	TREUB sc Dut	Mendeleyev,	DMITRY sc,e Rus
Melchior,	LAURITZ tenor Am	Mendelsohn,	JANE w Am
Meldrum,	WENDEL tv+	Mendelssohn,	ERICH ac Am
Melendez,	BILL d	Mendelssohn,	FELIX pian,cn,c Ger
Melendez,	JOHN tv	Mendelssohn,	MOSES ph Ger
Melgar,	GABRIEL tv	Mendenhall,	DAVID tv+
Meli,	GIOVANNI md,po It	Mendes,	CATULLE w Fr
Melies,	GEORGES d Fr	Mendoza,	DANIEL boxer Br
Melinda	CULEA tv	Mendoza,	INIGO po Sp
Melinda	DILLON	Mendoza,	MARK mr-bass Am
Melinda	NAUD tv	Menen,	AUBREY w Br
Meline,	FELIX st Fr	Menendez Pidal, RAMON h Sp
Melis,	JOSE m,cn,tv Am	Meng	FEI
Melissa	GILBERT tv+	Meng-tzu	--- ph China
Melissa	LEO	Mengatti,	JOHN tv+
Melissa	MARTIN tv	Menger,	CARL von ec,e Aus
Melissa	MOORE	Menges,	JOYCE tv
Melissa	REEVES tv	Mengs,	ANTON p Ger
Mell,	MARISA	Menighan,	KELLEY tv
Mellencamp,	JOHN mr-guit,s,ws	Menjou,	ADOLPHE tv+
Mellini,	SCOTT tv	Menken,	ADAH la Am
Mellon,	ANDREW id,f Am	Menken,	ALAN c Am
Melmacknan,	ALF tv	Menninger,	KARL ps Am
Melo,	FRANCISCOar,h,po Port	Menno ter BRAAK ct Dut
Melonie	HALLER tv	Menotti,	GIAN-CARLO p-m'50'55
Melora	HARDIN	Menou,	ABD ar Fr
Melora	WALTERS	Menshikov,	OLEG
Melton,	BILL b,hr'71	Menuhin,	YEHUDI violin Am
Melton,	JAMES tv	Menzel,	ADOLPH p,illus Ger
Melton,	SID tv+	Menzies,	HEATHER
Melvil	DEWEY e,library Am	Menzies,	ROBERT(Sir)st Aust
Melville	COOPER	Merald	KNIGHT mr-s Am
Melville	RUICK tv	Merande,	DORO tv+
Melville,	HERMAN w,po Am	Mercati,	MICHELE md It
Melville,	SAM tv+	Mercator,	GERARDUS geog Belg
Melvin	BELLI l Am	Merce	CUNNINGHAM ba Am
Melvin	CALVIN sc Am	Merce,	ANTONIA ba Arg
Melvin	FRANK d	Mercedes	LACKEY w Am
Melvin	Van PEEBLES tv+	Mercedes	RUEHL
Melvin,	ALLAN tv	Mercer,	BERYL
Melvin,	HAROLD m-soul	Mercer,	CECIL w Br
Melvin,	MURRAY	Mercer,	FRANCES tv
Mehmed	FAUD PASA st Turk	Mercer,	JOHNNY lyriics Am
Melvin,	MURRAY	Mercer,	MABEL s Am
Melvin,	SUSAN tv	Mercer,	MARIAN tv
Melvyn	BRAGG w Br	Merchant,	JIMMY mr-s Am
Melvyn	DOUGLAS tv+	Merchant,	NATALIE mr,s Am
Mem de	SA st Port	Merchant,	VIVIEN
Memling,	HANS p Belg	Mercie,	ANTONIN su Fr
Memmoli,	GEORGE tv	Mercier,	DESIRE r,ph Belg
Mena,	JUAN de po Sp	Mercier,	HONORE st Can
Mena,	PEDRO de su Sp	Mercier,	MICHELE
Menachem	BEGIN st Israel	Merck,	JOHANN w,ct Ger

Mercouri,	MELINA
Mercy	WARREN w Am
Mercy,	FRANZ von ar Aus
Meredith	MacRAE tv+
Meredith	MARON tv
Meredith	WILLSON mj,cn,c,tv Am
Meredith,	BURGESS tv+
Meredith,	DON tv+
Meredith,	GEORGE po,w,ct Br
Meredith,	IRIS
Meredith,	JUDI tv
Meredith,	LUCILLE tv
Meredith,	WILLIAM p-q'88
Merenda,	LUC
Merezhkovsky,	DMITRY w,po Rus
Mergenthaler,	OTTMAR i Am
Merhi,	JALAL
Merhi,	JOSEPH d
Merian	COOPER w,pr Am
Merie	EARLE tv
Meril,	MACHA
Merimee,	PROSPER w Fr
Mering,	JOSEPH von md,e Ger
Meriwether LEWIS x Am	
Meriwether,	LEE tv+
Meriwether,	LOUISE w Am
Merkel,	UNA
Merkin,	DAPHNE w,j Am
Merkys,	ANTANAS st,ar Lith
Merle	HAGGARD s-cnt Am
Merle	OBERON
Merle	PARK ba Br
Merle	TRAVIS s-cnt Am
Merle	TUVE sc,e Am
Merleau-Ponty,	MAURICE ph,e,w Fr
Merlin	OLSEN fb,hf,tv+
Merlin,	JAN tv+
Merman,	ETHEL la,s+ Am
Merna	KENNEDY
Merriam	GEORGE id-print,pb Am
Merriam,	CHARLES id-print,pb
Merrick	LEONARD w Br
Merrick,	LYNN
Merrifield,	BRUCE n-c'84
Merrill	OSMOND s,tv Am
Merrill,	BOB lyrics Am
Merrill,	BUDDY m-guit,tv Am
Merrill,	DINA
Merrill,	GARY tv+
Merrill,	JAMES w,p-q'77
Merrill,	ROBERT tv
Merrill,	STUART po Am
Merriman,	RANDY tv
Merritt	BUTRICK tv+
Merritt	FERNALD sc Am
Merritt,	ANNA p Am
Merritt,	THERESA tv
Merrow,	JANE
Merry	ANDERS tv+
Merry	CLAYTON tv
Merry	MARTIN tv

Merton	MILLER ec Am
Merton,	JOHN
Merton,	ROBERT n-e'97
Merton,	THOMAS r,po,w Am
Merton,	ZIENIA tv
Merulo,	CLAUDIO organ,c It
Merv	GRIFFIN tv-pr Am
Mervyn	JOHNS
Mervyn	LeROY d
Mervyn	PEAKE w,illus Br
Merwin,	WILLIAM(W.S,)p-q'71
Meryl	STREEP
Mesdag,	HENDRIK p Dut
Meshach	TAYLOR tv+
Meshech	WEARE l,st Am
Mesmer,	FRANZ md Ger
Messerschmitt,WILLYds-aero,idGer	
Messiaen,	OLIVIER c,e Fr
Messick,	DON tv
Messier,	CHARLES astr Fr
Messier,	MARK ho-m'90'2
Messina,	JIM mr-guit,s Am
Messinger,GERTRUDE	
Mesta,	PEARLE hostess Am
Mestre,	ERNESTO w Am
Mestrovic,IVAN su Yu	
Meta	GOLDING tv
Metalious,GRACE w Am	
Metaxas,	IOANNIS ar,st Gr
Metcalf,	LAURIE tv+
Metcalf,	MARK
Metcalfe,	BURT tv
Metchik,	AARON tv
Metchnikoff, ELIE n-m'08	
Metge,	BERNAT po Sp
Metheny,	PAT mj-guitar Am
Methot,	MAYO
Metrano,	ART tv+
Metraux,	ALFRED an,w Swi
Metsu,	GABRIEL p Dut
Mettey,	LYNETTE tv
Metzler,	JIM
Meulen,	ADAM van der p Belg
Meurisse,	PAUL
Mew,	CHARLOTTE po Br
Meyer	LEVIN w,j Am
Meyer	LONDON labor Am
Meyer,	ADOLF ps,e Am
Meyer,	ANNIE e,w Am
Meyer,	CONRAD po,w Swi
Meyer,	EDUARD h,e Ger
Meyer,	JOSEPH c Am
Meyer,	NICHOLAS d,w Am
Meyer,	RAY bbc hf
Meyer,	RUSS d
Meyer,	TORBEN
Meyer,	VIKTOR sc,e Ger
Meyerbeer GIACOMO c Ger	
Meyerheim,EDUARD p Ger	
Meyerhof,	OTTO n-m'22
Meyerink,	VICTORIA tv/fs

Meyers,	ANN bb hf	Michael	DANTE
Meyers,	ARI tv+	Michael	DATTA po Bengal
Meyers,	AUGIE mr-keybds Am	Michael	DELANO tv+
Meyers,	MIKE	Michael	DeLUISE tv
Meynell,	ALICE po,w Br	Michael	Des BARRES tv+
Meynell,	WILFRID j,w Br	Michael	DONAHUE tv
Meyrink,	GUSTAV w Ger	Michael	DORN tv+
Meyrink,	MICHELLE	Michael	DORRIS w Am
Mezzogiorno,	VITTORIO	Michael	DOUGLAS tv+
Mia	FARROW tv+	Michael	DRAYTON po Br
Mia	KORF tv	Michael	DUNN
Mia	SARA	Michael	EISNER tv
Miall,	EDWARD r,j Br	Michael	ELPHICK
Miall,	TERRY mr-drums Br	Michael	EMIL
Miao,	CORA	Michael	ENSIGN tv+
Miao,	NORA	Michael	FAIRMAN tv
Michael	ANSARA	Michael	FARADAY sc Br
Michael	ANTHONY mr-bass Am	Michael	FEMINA
Michael	APAFI st Transyl	Michael	FISHMAN tv
Michael	APTED d	Michael	FOREST
Michael	ARLEN w Br	Michael	FRAYN j,w Br
Michael	BALCON(Sir)pr-films	Michael	GALABRU
Michael	BALFE s,c Irish	Michael	GAMBON
Michael	BALFOUR tv+	Michael	GAZZZO
Michael	BEACH tv+	Michael	GENET tv
Michael	BECK tv+	Michael	GEORGE mr,s Br
Michael	BEER w Ger	Michael	GILBERT w Br
Michael	BENNETT ba Am	Michael	GOODROW tv
Michael	BERGER tv	Michael	GOODWIN tv+
Michael	BIEHN	Michael	GOTHARD
Michael	BOATMAN tv	Michael	GOUGH
Michael	BOLTON s-pop Am	Michael	GREENE
Michael	BOND w Am	Michael	GROSS tv+
Michael	BOWEN	Michael	GWYNNE
Michael	BRANDON	Michael	HALL tv
Michael	BROWN mr-kbds Am	Michael	HARLAND tv
Michael	BRUCE po,e Scot	Michael	HARVEY tv
Michael	BUFFER tv	Michael	HIGGINS
Michael	BURNS tv+	Michael	HOGAN
Michael	BUTOR w Fr	Michael	HORDERN
Michael	CAINE	Michael	HORSE tv+
Michael	CALLAN tv+	Michael	HORTON tv
Michael	CARTER tv	Michael	HUGHES tv
Michael	CASHIN(Sir)st Can	Michael	INNES w Br
Michael	CEVERIS tv+	Michael	JACKSON mr-s+ Am
Michael	CHAN	Michael	JAYSTON
Michael	CHIKLIS tv	Michael	JETER tv+
Michael	CHRISTY tv	Michael	JORDAN bb
Michael	CIMINO d	Michael	KEATON
Michael	CLARKE mr-drm Am	Michael	KEENS tv
Michael	COLE tv+	Michael	KERR l,st Am
Michael	COLLINS as Am	Michael	KIRBY
Michael	CONNER w Am	Michael	KITCHEN
Michael	CONRAD tv+	Michael	KNIGHT tv+
Michael	COSTA(Sir)cn,c Br	Michael	LANDON tv+
Michael	CRAIG	Michael	LEARNED tv+
Michael	CRAWFORD	Michael	LEHMANN d
Michael	CUDAHY id-meats Am	Michael	LEMBECK tv+
Michael	CULVER	Michael	LERNER
Michael	CURTIZ d	Michael	LINK tv
Michael	DAHL p Swe	Michael	LIPTON tv

Michael	LOMBARD tv	Michael	TESSIER tv
Michael	MacRAE	Michael	THOMA tv
Michael	MADSEN	Michael	THOMAS cn
Michael	MAZES tv	Michael	TODD tv
Michael	McCLURE po,w Am	Michael	TOLAN tv+
Michael	McDONALDm-kbds,s,w Am	Michael	TUCCI tv
Michael	McDONALD tv	Michael	TUCHNER d
Michael	McGUIRE	Michael	TUCKER tv+
Michael	McKEAN tv+	Michael	VENTRIS ac Br
Michael	McMANUS tv	Michael	WARREN
Michael	MEDWIN	Michael	WELDON tv
Michael	MONARCH, mr-guit Am	Michael	WHALEN
Michael	MORGAN tv+	Michael	WILDING tv+
Michael	MURPHY	Michael	WINCOTT
Michael	NADER tv+	Michael	WINNER d
Michael	NORELL tv	Michael	WINSLOW
Michael	NOURI tv+	Michael	WOLFF m,cn,tv Am
Michael	O'CLERY h Ir	Michael	WOODS
Michael	O'KEEFE	Michael	WRIGHT tv+
Michael	O'LEARY tv	Michael	YAMA tv
Michael	O'SHEA tv+	Michael	YORK tv+
Michael	OLIVER	Michael D.ROBERTS tv+	
Michael	ONTKEEN tv+	Michael J.FOX tv+	
Michael	OVITZ bus Am	Michael Jai WHITE	
Michael	OWENS i,id-glass Am	Michael, GEORGE s,tv Br	
Michael	PACHER p Ger	Michael, GERTRUDE	
Michael	PALIN	Michael, MIKHAIL st-czar Rus	
Michael	PALMER w Am	Michael, RALPH tv+	
Michael	PARE tv+	Michael-James WIXTED tv	
Michael	PARKS tv+	Michaelangelo ANTONIONI d	
Michael	PATAKI	Michaelis,DARIO	
Michael	PATE	Michaels, AL tv-spts j Am	
Michael	POLLARD	Michaels, JANNA tv	
Michael	POWELL d+	Michaels, JEANNA tv	
Michael	PRAED tv+	Michaels, LORNE tv pr	
Michael	PUPIN sc,i Am	Michaels, RAY tv	
Michael	REED tv	Michaels, RICHARD d	
Michael	RENNIE tv+	Michaelson, KARI tv	
Michael	RICH tv	Michal BAT-ADAM	
Michael	RIPPER	Michalske,MIKE fb hf	
Michael	RITCHIE d	Michaux, HENRI po,p Fr	
Michael	ROOKER	Miche, JEAN r Fr	
Michael	RUDDER tv	Michel AUCLAIR	
Michael	SADLER st,ref Br	Michel AUMONT	
Michael	SALCIDO tv	Michel BLANC	
Michael	SARS sc,e Nor	Michel BOUQUET	
Michael	SCHULTZ d	Michel BUTOR w Fr	
Michael	SCOLARI tv	Michel COLOMBE su Fr	
Michael	SCOT astrology Scot	Michel De YOUNG j,pb Am	
Michael	SHAARA w Am	Michel FOKINE ba Am	
Michael	SHEA tv	Michel MENARD fur trade Am	
Michael	SHEPLEY tv+	Michel NEY ar Fr	
Michael	SKLAR tv	Michel PICCOLI	
Michael	SMITH sc Can	Michel ROLLE math Fr	
Michael	SMITH tv	Michel SEDAINE w Fr	
Michael	SOMES ba Br	Michel SIMON	
Michael	SPINKS boxer Am	Michel de KLERK ac Dut	
Michael	SPOUND tv	Michel, CLAUDE su Fr	
Michael	ST. GERARD tv+	Michel, FRANNY tv	
Michael	SUTTON tv	Michel, HARTMUT n-c'88	
Michael	TALBOTT tv	Michelangelo---su,ac,p,po It	

Michele	CARAFA c It	Middleton,CHARLES	
Michele	CAREY tv+	Middleton,NOELLE	
Michele	LEE tv+	Middleton,RAY	
Michele	MERCATI md It	Middleton,ROBERT tv+	
Michele	MERCIER	Middleton,THOMAS w Br	
Michele	MORGAN	Middleton,TOM tv	
Michele	PEZZA robber It	Midgley, RICHARD tv	
Michele	PLACIDO	Midgley, THOMAS Jr sc,id Am	
Michele	SOAVI d	Midkiff, DALE	
Michele,	BRIDGET tv	Midler, BETTE g-r'89 Am	
Michelet, JULES h Fr		Midori --- violin Japan	
Michelin, ANDRE id-tires,f Fr		Midori ITO sk Japan	
Micheline PRESLE		Midori Ito --- sk Japan	
Michell, KEITH tv+		Mie HAMA	
Michelle	BAUER	Mies van der Rohe, LUDWIG ac Am	
Michelle	BENNETT tv	Mifflin, GEORGE pb Am	
Michelle	GREENE tv+	Mifune, TOSHIRO	
Michelle	JOHNSON	Migne, JACQUES r,ed Fr	
Michelle	LITTLE	Mignon, ABRAHAM p Dut	
Michelle	MEYRINK	Miguel CARO st Colom	
Michelle	NICHOLS tv+	Miguel DELIBES w Sp	
Michelle	SEPE tv	Miguel ESLAVA c Sp	
Michelle, ANNE		Miguel FERRER	
Michelle, JANEE		Miguel MIHURA w Sp	
Michelman,KEN tv		Miguel MIRAMON ar Mex	
Michels, ROBERT ec,e Ger		Miguel NUNEZ Jr tv	
Michelson,ALBERT sc Am		Miguel PINERO	
Michelson,AMY tv		Miguel de UNAMUNO ph,po,w Sp	
Michenaud,GERALD tv		Mihalache,ION st Rom	
Michener, JAMES A. p-f'48		Mihalik, RED bbr hf	
Michi, MARIA		Mihaly BABITS w Hung	
Michiel RUYTER navy Dut		Mihaly HORVATH r,st Hung	
Michiel van COXIE p Belg		Mihaly KAROLYI st Hung	
Michiyo ARATAMA		Mihashi, PATSUYA	
Mick	AVORY mr-drm Br	Mihura, MIGUEL w Sp	
Mick	BOX ws Br	Miiko TAKA	
Mick	FORD	Mika WALTARI w Finn	
Mick	JAGGER mr+ Br	Mikan, GEORGE bb hf	
Mick	JONES mr-guit,s Br	Mike ALLSUP mr-guit Am	
Mick	MARS mr-guit Am	Mike BARSON mr-kbds Br	
Mick	McNEIL mr-kbds Br	Mike BOSSY ho	
Mick	RALPHS mr-guit Br	Mike CONNORS tv+	
Mick	TALBOT mr-kbds Br	Mike CUELLAR b	
Mick	TUCKER mr-drm Br	Mike CURB tv	
Mickey	BAKER s Am	Mike DITKA fb,fbc,tv	
Mickey	DANIELS	Mike DONAHUE tv	
Mickey	DEEMS tv	Mike DOUGLAS tv	
Mickey	DOLENZ mr-drm,s,tv Am	Mike ESPY st Am	
Mickey	FREEMAN tv	Mike EVANS tv	
Mickey	JONES drm,tv Am	Mike FARRELL d,w+ Am	
Mickey	MANNERS tv	Mike FINK frontier Am	
Mickey	MANTLE b hf	Mike GIBBINS mr-drm Welsh	
Mickey	ROONEY tv+	Mike GILES mr-drm Br	
Mickey	ROURKE	Mike HAYNES fb	
Mickey	SHOLDAR tv	Mike HENRY	
Mickey	VIRTUE mr-kbds Br	Mike HUGG mr-drm Br	
Mickey	WALKER boxer Am	Mike JOYCE mr-drm Br	
Mickey	WELCH b hf	Mike KELLIN	
Mickey	WRIGHT g Am	Mike LANE	
Micky	HART mr-drm,ws Am	Mike LEIGH d	
Middlemass, FRANK		Mike LOVE mr-s Am	

Mike	MAZURKI tv+	Milano,	FRED s-tenor Am
Mike	MINOR tv	Milanov,	ZINKA sopr Yugo
Mike	MUSSINA b	Milburn	MORANTE
Mike	MYERS tv+	Milburn	STONE tv+
Mike	NESMITH s,guit,tv Am	Milch,	ERHARD fly Ger
Mike	NICHOLS d	Mildred	BAILEY s-blues Am
Mike	NOLAN mr-s Ir	Mildred	DUNNOCK
Mike	NORRIS	Mildred	NATWICK tv+
Mike	PATTON mr-s Am	Milena	DRAVIC
Mike	PENDER mr-guit,s Br	Miles	CHAPIN
Mike	PETERS mr-guit,s Welsh	Miles	DAVIS mj-trump,c Am
Mike	PIAZZA b	Miles	HALPIN tv
Mike	PINDER mr-kbds Br	Miles	MANDER
Mike	POST tv	Miles	O'KEEFE
Mike	PRESTON	Miles,	BERNARD
Mike	ROAD tv	Miles,	BETTY
Mike	ROBE d	Miles,	ELAINE tv
Mike	SAMMES s,cn,tv Am	Miles,	JACK p-b'96
Mike	SCHMIDT b hf	Miles,	JOANNA
Mike	SCOTT b	Miles,	JOSEPHINE po,w Am
Mike	SCOTT mr-guit,s Scot	Miles,	RICHARD tv
Mike	SMITH mr-kbds,s Br	Miles,	SARAH
Mike	SNYDER tv	Miles,	SYLVIA
Mike	STARR	Miles,	VERA
Mike	STOKER tv	Milestone,	LEWIS o-d'30
Mike	STOLLER c Am	Miley,	BUBBER mj-trump Am
Mike	TYSON boxer Am	Milford,	JOHN tv
Mike	VICKERS mr-guit Br	Milford,	PENELOPE
Mike	WAGNER tv	Milhaud,	DARIUS c Fr
Mike	WALLACE tv-j Am	Milian,	TOMAS
Mike D.	--- m-rap Am	Mill,	HUGH geog,weather Scot
Mikels,	TED d	Mill,	JAMES ec,ph,h Scot
Mikey	CRAIG mr-bass Br	Mill,	JOHN ec,ph Br
Mikhail	GLINKA c Rus	Millais,	JOHN(Sir)p
Mikhail	KALININ st Rus	Milland,	RAY o-a'45,tv+
Mikhail	KATKOV j,ed Rus	Millar,	GAVIN d
Mikhail	MICHAEL st-czar Rus	Millar,	MARJIE tv
Mikhail	TAL chess Rus	Millard	HARMON ar,fly Am
Mikhalkov,	NIKITA d	Millard	MITCHELL
Miki,	NORIHEI	Millard	THOMAS mj,cn,c Am
Mikita,	STAN ho-m'67'8	Millay,	EDNA ST.VINCENTp-q'23
Mikkelsen,	VERN bb hf	Miller	HUGGINS b hf
Mikki	JAMISON tv	Miller,	ALICE w Am
Miklas,	WILHELM st Aus	Miller,	ALLAN tv+
Miklos	JOSIKA W Hung	Miller,	ANN ba+ Am
Miklos	KALLAY st Hung	Miller,	ARTHUR p-d'49
Miklos	ZRINYI ar Hung	Miller,	AUBREE
Miko	HUGHES	Miller,	BARRY tv+
Miko	MAYAMA tv	Miller,	CAROLINE p-f'34
Mikolaj	REJ w Pol	Miller,	CHARLES mr-sax Am
Mikoyan,	ANASTAS st Rus	Miller,	CHERYL bb hf
Mikszath,	KALMAN w Hung	Miller,	CHERYL tv+
Mikuni,	RENTARO	Miller,	DAN tv
Mil	MASCARAS	Miller,	DAVID d
Mila	PARELY	Miller,	DEAN tv
Milan	HODZA st Cz	Miller,	DENISE tv
Milan	KUNDERA w Cz	Miller,	DENNIS tv+
Milan	WILLIAMS mr-kbds,drm	Miller,	DENNY(Scott)tv+
Milan,	LITA	Miller,	DICK tv+
Milan,	LUIS m-vihuela,c Sp	Miller,	EVE
Milano,	ALYSSA tv+	Miller,	F.E.

Miller,	GEORGE d	Mills,	DONNA tv+
Miller,	GLENN mj,cn,tv+	Mills,	HAYLEY
Miller,	HARRIET birds,w Am	Mills,	JOHN o-s'70
Miller,	HENRY la,d Am	Mills,	JULIET tv+
Miller,	HENRY w Am	Mills,	MORT tv
Miller,	JASON p-d'73+	Mills,	STEPHANIE
Miller,	JEREMY tv+	Millward,	MIKE mr-guit,s Br
Miller,	JERRY mr-guit Am	Milman,	HENRY po,r,e,h Br
Miller,	JOAQUIN po,w Am	Milne,	ALAN(A.A.)w,po Br
Miller,	JOHN A. w Am	Milne,	EDWARD astr,e Br
Miller,	JOHN geol,e Am	Milner,	ALFRED st Br
Miller,	JOSHUA	Milner,	MARTIN tv+
Miller,	KRISTINE	Milner,	WAYNE fb hf
Miller,	LARA tv	Milo	O'SHEA
Miller,	LARRY	Milo,	SANDRA
Miller,	LEE tv	Milo,	TITUS st Ro
Miller,	LINDA tv+	Milos	FORMAN tv+
Miller,	LORRAINE	Milosz,	CZESLAW po,n-l'80
Miller,	MARK tv+	Milsap,	RONNIE s Am
Miller,	MARTIN	Milstein,	CESAR n-m'84
Miller,	MARVIN tv+	Milstein,	NATHAN violin Am
Miller,	MAX w Am	Milt	GROSS cr Am
Miller,	MAXINE tv	Milt	HINTON mj-bass Am
Miller,	MERTON n-e'90	Milt	JACKSON mj-vibes. Am
Miller,	MINDI tv	Milt	KAMEN cm,tv Am
Miller,	MITCH m,s,cn.tv Am	Milt	SCHMIDT ho
Miller,	PATSY	Miltiz,	KARL von r Ger
Miller,	PENELOPE	Milton	AGER ws Am
Miller,	PERRY p-h'66	Milton	AVERY p Am
Miller,	RALPH bbc hf	Milton	BERLE cm,tv+ Am
Miller,	REBECCA	Milton	DELUGG tv
Miller,	REGGIE bb	Milton	FROME tv+
Miller,	ROBYN tv	Milton	HERSHEY id-candy Am
Miller,	ROGER s-cnt,cn Am	Milton	MARGAI(Sir)st S.Leone
Miller,	SCOTT tv	Milton	SELZER tv+
Miller,	SID tv	Milton,	JOHN po,w Br
Miller,	STEVE mr-guit,s Am	Milton,	NADIA
Miller,	SUE w Am	Milyukov,	PAVEL st,h,e Rus
Miller,	TY tv	Mimi	DILLARD tv
Miller,	WALTER	Mimi	GIBSON
Miller,	WALTER Jr.w scifi Am	Mimi	KENNEDY tv
Millerick,	KERRY tv	Mimi	KUZYK tv+
Milles,	CARL su Am	Mimi	LESSEOS
Millet,	JEAN p Fr	Mimi	MAYNARD
Millett,	KATE fe	Mimi	ROGERS
Millhollin,	JAMES tv	Mimi	SHERATON ct-food Am
Millian,	ANDRA tv+	Mimieux,	YVETTE
Millicent	FENWICK tv	Mimsy	FARMER
Millicent	MARTIN tv+	Mina	KOLB tv
Millie	PERKINS	Mince,	JOHNNY mj-clari Am
Milligan,	ANDY d	Minciotti,	ESTER
Milligan,	SPIKE	Mindy	CARSON tv
Millikan,	ROBERT n-p'23	Mindy	CLARKE
Millin,	SARAH w S.Afr	Mindy	COHN tv
Millis,	HARRY ec,e Am	Mindy	MILLER tv
Mills	WATSON tv+	Mineo,	SAL
Mills Bros.,	THE s Am	Miner,	JAN tv+
Mills,	ALLEY tv+	Miner,	JOHN(Jack) nature Can
Mills,	ALLISON tv	Minerva	URECAL tv
Mills,	BERTRAM circus Br	Ming	SHUM d
Mills,	CLARK su Am	Minghella,	ANTHONY o-d'96

Mingus,	CHARLES mj-bass,c Am		Miss	READ w Br
Mink	STOLE		Missy	FRANCIS tv
Minkus,	BARBARA tv		Missy	GOLD tv
Minna	GOMBELL		Mistal,	KAREN tv+
Minnabess	LEWIS tv		Mister	ROGERS tv-host,pr Am
Minnelli,	LIZA o-a'72		Mistral,	FREDERIC po,n-1'04
Minnelli,	VINCENTE d		Mistral,	GABRIELA po,n-1'45
Minnesota	FATS pool Am		Mistral,	JORGE
Minnie	DRIVER		Misty	ROWE tv+
Minnie	FISKE la Am		Misumi,	KENJI d
Minnie	GENTRY		Mitch	GAYLORD gy Am
Minnie	HAUK sopr Am		Mitch	LEIGH c Am
Minnie	PEARL cm,tv Am		Mitch	MARGO s-tenor Am
Minns,	BYRON tv		Mitch	MILLER s,cn,tv Am
Minor	WATSON		Mitch	RYDER mr-s Am
Minor	WHITE fo,e Am		Mitch	VOGEL tv
Minor,	MIKE tv		Mitchel,	ORMSBY astr Am
Minoru	CHIAKI		Mitchell	AYRES mj,cn Am
Minos,	BOB		Mitchell	LEWIS
Minot,	GEORGE n-m'34		Mitchell	PARISH lyrics Am
Minot,	SUSAN w Am		Mitchell	RYAN tv+
Minta	DURFEE		Mitchell,	BELLE
Minter,	KELLY		Mitchell,	BOBBIE tv
Minton,	THOMAS id-pottery Br		Mitchell,	BOBBY fb hf
Mintz,	ELI tv		Mitchell,	BRIAN tv
Miou Miou	---		Mitchell,	CAMERON tv+
Miquel,	JOHANNES von st Ger		Mitchell,	CHUCK"Porky"
Mir	NAVA'I po Turk		Mitchell,	DON tv
Mira Sorvino	---		Mitchell,	GORDON
Mira,	BRIGITTE		Mitchell,	GRANT
Mirabeau	LAMAR st Am		Mitchell,	GUY s Am
Mirabella,	GRACE ed,pb Am		Mitchell,	JAMES sc,w,h Scot
Miracle,	IRENE		Mitchell,	JOHN labor Am
Miramon,	MIGUEL ar Mex		Mitchell,	JONI mr-s Can
Miranda	OTTO la+ Austra		Mitchell,	KEITH tv+
Miranda	RHYNE		Mitchell,	KEVIN b-mv'89,hr'89
Miranda,	CARMEN s+ Braz-Am		Mitchell,	LEONA soprano+
Miranda,	ISA		Mitchell,	LIZ mr-s Jamaica
Miranda,	ROBERT		Mitchell,	MARGARET p-f'37
Mirbeau,	OCTAVE j,w Fr		Mitchell,	MARIA astr Am
Mircea	ELIADE ph,w Rom		Mitchell,	MILLARD
Mireille	DARC		Mitchell,	MITCH mr-drm Br
Mireille	PERRIER		Mitchell,	NEIL mr-kbds Scot
Mirella	FRENI s-opera It		Mitchell,	PETER n-c'78
Miriam	BOYER		Mitchell,	SASHA tv+
Miriam	FLYNN tv		Mitchell,	SCOEY tv+
Miriam	HOPKINS		Mitchell,	SHIRLEY tv
Miro,	GABRIEL w Sp		Mitchell,	SILAS md,w Am
Miro,	JOAN p Sp		Mitchell,	STEVE tv
Miron	COSTIN po Moldavia		Mitchell,	THOMAS o-s'39
Miron	CRISTEA r Rom		Mitchell,	WARREN
Mirren,	HELEN		Mitchell,	WESLEY ec,e,w Am
Mirtha	IBARRA		Mitchell,	YVONNE
Mirza	BEDIL po India		Mitchell-Smith, ILAN	
Mirza	GHALIB po India		Mitchison,NAOMI(Lady)w,po Br	
Mischa	AUER		Mitchum,	BENTLEY
Mischa	ELMAN viol Am		Mitchum,	CHRIS
Mises,	LUDWIG von ec,e,w Am		Mitchum,	JACK tv
Mises,	RICHARD von math,e Am		Mitchum,	JIM
Misha	McK tv		Mitchum,	JOHN
Mishima,	YUKIO w Japan		Mitchum,	ROBERT

Mitford,	JESSICA w Am
Mitford,	MARY w Br
Mitford,	NANCY w Br
Mitre,	BARTOLOME ar,st,w Arg
Mitropoulos,	DIMITRI cn,c Am
Mittelholzer,	EDGAR w Guyana
Mitzi	GAYNOR
Mitzi	HOAG tv
Mitzi	KAPTURE tv+
Mitzi	McCALL tv
Mitzie	GREEN
Miuccia	PRADA ds It
Mix,	ART
Mix,	RON fb hf
Mix,	RUTH
Mix,	TOM la+ Am
Miya,	JO ANNE tv
Miyamoto,	NOBUKO
Miyori,	KIM tv+
Miyoshi	UMEKI tv+
Mize,	JOHNNY b hf
Mizner,	ADDISON ac Am
Mizoguchi,	KENJI d
Mizra	BEDIL po India
Mlle	RACHEL la Fr
Mlle.	MARS la Fr
Mme. de	STAEL w Fr
Mo	VAUGHN b
Moa	MARTINSON w Swe
Moar,	ANDREA tv
Moberg,	VILHELM w Swe
Mobius,	AUGUST astr,e,w Ger
Mobley,	MARY tv+
Mobutu,	SESE SEKO st Zaire
Mockel,	ALBERT po,ct Belg
Moctezuma,	CARLOS LOPEZ
Modibo	KEITA st Mali
Modigliani,	AMADEO p,su It
Modigliani,	FRANCO n-e'85
Modine,	MATTHEW
Modjeska,	HELENA la Am
Modot,	GASTON
Modugno,	DOMONICO s g-r'58
Moe	BERG b
Moe	COHEN mj-sax Am
Moe	HOWARD
Moe,	JORGEN po,folklre Nor
Moe,	TOMMY ski,o-g'94
Moen,	ANDREA tv
Moeran,	ERNEST c Br
Moffat,	DAVID id,f Am
Moffatt,	DONALD
Moffett,	D.W.
Moffo,	ANNA sopr Am
Mofolo,	THOMAS w Bantu
Mogila,	PETER r Rus
Mohammad	BAHAR po Iran
MohammedReza	PAHLEVI(Shah)st Ira
Mohl,	HUGO von sc,e Ger
Mohn,	HENRIK weather Nor
Mohner,	CARL

Moholy-Nagy	LASZLO p,fo Hung
Mohr,	GERALD tv+
Mohr,	JOSEPH r,po Aus
Mohs,	FRIEDRICH minerals Ger
Mohyeddi,	ZIA
Moinaux,	GEORGES w-humor Fr
Moir,	DAVID md,po,w Scot
Moir,	RICHARD
Moira	KELLY
Moira	SHEARER ba+ Scot-Br
Moise	AMYRAUT re,e Fr
Moise	TSHOMBE st Congo
Moises	ALOU b
Moissan,	HENRI n-c'06
Moissi,	ALEXANDER la It
Mojo	NIXON
Mokae,	ZAKES
Mola,	EMILIO ar Sp
Mola,	PIER p It
Mole,	MATHIEU l,st Fr
Moley,	RAYMOND j,e,st Am
Moliere	--- w,la Fr
Molina	ALFRED
Molina,	ANGELA
Molina,	MARIO n-c'95
Molinaro,	AL tv
Moll,	RICHARD tv+
Molland,	JOEY mr-kbds,s Br
Moller,	GEORG ac Ger
Moller,	POUL w Dan
Mollet,	GUY st Fr
Mollie	O'MARA
Mollien,	GASPARD x,st Fr
Molly	CHEEK tv
Molly	HAGAN tv+
Molly	McCLURE
Molly	McGEE cm/Fibber Am
Molly	PICON tv+
Molnar,	FERENC w Hung
Molotov,	VYACHESLAV st Rus
Moltke,	ADAM st Dan
Moltke,	HELMUTH von ar Ger
Molza,	FRANCESCO po It
Momaday,	N. SCOTT p-f'69
Mommsen,	THEODOR n-l'02, h
Moms	MABLEY
Mona	BARRIE
Mona	BRUNS tv
Mona	FREEMAN
Mona	MARIS
Mona	Van DUYN po Am
Monarch,	MICHAEL mr-guit Am
Monarque,	STEVEN tv
Monash,	JOHN(Sir)eng,ar Aust
Moncey,	BON de ar Fr
Mond,	LUDWIG sc,id Br
Mond,	STEVEN tv
Mondale,	WALTER(Fritz)st Am
Mondello,	TOOTS mj-sax Am
Mondesi,	RAUL b-gg'97
Mondo,	PEGGY tv

Mondragon, JORGE	Monteros, ROSENDA
Mondrian, PIET p Dut	Montes, ISMAEL st Boliv
Monet, CLAUDE p Fr	Montessori, MARIA e It
Moneta, ERNESTO n-x'07	Montet, PIERRE h-Egypt,e,w Fr
Monette, RICHARD	Monteux, PIERRE cn Am
Money, EDDIE s Am	Monteverdi, CLAUDIO c It
Monge, GASPARD math,sc.e Fr	Montez, LOLA ba,w Am
Mongo BETI w Cameroon	Montez, MARIA
Monica EVANS tv	Montgolfier, JACQUES i Fr
Monica MOORE tv	Montgolfier, JOSEPH i,balloons Fr
Monica SELES t Cz	Montgomery CLIFT
Monica VITTI	Montgomery TULLY d
Monica, CORBETT tv	Montgomery,BARBARA tv
Monier, JOSEPH i Fr	Montgomery,BELINDA tv+
Monique LANIER tv	Montgomery,ELIZABETH tv+
Monique VanDeVEN	Montgomery,GEORGE tv+
Moniz, ANTONIO n-m'49	Montgomery,JOHN MICHAEL s-cnt Am
Moniz, WENDY tv	Montgomery,JULIA
Monk, ART fb	Montgomery,LEE
Monk, MARIA imposter,w Can	Montgomery,LUCY MAUD(L.M.)w Can
Monk, THELONIUS mj,c,cn Am	Montgomery,MELBA s-cnt Am
Monkhouse,ALLAN w Br	Montgomery,RAY tv
Monnet, JEAN.ec,st Fr	Montgomery,ROBERT
Monod, JACQUES n-m'65	Montgomery,SY w Am
Monoson, LAWRENCE	Montgomery,WES mj-guit Am
Monrad, DITLEV r,st Dan	Montherlant, HENRY de w Fr
Monro, HAROLD po,ed Br	Monti, VINCENZO po,e It
Monroe, BILL j,tv Am	Montiel, SARA
Monroe, DEL tv	Montini, LUIGI
Monroe, EARL bb hf	Montoya, CARLOS m-flamenco Sp
Monroe, HARRIET ed,po Am	Montrose, BELLE tv
Monroe, JAMES 5th pres	Montserrat CABALLE s
Monroe, MARILYN	Montt, MANUEL st Chile
Monroe, VAUGHN mj,s Am	Monty HALL tv
Monson, WILLIAM(Sir)navy	Monty MARGETTS tv
Montagu CORRY st,f Br	Monty WOOLLEY
Montagu LOVE	Mony REY
Montagu, EDWIN st Br	Monzie, ANATOLE de st,pb Fr
Montagu, MARY(Lady)po,w Br	Moodie, SUSANNAH w Can
Montague, MONTE	Moody, BLAIR tv
Montagut, FRANCOIS tv	Moody, DWIGHT r Am
Montaigne,MICHEL de ph,w Fr	Moody, JOHN analyst-f,w Am
Montalban,RICARDO tv+	Moody, KING tv+
Montale, EUGENIO po,n-l'75	Moody, LYNNE tv+
Montalvo, JUAN w Ecu	Moody, RON
Montana, JOE fb-m'89,tv	Moody, WILLIAM po,w Am
Montana, KARLA	Moon Unit ZAPPA s Am
Montana, MONTE	Moon, KEITH
Montand, YVES s+ Fr	Moon, WARREN fb-m'90
Monte BLUE	Moon, WILLIAM i Br
Monte HALE	Mooney, DEBRA tv
Monte HAWLEY	Mooney, EVIN mr-bass Br
Monte IRVIN b hf	Mooney, THOMAS labor Am
Monte MARKHAM tv+	Moore, ALVY tv+
Monte MONTANA	Moore, ARCHIE boxer+ Am
Monte, PHILIPPE de c Belg	Moore, BARBARA tv
Montel WILLIAMS tv-host Am	Moore, BRIAN w Can
Montemezzi, ITALO c It	Moore, CANDY tv+
Montenaro,TONY Jr. tv	Moore, CLAYTON tv+
Montenegro, SASHA	Moore, CLEMENT po,e Am
Montepin, XAVIER de w Fr	Moore, COLLEEN

Moore,	CONSTANCE tv+	Mordecai	RICHLER w Can
Moore,	DEL tv	Mordente,	LISA tv
Moore,	DEMI	Mordente,	TONY ba,tv Am
Moore,	DENNIS	More,	ANTHONY(Sir)p Dut
Moore,	DICKIE	More,	HANNAH w,r Br
Moore,	DOUGLAS p-m'51	More,	HENRY ph,po Br
Moore,	DUDLEY	More,	KENNETH
Moore,	G.E. ph,e Br	More,	PAUL w,ct,e Am
Moore,	GAR	More,	THOMAS(Sir)st,po,w
Moore,	GARRY tv	Moreau,	GUSTAVE p Fr
Moore,	GEORGE w,po,ct Ir	Moreau,	JEANNE
Moore,	GRACE s opera+ Am	Moreau,	LOUIS p Fr
Moore,	HENRY su Br	Moreau,	MARSHA tv
Moore,	IDA tv	Moreell,	BEN navy Am
Moore,	JOANNA	Moreelse,	PAULUS p Dut
Moore,	JUANITA	Morehouse,	DANIEL astron Am
Moore,	JULIA po Am	Moreland,	MANTAN
Moore,	JULIANNE	Morell,	ANDRE
Moore,	KIERON	Morell,	OTTOLINE(Lady)hostess
Moore,	LANNY fb-m'64 hf	Moreno,	ANTONIO
Moore,	LORRIE w Am	Moreno,	BELITA tv
Moore,	MARIANNE p-q'52	Moreno,	BUDDY mj-guitat,s Am
Moore,	MARY TYLER cm,tv+ Am	Moreno,	MARIANO st Arg
Moore,	MATT	Moreno,	RITA o-s'61 tv+
Moore,	MELBA s-r&b+ Am	Morenz,	HOWIE ho-m'28'31'2
Moore,	MELISSA	Morey	AMSTERDAM cm,tv+ Am
Moore,	MONICA tv	Morey	BUNIN pupp,tv Am
Moore,	ROGER tv+	Morey,	BILL tv
Moore,	RUDY	Morfogen,	GEORGE
Moore,	SAM s Am	Morgan	BRITTANY tv+
Moore,	SHEMAR tv	Morgan	BUKELEY b hf
Moore,	STANFORD n-c'72	Morgan	CONWAY
Moore,	TERRY tv+	Morgan	EDWARD tv
Moore,	THOMAS po Ir	Morgan	FREEMAN
Moore,	THOMAS STURGE po,h Br	Morgan	JONES tv
Moore,	TIM tv	Morgan	LLWYD w Welsh
Moore,	VICTOR	Morgan	RUSSELL p Am
Moorehead,	ALAN j,h Austra	Morgan	STEVENS tv+
Moores,	DICK cr Am	Morgan	WALLACE
Moorhead,	AGNES tv+	Morgan	WHITE tv
Moorhead,	NATALIE	Morgan,	AL s,piano,tv
Moose	KRAUSE bb hf	Morgan,	CHARLES w,ct Br
Moosie	DRIER tv+	Morgan,	CINDY tv
Mor	JOKAI w Hung	Morgan,	CONWY sc,ps,e,w Br
Mora,	PHILIPPE d	Morgan,	DEBBI
Moraes,	DOM po,j India	Morgan,	DENNIS tv+
Morales,	ESAI	Morgan,	EDWARD P. tv
Morales,	LUIS de p Sp	Morgan,	FRANK
Moran,	DEE	Morgan,	HARRY tv+
Moran,	ERIN tv+	Morgan,	HELEN
Moran,	JACKIE	Morgan,	HENRY tv+
Moran,	LOIS tv	Morgan,	HENRY(Sir)buccaneer
Morand,	PAUL st,w Fr	Morgan,	J. PIERPONT f,f Am
Morandi,	GIORGIO p It	Morgan,	JANE tv
Moranis,	RICK tv+	Morgan,	JAYE P. s,tv+ Am
Morante,	ELSA w,po It	Morgan,	JOE b-mv'75'6 hf,tv
Morante,	MILBURN	Morgan,	JUNIUS banker,f Am
Moratin,	LEANDRO de w Sp	Morgan,	MARION s,tv Am
Moravia,	ALBERTO w It	Morgan,	MARLO w Am
Mordecai	BROWN(3 Finger)b	Morgan,	MICHAEL tv+
Mordecai	NOAH j,ed Am	Morgan,	MICHELE

Morgan,	NANCY	Morris,	ERROL d
Morgan,	RALPH	Morris,	GARRETT tv+
Morgan,	READ tv	Morris,	GARY s-cnt,tv Am
Morgan,	ROBIN tv	Morris,	GEORGE j,po Am
Morgan,	SEAN tv	Morris,	GREG tv
Morgan,	SYDNEY(Lady)po Ir	Morris,	HAVILAND
Morgan,	THOMAS n-m'33	Morris,	HOWARD tv+
Morgan,	WESLEY tv	Morris,	JAN j,w Br
Morgenstern LINA reform,w Ger		Morris,	JUDY
Mori Ogai --- md,w Japan		Morris,	JULIANNE tv
Mori,	KYOKO w Am	Morris,	KIRK
Mori,	MASSAYUKI	Morris,	LESLIE tv
Mori,	TOSCHIA	Morris,	PHIL tv
Moriarity,ERIN tv		Morris,	STEPHEN mr-drm Br
Moriarty, CATHY		Morris,	THOMAS(Old Tom)g Scot
Moriarty, MICHAEL tv+		Morris,	WAYNE
Morice,	CHARLES w Fr	Morris,	WILLIAM at,ac,po,w Br
Moricz,	ZSIGMOND w Hung	Morris,	WRIGHT w Am
Morier,	JAMES st Br	Morris-Jones,JOHN(Sir)po,e Welsh
Morike,	EDUARD po Ger	Morrisey, BILL guit,s,w Am
Morin,	ALBERTO tv	Morrison WAITE l,ch just Am
Morin,	PAUL po Can	Morrison, BRIAN tv
Morini,	ERIKA violin	Morrison, SAMMY
Morison,	PATRICIA	Morrison, SHELLEY tv+
Morison,	SAMUEL p-b'43'60	Morrison, STERLING mr-bass,s Am
Morisot,	BERTHE p Fr	Morrison, TONI p-f'88,n-l'93
Morita,	Pat tv+	Morrison, VAN mr,s Ir
Moritz	DROBISCH math ph Ger	Morriss, ANN tv
Moritz	PASCH math,e Ger	Morrissey --- mr-s Br
Moritz	SCHIFF md,e Ger	Morrow, BOBBY o-g'56
Moritz	SCHLICK ph,e Ger	Morrow, BYRON tv
Moritz von HIRSCH bus,f Ger		Morrow, DWIGHT l,banker,st Am
Moritz von SCHWIND p Ger		Morrow, JEFF tv+
Moritz,	LOUISA	Morrow, JOSHUA tv
Morland,	GEORGE p,engr Br	Morrow, KAREN tv
Morley	SAFER tv-j Am	Morrow, LIZA mj-s Am
Morley,	CHRISTOPHER w,ed Am	Morrow, MARI tv
Morley,	JOHN st,w Br	Morrow, PATRICIA tv
Morley,	KAREN	Morrow, ROB tv
Morley,	ROBERT	Morrow, VIC tv+
Moro,	ALDO st,e It	Morse, BARRY tv+
Moro,	ALICIA	Morse, DAVID tv+
Moro,	CESAR po Peru	Morse, HELEN
Moroni	OLSEN	Morse, ROBERT tv+
Moroni,	GIOVANNI p It	Morse, SAMUEL(S.F.B.)p,i,eAm
Morphy,	PAUL chess Am	Morse, TERRY d
Morrell,	EARL fb-m'68	Mort COOPER b
Morrell,	OTTOLINE(Lady)hostess	Mort GREENE tv
Morrie	RYSKIND w Am	Mort LINDSEY m,cn,tv Am
Morrill,	PRISCILLA tv+	Mort MILLS tv
Morris	ANKRUM	Mort SAHL cm Can
Morris	BADGRO(Red)fb hf	Mort WALKER cr Am
Morris	JASTROW e,w Am	Mortara, EDGAR r It
Morris	JESUP mer,f Am	Morten HARKET mr-s Nor
Morris	LOUIS p Am	Morten NIELSEN po Dan
Morris	STOLOFF c Am	Mortensen,VIGGO
Morris	WEST w Aust	Mortimer ADLER e,ph Am
Morris,	ANITA	Mortimer, JOHN w Br
Morris,	BARBOURA	Morton DOWNEY Jr. tv-host+
Morris,	CHESTER	Morton DOWNEY tv
Morris,	CLARA la Am	Morton PRINCE md,ps,w Am

Morton,	BOB tv	Motilal	NEHRU(Pandit)st India
Morton,	CLIVE	Motley	CRUE mr Am
Morton,	GREG tv	Motley,	JOHN h Am
Morton,	HOWARD tv	Motley,	MARION fb hf
Morton,	JELLY ROLL mj,c+ Am	Motley,	WILLARD w Am
Morton,	JOE tv+	Moton,	ROBERT e,w Am
Morton,	JOY id-salt,mer Am	Mott,	FRANK e,j,w Am
Morton,	LEVI banker,st Am	Mott,	JOHN n-x'46
Morton,	SARAH po Am	Mott,	LUCRETIA fe Am
Morton,	THOMAS colonizer,w Am	Mott,	NEVILLE(Sir)n-p'77
Mosby,	JOHN ar,st,w Am	Motta,	GIUSEPPE st Swi
Mosca,	GAETANO polit-sc,e It	Motta,	ZEZE
Moscheles,IGNAZ piano Ger		Motteux,	PETER w Br
Moscicki, IGNACY sc,st Pol		Mottl,	FELIX c,cn Aus
Moscovich,MAURICE		Mottola,	TONY m,cn,tv Am
Mosel,	TAD p-d'61	Mottram,	RALPH w Br
Moseley,	BILL	Motzu	--- ph China
Mosen,	JULIUS po,w Ger	Motzu,	MASTER MO ph China
Moser,	GUSTAV von w Ger	Mouhot,	HENRI x Fr
Moser,	JUSTUS h,l Ger	Moulay	HASAN st Morocco
Moses	BEACH j,i Am	Moulder-Brown, JOHN	
Moses	DROPSIE l Am	Moulding, COLIN mr-Bass,s Br	
Moses	EZEKIEL su Am	Moulton,	FOREST astr Am
Moses	FARMER i Am	Mount,	DAVE mr-drm,s Br
Moses	GASTER r,e Br	Mount,	WILLIAM p Am
Moses	GOMBERG sc,e Am	Mountain, JOHNNY tv	
Moses	GUNN tv+	Mountbatten, LOUIS navy,st Br	
Moses	MALONE bb hf	Mourning, ALONZO bb	
Moses	ROGERS mariner Am	Mouron,	ADOLPHE at,ds,ads Fr
Moses	TYLER h,ref,e Am	Mousie	GARNER tv
Moses	WADDEL e Am	Movita	---
Moses,	ANNA(Grandma)p Am	Mowat,	FARLEY w Can
Moses,	GRANDMA p Am	Mowatt,	ANNA w,la Am
Moses,	MARK tv+	Mowbray,	ALAN tv+
Moses,	ROBERT st Am	Mower,	PATRICK
Moses,	WILLIAM tv+	Moxam	WHITNEY mj-guit,cn Can
Moshe	DAYAN st Isr	Moxey,	JOHN d
Moshe	SHARETT st Isr	Moxley,	BRAD mj,piano Can
Mosley,	BOB mr-bass Am	Moyer,	PAUL tv
Mosley,	OSWALD(Sir)st	Moyers,	BILL w,tv-j Am
Mosley,	ROGER tv+	Moyet,	ALISON mr-s Br
Mosley,	WALTER w Am	Moyle,	ALLAN d
Moss	HART w Am	Moyna	MacGILL
Moss,	ARNOLD	Moynihan, PAT st Am	
Moss,	CARRIE tv	Mozart,	LEOPOLD viol,c Aus
Moss,	JON mr-drm Br	Mozart,	WOLFGANG c Aus
Moss,	KATE mo Br	Mpadi,	SIMON r Congo
Moss,	RON tv+	Mphahlele,EZEKIEL w,ct S.Afr	
Moss,	STEWART tv+	Mr. T.	--- (Tero)tv
Mossbauer,RUDOLF n-p'61		Mrozek,	SLAWOMIR w Pol
Mossen,	BRAD tv	Mrs. Aphra BEHN w Br	
Mossman,	DOUG tv	Mrs. Henry WOOD w Br	
Most,	DONNY tv	Mrs. Leslie CARTER la Am	
Mostel,	JOSH	Mrs.Humphrey WARD w Br	
Mostel,	ZERO s+ Am	Muammar	QADDAFI st Libya
Moten,	BENNIE mj piano,c Am	Mubarak,	ALI st Egypt
Mother	JONES labor Am	Muburak,	HOSNI st Egypt
Mother	TERESA r Albania	Mubarak,	MUHAMMAD st Egypt
Mother Ann LEE r-Shakers Am		Mucha,	ALPHONSE p,illus Cz
Mother Maybell CARTER tv		Muck,	CARL cn Ger
Motherwell, ROBERT p Am		Mudd,	ROGER tv-j Am

Muddy	WATERS mj-blues,s Am	Munch,	EDVARD p Nor
Mueller,	ERWIN sc,e Am	Munch,	PETER h,st Dan
Mueller,	MAUREEN tv	Munchhausen BORRIES von ws Ger	
Mueller	OTTO p Ger	Munchkin,	RICHARD W. d
Mueller-Stahl, ARMIN		Munday,	ANTHONY po,w Br
Muench,	ALOISIUS r Am	Mundhra,	JAG d
Muff	WINWOOD m-bass,s Br	Mundt,	THEODOR w,ct Ger
Muffat,	GEORG c Ger	Mundy,	AL(Big Al)mj,c,cn
Mugge,	THEODOR w Ger	Mune,	IAN
Muggeridge, MALCOLM w Br		Mung	LING tv
Muggsy	SPANIER mj-corn,c Am	Mungo	PARK x Scot
Muhammad	ALI boxer+ Am	Mungo	PONTON i Scot
Muhammad	IQBAL(Sir)po,ph India	Muni,	PAUL la+,o-a'36
Muhammad	MUBARAK st Egypt	Munk,	KAJ w,r Dan
Muir,	EDWIN po,ct Scot	Munn,	BILLY mj-piano Br
Muir,	GAVIN tv+	Munne,	PEP
Muir,	JOHN natur,w Am	Munonye,	JOHN w Nigeria
Muirhead	BONE(Sir)p Scot	Munro,	ALICE w Can
Mujibur	RAHMAN st Bengal	Munro,	C. PETE tv
Mulcahy,	RICHARD st Irish	Munro,	CAROLINE
Muldaur,	DIANA tv+	Munro,	HECTOR w Scot
Muldoon,	PATRICK tv	Munro,	JANET
Mulford,	CLARENCE w Am	Munro,	NEIL w,j,ct Scot
Mulgrew,	KATE tv+	Munsel,	PATRICE s,tv Am
Mulhall,	JACK	Munsell,	ALBERT p Am
Mulhare,	EDWARD tv+	Munsey,	FRANK pb Am
Mulhern,	MATT tv	Munson,	ONA
Mulkey,	CHRIS tv+	Munson,	THURMAN b-mv'76
Mull,	MARTIN tv+	Munson,	WARREN tv
Mullally,	MEGAN tv	Munsterberg, HUGO ps Am	
Mullaney,	JACK tv+	Munthe,	AXEL md,w Swe
Mullavey,	GREG tv+	Munthe,	GERHARD p,illus Nor
Mullen,	LARRY Jr mr-drm Ir	Muppets,	JIM HANSEN'S tv+
Muller,	EDUARD st Swi	Murad,	FERID n-m'98
Muller,	GEORG ps,e Gert	Murat	YOUNG(Chic)cr Am
Muller,	HARRISON	Murat,	JOACHIM ar Fr
Muller,	HERMANN n-m'46	Murayama,	NOE
Muller,	JOHANN astr Ger	Murdoch,	IRIS(Dame)w Br
Muller,	K. ALEX n-p'87	Murdoch,	JAMES la Am
Muller,	KATHRYN puppets, tv	Murdoch,	RUPERT me Aust
Muller,	MARCIA w Am	Murdock	McQUARRIE
Muller,	PAUL	Murdock,	GEORGE tv+
Muller,	PAUL n-m'48	Murdock,	JACK tv
Muller,	SOPHUS sc,h,w Dan	Murdock,	JAMES tv
Muller,	WENZEL c Ger	Mure,	WILLIAM(Sir)po Scot
Muller,	WILHELM po Ger	Muret,	MARC po,e Fr
Mullican,	MOON m-cnt Am	Murfree,	MARY w Am
Mulligan,	GERRY mj,sax,c Am	Murger,	HENRI w Fr
Mulligan,	RICHARD tv+	Muriel	EVANS
Mulligan,	ROBERT d	Muriel	SPARK w,po,ct Scot
Mulliken,	ROBERT n-c'66	Murieta,	JOAQUIN outlaw Mex
Mullis,	KARY n-c'93	Murillo,	BARTOLOME p Sp
Mulqueen,	KATHLEEN tv	Murillo,	GERARDO p,w Mex
Mulroney,	DERMOT	Murnau,	FRIEDRICH(F.W.)d Ger
Mulrooney, JOHN tv		Murney,	CHRISTOPHER
Mumford,	LEWIS e,ph,w Am	Murphy,	ARTHUR la,w Ir
Mummert,	DANNY	Murphy,	AUDIE
Mumy,	BILLY tv+	Murphy,	BARRI
Mun,	ALBERT de st,w Fr	Murphy,	BEN tv+
Mun,	THOMAS w Br	Murphy,	BRITTANY tv
Munch,	CHARLES cn Fr	Murphy,	CALVIN bb hf

Murphy,	DALE b-mv'82'3,hr'84'5	Mussorgsky,	MODEST c Rus
Murphy,	EDDIE cm,tv+ Am	Mustafa	KAMIL st Egypt
Murphy,	GEORGE tv+	Mustafa	NAIMA h Turk
Murphy,	HARRY tv	Mustel,	VICTOR i,id Fr
Murphy,	HORACE	Mustin,	BURT tv
Murphy,	ISAAC jockey Am	Muti,	ORNELLA
Murphy,	JOHN p Am	Muti,	RICCARDO c It
Murphy,	KRISTA tv	Mutis,	JOSE md Sp
Murphy,	MARY	Mutombo,	DIKEMBE bb
Murphy,	MAURICE	Mutt	CAREY(Thomas)mj-cn Am
Murphy,	MICHAEL	Muzzey,	DAVID h,e Am
Murphy,	ROBERT st Am	Muzzy	MARCELLINO mj,cn
Murphy,	ROSEMARY tv+	Myer,	ALBERT ar Am
Murphy,	SCOTT tv	Myers,	CARMEL
Murphy,	STRETCH bb hf	Myers,	HARRY
Murphy,	TERI tv	Myers,	LEOPOLD w Br
Murphy,	TIMOTHY tv	Myers,	LOU tv
Murphy,	TURK mj-tromb,c Am	Myers,	MIKE tv+
Murphy,	WILLIAM n-m'34	Myers,	PAMELA tv
Murray	HAMILTON tv+	Myers,	PAULINE tv
Murray	LANGSTON tv+	Myers,	RUSSELL cr Am
Murray	MELVIN	Myers,	SUSAN tv+
Murray,	ANNE s Can	Myerson,	BESS tv
Murray,	BARBARA	Mykel	WILLIAMSON tv+
Murray,	BILL tv+	Myles,	HOWARD tv
Murray,	CHARLES po,eng Scot	Mynie	SUTTON mj-sax,cn Can
Murray,	DAVE mr-guit Br	Myra	HESS(Dame)piano Br
Murray,	DON tv+	Myra	TAYLOR mj-s Am
Murray,	EDDIE b,rbi'81	Myrdal,	ALVA n-x'82
Murray,	GILBERT w,e,h Br	Myrdal,	GUNNAR n-e'74
Murray,	JAMES	Myriem	ROUSSEL
Murray,	JAN tv	Myrna	DELL tv+
Murray,	JOEL tv+	Myrna	FAHEY tv
Murray,	JOHN ed,ct Br	Myrna	LOY
Murray,	JOSEPH E. n-m'90	Myrna	STONE w Am
Murray,	KEN tv+	Myron	--- su Gr
Murray,	LINDLEY l,mer,w Am	Myron	COHEN cm Am
Murray,	PEG tv	Myron	FLOREN accordi,tv Am
Murray,	PHILIP labor Am	Myron	HEALEY
Murrow,	EDWARD R. j,tv-j Am	Myron	HERRICK st Am
Murry,	JOHN w,ct,ed Br	Myron	NATWICK tv
Murvyn	VYES	Myron	SCHOLES ec Am
Mus,	PAUL w,e Fr	Myron	SUTTON(Mynie)mj,cn Can
Musante,	TONY tv+	Myron	WALLACE tv
Musaus,	JOHANN w Ger	Myyra,	JONNI o-g'20'24
Musberger,	BRENT tv-j,sports		

Muscat,	ANGELO tv		
Muse,	CLARENCE tv+		
Musgrave,	THEA c,cn Am		
Musial,	STAN b,6x bat champ &		
Musial,	STAN b-mv'43'8, hf		
Musil,	ROBERT von w Ger		
Musketeer	ARAMIS fc		
Musketeer	ATHOS fc		
Musketeer	PROTHOS fc		
Musketeers	THE THREE fc		
Mussert,	ANTON eng,st Dut		
Musset,	ALFRED de po,w Fr		
Mussina,	MIKE b-gg'97		
Musso,	JOE fb hf	N'Kena,	DAVID
Mussolini,	BENITO st It	Nabokov,	VLADIMIR w,po Am

Nabors Kids, THE tv		Nancy	EVANS tv
Nabors,	JIM s,tv+ Am	Nancy	FISH
Nabuco,	JOAQUIM st,w Braz	Nancy	FOX tv
Nacio	BROWN c Am	Nancy	GATES
Nadel,	SIEGFRIED an,e,w Aus	Nancy	GUILD tv+
Nadelman, ELIE su Am		Nancy	HADLEY tv
Nader,	GEORGE tv+	Nancy	HALE tv
Nader,	MICHAEL tv+	Nancy	KELLY
Nader,	RALPH ct,w Am	Nancy	KOVAK
Nadia	MILTON	Nancy	KULP tv+
Nadia	NERINA ba Br	Nancy	KWAN
Nadine	VanDerVELDE	Nancy	LANE tv
Nadja	TILLER	Nancy	LEWIS tv
Nadoja	PAMPA po India	Nancy	MALONE tv
Nagai Kafu --- w Japan		Nancy	McKEON tv+
Nagel,	ANNE	Nancy	MITFORD w Br
Nagel,	CONRAD	Nancy	MORGAN
Nageli,	KARL sc,e Swi	Nancy	OLSON
Nagisa	OSHIMA d	Nancy	PARSONS
Nagle,	NANO r,e Ir	Nancy	REAGAN - Ron's wife
Nagurski, BRONKO fb hf		Nancy	RENNICK tv
Nagy,	IMRE st Hung	Nancy	SAVOCA d
Nagy,	IVAN ba,d+ Am	Nancy	SINATRA s+ Am
Nahl,	JOHANN su Ger	Nancy	STEEN tv
Nahum	SOKOLOW w,r Pol	Nancy	TAYLOR tv
Nahum	TATE po,w Br	Nancy	TRAVIS
Nai	BONET	Nancy	VAWTER tv
Naidu,	AJAY	Nancy	WALKER tv+
Naidu,	SAROJINI po India	Nancy	WILSON s-r&b Am
Naima,	MUSTAFA h Turk	Nanette	FABRAY tv+
Naipaul,	V.S. w W.Indies	Naniwa,	CHIEKO
Nairne,	CAROLINA ws Scot	Nano	NAGLE r,e Irish
Naish,	J. CARROL tv+	Nansen,	FRIDTJOF x,n-x'22
Naismith, JAMES i-bb,bbc,e Am		Nanton,	JOE (TrickySam)mj-trom
Naismith, LAURENCE tv+		Naomi	CAMPBELL mo Br
Najera,	RICK tv	Naomi	CHANCE
Najimy,	KATHY	Naomi	JUDD s-cnt Am
Nakadai,	TATSUYA	Naomi	STEVENS tv
Nakahara, KELLYE tv		Naoya	KOJIMA ba Jap
Nakamura, GANJIRO		Napaul,	NERIAH
Nakian,	REUBEN su Am	Naphtali	IMBER po Israel
Nalder,	REGGIE	Napier,	ALAN tv+
Naldi,	NITA	Napier,	CHARLES
Namath,	JOE fb hf+	Napier,	MacVEY l,ed Scot
Namier,	LEWIS(Sir)h,e	Naples,	TONI
Namik	KEMAL j,w Turk	Napoleon	LAJOIE(Larry)b hf
Nan	GREY	Napoleon	REBER c Fr
Nan	LESLIE tv+	Napoleon	WHITING tv
Nan	MARTIN	Naquib	MAHFOUZ w Egypt
Nan	WOODS tv+	Narayan,	JAYA st India
Nana	BRYANT tv+	Narayan,	R.K. w India
Nance	O'NEILL	Narciso	CAMPERO ar,st Bol
Nance,	JACK tv+	Nardini,	TOM tv+
Nanci	HAMMOND tv	Nares,	GEORGE(Sir)navy
Nancy	ALLEN	Narita,	RICHARD tv
Nancy	AMES tv	Narita,	ROB tv
Nancy	BELL tv	Narizzano, SILVIO d
Nancy	CARR tv	Narvaez,	RAMON ar Sp
Nancy	CARROLL tv+	Narz,	JACK tv
Nancy	CONRAD tv	Naschy,	PAUL
Nancy	DAVIS	Nash,	BRIAN mr-guit,tv Br

Nash,	GRAHAM mr-guit Br		Naude,	GABRIEL md,h Fr
Nash,	JOE tv		Nauffts,	GEOFFREY tv
Nash,	NOREEN tv+		Naughton,	DAVID tv+
Nash,	OGDEN po,w Am		Naughton,	JAMES tv+
Nash,	PAUL p,fo Br		Naum	GABO su Am
Nash,	WALTER(Sir)st N.Z.		Naumann,	KARL geol Ger
Nashe,	THOMAS w Br		Naunton	WAYNE
Nasi,	JOSEPH st,f Port		Nava'i,	MIR po Turk
Nasif	YAZIJI scholar Leb		Navarez,	RAMON ar Sp
Nasmyth,	ALEXANDER p Scot		Navarro,	RAMON
Nassau	SENIOR ec,e Br		Navarro,	THEODORE(Fats)mj Am
Nasser,	GAMAL st Egypt		Navez,	FRANCOIS p Belg
Nast,	CONDE pb Am		Naville,	EDOUARD an Swi
Nast,	THOMAS cr Am		Navin,	JOHN P. Jr. tv
Nastase,	ILIE t Rom		Navratilova,	MARTINA t Am
Nastassia	KINSKI		Naya	RIVERA tv
Nat	HOLMAN bb hf		Nazarro,	CLIFF
Nat	TURNER slave		Nazim	HIKMET po,j Turk
Nat King	COLE s,tv+ Am		Nazimova,	ALLA
Natalia	NEGODA		Nazzari,	AMADEO
Natalie	COLE s,tv+ Am		Neagle,	ANNA
Natalie	NEVINS s,tv Am		Neagle,	JOHN p Am
Natalie	SCHAFER tv+		Neal	DOUGHTY mr-kbds Am
Natalie	TRUNDY		Neal	DOW temperance Am
Natalie	WEST tv		Neal	SCHON mr-guit Am
Natalie	WOOD tv+		Neal,	DYLAN tv
Natasha	WAGNER		Neal,	KELLY tv
Natavidad,	FRANCESCA(Kitten)		Neal,	PATRICIA o-a'63
Nathalie	BAYE		Neal,	TOM
Nathalie	DELON		Neale	FRASER t Aust
Nathan	ADLER r Br		Neale,	EDWARD ref Br
Nathan	BAILEY w-dicts Br		Neale,	GREASY fb hf
Nathan	COOK tv		Nealon,	KEVIN tv+
Nathan	DANE l,w Am		Neame,	CHRISTOPHER
Nathan	FIELD la,w Br		Neame,	RONALD d
Nathan	FILLION tv		Neander,	JOHANN h,r Ger
Nathan	FINKEL e Isr		Nechuv,	IVAN w Ukriane
Nathan	HALE st,hero Am		Neckar,	VACLAV
Nathan	LANE		Necker,	JACQUES f,st,w Fr
Nathan	PURDEE tv		Ned	BEATTY tv+
Nathan	WATT tv		Ned	BROOKS tv
Nathan,	STEVE tv		Ned	GLASS tv+
Nathanael	WEST w Am		Ned	HARVEY m,cn,tv Am
Nathaniel	CURRIER lithos Am		Ned	KELLY outlaw Aust
Nathaniel	GORHAM st Am		Ned	LUD(D)rioter Br
Nathaniel	OWINGS ac Am		Ned	ROMERO tv+
Nathaniel	PARKER		Ned	ROREM c Am
Nathaniel	SHALER geol Am		Ned	SPARKS
Nathaniel	TAYLOR tv		Ned	VAUGHN tv
Nathaniel	WILLIS ed,w Am		Nedbal,	OSKAR viol,cn,c Cz
Nathans,	DANIEL n-m'78		Nedim,	AHMED po Turk
Nathenson,	ZOE		Nedra	TALLEY s Am
Nation,	CARRY fe(wctu)Am		Nedra	VOLZ tv
Natoli,	SARAH tv		Nedwell,	ROBIN tv
Natorp,	PAUL ph,e Ger		Needham,	CONNIE tv
Natsume Soseki	--- w Japan		Needham,	HAL d
Natta,	GIULIO n-c'63		Needham,	TRACEY tv
Nattier,	JEAN p Fr		Neefe,	CHRISTIAN c Ger
Natwick,	MILDRED tv+		Neel,	LOUIS n-p'70
Natwick,	MYRON tv		Neeley,	TED
Naud,	MELINDA tv		Neeme	JARVI cn

Neenan,	AUDRIE J. tv	Nelson	LEIGH tv+
Neer,	AART van der p Dut	Nelson	MANDELA st S.Afr
Neeson,	LIAM	Nelson	McDOWELL
Nef,	JOHN sc,e Am	Nelson	RIDDLE mj,cn,tv+Am
Neff,	HILDEGARDE	Nelson,	ANN tv+
Negoda,	NATALIA	Nelson,	BARRY tv+
Negri,	ADA po,w It	Nelson,	BOB
Negri,	POLA	Nelson,	BOBBY
Negrin,	JUAN st,e Sp	Nelson,	BYRON g Am
Negron,	CHUCK mr-s Am	Nelson,	CHRISTINE tv
Negron,	TAYLOR	Nelson,	CRAIG T. tv+
Nehemiah	PERSOFF	Nelson,	DAVID tv+
Neher,	EDWIN n-m'91	Nelson,	DON bb,bbc
Neher,	SUSAN tv	Nelson,	ED tv+
Nehru,	JAWAHARLAL st India	Nelson,	FRANK tv
Nehru,	MOTILAL(Pandit)stInd	Nelson,	GARY d
Neihardt,	JOHN po,e Am	Nelson,	GENE s+
Neil	DIAMOND mj-s,w	Nelson,	HARRIET tv
Neil	GUNN w Scot	Nelson,	HAYWOOD tv
Neil	INNES mr-kbds,s Br	Nelson,	HORATIO navy Br
Neil	JONES mr-guit Welsh	Nelson,	JERRY tv
Neil	McCALLUM tv	Nelson,	JESSICA tv
Neil	MUNRO w,j,ct Scot	Nelson,	JIMMY tv
Neil	PEART mr-drm Can	Nelson,	JOHN ALLEN tv+
Neil	SCHWARTZ tv	Nelson,	JOHN tv
Neil	SEDAKA s-pop,ws Am	Nelson,	JUDD
Neil	SHEEHAN w Am	Nelson,	KENNETH tv
Neil	SIMON w Am	Nelson,	LLOYD
Neil	TENNANT mr-s Br	Nelson,	LORI
Neil	YOUNG mr Can	Nelson,	OZZIE mj,s,cn,tv+Am
Neil Patrick HARRIS tv+		Nelson,	PETER tv+
Neil,	VINCE mr-s Am	Nelson,	RALPH d
Neill,	NOEL tv+	Nelson,	RICKY m,tv+ Am
Neill,	ROY d	Nelson,	RUTH
Neill,	SAM	Nelson,	SANDRA tv
Neilson,	JAMES d	Nelson,	SANDY mj,mr-drm
Neilson,	JULIA la Br	Nelson,	TRACY
Neilson,	WILLIAM e,w Am	Nelson,	WILLIE s-cnt,ws+ Am
Neiman,	LEROY p Am	Nemec,	CORIN(Corky)tv+
Neise,	GEORGE tv	Nemerov,	HOWARD w,p-q'78
Nekrasov,	NIKOLAY po,ed Rus	Nemes,	LES mr-bass Br
Nekrasov,	VIKTOR ar,w Rus	Nemes,	SCOTT tv
Nelkin,	STACEY	Nemo,	GINA tv
Nell	CARTER s,tv+ Am	Neneh	CHERRY s-pop,rap Swe
Nell	GWYN la Br	Nenni,	PIETRO st It
Nell	O'DAY	Nepos,	JULIUS st-emp Rom
Nell,	WILLIAM w Am	Nera	WHITE bb hf
Nellie	FISHER ba,tv Am	Neri,	PHILIP r,mystic It
Nellie	FOX b hf	Neri,	ROSALBA(Sara Bay)
Nellie	MELBA(Dame)s Austra	Neriah	NAPAUL
Nellie	ROSS st Am	Nerina,	NADIA ba Br
Nelligan,	EMILE po Can	Nerman,	DAVID tv
Nelligan,	KATE	Nernst,	WALTHER n-c'20
Nello	SANTI cn Am	Nero	WOLFE fc
Nelly	SACHS po,w Ger	Nero,	FRANCO
Nels	STEWART ho	Nero,	PETER mj-piano Am
Nels	VanPATTEN	Nero,	TONI
Nelson	ALDRICH st Am	Neruda,	JAN po,w,j,ct Cz
Nelson	ALGREN w Am	Neruda,	PABLO n-l'71, po
Nelson	CASE tv	Nervi,	PIER eng,ac It
Nelson	EDDY s+ Am	Nervo,	AMADO de po Mex

Nesbit,	EDITH w,po Br	Newman,	JOHN r,w Br
Nesbitt,	CATHLEEN tv+	Newman,	LARAINE
Nesbitt,	JOHN tv	Newman,	NICHOLAS tv
Nesby,	ANN s-soul Am	Newman,	PAUL o-a'86,d,tv+
Nesimi,	SEYID po,mystic Turk	Newman,	PHYLLIS tv+
Nesmith,	MIKE s,guit,tv Am	Newmar,	JULIE tv+
Nessen,	RON press secy Am	Newmark,	MATTHEW tv
Nestle,	HENRI id-chocolat Swi	Newnes,	GEORGE(Sir)pb
Nestor	PAIVA	Newsom,	DAVID tv
Netherly,	PENDRANT tv	Newsom,	TOMMY tv
Netherton,	TOM m,tv	Newton	ROWELL l,st Can
Neto,	ANTONIO st,po Angola	Newton,	CONNIE NEEDHAM tv
Nettles,	GREG b,hr'76	Newton,	HUBERT astr,e Am
Nettleton,	LOIS tv+	Newton,	ISAAC(Sir)sc,math,e
Neuber,	FRIEDERIKE la Ger	Newton,	JOHN tv+
Neuhof,	THEODOR von ar,st Ger	Newton,	JUICE s-cnt Am
Neumann,	DOROTHY tv	Newton,	RICHARD tv
Neumann,	JENNY	Newton,	ROBERT
Neumann,	JOHN von math Am	Newton,	WAYNE
Neumann,	KURT d	Newton-John,	OLIVIA
Neurath,	OTTO ph,w Ger	Nexo,	MARTIN w Dan
Neutra,	RICHARD ac Am	Ney	LATORRACA
Neuwirth,	BEBE tv+	Ney,	ELISABET su Am
Neva'i,	ALI po Turk	Ney,	MICHEL ar Fr
Nevan	ROWE	Nezval,	VITEZSLAV po,w Czec
Nevelson,	LOUISE su Am	Ngaio	MARSH(Dame)w N.Zea
Nevers,	ERNIE b,fb hf	Ngata,	APIRANA(Sir)st N.Z.
Nevil	NORWAY w Br	Ngor,	HAING S. o-s'84
Nevil	SHUTE w Br	Ngugi wa Thiong'o	--- w Kenya
Neville	BRAND tv+	Ngugi,	JAMES w Kenya
Neville	MOTT(Sir)sc	Nguyen,	DUSTIN tv+
Neville,	AARON s-pop Am	Nia	LONG
Neville,	ART mr-kbds,s Am	Nia	PEEPLES tv+
Neville,	CHARLES mr-sax Am	Niall	MacGINNIS
Neville,	CYRIL mr-drm,s Am	Niblo,	FRED d
Neville,	JOHN tv+	Niblo,	WILLIAM bus Am
Nevin,	DAVID w Am	Nicanor	PARRA po Chile
Nevin,	ETHELBERT c Am	Nicassio,	JOEAL tv
Nevins,	ALLAN p-b'33'37	Niccolo	PISANI navy It
Nevins,	CLAUDETTE tv+	Niccolo	SALVI su It
Newbern,	GEORGE	Niccolo dell'ABBATE p It	
Newbery,	JOHN pb Br	Niccolo di MASSIO p It	
Newbolt,	HENRY(Sir)po	Niceto	ACALA ZAMORA st Sp
Newby,	P.H. w Br	Nichelle	NICHOLS
Newcomb,	DON b-cy-mv'56-1st cy	Nichol,	AL mr-guit,kbds,s
Newcomb,	SIMON astr Am	Nicholas	BIDDLE f Am
Newcombe,	JOHN t Aust	Nicholas	CLAY
Newell	WYETH p,illus Am	Nicholas	COSTER tv+
Newell,	WILLIAM	Nicholas	COUSTOU su Fr
Newfield,	SAM d	Nicholas	DANTE w Am
Newhart,	BOB cm,tv+	Nicholas	EVANS w Br
Newhouser,	HAL b-mv'44'45 hf	Nicholas	GAGE w Am
Newill,	JAMES	Nicholas	GUEST
Newlan,	PAUL tv	Nicholas	HAMMOND
Newland,	JOHN tv	Nicholas	LEA tv
Newley,	ANTHONY c+ Br	Nicholas	MEYER d,w Am
Newlove,	JOHN po Can	Nicholas	NEWMAN tv
Newman,	BARNETT p Am	Nicholas	PRYOR tv+
Newman,	BARRY tv+	Nicholas	RAY d+
Newman,	EDWIN tv-host Am	Nicholas	ROWE pol'1715-,w Br
Newman,	ERNEST ct-music Br	Nicholas	SHIELDS

Nicholas	SPARKS w Am	Nicolae	RADESCU ar,st Rom
Nicholas	UDALL w,e Br	Nicolaes	MAES(or Maas)p Dut
Nicholas	WORTH	Nicolaes	TULP md,sc,e Dut
Nicholas Murray BUTLER e Am		Nicolai	GEDDA tenor Swe
Nicholas, DENISE tv+		Nicolai,	OTTO c,cn Ger
Nicholas, PAUL		Nicolaou,	TED d
Nichols,	ANNE w Am	Nicolas	APPERT chef,i Fr
Nichols,	BARBARA tv+	Nicolas	BOILEAU po,ct It
Nichols,	BRITT	Nicolas	BRIOT engr Fr
Nichols,	EDWARD sc,e Am	Nicolas	CAGE
Nichols	GEORGE	Nicolas	CONTE sc Fr
Nichols,	KID b hf	Nicolas	GOMBERT c Belg
Nichols,	MIKE d	Nicolas	GUILLEN po Cuba
Nichols,	NICHELLE tv+	Nicolas	ISOUARD c Fr
Nichols,	PETER w Br	Nicolas	LEMERY sc,e,w Fr
Nichols,	RED mj-cornet,cn Am	Nicolas	POUSSIN p Fr
Nichols,	STEPHEN tv	Nicolas	RESTIF w Fr
Nichols,	TAYLOR tv	Nicolas	ROEG d
Nicholson,BEN p Br		Nicolas	SUROVY tv+
Nicholson,JACK o-s'83,o-a'75'98		Nicolas de SOULT ar,st Fr
Nicholson,SETH astron Am		Nicolas de STAEL p Fr
Nick	ADAMS tv+	Nicolas-F. APPERT chef,i Fr
Nick	CARTER fc-sleuth	Nicolay	ARZHAK w Rus
Nick	CASTLE ba,d,tv Am	Nicolay	ERDMAN w Rus
Nick	CHARLES fc-sleuth	Nicolay,	JOHN bio Am
Nick	CORRI	Nicole	BERGEN
Nick	DeMAURO tv	Nicole	DUBUC tv
Nick	DENNIS tv	Nicole	EGGERT tv+
Nick	FALDO g Br	Nicole	GARCIA
Nick	FORTUNE mr-bass Am	Nicole	KIDMAN
Nick	HEYWARD mr-guit,s Br	Nicole	MAUREY
Nick	MANCUSO tv+	Nicolet,	JEAN x Fr
Nick	MASON mr-drm Br	Nicolle,	CHARLES n-m'28
Nick	MASSI mr-bass,s Am	Nicolo	AMATI violins,e It
Nick	NOLTE	Nicolodi, DARIA
Nick	O'DEMUS tv	Nicolson, HAROLD(Sir)j,ct,h
Nick	RAMUS tv+	Niebuhr,	REINHOLD r,w Am
Nick	RHODES mr-kbds Br	Niehaus,	CHARLES su Am
Nick	STEWART tv	Niekro,	PHIL b hf
Nick	TATE tv+	Niel	GOW viol,c Scot
Nick	Van EXEL bb	Niel	YOUNG mr+ Can
Nicklaus, JACK g Am		Niels	ABEL math Nor
Nickolas ASHFORD s Am		Niels	BOHR sc Dan
Nickolas GRACE		Niels	FINSEN md Dan
Nicks,	STEVIE mr-s Am	Niels	GADE c Dan
Nickson-Soul,JULIA		Niels	JERNE md Dan
Nicky	HEADON mr-drm Br	Niels	JUEL navy Dan
Nicky	KATT tv	Niels	STENSEN geol,sc Dan
Nicky	ROSE tv	Nielsen,	ARTHUR bus,survey Am
Nicodemus TESSIN ac Swe		Nielsen,	ASTA
Nicol,	ABIOSEH po,w S.Leone	Nielsen,	BRIGITTE
Nicol,	ALEX	Nielsen,	CARL c Dan
Nicol,	WILLIAM sc,i Scot	Nielsen,	LESLIE tv+
Nicola	COWPER	Nielsen,	MORTEN po Dan
Nicola	PASIC st Serb	Nielsen,	RICK mr-guit,s Am
Nicola	PISANO su It	Niemeyer, OSCAR ac Braz
Nicola	PORPORA c It	Niemi,	LISA tv+
Nicola	SACCO radical Am	Niepce,	JOSEPH sc Fr
Nicolaas BEETS r,w,e Dut		Nievo,	IPPOLITO w,po It
Nicolaas LOUW po,w S.Afr		Nifo,	AGOSTINO ph,e It
Nicolae	IORGA h,e,st Rom	Nigel	BALCHIN w Br

Nigel	BRUCE	Nilsson,	ROB d+
Nigel	GREEN	Nimitz,	CHESTER navy Am
Nigel	HAVERS	Nimoy,	LEONARD w,d,tv+ Am
Nigel	PATRICK	Nims,	JOHN po Am
Nigel	PLANER	Nimzowitsch,	ARON chess Rus
Nigel	STOCK	Nin,	ANAIS w Am
Nigel	TERRY	Nina	BARA tv+
Nigel	TWIST mr-drm Br	Nina	EFIMOVA pupp Rus
Nigel de	BRULIER	Nina	FOCH tv+
Niggli,	PAUL sc,e Swi	Nina	RICCI ds Fr
Nigh,	JANE tv+	Nina	SIMONE s Am
Nigh,	WILLIAM d	Nina	WAYNE tv+
Night Train LANE fb hf		Nina	WILCOX tv
Nightingale, FLORENCE nurse Br		Nina Mae	McKINNEY
Nigo de	SANTILLANA po Sp	Ninetto	DAVOLI
Nigra,	CHRISTINA tv	Nino	BIXIO ar,st It
Nijhoff,	MARTINUS po Dut	Nino	ROTA c It
Nijinska,	BRONISLAWA ba Rus	Nino,	PEDRO x Sp
Nijinsky,	FOMICH ba Rus	Nipar,	YVETTE tv+
Nijinsky,	VASLAV ba Rus	Nipper,	WILL tv
Nijlen,	JAN van po Belg	Nipsey	RUSSELL cm,tv+ Am
Nikisch,	ARTHUR m,cn Hung	Nirenberg,	MARSHALL n-m'68
Nikitin,	AFANSAY w Rus	Nisard,	DESIRE j,ct Fr
Nikitin,	IVAN po Rus	Nisbett,	LOUISA la Br
Nikki	COGHILL	Nissenson,	HUGH w Am
Nikki	SIXX mr-bass Am	Nita	NALDI
Nikki	SWASEY tv	Nita	TALBOT tv+
Niklas,	JAN	Nitikin	AFANSAY w Rus
Niklaus	FLUE l,hero Swi	Nitikin,	IVAN po Rus
Niklaus	MANUEL p,engr Swi	Nitschke,	RAY fb hf
Nikola	TESLA i,eng Am	Nitti,	FRANCESCO ec,st It
Nikolai	SEMENOV sc Rus	Nittis,	GIUSEPPE de p It
Nikolais,	ALWIN ba Am	Niven,	DAVID o-a'58, tv+
Nikolaus	LENAU po Aus	Niven,	FREDERICK w Scot
Nikolay	GOGOL w Rus	Niven,	KIP
Nikolay	LENIN st Rus	Niverson,	ELAINE ba,tv Am
Nikolay	LESKOV w Rus	Nix,	MARTHA tv
Nikolay	MARR arc Rus	Nixon,	CYNTHIA
Nikolay	MEDTNER piano,c Rus	Nixon,	MARION
Nikolay	NOVIKOV j,f Rus	Nixon,	MARNI mj-s Am
Nikolay	POGODIN w Rus	Nixon,	MOJO
Nikolay	RAYNOV po,h-art Bulg	Nixon,	RICHARD M.37th pres
Nikolay	ROERICH p Rus	Nixon-Soul, JULIA	
Nikolay	SEMENOV sc,e Rus	Niza,	MARCOS de r,x Fr
Nikolay	VATUTIN ar Rus	Nizer,	LOUIS l Am
Nikolay	VAVILOV sc,e Rus	Noah	BEERY Jr. tv+
Nikolay	YEZHOV st Rus	Noah	BEERY Sr.
Nil	SORSKY r Rus	Noah	GORDON w Am
Nile	RODGERS mr-guit Am	Noah	KEEN tv
Niles,	HEZEKIAH ed Am	Noah	PORTER r,e,ed Am
Niles,	WENDELL tv	Noah	SWAYNE l,supr ct Am
Nils	ASTHER	Noah	TAYLOR
Nils	DALEN i,sc Swe	Noah	WEBSTER w,dictionry Am
Nils	DUNER astr Swe	Noah,	MORDECAI j,ed Am
Nils	EDEN st,h Swe	Noah,	YANNICK t Fr
Nils	LOFGREN m-guit,s,c	Noailles,	ANNA de po,w Fr
Nils	VOGT w,po Nor	Noam	CHOMSKY linguist Am
Nilson,	LARS sc,e Swe	Noam	PITLIK tv
Nilsson,	ANNA	Noam	ZYLBERMAN
Nilsson,	BIRGIT sopr Swe	Nobel,	ALFRED i,id,f Swe
Nilsson,	MAJ-BRITT	Nobile,	UMBERTO x,eng-aero It

Noble	JOHNSON	Noot,	JAN po Dut
Noble	SISSLE	Nora	BAYES la,s Am
Noble,	CHELSEA tv	Nora	DUNN cm,tv+ Am
Noble,	JAMES tv+	Nora	EPHRON d,w Am
Noble,	RAY mj,cn,c Br-Am	Nora	MARLOWE tv
Noble,	TRISHA tv+	Nora	MIAO
Nobre,	ANTONIO po Port	Nora	ROBERTS w Am
Nobuo	KANEKO	Nora Okja	KELLER w Am
Nocard,	EDMOND vet,sc Fr	Norbert	JOKL e,w Czech
Nock,	ALBERT w Am,	Norbert	WEISSER
Noddy	HOLDER mr-guit,s Br	Norbert	WIENER math,e,w Am
Noe	MURAYAMA	Norby,	GHITA
Noel	BLACK d	Norden,	CARL i Dut
Noel	BOUTON ar Fr	Norden,	TOMMY tv
Noel	COWARD(Sir)c,w,la	Nordhoff,	CHARLES w Am,
Noel	FRANCIS	Nordica,	LILLIAN sopr Am
Noel	MADISON	Nordstrom,	LUDVIG w Swe
Noel	NEILL tv+	Noreen	NASH tv+
Noel	NOSSECK d	Norell,	MICHAEL tv
Noel	REDDING mr-bass Br	Norihei	MIKI
Noel,	CHRIS tv	Norkey	TENZING sherpa guide
Noel,	MAGALI	Norm	CASH tv
Noel,	NOELIA	Norm	CROSBY cm Am
Noel-Baker,	PHILIP n-x'59	Norma	CRANE tv+
Noelia	NOEL	Norma	JEAN tv
Noelle	PARKER	Norma	MARLOWE tv
Noguchi,	HIDEYO sc,e Am	Norma	SHEARER
Noguchi,	ISAMU su Am	Norma	VARDEN tv+
Nohl,	MARY w Am	Norma	ZIMMER tv
Noir,	VICTOR j Fr	Norman	ALDEN tv+
Noiret,	PHILIPPE	Norman	ANGELL(Sir)w.ed,i
Nokie	EDWARDS mr-guit Am	Norman	BORLAUG st Am
Nol,	LON st Cambodia	Norman	BOWEN sc Am
Nolan	RYAN b	Norman	BROOKES(Sir)t Aust
Nolan,	BARRY tv	Norman	BURTON tv+
Nolan,	BOB	Norman	COOK mr-s Br
Nolan,	JAMES tv	Norman	COUSINS j,ed Am
Nolan,	JEANETTE tv+	Norman	DOUGLAS w Br
Nolan,	KATHY tv	Norman	FELL tv+
Nolan,	LLOYD tv+	Norman	FELTON pr-tv Am
Nolan,	MIKE mr-s Ir	Norman	FISHER(Sir)st
Nolan,	TOM tv+	Norman	HAPGOOD ed,w Am
Nolan,	TOMMY tv	Norman	HASSAN mr-drm Br
Nolde,	EMIL p Ger	Norman	JEWISON d
Noley	THORNTON	Norman	JOIO c Am
Nolhac,	PIERRE de w Fr	Norman	JOLLEY tv
Noll,	CHUCK fb hf	Norman	KAYE
Nollet,	JEAN sc,e Fr	Norman	KIRK st N.Zea
Nolte,	NICK	Norman	KUHLKE mr-drm Br
Nomellini,	LEO fb hf	Norman	LEAR pr Am
Nomkeena,	KEENA tv	Norman	LINDSAY p,cr,w Austra
Nona	HENDRIX s Am	Norman	LLOYD
Noon,	FIROZ(Sir)st Pakis.	Norman	LUBOFF s,cn Am
Noon,	JEFF w,m,p Br	Norman	MAEN ba,tv Am
Noonan,	FRED fly Am	Norman	MAILER w Am
Noonan,	PEGGY w-Pres.spchs	Norman	McLEOD d
Noonan,	TOMMY	Norman	O'NEILL c Br
Noone,	JIMMY mj-reeds Am	Norman	PARIS tv
Noone,	KATHLEEN tv	Norman	PARKER tv+
Noone,	PETER mr-s Br	Norman	RAMSEY sc Am
Noot,	HENRI van der st Bel	Norman	ROSE tv

Norman	SELBY (Kid McCoy) boxer	Novalis	--- po,w Ger
Norman	TAUROG d	Novarro,	RAMON
Norman	THOMAS r,ref Am	Novatna,	JANA t Cz
Norman	TOKAR d	Novello,	DON tv+
Norman Bel GEDDES ds,ac Am		Novello,	IVOR la,w.c+ Br
Norman Vincent PEALE r,w Am		Novello,	JAY tv+
Norman,	B.G. tv	Noverre,	JEAN ba Fr
Norman,	GEOFFREY w Am	Novikov,	NIKOLAY j,f Rus
Norman,	GREG g Aust	Novotny,	ANTONIN st Cz
Norman,	HOWARD w Am	Novy,	FREDERICK sc Am
Norman,	MARSHA p-d'83	Nowlan,	ALDEN po,w Can
Norman,	ZACK	Noy,	ZACHI
Normand,	MABEL la+ Am	Noyce,	PHILLIP d
Norn	URTH fc	Noyce,	ROBERT eng,i,id Am
Norris,	AARON d	Noyes,	ALFRED po,w Br
Norris,	CHARLES w Am	Noyes,	ARTHUR sc,e Am
Norris,	CHRISTOPHER tv	Noyes,	JOHN ref,w Am
Norris,	CHUCK tv+	Noyes,	La VERNE id,i Am
Norris,	EDWARD	Noyes,	TYLER tv
Norris,	FRANK w Am	Nucatola,	JOHN bbr hf
Norris,	FRED tv	Nucci,	DANNY tv+
Norris,	GEORGE st Am	Nugent,	EDDIE
Norris,	KATHLEEN w Am	Nugent,	JOHN la,w Am
Norris,	LEE tv	Nugent	JUDY tv
Norris,	MIKE	Nugent,	LAVAL ar Ir
Norrish,	RONALD n-c'67	Nugent,	TED mr-guit Am
North,	ALAN tv+	Nuland,	SHERWIN w Am
North,	ALEX c Am	Numa	DROZ j,st Swi
North,	DOUGLASS n-e'93	Numan,	GARY mr-s Br
North,	JAY tv+	Nunes,	PEDRO math Port
North,	OLIVER ar,st Am	Nunez,	CHARLES tv
North,	SHEREE ba,tv+ Am	Nunez,	DANNY tv
North,	SIMEON id-guns Am	Nunez,	MIGUEL Jr tv
North,	TED	Nunez,	RAFAEL st Colom
Northrop,	JOHN n-c'46	Nunez,	VICTOR d
Northrop,	WAYNE tv	Nunn,	ALICE tv
Northrup	FRYE ct,w Can	Nunn,	BILL
Northup,	HARRY tv	Nunn,	SAM st Am
Norton,	ALEX	Nunn,	TERI
Norton,	CAROLINE w Br	Nuno,	JAIME cn,c Sp
Norton,	CHARLES e,w Am	Nureyev,	RUDOLF ba+ Rus
Norton,	CLIFF cm,tv Am	Nurmi,	PAAVO og's'20'4'8 Finn
Norton,	KEN boxer,tv+ Am	Nuesslein-Vol., CHRISTIANE n-m'95	
Norton,	RICHARD	Nutt,	GRADY(Rev.)tv
Norton,	THOMAS l,po Br	Nuttall,	ZELIA arc Am
Norton-Taylor, JUDY tv+		Nutter,	MAYF
Norval	BAPTIE sk Am	Nutter,	RIK von
Norvo,	RED mj-vibes,cn Am	Nuvolari,	TAZIO racecars It
Norway,	NEVIL w Br	Nuyen,	FRANCE tv+
Norwid,	CYPRIAN w Pol	Nwapa,	FLORA w Nigeria
Norworth,	JACK lyrics Am	Nydia	WESTMAN tv+
Noske,	GUSTAV st Ger	Nye,	EDGAR w-humor Am
Nosseck,	NOEL d	Nye,	LOUIS cm,tv+
Noth,	CHRISTOPHER tv+	Nye,	RUSSELL p-d'45
Noth,	MARTIN r,e,w Ger	Nykvist,	SVEN movie camera.,d
Nouri,	MICHAEL tv+	Nyman,	LENA
Nova	PILBEAM	Nyree Dawn PORTER tv	
Novack,	SHELLY tv		
Novack,	KIM tv	**NO "O" NATIONALITY CODES**	
Novack,	VITEZSLAV v Cz		
Novakovic,STOJAN w Serbia			

"O" NAME DESIGNATION CODES

o-a	OSCAR BEST ACTOR
	OR ACTRESS
o-d	OSCAR BEST DIRECTOR
o-g	OLYMPIC GAMES GOLD MEDAL
o-p	OSCAR BEST PICTURE
o-s	OSCAR BEST SUPPORTING
	ACTOR OR ACTRESS

NO "O" NATIONALITY CODES

"O's"

O'Brian,   HUGH tv+
O'Brian,   PATRICK w Br
O'Brien,   AUSTIN
O'Brien,   CONAN tv
O'Brien,   CONOR h,st Ir
O'Brien,   DAVE
O'Brien,   EDMOND o-s'54,tv+
O'Brien,   EDNA w Ir
O'Brien,   EDWARD w,ed Am
O'Brien,   FLANN w Ir
O'Brien,   GEORGE
O'Brien,   JOAN
O'Brien,   MARGARET
O'Brien,   PARRY o-g'52'56
O'Brien,   PAT
O'Brien,   RORY tv
O'Brien,   TIM w Am
O'Brien,   TOM
O'Brien,   VIRGINIA
O'Brien-Moore, ERIN tv
O'Bryan,   PAT
O'Casey,   SEAN w Ir
O'Clery,   MICHAEL h Ir
O'Connell, ARTHUR tv+
O'Connell, DANIEL st Ir
O'Connell, DEIDRE
O'Connell, HELEN mj,s Am
O'Connell, JERRY tv+
O'Connor, BUDDY ho-m'48
O'Connor, CARROLL tv+
O'Connor, DONALD tv+
O'Connor, EDWIN p-f'62
O'Connor, FEARGUS st Ir
O'Connor, FLANNERY w Am
O'Connor, FRANK w Ir
O'Connor, GLYNNIS
O'Connor, HUGH tv
O'Connor, KEVIN
O'Connor, SANDRA DAY supr.ct
O'Connor, SINEAD s Ir
O'Connor, THOMAS j Ir
O'Connor, TIM tv+
O'Connor, UNA
O'Curry,   EUGENE antiq Ir
O'Day,   ANITA mj-s Am
O'Day,   NELL
O'Dea,   DENIS
O'Dell,   BRYAN tv
O'Dell,   TONY tv
O'Demus, NICK tv
O'Donnell, CATHY

O'Donnell, CHRIS
O'Donnell, COLLIN tv
O'Donnell, LILLIAN w Am
O'Donnell, ROSIE la,tv+ Am
O'Donovan, MICHAEL w,IRA Ir
O'Donovan, WILLIAM su Am
O'Doul,   LEFTY b
O'Dowd,   BERNARD po Aust
O'Driscoll, MARTHA
O'Duffy,   EOIN ar-IRA Ir
O'Dwyer, WILLIAM st Am
O'Faolain, SEAN w Ir
O'Farrell, BERNADETTE tv
O'Flaherty, LIAM w Ir
O'Flynn,   DAMIAN tv+
O'Gorman, JUAN ac,p Mex
O'Grady,   DESMOND po Ir
O'Grady,   GAIL
O'Grady,   LANI tv
O'Halloran, JACK
O'Halloran, MICHAEL tv
O'Hanlon, GEORGE Jr. tv+
O'Hanlon, GEORGE tv
O'Hara,   BRIAN mr-guit,s Br
O'Hara,   CATHERINE tv+
O'Hara,   FRANK po,ct-art,Am
O'Hara,   GEOFFREY c,ws
O'Hara,   JENNY tv+
O'Hara,   JOHN w Am
O'Hara,   MARY w Am
O'Hara,   MAUREEN
O'Herlihy, DAN tv+
O'Herlihy, GAVAN tv+
O'Herlihy, MICHAEL d
O'Higgins, HARVEY j,w Am
O'Keefe,   DENNIS tv+
O'Keefe,   JODI tv
O'Keefe,   MICHAEL
O'Keefe,   MILES
O'Keefe,   PAUL tv
O'Keefe,   WALTER tv
O'Keeffe, GEORGIA p Am
O'Kelly   ISLEY s Am
O'Kelly,   SEAN st Ir
O'Kelly,   SEUMAS w,ed Ir
O'Leary,   MICHAEL tv
O'Leary,   WILLIAM tv+
O'Loughlin, GERALD S. tv+
O'Malley, J. PAT tv+
O'Malley, PAT
O'Mara,   KATE tv+
O'Mara,   MOLLIE
O'More,   RORY re Ir
O'Morrison, KEVIN tv
O'Neal,   FREDERICK tv
O'Neal,   GRIFFIN
O'Neal,   KEVIN tv
O'Neal,   PATRICK tv+
O'Neal,   RON tv+
O'Neal,   RYAN tv+
O'Neal,   SHAQUILLE bb

O'Neal,	TATUM o-s'73
O'Neil,	BARBARA
O'Neill	MAIRE
O'Neill,	DICK tv+
O'Neill,	ED tv+
O'Neill,	EILEEN tv
O'Neill,	EUGENE n-1'36,p-d'57 &
O'Neill,	EUGENE p-d'20'22'28
O'Neill,	F.J. tv
O'Neill,	JENNIFER tv+
O'Neill,	JIMMY tv
O'Neill,	NANCE
O'Neill,	NORMAN c Br
O'Neill,	PAUL b,bat'94
O'Neill,	REMY
O'Neill,	ROSE illus,w Am
O'Neill,	THOMAS(Tip)st Am
O'Nolan,	BRIAN w Ir
O'Quinn,	TERRY
O'Reilly,	BILL tv
O'Reilly,	CYRIL
O'Reilly,	HARRY tv
O'Reilly,	JOHN po,ed Am
O'Ross,	ED
O'Rourke,	HEATHER tv+
O'Rourke,	JAMES b hf
O'Shea,	MICHAEL tv+
O'Shea,	MILO
O'Shea,	TESSIE s,tv
O'Sullivan,	GILBERT ws Ir
O'Sullivan,	MAUREEN
O'Sullivan,	MAURICE w Ir
O'Sullivan,	RICHARD tv
O'Toole,	ANNETTE
O'Toole,	MARK mr-bass Br
O'Toole,	PETER
O.	HENRY w Am
O.E.	HASSE
O.J.	SIMPSON fb hf,tv+
O.P.	HEGGIE
Oakes	AMES f,id,st Am
Oakes	AMES sc,e Am
Oakes,	RANDI tv
Oakey,	PHILIP mr-s Br
Oakie,	JACK
Oakland,	SIMON tv+
Oakley,	ANNIE markswoman Am
Oakley,	BERRY mr-bass Am
Oakman,	WHEELER
Oates,	JOHN mr-guit,s Am
Oates,	JOYCE CAROL w,po,ct
Oates,	LAWRENCE x Br
Oates,	SIMON
Oates,	TITUS impostor Br
Oates,	WARREN tv+
Obando,	JOSE st Colom
Obbe	PHILIPS r Dut
Obed	HUSSEY i Am
Ober,	PHILIP tv+
Oberdiear,	KAREN tv
Oberon,	MERLE
Obraztsova,	ELENA mezzo Rus
Obregon,	ALVARO ar,st Mex
Obregon,	RODRIGO
Ocampo,	FLORIAN h Sp
Ocasek,	RIC mr-guit,s Am
Occam,	WILLIAM of ph,r Br
Occhipinti, ANDREA	
Ocean,	BILLY s-folk,mr,w
Ochoa,	EUGENIO de w,ed Sp
Ochoa,	SEVERO n-m'59
Ochs,	ADOLPH pb,ed Am
Ochs,	PETER st Swi
Ochs,	SIEGFRIED cn,c Ger
Ochsenknecht,UWE	
Octave	CHANUTE eng,id Am
Octave	MIRBEAU j.w Fr
Octave	PIRMEZ w Belg
Octavia	HILL ref Br
Octavian	GOGA w,st Rom
Octavio	PAZ po,w Mex
Octavus	COHEN w Am
Odd	HASSEL sc Nor
Oded	KOTLER
Odell,	JONATHAN ar,w Am
Odessa	CLEVELAND tv
Odessa,	DEVON tv
Odet de	LAUTREC ar Fr
Odets,	CLIFFORD w Am
Odette	JOYEUX
Odile	VERSOIS
Odilon	BARROT st Fr
Odilon	REDON p,engr Fr
Odon von	HORVATH w Ger
Odum,	HOWARD soc,e Am
Odysseus	ELYTIS po Gr
Oe,	KENZABURO w Japan
Oeben,	JEAN id-furnit. Fr
Oehlenschlaeger, ADAM po,w Dan	
Oertel,	HANNS e,w Ger
Oerter,	AL 4x o-g'56 &
Oerter,	AL o-g'60'4'8
Oeser,	ADAM p Ger
Ofelia	MEDINA
Offenbach,JACQUES c Fr	
Officer Marete EDILLO tv	
Ogata,	KEN
Ogburn,	WILLIAM soc Am
Ogden	NASH po,w Am
Ogden	ROOD sc Am
Ogden,	AARON l,st Am
Ogden,	CHARLES(C.K.)ps,w Br
Ogden,	ROLLO j,ed Am
Oge,	JACQUES re Haiti
Ogier,	BULLE
Ogilvy,	IAN
Oglethorpe, JAMES ar,f Br	
Oglivie,	BEN b,hr'80
Oh,	SANDRA
Oh,	SOON-TECK
Ohana,	CLAUDIA
Ohlin,	BERTIL n-e'77

Ohm,	GEORG sc,e Ger	Olga	SUAREZ tv
Ohman,	PHIL mj-piano,cn Am	Olga	ZUBARRY
Ohmart,	CAROL	Olid,	CRISTOBAL de ar Sp
Oil Can	TIANT b	Olier,	JEAN r Fr
Oistrakh,	DAVID viol Rus	Oliphant,	PATRICK p-x'67
Ojeda,	ALONSO de x Sp	Olin	DOWNES ct-music Am
Ojetti,	UGO w,ct-art It	Olin	HOWLAND
Okada,	EIJI	Olin	HOWLIN tv
Okara,	GABRIEL po,w Niger	Olin,	KEN tv+
Okazaki,	BOB tv	Olin,	LENA
Oken,	LORENZ ph,natur Ger	Oliva,	TONY b,bat'64
Okigbo,	CHRISTOPHER po Niger	Olive	BLAKENEY tv+
Oklahoma Wranglers--- m,tv Am		Olive	CAREY tv
Okot	p'BITEK po Uganda	Olive	DUNBAR tv
Okudzhava,BULAT po,w Rus		Olive	PROUTY w Am
Okumoto,	YUJI	Oliver	BLAKE tv
Ola	HANSSON w Swe	Oliver	CLARK tv+
Olaf	BULL po Nor	Oliver	ELTON h,e Br
Olaf	STAPLEDON ph,w Br	Oliver	EVANS i Am
Olaf,	PIERRE tv	Oliver	GIBBS sc Am
Olafur	THORS st Iceland	Oliver	GOGARTY md,w Ir
Olajuwon,	HAKEEM bb-m'94	Oliver	HARDY cm+ Am
Olan	SOULE tv	Oliver	HERFORD w,illus Am
Oland,	WARNER	Oliver	La FARGE an,w Am
Olaudah	EQUIANO w Africa	Oliver	LODGE(Sir)sc,e,w
Olaus	PETRI r Swe	Oliver	NORTH ar,st Am
Olav	AUKRUST po Nor	Oliver	ONIONS w Br
Olav	DUUN w Nor	Oliver	OPTIC w,ed Am
Olbers,	HEINRICH md,astr Ger	Oliver	PERRY navy Am
Olbrychski, DANIEL		Oliver	PLATT
Olcott,	CHAUNCEY la,s,c Am	Oliver	POLLOCK mer Am
Old Grog	VERNON navy Br	Oliver	REED
Old Tom	MORRIS g Scot	Oliver	SACKS w Am
Oldberg,	ARNE c Am	Oliver	STONE d
Oldenbourg, ZOE w Fr		Oliver	TOBIAS
Oldfield, ANNE la Br		Oliver Wendall HOLMES Jr l Am	
Oldfield, BARNEY racecars Am		Oliver Wendall HOLMES Sr w,e Am	
Oldfield, ERIC		Oliver,	AL b,rbi'82
Oldfield, MIKE mr-bass,c Br		Oliver,	BARRET
Oldham,	RICHARD geol Br	Oliver,	DAVID tv
Oldman,	GARY	Oliver,	EDNA MAY
Olds,	RANSOM ELI i,id Am	Oliver,	GORDON
Ole	BULL viol Nor	Oliver,	KING mj-cornet,c Am
Ole	OLSEN cm+	Oliver,	MARY p-q'84
Ole	ROLVAAG w,e Am	Oliver,	MICHAEL
Ole	ROMER astr Dan	Oliver,	PAUL i Am
Ole	WORM md,sc Dan	Oliver,	ROCHELLE
Ole-Thorsen, SVEN		Oliver,	STEPHEN tv+
Oleg	CASSINI ds Fr	Oliver,	SUSAN
Oleg	TABAKOV	Oliver,	SY mj-arranger,c Am
Olek	KRUPA	Olivia	BARASH tv+
Olerud,	JOHN b,bat'93	Olivia	BROWN tv
Olesha,	YURY w Rus	Olivia	COLE tv+
Oleta	ADAMS s-soul,ws Am	Olivia	D'ABO tv+
Oley	SPEAKS	Olivia	DIONNE quints' Dad
Olga	FORSH w Rus	Olivia	HUSSEY
Olga	JAMES tv	Olivia	PASCAL
Olga	KORBUT gy Rus	Olivier	GLOUX w Fr
Olga	LINDO	Olivier	PIERRE tv
Olga	RUSSELL tv	Olivier,	LAURENCE(Sir)la+ &
Olga	SAN JUAN	Olivier,	LAURENCE(Sir)o-a'48

Oliviero,	SILVIO	Opie,	AMELIA w Br
Ollie	MATSON fb hf	Opie,	PETER folklore Br
Ollivier,	EMILE st Fr	Opitz,	MARTIN po,ct Ger
Qlmedo,	ALEX t Am	Oppel,	ALBERT geol,e Ger
Olmedo,	JOSE st Ecu	Oppen,	GEORGE p-q'69
Olmos,	EDWARD tv+	Oppenheim,E.	PHILLIPS w Br
Olmsted,	FREDERICK ac-lskp Am	Oppenheimer,	ALAN tv+
Olmsted,	GERTRUDE	Oppenheimer,	ROBERT sc,e Am
Olney,	RICHARD st Am	Opper,	DON
Olof	RUDBECK sc-md Swe	Opper,	FREDERICK illus,cr Am
Olof von	DALIN po,h Swe	Oppert,	JULES h-orient Fr
Olsen,	ASHLEY tv	Oprah	WINFREY tv-host+
Olsen,	JOHNNY tv	Optic,	OLIVER w,ed Am
Olsen,	MARY-KATE tv	Oquendo,	ANTONIO de s Sp
Olsen,	MERLIN fb hf,tv+	Orage,	ALFRED ed Br
Olsen,	MORONI	Oral	ROBERTS r,tv Am
Olsen,	OLE cm+	Oran	PAGE(Hot Lips)mj,cn
Olsen,	SUSAN tv	Orane	DEMAZIS
Olson,	CHARLES po,e Am	Orange	SCOTT r,abolit Am
Olson,	ERIC tv	Orange,	WALTER mr-drm,s
Olson,	JAMES	Orazio	VECCHI c It
Olson,	NANCY	Orbach,	JERRY
Olympe	MANCINI mistress Fr	Orbison,	ROY mr,tv+ Am
Olympia	DUKAKIS	Orcagna,	ANDREA p,su,ac It
Olympio,	SYLVANUS st Togo	Orchard,	JOHN tv
Om	PURI	Orczy,	EMMUSKA w Br
Oman,	CHARLES(Sir)h	Orde	WINGATE ar Br
Omar	BRADLEY ar Am	Ordonez,	RAY b-gg'97
Omar	EPPS	Orfei,	LIANA
Omar	KAHAYYAM po Persia	Orff,	CARL c Ger
Omar	SHARIF	Orfila,	MATTHIEU sc Fr
Omar	VIZQUEL b	Oriana	FALLACI j,w It
Omar Khayyam	---po,astron Pers	Oriani,	ALFREDO po,w It
Omen,	JUDD	Oribe,	MANUEL ar,st Urug
Omer,	JEAN mj,cn Belg	Origen	--- w,e,r Gr
Omero	ANTONUTTI	Orkin,	DICK tv
Omri	KATZ tv+	Orlandersmith,	DAEL w Am
Ona	MUNSON	Orlando	CEPEDA b hf
Ona,	PEDRO de po Chile	Orlando	GIBBONS organ,c Br
Onassis,	ARISTOTLE(Ari)f Gr	Orlando di	LASSO c Belg
Onate,	JUAN de x Sp	Orlando,	TONY s,tv Am
Oncken,	HERMANN h,e Ger	Orlando,	VITTORIO st It
Ondaatje,	MICHAEL w Can	Orlandt,	KEN tv
Ondra,	ANNY	Orley,	BENAERT van p Belg
Onetti,	JUAN w Uruguay	Orlik,	EMIL p,etch Ger
Onions,	CHARLES ed-dicts. Br	Ormandy,	EUGENE cn Am
Onions,	OLIVER w Br	Ormond,	JULIA tv+
Onna	WHITE ba Am	Ormsby	MITCHEL astr Am
Onnie	McINTYRE mr-guit Scot	Ornella	MUTI
Ono,	YOKO s+	Ornette	COLEMAN mj-sax Am
Onorati,	PETER tv+	Oronce	FINE math Fr
Onsager,	LARS n-c'68	Orozco,	JOSE p Mex
Onslow	STEVENS tv+	Orpen,	WILLIAM(Sir) p
Onslow,	GEORGES c Fr	Orr,	BENJAMIN mr-bass,s
Ontkean,	MICHAEL tv+	Orr,	BOBBY ho-m'70'1'2
Oona	CHAPLIN(Ch's Wife)	Orr,	CAREY p-x'61
Oost,	JAKOB van p Belg	Orr,	JOHN B.(Lord)n-x'49
Opatoshu,	DAVID	Orrente,	PEDRO p Sp
Opel,	FRITZ von id-cars Ger	Orrin	HATCH st Am
Ophuls,	MAX d	Orrison,	JACK tv
Opie	READ w Am	Orry,	JEAN ec Fr

Orser,	BRIAN sk Can	Oskar	HERTWIG sc-md e Ger
Orsi,	GINGER tv	Oskar	LOERKE po Ger
Orsi,	LEIGH tv	Oskar	NEDBAL viola,cn,c Cz
Orsi,	PAOLO arc It	Oskar	STRAUS c Fr
Orsini,	FELICE re It	Oskar	WERNER
Orsini,	UMBERTO	Oskar,	LEEmr-harmonica Den
Orson	BEAN tv+	Osler,	WILLIAM(Sir)md Can
Orson	WELLES pr,d+ Am	Oslin,	K.T. s+ Am
Orson Scott CARD w Am		Osmena,	SERGIO st Phil
Orsted,	HANS sc Dan	Osmond,	ALAN s,tv Am
Ortega y Gasset, JOSE ph,w,ct Sp		Osmond,	CHRISTIAN tv
Ortega,	ARMANDO tv	Osmond,	CLIFF
Orteig,	RAYMOND restaur.Am	Osmond,	DONNIE s,tv+ Am
Orth,	FRANK tv	Osmond,	ERIC tv
Ortiz,	ROBERTO st Arg	Osmond,	JAY s,tv Am
Orton,	JOE w,ct Br	Osmond,	JIMMY s, tv
Orville	PLATT st Am	Osmond,	KEN tv
Orville	VICTOR w,pb Am	Osmond,	MARIE s,tv+ Am
Orville	WRIGHT i,aviation	Osmond,	MERRILL s,tv Am
Orwell,	GEORGE w,ct Br	Osmond,	TRAVIS s,tv Am
Ory,	KID mj-tromb Am	Osmond,	WAYNE s,tv Am
Orzabal,	ROLANDmr-guit Br	Osser,	GLENN m,cn,tv
Osa	JOHNSON x Am	Ossie	DAVIS tv+
Osa	MASSEN	Ossietzky,CARL von w, n-x'35	
Osbert	SITWELL(Sir)po,w	Ossip	ZADKINE su Rus
Osborn,	FAIRFIELD w Am	Ostade,	ADRIAEN van p Dut
Osborn,	HENRY sc,e Am	Ostaijen,	PAUL van po,ct Belg
Osborn,	LYN tv+	Ostberg,	RAGNAR ac Swe
Osborn,	SHERARD x,navy Br	Ostenso,	MARTHA w Am
Osborn,	VIRGINIA s,tv Am	Osterhage,JEFFREY(Jeff)tv+	
Osborne	MAVOR md,w Scot	Osterwald,BIBI	
Osborne,	BUD	Ostrovsky,NIKOLAY w Rus	
Osborne,	GEORGE piano,c Ir	Ostwald,	WILHELM n-c'09
Osborne,	JEFFREY mr-drm,s,w	Osuna,	RAFAEL t
Osborne,	JOHN w Br	Oswald	AVERY sc,e Am
Osborne,	VIVIENNE	Oswald	HEER sc,w Swi
Osbourne,	OZZY	Oswald	KULPE ph,ps,w Ger
Oscar	CARGILL ct,e,ed Am	Oswald	MOSLEY(Sir)st
Oscar	De la HOYA boxer Am	Oswald	VEBLEN math,e,w Am
Oscar	De La RENTA ds Am	Oswald	VILLARD j,ed,pb Am
Oscar	EWING tv	Oswald de ANDRADE po,w Braz	
Oscar	HOMOLKA	Oswald,	LEE HARV.assasn-JFK
Oscar	LEVANT piano,c Am	Oswaldo	ARANHA l,st Braz
Oscar	LEVENE tv	Otake,	SHOJI
Oscar	LEWIS an,w Am	Oteri,	CHERI tv
Oscar	McINTYRE j,w Am	Otescu,	ION c Rom
Oscar	POLK	Othmar	SCHOECK c Swi
Oscar	SANCHEZ st CostaR	Othniel	MARSH sc,e Am
Oscar	SONNECK m,library	Othon	FRIESZ p Fr
Oscar	STRAUS c Fr	Otis	HARLAN
Oscar	WILDE po,w Irish	Otis	REDDING s-soul,c Am
Oscar,	HENRY	Otis	SKINNER la Am
Oscarson, PER		Otis	WILLIAMS mr-s Am
Osgood	PERKINS	Otis	YOUNG tv+
Osgood,	CHARLES tv-j Am	Otis,	AMOS b
Osgood,	FRANCES po Am	Otis,	BASS p Am
Oshima,	NAGISA d	Otis,	CARRE mo+ Am
Osip	MANDELSTAM po Rus	Otis,	ELISHA i,id Am
Oskar	BARNACK eng Ger	Otis,	HARRISON ar,j Am
Oskar	BRAATEN w Nor	Otis,	JAMES l-colonial Am
Oskar	FRIED c,cn Ger	Otis,	JOHNNY m-r&b,drm,w

Otlet,	PAUL l Belg		Ovitz,	MICHAEL bus Am
Otsuki,	TAMAYO tv		Owen	BUSH
Ott,	MEL b hf		Owen	DAVIS w Am
Otto	BISMARK st Ger		Owen	EDWARDS(Sir)w,eWel
Otto	BRAHM ct,d Ger		Owen	JONES ac Br
Otto	BRAUN st Ger		Owen	TEALE
Otto	BROWER d		Owen	WISTER w Am
Otto	DIELS sc Ger		Owen	YOUNG id-GE Am
Otto	DIX p Ger		Owen,	BILL
Otto	ENDER st Aus		Owen,	DANIEL w Welsh
Otto	GESSLER st Ger		Owen,	GORONWY r,po Welsh
Otto	GIERKE l,e Ger		Owen,	JAY tv
Otto	GRAHAM fb hf		Owen,	RANDY m-guit,s Am
Otto	HAHN sc Ger		Owen,	REGINALD
Otto	HARBACH w Am		Owen,	ROBERT id,f,f Welsh
Otto	JAHN sc,w,ct Ger		Owen,	SEENA
Otto	KAHN banker,f Am		Owen,	STEVE fb hf
Otto	KRUGER tv+		Owen,	WILFRED po Br
Otto	LOEWI sc,md,e Am		Owens,	ALVIS(Buck)s-cnt,tv
Otto	LUDWIG w Ger		Owens,	GARY tv+
Otto	LUMMER sc,e Ger		Owens,	GEOFFREY tv
Otto	MUELLER p Ger		Owens,	JESSE 4x o-g'36
Otto	NEURATH ph,w Ger		Owens,	MICHAEL i,id-glass Am
Otto	NICOLAI c,cn Ger		Owens,	PATRICIA
Otto	PENZLER w Am		Owens,	SHIRLEY mr-s Am
Otto	RANK ps,ed Aus		Owensby	EARL
Otto	SANDER		Owings,	NATHANIEL ac Am
Otto	SCHMIDT w Ger		Oxenberg,	CATHERINE
Otto	SHMIDT sc,e,x Rus		Oxnam,	GARFIELD r,e,w Am
Otto	SINDING p Nor		Oz,	AMOS w Israel
Otto	SOGLOW cr Am		Oz,	FRANK puppets,d,tv+
Otto	STERN sc,e Am		Ozawa,	SEIJI cn
Otto	WAGNER ac Aus		Ozenfant,	AMEDEE p Fr
Otto	WALLACH sc,e Ger		Ozick,	CYNTHIA w Am
Otto	WARBURG sc,e Ger		Ozker,	ERIN pupp tv
Otto van	VEEN p Dut		Ozzie	NELSON mj-s,cn,tv+
Otto von	PACK st Ger		Ozzie	SMITH b
Otto,	JIM fb hf		Ozzy	OSBOURNE
Otto,	MIRANDA la+ Aust			
Otto,	RUDOLF ph,e,st Ger		**"P" NAME DESIGNATION CODES**	
Ottoline	MORRELL(Lady)hosts		p	PAINTER
Otway,	THOMAS w,po Br		pb	PUBLISHER
Otwell,	DAVID tv		ph	PHILOSOPHER
Otwell,	ROGER tv		po	POET
Oud,	JACOBUS ac Dut		pol	POET LAUREATE BRITISH
Oudry,	JEAN p,illus Fr		pr	PRODUCER
Oursler,	FULTON j,w Am		ps	PSYCHIATRIST OR
Oury,	GERARD			PSYCHOANALYST
Ousley,	DINA tv		pupp	PUPPET(S)
Ouspenskaya,	MARIA		p-b	PULITZER PRIZE-BIOGRAPHY
Outerbridge,	PETER		p-c	PULITZER PRIZE-CRITICISM
Ouvard,	GABRIEL bus,f Am		p-d	PULITZER PRIZE-DRAMA
Ovens,	JURGEN p Dan		p-e	PULITZER PRIZE-EDITORIAL
Overall,	PARK		p-f	PULITZER PRIZE-FICTION
Overbury,	THOMAS(Sir)po,w		p-h	PULITZER PRIZE-HISTORY
Overend	WATTS mr-bass Br		p-m	PULITZER PRIZE-MUSIC
Overland,	ARNULF po,w Nor		p-n	PULITZER PRIZE-NON FICTION
Overman,	LYNNE		p-p	PULITZER PRIZE-PHOTOGRAPHY
Overton,	FRANK tv+		p-q	PULITZER PRIZE-POETRY
Overton,	RICK		p-r	PULITZER PRIZE-REPORTING
Ovid	--- po Ro		p-x	PULITZER PRIZE-CARTOONING

"P" NATIONALITY CODES	
P.Rico - PUERTO RICAN	
Parag - PARAGUAYAN	
Phil - PHILLIPPINO	
Pol - POLISH	
Port - PORTUGESE	
"P's"	

P'Bitek,	OKOT po Uganda
P.D.	JAMES w Br
P.H.	NEWBY w Br
P.J.	PROBY s Am
P.J.	SOLES
P.K.	PAGE po,ed Can
P.L.	TRAVERS w Aust
P.R.	PAUL tv
Paap,	WILLEM w Dut
Paar,	JACK tv-host+ Am
Paavo	NURMI runner Finn
Pablo	CASALS cello,c Sp
Pablo	NERUDA po,st Chile
Pablo	PICASSO p,su Sp
Pabst,	GEORGE d-films Ger
Paca,	WILLIAM l,re ldr Am
Pace,	JUDY tv+
Pace,	TOM
Pacher,	MICHAEL p Ger
Pacini,	GIOVANNI c It
Pacino,	AL o-a'92
Pacius,	FREDRIK viol,c Finn
Pack,	OTTO von st Ger
Packard,	DAVID id,w Am
Packard,	JAMES eng-cars,i Am
Packer,	DAVID
Packer,	DORIS tv
Packer,	JERRY tv
Pacula,	JOANNA
Padden,	SARAH
Paderewski,	IGNACY piano,c Pol
Padilla,	MANUEL Jr. tv
Padovani,	LEA
Padriac	COLUM po,w Ir
Paer,	FERDINANDO c It
Paes,	SIDONIO st Port
Paez,	JOSE ar,st Venz
Paganini,	NICOLO viol,c
Page	FORSYTHE tv
Page	HANNAH
Page,	ALAN fb-d'73 hf
Page,	ANITA
Page,	ANTHONY d
Page,	EARLE(Sir)st Aust
Page,	GENEVIEVE
Page,	GERALDINE la+,o-a'85
Page,	HARRISON tv+
Page,	JIMMY mr-guit Br
Page,	La WANDA tv+
Page,	ORAN(HotLips)mj,cn Am
Page,	P.K. po,ed Can
Page,	PAT bb hf
Page,	PATTI s,tv+ Am

Page,	RUTH ba Am
Page,	THOMAS w,st Am
Page,	WALTER j,st Am
Page,	WILLIAM p Am
Pagels,	ELAINE w Am
Paget,	ALFRED
Paget,	DEBRA
Paget,	JAMES(Sir)md,sc
Paget,	VIOLET w,ct-art Br
Pagett,	GARY tv
Pagnol,	MARCEL w,d Fr
Pahlevi,	MOHAMMED REZA st Iran
Pahlevi,	REZA SHAH(MR's father)
Pai,	SUE tv
Paice,	IAN mr-drm Br
Paich,	DAVID mr-kbds,s Am
Paich,	MARTY m,cn,tv Am
Paige	BARDOLPH tv
Paige	MALONEY tv
Paige,	JANIS tv+
Paige,	ROBERT tv+
Paige,	SATCHEL b hf
Pain,	DIDIER
Paine,	ALBERT w,ed Am
Paine,	HEIDI
Paine,	JOHN organ,e,c Am
Paine,	THOMAS ph,w,re Am
Paine,	TOM w Am
Painter,	WILLIAM w Br
Pais,	ETTORE h,e It
Paiva,	NESTOR
Pajol,	CLAUDE ar Fr
Pajou,	AUGUSTIN su Fr
Pakula,	ALAN d
Pal	TELEKI geog,st Hung
Pal,	BIPIN j India
Palade,	GEORGE n-m'74
Palamas,	KOSTIS(Koster)po Gr
Palance,	HOLLY tv+
Palance,	JACK o-s'91,tv+
Palander,	LOUIS navy,x Swe
Palermo,	GEORGE tv
Pales Matos,	LUIS po P.Rico
Paley,	GRACE w Am
Paley,	WILLIAM r,ph Br
Paley,	WILLIAM tv-exec Am
Palgrave,	FRANCIS(Sir)po,ct
Palillo,	RON tv+
Palin,	MICHAEL
Palisa,	JOHANN astr Aus
Palladio,	ANDREA ac It
Pallas,	PETER sc Ger
Pallen,	CONDE ed Am
Pallette,	EUGENE
Pallotti,	GABRIELLA
Palm,	ANDERS d
Palm,	JOHANN book mer,pb Ger
Palma,	BRIAN de d
Palma,	JACOPO p It
Palma,	RICARDO w Peru
Palme,	ULF

Palmeiro	RAFAEL b	Pankow,	JAMES m-tromb Am
Palmer	COX illus,w Am	Pankow,	JOHN tv+
Palmer,	ARNOLD(Arnie)g Am	Pannini,	GIOVANNI p It
Palmer,	AUSTIN handwritng Am	Panofsky,	ERWIN h-art Am
Palmer,	BETSY tv+	Panova,	VERA w Rus
Palmer,	BUD tv	Panozzo,	CHUCK mr-bass Am
Palmer,	CARL mr drm Br	Panozzo,	JOHN mr-drm Am
Palmer,	DANIEL chiropract Am	Pantoliano,	JOE
Palmer,	ERASTUS su Am	Paola	STOPPA
Palmer,	HELEN w Am	Paoli,	PASQUALE st It
Palmer,	HORATIO c,e Am	Paolo	FRISI sc,astr It
Palmer,	JIM b-cy'73'5'6 hf,tv	Paolo	GIOVIO bio,h It
Palmer,	LILLI tv+	Paolo	ORSI arc It
Palmer,	LIZA tv	Paolo	ROLLI po,lyrics It
Palmer,	MICHAEL w Am	Paolo	RUFFINI math,sc,e It
Palmer,	POTTER mer Am	Paolo	SEGANTI tv
Palmer,	ROBERT s,ws Br	Paolo	TAVIANI d
Palmer,	VANCE w,po Aust	Paolo	UCCELLO p It
Palmgren,	SELIM piano,c Finn	Paolo	VERONESE p It
Palminteri,	CHAZZ	Papa Dee	ALLEN mr-kbds,s Am
Palomino,	CARLOS	Papas,	IRENE tv+
Palou,	FRANCISCO r Sp	Papas,	LASLO
Paltrow,	GWYNETH o-a'99	Papen,	FRANZ von st,ar Ger
Paluzzi,	LUCIANNA	Papenfuss,	TONY tv
Pam	DAWBAR tv+	Papin,	DENIS sc Fr
Pam	FREEMAN tv	Pappas,	IKE
Pam	GRIER	Paquin,	ANNA o-s'93
Pam	STONE tv	Par	LAGERKVIST n-l'51
Pam	TILLIS s Am	Parady,	HERSHA tv
Pamela	BEAIRD tv	Paramore,	KIRI
Pamela	BLAKE	Parazaider,	WALTER m-sax Am
Pamela	BRITTON tv+	Pardo Bazan,	EMILIA w Sp
Pamela	BROWN	Pardo,	DON tv
Pamela	DIXON	Pardo,	MANUEL st Peru
Pamela	GIDLEY	Pare,	AMBROISE md Fr
Pamela	HENSLEY tv+	Pare,	MICHAEL tv+
Pamela	JOHNSON w,ct Br	Parec,	MARIE-JOSE o-g'92'96
Pamela	JONES tv	Pareja,	JUAN de p Sp
Pamela	LEE tv	Parely,	MILA
Pamela	LUDWIG	Pareto,	VILFREDO ec It
Pamela	MARTIN tv+	Paretsky,	SARA w
Pamela	MYERS tv	Parez,	TONY b
Pamela	REED tv+	Parfitt,	JUDY tv+
Pamela	RODGERS tv	Parfitt,	RICK mr-guit,s Br
Pamela	SEGALL tv+	Parini,	GIUSEPPE po It
Pamela	TIFFIN	Parini,	JAY w Am
Pamelyn	FERDIN tv	Paris	VAUGHAN
Pampa,	NADOJA po India	Paris,	ALEXIS e,ed Fr
Pamus,	JEROME(Doc)c Am	Paris,	JERRY d,tv
Pan,	YANG PAN	Paris,	MATTHEW h Br
Panama	FRANCIS mj-drm,cn Am	Paris,	NORMAN tv
Panayotis	POTAGOS md Gr	Parish,	MITCHELL lyrics Am
Pancho	VILLA bandit,re Mex	Park	OVERALL
Pandit Motilal	NEHRU st India	Park,	MAUD ref,fe Am
Pando,	JOSE ar,st Bolivia	Park,	MERLE ba Br
Paneth,	FRIEDRICH sc,e Aus	Park,	MUNGO x Scot
Pang,	TIEN	Park,	REG
Pangborn,	FRANKLIN	Park,	ROBERT j,e,w Am
Panhard,	RENE eng-cars Fr	Park,	STEVE tv
Panico,	LOUIS mj-trump,cn Am	Park,	VINCENT w Am
Pankin,	STUART tv+	Park-Lincoln,	LAR tv

Parke,	DOROTHY tv		Parodi,	DOMINIQUE po,w Fr
Parker	JACOBS tv		Parr,	CATHERINE wf-Henry8th
Parker,	ALAN d		Parra,	NICANOR po Chile
Parker,	CECIL		Parra,	TERESA de la w Venz
Parker,	CECILIA		Parran,	THOMAS Jr md,st Am
Parker,	CHARLIE(Bird)sax,c Am		Parratt,	WALTER(Sir)organ,c
Parker,	CLARENCE(Ace)fb hf		Parri,	FERRUCCIO st It
Parker,	COREY		Parrington, VERNON.e,p-h'28
Parker,	DAVE b-mv'78,rbi'85		Parris,	SAMUEL r Am
Parker,	DOROTHY w,po,ct Am		Parrish	MAYNARD ba Am
Parker,	ELEANOR tv+		Parrish,	ANNE w Am
Parker,	ELLEN tv		Parrish,	HELEN
Parker,	F. WILLIAM tv		Parrish,	JUDY tv
Parker,	FESS tv+		Parrish,	JULIE tv+
Parker,	FRANK tv		Parrish,	LESLIE
Parker,	GILBERT(Sir)w,ed Can		Parrish,	MAXFIELD p,illus Am
Parker,	GRAHAM mr-s Br		Parros,	PETER tv
Parker,	HORATIO c,e Am		Parry	O'BRIEN o-g'52'56
Parker,	HYDE(Sir)navy		Parry,	CHARLES(Sir)c,h-m,e
Parker,	JACOB tv		Parry,	JOSEPH c Welsh
Parker,	JAMESON tv+		Parry,	WILLIAM(Sir)x
Parker,	JEAN		Parsegian,ARA fbc
Parker,	JIM fb hf		Parsons,	ELSIE an,w Am
Parker,	LARA		Parsons,	ESTELLE o-s'67
Parker,	LEW tv		Parsons,	KARYN tv
Parker,	MAGGI tv		Parsons,	LOUELLA j-column Am
Parker,	MARY-LOUISE		Parsons,	NANCY
Parker,	NATHANIEL		Parsons,	PERCY
Parker,	NOELLE		Parsons,	TALCOTT soc,e Am
Parker,	NORMAN tv+		Parsons,	WILLIAM astr Ir
Parker,	PENNEY tv		Partch,	HARRY c Am
Parker,	RAY Jr s,ws Am		Parton,	DOLLY s-cnt,tv+ Am
Parker,	ROBERT w Am		Parton,	JAMES w Am
Parker,	SACHI		Partridge,ANDY mr-guit,s Malta
Parker,	SARAH tv+		Partridge,ERIC dictionary Br
Parker,	SUNSHINE tv+		Pascal,	BLAISE sc,ph,w Fr
Parker,	SUZY		Pascal,	CHRISTINE
Parker,	THEODOREr,w,abolit Am Pascal,	OLIVIA
Parker,	WARREN tv		Pascale	SALKIN
Parker,	WES b,6xgg winner		Pasch,	MORITZ math,e Ger
Parkes,	ALEXANDER sc,i Br		Pascin,	JULES p Fr
Parkhurst,HELEN tv		Pascoli,	GIOVANNI e,po It
Parkins,	BARBARA tv+		Pascuale	VILLARI h It
Parkman,	FRANCIS h Am		Pasdar,	ADRIAN
Parks,	BERT tv+		Pasek,	JAN ar Pol
Parks,	HILDY tv		Pasic,	NICOLA st Serb
Parks,	LARRY		Pasley,	CHARLES(Sir)ar,eng
Parks,	LILLIAN w		Pasolini,	PIER po,w,d It
Parks,	MICHAEL tv+		Pasquale	AMATO bari It
Parks,	ROSA civil rts Am		Pasquale	FIORE l,w It
Parks,	TIM w Am		Pasquale	PAOLI st It
Parks,	TRINA		Pasquier	QUESNEL r Fr
Parler,	PETR ac Ger		Pass,	CYNDI
Parley	BAER tv+		Pass,	JOE mj-guit Am
Parley,	PETER w Am		Passer,	IVAN d
Parlo,	DITA		Passy,	FREDERIC n-x'01
Parmenides --- ph Gr		Pasta,	GIUDITTA sopr It
Parnell,	CHARLES ref Ir		Pasternak,BORIS w,po Rus
Parnell,	EMORY tv+		Pasteur,	LOUIS sc,e,md Fr
Parnell,	JACK tv		Pastor,	ANTONIO(Tony)la Am
Parnell,	THOMAS po,r Ir		Pastor,	LUDWIG von h,e Ger

Pastorelli,	ROBERT tv+	Patino,	SIMON tin mines Bol
Pastrano,	WILLIE	Patman,	WRIGHT st Am
Pat	BENATAR mr,s Am	Patmore,	COVENTRY po Br
Pat	BOONE s,tv+ Am	Paton,	ALAN w S.Afr
Pat	BRADY s,tv+ Am	Paton,	ANGELA tv
Pat	BRESLIN tv	Patric	KNOWLES
Pat	BUTTRAM tv+	Patric,	JASON
Pat	CARDI tv	Patrice	COLIHAN tv
Pat	CARROLL tv+	Patrice	KOELSCH w Am
Pat	COLBERT tv	Patrice	MUNSEL s,tv Am
Pat	COLLINS tv	Patrice	WYMORE
Pat	CONROY w Am	Patricia	BARRY
Pat	CONWAY(female)tv	Patricia	BENNETT s Am
Pat	CONWAY(male) tv+	Patricia	BENOIT tv
Pat	COOPER	Patricia	BLAIR tv
Pat	CORLEY tv+	Patricia	BRIGHT cm,tv Am
Pat	CROWLEY	Patricia	CROWLEY tv
Pat	DAY jockey Am	Patricia	CUTTS tv
Pat	DELANY tv	Patricia	DANE
Pat	EMERY tv	Patricia	DONAHUE tv
Pat	ENGLUND tv	Patricia	ELLIS
Pat	FINLEY tv	Patricia	HARTY tv
Pat	FINN tv	Patricia	HAYES
Pat	GAYE tv	Patricia	HODGE
Pat	GLEASON	Patricia	HUSTON tv
Pat	HENTGEN b	Patricia	IRELAND fe Am
Pat	HINGLE	Patricia	KOTERO(Apollonia)tv
Pat	HOGAN	Patricia	MALLORY(Boots)
Pat	KLOUS tv	Patricia	McKINNON tv
Pat	McNULTY tv	Patricia	MEDINA
Pat	MEIKLE tv	Patricia	MORISON
Pat	METHENY mj-guit Am	Patricia	MORROW tv
Pat	MORITA tv+	Patricia	NEAL
Pat	O'BRIEN	Patricia	OWENS
Pat	O'BRYAN	Patricia	ROC
Pat	O'MALLEY	Patricia	SMITH tv+
Pat	PAGE bb hf	Patricia	STEVENS tv
Pat	PAULSEN tv+	Patricia	THOMSON tv
Pat	PRIEST tv+	Patricia	WETTIG tv+
Pat	QUINN	Patrick	ALLEN
Pat	RENELLA	Patrick	BARR
Pat	RILEY bb,bbc	Patrick	BAUCHAU
Pat	SAJAK tv-host Am	Patrick	BERGIN
Pat	WOODELL tv+	Patrick	BREEN tv+
Pat	WRIGHT s Am	Patrick	CASSIDY
Pataki,	MICHAEL	Patrick	CRONIN tv
Patch	MacKENZIE	Patrick	DELANY eng,i Am
Patch,	ALEXANDER ar-Gen Am	Patrick	DEMPSEY
Patch,	WALLY	Patrick	DEWAERE
Patchen,	KENNETH po,w Am	Patrick	DUFFY tv+
Pate,	MICHAEL	Patrick	DUNCAN(Sir) st S.Afr
Pater,	JEAN p Fr	Patrick	EWING bb
Pater,	WALTER w,ct Br	Patrick	GEDDES(Sir)sc,e Scot
Paterno,	JOE fbc	Patrick	HENRY st,orator Am
Paterson,	ANDREW po,j Aust	Patrick	HOLT
Paterson,	BILL	Patrick	HORGAN tv
Paterson,	GERRY mr-drm Can	Patrick	HURLEY st Am
Pathe,	CHARLES pr-films Fr	Patrick	LAIDLAW(Sir)md
Pathe,	EMILE pr-films Fr	Patrick	MACNEE
Patience	WRIGHT su Am	Patrick	MAGEE
Patinkin,	MANDY	Patrick	MANSON(Sir)sc,e

Patrick	McCAULEY mr-drm Ir	Patti	TIPPO tv
Patrick	McGOOHAN tv+	Patti,	ADELINA sopr Am
Patrick	McVEY tv+	Pattie,	JAMES frontier Am
Patrick	MOWER	Pattinson,LES mr-bass Br
Patrick	MULDOON tv	Pattison, MARK w,e Br
Patrick	O'BRIAN w Br	Patton,	GEORGE(Bld&Guts)ar Am
Patrick	O'NEAL tv+	Patton,	MIKE mr-s Am
Patrick	PEARSE w,patriot Ir	Patton,	WILL
Patrick	ROY ho	Patty	BERG g Am
Patrick	RUTHVEN ar Scot	Patty	DUKE tv+
Patrick	RYECART	Patty	HILL e Am
Patrick	SIMMONS m-guit,s Am	Patty	SHEPARD
Patrick	STEWART tv+	Patty	SMYTH s Am
Patrick	STUART tv	Paul	AARON d
Patrick	SUSKIND w Ger	Paul	ADAM w Fr
Patrick	SWAYZE tv+	Paul	ALER r,e Belg
Patrick	TOVATT tv	Paul	ALLEN po Am
Patrick	WAYNE	Paul	ALMOND d
Patrick	WHITE w Aust	Paul	ANKA s+ Can
Patrick	WHYTE tv	Paul	ARENE w,po Fr
Patrick	WYMARK	Paul	ARIZIN bb hf
Patrick,	BUTCH tv	Paul	BARRAS re,ar Fr
Patrick,	DENNIS tv+	Paul	BARRERE mr-guit Am
Patrick,	GAIL	Paul	BARTEL d+
Patrick,	JOAN tv	Paul	BARTH e,w Ger
Patrick,	JOHN p-d'54	Paul	BAUDRY p Fr
Patrick,	LEE tv+	Paul	BERG sc Am
Patrick,	LORY tv	Paul	BERT md,e,st Fr
Patrick,	NIGEL	Paul	BIRCH tv+
Patrick,	ROBERT	Paul	BLOUET w Fr
Patrika	DARBO tv+	Paul	BOGART d
Pats,	KONSTANTIN st Estonia	Paul	BOURGET w.ct Fr
Patsuya	MIHASHI	Paul	BOWLES w
Patsy	CLINE s-cnt Am	Paul	BOYER sc,e,n-c'97
Patsy	GARRETT tv+	Paul	BRIL p Belg
Patsy	KELLY	Paul	BROCA md,an FR
Patsy	KENSIT	Paul	BROWN fbc
Patsy	LEE tv	Paul	BRYANT(Bear)fbc
Patsy	MILLER	Paul	BURKE tv+
Patten,	BART tv	Paul	BUTLER tv+
Patten,	EDWARD s-pop Am	Paul	CARR tv+
Patten,	GILBERT w Am	Paul	CARRACK mr-s,ws Br
Patten,	LUANNA	Paul	CARUS ed,ph Am
Patterson, ELIZABETH tv+	Paul	CEZANNE p Fr
Patterson, FLOYD boxer Am	Paul	CLAUDEL w,po,st Fr
Patterson, HANK tv	Paul	CLEMENS
Patterson, JAY	Paul	COMI tv
Patterson, LEE tv+	Paul	COOK mr-drm Br
Patterson, LORNA tv	Paul	CORNU eng Fr
Patterson, MELODY tv	Paul	COUFOS
Patterson, NEVA tv+	Paul	COWSILL mr-kbds,s Am
Patterson, ORLANDO w Jamaica	Paul	CRESTON c Am
Patterson, RICHARD NORTH w	Paul	CRET ac Am
Patti	COHOON tv	Paul	CRUTZEN sc Dut
Patti	DAVIS tv	Paul	DAVIS mr-kbds Br
Patti	HANSEN	Paul	DESMOND mj-sax Am
Patti	LaBELLE s-pop,soul+	Paul	DIRAC sc Br
Patti	LuPONE s,tv+ Am	Paul	DIXON tv
Patti	McCARTY	Paul	DOOLEY tv+
Patti	PAGE s,tv+ Am	Paul	DOUGLAS tv+
Patti	SMITH s,ws Am	Paul	DOUMER st Fr

Paul	DRUDE sc,e Ger	Paul	LEDER d
Paul	DUBOIS su Fr	Paul	LEMAT
Paul	DUBOV	Paul	LINKE tv
Paul	DUKAS c Fr	Paul	LUKAS la+ Am
Paul	DUNBAR po Am	Paul	LYNDE tv+
Paul	DUVAL w Fr	Paul	MANTEE tv+
Paul	EBER r,e Ger	Paul	MAURIAT mj,cn,c Br
Paul	EHRLICH sc-md Ger	Paul	MAXEY tv
Paul	EIDING tv	Paul	McCARTNEY mr,c+
Paul	ELUARD po Fr	Paul	McCRANE tv+
Paul	ERNST w,ct Ger	Paul	McGANN
Paul	FEVAL w Fr	Paul	MORAND st.w Fr
Paul	FIX tv+	Paul	MORE ct,e,ed Am
Paul	FLORY sc Am	Paul	MORIN po Can
Paul	FONCK fly Fr	Paul	MORPHY chess Am
Paul	FORD tv+	Paul	MOYER tv
Paul	FORT po Fr	Paul	MULLER sc Swi
Paul	FRANKL ct-art,h Ger	Paul	MUNI la+ Am
Paul	FREEMAN	Paul	MUS w,e Fr
Paul	FREES tv+	Paul	NASCHY
Paul	FUSCO tv	Paul	NASH p,fo Br
Paul	GALLICO j,w Am	Paul	NATORP ph,e Ger
Paul	GANUS	Paul	NEWLAN tv
Paul	GAUGUIN p Fr	Paul	NEWMAN tv+
Paul	GEARY tv	Paul	NIGGLI sc,e Swi
Paul	GIUSTI	Paul	O'KEEFE tv
Paul	GLASER tv+	Paul	O'NEILL b,bat'94
Paul	GLEASON	Paul	OLIVER i Am
Paul	GRAETZ	Paul	OTLET l Belg
Paul	GREEN w Am	Paul	PICERNI tv+
Paul	GROSS	Paul	POIRET ds Fr
Paul	HAMPTON	Paul	POTTER p Dut
Paul	HANSARD tv	Paul	PRICE tv
Paul	HARTMAN tv	Paul	RADIN an,e,w Am
Paul	HARVEY tv+	Paul	RAYNAL w Fr
Paul	HAYNE po Am	Paul	REED tv
Paul	HEATON mr-guit,s Br	Paul	REISER tv+
Paul	HECHT tv+	Paul	REUBENS(PeeWeeHerman)
Paul	HENREID	Paul	REVERE mr-kbds Am
Paul	HEYSE w Ger	Paul	REVERE st,at-silv Am
Paul	HOGAN	Paul	REYNAUD st Fr
Paul	HOLBACH pb Fr	Paul	RHYS
Paul	HORGAN w Am	Paul	RICHTER
Paul	HURST	Paul	RIVET sc,w Fr
Paul	HYMANS st Belg	Paul	ROBESON s+ Br
Paul	JACKSON tv	Paul	RODGERS mr-s Br
Paul	JESSUP tv	Paul	ROGERS
Paul	JONES m-harmonic,s Br	Paul	RUDD tv+
Paul	KANE p Can	Paul	RYDER mr-bass Br
Paul	KANTNER mr-guit Am	Paul	SAND tv+
Paul	KARRER sc,e Swi	Paul	SANDBY p,engr Br
Paul	KELLY	Paul	SCARRON po,w Fr
Paul	KLEE p Swi	Paul	SCOTT tv
Paul	KLENAU c,cn Dan	Paul	SCOTT w Br
Paul	KOSLO tv+	Paul	SHAFFER cm,tv Am
Paul	KOSSOFF mr-guit Br	Paul	SHENAR
Paul	KRASNY d	Paul	SHOREY r,w Am
Paul	KREPPEL tv	Paul	SIGNAC p Fr
Paul	KRUGER(Oom)st S.Afr	Paul	SIMON m+ Am
Paul	LANGTON tv+	Paul	SIMONON mr-bass Br
Paul	LEBAUDY id Fr	Paul	SMITH

Paul	SORVINO tv+	Paula	KELLY s Am
Paul	SPAAK st Belg	Paula	KELLY tv+
Paul	SPARER tv	Paula	McCLURE tv
Paul	SPECHT mj-viol,cn Am	Paula	RAYMOND
Paul	STANLEY mr-guit,s Am	Paula	VOGEL w Am
Paul	STARR w Am	Paula	ZAHN tv-j Am
Paul	STEIN d	Paulding,	JAMES w,h Am
Paul	STEVENS	Paulette	DUBOST
Paul	STEWART	Paulette	GODDARD
Paul	STORR goldsmith Br	Pauley,	JANE tv-j Am
Paul	STOUT tv	Pauli,	WOLFGANG n-p'89
Paul	STRAND fo Am	Paulie	FREED mj-piano Am
Paul	SYLVAN tv	Paulin,	SCOTT
Paul	SZEP cr Am	Pauline	BETZ t Am
Paul	TERRY	Pauline	DEJAZET la Fr
Paul	THEROUX w Am	Pauline	JOHNSON po Can
Paul	TILLICH r,ph,e Am	Pauline	KAEL ct-movies Am
Paul	TRINKA tv	Pauline	MYERS tv
Paul	TRIPP tv	Pauline	SMITH w S.Afr
Paul	TULANE mer,r-Tulane U.	Pauline	TARN po Fr
Paul	TULLEY tv	Pauline	VIARDOT mezzo Fr
Paul	VALERY po,ct Fr	Pauling,	LINUS n-c'54,n-x'62
Paul	VALLEY tv	Paulo	COELHO w Braz
Paul	VIEILLE eng Fr	Paulsen,	PAT tv+
Paul	WALDEN sc,e Lat	Paulus	BUYS st Dut
Paul	WALKER tv	Paulus	CUA w,e Vietnam
Paul	WALLACE tv	Paulus	MOREELSE p Dut
Paul	WANER b hf	Pauly	SHORE
Paul	WEBSTER lyrics Am	Pauly,	AUGUST ed Ger
Paul	WEGENER d+	Pavan,	MARISA
Paul	WEISS sc Am	Pavarotti,	LUCIANO tenor+ It
Paul	WELLER mr-guit,s Br	Pavel	PESTEL ar,re Rus
Paul	WENDKOS d	Pavel	SAFARIK w Cz
Paul	WESTON mj,c,cn,tv Am	Pavelic,	ANTE st Croat
Paul	WILSSON tv	Pavese,	CESARE po,w,ed It
Paul	YOUNG s,ws Br	Pavie,	AUGUSTE st,x Fr
Paul	ZINDEL w Am	Pavlov,	IVAN n-m'04
Paul de	KRUIF sc,w Am	Pavlova,	ANNA ba Rus
Paul van	ZEELAND ec,st Belg	Paxinou,	KATINA o-s'43
Paul von	HINTZE navy,st Ger	Paxton,	BILL
Paul von	JANKO piano,i Hung	Paxton,	GEORGE mj-sax,cn Am
Paul von	REUTER j Ger	Paxton,	JOSEPH(Sir)ac
Paul(us)	BRIL(L) p Belg	Paycheck,	JOHNNY s-pop Am
Paul,	ADRIAN tv+	Payen,	ANSELME sc Fr
Paul,	ALEXANDRA	Payer,	JULIUS von x,p Aus
Paul,	ALICE fe Am	Paymar,	JIM tv
Paul,	DAVID	Paymer,	DAVID tv+
Paul,	DON	Payn,	JAMES w Br
Paul,	ELLIOT w Am	Payne,	BILL mr-kbds Am
Paul,	EUGENIA tv	Payne,	BRUCE
Paul,	KEGAN pb,w Br	Payne,	CARL ANTHONY II tv
Paul,	KURT tv	Payne,	FREDA s-r&b Am
Paul,	LES mj-guit Am	Payne,	JACK mj,cn Br
Paul,	P.R. tv	Payne,	JOHN la,w Am
Paul,	PETER mj+ Am	Payne,	JOHN tv+
Paul,	RICHARD tv+	Payne,	LAURENCE
Paul,	WOLFGANG sc,e Ger	Pays,	AMANDA tv+
Paul-Marie	LAPOINTE po Can	Payton,	BARBARA
Paula	ABDUL mr,ba,s Am	Payton,	DENIS m-sax Br
Paula	DREW tv	Payton,	GARY bb
Paula	FOX w Am	Payton,	LAWRENCE mr-s Am

Payton,	WALTER fb-m'77'85 hf	Pedro	CABRAL x Port
Payton-France,	JO MARIE tv	Pedro	INFANTE
Paz,	OCTAVIO n-l'90	Pedro	NINO x Sp
Peabo	BRYSON s-pop Am	Pedro	NUNES math Port
Peabody,	DICK tv	Pedro	ORRENTE p Sp
Peabody,	ENDICOTT e Am	Pedro	PRADO w Chile
Peabody,	GEORGE mer,f Am	Pedro	RAMIREZ ar,st Arg
Peach,	CHARLES geol Br	Pedro	ROLDAN su,p,ac Sp
Peacock,	THOMAS w,po Br	Pedro	SALINAS po,w,ct Sp
Peake,	MERVYN w,illus Br	Pedro	SANCHEZ
Peaker,	E.J. tv	Pedro de	ALARCON w sp
Peale,	CHARLES p Am	Pedro de	CORDOBA
Peale,	NORMAN VINCENT r,w Am	Pedro de	MENA su Sp
Peale,	REMBRANDT p Am	Pedro de	ONA po Chi+le
Pean,	JULES md Fr	Pee Wee	KING s-cnt,c Am
Peano,	GIUSEPPE math,e It	Pee Wee	REESE b hf
Peanuts	HUCKO tv	Pee Wee	RUSSELL mj-clarin Am
Pearce,	ALICE tv	Peek,	DAN m-guit,s Am
Pearce,	MARY	Peel,	ROBERT(Sir) st
Pearl	BAILEY s,tv+ Am	Peele,	GEORGE w,po Br
Pearl	BUCK w Am	Peeples,	NIA tv+
Pearl	CRAIGIE w Br	Peerce,	JAN tenor Am
Pearl	PRIMUS ba Am	Peerce,	LARRY d
Pearl	WHITE la Am	Peete,	CALVIN g Am
Pearl,	BARRY tv	Peg	LYNCH tv
Pearl,	MINNIE cm,tv Am	Peg	MURRAY tv
Pearl,	RAY mj,cn Am	Peggy	CASS tv+
Pearle	MESTA hostess Am	Peggy	CASTLE tv+
Pears,	PETER tenor Br	Peggy	CUMMINS
Pearse,	PATRICK w,patriot Ir	Peggy	FEURY
Pearson,	DELROY mr-s Br	Peggy	FLEMING sk Am
Pearson,	DENIECE mr-s Br	Peggy	GARNER
Pearson,	DORIS mr-s Br	Peggy	KING tv
Pearson,	DREW w,j,tv Am	Peggy	KNUDSEN
Pearson,	KARL math,e Br	Peggy	LEE s,tv Am
Pearson,	LESTER n-x'57	Peggy	LENNON s,tv Am
Pearson,	LORRAINE mr-s Br	Peggy	LIPTON tv+
Pearson,	MAURICE s,tv Am	Peggy	MONDO tv
Pearson,	STEDMAN mr-s Br	Peggy	NOONAN w-Pres spchs
Pearson,	WEETMAN bus Br	Peggy	POPE tv
Peart,	NEIL mr-drm Can	Peggy	REA tv+
Peary,	HAROLD(Hal)	Peggy	RYAN tv+
Peary,	ROBERT x Am	Peggy	STEWART
Pease,	FRANCIS astr Am	Peggy	WALKER tv
Peattie,	DONALD natural Am	Peggy	WOOD tv+
Pecheur,	SIERRA	Pegler,	WESTBROOK j Am
Peck,	ANNIE mtn climber Am	Pegoud,	ADOLPHE fly-acrobat Fr
Peck,	AUSTIN tv	Peguy,	CHARLES po,w Fr
Peck,	BOB	Pehr	KALM sc Swe
Peck,	CECILIA	Pei,	IEOH MING(I.M.)ac Am
Peck,	GREGORY o-a'62	Peider	LANSEL po,w It
Peck,	J. EDDIE tv+	Peine,	VIRGINIA tv
Peck,	TONY	Peirce,	CHARLES sc,ph Am
Peckham,	RUFUS l,supr ct Am	Peirce,	ROBERT tv
Peckinpah,	SAM d	Pekkanen,	TOIVO w Finn
Pedersen,	CHARLES n-c'87	Peldon,	COURTNEY tv
Pedersen,	HOLGER w Dan	Pele,	EDSON soccer+ Braz or
Pederson,	KNUT w Nor	Pele,	PEROLA NEGRA soccer
Pedi,	TOM tv	Pelham	HUMFREY md,c Br
Pedrell,	FELIPE c Sp	Pelikan,	LISA
Pedro	ALARCON w Sp	Pelissier,	AIMABLE ar Fr

Pell, JOHN math,e Br	Penzias, ARNO n-p'78
Pellegrin,RAYMOND	Penzler, OTTO w Am
Pellicer, PILAR	Pep MUNNE
Pellicer, PINA	Pepa --- m rap Am
Pellico, SILVIO w It	Pepe LE PEW fc
Pellonpaa, MATTI	Pepe SERNA
Pelloux, LUIGI ar,st It	Peppard, GEORGE tv+
Pellow, MARTI mr-s Scot	Pepper, ART mj-alto sax Am
Pelton, LESTER i-turbine Am	Pepper, BARBARA tv+
Peluce, MEENO tv	Pepper, CLAUDE st Am
Peluffo, ANA LOUISA	Pepper, CYNTHIA tv
Peluso, LISA tv	Pepys, SAMUEL st,w Br
Pemberton,MAX(Sir)w	Per BRAHE ar,st Swe
Pembroke, GEORGE	Per HANSSON st Swe
Pena, AFONSO st Braz	Per OSCARSON
Pena, ALEJANDRO b	Per Teodor CLEVE sc,e Swe
Pena, ELIZABETH tv+	Pera, MARILIA
Pena, GEORGE de la	Pera, RADAMES tv
Pena, JULIO	Percier, CHARLES ac Fr
Penck, ALBRECHT geog,e Ger	Percival LOWELL astr Am
Pencz, GEORG p,engr Ger	Percy ADLON d
Pendarvis,PAUL mj,cn Am	Percy BATES(Sir)ships
Pender, MIKE mr-guit,s Br	Percy FAITH mj,cn Am
Pendergrass, TEDDY s-r&b,ws Am	Percy GARDNER arc,e Br
Pendleton, AUSTIN	Percy HARRIS(Bud)tv
Pendleton, BRIAN mr-guit Br	Percy HELTON tv
Pendleton, NAT	Percy HERBERT tv+
Pendleton, TERRY b-mv'91,bat'91	Percy JULIAN sc,e,id Am
Penelope KEITH tv+	Percy MacKAYE po,w Am
Penelope MILFORD	Percy MARMONT
Penelope MILLER	Percy PARSONS
Penelope WARD	Percy RAYMOND sc,e Am
Penelope WILTON	Percy SHELLEY po Br
Penghlis, THAAO tv+	Percy SLEDGE mr-s Am
Penhaligon, SUSAN	Percy WENRICH c Am
Penhall, BRUCE tv+	Percy, EILEEN
Penina SEGALL tv	Percy, ESME
Peniston, CECE s-soul,rock Am	Percy, WALKER w Am
Penn, ARTHUR d	Perdomo, WILLIAM w Am
Penn, CHRISTOPHER	Pereda, ANTONIO p Sp
Penn, SEAN d+	Pereda, JOSE de w Sp
Penn, WILLIAM r,st,w Br	Peredes, MARISA
Pennell, JON tv	Perelman, S.J. w-humor Am
Pennell, JOSEPH etch Am	Peres, SHIMON st Isr n-x'94
Pennell, LARRY tv	Peretz, ISAAC w Pol
Penney, JAMES mer Am	Peretz, SUSAN tv
Pennington, MARLA tv	Perey, MARGUERITE sc,e Fr
Pennock, HERB b hf	Perez PRADO mj,cn Cuban-Am
Penny EDWARDS	Perez de Ayala,RAMON w,po,ct,j Sp
Penny FULLER	Perez de Hita, GINES w,ar Sp
Penny GERARD tv	Perez Galdos, BENITO w Sp
Penny JOHNSON tv	Perez, JOSE st Chile
Penny PARKER tv	Perez, JOSE tv+
Penny PEYSER tv+	Perez, ROSIE ba,tv+ Am
Penny SANTON tv	Perez, SANTIAGO st Colomb
Penny, DON tv	Perez, TONY b
Penny, JOE tv+	Perfall, KARL von c Ger
Penny, SYDNEY tv+	Peri GILPIN tv
Penrose, BOIES st Am	Peri, JACOPO c It
Penry, JOHN w,pb Welsh	Perick, CHRISTOF cn Ger
Pentti ESKOLA sc,e Finn	Perier, CASIMIR st Fr

Perier,	FRANCOIS	Perry,	JOE mr-guit Am
Perkin	WARBECK imposter Belg	Perry,	JOHN tv
Perkin,	WILLIAM(Sir)sc,id	Perry,	JOSEPH tv
Perkins,	ANTHONY	Perry,	LUKE tv+
Perkins,	CARL s,ws,tv+ Am	Perry,	MATTHEW navy,st Am
Perkins,	ELIZABETH	Perry,	MATTHEW tv
Perkins,	FRANCES st-labor Am	Perry,	OLIVER navy Am
Perkins,	JACK tv	Perry,	RALPH ph,e,p-b'36
Perkins,	JACOB i Am	Perry,	ROD tv+
Perkins,	JUSTIN r Am	Perry,	ROGER tv+
Perkins,	KENT tv	Perry,	ROLAND p,su Am
Perkins,	MARLIN zoos,tv Am	Perry,	STEVE mr-s Am
Perkins,	MAXWELL ed Am	Perry,	STEVE w Am
Perkins,	MILLIE	Perry,	WM.(Refrigerator)fb
Perkins,	OSGOOD	Perry,	WOLFE tv
Perkins,	RED mj,cn Am	Perry,	YVONNE tv
Perkins,	RON tv	Perschy,	MARIA
Perla	CRISTAL	Perse,	St.JOHN po,st,n-1'60
Perle,	GEORGE p-m'86	Pershing,	JOHN(Gen.)p-h'32
Perley,	GEORGE(Sir)bus,st Can	Persius	--- po Ro
Perlich,	MAX	Persky,	LISA JANE
Perlman,	ITZHAK viol Isr	Persoff,	NEHEMIAH
Perlman,	MICHAEL	Persson,	ESSY
Perlman,	RHEA tv+	Pert	KELTON
Perlman,	RON tv+	Pertz,	GEORG h Ger
Perlow,	BOB tv	Perugorria,	JORGE
Pernell	ROBERTS tv+	Perutz,	MAX n-c'62
Pero da	COVILHA x Port	Pervis	JACKSON mr-s Am
Perola Negra PELE(Edson)soccer+		Pesci,	JOE o-s'90
Peron,	EVA st Arg	Pescow,	DONNA tv+
Peron,	JUAN st-dictator Arg	Peshkov,	ALEKSEY w Rus
Perosi,	LORENZO r,c It	Pesne,	ANTOINE p Fr
Perot,	HENRY ROSS f Am	Pessoa,	EPITACIO da st,l Braz
Perrault,	CHARLES w,ct Fr	Pessoa,	FERNANDO po Port
Perreau,	GIGI tv+	Pestel,	PAVEL ar,re Rus
Perret,	AUGUSTE ac Fr	Peta	TOPPANO
Perrier,	MIREILLE	Petau,	DENIS r Fr
Perrin,	AMI st Swi	Pete	AGNEW mr-bass,s Scot
Perrin,	JACK	Pete	BIRRELL mr-bass Br
Perrin,	JACQUES	Pete	DEXTER w Am
Perrin,	JEAN n-p'26	Pete	DUNN tv
Perrin,	PIERRE po Fr	Pete	HAM mr-guit,s Welsh
Perrine,	VALERIE	Pete	HENRY fb hf
Perron,	CHARLES w,ct Dut	Pete	PIHOS fb hf
Perrot,	GEORGES arc Fr	Pete	QUAIFE mr-bass Br
Perry	CARTER	Pete	ROSE b
Perry	COMO s,tv+ Am	Pete	ROZELLE fbc,commish hf
Perry	ELLIS ds-perfumes Am	Pete	SALEMI mj-tromb Am
Perry	KING tv+	Pete	SAMPRAS t Am
Perry	LANG	Pete	SCHRUM tv
Perry	LOPEZ	Pete	SEEGER s-folk,ws Am
Perry	MILLER h Am	Pete	SHELLEY mr-guit,s Br
Perry,	ANNE w Br	Pete	STAMPER tv
Perry,	ANTOINETTE la Am	Pete	STAPLES mr-bass Br
Perry,	BARBARA tv	Pete	WALKER d
Perry,	BLISS e,ct Am	Pete	YORK mr-drm Br
Perry,	FELTON tv+	Pete,	PIUTE tv
Perry,	FRANK d	Peter	ARNE
Perry,	GAYLORD b-cy'72'8,hf	Peter	ARNO cr Am
Perry,	JIM b-cy'70	Peter	ARTEDI sc Swe
Perry,	JOE fb hf	Peter	ASHER s Br

Peter	BARTON tv+	Peter	HANSON tv
Peter	BAY cn Am	Peter	HASKELL tv+
Peter	BEHRENS ac Ger	Peter	HAYES tv+
Peter	BENNETT tv	Peter	HEHIR
Peter	BENOIT(Pierre)c Belg	Peter	HOEG w Dan
Peter	BERG	Peter	HOOK mr-bass Br
Peter	BERGMAN tv	Peter	HOOTEN
Peter	BONERZ	Peter	HORTON tv+
Peter	BOWLES	Peter	HURD p Am
Peter	BOYLE tv+	Peter	HYAMS d
Peter	BRECK tv+	Peter	ILLING
Peter	BROOKS tv	Peter	JACKSON boxer W.Indi
Peter	BROWN tv+	Peter	JASON
Peter	BUCK mr-guit Am	Peter	JEFFREY
Peter	BULL	Peter	JURASIK tv+
Peter	CAPALDI	Peter	KASTNER
Peter	CARSTEN	Peter	KRAUSE tv
Peter	CELLIER	Peter	LACY ar Ir
Peter	CETERA s Am	Peter	LALOR eng,st Aust
Peter	CHEYNEY w Br	Peter	LAWFORD tv+
Peter	COOK tv+	Peter	LEEDS tv
Peter	COOPER id,f Am	Peter	LELY(Sir)p
Peter	COSTA tv	Peter	LENZ p,ac,su,r Ger
Peter	COYOTE	Peter	LEWIS mr-guit,s Am
Peter	CRISS mr-drm,s Am	Peter	LOMBARD ph,w It
Peter	CULLEN tv	Peter	LOONEY tv
Peter	CUSHING	Peter	LORRE
Peter	DAVIES w Am	Peter	LUPUS tv+
Peter	De VRIES w Am	Peter	MAAS w Am
Peter	De WINT p Br	Peter	MacKENZIE tv
Peter	DEBYE sc Am	Peter	MacNICHOL
Peter	DeLUISE	Peter	MARTIN ba
Peter	DEUEL tv	Peter	MATZ cn, tv
Peter	DONALD tv	Peter	MAUSER i-guns Ger
Peter	DONAT tv+	Peter	MAYLE w Am
Peter	DYNELEY	Peter	McENERY
Peter	EGAN	Peter	MEDAWAR(Sir)md,e
Peter	EGGE w Nor	Peter	MOTTEUX w Br
Peter	EMERSON fo Br	Peter	MUNCH h,st Dan
Peter	EVANS tv	Peter	NELSON tv+
Peter	EYRE	Peter	NERO mj-piano Am
Peter	FABERGE jeweler Rus	Peter	NICHOLS w Br
Peter	FALK tv+	Peter	NOONE mr s Br
Peter	FINCH	Peter	O'TOOLE
Peter	FIRTH	Peter	OCHS st Swi
Peter	FONDA	Peter	ONORATI tv+
Peter	FORCE h,id,st Am	Peter	OPIE folklore Br
Peter	FORD tv	Peter	PALLAS sc Ger
Peter	FOX tv+	Peter	PARLEY w Am
Peter	FUNT tv	Peter	PARROS tv
Peter	GABB tv	Peter	PAUL mj+ Am
Peter	GABRIEL s Br	Peter	PEARS tenor Br
Peter	GENNARO tv	Peter	PHELPS tv+
Peter	GILL mr-drm Br	Peter	POTTER tv
Peter	GOETZ tv+	Peter	QUINCE po Am
Peter	GRAVES tv+	Peter	RECKELL tv
Peter	GREENE	Peter	RICHMAN tv+
Peter	HAMMOND tv	Peter	RIEGERT
Peter	HANDKE w,po Aus	Peter	ROBBINS tv
Peter	HANLEY tv	Peter	ROGET md,w Br
Peter	HANSEN tv	Peter	RUBENS p Belg

Peter	SASDY d	Peterson,	VICKI mr-guit,s Am
Peter	SCHUCK tv	Peterson,	VIRGILIA tv
Peter	SCOLARI tv+	Peterson,	WAYNE p-m'92
Peter	SCOTT(Sir)p-wildlife	Petersson,TOM mr-bass,s Am	
Peter	SELLERS	Petigru,	JAMES l,st Am
Peter	SHAFFER w Br	Petion,	ALEXANDRE ar,st Haiti
Peter	SIMMONS tv	Petipa,	MARIUS ba Fr
Peter	SNELL o-g'60'64	Petit,	ALEXIS sc Fr *Roland(dancer)*
Peter	STRAUSS tv+	Peto,	JOHN p Am
Peter	TAYLOR w Am	Petofi,	SANDOR po Hung
Peter	TORK mr-kbds,s Am	Petr	PARLER ac Ger
Peter	USTINOV w,d+ Br	Petrarch	--- po It
Peter	VALDES(Pierre)r Fr	Petre,	GIO
Peter	VAUGHAN	Petri,	OLAUS r Swe
Peter	VIERECK po Am	Petrie,	CARROLL st@UN Am
Peter	VOGT tv	Petrie,	DANIEL d
Peter	WEIR d	Petrie,	DONALD d
Peter	WEISS w Ger	Petrie,	FLINDERS(Sir)arc
Peter	WELLER	Petrie,	GEORGE tv
Peter	WERNER d	Petrie,	HAY
Peter	WHITE tv	Petroski,	HENRY w Am
Peter	WHITNEY tv+	Petrus	CHRISTUS p Belg
Peter	WIDENER bus-meat Am	Petrus	CUYPERS ac Dut
Peter	YARROW mj,s,c,w Am	Petrus	JOUBERT(Piet)ar S.Afr
Peter	YATES d	Petter	DASS po Nor
Peter Lee LAWRENCE		Pettet,	JOANNA tv+
Peter Paul RUBENS tv		Pettie,	GEORGE w Br
Peter van EYCK		Pettiet,	CHRISTOPHER tv
Peter von WINTER c Ger		Pettiford,OSCAR mj-bass Am	
Peterkin, JULIA M. p-f'29		Pettit,	BOB bb-m'56'9,hf
Peterman, STEVEN tv		Petty,	LORI tv+
Peters,	BERNADETTE tv+	Petty,	RICHARD racecar Am
Peters,	BROCK	Petty,	TOM guit,s Am
Peters,	CARL x Ger	Petty,	WILLIAM(Sir)ec,e
Peters,	CURTIS cr Am	Pettyjohn,ANGELIQUE	
Peters,	DEEDY tv	Petula	CLARK s-pop+
Peters,	HOUSE	Pevney,	JOSEPH d
Peters,	JEAN	Pevsner,	ANTOINE su,p Fr
Peters,	KELLY tv	Pey de	GARROS po Fr
Peters,	LUAN	Peyre,	JOSEPH w Fr
Peters,	MIKE mr-guit,s Welsh	Peyrefitte, ROGER w Fr	
Peters,	PHIL tv	Peyser,	PENNY tv+
Peters,	RALPH	Pezza,	MICHELE robber It
Peters,	SCOTT tv	Pfaff,	JOHANN math,e Ger
Peters,	WERNER	Pfeiffer, BOB tv	
Petersen, CHRIS tv+		Pfeiffer, DEDEE	
Petersen, PAT tv+		Pfeiffer, MICHELLE tv+	
Petersen, PATTY tv		Pfenning, WESLEY ANN tv	
Petersen, PAUL tv		Pfisterer,ALBAN mr-drm,kbds Swi	
Petersen, WILLIAM		Pflug,	JO ANN tv+
Peterson, AMANDA tv+		Pforr,	FRANZ p Ger
Peterson, ARTHUR tv		Phaedrus	--- ph Gr
Peterson, CASSANDRA		Phaer,	THOMAS l,md Br
Peterson, DEBBI mr-drm,s Am		Phair,	LIZ s-pop Am
Peterson, DOLORES tv		Phal,	LOUIS boxer Senegal
Peterson, EUGENE tv		Phayre,	ARTHUR st,ar Br
Peterson, KRISTINE d		Phelan,	JOE
Peterson, MAGGIE tv		Phelps,	CLAUDE(Jackie)tv
Peterson, OSCAR mj-piano,c Can		Phelps,	JILL tv pr
Peterson, STEWART		Phelps,	PETER tv+
Peterson, SYLVIA mr-s Am		Phidias	--- su Gr

Phifer,	MEKHI		Philip	HALL tv+
Phil	BROWN		Philip	HENCH md Am
Phil	BRUNS tv		Philip	HITTI h,e Am
Phil	BUCKMAN tv		Philip	HOFFMAN
Phil	CAREY tv+		Philip	HONE bus,w Am
Phil	COLLEN mr-guit Br		Philip	HOWARD l,w Am
Phil	COLLINS mr-drm,s+		Philip	JOHNSON ac Am
Phil	DANIELS		Philip	LARKIN po,w Br
Phil	DONAHUE tv-host Am		Philip	LOEB tv
Phil	EVERLY s-cnt Am		Philip	MacKENZIE tv
Phil	FOSTER tv+		Philip	McKEON tv
Phil	GORDON tv		Philip	MURRAY labor Am
Phil	HARRIS mj-s,cn,cm+ Am		Philip	NERI r,mystic It
Phil	HARTMAN tv+		Philip	NOEL-BAKER st Br
Phil	JOANOU d		Philip	OAKEY mr-s Br
Phil	JONES tv		Philip	OBER tv+
Phil	KARLSON d		Philip	PHYSICK md Am
Phil	LEEDS tv+		Philip	PROCTOR tv
Phil	LESH mr-bass Am		Philip	RAHV ct,w Am+
Phil	LYNOTTmr-bass,s Ir		Philip	REED
Phil	MAHRE ski Am		Philip	ROTH w Am
Phil	MARGO s-basso Am		Philip	RUDD mr-drm Aust
Phil	MAY mr-s Br		Philip	SAVILLE d
Phil	MORRIS tv		Philip	SHELBY w Am
Phil	NIEKRO b hf		Philip	SIDNEY(Sir)po,st
Phil	OHMAN mj-piano,cn Am		Philip	SIMMS tv
Phil	PETERS tv		Philip	STEER p Br
Phil	ROMAN d		Philip	THOMAS tv+
Phil	ROSEN d		Philip	TONGE tv
Phil	ROTH tv		Philip	Van ZANDT
Phil	SILVERS tv+		Philip	WATTS(Sir)ac-naval
Phil	SIMMS b hf		Philip	WYLIE w Am
Phil	STONG w Am		Philipp	LENARD sc,e,w Ger
Phil	TEAD		Philipp	VEIT p Ger
Philander	KNOX l,st Am		Philipp von ZESEN w Ger	
Philbin,	JOHN		Philipp,	KAREN tv
Philbin,	MARY		Philippa	CARR w Br
Philbin,	REGIS tv-host,w Am		Philippe	BRIDEL r,w Swi
Philby,	HARRY x Br		Philippe	CAUBERE
Philece	SAMPLER tv		Philippe	GERARD
Philibert	DELORME ac Fr		Philippe	HALSMAN fo Am
Philip	AHN		Philippe	MORA d
Philip	ARMOUR id-meats Am		Philippe	NOIRET
Philip	ASTLEY horses,ar Am		Philippe	PINEL md Fr
Philip	BAILEY mr-drms Am		Philippe de GASPE l,w Can	
Philip	BALSLEY s Am		Philippe de MONTE c Belg	
Philip	BARRY tv		Philips,	AMBROSE po,w Br
Philip	BARRY w Am		Philips,	EMO cm+ Am
Philip	BROWN tv+		Philips,	LEE d
Philip	BRUNS		Philips,	OBBE r Dut
Philip	CAREY(Phil)tv+		Phill	LEWIS
Philip	CASNOFF tv+		Phillip	ABBOTT tv+
Philip	CLARK tv		Phillip	ALLEN tv
Philip	DAVIS		Phillip	BORSOS d
Philip	DORN		Phillip	BOSCO
Philip	EMBURY r Am		Phillip	HENCH md Am
Philip	FRENEAU po Am		Phillip	LEVINE po Am
Philip	GLASS c Am		Phillip	NOYCE d
Philip	GOSSE sc-marine Br		Phillip	PINE tv+
Philip	GOVE dictionary Am		Phillip	RHEE
Philip	GUEDALLA w		Phillip	SCHAFF r,w Am

Phillip	SHARP md Am		Phyllis	NEWMAN tv+
Phillip	TERRY		Phyllis	THAXTER
Phillip,	ANDY bb hf		Physick,	PHILIP md Am
Phillippe	LeROY		Pia	ZADORA s+ Am
Phillippe,	ANDRE tv		Piaf,	EDITH s Fr
Phillips	HOLMES		Piaget,	JEAN ps,e Swi
Phillips,	BARNEY tv+		Piaggia,	CARLO x It
Phillips,	BERT p Am		Pialat,	MAURICE d
Phillips,	CARMEN tv		Piat,	JEAN
Phillips,	CHYNNA s+ Am		Piatt,	DONN j,ed Am
Phillips,	DAVID j,w Am		Piatt,	JOHN j,po Am
Phillips,	ETHAN tv+		Piazza,	BEN tv+
Phillips,	HARRY GEORGE tv		Piazza,	MARGUERITE tv
Phillips,	JAYNE ANNE w Am		Piazza,	MIKE b
Phillips,	JOHN s-pop,rock Am		Pica,	TONY
Phillips,	JOSEPH C. tv		Picabia,	FRANCIS p Fr
Phillips,	JULIANNE tv+		Picabo	STREET ski Am
Phillips,	KATHY tv		Picard,	CHARLES math,e Fr
Phillips,	LESLIE		Picard,	EDMOND l,w Belg
Phillips,	LOU		Picard,	JEAN astr Fr
Phillips,	MacKENZIE		Picardo,	ROBERT tv+
Phillips,	MACKENZIE tv		Picasso,	PABLO p,su,Sp
Phillips,	MICHELLE tv+		Picasso,	PALOMA at Sp
Phillips,	NANCY cm,tv Am		Piccard,	AUGUSTE sc Swi
Phillips,	PEG tv		Piccoli,	MICHEL
Phillips,	SIAN		Picerni,	PAUL tv+
Phillips,	STONE tv		Pichel,	IRVING d+
Phillips,	WENDELL abolit,ref Am		Pichler,	KAROLINE w Aus
Phillips,	WENDY tv+		Pichon,	STEPHEN j,st Fr
Phillips,	WILLIAM n-p'97		Pickard,	SORRELS
Phillpotts,	EDEN w Br		Pickens,	JAMES Jr tv
Philly Joe	JONES mj-drm Am		Pickens,	SLIM tv+
Philo Judaeus	--- ph Jewish		Pickett,	CINDY tv+
Philpot,	ANDREW tv		Pickett,	JOSEPH p Am
Philthy Animal	---mr-drm Br		Pickett,	WILSON s,ws Am
Phineas	QUIMBY healer Am		Pickford,	MARY o-a'28
Phineas	T.BARNUM circus Am		Pickles,	CHRISTINA tv
Phipps,	MAX		Pickup,	RONALD
Phipps,	WILLIAM tv+		Pico	IYER w Br
Phoebe	CARY po Am		Picon,	JACINTO w,ct-art Sp
Phoebe	CATES		Picon,	MOLLY tv+
Phoebe	LEGERE		Picone,	EVAN ds
Phoebus	LEVENE sc Am		Picot,	AUGUSTE ar Fr
Phoenix,	RIVER tv+		Picou,	ALPHONSE mj-clar,cn
Phrynicus	--- w Gr		Pictet,	RAOUL sc,e Swi
Phyfe,	DUNCAN id-cabinets Am		Picton,	THOMAS(Sir)ar
Phylicia	RASHAD tv		Pidgeon,	WALTER
Phyllida	LAW		Pie	TRAYNOR b hf
Phyllis	AVERY tv		Piekarski,	JULIE tv
Phyllis	BOTTOME w Br		Pier	ANGELI
Phyllis	BROOKS		Pier	MOLA p It
Phyllis	CALVERT		Pier	NERVI eng, ac It
Phyllis	CERF tv		Pierce	BROSNAN tv+
Phyllis	COATES tv+		Pierce	EGAN w-sports Br
Phyllis	DAVIS tv		Pierce,	FRANKLIN 14th pres
Phyllis	DILLER cm,tv+ Am		Pierce,	GEORGE WASH. sc,e Am
Phyllis	GEORGE tv		Pierce,	GILBERT st,w Am
Phyllis	KIRK tv+		Pierce,	MAGGIE tv
Phyllis	LOGAN		Pierce,	STACK
Phyllis	McGINLEY po W Am		Pierce,	WEBB s-cnt,c+ Am
Phyllis	McGUIRE tv		Piercy,	MARGE po,w Am

Pierino	BELLI ar,l It	Pierre de	LACLOS w Fr
Pierne,	GABRIEL cn,c Fr	Pierre de	LARIVEY w Fr
Piero della Francesca---p It		Pierre de	NOLHAC w Fr
Pierpaoli,WALTER w Am		Pierre de	RONSARD po Fr
Pierpoint,ERIC tv		Pierre,	OLIVIER tv
Pierre	AZAIS ph,w Fr	Piers	ANTHONY w scifi Br-Am
Pierre	BAYLE ph,ct Fr	Pierson,	FRANK d
Pierre	BECKX r Belg	Pierson,	KATE mr-organ,s Am
Pierre	BELON sc Fr	Piet	CRONJE re S.Afr
Pierre	BENOIT w Fr	Piet	HEIN navy Dut
Pierre	BENOIT(Peter)c Belg	Piet	JOUBERT ar-Boer S.Afr
Pierre	BERTON m,cn Fr	Pieter	BOUTENS po Dut
Pierre	BONNARD p Fr	Pieter	BRUEGEL p Belg
Pierre	BOULEZ c Fr	Pieter	BRUEGEL(Youngr)p Belg
Pierre	BRAZZA x Fr	Pieter	CAMPER md,e Dut
Pierre	BRICE	Pieter	GEYL h,e Dut
Pierre	CARDIN ds Fr	Pieter	HOOFT h,po,w Dut
Pierre	CURIE sc Fr	Pieter	LASTMAN p Dut
Pierre	DARU ar,h Fr	Pieter	RETIEF(Piet)ar,st S.Afr
Pierre	De SMET r Am	Pieter	ZEEMAN sc,e Dut
Pierre	Du BUAT eng Fr	Pieter de HOOCH p Dut
Pierre	DUHEM sc,ph,Fr	Pieter van BLOEMEN p Belg
Pierre	DUMONT su Fr	Pieter van LAER p Dut
Pierre	FAILLY ar Fr	Pieter Willem BOTHA st S.Afr
Pierre	FERMAT math,st Fr	Pietro	ARETINO w It
Pierre	FRESNAY	Pietro	BEMBO r,h It
Pierre	GUA(ST)colonizer Fr	Pietro	BERNINI su It
Pierre	HETZEL pb Fr	Pietro	COSSA w It
Pierre	HULIN ar Fr	Pietro	LONGHI p It
Pierre	JALBERT tv	Pietro	NENNI st It
Pierre	JANET ps,md Fr	Pietro	SARPI r,h,sc It
Pierre	JOUVE po,w,ct Fr	Pietro	SECCHI astron,e It
Pierre	JULIEN su Fr	Pietro	VERRI ec,j,w It
Pierre	LAPLACE astr,st Fr	Pigalle,	JEAN su Fr
Pierre	LAVAL st Fr	Pigeon,	CORKY tv
Pierre	LOTI w Fr	Pigg,	ALEXANDRA
Pierre	LOUIS po,w Fr	Pigmeat	MARKHAM tv
Pierre	LOUYS w,po Fr	Pigot,	GEORGE mer,st Br
Pierre	MONTET h-Egypt,e,w Fr	Pigott,	RICHARDj,forger Ir
Pierre	MONTEUX cn Am	Pigott-Smith, TIM
Pierre	OLAF tv	Pigou,	ARTHUR ec,e Br
Pierre	PERRIN po Fr	Pihos,	PETE fb hf
Pierre	PRIEUR l,st Fr	Pike,	ZEBULON ar,x Am
Pierre	PUGET ac,su Fr	Pilar	PELLICER
Pierre	RENOIR	Pilar	VELASQUEZ
Pierre	RENOIR p Fr	Pilate,	PONTIUS l Ro
Pierre	REVERDY po,w Fr	Pilatus,	ROBERT mr-s Am
Pierre	RICHARD	Pilbeam,	NOVA
Pierre	RODE viol,e Fr	Pilnyak,	BORIS w Rus
Pierre	ROUX md,sc Fr	Pilon,	DANIEL
Pierre	SOULE st Am	Pilon,	GERMAIN su Fr
Pierre	TRUDEAU st Can	Piloty,	KARL von p Ger
Pierre	VALDES r Fr	Pina	AMENTA d
Pierre	VERNIER math,st,i Fr	Pinal,	SILVIA
Pierre	VIRET r Swi	Pincay,	LAFFIT Jr jockey Am
Pierre	WATKIN	Pinchot,	BRONSON tv+
Pierre	WEISS sc,e Fr	Pinchot,	GIFFORD forests,st Am
Pierre	WOLFF w Fr	Pindar	--- po Gr
Pierre d' AILLY r,e Fr		Pinder,	MIKE mr-kbds Br
Pierre de GENNES sc Fr		Pine,	PHILLIP tv+
Pierre de La RUE c Belg		Pine,	ROBERT p Br-Am

Pine,	ROBERT tv+	Pitoeff,	SACHA
Pinel,	PHILIPPE md Fr	Pitofsky,	PETER tv
Pinero,	ARTHUR(Sir)la,w	Pitoni,	GIUSEPPE c It
Pinero,	MIGUEL	Pitoniak,	ANNE tv+
Pinetop	SMITH mj-s Am	Pitot,	HENRI eng Fr
Pinette,	JOHN tv	Pitt,	BRAD
Ping,	WANG	Pitt,	INGRID
Pinhas	LAVON st Isr	Pitt,	WILLIAM(Elder)st Br
Pinker,	STEVEN w Am	Pitta,	MARK tv
Pinkerton,	ALLAN detective Am	Pitti,	CARL
Pinkett,	JADA tv+	Pittman,	ROBERT tv
Pinkham,	LYDIA id-medicine Am	Pitts,	ZASU tv+
Pinkhard,	RON tv	Piute	PETE tv
Pinkney,	BILL mr-bass Am	Piven,	JEREMY tv+
Pinky	LEE	Pizi(Gall)	--- Indian Chief Am
Pinky	TOMLIN tv	Plaatje,	SOLOMON w,st S.Afr
Pinsent,	GORDON	Place,	MARY tv+
Pinsent,	LEAH	Placido	DOMINGO tenor+ It
Pinsker,	LEO md Rus	Placido,	MICHELE
Pinski,	DAVID w Am	Plaidy,	JEAN w Br
Pinsky,	ROBERT w Am	Plain,	BELVA w Am
Pintauro,	DANNY tv+	Plana,	TONY
Pinter,	HAROLD w Br	Planck,	MAX n-p'18
Pinto,	ANIBAL st Chile	Planer,	NIGEL
Pinto,	FERNAO w Port	Plank,	ED b hf
Pintoff,	ERNIE d	Plank,	SCOTT
Pinza,	EZIO s+ It	Plant,	JACK mj-s Br
Pinzon,	MARTIN x Sp	Plant,	ROBERT mr-s Br
Pio	BAROJA w Sp	Plante,	CAROL-ANN tv
Piotr	SKARGA r,w Pol	Plante,	JACQUES ho-m'62
Piotr Ilich TCHAIKOVSKY c		Platen,	AUGUST von po,w Ger
Piozzi,	HESTER w Br	Plath,	SYLVIA p-q'82
Piper	LAURIE tv+	Plato	--- ph,w Gr
Pippa	STEELE	Plato,	DANA tv+
Pippin,	HORACE p Am	Platonov,	ANDREY w,po,ct Rus
Pirandello, LUIGI n-l'34		Platt	SPENCER calligr Am
Pire,	GEORGES n-x'58	Platt,	EDWARD tv+
Pirmez,	OCTAVE w Belg	Platt,	HOWARD tv
Pirner,	DAVE mr-s Am	Platt,	OLIVER
Piron,	ALEXIS po,w Fr	Platt,	ORVILLE st Am
Pirro	LIGORIO ac It	Player,	JESSICA tv
Pirro,	MARK d	Pleasence,	ANGELA
Pirroni,	MARCO mr-guit Br	Pleasence,	DONALD tv+
Pisani,	NICCOLO navy It	Plehve,	VYACHESLAV st Rus
Pisano,	GIOVANNI su It	Pleshette,JOHN tv+	
Pisano,	NICOLA su It	Pleshette,SUZANNE tv+	
Pisarev,	DMITRY w,j Rus	Plessis,	ARMAND ar,st Fr
Piscator,	ERWIN pr,d-stage Ger	Pleyel,	IGNAZ c,id-pianos Aus
Piscopo,	JOE tv+	Plimpton,	GEORGE
Pisemsky,	ALEKSEY w Rus	Plimpton,	MARTHA
Pisier,	MARIE	Plomer,	WILLIAM w S.Afr
Pissarro,	CAMILLE p Fr	Plone,	ALLEN d
Pistilli,	LUIGI	Plowright,JOAN	
Piston,	WALTER p-m'48,'61	Plucker,	JULIUS math,sc,e Ger
Pisu,	MARIO	Plumb,	EVE tv+
Pitirim	SOROKIN sociology Am	Plumb,	J.H. h Br
Pitkin,	WALTER w Am	Plumer,	HERBERT ar Br
Pitlik,	NOAM tv	Plummer,	AMANDA
Pitman,	ISAAC(Sir)e,i	Plummer,	CHRISTOPHER
Pitney,	GENE s,ws Am	Plummer,	GLENN
Pitney,	MAHLON l,st Am	Plumpe,	FRIEDRICH d Ger

Plunkett,	EDWARD w Irish		Polo,	MARCO x,w It
Plutarch	--- bio Gr		Polo,	TERI
Plutarco	CALLES ar,st Mex		Polykarp,	KUSCH sc,e Am
Po	BRONSON w Am		Pomare,	MAUI(Sir)md,st Maori
Po Chu-i	--- po China		Ponce de Leon,	JUAN x Sp
Pocci,	FRANZ von at,m,po Ger		Ponce,	DANNY tv
Pocock,	REGINALD sc Br		Ponce,	MANUEL c Mex
Podesta,	ROSSANA		Ponchielli,	AMILCARE c It
Podewell,	CATHY tv		Pond,	JAMES mgr-lectures Am
Podhoretz,	NORMAN ed,ct,w Am		Pons,	BEA tv
Poe,	EDGAR ALLAN w Am		Pons,	JEAN astr Fr
Poel,	WILLIAM la,pr Br		Pons,	LILY sopr+ Am
Poelzig,	HANS ac Ger		Ponselle,	ROSA s-opera Am
Poerio,	ALESSANDRO po It		Pontano,	GIOVANNI po,st It
Pogodin,	NIKOLAY w Rus		Ponte,	ANTONIO da ac It
Pogue,	KEN tv+		Ponti,	CARLO pr It
Pohl,	FREDERIK w-scifi Am		Pontiac	--- Am Indian Chief
Pohl,	FREDERIK w-scifi Am		Pontius	PILATE l Ro
Pohl,	RICHARD w Ger		Ponton,	MUNGO i Scot
Pohlmann,	ERIC		Ponton,	YVAN
Poincare,	JULES math,e Fr		Pontoppidan,	HENRIK n-l'17
Poindexter,	LARRY tv+		Pontormo,	JACOPO da p It
Poindexter,	RON ba,tv Am		Ponzini,	ANTONY tv
Pointer,	ANITA s Am		Poole,	BRIAN mr-s Br
Pointer,	BONNIE s Am		Poole,	ERNEST p-f'18
Pointer,	JUNE s Am		Poole,	JOHN w Am
Pointer,	PRISCILLA tv+		Poole,	LYNN tv
Pointer,	RUTH s Am		Poor,	CHARLES astr Am
Poire,	EMMANUEL illus Fr		Poor,	HENRY ec,w Am
Poiret,	PAUL ds Fr		Poot,	HUBERT po Dut
Poise,	FERDINAND c Fr		Pop	ANSON b,bmg hf
Poisson,	SIMEON math,e Fr		Pop	GATES bb hf
Poitier,	SIDNEY o-a'63,d+		Pop	LLOYD b hf
Pol,	WINCENTY po Pol		Pop	WARNER fbc Am
Pola	NEGRI		Pop,	IGGY s,w-song Am
Polanski,	ROMAN d+		Popcorn,	FAITH consultant Am
Polanyi,	JOHN n-c'86		Pope,	ALBERT bikes,cars Am
Polesie,	HERB tv		Pope,	ALEXANDER po,w Br
Polic,	HENRY II, tv		Pope,	CARMELITA tv
Polinsky,	ALEXANDER tv		Pope,	JOHN ac Am
Polito,	JON tv+		Pope,	PEGGY tv
Polito,	LINA		Pople,	JOHN sc,e,n-c'98
Polk,	JAMES 11th Pres		Popov,	ALEKSANDR sc,eng Rus
Polk,	LEONIDAS r,ar-CSA Am		Popper,	KARL ph,e Br
Polk,	OSCAR		Popwell,	ALBERT tv
Pollack,	BEN mj-drm,cn Am		Porcaro,	STEVE mr-kbds,s Am
Pollack,	ROBERT tv		Porcel,	JORGE
Pollack,	SYDNEY d+		Porfirio	DIAZ ar,st Mex
Pollak,	CHERYL		Porpora,	NICOLA c It
Pollak,	KEVIN tv+		Porras,	BELISARIO st Panama
Pollan,	TRACY tv+		Porta,	CARLO po It
Pollard,	JIM bb hf		Portaas,	HERMAN po Nor
Pollard,	MICHAEL		Portal,	CHARLES fly,st Br
Pollard,	SNUB		Porter	HALL
Pollock,	JACKSON p Am		Porter	WAGONER m-cnt,tv Am
Pollock,	OLIVER mer Am		Porter,	ALISAN tv
Polly	BERGEN tv+		Porter,	ARTHUR tv
Polly	DRAPER tv+		Porter,	COLE c,lyrics Am
Polly	ROWLES tv+		Porter,	DON tv+
Polly	WALKER		Porter,	EDWIN d,cameraman Am
Polly	YOUNG		Porter,	ELEANOR w Am

Porter,	ELIOT fo Am
Porter,	ERIC
Porter,	GENE w Am
Porter,	GEORGE(Sir)n-c 67
Porter,	HAL w Aust
Porter,	JANE w Br
Porter,	KATHERINE p-f'66
Porter,	NOAH r,e,ed Am
Porter,	NYREE DAWN tv
Porter,	QUINCY p-m'54
Porter,	RODNEY n-m'72
Porter,	TODD tv
Porter,	WILLIAM w Am
Porthan,	HENRIK e Finn
Portman,	ERIC
Portnow,	RICHARD
Portola,	GASPAR de ar Sp
Portz,	CHUCK mr-bass Am
Posada,	JOSE at Mex
Posey,	THOMAS ar,st Am
Post,	CHARLES id-foods Am
Post,	EMIL math,e Am
Post,	EMILY j,w Am
Post,	MARKIE tv+
Post,	MIKE tv
Post,	SASKIA
Post,	TED d
Post,	WILEY fly Am
Post,	WILLIAM Jr tv+
Postlethwaite, PETER
Poston,	TOM tv+
Potagos,	PANAYOTIS md Gr
Potel,	VICTOR
Potocki,	WACLAW po Pol
Potok,	CHAIM w Am
Pott,	AUGUST e,w Ger
Potter	PALMER mer Am
Potter	STEWART l-supr ct Am
Potter,	BEATRIX w,illus Br
Potter,	CAROL tv
Potter,	CLIFF tv
Potter,	EDWARD su Am
Potter,	H.C. d
Potter,	JERRY tv
Potter,	MADELEINE
Potter,	MARTIN
Potter,	PAUL p Dut
Potter,	PETER tv
Potter,	STEWART l,supr ct Am
Pottier,	EUGENE ws,st Fr
Pottinger,STANLEY w Am
Potts,	ANNIE tv+
Potts,	CLIFF tv+
Pouchet,	FELIX e,nature Fr
Pouget,	ELY
Poul	MOLLER w Dan
Poul	STEMANN st Dan
Poulenc,	FRANCIS c Fr
Pound,	DUDLEY(Sir)navy
Pound,	EZRA po Am
Pound,	ROSCOE e,w Am

Pounder,	CCH tv+
Poundstone, PAULA cm+ Am
Poussin,	NICOLAS p Fr
Povich,	MAURY tv-host Am
Powel	CROSLEY id-radios Am
Powell,	ADAM CLAYTON r,st Am
Powell,	ANGELA tv
Powell,	ANTHONY w Br
Powell,	BILLY mr-kbds Am
Powell,	BOOG b
Powell,	BUD-mj piano,cn Am
Powell,	CECIL n-p'50
Powell,	COLIN ar,w Am
Powell,	DAWN w Am
Powell,	DICK tv+
Powell,	ELEANOR
Powell,	JANE tv+
Powell,	JOHN geol,x Am
Powell,	JOHN(Boog)b-mv'70
Powell,	LEE
Powell,	MEL p-m'90
Powell,	MICHAEL d+
Powell,	RANDOLPH tv
Powell,	ROBERT
Powell,	SCOTT(Tony Santini)tv
Powell,	SUE m-cnt,tv Am
Powell,	TEDDY mj,cn Am
Powell,	WILLIAM
Power,	JOHN d
Power,	LEONEL c Br
Power,	TARYN
Power,	TYRONE
Power,	TYRONE Jr.
Power,	TYRONE Sr.
Powers	BOOTHE
Powers,	ALEXANDRA
Powers,	BEN tv
Powers,	HIRAM su Am
Powers,	JIMMY tv
Powers,	LEONA tv
Powers,	MALA tv+
Powers,	STEFANIE tv+ or
Powers	STEPHANIE tv+
Powers,	TOM
Powers,	VICKI
Powers,	WAYNE tv
Powys,	J.C. w,po Br
Powys,	T.F. w Br
Poynter,	EDWARD(Sir)p
Pozzo,	ANDREA dal r,ac,p It
Pr'ss Ann --- daut. Qn. Eliz.II
Pr'ss Beatrice---daut. Pr.Andrew
Pr'ss Caroline-daut. Pr'ss Grace
Pr'ss Diana---ex-wf Pr. Charles
Pr'ss Eugenie---daut. Pr. Andrew
Pr. Henry---son Pr Chas-Diane
Pr. Philip--hus. Qn. Eliz II
Pr. William-son Pr Chas-Diane
Prada,	MIUCCIA ds It
Prado,	LILIA
Prado,	MARIANO ar,st Peru

Prado,	PEDRO w Chile
Prado,	PEREZ m, cn Cuban-Am
Praed,	MICHAEL tv+
Praed,	WINTHROP po,st Br
Praga,	EMILIO po It
Praise-God	BARBON r Br
Prandtl,	LUDWIG sc-airflow Ger
Prano,	LOU mj-s Am
Prasad,	RAJENDRA l,st India
Pratt,	BABE ho-m'44
Pratt,	DEBORAH tv
Pratt,	E.J. po,e Can
Pratt,	FRANCIS i,id Am
Pratt,	SILAS c Am
Pratt,	WALDO m,e,r Am
Preacher	ROE b
Preece,	WILLIAM(Sir)eng
Pregl,	FRITZ n-c'23
Preiss,	WOLFGANG
Prejean,	ALBERT
Prelog,	VLADIMIR sc Swi
Preminger,	OTTO d+
Prendergast,	MAURICE p Am
Prendes,	LUIS
Prentis	HANCOCK tv
Prentiss,	ED tv
Prentiss,	PAULA tv+
Pres	YOUNG mj-sax Am
Preserved	SMITH h Am
Presle,	MICHELINE
Presley,	ELVIS AARON s,tv+ Am
Presley,	PRISCILLA tv+
Presley,	REG mr-s Br
Presnell,	HARVE
Pressburger,	EMERIC d+
Pressman,	LAWRENCE tv+
Pressman,	MICHAEL d
Presson,	JASON
Prestidge,	MEL tv
Preston	FOSTER tv+
Preston	STURGES d,w Am
Preston,	BILLY
Preston,	DAVID tv
Preston,	J.A. tv+
Preston,	KELLY
Preston,	MIKE
Preston,	RICHARD w Am
Preston,	ROBERT s,tv+
Preston,	WAYDE tv+
Preti,	MATTIA p It
Pretre,	GEORGES cn Fr
Pretto,	ROGERT tv
Preuss,	HUGO l,st Ger
Prevert,	JACQUES po,w Fr
Previn,	ANDRE cn Am
Prevost,	ABBE w Fr
Prevost,	EUGENE w Fr
Prevost,	MARIE
Prey,	HERMANN bari
Preyer,	WILHELM md,ps Ger
Price,	ALAN mr-kbds Am

Price,	ALLEN tv
Price,	DENNIS
Price,	HAL
Price,	LEONTYNE sopr Am
Price,	LINDSAY tv
Price,	LLOYD mr,s Am
Price,	MARC tv+
Price,	PAUL tv
Price,	REYNOLDS w Am
Price,	RICHARD w,ph Welsh
Price,	ROGER tv
Price,	STANLEY
Price,	UVEDALE(Sir)ac-land
Price,	VINCENT tv+
Prickett,	MAUDIE tv
Pride,	CHARLEY s-cnt Am
Priest,	PAT tv+
Priest,	STEVE mr-bass Br
Priestley,	J.B. w Br
Priestley,	JOSEPH r,sc Br
Priestly,	JASON tv+
Prieur,	PIERRE l,st Fr
Prigogine,	ILYA n-c'77
Prim,	SUZY
Prima,	LOUIS mj-trum,cn,c Am
Prime,	HARRY mj-s Am
Prime,	JAMES mr-kbds Scot
Primo	CARNERA boxer Am
Primo	LEVI w,po It
Primus,	BARRY tv+
Primus,	PEARL ba Am
Prince	--- mr,s Am
Prince Mark D	--- m-rap Am
Prince,	BOB tv
Prince,	CLAYTON tv
Prince,	FAITH
Prince,	HAROLD d
Prince,	JACK s,tv Am
Prince,	JONATHAN tv+
Prince,	MORTON md,ps,w Am
Prince,	WILLIAM tv+
Princip,	GAVRILO assassin Serb
Principal,	VICTORIA tv+
Prine,	ANDREW tv+
Pringle,	AILEEN
Pringle,	JOAN tv
Prinsloo,	SANDRA
Prinze,	FREDDIE tv
Prior,	DAVID d
Prior,	EDWARD ac,e Br
Prior,	MATTHEW po,st Br
Prior,	TED
Priscilla	ALDEN(pilgrim) Am
Priscilla	BARNES tv+
Priscilla	LANE mj-s+ Am
Priscilla	MORRILL tv+
Priscilla	POINTER tv+
Priscilla	PRESLEY tv+
Priscilla	WEEMS tv
Pritchard,	BARRY mr-guit,s Br
Pritchard,	HANNAH la Br

Pritchett, FLORENCE tv
Pritchett, V.S.(Sir)w,ct
Prival, LUCIEN
Proby, P.J. s Am
Prochnow, JUERGEN
Prochorov,ALEKSANDER n-p'64
Proclus --- ph Gr
Procopius --- h Byzantine
Procter, BRYAN po Br
Proctor, PHILIP tv
Profiat DURAN r Fr-Jew
Prohaska, JANOS tv
Prohut, LOU tv
Prokofiev,SERGEY c Rus
Prosky, ROBERT tv+
Prosper JOLYOT po Fr
Prosper MERIMEE w Fr
Protic, STOJAN ed,st Yugo
Proulx, E. ANNIE p-f'94
Proust, MARCEL w Fr
Prout, EBENEZER c Br
Prouty JED
Prouty, OLIVE w Am
Proval, DAVID
Provenza, PAUL tv
Provine, DOROTHY tv+
Provost, JON tv+
Prowse, DAVID
Prud'homme,CAMERON tv
Pruitt Taylor VINCE
Prunell, JESSICA tv
Prunella SCALES
Prutz, ROBERT w Ger
Pryce, JONATHAN
Prynne, WILLIAM w Br
Pryor, NICHOLAS tv+
Pryor, RAIN tv
Pryor, RICHARD tv+
Pryor, ROGER
Prysock, RED mj-sax Am
Przhevalsky, NIKOLAY x Rus
Puccini, GIACOMO c It
Puckett, KIRBY b,rbi'94
Pud GALVIN b hf
Puente, TITO mj-drm,cn+ Am
Puenzo, LUIS d
Puett, TOMMY tv
Puget, PIERRE ac,su Fr
Pugh, WILLARD
Pugin, AUGUSTUS ac,arc Fr
Puglia, FRANK
Pugliese, AL tv
Puglisi, ALDO
Puig, MANUEL w Arg
Pulitzer, JOSEPH j(prizes) Am
Pullen, DON mj-piano Am
Pulliam, KESHIA KNIGHT tv
Pullman, BILL
Pullman, GEORGE i-rr cars Am
Pulver, LILO(Liselotte)
Pun, KONG

Punnett, REGINALD sc,e,ed Br
Pupi AVATI d
Pupi CAMPO mj-cn,tv Am
Pupin, MICHAEL sc,i Am
Purcell, DICK
Purcell, EDWARD n-p'52
Purcell, HENRY c Br
Purcell, LEE
Purcell, SARAH tv-hostess Am
Purcill, KAREN tv
Purdee, NATHAN tv
Purdom, EDMUND
Purdue, JOHN mer,f Am
Purdy, AL po Can
Purdy, JAMES w Am
Puri, OM
Purl, LINDA tv+
Pursh, FREDERICK sc,w Am
Purviance,EDNA
Pusey, E.B. r,e,w Br
Pushkin, ALEKSANDR po,w Rus
Pustil, JEFF tv
Putnam, ANNE witch trials Am
Putnam, GEORGE tv
Putte, ISAAC van de st Dut
Putti, LYA de s Ger
Puvis de Chavannes --- p Fr
Puzo, MARIO w Am
Pyat, FELIX w,st Fr
Pye, HENRY pol'1790+
Pyl, JEAN tv
Pyle, DENVER s,tv+ Am
Pyle, ERNEST(Ernie)j Am
Pyle, GOMER fc
Pyle, HOWARD illus,w Am
Pym, BARBARA w Br
Pym, JOHN st Br
Pynchon, THOMAS w Am
Pyotr BAGRATION ar Rus
Pyotr LAVROV re,ed Rus
Pythagoras --- ph, math Gr
Pyun, ALBERT d

**NO NAME DESIGNATION CODES
OR NATIONALITY CODES
BEGIN WITH "Q's"**

"Q's"
Q --- e,w Br
Qaddafi, MUAMMAR st Libya
Quade, JOHN
Quadros, STEPHEN
Quaid, DENNIS
Quaid, RANDY tv+
Quaife, PETE mr-bass Br
Qualen, JOHN
Quan, JOHATHAN KE tv+
Quant, MARY ds(minis)Br
Quantz, JOHANN flute,c Ger
Quare, DANIEL id-clocks Br
Quarless, FRANCIS po Br

Quarry,	ROBERT tv+
Quasimodo,	SALVATOR po,n-l'59
Quatro,	SUZI mr
Quay,	MATTHEW st Am
Quayle,	ANNA
Quayle,	ANTHONY(Sir)d,la,tv+
Quayle,	DAN st,ex-vp Am
Quayle,	MARILYN l,w,Dan's wife
Queen	KONG
Queen Latifah	--- m-rap,tv Am
Queen,	ELLERY w Am
Queenan,	JOE w Am
Queenie	LEONARD
Queiros,	RACHEL de w,j Braz
Queler,	EVE cn Am
Queneau,	RAYMOND w,po,ct Fr
Quennell,	PETER w,ed,bio,po Br
Quental,	ANTERO de po Port
Quentin	MASSYS p Belg
Querard	JOSEPH w Fr
Querido,	ISRAEL w Dut
Quesnay,	FRANCOIS md,e Fr
Quesnel,	PASQUIER r Fr
Questel,	MAE
Quevedo,	FRANCISCO de w,po Sp
Quick,	ARMAND sc-md,e Am
Quick,	DIANA
Quidde,	LUDWIG h, n-x'27
Quidor,	JOHN p Am
Quigley,	CHARLES
Quigley,	ERNEST bbr, hf
Quigley,	LINNEA
Quigley,	RITA
Quill,	TIM
Quillan,	EDDIE tv+
Quiller-Couch,ARTHUR(Sir)e,w	
Quilley,	DENIS
Quilter,	ROGER c Br
Quimby,	PHINEAS healer Am
Quin	KESSLER
Quin,	JAMES la Ir
Quince,	PETER po Am
Quincke,	GEORG sc,e Ger
Quincy	HOWE tv
Quincy	JONES mj,pr Am
Quincy	PORTER c Am
Quincy	WRIGHT sc-politics Am
Quincy,	JOSIAH l,st Am
Quindlen,	ANNA j,w Am
Quine,	DON tv
Quine,	RICHARD d, tv+
Quine,	WILLARD ph Am
Quinet,	EDGAR w,st Fr
Quinlan,	KATHLEEN
Quinlan,	ROBERTA tv
Quinlan,	SIOBHAN tv
Quinn	CUMMINGS tv+
Quinn	MARTIN tv
Quinn	REDEKER
Quinn,	AIDAN
Quinn,	ANTHONY o-s'52'56

Quinn,	BILL tv+
Quinn,	CARMEL tv
Quinn,	DEREK mr-guit Br
Quinn,	FRANCESCO
Quinn,	J.C.
Quinn,	LOUIS tv+
Quinn,	PAT
Quinn,	SALLY w Am
Quinn,	SUSAN bio,w,e Am
Quinn,	TEDDY tv
Quintana,	MANUEL w,st Sp
Quintin	BRAND(Sir)fly
Quintin	CRAUFURD w Scot
Quintin	HOGG ref,f Br
Quintus	ENNIUS po Ro
Quirino,	ELPIDIO st Phil
Quiroga,	HORACIO w Urug
Quisling,	VIDKUN ar,traitor Nor
Quivers,	ROBIN w,radio,tv+ Am
Quo,	BEULAH

"R" NAME DESIGNATION CODES

r		RELIGIONIST
rbi	b	RUNS-BATTED-IN LEADER
re		REVOLUTIONARY
ref		REFORMER
r&b		RYTHYM & BLUES(MUSIC)
ru		RUNNER

'R" NATIONALITY CODES

Ro	-	ROMAN
Rom	~	ROMANIAN
Rus	-	RUSSIAN

"R's"

R.A.K.	MASON po,ed,w N.Zea
R.B.	GREAVES m-r&b Am
R.D.	LAING ps,w Scot
R.H.	TAWNEY h-ec Br
R.H.	THOMSON
R.K.	NARAYAN w India
R.S.	THOMAS po Welsh
R. Buckminster	FULLER ac,eng
R. Lee	ERMEY
Raab,	JULIUS st Aus
Raab,	KURT
Raabe,	WILHELM po,w Ger
Rabal,	FRANCESCO
Rabaud,	HENRI c,cn Fr
Rabbit,	EDDIE s,ws Am
Rabe,	DAVID w Am
Rabi,	ISIDOR n-p'44
Rabin,	LEAH(Y's wife) Isr
Rabin,	YITZHAK n-x'94
Rabindranath	TAGORE w India
Rabinowitz,	SHOLEM w Rus
Rabinowitz,	SIMA po Am
Rachel	CARSON w,sc Am
Rachel	DUNCAN tv
Rachel	JACOBS tv
Rachel	KEMPSON
Rachel	ROBERTS tv+
Rachel	TICOTIN tv+

Rachel	WARD	Rahv,	PHILIP ct,w Am
Rachel de	QUEIROS w,j Braz	Raikes,	ROBERT pb,ref Br
Rachel,	MLLE la Fr	Railsback,	STEVE
Rachins,	ALAN tv+	Raimi,	SAM d
Rachmaninoff,	SERGEY pia,cn,c Rus	Raimi,	THEODORE
Racimo,	VICTORIA tv+	Raimund,	FERDINAND la,w Aus
Racine,	JEAN w Fr	Rain	PRYOR tv
Rackham,	ARTHUR illus Br	Rainbeaux	SMITH
Rad	DALY tv	Raine,	KATHLEEN po Br
Radames	PERA tv	Rainer	RILKE po Ger
Radbourn,	CHARLIE b hf	Rainer,	LUISE o-a'36'37
Radcliffe,	ANN w Br	Raines,	CRISTINA tv+
Radclyffe	HALL w Br	Raines,	ELLA tv+
Radek,	KARL st Rus	Raines,	REVA tv
Raden	KARTINI fe Java	Raines,	STEVE tv
Raden	SOETOMO md,st Java	Raines,	TIM b.bat'86
Radescu,	NICOLAE ar,st Rom	Rainey,	FORD tv+
Radford,	BASIL	Rainey,	GERTRUDE(Ma)mj,s Am
Radic,	STJEPAN st Croat	Rainey,	HENRY st Am
Radiguet,	RAYMOND w,po Fr	Rains,	CLAUDE
Radin,	PAUL an,e,w Am	Rainwater,	GREGG tv
Radko	DIMITRIEV r Bulg	Rainwater,	JAMES n-p'75
Radlov,	VASILY e,philolog Rus	Rainwater,	MARVIN tv
Radner,	GILDA tv+	Rainy,	ROBERT r Scot
Radomir	PUTNIK ar Serb	Rais,	GILLES de ar Fr
Rae Dawn	CHONG	Raisa	GORBECHEV M's wfe Rus
Rae,	CHARLOTTE tv+	Raisch,	BILL tv
Rae,	JOHN x Scot	Raisuli,	AHMAD brigand Morocco
Raeburn,	BOYD mj,cn Am	Raitt,	BONNIE s Am
Raeburn,	HENRY(Sir)p Scot	Raja	RAO w India
Raeder,	ERICH navy,Nazi Ger	Rajendra	PRASAD l,st India
Raemaekers,	LOUIS cr Dut	Rajiv	GANDHI fly,st India
Raf	VALLONE	Rakoff,	ALVIN d
Rafael	ALBERTI po,w Sp	Rakosi,	CARL po Am
Rafael	CAMPOS tv+	Rakosi,	MATYAS st Hung
Rafael	INCLAN	Raleigh	BOND tv
Rafael	NUNEZ st Colom	Raleigh,	WALTER(Sir)x,po,w
Rafal	ZEILINSKI d	Ralf	HAROLDE
Rafelson,	BOB d	Ralf	HUTTER mr-kbd,s Ger
Raff,	JOACHIM c Ger	Rall,	TOMMY
Raffaello	dal COLLE p It	Ralna	HOVIS tv
Rafferty,	BILL tv	Ralph	ALLEN f Br
Rafferty,	CHIPS	Ralph	BAKSHI d,w,animat Am
Rafferty,	FRANCES tv+	Ralph	BATES
Rafferty,	GERRY s,ws Scot	Ralph	BELLAMY tv+
Raffi	--- s,ws Egypt	Ralph	BROWN
Raffill,	STEWART d	Ralph	BUNCHE st,e Am
Raffin,	DEBORAH	Ralph	BYRD tv+
Rafn,	CARL philolog Dan	Ralph	CARTER tv
Raft,	GEORGE tv+	Ralph	CRAM ac,w,e Am
Raggio,	LISA tv	Ralph	De PALMA car racer Am
Ragin,	JOHN tv	Ralph	EARLE p Am
Ragland,	RAGS	Ralph	EDWARDS tv
Ragnar	FRISCH ec, e Nor	Ralph	ELLIS mr-guit,s Br
Ragnar	GRANIT md Swe	Ralph	ELLISON w Am
Ragnar	OSTBERG ac Swe	Ralph	EMERY tv
Rags	RAGLAND	Ralph	FIENES
Ragsdale,	WILLIAM tv+	Ralph	FORBES
Rahbek,	KNUD po,w,ct Dan	Ralph	FREEMAN(Sir)eng
Rahman,	MUJIBUR st Bengal	Ralph	GARR b
Rahner,	KARL r,e Ger	Ralph	GRAVES

Ralph	GURLEY f Am	Ramon de la SAGRA sc,re Sp	
Ralph	HART tv	Ramon yCajal,SANTIAGO n-m'06	
Ralph	HODGSON po Br	Ramon,	GASTON sc Fr
Ralph	IZARD re Am	Ramona	BURNETT tv
Ralph	KINER b hf	Ramone,	DEE DEE mr-bass Am
Ralph	LAUREN ds Am	Ramone,	JOEY mr-s Am
Ralph	LEWIS	Ramone,	JOHNNY mr-guit Am
Ralph	LINTON an,e,w Am	Ramone,	TOMMY mr-drm Hung
Ralph	LOCKE tv	Ramos,	GRACILIANO w Braz
Ralph	MACCHIO tv+	Ramos,	LARRY Jr mr-guit,s Am
Ralph	MANZA tv	Ramos,	RUDY tv+
Ralph	MEEKER	Rampling,	CHARLOTTE
Ralph	MICHAEL tv+	Ramsay,	ALLAN po Scot
Ralph	MILLER bbc hf	Ramsay,	ANNE ELIZABETH tv
Ralph	MORGAN	Ramsay,	JACK bbc hf
Ralph	MOTTRAM w Br	Ramsay,	REMAK
Ralph	NADER ct,w Am	Ramsay,	WILLIAM(Sir)n-c'04
Ralph	NELSON d	Ramsden,	JESSE id-astr Br
Ralph	PERRY ph,e Am	Ramsey	LEWIS mj-piano
Ralph	PETERS	Ramsey,	AL mr-guit Am
Ralph	REED tv	Ramsey,	ANNE
Ralph	ROSE o-g'04'08	Ramsey,	FRANK bb hf
Ralph	SANFORD tv+	Ramsey,	LOGAN tv+
Ralph	STORY tv	Ramsey,	NORMAN n-p'89
Ralph	THOMAS d	Ramus,	NICK tv+
Ralph	TRUMAN	Ramuz,	CHARLES w Swi
Ralph	TURNER h,e Am	Ramy	ZADA tv+
Ralph	UPSON eng-aero Am	Ran,	SHULAMIT p-m'91
Ralph	WAITE tv+	Rana	SINGH st Hindu
Ralph	WILCOX tv	Ranade,	MAHADEV l India
Ralph	WOOD id-pottery Br	Rance	HOWARD tv+
Ralph Waldo EMERSON po Am		Rance,	ARMAND r Fr
Ralph,	JESSIE	Rand	BROOKS
Ralph,	SHERYL tv+	Rand,	AYN w Am
Ralphs,	MICK mr-guit Br	Rand,	SALLY ba Am
Ralston,	BOB piano,org,tv Am	Randa	HAINES d
Ralston,	ESTHER	Randal	KLEISER d
Ralston,	JOBYNA	Randall	CARVER tv
Ralston,	VERA	Randall	COBB(Tex)
Rama	LENZ w,cults Am	Randall	JARRELL po,w,ct Am
Raman,	CHANDRASEK n-p'30	Randall,	ANN tv
Rambal,	ENRIQUE	Randall,	BOB tv
Rambeau,	MARJORIE	Randall,	ETHAN
Rambert,	MARIE(Dame)ba Br	Randall,	JACK
Rambo,	DACK tv+	Randall,	JAMES j,ws Am
Rameau,	JEAN c Fr	Randall,	STUART tv
Ramee,	MARIE de la w Br	Randall,	SUE tv
Ramer,	HENRY	Randall,	TONY tv+
Ramirez,	PEDRO ar,st Arg	Randee	HELLER tv+
Ramiro de MAEZTU w Sp		Randell,	RON tv
Ramis,	HAROLD d,w,tv+ Am	Randi	BRAZEN tv
Ramler,	KARL po Ger	Randi	BROOKS
Ramon	BIERI tv+	Randi	OAKES tv
Ramon	FRANCO tv+	Randle,	THERESA
Ramon	FREIRE ar,st Chile	Randolf,	ANDERS
Ramon	LLULL po Sp	Randolph	BOURNE w,ct Am
Ramon	NARVAEZ ar Sp	Randolph	POWELL tv
Ramon	NAVARRO	Randolph	ROBERTS tv
Ramon	SENDER w Sp	Randolph	SCOTT
Ramon	VINAY tenor	Randolph	STOW w,po Austra
Ramon de la CRUZ w Sp		Randolph,	AMANDA tv

Randolph,	ASA labor Am	Rasey,	JEAN tv
Randolph,	BOOTS m-sax Am	Rash,	STEVE d
Randolph,	CHASE tv	Rashad,	AHMAD fb tv-spts Am
Randolph,	JANE	Rashad,	PHYLICIA tv
Randolph,	JOHN	Rasin,	ALOIS st Cz
Randolph,	JOYCE tv	Rask,	RASMUS h-east,e Dan
Randolph,	LILLIAN tv	Raskin,	DAMON tv
Random,	BOB tv	Rasmus	RASK h-orient,e Dan
Randone,	SALVO	Rasmussen,	KNUD x Dan
Rands,	BERNARD p-m'84	Rasp,	FRITZ
Randy	BACHMAN mr-guit,s Can	Raspe,	RUDOLPH w Ger
Randy	BOONE tv	Rassam,	HORMUZD arc Turk
Randy	CROWDER tv	Rasulala,	THALMUS tv+
Randy	GRAFF tv	Rat	SCABIES mr-drm Br
Randy	JONES b	Ratana,	TAHUPOTIKIst,r Maori
Randy	KIRBY tv	Ratdolt,	ERHARD id-print Ger
Randy	MEIER tv	Rateau,	CAMILLE eng,i Fr
Randy	MEISNER mr-bass,s Am	Rathbone,	BASIL
Randy	OWEN m-guit,s Am	Rather,	DAN tv-j,anchor Am
Randy	QUAID tv+	Rathke,	MARTIN md-sc Ger
Randy	SPARKS s,cn,tv Am	Ratia,	ARMI ds-textile Finn
Randy	STUART tv+	Ratliffe,	GARETTE tv
Randy	TRAVIS s-cnt Am	Ratoff,	GREGORY d+
Randy	WAYNE s	Ratray,	DEVIN
Randy	WHIPPLE tv	Rattigan,	TERENCE(Sir)w
Randy	WHITE fb hf	Rattle,	SIMOM(Sir)cn
Rank,	JOSEPH id,pr-films Br	Rattray,	HEATHER
Rank,	OTTO ps,ed Aus	Ratzel,	FRIEDRICHgeog,e Ger
Ranke,	LEOPOLD von h,e Ger	Ratzenberger,	JOHN tv+
Rankin,	ARTHUR	Rau,	ANDREA
Rankin,	JEANETTE 1st fe congr	Rau,	BENEGAL(Sir)l,st Indi
Ransom	SHERMAN tv	Rau,	SANTHA RAMA w
Ransom Eli OLDS i,id-cars Am		Rauffe,	ALIDA
Ransom,	JOHN po,ct Am	Raul	JULIA
Ransome,	ARTHUR w Br	Raul	MONDESI b
Rantzau,	JOHAN ar Ger	Raupach,	ERNST w Ger
Ranulf	HIGDEN r Br	Ravazza,	CARL mj,cn Am
Ranvier,	LOUIS md-sc Fr	Ravel,	MAURICE c Fr
Rao,	RAJA w India	Raven,	ELSA tv
Raoul	DUFY p,ds Fr	Raven-Symone	--- tv
Raoul	PICTET sc,e Swi	Ravera,	GINA
Raoul	TRUJILLO	Ravi	SHANKAR m India
Raoul	WALSH d+	Rawlings,	MARJORIE p-f'39
Raoult,	FRANCOIS sc,e Fr	Rawlinson,	BRIAN tv
Raphael	--- p It	Rawlinson,	HERBERT
Raphael	CAMPOS	Rawls,	LOU s-r&b Am
Raphael	SBARGE	Rawson,	ARTURO ar Arg
Raphael	SEMMES navy Am	Ray	ALDO m+ Am
Raphael,	SALLY JESSY tv &	Ray	ANTHONY mj,cn,tv Am
Raphael,	SALLY J. --hostess	Ray	ARCEL mgr-boxing Am
Rapp,	ANTHONY	Ray	AUSTIN d
Rapp,	BARNEY mj,cn Am	Ray	BAKER tv+
Rapp,	DANNY mr-s Am	Ray	BAKER w,Am
Rapp,	GEORGE r Am	Ray	BARR tv
Rappaport,	DAVID tv+	Ray	BARRETT
Rappaport,	MICHAEL	Ray	BENNETT
Rapper,	IRVING d	Ray	BERWICK tv
Raquel	WELCH	Ray	BLOCH mj Am
Ras,	EVA	Ray	BOLGER ba,tv+ Am
Rasch,	ALBERTINA ba Am	Ray	BORQUE ho
Rasche,	DAVID tv+	Ray	BROOKS

Ray	BROWN mj-bass Am	Ray,	NICHOLAS d+
Ray	CARTER tv	Ray,	RENE
Ray	CHARLES piano,c+	Ray,	SATYAJIT pr-films Ind
Ray	CLARK s-cnt,tv Am	Rayburn,	GENE tv
Ray	COLLINS tv+	Rayburn,	SAMUEL(Sam)st Am
Ray	COMBS tv	Raye	BIRK tv
Ray	DANTON tv+	Raye,	MARTHA s,tv+ Am
Ray	EBERLE mj,s,cn Am	Rayet,	GEORGES astr Fr
Ray	ENNIS mr-guit,s Br	Rayleigh,	LORD n-p'04
Ray	ENRIGHT d	Raymond	ALLEN tv
Ray	EWRY 8xo-g'00'04'08	Raymond	ARON ph Fr
Ray	FERRELL tv	Raymond	BAILEY tv+
Ray	FORREST tv	Raymond	BARRY
Ray	FULMER tv	Raymond	BRAMLEY tv
Ray	GANDOLF tv	Raymond	BURR tv+
Ray	JONES mr-bass Br	Raymond	DITMARS sc Am
Ray	KELLOGG tv	Raymond	DODGE ps,e Am
Ray	KROC hamburgers Am	Raymond	HADDON tv
Ray	LAWLER w Aust	Raymond	HATTON
Ray	LEONARD boxer Am &	Raymond	HUNTLEY
Ray	LEONARD=Sugar Ray	Raymond	LOEWY id-design Am
Ray	LIOTTA	Raymond	MASSEY tv+
Ray	LONNEN	Raymond	MOLEY j,e,st Am
Ray	MALONE tv	Raymond	ORTEIG restaurnt Am
Ray	MANCINI(Boom Boom)	Raymond	QUENEAU w,po Fr
Ray	McANALLY	Raymond	SCOTT m,cn,tv Am
Ray	MEYER bbc hf	Raymond	SINGER tv
Ray	MILLAND	Raymond	SOUSTER po,ed Can
Ray	NOBLE mj,cn,c Br-Am	Raymond	ST.JACQUES tv+
Ray	ORDONEZ b	Raymond	SWING j Am
Ray	PARKER Jr s,ws Am	Raymond	WALBURN
Ray	PEARL mj,cn Am	Raymond,	ALEX cr Am
Ray	SANDERS tv	Raymond,	BILL
Ray	SAWYER mr-s Am	Raymond,	CANDY
Ray	SCHALK b hf	Raymond,	CYRIL
Ray	SERRA	Raymond,	GARY tv+
Ray	SHARKEY	Raymond,	GENE tv+
Ray	STEVENS s-pop,folk	Raymond,	GUY tv
Ray	STILES mr-bass,s Br	Raymond,	LINA
Ray	TAYLOR d+	Raymond,	PAULA
Ray	TEAL tv+	Raymond,	PERCY sc,e Am
Ray	THOMAS mr-flute,s Br	Raynal,	PAUL w Fr
Ray	VITTE tv+	Rayner	GODDARD l Br
Ray	WALKER	Rayner,	CHUCK ho-m'50
Ray	WALSTON tv+	Raynov,	NIKOLAY po,p,h-art
Ray	WISE tv+	Raz,	KAVI tv
Ray	WOOD tv	Razaf,	ANDY lyrics Am
Ray Charles Singers, THE Am		Razi,	ABU md,ph Persia
Ray,	ALDO	Razin,	STEPAN rebel Rus
Ray,	ANDREW	Rea,	CHRIS s,ws Br
Ray,	CHARLES	Rea,	GARDNER cr Am
Ray,	CONNIE tv	Rea,	PEGGY tv+
Ray,	DIXY sc,st Am	Rea,	STEPHEN tv+
Ray,	FRED OLEN d	Read	MORGAN tv
Ray,	GENE tv	Read,	ALBERT navy Am
Ray,	HUGH(Shorty) fb hf	Read,	HERBERT(Sir)po,ct
Ray,	JAMES EARL killd MLK	Read,	JAMES
Ray,	JOHNNIE s Am	Read,	MISS w Br
Ray,	LEAH	Read,	OPIE w Am
Ray,	MAN p,fo Am	Reade,	CHARLES w Br
Ray,	MARGUERITE tv	Reading,	DONNA tv

Reagan,	NANCY(wf-Ronald)+	Redding,	OTIS s-soul,c Am
Reagan,	RONALD 40th pres+	Reddy,	HELEN s,tv+ Austra
Realdo	COLOMBO md It	Redeker	QUINN
Reason,	REX tv+	Redfield,	JAMES w Am
Reasoner,	HARRY tv-j,anchor	Redfield,	ROBERT an,e Am
Reaumur,	RENE sc Fr	Redfield,	WILLIAM
Reb	BROWN	Redford,	ROBERT o-d'80,d+
Reb	RUSSELL	Redglare,	ROCKETS
Reba	McENTIRE s-cnt+ Am	Redgrave,	CORIN
Reba	WATERS tv	Redgrave,	JEMMA
Rebbot,	SADY	Redgrave,	LYNN tv+
Rebecca	BALDING tv	Redgrave,	MICHAEL(Sir)la+
Rebecca	DAVIS w Am	Redgrave,	VANESSA o-s'77
Rebecca	DeMORNAY	Redi,	FRANCESCO md,po It
Rebecca	FELTON st,w Am	Reding,	ALOYS st Swi
Rebecca	FRITH la+ Aust	Reding,	ITAL st Swi
Rebecca	HOLDEN tv+	Reding,	JULI
Rebecca	JENKINS	Redlich,	JOSEPH l,st Aus
Rebecca	MILLER	Redman,	DEWEY mj-sax,cn Am
Rebecca	RIGG	Redman,	DON mj-reeds,cn Am
Rebecca	SCHULL tv	Redman,	JOSHUA mj sax Am
Rebecca	SOBEL tv	Redmond,	LIAM
Rebecca	WEST(Dame)w,ct,j,fe	Redmond,	MARGE tv
Rebecca	YORK tv	Redmond,	MARKUS tv
Reber,	NAPOLEON c Fr	Redon,	ODILON p,engr Fr
Rebhorn,	JAMES	Redpath,	JAMES j Am
Rebikov,	VLADIMIR c Rus	Redvers	BULLER(Sir)ar
Recasner,	MARIE-ALISE tv	Reed	DIAMOND
Reckell,	PETER tv	Reed	HADLEY tv+
Reclus,	JEAN geog,w Fr	Reed	HOWES
Recto,	CLARO st Phil	Reed	RUDY
Red	ADAIR oil fires Am	Reed	SMOOT st Am
Red	BARBER j-sp,tv Am	Reed,	ALAN Jr. tv+
Red	BENSON tv	Reed,	ALBERT tv
Red	BUTTONS cm,tv+ Am	Reed,	CAROL(Sir)d
Red	FOLEY s-cnt Am	Reed,	DONNA o-s'53,tv+
Red	GARLAND mj-piano Am	Reed,	ISAAC ed Br
Red	GRANGE fb hf	Reed,	ISHMAEL w po Am
Red	HOLZMAN bbc hf	Reed,	JERRY s+ Am
Red	HYMIE mj-trump Am	Reed,	JOHNj,po,radical Am
Red	INGLES mj-sax Am	Reed,	LADY
Red	MIHALIK bbr hf	Reed,	LOU mr,s,ws+ Am
Red	NICHOLS mj-corn,cn Am	Reed,	LUCILLE s,tv Am
Red	NORVO mj-vibes Am	Reed,	MARSHALL(1950's)tv
Red	PERKINS mj,cn Am	Reed,	MARSHALL(1970's)tv
Red	PRYSOCK mj-sax Am	Reed,	MAXWELL
Red	RODNEY mj-trump Am	Reed,	MICHAEL tv
Red	RUFFING b hf	Reed,	OLIVER
Red	SKELTON cm,tv+	Reed,	PAMELA tv+
Red	SMITH tv	Reed,	PAUL tv
Red	SOVINE s	Reed,	PHILIP
Red	WEST	Reed,	RALPH tv
Red Cloud	--- Am Indian Chief	Reed,	REX tv
Red Eagle	--- Am Indian Chief	Reed,	ROBERT tv+
Red Jacket	--- Am Indian Chief	Reed,	SHANNA tv+
Redanty	MARISA tv	Reed,	STANLEY l,supr ct
Redd	FOXX cm,tv+ Am	Reed,	TRACY tv+
Reddin,	ELIZABETH tv	Reed,	WALTER
Redding,	CHAD tv	Reed,	WALTER ar,md Am
Redding,	EARL tv	Reed,	WILLIS bb-m'70 hf
Redding,	NOEL mr-bass Br	Reed-Hall,	ALAINA tv

Reems,	HARRY porn actor Am
Rees,	ANGHARAD
Rees,	LANNY tv
Rees,	ROGER tv+
Reese,	DELLA s,tv+ Am
Reese,	LIZETTE po Am
Reese,	PEE WEE b hf
Reese,	TOM tv
Reeve,	CHRISTOPHER
Reeve,	CLARA w Br
Reeve,	TAPPING l,e Am
Reeves,	DAN fb hf
Reeves,	DEL s Am
Reeves,	GEORGE tv+
Reeves,	JIM s-cnt Am
Reeves,	KEANU
Reeves,	MARTHA mr-s Am
Reeves,	MELISSA tv
Reeves,	SASKIA
Reeves,	SCOTT tv+
Reeves,	STEVE
Reeves,	WILLIAM j,st N.Zea
Refrigerator PERRY fb	
Reg	LYE
Reg	PARK
Reg	PRESLEY mr-s Br
Regalbuto, JOE tv+	
Regan,	DONALD st Am
Regan,	ELLEN tv
Regan,	MARGIE tv
Regan,	MARY
Regas,	JACK tv
Regehr,	DUNCAN tv+
Regelson, WILLIAM md,w Am	
Regent,	BENOIT
Reger,	MAX c,e Ger
Reggiani,	SERGE
Reggie	JACKSON b hf
Reggie	MILLER bb
Reggie	NALDER
Reggie	WHITE fb
Regina	CARROL
Regina	GROVES tv
Regina	KING tv
Regina	KRUEGER tv
Regina	TAYLOR tv
Reginald	BRETT st Br
Reginald	De KOVEN c Am
Reginald	DENNY
Reginald	DOHERTY t Br
Reginald	GIBBONS po Am
Reginald	HUDLIN d,pr
Reginald	MARSH p Am
Reginald	McKENNA st Br
Reginald	OWEN
Reginald	POCOCK sc Br
Reginald	PUNNETT sc,e,ed Br
Regis	HUC r Fr
Regis	PHILBIN tv-host,w Am
Regis	TOOMEY tv+
Regnard,	JEAN w Fr

Regnier,	HENRI de po,ct,w Fr
Rehan,	ADA la+ Am
Rehnquist, WILLIAM.l,ch just Am	
Reich,	WILHELM ps,e Aus
Reicha,	ANTON c Cz
Reichenbach, HANS ph,e Ger	
Reichstein, THADEUS n-m'50	
Reid	SMITH tv
Reid	WHITELAW j,st Am
Reid,	ALASTAIR d
Reid,	BERYL
Reid,	CARL tv+
Reid,	CHRISTOPHER
Reid,	DAPHNE tv
Reid,	DON s-cnt,folk Am
Reid,	ELLIOT tv+
Reid,	FIONA
Reid,	FORREST w,ct Ir
Reid,	FRANCES tv
Reid,	GEORGE (Sir) st Aust
Reid,	HAROLD m-pop,cnt Am
Reid,	HARRY geol,e Am
Reid,	JIM mr-guit,s Scot
Reid,	KATE tv+
Reid,	MAYNE w Ir
Reid,	TIM II tv
Reid,	TIM tv+
Reid,	WHITELAW j,st Am
Reid,	WILLIAM mr-guit,s
Reidy,	AFFONSO ac Braz
Reil,	JOHANN md Ger
Reille,	HONORE ar Fr
Reilly,	CHARLES tv
Reilly,	HUGH tv+
Reilly,	JOHN tv+
Reilly,	TOM tv+
Reimers,	ED tv
Reina	KING tv
Reiner,	CARL d,tv+
Reiner,	FRITZ cn Am
Reiner,	ROB d,tv+
Reiner,	TRACY
Reinhard	KEISER c Ger
Reinhard	SCHEER navy Ger
Reinhard	SORGE w,po Ger
Reinhardt,	AD p Am
Reinhardt, DJANGO mj-gyps guit Fr	
Reinhardt, MAX d,mgr Aus	
Reinhart	DOZY h,e Dut
Reinhold	NIEBUHR r,w Am
Reinhold,	JUDGE
Reinken,	JOHANN organ,c Ger
Reinking,	ANN ba+ Am
Reinl,	HARALD d
Reis,	JOHANN sc Ger
Reiser,	PAUL tv+
Reiser,	PAUL w
Reisner,	GEORGE arc Am
Reith,	JOHN (Sir) eng-BBC
Reitman,	IVAN d,pr Cz
Rej,	MIKOLAJ w Pol

Rekert,	WINSTON tv+	Renee	FLEMING s-opera Am
Relly,	JAMES r Br	Renee	HOUSTON
Remak	RAMSAY	Renee	JONES tv
Remak,	ROBERT md,sc Ger	Renee	TAYLOR tv+
Remar,	JAMES	Renella,	PAT tv
Remarque,	ERICH j,w Ger	Renfro,	BRAD
Rembrandt	--- p,etch Dut	Renfro,	BRYAN tv
Rembrandt	PEALE p Am	Reni	SANTONI tv+
Remick,	LEE	Reni	GUIDO p It
Remington	STEELE fc-tv	Rennard,	DEBORAH tv+
Remington,	FREDERIC p,su Am	Renner,	KARL st Aus
Remizov,	ALEKSEY w Rus	Rennick,	NANCY tv
Remnick,	DAVID p-n'94	Rennie,	JOHN eng Scot
Remsen,	BERT tv+	Rennie,	MICHAEL tv+
Remsen,	IRA sc,e Am	Renny	HARLIN d
Remue,	CHARLES mj,cn Belg	Reno,	JANET st(DA) Am
Remy	LAURENT	Reno,	JESSE ar Am
Remy	O'NEILL	Reno,	KELLY
Remy de	GOURMONT w Fr	Renoir,	AUGUSTE p Fr
Remy,	ALBERT	Renoir,	JEAN d Fr
Ren	WOODS tv	Renoir,	PIERRE
Rena	SOFER tv	Renoir,	PIERRE p Fr
Renaldo	BENSON s Am	Renshaw,	ERNEST t Br
Renaldo,	DUNCAN tv+	Renshaw,	WILLIAM t Br
Renan,	ERNEST cr,w Fr	Rentaro	MIKUNI
Renan,	JOSEPH ph,ct,w Fr	Renwick,	JAMES ac Am
Renard,	ALPHONSE geol Belg	Renzi,	EVA
Renard,	JULES w Fr	Renzi,	MAGGIE
Renata	SCOTTO s It	Renzo	CESANA tv+
Renata	TEBALDI s-opera It	Repin,	ILYA p,e Rus
Renato	BRUSON bari Braz	Repnin,	ANIKITA ar Rus
Renato	GUTTUSO p It	Repplier,	AGNES w Am
Renato	VANNI	Repton,	HUMPHREY ac-land Br
Renault,	LOUIS id-cars Fr	Reri	GRISTS s-opera,ba
Renault,	LOUIS n-x'07	Resin,	DAN tv+
Renault,	MARY w S.Afr	Resnais,	ALAIN d
Renay,	LIZ	Ressam	LEVNI p Turk
Rendell,	RUTH w Br	Ressel,	JOSEF i Aus
Rene	BEHAINE w Fr	Restif,	NICOLAS w Fr
Rene	CASSIN l,st Fr	Reston,	JAMES j,w Am
Rene	CHAR po Fr	Reta	SHAW tv+
Rene	CLAIR w,d+ Fr	Rethel,	ALFRED p Ger
Rene	CLEMENT d	Reti,	RICHARD chess Hung
Rene	COTY st Fr	Reti,	RUDOLPH ct-music
Rene	DOUMIC w,ct Fr	Retief,	PIETER(Piet)st S.Afr
Rene	DUBOS sc,e,w Am	Rettig,	TOMMY tv+
Rene	GHIL po Fr	Rettino,	SHERRIL tv
Rene	GOBLET st Fr	Retz,	GILLES de ar,st Fr
Rene	HAUY sc,e Fr	Retzius,	ANDERS an,md Swe
Rene	LALIQUE id-glass Fr	Reuben	GRUNDY tv
Rene	LAVAN tv	Reuben	NAKIAN su Am
Rene	LECOSTE t Am	Reubens,	PAUL(PeeWee Herman)
Rene	MARAN w Fr	Reuter,	ERNST st Ger
Rene	PANHARD eng-cars Fr	Reuter,	PAUL von j Ger
Rene	RAY	Reuther,	WALTER labor Am
Rene	REAUMUR sc Fr	Reva	RAINES tv
Rene	RUSSO	Revell,	VILJO ac Finn
Rene	VIVIANI st Fr	Reverdy	JOHNSON st Am
Rene de	La SALLE(Sieur)x Fr	Reverdy,	PIERRE po,w Fr
Renee	ADOREE	Revere,	ANNE o-s'45
Renee	ESTEVEZ	Revere,	PAUL mr-kbds Am

Revere,	PAUL st,at-silver Am
Revier,	DOROTHY
Revill,	CLIVE
Revius,	JACOBUS w Dut
Rex	ALLEN
Rex	BEACH w Am
Rex	BELL
Rex	INGRAM
Rex	LEASE
Rex	REASON tv+
Rex	REED tv
Rex	ROBBINS tv
Rex	SMITH
Rex	STOUT w Am
Rex	WARNER w,po,ct Br
Rexford	TUGWELL ec,e,w Am
Rexroth,	KENNETH po,ct,w Am
Rey,	ALEJANDRO tv+
Rey,	ALVINO m,cn,tv Am
Rey,	BRUNO
Rey,	FERNANDO
Rey,	MONY
Reyes,	ALFONSO w, po Mex
Reyes,	ERNIE Jr. tv
Reyes,	KAMAR
Reyles,	CARLOS w Urug
Reymont,	WLADYSLAW n-l'24
Reynaldo	HAHN c Venz
Reynaud,	PAUL st Fr
Reynolds	PRICE w Am
Reynolds	ROGER c Am
Reynolds,	BURT tv+
Reynolds,	DEBBIE s+ Am
Reynolds,	GENE
Reynolds,	JAMES D. tv
Reynolds,	JOSHUA(Sir)p
Reynolds,	KATHRYN tv
Reynolds,	MARJORIE tv+
Reynolds,	QUENTIN tv
Reynolds,	SIMON tv
Reynolds,	VERA
Reynolds,	WILLIAM tv+
Reza	BADIYI d
Reza Shah	PAHLEVI(father-M.R.)
Reznikoff,	CHARLES po,w Am
Reznor,	TRENT mr-s Am
Rhames,	VING
Rhea	PERLMAN tv+
Rhee,	PHILLIP
Rhee,	SIMOM
Rhee,	SYNGMAN st Korea
Rhett,	ROBERT st Am
Rhijnvis	FEITH w Dut
Rhine,	JOSEPH ps,e Am
Rhoades,	BARBARA tv+
Rhodes,	CECIL st,f S.Afr
Rhodes,	CYNTHIA
Rhodes,	DONNELLY
Rhodes,	ERIK
Rhodes,	GEORGE tv
Rhodes,	HARI tv+

Rhodes,	NICK mr-kbds Br
Rhodes,	RICHARD p-n'88
Rhonda	FLEMING
Rhue,	MADLYN tv
Rhyne,	MIRANDA
Rhys	DAVIES w Welsh
Rhys	WILLIAMS
Rhys,	ERNEST ed,w Br
Rhys,	JEAN w Br
Rhys,	PAUL
Rhys-Davis,	JOHN
Riad	SOLH BEY st Lebanon
Rialson,	CANDICE
Ribalta,	FRANCISCO p Sp
Ribault,	JEAN navy Fr
Ribbentrop,	JOACHIMst Nazi Ger
Ribeiro,	ALFONSO tv+
Ribera,	JOSE de p Sp
Ribisi,	VONNI tv
Ribot,	THEODULE ps,e Fr
Ric	LEE mr-drm Br
Ric	OCASEK mr-guit,s Am
Ric	YOUNG
Ricarda	HUCH w,po Ger
Ricardo	ALFARO st Panama
Ricardo	CORTEZ
Ricardo	FREDA d
Ricardo	PALMA w Peru
Ricardo,	DAVID ec,st Br
Riccardo	MUTI c It
Riccati	JACOPO math It
Ricci,	CHRISTINA
Ricci,	MATTEO r It
Ricci,	NINA ds Fr
Riccio,	ANDREA su It
Rice,	ALICE w Am
Rice,	ANNE w Am
Rice,	DAN clown Am
Rice,	ELMER p-d'29
Rice,	FLORENCE
Rice,	FRANK
Rice,	GIGI tv
Rice,	GRANTLAND j-sports
Rice,	HOWARD tv
Rice,	JERRY fb-m'87
Rice,	JIM b-mv'78,hr &
Rice,	JIM hr'77'8'83
Rice,	ROSEMARY tv
Rice,	SAM b hf
Rich	HALL tv+
Rich	LITTLE cm,tv+ Am
Rich,	ADAM tv
Rich,	ADRIENNE po Am
Rich,	BARNABE ar,w Br
Rich,	BUDDY mj-drm,cn Am
Rich,	CHARLEY w-cnt,s Am
Rich,	CHRISTOPHER tv+
Rich,	CLAUDE
Rich,	DAVID LOWELL d
Rich,	DON tv
Rich,	ELI

Rich,	IRENE	Richard	DAVIS j,w Am
Rich,	JOHN(Lun) la,mgr Br	Richard	DAWSON tv+
Rich,	KATIE tv	Richard	DEACON tv+
Rich,	MICHAEL tv	Richard	DEHMEL po,w Ger
Richard	ABEGG sc,e Ger	Richard	DENNETT w Br
Richard	ADLER c Am	Richard	DENNING tv+
Richard	ALDRICH d	Richard	DERING organ,c Br
Richard	ARLEN	Richard	DERR
Richard	AVEDON fo Am	Richard	DIX
Richard	BACHMAN w Am	Richard	DIXON po Br
Richard	BAXTER w, r Br	Richard	DONNER d
Richard	BELZER tv+	Richard	DOYLE cr,p Br
Richard	BENNETT la,pr Am	Richard	DUNLAP tv-pr
Richard	BENTLEY r,ct Br	Richard	DYSART tv+
Richard	BERGMAN tv	Richard	EASTHAM tv
Richard	BERRY	Richard	EDER ct-books Am
Richard	BEYMER tv+	Richard	EDSON tv+
Richard	BISSELL w Am	Richard	EGAN
Richard	BONG ar,fly Am	Richard	ELLMANN ct,e Am
Richard	BOONE tv+	Richard	ELY ec,e Am
Richard	BOURKE(Sir)ar	Richard	ERDMAN tv+
Richard	BOWKER ed,w Am	Richard	ERNST sc Swi
Richard	BRIERS	Richard	EVANS tv
Richard	BRIGHT	Richard	EWELL ar Am
Richard	BROME w Br	Richard	EYER tv+
Richard	BROOKS d, tv+	Richard	FEYNMAN sc Am
Richard	BULL tv+	Richard	FINCH mr-bass Am
Richard	BURBAGE la Br	Richard	FLINT glaciers Am
Richard	BURTON	Richard	FORD w Am
Richard	BUSBY r,e Br	Richard	FORONJY
Richard	BUTLER mr-s,lyrics	Richard	FOX pb Am
Richard	BYRD x Am	Richard	FRANK tv
Richard	CAREW po Br	Richard	GABAI
Richard	CARLILE pb,ref Br	Richard	GERE
Richard	CARLSON tv+	Richard	GERING tv
Richard	CARLYLE tv	Richard	GRANT
Richard	CARTE m Br	Richard	GREENE tv+
Richard	CASEY st Austra	Richard	GRIECO tv+
Richard	CHAVES tv+	Richard	GUYON mercenary Br
Richard	CHURCH po,w,ct Br	Richard	HARRIS
Richard	CLAIR tv	Richard	HATCH tv+
Richard	COBDEN st,ec Br	Richard	HAYDN
Richard	COLLA d	Richard	HAYES tv
Richard	COLLIER tv	Richard	HELL mr-bass Am
Richard	COMAR tv	Richard	HERD tv+
Richard	COMPTON d	Richard	HILL tv+
Richard	CONTE	Richard	HOE i,id Am
Richard	COOGAN tv	Richard	HOOKER tv
Richard	CORRELL tv	Richard	HOPE
Richard	COSWAY p Br	Richard	HOVEY po Am
Richard	COX	Richard	HOWARD po Am
Richard	CRAMER	Richard	HUGHES w Br
Richard	CRANE	Richard	HUNT tv
Richard	CRASHAW po Br	Richard	JAECKEL tv+
Richard	CRENNA tv+	Richard	JEBB(Sir)e,w Scot
Richard	CROKER(Boss)st Am	Richard	JENKINS
Richard	CROOKS tenor Am	Richard	JOHNSON
Richard	DALEY st Am	Richard	JORDAN
Richard	DANA w,l Am	Richard	KANTOR tv
Richard	DAVALOS	Richard	KARN tv
Richard	DAVIES mr-kbds,s Br	Richard	KARRON tv

Richard	KEITH tv	Richard	SEFF tv
Richard	KIEL	Richard	SHEIL w,st Ir
Richard	KILEY tv+	Richard	SIMMONS health,tv
Richard	KIND tv	Richard	SIMON pb Am
Richard	KING rancher Am(TX)	Richard	SINATRA tv
Richard	KIRWAN sc Ir	Richard	SORGE j,spy Ger
Richard	KLINE tv	Richard	SQUIRES(Sir)st Can
Richard	KUHN sc Aus	Richard	STAHL tv+
Richard	LANE	Richard	STARK tv
Richard	LANG d	Richard	STEELE tv
Richard	LAWSON tv+	Richard	STEELE(Sir)w
Richard	LENZ tv	Richard	STERBAN m-bass,s Am
Richard	LESTER d	Richard	STERN j,ed,w Am
Richard	LEWIS tv+	Richard	STONE(Sir)ec
Richard	LONG tv+	Richard	STRAUSS c,cn Ger
Richard	LOO	Richard	SYNGE sc Br
Richard	LYNCH tv+	Richard	TANDY mr-bass Br
Richard	MARIN(Cheech)	Richard	TAUBER tenor Aus
Richard	MARION tv	Richard	TAYLOR sc Can
Richard	MARTIN	Richard	THOMAS tv+
Richard	MARX s,ws Am	Richard	THORPE d
Richard	MASUR tv+	Richard	TODD
Richard	McKENZIE tv	Richard	TRAVIS
Richard	MIDGLEY tv	Richard	TRENCH r,po Ir
Richard	MILES tv	Richard	TUCKER
Richard	MOIR	Richard	TURPINhighwayman Br
Richard	MOLL tv+	Richard	TYLER tv
Richard	MONETTE	Richard	TYSON tv+
Richard	MULCAHY st Ir	Richard	UPJOHN ac Am
Richard	MUNCHKIN d	Richard	VENTURE
Richard	NARITA tv	Richard	VOSS w Ger
Richard	NEUTRA ac Am	Richard	WAGNER c Ger
Richard	NEWTON tv	Richard	WALLACE d
Richard	NORTON	Richard	WATTIS tv+
Richard	OLDHAM geol Br	Richard	WEBB
Richard	OLNEY st Am	Richard	WERNICK c Am
Richard	PAUL tv+	Richard	WESSELL tv
Richard	PETTY car race Am	Richard	WHITING c Am
Richard	PIGOTT j,forger Ir	Richard	WIDMARK tv+
Richard	PIPES w Am	Richard	WIESE tv
Richard	PORTNOW	Richard	WILBUR po Am
Richard	PRESTON w Am	Richard	WILSON p Welsh
Richard	PRICE w,ph Welsh	Richard	WRIGHT w Am
Richard	PRYOR tv+	Richard	WYLER tv
Richard	QUINE tv+	Richard	YATES st Am
Richard	RETI chess Hung	Richard	YOUNG
Richard	RHODES w Am	Richard	ZOUCHE l,e Br
Richard	RIEHLE	Richard B.	SHULL tv+
Richard	ROBER	Richard E.BYRD navy,x Am	
Richard	ROBERTS md Br	Richard F.BURTON(Sir)x,w	
Richard	RODGERS c,w Am	Richard Paul EVANS w Am	
Richard	ROMANUS tv+	Richard von MISES math,e Am	
Richard	ROTHE r,e Ger	Richard,	CLIFF mr-drm,s India
Richard	RUSH d	Richard,	DARRYL tv
Richard	RUST tv+	Richard,	MAURICE ho-m'47
Richard	SANDERS tv+	Richard,	PIERRE
Richard	SAVAGE po Br	Richards,	ADDISON tv+
Richard	SCARRY w Am	Richards,	ANN
Richard	SCHAAL tv	Richards,	ARIANA
Richard	SEARS mer Am	Richards,	BEAH tv+
Richard	SEARS t Am	Richards,	CAROL tv

Richards, DANNY Jr. tv	Richmond, STEVE tv
Richards, DICKIN Jr n-m'56	Richmond, WARNER
Richards, EVAN	Richrath, GARY mr-guit Am
Richards, GRANT tv	Richter, BURTON n-p'76
Richards, I.A. ct,e,po Br	Richter, CHARLES sc,e Am
Richards, JEFF tv+	Richter, CONRAD p-f'51
Richards, KEITH mr-guit Br	Richter, DEBORAH
Richards, KIM tv+	Richter, FRANZ c Ger
Richards, LISA	Richter, HANS p,pr-films Am
Richards, LOU tv	Richter, HANS(Janos)cn Ger
Richards, MICHAEL tv+	Richter, JASON
Richards, PAUL tv	Richter, JEAN w Ger
Richards, RENEE(Dr.)t Am	Richter, PAUL
Richards, ROBERT o-g'52'56	Richthofen, MANFRED fly Ger &
Richards, ROBYN tv	Richthofen, MANFRED=RedBaron
Richards, THEODORE n-c'14	Rick ALLEN mr-drm Br &
Richardson, BURTON tv	Rick ALLEN=1 armed
Richardson, DOROTHY w Br	Rick ASTLEY s,ws Br
Richardson, ETHEL w Austra	Rick AVILES
Richardson, HENRY ac Am	Rick BARRY bb hf
Richardson, HENRY HANDEL w	Rick DANKO mr-bass,s Can
Richardson, IAN	Rick DEAN
Richardson, JACK	Rick DEES tv
Richardson, JACKIE tv	Rick FITTS tv+
Richardson, JAY	Rick GIANASI
Richardson, JOELY	Rick HURST tv
Richardson, JOHN	Rick HUXLEY mr-guit Br
Richardson, LEE	Rick JAMES s-funk,ws Am
Richardson, MICHAEL tv	Rick JASON tv+
Richardson, MIRANDA	Rick LAWLESS tv
Richardson, NATASHA	Rick MORANIS tv+
Richardson, OWEN(Sir)n-p'28	Rick NAJERA tv
Richardson, PATRICIA tv	Rick NIELSEN mr-guit,s
Richardson, RALPH(Sir)la+	Rick OVERTON
Richardson, SALLI	Rick PARFITT mr-guit,s
Richardson, SAMUEL w Br	Rick SAVAGE mr-bass Br
Richardson, SUSAN tv	Rick SLOANE d
Richardson, SY	Rick VALLIN
Richardson, TONY d-stage+ Br	Rick WEST mr-guit Br
Riche, GASPARD math,eng Fr	Rick WRIGHT mr-kbds Br
Richer, JEAN astr Fr	Rickards, TONY
Richet, CHARLES n-m'13	Rickenbacker,EDWARD fly,id Am
Richfield,EDWIN tv	Rickert, EDITH e,w Am
Richie ASHBURN b hf	Rickey KELMAN tv
Richie FURAY mr-guit,s Am	Rickey, BRANCH bmg hf
Richie HAVENS s-folk+ Am	Ricki LAKE tv+
Richie, LIONEL s,ws Am	Rickie JONES mj&mr-s,ws Am
Richier, LIGIER su Fr	Rickles, DON cm,tv+
Richings, JULIAN tv	Rickman, ALAN
Richler, MORDECAI w Can	Rickover, HYMAN navy-Adm Am
Richman, BOOMIE mj-sax Am	Ricky BELL mr,s Am
Richman, CARYN tv	Ricky COONCE drm Am
Richman, JEFFREY tv	Ricky DER tv
Richman, JONATHAN s Am	Ricky GOLDIN
Richman, PETER tv+	Ricky MARTIN tv
Richmond LATTIMORE po Am	Ricky NELSON m,tv+ Am
Richmond, BRANSCOMBE tv+	Ricky ROSS mr-s Scot
Richmond, DEON tv	Ricky SEGALL tv
Richmond, FIONA	Ricky VERA tv
Richmond, KANE	Rico CARTY b
Richmond, MITCH bb	Ridder, ALFONS De w Dut

Riddick	BOWE boxer Am	Rimmer,	WILLIAM p,su Am
Riddle,	JIMMY tv	Rimsky-Korsakov,NIKOLAY c,e	
Riddle,	NELSON mj,cn,tv+Am	Rinard,	FLORENCE tv
Ride,	SALLY as Am	Rincon,	EMANUELE c It
Rider,	FREEMONT ed,pb Am	Rinehart,	MARY w Am
Ridgeley,	ANDREW mr-guit Br	Ring	LARDNER w Am
Ridgely,	JOHN	Ring,	THERESA tv
Ridgely,	ROBERT tv+	Ringer,	SYDNEY md Br
Ridges,	STANLEY	Ringling,	ALFRED circus Am
Ridgway,	MATTHEW ar Am	Ringling,	CHARLES circus Am
Ridgway,	ROBERT birds Am	Ringling,	JOHN circus Am
Riding,	LAURA po,ct,w Am	Ringling,	OTTO circus Am
Ridley	SCOTT d	Ringo	STARRmr-drm,s,c+ Br
Ridley,	HENRY sc Br	Ringo,	JIM fb hf
Riecke,	CARL sc,e Ger	Ringwald,	MOLLY tv+
Riefenstahl, LENI d+		Rinna,	LISA tv
Rieffel,	LISA tv	Rioja,	FRANCISCO de po Sp
Rieger,	FRANTISEK st Cz	Riordan,	MARJORIE
Riegert,	PETER	Rip	TAYLOR tv+
Riehl,	ALOIS ph,e Ger	Rip	TORN
Riehle,	RICHARD	Ripkin,	CAL Jr b-mv'83'91
Riel,	LOUIS re Can	Ripley,	GEORGE r,ed,ct Am
Riemann,	GEORG math,e Ger	Ripley,	JOE tv
Riemann,	HUGO h-music,ct Ger	Ripley,	ROBERT.cr Am &
Rienzo,	COLA di re It	Ripley,	ROBT.=Blieve it or-
Riesz,	FRIGYES math,e Hung	Ripper,	MICHAEL
Rietveld,	GERRIT ac,ds-furn Dut	Rippy,	LEON
Rietz,	JULIUS c,cn Ger	Riqueti,	HONORE st Fr
Rif	HUTTON tv	Risdon,	ELISABETH
Rifkin,	JEREMY w Am	Rise	STEVENS s,tv+ Am
Rifkin,	RON tv+	Risley,	HERBERT(Sir)an,st
Rigaud,	ANDRE ar,re Haiti	Risso,	GIOVANNI sc It
Rigaud,	HYACINTHE p Fr	Rist,	JOHANN po Ger
Rigaud,	JORGE	Rist,	ROBBIE tv+
Rigby,	CATHY gy Am	Ristic,	JOVAN st Serb
Rigdon,	SIDNEY r Am	Risto	RYTI st Finn
Rigg,	DIANA tv+	Ristori,	ADELAIDE la It
Rigg,	REBECCA	Rita	CORDAY
Riggins,	JOHN fb hf	Rita	DOVE po Am
Riggs,	BOBBY t Am	Rita	GAM
Righi,	AUGUSTO sc,e It	Rita	JOHNSON
Rigoberta MENCHU st Guat		Rita	KARIN
Riha,	BOBBY tv	Rita	MACEDO
Riis,	JACOB j,w,ref Am	Rita	MORENO tv+
Rijn,	BRAD	Rita	QUIGLEY
Rik	ELSWIT mr-guit,s Am	Rita	RUDNER cm Am
Rik	MAYALL	Rita	TAGGART
Rik	SMITS bb	Rita Mae	BROWN w Am
Rik von	NUTTER	Ritch,	STEVEN tv
Riker,	ROBIN tv+	Ritchard,	CYRIL
Rikki	MARIN	Ritchey,	GEORGE astr Am
Riley,	ELAINE	Ritchie	VALENS mr-s Am
Riley,	JACK tv+	Ritchie,	MICHAEL d
Riley,	JAMES WHITCOMBpo,j	Ritschl,	FRIEDRICH w Ger
Riley,	JEANNINE	Ritsos,	YANNIS po Gr
Riley,	PAT bb,bbc	Ritt,	MARTIN d+
Rilke,	RAINER po Ger	Ritten,	EDDIE mj-tromb Am
Rilla,	WALTER	Ritter,	CARL geog Ger
Rimbaud,	ARTHUR po Fr	Ritter,	JOHN tv+
Rimes,	LeANN s-cnt Am	Ritter,	TEX s-cnt+ Am
Rimmer,	SHANE	Ritter,	THELMA

Ritterbusch,	DALE w Am		Robbins,	FREDERICK n-m'54
Rittner,	TADEUSZ w Pol		Robbins,	GALE
Ritz,	CESAR hotels Swi		Robbins,	HAROLD w Am
Ritza	BROWN		Robbins,	JEROME o-d'61,ba Am
Riva	SPIER		Robbins,	MARTY m-cnt,tv+ Am
Rivas,	ANGEL po,w Sp		Robbins,	PETER tv
Rivas,	CARLOS		Robbins,	REX tv
Rivelles,	AMPARO		Robbins,	TIM d,w+ Am
River	PHOENIX tv+		Robbins,	TOM ALAN tv
Rivera,	CHITA s,tv+ Am		Robbins,	TOM w Am
Rivera,	CRAIG tv		Robby	BENSON
Rivera,	DIEGO p Mex		Robby	KIGER tv+
Rivera,	GERALDO tv-host Am		Robe,	MIKE d
Rivera,	JOSE w,po Colom		Rober,	RICHARD
Rivera,	NAYA tv		Roberge,	SEAN tv
Rivera-Batisse, CHANTAL tv			Robert	ADAM ac Scot
Rivero,	GEORGE		Robert	AITKEN astr Am
Rivero,	JORGE		Robert	AITKEN su Am
Rivero,	JULIAN		Robert	ALDA tv+
Rivers,	JOAN tv+		Robert	ALLEN
Rivers,	JOHNNY mr,s Am		Robert	ALLOTT po,ed Br
Rivers,	LARRY p,su Am		Robert	ALTMAN d
Rivers,	THOMAS sc-md Am		Robert	ARDREY w Am
Rivet,	PAUL sc,w Fr		Robert	ARTHUR
Rixey,	EPPA b hf		Robert	AYTON(Sir)po Scot
Rizal,	JOSE st,w Phil		Robert	BARANY md,e Aus
Rizzio,	DAVID m It		Robert	BARCLAY r,w Scot
Rizzo,	GIANNI		Robert	BARRATT
Rizzuto,	PHIL b-mv'50 hf,tv		Robert	BARRON
Roach,	BERT		Robert	BEATTY
Roach,	HAL d		Robert	BELL mr,s Am
Roach,	MAX mj-drm Am		Robert	BELTRAN
Road,	MIKE tv		Robert	BENNETT c,cn Am
Roald	DAHL w Br		Robert	BENTON d
Roarke,	ADAM		Robert	BEVERLY h Am
Roarke,	JOHN tv		Robert	BLAKE tv+
Rob	DAVIS mr-s Br		Robert	BLY po,ed Am
Rob	ESTES tv		Robert	BOLT w Br
Rob	GRILL mr-bass,s Am		Robert	BONNER pb Am
Rob	HALFORD mr-s Br		Robert	BOSCH eng,id Ger
Rob	KNEPPER		Robert	BOYLE sc Br
Rob	LOWE		Robert	BRAY tv
Rob	MORROW tv		Robert	BRESSON d,w Fr
Rob	NARITA tv		Robert	BRIDGES po Br
Rob	NILSSON d+		Robert	BROOM sc S.Afr
Rob	REINER d,tv+		Robert	BROWN tv+
Rob	STONE tv		Robert	BROWNE tv
Robards,	GLENN tv		Robert	BRUCE king Scot
Robards,	JASON Jr o-s'76,'77		Robert	BUNSEN sc,i Ger
Robards,	JASON Sr.		Robert	BURKE
Robards,	SAM tv+		Robert	BURNS
Robb	WELLER tv		Robert	BURNS po Scot
Robb,	CHARLES st Am		Robert	BURTON
Robbe-Grillet, ALAIN w,ct Fr			Robert	BURTON r,w Br
Robbia,	LUCA della su It		Robert	BUTLER d
Robbie	BACHMAN mr-drm Can		Robert	BUTLER w Am
Robbie	KRIEGER mr-guit Am		Robert	CABAL tv
Robbie	RIST tv+		Robert	CAMBERT c Fr
Robbins,	BARBARA tv		Robert	CAMPIN p Belg
Robbins,	CINDY tv		Robert	CAPA fo Am
Robbins,	FRED tv		Robert	CARNEY navy Am

Robert	CARROLL tv	Robert	GINTY tv+
Robert	CARVER c Scot	Robert	GIST tv+
Robert	CASEY tv	Robert	GODDARD sc Am
Robert	CHAPMAN tv	Robert	GORMAN tv+
Robert	CHAVEZ tv	Robert	GOTHIE tv
Robert	CLARKE	Robert	GOULET s+ Am
Robert	CLARKE w Am	Robert	GRAVES po,w,ct Br
Robert	CLARY tv+	Robert	GRAY tv
Robert	CLIVE st Br	Robert	GRAY x Am
Robert	CLOUSE d	Robert	GREENE po,w Br
Robert	COCHRAN	Robert	GUNTON tv+
Robert	COFFIN po,w,e Am	Robert	HANLEY tv
Robert	COLBERT tv	Robert	HARDY
Robert	COLEBY	Robert	HARLAND tv
Robert	COLES w Am	Robert	HARPER tv+
Robert	CONRAD tv+	Robert	HARRIS tv
Robert	COOTE tv+	Robert	HAYDEN po Am
Robert	CRAY m-r&b,s,ws Am	Robert	HAYS tv+
Robert	CREELEY w,po Am	Robert	HEGYES tv+
Robert	CROSBY w Am	Robert	HENRI p Am
Robert	CULP tv+	Robert	HENRY (Buzzy)
Robert	DALTON outlaw Am.	Robert	HERRICK po Br
Robert	DAVI	Robert	HERRICK w Am
Robert	DAY d	Robert	HICHENS w Br
Robert	De NIRO	Robert	HILL ba Am
Robert	DESNOS po Fr	Robert	HILL d
Robert	DETT cn,c Am	Robert	HILLYER po Am
Robert	DIX	Robert	HOE id Am
Robert	DODSLEY po,w Br	Robert	HOGAN tv+
Robert	DOLLAR ships Am	Robert	HOLLEY sc Am
Robert	DONAT	Robert	HOMANS
Robert	DONNER tv+	Robert	HOOKE sc Br
Robert	DoQUI tv+	Robert	HOOKS tv+
Robert	DOUGLAS	Robert	HORTON tv+
Robert	DOWDELL tv	Robert	HOY tv
Robert	DOWNEY d	Robert	HUBER sc Ger
Robert	DOWNEY Jr. tv+	Robert	HUTTON
Robert	DUN mer,f Am	Robert	ITO tv+
Robert	DUNCAN po Am	Robert	JOFFREY ba Am
Robert	DUVALL	Robert	JOHNSON s-blues Am
Robert	EITNER h-music Ger	Robert	JONES (Bobby) g Am
Robert	ELLIOTT	Robert	JORDAN tv
Robert	ELLIS	Robert	JOY
Robert	EMMET st Iri	Robert	KAJANUS c Finn
Robert	ENGLUND tv+	Robert	KARNES tv
Robert	FAYRFAX c Br	Robert	KEANE
Robert	FEKE p Am	Robert	KEITH
Robert	FILMER (Sir) w	Robert	KELLY po,ed Am
Robert	FLEMYNG	Robert	KENNEDY st Am
Robert	FOGEL ec Am	Robert	KENT
Robert	FORSTER	Robert	KIDSTON sc Br
Robert	FOULIS mer-bks Scot	Robert	KLEIN cm,tv+ Am
Robert	FOULK tv	Robert	KOCH md,sc Ger
Robert	FRANZ organ,c Ger	Robert	KOCH tv
Robert	FRAZER	Robert	KORTMAN (Bob)
Robert	FRIPP mr-guit Br	Robert	LAMM mr-kbds,s Am
Robert	FROST po Am	Robert	LANSING tv+
Robert	FUEST d	Robert	LEONARD
Robert	FULLER tv+	Robert	LEONARD d
Robert	FULTON eng,i Am	Robert	LEVINE tv
Robert	GARNIER w Fr	Robert	LEWIS d

Robert	LEWIS tv-host Am	Robert	REMAK md,sc Ger
Robert	LEY st-Nazi Ger	Robert	RHETT st Am
Robert	LIEB tv	Robert	RIDGELY tv+
Robert	LIPTON tv	Robert	RIDGWAY birds Am
Robert	LOGAN tv	Robert	ROGERS frontier,ar
Robert	LOGGIA tv+	Robert	RUARK w Am
Robert	LOWELL po,e Am	Robert	RUSLER
Robert	LOWERY	Robert	RYAN tv+
Robert	LOWIE an,e Am	Robert	SAMPSON
Robert	LOWTH r,e Br	Robert	SCOTT navy,x Br
Robert	LUCAS Jr ec Am	Robert	SERVICE w,po Can
Robert	LUDLUM w Am	Robert	SHAW
Robert	LURIE(Bob)bmg	Robert	SHAYNE tv+
Robert	LYND soc,e Am	Robert	SHIELDS mime,tv Am
Robert	LYONS	Robert	SIMON tv+
Robert	MacIVER soc,e Am	Robert	SIODMAK d
Robert	MacNEIL tv-j Am	Robert	SMALLS navy,st Am
Robert	MANDAN tv+	Robert	SMIRKE(Sir)ac
Robert	MANNYNG po,h Br	Robert	SMITH mr-guit,s Br
Robert	McKIM	Robert	SOLOW ec Am
Robert	McNAMARA st,w,e Am	Robert	SOUTHEY po Br
Robert	MENZIES(Sir)st Aust	Robert	SPROUL e-u.Cal Am
Robert	MERRILL tv	Robert	STACK tv+
Robert	MERTON ec Am	Robert	STOBO ar Scot
Robert	MICHELS ec,e Ger	Robert	STONE w Am
Robert	MIRANDA	Robert	STOUT(Sir)st N.Zea
Robert	MITCHUM	Robert	STRAUSS
Robert	MORLEY	Robert	STROUD birds,murder
Robert	MORSE tv+	Robert	SURTEES w,j-spts Br
Robert	MOSES st Am	Robert	TAFT st Am
Robert	MOTON e,w Am	Robert	TANSEY d
Robert	MURPHY st Am	Robert	TAYLOR tv+
Robert	MUSIL w Ger	Robert	TESSIER
Robert	NEWTON	Robert	TROUT tv
Robert	NOYCE eng,i,id Am	Robert	URICH tv+
Robert	OWEN id,f,f Welsh	Robert	VAUGHN tv+
Robert	PAIGE tv+	Robert	VIHARO tv+
Robert	PALMER s,ws Br	Robert	WAGNER tv+
Robert	PARK j,e,w Am	Robert	WALDEN tv+
Robert	PARKER w Am	Robert	WALKER
Robert	PATRICK	Robert	WALKER Jr.
Robert	PEARY x Am	Robert	WALPOLE(Sir)st
Robert	PEEL(Sir)st	Robert	WARD c Am
Robert	PEIRCE tv	Robert	WARREN w,po Am
Robert	PICARDO tv+	Robert	WARWICK
Robert	PILATUS mr-s Am	Robert	WEBBER tv+
Robert	PINE p Br-Am,	Robert	WEIR p Am
Robert	PINE tv+	Robert	WILCOX
Robert	PINSKY w Am	Robert	WILKE tv
Robert	PITTMAN tv	Robert	WILSON la,w Br
Robert	PLANT mr-s Br	Robert	WILSON sc Am
Robert	POLLACK tv	Robert	WISE d
Robert	POWELL	Robert	WOLDERS tv
Robert	PRESTON s,tv+	Robert	WOODS tv
Robert	PROSKY tv+	Robert	WOOLSEY
Robert	PRUTZ w Ger	Robert	WRIGHT bus-NBC Am
Robert	QUARRY tv+	Robert	WUHL
Robert	RAIKES pb,ref Br	Robert	WYLIE p Am
Robert	RAINY r Scot	Robert	YERKES po,e,w Am
Robert	REDFORD	Robert	YOUNG d
Robert	REED tv+	Robert	YOUNG tv+

Robert	Z'DAR	Robertson,	DAVIES w Can
Robert	ZAEHNER h,e Br	Robertson,	DENNIS tv
Robert	ZUPPKE fbc Am	Robertson,	FRANCOIS tv
Robert de BORRON po Fr		Robertson,	KIMMY tv
Robert E. LEE ar Am		Robertson,	OSCAR bb-m'64 hf
Robert F LOGAN		Robertson,	PAT r,tv Am
Robert Lewis TAYLOR w Am		Robertson,	ROBBIE mr-guit,s
Robert N. BUTLER w Am		Robertson,	WILLIAM h Scot
Roberta	COLLINS	Robeson,	KENNETH w
Roberta	FLACK m Am	Robeson,	PAUL s+ Am
Roberta	HAYNES	Robey,	GEORGE(Sir)cm,la
Roberta	LEE tv	Robey,	LOUISE tv
Roberta	QUINLAN tv	Robie,	WENDY tv
Roberta	SHORE tv	Robin	COOK w Am
Roberta	VASQUEZ	Robin	DUKE tv+
Roberto	ALOMAR b	Robin	GAMMELL
Roberto	ARDIGO ph,e It	Robin	GIBB mr-s Br
Roberto	AVILA b	Robin	GIVENS tv+
Roberto	BENIGNI d+	Robin	GREER tv
Roberto	BRACCO w It	Robin	HARRIS
Roberto	DURAN boxer Am	Robin	HUGHES tv
Roberto	ORTIZ st Arg	Robin	IGNICO tv
Roberto,	ALAGNA tenor Fr-It	Robin	LEACH tv
Roberts	BLOSSOM	Robin	LIVELY tv+
Roberts,	ALAN d	Robin	MATTSON
Roberts,	ANDY tv	Robin	MORGAN tv
Roberts,	ARTHUR	Robin	NEDWELL tv
Roberts,	CHARLES(Sir)po,w Can	Robin	QUIVERS w,radio,tv+
Roberts,	COKIE tv-news Am	Robin	RIKER tv+
Roberts,	DAVIS tv	Robin	ROBERTS b hf
Roberts,	DES	Robin	ROSE tv
Roberts,	DORIS tv+	Robin	SPRY d
Roberts,	ELIZABETH w Am	Robin	THOMAS tv+
Roberts,	ERIC	Robin	TROWER mr-guit Br
Roberts,	FRANCESCA tv+	Robin	WRIGHT
Roberts,	GILBERT(Sir)eng	Robin	YOUNG tv
Roberts,	GLENN carrace Am	Robin	YOUNT b
Roberts,	JIM tv	Robin	ZANDER mr-guit,s Am
Roberts,	JULIA	Robin,	DIANE tv
Roberts,	KEITH ba Am	Robin,	LEO lyrics Am
Roberts,	KENNETH w Am	Robins,	LAILA tv+
Roberts,	LOIS tv	Robinson	JEFFERS po Am
Roberts,	LYNN(Mary Hart)	Robinson,	ANDREW(Andy)
Roberts,	MICHAEL D. tv+	Robinson,	BARTLETT tv
Roberts,	NORA w Am	Robinson,	BILL(Bojangles)ba
Roberts,	ORAL r,tv Am	Robinson,	BROOKS b-mv'64 hf
Roberts,	PERNELL tv+	Robinson,	BUMPER tv
Roberts,	RACHEL tv+	Robinson,	CHARLES tv+
Roberts,	RANDOLPH tv	Robinson,	CHRIS mr-guit,s,tv+
Roberts,	RICHARD n-m'93	Robinson,	CYNTHIA trump Am
Roberts,	ROBIN b hf	Robinson,	DAR
Roberts,	ROY tv+	Robinson,	DAVID bb-m'95
Roberts,	STEPHEN tv	Robinson,	DOUG tv
Roberts,	TANYA tv+	Robinson,	EDWARD G.
Roberts,	TONY tv+	Robinson,	EDWIN p-q'22'25'28
Roberts,	TRACY tv	Robinson,	FRAN tv
Roberts,	WINK	Robinson,	FRANCES
Roberts,	XAVIER id-dolls Am	Robinson,	FRANK b-mv'61'66,hf
Robertson,	BRIAN mr-guit Scot	Robinson,	HOLLY tv
Robertson,	CLIFF o-a'68,tv+	Robinson,	HUBBELL tv
Robertson,	DALE tv+	Robinson,	JACKIE b-mv'49, hf

Robinson,	JAMES h,e Am	Rod	BROGAN tv
Robinson,	JAY	Rod	CAMERON tv+
Robinson,	JOE	Rod	CAREW b
Robinson,	JOEL tv	Rod	COLBIN tv
Robinson,	LAURA tv	Rod	DANIEL d
Robinson,	LENNOX w Ir	Rod	GIST tv
Robinson,	RICH mr-guit Am	Rod	HOLCOMB d
Robinson,	ROBERT(Sir) n-c'47	Rod	La ROCQUE
Robinson,	RUSSELL PHILLIP tv	Rod	McCARY tv+
Robinson,	SMOKEY mr,s,s Am	Rod	McKUEN po Am
Robinson,	SUGAR RAY boxer Am	Rod	PERRY tv+
Robinson,	WILBERT b hf	Rod	SERLING w,tv Am
Roble,	CHET tv	Rod	STEIGER
Robles Emmanuel --- w Fr		Rod	STEWART s,ws3 Br
Robles,	GARCIA n-x'82	Rod	TAYLOR tv+
Robles,	GERMAN	Rod,	EDOUARD w Swi
Robley	EVANS navy Am &	Rodann,	ZIVA
Robley	EVANS=Fighting Bob	Rodd,	MARCIA tv+
Robson,	FLORA	Roddam,	FRANC d
Robson,	GREER	Roddy	BOTTUM mr-kbds Am
Robson,	MARK d	Roddy	DOYLE w Br
Robson,	MAY la+ Am	Roddy	FRAME mr-guit,s Scot
Robson,	WAYNE	Roddy	McDOWALL tv+
Robustelli, ANDY fb hf		Roddy	PIPER
Robusti,	JACOPO p It	Roddy-Maude ROXBY tv	
Robyn	--- s-pop,ws Swe	Rode,	EBBE
Robyn	DOUGLASS tv+	Rode,	HELGE po,w,ct Dan
Robyn	GIBBES	Rode,	PIERRE violin,e Fr
Robyn	MILLER tv	Roderick	COOK tv+
Robyn	RICHARDS tv	Roderick	WALLACE b hf
Roc,	PATRICIA	Rodgers,	JIMMIE s-cnt,c Am
Roca,	JULIO ar,st Arg	Rodgers,	NILE mr-guit Am
Rocco	SISTO	Rodgers,	PAMELA tv
Rocco,	ALEX tv+	Rodgers,	PAUL mr-s Br
Rocco,	MARE d	Rodgers,	RICHARD c,p-d'50
Roche,	EUGENE tv+	Rodin,	AUGUSTE su Fr
Roche,	SUZZY	Rodina,	IRINA sk Rus
Rochefort,JEAN		Rodman,	DENNIS bb,w Am
Rochelle	HUDSON tv+	Rodman,	THOMAS ar Am
Rochelle	OLIVER	Rodney	GRANT
Rochelle, CLAIRE		Rodney	HARVEY
Rochester,JOHN po Br		Rodney	LAY tv
Rock	HUDSON tv+	Rodney	PORTER sc,e Br
Rock,	CHRIS tv+	Rodney	SLATER m-sax,trump
Rock,	JOHN md,e Am	Rodney,	CAESAR re,st Am
Rockefeller, JOHN D.Sr f,f Am		Rodney,	RED mj-trump Am
Rockefeller, NELSON st Am		Rodo,	JOSE ph,w Urug
Rocket,	CHARLES tv+	Rodolfo	USIGLI w Mex
Rockne,	KNUTE fbc	Rodolphe	BRESDIN etch Fr
Rockwell	KENT p,illus Am	Rodrigo	OBREGON
Rockwell, JACK		Rodriguez, ALEX b,bat'96	
Rockwell, NORMAN illus Am		Rodriguez, ESTELITA	
Rockwell, ROBERT tv+		Rodriguez, IVAN b-gg'97	
Rockwell, ROCKY tv		Rodriguez, MARCO	
Rocky	AOKI	Rodriguez, PAUL tv+	
Rocky	CARROLL tv	Rodriguez, PERCY tv	
Rocky	COLE tv	Rodzinski, ARTUR cn Pol-Am	
Rocky	LANE	Roe,	CHUBBY CHUCK cm,tv
Rocky	SHAHAN tv	Roe,	EDWIN(Sir)id-planes
Rod	ALLEN mr-bass,s Br	Roe,	ELWIN(Preacher)b
Rod	ARGENT mr-kbds Br	Roe,	TOMMY s,ws Am

Roebling,	JOHN eng,id Am	Roger	YOUNG d
Roebuck	DANIEL	Roger Martin du GARD w Fr	
Roebuck,	JOHN md,i Br	Rogers	HORNSBY b hf
Roeg,	NICOLAS d	Rogers,	BRUCE ds-books,pb
Roemer,	FRIEDRICH geol,e Ger	Rogers,	CARL ps,e Am
Roentgen,	WILHELM n-p'01	Rogers,	CHARLES"Buddy"
Roerich,	NIKOLAY p Rus	Rogers,	EDITH st Am
Roethke,	THEODORE p-q'54	Rogers,	GINGER o-a'40
Roeves,	MAURICE	Rogers,	HENRY id-oil,f Am
Roger	ADAMS sc,e Am	Rogers,	IVAN
Roger	ASCHAM e,w Br	Rogers,	JAIME ba,tv Am
Roger	BACON sc,ph,w,e Br	Rogers	JEAN
Roger	BALDWIN ref Am	Rogers,	JIMMY
Roger	BALL m-sax Scot	Rogers,	KASEY tv
Roger	BOWEN tv+	Rogers,	KENNY s-cnt,tv+
Roger	CARMEL tv+	Rogers,	MARIANNE tv
Roger	CHAFFEE as Am	Rogers,	MIMI
Roger	CHAPMAN s Br	Rogers,	MISTER tv-host,pr
Roger	CLEMENS b	Rogers,	MOSES mariner Am
Roger	COE miler Br	Rogers,	PAUL
Roger	CONNOR b hf	Rogers,	ROBERT frontier,ar
Roger	CORMAN	Rogers,	ROY s,tv+ Am
Roger	CRAIG fb	Rogers,	SAMUEL po Br
Roger	DALTREY	Rogers,	STEVEN tv
Roger	DALTREY mr-s Br	Rogers,	SUZANNE tv
Roger	DAVIS tv+	Rogers,	TRISTAN tv
Roger	EBERT ct-films,tv	Rogers,	WAYNE tv+
Roger	EWING tv	Rogers,	WILL humor,w+ Am
Roger	FENTON fo Br	Rogers,	WILL Jr.
Roger	FISHER mr-guit Am	Rogert	PRETTO tv
Roger	FRY p, ct Br	Roget,	PETER md,w Br
Roger	GLOVER mr-bass Welsh	Rogier van der WEYDEN p Belg	
Roger	HODGSON mr-guit Br	Rogier,	CHARLES st Br
Roger	HOWARTH tv	Rogoberto JIMINEZ tv	
Roger	KINGDOM o-g'84'88	Rohde,	RUTH st Am
Roger	LAVERN mr-kbds Br	Roheim,	GEZA ps Hung
Roger	LIVESY	Rohlfs,	CHARLES ds-furn Am
Roger	MARIS b	Rohlfs,	CHRISTIAN p Ger
Roger	McGUINN mr-guit,s &	Rohm,	ERNST ar Ger
Roger	McGUINN = Jim	Rohm,	MARIA
Roger	MILLER s-cnt.cn Am	Rohmer,	ERIC d,w Fr
Roger	MOORE tv+	Rohner,	CLAYTON
Roger	MOSLEY tv+	Rohrer,	HEINRICH n-p'86
Roger	MUDD tv-j Am	Rojas,	FERNANDO de w Sp
Roger	OTWELL tv	Rojas,	MANUEL w Chile
Roger	PERRY tv+	Rojo,	GUSTAVO
Roger	PRICE tv	Roker,	AL tv-host
Roger	PRYOR	Roker,	ROXIE tv
Roger	QUILTER c Br	Roland	BARTHES ct,w Fr
Roger	REES tv+	Roland	BERTIN
Roger	SHERMAN l,st Am	Roland	CULVER
Roger	SMITH tv+	Roland	DIXON an,e Am
Roger	SPERRY md Am	Roland	GARROS fly Fr
Roger	TANEY 1st ch just	Roland	GIFT mr-s Br
Roger	TAYLOR mr-drm Br	Roland	GIGUERE po,p Can
Roger	TORREY tv	Roland	GOT
Roger	VADIM d	Roland	HAYES tenor Am
Roger	VERCEL w Fr	Roland	JOFFE d
Roger	VITRAC w Fr	Roland	LaSTARZA tv
Roger	WATERS mr-bass,s Br	Roland	ORZABAL mr-guit Br
Roger	WILSON tv+	Roland	PERRY p,su Am

Roland	WINTERS tv+		Rommel,	ERWIN ar Ger &
Roland	YOUNG		Rommel,	ERWIN = Desert Fox
Roland,	GILBERT		Romney	BRENT
Roland,	GYLIAN		Romney,	GEORGE p Br
Roland,	WILL tv		Romolo	GESSI ar,x It
Roldan,	PEDRO su,p,ac Sp		Romolo	VALLI
Roldano	LUPI		Romulo,	CARLOS ar,st,j Phil
Rolf	HOPPE		Romy	WINDSOR
Rolf,	TUTTA		Ron	CAREY tv+
Rolfe	SEDAN tv		Ron	CARTER mj-bass Am
Rolfe,	FREDERICK w Br		Ron	CASTRO tv
Rolfe,	GUY		Ron	CEY b
Rolland,	ROMAIN n-l'15		Ron	COCHRAN tv
Rolle,	ESTHER tv+		Ron	DARLING b
Rolle,	MICHEL math Fr		Ron	DEAN tv+
Rolli,	PAOLO po,lyrics It		Ron	ELY tv+
Rollie	FINGERS b hf		Ron	FASSLER tv
Rollin	KIRBY cr Am		Ron	FAZIO
Rolling Stones THE mr Am			Ron	GLASS tv+
Rollini,	ADRIAN mj-sax Am		Ron	GUIDRY b
Rollins,	AL ho-m'54		Ron	HARPER tv
Rollins,	HOWARD Jr tv+		Ron	HAYES tv
Rollins,	SONNY mj-sax Am		Ron	HENDREN tv
Rollo	MAY ps,w Am		Ron	HOWARD tv+
Rollo	OGDEN j,ed Am		Ron	LEIBMAN tv+
Rolls,	CHARLES fly,id-cars		Ron	MASAK tv+
Rolston	MARK		Ron	McLARTY tv+
Rolvaag,	OLE w,e Am		Ron	MIX fb hf
Roma	DOWNEY		Ron	MOODY
Romain	GARY w Fr		Ron	MOSS tv+
Romain,	ROLAND w Fr		Ron	NESSON j,press secy
Romains,	JULES w,po Fr		Ron	O'NEAL tv+
Roman	DMOWSKI st Pol		Ron	PALLILO tv+
Roman	GABRIEL fb		Ron	PERKINS tv
Roman,	GREG tv		Ron	PERLMAN tv+
Roman,	JOHAN viol,c Swe		Ron	RIFKIN tv+
Roman,	JOSEPH tv		Ron	RYAN tv
Roman,	LAUREN tv		Ron	SILVER tv+
Roman,	LETICIA		Ron	SOBLE tv
Roman,	LULU tv		Ron	TAYLOR tv
Roman,	PHIL d		Ron	TOMME tv
Roman,	RUTH tv+		Ron	TOWNSON mr-s Am
Romance,	VIVIANE		Ron	VanCLIFF
Romand,	BEATRICE		Ron	VAWTER
Romano,	ANDY tv+		Ron	WICKENS mj-drm,cn
Romano,	TONY tv		Ron	WOOD mr-guit Br
Romanus,	RICHARD tv+		Ron	ZIEGLER pr.secy-RLN
Romay,	LINA		Rona	BARRETT j,tv Am
Rombauer,	IRMA w-cookbk Am		Rona	JAFFE ct,w,tv Am
Romberg,	SIGMUND c Am		Ronald	BELL m-sax Am
Rome,	HAROLD c Am		Ronald	BUSHY mr-drm Am
Rome,	SYDNE		Ronald	COASE ec Br-Am
Romer,	ALFRED sc,e Am		Ronald	COLMAN tv+
Romer,	OLE astr Dan		Ronald	FANGEN w,ct Nor
Romero,	CARLOS tv		Ronald	FIRBANK w Br
Romero,	CESAR tv+		Ronald	HOWARD tv+
Romero,	CHANDA		Ronald	JOSEPH tv
Romero,	GEORGE d		Ronald	KEITH tv
Romero,	MATIAS ec,st Mex		Ronald	KESSLER w Am
Romero,	NED tv+		Ronald	LACEY
Romine,	CHARLES tv		Ronald	LAPREAD mr-bass Am

Ronald	LEWIS	Rosa	BONHEUR p Fr
Ronald	NEAME d	Rosa	PARKS civil rghts
Ronald	NORRISH sc Br	Rosa,	SALVATOR p,po It
Ronald	PICKUP	Rosalba	NERI
Ronald	REAGAN 40th Pres+	Rosales,	LUIS po,ct Sp
Ronald	ROSS(Sir)md Br	Rosalia de CASTRO w Sp
Ronald	STARR tv	Rosalind	ASHFORD mr,s Am
Ronalda	DOUGLAS tv	Rosalind	CASH
Rondo	HATTON	Rosalind	CHAO tv+
Ronet,	MAURICE	Rosalind	RUSSELL
Roni	STONEMAN tv	Rosalyn	YALOW md-sc Am
Ronne	TROUP tv	Rosamond	LEHMANN w Br
Ronne,	FINN x Am	Rosamond	SMITH w Am
Ronnie	BARKER	Rosana	De SOTO
Ronnie	BOND mr-drm Br	Rosanna	ARQUETTE
Ronnie	BURNS tv	Rosanna	HUFFMAN tv
Ronnie	DIO mr-s Am	Rosanne	CASH s-cnt Am
Ronnie	EDWARDS tv+	Rosanne	KATON
Ronnie	LANE mr-bass Br	Rosario,	BERT tv
Ronnie	LOTT fb	Rosario,	JOE tv
Ronnie	MILSAP s Am	Rosas,	JUAN de dictat Arg
Ronnie	SCHELL tv	Rosato,	TONY tv+
Ronnie	STEVENS tv	Rosay,	FRANCOISE
Ronny	COX tv+	Roscoe	ATES
Ronny	GRAHAM tv+	Roscoe	BORN tv+
Ronsard,	PIERRE de po Fr	Roscoe	KARNS tv+
Ronstadt,	LINDA s+ Am	Roscoe	POUND e,w Am
Rontgen,	WILHELM n-p'01	Roscoe	TANNER t Am
Rood,	OGDEN sc Am	Roscoe Lee BROWNE tv+
Roodt,	DARRELL d	Roscoe,	WILLIAM h,l Br
Rooke,	GEORGE(Sir)navy	Rose	COGHLAN la Am
Rooker,	MICHAEL	Rose	COOKE w Am
Roone	ARLEDGE tv exec Am	Rose	HOBART
Rooney,	ANDREW(Andy)tv-j Am	Rose	MARIE tv
Rooney,	ART fb hf	Rose	O'NEILL illus,w Am
Rooney,	MICKEY tv+	Rose	THORPE w Am
Roos,	SJOERD ds-books Dut	Rose Marie ---
Roosevelt BROWN fb hf		Rose,	AXL mr,s Am
Roosevelt GRIER fb,tv+		Rose,	BILLY pr Am
Roosevelt, BUDDY		Rose,	DAVID cn,ws,tv Am
Roosevelt, ELEANOR fe,w Am &		Rose,	FRED ws-cnt,s Am
Roosevelt, ELEANOR = FDR's wf		Rose,	GABRIELLE
Roosevelt, FRANKLIN D.32nd pres		Rose,	GEORGE
Roosevelt, SARA(FDR's mother)		Rose,	JAMIE tv+
Roosevelt, THEODORE 26th pres&		Rose,	JANE tv
Roosevelt, THEODORE n-x'06		Rose,	JUDD tv
Roosma,	JOHN bb hf	Rose,	LAURIE
Root,	AMANDA	Rose,	NICKY tv
Root,	ELIHU st,n-x'12	Rose,	NORMAN tv
Root,	GEORGE c,e Am	Rose,	PETE b-mv'73,2xgg's
Ropartz,	JOSEPH c Fr	Rose,	RALPH o-g'04'08
Roper,	ELMO j polls Am	Rose,	ROBIN tv
Roper,	WILLIAM bio Br	Rose,	VINCENT c Am
Rops,	FELICIEN p Belg	Roseanne ARNOLD(Barr)tv+
Rore,	CIPRIANO de c Belg	Roseanne BARR tv+
Rorem,	NED p-m'76	Rosel	ZECH
Rori	KING tv	Rosellen	BROWN w Am
Rorke,	HAYDEN tv+	Rosemarie JACKSON tv
Rory	CALHOUN tv+	Rosemary	ALTEA w Am
Rory	O'BRIEN tv	Rosemary	CLOONEY s,tv+ Am
Rory	O'MORE re Ir	Rosemary	DeCAMP tv+

Rosemary	FORSYTH	Ross,	WILLIAM(Sir)ph,ctScot
Rosemary	HARRIS tv+	Rossana	PODESTA
Rosemary	LANE mj-s Am	Rossana	YANNI
Rosemary	LEACH	Rossano	BRAZZI tv+
Rosemary	MURPHY tv+	Rossby,	CARL weather,e Am
Rosemary	RICE tv	Rossellini, ISABELLA	
Rosen	AL b-mv'53	Rossellini, ROBERTO d,pr It	
Rosen,	DANIEL tv	Rossetti, CHRISTINA po Br	
Rosen,	PHIL d	Rossetti, DANTE po, p Br	
Rosenberg, ALAN		Rossetti, WILLIAM ct,w Br	
Rosenberg, ALFRED w Nazi Ger		Rossi,	BRUNO sc Am
Rosenberg, ETHEL(wife-J)spy		Rossi,	FRANCIS mr-guit,s Br
Rosenberg, ISAAC po,p Br		Rossi,	GIOVANNI arc It
Rosenberg, JULIUS spy Am		Rossi,	LEO
Rosenberg, STUART d		Rossi,	LUKE tv
Rosenberg, TINA p-n'96		Rossi,	VITTORIO tv
Rosenbloom, MAXIE boxer Am &		Rossi-Stuart, GIACOMO(Jack)	
Rosenbloom, MAXIE=Slapsie		Rossington, GARY mr-guitar Am	
Rosencrantz, ZACHARY tv		Rossini, GIOACCHINO c It	
Rosenda	MONTEROS	Rossiter, LEONARD	
Rosenfield, ISADORE md,w Am		Rossitto, ANGELO	
Rosenfield, JOE(Big Joe)tv		Rossner, JUDITH w Am	
Rosengarden, BOBBY tv		Rosso,	GIOVANNI p It
Rosenwald,JULIUS mer,f Am		Rosso,	MEDARDO su It
Rosetta	LeNOIRE tv	Rossovich,RICK	
Roshan	SETH	Rostand, EDMOND w Fr	
Rosie	DALEY chef,w-ck bks	Rosten, LEO e,w-humor Am	
Rosie	O'DONNELL la,tv+ Am	Rosvaenge,HELGE tenor	
Rosie	PEREZ ba,tv+ Am	Roswell, MAGGIE tv	
Rosie	STONE mr-kbds,s Am	Roswitha --- po,w Ger	
Rosita	ARENAS	Roszak, THEODORE su Am	
Roslin,	ALEXANDER p Swe	Rota,	NINO c It
Rosner,	ADY mj,cn Pol	Rote,	KYLE tv
Rosollino,FRANK mj-tromb Am		Roter,	DIANE tv
Ross	FORD tv	Roth,	ALAN m,cn,tv Am
Ross	HAGEN tv+	Roth,	BOBBY d
Ross	MARTIN tv+	Roth,	DAVID mr-s Am
Ross	PEROT f Am	Roth,	HENRY w Am
Ross	SHAFER tv	Roth,	JACK tv
Ross	VALORY mr-bass Am	Roth,	JOE d
Ross	YOUNGS b hf	Roth,	LILLIAN
Ross,	ANNIE	Roth,	PHIL tv
Ross,	BETSY(US flag)Am	Roth,	PHILIP p-f'98
Ross,	CHELCIE	Roth,	TIM
Ross,	DIANA s+ Am	Rothe,	RICHARD r,e Ger
Ross,	DUNCAN tv	Rothery, STEVE mr-guit Br	
Ross,	EARL tv	Rothko, MARK p Am	
Ross,	GENE	Rothrock, CYNTHIA	
Ross,	HAROLD ed Am	Rothschild, MAYER f Ger	
Ross,	HERBERT d	Rothschild, NATHAN f Ger	
Ross,	JAMES(Sir)x Scot	Rothschild, SIGMUND tv	
Ross,	JERRY tv	Rothwell, RIC mr-drm Br	
Ross,	JOE tv	Rotrou, JEAN de w Fr	
Ross,	KATHARINE tv+	Rottlaender, YELLA	
Ross,	LANNY tv	Rouault, GEORGES p Fr	
Ross,	MARION tv+	Rouher, EUGENE st Fr	
Ross,	NELLIE st Am	Roumain, JACQUES w,st Haiti	
Ross,	RICKY mr-s Scot	Roundtree,RICHARD tv+	
Ross,	RONALD(Sir)n-m'02	Rountree, MARTHA tv	
Ross,	SHAVAR tv+	Rourke, CONSTANCE h Am	
Ross,	SINCLAIR w Can	Rourke, MICKEY	

Rous,	FRANCIS n-m'66	Roy	ORBISON mr,tv+ Am
Rouse,	CHRISTOPHER p-m'93	Roy	ROBERTS tv+
Roush,	EDD b hf	Roy	ROGERS s,tv+ Am
Rousseau,	HENRI p Fr	Roy	STUART tv
Rousseau,	JEAN ph,w Fr	Roy	THINNES tv+
Roussel,	ALBERT c Fr	Roy	THOMSON me-exec Br
Roussel,	MYRIEM	Roy	WILKINS cvl rts,ed
Roussin,	ANDRE w Fr	Roy	WOOD mr-guit,s Br
Routh,	EDWARD math,e Br	Roy	WORTERS ho
Rouvel,	CATHERINE	Roy Chapman ANDREWS sc,x,w Am
Rouvier,	MAURICE st Fr	Roy M.	COHN l Am
Rouvroy,	CLAUDE de ref Fr	Roy,	ARUNDHATI w India
Roux,	PIERRE md,sc Fr	Roy,	GABRIELLE w Can
Roux,	WILHELM sc,e Ger	Roy,	JOSEPH ct Can
Rovetta,	GEROLAMO w It	Roy,	PATRICK ho
Rowan,	DAN cm,tv Am	Roya	MEGNOT tv
Rowe,	MISTY tv+	Royal	DANO
Rowe,	NEVAN	Royal	HOUSE i Am
Rowe,	NICHOLAS pol'1715-	Royal,	ALLAN tv
Rowe,	VERNE tv	Royall	TYLER l,w Am
Rowell,	NEWTON l,st Can	Royall,	ANNE w,j Am
Rowland	HILL r Br	Royce	BRIER j Am
Rowland	LEE d	Royce	KENDALL s Am
Rowland,	HENRY sc,e Am	Royce,	HENRY(Sir)id-cars
Rowland,	KEVIN mr-guit,s Br	Royce,	JOSIAH ph,e,w Am
Rowland,	SHERWOOD n-c'95	Royce,	LIONEL
Rowlands,	GENA tv+	Roylance,	PAMELA tv
Rowlandson, MARY pioneer,w Am	Royle,	SELENA
Rowlandson, THOMAS at,cr Br	Roz	KELLY
Rowles,	POLLY tv+	Roz	RYAN tv
Rowley,	CYNTHIA ds Am	Rozanov,	VASILY w,ct,ph Rus
Rowley,	WILLIAM la,w Br	Rozario,	BOB tv
Rowse,	A.L. ct,po Br	Rozelle,	PETE fbc hf
Rowson,	SUSANNA la,w,e Am	Rozewicz,	TADEUSZ po,w Pol
Roxana	ZAL	Ruark,	ROBERT w Am
Roxann	BIGGS	Rubbia,	CARLO n-p'84
Roxanne	--- tv	Rube	GOLDBERG cr Am
Roxanne	BROOKS tv	Rube	WADDELL b hf
Roxanne	HART	Ruben	BLADES
Roxby,	RODDY-MAUDE tv	Ruben	DARIO po Nicar
Roxie	ROKER tv	Ruben	SIERRA b
Roy	ACUFF s-cnt Am	Ruben,	JOSEPH d
Roy	BAKER d	Ruben,	KATT SHEA d+
Roy	BARGY piano,cn,tv	Ruben,	TOM tv
Roy	BENTLEY po Am	Rubens,	ALMA
Roy	CHAPIN id Am	Rubens,	PETER p Belg
Roy	Del RUTH d	Rubes,	JAN
Roy	DOTRICE tv+	Rubey,	WILLIAM geol,e Am
Roy	DRUSKY s-cnt Am	Rubik,	ERNO i(the cube)Hun
Roy	ENGLE tv	Rubin,	BENNY tv+
Roy	FOX mj-cornet,cn Br	Rubin,	JENNIFER
Roy	FULLER po,w Br	Rubinek,	SAUL
Roy	GOLDMAN tv	Rubini,	GIULIA
Roy	HARRIS c Am	Rubinstein, ANTON piano,c Rus
Roy	HAY mr-guit,kbds Br	Rubinstein, ARTHUR piano Am
Roy	HAYNES mj-drm Am	Rubinstein, HELENA cosmetics Am
Roy	HOWARD j Am	Rubinstein, JOHN tv+
Roy	INNIS cvl rghts	Rubinstein, ZELDA
Roy	JENSON tv+	Rublyov,	ANDREY p Rus
Roy	KINNEAR	Ruby	DEE tv+
Roy	NEILL d	Ruby	KEELER

Ruby,	HARRY c Am	Ruffin,	EDMUND agricult Am
Ruck,	ALAN tv+	Ruffing,	RED b hf
Rucker,	DENNIS tv	Ruffini,	PAOLO math,sc,e It
Ruckert,	FRIEDRICH po Ger	Ruffo,	FABRIZIO r,ar It
Rudbeck,	OLOF sc-md Swe	Rufino	CUERVO w Colom
Rudd,	PAUL tv+	Rufino	TAMAYO p Mex
Rudd,	PHILIP mr-drm Aust	Rufus	CHOATE l,st Am
Rudder,	MICHAEL tv	Rufus	GILBERT md,i Am
Rude,	FRANCOIS su Fr	Rufus	JONES e,r Am
Rudi	DAVIES	Rufus	KING st Am
Rudkin,	DAVID w Br	Rufus	PECKHAM l,sup ct Am
Rudley,	HERBERT tv+	Rufus	PUTNAM pioneer Am
Rudner,	RITA cm Am	Ruge,	ARNOLD w Ger
Rudolf	ABEL spy Rus	Rugg,	HAROLD e,ed Am
Rudolf	BARTSCH w Aus	Ruggiero	BONGHI w,st It
Rudolf	BING opera-mgr Am	Ruggles,	CARL c Am
Rudolf	BRUN st Swi	Ruggles,	CHARLIE tv+
Rudolf	CARNAP ph,e Am	Ruginis,	VYTO
Rudolf	DIESEL i Ger	Ruhl,	JIM tv
Rudolf	DITZEN w Ger	Ruick,	BARBARA tv+
Rudolf	EUCKRN ph,e Ger	Ruick,	MELVILLE tv
Rudolf	FRIML piano,c Am	Ruisdael,	JACOB van p Dut
Rudolf	HALLEY tv	Ruisdael,	SALOMON van p
Rudolf	HAYM ph,h,e Ger	Ruiz,	ISAAC tv
Rudolf	KITTEL e,h Ger	Ruiz,	JUAN po Sp
Rudolf	LABAN ba Hung	Rukeyser,	MURIEL po,w Am
Rudolf	LOTZE ph,e Ger	Rule,	JANICE
Rudolf	NUREYEV ba+ Rus	Rulfo,	JUAN w Mex
Rudolf	OTTO ph,e,st Ger	Rumann,	SIG
Rudolf	SERKIN piano Am	Rumer	GODDEN w Br
Rudolf	SLANSKY st Cz	Rumpf,	GEORG sc Ger
Rudolf	SLATIN ar Aus	Rumsey,	JAMES i Am
Rudolf	VIRCHOW md-sc,st Ger	Runacre,	JENNY
Rudolf	WOLF astr Swi	Runciman,	STEVEN(Sir)h
Rudolf von	GNEIST l,st Ger	Rundgren,	TODD s,ws Am
Rudolph	DIRKS cr Am	Rundle	CIS tv
Rudolph	GANZ c,cn Am	Runeberg,	JOHAN po Finn
Rudolph	MARCUS sc Am	Runge,	FRIEDLIEB sc Ger
Rudolph	MATE d	Running Fox,	JOSEPH (Joe)
Rudolph	RASPE w Ger	Runyon,	DAMON j,w Am
Rudolph	RETI ct-music Serb	Runyon,	JENNIFER tv+
Rudolph	VALENTINO	Rupert	BROOKE po Br
Rudolph,	ALAN d	Rupert	CROSSE tv
Rudolph,	WILMA 3x o-g'60	Rupert	DAVIES
Rudulf	HESS st Nazi Ger	Rupert	EVERETT
Rudulph	EVANS su Fr	Rupert	GRAVES
Rudy	GATLIN s Am	Rupert	MURDOCH me Aust
Rudy	MOORE	Rupp,	ADOLPH bbc hf
Rudy	RAMOS tv+	Ruppell,	WILHELM sc,x Ger
Rudy	SOLARI tv	Ruppert,	JACOB,id-beer,bmg Am
Rudy	VALLEE mj-s,cn+ Am	Rusedski,	GREG t Br
Rudy	WIEBE w Can	Rush	LIMBAUGH radio Am
Rudy	WIEDOFT mj-sax Am	Rush,	BARBARA tv+
Rudy,	REED	Rush,	DEBRA tv
Rudyard	KIPLING w,po Br	Rush,	GEOFFREY o-a'96
Rue,	SARA tv	Rush,	MAGGIE tv
Rueda,	LOPE de w Sp	Rush,	RICHARD d
Ruediger	VOGLER	Rush,	WILLIAM su Am
Ruehl,	MERCEDES o-s'91	Rushdie,	SALMAN w,ct India
Rufe	DAVIS tv	Rushing,	JIMMY mj,s Am
Ruffin,	DAVID mr-s Am	Rushton,	JARED

Rusie,	AMOS b hf		Russell,	KIMBERLY tv
Rusinol,	SANTIAGO p,w Sp		Russell,	KURT
Rusk,	DEAN st Am		Russell,	LEON s-cnt,r&b Am
Rusk,	THOMAS st Am		Russell,	LILLIAN s,la Am
Ruska,	ERNEST n-p'86		Russell,	MARK humor tv
Ruskin,	JOHN w,ct-art Br		Russell,	MORGAN p Am
Ruskin,	JOSEPH		Russell,	NIPSEY cm,tv+ Am
Ruskin,	SHIMEN tv		Russell,	OLGA tv
Rusler,	ROBERT		Russell,	PEE WEE mj-clar Am
Russ	BENDER		Russell,	REB
Russ	CASE tv		Russell,	ROSALIND
Russ	COLUMBO mj,c Am		Russell,	THERESA
Russ	CONWAY tv		Russell,	WILLIAM tv+
Russ	GIGUERE mr-guit,s		Russell,	WILLIAM(Sir)j
Russ	HODGES b,tv		Russo,	JAMES
Russ	MEYER d		Russo,	RENE
Russ	TAMBLYN tv+		Rust,	RICHARD tv+
Russ,	WILLIAM tv+		Rustin,	BAYARD civil rts Am
Russek,	JORGE		Rusty	GILL tv
Russek,	LEE tv		Rusty	HAMER tv
Russel	CROUSE w Am		Rusty	STEVENS tv
Russel,	DEL tv		Rusty	YOUNG m-steel guit
Russell	ALGER st Am		Ruta	LEE tv+
Russell	ARMS s,tv+		Rutanya	ALDA
Russell	BANKS w Am		Rutger	HAUER
Russell	COLLINS		Ruth	ASAWA su Am
Russell	CROWE		Ruth	BROWN tv
Russell	GLEASON		Ruth	BUZZI cm,tv+ Am
Russell	HAYDEN		Ruth	COLLINS
Russell	HICKS		Ruth	COX tv+
Russell	HOPTON		Ruth	ENDERS tv
Russell	HULSE sc Am		Ruth	GATES tv
Russell	JOHNSON tv+		Ruth	GAYLOR mj-s Am
Russell	MYERS cr Am		Ruth	GORDON la,w+ Am
Russell	NYE w Am		Ruth	HALL
Russell	SAGE mer,f,st Am		Ruth	HUSSEY
Russell	SIMPSON		Ruth	McDEVITT tv+
Russell	THORSON tv		Ruth	McKENNEY w Am
Russell	TODD tv+		Ruth	MIX
Russell	VARIAN sc,i,e Am		Ruth	NELSON
Russell	WONG		Ruth	PAGE ba Am
Russell,	BERTRAND n-l'50		Ruth	POINTER s Am
Russell,	BETSY		Ruth	RENDELL w Br
Russell,	BILL bb-m'58'61 &		Ruth	ROHDE st Am
Russell,	BILL bb-m'62'3'5 hf		Ruth	ROMAN tv+
Russell,	BING		Ruth	ST. DENIS ba,e Am
Russell,	BOB tv		Ruth	STUART w Am
Russell,	CONNIE tv		Ruth	TERRY
Russell,	DON tv		Ruth	WARRICK tv+
Russell,	ELIZABETH		Ruth	YORKE tv
Russell,	GAIL		Ruth,	GEORGE HERMAN b &
Russell,	GEORGE mj-piano,c		Ruth,	GEO. HER. = Babe hf
Russell,	GEORGE w Ir		Rutherford,	ANGELO tv
Russell,	GRAHAM mr-s Br		Rutherford,	ANN
Russell,	HAROLD o-s'46		Rutherford,	ERNEST n-c'08
Russell,	HONEY bb hf		Rutherford,	JOHNNY carrace Am
Russell,	JANE		Rutherford,	MARGARET o-s'63
Russell,	JEANNIE tv		Rutherford,	PAUL mr-s Br
Russell,	JOHN tv+		Ruthven,	PATRICK ar Scot
Russell,	KAREN		Rutledge,	JOHN l,ch just Am
Russell,	KEN d		Ruttan,	SUSAN tv+

Ruvinskis,WOLF		
Ruyak,	BETH tv	
Ruysch,	RACHEL p Dut	
Ruysdael,	BASIL	
Ruyter,	MICHIEL navy Dut	
Ruz	CASTRO=Fidel st Cuba	
Ruzicka,	LEOPOLD n-c'39	
Ry	COODER m-r&b,guit,c	
Ryan	FRANCIS tv	
Ryan	JESSUP tv	
Ryan	McDONALD tv	
Ryan	O'NEAL tv+	
Ryan,	BUDDY fb	
Ryan,	DAVE(Chico)tv	
Ryan,	ELIZABETH t Am	
Ryan,	FRAN tv+	
Ryan,	IRENE tv	
Ryan,	JAMES	
Ryan,	JOAN j,w Am	
Ryan,	JOHN P. tv+	
Ryan,	LISA tv	
Ryan,	MARISA tv	
Ryan,	MEG	
Ryan,	MITCHELL tv+	
Ryan,	NOLAN b hf	
Ryan,	PEGGY tv+	
Ryan,	ROBERT tv+	
Ryan,	RON tv	
Ryan,	ROZ tv	
Ryan,	SHEILA	
Ryan,	STEVE tv	
Ryan,	TIM tv+	
Ryan,	TOM cr Am	
Rydberg,	ABRAHAM w Swe	
Rydell,	BOBBY tv	
Rydell,	CHRISTOPHER	
Rydell,	MARK d	
Ryder,	ALBERT p Am	
Ryder,	EDDIE tv	
Ryder,	MITCH mr-s Am	
Ryder,	PAUL mr-bass Br	
Ryder,	SHAUN mr-s Br	
Ryder,	WINONA	
Ryecart,	PATRICK	
Ryerson,	ANN tv	
Rykov,	ALEKSEY st Rus	
Ryle,	GILBERT ph,ed Br	
Ryle,	MARTIN(Sir) n-p'74	
Ryleyev,	KONDRATY po,re Rus	
Ryo	IKEBE	
Ryskind,	MORRIE p-d'32	
Ryti,	RISTO st Finn	
Ryu,	CHISHU	
Rzewuski,	HENRYK w Pol	

Remember:

All Pulitzer Prize Winners
  Are American.

All Poets Laureate(in this
  book) are British.

"S" NAME DESIGNATION CODES

s	SINGER
sc	SCIENTIST
sk	SKATER
ski	SKIER
soc	SOCIOLOGIST
sopr	SOPRANO
sp	SPORTSMAN-not b,bb,fb ho or t
st	STATESMAN or GOVERNMENT FIGURE
su	SCULPTOR
supr ct	U.S. SUPREME COURT
sw	SWIMMER

"S" NATIONALITY CODES

S.Afr	-	SOUTH AFRICAN
S.Leon	-	SIERRA LEONEAN
Salv	-	SALVADOREAN
Scot	-	SCOTTISH
Sp	-	SPANISH
Swe	-	SWEDISH
Swi	-	SWISS

"S's"

S.E.	HINTON w Am
S. Marc	JORDAN tv
S. Roy	LUBY d
S.F.B.	MORSE i,p,e Am
S.N.	BEHRMAN w Am
S.S.	McCLURE ed,pb Am
S.W.	WAYANS tv
S.Z.	SAKALL
Sa'd	ZAGHLUL l,j,st Egypt
Sa'di	--- po Persia
Sa,	MEM de st port
Saada,	ANTUN agitator Syria
Saam,	BYRUM tv
Saarinen,	EERO ac(son) Am
Saarinen,	ELIEL ac(father)Finn
Saavedra Lamas,	CARLOS n-x'36
Sab	SHIMONO
Sabatier,	PAUL n-c'12
Sabatini,	GABRIELA t Arg
Sabatini,	RAFAEL w It
Sabato,	ANTONIO
Sabato,	ANTONIO Jr tv
Sabato,	BO
Sabato,	ERNESTO w Arg
Sabean,	BRIAN bmg
Sabella,	ERNIE tv
Saberhagen,	BRET b-cy'85'9
Sabin,	ALBERT md Am
S.E.	HINTON w Am
S. Marc	JORDAN tv
S. Roy	LUBY d
S.F.B.	MORSE i,p,e Am
S.N.	BEHRMAN w Am
Sabu	---
Sacagawea	--- Am Indian guide

Sacasa,	JUAN st Nica	Sailer,	ANTON(Toni)3x o-g'56
Sacchetti,	FRANCO po,w It	Sain,	JOHNNY b
Sacchi,	ANDREA p It	Saint	TERESA r,w Sp
Sacchis,	GIOVANNI p It	Saint Laurentt, YVES ds
Sacco,	NICOLA radical Am	Saint,	EVA MARIE o-s'54
Sacco,	TONY mj-s Am	Saint,	H.F. w-scifi Br
Sacha	GUITRY w,la Fr	Saint-Amant, MARC po Fr
Sacha	PITOEFF	Saint-Beuve, CHARLES ct,w Fr
Sacher-Masoch,LEOPOLD von w Aus	Saint-Denys-Garneau,HECTOR po
Sacheverell SITWELL po,w Br	Saint-Exupery,ANTOINE de flyer,w
Sachi	PARKER	Saint-Gaudens,AUGUSTUS su Am
Sachiko	HIDARI	Saint-Just, LOUIS re Fr
Sachs,	CURT musicology,e Am	Saint-Saens, CAMILLE c Fr
Sachs,	HANS po,w,s Ger	Saint-Simon, CLAUDE ph,reform Fr
Sachs,	JULIUS von sc,e Ger	Saintsbury, GEORGE ct Br
Sachs,	LEONARD bbc hf	Sais,	MARIN
Sachs,	NELLY n-l'66,po	Sajak,	PAT tv-host Am
Sachs,	WILLIAM d	Sakall,	S.Z.
Sacino,	ANDREA tv	Sakata,	HAROLD
Sackler,	HOWARD p-d'69	Saker,	ALFRED r Br
Sacks,	OLIVER w Am	Sakharov, ANDREI sc,n-x'75
Sackville,THOMAS po,st Br	Saki	--- w Scot
Sackville-West,VICTORIA w,po Br	Sakic,	JOE ho
Sada	THOMPSON tv+	Sakmann,	BERT n-m'91
Sada,	KEIJI	Saks,	GENE d+
Sadat,	ANWAR st n-x'78	Sal	BANDO b
Saddam	HUSSEIN st Iraq	Sal	JENCO tv
Sade	--- s Nigeria	Sal	LANDI
Sade,	DONATIEN(Marquis de)w	Sal	LOPEZ
Sadi	--- po Persia	Sal	MAGLIE b
Sadi	CARNOT sc,eng Fr	Sal	MINEO
Sadie	FROST	Sal	SUSSMAN mj-guit Am
Sadler,	LAURA	Sal	VISCUSO tv+
Sadler,	MICHAEL st,ref Br	Sal	VIVIANO
Sadlier,	DENIS pb Am	Sala,	GEORGE w Br
Sadowsky, ADAM tv	Salacrou, ARMAND w Fr
Sady	REBBOT	Salam,	ABDUS n-p'79
Saeed	JAFFREY	Salamon,	JULIE w Cz-Am
Saenz,	MANUELA mistress Ecu	Salata,	GREGORY tv
Safarik,	PAVEL w Cz	Salazar,	ABEL
Safer,	MORLEY tv-j Am	Salazar,	ALBERTO marathons Cuba
Safire,	WILLIAM p-c'78	Salcido,	MICHAEL tv
Safranski,EDDIE m,cn,tv Am	Salda,	FRANTISEK ct,po,w Cz
Sagal,	BORIS d	Saldana,	THERESA tv+
Sagal	JEAN tv	Sale,	CHIC
Sagal,	KATEY tv+	Sale,	VIRGINIA tv
Sagal,	LIZ tv	Salem,	JESSICA tv
Sagan	LEWIS tv	Salem,	KARIO tv+
Sagan,	CARL n-p'78	Salemi,	PETE mj-tromb Am
Sagan,	FRANCOISE w Fr	Salenger, MEREDITH
Sage,	RUSSELL mer,f,st Am	Salerno,	CHARLENE tv
Sagebrecht, MARIANNE	Sales,	CLIFFORD tv
Sager,	RAY	Sales,	SOUPY tv
Saget,	BOB tv	Salieri,	ANTONIO c It
Sagoes,	KEN tv+	Salim,	HADJI st,r Indonesia
Sagra,	RAMON de la sc,re Sp	Salinas,	PEDRO po,w,ct Sp
Saha,	MEGHNAD astr,e India	Saline,	CAROL j,w Am
Sahagun,	ELENA	Salinger, DIANE
Sahara,	KENJI	Salinger, J.D. w Am
Sahl,	MORT cm Can	Salinger, MATT
Sahm,	DOUG mr-guit,s Am	Salk,	JONAS md Am

Salkin,	PASCALE	Sam	GROOM tv+
Salle,	MARIE ba Fr	Sam	HARDY
Sallee	ELYSE	Sam	HOPKINS mj-guit Am
Salli	FLYNN s,tv Am	Sam	HOUSTON ar,st Am
Salli	RICHARDSON	Sam	HUFF fb hf
Sallie	BROPHY tv	Sam	JAFFE tv+
Sallie	LAW nurse-CSA Am	Sam	JONES
Sallust	--- h Roman	Sam	JONES bb hf
Sally	BLANE	Sam	JONES tv
Sally	EILERS	Sam	LAWS tv
Sally	FIELD tv+	Sam	LEVENE
Sally	FORREST	Sam	McMURRAY tv
Sally	FRASER	Sam	MOORE s Am
Sally	GEESON	Sam	NEILL
Sally	GRAY	Sam	NUNN st Am
Sally	QUINN w Am	Sam	RAIMI d
Sally	RAND ba Am	Sam	RAYBURN st Am
Sally	RIDE as Am	Sam	RICE b hf
Sally Ann HOWES		Sam	ROBARDS tv+
Sally JessyRAPHAEL tv-hostess Am		Sam	SHEPARD w+ Am
Salman	RUSHDIE w,ct India	Sam	SNEAD g Am
Salmi,	ALBERT tv+	Sam	TAYLOR d
Salmon	CHASE st,l Am	Sam	WOOD d
Salome	JENS tv+	Samain,	ALBERT po Fr
Salomon	ANDREE eng,x Swe	Samantha	EGGAR
Salomon	GESSNER po Swi	Samantha	FOX s-pop Br
Salomon de BROSSE ac Fr		Samantha	MATHIS
Salomon,	ERICH fo Ger	Sambrel,	ALDO
Salomon,	HAYM mer,f Am	Sami	FREY
Salonen,	ESA-PEKKA cn	Samm-Art	WILLIAMS
Salonga,	LEA s,tv+ Phil	Sammee	TONG tv
Salsman,	MARK w Am	Sammes,	MIKE s,cn,tv Am
Salt	--- m rap Am	Sammi	DAVIS-VOSS tv+
Salt,	JENNIFER tv+	Sammi	SMITH s Am
Salt,	TITUS(Sir)id	Sammie	WINMILL tv
Salten,	FELIX w Hung	Samms,	EMMA tv+
Salter,	HARRY m,cn,tv Am	Sammy	BAUGH fb hf
Saltus,	EDGAR w Am	Sammy	CAHN lyrics Am
Saltykov,	MIKHAIL w Rus	Sammy	DAVIS Jr. cm,s,tv+ Am
Salvador	DALI p,etch Sp	Sammy	FAIN c Am
Salvador	LURIA sc Am	Sammy	HAGAR mr-guit,s Am
Salvator	ROSA p,po It	Sammy	JACKSON tv+
Salvatore FARINA w It		Sammy	KAHN lyrics Am
Salvatore VIGANO ba It		Sammy	KAYE mj-clarinet,cn Am
Salvatori,RENATO		Sammy	SNYDERS tv
Salvi,	NICCOLO su It	Sammy	SOSA b
Salviati,	ANTONIO at-mosaics It	Sammy	SPEAR m,cn,tv Am
Salvo	RANDONE	Sammy	WATKINS mj,cn Am
Sam	BARRY bbc hf	Samo	HUNG
Sam	BASS outlaw Am	Samoset	---Am Indian Leader
Sam	BEHRENS tv+	Sampler,	PHILECE tv
Sam	BOTTOMS	Samples,	ALVIN(Junior)tv
Sam	CASPIN mj-trump Am	Sampley,	JAMESON tv
Sam	COOKE s-gospel,r&b Am	Sampras,	PETE t Am
Sam	COWLING tv	Sampson,	ROBERT tv+
Sam	ELLIOTT tv+	Sampson,	WILL tv+
Sam	ERVIN st Am	Sampson,	WILLIAM navy Am
Sam	FLINT	Sams,	JEFFREY
Sam	FOSS ed,po Am	Samuel	ADAMS w.j Am
Sam	FREED tv	Samuel	AGNON w Isr
Sam	GOODEN mr-s Am	Samuel	ARGALL(Sir)adventure

Samuel	ARNOLD organ,c Br	Samuelson,PAUL n-e'70
Samuel	AVERY at,e Am	Samuelsson,BENGT n-m'82
Samuel	BARBER c Am	Samwell-Smith, PAUL mr-bass Br
Samuel	BECKETT w Ir	San Giacomo, LAURA
Samuel	BEMIS h,e Am	San Juan, OLGA
Samuel	BUTLER po Br	Sanborn, DAVID tv
Samuel	BUTLER po(d 1680)Br	Sanborn, JAMES bus-spices Am
Samuel	BUTLER w Br	Sanchez Vicario, ARANTXA t Sp
Samuel	CLEMENS w Am	Sanchez, BLANCA
Samuel	COLMAN p Am	Sanchez, JAIME
Samuel	COLT i,id Am	Sanchez, OSCAR n-x'87
Samuel	COOPER p Br	Sanchez, PEDRO
Samuel	CRISP w Br	Sanchez, SONIA po,w Am
Samuel	CUNARD(Sir)ships	Sand, GEORGE w Fr
Samuel	DANIEL po Br	Sand, PAUL tv+
Samuel	FOOTE la,w Br	Sanda, DOMINIQUE
Samuel	FROLER	Sandahl BERGMAN
Samuel	FULLER d+	Sanday, WILLIAM r,e Br
Samuel	GOLDWYN pr-films Am	Sandberg, RYNE b-mv'84,hr'90
Samuel	GOMPERS labor Am	Sandburg, CARL p-h'40,p-q'51
Samuel	GRAFTON tv	Sandby, PAUL p,engr Br
Samuel	HARTLIB ref Br	Sande, WALTER tv+
Samuel	HEARNE x Br	Sandeau, LEONARD w Fr
Samuel	HENZI re Swi	Sandel, CORA w Nor
Samuel	HINDS	Sander VANOCUR tv+
Samuel	HOAR l,st Am	Sander, OTTO
Samuel	HOUSTON ar,st Am	Sanders, BARRY fb-m'97
Samuel	HOWE md,e,ref Am	Sanders, BEVERLY tv
Samuel	INSULL id-elec Am	Sanders, GEORGE o-s'50
Samuel	JACKSON	Sanders, HARLAND(Col.)KFC Am
Samuel	JOHNSON ph,e Am	Sanders, JAY O. tv+
Samuel	JOHNSON(Dr.)l,e po Br	Sanders, LAWRENCE w Am
Samuel	KRESS mer Am	Sanders, LEON fb-d'94
Samuel	LANGLEY astr,e Am	Sanders, LUGENE tv
Samuel	LAWS e Am	Sanders, RAY tv
Samuel	LOVER w,ws Ir	Sanders, RICHARD tv+
Samuel	LOYD puzzles Am	Sanders, TERRY tv
Samuel	MORISON h Am	Sanderson,MARTYN
Samuel	MORSE(S.F.B.)p,i,e Am	Sanderson,WILLIAM tv+
Samuel	PARRIS r Am	Sandford, JOHN w Am
Samuel	PEPYS w,st Br	Sandi JENSEN tv
Samuel	RAYBURN st Am	Sandie SHAW s-pop Br
Samuel	ROGERS po Br	Sandino, AUGUSTO re Nica
Samuel	SCHEIDT organ,c Ger	Sandler, ADAM cm,tv Am
Samuel	SCUDDER sc,ed Am	Sandler, ALBERT mj-viol,cn Br
Samuel	SEABURY r Am	Sandler, BOBBY tv
Samuel	SELVON w Trinidad	Sandor PETOFI po Hung
Samuel	SEWALL mer,l,w Am	Sandor STERN d
Samuel	SLATER id Am	Sandor WEKERLE st Hung
Samuel	SMILES w Scot	Sandoval, MIGUEL tv+
Samuel	SUGDEN sc,e Br	Sandow, EUGENE strongman Am
Samuel	TELEKI x Hung	Sandoz, MARI bio,h Am
Samuel	TING sc Am	Sandra BROWN ba Am
Samuel	TUKE(Sir)ar,w	Sandra BROWN w Am
Samuel	WESLEY organ,c Br	Sandra BULLOCK tv+
Samuel	WHITSON tv	Sandra DEE tv+
Samuel	WILSON id-meat Am	Sandra DORNE
Samuel	WRIGHT tv	Sandra EGO tv
Samuel,	HERBERT(Sir)st	Sandra GOULD tv
Samuel,	JOANNE	Sandra KEARNS tv
		Sandra KERNS tv

Sandra	KNIGHT		Santiago,	SAUNDRA tv
Sandra	MILO		Santillana,	INIGO de po Sp
Sandra	NELSON tv		Santini,	GIULIANA tv
Sandra	OH		Santini,	TONY tv
Sandra	SMITH tv		Santo	---
Sandra	SPENCE tv		Santon,	PENNY tv
Sandra Day O'CONNOR supr.ct Am			Santoni,	RENI tv+
Sandrelli,STEFANIA			Santos,	EDUARDO st,pb Colom
Sandrich, MARK d			Santos,	JOE tv+
Sandro	GIGLIO		Santos,	MAXIMO st Urug
Sands,	BILLY tv		Santos-Dumont,ALBERTO fly Brz	
Sands,	DIANA		Santschi,	THOMAS
Sands,	JULIAN		Sanudo,	MARINO h It
Sandy	ALOMAR b		Sanz,	JORGE
Sandy	BARON		Saperstein, ABE bbc	
Sandy	BROOKE		Sapir,	EDWARD an,e Am
Sandy	DENNIS		Sappho	--- po Gr
Sandy	DESCHER tv+		Sapru,	TEJ(Sir)l,st India
Sandy	DUNCAN tv+		Sara	ALLGOOD
Sandy	FAISON tv		Sara	GILBERT tv+
Sandy	KENYON tv		Sara	HADEN
Sandy	KOUFAX b,tv hf		Sara	LANE tv+
Sandy	McPEAK		Sara	MONTIEL
Sandy	NELSON mj,mr-drm Am		Sara	RUE tv
Sandy	STEWART tv		Sara	SEEGAR tv
Sandy	WARD tv+		Sara Bay	NERI
Sandy,	GARY tv		Sara,	MIA
Sandys,	EDWIN r Br		Sarafian, DERAN d	
Sandys,	JOHN(Sir)h,e		Sarafian, RICHARD d	
Saneev,	VIKTOR o-g'68'72'76		Sarah	ABRELL tv
Sanford	CLUETT eng,id Am		Sarah	ADAMS po,hyms Br
Sanford	DOLE l,st Am		Sarah	DALLIN mr-s Br
Sanford	JENSEN tv		Sarah	DOUGLAS tv+
Sanford,	CHARLES m,cn,tv Am		Sarah	ELLIOTT w Am
Sanford,	ERSKINE		Sarah	GRIMKE fe Am
Sanford,	ISABEL tv+		Sarah	HALE w,ed Am
Sanford,	RALPH tv+		Sarah	KENNEDY tv
Sangallo,	ANTONIO ac It		Sarah	KNIGHT bus,w Am
Sangallo,	GIULIANO da ac,su It		Sarah	LYND po Br
Sanger,	EUGEN eng-rocket Aus		Sarah	MILES
Sanger,	FREDERICK n-c'58'80		Sarah	MILLIN w S.Afr
Sanger,	MARGARET fe Am		Sarah	MORTON po Am
Sangster, CHARLES po Can			Sarah	NATOLI tv
Sangster, MARGARET w Am			Sarah	PADDEN
Sankey,	IRA r,w-hyms Am		Sarah	PARKER tv+
Sankey,	JOHN l,st Br		Sarah	PURCELL tv-hostess Am
Sannazzaro, JACOPO po It			Sarah	SELBY tv+
Sansberry,HOPE tv			Sarah	SIDDONS la Br
Sansom,	ART cr Am		Sarah	TRIGGER
Sansom,	WILLIAM w Br		Sarah	VAUGHAN(Sassy)mj,s Am
Sanson,	CHARLES executioner Fr		Sarah	WHITMAN po Am
Santa Anna, ANTONIO ar,st Mex			Sarah	WOOLSEY w Am
Santana,	CARLOS mr-guit,s Mex		Sarah Orne JEWETT w Am	
Santayana,GEORGE ph,w,po,ct Am			Saramago,	JOSE n-l'98
Santha Rama RAU w			Sarandon,	CHRIS
Santi,	NELLO cn Am		Sarandon,	SUSAN o-a'95
Santiago	PEREZ st Colomb		Sarasin,	JEAN po Fr
Santiago	RUSINOL p,w Sp		Sarazen,	GENE g Am
Santiago, BENITO b,gg'88			Sardar	DAUD KHAN st Afgan
Santiago, CIRIO H. d			Sardou,	VICTORIEN w Fr
Santiago, HERMAN mr-s Am			Sarelle	LEILANI

Sarg,	TONY marionettes Am	Sauveur,	ALBERT sc,e Am
Sargent,	DICK tv+	Savage,	ANN
Sargent,	JOHN p Am	Savage,	ARTHUR id-arms Am
Sargent,	JOSEPH d	Savage,	BEN tv+
Sargeson,	FRANK w N.Zea	Savage,	BOOTH tv
Sari	MARITZA	Savage,	BRAD tv
Saris,	JOHN mer,mariner Br	Savage,	EDWARD p,engr Am
Sarita	CHOUDRAY	Savage,	FRED tv+
Sarkar,	JADUNATH(Sir)h,e In	Savage,	JOHN
Sarmiento,	FELIX po,w Nica	Savage,	RICHARD w,po Br
Sarnoff,	DAVID id-RCA Am	Savage,	RICK mr-bass Br
Sarojini	NAIDU po India	Saval,	DANY
Saroyan,	WILLIAM w Am	Savalas,	CANDACE tv
Sarpi,	PIETRO r,h,sc It	Savalas,	GEORGE tv
Sarrail,	MAURICE ar Fr	Savalas,	TELLY tv+
Sarraut,	ALBERT st Fr	Savant,	DOUG tv+
Sarrazin,	MICHAEL	Savarkar,	VIR st,re India
Sars,	MICHAEL sc,e Nor	Savart,	FELIX md,sc,e Fr
Sartain,	GAILARD tv+	Savary,	ANNE ar,st Fr
Sartain,	JOHN engr Am	Saveli,	LUCA st Ro
Sarti,	GIUSEPPE c It	Savery,	THOMAS eng-ar Br
Sarto,	ANDREA del p It	Saviano,	JOSH tv
Sarton,	GEORGE h-science,e Am	Savidge,	JENNIFER tv
Sarton,	MAY po,w Am	Savile,	HENRY(Sir)e
Sartre,	JEAN ph,w,ct,e Fr	Saville,	PHILIP d
Sarzec,	GUSTAVE archeol,st Fr	Saville,	VICTOR d
Sasaki,	KATSUHIKO	Savina	GERSAK
Sasdy,	PETER d	Savini,	TOM
Sasha	JENSEN	Savitch,	JESSICA tv-j,anchor Am
Saskia	POST	Savoca,	NANCY d
Saskia	REEVES	Savold,	LEE boxer Am
Sasser,	JIM st(sen-TN)	Saw,	U st Burma
Sassoon,	CATYA"Cat"	Sawallisch,	WOLFGANG cn
Sassoon,	SIEGFRIED po,bio Br	Sawyer,	BUZ fc
Sassoon,	VIDAL hair stylist Br	Sawyer,	DIANE tv-j,host Am
Sassy	VAUGHN(Sarah)mj-s Am	Sawyer,	JOE tv
Sastre,	ALFONSO w Sp	Sawyer,	JOSEPH
Sastri,	LINA	Sawyer,	RAY mr-s Am
Sastri,	VALANGIMAN st India	Sax,	ANTOINE id-mus.insts
Satana,	TURA	Sax,	GUNNE ds Am
Satchel	PAIGE b hf	Saxon,	JOHN tv+
Satie,	ERIK c Fr	Saxton,	JOSEPH i Am
Sato,	EISAKU n-x'74	Say,	JEAN ec.ed Fr
Sato,	KEI	Say,	THOMAS sc,e Am
Satyajit	RAY pr-films India	Sayer,	LEO s,ws Br
Satyendra	SINHA(Sir)l,st India	Sayers,	DOROTHY w Br
Sauer,	CARL geog,e Am	Sayers,	GALE fb hf
Sauer,	HANK b-mv'52	Sayers,	TOM boxer Br
Saul	ALINSKY reformer Am	Sayle,	ALEXEI
Saul	BELLOW w Am	Sayles,	JOHN d+
Saul	RUBINEK	Saylor,	SYD tv+
Saunders,	JIMMY mj-piano Am	Sayno,	BIOU sopr
Saunders,	LEW tv	Sayre,	LEWIS md,e Am
Saunders,	LORI tv	Sayyid	AMIR ALI l,w India
Saunders,	MARY JANE tv	Sayyid	HASAN r Somali
Saunders,	NICHOLAS tv	Sazonov,	SERGEY st Rus
Saundra	SHARP tv	Sbarge,	RAPHAEL
Saura,	CARLOS d	Sbragia,	MATTIA
Sauser,	FREDERIC w,po Swi	Scabies,	RAT mr-drm Br
Sautet,	CLAUDE d	Scacchi,	GRETA
		Scaggs,	BOZ mr-guitar,s,w-songs

Scala,   GIA
Scales,   PRUNELLA
Scalia,   JACK tv+
Scaligero,GIULIO ct It
Scannell,   KEVIN tv+
Scannell,   SUSAN tv
Scarabelli, MICHELLE tv+
Scarborough, CHUCK tv
Scarface   CAPONE(Al)gangster Am
Scarfe,   ALAN tv+
Scarpa,   ANTONIO md It
Scarpelli,GLENN tv
Scarron,   PAUL w,po Fr
Scarry,   RICHARD w
Scarwid,   DIANA
Sceve,   MAURICE po Fr
Scewcroft,BRENT st
Schaaf,   LILLIAN tv
Schaal,   RICHARD tv
Schaal,   WENDY tv+
Schaalow,   ARTHUR n-p'81
Schacher,   MEL mr-bass Am
Schacht,   HJALMAR f-banker Ger
Schack   KROGH md Dan
Schackelford,MICHAEL DAVID tv
Schacter,   FELICE tv
Schadler,   JAY tv
Schadow,   JOHANN su Ger
Schaefer,   ARMAND d
Schaefer,   GEORGE d
Schaefer,   LAUREL tv
Schaeffer,REBECCA tv+
Schafer,   NATALIE tv+
Schafer,   WILHELM w Ger
Schaff,   PHILLIP r,w Am
Schaffner, FRANKLIN o-d'70
Schalk,   RAY b hf
Schallert,WILLIAM tv+
Schally,   ANDREW n-m'77
Schaper,   JOHANN ceramics Ger
Scharf,   SABRINA
Scharf,   WALTER c Am
Scharwenka, FRANZ piano,c,e Ger
Scharwenka, LUDWIG piano,c Ger
Schary,   DORE pr-films Am
Schatzberg, JERRY d
Schayes,   ADOLPH(Dolph)bb hf
Schedeen,   ANNE tv
Scheele,   CARL sc Swe
Scheer,   REINHARD navy Ger
Scheider,   ROY
Scheidt,   SAMUEL organ,c Ger
Schein,   JOHANN c Ger
Scheler,   MAX ph,e Ger
Schell,   CATHERINE tv+
Schell,   MARIA
Schell,   MAXMILLIAN o-a'61,tv+
Schell,   RONNIE tv
Schellenberg, AUGUST
Schenkel,   CARL d
Schenkkan,ROBERT p-d'92

Schepisi,   FRED d
Scherer,   WILHELM e,w Ger
Schermie,   JOE mr-bass Am
Schiaffino, ROSANNA
Schiaparelli, ELSA ds Fr
Schiavelli, VINCENT tv+
Schick,   BELA md,e Am
Schick,   GEORGE tv
Schiele,   EGON p Aus
Schiff,   JACOB banker,f Am
Schiff   MARTY tv
Schiff,   MORITZ md,e Ger
Schiffer,   CLAUDIA mo Ger
Schifrin,   LALO mj Am
Schildkraut, JOSEPH o-s'37
Schilling,VIVIAN
Schilling,WILLIAM G. tv
Schine,   CATHLEEN w Am
Schiner,   MATTHAUS r Swi
Schipa,   TITO tenor
Schlaf,   JOHANNES w Ger
Schlatter,CHARLIE
Schlegel,   AUGUST von e,po,ct Ger
Schlemmer,OSKAR p,su Ger
Schlesinger, ARTHUR.Jr p-h'46 &
Schlesinger, ARTHUR.Jr p-b'66
Schlesinger, JOHN o-d'69
Schlesinger, RICHARD tv
Schley,   WINFIELD navy Am
Schlich,   WILLIAM(Sir)forester,e
Schlick,   MORITZ ph,e Ger
Schlitt,   CAROLINE tv
Schlondorff, VOLKER d
Schluter,   ANDREAS su,ac Ger
Schmid,   EDUARD w Ger
Schmidt,   ERNEST bb hf
Schmidt,   JOE fb hf
Schmidt,   JOZEF o-g'60'64
Schmidt,   MIKE b-mv'80'1'6 hf
Schmidt,   MILT ho-m'51
Schmidt,   OTTO w Ger
Schmitt,   FLORENT c Fr
Schmitz,   ETTORE w It
Schmitz,   SYBILLE
Schmock,   JONATHAN tv
Schmoeller, DAVID d
Schnabel,   ARTUR piano,c Am
Schnabel,   STEFAN
Schneider, DANIEL J. tv
Schneider, FRED mr-kbds,s Am
Schneider, JOHN tv+
Schneider, MARIA
Schneider, ROB tv+
Schneider, ROMY
Schneider, TAWNY tv
Schnetzer, STEPHEN tv
Schnitzler, ARTHUR md,w Aus
Schober,   JOHANN st Aus
Schoeck,   OTHMAR c Swi
Schoeffling, MICHAEL
Schoelen,   JILL

Schoenberg, ARNOLD e,c Am
Schoendienst, RED b,bmg hf
Scholem, GERSHOM w Isr
Scholes, MYRON n-e'97
Scholz, ALFRED c
Scholz, TOM mr-guit,kbds Am
Schommer, JOHN bb hf
Schon, NEAL mr-guit Am
Schoner, JOHANNES astr,geog Ger
Schongauer, MARTIN p,engr Ger
Schoolcraft, HENRY x,sc,w Am
Schopenhauer, ARTHUR ph Ger
Schorer, MARK w,ct Am
Schorr, DANIEL tv-j Am
Schorr, LONNIE tv
Schorske, CARL p-n'81
Schrader, PAUL d
Schramm, DAVID tv
Schramm, TEX fb hf
Schreck, VICKI tv
Schreiber,AVERY tv+
Schreiner,OLIVE w S.Afr
Schrieffer, JOHN n-p'72
Schriver, PAM t Am
Schroder, CARL c,cn Ger
Schroder, RICK tv+
Schrodinger, ERWIN n-p'33
Schroeder,BARBET d
Schrum, PETE tv
Schubert, FRANZ c,e Aus
Schubert, KARIN
Schuck, JOHAN h-lit,e Swe
Schuck, JOHN tv+
Schuck, PETER tv
Schulberg,BUDD w Am
Schull, REBECCA tv
Schulman, EMILY tv
Schulte, JOHANN e Ger
Schultz, CARL d
Schultz, DWIGHT tv+
Schultz, KEVIN tv
Schultz, MICHAEL d
Schultz, THEODORE n-e'79
Schulz, CHARLES cr Am
Schulze, ALFRED p Fr
Schulze, GOTTLOB ph,e Ger
Schumacher, JOEL d
Schumacher, JULIE w Am
Schumacher, MICHAEL carrace Am
Schuman, WILLIAM p-m'43
Schumann, CLARA piano,c Ger
Schumann, ROBERT c Ger
Schunzel, REINHOLD
Schur, FRIEDRICH math,e Ger
Schurman, JACOB e,st,w Am
Schurz, CARL ar,st,ref Am
Schuster, HAROLD d
Schutz, HEINRICH c Ger
Schuyler, JAMES w,p-q'81
Schwab, CHARLES bus-broker Am
Schwab, CHARLES id-steel Am

Schwantner, JOSEPH p-m'79
Schwartz, AARON tv
Schwartz, ARTHUR c Am
Schwartz, DELMORE po,w,ct Am
Schwartz, DOROTHY tv
Schwartz, MELVIN n-p'88
Schwartz, NEIL tv
Schwarz, GERARD cn Am
Schwarz-Bart, ANDRE w Fr
Schwarzenegger, ARNOLD
Schwarzkopf, NORMAN ar-ret. Am
Schweig, ERIC
Schweitzer, ALBERT ph,m,md,n-x'52
Schwimmer,ROSIKA fe Hung
Schwind, MORITZ von p Ger
Schwinger,JULIAN n-p'65
Schygulla, HANNA
Schyuler FISK
Scilla GABEL
Sciorra, ANNABELLA
Scipio, GNAEUS ar Ro
Scob, EDITH
Scoey MITCHELL tv+
Scofield, PAUL o-a'66
Scogan, HENRY po Br
Scoggins, TRACY tv+
Scola, ETTORE d
Scolari, MICHAEL tv
Scolari, PETER tv+
Scooler, ZVEE
Scoop JACKSON st Am
Scopes, JOHN e Am
Scorsese, MARTIN d+
Scot, MICHAEL astrology Scot
Scott BAIO tv+
Scott BAKULA
Scott BLOOM tv
Scott BRADY tv+
Scott BREMMER tv
Scott COFFEY
Scott COLOMBY
Scott ENGEL mr-s Am
Scott FORBES tv
Scott GLENN
Scott GORHAM mr-guit Am
Scott GRIMES
Scott HOXBY tv
Scott HYLANDS tv+
Scott JACOBY
Scott JOPLIN mj-piano,c Am
Scott La ROSE tv
Scott LaFARO mj-bass Am
Scott LANE tv
Scott McGINNIS tv+
Scott MELLINI tv
Scott MILLER tv
Scott MURPHY tv
Scott NEMES tv
Scott PAULIN
Scott PETERS tv
Scott PLANK

Scott	POWELL tv	Scott,	SUSAN
Scott	REEVES tv+	Scott,	SYNDA tv
Scott	SHANNON tv	Scott,	TIMOTHY tv+
Scott	TUROW w Am	Scott,	TOM tv
Scott	WEINGER tv	Scott,	TONY d
Scott	WILSON	Scott,	WALTER(Sir)w,po Scot
Scott Thomas, KRISTIN		Scott,	WILLARD tv-weather Am
Scott,	ALAN tv	Scott,	ZACHARY tv+
Scott,	ALEX	Scott-Heron, GIL m-rap	
Scott,	ANDY mr-guit Welsh	Scott-Peck, M. w Am	
Scott,	BILL tv	Scotti,	VITO tv+
Scott,	BON mr-s Scot	Scotto,	RENATA s It
Scott,	BONNIE tv	Scotty	BECKETT
Scott,	BRENDA tv+	Scowcroft,BRENT(Gen.) ar,st	
Scott,	CAMPBELL	Screamin Scott SIMON	
Scott,	CYRIL piano,c Br	Scribe,	AUGUSTIN w Fr
Scott,	DARIECK w Am	Scribner, CHARLES pb Am	
Scott,	DAWAN tv	Scrimm,	ANGUS
Scott,	DEBRALEE tv+	Scripps,	ELLEN ed,pb,f Am
Scott,	DEVON tv	Scripps,	JAMES pb Am
Scott,	DIANA tv	Scroggins,BOBBY tv	
Scott,	DRED slave	Scrope,	GEORGE geol Br
Scott,	DUNCAN po,w Can	Scruggs,	EARL m-bluegrass Am
Scott,	ERIC tv+	Scruggs,	LANGHORN tv
Scott,	EVELYN tv	Scruggs,	LINDA tv
Scott,	F.R. po,l Can	Scudder,	SAMUEL sc,ed Am
Scott,	FRANK piano,tv Am	Scudery,	MADELEINE de w Fr
Scott,	FRED tv+	Scullin,	JAMES st Austra
Scott,	GEOFFREY tv+	Seaborg,	GLENN n-c'51
Scott,	GEORGE b,hr'75	Seabury,	SAMUEL r Am
Scott,	GEORGE C. d,tv+	Seagal,	STEVEN
Scott,	GEORGE(Sir)ac	Seagram,	LISA tv
Scott,	GORDON	Seagren,	BOB tv
Scott,	HARRIS w Am	Seagrove,	JENNY
Scott,	HOWARD mr-guit,s Am	Seale,	BOBBY blk panther Am
Scott,	JACQUELINE tv	Seale,	DOUGLAS tv+
Scott,	JACQUES tv	Seales,	FRANKLYN tv+
Scott,	JEAN tv	Seals,	JIM mr-guit,sax,s Am
Scott,	JOE tv	Sealy	FOURDRINIER i Br
Scott,	JOSEPH tv	Seaman	KNAPP agriculture Am
Scott,	JUDSON tv	Seaman,	ELIZABETH j Am
Scott,	JUSTIN w Am	Seamus	HEANEY po,w Ir
Scott,	KATHRYN	Sean	ASTIN
Scott,	LARRY tv+	Sean	BEAN
Scott,	LIZBETH	Sean	CONNERY
Scott,	LUCIEN tv	Sean	FLANERY
Scott,	MARGARETTA	Sean	HALL tv
Scott,	MARTHA tv+	Sean	HOPPER mr-kbds Am
Scott,	MIKE b-cy'86	Sean	KANAN tv+
Scott,	MIKE mr-guit,s Scot	Sean	MacBRIDE st Ir
Scott,	ORANGE r,abolit Am	Sean	MANNING tv
Scott,	PAUL tv	Sean	McCANN tv+
Scott,	PAUL w Br	Sean	McCLORY tv+
Scott,	PETER(Sir)p-wildlife	Sean	MORGAN tv
Scott,	PIPPA tv+	Sean	O'CASEY w Ir
Scott,	RANDOLF	Sean	O'KELLY st Ir
Scott,	RAYMOND m,cn,tv Am	Sean	PENN d+
Scott,	RIDLEY d	Sean	ROBERGE tv
Scott,	ROBERT navy,x Br	Sean	SIX tv
Scott,	SELINA tv	Sean	YOUNG
Scott,	SIMON tv	Sean de	VERITCH tv

Searl,	JACKIE		Seganti,	PAOLO tv
Searle,	FREDERICK j,w Br		Segar,	ELZIE cr Am
Sears,	BARRY w Am		Seger	ELLIS mj-piano,s,cn Am
Sears,	RICHARD mer Am		Seger,	BOB s,ws Am
Sears,	RICHARD t Am		Seghers,	ANNA w Ger
Season	HUBLEY		Segner,	JOHANN sc,e Ger
Seaton,	GEORGE d		Segovia,	ANDRES guit,Sp
Seaton,	WILLIAM j,ed Am		Segrais,	JEAN po Fr
Seattle	--- Am Indian Chief		Segre,	EMILIO n-p'59
Seau,	JUNIOR fb-d'92		Seguin,	MARC eng Fr
Seaver,	TOM b-cy'69'73'75 hf		Seidelman,	ARTHUR d
Seay,	JAMES		Seidl,	JOHANN j,po Aus
Seba	SMITH w-satire,ed Am		Seifert,	JAROSLAV po,j Cz
Sebastian	BRANT po Ger		Seigel,	IRMA tv
Sebastian	CABOT tv+		Seigner,	LOUIS
Sebastian	CABOT x It		Seiji	OZAWA cn
Sebastian	COE runner Br		Seinfeld,	JERRY cm,tv+ Am
Sebastian	ERARD id Fr		Seipel,	IGNAZ r,st Aus
Sebastian	SHAW		Seiter,	WILLIAM d
Sebastian,	DOROTHY		Seitz,	GEORGE d
Sebastian,	FERD d		Seitz,	JOHN
Sebastian,	JOHN mr-guitr,s Am		Seitz,	KARL st Aus
Sebastiano	CONCA p It		Sela	WARD tv+
Sebastiano	SERLIO ac,p It		Selander,	LESLEY d
Sebastiano	ZIANI l,st It		Selassie,	HAILE st Ethiopia
Sebastien	VAUBAN ar-eng Fr		Selby,	DAVID tv+
Seberg,	JEAN		Selby,	HUBERT Jr w Am
Secada,.	JON		Selby,	NORMAN boxer Am &
Secchi,	PIETRO astr,e It		Selby,	NORMAN=Kid McCoy
Secondari,	JOHN H. tv		Selby,	SARAH tv+
Secor,	KYLE		Selden,	GEORGE l,i Am
Seda,	JON		Selden,	JOHN l,w Br
Sedaine,	MICHEL w Fr		Seldes,	GILBERT j,w Am
Sedaka,	NEIL s-pop,ws Am		Selena	ROYLE
Sedan,	ROLFE tv		Seles,	MONICA t Cz
Seddon,	KING DICK st N.Zea		Selfridge,	HARRY mer Br
Seddon,	MARGARET		Selig,	BUD bmg, commiss
Sedgwick,	EDIE		Selim	PALMGREN piano,c Finn
Sedgwick,	EDWARD d		Selina	SCOTT tv
Sedgwick,	KYRA		Selkirk,	ALEXANDER mariner Scot
Sedran,	BARNEY bb hf		Sellars,	ELIZABETH
See,	THOMAS astron,e Am		Sellecca,	CONNIE tv+
Seebeck,	THOMAS sc Ger		Selleck,	TOM tv+
Seebohm,	FREDERIC h-ec Br		Sellers,	ISAIAH river pilot Am
Seeckt,	HANS von ar,w Ger		Sellers,	PETER
Seegar,	SARA tv		Sellon,	CHARLES
Seeger,	ALAN po Am		Selma	DIAMOND tv+
Seeger,	PETE s-folk,ws Am		Selman	WAKSMAN sc Am
Seel,	CHARLES tv		Selmer	JACKSON tv+
Seeley,	JOHN(Sir)h		Selmi,	FRANCESCO md-sc It
Seena	OWEN		Selmon,	LEE fb-d'79 hf
Seers,	EUGENE w,ct Can		Selous,	FREDERICK hunter,x Br
Seferis,	GIORGOS po,s,n-l'63		Selti,	GEORGE c
Seff,	RICHARD tv		Selvon,	SAMUEL w Trinidad
Segal,	ERICH w Am		Selwyn,	GEORGE r Br
Segal,	GEORGE p,su Am		Selzer,	MILTON tv+
Segal,	LORE po,w Am		Selznick,	DAVID pr
Segal,	ZOHRA		Sem	BENELLI w It
Segall,	PAMELA tv+		Semenov,	ALEXI mj,cn Rus
Segall,	PENINA tv		Semenov,	NIKOLAI n-c'56
Segall,	RICKY tv		Semler,	JOHANN r,e Ger

Semmes,	RAPHAEL navy Am	Seth	BOYDEN i,id Am
Semper,	GOTTFRIED ac Ger	Seth	GREEN
Semyonova,	ULYONA bb hf	Seth	JAFFE
Sen	YUNG	Seth	JUSTMAN mr-kbds,s Am
Sen Yung,	VICTOR tv	Seth	KALWITZ c Ger
Sen,	APARNA	Seth	LOW mer,st,e Am
Sendak,	MAURICE w,illus Am	Seth	LUTHER ref Am
Sender,	RAMON w Sp	Seth	THOMAS id-clocks Am
Seneca,	JOE	Seth	WARD r,astr Br
Senfl,	LUDWIG c Swi	Seth	WARNER ar-re Am
Senghor,	LEOPOLD po,st Sengal	Seth,	ROSHAN
Senior,	NASSAU ec,e Br	Seton,	ANYA w Am
Sennett,	MACK pr,d+ Am	Seton,	ERNEST THOMP.sc,w,p Am
Senoa,	AUGUST w Croat	Seton-Watson, HUGH h Br	
Sensible,	CAPTAIN mr-bass Br	Setsuko	HARA
Senta	BERGER	Settle,	ELKANAH w Br
Sepe,	MICHELLE tv	Seumas	O'KELLY w,ed Ir
Septimus	WINNER ws Am	Seurat	GEORGES p Fr
Serao,	MATILDE w,j It	Seuss,	DR. w,illus Am
Seraphine,	DANNY drm Am	Sevareid,	ERIC tv-j Am
Serato,	MASSIMO	Seve	BALLESTEROS g Sp
Serene	HEDIN	Seven Ann McDONALD tv	
Sereno	WATSON sc Am	Seven,	JOHNNY tv
Serge	GAINSBOURG	Severence,	JOAN
Serge	LIFAR ba Fr	Severin,	FERNAND po Belg
Serge	REGGIANI	Severinsen, DOC cn,tv Am	
Sergeant,	WILL mr-guit Br	Severn	DARDEN
Sergei	AKSAKOV w Rus	Severn,	JOSEPH p Br
Sergei	BELOV bb hf	Severo	OCHOA sc,e Am
Sergei	BUBKA pole vault Ukr	Sevier,	JOHN ar,st Am
Sergei	ESENIN po Rus	Sevigne,	MARIE de w Fr
Sergei	FEDEROV ho	Sewall	WRIGHT md-sc.e Am
Sergey	KIROV st Rus	Sewall,	SAMUEL mer,l,w Am
Sergey	LEBEDEV sc,e Rus	Sewell,	ANNA po,w Br
Sergey	SAZONOV st Rus	Sewell,	JOE b hf
Sergey	TANEYEV c Rus	Sewell,	VERNON d
Sergey	WITTE st Rus	Sexton,	ANNE p-q'67
Sergey	YESENIN(Esenin)po,w Ru	Sextus	BURRUS ar Ro
Sergio	FANTONI	Sextus	FESTUS w Ro
Sergio	LEONE d	Seyffertitz, GUSTAV von	
Sergio	MARTINO d	Seyid	NESIMI po,mystic Turk
Sergio	OSMENA st Phil	Seyler,	ATHENE
Serkin,	RUDOLF piano Am	Seymor,	LYNN ba Can
Serling,	ROD w,tv Am	Seymour	CASSEL tv+
Serlio,	SEBASTIANO ac,p It	Seymour,	ALAN w Aust
Serna,	ASSUMPTA tv+	Seymour,	ANNE tv+
Serna,	PEPE	Seymour,	CAROLYN
Sernas,	JACQUES	Seymour,	DAN tv+
Serov,	ALEKSANDR c Rus	Seymour,	DAVID fo-j Am.
Serra,	JUNIPERO missionary Sp	Seymour,	JANE
Serra,	RAY	Seymour,	JANE('50'S) tv
Serrano,	JULIETA	Seymour,	STEPHANIE mo am
Serrato,	JOSE st Urug	Seyrig,	DELPHINE
Serrault,	MICHEL	Shaara,	JEFF w Am
Servais,	JEAN	Shaara,	MICHAEL p-f'75
Server,	ERIC tv	Shackelford, LYNN tv	
Service,	ROBERT w.po Can	Shackelford, TED tv+	
Servius	GALBA st Roman	Shad	COLLINS mj-trump Am
Sese Seko MOBUTU st Zaire		Shadel,	BILL tv
Sessions,	ALMIRA	Shadix,	GLENN
Sessions,	ROGER p-m'82	Shadwell,	THOMAS w,pol 1688-92

Shafer,	ROSS tv
Shaffer,	PAUL cm,tv Am
Shaffer,	PETER w Br
Shafter,	WILLIAM ar Am
Shah,	JAMAL
Shahan,	ROCKY tv
Shahn,	BEN p,fo Am
Shakespeare,	WILLIAM po,w Br
Shakman,	MATT tv
Shakur,	TUPAC m-rap+ Am
Shalane	McCALL tv
Shaler,	NATHANIEL geol Am
Shalit,	GENE ct,tv Am
Shalom	ALEICHEM w Rus-Am
Shamata,	CHUCK
Shana	LANE-BLOCK tv
Shandling,	GARRY tv
Shane	BRIANT
Shane	MacGOWAN mr-guit,s Br
Shane	RIMMER
Shane,	JIM tv
Shani	WALLIS
Shankar,	RAVI m India
Shankar,	UDAY ba India
Shanks,	DON tv+
Shanna	REED tv+
Shannen	DOHERTY tv+
Shannon	TWEED tv+
Shannon	WHIRRY
Shannon	WILCOX tv+
Shannon,	DEL mr Am
Shannon,	HARRY
Shannon,	SCOTT tv
Shantz,	BOBBY b-mv'52
Shapiro,	JORDANA(Bink)tv
Shapiro,	KARL ct,e,p-q'45
Shapley,	HARLOW astr,e Am
Shaquille	O'Neal bb
Sharbutt,	DEL tv
Sharett,	MOSHE st Isr
Shari	EUBANK
Shari	LEWIS pupp Am
Shari	SABO tv
Sharif,	OMAR
Sharkey,	FEARGAL mr-s Ir
Sharkey,	RAY
Sharma,	BARBARA tv
Sharman,	BILL bb hf
Sharmila	TAGORE
Sharon	ACKER tv+
Sharon	CASE tv
Sharon	FARRELL
Sharon	GLESS tv+
Sharon	SOLWITZ w Am
Sharon	SPELMAN tv
Sharon	STONE
Sharon	TATE tv+
Sharp,	BECKY fc
Sharp,	CECIL m,e Br
Sharp,	DAVE mr-guit Br
Sharp,	DON d

Sharp,	IAN d
Sharp,	PHILLIP n-m'93
Sharp,	SAUNDRA tv
Sharp,	THOM tv
Sharpe,	ALFRED(Sir)adventur,st
Sharpe,	CORNELIA
Sharpe,	DAVID
Sharpe,	KAREN tv
Sharpe,	WILLIAM n-e'90
Sharples,	JAMES p,i Am
Sharpton,	AL st,ref,r Am
Shashi	KAPOOR
Shastri,	LAL st India
Shatner,	WILLIAM tv+
Shattuck,	SHARI
Shaud,	GRANT tv+
Shaughnessy,	MICKEY
Shaun	CASSIDY tv+
Shaun	RYDER mr-s Br
Shaun	WEISS
Shavar	ROSS tv+
Shavelson,	MELVILLE d
Shaver,	HELEN
Shaw,	ALBERT ed Am
Shaw,	ANNA r,md,fe Am
Shaw,	ARTIE mj,cn Am
Shaw,	FIONA
Shaw,	GEORGE BERNARD n-l'25
Shaw,	HENRY w Am
Shaw,	IRWIN w Am
Shaw,	LEMUEL l Am
Shaw,	MARTIN organ,c,ed Br
Shaw,	MARTIN tv+
Shaw,	RETA tv+
Shaw,	ROBERT
Shaw,	SANDIE s-pop Br
Shaw,	SEBASTIAN
Shaw,	STAN tv+
Shaw,	STEVE tv
Shaw,	SUSAN tv+
Shaw,	WARREN carrace Am
Shaw,	WILLIAM(Sir)weather,e
Shawlee,	JOAN tv+
Shawn	BLACK ba Am
Shawn	ELLIOTT
Shawn	KEMP bb
Shawn	SMITH
Shawn	WAYANS(S.W.)tv
Shawn,	DICK
Shawn,	TED ba Am
Shawn,	WALLACE
Shawnee	SMITH
Shawqi,	AHMAD w Egypt
Shay,	EPHRAIM i-rrs Am
Shaye	COGAN tv
Shaykh	JUNAYD r Persia
Shayne,	CARI tv
Shayne,	ROBERT tv+
Shays,	DANIEL ar-re Am
Shea	FARRELL tv
Shea,	GLORIA

Shea,	JOE tv		Sheldon,	SIDNEY w,pr Am
Shea,	JOHN		Shelford,	VICTOR sc,e Am
Shea,	MICHAEL tv		Shell,	ART fb hf
Shean,	AL cm,la+ Am		Shellan,	STEPHEN
Shear,	AL		Shelley	BERMAN tv+
Shearer,	HARRY tv+		Shelley	BURTON tv
Shearer,	MOIRA ba+ Scot-Br		Shelley	DUVALL
Shearer,	NORMA o-a'30		Shelley	FABARES tv+
Shearin,	JOHN tv		Shelley	HACK tv+
Shearing,	GEORGE mj-piano,c Am		Shelley	LONG tv+
Sheb	WOOLEY s-cnt+ Am		Shelley	WINTERS
Sheckley,	ROBERT w-scifi Am		Shelley	WYANT
Shecky	GREENE tv+		Shelley,	BARBARA
Sheed,	FRANCIS pb Br		Shelley,	JOSHUA tv
Sheed,	WILFRED w,j Am		Shelley,	MARY w Br
Sheedy,	ALLY		Shelley,	PERCY po Br
Sheehan,	DOUGLAS tv		Shelley,	PETE mr-guit,s Br
Sheehan,	FRAN mr-bass Am		Shelly	NOVACK tv
Sheehan,	NEIL p-n'89		Shelly,	ADRIENNE
Sheehan,	SUSAN p-n'83		Shelly,	CAROL tv
Sheehy,	GAIL w Am		Shelton,	DEBORAH tv+
Sheeler,	CHARLES p,fo Am		Shelton,	EVERETT bbc hf
Sheen,	CHARLIE		Shelton,	GEORGE tv
Sheen,	FULTON(Bishop)r,tv Am		Shemar	MOORE tv
Sheen,	MARTIN		Shemp	HOWARD
Sheena	EASTON s.tv+ Scot		Shenar,	PAUL
Sheets,	CHAD		Shenkarow,JUSTIN tv	
Sheffer	CRAIG		Shenstone,WILLIAM po Br	
Sheffield,GARY b,bat'92			Shep	FIELDS mj-sax,cn Am
Sheffield,JAY tv			Shepard,	ALAN as(1st Amer.)
Shehu,	MEHMET st Albania		Shepard,	BOB tv
Sheil,	RICHARD w,st Ir		Shepard,	ERNEST illus,cr Br
Sheila	ALLEN		Shepard,	JEWEL
Sheila	BROMLEY tv+		Shepard,	KIKI tv
Sheila	FRAZIER		Shepard,	PATTY
Sheila	GISH		Shepard,	SAM p-d'79+
Sheila	JAMES tv		Shepherd,	CYBILL tv+
Sheila	KEITH		Shepherd,	ELIZABETH
Sheila	KELLEY tv+		Shepherd,	JACK
Sheila	LARKIN tv		Shepley,	MICHAEL tv+
Sheila	McCARTHY		Sheppard	STRUDWICK
Sheila	RYAN		Sheppard,	DELIA
Sheila	TERRY		Shera,	MARK tv
Sheila	WELLER w Am		Sherard	OSBORN navy,x Br
Sheila E.	--- mr-drums,s Am		Sheraton,	MIMI ct-food Am
Sheiner,	DAVID tv		Sheraton,	THOMAS ds furniture Br
Sheinkopf,DAVID tv			Shere	HITE w Am
Shel	SILVERSTEIN ws Am		Sheree	NORTH ba,tv+ Am
Shelagh	DELANY w Br		Sheree	WILSON tv+
Shelby	FIDDIS		Sheridan	Le FANU w Ir
Shelby	HEARON w Am		Sheridan,	ANN tv+
Shelby,	EVAN ar-militia Am		Sheridan,	BONNIE tv
Shelby,	PHILIP w Am		Sheridan,	DAN tv
Sheldon	CHENEY ct,ed Am		Sheridan,	DINAH
Sheldon	GLUECK sc,e Am		Sheridan,	JAMEY tv+
Sheldon	HARNICK w Am		Sheridan,	JIM d,w Am
Sheldon	LEONARD tv+		Sheridan,	LIZ tv
Sheldon,	CHARLES r,w Am		Sheridan,	NICOLLETTE tv+
Sheldon,	EDWARD w Am		Sheridan,	RICHARD w,st Ir
Sheldon,	GENE tv+		Sherilyn	FENN tv+
Sheldon,	JACK tv		Sherk,	JERRY fb-d'76

Sherl	STERN tv
Sherlock	HOLMES fc-sleuth
Sherman	ALEXIE w Native Am
Sherman	EDWARDS c Am
Sherman	HEMSLEY tv+
Sherman	HOWARD tv
Sherman,	ALLAN cm,lyrics Am
Sherman,	BOBBY tv
Sherman,	FRED tv
Sherman,	GARY d
Sherman,	GEORGE d
Sherman,	JAMES st,l,US vp Am
Sherman,	JOHN st l Am
Sherman,	LOWELL d+
Sherman,	RANSOM tv
Sherman,	ROGER l,st Am
Sherman,	WILLIAM ar-general Am
Sherr,	LYNN tv
Sherri	STONER
Sherrie	KRENN tv
Sherriff,	ROBERT w Br
Sherril	RETTINO tv
Sherrington,	CHARLES(Sir)n-m'32
Sherry	BOUCHER tv
Sherry	JACKSON tv+
Sherry	LANSING bus-movies Am
Sherry	STEINER
Sherry,	BOB tv
Sherry,	DIANE tv
Sherwin	NULAND w Am
Sherwood	ROWLAND sc Am
Sherwood,	ANTHONY tv
Sherwood,	BOBBY tv
Sherwood,	MADELINE tv+
Sherwood,	ROBERT p-d'36'39
Sheryl	CROW s-pop,ws Am
Sheryl	LEE tv+
Sheryl	RALPH tv+
Shevchenko,	TARAS po Ukraine
Shevtsov,	GEORGE la+ Aust
Sheybal,	VLADEK
Sheykh	HEYDAR r Persia
Shield,	WILLIAM c Br
Shields,	ARTHUR
Shields,	BROOKE
Shields,	CAROL p-f'95
Shields,	FRED tv
Shields,	NICHOLAS
Shields,	ROBERT mime,tv Am
Shigekuni,	JULIE w Am
Shigeta,	JAMES
Shilling,	MARION
Shilo,	SHMUEL
Shiloah,	YOSEPH
Shima	IWASHITA
Shimazaki	Toson --- po,w Japan
Shimen	RUSKIN tv
Shimon	PERES st Isr
Shimono,	SAB
Shimura,	TAKASHI

Shin'	ICHIRO TOMONAGA sc Jap
Shing,	CHEN
Shinn,	EVERETT p Am
Shintaro	KATSU
Shipler,	DAVID p-n'87
Shipp,	JOHN WESLEY tv+
Shippen,	EDWARD st Am
Shipwreck	KELLY(Alvin)stuntman
Shirakawa,	YUMI
Shiras,	GEORGE l,supr ct Am
Shire,	TALIA
Shirer,	WILLIAM j,h Am
Shirl	CONWAY tv
Shirley	ALSTON s Am
Shirley	BOOTH tv+
Shirley	CASE w,e Am
Shirley	EATON
Shirley	ELLIS s-cnt Am
Shirley	FIELD
Shirley	GRAU w Am
Shirley	GREY
Shirley	HARMER tv
Shirley	JACKSON w Am
Shirley	JONES tv+
Shirley	KNIGHT
Shirley	LANG tv
Shirley	MacLAINE
Shirley	OWENS mr-s Am
Shirley	STOLER
Shirley	TEMPLE
Shirley,	ANNE
Shirley,	J. DALLAS bbr hf
Shirley,	JAMES w Br
Shirriff,	CATHERINE tv+
Shklovsky,	VIKTOR po,w,ct Rus
Shmidt,	OTTO sc,e,x Rus
Shmuel	AGNON w Isr
Shmuel	SHILO
Sho	KOSUGI
Shockley,	WILLIAM n-p'56
Shoemaker,	WILLIE jockey Am
Shoenberg,	ISAAC(Sir)eng-elect
Shoji	OTAKE
Sholdar,	MICKEY tv
Sholder,	JACK d
Sholem	ASCH w Pol-Am
Sholes,	CHRISTOPHER i-typewr Am
Sholokov,	MIKHAIL n-l'65
Shor,	DAN tv+
Shor,	TOOTS restruanteer Am
Shore,	DANNY tv
Shore,	DINAH
Shore,	EDDIE ho-m'33'5'6'8
Shore,	ELAINE tv
Shore,	PAULY
Shore,	ROBERTA tv
Shore,	SIG d
Shorey,	PAUL r,w Am
Shorrock,	GLENN mr-s Br
Short,	DOROTHY
Short,	JAMES id-optics Scot

Short,	JOHN tv	Sidney	CATLETT mj-drums Am
Short,	MARTIN tv+	Sidney	CLUTE tv
Short,	WALTER ar Am	Sidney	COLVIN(Sir)ct,e
Shorty	RAY fb hf	Sidney	FAY h,e Am
Shortz,	WILL ed-xword,radio	Sidney	FIRMAN mj,cn Br
Shostakovich, DMITRY c Rus		Sidney	FURIE d
Shotwell, JAMES st,h Am		Sidney	HAYERS d
Shoup,	GEORGE mer,st Am	Sidney	HOOK ph,e Am
Show,	GRANT tv	Sidney	HOWARD w Am
Shower,	KATHY	Sidney	JAMES
Shrapnel,	HENRY ar,i Br	Sidney	LANIER po,e Am
Shreeve,	BOB tv	Sidney	LEE(Sir)j,ed,w
Shreve,	HENRY mariner Am	Sidney	LIPTON mj,cn Br
Shrimpton,JEAN mo Br		Sidney	LUMET d,w Am
Shriner,	HERB w,radio,tv Am	Sidney	POITIER d+
Shriner,	KIN tv+	Sidney	RIGDON r Am
Shriner	WIL tv	Sidney	SHELDON w,pr Am
Shriver,	MARIA tv-j Am	Sidney	TOLER
Shroyer,	SONNY tv	Sidney	WEBB ec,h,e Br
Shudi,	BURKAT id-harpsich Br	Sidney,	ALGERNON martyr Br
Shue,	ANDREW tv	Sidney,	GEORGE d
Shue,	ELISABETH	Sidney,	PHILIP(Sir)po,st
Shug	FISHER	Sidney,	SYLVIA
Shukshin, VASILY w Rus		Sidonie	COLETTE w Fr
Shula,	DON fbc	Sidonio	PAES st Port
Shulamit RAN c Am		Siebe,	AUGUSTUS i Ger
Shull,	GEORGE sc,e Am	Siebert,	BABE ho-m'37
Shull,	RICHARD	Siebert,	CHARLES tv
Shum,	MINA d	Siebold,	CARL von sc,e Ger
Shusaku	ENDO w Japan	Siefert,	JAROSLAV n-l'84
Shuster,	WILLIAM l,pb,f Am	Sieg,	EMIL e Ger
Shute,	HENRY w-humor Am	Siegbahn, KAI MANNE n-p'81	
Shute,	NEVIL w Br	Siegbahn, KARL n-p'24	
Si	JENKS	Siegel,	DON d+
Si	ZENTNER mj,cn Am	Siegel,	JAY bari Am
Sian	PHILLIPS	Siegel,	JERRY cr Am
Sibbald,	LAURIE tv	Siegel,	MATTHEW tv
Sibbett,	JANE tv	Siegen,	LUDWIG von p,engr Ger
Sibelius,	JEAN c Finn	Siegfried ARNO	
Sibley,	ANTOINETTE ba Br	Siegfried LENZ w Ger	
Sibley,	HENRY pioneer,st Am	Siegfried NADEL an,e,w Aus	
Sibley,	HIRAM bus-telegr Am	Siegfried OCHS cn,c Ger	
Sickel,	THEODOR von h,e Ger	Siegfried SASSOON po,bio Fr	
Sickert,	WALTER p,etch Br	Siegmann, GEORGE	
Sickles,	DANIEL ar,st Am	Siegmeister, ELIE c Am	
Sid	ABEL ho	Siemaszko,CASEY	
Sid	CAESAR mj-sax,tv+ Am	Siemaszko,NINA	
Sid	GILLMAN fb hf	Siemens,	CHARLES(Sir)i
Sid	HAIG	Siemens,	ERNST von id Ger
Sid	LUCKMAN fb hf	Sienkiewicz, HENRYK n-l'05	
Sid	McCOY tv	Siepi,	CESARE basso It
Sid	MELTON tv+	Sierra	PECHEUR
Sid	MILLER tv	Sierra,	GREGORY tv+
Sid	STONE tv	Sierra,	MARGARITA tv
Sid	TOMACK tv	Sierra,	RUBEN b,rbi'89
Sid	WEISS mj-bass Am	Sieur de La SALLE x Fr	
Sidaris,	ANDY d	Sievers,	FREDERICK su Am
Siddons,	SARAH la Br	Sieyes,	EMMANUEL re Fr
Sidney	ALTMAN sc Am	Sig	RUMANN
Sidney	BECHET mj-sax Am	Sig	SHORE d

Sigel,	BARBARA tv	Silverstein, SHEL ws Am
Sigel,	FRANZ ar,ed,pb Am	Silverstone, ALICIA tv+
Sigmund	FREUD md,ps Aus	Silvestre,ARMANDO
Sigmund	ROMBERG c Am	Silvestre,FLOR
Sigmund	SPAETH m,ed,w Am	Silvia PINAL
Signac,	PAUL p Fr	Silvia SOLAR
Signe	HASSO	Silvio PELLICO w It
Signoret,	SIMONE o-a'59	Sim, ALASTAIR
Signy	COLEMAN tv	Sima RABINOWITZ po Am
Sigonio,	CARLO h It	Sima, JAN mj,cn Cz
Sigourney WEAVER		Simcoe, JOHN ar,st Br
Sigrid	GURIE	Simenon, GEORGES w Fr
Sigrid	UNDSET w Nor	Simeon DURAN r Sp-Jew
Sigrid	VALDIS tv	Simeon NORTH id-guns Am
Sigsbee,	CHARLES navy Am	Simeon POISSON math,e Fr
Sigurd	HOEL w Nor	Simeone, HARRY m,cn,tv Am
Sigurd	WALLEN	Simic, CHARLES p-q'90
Sigurdsson, JON st,w Iceland		Simmel, GEORG ph,e Ger
Sikes,	CYNTHIA tv+	Simmons AL b hf
Sikking,	JAMES tv+	Simmons, ALEXAUNDRIA tv
Siklos,	ALBERT cello,c Hung	Simmons, EDWARD p Am
Sikorsky,	IGOR eng-aero,id Am	Simmons, FURNIFOLD st Am
Silas	DEANE r,st Am	Simmons, GENE
Silas	HOCKING r,w Br	Simmons, GENE mr-bass,s Isr
Silas	MARNER fc	Simmons, JEAN
Silas	MITCHELL md,w Am	Simmons, JOSEPH m-rap Am
Silas	PRATT c Am	Simmons, PATRICK m-guit,s Am
Silas,	CAROLYN tv	Simmons, PETER tv
Silbar,	ADAM tv	Simmons, RICHARD health,tv Am
Silberg,	JOEL d	Simms, GINNY
Silberg,	TUSSE	Simms, LARRY
Silenti,	VIRA	Simms, LU ANN tv
Siles,	HERNANDO st Bol	Simms, PHIL fb-m'86
Sillanpaa,FRANS n-l'39		Simms, PHILIP tv
Sillitoe,	ALAN w Br	Simms, WILLIAM w,po Am
Sills,	BEVERLY sopr Am	Simnel, LAMBERT imposter Br
Silo,	SUSAN tv	Simom, JULES ph,st,e Fr
Siloe,	GIL de su Sp	Simon ANDREW
Silone,	IGNAZIO w It	Simon BOLIVAR st Venz
Silva,	ADHEMAR da o-g'52'56	Simon CALLOW
Silva,	ANTONIO da w Port	Simon CUFF tv
Silva,	GENO	Simon DACH po Ger
Silva,	HENRY	Simon DUBNOW h Rus-Jew
Silva,	JOSE po Colom	Simon ESTES s,bari Am
Silva,	TRINIDAD tv+	Simon FLEXNER md,e Am
Silvana	MANGANO	Simon GIRTY ar,re Am
Silvela,	FRANCISCO st Sp	Simon GRAY w Br
Silver,	DANIEL tv	Simon ISLIP r Br
Silver,	FAWN	Simon JONES
Silver,	HORACE mj-piano,cn Am	Simon KENTON ar-scout Am
Silver,	JEFF tv	Simon KIRKE mr-drm Welsh
Silver,	JOAN d	Simon KUZNETS ec,e Am
Silver,	JOE tv+	Simon LAKE ac-naval Am
Silver,	MARISA d	Simon LEBON mr-s Br
Silver,	RON tv+	Simon MPADI r Congo
Silvera,	FRANK tv+	Simon NEWCOMB astr,math Am
Silverheels, JAY tv+		Simon OAKLAND tv+
Silverman,JONATHAN tv+		Simon OATES
Silvers,	CATHY tv	Simon PATINO tin mines Bol
Silvers,	PHIL tv+	Simon RATTLE(Sir)cn
Silverstein, JOSEPH viol,cn Am		Simon RHEE

Simon	SCOTT tv		Sinclair,	MADGE tv+
Simon	STEVIN math,st Dut		Sinclair,	UPTON p-f'43
Simon	TEMPLAR fc		Sinden,	DONALD
Simon	VOUET p Fr		Sinding,	OTTO p Nor
Simon	WARD		Sinead	CUSACK
Simon	WILLARD id-clocks Am		Sinead	O'CONNOR s Ir
Simon	WINCER d		Sinetar,	MARSHA w Am
Simon	YAM		Sing,	CHEN
Simon & Garfunkel--g-r's'68'70			Sing,	MAI TAI tv
Simon de GRAAFF st Dut			Singer,	ISAAC B. n-1'78
Simon van der MEER sc Dut			Singer,	ISAAC M. i,id Am
Simon,	CARLY s,ws,w Am		Singer,	ISRAEL w,j Am
Simon,	CLAUDE n-1'85		Singer,	LORI tv+
Simon,	HERBERT n-e'78		Singer,	MARC tv+
Simon,	JOHN(Sir)st,l		Singer,	RAYMOND tv
Simon,	MICHEL		Singer,	STUFFY tv
Simon,	NEIL p-d'91		Singh,	KHUSHWANT h,w India
Simon,	PAUL m+ Am		Singh,	RANA st Hindu
Simon,	RICHARD pb Am		Singletary, MIKE fb-d'88	
Simon,	ROBERT tv+		Singleton, DORIS tv	
Simon,	SCOTT(Screamin)tv		Singleton, PENNY	
Simon,	SIMONE		Singleton, STEPHEN m-sax Br	
Simon,	SYLVAN d		Singleton, ZUTTY mj-drms Am	
Simonds	D'EWES(Sir)h		Sinha,	SATYENDRA(Sir)1.st Ind
Simone	MARTINI p It		Sinise,	GARY
Simone	SIMON		Sinyavsky,ANDREY w,ct Rus	
Simone	WEIL ph,w Fr		Siobhan	McKENNA
Simone de BEAUVOIR w Fr			Siobhan	QUINLAN tv
Simone,	NINA s Am		Siodmak,	ROBERT d
Simoneau, YVES d			Sioux,	SIOUXSIE mr-s Br
Simonon,	PAUL mr-bass Br		Siouxsie	SIOUX mr-s Br
Simonov,	KONSTANTIN w,j,ed Rus		Siqueiros,DAVID p Mex	
Simonson, LEE ds-stage sets Am			Sirk,	DOUGLAS d
Simovic,	DUSAN ar,st Yugo		Sirola,	JOSEPH tv
Simpson,	ADELE ds Am		Sirott,	BOB tv
Simpson,	BART fc		Sirry	STEFFEN tv
Simpson,	DANONE tv		Sirtis,	MARINA tv+
Simpson,	GEORGE(Sir)x Can		Sisk,	LAURA
Simpson,	JEREMIAH st Am		Siskel & Ebert ct-films,tv Am	
Simpson,	JIM tv		Siskel,	GENE ct-films tv
Simpson,	LOUIS p-q'64		Sisler,	GEORGE b hf
Simpson,	O.J.fb-m'73,hf, tv+		Sisley,	ALFRED p Fr
Simpson,	RUSSELL		Sissle,	NOBLE
Simpson,	WALLIS(Duch-Windsor)Am		Sissy	SPACEK
Simrock,	KARL w,e Ger		Sisto,	ROCCO
Sims,	GEORGE j,w Br		Sitte,	CAMILLO ac Aus
Sims,	JOAN		Sitter,	WILLEM de astr Dut
Sims,	ZOOT mj-reeds Am		Sitwell,	EDITH(Dame)po,w Br
Sinasi,	IBRAHIM w,j Turk		Sitwell,	FRANCIS(Sir)po,w
Sinatra,	FRANK g-r'59 &		Sitwell,	GEORGE(Sir)w
Sinatra,	FRANK s,o-s'53,tv+		Sitwell,	SACHEVERELL po,w Br
Sinatra,	FRANK Jr.		Six,	SEAN tv
Sinatra,	NANCY s+ Am		Sixx,	NIKKI mr-bass Am
Sinatra,	RICHARD tv		Sizemore,	TOM
Sinbad	--- cm,tv Am		Sjahrir,	SUTAN st Indonesia
Sinclair	LEWIS w Am		Sjoberg,	BIRGER po Swe
Sinclair	ROSS w Can		Sjoberg,	ERIK po Swe
Sinclair,	DIANE ba,tv Am		Sjoerd	ROOS ds-books Dut
Sinclair,	ERIC tv		Sjostrom,	VICTOR d+ Swe
Sinclair,	HARRY id-oil Am		Sjowall,	MAJ w Swe
Sinclair,	HUGH		Skaggs,	JIMMIE F.

Skala,	LILIA	Slayton,	DONALD(Deke)as Am
Skarbek	FRYDERYK w,ec Pol	Sledge,	DEBBIE mr-s Am
Skarga,	PIOTR r,w Pol	Sledge,	JONI mr-s Am
Skarsgard,STELLAN		Sledge,	KATHY mr-s Am
Skeat,	WALTER philology,e Br	Sledge,	KIM mr-s Am
Skeets	GALLAGHER	Sledge,	PERCY mr-s Am
Skelton,	JOHN po Br	Slessor,	KENNETH po,j Aust
Skelton,	RED cm,tv+ Am	Slevogt,	MAX p Ger
Skene,	WILLIAM h Scot	Slezak,	LEO tenor Cz
Skerritt,	TOM tv+	Slezak,	WALTER tv-j+
Skinnay	ENNIS mj-drm,cn Am	Slick,	GRACE mr-s Am
Skinner,	B.F. ps,e,w Am	Slide	HAMPTON mj Am
Skinner,	CONSTANCE w Am	Slim	KING m-cnt,cn,tv Am
Skinner,	CORNELIA OTIS la,w Am	Slim	PICKENS tv+
Skinner,	EDNA tv	Slim	WHITMAN s-cnt,pop Am
Skinner,	OTIS la,w Am	Slim	WILSON m-cnt,cn,tv Am
Skip	BURTON tv	Slim,	WILLIAM ar,st Br
Skip	HINNANT tv	Slipher,	VESTO astr Am
Skip	HOMIER tv+	Sliwa,	CURTIS Guardian Angels
Skip	YOUNG tv	Sloan	WILSON w Am
Skipper	DAWES tv	Sloan,	ALFRED id-GM Am
Skipworth,ALISON		Sloan,	JOHN p Am
Sklar,	MICHAEL tv	Sloane,	BOB tv
Skoda,	EMIL von id,eng Cz	Sloane,	ESTELLE tv
Skolem,	THORALF math,e Nor	Sloane,	EVERETT
Skolimowski, JERZY d		Sloane,	HANS(Sir)sc,md
Skomorovsky, JAKOV mj,cn Rus		Sloane,	RICK d
Skou,	JENS sc,e,n-c'97	Sloat,	JOHN navy Am
Skouras,	SPYROS bus-films Am	Slocum,	HENRY ar Am
Skram,	BERTHA w Nor	Slonimsky,NICOLAS c Am	
Skrovan,	STEVE tv	Slotky,	ANNA tv
Skunk	BAXTER mr-guit Am	Slowacki,	JULIUSZ po,w Pol
Skvorecky,JOSEF w,pb Cz		Slowik,	MATTHEW tv
Skye,	IONE	Sloyan,	JAMES tv+
Slade,	DEMIAN tv	Sluter,	CLAUS su Dut
Slade,	MARK tv	Sly	STONE mr-keybds,guit,s ì
Slam	STEWART mj-bass Am	Small,	ALBION sociology,e Am
Slammin' Sam SNEAD g Am		Smalls,	ROBERT navy,st Am
Slansky,	RUDOLF st Cz	Smaniotto,SOLOMON tv	
Slap Rags WHITE mj,cn Can		Smart,	CHRISTOPHER po,j Br
Slappy	WHITE tv+	Smart,	JEAN tv+
Slapsie Maxie ROSENBLOOM boxer A	Smart,	MAXWELL fc	
Slash	--- mr-guit Br	Smeal,	ELEANOR fe-NOW Am
Slate,	HENRY tv	Smeaton,	JOHN eng Br
Slate,	JEREMY tv+	Smedley	BUTLER Ar Am
Slaten,	TROY tv	Smedley,	FRANK w Br
Slater	MARTIN bb hf	Smellie,	WILLIAM md,w Scot
Slater,	BILL tv	Smetana,	BEDRICH c Cz
Slater,	CHRISTIAN	Smetona,	ANTANAS st Lith
Slater,	HELEN	Smiar,	BRIAN tv
Slater,	RODNEY m-sax,trump Br	Smibert,	JOHN p Am
Slater,	SAMUEL id Am	Smight,	JACK d
Slatin,	RUDOLF ar Aus	Smight,	JOYCE tv
Slatkin,	LEONARD cn Am	Smiles,	SAMUEL w Scot
Slats	GILL bbc hf	Smiley	BURNETTE tv+
Slattery,	RICHARD X. tv	Smiley,	JANE p-f'92
Slaughter,ENOS b hf		Smirke,	ROBERT(Sir)ac
Slaughter,TOD		Smirnoff,	YAKOV
Slavens,	DARLA	Smith	BALLEW mj-s,cn+ Am
Slawek,	WALERY st Pol	Smith,	A. THOMAS
Slawomir	MROZEK w Pol	Smith,	A.J.M. po,ct Can

Smith,	ADAM ec,e,ph Scot	Smith,	KURTWOOD tv+
Smith,	ADRIAN mr-guit Br	Smith,	LANE tv+
Smith,	ALEXIS tv+	Smith,	LARRY mr-drm Br
Smith,	ALFRED(Al) st Am	Smith,	LEE b
Smith,	ALLISON tv	Smith,	LEE w Am
Smith,	ARCHIE tv	Smith,	LELAND tv
Smith,	ART	Smith	LEONARD tv
Smith,	ASHBEL md,st Am	Smith,	LEWIS
Smith,	BESSIE s-blues Am	Smith,	LILLIAN w Am
Smith,	BILLY ho	Smith,	LIZ j-gossip+ Am
Smith,	BOB tv	Smith,	LOIS
Smith,	BOBBIE mr-s Am	Smith,	MADELINE tv+
Smith,	BRUCE fb-d'90'3	Smith,	MADOLYN
Smith,	BUBBA fb+	Smith,	MAGGIEo-a'69,o-s'78
Smith,	C. AUBREY(Sir)	Smith,	MARTHA tv
Smith,	CAMERON tv	Smith,	MARTIN w Am
Smith,	CARL tv	Smith,	MEL
Smith,	CEDRIC	Smith,	MICHAEL n-c'93
Smith,	CHARLES MARTIN	Smith,	MICHAEL tv
Smith,	CHERYL(Rainbeaux)	Smith,	MIKE mr-kbds,s Br
Smith,	CLARENCE(Pinetop)s Am	Smith,	OZZIE b,gg'81
Smith,	CLAYDES mr-guit Am	Smith,	PATRICIA tv+
Smith,	CONNIE	Smith,	PATTI s,ws Am
Smith,	COTTER tv+	Smith,	PAUL
Smith,	CURT mr-bass,s Br	Smith,	PAULINE w S.Afr
Smith,	CYRIL tv	Smith,	PRESERVED h Am
Smith,	DAVID c,e Am.	Smith,	RED tv
Smith,	DAVID su Am	Smith,	REID tv
Smith,	DEAN bbc hf	Smith,	REX
Smith,	DWAN tv	Smith,	ROBERT mr-guit,s Br
Smith,	E.E.(Doc)w-scifi Am	Smith,	ROGER tv+
Smith,	EBONIE tv	Smith,	ROSAMOND w Am
Smith,	EMMITT fb-m'93	Smith,	SAMMI s Am
Smith,	ERNEST w Br	Smith,	SANDRA tv
Smith,	EVELYN w	Smith,	SEBA w,po,ed Am
Smith,	FLORENCE w Br	Smith,	SHAWN
Smith,	FRANCIS(Sir)i-propelle:	Smith,	SHAWNEE
Smith,	G.E. m,cn,tv Am	Smith,	SOPHIA f Am
Smith,	GIL tv	Smith,	STAN t Am
Smith,	H. ALLEN w-humor Am	Smith,	STEVE bb
Smith,	HAL tv	Smith,	STEVE s,tv Am
Smith,	HAMILTON n-m'78	Smith,	STEVIE po,w Br
Smith,	HEATHER tv	Smith,	SYDNEY cr Am
Smith,	HILLARY tv	Smith,	TARAN tv
Smith,	HOKE st Am	Smith,	THORNE w humor Am
Smith,	HOLLAND mariner Am	Smith,	TOUKIE A. tv
Smith,	HOWARD K. tv-j,anchor	Smith,	WILBUR w S.Afr
Smith,	HURRICANE mj,cn Br	Smith,	WILL tv+
Smith,	J. BRENNAN tv	Smith,	WILLIAM
Smith,	JACK tv	Smith,	WILLIAM geol Br
Smith	JACKIE fb hf	Smith,	WILLIE mj --sax Am
Smith,	JACLYN tv+	Smith,	WILLIE(Lion)mj-piano Am
Smith,	JEDEDIAH fur trade,x	Smith,	XANTHUS p Am
Smith,	JEFF tv-frugal gourm	Smith,	YEARDLEY tv+
Smith,	JEROME mr-guit Am	Smith-Cameron, J. tv	
Smith,	JOHN colonist,x Am	Smithee,	ALAN d
Smith,	JOHN tv	Smithers,	JAN tv+
Smith,	JOSEPH r-Morman Am	Smers,	WILLIAM tv+
Smith,	KATE s+ Am	Smithhart,PEGGY tv	
Smith,	KEELY s-pop Am	Smithson, JAMES sc,f Br	
Smith,	KENT tv+	Smitrovich, BILL tv+	

Smits,	JIMMY tv+	
Smits,	RIK bb	
Smits,	SONJA	
Smollett,	TOBIAS w,md Scot	
Smoltz,	JOHN b-cy'96	
Smoot,	REED st Am	
Smothers Brothers, THE tv+ Am		
Smothers,	DICK cm,tv+ Am	
Smothers,	TOM cm,tv+ Am	
Smuts,	JAN st S.Afr	
Smyth,	ETHEL(Dame)c,w,fe Br	
Smyth,	HENRY sc Am	
Smyth,	PATTY s Am	
Snary,	BILL tv	
Snead,	SAM(Slammin') g Am	
Sneed,	FLOYD mr-drm Can	
Snel,	WILLEBRORD astr Dut	
Snell,	GEORGE n-m'80	
Snell,	PETER o-g'60'64	
Snellen,	HERMAN md-eyes Dut	
Snider,	DUKE b hf	
Snipes,	WESLEY	
Snitz	EDWARDS	
Snodgrass,	CARRIE	
Snodgrass,	W.D. p-q'60	
Snooky	LANSON s,tv Am	
Snooky	YOUNG mj-trump Am	
Snoop Doggy Dogg --- m-rap Am		
Snorri Sturluson --- h Iceland		
Snow,	C.P. w,sc,st Br	
Snow,	EDGAR j,w Am	
Snow,	HANK s-cnt,tv Am	
Snow,	J.T. b-gg'97	
Snow,	LORENZO r Am	
Snub	POLLARD	
Snyder,	ARLEN	
Snyder,	DREW	
Snyder,	GARY w,p-q'75	
Snyder,	JOHN tv	
Snyder,	MIKE tv	
Snyder,	SUZANNE	
Snyder,	TOM tv	
Snyders,	FRANS p Dut	
Snyders,	SAMMY tv	
Soane,	JOHN(Sir)ac	
Soavi,	MICHELE d	
Sobel,	BARRY tv+	
Sobel,	MARK d	
Sobel,	REBECCA tv	
Soble,	RON tv	
Socas,	MARIA	
Socrates	--- ph Gr	
Soddy,	FREDERICK n-c'21	
Sode,	LAURA tv	
Soden,	HERMAN von r,e Ger	
Soderberg,	HJALMAR w Swe	
Soderblom,	NATHAN n-x'30	
Sodoma	--- p It	
Sodsai,	SONDI tv	
Soetomo,	RADEN md,st Java	
Sofaer,	ABRAHAM	

Sofer,	RENA tv	
Sofia	COPPOLA	
Soglow,	OTTO cr Am	
Sohr,	MARTIN m,c Ger	
Sojourner TRUTH r,ref Am		
Sokollu,	MEHMED st Turk	
Sokoloff,	VLADIMIR	
Sokolow,	NAHUM w,r Pol	
Sol	HUROK impressario Am	
Solar,	SILVIA	
Solari,	ANTONIO p It	
Solari,	RUDY tv	
Solari,	TOM tv	
Solder,	FLO tv	
Soleil Moon FRYE tv		
Soler,	ANDRES	
Soler,	ANTONIO c Sp	
Soler,	FERNANDO	
Soles,	P.J.	
Solf,	WILHELM st Ger	
Solh Bey,	RIAD st Lebanon	
Solis,	JAVIER	
Solo,	HAN fc starwars	
Sologub,	FYODOR w,po Rus	
Solomon	ADRET r Sp	
Solomon	BURKE s-cnt,r&b,ws Am	
Solomon	JUNEAU st Am	
Solomon	PLAATJE w,st S.Afr	
Solomon,	BRUCE tv	
Solomon,	MARCIA tv	
Solomos,	DHIONISIOS po Gr	
Solon	BAILEY astr Am	
Solow,	ROBERT n-e'87	
Solti,	GEORG cn Hung	
Solvay,	ERNEST sc,i,id,f Belg	
Solveig,	DOMMARTIN	
Solwitz,	SHARON w Am	
Solzhenitsyn, ALEKSAN n-l'70		
Somer,	YANTI	
Somers,	BRETT tv	
Somers,	GEORGE(Sir)navigator	
Somers,	KRISTI	
Somers,	SUZANNE tv+	
Somerville, E.A.O. w Ir		
Somes,	MICHAEL ba Br	
Sommars,	JULIE tv+	
Sommer,	ELKE	
Sommer,	FERDINAND e,w Ger	
Sommer,	JOSEF	
Sommerfeld, HELGA		
Sommers,	JIMMY tv	
Sommers,	JOANIE s Am	
Sommo,	JUDAH w It	
Somoza,	ANASTASIO st-ar Nica &	
Somoza,	ANASTASIO=Tacho	
Sondergaard, GALE o-s'36		
Sondheim,	STEPHEN p-d'85,c	
Sondi	SODSAI tv	
Sondra	CURRIE	
Sondra	LOCKE	
Sonia	BRAGA	

Sonia	SANCHEZ po,w Am	Sosebee,	TOMMY tv
Sonja	BULLATY fo Am	Sosnik,	HARRY m,cn,tv Am
Sonja	HENIE sk+ Nor	Sosthenes BEHN id Am
Sonja	SMITS	Sotheby,	JOHN mer-auctions Br
Sonja	ZIEMANN	Sothern,	ANN tv+
Sonneck,	OSCAR m,library Am	Sothern,	EDWARD la Am
Sonny	BONO s,st,tv+ Am	Soto,	FERNANDO
Sonny	BUPP	Soto,	HERNANDO de x Sp
Sonny	CHIBA	Soto,	HUGO
Sonny	CURTIS mr-guit Am	Soto,	MARCO st Honduras
Sonny	DAVIS	Soto,	TALISA
Sonny	FOX tv	Soul,	DAVID tv+
Sonny	GRAHAM tv	Soulas,	JOSIAS de la Fr
Sonny	JAMES s-cnt+ Am	Soule,	OLAN tv
Sonny	LANDHAM	Soule,	PIERRE st Am
Sonny	LISTON boxer Am	Soult,	NICOLAS de ar,st Fr
Sonny	ROLLINS mj-sax Am	Soumitra CHATTERJEE
Sonny	SHROYER tv	Soupault,	PHILIPPE po,w,ct Fr
Sonny	STITT mj-sax Am	Soupy	SALES tv
Sonny	TUFTS	Sousa,	JOHN PHILLIP m,c,cn Am
Sonny & Cher --- tv Am	Sousa	TOME de ar,st Port
Sontag,	SUSAN w,ph,pr-films Am	Souster,	RAYMOND po,ed Can
Soo,	JACK tv+	Soutar,	WILLIAM po Scot
Soodik,	TRISH tv	Soutendijk, RENEE
Soon-Teck OH	Souter,	DAVID l-Supr Ct Am
Sophia	LOREN	Southern,	TERRY w,w-films Am
Sophia	SMITH f Am	Southey,	ROBERT pol 1813-43
Sophie	LORAIN tv	Southwell, ROBERT po,w,r Br
Sophie	TUCKER s+ Am	Soutine,	CHAIM p Fr
Sophie	WARD	Soutsos,	ALEXANDROS po Gr
Sophie von La ROCHE w Ger	Sova,	ANTONIN w Czech
Sophus	BUGGE e Nor	Sovine,	RED s
Sophus	CLAUSSEN po Dan	Sower,	CHRISTOPHER pb Am
Sophus	LIE math,e Nor	Sowerby,	LEO p-m'46
Sophus	MULLER sc,h,w Dan	Soyinka,	WOLE n-l'86,po
Sopwith,	THOMAS(Sir)ds,id-plane Sozzini,	LELIO r It
Sor Juana de CRUZ po Mex	Spaak,	CATHERINE
Sor,	FERNANDO guit,c Sp	Spaak,	PAUL st Belg
Soral,	AGNES	Spaatz,	CARL airforce Am
Sorby,	HENRY geol Br	Space	ARTHUR tv+
Sordi,	ALBERTO	Spacek,	SISSY o-a'80
Sorel,	GEORGES ref,w Fr	Spacey,	KEVIN o-s'95,tv+
Sorel,	LOUISE tv+	Spada,	LEONELLO p It
Sorensen, LINDA	Spade,	DAVID tv+
Sorensen, RICKIE tv	Spader,	JAMES
Sorensen, SOREN sc Dan	Spaeth,	SIGMUND m,ed,w Am
Sorg,	ANN tv	Spahn,	WARREN b-cy'57,hf
Sorge,	REINHARD w.po Ger	Spain,	FAY
Sorge,	RICHARD j,spy Ger	Spalding GRAY
Sorin,	EDWARD r,e Am	Spalding,	ALBERT b hf
Sorkin,	ARLEEN tv+	Spalding,	ALBERT viol,c,w Am
Sorkin,	DAN tv	Spall,	TIMOTHY
Sorokin,	PITIRIM soc Am	Spang,	LAURETTE tv
Sorrell	BOOKE tv+	Spanger	BARRY la Irish
Sorrells	BOB tv	Spanier,	MUGGSY mj-cornet,c Am
Sorrels	PICKARD	Spano,	JOE tv+
Sorrentino, GILBERT po,w Am	Spano,	VINCENT
Sorsky,	NIL r Rus	Sparer,	PAUL tv
Sorvino,	MIRA o-a'95	Spark,	MURIEL w,po,ct Scot
Sorvino,	PAUL tv+	Sparks,	DANA tv
Sosa,	SAMMY b	Sparks,	DAVID tv

Sparks, DON tv	Spinks, MICHAEL boxer,o-g'76
Sparks, JARED h,ed,e Am	Spinola, AMBROGIO di ar It
Sparks, NED	Spinoza, BARUCH ph Dut
Sparks, NICHOLAS w Am	Spiro AGNEW st Am
Sparks, RANDY s,cn,tv Am	Spiros FOCAS
Sparky LYLE b	Spitalny, PHIL mj,c,cn Am
Sparky MARCUS tv	Spitta, JULIUS e-music Ger
Spaulding,KEN ba,tv Am	Spitteler,CARL po, n-l'19
Speaker, TRIS b hf	Spitz, MARK sw, 7x o-g'72
Speakman, JEFF	Spivak, CHARLIE mj,cn Am
Speaks, OLEY	Spivak, LAWRENCE tv
Spear, SAMMY m,cn,tv Am	Spock, BENJAMIN md,w Am
Specht, PAUL mj-viol,cn Am	Spode, JOSIAH id pottery Br
Spector, ARLEN st Am	Spohr, LOUIS viol,c,cn Ger
Spee, GRAF von navy Ger	Spooner, JOHN l,st Am
Speed, CAROL	Spooner, WILLIAM e Br
Speer, ALBERT ac,st,Nazi Ger	Spotted Tail --- Am Indian Chief
Speicher EUGENE p Am	Spottiswoode, ROGER d
Speir, DONA	Spound, MICHAEL tv
Speke, JOHN x Br	Spradlin, G.D.
Spell, GEORGE	Spradling,CHARLIE
Spelling, AARON pr	Sprague, FRANK eng-elect,i Am
Spelling, TORI tv	Spranger, BARRY la Ir
Spelman, SHARON tv	Sprat, THOMAS r,w Br
Spemann, HANS n-m'35	Spreckels,CLAUS id-sugar Am
Spence, BASIL(Sir)ac	Sprigg, JOHN(Sir)st S.Afr
Spence, BRUCE	Spring, HOWARD w Br
Spence, SANDRA tv	Springfield, DUSTY s-folk,pop Br
Spencer BENNET d	Springfield, RICK s,tv Aust
Spencer DAVIS mr-guit Welsh	Springs, ELLIOT fly,id,w Am
Spencer DRYDEN mr-drm Am	Springsteen, BRUCE mr,c Am
Spencer TRACY	Springsteen, PAMELA
Spencer, BUD	Springsteen, R.G. d
Spencer, DANIELLE tv	Sproul, ROBERT e-U.Cal Am
Spencer, HERBERT ph,ed,w Br	Spry, ROBIN d
Spencer, JOHN tv+	Spurr, JOSIAH geol Am
Spencer, La VYRLE w	Spyri, JOHANNA w Swi
Spencer, PLATT calligr Am	Spyros SKOURAS bus-films Am
Spencer, STANLEY(Sir)p	Squibb, EDWARD md,id-drugs Am
Spender, STEPHEN po Br	Squier, BILLY mr-s Am
Spengler, OSWALD ph,w Ger	Squier, EPHRAIM arc,st Am
Spengler, VOLKER	Squire WHIPPLE eng-bridges Am
Spenser, EDMUND po Br	Squire, CHRIS mr-bass Br
Sperber, WENDIE JO tv+	Squire, J.C.(Sir)po,ed
Sperry, ELMER eng,id,i Am	Squire, JOHN mr-guit Br
Sperry, ROGER n-m'81	Squires, RICHARD(Sir)st Can
Speyer, LEONORA p-q'27	Ssuma Ch'ien --- h China
Spheeris, PENELOPE d	St. Clair,BOB fb hf
Spiegelman, ART w Am	St. Cyr, LILI
Spielberg,DAVID tv+	St. Denis,RUTH ba Am
Spielberg,STEVEN o-d'93'99	St. Francis XAVIER missionary Sp
Spier, LESLIE an,e Am	St. Gerard,MICHAEL tv+
Spier, RIVA	St. Jacques, RAYMOND tv+
Spike JONES mj-drm,cn,tv+ Am	St. James,SUSAN tv+
Spike LEE d+	St. John ERVINE w Ir
Spillane, MICKEY w Am	St. John PERSE po,st Fr
Spinden, HERBERT an Am	St. John, AL(Fuzzy)
Spinell, JOE	St. John, BETTA
Spiner, BRENT tv+	St. John, HENRY w Br
Spingarn, JOEL ct Am	St. John, HOWARD tv+
Spinks, LEON boxer Am	St. John, JANICE tv

St. John, JILL		Stan	FRITTS m,cn,tv Am
St. John, KRISTOFF tv		Stan	GETZ mj-sax Am
St. Johns,ADELA j Am		Stan	IVAR tv
St. Laurent, YVES ds		Stan	JONES fb hf
St. Leger,BARRY ar Br		Stan	JONES tv
St. Onge, GUYLAINE tv		Stan	KENTON mj,c,cn Am
St. Polis,JOHN		Stan	LAUREL cm+ Am
St. Thomas AQUINAS ph It		Stan	LEE w,pr Am
St. Vincent Millay, EDNA po		Stan	LOMAX tv
St. Vrain,CERAN de fur trader Am		Stan	LYNCH mr-drm Am
Staahl, JIM tv		Stan	MIKITA ho
Stabile, DICK mj-sax,cn Am		Stan	MUSIAL(The Man)b hf
Stabler, KEN fb-m'74		Stan	SHAW tv+
Stacey NELKIN		Stan	SMITH t Am
Staci KEANAN tv		Stan	WATTS bbc hf
Stack PIERCE		Stanczak, WADECK
Stack, ROBERT tv+		Stand WATIE st Amer. Indian
Stacy GALINA tv		Stander, LIONEL tv+
Stacy HARRIS tv		Standing, GUY
Stacy KEACH tv+		Standing, JOHN
Stacy TRAVIS tv+		Standish, MILES pilgrim Am
Stacy, CHRIS tv		Stanford MOORE sc Am
Stacy, JAMES		Stanford WHITE ac Am
Stadlen, LEWIS tv		Stanford, CHARLES(Sir)c,cn,e
Stael, ANNE(Mme de)w Fr		Stanford, LELAND id-rrs,f Am
Stael, NICOLAS de p Fr		Stang, ARNOLD cm,tv+ Am
Staff, LEOPOLD po,w Pol		Stang, FREDERICK l,st Nor
Stafford REPP tv		Stanis, BERNNADETTE tv
Stafford, JEAN p-f'70		Stanislaw LEM w-scifi Pol
Stafford, JESSE mj,cn Am		Stanislaw STASZIC w Pol
Stafford, JIM s,ws Am		Stanko VRAZ po Croat
Stafford, JIM tv+		Stanley ANDREWS tv+
Stafford, JO s,tv Am		Stanley BAKER
Stafford, MARIAN tv		Stanley COHEN md Am
Stafford, MICHELLE tv		Stanley De SANTIS tv
Stafford, NANCY tv		Stanley DONEN d
Stafford, WILLIAM po,ed Am		Stanley ELKIN w Am
Stagg, AMOS ALONZO fbc		Stanley FAFARA tv
Stahl, LESLIE tv-j Am		Stanley GROVER tv
Stahl, RICHARD tv+		Stanley KETCHEL boxer Am
Stainer, JAKOB viol mkr Aus		Stanley KUBRICK d,pr,w Am
Stainer, JOHN(Sir)organ,c		Stanley KUNITZ po,ed Am
Stait, BRENT		Stanley PRICE
Staley, JAMES tv+		Stanley REED l,supr ct Am
Staley, JOAN tv		Stanley RIDGES
Stalin, JOSEPH st Rus		Stanley SPENCER(Sir)p
Stallone, FRANK		Stanley TUCCI tv+
Stallone, SYLVESTER d+		Stanley UNWIN(Sir)pb
Stalmaster, LYN tv		Stanley WEYMAN w Br
Stamitz, JOHANN viol,c Ger		Stanley, CHRIS tv
Stamos, JOHN tv+		Stanley, FLORENCE tv+
Stamp, TERENCE		Stanley, FRANCIS i,id-steam car
Stampa, GASPARA po It		Stanley, HENRY(Sir)j,x
Stamper, PETE tv		Stanley, KIM tv+
Stan BARSTOW w Br		Stanley, LOUISE
Stan BENDERS mj-pian,cn Bel		Stanley, PAUL mr-guit,s Am
Stan BROCK tv+		Stanley, WENDELL n-c'46
Stan DRAKE cr Am		Stansfield, LISA s Br
Stan EGI		Stanton, BOB tv
Stan FOSTER tv		Stanton, ELIZABETH fe Am
Stan FREBERG cm,tv Am		Stanton, HARRY

Stanton,   JACK tv
Stanton,   JOHN
Stanwyck, BARBARA tv+
Stapel,   HUUB
Stapledon,OLAF ph,w Br
Staples,   PETE mr-bass Br
Stapleton,JEAN tv+
Stapleton,MAUREEN o-s'81
Star   JASPER
Starbuck, JAMES tv
Stargell, WILLIE b-mv'79 &
Stargell, WILLIE hr'71'3 hf
Stark   YOUNG w,ed,ct Am
Stark,   CHARLES tv
Stark,   FREYA(Dame)w Br
Stark,   HAROLD navy Am
Stark,   JOHANNES n-p'19
Stark,   KOO
Stark,   RICHARD tv
Starke,   TODD tv
Starkey,   JAMES po,ed Irish
Starletta DuPOIS
Starley,   JAMES i Br
Starr   ANDREEFF
Starr,   BART fb-m'66,fbc hf
Starr,   BELLE outlaw Am
Starr,   DON tv
Starr,   ELLEN fe Am
Starr,   KAY mj-s Am
Starr,   KENNETH l Am
Starr,   MIKE
Starr,   PAUL p-n'84
Starr,   RINGO mr-drm,s,c+
Starr,   RONALD tv
Starrett, CHARLES
Starrett, JACK d+
Stas,   JEAN sc,e Belg
Stassen,   HAROLD st Am
Staszic,   STANISLAW w Pol
Statler Brothers, THE s,tv Am
Statler,   ELLSWORTH hotels Am
Staubach, ROGER fb hf
Staudinger, HERMANN n-c'53
Staudt,   KARL math,e Ger
Stauffer, TEDDY mj,cn Swi
Staunton, IMELDA
Stautner, ERNIE fb hf
Stax,   JOHN mr-bass Br
Stead,   CHRISTINA w Aust
Stead,   WILLIAM j Br
Steadman, ALISON
Steadman, LYNDA
Steady Eddie LOPAT b
Stearns,   CHRISTOPHER tv
Stearns,   JOHNNY tv
Stearns,   MARY tv
Steber,   ELEANOR sopr Am
Steckler, RAY d
Stedman   PEARSON mr-s Br
Stedman,   EDMUND po,ct,bus Am
Steeg,   THEODORE st Fr

Steegmuller, FRANCIS w,ct Am
Steel,   ALAN
Steel,   AMY tv+
Steel,   ANTHONY
Steel,   DANIELLE w Am
Steel,   JEAN tv
Steel,   JOHN mr-drm Br
Steel,   SUSAN tv
Steele,   BARBARA
Steele,   BOB tv+
Steele,   DAVID mr-kbds,bass Br
Steele,   JADRIEN
Steele,   KAREN
Steele,   PIPPA
Steele,   REMINGTON fc-tv
Steele,   RICHARD tv
Steele,   RICHARD(Sir)w
Steele,   STEPHANIE tv
Steele,   TED tv
Steele,   TOMMY guitar,s+ Br
Steele,   WILBUR w Am
Steen,   JAN p Dut
Steen,   JESSICA tv+
Steen,   MARGUERITE w Br
Steen,   NANCY tv
Steenburgen, MARY o-s'80
Steendam, JACOB po,mer Dut
Steep   WADE mj-piano,cn Can
Steer,   PHILIP p Br
Stefan   BANACH math Pol
Stefan   EDBERG t Swe
Stefan   GEORGE po Ger
Stefan   ZWEIG w Aus
Stefan,   JOSEF sc,e Aus
Stefan,   VIRGINIA tv
Stefanie POWERS tv+
Stefano della BELLA ds,eng It
Steffen,   ALBERT w Swi
Steffen,   ANTHONY
Steffen,   SIRRY tv
Steffens, LINCOLN j,ed Am
Steffi   DUNA
Steffi   GRAF t Ger
Stegers,   BERNICE
Stegner,   WALLACE p-f'72
Steichen, EDWARD JEAN fo Am
Steiger,   ROD o-a'67
Stein,   AUREL(Sir)arc
Stein,   CHRIS mr-guit Am
Stein,   EDITH r,ph Ger
Stein,   FRED tv
Stein,   GERTRUDE w Am
Stein,   HERBERT e,w
Stein,   JOHANN id-pianos Ger
Stein,   MARK mr-organ,s Am
Stein,   PAUL d
Stein,   WILLIAM n-c'72
Steinbeck,JOHN p-f'40,n-l'62
Steinberg,SAUL at drawings Am
Steinberger, JACK n-p'88
Steindl,   EMMERICH von ac Hung

Steinem,	GLORIA fe Am	Stephen	HAWKING w Br
Steiner,	GEORGE ct,w Am	Stephen	HEREK d
Steiner,	JOHN	Stephen	HOPKINS d
Steiner,	MAX c Am	Stephen	KEEP tv
Steiner,	SHERRY	Stephen	KING w Am
Steinfeld,ANDY tv		Stephen	LACK
Steinfeld,PETE tv		Stephen	LANG tv+
Steinle,	EDWARD von p Aus	Stephen	LANGTON r,st Br
Steinmetz,CHARLES eng-elect,e Am		Stephen	LEACOCK ec.e,humor Can
Steinmetz,CHRISTIAN bb hf		Stephen	LEE
Steinmiller, ROBERT Jr.		Stephen	LONG ar,x Am
Steinway, HENRY id-pianos Am		Stephen	MACHT tv+
Steis,	WILLIAM	Stephen	MATHER id,conserv Am
Stella	ADLER la,e Am	Stephen	McHATTIE tv+
Stella	STEVENS tv+	Stephen	McNALLY tv+
Stella,	JOSEPH p Am	Stephen	MENDEL tv
Stellan	SKARSGARD	Stephen	MORRIS mr-drm Br
Steller,	GEORG sc,x Ger	Stephen	NICHOLS tv
Stemann,	POUL st Dan	Stephen	OLIVER tv+
Sten,	ANNA	Stephen	PICHON j,st Fr
Stendhal	--- w,ct Fr	Stephen	QUADROS
Stenerud,	JAN fb hf	Stephen	REA tv+
Stengel,	CASEY b,bmg hf	Stephen	ROBERTS tv
Stensen,	NIELS geol,sc Dan	Stephen	SHELLAN
Stensgaard, YUTTE		Stephen	SPENDER po Br
Stepan	RAZIN rebel Rus	Stephen	STILLS mr-guit,s Am
Stepanek, KAREL		Stephen	STORACE c Br
Stepfanie RAMER tv		Stephen	TALBOT tv
Stephan	BURNS tv	Stephen	WILCOX i,id-boilers Am
Stephane AUDRAN		Stephen	YOUNG tv+
Stephanie BEACHAM tv+		Stephen Vincent BENET po Am	
Stephanie EDWARDS tv		Stephen,	LESLIE(Sir)w
Stephanie FARACY tv+		Stephenie DUNNHAM tv	
Stephanie HODGE tv		Stephenie PWOERS tv+	
Stephanie JAMES tv		Stephens, GARN tv	
Stephanie MILLS		Stephens, HARVEY	
Stephanie POWERS tv+		Stephens, JAMES tv+	
Stephanie SEYMOUR mo Am		Stephens, LARAINE tv	
Stephanie STEELE tv		Stephens, ROBERT	
Stephansson, STEPHAN po,w Can		Stephenson, HENRY	
Stephen	ALBERT c Am	Stephenson, JAMES	
Stephen	AUSTIN colonizer-TX Am	Stephenson, JOHN tv	
Stephen	BADIN r Am	Stephenson, PAMELA tv+	
Stephen	BALDWIN tv+	Stephenson, SKIP tv	
Stephen	BLADD mr-drm,s Am	Stepin	FETCHIT
Stephen	BOYD	Sterban,	RICHARD m-bass,s Am
Stephen	BROOKS tv	Sterling	HAYDEN
Stephen	CAFFREY tv+	Sterling	MACER Jr tv
Stephen	COLLINS tv+	Sterling	YOUNG mj,cn Am
Stephen	CRANE po,w Am	Sterling, FORD	
Stephen	DORFF	Sterling, GEORGE po Am	
Stephen	DOUGLAS st Am	Sterling, JAN	
Stephen	EARLY j,st Am	Sterling, ROBERT tv+	
Stephen	ELLIOTT tv+	Sterling, TISHA	
Stephen	FOSTER ws Am	Stern,	BILL tv
Stephen	FREARS d	Stern,	DANIEL
Stephen	FRY w Br	Stern,	HAROLD mj,cn Am
Stephen	FURST tv+	Stern,	HOWARD w,tv
Stephen	GIRARD mer,f Am	Stern,	ISAAC viol+ Rus-Am
Stephen	GWYNN w,po,j Ir	Stern,	OTTO n-p'43
Stephen	HAVEN w Am	Stern,	RICHARD j,ed,w Am

Stern,	SANDOR d	Steve	NATHAN tv
Stern,	SHERL tv	Steve	OWEN fb hf
Stern,	STEVEN d	Steve	PARK tv
Stern,	WES	Steve	PERRY mr-s Am
Sternberg,	LEV an,e Rus	Steve	PERRY w Am
Sterne,	LAURENCE w,r Br	Steve	PORCARO mr-kbds,s Am
Sterne,	MAURICE p,su Am	Steve	PRIEST mr-bass Br
Sternhagen,	FRANCES	Steve	RAINES tv
Sternig,	ELEANOR w Am	Steve	RASH d
Sternoff,	BILL tv	Steve	REEVES
Stesichorus	--- po Gr	Steve	ROTHERY mr-guit Br
Stetson,	JOHN id-hats Am	Steve	RYAN tv
Stettinius,	EDWARD id,f Am	Steve	SHAW tv
Steve	ALLEN tv+	Steve	SKROVAN tv
Steve	ANTIN	Steve	SMITH bb
Steve	BARNETT d	Steve	SMITH s,tv Am
Steve	BISLEY	Steve	STONE b
Steve	BOND	Steve	TANNEN tv
Steve	BOONE mr-bass,s Am	Steve	Van BUREN fb hf
Steve	BRODIE tv+	Steve	WARINER s-cntry Am
Steve	BURTON tv	Steve	WILSON tv
Steve	BUSCEMI	Steve	WINWOOD mr,s,ws Br
Steve	CARLTON b	Steve	WITTING tv
Steve	CHASE	Steve	YOUNG fb
Steve	CLARK	Steven	BAUER tv+
Steve	CLARK mr-guit Br	Steven	BERKOFF
Steve	COCHRAN	Steven	BOCHCO pr-tv,w Am
Steve	CROPPER mr-guit Am	Steven	BORN tv
Steve	DELANEY tv	Steven	CHU sc Am
Steve	DITKO cr Am	Steven	HAGUE tv
Steve	DUNLOP tv	Steven	HILL tv+
Steve	DUNNE tv+	Steven	HIRSCH tv
Steve	EARLE s-cnt,ws Am	Steven	JONES tv
Steve	EDWARDS tv	Steven	KEATS
Steve	FINLEY b	Steven	MOND tv
Steve	FORREST tv+	Steven	PINKER w Am
Steve	FOX tv	Steven	RITCH tv
Steve	FRANKEN tv+	Steven	ROGERS tv
Steve	GARVEY b-m,74	Steven	SEAGAL d+
Steve	GATLIN s Am	Steven	STERN d
Steve	GERAY	Steven	TERRELL tv+
Steve	GORHAM mr-drm Am	Steven	TYLER mr Am
Steve	HARLEY mr-s Br	Steven	VIDLER
Steve	HARMON tv	Steven	WEBER
Steve	HOWE mr-guit,s Br	Steven	WRIGHT cm+ Am
Steve	JAMES	Steven Vincent BENET po Am	
Steve	JOBS id Am	Steven,	CARL tv
Steve	JONES mr-guit Br	Stevens,	ALBERT fo-aerial Am
Steve	KAHAN tv+	Stevens,	ANDREW tv+
Steve	KANALY tv+	Stevens,	BRINKE
Steve	KATZ mr-guit,harm,s Am	Stevens,	CAT s,ws Br
Steve	KELLEY tv	Stevens,	CONNIE tv+
Steve	KMETKO rv	Stevens,	CRAIG tv+
Steve	KROFT tv	Stevens,	FISHER
Steve	LARGENT fb, hf	Stevens,	GEORGE d
Steve	LONDON tv	Stevens,	INGER tv+
Steve	MAHRE ski Am	Stevens,	JAMES w Am
Steve	MARTIN tv+	Stevens,	JOHN i Am
Steve	MARTINI w Am	Stevens,	JULIE tv
Steve	McQUEEN tv+	Stevens,	K.T.
Steve	MILLER mr-guit,s Am	Stevens,	MARK tv+

Stevens, MORGAN tv+	Stewart, POTTER l-supr ct Am
Stevens, NAOMI tv	Stewart, ROD s,ws Br
Stevens, ONSLOW tv+	Stewart, SANDY tv
Stevens, PATRICIA tv	Stewart, SLAM mj-bass Am
Stevens, PAUL	Stewart, TRISH tv+
Stevens, RAY s-pop,folk Am	Steyn, MARTHINUS l,st S.Afr
Stevens, RISE s+ Am	Stickney, TIMOTHY D. tv
Stevens, RONNIE tv	Stieb, DAVE b
Stevens, RUSTY tv	Stieglitz,ALFRED fo,ed Am
Stevens, STELLA tv+	Stieler, JOSEPH p Ger
Stevens, THADDEUS l,st Am	Stiers, DAVID tv+
Stevens, WALLACE p-q'55	Stifter, ADALBERT w Aus
Stevens, WARREN tv+	Stig DAGERMAN w Swe
Stevens, WILLIAM tv	Stigler, GEORGE n-e'82
Stevenson, ADLAI EWING st,w Am	Stiglitz, HUGO
Stevenson, DON mr-drm Am	Stignani, EBE mezzo
Stevenson, JIM tv	Stiles, EZRA r Am
Stevenson, McLEAN tv+	Stiles, RAY mr-bass,s Br
Stevenson, PARKER tv+	Still, ANDREW md Am
Stevenson, ROBERT d	Still, CLYFFORD p Am
Stevenson, ROBERT LOUIS w,po Sco	Still, WILLIAM c,arranger Am
Stevenson, ROBERT tv+	Stiller, BEN
Stevie NICKS mr,s Am	Stiller, JERRY tv+
Stevie SMITH po,w Br	Stiller, MAURITZ d+ Swe
Stevie WONDER s,ws+ Am	Stills, STEPHEN mr-guit,s Am
Stevie Ray VAUGHN mj,guit Am	Stilwell, JOSEPH(VinegarJoe)ar Am
Stevin, SIMON math,st Dut	Stimson, HENRY st Am
Steward, JULIAN an,e,w Am	Stimson, JULIA nurse Am
Stewart ALSOP j,w Am	Stine, CHARLES sc Am
Stewart COSS tv	Sting --- s,ws+ Br
Stewart GRANGER tv+	Stinnes, HUGO id Ger
Stewart MOSS tv+	Stirling, JAMES(Sir)ac
Stewart POTTER l,supr ct Am	Stirling, LINDA
Stewart RAFFILL d	Stitt, SONNY mj-sax Am
Stewart WHITE w Am	Stjepan RADIC st Croat
Stewart, AL s,ws Scot	Stobo, ROBERT ar Scot
Stewart, ALEXANDRA	Stock, AMY tv
Stewart, ATHOLE	Stock, BARBARA tv+
Stewart, BYRON tv+	Stock, JESSE tv
Stewart, CATHERINE	Stock, NIGEL
Stewart, CHARLOTTE tv+	Stockhausen, KARLHEINZ c Ger
Stewart, DAVE mr-kbds,guit Br	Stockton, FRANK w,ed Am
Stewart, DOUGLAS po,w,ct Aust	Stockton, JOHN bb
Stewart, DUGALD ph Scot	Stockwell,DEAN tv+
Stewart, ELEANOR	Stockwell,GUY tv+
Stewart, ERIC mr-guit,s Br	Stockwell,JOHN
Stewart, EVELYN	Stoddard, RICHARD po,ct Am
Stewart, FRANK	Stojan PROTIC ed,st Yugo
Stewart, J.I.M. w,ct Br	Stojko, ELVIS sk Can
Stewart, JACKIE carrace Scot	Stoker, ABRAHAM(Bram)w Ir
Stewart, JAMES o-a'40,tv+	Stoker, AUSTIN
Stewart, JAY tv	Stoker, MIKE tv
Stewart, MARTHA w,tv Am	Stokes, FREDERICK(Sir)i,eng
Stewart, MARY(Lady)w Br	Stokey, SUSAN
Stewart, MEL tv	Stokowski,LEOPOLD cn Am
Stewart, NELS ho-m'30	Stole, MINK
Stewart, NICK tv	Stoler, SHIRLEY
Stewart, PATRICK tv+	Stoll, CLIFFORD w Am
Stewart, PAUL	Stoller, MIKE c Am
Stewart, PAUL tv	Stoloff, MORRIS c Am
Stewart, PEGGY	Stoltz, ERIC

Stolze,	LENA		Stossel,	LUDWIG tv+
Stone,	ANDREW d		Stothard,	THOMAS p,illus Br
Stone,	BARTON r Am		Stout,	PAUL tv
Stone,	CAROL tv		Stout,	REX w Am
Stone,	CHRISTOPHER tv+		Stout,	ROBERT(Sir)st N.Zea
Stone,	DANTON		Stow,	JOHN h Br
Stone,	DEE WALLACE tv+		Stow,	RANDOLPH w,po Aust
Stone,	EDWARD ac Am		Stowe,	HARRIET BEECHER w Am
Stone,	FREDDIE mr-guit Am		Stowe,	MADELINE
Stone,	GEORGE		Stoyan	DANEV st Belg
Stone,	HARLAN l-chief just Am		Stoyanov,	MICHAEL tv
Stone,	HAROLD tv+		Strachey,	LYTTON h,bio Br
Stone,	I.F. j,w Am		Stracke,	WIN tv
Stone,	IRVING w,bio Am		Straeter,	TED mj-piano,cn Am
Stone,	KATHERINE w Am		Straight,	BEATRICE o-s'76
Stone,	LEONARD tv		Straight,	CHARLIE mj-piano,cn Am
Stone,	LEW mj-piano,cn Br		Strain,	JULIE
Stone,	LEWIS		Strait,	GEORGE s-cnt Am
Stone,	LUCY fe Am		Strand,	MARK po,ed Am
Stone,	MILBURN tv+		Strand,	PAUL fo Am
Stone,	MYRNA w Am		Strang,	HARRY
Stone,	OLIVER d		Strang,	JESSE r Am
Stone,	PAM tv		Strange,	GLENN tv+
Stone,	RICHARD(Sir)n-e'84		Strangis,	JUDY tv
Stone,	ROB tv		Straparola,	GIOVAN w It
Stone,	ROBERT w Am		Strasberg,	LEE d+,e
Stone,	ROSIE mr-kbds,s Am		Strasberg,	SUSAN tv+
Stone,	SHARON		Strasser,	ROBIN tv+
Stone,	SID tv		Strassman,	MARCIA tv+
Stone,	SLY mr-kbds,guit,s Am		Stratemeyer,	EDWARD w Am
Stone,	STEVE b-cy'80		Stratford	JOHNS
Stone,	STEVE tv		Stratford,	TRACY tv
Stone,	SUZANNE tv		Strathairn,	DAVID tv+
Stoneman,	RONI tv		Stratton,	ALBERT tv
Stoner,	SHERRI		Stratton,	DAVID tv
Stonewall	JACKSON ar-CSA Am		Stratton,	DENNIS mr-guit Br
Stoney	JACKSON tv+		Stratton,	GIL Jr. tv
Stoney,	GEORGE sc.e Ir		Stratton,	W.K. tv
Stong,	PHIL w Am		Straus,	ISIDOR mer Am
Stony	HARRIS tv		Straus,	OSCAR c Fr
Stopes,	MARIE sc,fe,w Br		Strauss,	DAVID ph,r Ger
Stoppa,	PAOLA		Strauss,	JOHANN c-waltz,cn Aus
Stoppard,	TOM w Br		Strauss,	JOHANN(father)c Aus
Storace,	STEPHEN c Br		Strauss,	JOSEF c Aus
Storch,	LARRY tv+		Strauss,	LEVI id-blue jeans Am
Stordahl,	AXEL m,cn,tv Am		Strauss,	PETER tv+
Storey,	DAVID w Br		Strauss,	RICHARD c,cn Ger
Storke,	ADAM		Strauss,	ROBERT
Storm,	GALE tv+		Stravinsky,	IGOR c Am
Storm,	TEMPEST stripper Am		Strawberry,	DARRYL b,hr'88
Storm,	THEODOR po,w Ger		Strayer,	FRANK d
Stormer,	FREDRIK math,sc,e Nor		Strayhorn,	BILLY mj-piano,c Am
Stormer,	HORST n-p'98		Streep,	MERYL o-s'79,o-a'82
Storni,	ALFONSINA po Arg		Street,	DAVE tv
Storr,	PAUL goldsmith Br		Street,	DELLA fc
Storrs,	SUZANNE tv		Street,	GEORGE ac Br
Story,	ISAAC po Am		Street,	PICABO ski,o-g'98
Story,	RALPH tv		Streisand,	BARBRA o-a'68,s,tv+ Am
Story,	WILLIAM su Am		Stresemann,	GUSTAV n-x'26
Stoss,	VIET su Ger		Stretch	MURPHY bb hf
Stossel,	JOHN tv		Stribling,	T.S. p-f'33

Strickland,	AMZIE tv	Stuart,	MAXINE tv+
Strickland,	GAIL tv+	Stuart,	MEL d
Strickland,	KEITH mr-drums Am	Stuart,	PATRICK tv
Strindberg,	AUGUST w,po	Stuart,	RANDY tv+
Stringer,	ARTHUR w Am	Stuart,	ROY tv
Stringfellow	BARR e Am	Stuart,	RUTH w Am
Stritch,	ELAINE s,tv+ Am	Stubbs,	GEORGE p Br
Strock,	HERBERT d	Stubbs,	IMOGEN
Strode,	WOODY	Stubbs,	LEVI mr-s Am
Stroheim,	ERICH von d	Stubbs,	WILLIAM r,h Br
Stroll,	EDSON tv	Stubby	FOUTS(Tom)tv
Strom	THURMOND st Am	Stubby	KAYE tv+
Strom,	EARL bbr hf	Stuck,	FRANZ von p,su Ger
Stromsoe,	FRED tv	Stuckenberg, VIGGO po Dan	
Stromstedt,	ULLA tv	Studebaker, CLEMENT id-wagons Am	
Strong,	BENNY mj-drm,cn Am	Student,	KARL ar Nazi Ger
Strong,	BOB mj-sax,cn Am	Studi,	WES
Strong,	KEN fb hf	Studs	TERKEL pub ownr,w,tv+Am
Strong,	LEONARD w,po Ir	Study,	EDUARD math,e Ger
Stronheim, ERICH von d+		Stuffy	SINGER tv
Stroock,	GLORIA tv	Stuhr,	JERZY
Strother	MARTIN tv+	Stumpf,	CARL ph.ps,e Ger
Stroud,	DON tv+	Sturdee,	DOVETON(Sir)navy
Stroud,	EDDIE mj,cn Can	Sturge,	JOSEPH ref,f Br
Stroud,	ROBERT birds,murderer	Sturges,	JOHN d
Strouse,	CHARLES c Am	Sturges,	PRESTON d,w Am
Strozzi,	BERNARDO p,engr It	Sturgkh,	KARL von st Aus
Strube,	GUSTAV cn,c Am	Sturm,	JACQUES math,e Fr
Strudwick, SHEPPARD		Sturmer,	BORIS st Rus
Strugatsky, ARKADY w-scifi Rus		Stursa,	JAN su Cz
Strugatsky, BORIS w-scifi Rus		Sturt,	CHARLES x Br
Strummer,	JOE mr-guit,s Turk	Sturzo,	LUIGI r,st It
Strunk,	JUD tv	Stutz,	HARRY id-cars Am
Struthers	BURT w Am	Stydahar	JOE fb hf
Struthers, SALLY tv+		Styles	BRIDGES st Am
Strutt,	JOHN n-p'04	Stymie	BEARD
Struychen CAROL		Styne,	JULE c Am
Strykert,	RON mr-guit Aust	Styron,	WILLIAM p-f'68
Stu	COOK m-folk,drm Am	Suarez,	HECTOR
Stu	ERWIN tv+	Suarez,	JOSE
Stu	GILLIAM tv	Suarez,	OLGA tv
Stuart	ADAMSON mr-guit,s Br	Subasic,	IVAN st Yugo
Stuart	CLOETE w S.Afr	Subhas	BOSE st India
Stuart	DAVIS p Am	Subrahmanyan,CHANDRASEKHAR n-p'83	
Stuart	ERWIN(Stu)tv+	Suchet,	DAVID
Stuart	FRATKIN tv+	Suchet,	LOUIS ar Fr
Stuart	HEISLER d	Suckert,	KURT j,w It
Stuart	MERRILL po Am	Suckling,	JOHN(Sir)po
Stuart	PANKIN tv+	Sucre,	ANTONIO de ar,re Venz
Stuart	RANDALL tv	Sudermann,HERMANN w Ger	
Stuart	WHITMAN tv+	Sudie	BOND
Stuart	WILSON	Sue	BENDER w Am
Stuart	WOOD mr-guit Scot	Sue	BENNETT tv
Stuart,	BARBARA tv	Sue	BUGDEN tv
Stuart,	CASSIE	Sue	COWSILL mr-s Am
Stuart,	CHAD mr-guit,s Br	Sue	GRAFTON w Am
Stuart,	GILBERT p Am	Sue	LLOYD
Stuart,	GLORIA	Sue	LYON
Stuart,	HAMISH mr-guit,s Scot	Sue	MILLER w Am
Stuart,	JESSE po,w Am	Sue	PAI tv
Stuart,	JOHN	Sue	POWELL m-cnt,tv

Sue	RANDALL tv	Sunny	JOHNSON
Sue Ane	LANGDON tv+	Sunset	CARSON
Sue,	EUGENE w Fr	Sunshine	PARKER tv+
Sues,	ALAN cm,tv Am	Supan,	ALEXANDER geog,ed,e Ger
Suess,	EDUARD geol,e,w Aus	Supervielle,	JULES po,w Fr
Sugai,	ICHIRO	Supilo,	FANO st Croat
Sugar	DAWN	Supiran,	JERRY tv
Sugar Ray	LEONARD boxer Am	Sure!,	AL B. tv
Sugden,	SAMUEL sc,e Br	Surovy,	NICOLAS tv+
Sugimura,	HARUKO	Surrey,	HENRY po Br
Suhor,	YVONNE tv	Surtees,	ROBERT w,j-spts Br
Sui,	ANNA ds Am	Susan	ANSPACH
Suimmers,	YALE tv	Susan	ANTON s+ Am
Suits,	WENDY tv	Susan	BLAKELY tv+
Suk,	JOSEF viol,c Cz	Susan	BUCKNER tv
Sukowa,	BARBARA	Susan	CABOT
Sulaitis,	D.S. w Am	Susan	CLARK tv+
Sullavan,	MARGARET	Susan	DEY tv+
Sullivan,	ANDREW w Br-Am	Susan	DOUGHTY ceramics Br
Sullivan,	ANN tv	Susan	DUMBRYS w Am
Sullivan,	ARTHUR(Sir)organ,c	Susan	DUVALL tv
Sullivan,	BARRY tv+	Susan	GEORGE tv+
Sullivan,	BIG JIM tv	Susan	HAHN po Am
Sullivan,	BRAD tv+	Susan	HART
Sullivan,	DON	Susan	HASKELL tv
Sullivan,	ED tv+	Susan	HAYWARD
Sullivan,	FRANCIS L.	Susan	HOGAN tv+
Sullivan,	FRANK j,w-humor Am	Susan	HOWARD tv+
Sullivan,	JOHN L. boxer Am	Susan	HUNT tv
Sullivan,	KATHY tv	Susan	JAFFE ba Am
Sullivan,	KITTY tv	Susan	KIGER
Sullivan,	LIAM tv	Susan	LANIER tv
Sullivan,	LOUIS ac Am	Susan	LUCCI tv+
Sullivan,	MARK j,h Am	Susan	MELVIN tv
Sullivan,	ROBERT tv	Susan	MINOT w Am
Sullivan,	SUSAN tv+	Susan	MYERS tv+
Sully	BOYER	Susan	NEHER tv
Sully,	THOMAS p Am	Susan	OLIVER
Sully Prudhomme, R. n-l'01,po		Susan	OLSEN tv
Sulzer,	WILLIAM st Am	Susan	PERETZ tv
Sumac,	YMA s Peru	Susan	QUINN bio,w,e Am
Summer,	CREE tv	Susan	RUTTAN
Summer,	DONNA s Am	Susan	SCOTT
Summers,	ANDY mr-guitar,s Fr	Susan	SHAW tv+
Summers,	HOPE tv	Susan	SHEEHAN w Am
Summerville,	SLIM	Susan	SILO tv
Sumner	WELLES st Am	Susan	SONTAG w,ph,pr-films Am
Sumner,	BARNEY mr-guit,s Br	Susan	ST. JAMES tv+
Sumner,	CHARLES st Am	Susan	STEEL tv
Sumner,	JAMES n-c'46	Susan	STOKEY
Sumner,	WILLIAM ec,e Am	Susan	SWIFT tv
Sumter,	THOMAS ar-re Am	Susan	TOLSKY tv
Sun Ra	--- mj-piano,cn,c	Susan	TYRELL
Sun Yat-sen	--- st China	Susan	URSITTI
Sunday,	BILLY r Am	Susan	WALTERS tv+
Sundberg,	CLINTON	Susan	WALTHER tv
Sundquist,	BJORN	Susan	WARNER w Am
Sundquist,	GERRY	Susan B.	ANTHONY fe Am
Sundstrom,	CEDRIC d	Susanna	HOFFS mr-guit,s Am.
Sundstrom,	FLORENCE tv	Susanna	ROWSON la,w,e Am
Sune	BERGSTROM md Swe	Susannah	MOODIE w Can

Susannah	YORK		Sven	HEDIN geog,x Swe
Susanne	LANGER ph,e,w Am		Sven	NYKVIST movie camera,d
Suse,	HEINRICH mystic Ger		Sven	OLE-THORSEN
Susette	La FLESCHE reform Am		Sven	WOLLTER
Susi,	CAROL ANN tv		Svend	AAGESEN h Dan
Susie	BRIGHT w Am		Svenson,	BO tv+
Susie	GARRETT tv		Sverak,	ZDENEK
Suskind,	PATRICK w Ger		Sverdrup,	OTTO x Nor
Susman,	TODD tv+		Svevo,	ITALO w It
Suss,	HANS p Ger		Svoboda,	LUDVIK ar,st Cz
Susskind,	DAVID tv		Swackhamer,	E.W. d
Sussman,	SAL mj-guitAm		Swaggart,	JIMMY r,tv Am
Sutan	SJAHRIR st Indonesia		Swaim,	CASKEY tv
Sutcliffe,	RICK b-cy'84		Swain,	MACK
Sutherland,	DONALD		Swamp Fox	MARION(Francis)ar Am
Sutherland,	EARL n-m'71		Swan,	JOSEPH(Sir)sc
Sutherland,	EDWARD d		Swann,	LYNN fb,tv
Sutherland,	GRAHAM p,etch,engr B:	Swann,	WILLIAM sc,e Am
Sutherland,	JOAN(Dame)sopr. Aust	Swanson,	GARY
Sutherland,	KIEFER		Swanson,	GLORIA
Sutorius,	JAMES tv+		Swanson,	JACKIE tv
Sutro,	ADOLPH eng-mines Am		Swanson,	KRISTY tv+
Sutter,	BRUCE b-cy'79		Swanton,	JOHN an Am
Sutter,	JOHN pioneer Am		Swarowsky	HANS c Aus
Suttner,	BERTHA von w,n-x'05		Swarthout,	GLADYS sopr
Sutton	VANE w Br		Swartz,	TONY tv
Sutton,	DUDLEY		Swasey,	NIKKI tv
Sutton,	FRANK tv		Swayne,	NOAH 1,supr ct Am
Sutton,	GRADY tv+		Swayze,	DON
Sutton,	JOHN		Swayze,	JOHN CAMERON tv-news
Sutton,	LISA tv		Swayze,	PATRICK tv+
Sutton,	MICHAEL tv		Sweatman,	WILBUR C.mj-pia,c,cn Am
Sutton,	MYRON(Mynie)mj,cn Can	Swedenborg,	EMANUEL sc,ph,r,w Swe
Sutton	WILLIE robber-banks Am	Sweelinck,	JAN organ,c Dut
Suvorin,	ALEKSEY j,pb Rus		Sweeney,	ALISON tv
Suzanna	LEIGH		Sweeney,	BOB tv+
Suzanna	LOVE		Sweeney,	D.B.
Suzanne	CHILDS tv		Sweeney,	JULIA tv+
Suzanne	CROUGH tv		Sweeney,	TERRY tv
Suzanne	DOUGLAS tv		Sweet,	BLANCHE
Suzanne	HUNT tv		Sweet,	DOLPH tv+
Suzanne	LEDERER tv+		Sweet,	GARY
Suzanne	LENGLEN t Fr		Sweet,	KATIE tv
Suzanne	ROGERS tv		Sweet,	MATTHEW s,ws Am
Suzanne	SNYDER		Sweetin,	JODIE tv
Suzanne	SOMERS tv+		Swenson,	INGA tv+
Suzanne	STONE tv		Swenson,	KARL tv
Suzanne	STORRS tv		Swenson,	MAY po Am
Suzanne	VEGA s-folk,ws Am		Swickard,	JOSEF
Suzi	QUATRO mr		Swift,	GUSTAVUS id-meat Am
Suzman,	JANET		Swift,	HOMER md Am
Suzy	AMIS		Swift,	JONATHAN r,po,w Br
Suzy	CHAFFEE ski Am		Swift,	SUSAN tv
Suzy	DELAIR		Swilling,	PAT fb-d'91
Suzy	KENDALL		Swinburne,	NORA
Suzy	PARKER		Swing,	RAYMOND j Am
Suzy	PRIM		Swinnerton,	FRANK w,ct Br
Suzzy	ROCHE		Swinton,	TILDA
Svatopluk	CECH po, w Cz		Swit,	LORETTA(Hot Lips) tv+
Svedberg,	THEODOR(The)n-c'26		Switzer,	CARL(Alfalfa)
Sveltana	BOUSOVA ba Lith-Br		Swofford,	KEN tv+

Swoozie	KURTZ tv+
Swope,	GERARD eng,id-GE Am
Swope,	TOPO
Sy	OLIVER mj-arrger,c Am
Sybel,	HEINRICH von h Ger
Sybil	DANNING
Sybil	JASON
Sybille	SCHMITZ
Syd	BARRETT mr-guit,s Br
Syd	CROSSLEY
Syd	SAYLOR tv+
Sydne	ROME
Sydney	CHAPLIN
Sydney	DOBELL po,ct Br
Sydney	KYTE mj-viol,cn Br
Sydney	LASSICK
Sydney	MORGAN(Lady)po Ir
Sydney	PENNY tv+
Sydney	POLLACK tv+
Sydney	RINGER md Br
Sydney	SMITH cr Am
Sydney	WALSH tv+
Sydney,	BASIL
Sydow,	MAX von
Sykes,	MARK(Sir)st
Sylva	KOSCINA
Sylvain	LEVI h,e Fr
Sylvan	SIMON d
Sylvan,	PAUL tv
Sylvanus	OLYMPIO st Togo
Sylvanus	THAYER ar,e Am
Sylver	GREGORY tv
Sylvester	STALLONE d+
Sylvester,HAROLD tv+	
Sylvester,WILLIAM	
Sylvia	CHASE tv
Sylvia	FIELD tv
Sylvia	KRISTEL
Sylvia	LEWIS tv
Sylvia	MILES
Sylvia	PLATH po,e Am
Sylvia	SIDNEY
Sylvia	SYMS s+ Am
Sylvia	WARNER w,po Br
Sylvian,	DAVID mr-guit,s Br
Sylvie	Van Den ELSEN
Symington, STUART id,st Am	
Symonds,	JOHN po,w,h Br
Symons,	ARTHUR ct,bio Br
Symons,	JULIAN po,ct Br
Syms,	SYLVIA s+ Am
Synda	SCOTT tv
Synge,	JOHN w Ir
Synge,	RICHARD n-c'52
Syngman	RHEE st Korea
Syreeta	WRIGHT s,ws Am
Szabo,	ISTVAN d
Szabo,	LASZLO
Szapolowska, GRAZYNA	
Szarabajka, KEITH tv+	
Szell,	GEORGE cn Am

Szent-Gyorgyi,ALBERT von n-m'37	
Szep,	PAUL p-x'74,'77
Szeryng,	HENRYK violin Mex
Szilard,	LEO sc Am
Szold,	HENRIETTA r,pb Am
Szwarc,	JEANNOT d

"T" NAME DESIGNATION CODES

t		TENNIS PLAYER
tv		TELEVISION ACTOR

"T" NATIONALITY CODES

Transyl	-	TRANSYLVANIAN
Turk	-	TURKISH

"T's"

T'ao Ch'ien --- po	
T'Keyah	KEYMAH tv
T-Bone	WALKER mj,guit Am
T.,	MR. tv
T.F.	POWYS w Br
T.H.	WHITE w Br
T.K.	CARTER tv+
T.P.	McKENNA
T.S.	ELIOT po,w Br
T.W.	KING tv
Ta-Tanisha --- tv	
Taaffe,	EDUARD st Aus
Tab	HUNTER tv+
Tabakov,	OLEG
Taban Io	LIYONG po Uganda
Tabor,	ERON
Tache,	ETIENNE(Sir)st,md Can
Tachik,	CHRISTINE w Am
Tacho	SOMOZA st-ar Nica
Tacitus,	CORNELIUS st Ro
Tacker,	FRANCINE tv
Tackitt,	WESLEY tv
Tad	MOSEL w Am
Tadd	DAMERON mj-piano,c Am
Taddeo	GADDI p It
Taddeo	ZUCARRI p It
Tadeusz	RITTNER w Pol
Taft,	ALPHONSO l,st Am
Taft,	LORADO su Am
Taft,	ROBERT st Am
Taft,	WM. HOWARD 27th Pres
Tagawa,	CARY-HIROYUKI
Taggart,	RITA
Taglioni,	MARIE ba It
Tagore,	RABINDRANATH n-l'13
Tagore,	SHARMILA
Tahnee	WELCH
Tahupotiki RATANA st,r Maori	
Taiji	TONOYAMA
Taina	ELG
Taine,	HIPPOLYTE ph,ct,w Fr
Tainter,	CHARLES i Am
Tairov,	ALEKSANDR pr Rus
Tait,	ARCHIBALD r Scot

Tait,	PETER sc,math,e Scot		Tan,	TIN
Taj	JOHNSON tv		Tanaka,	KAKUEI st eng Jap
Taj Mahal	--- s,ws Am		Tanaka,	KINUYO
Taka,	MIIKO		Tanaka,	TORU
Takakura,	KEN		Tandy,	JAMES re Ir
Takamine,	HIDEKO		Tandy,	JESSICA o-a'89
Takashi	SHIMURA		Tandy,	RICHARD mr-bass Br
Take	IONESCU st Rom		Taney,	ROGER 1st ch just Am
Takei,	GEORGE tv+		Taneyev,	SERGEY c Rus
Tal,	MIKHAIL chess Rus		Tanguay,	EVA la,cm Am
Talbot,	ARTHUR eng,e Am		Tanguy,	YVES p Am
Talbot,	LYLE tv+		Tani Phelps GUTHRIE	
Talbot,	MARY ar(disguised)Br		Tani,	YOKO
Talbot,	MICK mr-kbds Br		Tannen,	STEVE tv
Talbot,	NITA tv+		Tannen,	WILLIAM tv+
Talbot,	SILAS navy Am		Tanner,	HENRY p Am
Talbot,	STEPHEN tv		Tanner,	MARY tv
Talbott,	GLORIA		Tanner,	ROSCOE t Am
Talbott,	MICHAEL tv		Tanner,	VAINO st Finn
Talcott	PARSONS soc,e Am		Tannis	VALLELY tv
Talent,	ZIGGY tv		Tansey,	ROBERT d
Talese,	GAY w Am		Tantoo	CARDINAL
Talia	BALSAM		Tanucci,	BERNARDO st It
Talia	SHIRE		Tanya	FENMORE tv+
Taliaferro, HAL			Tanya	HARDING sk Am
Taliesin JAFFE tv			Tanya	ROBERTS tv+
Talisa	SOTO		Tanya	TUCKER s-pop+ Am
Tallchief,MARIA ba Am			Tanya Falan WELK tv	
Talley,	GARY mr-guit Am		Tao,	WANG
Talley,	NEDRA s-Am		Tapley,	COLIN tv
Tallien,	JEAN re,st Fr		Tapp,	GORDIE tv
Tallis,	THOMAS organ,c Br		Tappan,	ARTHUR mer,anti-slave
Talma,	FRANCOIS la Fr		Tapping	REEVE l,e Am
Talmadge, CONSTANCE			Tara	BUCKMAN tv
Talmadge, NORMA			Tara	MacGOWAN
Talmadge, RICHARD			Taran	SMITH tv
Talman,	WILLIAM tv+		Tarantino,QUENTIN d+	
Talton,	ALIX tv		Taras	SHEVCHENKO po
Tam,	JACOB r Fr		Tarbell,	IDA w,ed Am
Tamar	YOUNG tv		Tarde,	JEAN soc Fr
Tamara	DOBSON		Tardieu,	ANDRE st Fr
Tamayo	OTSUKI tv		Tari,	LE tv
Tamayo,	RUFINO p Mex		Tariq,	AZIZ st Iraq
Tamba,	TETSURO		Tarjei	VESAAS w Nor
Tamblyn,	RUSS tv+		Tarkenton,FRAN fb-m'75 hf,tv	
Tambor,	JEFFREY tv+		Tarkington, BOOTH p-f'19'22	
Tamerlis,	ZOE		Tarkington, ROCKNE	
Tamiris,	HELEN ba,e Am		Tarkovsky,ANDREI d	
Tamiroff,	AKIM		Tarn,	PAULINE po Fr
Tamiya,	JIRO		Tarr,	JUSTIN tv
Tamiyo	KUSAKARI		Tarses,	JAY tv
Tamlyn	TOMITA		Tarso,	IGNACIO
Tamm,	IGOR n-p'58		Tartini,	GIUSEPPE viol,c It
Tammii,	TOM tv		Tartt,	DONNA w Am
Tammy	GRIMES		Taryn	POWER
Tammy	LAUREN tv		Tashiro,	SHIRO sc,e Am
Tammy	LOCKE tv		Tashlin,	FRANK d
Tammy	WYNETTE s-cnt Am		Tashman,	LILYAN
Tammy-Faye BAKKER r,tv Am			Tasia	VALENZA
Tan	DUN c,cn Am		Tasker	BLISS ar Am
Tan,	AMY w Am		Tasman,	ABEL x Dut

Tassie,	JAMES jeweler Scot	Taylor,	DON
Tasso,	TORQUATO po It	Taylor,	DON d
Tassoni,	ALESSANDRO po,w It	Taylor,	DUB tv+
Tata,	JAMSETJI id India	Taylor,	EDWARD r,po Am
Tata,	JOE(Joey)tv	Taylor,	ELIZABETH o-a'60'66 &
Tate	DONOVAN	Taylor,	ELIZABETH tv+
Tate,	ALLEN po,ct,bio Am	Taylor,	ELIZABETH w Br
Tate,	HENRY(Sir)id-sugar,f	Taylor,	ESTELLE
Tate,	JAMES p-q'92	Taylor,	FORREST tv+
Tate,	JEFFREY cn Br	Taylor,	FRED bbc,hf
Tate,	LARENZ tv+	Taylor,	GARRETT
Tate,	LAURA	Taylor,	HENRY p-q'86
Tate,	NAHUM w,po Br	Taylor,	HENRY(Sir)po
Tate,	NICK tv+	Taylor,	LARRY mr-bass Am
Tate,	SHARON tv+	Taylor,	HOLLAND tv+
Tati,	JACQUES d+	Taylor,	JACK
Tatlin,	VLADIMIR p,su,ac Rus	Taylor,	JAMES s-folk AM
Tatsuya	NAKADAI	Taylor,	JIM fb-m'62,hf
Tatum	O'NEAL	Taylor,	JOAN tv+
Tatum,	ART mj-piano,cn Am	Taylor,	JOHN mr-bass Br
Tatum,	EDWARD n-m'58	Taylor,	JOHN w,po Br
Taube,	HENRY n-c'83	Taylor,	JOHN HENRY g Br
Tauber,	RICHARD tenor Aus	Taylor,	JOSEPH la Br
Taunay,	ALFREDO w,h Braz	Taylor,	JOSEPH n-p'93
Taupin,	BERNIE lyrics Br	Taylor,	JOSH tv
Taurean	BLACQUE tv+	Taylor,	JUD tv
Taurog,	NORMAN d	Taylor,	JUDD d
Tausen,	HANS r,ref Dan	Taylor,	JUNE va,tv Am
Taussig,	HELEN md,sc,e Am	Taylor,	KEITH tv
Taviani,	PAOLO d	Taylor,	KELLI tv
Taviani,	VITTORIO d	Taylor,	KENT tv+
Tawfiq al-	HAKIM w Egypt	Taylor,	KIT
Tawney,	R.H. h-ec Br	Taylor,	LARRY mr-bass Am
Tawny	FERE	Taylor,	LAURETTE la Am
Tawny	KITAEN tv+	Taylor,	LAURENCE fb-d'86
Tawny	SCHNEIDER tv	Taylor,	LILI
Taxier,	ARTHUR tv	Taylor,	MARC tv
Tay	GARNETT d	Taylor,	MARC SCOTTtv
Tayback,	VIC tv+	Taylor,	MARJORIE
Taylor	DAYNE s-pop,soul Am	Taylor,	MARY tv
Taylor	FRY tv+	Taylor,	MAXWELL ar,st Am
Taylor	HOLMES	Taylor,	MESHACH tv+
Taylor	LACHER tv	Taylor,	MYRA mj-s Am
Taylor	NEGRON	Taylor,	NANCY tv
Taylor	NICHOLS tv	Taylor,	NATHANIEL tv
Taylor,	A.J.P. h,e Br	Taylor,	NOAH
Taylor,	ANDY mr-guit Br	Taylor,	PETER w Am
Taylor,	ART mj-drm,cn Am	Taylor,	RAY d+
Taylor,	BAYARD w Am	Taylor,	REGINA tv
Taylor,	BAZ d	Taylor,	RENEE tv+
Taylor,	BENEDICT	Taylor,	RICHARD n-p'90
Taylor,	BERT(B.L.T.)j Am	Taylor,	RIP tv+
Taylor,	BILLY mj-piano,cn Am	Taylor,	ROBERT LEWIS p-f'59
Taylor,	BUCK tv+	Taylor,	ROBERT tv+
Taylor,	CECIL mj-pian,cn Am	Taylor,	ROD tv+
Taylor,	CHARLIE fb hf	Taylor,	ROGER mr-drm Br
Taylor,	CLARICE tv	Taylor,	RON tv
Taylor,	CLIVE mr-bass Welsh	Taylor,	SAM d
Taylor,	DEBORAH tv	Taylor,	TOM tv
Taylor,	DEEMS c,ct,tv Am	Taylor,	TOM w Br
Taylor,	DICK mr-guit Br	Taylor,	VALERIE tv

Taylor,	VAUGHN tv+	Ted	TURNER tv-exec Am
Taylor,	ZACHARY 12th pres	Ted	WASS tv+
Taylor,	ZACK	Ted	WEEMS mj,cn Am
Taylor-Young, LEIGH tv+		Ted	ZEIGLER tv
Taymor	JULIE d,ba Am	Ted de	CORSIA tv+
Tayri,	ANDRE ba,tv Am	Tedder,	ARTHUR fly Br
Tchaikovsky, PIOTR ILICH c Rus		Teddy	POWELL mj,cn Am
Tcheky	KARYO	Teddy	QUINN tv
Tchelichev, PAVEL p Am		Teddy	WILSON mj-piano,c+ Am
Tcherkasskaya, MARIANNA ba Am		Tedrow,	IRENE tv+
Tchicaya U TAM'SI po Congo		Teefy,	MAUREEN
Te Kanawa,KIRI(Dame)c N.Zea		Teen,	HAROLD fc
Teach,	EDW.(Blackb'rd)pirate	Teena	MARIE mr s
Tead,	PHIL	Tefkin,	BLAIR tv+
Teagarden,JACK mj-tromb,s Am		Teggart,	FREDERICK h,e Am
Teague,	BERTHA bbc hf	Tegner,	ESAIAS r,po,e Swe
Teague,	LEWIS d	Teich,	AARON
Teague,	WALTER id-ds Am	Tej	SAPRU(Sir)l,st India
Teal,	RAY tv+	Tekulve,	KENT b
Teala	LORING	Teleki,	PAL geog,st Hung
Teale,	EDWIN p-n'66	Teleki,	SAMUEL x Hung
Teale,	OWEN	Telemann,	GEORG c Ger
Tearle,	CONWAY	Telesio,	BERNARDINO ph It
Teasdale, SARA po Am		Telford,	THOMAS eng Scot
Teasdale, VERREE		Tell,	WILHELM(Wm.)hero Swi
Tebaldi,	RENATA s-opera It	Teller,	EDWARD sc Am
Tecumseh	--- Am Indian Chief	Tellez,	GABRIEL de w Sp
Ted	ADAMS	Tellier	CHARLES eng Fr
Ted	BESSELL tv+	Telly	SAVALAS tv+
Ted	BROWN tv	Telma	HOPKINS mr-s,tv+ Am
Ted	CASSIDY tv+	Temin,	HOWARD n-m'75
Ted	COLLINS tv	Tempest	STORM stripper Am
Ted	DANSON tv+	Tempestt	BLEDSOE tv
Ted	FIO RITOmj-kbds,cn Am	Templar,	SIMON fc
Ted	GEHRING tv	Temple,	HENRY st Br
Ted	GRANT m-cnt,tv Am	Temple,	JULIEN d
Ted	HEALY	Temple,	SHIRLEY tv+
Ted	HEATH mj-tromb Br	Templeton,ALEC mj-piano Am
Ted	HUGHES po Br	Tench,	BENMONT mr-kbds Am
Ted	JORDAN tv	Tench,	WATKIN ar,w Br
Ted	KENNEDY ho	Tencin,	CLAUDINE w,mistrss Fr
Ted	KENNEDY st Am	Tendler,	JESSE tv
Ted	KNIGHT tv+	Teniers,	DAVID(Elder)p Belg
Ted	KOPPEL tv-j Am	Teniers,	DAVID(Younger)p Belg
Ted	LANGE tv+	Tenison.	THOMAS r Br
Ted	LEPLAT	Tennant,	KYLIE w Aust
Ted	LEVINE tv+	Tennant,	NEIL mr-s Br
Ted	LEWIS mj-clari,s,cn Am	Tennant,	VICTORIA
Ted	LYONS b hf	Tennessee Ernie FORD s Am
Ted	MACK tv-host Am	Tenney,	JON tv+
Ted	MARCOUX	Tenney,	KEVIN d
Ted	McGINLEY tv+	Tenniel,	JOHN(Sir)illus,cr
Ted	MIKELS d	Tennille,	TONI s,tv Am
Ted	NEELEY	Tennyson,	ALFRED pol 1850-92 Br
Ted	NORTH	Tenzing,	NORKEY sherpa guide
Ted	NUGENT mr-guit Am	Teofilo	BRAGA w,e Port
Ted	POST d	Teofilo	FOLENGO po,r It
Ted	PRIOR tv+	Ter Borch GERARD(Terborch)p Dut
Ted	SHAWN ba Am	Terao,	AKIRA
Ted	STEELE tv	Terbrugghen, HENDRIK p Dut
Ted	TILLER tv	Terence	--- w Ro

Terence	D'ARBY s-r&b,ws Am	Terry	MIALL mr-drm Br
Terence	DeMARNEY tv	Terry	MOORE tv+
Terence	FISHER d	Terry	MORSE d
Terence	HILL	Terry	O'QUINN
Terence	KILBURN	Terry	SANDERS tv
Terence	KNOX tv+	Terry	SWEENEY tv
Terence	STAMP	Terry	TWEED tv+
Terence	WHITE w Br	Terry	WALKER
Terence	YOUNG d	Terry	WILLS tv
Teresa	BREWER s Am	Terry	WILSON tv
Teresa	GANZEL tv	Terry	WOLLMAN tv
Teresa	GIMPERA	Terry,	ALFRED ar Am
Teresa	GRAVES tv	Terry,	BILL b hf
Teresa	THORNE tv	Terry,	BOB
Teresa	WRIGHT	Terry,	ELI id-clocks Am
Teresa de la PARRA w Venz		Terry,	ELLEN(Dame)la Br
Teresa,	MOTHER r,n-x'79	Terry,	JOHN
Teresa,	SAINT r,w Sp	Terry,	MARY tv
Terfel,	BRYN bari Welsh	Terry,	NIGEL
Terhune,	ALBERT w,ed Am	Terry,	PAUL
Terhune,	MAX	Terry,	PHILLIP
Teri	AUSTIN tv	Terry,	RUTH
Teri	COPLEY	Terry,	SHEILA
Teri	GARR tv+	Terry-Costin, KIM tv	
Teri	HATCHER tv+	Terry-Thomas --- cm+ Br	
Teri	MURPHY tv	Terzieff, LAURENT tv+	
Teri	NUNN	Tesh,	JOHN tv
Teri	POLO	Tesla,	NIKOLA eng,i Am
Teri	WEIGEL	Tesreau,	KRISTA tv
Terkel,	STUDS p-n'85+	Tess	HARPER
Terlesky,	JOHN	Tessa	HUMPHRIES
Terman,	LEWIS ps,e,w Am	Tessie	O'SHEA s,tv
Termier,	PIERRE geol,e Fr	Tessier,	MICHAEL tv
Terra,	GABRIEL l,st Urug	Tessier,	ROBERT
Terrance	MANN	Tessin,	NICODEMUS ac Swe
Terray,	JOSEPH r,st Fr	Testi,	FABIO
Terrell,	STEVEN tv+	Tetens,	JOHANNES math,ph Ger
Terri	AUSTIN	Tetley,	WALTER tv
Terri	GARBER tv	Tetrazzini, LUISA sopr It	
Terri	GARDNER tv	Tetsuro	TAMBA
Terri	GIBBS s-cnt Am	Tevfik,	MEHMED po Turk
Terri	IVENS tv	Tevis,	LLOYD bus,f Am
Terri	TREAS	Tewes,	LAUREN tv+
Terri	WOOD tv	Tex	AVERY cr Am
Terrio,	DENEY tv	Tex	BENEKE mj.cn Am
Terriss,	WILLIAM la Br	Tex	COBB
Terry	CARTER tv+	Tex	McCRARY tv
Terry	DONAHOE tv	Tex	RITTER s-cnt+ Am
Terry	FARRELL	Tex	SCHRAMM fb hf
Terry	FROST	Texas	GUINAN(Mary)s Am
Terry	GILLIAM d,w+ Am	Tey,	JOSEPHINE w Scot
Terry	HALL mr-s Br	Teyte,	MAGGIE soprano Br
Terry	HUGHES d	Thad	COCHRAN st Am
Terry	JONES	Thad	JONES mj-trump Am
Terry	KATH mr-guit Am	Thaddeus	CAHILL i Am
Terry	KINNEY	Thaddeus	STEVENS l,st Am
Terry	KIRKMAN mr-kbds,s Am	Thal,	ERIC
Terry	KISER tv+	Thalberg,	IRVING film-exec Am
Terry	LEWIS pr-music Am	Thales	--- ph Gr
Terry	McGOVERN tv	Thall,	BILL tv
Terry	McMILLAN w Am	Thant,	U secy gen@UN Burma

Tharaud,	JEROME j,w Fr
Tharp,	TWYLA ba Am
Thatcher,	BECKY fc
Thatcher,	MARGARET PrimeMin. Br
Thatcher,	TORIN
Thaw,	JOHN
Thaxter,	CELIA po Am
Thaxter,	PHYLLIS
Thayer	DAVID
Thayer,	ABBOTT p Am
Thayer,	BRYNN
Thayer,	MAX
Thayer,	SYLVANUS ar,e Am
Thayer,	TINA
The	EDGE mr-guit Welsh
The	SVEDBERG sc,e Swe
Thea	GREGORY
Thea	MUSGRAVE c,cn Am
Theda	BARA
Theile,	JOHANN c Ger
Theiler,	MAX n-m'51
Theismann,	JOE fb-m'83,tv
Theiss,	BROOKE tv
Thel	ROSENBERG spy Am
Thelen,	JODI tv
Thelma	RITTER
Thelma	TODD
Thelonius	MONK mj,c,cn Am
Thenard,	LOUIS sc,e Fr
Theobald	BOHM flute,c Ger
Theodor	ADORNO ph,ct Ger
Theodor	BENFEY e Ger
Theodor	BOVERI sc,p Ger
Theodor	DAUBLER po Ger
Theodor	HERZL r,j Hung
Theodor	HEUSS st,j,w Ger
Theodor	HIPPEL w Ger
Theodor	LIPPS ph,e Ger
Theodor	MOMMSEN h Ger
Theodor	MUGGE w Ger
Theodor	MUNDT w,ct Ger
Theodor	STORM po,w Ger
Theodor von	KARMAN sc,eng Am
Theodor von	NEUHOF ar,st Ger
Theodor von	SICKEL h,e Ger
Theodore	BIKEL s+ Aus
Theodore	BILBO st Am
Theodore	DREISER w Am
Theodore	DUBOIS organ,c Fr
Theodore	GRANIK tv
Theodore	NAVARRO mj Am
Theodore	PARKER r,w,abolit Am
Theodore	RAIMI
Theodore	ROETHKE po Am
Theodore	ROSZAK su Am
Theodore	SCHULTZ ec Am
Theodore	STEEG st Fr
Theodore	THOMAS cn Am
Theodore	VAIL id-AT&T Am
Theodor	WELD ref Am
Theodore	WHITE j,w Am

Theodore	WILSON tv
Theodore de	BEZE r,l,po Fr
Theodore	SeussGEISEL(Dr.Seuss)w
Theodore von	ELTZ
Theodule	RIBOT ps,e Fr
Theognis	--- po Gr
Theophile	GAUTIER po, w Fr
Theophile de	VIAU po Fr
Theorell,	AXEL(Hugo)n-m'55
Theresa	MERRITT tv
Theresa	RANDLE
Theresa	RING tv
Theresa	RUSSELL
Theresa	SALDANA tv+
Therese	LIOTARD
Theroux,	PAUL w Am
Thesiger,	ERNEST
Thespis	--- po Gr
Thibault,	JACQUES w Fr
Thibaut,	ANTON l,e Ger
Thibeault,	DEBI
Thicke,	ALAN tv+
Thierry,	AUGUSTIN h Fr
Thiers,	LOUIS st,h Fr
Thigpen,	LYNNE tv+
Thill,	GEORGES tenor Br
Thinnes,	ROY tv+
Thirkell,	ANGELA w Br
Thistlethwaite,	ANTHONY mr-sax Br
Thokoly,	IMRE re Hung
Thom	BRAY tv
Thom	GUNN po Br
Thom	MATHEWS
Thom	SHARP tv
Thoma,	HANS p Ger
Thoma,	LUDWIG j,w Ger
Thoma,	MICHAEL tv
Thomas	AIRD po Scot
Thomas	ALDRICH po,w,j Am
Thomas	AMORY w Br
Thomas	ANDREWS sc,e Ir
Thomas	AQUINAS(St.)ph It
Thomas	ARCHER ac Br
Thomas	ARNE c Br
Thomas	ARNOLD e Br
Thomas	ASTLE h Br
Thomas	AUDLEY st Br
Thomas	BABSON tv
Thomas	BALL su Am
Thomas	BARLOW bb hf
Thomas	BEDDOES w,po Br
Thomas	BEECHAM(Sir)cn
Thomas	BEER w Am
Thomas	BENTON p Am
Thomas	BERGER w Am
Thomas	BEWICK illus Br
Thomas	BLOUNT h,w Fr
Thomas	BODLEY(Sir)st,e
Thomas	BROCK(Sir) su
Thomas	BROWN tv
Thomas	BROWNE(Sir)w

Thomas	BURKE w Br	Thomas	KINGO po,r Dan
Thomas	BUXTON(Sir)f,id	Thomas	KYD w Br
Thomas	CAHILL w Am	Thomas	LINLEY viol,c Br
Thomas	CALABRO tv	Thomas	LIPTON(Sir)id,yachts
Thomas	CAMPION po,c Br	Thomas	LODGE po,w Br
Thomas	CAREW po Br	Thomas	MacINNES w Can
Thomas	CAREY(Mutt)mj,cn Am	Thomas	MALORY(Sir)w
Thomas	CARLYLE w,h Scot	Thomas	MALTHUS ec,e,w Br
Thomas	CARR d+	Thomas	MANN w Ger
Thomas	CARTER tv+	Thomas	MBOYA st Kenya
Thomas	CECH sc Am	Thomas	McGEE st,w Can
Thomas	CHAPAIS(Sir)l,st Can	Thomas	McGUANE w Am
Thomas	CHONG	Thomas	McKEAN st,l Am
Thomas	CHUBB w Br	Thomas	MEIGHAN
Thomas	COLE p Am	Thomas	MERTON po,w,r Am
Thomas	COOK tourist agent Br	Thomas	MIDGLEY Jr sc,id Am
Thomas	COOKE po,j Br	Thomas	MINTON id-pottery Br
Thomas	COSTAIN w Can	Thomas	MOFOLO w Bantu
Thomas	D'URFEY c,w Br	Thomas	MOONEY labor Am
Thomas	DAVIS po Ir	Thomas	MOORE po Ir
Thomas	DEKKER w Br	Thomas	MORAN p Am
Thomas	DEWEY l,st Am	Thomas	MORE(Sir)st,po,w
Thomas	DEWING p Am	Thomas	MORGAN sc,e Am
Thomas	DIBDIN bio Br	Thomas	MORRIS g Scot
Thomas	DOGGETT la Ir	Thomas	MORTON colonizer,w Am
Thomas	DORGAN cr,j Am	Thomas	MUN w Br
Thomas	DUNCAN p Scot	Thomas	NASHE w Br
Thomas	DUNHILL c,e Br	Thomas	NAST cr Am
Thomas	DURANT id-rrs Am	Thomas	NORTON l,po Br
Thomas	DYKERS tv	Thomas	O'CONNOR j Ir
Thomas	EAKINS p Am	Thomas	O'NEILL(Tip)st Am
Thomas	ELYOT(Sir)st,w	Thomas	OTWAY w,po Br
Thomas	EMLYN r Br	Thomas	PAGE w,st Am
Thomas	EMMET l,st Ir	Thomas	PAINE ph,w,re Am
Thomas	ENGLISH md,l,w Am	Thomas	PARNELL po,r Ir
Thomas	FULLER r,w Br	Thomas	PARRAN Jr md,st Am
Thomas	GIBSON	Thomas	PEACOCK w,po Br
Thomas	GIRTIN p Br	Thomas	PHAER l,md Br
Thomas	GODFREY math,i Am	Thomas	PICTON(Sir)ar
Thomas	GOMEZ	Thomas	POSEY ar,st Am
Thomas	GRAHAM sc,e Scot	Thomas	PYNCHON w Am
Thomas	GRAY po Br	Thomas	RIVERS sc-md Am
Thomas	GRESHAM(Sir)f	Thomas	RODMAN ar Am
Thomas	GRIFFITH	Thomas	RUSK st Am
Thomas	HARDY w,po Br	Thomas	SAVERY eng-ar Br
Thomas	HEARNS box Am	Thomas	SAY sc,e Am
Thomas	HELWYS r Br	Thomas	SEE astr,e Am
Thomas	HEYWOOD w Br	Thomas	SEEBECK sc Ger
Thomas	HILL tv	Thomas	SOPWITH(Sir)id-planes
Thomas	HOBBES ph Br	Thomas	SPRAT r,w Br
Thomas	HOBY(Sir)st	Thomas	SULLY p Am
Thomas	HOOD po,ed Br	Thomas	SUMTER ar-re Am
Thomas	HOVING tv	Thomas	TOFT potter Br
Thomas	HUGHES l,ref,w Br	Thomas	TOMPION id-clocks Br
Thomas	HULME ct,ph,po Br	Thomas	TOUT h Br
Thomas	HUXLEY sc,e Br	Thomas	USK w Br
Thomas	INCE d,pr Am	Thomas	WADE(Sir)ar,st
Thomas	INSKIP st,l Br	Thomas	WAITES
Thomas	JACKSON ar-CSA am	Thomas	WAKLEY sc Am
Thomas	JONES su Am	Thomas	WALLER(Fats) mj Am
Thomas	KEN r,w-hymns Br	Thomas	WARTON h,ct,po Br

Thomas	WEELKES organ,c Br	Thompkins,RUSSELL Jr mr-s Am
Thomas	WELLER md Am	Thompson, ANDREA tv
Thomas	WILSON	Thompson, BRIAN tv+
Thomas	WOLFE w Am	Thompson, CAT bb hf
Thomas	WRIGHT d	Thompson, CHARLES tv
Thomas	WYATT(Sir)po,st	Thompson, CHUCK tv
Thomas a Becket --- r Br		Thompson, D'ARCY(Sir)sc,e Scot
Thomas a Kempis --- r, w Ger		Thompson, DALEY o-g'80'84
Thomas Alva EDISON i Am		Thompson, DAVID fur trade,x Can
Thomas Aquinas, SAINT r,ph It		Thompson, DOROTHY j Am
Thomas de LALLY w Fr		Thompson, EMMA o-a'92
Thomas Sturge MOORE po,h Br		Thompson, FRANCIS po Br
Thomas, AMBROISE c Fr		Thompson, FRED DALTON
Thomas, AUGUSTUS w Am		Thompson, HILARY tv
Thomas, B.J. s-pop Am		Thompson, J. LEE d
Thomas, BETTY tv+		Thompson, JACK
Thomas, BRUCE tv		Thompson, JEAN w Am
Thomas, CALVIN tv		Thompson, JENN tv
Thomas, D.M. po,w Welsh		Thompson, JOANN tv
Thomas, DAMIEN		Thompson, KAY mj-d Am
Thomas, DANNY tv+		Thompson, LARRY tv
Thomas, DAVE tv+		Thompson, LEA
Thomas, DEBI sk Am		Thompson, LINDA tv
Thomas, DICK tv		Thompson, MARSHALL tv+
Thomas, DYLAN po,w Welsh		Thompson, PAUL mr-drm Br
Thomas, E. DONNALL n-m'90		Thompson, REX
Thomas, EDWARD po,ct Br		Thompson, SADA tv+
Thomas, ERNEST tv		Thompson, SAM b hf
Thomas, FRANK b-mv'93'94		Thompson, TRACY w Am
Thomas, FRANK Jr tv+		Thompson, WILLIAM(Bendigo)boxBr
Thomas, FRANK tv		Thoms, WILLIAM antiquary Br
Thomas, FRANKIE tv		Thomsen, JULIUS sc,e Dan
Thomas, GERALD d		Thomsen, VILHELM philology Dan
Thomas, GORMAN b,hr'79'82		Thomson, DORRIE tv
Thomas, HEATHER tv+		Thomson, DOUGIE mr-bass Scot
Thomas, HELEN j Am		Thomson, ELIHU eng-elect,i Am
Thomas, HENRY		Thomson, GEORGE(Sir)n-p'37
Thomas, HOWARD tv		Thomson, GORDON tv
Thomas, HUGH w,h Br		Thomson, JAMES po (d 1882)Scot
Thomas, ISIAH bb		Thomson, JAMES po(d 1748)Scot
Thomas, JAMESON		Thomson, JOHN sc,e Scot
Thomas, JAY tv+		Thomson, JOSEPH(Sir)n-p'06
Thomas, LOWELL j,w Am		Thomson, KENNETH
Thomas, MARLO tv+		Thomson, KIM
Thomas, MARTHA e Am		Thomson, PATRICIA tv
Thomas, MARY mr-s Am		Thomson, R.H.
Thomas, MICHAEL TILSON cn		Thomson, ROY me-exec Br
Thomas, MILLARD mj,cn,c Am		Thomson, TOM p Can
Thomas, NORMAN r,ref Am		Thomson, VIRGIL p-m'49
Thomas, PHILLIP tv+		Thomson, WILLIAM math,sc,i Br
Thomas, R.S. po Welsh		Thon, MELANIE w Am
Thomas, RALPH d		Thonet, MICHAEL id-furnit Ger
Thomas, RAY mr-flte,harmo,s Br	Thor, JEROME tv
Thomas, RICHARD tv+		Thor, JON
Thomas, ROBIN tv+		Thora --- tv
Thomas, SETH id-clocks Am		Thora BIRCH
Thomas, THEODORE cn Am		Thora HIRD
Thomas, THURMAN fb-m'91		Thoralf SKOLEM math,e Nor
Thomas, WILLIAM Jr. tv		Thore EHRLINGmj-tru,cn,cSwe
Thome, FRANCIS c Fr		Thoreau, HENRY po, w Am
Thomerson,TIM tv+		Thorek, MAX md,w Am

Thorez,	MAURICE st Fr		Ti	LUNG
Thorild,	THOMAS j,po Swe		Tia	CARRERE
Thorley	WALTERS		Tiant,	LUIS(Oil Can)b
Thorn,	FRANKIE		Tibaldi,	PELLEGRINO p,ac It
Thorn,	TRACEY mr-s Br		Tibbett,	LAWRENCE bari Am
Thorndike,ASHLEY e,w Am			Tiberio	FIORILLO la It
Thorndike,SYBIL(Dame)la+			Tibullus,	ALBIUS po Ro
Thorne	SMITH w-humor Am		Tich	--- mr-guit Br
Thorne,	DYANNE		Tichy,	GERARD
Thorne,	GARY tv		Tickell,	THOMAS po Br
Thorne,	GEOFFREY tv		Ticker	FREEMAN piano,tv Am
Thorne,	TERESA tv		Ticknor,	GEORGE e,h Am
Thorne-Smith, COURTNEY tv+			Ticotin,	RACHEL tv+
Thornhill,JAMES(Sir)p			Tieck,	LUDWIG w Ger
Thornton	BURGESS w Am		Tiegs,	CHERYL mo,w Am
Thornton	WILDER w,e Am		Tiele,	CORNELIS r,e Dut
Thornton,	BILLY BOB d+		Tien	PANG
Thornton,	BLAIR mr-guit Can		Tiepolo,	GIOVANNI p It
Thornton,	LAWRENCE w Am		Tierney,	GENE
Thornton,	NOLEY		Tierney,	LAWRENCE
Thornton,	SIGRID tv+		Tierney,	MAURA
Thornton,	WILLIAM ac Am		Tietjens	EUNICE w Am
Thornycroft, HAMO(Sir)su			Tietz,	JOHANN astr,e Ger
Thorogood, GEORGE mr-guit,s Am			Tiffany	--- s Am
Thorold	DICKINSON d		Tiffany	BOLLING
Thorp,	JOHN iAm		Tiffany	LUBRAN tv
Thorpe,	JERRY d		Tiffany,	CHARLES jeweler Am
Thorpe,	JIM o-g'12,fb hf+		Tiffany,	LOUIS ds-jewelry Am
Thorpe,	RICHARD d		Tiffin,	PAMELA
Thorpe,	ROSE w Am		Tige	ANDREWS tv
Thors,	OLAFUR st Iceland		Tiger	WOODS g Am
Thorson,	LINDA tv		Tighe,	KEVIN tv+
Thorson,	RUSSELL tv		Tiiu	LEEK tv
Thorstein VEBLEN ec,ph,e Am			Tikkanen,	ESA ho
Thorton	WILDER w Am		Tilak,	BAL ed,e,ref India
Thorvaldsen, BERTEL su Dan			Tilbrook,	GLENN mr-guit,s Br
Thou,	JACQUES st,h Fr		Tilbury,	ZEFFIE
Thrale,	HESTER confidante Br		Tilda	SWINTON
Thrane,	MARCUS j,e Nor		Tilden,	WILLIAM(Big Bill)t Am
Three Stooges, THE cm+ Am			Tildy,	ZOLTAN st Hung
Threfall,	DAVID		Tilghman,	TENCH ar-re Am
Thring,	EDWARD e Br		Till,	ERIC d
Throne,	MALACHI tv		Tiller,	NADJA
Thue,	AXEL math,e Nor		Tiller,	TED tv
Thuille,	LUDWIG c Aus		Tilley,	CECIL minerals,e Br
Thulin,	INGRID tv+		Tilley,	VESTA s,impersonat Br
Thundercloud, CHIEF Am Indian			Tillich,	PAUL r,ph,e Am
Thurber,	JAMES w,cr Am		Tillis,	MEL s,ws Am
Thuret,	GUSTAVE sc Fr		Tillis,	PAM s Am
Thurloe,	JOHN st Br		Tillotson,JOHNNY s-cnt Am	
Thurlow	WEED j,ed,st Am		Tillstrom,BURR tv	
Thurman	MUNSON b		Tilly,	JENNIFER
Thurman	THOMAS fb		Tilly,	MEG
Thurman,	BILL		Tilton,	CHARLENE tv+
Thurman,	UMA		Tilton,	MARTHA mj,s+ Am
Thurmond,	NATE bb hf		Tilyou,	GEORGE bus Am
Thurmond,	STROM st Am.		Tilzer,	ALBERT von c Am
Thurston	HALL tv+		Tilzer,	HARRY von c Am
Thurston,	CAROL tv+		Tim	ALLEN tv
Thynne,	THOMAS st Br		Tim	BOGERT mr-bass Am
Thyssen,	FRITZid-steel Nazi Ger	Tim	BURTON d

Tim	CHOATE	Tina	BROWM ed Am
Tim	CONWAY tv+	Tina	COLE tv
Tim	CURRY	Tina	GAYLE tv
Tim	DALY tv+	Tina	LIFFORD tv+
Tim	FARRELL tv	Tina	LOUISE tv+
Tim	FINN mr-kbds,s N.Zea	Tina	THAYER
Tim	GRIMM tv	Tina	TURNER s+ Am
Tim	GUINEE	Tina	YOTHERS tv
Tim	HARRIS fb	Tinayre,	MARCELLE w Fr
Tim	HOLT	Tinbergen,JAN n-e'69
Tim	HUNTER d	Tinbergen,NIKOLAAS n-m'73
Tim	JONES tv	Tinel,	EDGAR piano,c Belg
Tim	MAIER tv+	Ting,	SAMUEL n-p'76
Tim	MARA fb hf	Tingwell,	CHARLES
Tim	McCARVER b,tv Am	Tinker to Evers to Chance b
Tim	McCOY	Tinker,	CHAUNCEY e Am
Tim	McGraw s-cnt Am	Tinker,	JOE b hf
Tim	McINTIRE tv+	Tinne,	ALEXANDRINE x Dut
Tim	MEADOWS tv	Tino	INSANA
Tim	MOORE tv	Tino	MARTINEZ b
Tim	O'BRIEN w Am	Tinti,	GABRIELE
Tim	O'CONNOR tv+	Tiny	GRIMES mj Am
Tim	PARKS w Am	Tiny	LISTER
Tim	QUILL	Tiny	LITTLE Jr piano,tv Am
Tim	RAINES b	Tiny	TIM fc
Tim	REID II tv	Tiomkin,	DIMITRI piano,c Am
Tim	REID tv+	Tip	O'NEILL st Am
Tim	ROBBINS d,w+ Am	Tipaldi,	ANDY mj-banjo,cn Can
Tim	ROTH	Tippett,	ANDRE fb-d'85
Tim	RUSSERT tv host	Tippi	HEDREN
Tim	RYAN tv+	Tippo,	PATTI tv
Tim	TOPPER tv	Tippy	WALKER
Tim	WHELAN d	Tiptoft,	JOHN st Br
Tim,	TINY fc	Tipton,	GLENN mr-guit Br
Timken,	HENRY id-bearings Am	Tisa	FARROW
Timmermans, FELIX w,po Belg	Tisch,	LAURENCE tv exec Am
Timotheus	--- po Gr	Tiselius, ARNE n-c'48
Timothy	ALUKO w Nigeria	Tisha	CAMPBELL tv+
Timothy	ARTHUR w Am	Tisha	STERLING
Timothy	BOTTOMS	Tisi,	BENVENUTO p It
Timothy	BRENT	Tiso,	JOSEF r,st Slovak
Timothy	BROWN tv+	Tissot,	JAMES p,engr Fr
Timothy	CAREY	Tisza,	KALMAN st Hung
Timothy	CARHART	Tita	BELL tv
Timothy	DALTON tv+	Titchener,EDWARD ps Am
Timothy	DALY tv+	Titian	--- p It
Timothy	DALY(Tim)tv+	Titl,	ANTON c Ger
Timothy	DEXTER mer,f Am	Tito	--- st Yugo
Timothy	DWIGHT po,e Am	Tito	BROZ st Yugo
Timothy	FARRELL	Tito	GOBBI bari It
Timothy	GIBBS tv+	Tito	GUIZAR
Timothy	HUTTON	Tito	JACKSON mr-s Am
Timothy	KEEFE b hf	Tito	JUNCO
Timothy	MURPHY tv	Tito	PUENTE mj,cn+ Am
Timothy	SCOTT tv+	Tito	SCHIPA tenor
Timothy	SPALL	Tito	VANDIS
Timothy	Van PATTEN tv+	Tittle,	Y.A. fb-m'61'3 hf
Timothy	WEST	Titus	MILO st Ro
Timrod,	HENRY po,j Am	Titus	OATES impostor Br
Tin	TAN	Titus	SALT(Sir)id
Tina	AUMONT	Tiziano	VECELLI p It

Tobe	HOOPER d		Toles,	TOM p-x'90
Tobey,	DAVID bbr hf		Tolkan,	JAMES
Tobey,	KEN tv		Tolkien	J.R.R. w Br
Tobey,	KENNETH		Tollens,	HENDRIK po Dut
Tobey,	MARK p Am		Toller,	ERNST w,po Ger
Tobias	ASSER l,e Dut		Tolo,	MARILU
Tobias	LEAR st Am		Tolsky,	SUSAN tv
Tobias	MATTHAY piano,c e Br		Tolstoy,	ALEKSEY w Rus
Tobias	SMOLLETT w Scot		Tolstoy,	LEV(Leo)w Rus
Tobias	WOLFF w Am		Tolstoy,	PYOTR st Rus
Tobias,	GEORGE tv+		Tom	ARNOLD tv+
Tobias,	HARRY c Am		Tom	ATKINS tv+
Tobias,	OLIVER		Tom	BAILEY mr-kbds,S Br
Tobin,	DAN tv+		Tom	BAKER
Tobin,	JAMES n-e'81		Tom	BELL tv+
Tobolowsky, STEPHEN			Tom	BOSLEY
Toch,	ERNEST(Ernst)p-m'56		Tom	BOWER tv+
Tochi,	BRIAN tv+		Tom	BROKAW tv-j,anchor+
Tocqueville, ALEXIS de h,w,st Fr			Tom	BROWN tv+
Tod	BARTON tv		Tom	BUTLER
Todd	ALLEN		Tom	BYRD tv
Todd	BRIDGES tv+		Tom	CLANCY w Am
Todd	CRESPI tv		Tom	CLARK st Am
Todd	FERRELL tv		Tom	CLEGG d
Todd	FIELD		Tom	CONTI
Todd	GRAFF		Tom	CONWAY tv+
Todd	KARNS tv		Tom	CRIBB boxer Br
Todd	PORTER tv		Tom	CRUISE
Todd	STARKE tv		Tom	D'ANDREA tv+
Todd	SUSMAN tv+		Tom	DRAKE
Todd,	ALEXANDER{Sir)n-c'57		Tom	DUGAN
Todd,	ANN tv+		Tom	EPLIN tv
Todd,	BEVERLY tv+		Tom	EWELL tv+
Todd,	BOB tv		Tom	FADDEN tv
Todd,	DANIEL tv		Tom	FEARS fb hf
Todd,	HALLIE tv		Tom	FOUTS(Stubby) tv
Todd,	JAMES tv+		Tom	GLAVIN b
Todd,	JOSEPH tv		Tom	GOLA bb hf
Todd,	MICHAEL tv		Tom	GRIES d
Todd,	RICHARD		Tom	HALL s Am
Todd,	RUSSELL tv+		Tom	HALLICK
Todd,	THELMA		Tom	HANKS tv+
Todd,	TONY		Tom	HELMORE
Todor	ALEKSANDROV re Rus		Tom	HODGES tv+
Todt,	FRITZ eng-ar Ger		Tom	HOWARD tv
Toe	BLAKE ho		Tom	HULCE
Toft,	THOMAS potter Br		Tom	JONES s-pop Welsh
Tognazzi, UGO			Tom	KEENE
Togo Heihachiro--- navy Jap			Tom	KENNEDY
Toivo	PEKKANEN w Finn		Tom	La GRUE tv
Tojo Hideki --- ar, st Jap			Tom	LANDRY fbc hf
Tokar,	NORMAN d		Tom	LESTER tv
Tokuda,	MARILYN		Tom	LIGON
Tolan,	MICHAEL tv+		Tom	LONDON
Toland,	JOHN p-n'71		Tom	MASON tv+
Tolbert	LANSTON i Am		Tom	MBOYA st Kenya
Tolbert,	BERLINDA tv		Tom	MIX la+ Am
Tolbert,	WILLIAM st Liberia		Tom	NARDINI tv+
Toledo,	PEDRO de ar Sp		Tom	NEAL
Tolentino,JOAN tv			Tom	NOLAN tv+
Toler,	SIDNEY		Tom	O'BRIEN

Tom	PACE	Tomlinson,	CHARLES po,ct Br
Tom	PAINE w Am	Tomlinson,	DAVID
Tom	PEDI tv	Tomlinson,	HENRY j,ed,w Br
Tom	PETTY guit,s Am	Tommaso	BAI tenor,c It
Tom	POSTON tv+	Tommaso de VIO r It	
Tom	POWERS	Tomme,	RON tv
Tom	REESE tv	Tommie	AGEE b
Tom	REILLY tv+	Tommie	LOY mj-trump Am
Tom	ROBBINS tv	Tommy	BENFORD mj-drm Am
Tom	ROBBINS w Am	Tommy	BERNARD tv
Tom	RUBEN tv	Tommy	BURNS boxer Can
Tom	RYAN cr Am	Tommy	BUSH tv
Tom	SAVINI	Tommy	DEVITO mr-guit.s Am
Tom	SAYERS boxer Br	Tommy	DORSEY mj,cn,tv+ Am
Tom	SCHOLZ mr-guit Am	Tommy	FARRELL tv+
Tom	SCOTT tv	Tommy	GERUN mj,cn Am
Tom	SEAVER b hf	Tommy	IVO tv
Tom	SELLECK tv+	Tommy	JAMES mr-s Am
Tom	SNYDER tv	Tommy	KIRK
Tom	SOLARI tv	Tommy	LASORDA bmg hf
Tom	TAMMII tv	Tommy	MOE ski Am
Tom	TAYLOR tv	Tommy	NEWSOM tv
Tom	TAYLOR w Br	Tommy	NOLAN tv
Tom	THOMSON p Can	Tommy	NOONAN
Tom	TOLES cr Am	Tommy	NORDEN tv
Tom	TOWLES	Tommy	PUETT tv
Tom	TRYON	Tommy	RALL
Tom	TULLY tv+	Tommy	RAMONE mr-drm Hung
Tom	TYLER	Tommy	RETTIG tv+
Tom	VERICA	Tommy	ROE s,ws Am
Tom	VILLARD	Tommy	SHAW mr-guit Am
Tom	WAITS s,c+ Am	Tommy	SOSEBEE tv
Tom	WATSON g Am	Tommy	STEELE guit,s+ Br
Tom	WIGGIN tv	Tommy	TUNE ba,d,tv+ Am
Tom	WILLETT tv	Tommy Lee JONES	
Tom	WILSON cr Am	Tomonaga,	SHIN'ICHIRO n-p'65
Tom	WOLFE j,w Am	Tompion,	THOMAS id-clocks Br
Tom	WOPAT b,tv+	Tompkins,	ANGEL tv+
Tom	YAWKEY b hf	Tompkins,	JOAN tv
Tom,	LAUREN	Tompson,	BENJAMIN e,po Am
Tomack,	SID tv	Tone	LOC
Tomas	ARANA	Tone,	FRANCHOT tv+
Tomas	BAT'A id Cz	Tone,	WOLFE rebel Irish
Tomas	MASARYK st,ph Cz	Tone-Loc	--- m-rap Am
Tomas	MILIAN	Tonegawa,	SUSUMU n-m'87
Tomas de	IRIARTE po sp	Tong,	KAM tv
Tomas M.	DYKERS tv	Tong,	SAMMEE tv
Tomasina,	JEANA	Tonge,	PHILIP tv
Tombaugh,	CLYDE astr Am	Toni	BASIL s+ Am
Tombs,	HENRY(Sir)ar	Toni	BRAXTON s-r&b Am
Tome de	SOUSA ar,st Port	Toni	GILMAN tv
Tomei,	CONCETTA tv+	Toni	HUDSON
Tomei,	MARISA o-s'92,tv+	Toni	KALEM
Tomelty,	FRANCES	Toni	NAPLES
Tomikawa,	AKIHIRO	Toni	NERO
Tomita,	TAMLYN	Toni	SAILER ski Aus
Tomkins,	THOMAS organ,c Br	Toni	TENNILLE s,tv Am
Tomkis,	THOMAS w Br	Toni	YUSKIS ba,tv Am
Tomlin,	BRADLEY p Am	Tonisson,	JAAN l,ed,st Estonia
Tomlin,	LILY tv+	Tonja	WALKER tv
Tomlin,	PINKY tv	Tonnies,	FERDINAND soc Ger

Tono,	EIJIRO	Tony	ROMANO tv
Tonoyama,	TAIJI	Tony	ROSATO tv+
Tonson,	JACOB pb Br	Tony	SACCO mj-s Am
Tonti,	LORENZO banker Fr	Tony	SANTINI tv
Tony	ANHOLT tv	Tony	SARG pupp Am
Tony	ARMAS b	Tony	SCOTT d
Tony	AUTH cr Am	Tony	SWARTZ tv
Tony	BANKS mr-kbds Br	Tony	TODD
Tony	BARRY	Tony	WILSON mr-bass,s Trin
Tony	BECKER tv	Tony	ZALE boxer
Tony	BELLAMY mr-guit,s Am	Tonya	CROWE tv
Tony	BENNETT s,tv+ Am	Tonya	WILLIAMS tv
Tony	BILL	Tooke,	HORNE st-re Br
Tony	BONNER	Toole,	JOHN p-f'81
Tony	BRITTON	Toombs,	ROBERT st Am
Tony	BURTON	Toomer,	JEAN w Am
Tony	BUTLER r-bass Br	Toomey,	REGIS tv+
Tony	CANADEO fb hf	Toorop,	JAN p Dut
Tony	CURTIS tv+	Tootoosis,	GORDON
Tony	DAKOTA tv	Toots	MONDELLO mj-sax Am
Tony	DANZA tv+	Toots	SHOR ny restruant Am
Tony	De COSTA tv	Topelius,	ZACHRIS w Finn
Tony	DeSIMONE m,tv Am	Topffer,	RODOLPHE p,w Swi
Tony	DORSETT fb hf	Topham,	ANTHONY mr-guit Br
Tony	DOW tv+	Topo	SWOPE
Tony	EASEN fb	Topol,	CHAIM
Tony	GANIOS	Toppano,	PETA
Tony	GARNIER ac Fr	Topper,	TIM tv
Tony	GOLDWYN	Tor	JOHNSON
Tony	GWYNN b,6xbat'89-96	Torben	MEYER
Tony	HADLEY mr-s Br	Torbern	BERGMAN sc Swe
Tony	HICKS mr-guit Br	Torelli,	GIACOMO ds-stage It
Tony	IOMMI mr-guit Br	Tori	AMOS mr-s Am
Tony	JACKSON mr-bass,s Br	Tori	BRENNO tv
Tony	JOHNSON tv+	Tori	SPELLING tv
Tony	KENDALL	Torin	THATCHER
Tony	KING tv+	Tork,	PETER mr-kbds,s Am
Tony	KUBEC b,tv	Tork,	PETER tv
Tony	KUSHNER w Am	Torme,	MEL s+ Am
Tony	La TORRE tv	Torn,	RIP
Tony	LAZZERI b hf	Torocsik,	MARI
Tony	LEMA g Am	Torpey,	ERIN tv
Tony	LEUNG	Torquato	TASSO po It
Tony	LoBIANCO	Torquet,	EUGENE w Fr
Tony	LONGO tv+	Torre,	JOE b-mv'71,rbi'71
Tony	LOREA	Torrence,	DEAN s Am
Tony	MARTIN tv+	Torrence,	ERNEST
Tony	MARVIN tv	Torrens,	ROBERT(Sir)ar,ec
Tony	MOTTOLA m,cn,tv Am	Torrent,	ANA
Tony	MUSANTE tv+	Torres,	LIZ tv+
Tony	O'DELL tv	Torres,	LUIS x Sp
Tony	OLIVA b	Torrey,	CHARLES h,e Am
Tony	ORLANDO s,tv Am	Torrey,	ROGER tv
Tony	PAREZ b	Torsvan,	BERWICK w Ger
Tony	PASTOR la Am	Toru	TANAKA
Tony	PECK	Torvay,	JOSE
Tony	PEREZ b	Tory,	GEOFFROY p Fr
Tony	PICA	Toscanini,	ARTURO cn It
Tony	PLANA	Toschia	MORI
Tony	RANDALL tv+	Toshiro	MIFUNE
Tony	ROBERTS tv+	Tosten	WIESEL md Am

Toth,	ANDRE de d	Tracy	WALTER
Toth,	LESLIE	Tracy	WELLS tv
Toth,	SUSAN ALLEN w	Tracy,	EMERSON
Totie	FIELDS cm,la Am	Tracy,	HONOR w Br
Toto	---	Tracy,	JILL tv
Toto	BRUGNON t Fr	Tracy,	LEE tv+
Totter,	AUDREY tv+	Tracy,	SPENCER o-a'37'38,tv+
Tough,	DAVE mj-drm Am	Tracy,	WILLIAM
Toukie	SMITH tv	Traetta,	TOMMASO c It
Toulet,	PAUL w Fr	Trafton,	GEORGE fb hf
Touliatos,	GEORGE tv+	Traherne,	THOMAS r,po Br
Toulouse-Lautrec --- p Fr		Traill,	CATHERINE w Can
Toulouse-Lautrec, HENRI p Fr		Train,	GEORGE mer Am
Tourgee,	ALBION w Am	Trainor,	MARY
Tourjee,	EBEN m Am	Trakl,	GEORG po Aus
Tourneur,	CYRIL w Br	Tranelli,	DEBORAH tv
Tourneur,	JACQUES d	Tranum,	CHUCK tv
Tourneur,	MAURICE d	Trapp,	MARIA s Am
Tourte,	FRANCOIS viol bows Fr	Trask,	DIANA tv
Toussaint,	BETH tv	Traube,	ISIDOR sc,e Ger
Toussaint,	LORRAINE	Traubel,	HELEN sopr+ Am
Tout,	THOMAS h Br	Traun,	OTTO ar Aus
Toutin,	JEAN p Fr	Travanti,	DANIEL J. tv+
Tova,	LUPITA	Traven,	B. w Ger
Tovah	FELDSHUH	Travers,	BEN w Br
Tovatt,	PATRICK tv	Travers,	BILL
Tovey,	DONALD(Sir)c,w	Travers,	BRIAN mr-sax Br
Towers,	CONSTANCE	Travers,	HENRY
Towles,	TOM	Travers,	JEROME g Am
Town,	ITHIEL ac Am	Travers,	MORRIS sc,e Br
Towne,	ALINE	Travers,	P.L. w Austra
Townes,	CHARLES n-p'64	Travis	FINE tv
Townsend,	BARBARA tv	Travis	JACKSON b hf
Townsend,	JILL tv+	Travis	McKENNA tv
Townsend	ROBERT	Travis	OSMOND s,tv Am
Townshend,	PETE mr-guit+ Br	Travis	TRITT s-cnt,ws Am
Townson,	RON mr-s Am	Travis,	JUNE
Toyah	WILCOX	Travis,	MERLE s-cntry Am
Toynbee,	ARNOLD h,e Br	Travis,	NANCY
Tozzer,	ALFRED an,e,w Am	Travis,	RANDY s-cnt Am
Tozzi,	FAUSTO	Travis,	RICHARD
Tozzi,	FEDERIGO w It	Travis,	STACEY
Tracey	GOLD tv	Travolta,	JOEY
Tracey	MANN	Travolta,	JOHN
Tracey	NEEDHAM tv	Tray	LOREN
Tracey	THORN mr-s Br	Traynor,	PIE b hf
Tracey	ULLMAN tv+	Treacher,	ARTHUR tv+
Tracey	WALTER tv+	Treas,	TERRI tv+
Tracey,	IAN	Treat	WILLIAMS
Trachta,	JEFF tv	Trebek,	ALEX tv-host Am
Traci	LIN	Tree,	HERBERT(Sir) la
Traci	LIND	Treece,	HENRY po,w Br
Traci	LORDS	Treen,	MARY tv+
Tracy	CHAPMAN s-flk,ws Am	Trelawny,	EDWARD bio Br
Tracy	JOHNS tv	Tremayne,	LES tv+
Tracy	KIDDER w Am	Trench,	RICHARD r,po Ir
Tracy	NELSON	Trenchard-Smith, BRIAN d	
Tracy	POLLAN tv+	Trendler,	ROBERT m,cn,tv Am
Tracy	REED tv+	Trent	LEHMAN tv
Tracy	REINER	Trent	LOTT st Am
Tracy	ROBERTS tv	Trent	REZNOR mr,s Am

Trent,	BUCK tv		Trolle,	GUSTAV r Swe
Trepov,	FYODOR st-police Rus		Trollope,	ANTHONY w Br
Trese,	ADAM		Trollope,	FRANCES w Br
Tresham,	FRANCIS conspiratr Br		Trollope,	JOANNA w Br
Tresvant,	RALPH mr-s Am		Trollope,	THOMAS w Br
Treub,	MELCHIOR sc Dut		Tromp,	MAARTEN navy Dut
Trevelyan,G.M. h Br			Trotsky,	LEON re,w Rus
Trevelyan,GEORGE OTTO(Sir)h,st			Trotter,	JOHN SCOTT m,cn,tv Am
Trevino,	LEE g Am		Trotter,	WILFRED md Br
Trevino,	VIC		Trottier,	BRYAN ho-m'79
Trevor	BULLOCK tv		Troughton,PATRICK	
Trevor	HOWARD		Troup,	BOBBY tv
Trevor,	CLAIRE o-s'48		Troup,	RONNE tv
Trevor,	WILLIAM w Ir		Trout,	ROBERT tv
Trevor-Roper, H.R. e,h Br			Trowbridge, CHARLES	
Trewavas, PETER mr-kbds Br			Trower,	ROBIN mr-guit Br
Trey	WILSON		Troy	AIKMAN fb
Tricia	CAST tv		Troy	BEYER tv+
Tricia	FISHER		Troy	CURVEY Jr tv
Tricky Sam NANTON mj-tromb Am			Troy	DONAHUE tv+
Triesault,IVAN			Troy	EVANS tv+
Trieste,	LEOPOLDO		Troy	SLATEN tv
Trifonov,	YURY w Rus		Troyat,	HENRI w,bio Fr
Trigger	--- Tonto's horse		Troyon,	CONSTANT p Fr
Trigger,	SARAH		Trudeau,	GARRY cr Am
Trigo,	FELIPE w Sp		Trudeau,	PIERRE st Can
Trikonis, GUS d			True,	JIM
Trilling, LIONEL ct,w,e Am			Truex,	ERNEST tv+
Trimble,	DAVID st, n-x'98		Truffaut,	FRANCOIS d+
Trimble,	ROBERT l,supr ct Am		Truinet,	CHARLES w Fr
Trina	PARKS		Trujillo,	RAOUL
Trini	ALVARADO		Truman	BRADLEY tv
Trini	LOPEZ s Am		Truman	CAPOTE w Am
Trinidad	SILVA tv+		Truman,	HARRY S. 33rd Pres.
Trinka,	PAUL tv		Truman,	MARGARET w Am
Trintignant, JEAN-LOUIS			Truman,	RALPH
Triolet,	ELSA w Fr		Trumbic,	ANTE st Croat
Tripp,	LOUIS		Trumbo,	DALTON w,w-films Am
Tripp,	PAUL tv		Trumbull,	JOHN p (d 1843) Am
Trippe,	JUAN bus-airline Am		Trumbull,	JOHN po,l (d 1831)Am
Trippi,	CHARLIE fb hf		Trump,	DONALD f Am
Tripplehorn, JEANNE tv			Trump,	IVANA(D's ex-wife) Am
Tris	COFFIN		Trump,	MARLA(D's wife'94-)Am
Tris	SPEAKER b hf		Trundy,	NATALIE
Trish	SOODIK tv		Trunk,	YEHIEL w Pol
Trish	STEWART tv+		Trusel,	LISA tv
Trish	VanDEVERE		Truth,	SOJOURNER r,ref Am
Trisha	NOBLE tv+		Truxtun,	THOMAS navy Am
Trissenaar, ELISABETH			Trygve	LIE secy gen@UN Nor
Trissino, GIAN po, w It			Tryon,	TOM
Trist,	NICHOLAS st Am		Tryon,	WILLIAM st Br
Tristan	BERNARD w Fr		Ts'ao Chan --- w China	
Tristan	ROGERS tv		Tsai	CHIN
Tristan	TZARA po,w Fr		Tsankov,	ALEKSANDUR st Bulg
Tristano, LENNIE mj-piano,c Am			Tschirky,	OSCAR maitre d' Am
Tristao da CUNHA x Port			Tschudi,	GILG h Swi
Tristram	COFFIN		Tse	LAN
Tritt,	TRAVIS s-cnt,ws Am		Tse-tung,	MAO st China
Troell,	JAN d		Tselikovskaya, LUDMILA	
Trofim	LYSENKO sc,e Rus		Tshombe,	MOISE st Congo
Troland,	LEONARD ps,sc,i Am		Tsu,	IRENE

Tsuchiya,   YOSHIO
Tsui,   DANIEL n-p'98
Tsukiyama,GAIL w Am
Tsung-Dao LEE sc Am
Tsvetayevna, MARINA po Rus
Tu Fu   --- po China
Tubb,   BARRY
Tubb,   ERNEST s-cnt Am
Tubman,   HARRIET abolition Am
Tubman,   WILLIAM st Liberia
Tucci,   CHRISTINE tv
Tucci,   MARIA
Tucci,   MICHAEL tv
Tucci,   STANLEY tv+
Tuchman,   BARBARA p-n'63'72
Tuchner,   MICHAEL d
Tucker,   BENJAMIN j,anarchy Am
Tucker,   CHRIS
Tucker,   DEBORAH tv
Tucker,   FORREST tv+
Tucker,   JIM mr-guit Am
Tucker,   MICHAEL tv+
Tucker,   MICK mr-drm Br
Tucker,   RICHARD
Tucker,   RICHARD tenor Am
Tucker,   SOPHIE s+ Am
Tucker,   TANYA s-pop+ Am
Tuckey,   JAMES x Br
Tudor,   ANTONY ba Br
Tuesday   WELD tv+
Tufano,   DENNIS mr-guit,s Am
Tufeld,   DICK tv
Tuffy   LEEMANS fb hf
Tufts,   CHARLES f Am
Tufts,   SONNY
Tugwell,   REXFORD ec,e,w Am
Tuke,   SAMUEL(Sir)ar,w
Tulane,   PAULmer,f-TulaneU. Am
Tulasne,   LOUIS sc Fr
Tull,   JETHRO farms,i Br
Tulley,   PAUL tv
Tulloch,   JOHN r Scot
Tully   MARSHALL
Tully,   JIM w Am
Tully,   MONTGOMERY d
Tully,   TOM tv+
Tulp,   NICOLAES md,sc,e Dut
Tulsidas   --- po India
Tun   ABDUL RAZAK st Malay
Tune,   TOMMY ba,d,tv+ Am
Tunnell,   EMLEN fb,hf
Tunney,   GENE boxer Am
Tupac   SHAKUR m-rap,w+ Am
Tupolev,   ANDREY eng-aero Rus
Tupper,   CHARLES(Sir)st Can
Tura   SATANA
Tura,   COSME p It
Turati,   FILIPPO socialist It
Turbo B   --- m-rap Am
Turgenev,   IVAN w Rus
Turgot,   ANNE-ROBERT st,ec Fr

Turhan   BEY
Turina,   JOAQUIN c Sp
Turing,   ALAN math,e Br
Turk   EDWARDS fb hf
Turk   MURPHY mj-tromb,c Am
Turkel   ANN
Turkel,   JOE
Turley,   BOB b-cy'58
Turlington, CHRISTY mo Am
Turman,   GLYNN tv+
Turnbeaugh, BRENDA tv
Turnbeaugh, WENDY tv
Turnbull,   JOHN
Turner,   BIG JOE s-r&b Am
Turner,   C.F. m-bass,s Can
Turner,   CLYDE(Bulldog)fb, hf
Turner,   FREDERICK p-h'33
Turner,   IKE s,ws Am
Turner,   JANINE tv+
Turner,   JIM tv+
Turner,   JOE mj,s-blues Am
Turner,   JOSEPH p Br
Turner,   KATHLEEN
Turner,   LANA tv+
Turner,   LONNIE mr-bass,s Am
Turner,   NAT slave leader Am
Turner,   RALPH h,e Am
Turner,   TED tv exec Am
Turner,   TINA s+ Am
Turner,   ZEKE m-cnt,tv Am
Turow,   SCOTT w Am
Turpin,   BEN
Turpin,   RICHARD highwayman Br
Turturro,   AIDA
Turturro,   JOHN
Tushingham, RITA
Tusi,   NASIR ad- ph,sc Pers
Tussaud,   MARIE(Mdm)wax figs Swi
Tusse   SILBERG
Tusser,   THOMAS farms Br
Tutin,   DOROTHY
Tutta   ROLF
Tuttle,   ASHLEY ba Am
Tuttle,   LURENE tv+
Tutu,   DESMOND r,n-x'84
Tutuola,   AMOS w Nigeria
Tuve,   MERLE sc,e Am
Tuwhare,   HONE po N.Zea
Tuwim,   JULIAN po Pol
Tuxen,   RIK mj,cn Dan
Twachtman,JOHN p Am
Twain,   MARK w Am
Tweed,   SHANNON tv+
Tweed,   TERRY tv+
Tweed,   WILLIAM(Boss)st Am
Twelvetrees, HELEN la+
Twiggy   --- mo+ Br
Twist,   NIGEL mr-drm Br
Twitty,   CONWAY s-cnt+ Am
Twomey,   ANNE

Tworkov,	JACK p Am
Twort,	FREDERICK sc Br
Twyla	THARP ba Am
Twyman,	JACK bb hf
Twysden,	ROGER(Sir)w,st
Ty	COBB b hf
Ty	HARDIN tv+
Ty	MILLER tv
Tyard,	PONTUS de po Fr
Tycho	BRAHE astr Dan
Tye,	CHRISTOPHER c Br
Tyler	BANKS tv
Tyler	DENNETT h,e Am
Tyler	NOYES tv
Tyler,	ANNE p-f'89
Tyler,	BENNET r,e Am
Tyler,	BEVERLY s Am
Tyler,	BONNIE s Welsh
Tyler,	CORY tv
Tyler,	JOHN 10th Pres
Tyler,	KIM tv
Tyler,	LIV
Tyler,	LYON e Am
Tyler,	MOSES h,ref,e Am
Tyler,	RICHARD tv
Tyler,	ROYALL l,w Am
Tyler,	STEVEN mr Am
Tyler,	TOM
Tyler,	WAT re Br
Tyler,	WILLIE cm,tv Am
Tylo,	HUNTER tv
Tylor,	EDWARD(Sir)an,e,w
Tynan,	KATHARINE po,w Ir
Tynan,	KENNETH ct-drama Br
Tyndall,	JOHN sc,e Ir
Tyne	DALY tv+
Tyner,	CHARLES tv+
Tyner,	McCOY mj-piano,cn Am
Tynyanov,	YURY ct,w Rus
Typhoid Mary	MALLON carrier Am
Tyra	BANKS mo,tv+ Am
Tyra	FERRELL tv+
Tyrell,	SUSAN
Tyrone	POWER
Tyrone	POWER Jr.
Tyrone	POWER Sr.
Tyrrell,	ANN tv
Tyrrell,	GEORGE r Ir
Tyrus	COBB(Ty) b hf
Tyson,	CATHY
Tyson,	CICELY tv+
Tyson,	MIKE boxer Am
Tyson,	RICHARD tv+
Tytler,	JAMES w Scot
Tytler,	PATRICK h Scot
Tyus,	WYOMIA runnr o-g'64'8
Tyutchev,	FYODOR po Rus
Tzara,	TRISTAN po,w Fr
Tzi	MA

THERE ARE NO "U" NAME
DESIGNATION CODES

"U" NATIONALITY CODE
Urug - URUGUAYAN

"U's"

U	SAW st Burma
U	THANT secy gen@UN Burma
U Tam'si,	TCHICAYA po Congo
U'Ren,	WILLIAM l,ref Am
Uberti,	FARINATA noble It
Uccello,	PAOLO p It
Udall,	NICHOLAS w,e Br
Uday	SHANKAR ba India
Udenio,	FABIANA
Udet,	ERNST fly,ar Ger
Udo	KIER
Udrzal,	FRANTISEK st Cz
Uecker,	BOB b,tv+ Am
Ueland,	OLE st Nor
Ufford,	ROBERT de ar Br
Ugarte,	MANUEL w Arg
Uggams,	LESLIE s,tv+ Am
Ugo	BASSI r It
Ugo	BETTI po,w It
Ugo	FOSCOLO w,po It
Ugo	OJETTI w,ct-art It
Ugo	TOGNAZZI
Ugo da	CARPI at It
Ugolino	VIVALDI mer It
Uhde,	FRITZ von p Ger
Uhland,	LUDWIG po Ger
Uhlen,	GISELA
Uhry,	ALFRED p-d'88
Ula	HOLT
Ulbricht,	WALTER st E.Ger
Ulf	PALME
Ulf	Von EULER md Swe
Uli	EDEL d
Ulie	PIEKARSKI tv
Ulises	DUNMONT
Ulla	JACOBSSON
Ulla	STROMSTEDT tv
Ulli	LOMMEL d+
Ullman,	TRACEY tv+
Ullmann,	LIV
Ulloa,	ANTONIO de navy,sc Sp
Ullrich	HAUPT
Ulmanis,	KARLIS st Lat
Ulmer,	EDGAR d
Ulric,	LENORE
Ulrich	BONER r,w Swi
Ulrich	GERING pb Swi
Ulrich	HAN print Aus
Ulrich	WILLE ar Swi
Ulrich	ZWINGLI r,ref Swi
Ulrich von	HUTTEN noble Ger
Ulrici,	HERMANN ph,e Ger
Ulrika	CANTH fe,w Finn
Ulvaeus,	BJORN mr-guit,s Swe

Uma	THURMAN
Umbers,	MARGARET
Umberto	LENZI d
Umberto	NOBILE eng-aero,x It
Umberto	ORSINI
Umberto,	ECO w It
Umeki,	MIYOSHI tv+
Una	MERKEL
Una	O'CONNOR
Unamuno,	MIGUEL de ph,po,w Sp
Uncle Dave MACON mj,s Am
Uncle Joe CANNON st Am
Unden,	BO OSTEN st,e Swe
Underhill,	EVELYN w Br
Underwood,	BLAIR tv+
Underwood,	JAY
Underwood,	OSCAR st Am
Undset,	SIGRID n-l'28
Une	WILKINSON
Unger,	DEBORAH
Unitas,	JOHNNY fb-m'57'67 hf
Unruh,	FRITZ von w Ger
Unruh,	JESSE st-Calif Am
Unseld,	WES bb-m'69 hf
Unser,	AL carrace Am
Unser,	BOBBY carrace Am
Untermeyer, LOUIS po,tv Am
Unwin,	STANLEY(Sir)pb
Updike,	JOHN p-f'82'91
Upfield,	ARTHUR w Aust
Upjohn,	RICHARD ac Am
Uppdal,	KRISTOFER w Nor
Upshaw,	DAWN sopr Am
Upshaw,	GENE fb hf
Upson,	RALPH eng-aero Am
Upton	SINCLAIR ref,w Am
Upton,	EMORY ar,w Am
Urban	FABER b hf
Urban,	JOSEPH ac Am
Ure,	MARY
Urecal,	MINERVA tv
Urena,	FABIO
Urey,	HAROLD n-c'34
Urfe,	HONORE d' w Fr
Uri	GELLER magic Aus
Uriah	HEEP fc
Uriah	LEVY navy Am
Uriburu,	JOSE ar,st Arg
Urich,	ROBERT tv+
Uriel da	COSTA r,w Port
Uris,	LEON w Am
Urquhart,	GORDON tv+
Urquhart,	ROBERT
Urquhart,	THOMAS(Sir)w
Urquiza,	JUSTO ar,st Arg
Urs	GRAF at,engr Swi
Ursitti,	SUSAN
Ursula	ANDRESS
Ursula	HEGI w Am
Ursula	HOWELLS
Ursula	JEANS

Ursula	Le GUIN w-scifi Am
Urth,	NORN fc
Usakhgil,	HALID w Turk
Usigli,	RODOLFO w Mex
Usk,	THOMAS w Br
Uslar Pietri, ARTURO w Venz
Uspensky,	GLEB w Rus
Ussher,	JAMES r,e,w Irish
Ustinov,	DMITRY st Rus
Ustinov,	PETER o-s'60'64
Uta	HAGEN
Utay,	WILLIAM tv
Utesov,	LEONID mj,cn Rus
Utley,	GARRICK tv-j,anchor Am
Utrillo,	MAURICE p Fr
Uttal,	JAI m,cn India
Uvedale	PRICE(Sir)ac-land
Uxor	CAESER Julius' wife
Uys,	JAMIE d
Uz,	JOHANN po Ger

"V" NAME DESIGNATION CODES
     viol - VIOLIN

"V" NATIONALITY CODE
     Venz - VENEZUELAN

"V's"

V.S.	NAIPAUL w W.Indies
Vaananen,	KARI
Vaccaro,	BRENDA
Vachel	LINDSAY po Am
Vachell,	HORACE w Br
Vaclav	HAVEL w,po Cz
Vaclav	JEBAVY po Cz
Vaclav	NECKAR
Vade,	JEAN po,w Fr
Vadim,	ROGER d
Vadino	VIVALDI mer It
Vadis,	DAN
Vagn	EKMAN sc-oceans Swe
Vail,	ALFRED id-telegrph Am
Vail,	THEODORE id-AT&T Am
Vailland,	ROGER w Fr
Vaino	TANNER st Finn
Val	AVERY
Val	FITCH sc Am
Val	KILMER
Valangiman SASTRI st India
Valberg,	BRIGITTA
Valcour	AIME farmer Am
Valdes,	GABRIEL de po Cuba
Valdes,	PETER(Pierre) r Fr
Valdez,	LUIS d
Valdimer	KEY sc-politics Am
Valdis,	SIGRID tv
Vale,	JERRY s-pop Am
Vale,	VIRGINIA
Valens,	RITCHIE mr-s Am

Valente, JOSE po Sp	Van Damme,JEAN-CLAUDE
Valentin KATAYEV w Rus	Van de Venter, FRED tv
Valentina CORTESE	Van den Elsen, SYLVIE
Valentine DYALL	Van der Meer,JAN p Dut
Valentine, HILTON mr-guit Br	Van der Post,LAURENS w S.Afr
Valentine, KAREN tv+	Van der Rohe,MIES ac Am
Valentine, SCOTT tv+	Van Der Velde, NADINE
Valentino, RUDOLPH	Van DeVen, MONIQUE
Valenza, TASIA	Van Devere, TRISH
Valenzuela, FERNANDO b-cy'81	Van Doren, CARL ed,ct,bio Am
Valera y Alcala G.,JUAN w,ct Sp	Van Doren, MAMIE
Valeria GOLINO	Van Doren, MARK w,e,p-q'40
Valerie CURTIN	Van Dorn, EARL ar Am
Valerie HARPER tv+	Van Dusen, GRANVILLE
Valerie HOBSON	Van Duyn, MONA p-q'91
Valerie PERRINE	Van Dyck, ANTHONY(Sir)p Belg
Valerie TAYLOR tv	Van Dyck, JENNIFER tv
Valery LARBAUD w Fr	Van Dyke, BARRY tv+
Valery, PAUL po,ct Fr	Van Dyke, CONNY
Valeska GERT	Van Dyke, DICK tv+
Valez, EDDIE	Van Dyke, HENRY r,w Am
Valie EXPORT d	Van Dyke, HILARY tv
Valk, FREDERICK	Van Dyke, JERRY tv+
Valla, LORENZO w It	Van Dyke, WOODBRIDGE d
Vallance, LOUISE tv	Van Eman, CHARLES tv
Valle-Inclan, RAMON del w Sp	Van Eps, GEORGE mj-guit Am
Vallee, MARCEL	Van Exel, NICK bb
Vallee, RUDY mj-s,cn+ Am	Van Eyck, PETER
Vallejo, CESAR po Peru	Van Eyssen, JOHN
Vallejo, MARIANO ar,st Am	Van Fleet, JO o-s'55
Vallely, JAMES tv	Van Gogh, VINCENT p Dut
Vallely, TANNIS tv	Van Halen, ALEX mr-drums Dut
Valles, JULES j,socialist Fr	Van Halen, EDDIE mr s Dut
Valley, MARK tv	Van Hentenryck, KEVIN
Valley, PAUL tv	Van Heusen, JIMMY c Am
Valli, ALIDA	Van Hise, CHARLES geol,e Am
Valli, FRANKIE s+ Am	Van Horne, HARRIET tv
Valli, JUNE tv	Van Kamp, MARETE tv+
Valli, ROMOLO	Van Loon, HENDRIK h,w Am
Valli, VIRGINIA	Van Nessa CLARKE tv
Vallin, RICK	Van Pallandt, NINA
Vallone, RAF	Van Patten, DICK tv+
Valois, CHARLES de ar Fr	Van Patten, JAMES tv+
Valory, ROSS mr-bass Am	Van Patten, JOYCE tv+
Van CLIBURN piano Am	Van Patten, NELS
Van HEFLIN tv+	Van Patten, TIMOTHY tv+
Van JOHNSON tv+	Van Patten, VINCENT tv+
Van WILLIAMS tv	Van Peebles, MARIO tv+
Van Allen,JAMES sc Am	Van Peebles, MELVIN tv+
Van Alstyne, EGBERT c Am	Van Sloan, EDWARD
Van Ammelrooy, WILLEKE	Van Spee, GRAF navy,st Ger
Van Ark, JOAN tv+	Van Steeden, PETER m,cn,tv Am
Van Atta, LEE	Van Valkenburgh, DEBORAH tv+
Van Bergen, LEWIS	Van Vechten, CARL ct,w Am
Van Brocklin, NORM fb-m'60 hf	Van Vleck, JOHN n-p'77
Van Buren, ABIGAIL(Ask Abby}j Am	Van Wyck BROOKS h Am
Van Buren, MARTIN 8th pres	Van Zandt, BILLY tv
Van Buren, STEVE fb hf	Van Zandt, DONNIE mr-guit,s Am
Van Cleef, LEE	Van Zandt, PHILIP
Van Cliff, RON	Van't Hoff, JACOBUS n-c'01
Van Dam, JOSE baritone Belg	Van, BILLY tv

Van,	BOBBY	Vasconcelos,	JOSE e,ph,w Mex
Van,	GAREWOOD mj,cn Am	Vasek,	VLADIMIR po Czech
Van,	GLORIA tv	Vasily	BARTOLD an Rus
Van,	JACKIE s,tv Am	Vasily	BLUCHER ar Rus
Vanbrugh,	JOHN(Sir)w,ac	Vasily	BYKOV w Rus
Vance	PALMER po,w Aust	Vasily	RADLOV e,philolog Rus
Vance,	COURTENEY	Vasily	ROZANOV w.ct.ph Rus
Vance,	DANITRA tv+	Vasquez,	ROBERTA
Vance,	DAZZY b hf	Vassar,	MATTHEW id-beer,f Am
Vance,	ETHEL tv,	Vassey,	KIN guit,tv Am
Vance,	LOUIS w Am	Vassilli	KARIS
Vance,	VIVIAN tv	Vattel,	EMMERICH von l Swi
Vance,	ZEBULON st,ar-CSA Am	Vatutin,	NIKOLAY ar Rus
Vancouver,	GEORGE navy,x Br	Vauban,	SEBASTIEN ar-eng Fr
Vancura,	VLADISLAV md,w Cz	Vaucher,	JEAN sc,r,e Swi
Vanda,	HARRY mr-guit Dut	Vaugelas,	CLAUDE e,w Fr
Vandenberg,	ARTHUR ed,st Am	Vaughan Williams,	RALPH c Br
Vanderbilt,	CORNELIUS id Am	Vaughan,	HENRY po Br
Vanderbilt,	GLORIA ds Am	Vaughan,	PARIS
VanderPyl,	JEAN tv	Vaughan,	PETER
Vandis,	TITO	Vaughan,	SARAH(Sassy)mj,s Am
Vandivier,	FUZZY bb hf	Vaughn	MEADER m Am
Vandross,	LUTHER s-r&b Am	Vaughn	MONROE mj,s Am
Vane,	HENRY(Sir)st	Vaughn	TAYLOR tv+
Vane,	JOHN n-m'82	Vaughn,	ALBERTA
Vane,	SUTTON w Br	Vaughn,	ARKY b hf
Vanel,	CHARLES	Vaughn,	COUNTESS tv
Vanessa	ANGEL mo+ Am	Vaughn,	DENNY m,cn,tv Am
Vanessa	BROWN tv+	Vaughn,	HEIDI
Vanessa	MARCIL tv	Vaughn,	MO b-mv'95
Vanilla	ICE m-rap Am	Vaughn,	NED tv
Vanity	---	Vaughn,	ROBERT tv+
Vanna	WHITE tv+	Vaughn,	STEVIE RAY mj,guit Am
Vannelli,	GINO s,ws Can	Vautier,	BENJAMIN p,illus Swi
Vannevar	BUSH eng-elec Am	Vaux,	CALVERT ac-landscp Am
Vanni,	RENATO	Vavilov,	NIKOLAY sc,e Rus
Vanocur,	SANDER tv+	Vawter,	NANCY tv
Vanzina,	CARLO d	Vawter,	RON
Varchi,	BENEDETTO h It	Vazov,	IVAN po,w,st Bulg
Varda,	AGNES d	Ve Sota,	BRUNO
Varden,	NORMA tv+	Veber,	FRANCIS d
Vardon,	HARRY g Br	Veblen,	OSWALD math,e,w Am
Vare,	DANIELE st,w It	Veblen,	THORSTEIN ec,ph,e Am
Varela,	JAY tv	Vecchi,	ORAZIO c It
Varen,	BERNHARD geog Ger	Vecelli,	TIZIANO p It
Varese,	EDGARD c Am	Ved	MEHTA j,w India
Vargas Llosa,	MARIO w Peru	Veda Ann	BORG
Vargas,	GETULIO st Braz	Vedder,	EDDIE mr,s Am
Vargas,	LUIS de p Sp	Vedder,	ELIHU p,illus Am
Varian,	RUSSELL sc,i,e Am	Vedel,	ANDERS h Dan
Varley,	BEATRICE tv+	Vee,	BOBBY s,ws Am
Varley,	JOHN p Br	Veeck,	BILL bmg hf
Varmus,	HAROLD n-m'89	Veen,	OTTO van p Dut
Varnay,	ASTRID s-opera	Vega,	ISELA
Varney,	JIM tv+	Vega,	LOPE de w,po Sp
Varnum,	JAMES l,ar-re Am	Vega,	SUZANNE s-folk Am
Varolio,	COSTANZO md,e It	Vegio,	MAFFEO r,w It
Varsi,	DIANE	Veidt,	CONRAD
Vasari,	GIORGIO p,ac,h-art It	Veit,	PHILIPP p Ger
Vasco da	GAMA x Port	Veit,	STOSS p,su
Vasco N. de	BALBOA x sp	Vela,	VINCENZO su It

Velasco, LUIS de st Sp	Verna BLOOM
Velasquez,LORENA	Verna FELTON tv+
Velasquez,PILAR	Verna HILLIE
Velazquez,DIEGO p Sp	Verne ROWE tv
Velde, ESAIAS van de p Dut	Verne, JULES w Fr
Velde, HENRY ac Belg	Verne, KAREN
Velez de Guevara, LUIS w Sp	Vernee WATSON
Velez, EDDIE tv+	Verner, KARL philology Dan
Velez, LUPE	Verney CAMERON x Br
VelJohnson, REGINALD tv	Vernier, PIERRE math,st,i Fr
Velvet BRUEGEL(Jan)p Belg	Vernon CASTLE ba,fly Br-Am
Venable, EVELYN	Vernon DALHART s-cnt Am
Vendela --- mo Swe	Vernon DENT
Venn, JOHN e,w Br	Vernon DUKE c Am
Venner, ELSIE fc	Vernon LAW b
Vennera, CHICK	Vernon SEWELL d
Venora, DIANE	Vernon WATKINS po Welsh
Ventham, WANDA	Vernon WEDDLE tv
Ventris, MICHAEL ac Br	Vernon WELLS
Ventura JESSE	Vernon, EDWARD(OldGrog)nav Br
Ventura, LINO	Vernon, HARVEY tv
Venture, RICHARD	Vernon, HOWARD
Venturi, ADOLFO h-art It	Vernon, IRENE tv
Venus WILLIAMS t Am	Vernon, JOHN
Venuti, JOE mj-viol Am	Vernon KATE tv+
Venyamin KAVERIN w Rus	Vernon, LILLIAN bus Am
Vera FIGNER re,w Rus	Vernon, WALLY
Vera FISCHER	Veronese, PAOLO p It
Vera LYNN mj-s Br	Veronica HAMEL tv+
Vera MILES	Veronica HURST
Vera PANOVA w Rus	Veronica LAKE
Vera RALSTON	Verrell, CEC
Vera WANG ds Am	Verri, PIETRO ec,j,w It
Vera, BILLY m,cn,tv+ Am	Verrill, ADDISON sc,e Am
Vera, RICKY tv	Verrill, ALPHEUS x Am
Vera, VICTORIA	Verrio, ANTONIO p It
Vera-Ellen ---	Verrocchio, ANDREA del su,p,at It
Vercel, ROGER w Fr	Versace, GIANNI ds It
Vercors --- w Fr	Versalles,ZOILO b-mv'65
Verde, CESARIO po Port	Versois ODILE
Verden ALLEN mr-kbds Br	Verwey, ALBERT po,ct Dut
Verdi, GIUSEPPE c It	Very, JONES po,w Am
Verdine WHITE mr-bass,s Am	Vesaas, TARJEI w Nor
Verdon, GWEN ba+ Am	Vesey, DENMARK re Am
Verdu, MARIBEL	Vespucci, AMERIGO x It
Verdugo, ELENA tv+	Vesta TILLEY s,impersonat Br
Vere CHILDE h,e Aust	Vestine, ERNEST sc,e Am
Vere, FRANCIS(Sir)ar	Vestine, HENRY mr-guit Am
Vereen, BEN tv+	Vesto SLIPHER astron Am
Verga, GIOVANNI w It	Vestris, LUCIA la,s,pr Br
Vergil --- po Ro	Vian, BORIS w Fr
Verhaeren,EMILE po Belg	Vianney, JEAN r Fr
Verhoeven,PAUL d	Viardot, PAULINE mezzo Fr
Verica TOM	Viau, THEOPHILE de po Fr
Verissimo,ERICO w Braz	Viaud, LOUIS navy,w Fr
Veritch, SEAN de tv	Vic DAMONE s,tv+ Am
Verjus, LOUIS st Fr	Vic DIAZ
Verlaine PAUL po Fr	Vic DUNLOP tv+
Verlaine, TOM mr-guit,s Am	Vic MORROW tv+
Vermeer, JAN p Dut	Vic TAYBACK tv+
Vermeylen,AUGUSTE w,ct Belg	Vic TREVINO

Vice,	LISA w Am		Victoria	RACIMO tv+
Vicente,	GIL w Port		Victoria	TENNANT
Vichard,	CESAR h Fr		Victoria	VERA
Vick,	JAMES sc,bus,pb Am		Victoria	YOUNG tv
Vickers,	EDWARD id-steel Br		Victoria,	TOMAS LUIS de c Sp
Vickers,	MIKE mr-guit Br		Victortien SARDOU w Fr	
Vickery,	HOWARD navy Am		Vida	BLUE b
Vicki	BAUM w Am		Vida	HOPE
Vicki	BIRD tv		Vida,	GIROLAMO (Marco) po It
Vicki	POWERS		Vidal	SASSOON hair style Br
Vicki	SCHRECK tv		Vidal,	GORE w+
Vicki	VOLANTE		Vidal,	HENRI
Vico,	GIAMBATTISTA ph,e It		Vidalin,	JON r Iceland
Victor	ADLER st Aus		Vidler,	STEVEN
Victor	ARDEN m-pian,mj,cn Am		Vidocq,	FRANCOIS police Fr
Victor	ARGO		Vidor,	CHARLES d
Victor	BABES md,sc,e Rom		Vidor,	FLORENCE
Victor	BARBEE ba Am		Vidor,	KING d
Victor	BERGER ed,st Am		Viebig,	CLARA w Ger
Victor	BORGE cm,tv+ Dan		Vieille,	PAUL eng Fr
Victor	BUONO		Vieira,	ANTONIO r,st,w Port
Victor	CAMPOS tv		Vieira	ASIA
Victor	COUSIN ph Fr		Viereck,	GEORGE w Am
Victor	DUNLOP tv+		Viereck,	PETER p-q'49
Victor	DURUY h,e Fr		Viet	STOSS su Ger
Victor	FLEMING d		Viete,	FRANCOIS math,l Fr
Victor	FRANCEN		Vigano,	SALVATORE ba It
Victor	FRENCH tv+		Viger,	DENIS st Can
Victor	GRUEN ac Am		Viggo	HORUP j,st Dan
Victor	HANSON bb hf		Viggo	MORTENSEN
Victor	HERBERT cn,c Am		Viggo	STUCKENBERG po Dan
Victor	HESS sc,e Am		Vigneaud,	VINCENT du n-c'55
Victor	HORTA ac Belg		Vignola,	GIACOMO da ac It
Victor	HUGO w,po Fr		Vigny,	ALFRED de po,w Fr
Victor	JORY tv+		Vigoda,	ABE tv+
Victor	KILIAN tv+		Viharo,	ROBERT tv+
Victor	LANOUX		Vijay	AMITRAJ t,tv+ India
Victor	LAWSON j,pb Am		Vikki	CARR
Victor	LOVE		Vikram	CHANDRA w India
Victor	MADDERN tv		Viktor	CHERNOV j,st Rus
Victor	MATURE		Viktor	DANKL ar Aus
Victor	MAUREL bari Fr		Viktor	DYK w Cz
Victor	McLAGLEN		Viktor	HENSEN md-sc,e Ger
Victor	MOORE		Viktor	KAPLAN i Aus
Victor	MUSTEL i,id Fr		Viktor	MEYER sc,e Ger
Victor	NOIR j Fr		Viktor	SANEEV o-g'68'72'76
Victor	NUNEZ d		Vilar,	JEAN la,d Fr
Victor	POTEL		Vile,	WILLIAM cabinets Br
Victor	SEN YUNG tv		Vilfredo	PARETO ec It
Victor	WONG		Vilhelm	BUHL st Dan
Victor	YOUNG mj,pop,cn,c Am		Vilhelm	MOBERG w Swe
Victor Sen YUNG			Viljo	REVELL ac Finn
Victor,	KATHERINE		Villa,	FRANCISCO (Pancho) reMx
Victor,	ORVILLE w,pb Am		Villa,	LUCHA
Victoria	ABRIL		Villa-Lobos,	HEITOR c Braz
Victoria	CARROLL tv		Villard,	HENRY j,bus-rrs,f Am
Victoria	CATLIN tv+		Villard,	OSWALD j,ed,pb Am
Victoria	FOYT		Villard,	TOM
Victoria	HALLMAN tv		Villari,	PASCUALE h It
Victoria	HOLT w Br		Villars,	CLAUDE st,ar Fr
Victoria	JACKSON		Villaume,	ASTRID

Villaverde,	MANOLO tv	Vinson,	FREDERICK l,ch just Am
Villechaize,	HERVE tv+	Vinson	GARY tv
Villele,	JOSEPH st Fr	Vinson,	HELEN
Villena,	ENRIQUE de w Sp	Vinson,	JACKIE tv
Villeret,	JACQUES	Vint,	ALAN
Villers,	JAMES	Vint,	BILL
Villon,	FRANCOIS po Fr	Vint,	JESSE
Villon,	JACQUES p Fr	Vintas,	GUSTAV
Vilmorin,	LOUISE de w,po Fr	Vinton	FREEDLY tv
Vin	BAKER bb	Vinton	HAYWORTH tv
Vinay,	RAMON tenor	Vinton,	BOBBY tv+
Vincas	KREVE w,po,e Lith	Vio,	TOMMASO de r It
Vince	BARNETT	Viola	ALLEN la Am
Vince	CLARKE mr-kbds Br	Viola,	FRANK b-cy'88
Vince	CONTI tv	Violet	HUNT bio,w Br
Vince	EDWARDS tv+	Violet	JACOB w,po Scot
Vince	GILL s-cnt Am	Violet	MARTIN w Ir
Vince	HOWARD tv	Violet	PAGET w,ct-art Br
Vince	MARTELL mr-guit Am	Violetta	ELVIN ba Br
Vince	NEIL mr-s Am	Violette	LEDUC w Fr
Vince	WELNICK mr-kbds Am	Violle,	JULES sc,e Fr
Vince,	PRUIT TAYLOR	Viollet-le-Duc,	EUGENE ac Fr
Vincent	ALSOP r Br	Viotti,	GIOVANNI viol,cn It
Vincent	AURIOL st Fr	Vir	SAVARKAR st,re
Vincent	BALL	Vira	SILENTI
Vincent	BENDIX id,i Am	Virchow,	RUDOLF md-sc,st,e Ger
Vincent	BUFANO tv	Viren,	LASSE 4x o-g'72'76
Vincent	KLYN	Viret,	PIERRE r Swi
Vincent	LOPEZ mj,cn,tv Am	Virgil	--- po Ro
Vincent	McEVEETY d	Virgil	FOX organ Am
Vincent	PARK w Am	Virgil	FRYE
Vincent	PRICE tv+	Virgil	THOMSON c,ct Am
Vincent	ROSE c Am	Virgil	VOGEL d
Vincent	SPANO	Virginia	APGAR md,e Am
Vincent	Van GOGH p Dut	Virginia	BRUCE
Vincent	Van PATTEN tv+	Virginia	BURTON w Am
Vincent	WINTER	Virginia	CAPERS tv+
Vincent	YOUMANS c Am	Virginia	CURTIS tv
Vincent d'INDY c Fr		Virginia	DARE 1st child in Am
Vincent van GOGH p Dut		Virginia	FIELD
Vincent,	CHUCK d	Virginia	GIBSON tv+
Vincent,	FRANK	Virginia	GORDON tv
Vincent,	JAN-MICHAEL tv+	Virginia	GORSKI tv
Vincent,	JUNE	Virginia	GRAHAM tv
Vincent,	VIRGINIA tv	Virginia	GREGG tv+
Vincenzo	BELLINI c It	Virginia	GREY
Vincenzo	CAMPI p It	Virginia	HAWKINS tv
Vincenzo	CIAMPI c It	Virginia	HEWITT tv
Vincenzo	FOPPA p It	Virginia	HUSTON
Vincenzo	MONTI po,e It	Virginia	MADSEN
Vincenzo	VELA su It	Virginia	MAYO
Vincenzo di CATENA p It		Virginia	McKENNA
Vinci,	LEONARDO c It	Virginia	O'BRIEN
Vinegar Joe STILWELL ar Am		Virginia	OSBORN s,tv Am
Vines,	H. ELLSWORTH t Am	Virginia	PEINE tv
Vines	RHAMES	Virginia	SALE tv
Ving,	LEE	Virginia	STEFAN tv
Vinje,	AASMUND po,j,ref Nor	Virginia	VALE
Vinnie	HOXIE su Am	Virginia	VALLI
Vinogradoff,	PAUL(Sir)l,h	Virginia	VINCENT tv
Vinson,	CARL st Am	Virginia	WADE t Br

Virginia	WEIDLER	Vladimov,	GEORGY w Rus
Virginia	WOOLF w,ct Br	Vladislav	VANCURA md,w Cz
Virna	LISI	Vladislav	VOLKOV as Rus
Virtanen,	ARTTURI n-c'45	Vlady,	MARINA
Virtue,	MICKEY mr-kbds Br	Vlaminck,	MAURICE de p Fr
Virues,	CRISTOBAL de po Sp	Vlasta	VRANA tv+
Vischer,	FRIEDRICH po,ct,e Ger	Voet,	GIJSBERT r,e Dut
Visconti,	LUCHINO d	Vogau,	BORIS w Rus
Viscuso,	SAL tv+	Vogel,	CHARLES c Fr
Vital,	HAYYIM r Palestine	Vogel,	JULIUS(Sir)st N.Zea
Vitali,	GIOVANNI c It	Vogel,	MITCH tv
Vitali,	KEITH	Vogel,	PAULA p-d'98
Vitet,	LOUIS w,st Fr	Vogel,	VIRGIL d
Vitezslav	NEZVAL po,w Cz	Vogl,	JOHANN po Aus
Vitezslav	NOVAK c Cz	Vogler,	GEORG organ,c,w Ger
Vito	D'AMBROSIO tv	Vogler,	RUEDIGER
Vito	SCOTTI tv+	Vogt,	JOHAN geol,e Nor
Vitrac,	ROGER w Fr	Vogt,	NILS w,po Nor
Vitruvius,	--- ac,eng Ro	Vogt,	PETER tv
Vitte,	RAY tv	Vogue,	EUGENE w,st Fr
Vitti,	MONICA	Vohrer,	ALFRED d
Vittoria	COLONNA po It	Vohs,	JOAN tv+
Vittorini,	ELIO w,ct It	Voight,	JON
Vittorio	ALFIERI w,po It.	Voigt,	WOLDEMAR sc,e Ger
Vittorio	De SICA d+	Voisin,	GABRIEL id-planes Fr
Vittorio	GASSMAN	Voit,	CARL von ps,e Ger
Vittorio	ORLANDO st It	Voland,	HERB tv
Vittorio	ROSSI tv	Volante,	VICKI
Vittorio	TAVIANI d	Voldstad,	JOHN tv
Vitus	BERING x Dan	Volkov,	FYODOR la Rus
Viva	---	Volkov,	VLADISLAV as Rus
Vivaldi,	ANTONIO viol,c,e It	Vollard,	AMBROISE mer-art,pb Fr
Vivaldi,	UGOLINO mer It	Volman,	MARK mr-sax,s Am
Vivaldi,	VADINO mer It	Volonte,	GIAN MARIA
Viveka	DAVIS	Volstead,	ANDREW st,l Am
Vives,	AMADEO c Sp	Volta,	ALLESSANDRO sc,e It
Vives,	VIVIANE tv	Voltaire	--- ph,h,po Fr
Vivi	JANNIS tv	Volter	KILPI w Finn
Vivian	BLAINE tv+	Volz,	NEDRA tv
Vivian	SCHILLING	Von Dohlen,	LENNY
Vivian	VANCE tv	Von Euler,	ULF n-m'70
Vivian	WU	Von Glatz,	ILSE tv
Viviane	ROMANCE	Von Hoffman,	NICHOLAS tv
Viviane	VIVES tv	Von Leer,	HUNTER tv
Viviani,	RENE st Fr	Von Oy,	JENNA tv
Viviano,	SAL	Von Sternberg,	JOSEF d
Vivica	FOX	Vonck,	JEAN st Belg
Vivien	LEIGH	Vondel,	JOOST van den p,w Dut
Vivienne	OSBORNE	Vonetta	McGEE
Vivyan,	JOHN tv	Vonnegut,	KURT Jr w Am
Vizquel,	OMAR b-gg'97	Vonni	RIBISI tv
Vlacic,	MATIJA r,e Ger	Vonstade,	FREDERICA mezzo
Vlacq,	ADRIAAN math Dut	Voorhies,	LARK tv
Vladek	SHEYBAL	Vorgan,	GIGI tv
Vladimar	FOGEL	Vorhaus,	BERNARD d
Vladimir	MACEK st Yugo	Vorkov,	ZANDOR
Vladimir	NABOKOV w,po Am	Vorster,	BALTHAZAR st S.Afr
Vladimir	PRELOG sc Swi	Vos,	CORNELIS de p Belg
Vladimir	REBIKOV c Rus	Vos,	GERRIT philolog,e Dut
Vladimir	VASEK po Cz	Vos,	MAERTEN de p Belg
Vladimir Ilyich	LENIN re,st Rus	Voskovec,	GEORGE

Vosloo,	ARNOLD
Voss,	RICHARD w Ger
Vossoughi,	SHAHRAD tv
Vouet,	SIMON p Fr
Vought,	CHANCE ds-planes Am
Voyagis,	YORGO
Voysey,	CHARLES ac,ds Br
Voznesensky,	ANDREY po Rus
Vozoff,	LORINNE tv
Vrana,	VLASTA tv+
Vraz,	STANKO po Croat
Vreeland,	DIANA ed Am
Vries,	HUGO de sc,e Dut
Vries,	MATTHIJS de philolDut
Vsevolod	GARSHIN w Rus
Vsevolod	IVANOV w Rus
Vuckovich,	PETE b-cy'82
Vuillard,	EDOUARD p Fr
Vuitton,	LOUIS ds-luggage It
Vulpius,	CHRISTIAN w Ger
Vyacheslav	PLEHVE st Rus
Vyacheslav	MOLOTOV st Rus
Vyes,	MURVYN
Vyto	RUGINIS
Vyvyan	HOLLAND w Br

"W" NAME DESIGNATION CODE

w	WRITER
ws	SONG WRITER

"W" NATIONALITY CODE

W.Indies - WEST INDIAN

"W's"

W. Somerset	MAUGHAM w Br
W.C.	FIELDS cm+ Am
W.E.B.	Du BOIS civ rts.w Am
W.H.	DAVIES po Welsh
W.S.	GRAHAM po Scot
W.S.	MERWIN po Am
W.W.	GREG(Sir)w
Waaktaar,	PAUL mr-guit,s Nor
Waals,	JOHANNES v.der n-p'10
Wach,	JOACHIM r,e Am
Wachner,	LINDA bus Am
Wachter,	EDWARD bb hf
Waclaw	BERENT w Pol
Waclaw	POTOCKI po Pol
Waddel,	MOSES e Am
Waddell,	HELEN w Br
Waddell,	JACKIE tv
Waddell,	RUBE b hf
Wadding,	LUKE r Ir
Wade	BOGGS b
Wade	BOTELER
Wade	HAMPTON st,ar-CSA Am
Wade,	ADAM tv
Wade,	ERNESTINE tv
Wade,	HAROLD(Steep)mj,cn Can

Wade,	MARGARET bbc hf
Wade,	THOMAS(Sir)ar,st
Wade,	VIRGINIA t Br
Wadeck	STANCZAK
Wadkins,	LANNY g Am
Wagenheim,	CHARLES tv
Waggner,	GEORGE d
Waggoner,	LYLE tv+
Wagner,	BRUCE tv
Wagner,	ELIN w,j Swe
Wagner,	GORGEOUS GEO.wrestler
Wagner,	HONUS b hf
Wagner,	JACK tv+
Wagner,	LINDSAY tv+
Wagner,	LOU tv
Wagner,	MIKE tv
Wagner,	NATASHA
Wagner,	OTTO ac Aus
Wagner,	RICHARD c Ger
Wagner,	ROBERT tv+
Wagner,	WENDE tv
Wagner-Jauregg,	JULIUS n-m'27
Wagoner,	PORTER m-cnt,tv Am
Wahl,	KEN tv+
Wahlberg,	DONNIE mr-s Am
Wai,	CHAN
Wailer,	BUNNY mr-drm,s Jamai
Wain,	JOHN w,po,ct Br
Wainwright,	JAMES tv+
Waite	HOYT b hf
Waite,	JOHN s,ws Br
Waite,	MORRISON l,ch just Am
Waite,	RALPH tv+
Waites,	THOMAS
Waits,	TOM s,c+ Am
Waitz,	GEORG h Ger
Wajda,	ANDRZEJ pr-films Pol
Wake,	WILLIAM r Br
Wakely,	JIMMY
Wakley,	THOMAS sc Am
Waksman,	SELMAN n-m'52
Walberg,	GARRY tv
Walbrook,	ANTON
Walburn,	RAYMOND
Walcott,	DEREK n-l'92,po
Walcott,	GREGORY tv+
Wald,	GEORGE n-m'67
Wald,	JERRY mj,cn Am
Wald,	LILLIAN nurse Am
Waldemar	BROGGER geol Nor
Walden,	LYNETTE
Walden,	PAUL sc,e Latvia
Walden,	ROBERT tv+
Waldheim,	KURT secy gen@UN Aus
Waldis,	BURKARD po,w,r Ger
Waldo	FRANK w Am
Waldo	PRATT m,e,r Am
Waldo,	JANET tv
Waldziu	LIBERACE pian,c,tv Am
Walery	SLAWEK st Pol
Wales,	ETHEL

Wales,	WALLY		Wallace,	ALFRED sc,w Br
Walesa,	LECH st,n-x'83		Wallace,	BASIL
Waley,	ARTHUR h-orient Br		Wallace,	BERYL
Walgreen,	CHARLES mer-drugs Am		Wallace,	CHRIS tv
Walken,	CHRISTOPHER o-s'78		Wallace,	DAVID
Walker	EVANS fo Am		Wallace,	DAVID FOSTER w Am
Walker	PERCY w Am		Wallace,	DeWITT ed,pb Am
Walker	ALICE p-f'83		Wallace,	EDGAR w Br
Walker,	ALLAN tv		Wallace,	GEORGE
Walker,	ALLY		Wallace,	HENRY AGARD st-vp Am
Walker,	AMASA ec,e,st Am		Wallace,	JACK tv+
Walker,	ANTOINE bb		Wallace,	JEAN
Walker,	ARNETIA tv+		Wallace,	LEW(IS)l,ar,w Am
Walker,	BILL m-cnt,cn,tv Am		Wallace,	MARCIA tv+
Walker,	BILLY tv		Wallace,	MIKE tv-j Am
Walker,	CAROLSUE tv		Wallace,	MORGAN
Walker,	CHRIS tv		Wallace,	MYRON tv
Walker,	CLINT tv+		Wallace,	PAUL tv
Walker,	DAVID mr-kbds Am		Wallace,	RICHARD d
Walker,	DOAK fb hf		Wallace,	RODERICK b hf
Walker,	ELIZABETH(Tippy)tv		Wallach,	ELI
Walker,	EMERY(Sir)engr		Wallach,	OTTO n-c'10
Walker,	GEORGE p-m'96		Wallack,	HENRY la Am
Walker,	GILES d		Wallas,	GRAHAM sc-politics Br
Walker,	HELEN		Wallen,	SIGURD
Walker,	JIMMIE tv+		Wallenstein,	JUDITH w Am
Walker,	JIMMY st Am		Waller,	EDMUND po Br
Walker,	JOHN sc,e,n-c'97		Waller,	FATS mj-pia,s,cn,c Am
Walker,	JUNIOR mr-sax,s Am		Waller,	GORDON s Scot
Walker,	KATHRYN		Waller,	MAX po Belg
Walker,	LARRY b-gg'97		Walley,	DEBORAH tv+
Walker,	MARCY tv		Wallin,	JOHAN r,hymns Swe
Walker,	MARGARET po,w Am		Wallinger,	KARL mr-kbds Welsh
Walker,	MARY md,fe Am		Wallis	BUDGE(Sir)archeol
Walker,	MICKEY boxer Am		Wallis	SIMPSON(Duch.Windsor)
Walker,	MORT cr Am		Wallis,	HAL pr-films Am
Walker,	NANCY tv+		Wallis,	SHANI
Walker,	PAUL tv		Wallis,	WILSON an,w Am
Walker,	PEGGY tv		Wallon,	HENRI h,st,e Fr
Walker,	PETE d		Wally	AMOS choc cookies Am
Walker,	POLLY		Wally	BROWN tv+
Walker,	RAY		Wally	CAMPO
Walker,	ROBERT		Wally	COX tv+
Walker,	ROBERT Jr.		Wally	KURTH tv
Walker,	T-BONE mj,guit Am		Wally	LAMB w Am
Walker,	TERRY		Wally	PATCH
Walker,	TIPPY		Wally	SHIRRA as Am
Walker,	TONJA tv		Wally	VERNON
Wall,	MAX		Wally	WALES
Wallace	ATWOOD geol Am		Wally	WARD
Wallace	BEERY		Wally	WICKENS mj,cn Can
Wallace	FARD r Am		Walmsley,	JON tv
Wallace	FORD tv+		Walpole,	HORACE w,h Br
Wallace	FOX d		Walpole,	HUGH(Sir)w
Wallace	IRWIN w,bio,h Am		Walpole,	ROBERT(Sir)st
Wallace	MacDONALD		Walras,	LEON ec,e Fr
Wallace	SABINE sc Am		Walser,	MARTIN w Ger
Wallace	SHAWN		Walsh,	BILL fbc hf
Wallace	STEGNER w Am		Walsh,	BRIGID tv
Wallace	STEVENS po Am		Walsh,	DAVID bbr hf
Wallace Stone,	DEE		Walsh,	DERMOT

Walsh,	DYLAN tv	Walter	KING
Walsh,	ED b hf	Walter	KOENIG tv+
Walsh,	GEORGE	Walter	KOHN sc,e,n-c'98
Walsh,	GWYNYTH	Walter	LANDOR po,w,ct Br
Walsh,	J.T.	Walter	LANG d
Walsh,	JOE mr-guit,s Am	Walter	LANTZ cr Am
Walsh,	JOEY tv	Walter	LONG
Walsh,	JOHN tv	Walter	MACKEN w,la,d Ir
Walsh,	KAY	Walter	MAP w-satire,r Br
Walsh,	KEN	Walter	MATTHAU
Walsh,	M. EMMET	Walter	McGRAIL
Walsh,	RAOUL d+	Walter	MILLER
Walsh,	SYDNEY tv+	Walter	MILLER Jr w-scifi Am
Walsingham, FRANCIS (Sir) spymaster		Walter	MONDALE st Am
Walston,	RAY tv+	Walter	MOSLEY w Am
Walt	ALSTON bmg hf	Walter	NASH (Sir) st N.Zea
Walt	BELLAMY bb hf	Walter	O'KEEFE tv
Walt	FRAZIER bb hf	Walter	ORANGE mr-drm,s Am
Walt	KUHN p,illus,cr Am	Walter	PAGE j,st Am
Walt	WHITMAN po Am	Walter	PARRATT (Sir) organ,c
Walt	WILLEY tv	Walter	PATER w,ct Br
Waltari,	MIKA w Finn	Walter	PAYTON fb hf
Walter	ABEL tv+	Walter	PIDGEON
Walter	ADAMS astr Am	Walter	PISTON c Am
Walter	BAADE astr Ger	Walter	PITKIN w Am
Walter	BAGEHOT ec,ct,j Br	Walter	RALEIGH (Sir) x,w,po
Walter	BARNES mj-clar,cn Am	Walter	REED
Walter	BATE bio Am	Walter	REED ar,md Am
Walter	BECKER mr-bass Am	Walter	REUTHER labor Am
Walter	BESANT (Sir) w	Walter	RILLA
Walter	BRENNAN tv+	Walter	SANDE tv+
Walter	BROOKE tv	Walter	SCHARF c Am
Walter	BUCHER geol Am	Walter	SCOTT (Sir) po,w,h Scot
Walter	BYRON	Walter	SHORT ar Am
Walter	CAMP fbc	Walter	SICKERT p,etch Br
Walter	CATLETT	Walter	SKEAT philology,e Br
Walter	COMPTON tv	Walter	SLEZAK tv+
Walter	COY tv	Walter	TEAGUE id-ds Am
Walter	CRANE p Br	Walter	TETLEY tv
Walter	CRONKITE tv-j Am	Walter	WELLMAN j,x Am
Walter	EDGE st,pb Am	Walter	WHITE w,naacp Am
Walter	EDMONDS w Am	Walter	YUST j,ed Am
Walter	EGAN mr-s Am	Walter de la MARE 3w,po Br	
Walter	GILBERT sc Am	Walter Elias DISNEY pr Am	
Walter	GOTELL	Walter van CLARK w Am	
Walter	GRAUMAN d	Walter,	BRUNO cn Am
Walter	GREAZA tv	Walter,	JESSICA tv+
Walter	GRIFFIN sc Am	Walter,	TRACEY tv+
Walter	GROPIUS ac Ger	Walter,	TRACY
Walter	HAGEN g Am	Walters,	ALEXANDER tv
Walter	HAMPDEN la+ Am	Walters,	BARBARA tv-j Am
Walter	HAWORTH (Sir) sc,e	Walters,	BETTY LOU tv
Walter	HERLIHY tv	Walters,	BUCKY b-mv'39
Walter	HESS md,e Swi	Walters,	CHARLES d
Walter	HILL d	Walters,	JAMIE tv
Walter	HUSTON la+ Am	Walters,	JULIE
Walter	JAMES	Walters,	LAURIE tv+
Walter	JOHNSON b hf	Walters,	LUANA
Walter	KELLY cr Am	Walters,	MELORA
Walter	KERR w,ct-theatr Am	Walters,	SUSAN tv+
Walter	KIERNAN tv	Walters,	THORLEY

Walthall,	HENRY B.	Ward,	ROBERT p-m'62
Walthall,	ROMY tv	Ward,	SANDY tv+
Walther	BOTHE sc,e Ger	Ward,	SELA tv+
Walther	NERNST sc,e Ger	Ward,	SETH r,astr Br
Walther,	HANS-JURGEN cn Ger	Ward,	SIMON
Walther,	JOHANN organ,c Ger	Ward,	SOPHIE
Walther,	SUSAN tv	Ward,	WALLY
Walton,	BILL bb-m'78 hf	Warden,	JACK tv+
Walton,	DOUGLAS	Warder	ALLEE sc,e Am
Walton,	ERNEST n-p'51	Ware,	EFFERGEE mj-guit Am
Walton,	FRED d	Ware,	HERTA
Walton,	IZAAK bio,w-angler Br	Ware,	IRENE
Walton,	WILLIAM(Sir)c	Ware,	MARTYN mr-synthesr Br
Waltz,	JEAN cr,w Fr	Ware,	WILLIAM ac Am
Waltz,	LISA	Warfield,	EMILY
Wambaugh,	JOSEPH w Am	Warfield,	MARLENE tv
Wanamaker,	JOHN mer,st Am	Warfield,	MARSHA tv+
Wanamaker,	SAM	Warfield,	PAUL fb hf
Wanamaker,	ZOE	Warham,	WILLIAM r Br
Wanda	ACUNA tv	Warhol,	ANDY p,pr-films Am
Wanda	CANNON tv	Wariner,	STEVE s-cnt Am
Wanda	JACKSON tv	Waring,	EDWARD math,e Br
Wanda	LEWIS tv	Waring,	FRED mj,c,cn,tv Am
Wanda	McKAY	Waris	HUSSEIN d
Wanda	VENTHAM	Warlock,	BILLY tv+
Waner,	LLOYD b hf	Warming,	JOHANNES sc,e Dan
Waner,	PAUL b hf	Warne,	FREDERICK pb Br
Wang	PING	Warner	BAXTER
Wang	TAO	Warner	JONES tv
Wang Wei	--- po China	Warner	OLAND
Wang Yang-ming--- st, ph China		Warner	WOLF tv
Wang,	AN eng-computer,id Am	Warner,	CHARLES w,ed Am
Wang,	VERA ds Am	Warner,	DAVID
Wang,	WAYNE d	Warner,	ELEANOR tv
Wankel,	FELIX rotary engs Ger	Warner,	GLENN(Pop)fbc Am
Wanzer,	BOBBY bb hf	Warner,	H.B.
Warbeck,	DAVID	Warner,	HARRY exec-films Am
Warbeck,	PERKIN imposter Belg	Warner,	JACK
Warburg,	ABY h-art Ger	Warner,	JUDITH w Am
Warburg,	OTTO n-m'31	Warner,	JULIE
Warburton,JOHN		Warner,	MALCOLM-JAMAL tv
Ward	BOND	Warner,	REX w,po,ct Br
Ward	HUNT l,supr ct Am	Warner,	SETH ar-re Am
Ward,	AARON MONTGOMERY mer	Warner,	SUSAN w Am
Ward,	ANITA s Am	Warner,	SYLVIA w,po Br
Ward,	ARTEMAS ar-re Am	Warner,	WILLIAM p-n'77
Ward,	ARTEMUS w-humor,ed Am	Warnes,	JENNIFER s-pop,tv Am
Ward,	BARBARA ec,w Br	Warren	BEATTY tv+
Ward,	BILL mr-drm Br	Warren	BURGER l Am
Ward,	BURT tv+	Warren	CANN mr-drm Can
Ward,	DAVID d	Warren	CLARKE
Ward,	FRED	Warren	De la RUE astr,i Br
Ward,	JOHN b hf	Warren	DODDS mj-drm Am
Ward,	JONATHAN tv+	Warren	ENTNER mr-guit,s Am
Ward,	LYMAN	Warren	FROST tv+
Ward,	MAITLAND tv	Warren	GILES b hf
Ward,	MARY w Br	Warren	HULL tv+
Ward,	MEGAN	Warren	HYMER
Ward,	MRS. HUMPHRY w Br	Warren	JERRY d
Ward,	PENELOPE	Warren	MOON fb
Ward,	RACHEL	Warren	MUNSON tv

Warren	OATES tv+		Waters,	JOHN
Warren	PARKER tv		Waters,	JOHN d
Warren	SHAW carrace Am		Waters,	MUDDY mj-blues,s Am
Warren	SPAHN b hf		Waters,	REBA tv
Warren	STEVENS tv+		Waters,	ROGER mr-bass,s Br
Warren	WILLIAM		Waterston,SAM tv+	
Warren	ZEVON s,ws Am		Watford,	GWEN
Warren,	ANN tv		Watie,	STAND st Am Indian
Warren,	BOB tv		Watkin,	TENCH ar,w Br
Warren,	E. ALLEN		Watkin,	IAN
Warren,	EARL 1,ch justice Am		Watkin,	PIERRE
Warren,	HARRY ws,c Am		Watkins,	CARLENE tv
Warren,	JASON tv		Watkins,	JIM tv
Warren,	JENNIFER tv+		Watkins,	SAMMY mj,cn Am
Warren,	JOE tv		Watkins,	VERNON po Welsh
Warren,	JOSIAH ref Am		Watley,	JODY s Am
Warren,	LEONARD bari Am		Watling,	DEBORAH tv
Warren,	LESLEY ANN tv+		Watros,	CYNTHIA tv
Warren,	MERCY w Am		Watson,	ALBERTA tv+
Warren,	MICHAEL		Watson,	ANGELA tv
Warren,	ROBERT p-f'47 &		Watson,	BOBBY
Warren,	ROBERT p-q'58'79		Watson,	BRUCE mr-guit Can
Warrick,	RUTH tv+		Watson,	DEBBIE tv
Warrington HUDLIN d,pr			Watson,	ELKANAH bus-cattle Am
Warton,	JOSEPH ct,e Br		Watson,	JACK
Warton,	THOMAS pol 1785-90		Watson,	JAMES A. Jr. tv
Warwick	DAVIS		Watson,	JAMES n-m'62
Warwick	DEEPING w Br		Watson,	JOHN ps,e Am
Warwick,	CLINT mr-bass Br		Watson,	JOHN r,w Scot
Warwick,	DIONNE s-pop,gospl Am		Watson,	LARRY w Am
Warwick,	JAMES		Watson,	LUCILE
Warwick,	ROBERT		Watson,	MILLS tv+
Waser,	JOHANN st Swi		Watson,	MINOR
Washbourne, MONA			Watson,	SERENO sc Am
Washbrook,JOHNNY tv			Watson,	TOM g Am
Washburn,	BRYANT		Watson,	VERNEE
Washburn,	ISRAEL st Am		Watson,	WILLIAM tv+
Washburne,RICK			Watson,	WILLIAM(Sir)po
Washington ALLSTON p,w Am			Watson,	WYLIE
Washington IRVING w Am			Watt,	JAMES i,eng Scot
Washington Atlee BURPEE seeds Am			Watt,	JOACHIM von po Swi
Washington, BOOKER T. e,w Am			Watt,	NATHAN tv
Washington, DENZEL o-s'89,tv+			Watteau,	ANTOINE p Fr
Washington, DINAH s Am			Watterson,BILL cr Am	
Washington, GEORGE 1st Pres			Watterson,HENRY j,st Am	
Washington, KENNETH tv			Wattis,	RICHARD tv+
Wass,	TED tv+		Watts,	ALAN ph,r,e,w Am
Wasserman,JERRY tv			Watts,	ANDRE piano Ger
Wassermann, AUGUST von sc Ger			Watts,	CHARLIE mr-drm Br
Wassermann, JAKOB w Ger			Watts,	GEORGE p,su Br
Wasserstein, WENDY p-d'89			Watts,	ISAAC r,w-hymns Br
Wassily	LEONTIEF ec Am		Watts,	OVEREND mr-bass Br
Wasson,	CRAIG tv+		Watts,	PHILIP(Sir)ac-naval
Watanabe, GEDDE			Watts,	STAN bbc hf
Watanabe, KEN			Waugh,	ALEC w Br
Waterfield, BOB fb hf			Waugh,	AUBERON w,j Br
Waterman, DENNIS tv+			Waugh,	EVELYN w Br
Waterman, WILLARD tv+			Waugh,	HILLARY w Am
Waters,	CHERYL		Wavell.	ARCHIBALD ar Br
Waters,	CRYSTAL s-soul Am		Waxman,	AL tv+
Waters,	ETHEL s,tv+ Am		Wayans,	DAMON cm,tv+ Am

Wayans,	KEENAN IVORY tv+		Webb,	MATTHEW sw Br
Wayans,	KIM tv		Webb,	RICHARD
Wayans,	MARLON		Webb,	SIDNEY h,e,ref Br
Wayans,	SHAWN(S.W.)tv		Webb,	WILLIAM d
Waybill,	FEE mr-s Am		Webber,	ANDREW LLOYD pr Am
Wayde	PRESTON tv+		Webber,	ROBERT tv+
Waylon	JENNINGS s-cnt+ Am		Weber,	CARL von(Carl)c Ger
Wayne	BROWN cn		Weber,	ERNST sc,e Ger
Wayne	CRAWFORD		Weber,	JOE cm,pr Am
Wayne	FONTANA mr-s Br		Weber,	LAURA tv
Wayne	GRETZKY ho		Weber,	MAX h,e Ger
Wayne	HUSSEY mr-guit,s Br		Weber,	MAX p Am
Wayne	KING tv		Weber,	STEVEN tv+
Wayne	LONG tv		Webern,	ANTON von c Aus
Wayne	MAUNDER tv		Webster,	BEN mj-tenor sax Am
Wayne	MILNER fb hf		Webster,	DANIEL st,orator Am
Wayne	MORRIS		Webster,	JEAN w Am
Wayne	NEWTON		Webster,	JOHN w Br
Wayne	OSMOND s,tv Am		Webster,	MARGARET la,d Br
Wayne	POWERS tv		Webster,	NOAH w,dictionary Am
Wayne	ROBSON		Webster,	PAUL lyrics Am
Wayne	ROGERS tv+		Weddell,	JAMES x Br
Wayne	WANG d		Weddle,	VERNON tv
Wayne	WHEELER l,ref,st Am		Wedekind,	FRANK w,la Ger
Wayne,	ANTHONY(Mad)ar-re Am		Wedemeyer,	HERMAN tv
Wayne,	CARL mr-s Br		Wedgeworth,	ANN tv+
Wayne,	CAROL		Wedgwood,	C.V.(Dame)h Br
Wayne,	DAVID tv+		Wedgwood,	JOSIAH id-pottery Br
Wayne,	ETHAN tv		Wee Willie	KEELER b hf
Wayne,	JOHN o-a'69,tv+		Weeb	EUBANK fb
Wayne,	NAUNTON		Weed,	BUDDY tv
Wayne,	NINA tv+		Weed,	THURLOW j,ed,st Am
Wayne,	PATRICK		Weeks,	ANSON mj,cn,c Am
Weare	MESHECH l,st Am		Weeks,	LAURIE w Am
Weatherly,	SHAWN tv+		Weelkes,	THOMAS organ,c Br
Weathers,	CARL tv+		Weems,	MASON r,bio,w Am
Weatherwax,	KEN tv		Weems,	PRISCILLA tv
Weaver	LEVY tv		Weems,	TED mj-tromb,cn Am
Weaver,	BLUE mr-organ Welsh		Weenix,	JAN p Dut
Weaver,	DENNIS		Weetman	PEARSON bus Br
Weaver,	DOODLES		Wegener	PAUL d+
Weaver,	EARL b,tv		Wehner,	HEINZ mj,cn Ger
Weaver,	FRITZ		Weider,	JOHN mr-bass Br
Weaver,	JACKI		Weidler,	VIRGINIA
Weaver,	JOHN ba Br		Weidman,	CHARLES ba Am
Weaver,	LEE tv		Weidman,	JEROME p-d'60
Weaver,	SIGOURNEY		Weidoft,	RUDY mj-sax Am
Weaving,	HUGO		Weigel,	TERI
Webb	PIERCE s-cnt,c+ Am		Weigl,	JOSEPH c Aus
Webb,	ALAN		Weigle,	LUTHER r,e Am
Webb,	ASTON(Sir)ac		Weil,	ANDREW w Am
Webb,	BEATRICE h,e Br		Weil,	SIMONE ph,w Fr
Webb,	CHICK mj-drm,cn Am		Weill,	KURT c Am
Webb,	CHLOE tv+		Weinberg,	STEVEN n-p'79
Webb,	CLEMENT ph,e,w Br		Weinberger,	JAROMIR c Am
Webb,	CLIFTON		Weiner,	JONATHAN p-n'95
Webb,	GREG tv+		Weiner,	LEO c,e Hung
Webb,	JACK tv+		Weinger,	SCOTT tv
Webb,	JIMMY c Am		Weinmeister,	ARNIE fb hf
Webb,	LUCY tv		Weinstein,	NATHAN w Am
Webb,	MARY w Br		Weir,	BOB mr-guit Am

Weir,	PETER d		Wells,	DAWN tv+
Weir,	ROBERT p Am		Wells,	DOLORES
Weis,	GARY cm,tv		Wells,	HERBERT(H.G.)w,j Br
Weischaus,	ERIC n-m'95		Wells,	HORACE dentist Am
Weiser,	CONRAD Indian agt Am		Wells,	IDA BELLj,ed,ref Am
Weiss,	BERNHARD r,e Ger		Wells,	JACQUELINE
Weiss,	GEORGE b hf		Wells,	KITTY s-cnt Am
Weiss,	PAUL sc Am		Wells,	MARY m-pop,s Am
Weiss,	PETER w Ger		Wells,	MARY tv
Weiss,	PIERRE sc,e Fr		Wells,	TRACY tv
Weiss,	SHAUN		Wells,	VERNON
Weiss,	SID mj-bass Am		Wells,	WILLIE b hf
Weisser,	NORBERT		Welnick,	VINCE mr-kbds Am
Weissmuller,	JOHNNY sw+ Am		Welsh,	JOHN tv
Weist,	DWIGHT tv		Welsh,	KENNETH
Weitz,	BRUCE tv+		Welsh,	MARGARET tv+
Weizmann,	CHAIM sc,e,st Rus		Welter	ARIADNE
Wekerle,	SANDOR st Hung		Welti,	EMIL st Swi
Welch,	ADAM r,w Scot		Welty,	EUDORA p-f'73
Welch,	BOB b-cy'90		Wende	WAGNER tv
Welch,	BRUCE mr-guit Br		Wendel	MELDRUM tv+
Welch,	DENTON w Br		Wendell	BURTON tv+
Welch,	JONATHAN tv		Wendell	COREY tv+
Welch,	MICKEY b hf		Wendell	NILES tv
Welch,	RAQUEL		Wendell	STANLEY sc Am
Welch,	TAHNEE		Wendell	WILLKIE st Am
Welch,	WILLIAM sc-md,e Am		Wendell,	BARRETT e Am
Welcome,	BUDDY mj-sax Am		Wendell,	BILL tv
Weld,	THEODORE ref Am		Wendell,	LARA
Weld,	TUESDAY tv+		Wenders	WIM d+
Weldon	HEYBURN		Wendie Jo	SPERBER tv+
Weldon,	ANN tv		Wendkos,	PAUL d
Weldon,	MICHAEL tv		Wendt,	GEORGE tv+
Welk,	LAWRENCE m,cn,tv Am		Wendy	BARRIE tv+
Welk,	TANYA FALAN tv		Wendy	COX tv
Welker,	FRANK tv		Wendy	CREWSON tv+
Well,	CYNTHIA c Am		Wendy	CUTLER tv
Well,	DAVID ba Br		Wendy	DAVIS tv
Weller,	PAUL mr-guit,s Br		Wendy	FULTON tv
Weller,	PETER		Wendy	GAZELLE
Weller,	ROBB tv		Wendy	GIRARD tv
Weller,	SHEILA w Am		Wendy	HERON mj,pop-s Br
Weller,	THOMAS n-m'54		Wendy	HILLER
Welles,	GIDEON st,ed Am		Wendy	HUGHES
Welles,	GWEN		Wendy	MacDONALD
Welles,	JESSE tv		Wendy	MONIZ tv
Welles,	MEL		Wendy	ROBIE tv
Welles,	ORSON pr,d+ Am		Wendy	SCHAAL tv+
Welles,	SUMNER st Am		Wendy	SUITS tv
Wellesley,	ARTHUR(IronDuke)ar Br		Wendy	WILSON s Am
Wellington	MARA fbc hf		Wenrich,	PERCY c Am
Wellington,	ARTHUR(IronDuke)ar B		Went,	FRIEDRICH sc,e Dut
Wellman,	ALAN mj-trump,cn Can		Wentworth,	MARTHA
Wellman,	WALTER j,x Am		Wenzel	HOLLAR engr Cz
Wellman,	WILLIAM d		Wenzel	KAUNITZ st Aus
Wellman,	WILLIAM Jr.		Wenzel	MULLER c Ger
Wells,	CAROLE tv+		Wera	ENGELS
Wells,	CAROLYN w Am		Werfel,	FRANZ w,po Ger
Wells,	CLAUDETTE tv		Werff,	ADRIAEN van der p Dut
Wells,	CORY mr-s Am		Werle,	BARBARA tv
Wells,	DANNY tv		Werner	ARBER md Swi

Werner	BISCHOF fo Swi
Werner	HERZOG d+
Werner	KRAUSS
Werner	PETERS
Werner,	ALFRED n-c'13
Werner,	OSKAR
Werner,	PETER d
Werner,	ZACHARIAS w,po Ger
Wernher von BRAUN rockets Am	
Wernick,	RICHARD p-m'77
Wert,	GIACHES c Belg
Werth,	JOHANN von ar Ger
Wertimer,	NED tv
Wertmuller,	LINA pr, d
Wes	PARKER b
Wes	STERN
Wes	STUDI
Wes	UNSELD bb hf
Wes	WESTRUM b,bmg
Wescott	ABELL(Sir)ac
Wescott,	GLENWAY w,po Am
Wesker,	ARNOLD w Br
Wesley	ADDY tv+
Wesley	EURE
Wesley	LAU tv
Wesley	MORGAN tv
Wesley	SNIPES
Wesley	TACKITT tv
Wesley,	CHARLES r,w-hymns Br
Wesley,	JOHN r,w Br
Wesley,	KASSIE tv
Wesley,	SAMUEL organ,c Br
Wessel,	CASPAR math Nor
Wessel,	HORST w-song Ger
Wessell,	RICHARD tv
Wesson,	DANIEL i,id-guns Am
Wesson,	DICK tv+
West,	ADAM tv+
West,	ALVY mj-sax,cn Am
West,	ANTHONY w,ct Br
West,	BENJAMIN p Am
West,	BROOKS tv
West,	DOTTIE s+ Am
West,	JERRY bb,bbc hf
West,	JOHN mr-guit Am
West,	MAE
West,	MAURA tv
West,	MORRIS w Aust
West,	NATALIE tv
West,	NATHANAEL w Am
West,	REBECCA(Dame)j,fe Br
West,	RED
West,	RICK mr-guit Br
West,	TIMOTHY
Westbrook PEGLER j Am	
Westcott,	HELEN
Westergren, HAKAN	
Westerman, FLOYD(Red Crow)	
Westermarck, EDWARD ph,an,e Finn	
Westheimer, RUTH tv	
Westinghouse,GEORGE i Am	

Westly,	HELEN
Westman,	NYDIA tv+
Weston,	CELIA tv+
Weston,	EDWARD fo Am
Weston,	EDWARD walker Am
Weston,	ELLEN tv
Weston,	JACK tv+
Weston,	PAUL mj,c,cn,tv Am
Westover	RUSS cr Am
Westrum,	WES b,bmg
Wet,	CHRISTIAAN de st S.Afr
Wetering,	JANWILLEM v.de w Dut
Wetherell,VIRGINIA	
Wettig,	PATRICIA tv+
Wetton,	JOHN mr-bass,s Br
Wetzel,	LOUIS scout Am
Wexler,	HARRY weather Am
Weyden,	ROGIER van der p Belg
Weyerhaeuser,FREDERICK lumber Am	
Weyers,	MARIUS
Weygand,	MAXIME ar Fr
Weyl,	HERMANN math,e,w Ger
Weyman,	STANLEY w Br
Weymouth,	TINA mr-bass Am
Whale,	JAMES d
Whalen,	MICHAEL
Whaley,	FRANK
Whalin,	JUSTIN tv+
Whalley-Kilmer, JOANNE	
Wharton,	EDITH p-f'21
Wharton,	JOSEPH id Am
Wharton,	WILLIAM w Am
Whatley,	DIXIE tv
Whatley,	LIEM
Wheat,	ZACH b hf
Wheatley,	ALAN tv+
Wheatley,	PHILLIS po Am
Wheaton,	WIL tv+
Wheatstone, CHARLES(Sir)sc,i,e	
Whedon,	DANIEL r,e Am
Wheeler	OAKMAN
Wheeler,	BERT tv+
Wheeler,	BURTON st Am
Wheeler,	EARLE ar(Gen.) Am
Wheeler,	WAYNE l,ref,st Am
Wheeler-Nicholson, DANA	
Wheelock,	ELEAZAR r,e Am
Wheezer	HUTCHINS
Whelan,	ARLEEN
Whelan,	JILL tv
Whelan,	TIM d
Whelchel,	LISA tv+
Whewell,	WILLIAM ph,math,e Br
Whinnery,	BARBARA tv+
Whipp,	JOSEPH tv
Whipple,	GEORGE n-m'34
Whipple,	RANDY tv
Whipple,	SQUIRE bridges Am
Whirry,	SHANNON
Whislering Joe WILSON tv	
Whistler,	JAMES p Am

Whistler,	REX p,illus Br	White,	WM. ALLEN j,p-b'47
Whiston,	WILLIAM math Br	Whitehead,	ALFRED math,ph,e Br
Whit	BISSEL tv+	Whitehead,	PAXTON
Whit	BURNETT j,ed Am	Whitehead,	WILLIAM pol 1757 Br
Whitaker,	CHARLES(Slim)	Whitelaw,	BILLIE
Whitaker	FOREST	Whitelaw,	REID j,st Am
Whitaker,	JOHNNY tv+	Whiteman,	MARGO tv
Whitcomb,	IAN mr Br	Whiteman,	PAUL mj,cn,tv+ Am
White,	ALICE	Whitey	FORD b hf
White,	ALMA r Am	Whitfield	CONNOR
White,	ANDREW e,st Am	Whitfield,	LYNN tv+
White,	ANTONIA w,j Br	Whitford,	BRAD mr-guit Am
White,	BAILEY w Am	Whitford,	BRADLEY
White,	BARRY s-r&b,ws Am	Whiting,	ARCH tv
White,	BERNARD tv	Whiting	BARBARA tv
White,	BERNIE	Whiting,	JOHN w Br
White,	BETTY tv	Whiting,	MARGARET s,tv+ Am
White,	BILL b,7xgg's,tv	Whiting,	NAPOLEON s
White,	BYRON fb,l-supr ct Am	Whiting,	RICHARD c Am
White,	CANVASS eng Am	Whitley,	JOHN st Br
White,	CAROL	Whitlock,	BRAND j,st,w Am
White,	CAROLE ITA tv	Whitlock,	LLOYD
White,	CHRIS mr-bass Br	Whitlow,	JILL
White,	CHRISTINE tv	Whitman	MAYO tv
White,	DAVE mr-s Am	Whitman,	CHARLES sc,e Am
White,	DAVID tv+	Whitman,	KARI
White,	De VOREAUX tv	Whitman,	MARCUS pioneer,r Am
White,	DIZ	Whitman,	SARAH po Am
White,	E.B. w-humor Am	Whitman,	SLIM s
White,	EDWARD as Am	Whitman,	STUART tv+
White,	EDWARD l-ch jus Am	Whitman,	WALT po Am
White,	ELIJAH md,pioneer Am	Whitmire,	STEVE pupp,tv Am
White,	ELWYN w Am	Whitmore,	JAMES Jr tv+
White,	JACQUELINE	Whitmore,	JAMES tv+
White,	JALEEL tv	Whitney	BLAKE tv
White,	JESSE tv+	Whitney	HOUSTON mr,s Am
White,	JOHN tv	Whitney	KERSHAW tv
White,	KENNETH tv	Whitney	WHITE tv
White,	LESLIE an,e,w Am	Whitney	YOUNG civil rts Am
White,	MARK mr-guar Br	Whitney,	ANNE su Am.
White,	MICHAEL JAI	Whitney,	ASA i,id-rr cars Am
White,	MINOR fo,e Am	Whitney,	CHARLIE mr-guit Br
White,	MORGAN tv	Whitney,	ELI i Am
White,	NERA bb hf	Whitney,	GRACE tv
White,	ONNA ba tv	Whitney,	JAYNE mj-s Am
White,	PATRICK n-l'73	Whitney,	JOSIAH geol,e,w Am
White,	PEARL la Am	Whitney,	MARY astr,e Am
White,	PETER tv	Whitney,	MOXAM mj,guit,cn Can
White,	RANDY fb hf	Whitney,	PETER tv+
White,	REGGIE fb-d'87	Whitson,	SAMUEL tv
White,	SLAP RAGS mj,cn Can	Whittaker,	ROGER s Am
White,	SLAPPY tv+	Whittier,	JOHN GREENLEAF po Am
White,	STANFORD ac Am	Whitton,	MARGARET
White,	STEWART w Am	Whitty,	MAY
White,	T.H. w Br	Whitworth,	JAMES
White,	TERENCE w Br	Whoopi	GOLDBERG tv+
White,	THEODORE p-n'62	Whorf,	BENJAMIN linguist Am
White,	VANNA tv+	Whymper,	EDWARD engr,mtns Br
White,	VERDINE mr-bass,s Am	Whyte,	DAVID w Br
White,	WALTER w,naacp Am	Whyte,	PATRICK tv
White,	WHITNEY tv	Wickens,	RON(Darkie)mj,cn Can

Wickens,	WALLY mj,cn Dan	Wilcox,	STEPHEN id-boilers Am
Wickert,	ANTHONY tv	Wilcox,	TOYAH
Wickes,	MARY tv+	Wilcoxon,	HENRY
Wickham,	HENRY(Sir)x	Wild Bill	DONOVAN l,st Am
Wickman,	DICK mj,cn Am	Wild Bill	ELLIOTT
Wicksell,	KNUT ec,e Swe	Wild Bill	HICKOK ar,hero Am
Widal,	FERNAND md,e Fr	Wild,	EARL cm,tv
Widdoes,	JAMES tv	Wild,	JACK
Widdoes,	KATHLEEN	Wild,	JONATHAN thief Br
Wideman,	JOHN w Am	Wilde,	BRANDON de tv+
Widener,	PETER bus-meat Am	Wilde,	CORNEL
Widman,	JOHANNES math Ger	Wilde,	KIM s,ws Br
Widmann,	JOSEPH w Swi	Wilde,	OSCAR po.w Ir
Widmark,	RICHARD tv+	Wildenvey,	HERMAN po Nor
Widor,	CHARLES organ,c Fr	Wilder,	ALEC mj,cn,c Am
Wiebe,	RUDY w Can	Wilder,	ALEXANDER c Am
Wied,	GUSTAV w Dan	Wilder,	BILLY o-d'45'60
Wiedoft,	HERB mj-trump,cn Am	Wilder,	BURT sc,e Am
Wieland,	BOB tv	Wilder,	GENE
Wieland,	CHRISTOPH po,w Ger	Wilder,	JAMES tv+
Wieland,	HEINRICH n-c'27	Wilder,	LAURA w Am
Wien,	WILHELM n-p'11	Wilder,	THORNTON p-d'32'38 &
Wienbarg,	LUDOLF w Ger	Wilder,	THORNTON p-f'28
Wiener,	LEO e Am	Wilder,	YVONNE tv+
Wiener,	NORBERT math,e,w Am	Wilding,	MICHAEL tv+
Wiese,	RICHARD tv	Wildman,	JOHN
Wiesel,	ELIE w,n-x'86 Am	Wildsmith,	DAWN
Wiesel,	TOSTEN n-m'81	Wiles,	JASON tv
Wiesmeier,	LYNDA	Wiley	POST fly Am
Wiest,	DIANNE o-s'86,'94	Wiley,	HARVEYsc,ref,st Am
Wiggin,	KATE w,e Am	Wiley,	JAN
Wiggin,	TOM tv	Wilford	BRIMLEY tv+
Wiggins,	CHRIS tv+	Wilford	OWEN po Br
Wigginton,	RICHARD tv	Wilfred	LAWSON
Wigglesworth,	MICHAEL r,po Am	Wilfred	OWEN po Br
Wightman,	HAZEL t Am	Wilfred	SHEED w,j Am
Wightman,	ROBERT tv	Wilfrid	BLUNT w,po,st,x Br
Wigman,	MARY ba Ger	Wilfrid	CLARK(Sir)md,an,e
Wigmore,	JOHN l,e Am	Wilfrid	DOWNING tv
Wigner,	EUGENE n-p'63	Wilfrid	LAURIER(Sir)st Can
Wil	SHRINER tv	Wilfrid	LUCAS
Wil	WHEATON tv+	Wilfrid	MEYNELL j,w Br
Wilbert	ROBINSON b hf	Wilfrid	SHEED w,j Am
Wilbur	CROSS e,st Am	Wilgus,	WILLIAM eng Am
Wilbur	EVANS tv	Wilhelm	BACH m, c Ger
Wilbur	SMITH w S.Afr	Wilhelm	BUSCH po,illus Ger
Wilbur	STEELE w Am	Wilhelm	GRIMM w Ger
Wilbur	WRIGHT i,aviation Am	Wilhelm	HANKEL sc,e Ger
Wilbur,	JAY mj,cn Br	Wilhelm	HAUFF w,po Ger
Wilbur,	RICHARD p-q'57'89	Wilhelm	HIS md,e Ger
Wilby,	JAMES	Wilhelm	JUNKER x Ger
Wilbye,	JOHN c Br	Wilhelm	KEITEL ar-Nazi Ger
Wilcox,	ELLA j,po Am	Wilhelm	KOPPERS an,r,e,Ger
Wilcox,	FRANK tv+	Wilhelm	LEIBL p Ger
Wilcox,	HERBERT d	Wilhelm	MARX st Ger
Wilcox,	LARRY tv+	Wilhelm	MAUSER id-guns Ger
Wilcox,	MARY tv	Wilhelm	MAYBACH id-cars Am
Wilcox,	NINA tv	Wilhelm	MIKLAS st Aus
Wilcox,	RALPH tv	Wilhelm	MULLER po Ger
Wilcox,	ROBERT	Wilhelm	OSTWALD sc Ger
Wilcox,	SHANNON tv+	Wilhelm	PREYER md,ps Ger

Wilhelm	RAABE po,w Ger	Willard,	SIMON id-clocks Am
Wilhelm	REICH ps,e Aus	Willcocks,	WILLIAM(Sir)eng
Wilhelm	RONTGEN sc Ger	Wille,	ULRICH ar Swi
Wilhelm	ROUX sc,e Ger	Willebrord SNEL astr Dut	
Wilhelm	RUPPELL sc,x Ger	Willem	BARENTS x Dut
Wilhelm	SCHAFER w Ger	Willem	BLAEU math Dut
Wilhelm	SCHERER e,w Ger	Willem	DAFOE
Wilhelm	SOLF st Ger	Willem	DUDOK ac Dut
Wilhelm	TELL hero Swi	Willem	HEDA p Dut
Wilhelm	WIEN sc,e Ger	Willem	KALFF p Dut
Wilhelm	WUNDT ps.sc Ger	Willem	KLOOS po,ct Dut
Wilhelm,	CARL cn,c Ger	Willem	PAAP w Dut
Wilhelm,	HOYT b hf	Willem de KOONING p Am	
Wilhoite,	KATHLEEN	Willem de SITTER astr Dut	
Wilke,	ROBERT tv	Willems,	JAN po,ed Belg
Wilker,	JOSE	Willett,	TOM tv
Wilkerson,	GUY	Willette	JoANN tv
Wilkes,	CHARLES navy,x Am	Willey,	WALT tv
Wilkes,	DONNA tv+	William	ADAMS w,ed Am
Wilkes,	JOHN w,j,ref Br	William	AITKEN st,pb Br
Wilkie	COLLINS w Br	William	AITON sc Scot
Wilkie,	DAVID(Sir)p Scot	William	ARCHER w,ct Scot
Wilkins,	GEO.(Sir)x,fly Austra	William	ARKELL sc,e Br
Wilkins,	LENNY bb,bbc hf	William	ARROL(Sir)eng Scot
Wilkins,	MAURICE n-m'62	William	ASHLEY x,furs Am
Wilkins,	ROY civil rts,ed Am	William	ASHLEY(Sir)ec,e
Wilkinson,	ELLEN fe,st Br	William	ASTOR f,j Br
Wilkinson,	GEOFFREY(Sir)n-c'73	William	AYRTON eng,i Br
Wilkinson,	JUNE	William	AYTOUN po Scot
Wilkinson,	SIGNE p-x'92	William	BABELL organ,c Br
Wilkof,	LEE tv	William	BAFFIN x Br
Will	CLARK b	William	BAGLEY e Am
Will	COOK m,c Am	William	BAIKIE sc,md Scot
Will	CUPPY ct,humor Am	William	BALCOM c Am
Will	DURANT e,ph Am	William	BALDWIN
Will	FYFFE la+ Scot	William	BARNES po Br
Will	GEER tv+	William	BARR(Gen,.)l,st Am
Will	HAYS l,st Am	William	BARTRAM sc,x,w,Am
Will	HUNT tv	William	BECKLEY tv
Will	IRWIN j,w Am	William	BEECHEY(Sir)p
Will	KELLOGG cornflakes Am	William	BENDIX tv+
Will	NIPPER tv	William	BENET po,w Am
Will	PATTON	William	BENN st Br
Will	ROGERS humor,w+ Am	William	BENNETT(Sir)piano,c
Will	ROGERS Jr	William	BENSON navy Am
Will	ROLAND tv	William	BERGER
Will	SAMPSON	William	BERKE d
Will	SHORTZ ed-xword,radio	William	BISHOP fly Can
Will	SMITH tv+	William	BLAKE po,p Br
Willa	CATHER w Am	William	BLIGH navy Br
Willard	LIBBY sc,e Am	William	BOEING id-planes Am
Willard	MOTLEY w Am	William	BOGERT tv
Willard	PUGH	William	BONNEY outlaw Am
Willard	QUINE ph Am	William	BOOTH salv army Br
Willard	SCOTT tv-weather Am	William	BORAH st Am
Willard	WRIGHT w Am	William	BOYCE organ,c Br
Willard,	ARCHIBALD p Am	William	BOYD tv+
Willard,	EMMA e Am	William	BOYETT tv
Willard,	FRANK cr Am	William	BRANDE sc,w Br
Willard,	FRED tv+	William	BROOME po Br
Willard,	JESS boxer Am	William	BROWN w Am

William	BRYANT tv+	William	FOLMER i,id Am
William	BUDD md Br	William	FOSTER labor Am
William	BULLITT st,w Am	William	FOWLER sc Am
William	BURNS dective Am	William	FOWLER w Am
William	BURT i Am	William	FRAWLEY tv+
William	BURTON sc,id Am	William	FRITH p Br
William	BYRD organ,c Br	William	FRY c, ct Am
William	CANNON tv	William	GADDIS w Am
William	CASTLE md,e Am	William	GALLO tv
William	CAXTON id,mer Br	William	GARGAN tv+
William	CHASE p Am	William	GASS w,ph Am
William	CHING	William	GED at-gold Scot
William	CHURCH i Am	William	GIAQUE sc Am
William	CLANNY md,i Br	William	GIBSON illus Am
William	CLARK ar,x Am	William	GILBERT md,sc Br
William	CODY(BuffaloBill)hero	William	GILBERT(Sir)w
William	COLGATE id Am	William	GODWIN ph,w Br
William	COLLINS po Br	William	GOLDEN s-cnt Am
William	COMBE w Br	William	GOLDING w Br
William	CONRAD tv+	William	GOLDMAN w Am
William	CORBETT w,j Br	William	GORDON tv
William	CORY po Br	William	GORGAS ar,md Am
William	COWPER po Br	William	GOULD
William	COX w Ir	William	GQOBA w Bantu
William	CRAMP id-ships Am	William	GRACE mer,ships Am
William	CREMER(Sir)pacifist	William	GRAHAM d
William	CROFT organ,c Br	William	GREEN labor Am
William	CROOKES(Sir)sc	William	GROPPER p Am
William	CROTCH c Br	William	GUEST s-pop Am
William	CULLEN tv	William	GWINN tv
William	DANIELS tv+	William	HADOW(Sir)w
William	DAVIES po Welsh	William	HAINES
William	DAVIS geol,e Am	William	HARRIS ph,e Am
William	De MORGAN p,w Br	William	HART la+ Am
William	DEERING id Am	William	HARVEY md Br
William	DESMOND	William	HARVEY(Coin)ec,w Am
William	DEVANE tv+	William	HASTIE l.e,st Am
William	DINES weather Br	William	HAZEN ar Am
William	DOBSON p Br	William	HAZLITT w,ct Br
William	DODD h,e Am	William	HENLEY po,w,ed Br
William	DONOVAN l,st Am	William	HENRY
William	DUANE sc,e Am	William	HICKEY tv+
William	DUELL tv+	William	HICKS
William	DUER re,st Am	William	HOCKING ph,e Am
William	DUNBAR po Scot	William	HODGES w Am
William	DUNLAP p,w,h Am	William	HOGARTH p,eng Br
William	DURANT id-autos Am	William	HOLDEN
William	DYCE p Scot	William	HOME w Br
William	DYSON etch,cr Br	William	HOPPE billiards Am
William	ELLIOTT tv	William	HOPPER
William	EMPSON(Sir)po,ct	William	HOWELLS w,ct,po Am
William	ETTY p Br	William	HUDSON sc,w Br
William	EVARTS l,st Am	William	HUDSON tv+
William	EWART st Br	William	HUGGINS(Sir)astr
William	EYTHE	William	HUIE tv
William	FARGO f,bus Am	William	HULBERT b hf
William	FARLOW sc,e Am	William	HURT
William	FARNUM	William	INGE w Am
William	FARRER sc Br	William	JACOBS w Br
William	FAWCETT	William	JAMES ph,ps,e Am
William	FERREL weather Am	William	JENNEY ac Am

William	JEVONS ec,e Br	William	PALEY tv-exec Am
William	JOHNSON bb hf	William	PARRY(Sir)x
William	JOHNSON(Judi)b hf	William	PARSONS astr Ir
William	JORDAN tv+	William	PENN r,st,w Br
William	JUXON r,e Br	William	PERDOMO w Am
William	KATT tv+	William	PERKIN(Sir)sc,id
William	KEELER(WeeWillie)b hf	William	PERRY(Refrigerator)fb
William	KEITH p Am	William	PETTY(Sir)ec,e
William	KEMP cm,ba,la Br	William	PHIPPS tv+
William	KENNEDY w Am	William	PITT st Br
William	KENT p,ac Br	William	PLOMER w S.Afr
William	KER e Br	William	POEL la,mgr-theatr Br
William	KIDD(Capt.)pirate Br	William	PORTER w Am
William	KING mr-trump,kbds Am	William	POST Jr. tv+
William	KING st Can	William	POWELL
William	KNUDSEN id-cars Am	William	PREECE(Sir)eng
William	LANGER h,e Am	William	PRINCE tv+
William	LASSELL astr Br	William	PRYNNE w Br
William	LAUD r Br	William	RAMSAY(Sir)sc,e
William	LAW w Br	William	REEVES j,st,ec N.Zea
William	LEAHY navy,st Am	William	REID mr-guit,s Scot
William	LEAKE antiquary,w Br	William	RENSHAW t Br
William	LEAR eng,id-planes Am	William	RIMMER p,su Am
William	LECKY h Ir	William	ROPER bio Br
William	LEONARD po Am	William	ROSCOE h,l Br
William	LESCAZE ac Am	William	ROSS(Sir) ph,ct Scot
William	LESLIE tv	William	ROWLEY la,w Br
William	LEWIS tv	William	RUBEY geol,e Am
William	LOGAN(Sir)geol Can	William	RUSH su Am
William	LUCKING tv+	William	RUSS tv+
William	MACY mer Am	William	RUSSELL tv+
William	MARCY l,st Am	William	RUSSELL(Sir)j
William	MAYO md Am	William	SACHS d
William	McADOO id-rr,st Am	William	SAFIRE j Am
William	McFEELY w,bio Am	William	SAMPSON navy Am
William	McGUFFEY e,w Am	William	SANDAY r,e Br
William	McKINNEY tv	William	SANSOM w Br
William	McNAMARA	William	SAROYAN w Am
William	MERWIN po Am	William	SCHLICH(Sir)forests,e
William	MONSON(Sir)navy	William	SCHUMAN c Am
William	MOODY po,w Am	William	SEATON j,ed Am
William	MOON i Br	William	SEITER d
William	MORRIS at,ac,po,w Br	William	SHAFTER ar Am
William	MOSES tv+	William	SHARPE ec Am
William	MOUNT p Am	William	SHATNER tv+
William	MURE(Sir)po Scot	William	SHAW(Sir)weather,e
William	MURPHY md Am	William	SHERMAN ar-general Am
William	NELL w Am	William	SHIELD c Br
William	NEWELL	William	SHIRER j,h Am
William	NIBLO bus Am	William	SHUSTER l,pb,f Am
William	NICOL sc,i Scot	William	SIMMS w,po Am
William	NIGH d	William	SKENE h Scot
William	O'DWYER st Am	William	SLIM ar,st Br
William	O'LEARY tv+	William	SMELLIE md,w Scot
William	OGBURN soc Am	William	SMITH
William	ORPEN(Sir)p	William	SMITH geol Br
William	OSLER(Sir)md Can	William	SOUTAR po Scot
William	PAICA l,re leader Am	William	SPOONER e Br
William	PAGE p Am	William	STEAD j Br
William	PAINTER w Br	William	STEIN n-c'72
William	PALEY r,ph Br	William	STEIS

William	STEVENS tv	Williams,	WARREN
William	STILL c,arranger Am	Williams,	ADAM
William	STORY su Am	Williams,	ALLEN tv+
William	STUBBS r,h Br	Williams,	AMIR tv
William	STYRON w Am	Williams,	ANDREW tv
William	SULZER st Am	Williams,	ANDY s-pop,tv Am
William	SUMNER ec,e Am	Williams,	ANSON tv
William	SWANN sc.e Am	Williams,	BARBARA
William	TALMAN tv+	Williams,	BARRY tv+
William	TANNEN tv+	Williams,	BEN w Am
William	TELL hero Swi	Williams,	BERNIE b-gg'97
William	TERRISS la Br	Williams,	BERT cm,ws Am
William	THOMAS Jr tv	Williams,	BETTY n-x'76
William	THOMSON math,sc,i Br	Williams,	BILL dj,tv Am
William	TOLBERT st Liberia	Williams,	BILL tv+
William	TRACY	Williams,	BILLY b hf
William	TREVOR w Ir	Williams,	BILLY DEE
William	TUBMAN st Liberia	Williams,	BILLY m,tv Am
William	TWEED(Boss)st Am	Williams,	BOB dog act, tv
William	U'REN l,ref Am	Williams,	BRANDON tv
William	UTAY tv	Williams,	BRUCE tv
William	VILE cabinets Br	Williams,	CARA tv+
William	WAKE r Br	Williams,	CHARLES w po,ct Br
William	WALTON(Sir)c	Williams,	CHINO tv
William	WARE ac Am	Williams,	CHS.(Cootie)mj,c,tv Am
William	WARHAM r Br	Williams,	CINDY tv+
William	WARNER w Am	Williams,	CLARENCE III tv+
William	WATSON tv+	Williams,	CLIFF mr-guit Br
William	WATSON(Sir)po	Williams,	COOTIE mj-trump Am
William	WEBB d	Williams,	DENIECE s-pop,gosp Am
William	WELCH sc-md,e Am	Williams,	DICK ANTHONY tv+
William	WELLMAN d	Williams,	DON s-cnt Am
William	WELLMAN Jr.	Williams,	ED tv
William	WHARTON w Am	Williams,	EDY
William	WHEWELL ph,math,e Br	Williams,	ELEAZAR r Am
William	WHISTON math Br	Williams,	EMLYN w,la+ Welsh
William	WILGUS eng Am	Williams,	EPHRAIM ar Am
William	WILLS w,po Ir	Williams,	ESTHER sw+ Am
William	WILSON labor Am	Williams,	FRANCES E. tv
William	WINDOM tv+	Williams,	GENE mj-s,cn Am
William	WIRT l,st Am	Williams,	GLUYAS cr Am
William	WITNEY d	Williams,	GRANT tv+
William	WORKMAN md,x Am	Williams,	GUINN tv+
William	WYLER d	Williams,	GUY tv+
William	YANCEY st Am	Williams,	HAL tv+
William	YEATS po,w Ir	Williams,	HANK Jr s-cnt+ Am
William	ZABKA tv	Williams,	HANK Sr s-cnt+ Am
William	ZIPP	Williams,	HUGH
William	ZORACH su Am	Williams,	JASON
William	ZUCKERT tv	Williams,	JAYSON bb
William Allen WHITE j,w Am		Williams,	JESSE p-d'18
William C. HANDY mj,c Am		Williams,	JIM
William Cullen BRYANT w Am		Williams,	JoBETH
William H. BRAGG(Sir)sc		Williams,	JODY n-x'97
William Jennings BRYAN st Am		Williams,	JOHN
William L. BRAGG(Sir)sc		Williams,	JOHN A. w Am
William O. DOUGLAS j,w Am		Williams,	JOHN cn,c Am
William of CCAM(Ockham)ph,r Br		Williams,	KELLI
William of Malmesbury --- h Br		Williams,	KELLIE SHANYGNE tv
William Randolf HEARST pb Am		Williams,	KENNETH
William Speirs BRUCE x Scot		Williams,	KENT tv

Williams,	MAISIE mr-s W.Indies	Willingham,	CALDER w Am
Williams,	MARY LOU mj-pian,c Am	Willingham,	NOBLE tv+
Williams,	MASON tv	Willis	CARRIER eng,i Am
Williams,	MATT b,hr'94,rbi'90 &	Willis	HAWLEY st Am
Williams,	MATT many gg's	Willis	LAMB sc Am
Williams,	MILAN mr-kbds,drm Am	Willis	REED bb hf
Williams,	MONTEL tv-host Am	Willis,	ANDRA s,tv Am
Williams,	OTIS mr-s Am	Willis,	BAILEY geol,e Am
Williams,	PAUL	Willis,	BILL fb hf
Williams,	RAYMOND w,ct Br	Willis,	BRUCE tv+
Williams,	RHYS	Willis,	MATT
Williams,	RICHARD tv	Willis,	NATHANIEL ed,w Am
Williams,	ROBERT	Willkie,	WENDELL LEWIS st Am
Williams,	ROBERT P. tv	Willock,	DAVE tv
Williams,	ROBIN o-s'98,tv	Willock,	MARGARET tv
Williams,	ROGER r,w,st Am	Wills Moody,	HELEN t Am
Williams,	ROGER sc Am	Wills,	BOB m-cnt,viol Am
Williams,	SADLER sp	Wills,	CHILL tv+
Williams,	SAMM-ART	Wills,	GARRY p-n'93
Williams,	SPENCER Jr tv+	Wills,	LOU Jr tv
Williams,	STEVEN tv+	Wills,	MAURY b-mv'62,tv
Williams,	T. HARRY p-b'70	Wills,	WILLIAM w,po Ir
Williams,	TED b-mv'46'49 hf	Willson,	MEREDITH mj,cn,c,tv Am
Williams,	TENESSEE p-d'48'55	Willstatter,	RICHARD n-c'15
Williams,	TERRY guit,tv Am	Willy	BRANDT st Ger
Williams,	TONYA tv	Willy	DIXON ws Am
Williams,	TREAT	Willy	FRITSCH
Williams,	VAN tv	Willy	WELLS b hf
Williams,	VANESSA mo,s+ Am	Willys,	JOHN id-cars,st Am
Williams,	VENUS t Am	Wilma	RUDOLPH sprinter Am
Williams,	VIC b hf	Wilmer,	DOUGLAS
Williams,	WENDY O.s,entertn Am	Wilmot,	FRANK po Aust
Williams,	WILLIAM B. tv	Wilms,	ANDRE
Williams,	WILLIAM po Am	Wilson	PICKETT s,ws Am
Williams,	WM. CARLOS p-q'63	Wilson	WALLIS an,w Am
Williamson,	FRED d,tv+	Wilson,	AJITA
Williamson,	HENRY w Br	Wilson,	AL(BlindOwl)mr-guit,s
Williamson,	MARIANNE w Am	Wilson,	ALEXANDRA tv
Williamson,	MICHAEL p-n'90	Wilson,	ANGUS(Sir)w,bio
Williamson,	MYKEL tv+	Wilson,	ANN mr-s Am
Williamson,	NICOL	Wilson,	AUGUST p-d'87'90
Williamson,	PENELOPE w Am	Wilson,	BARRY mr-drm Br
Willie	AAMES tv+	Wilson,	BOB tv
Willie	BEST tv+	Wilson,	BRIAN GODFREY tv
Willie	BROWN fb hf	Wilson,	BRIAN mr-bass,kbds,s
Willie	DAVIS fb hf	Wilson,	CARL mr-guit,s Am
Willie	HOPPE billiards Am	Wilson,	CARNIE s Am
Willie	LANIER fb hf	Wilson,	CASSANDRA mj-s Am
Willie	LOMAN fc	Wilson,	CHARLES n-p'27
Willie	MAYS b hf	Wilson,	CINDY mr-guit,s Am
Willie	McCOVEY b hf	Wilson,	COLIN w,ct Br
Willie	McGEE b,bat'90	Wilson,	DAVID tv+
Willie	NELSON s-cnt+ Am	Wilson,	DEMOND tv
Willie	SMITH mj-sax Am	Wilson,	DICK tv
Willie	SMITH(Lion)mj-pian Am	Wilson,	DON mr-guit Am
Willie	SUTTON rob-banks Am	Wilson,	DON(The Dragon)tv+
Willie	TYLER cm,tv Am	Wilson,	DOOLEY piano,tv+
Willie	WELLS b hf	Wilson,	DOREEN tv
Willie	WILSON b	Wilson,	DOROTHY
Willie	WOOD fb hf		
Willinger,	JASON tv		

Wilson,	DOVER e,ed Br
Wilson,	EARL tv+
Wilson,	EDMUND ct,w,po Am
Wilson,	EDWARD p-n'79,'91
Wilson,	EILEEN s,tv Am
Wilson,	ELIZABETH tv+
Wilson,	ETHEL tv
Wilson,	ETHEL w Can
Wilson,	FLIP cm,tv+ Am
Wilson,	FRANK
Wilson,	GAHAN cr Am
Wilson,	GERALD mj-trump,cn Am
Wilson,	HACK b hf
Wilson,	HALSEY pb Am
Wilson,	HARRY w Am
Wilson,	JACKIE mr Am
Wilson,	JANE tv
Wilson,	JEANNIE tv
Wilson,	JIM tv
Wilson,	JOE (Whispering) tv
Wilson,	JOHN w Am
Wilson,	JOYCE mr-s Am
Wilson,	JOYCE tv
Wilson,	KENNETH n-p'82
Wilson,	LAMBERT
Wilson,	LANFORD p-d'80
Wilson,	LARRY fb-d'66 hf
Wilson,	LIONEL tv
Wilson,	LISLE tv
Wilson,	LOIS tv+
Wilson,	MARIE tv+
Wilson,	MARY mr-s Am
Wilson,	MARY LOUISE tv+
Wilson,	MELANIE tv
Wilson,	NANCY s-r&b Am
Wilson,	RICHARD p Welsh
Wilson,	ROBERT la,w Br
Wilson,	ROBERT n-p'78
Wilson,	ROGER tv+
Wilson,	SAMUEL id-meat Am
Wilson,	SCOTT
Wilson,	SHEREE tv+
Wilson,	SLIM m-cnt,cn,tv Am
Wilson,	SLOAN w Am
Wilson,	STEVE tv
Wilson,	STUART
Wilson,	TEDDY mj-piano,c+ Am
Wilson,	TERRY tv
Wilson,	THEODORE tv
Wilson,	THOMAS
Wilson,	TOM cr Am
Wilson,	TONY mr-bass,s Trinid
Wilson,	TREY
Wilson,	WENDY s Am
Wilson,	WHISPERING JOE tv
Wilson,	WILLIAM labor Am
Wilson,	WILLIE b,bat'82
Wilson,	WOODROW 28th Pres &
Wilson,	WOODROW n-x'19
Wilsson,	PAUL tv
Wilt	CHAMBERLAIN bb hf+

Wilton,	PENELOPE
Wilzak,	CRISSY tv
Wim	WENDERS d+
Wimberly,	BILL m-cnt,cn,tv Am
Wimmer,	BRIAN tv+
Win	ELLIOT tv
Win	STRACKE tv
Wincenty	POL po Pol
Wincenty	WITOS st Pol
Wincer,	SIMON d
Winchell,	PAUL tv
Winchell,	WALTER j-gossip,tv Am
Winchester,	OLIVER id-rifles Am
Wincott,	JEFF tv+
Wincott,	MICHAEL
Windaus,	ADOLF n-c'28
Winding,	KAI mj-tromb,c Am
Windom,	WILLIAM tv+
Windsor,	MARIE
Windsor,	ROMY
Winfield	SCHLEY navy Am
Winfield,	DAVE b,rbi'79 &
Winfield,	DAVE gg'79'80
Winfield,	PAUL tv+
Winfrey,	OPRAH tv-hostess+ Am
Wingate,	ORDE ar Br
Winger,	DEBRA
Wings	HAUSER
Wingy	MANONE mj-trump,cn Am
Winifred	ASHTON w Br
Winifred	HOLTBY w Br
Wink	MARTINDALE tv
Wink	ROBERTS
Winkel,	DIETRICH i Ger
Winkel,	LAMBERT philology Dut
Winkleman,	MICHAEL tv
Winkler,	ANGELA
Winkler,	CLEMENS sc,e Ger
Winkler,	HENRY tv+
Winkworth,	MARK tv
Winmill,	SAMMIE tv
Winn,	ANONA mj-s Br
Winn,	KITTY
Winner,	MICHAEL d
Winner,	SEPTIMUS ws Am
Winnick,	MAURICE mj-viol,cn Br
Winnicka,	LUCYNA
Winnie	ILLE POOH fc
Winninger,	CHARLES tv+
Winningham,	MARE
Winona	RYDER
Winona,	KIM tv
Winslet,	KATE
Winslow	HOMER p Am
Winslow,	EDWARD st-Plymouth Am
Winslow,	KELLEN fb hf
Winslow,	MICHAEL
Winslowe,	PAULA tv
Winsor	McCAY cr Am
Winsor,	JUSTIN h Am
Winston	GROOM w Am

Winston	REKERT tv+
Winston,	DAYNA tv
Winston,	HATTIE tv
Winston,	JIMMY mr-organ Br
Winston,	LESLIE tv
Winter,	ALEX
Winter,	EDGARm-r&b,mr-kbds Am
Winter,	EDWARD tv
Winter,	JAN de navy Dut
Winter,	JO de tv
Winter,	JOHNNY m-r&b,mr-guit
Winter,	LYNETTE tv
Winter,	MARIUS B. mj,cn Br
Winter,	PETER von c Ger
Winter,	VINCENT
Winters,	DAVID d
Winters,	DEBORAH
Winters,	GLORIA tv
Winters,	JONATHAN cm,tv+ Am
Winters,	ROLAND tv+
Winters,	SHELLEY o-s'59'65
Winters,	YVOR ct,po,e Am
Winterson,	JEANETTE w Br
Winthrop	AMES pr Am
Winthrop	PRAED po,st Br
Winthrop,	JOHN 1st gov Mass.
Winton,	ALEXANDER bikes,cars
Winwood,	ESTELLE
Winwood,	MUFF m-bass,s,ws Br
Winwood,	STEVE mr,s,ws Br
Wiremu	KINGI chf Maori,N.Zea
Wirt,	WILLIAM 1,st Am
Wirth,	BILLY
Wirth,	JOSEPH st Ger
Wirth,	LOUIS soc,e Am
Wisa	D'ORSO tv
Wisbar,	FRANK tv
Wise,	ALFIE tv
Wise,	BUDDY mj-sax Am
Wise,	HERBERT d
Wise,	JOHN baloons Am
Wise,	RAY tv+
Wise,	ROBERT o-d'61
Wiseman,	JOSEPH tv+
Wisenberg,S.L.	w Am
Wissler,	CLARK an Am
Wissowa,	GEORG w Ger
Wistar,	CASPAR 1st glass id Am
Wister,	OWEN w Am
Witcher,	GABE tv
Wither,	GEORGE po,w Br
Withers,	BERNADETTE tv
Withers,	BILL s-pop,guit Am
Withers,	GOOGIE
Withers,	GRANT
Withers,	JANE
Withers,	MARK tv
Witherspoon,	CORA
Witherspoon,	REESE
Witi	IHIMAERA w N.Zea
Witkiewicz, S.I.	w Pol

Witney,	WILLIAM d
Witos,	WINCENTY st Pol
Witt,	FRIEDRICH cello,c Ger
Witt,	KATARINA sk,o-g'84'88
Witte,	EMANUEL de p Dut
Witte,	SERGEY st Rus
Witter,	KAREN
Wittig,	GEORG n-c'79
Witting,	STEVE tv
Witz,	KONRAD p Ger
Wixted,	MICHAEL-JAMES tv
Wladimir	KOPPEN weather Ger
Wladyslaw	ANDERS ar Pol
Wladyslaw	REYMONT w Pol
Wladziu	LIBERACE pian,c,tv Am
Wodehouse,P.G. (Sir)w,j
Woestijne,KAREL v. de po,stBelg
Wohl,	DAVID tv+
Wohler,	FRIEDRICH sc,e Ger
Wojciechowicz, ALEX fb hf
Woldemar	VOIGT sc,e Ger
Wolders,	ROBERT tv
Wole	SOYINKA po,w Nigeria
Wolf	HUBER p Ger
Wolf	LARSEN tv
Wolf	RUVINSKIS
Wolf,	HUGO c Aus
Wolf,	KELLY
Wolf,	RUDOLF astr Swi
Wolf,	WARNER tv
Wolfe	PERRY tv
Wolfe	TONE rebel Ir
Wolfe,	CHARLES po Ir
Wolfe,	HUMBERT po Br
Wolfe,	IAN
Wolfe,	JAMES ar-Gen Br
Wolfe,	JANICE tv
Wolfe,	NERO fc
Wolfe,	THOMAS w Am.
Wolfe,	TOM j,w Am
Wolfert,	IRA w Am
Wolff,	CHRISTIAN ph,math Ger
Wolff,	DANIEL w Br
Wolff,	FRANK
Wolff,	GEOFFREY w Am
Wolff,	HUGH cn Am
Wolff,	MICHAEL m,cn,tv Am
Wolff,	PIERRE w Fr
Wolff,	TOBIAS w Am
Wolfgang	MOZART c Aus
Wolfgang	PAUL sc,e Ger
Wolfgang	PAULI sc,e Am
Wolfgang	PREISS
Wolfit,	DONALD
Wolfman Jack	--- tv+
Wolheim,	LOUIS
Woll,	MATTHEW labor Am
Wollaston,WILLIAM sc,md Br
Wollman,	TERRY tv
Wollstonecraft, MARY fe,w Br
Wollter,	SVEN

Wolpe,	LENNY tv	Woods,	TIGER g Am
Wolter	HOEVELL st Dut	Woodson,	CARTER h,e Am
Womack,	BOBBY s-r&b,gospel Am	Woodville,	KATE
Wonder,	STEVIE s,ws+ Am	Woodvine,	JOHN
Wong,	ANNA MAY	Woodward,	EDWARD tv+
Wong,	ARTHUR tv	Woodward,	JOANNE o-a'57
Wong,	B.D.	Woodward,	KEREN mr-s Br
Wong,	CARTER	Woodward,	LENORE tv
Wong,	RUSSELL	Woodward,	MORGAN tv+
Wong,	VICTOR	Woodward,	ROBERT n-c'65
Wontner,	ARTHUR	Woodward,	TIM
Woo,	JOHN d	Woody	ALLEN d, w+
Wood,	BARRY mj-s Am	Woody	BROWN tv+
Wood,	BRITT	Woody	GUTHRIE s-folk Am
Wood,	CLEMENT w Am	Woody	HAYES fbc Am
Wood,	CLIVE	Woody	HERMAN mj-clar,cn Am
Wood,	DANNY mr-s Am	Woody	STRODE
Wood,	DONNA s Am	Wool,	JOHN ar Am
Wood,	EDWARD st Br	Wooldridge,	SUSAN
Wood,	ELIJAH	Wooley,	SHEB s-cnt,c,tv Am
Wood,	GARFIELD id-boats Am	Woolf,	DANIEL w Br
Wood,	GRANT p Am	Woolf,	LEONARD w Br
Wood,	HARLEY	Woolf,	VIRGINIA w,ct Br
Wood,	HELEN tv	Woollcott,	ALEXANDER j,ct,w Am
Wood,	HENRY(Sir)cn,c	Woolley,	LEONARD(Sir)arc
Wood,	JANET	Woolley,	MARY e Am
Wood,	JOHN	Woolley,	MONTY
Wood,	KELLY tv	Woolpert,	PHIL bbc hf
Wood,	KINGSLEY(Sir)st	Woolsey,	ROBERT
Wood,	LANA tv+	Woolsey,	SARAH w Am
Wood,	LEONARD md,ar Am	Woolson,	CONSTANCE w Am
Wood,	MRS. HENRY w Br	Woolworth,	FRANK WINFIELD mer Am
Wood,	NATALIE tv+	Woosnam,	IAN g Br
Wood,	PEGGY tv+	Wooster,	DAVID ar-re Am
Wood,	RALPH id-pottery Br	Wopat,	TOM b,tv+
Wood,	RAY tv	Worde,	WYNKYN de printer Br
Wood,	ROY mr-guit,cello,s Br	Worden,	JOHN navy Am
Wood,	SAM d	Wordsworth,	DOROTHY w Br
Wood,	STUART mr-guit Scot	Wordsworth,	WILLIAM po Br
Wood,	TERRI tv	Work,	HENRY ws Am
Wood,	WILLIE fb hf	Workman,	WILLIAM md,x Am
Woodard,	ALFRE tv+	Worley,	JO ANNE tv
Woodard,	CHARLAINE	Worm,	OLE md,sc Dan
Woodbridge Van DYKE d		Woronov	MARY
Woodbury,	JOAN	Worters,	ROY ho-m'29
Woodcock,	GEORGE w,ed Can	Worth,	CONSTANCE
Woode,	MARGO	Worth,	IRENE
Woodell,	PAT tv+	Worth,	NICHOLAS
Wooden,	JOHN bb,bbc hf	Wortham	KRIMMER tv
Woodham-Smith, CECIL bio,h Br		Worthington,	CAROL tv
Woodland,	LAUREN tv	Wotton,	HENRY(Sir)st,po
Woodruff,	LARGO	Wouk,	HERMAN p-f'52
Woods,	BARBARA	Wrangel,	FERDINAND x Rus
Woods,	DONALD tv+	Wrangel,	PYOTR ar Rus
Woods,	HARRY	Wray,	FAY tv+
Woods,	JAMES	Wrede,	KARL ar Ger
Woods,	MARGARET w Br	Wren,	CHRISTOPHER(Sir)ac
Woods,	MICHAEL	Wren,	CLARE tv+
Woods,	NAN tv+	Wright	COBINA Jr.
Woods,	REN tv	Wright	KING tv+
Woods,	ROBERT tv	Wright	MORRIS w Am

Wright	PATMAN st Am	Wyatt,	JANE tv+
Wright,	ALMROTH (Sir) md,sc	Wyatt,	THOMAS (Sir) po,st
Wright,	AMY	Wycherley,	WILLIAM w Br
Wright,	CHARLES p-q'98	Wycherly,	MARGARET
Wright,	ELIZUR ref,e Am	Wyclif,	JOHN r,ref Br
Wright,	FANNY ref Am	Wyeth,	ANDREW p Am
Wright,	FRANK LLOYD ac Am	Wyeth,	KATYA
Wright,	GEORGE b hf	Wyeth,	NEWELL p,illus Am
Wright,	HAROLD w Am	Wyld,	HENRY w,lexicog,e Br
Wright,	HARRY b hf	Wyle,	GEORGE m,cn,tv Am
Wright,	HENRY ac Am	Wyler,	GRETCHEN tv+
Wright,	HENRY bmg	Wyler,	RICHARD tv
Wright,	HORATIO ar Am	Wyler,	WILLIAM o-d'42'46'59
Wright,	JACKIE tv	Wylie	WATSON
Wright,	JAMES p-q'72	Wylie,	ELINOR po,w Am
Wright,	JEFFREY	Wylie,	IDA w Br
Wright,	JENNY	Wylie,	PHILIP w Am
Wright,	JOHN tv	Wylie,	ROBERT p Am
Wright,	JOSEPH p Br	Wyllie,	MEG tv
Wright,	JUDITH po,ct Aust	Wyman,	BILL mr-bass Br
Wright,	LITTLE STEVIE mr-s Br	Wyman,	JANE o-a'48, tv+
Wright,	MACK d	Wyman,	JEFFRIES md,sc,e Am
Wright,	MARTHA tv	Wymark,	PATRICK
Wright,	MAX tv+	Wymore,	PATRICE
Wright,	MICHAEL tv+	Wyndham	LEWIS w,p Br
Wright,	MICKEY g Am	Wyndham,	ANNE tv
Wright,	ORVILLE i,aviation Am	Wyndham,	JOHN w scifi Br
Wright,	PAT s Am	Wyner,	GEORGE tv+
Wright,	PATIENCE su Am	Wynette,	TAMMY s-cntAm
Wright,	QUINCY sc-politics Am	Wynkyn de	WORDE printer Br
Wright,	RICHARD w Am	Wynn	IRWIN tv
Wright,	RICK mr-kbds Br	Wynn,	EARLY b-cy'59,hf
Wright,	ROBERT bus-NBC Am	Wynn,	ED cm,tv+ Am
Wright,	ROBIN	Wynn,	KEENAN tv+
Wright,	SAMUEL tv	Wynn,	MAY tv+
Wright,	SEWALL md-sc,e Am	Wynne,	ELLIS w Welsh
Wright,	STEVEN cm+ Am	Wynonna	--- s cnt Am
Wright,	SYREETA s,ws Am	Wynorski,	JIM d
Wright,	TERESA o-s'42	Wynter,	DANA
Wright,	THOMAS d	Wynters,	CHARLOTTE
Wright,	WILBUR aviation Am	Wynton	MARSALIS mj-trump Am
Wrightson,	EARL tv	Wyomia	TYUS o-g'64'68
Wrixon,	MARIS	Wyrtzen,	JACK tv
Wu,	VIVIAN	Wyss,	AMANDA
Wuhl,	ROBERT	Wyss,	JOHANN w,ph,e Swi
Wuhrer,	KARI	Wystan	AUDEN po Am
Wulff,	KAI	Wythe,	GEORGE l,st Am
Wullner,	FRANZ cn,c Ger		
Wunderlich,	FRITZ tenor Ger		
Wundt,	WILHELM ps,sc Ger	**"X" NAME DESIGNATION CODE**	
Wuorinen,	CHARLES p-m'70	x - EXPLORER	
Wurdemann,	AUDREY p-q'35		
Wurmser,	DAGOBERT von ar Aus		
Wurtz,	CHARLES sc,e Fr	**"X's"**	
Wurtzel,	ELIZABETH w Am	X	BRANDS tv
Wuttke,	HEINRICH h,st Ger	X,	ALFONSO w,po Rom
Wyant,	ALEXANDER p Am	Xander	BERKLEY
Wyant,	SHELLEY	Xanthus	SMITH p Am
Wyatt	EARP lawman Am	Xavier	CUGAT mj,cn,c+
Wyatt,	EATON p Am	Xavier	HERBERT w Aust
Wyatt	KNIGHT	Xavier	LEROUX c Fr

Xavier   ROBERTS id-dolls Am
Xavier de MONTEPIN w Fr
Xavier,   FRANCIS(St.)missn. Sp
Xenocrates --- ph Gr
Xenophon   --- h Gr
Xenophones --- ph Gr
Xiaoping, DENG st China

NO NAME DESIGNATION CODES
BEGIN WITH "Y's"

"Y" NATIONALITY CODE
Yugo   -   YUGOSLAVIAN

"Y's"
Y.A.   TITTLE fb hf
Yaconelli,FRANK
Yadin,   YIGAEL ar,st,sc Isr
Yagher,   JEFF
Yakima   CANUTT
Yakov   SMIRNOFF
Yakusho, KOJI
Yale   LARY fb hf
Yale,   ELIHU st Br
Yale,   LINUS i,id-locks Am
Yallen,   JACK lyrics Am
Yalom,   IRVIN ps,w Am
Yalow,   ROSALYN n-m'77
Yam,   SIMON
Yama,   MICHAEL tv
Yamada,   ISUZU
Yamaguchi,KRISTI sk Am
Yamamoto, ISOROKU navy-adm Jap
Yamamura, SO
Yamazaki, TSUTOMU
Yan,   MARTIN tv chef Am
Yancey,   WILLIAM st Am
Yancey,   JIMMY mj-piano Am
Yanez,   AUGUSTIN w Mex
Yang,   CHEN NING n-p'57
Yang Pan PAN
Yankovic, WEIRD AL s,spoofs Am
Yankovsky,OLEG
Yanne,   JEAN
Yanni   --- m-piano Gr-Am
Yanni,   ROSSANA
Yannick   NOAH t Fr
Yannis   RITSOS po Gr
Yanovsky, ZAL mr-guit,s Can
Yanti   SOMER
Yaphet   KOTTO
Yarborough, BARTON tv
Yarborough, CALE carrace Am
Yarborough, JEAN d
Yarlett, CLAIRE tv
Yarnall, CELESTE
Yarnell, BRUCE tv
Yarnell, LORENE tv
Yarrow,   PETER mj,s,c,w Am
Yasbeck, AMY

Yashin,   ALEKSANDR po,w Rus
Yastrzemski, CARL b-mv'67 hf
Yates,   CASSIE tv+
Yates,   PETER d
Yates,   RICHARD st Am
Yawkey,   TOM b hf
Yaziji,   NASIF scholar Lebanon
Yeager,   CHUCK test fly Am
Yeardley SMITH tv+
Yearwood, TRISHA s-cnt Am
Yeats,   WILLIAM po,n-l'23
Yedidia, MARIO
Yegor   KANKRIN st Ger
Yehiel   TRUNK w Pol
Yehoram   GAON
Yehuda   AMICHAI po,w Israel
Yehudi   MENUHIN viol Am
Yelena   BONNER st Rus
Yella   ROTTLAENDER
Yeltsin, BORIS st Rus
Yerby,   FRANK w Am
Yergin,   DANIEL p-n'92
Yerkes,   CHARLES f Am
Yerkes,   ROBERT ps,e,w Am
Yersin,   ALEXANDRE sc Swi
Yesenin, SERGEY po,w Rus
Yesso,   DON tv
Yester,   JIM mr-guit,s Am
Yeung,   BOLO
Yevgeny   KATAYEV w Rus
Yezhov,   NIKOLAY st Rus
Yftach   KATZUR
Yi,   CHANG
Yigael   YADIN ar,st,sc Isr
Yimou,   ZHANG d
Yip   HARBURG lyrics Am
Yitzhak   RABIN st Isr
Yma   SUMAC s Peru
Yoakam,   DWIGHT s-cnt Am
Yocum,   CLARK mj-s Am
Yoda,   YOSHIO tv
Yoel   LEVI cn Isr-Am
Yohn,   ERICA tv+
Yoko   ONO mr,s+
Yoko   TANI
Yolanda   JILOT
Yolande   DONLAN
Yom   HELLER r-rabbi Ger
Yonge,   Charlotte w,ed Br
Yootla   JOYCE
Yordan   YOVKOV w Bulg
Yorgo   VOYAGIS
Yakov   MALKIEL sc,w Am
Yasir   ARAFAT st Palestinian
Yo-Yo   MA cello Fr
Yogi   BERRA b hf
York,   ALVIN ar,hero Am
York,   DICK tv+
York,   DONALD(Donny)tv
York,   FRANCINE tv+
York,   JEFF tv+

York,	JOHN tv	Young,	SKIP tv
York,	KATHLEEN tv+	Young,	SNOOKY mj-trump Am
York,	MICHAEL tv+	Young,	STARK w,ed,ct Am
York,	PETE mr-drm Br	Young,	STEPHEN tv+
York,	REBECCA tv	Young,	STERLING mj,cn Am
York,	SUSANNAH	Young,	STEVE fb-m'92'94
Yorke,	HENRY w Br	Young,	TAMAR tv
Yorke,	RUTH tv	Young,	TERENCE d
Yorkin,	BUD d	Young,	VICTOR mj-pop,cn,c Am
Yorlin	MADERA tv	Young,	VICTORIA tv
Yoseph	SHILOAH	Young,	WHITNEY civil rts Am
Yoshio	YODA tv	Younger	BEVERLY tv
Yost,	FIELDING(HurrryUp)fbc	Younger,	COLE desparado Am
Yothers	TINA tv	Youngfellow, BARRIE tv	
Youmans,	VINCENT c Am	Younghusband, FRANC.E.(Sir)x,w	
Young MC	--- m-rap Br	Youngman, HENNY cm,tv+ Br	
Young,	ADEN	Youngquist, ARTHUR tv	
Young,	ALAN tv+	Youngs,	GAIL
Young,	ANGUS mr-guit Scot	Youngs,	JIM
Young,	ART cr,ref Am	Youngs,	ROSS b hf
Young,	BRIGHAM r Am	Yount,	ROBIN b-mv'82'89, hf
Young,	BURT	Youskevitch, IGOR	
Young,	CARLETON tv+	Yovkov,	YORDAN w Bulg
Young,	CHIC cr Am	Yowlachie,CHIEF	
Young,	CHRIS tv+	Ysaye,	EUGENE viol,cn,c Belg
Young,	CLARA	Yuan Tseh LEE sc Am	
Young,	CY b hf	Yue,	MARION tv
Young,	DANA tv	Yuji	OKUMOTO
Young,	DENTON(Cy)b hf	Yukawa,	HIDEKI n-p'49
Young,	DEY	Yukio	MISHIMA w Japan
Young,	EDWARD po,w Br	Yul	BRYNNER tv+
Young,	EDWARD x Br	Yule,	IAN
Young,	ELLA e Am	Yule,	JOE
Young,	EVE tv	Yulin,	HARRIS
Young,	FARON s+ Am	Yuly	DANIEL w Rus
Young,	FRANCIS w Br	Yumi	SHIRAKAWA
Young,	GEORGE mr-guit Scot	Yung,	SEN
Young,	GIG o-s'69,tv+	Yung,	VICTOR SEN
Young,	HEATHER tv	Yunus	EMRE po Turk
Young,	JAMES mr-guit Am	Yurka,	BLANCHE
Young,	JESSE mr-guit,s Am	Yury	GAGARIN as Rus
Young,	KAREN	Yury	KAZAKOV w Rus
Young,	LESTER(Pres)mj-sax,cn	Yury	LIBEDINSKY w Rus
Young,	LORETTA o-a'47,tv+	Yury	OLESHA w Rus
Young,	MAHONRI su,p,etch Am	Yury	TRIFONOV w Rus
Young,	MALCOLM mr-guit Scot	Yury	TYNYANOV ct,w Rus
Young,	MURAT(Chic)cr Am	Yusef	BULOS tv
Young,	NEIL mr+ Can	Yuskis	TONI ba,tv Am
Young,	OTIS tv+	Yust,	WALTER j,ed Am
Young,	OWEN id-GE Am	Yutang,	LIN w China
Young,	PAUL s,ws Br	Yutte	STENSGAARD
Young,	POLLY	Yuzo	KAYAMA
Young,	RIC	Yvan	PONTON
Young,	RICHARD	Yves	BOISSET d
Young,	ROBERT d,tv+	Yves	DELAGE sc,e Fr
Young,	ROBERT M. d	Yves	MONTAND s+ Fr
Young,	ROBIN tv	Yves	SIMONEAU d
Young,	ROGER d	Yves	TANGUY p Am
Young,	ROLAND	Yvette	GUILBERT s Fr
Young,	RUSTY m-steel guit Am	Yvette	MIMIEUX
Young,	SEAN	Yvette	NIPAR tv+

Yvon	DELBOS st Fr		Zamin,	BRUNO
Yvon,	ADOLPHE p Fr		Zamora,	ANTONIO de w,po Sp
Yvonne	BURCH tv		Zamora,	DEL
Yvonne	CRAIG tv+		Zamyatin,	YEVGENY w Rus
Yvonne	De CARLO tv+		Zanchi,	GIROLAMO r It
Yvonne	KING s,tv Am		Zander,	ROBIN mr-guitar,s Am
Yvonne	LIME tv		Zandor	VORKOV
Yvonne	PERRY tv		Zandt,	PHILIP van
Yvonne	SUHOR tv		Zane	GREY w Am
Yvonne	WILDER tv+		Zane	LASKY tv
Yvonne King BURCH tv			Zane,	BILLY
Yvor	WINTERS ct,po,e Am		Zane,	EBENEZER pioneer Am
			Zane,	LISA
			Zangwill,	ISRAEL w Br
NO NAME DESIGNATION CODES OR			Zann,	LENORE
NATIONALITY CODES BEGIN			Zanuck,	DARRYL pr-films Am
WITH "Z's"			Zapata,	EMILIANO re Mex
			Zappa,	DWEEZIL mr-guit+ Am
"Z's			Zappa,	FRANK mr+ Am
Z'Dar,	ROBERT		Zappa,	MOON UNIT s Am
Zabach,	FLORIAN tv		Zappala,	JANET tv
Zabka,	WILLIAM tv		Zara	CULLY tv
Zabriskie,	GRACE tv+		Zarco,	JOAO x Port
Zacconi,	LUDOVICO c It		Zaremba,	JOHN tv
Zach	GRENIER tv		Zarlino,	GIOSEFFO c It
Zach	WHEAT b hf		ZaSu	PITTS tv+
Zach,	FRANZ astr Ger		Zatopek,	EMILo-g'48,3X o-g's'52
Zachariah	ALLEN i Am		Zaturenska,	MARYA p-q'38
Zacharias	WERNER w.po Ger		Zayak,	ELAINE sk Am
Zachary	ROSENCRANTZ tv		Zayas,	ALFONSO
Zachary	SCOTT tv+		Zbigniew	HERBERT po Pol
Zachary	TAYLOR 12th Pres.		Zdenek	FIBICH c Czech
Zachery	BRYAN tv		Zdenek	MACAL cn Am
Zachi	NOY		Zdenek	SVERAK
Zachow,	FRIEDRICH orgn,c,e Ger		Zeami Motokiyo --- actor,w	
Zachris	TOPELIUS w Finn		Zebe	CARVER tv
Zack	NORMAN		Zebulon	PIKE x,ar Am
Zack	TAYLOR		Zebulon	VANCE st,ar-CSA Am
Zada,	RAMY tv+		Zech,	ROSEL
Zadkine,	OSSIP su Rus		Zecharaiah CHAFEE l,e Am	
Zadok,	ARNON		Zede,	GUSTAVE eng-naval Fr
Zadora,	PIA s+ Am		Zedlitz,	JOSEPH po,w Aus
Zaehner,	ROBERT h,e Br		Zedong,	MAO st China
Zagarino,	FRANK		Zee,	JOHN tv
Zaghlul,	SA'D l,j,st Egypt		Zeeland,	PAUL van ec,st Belg
Zaharias,	BABE DIDRIKSON g &		Zeeman,	PIETER n-p'02
Zaharias,	B. DIDRIKSON o-g's'32+		Zeffie	TILBURY
Zaharoff,	BASIL(Sir)mer-arms Fr		Zeffirelli,	FRANCO d
Zahle,	CARL st Dan		Zeigler,	HEIDI tv
Zahn,	ERNST w Swi		Zeigler,	TED tv
Zahn,	PAULA tv-j Am		Zeilinski,	RAFAL d
Zaimis,	ALEXANDROS st Gr		Zeiss,	CARL id-optics Ger
Zajc,	IVAN c Croat		Zeke	MANNERS mj-s,ws Am
Zakes	MOKAE		Zeke	TURNER m-cnt,tv Am
Zakir	HUSAIN st India		Zelaya,	JOSE st Nica
Zal	YANOVSKY mr-guit,s Can		Zelda	BARRON d
Zal,	ROXANA		Zelezny,	JAN o-g'92'96
Zale,	TONY boxer Am		Zelia	NUTTALL arc Am
Zaleski,	JOZEF po Pol		Zeljko	IVANEK
Zalman	KING d,tv+		Zell,	HARRY von radio,tv Am
Zamah	CUNNINGHAM TV		Zell,	MATTHAUS r,ref Ger

Zeller,   CARL c Aus
Zellweger,RENEE
Zelniker,   MICHAEL
Zelter,   CARL c,cn Ger
Zeman,   KAREL d
Zemeckis, ROBERT o-d'94
Zemurray, SAMUEL id-ships Am
Zena   MARSHALL
Zenger,   JOHN j Am
Zeno of Citium --- ph Gr
Zeno of Elea --- ph Gr
Zeno,   CARLO navy It
Zenobe   GRAMME eng,i Belg
Zentner,   SI mj,cn Am
Zeppelin, GRAF von ds-aero Ger
Zeppo   MARX la,cm+ Am
Zerbe,   ANTHONY tv+
Zerneck,   DANIELLE von
Zernike,   FRITS n-p'53
Zero   MOSTEL s+ Am
Zesen,   PHILIPP von w Ger
Zetkin,   CLARA fe,st Ger
Zetterling, MAI
Zeuner,   FREDERICK geol,e Br
Zeuner,   GUSTAV sc,eng Ger
Zeuss,   JOHANN h,philology Ger
Zeuxis   --- p Gr
Zevin,   ISRAEL j,w Am
Zevon,   WARREN s,ws Am
Zeze   MOTTA
Zhang   YIMOU d
Zhdanov,   ANDREY st Rus
Zhukov,   GEORGY ar,st Rus
Zhukovsky,VASILY po Rus
Zia   MOHYEDDI
Ziani,   SEBASTIANO l,st It
Zieff,   HOWARD d
Ziegfeld, FLORENZ pr-follies am
Ziegler,   KARL n-c'63
Ziegler,   RON press secy to RMN
Zielinski,BRUNO(Junior)tv
Ziemann,   SONJA
Zien,   CHIP tv
Zienia   MERTON tv
Zierer,   FRED mj-viol Am
Ziering,   IAN tv
Zieten,   HANS ar Prussia
Ziggy   MARLEY s,ws Jamaica
Ziggy   TALENT tv
Zilcher,   HERMANN c Ger
Zimbalist,EFREM Jr. tv+
Zimbalist,STEPHANIE tv+
Zimmer,   KIM tv
Zimmer,   NORMA tv
Zimmerman,CAPTAIN CARL tv
Zimmerman,HARRY m,cn,tv Am
Zimmermann, BERND c,e Ger
Zina   BETHUNE tv
Zindel,   PAUL p-d'71
Zinka   MILANOV sopr Yugo
Zinman,   DAVID cn

Zinn,   JOHANN sc Ger
Zinnemann, RED o-d'53'66
Zinsser,   HANS sc,e Am
Zipp,   WILLIAM
Zirkel,   FERDINAND minerals Ger
Zischler, HANNS
Ziskie,   DAN
Zitek,   JOSEF ac Cz
Zito,   JOSEPH d
Zittel,   KARL von geol,e Ger
Ziva   RODANN
Ziya,   MEHMED w,e,st Turk
Zizka,   JAN ar Ger
Zmed,   ADRIAN tv+
Zoe   AKINS po,w Am
Zoe   CALDWELL
Zoe   TAMERLIS
Zoe   WANAMAKER
Zohra   LAMPERT tv+
Zohra   SEGAL
Zola,   EMILE w Fr
Zollinger,ALBIN w,po Swi
Zollner,   CARL c Ger
Zollner,   HEINRICH c,cn,w Ger
Zoltan   KODALY c Hung
Zoltan   KORDA d
Zoltan   TILDY st Hung
Zona   GALE w Am
Zooey   HALL
Zoot   SIMS mj-reeds Am
Zora Neale HURSTON w Am
Zorach,   WILLIAM su Am
Zorich,   LOUIS tv+
Zorn,   ANDERS p,su,etch Swe
Zorrilla y Moral, JOSE po, w Sp
Zoshchenko, MIKHAIL w Rus
Zouche,   RICHARD l,e Br
Zrinyi,   MIKLOS ar Hung
Zsa Zsa   GABOR
Zsigmond MORICZ w Hung
Zsigmondy,RICHARD A. n-c'25
Zubarry,   OLGA
Zubin   MEHTA cn India
Zucarri,   TADDEO p It
Zucco,   GEORGE
Zucco,   JOCELYNE tv
Zucker,   DAVID d
Zuckert   WILLIAM tv
Zuckmayer,CARL w Ger
Zukofsky, LOUIS po,ed Am
Zukor,   ADOLPH pr-films Am
Zulfikar BHUTTO st Pakistan
Zuloaga,   IGNACIO p Sp
Zulu   --- tv
Zumpe,   JOHANN id-pianofrt Ger
Zumpt,   KARL w Ger
Zumwalt,   ELMO navy Am
Zuniga,   DAPHNE
Zunz,   LEOPOLD w Ger
Zuppke,   ROBERT fbc Am
Zurakowska, DIANIK

Zurara,   GOMES h Port
Zurke,   BOB mj-piano,cn Am
Zutaut,   BRAD
Zutty   SINGLETON mj-drm
Zvee   SCOOLER
Zweig,   ARNOLD w Ger
Zweig,   MARTIN w-invests,tv
Zweig,   STEFAN bio,w Aus
Zwick,   EDWARD d
Zwicky,   FRITZ astr,sc,e Swi
Zwillich,   ELLEN p-m'83
Zwingli,   HULDRYCH r,ref Swi
Zwingli,   ULRICH r,ref Swi
Zylberman,NOAM

CROSSWORD PROPER NAME FINDER

SECTION II - PARTS A & B

OPERATING INSTRUCTIONS FOR SECTION II

Section II is in two parts.   PART A consists of an alphabetical listing of persons in its first column, a "VEHICLE" in its middle column, and a "PRODUCT" in its third column. For example:

    Farr, Jamie   Series   M.A.S.H. tv

Most VEHICLES are self explanatory such as Ballet, Cartoon, Film, Hit, Hit Song, Opera, Play, Poem, Role, Series, Song, Title and others. Some VEHICLES are indicated by abbreviations such as "Comp", for Composition, "Invent", for Invention; others are not properly "vehicles" such as "Nee" to indicate the Birth Name of a person as:

    Garbo, Greta   Nee   GRETA GUSTAFSSON

Similar to Nee are Aka or "Also known as" and Pen Name.
Films or Movies are the most numerous entries in Section II. Some 4,000 movies were selected from the 50,000 said to have been produced in the world to date. The basis for movie selection is stated at the beginning of the alphabetical listing.

All Movies have their release year following the name.   This differentiates movie names from any other name category in Section II. Four star movies carry the four stars, ****, following the release year as:

    Bogart, Humphrey   Film   CASABLANCA '42****

Persons and products in categories other than movies were selected on the basis of appearance in a crossword puzzle as the first consideration.

If a Composer was selected because of a crossword puzzle reference to a single composition, other popular composition names of his may have been added anticipating future puzzle clues.

SECTION II, PART B is a reverse listing of PART A. The "PRODUCTS" of PART A are now listed alphabetically, with the person, or persons involved in a second column. The persons column in PART B lists first names first and surnames last.

In PART B, the "VEHICLE" column used in PART A is omitted. If there is doubt about the connection between the first Named "PRODUCT" and the named "PERSON", one would need to look him or her up in PART A to retrieve the "VEHICLE".

SECTION II, PART A

This section is not intended to be a complete guide to movie
actors or directors and their movies. Included are only:
1. MOVIES awarded FOUR STARS -- ****
2. MOVIES awarded 2 1/2 to 3 1/2 stars and also
    A) having SINGLE WORD NAMES, with or without
      an accompanying "THE","AN" or "A".
    B) having 14 or 15 LETTER NAMES, including
      or excluding an accompanying "THE","AN" or "A".
A survey of hundreds of weekday crossword puzzles published in
newspapers indicate that this selection should furnish answers to
at least 70% of the puzzle clues giving an actor or director and
requesting a movie name. A similar percentage should apply to the
reverse listing, giving movie names and requesting actors or
directors.

Entries other than movie actors, eg: writers, musicians, painters,
are similarly non inclusive of all the works by any individual
Products of these persons are NOT bound by rules as to title length.

Surname, Forename	Vehicle	PRODUCT ('YR)(****)
	or **PERSONS plus**	
Aaker, Lee	Series	THE ADVENTURES OF RIN TIN TIN
Aakjaer, Jeppe w	Title	CHILDREN OF WRATH
Abbott & Costello	Film	BUCK PRIVATES COME HOME '47
Abbott & Costello	Film	PARDON MY SARONG '42
Abbott & Costello	Film	THE NOOSE HANGS HIGH '48
Abbott & Costello	Film	THE TIME OF THEIR LIVES '46
Abbott & Costello	Musical	RIO RITA
Abbott, Bud	Films	See Abbott & Costello
Abbott, George w&d	Play	COQUETTE
Abdul, Paula mr	Hit Song	FOREVER YOUR GIRL
Abraham, F. Murray	Film	AMADEUS '84
Ackland, Joss	Film	SHADOWLANDS '85
Adam, Adolphe	Comp	GISELLE
Adams, Alice	Title	ALMOST PERFECT
Adams, Alice	Title	CARELESS LOVE
Adams, Brooke	Film	GAS, FOOD LODGING '92
Adams, Brooke	Film	THE UNBORN '91
Adams, Cecil	Title	THE STRAIGHT DOPE
Adams, Don	Series	GET SMART tv
Adams, Edie	Nee	ELIZABETH EDITH ENKE
Adams, Julie	Film	TARAWA BEACHHEAD '58
Adams, Nick	Film	YOUNG DILLINGER '65
Adams, Nick	Series	THE REBEL tv
Adams, William T.	Pen Name	OLIVER OPTIC
Ade, George	Title	FABLES IN SLANG
Adela	Charac	A PASSAGE TO INDIA
Adele	Charac	DIE FLEDERMAUS
Adjani, Isabelle	Film	ONE DEADLY SUMMER '83

Adoree, Renee	Film	THE BIG PARADE '25 ****
Aeorsmith mr	Hit	SWEET EMOTION
Aeschylus w	Title	SEVEN AGAINST THEBES
Aesop	Fable	THE FOX AND THE GRAPES
Agar, Herbert	Title	A TIME FOR GREATNESS
Agar, John	Film	FORT APACHE '48
Agar, John	Film	TARANTULA '55
Agee, James w	Title	A DEATH IN THE FAMILY
Agee, James w	Title	PERMIT ME VOYAGE
Ager, Milton	Comp	AIN'T SHE SWEET
Agoult,Marie-C. d'	Pen Name	DANIEL STERN
Agutter, Jenny	Film	AMY '81
Agutter, Jenny	Film	WALKABOUT '71
Aherne, Brian	Film	THE GREAT GARRICK '37
Aiello, Danny	Film	DO THE RIGHT THING '89
Aiello, Danny	Film	RUBY '92
Aiello, Danny	Film	THE FRONT '76 ****
Aiello, Danny	Film	THE STUFF '85
Aimee, Anouk	Film	JUSTINE '69
Aimee, Anouk	Film	LOLA '61
Akins, Claude	Series	LOBO tv
Akins, Claude	Series	MOVIN' ON tv
Akyroyd, Dan	Film	DRAGNET '87
Albee, Edward w	Play	THREE TALL WOMEN
Albee, Edward w	Play	TINY ALICE
Albert, Eddie	Film	AN ANGEL FROM TEXAS '40
Albert, Eddie	Nee	EDWARD ALBERT HEIMBERGER
Albert, Eddie	Series	GREEN ACRES tv
Albert, Edward	Film	ACCIDENTS '88
Albertson, Jack	Series	CHICO AND THE MAN tv
Alcayaga, Lucila Godoy	Pen Name	GABRIELA MISTRAL po
Alcott, Louisa May	Title	EIGHT COUSINS
Alcott, Louisa May	Title	LITTLE WOMEN
Alda, Alan	Film	BETSY'S WEDDING '90
Alda, Alan	Film	CALIFORNIA SUITE '78
Alda, Alan	Film	THE FOUR SEASONS '81
Alda, Alan	Nee	ALPHONSO D'ABRUZZO
Alda, Alan	Series	M*A*S*H tv
Alda, Robert	Film	RHAPSODY IN BLUE '45
Alden, Norman	Film	ANDY '65
Aleandro, Norma	Film	THE OFFICIAL STORY '85 ****
Alexander, Jane	Film	TESTAMENT '83
Alexander, Jane	Nee	JANE QUIGLEY
Alger, Horatio	Title	LUCK AND PLUCK
Alger, Horatio	Title	RAGGED DICK
Alicia, Ana	Series	FALCON CREST tv
Allan, Elizabeth	Film	A TALE OF TWO CITIES '35 ****
Allen, Fred	Film	WE'RE NOT MARRIED '52
Allen, Fred	Nee	JOHN SULLIVAN
Allen, Karen	Film	BACKFIRE '87
Allen, Karen	Film	RAIDERS OF THE LOST ARK '81 ****
Allen, Patrick	Film	THE TRAITORS '63
Allen, Steve	Film	DOWN MEMORY LANE '49
Allen, Tim	Series	HOME IMPROVEMENT tv
Allen, Woody	Film	BANANAS '71 ****
Allen, Woody d+	Film	MANHATTAN '79
Allen, Woody d+	Film	MIGHTY APHRODITE '95
Allen, Woody	Film	NEW YORK STORIES '89
Allen, Woody	Film	PLAY IT AGAIN, SAM '72
Allen, Woody	Film	SCENES FROM A MALL '91
Allen, Woody	Film	SLEEPER '73

Allen, Woody	Film	THE FRONT '76 ****
Allen, Woody	Film	ZELIG '83
Allen, Woody	Nee	ALLEN KONIGSBERG
Allen, Woody d+	Film	ANNIE HALL '77 ****
Allgood, Sara	Film	BLACKMAIL '29
Allyson, June	Film	INTERLUDE '57
Allyson, June	Film	REMAINS TO BE SEEN '53
Allyson, June	Film	THE OPPOSITE SEX '56
Allyson, June	Film	THE SHRIKE '55
Allyson, June	Film	TOO YOUNG TO KISS '51
Allyson, June	Nee	ELLA GEISMAN
Alman Bros.Band mr	Hit	RAMBLIN' MAN
Alterio, Hector	Film	THE OFFICIAL STORY '85 ****
Altman, Robert d	Film	THE PLAYER '92
Ameche, Don	Film	OSCAR '91
Ameche, Don	Film	PALS '87
Ameche, Don	Film	WING AND A PRAYER '44
Ameche, Don o-s	Film	COCOON '85
Ames, Leon	Series	LIFE WITH FATHER tv
Amis, Kingsley w	Title	LUCKY JIM
Ammelrooy, Willeke	Film	ANTONIA'S LINE '96
Amos, John	Film	COMING TO AMERICA '88
Anderson, Harry	Series	NIGHT COURT tv
Anderson, Judith	Film	INN OF THE DAMNED '74
Anderson, Loni	Series	WKRP IN CINCINNATI tv
Anderson, Robert	Play	TEA AND SYMPATHY
Anderson, Sherwood	Title	WINESBURG, OHIO
Anderson, Warner	Film	THE LINEUP '58
Anderson, Warner	Series	THE LINEUP tv
Anderson,Richard Dean	Series	MACGYVER tv
Andersson, Bibi	Film	THE GIRLS '68
Andersson, Bibi	Film	PERSONA '66
Andersson, Bibi	Film	WILD STRAWBERRIES '57 ****
Andrews, Dana	Film	FEARMAKERS '58
Andrews, Dana	Film	MY FOOLISH HEART '49
Andersson, Bibi	Film	WILD STRAWBERRIES '57 ****
Andress, Ursula	Role	SHE
Andrews Sisters	Hit Song	BEER BARREL POLKA
Andrews, Dana	Film	BERLIN CORRESPONDENT '42
Andrews, Dana	Film	BOOMERANG! '47
Andrews, Dana	Film	CRACK IN THE WORLD '65
Andrews, Dana	Film	CURSE OF THE DEMON '58
Andrews, Dana	Film	DUEL IN THE JUNGLE '54
Andrews, Dana	Film	FEARMAKERS '58
Andrews, Dana	Film	MY FOOLISH HEART '49
Andrews, Dana	Film	THE FROGMEN '51
Andrews, Dana	Film	THE IRON CURTAIN '48
Andrews, Dana	Film	THE OX-BOW INCIDENT '43 ****
Adjani, Isabelle	Film	ONE DEADLY SUMMER '83
Adoree, Renee	Film	THE BIG PARADE '25 ****
Aeorsmith mr	Hit	SWEET EMOTION
Aeschylus w	Title	SEVEN AGAINST THEBES
Aesop	Fable	THE FOX AND THE GRAPES
Agar, Herbert	Title	A TIME FOR GREATNESS
Agar, John	Film	FORT APACHE '48
Agar, John	Film	TARANTULA '55
Agee, James w	Title	A DEATH IN THE FAMILY
Agee, James w	Title	PERMIT ME VOYAGE
Ager, Milton	Comp	AIN'T SHE SWEET
Agoult,Marie-C. d'	Pen Name	DANIEL STERN
Agutter, Jenny	Film	AMY '81

Agutter, Jenny	Film	WALKABOUT '71
Aherne, Brian	Film	THE GREAT GARRICK '37
Aiello, Danny	Film	DO THE RIGHT THING '89
Aiello, Danny	Film	RUBY '92
Aiello, Danny	Film	THE FRONT '76 ****
Aiello, Danny	Film	THE STUFF '85
Aimee, Anouk	Film	JUSTINE '69
Aimee, Anouk	Film	LOLA '61
Akins, Claude	Series	LOBO tv
Akins, Claude	Series	MOVIN' ON tv
Akyroyd, Dan	Film	DRAGNET '87
Albee, Edward w	Play	THREE TALL WOMEN
Albee, Edward w	Play	TINY ALICE
Albert, Eddie	Film	AN ANGEL FROM TEXAS '40
Albert, Eddie	Nee	EDWARD ALBERT HEIMBERGER
Albert, Eddie	Series	GREEN ACRES tv
Albert, Edward	Film	ACCIDENTS '88
Albertson, Jack	Series	CHICO AND THE MAN tv
Alcayaga, Lucila Godoy Pen Name		GABRIELA MISTRAL po
Alcott, Louisa May	Title	EIGHT COUSINS
Alcott, Louisa May	Title	LITTLE WOMEN
Alda, Alan	Film	BETSY'S WEDDING '90
Alda, Alan	Film	CALIFORNIA SUITE '78
Alda, Alan	Film	THE FOUR SEASONS '81
Alda, Alan	Nee	ALPHONSO D'ABRUZZO
Alda, Alan	Series	M*A*S*H tv
Alda, Robert	Film	RHAPSODY IN BLUE '45
Alden, Norman	Film	ANDY '65
Aleandro, Norma	Film	THE OFFICIAL STORY '85 ****
Alexander, Jane	Film	TESTAMENT '83
Alexander, Jane	Nee	JANE QUIGLEY
Alger, Horatio	Title	LUCK AND PLUCK
Alger, Horatio	Title	RAGGED DICK
Alicia, Ana	Series	FALCON CREST tv
Allan, Elizabeth	Film	A TALE OF TWO CITIES '35 ****
Allen, Fred	Film	WE'RE NOT MARRIED '52
Allen, Fred	Nee	JOHN SULLIVAN
Allen, Karen	Film	BACKFIRE '87
Allen, Karen	Film	RAIDERS OF THE LOST ARK '81 ****
Allen, Patrick	Film	THE TRAITORS '63
Allen, Steve	Film	DOWN MEMORY LANE '49
Allen, Tim	Series	HOME IMPROVEMENT tv
Allen, Woody	Film	BANANAS '71 ****
Allen, Woody d+	Film	MANHATTAN '79
Allen, Woody d+	Film	MIGHTY APHRODITE '95
Allen, Woody	Film	NEW YORK STORIES '89
Allen, Woody	Film	PLAY IT AGAIN, SAM '72
Allen, Woody	Film	SCENES FROM A MALL '91
Allen, Woody	Film	SLEEPER '73
Allen, Woody	Film	THE FRONT '76 ****
Allen, Woody	Film	ZELIG '83
Allen, Woody	Nee	ALLEN KONIGSBERG
Allen, Woody d+	Film	ANNIE HALL '77 ****
Allgood, Sara	Film	BLACKMAIL '29
Allyson, June	Film	INTERLUDE '57
Allyson, June	Film	REMAINS TO BE SEEN '53
Allyson, June	Film	THE OPPOSITE SEX '56
Allyson, June	Film	THE SHRIKE '55
Allyson, June	Film	TOO YOUNG TO KISS '51
Allyson, June	Nee	ELLA GEISMAN
Alman Bros.Band mr	Hit	RAMBLIN' MAN

Alterio, Hector	Film	THE OFFICIAL STORY '85 ****
Altman, Robert d	Film	THE PLAYER '92
Ameche, Don	Film	OSCAR '91
Ameche, Don	Film	PALS '87
Ameche, Don	Film	WING AND A PRAYER '44
Ameche, Don o-s	Film	COCOON '85
Ames, Leon	Series	LIFE WITH FATHER tv
Amis, Kingsley w	Title	LUCKY JIM
Ammelrooy, Willeke	Film	ANTONIA'S LINE '96
Amos, John	Film	COMING TO AMERICA '88
Anderson, Harry	Series	NIGHT COURT tv
Anderson, Judith	Film	INN OF THE DAMNED '74
Anderson, Loni	Series	WKRP IN CINCINNATI tv
Anderson, Robert	Play	TEA AND SYMPATHY
Anderson, Sherwood	Title	WINESBURG, OHIO
Anderson, Warner	Film	THE LINEUP '58
Anderson, Warner	Series	THE LINEUP tv
Anderson,Richard Dean	Series	MACGYVER tv
Andersson, Bibi	Film	THE GIRLS '68
Andersson, Bibi	Film	PERSONA '66
Andersson, Bibi	Film	WILD STRAWBERRIES '57 ****
Andrews, Dana	Film	FEARMAKERS '58
Andrews, Dana	Film	MY FOOLISH HEART '49
Andersson, Bibi	Film	WILD STRAWBERRIES '57 ****
Astor, Mary	Film	THE HURRICANE '37
Atherton, Gertrude F.	Title	BLACK OXEN
Atkins, Eileen	Film	COLD COMFORT FARM '96
Attenborough, Richard	Film	DULCIMER STREET '48
Attenborough, Richard	Film	EIGHT O'CLOCK WALK '52
Attenborough, Richard d	Film	GANDHI '82
Attenborough, Richard	Film	SEANCE ON A WET AFTERNOON '64 ****
Attenborough, Richard	Film	THE ANGRY SILENCE '60
Attenborough, Richard	Film	THE MAN UPSTAIRS '58
Atwill, Lionel	Film	MURDERS IN THE ZOO '33
Atwill, Lionel	Film	THE HIGH COMMAND '37
Auber, Daniel-Franc. E,	Comp	FRA DIAVOLO
Auberjonois, Rene	Film	THE FEUD '90
Aubrey, James	Film	LORD OF THE FLIES '63
Audran, Stephane	Film	BABETTE'S FEAST '87 ****
Audran, Stephane	Film	LA FEMME INFIDELE '69
Audran, Stephane	Film	WEDDING IN BLOOD '73
Auel, Jean M.	Title	CLAN OF THE CAVE BEARS
Auel, Jean M.	Title	THE MAMMOTH HUNTERS
Aumont,Jean-Pierre	Film	LILI '53
Austen, Jane w	Title	EMMA
Austin, Col. Steve	Charac	THE SIX MILLION DOLLAR MAN tv
Austin, Teri	Series	KNOTTS LANDING tv
Auteuil, Daniel	Film	A FEW DAYS WITH ME '88
Auteuil, Daniel	Film	UN COEUR EN HIVER '92
Avalon, Frankie s	Song	DEDE DINAH
Avalon, Frankie s	Song	VENUS
Aykroyd, Dan	Film	CONEHEADS '93
Aykroyd, Dan	Film	THE BLUES BROTHERS '80
Ayres, Lew	Film	ALL QUIET ON THE WESTERN FRONT'30 ****
Ayres, Lew	Film	THE CAPTURE '50
Ayres, Lew	Film	YOUNG DR. KILDARE '38
Aznavour, Charles	Film	SHOOT THE PIANO PLAYER '60 ****
Aznavour, Charles	Film	THE HEIST '79
Bacall, Lauren	Film	DESIGNING WOMAN '57
Bacall, Lauren	Film	FLAME OVER INDIA '59
Bacall, Lauren	Film	HARPER '66

Bacall, Lauren	Film	THE BIG SLEEP '46 ****
Bacall, Lauren	Film	THE SHOOTIST '76
Bacall, Lauren	Nee	BETTY JOAN PERSKE
Bach, Johann Seb.	Comp	AIR ON THE STRING
Bach, Johann Seb.	Comp	BRANDENBURG CONCERTOS
Bach, Johann Seb.	Comp	THE WELL-TEMPERED CLAVIER
Bacon, Kevin	Film	FOOTLOOSE '84
Bacon, Kevin	Film	SLEEPERS '96
Baez, Joan	Film	WOODSTOCK '70
Bagnold, Enid w	Title	NATIONAL VELVET
Bain, Conrad	Series	DIFF'RENT STROKES tv
Bainter, Fay	Film	MARYLAND '40
Bainter, Fay	Film	THREE IS A FAMILY '44
Baio, Scott	Series	CHARLES IN CHARGE tv
Baker Joe Don	Film	MITCHELL '75
Baker, Carroll	Film	BRIDGE TO THE SUN '61
Baker, Carroll	Film	HARLOW '65
Baker, Carroll	Film	SYLVIA '65
Baker, Carroll	Film	THE MIRACLE '59
Baker, George	Cartoon	THE SAD SACK
Baker, George	Film	THE MOONRAKER '58
Baker, Joe Don	Film	FRAMED .75
Baker, Joe Don	Film	THE PACK '77
Baker, Josephine	Film	PRINCESSE TAM TAM '35
Baker, Kenny	Film	THE MIKADO '39
Baker, Stanley	Film	DINGAKA '65
Baker, Stanley	Film	ROBBERY '67
Baker, Stanley	Film	THE CONCRETE JUNGLE '60
Baker, Stanley	Film	THE LAST GRENADE '70
Bakst, Leon	Nee	LEV SAMOYLOVICH ROSENBERG
Bakula, Scott	Series	QUANTUM LEAP tv
Baldwin, Alec	Film	MALICE '93
Baldwin, Alec	Film	PRELUDE TO A KISS '92
Baldwin, James	Title	GO TELL IT ON THE MOUNTAIN
Baldwin, James	Title	JUST ABOVE MY HEAD
Ball, Lucille	Film	BEST FOOT FORWARD '43
Ball, Lucille	Film	FOREVER DARLING '56
Ball, Lucille	Film	SEVEN DAYS LEAVE 42
Ball, Lucille	Film	THE LONG, LONG TRAILER '54
Ball, Lucille	Film	VALLEY OF THE SUN '42
Ball, Lucille	Series	I LOVE LUCY tv
Ball, Lucille	Series	THE LUCY SHOW tv
Balsam, Martin	Film	TORA! TORA! TORA! '70
Balzac, Honore de	Title	PERE GORIOT
Balzac, Honore de	Title	THE BLACK SHEEP
Bancroft, Anne	Film	THE PUMPKIN EATER '64
Bancroft, Anne	Film	THE TURNING POINT '77
Bancroft, Anne	Filn	THE GRADUATE '67 ****
Bancroft, Anne	Nee	ANNA MARIA ITALIANO
Bancroft, George	Film	DOCKS OF NEW YORK '28
Band, The mr	Hit	THE WEIGHT
Banderas, Antonio	Film	DESPERADO '95
Bankhead, Tallulah	Film	DEVIL AND THE DEEP '32
Bankhead, Tallulah	Film	DIE! DIE! MY DARLING '65
Bankhead, Tallulah	Film	FAITHLESS '32
Bankhead, Tallulah	Film	LIFEBOAT '44
Banks, Leslie	Film	HENRY V '45 ****
Baraka,Imamu Amiri	Pen Name	LeROI JONES
Barber, Samuel c	Comp	ADAGIO FOR STRINGS
Barber, Samuel c	Comp	VANESSA
Bardot, Brigitte	Film	COME DANCE WITH ME '60

Bardot, Brigitte	Film	CONTEMPT '63
Bardot, Brigitte	Film	VIVA MARIA! '65
Bardot, Brigitte	Nee	CAMILLE JAVAL
Barenger, Tom	Film	SHATTERED '91
Barker, Lex	Films	TARZAN FILMS '49 - '53
Barrault, Jean-Louis	Film	CHILDREN OF PARADISE '45 ****
Barrie, Chuck	Tv Desig.	KING OF BAD TASTE
Barrie, James M.(Sir)	Title	PETER PAN
Barry, Gene	Film	THE HOUSTON STORY '56
Barry, Gene	Film	THE WAR OF THE WORLDS '53
Barry, Gene	Nee	EUGENE KLASS
Barry, Gene	Series	BAT MASTERSON tv
Barry, Gene	Series	BURKE'S LAW tv
Barry, Jack	Host	TIC TAC DOUGH tv
Barry, Tony	Film	GOODBYE PORK PIE '81
Barrymore, Diana	Film	NIGHTMARE '42
Barrymore, Ethel	Film	PINKY '49
Barrymore, John	Film	COUNSELLOR-AT-LAW '33 ****
Barrymore, John	Film	DINNER AT EIGHT '33 ****
Barrymore, John	Film	GRAND HOTEL '32 ****
Barrymore, John	Film	LONG LOST FATHER '34
Barrymore, John	Film	MOBY DICK '30
Barrymore, John	Film	REUNION IN VIENNA '33
Barrymore, John	Film	STATE'S ATTORNEY '32
Barrymore, John	Film	SVENGALI '31
Barrymore, John	Film	TEMPEST '28
Barrymore, John	Film	THE BELOVED ROGUE '27
Barrymore, John	Film	THE GREAT PROFILE '40
Barrymore, John	Film	THE INVISIBLE WOMAN '41
Barrymore, John	Film	TOPAZE '33
Barrymore, John	Film	TWENTIETH CENTURY '34 ****
Barrymore, Lionel	Film	LOOKING FORWARD '33
Barrymore, Lionel	Film	ON BORROWED TIME '39
Barrymore, Lionel	Film	SWEEPINGS '33
Barrymore, Lionel	Film	THE STRANGER'S RETURN '33
Barthelmess, Richard	Film	CENTRAL AIRPORT '33
Barthelmess, Richard	Film	FOUR HOURS TO KILL '35
Barthelmess, Richard	Film	MASSACRE '34
Barthelmess, Richard	Film	THE FINGER POINTS '31
Bartholomew, Freddie	Film	CAPTAINS COURAGEOUS '37 ****
Bartholomew, Freddie	Film	DAVID COPPERFIELD '35 ****
Bartholomew, Freddie	Film	LLOYDS OF LONDON '36
Bartok, Bela	Comp	MIKROKOSMOS
Bartok, Bela	Opera	DUKE BLUEBEARD'S CASTLE
Basehart, Richard	Film	HE WALKED BY NIGHT '48
Basehart, Richard	Film	HITLER '62
Basehart, Richard	Film	OUTSIDE THE WALL '50
Basehart, Richard	Film	TENSION '49
Basehart, Richrd	Series	VOYAGE TO THE BOTTOM OF THE SEA tv
Basinger, Kim	Film	NADINE '87
Basinger, Kim	Film	THE MARRYING MAN '91
Bates, Alan	Film	AN UNMARRIED WOMAN '78 ****
Bates, Alan	Film	BUTLEY '74 ****
Bates, Alan	Film	NIJINSKY '80
Bates, Alan	Film	QUARTET '81
Bates, Alan	Film	THE FIXER '68
Bates, Alan	Film	THE GUEST '64
Bates, Alan	Film	THE ROSE '79
Bates, Alan	Film	THE SHOUT '78
Bates, Kathy	Film	MISERY '90
Baur, Harry	Film	VOLPONE '39

Baxter, Anne	Film	GUEST IN THE HOUSE '44
Baxter, Anne	Film	SMOKY '46
Baxter, Anne	Film	THE BLUE GARDENIA '53
Baxter, Anne	Film	THE COME-ON '56
Baxter, Anne	Film	THE EVE OF ST. MARK '44
Baxter, Anne	Film	THE SPOILERS '55
Baxter, Anne	Film	THE SULLIVANS '44
Baxter, Warner	Film	42ND STREET '33 ****
Baxter, Warner	Film	JUST BEFORE DAWN '46
Baxter, Warner	Film	KIDNAPPED '38
Baxter, Warner	Film	KING OF BURLESQUE '35
Baxter, Warner	Film	PENTHOUSE '33
Baxter, Warner	Film	TO MARY---WITH LOVE '36
Baxter-Birney, Meredith	Series	FAMILY TIES tv
Baye, Nathalie	Film	A WEEK'S VACATION '80
Baye, Nathalie	Film	I MARRIED A SHADOW '82
Beach Boys, The	Hit Song	I GET AROUND
Beach Boys, The mr	Hit	GOOD VIBRATIONS
Beals, Jennifer	Film	FLASHDANCE '83
Beals, Jennifer	Film	THE BRIDE '85
Bean, Orson	Nee	DALLAS BURROWS
Beatles	Film	A HARD DAY'S NIGHT '64 ****
Beatles	Film	HELP! '65
Beatles	Hit Song	HERE COMES THE SUN
Beatles	Song	AND I LOVE HER
Beatles	Song	ANY TIME AT ALL
Beatles	Song	HARD DAY'S NIGHT
Beatles	Song	HEY JUDE
Beatles	Song	LET ME WHISPER IN YOUR EAR
Beatles	Song	P.S. I LOVE YOU
Beatles	Song	SARGEANT PEPPER'S LONELY HEART CLUB BAND
Beatles	Song	SHE'S A WOMAN
Beatles	Song	YELLOW SUBMARINE
Beatles	Song	YES IT IS
Beatty, Robert	Film	AGAINST THE WIND '48
Beatty, Warren	Film	BONNIE AND CLYDE '67 ****
Beatty, Warren	Film	BUGSY '91
Beatty, Warren	Film	LILITH '64
Beatty, Warren	Film	REDS '81
Beatty, Warren	Film	SHAMPOO '75
Beatty, Warren	Film	THE PARALLAX VIEW '74
Beck, Michael	Film	THE WARRIORS '79
Beckett, Samuel	Play	WAITING FOR GODOT
Bedelia, Bonnie	Film	HEART LIKE A WHEEL '83
Bedelia, Bonnie	Film	PRESUMED INNOCENT '90
Bedelia, Bonnie	Film	THE STRANGER '87
Bedelia, Bonnie	Nee	BONNIE CULKIN
Bee Gees, The	Album	ODESSA
Bee Gees, The	Hit	STAYING ALIVE
Beer, Jakob Liebmann	Aka	GIACOMO MEYERBEER c
Beerbohm, Max	Title	ZULEIKA DOBSON
Beery, Wallace	Film	A MESSAGE TO GARCIA '36
Beery, Wallace	Film	BEHIND THE FRONT '26
Beery, Wallace	Film	FLESH '32
Beery, Wallace	Film	RATIONING '44
Beery, Wallace	Film	THE BOWERY '33
Beery, Wallace	Film	THE CHAMP '31
Beery, Wallace	Film	THE MIGHTY BARNUM '34
Beery, Wallace	Film	TREASURE ISLAND '34
Beethoven, Ludwig van	Comp	FUR ELISE
Beethoven, Ludwig van	Comp	MISSA SOLEMNIS

Beethoven,Ludwig van	Comp	MOONLIGHT SONATA
Beethoven,Ludwig van	Comp	PATHETIQUE-Piano Sonata in D Minor
Beethoven,Ludwig van	Opera	FIDELIO(b's only opera)
Behan, Brendan w	Title	BORSTAL BAY
Behrman, S.N.	Play	THE BURNIGH GLASS
Bel Geddes,Barbara	Series	DALLAS tv
Belafonte, Harry	Song	DAYO
Belafonte, Harry	Song	THE BANANA BOAT SONG
BelGeddes, Barbara	Film	CAUGHT '49
Bell, Dan	Film	THE SHOT '96
Bell, Tom	Film	THE VIOLENT ENEMY '68
Bellamy, Edward w	Title	LOOKING BACKWARD
Bellamy, Ralph	Series	MAN AGAINST CRIME tv
Bellini, Vincenzo	Heroine	NORMA
Bellini, Vincenzo	Opera	NORMA
Belloc, Hilaire	Title	CAUTIONARY TALES
Bellow, Saul	Title	HENDERSON THE RAIN KING
Bellow, Saul	Title	THE ADVENTURES OF AUGIE MARCH
Belmondo,Jean-Paul	Film	A WOMAN IS A WOMAN '60
Belmondo,Jean-Paul	Film	BORSALINO '70
Belmondo,Jean-Paul	Film	CARTOUCHE '64
Belmondo,Jean-Paul	Film	STAVISKY '74
Belmondo,Jean-Paul	Film	THAT MAN FROM RIO '64
Belmondo,Jean-Paul	Film	THE BURGLARS '72
Belmondo,Jean-Paul	Film	THE FORGIVEN SINNER '61
Belmondo,Jean-Paul	Film	THE THIEF OF PARIS '67
Beltran, Robert	Film	LATINO '85
Benaderet, Bea	Series	PETTICOAT JUNCTION tv
Benchley, Peter	Title	JAWS
Bendix, William	Film	CRASHOUT '55
Bendix, William	Film	THE LIFE OF RILEY '48
Benetar, Paul mr	Hit	HIT ME WITH YOUR BEST SHOT
Benigni,Roberto d+	Film	THE MONSTER '96
Benjamin, Paul	Film	DISTANCE '75
Benjamin, Richard	Film	GOODBYE, COLUMBUS '69
Benjamin, Richard	Film	WESTWORLD '73
Bennett, Arnold	Title	THE OLD WIVES' TALE
Bennett, Constance	Film	LAW OF THE TROPICS '41
Bennett, Constance	Film	THE SCAR '48
Bennett, Constance	Film	TOPPER '37
Bennett, Joan	Film	I MET MY LOVE AGAIN '38
Bennett, Joan d+	Film	LITTLE WOMEN '33
Bennett, Joan	Film	THE MACOMBER AFFAIR '47
Bennett, Joan	Film	THE MAN I MARRIED '40
Bennett, Joan	Film	THE RECKLESS MOMENT '49
Bennett, Tony s	Nee	ANTHONY BENEDETTO
Benny, Jack	Film	COLLEGE HOLIDAY '36
Benny, Jack	Film	LOVE THY NEIGHBOR '40
Benny, Jack	Nee	BENJAMIN KUBELSKY
Benny, Jack	ThemeSng	LOVE IN BLOOM
Benson, George m	Hit Song	GIVE ME THE NIGHT
Benson, Robby	Film	JEREMY '73
Benson, Robby	Nee	ROBERT SEGAL
Berenger, Tom	Film	GETTYSBURG '93
Berenger, Tom	Film	PLATOON '86
Berg, Alan	Opera	LULU
Berg, Gertrude	Film	THE GOLDBERGS '50
Berg, Gertrude	Series	THE GOLDBERGS tv
Berg, Peter	Film	A MIDNIGHT CLEAR '92
Bergen, Candice	Film	BITE THE BULLET '75 ****
Bergen, Candice	Film	THE GROUP '66

Bergen, Candice	Series	MURPHY BROWN tv
Bergen, Frances	Film	EATING '90
Bergman, Ingmar d	Film	SECRETS OF WOMEN '52
Bergman, Ingmar d	Film	THE SEVENTH SEAL '57 ****
Bergman, Ingrid	Film	ANASTASIA '56 ****
Bergman, Ingrid	Film	CASABLANCA '42 ****
Bergman, Ingrid	Film	GASLIGHT '44
Bergman, Ingrid	Film	INDISCREET '58
Bergman, Ingrid	Film	SPELLBOUND '45
Bergman, Ingrid	Film	STRANGERS '53
Bergman, Ingrid	Film	THE VISIT '64
Bergman, Ingrid	Role	ILSA in Casablanca '42
Bergman, Ingrid	Role	MEIR in A Woman Called Golda '82
Berle, Milton	Film	OVER MY DEAD BODY '42
Berlin, Irving	Nee	ISRAEL BALINE
Berlin, Irving	Song	HE'S A RAGPICKER
Berling, Charles	Film	RIDICULE '96
Berlioz, Hector	Comp	HAROLD IN ITALY
Berlioz, Hector	Comp	SYMPHONIE FANTASTIQUE
Berman, Susan	Film	SMITHEREENS '82
Bernard, Crystal	Series	WINGS tv
Bernardi, Herschel	Series	ARNIE tv
Bernhardt, Sarah	Nee	HENRIETTE ROSINE BERNARD
Bernstein, Leonard	Comp	CHICHESTER PSALMS
Berridge,Elizabeth	Film	THE FUNHOUSE '81
Berry, Chuck mr	Hit	JOHNNY B. GOODE
Berry, Glen	Film	BEAUTIFUL THING '96
Berry, Ken	Series	F TROOP tv
Berry, Ken	Series	MAYBERRY R.F.D. tv
Best, Edna	Film	INTERMEZZO '39
Best, James	Film	THE KILLER SHREWS '59
Best, James	Film	VERBOTEN! '59
Beti, Mongo po & w	Aka	ALEXANDRE BIYIDI
Bettger, Lyle	Series	THE COURT OF LAST RESORT tv
Betz, Carl	Series	JUDD FOR THE DEFENSE tv
Beyle,Marie Henri	Pen Name	STENDHAL
Bialik, Mayim	Series	BLOSSOM tv
Bickford, Charles	Film	THE STORM '38
Biehn, Michael	Film	TIMEBOMB '91
Big Bopper, The mr	Hit	CHANTILLY LACE
Biggers, Earl Derr	Tille	CHARLIE CHAN MYSTERIES
Billings, Josh w	Aka	HENRY WHEELER SHAW
Billingsley, Peter	Film	A CHRISTMAS STORY '83
Billingsley, Peter	Film	THE DIRT BIKE KID '86
Billingsley, Ray	Cartoon	CURTIS
Billingsley,Barbara	Series	LEAVE IT TO BEAVER tv
Binchy, Maeve	Title	CIRCLE OF FRIENDS
Binns, Edward	Series	BRENNER tv
Binoche, Juliette	Film	BLUE '93
Binoche, Juliette	Film	RENDEZ-VOUS '85
Binoche, Juliette o-s	Film	THE ENGLISH PATIENT '96
Birch, Paul	Film	NOT OF THIS EARTH '57
Birkin, Jane	Film	DUST '85
Birney, David	Series	BRIDGET LOVES BERNIE tv
Bishop, Joey	Nee	JOSEPH GOTTLIEB
Bisset, Jacqueline	Film	THE DEEP '77
Bisset, Jacqueline	Film	THE GRASSHOPPER '70
Bisset, Jacqueline	Film	THE SUNDAY WOMAN '76
Bixby, Bill	Series	THE INCREDIBLE HULK tv
Bizet, Alexandre C.L.	Comp.	L'ARLESIENNE
Bizet, Alexandre C.L.	Opera	CARMEN

```
Black Sabbath   mr    Hit        PARANOID
Black, Karen          Film       NASHVILLE '75 ****
Black, Karen          Film       PYX '73
Black, Karen          Film       THE GRASS IS SINGING '81
Blackmore,R.D. w      Heroine    LORNA (Doone)
Blair, Betsy          Film       MARTY '55
Blair, Eric           Pen Name   GEORGE ORWELL
Blake, Jon            Film       LIGHTHORSEMEN '87
Blake, Julia          Film       TRAVELLING NORTH '87
Blake, Robert         Film       CORKY '72
Blake, Robert         Film       IN COLD BLOOD '67 ****
Blake, Robert         Nee        MICHAEL GUBITOSI
Blake, Robert         Series     BARETTA tv
Blake,James Hubert Pen Name   EUBIE BLAKE
Blind Faith           Hit        CAN'T FIND MY WAY HOME
Blixen, Baroness Karen Dinesen Pen Name ISAK DINESEN
Blocker, Dan          Series     BONANZA tv
Blondell, Joan        Film       A TREE GROWS IN BROOKLYN '45 ****
Blondell, Joan        Film       DAMES '34
Blondie mr            Hit        HEART OF GLASS
Blood, Sweat&Tears mr Hit   SPINNING WHEEL
Bloom, Claire         Film       SHADOWLANDS '85
Bloom, Verna          Film       MEDIUM COOL '69 ****
Bluteau, Lothaire     Film       JESUS OF MONTREAL '89
Blyth, Ann            Film       A WOMAN'S VENGEANCE '47
Blyth, Ann            Film       KISMET '55
Blythe, Betty         Film       SHE '21
Boardman, Eleanor     Film       THE CROWD '28 ****
Bogarde, Dirk         Film       A TALE OF TWO CITIES '58
Bogarde, Dirk         Film       ACCIDENT '67
Bogarde, Dirk         Film       CAST A DARK SHADOW '55
Bogarde, Dirk         Film       DADDY NOSTALGIA '90
Bogarde, Dirk         Film       DESPAIR '79
Bogarde, Dirk         Film       DESPERATE MOMENT '53
Bogarde, Dirk         Film       JUSTINE '69
Bogarde, Dirk         Film       KING AND COUNTRY '64
Bogarde, Dirk         Film       LIBEL '59
Bogarde, Dirk         Film       OUR MOTHER'S HOUSE '67
Bogarde, Dirk         Film       SEBASTIAN '68
Bogarde, Dirk         Film       SIMBA '55
Bogarde, Dirk         Film       THE DAMNED '69
Bogarde, Dirk         Film       THE MIND BENDERS '62
Bogarde, Dirk         Film       THE SERVANT '63
Bogarde, Dirk         Film       THE SPANISH GARDENER '56
Bogarde, Dirk         Film       VICTIM '61
Bogart, Humphrey      Charac     EARLE in High Sierra
Bogart, Humphrey      Film       CASABLANCA '42 ****
Bogart, Humphrey      Film       CONFLICT '45
Bogart, Humphrey      Film       HIGH SIERRA '41
Bogart, Humphrey      Film       IN A LONELY PLACE '50
Bogart, Humphrey      Film       KEY LARGO '48
Bogart, Humphrey      Film       KNOCK ON ANY DOOR '49
Bogart, Humphrey      Film       SABRINA '54
Bogart, Humphrey      Film       SAHARA '43
Bogart, Humphrey      Film       SIROCCO '51
Bogart, Humphrey      Film       THE AFRICAN QUEEN '51 ****
Bogart, Humphrey      Film       THE BIG SLEEP '46 ****
Bogart, Humphrey      Film       THE CAINE MUTINY '54 ****
Bogart, Humphrey      Film       THE ENFORCER '51
Bogart, Humphrey      Film       THE HARDER THEY FALL '56
Bogart, Humphrey      Film       THE MALTESE FALCON '41 ****
```

Bogart, Humphrey	Film THE	TREASURE OF THE SIERRA MADRE'48****
Bogart, Humphrey	Role	QUEEG in Mutiny On The Bounty'54
Bogart, Humphrey	Role	ROY "MAD DOG" EARLE
Bogart, Humphrey	Role	SPADE in Maltese Falcon '41
Bohringer, Richard	Film	THE GRAND HIGHWAY '87
Boileau, Nicolas	Aka	BOILEAU-DESPREAUX
Boland, Mary	Film	PEOPLE WILL TALK '35
Boland, Mary	Film	RUGGLES OF RED GAP '35 ****
Bolger, Ray	Film	BABES IN TOYLAND '61
Bolger, Ray	Film	THE DAYDREAMER '66
Bolt, Robert	Play	A MAN FOR ALL SEASONS
Bon Jovi mr	Hit	SLIPPERY WHEN WET
Bond, Cynthia	Film	DEF BY TEMPTATION '90
Bond, Gary	Film	OUTBACK '71
Bonds,Gary"U.S."mr	Hit	QUARTER TO THREE
Bonerz, Peter	Film	FUNNYMAN '67
Bonet, Lisa	Series	A DIFFERENT WORLD tv
Bonnaire, Sandrine	Film	VAGABOND '85
Bonney, William	Aka	BILLY THE KID
Bono, Sonny	Film	HAIRSPRAY '88
Booker T.and the MG's mr Hit		GREEN ONIONS
Boone, Pat	Song	THEE I LOVE
Boone, Richard	Film	THE BUSHIDO BLADE '79
Boone, Richard	Series	HAVE GUN WILL TRAVEL tv
Booth, Shirley	Film	ABOUT MRS. LESLIE '54
Booth, Shirley	Film	THE MATCHMAKER '58
Booth, Shirley	Series	HAZEL tv
Borchers, Cornell	Film	THE DIVIDED HEART '54
Borge, Victor	Nee	BORGE ROSENBAUM
Borglum, Gutzon su	Works	FACES CARVED ON MT. RUSHMORE
Borgnine, Ernest	Film	MARTY '55
Borgnine, Ernest	Series	McHALES NAVY tv
Borgnine, Ernest	Film	THE WILD BUNCH '69 ****
Borodin, Aleksandr P.	Opera	PRINCE IGOR
Bostic, Earl mr	Hit	FLAMINGO
Boswell, James w	Title	THE LIFE OF SAMUEL JOHNSON
Bottoms, Joseph	Film	THE DOVE '74
Bottoms, Timothy	Film	THE DRIFTER '88
Bottoms, Timothy	Film	THE LAST PICTURE SHOW '71 ****
Boulting, Roy	Film	CREST OF THE WAVE '54
Bow, Clara	Film	DANCING MOTHERS '26
Bow, Clara	Film	HULA '28
Bow, Clara	Film	WINGS '27
Bow, Clara	Film	IT '27
Bowen, Elizabeth	Title	THE DEATH OF THE HEART
Bowie, David	Nee	DAVID ROBERT JONES
Bowie, David mr	Hit	LET'S DANCE
Bowles, Paul	Title	THE SHELTERING SKY
Boxleitner, Bruce	Series	SCARECROW AND MRS. KING tv
Boyce, Alan	Film	PERMANENT RECORD '88
Boyd, Stephen	Film	FANTASTIC VOYAGE '66
Boyd, Stephen	Film	THE THIRD SECRET '64
Boyd, William	Film	POWER '28
Boyd, William	Series	HOPALONG CASSIDY tv
Boyer, Charles	Film	A WOMAN'S VENGEANCE '47
Boyer, Charles	Film	ALGIERS '38
Boyer, Charles	Film	FANNY '61
Boyer, Charles	Film	FLESH AND FANTASY '43
Boyer, Charles	Film	GASLIGHT '44
Boyer, Charles	Film	HOLD BACK THE DAWN '41
Boyer, Charles	Film	LUCKY TO BE A WOMAN '56

Boyer, Charles	Film	MAYERLING '36
Boyer, Charles	Film	NANA '55
Boyer, Charles	Film	THE EARRINGS OF MADAME de...'53****
Boyer, Charles	Film	THE FIRST LEGION '51
Boyer, Charles	Film	TOVARICH '37
Boyle, Lara Flynn	Film	THREESOME '94
Boyle, Peter	Film	JOE '70
Bracken, Eddie	Film	HAIL THE CONQUERING HERO '44 ****
Bracken, Eddie	Film	OUT OF THIS WORLD '45
Bracken, Eddie	Film	THE MIRACLE OF MORGAN'S CREEK'44****
Braddock, Mickey	Series	CIRCUS BOY tv
Brady, Scott	Film	I WAS A SHOPLIFTER '50
Brady, Scott	Film	MOHAWK '56
Brady, Scott	Film	UNDERTOW '49
Brady, Scott	Series	SHOTGUN SLADE tv
Braine, John	Title	ROOM AT THE TOP
Branagh, Kenneth	d+Film	HAMLET '96
Branagh, Kenneth	Film	HENRY V '89
Brand, Neville	Series	LAREDO tv
Brandauer, Klaus Maria	Film	HANUSSEN '88
Brandauer, Klaus Maria	Film	MEPHISTO '81
Brando, Marlon	Film	A STREETCAR NAMED DESIRE '51 ****
Brando, Marlon	Film	BURN ! '69
Brando, Marlon	Film	DESIREE '54
Brando, Marlon	Film	DON JUAN deMARCO '95
Brando, Marlon	Film	ON THE WATERFRONT '54 ****
Brando, Marlon	Film	ONE EYED JACKS '61
Brando, Marlon	Film	SAYONARA '57
Brando, Marlon	Film	THE APPALOOSA '66
Brando, Marlon	Film	THE CHASE '66
Brando, Marlon	Film	THE FRESHMAN '90
Brando, Marlon	Film	THE FUGITIVE KIND '59
Brando, Marlon	Film	THE GODFATHER '72
Brando, Marlon	Film	THE MEN '50
Brando, Marlon	Film	THE UGLY AMERICAN '63
Brando, Marlon	Film	VIVA ZAPATA! '52 ****
Brandt, Willy	Nee	KARL HERBERT FRAHM
Branneman, Amy	Series	NYPD BLUE tv
Bread mr	HitSong	IT DON'T MATTER TO ME
Breathed, Berke	Cartoon	BLOOM COUNTY
Breck, Peter	Film	BENJI '74
Breck, Peter	Series	BLACK SADDLE tv
Brennan, Eileen	Film	CLUE '85
Brennan, Walter	Film	THE GNOME-MOBILE '67
Brennan, Walter	Series	THE GUNS OF WILL SONNETT tv
Brennan, Walter	Series	THE REAL MCCOYS tv
Brent, George	Film	JEZEBEL '38
Brent, George	Film	THE GOLDEN ARROW '36
Breslin, Patricia	Film	HOMICIDAL '61
Brian, David	Film	BREAKTHROUGH '50
Brian, David	Film	INSIDE STRAIGHT '51
Brice, Fanny	Nee	FANNY BORACH
Bridges, Beau	Film	THE FIFTH MUSKETEER '79
Bridges, Beau	Film	THE LANDLORD '70
Bridges, Jeff	Film	FEARLESS '93
Bridges, Jeff	Film	HEARTS OF THE WEST '75
Bridges, Jeff	Film	STARMAN '84
Bridges, Jeff	Film	TEXASVILLE '90
Bridges, Jeff	Film	THE LAST AMERICAN HERO '73
Bridges, Jeff	Film	THE LAST PICTURE SHOW '71 ****
Bridges, Lloyd	Film	TRAPPED '49

Bridges, Lloyd	Mini Sers	ROOTS tv
Brimley, Wilford	Series	OUR HOUSE tv
Brisette, Tiffany	Series	SMALL WONDER tv
Brisson, Carl	Film	THE RING '27
Britt, Mai	Film	THE UNFAITHFULS '60
Britten, Benjamin	Comp	WAR REQUIEM, opus 66
Britten, Benjamin	Opera	BILLY BUDD
Britton, Pamela	Series	BLONDIE tv
Britton, Tony	Film	THE RISK '60
Broderick, Matthew	Film	GLORY '89 ****
Broderick, Matthew	Film	WARGAMES '83
Brodie, Steve	Film	DESPERATE '47
Brolin, Josh	Film	THE GOONIES '85
Bromfield, John	Series	THE SHERIFF OF COCHISE tv
Bronson, Charles	Film	BREAKHEART PASS '76
Bronson, Charles	Film	BREAKOUT '75
Bronson, Charles	Film	MACHINE-GUN KELLY '58
Bronson, Charles	Film	RIDER ON THE RAIN '70
Bronson, Charles	Film	TELEFON '77
Bronson, Charles	Film	THE FAMILY '70
Bronson, Charles	Film	THE MECHANIC '72
Bronson, Charles	Film	THE STONE KILLER '73
Bronson, Charles	Nee	CHARLES BUCHINSKI
Bronstein,Lev Davidovich	Aka	LEON TROTSKY
Bronte, Anne	Pen Name	ACTON BELL w
Bronte, Charlotte	Pen Name	CURRER BELL w
Bronte, Emily	Heroine	JANE EYRE
Bronte, Emily	Pen Name	ELLIS BELL w
Bronte, Emily	Title	WUTHERING HEIGHTS
Brook, Claudio	Film	SIMON OF THE DESERT '65 ****
Brook, Clive	Film	CAVALCADE '33 ****
Brook, Clive	Film	SHERLOCK HOLMES '32
Brooks, Albert	Nee	ALBERT EINSTEIN
Brooks, Louise	Film	PANDORA'S BOX '28 ****
Brooks, Mel	Film	BLAZING SADDLES '74
Brooks, Mel d+	Film	SPACEBALLS '87
Brooks, Mel	Nee	MELVIN KAMINSKY
Brosnan, Pierce	Film	GOLDENEYE '95
Brosnan, Pierce	TitleRole	REMINGTON STEELE tv
Brown, Blair	Film	STRAPLESS '89
Brown, Bryan	Film	STIR '80
Brown, James mr	Hit	PAPA'S GOT A BRAND NEW BAG
Brown, Jim	Film	FINGERS '78
Brown, Jim	Film	KENNER '69
Brown, Jim	Film	THREE THE HARD WAY '74
Brown, Joe E.	Film	BROADMINDED '31
Brown, Joe E.	Film	CHATTERBOX '43
Brown, Joe E.	Film	SIX DAY BIKE RIDER '34
Brown, Joe E.	Film	THE GLADIATOR '78
Brown, Joe E.	Film	THE TENDERFOOT '32
Brown, John Mack	Film	THE GREAT MEADOW '31
Brown, Judy	Film	THE BIG DOLL HOUSE '71
Brown, Robert	Series	HERE COME THE BRIDES tv
Brown,Georg Stanford	Series	THE ROOKIES tv
Browne, Charles F.	Pen Name	ARTEMUS WARD
Browne, Dik	Cartoons	HAGAR THE HORRIBLE and HI AND LOIS
Browne, Jackson mr	Hit	DOCTOR MY EYES
Browning, Robert	Poem	RABBI BEN EZRA
Bruce, Virginia	Film	DANGEROUS CORNER '34
Bruce, Virginia	Film	THE INVISIBLE WOMAN '41
Bruller, Jean	Pen Name	VERCORS

Bryant, William Cullen	Poem	TO A WATERFOWL
Brynner, Yul	Film	CATLOW '71
Brynner, Yul	Film	SOLOMON AND SHEBA '59
Brynner, Yul	Film	SURPRISE PACKAGE '60
Brynner, Yul	Film	THE BUCCANEER '58
Brynner, Yul	Film	THE JOURNEY '59
Brynner, Yul	Film	THE SOUND AND THE FURY '59
Brynner, Yul	Film	THE TEN COMMANDMENTS '56 ****
Brynner, Yul	Film	THE ULTIMATE WARRIOR '75
Buchholz, Horst	Film	NINE HOURS TO RAMA '63
Buck, Pearl	Heroine	OLAN
Buck, Pearl	Nee	PEARL SYDENSTRICKER
Buck, Pearl	Title	A HOUSE DIVIDED
Buck, Pearl	Title	DRAGON SEED
Buck, Pearl	Title	SONS
Buck, Pearl	Title	THE GOOD EARTH
Buck, Pearl	Title	THE LIVING REED
Buell, Marjorie	Cartoon	LITTLE LULU
Buffalo Bill	Nee	WILLIAM F. CODY
Buffalo Springfield	mr Hit	FOR WHAT IT'S WORTH
Buffet, Jimmy	Song	MARGARITAVILLE
Bugaev, Boris	Pen Name	ANDREY BELY
Bujold, Genevieve	Film	COMA '78
Bunyan, John	Title	PILGRIMS PROGRESS
Buono, Victor	Film	THE STRANGLER '64
Burgess, Anthony	Pen Name	JOSEPH KELL
Burgess, Anthony	Title	1985
Burgess, Anthony	Title	A CLOCKWORK ORANGE
Burgess, Anthony	Title	THIS MAN AND MUSIC
Burgess, Meredith	Film	OF MICE AND MEN '39 ****
Burghoff, Gary	Flm Role	RADAR in Mash '70
Burke, Charlotte	Film	PAPERHOUSE '88
Burke, Delta	Sitcom	DESIGNING WOMEN tv
Burlinson, Tom	Film	WINDRIDER '86
Burnett, Carol	Film	A WEDDING '78
Burnett, Carol	Film	ANNIE '82
Burnett, Carol	Film	H.E.A.L.T.H. '79
Burnett, Carol	Film	THE FOUR SEASONS '81
Burney, Fanny	Aka	MADAME d'ARBLAY
Burns, George	Nee	NATHAN BIRNBAUM
Burr, Raymond	Film	DESIRE IN THE DUST '60
Burr, Raymond	Series	IRONSIDE tv
Burr, Raymond	Series	PERRY MASON tv
Burstyn, Ellen	Film	RESURRECTION '80
Burstyn, Ellen	Film	THE BABY-SITTERS CLUB '95
Burstyn, Ellen	Film	THE CEMETARY CLUB '92
Burstyn, Ellen	Film	THE EXORCIST '75
Burstyn, Ellen	Nee	EDNA GILHOOLEY
Burton, LeVar	Mini Ser.	ROOTS tv
Burton, Richard	Film	ABSOLUTION '81
Burton, Richard	Film	BECKET '64 ****
Burton, Richard	Film	EQUUS '77
Burton, Richard	Film	LOOK BACK IN ANGER ''58
Burton, Richard	Film	MASSACRE IN ROME '73
Burton, Richard	Film	PRINCE OF PLAYERS '55
Burton, Richard	Film	THE BRAMBLE BUSH '60
Burton, Richard	Film	THE COMEDIANS '67
Burton, Richard	Film	THE ROBE '53
Burton, Richard	Film	WHERE EAGLES DARE '69
Burton, Richard	Nee	RICHARD JENKINS
Burton, Richard	StgPlay	EQUUS b'dway

Busey, Gary	Film	CARNY '80
Busey, Gary	Film	INSIGNIFICANCE '85
Busey, Gary	Film	ROOKIE OF THE YEAR '93
Busey, Gary	Film	THE BUDDY HOLLY STORY '78
Bushman, Francis X.	Film	BEN HUR '26
Butler, Samuel	Title	THE WAY OF ALL FLESH
Buttons, Red	Film	SAYONARA '57
Buttons, Red	Nee	AARON CHWATT
Byington, Spring	Series	DECEMBER BRIDE tv
Byrd, Richard E. (Adm.)	Title	ALONE
Byrds, The mr	Hit	TURN! TURN! TURN!
Byrne, Gabriel	Film	MILLER'S CROSSING '90
Byrne, Gabriel	Film	SHIPWRECKED '90
Byron, Geo. Gordon (Lord)	Poem	CHILDE HAROLD
Byron, Geo. Gordon (Lord)	Poem	DON JUAN
Byron, Geo. Gordon (Lord)	Poem	THE BEPPO
Caan, James	Film	COUNTDOWN '68
Caan, James	Film	GARDENS OF STONE '87
Caan, James	Film	MISERY '90
Caan, James	Film	ROLLERBALL '75
Caan, James	Film	SLITHER '73
Caan, James	Film	THE GODFATHER '72
Caan, James	Film	THIEF '81
Cabot, Bruce	Film	KING KONG ,33 ****
Caesar, Sid	Film	TEN FROM YOUR SHOW OF SHOWS '73****
Cage, Nicolas	Film	LEAVING LAS VEGAS '96
Cage, Nicolas	Film	MOONSTRUCK '87
Cage, Nicolas	Film	RAISING ARIZONA '87
Cage, Nicolas	Nee	NICHOLAS COPPOLA
Cagney, James	Film	CITY FOR CONQUEST '40
Cagney, James	Film	COME FILL THE CUP '51
Cagney, James	Film	FOOTLIGHT PARADE '33
Cagney, James	Film	GMEN ("G"MEN) '35
Cagney, James	Film	ONE, TWO, THREE '61 ****
Cagney, James	Film	PICTURE SNATCHER '33
Cagney, James	Film	RAGTIME '81
Cagney, James	Film	THE GALLANT HOURS '60
Cagney, James	Film	THE MAYOR OF HELL '33
Cagney, James	Film	THE OKLAHOMA KID '39
Cagney, James	Film	THE PUBLIC ENEMY '31
Cagney, James	Film	THE ROARING TWENTIES '39
Cagney, James	Film	WEST POINT STORY '50
Cagney, James	Film	WHAT PRICE GLORY ,52
Cagney, James d	Film	SHORT CUT TO HELL '57
Cain, James M.	Title	MILDRED PIERCE
Cain, James M.	Title	THE POSTMAN ALWAYS RINGS TWICE
Caine, Michael	Film	ALFIE '66
Caine, Michael	Film	BATTLE OF BRITAIN '69
Caine, Michael	Film	GAMBIT '66
Caine, Michael	Film	PULP '72
Caine, Michael	Film	SLEUTH '72 ****
Caine, Michael	Film	THE EAGLE HAS LANDED '77
Caine, Michael	Film	THE FOURTH PROTOCOL '87
Caine, Michael	Film	THE IPCRESS FILE '65
Caine, Michael	Film	TOO LATE THE HERO '70
Caine, Michael	Film	ZULU '64
Caine, Michael	Nee	MAURICE MICKLEWHITE
Caine, Michael	TitleRole	ALFIE '66
Caldwell, Erskine	Title	TOBACCO ROAD
Calhoun, Rory	Film	A FACE IN THE RAIN '63
Calhoun, Rory	Film	AIN'T MISBEHAVIN' '55

Calhoun, Rory	Film	THE LOOTERS '55
Callan, Michael	Film	THE INTERNS '62
Callas, Maria	Nee	MARIA KALOGEROPOULOS
Calvert, Phyllis	Film	HER PANELLED DOOR '51
Calvert, Phyllis	Film	IT'S NEVER TOO LATE '56
Calvert, Phyllis	Film	THEY WERE SISTERS '45
Cambridge, Godfrey	Film	THE PRESIDENT'S ANALYST '67 ****
Cameron, Rod	Film	STAMPEDE '49
Camp, John	Pen name	JOHN SANDFORD
Campbell, Bill	Film	THE ROCKETEER '91
Campbell, Neve	Film	SCREAM '96
Campion, Jane d	Film	AN ANGEL AT MY TABLE '90
Campion, Jane d	Film	THE PIANO '93
Camus, Albert	Title	THE PLAGUE
Camus, Albert	Title	THE STRANGER
Canned Heat mr	Hit	GOING UP THE COUNTRY
Cannon, Dyan	Film	HONEYSUCKLE ROSE '80
Cannon, Dyan	Film	SUCH GOOD FRIENDS '71
Cantor, Eddie	Film	IF YOU KNEW SUSIE '48
Cantor, Eddie	Film	THE KID FROM SPAIN '32
Cantor, Eddie	Film	WHOOPEE! '30
Cantor, Eddie	Hit Song	BYE BYE BLACKBIRD
Capek, Karel	Title	R.U.R.
Capote, Truman	Title	THE GRASS HARP
Capp, Al	Cartoon	LI'L ABNER
Captain and Tennille, The	Hit Song	DO THAT TO ME ONE MORE TIME
Cara, Irene	File	FAME '80
Carafotes, Paul	Film	CHOICES '81
Carey, Macdonald	Film	OUTLAW TERRITORY '53
Carle, Frankie	Comp	SUNRISE SERANADE
Carlo, Yvonne de	Film	CASBAH '48
Carlo, Yvonne de	Film	PASSION '54
Carlo, Yvonne de	Film	TOMAHAWK '51
Carlo, Yvonne de	Nee	PEGGY MIDDLETON
Carlson, Richard	Film	BEYOND TOMORROW '40
Carlson, Richard	Film	THE MAGNETIC MONSTER '53
Carlson, Richard	Film	WINTER CARNIVAL '39
Carlson, Richard	Series	I LED THREE LIVES tv
Carmichael, Hoagy	Song	OLE BUTTERMILK SKY
Carmichael, Hoagy	Song	STARDUST
Carmichael, Ian	Film	I'M ALL RIGHT JACK '59
Carney, Art	Series	THE HONEYMOONERS tv
Caron, Leslie	Film	CONTRACT '80
Caron, Leslie	Film	DOCTOR'S DILEMMA '58
Caron, Leslie	Film	FANNY '61
Caron, Leslie	Film	GABY '56
Caron, Leslie	Film	GIGI '58 ****
Caron, Leslie	Film	LILI '53 ****
Caron, Leslie	Film	THE GLASS SLIPPER '55
Caron, Leslie	Film	THE L-SHAPED ROOM '63
Caron, Leslie	Film	THE SUBTERRANEANS '60
Carr, Thomas	Film	SULLIVAN'S EMPIRE '67
Carr, Vikki	Nee	FLORENCIA CASILLAS
Carradine, David	Film	Q '82
Carradine, David	Series	KUNG FU tv
Carradine, David d+	Film	AMERICANA '81
Carradine, John	Film	THE SCARECROW '82
Carradine, Keith	Film	THE BACHELOR '91
Carradine, Keith	Film	THE DUELLISTS '77
Carradine, Keith	Film	THE INQUIRY '87
Carradine, Keith	Film	THE MODERNS '88

Carrere, Tia	Film	WAYNE'S WORLD '92
Carrey, Jim	Film	LIAR LIAR '97
Carrey, Jim	Film	THE MASK '94
Carriere, Mathieu	Film	A WOMAN IN FLAMES '82
Carroll, Diahann	Film	CLAUDINE '74
Carroll, Diahann	Nee	CAROL DIAHANN JOHNSON
Carroll, Diahann	Series	JULIA tv
Carroll, Lewis	Title	ALICE'S ADVENTURES IN WONDERLAND
Carroll, Madeleine	Film	BLOCKADE '38
Carroll, Madeleine	Film	THE PRISONER OF ZENDA '37 ****
Carroll, Madeeline	Film	THIRTY-NINE(39) STEPS '35 ****
Carroll, Madeleine	Film	THE WORLD MOVES ON '34
Carroll, Nancy	Film	LAUGHTER '30
Cars, The mr	Hit	SHAKE IT UP
Carson Jeannie	Film	MAD LITTLE ISLAND '57
Carson, Jack	Film	MY DREAM IS YOURS '49
Carson, Jack	Film	THE GOOD HUMOR MAN '50
Carson, Rachel L.	Title	THE SEA AROUND US
Carstensen, Margit	Film	CHINESE ROULETTE '76
Carter, Cinnamon	Series	MISSION IMPOSSIBLE tv
Carter, Helena Bonham	Film	GETTING IT RIGHT '89
Carter, Janis	Film	THE MISSING JUROR '44
Carter, Lynda	Series	WONDER WOMAN tv
Carter, Nell	Series	GIMME A BREAK tv
Carver, Brent	Film	LILIES '97
Casey, Bernie	Film	BROTHERS '77
Cash, Johnny	HitSong	I WALK THE LINE
Cassavetes, John	Film	EDGE OF THE CITY '57 ****
Cassavetes, John	Film	ROSEMARY'S BABY '68 ****
Cassavetes, John	Film	THE KILLERS '64
Cassel,Jean-Pierre	Film	THE KILLING GAME '67
Cassidy, Shaun	Series	THE HARDY BOYS MYSTERIES tv
Cates, Phoebe	Film	SHAG '89
Cather, Willa	Title	DEATH COMES TO THE ARCHBISHOP
Catlin, Mrs Geo. Edw. Gordon	Pen Name	VERA BRITTAIN w
Cazale, John	Film	THE CONVERSATION '74 ****
Cazenove, Christopher	Film	THE FANTASIST '86
Chad, Everett	Mini Ser	CENTENNIAL tv
Chagall, Marc	Painting	THE JUGGLER
Challans, Mary	Pen Name	MARY RENAULT
Chamberlain, Margaret	Film	TUCK EVERLASTING '80
Chamberlain, Richard	Film	THE THREE MUSKETEERS '74
Chamberlain, Richard	Film	TWILIGHT OF HONOR '63
Chamberlain, Richard	Series	DR. KILDARE tv
Chambers, Marylin	Film	RABID '77
Champion, Marge	Film	GIVE A GIRL A BREAK '53
Chan, Jackie	Film	SUPERCOP '96
Chandler, Jeff	Film	DEPORTED '50
Chandler, Jeff	Film	RED BALL EXPRESS '52
Chandler, Jeff	Film	SIGN OF THE PAGAN '54
Chandler, Jeff	Film	THE JAYHAWKERS '59
Chandler, Jeff	Film	THE PLUNDERERS '60
Chandler, Jeff	Film	THE SPOILERS '55
Chandler, Jeff	Film	YANKEE BUCCANEER '52
Chandler, Raymond	Title	FAREWELL MY LOVELY
Chaney, Lon Jr.	Film	OF MICE AND MEN '39 ****
Chaney, Lon Jr.	Film	THE MUMMY'S CURSE '44
Chaney, Lon Jr.	Film	THE WOLFMAN '41
Chaney, Lon Sr.	Film	THE SHOCK '23
Chaney, Lon Sr.	Film	THE UNHOLY THREE '25
Chaney, Lon Sr.	Film	THE UNHOLY THREE '30

Chaney, Lon Sr.	Film	WEST OF ZANZIBAR '28
Chaplin, Charlie	Film	CHARLIE CHAPLIN CAVALCADE '38 ****
Chaplin, Charlie	Film	CHARLIE CHAPLIN FESTIVAL '38 ****
Chaplin, Charlie d+	Film	LIMELIGHT '52
Chaplin, Charlie d+	Film	THE CIRCUS '28
Chaplin, Charlie	Film	THE CURE '17
Chaplin, Charlie d+	Film	THE KID '21
Chaplin, Charlie d+	Film	A KING IN NEW YORK '57
Chaplin, Charlie d+	Film	CITY LIGHTS '31 ****
Chaplin, Charlie d+	Film	MODERN TIMES '36 ****
Chaplin, Charlie d+	Film	THE GOLD RUSH '25 ****
Chaplin, Charlie plus	Film	WHEN COMEDY WAS KING '60 ****
Chaplin, Geraldine	Film	REMEMBER MY NAME '78
Chapman, John	Aka	JOHNNY APPLESEED
Chapman, Marguerite	Film	THE GREEN PROMISE '49
Chapman, Tracy mr	Hit	FAST CAR
Charisse, Cyd	Film	BRIGADOON '54
Charisse, Cyd	Nee	TULA FINKLEA
Charles, Ray	Nee	RAY CHARLES ROBINSON
Charles, Ray mr	Hit	GEORGIA ON MY MIND
Chartier, Emile	Pen Name	ALAIN
Chase, Chevy	Film	FLETCH '85
Chatterton, Ruth	Film	CHARMING SINNERS '29
Chatterton, Ruth	Film	DODSWORTH '36 ****
Chatterton, Ruth	Film	FEMALE '33
Checker, Chubby	Nee	ERNEST EVANS
Checkers, Chubby mr	Hit	THE TWIST
Cheever, John	Title	THE WAPSHOT CHRONICLES
Chekov, Anton P.	Play	THE CHERRY ORDHARD
Chekov, Anton P.	Play	THE THREE SISTERS
Chekov, Anton P.	Play	UNCLE VANYA
Cher	Film	CHASTITY '69
Cher	Film	FAITHFUL '96
Cher	Film	MASK '85
Cher	Film	MERMAIDS '90
Cher	Film	MOONSTRUCK '87 ****
Cher	Hit Song	DARK LADY
Cher	Nee	CHERILYN SARKISIAN
Cherkassov, Nikolai	Film	ALEXANDER NEVSKY '38 ****
Cherkassov, Nikolai	Film	IVAN THE TERRIBLE,
		PART ONE '43 ****
Chester, Craig	Film	SWOON '92
Chevalier, Anna	Film	TABU '31
Chevalier, Maurice	Film	FANNY '61
Chevalier, Maurice	Film	GIGI '58 ****
Chevalier, Maurice	Film	LOVE ME TONIGHT '32 ****
Chevalier, Maurice	Film	ONE HOUR WITH YOU '32
Chiba, Sonny	Film	VIRUS '80
Chicago mr	Hit	SATURDAY IN THE PARK
Chiklis, Michael	Series	THE COMMISH tv
Childress, Alvin	Series	AMOS 'N' ANDY tv
Chinh, Kieu	Film	THE JOY LUCK CLUB '93
Chipmunks, The	Hit Song	ALVIN'S HARMONICA
Chong, Rae Dawn	Film	THE BORROWER '91
Chopin, Frederic	Comp	LES SYLPHIDES
Chordettes, The	Hit Song	MISTER SANDMAN
Christie, Agatha	Nee	AGATHA MARY CLARISSA MILLER
Christie, Agatha	Title	TEN LITTLE INDIANS
Christie, Dick	Series	SMALL WONDER tv
Christie, Julie	Film	DARLING '65
Christie, Julie	Film	PETULIA '68 ****

Christie, Julie	Film	SHAMPOO '75
Christie, Julie	Role	LARA in Dr. Zhivago
Christo at	Painting	THE UMBRELLAS
Churchill, Sir Winston	Nee	LEONARD SPENCER CHURCHILL
Cilea, Francesco	Opera	L'ARLESIANA
Citti, Franco	Film	DECAMERON '70
Clancy, Tom	Title	PATRIOT GAMES
Clancy, Tom	Title	RED STORM RISING
Clapton, Eric mr	Hit	LAYLA
Clark, Dane	Film	HIGHLY DANGEROUS '51
Clark, Dane	Film	MOONRISE '48
Clark, Dick	Series	AMERICAN BANDSTAND tv
Clark, Petula	Film	NEVER NEVER LAND '80
Clarke, Robert	Film	THE MAN FROM PLANET X '51
Clavell, James	Title	NOBLE HOUSE
Clavell, James	Title	SHOGUN
Clavell, James	Title	TAI-PAN
Clay, Henry	Quote	I WOULD RATHER BE RIGHT THAN PRESIDENT
Clay, Nicholas	Film	THE DARWIN ADVENTURE '72
Clayburgh, Jill	Film	AN UNMARRIED WOMAN '78 ****
Clayburgh, Jill	Film	LUNA '79
Cleese, John	Film	CLOCKWISE '86
Clemens, Samuel	Pen Name	MARK TWAIN
Clement, Aurore	Film	LACOMBE, LUCIEN '74 ****
Clement, Dick	Film	BULLSHOT '83
Clements, John	Film	SHIPS WITH WINGS '42
Clements, John	Film	THE FOUR FEATHERS '39 ****
Clift, Montgomery	Film	A PLACE IN THE SUN '51
Clift, Montgomery	Film	THE DEFECTOR '66
Clift, Montgomery	Film	FREUD '62
Clift, Montgomery	Film	FROM HERE TO ETERNITY '53 ****
Clift, Montgomery	Film	RED RIVER '48 ****
Clift, Montgomery	Film	THE SEARCH '48 ****
Cline, Patsy	Nee	VIRGINIA PATTERSON HENSLEY
Cline, Patsy	Song	CRAZY
Clive, Colin	Film	FRANKENSTEIN '31
Close, Glenn	Film	IMMEDIATE FAMILY '89
Cluzet, Francois	Film	CHOCOLAT '88
Cluzet, Francois	Film	COCKTAIL MOLOTOV '80
Cluzet, Francois	Film	OLIVIER OLIVIER '92
Coasters, The mr	Hit	YAKETY YAK
Cobb, Lee J.	Nee	LEO JACOBY
Cobb, Lee J.	Series	THE VIRGINIAN tv
Cobb, Lee J.	Film	TWELVE(12) ANGRY MEN '57 ****
Cobbett, William	Pen Name	PETER PORCUPINE
Coburn, Charles	Film	PEGGY '50
Coburn, Charles	Film	THE HIGHWAYMAN '51
Coburn, James	Film	THE BALTIMORE BULLET '80
Coburn, James	Film	THE CAREY TREATMENT '72
Coburn, James	Film	THE HONKERS '72
Coburn, James	Film	THE LAST OF SHEILA '73
Coburn, James	Film	THE PRESIDENT'S ANALYST '67 ****
Coca, Imogene	Film	TEN FROM YOUR SHOW OF SHOWS '73 ****
Cochran, Eddie mr	Hit	SUMMERTIME BLUES
Cochran, Steve	Film	THE WEAPON '56
Cocteau, Jean d	Film	BEAUTY AND THE BEAST '46 ****
Cody, Buffalo Bill	Nee	WILLIAM F. CODY
Coen, Joel d	Film	FARGO '96
Cohan, George M.	Play	SEVEN KEYS TO BALDPATE
Cohan, George M.	Song	I'M A POPULAR MAN
Cohan, George M.	Song	OVER THERE

Cohn, Mindy	Series	THE FACTS OF LIFE tv
Colbert, Claudette	Film	CLEOPATRA '34
Colbert, Claudette	Film	FAMILY HONEYMOON '48
Colbert, Claudette	Film	I MET HIM IN PARIS '37
Colbert, Claudette	Film	IMITATION OF LIFE '34
Colbert, Claudette	Film	IT HAPPENED ONE NIGHT '34 ****
Colbert, Claudette	Film	OUTPOST IN MALAYA '52
Colbert, Claudette	Film	REMEMBER THE DAY '41
Colbert, Claudette	Film	SKYLARK '41
Colbert, Claudette	Film	SO PROUDLY WE HAIL! '43
Colbert, Claudette	Film	THE BRIDE COMES HOME '35
Colbert, Claudette	Film	THE PALM BEACH STORY '42
Colbert, Claudette	Film	THE SECRET HEART '46
Colbert, Claudette	Film	TOVARICH '37
Colbert, Claudette	Nee	LILY CHAUCHOIN
Cole, Gary	Series	MIDNIGHT CALLER tv
Cole, Michael	Film	NICKEL MOUNTAIN '85
Cole, Michael	Series	THE MOD SQUAD tv
Cole, Nat King	Hit Song	UNFORGETTABLE
Coleman, Dabney	Series	DREXELL'S CLASS tv
Coleman, Gary	Film	ON THE RIGHT TRACK '81
Collins, Phil	Film	BUSTER '88
Collyer, Bud	Host	TO TELL THE TRUTH tv
Colman, Ronald	Film	A TALE OF TWO CITIES '35 ****
Colman, Ronald	Film	ARROWSMITH '31
Colman, Ronald	Film	BULLDOG DRUMMOND '29
Colman, Ronald	Film	KISMET '44
Colman, Ronald	Film	LOST HORIZON '37 ****
Colman, Ronald	Film	RAFFLES '30
Colman, Ronald	Film	TALK OF THE TOWN '42 ****
Colman, Ronald	Film	THE LATE GEORGE APLEY '47
Colman, Ronald	Film	THE LIGHT THAT FAILED '39
Colman, Ronald	Film	THE PRISONER OF ZENDA '37****
Colman, Ronald	Film	THE UNHOLY GARDEN '31
Como, Perry	Hit Song	PAPA LOVES MAMBO
Compson, Betty	Film	DOCKS OF NEW YORK '28 ****
Congreve, William	Play	THE WAY OF THE WORLD
Connelly, Jennifer	Film	CREEPERS '84
Connelly, Marc	Charac	LAWD in The Green Pastures
Connelly, Marc	Play	THE GREEN PASTURES
Connery, Sean	Film	CUBA '79
Connery, Sean	Film	DR. NO '62
Connery, Sean	Film	FAMILY BUSINESS '89
Connery, Sean	Film	GOLDFINGER '64
Connery, Sean	Film	MARNIE '64
Connery, Sean	Film	OPERATION SNAFU '61
Connery, Sean	Film	OUTLAND '81
Connery, Sean	Film	ROBIN AND MARIAN '76
Connery, Sean	Film	THE HILL '65
Connery, Sean	Film	THE PRESIDIO '88
Connery, Sean	Film	THE ROCK '96
Connery, Sean	Film	THE UNTOUCHABLES '87 ****
Connery, Sean	Film	THE WIND AND THE LION '75
Connery, Sean	Film	THUNDERBALL '65
Connery, Sean	Film	ZARDOZ '74
Connors, Chuck	Film	FLIPPER '63
Connors, Chuck	Film	GERONIMO '62
Connors, Chuck	Film	SYNANON '65
Connors, Chuck	Series	BRANDED tv
Connors, Michael	Nee	KREKER OHANIAN
Connors, Mike	Series	MANNIX tv

```
Conrad, Bob            Series     HAWAIIAN EYE tv
Conrad, Joseph         Title      HEART OF DARKNESS
Conrad, Joseph         Title      LORD JIM
Conrad, Joseph         Title      NOSTROMO
Conrad, Joseph         Title      THE SECRET AGENT
Conrad, Robert         Nee        CONRAD ROBERT FALK
Conrad, Robert         Series     BAA BAA BLACKSHEEP tv
Conrad, Robert         Series     CENTENNIAL tv
Conrad, Robert         Series     THE WILD WILD WEST tv
Conrad, William        Series     CANNON tv
Conrad, William        Series     JAKE AND THE FAT MAN tv
Constantine, Eddie  Film          THE THIRD GENERATION '79
Conte, Richard         Film       HOLLYWOOD STORY '51
Conte, Richard         Film       THE BROTHERS RICO '57
Conte, Richard         Film       THE FIGHTER '52
Conte, Richard         Film       THE RAIDERS '52
Conte, Richard         Film       THE SLEEPING CITY '50
Conte, Richard         Film       THIEVES' HIGHWAY '49
Converse-Roberts, Wm. Film   ON VALENTINE'S DAY '86
Conway, Gary           Series     LAND OF THE GIANTS tv
Conway, Shirl          Series     THE NURSES tv
Conway, Tim            Film       THE PRIVATE EYES '80
Conway, Tom            Film       THE FALCON IN MEXICO '44
Conway, Tom            Series     MARK SABER tv
Coogan, Jackie         Film       HUCKLEBERRY FINN '31
Coogan, Keith          Film       CHEETAH '89
Cook, Donald           Film       CONFIDENTIAL '35
Cook, Robin            Title      COMA
Cooke, Sam mr          Hit Song   YOU SEND ME
Cooper, Alice          Nee        VINCENT FURNIER
Cooper, Alice    mr    Hit        SCHOOL'S OUT
Cooper, Chris          Film       MATEWAN '87
Cooper, Gary           Film       A FAREWELL TO ARMS '32
Cooper, Gary           Film       ALONG CAME JONES '45
Cooper, Gary           Film       CLOAK AND DAGGER '46
Cooper, Gary           Film       DALLAS '50
Cooper, Gary           Film       DESIRE '36
Cooper, Gary           Film       FRIENDLY PERSUASION '56 ****
Cooper, Gary           Film       HIGH NOON '52 ****
Cooper, Gary           Film       HIS GIRL FRIDAY ****
Cooper, Gary           Film       MOROCCO '30
Cooper, Gary           Film       MR. DEEDS GOES TO TOWN'36****
Cooper, Gary           Film       PRIDE OF THE YANKEES '42 ****
Cooper, Gary           Film       THE FOUNTAINHEAD '49
Cooper, Gary           Film       THE HANGING TREE '59
Cooper, Gary        Film THE LIVES OF A BENGAL LANCER'35****
Cooper, Gary           Film       THE PLAINSMAN '36
Cooper, Gary           Film       THE VIRGINIAN '29
Cooper, Gary           Film       THE WEDDING NIGHT '35
Cooper, Gary           Film       THE WESTERNER '40
Cooper, Gary           Film       UNCONQUERED '47
Cooper, Gary           Role       DEEDS in Mr. Deeds Goes to Town
Cooper, Jackie         Film       BOY OF THE STREETS '37
Cooper, Jackie         Film       DINKY '35
Cooper, Jackie         Film       SEVENTEEN '40
Cooper, Jackie         Film       SOOKY '31
Cooper, Jackie         Series     HENNESEY tv
Cooper, Jackie         Series     THE PEOPLE'S CHOICE tv
Cooper, Jms. Fennimore Title LAST OF THE MOHICANS
Cooper, Jms. Fennimore Title THE PATHFINDER
Copland, Aaron         Comp       APPALACHIAN SPRING
```

Copland, Aaron	Comp	EL SALON MEXICO
Corbin, Barry	Series	NORTHERN EXPOSURE tv
Corey, Wendell	Film	THE BOLD AND THE BRAVE '56
Corey, Wendell	Film	THE WILD BLUE YONDER '51
Cornwell, David John M. Pen Name JOHN le CARRE		
Correll, Charles	RadioSer	AMOS 'N' ANDY radio
Cort, Bud	Film	GAS-S-S-S '70
Cort, Bud	Film	HAROLD AND MAUDE '72
Cortez, Ricardo	Film	THE TORRENT '26
Cos,William Trevor Pen Name WILLIAM TREVOR		
Cosell, Howard	Nee	HOWARD COHEN
Costello, Elvis mr Hit		ALISON
Costello, Elvis mr Nee		DECLAN MACMANUS
Costello, Lou	Films	See Abbott and Costello
Costello, Lou	Nee	LOUIS CRISTILLO
Costner, Kevin	Charac	NESS in the Untouchables tv
Costner, Kevin	Film	AMERICAN FLYERS '85
Costner, Kevin	Film	DANCES WITH WOLVES '90 ****
Costner, Kevin	Film	FANDANGO '85
Costner, Kevin	Film	JFK '91
Costner, Kevin	Film	THE BODYGUARD '92
Costner, Kevin	Film	THE UNTOUCHABLES '87
Costner, Kevin	Film	WATERWORLD '95
Cotten, Joseph	Film	LATITUDE ZERO '69
Cotten, Joseph	Film	SEPTEMBER AFFAIR '50
Cotten, Joseph	Film	SHADOW OF A DOUBT '43
Cotten, Joseph	Film	THE MAGNIFICENT AMBERSONS'42****
Cotten, Joseph	Film	UNTAMED FRONTIER '52
Cougar, John	Song	HURTS SO GOOD
Couric, Katie	tv Show	TODAY SHOW
Cousteau,Jacque-Yves d+ Film THE SILENT WORLD '56		
Cousteau,Jacques d Film		WORLD WITHOUT SUN '64 ****(doc)
Coward, Noel	Film	IN WHICH WE SERVE '42
Coward, Noel	Film	THE ASTONISHED HEART '50
Coward, Noel	Play	BLITHE SPIRIT
Coward, Noel c	Operetta	BITTERSWEET
Cox, Ronny	Series	APPLE'S WAY tv
Cox, Wally	Series	MR. PEEPERS tv
Cox,William Trevor Pen Name WILLIAM TREVOR		
Coyote, Peter	Film	HEARTBREAKERS '84
Coyote, Peter	Film	KIKA '93
Coyote, Peter	Film	OUT '88
Coyote, Peter	Nee	PETER COHON
Crabbe, Buster	Film	KING OF THE JUNGLE '33
Crabtree, Arthur	Film	QUARTET '49 ****
Crain, Jeanne	Film	A LETTER TO THREE WIVES'49****
Craig, Michael	Film	PAYROLL '61
Craig, Michael	Film	THE IRISHMAN '78
Crain, Jeanne	Film	MARGIE '46
Crain, Jeanne	Film	PINKY '49
Crane, Bob	Series	HOGAN'S HEROES tv
Crawford, Christina Title		MOMMIE DEAREST
Crawford, Joan	Film	ABOVE SUSPICION '43
Crawford, Joan	Film	CHAINED '34
Crawford, Joan	Film	DANCE, FOOLS, DANCE '31
Crawford, Joan	Film	GOODBYE, MY FANCY '51
Crawford, Joan	Film	HUMORESQUE '46
Crawford, Joan	Film	MANNEQUIN '37
Crawford, Joan	Film	PAID '31
Crawford, Joan	Film	POSSESSED '47
Crawford, Joan	Film	RAIN '32

```
Crawford, Joan         Film      STRAIT-JACKET '64
Crawford, Joan         Film      THE SHINING HOUR '38
Crawford, Joan         Film      THE WOMEN '39
Crawford, Joan         Nee       LUCILLE LeSUEUR
Crawford, John         Film      IMPERSONATOR '61
Crawford, Michael      Nee       MICHAEL DUMBELL-SMITH
Crawford,Broderick     Film      ALL THE KING'S MEN '49 ****
Crawford,Broderick     Series    HIGHWAY PATROL tv
Crayencour, Marguerite de Pen Name MARGUERITE YOURCENAR
Cream  mr              Hit       SUNSHINE OF YOUR LOVE
Creedence Clearwater Revival  mr Hit PROUD MARY
Crenna, Richard        Series    ALL'S FAIR tv
Crenna, Richard        Series    THE REAL McCOYS tv
Crenna,Richard         Film      THE EVIL '78
Crichton, Michael      Title     CONGO
Crisp, Donald          Film      GREYFRIARS BOBBY '61
Crompton, Samuel       Invent.   SPINNING MULE
Cronyn, Hume           Play      THE GIN GAME
Crosby, Bing           Film      BIRTH OF THE BLUES '41
Crosby, Bing           Film      DIXIE '43
Crosby, Bing           Film      DOUBLE OR NOTHING '37
Crosby, Bing           Film      GOING HOLLYWOOD '33
Crosby, Bing           Film      GOING MY WAY '44 ****
Crosby, Bing           Film      MISSISSIPPI '35
Crosby, Bing           Film      PARIS HONEYMOON '39
Crosby, Bing           Film      ROAD TO SINGAPORE '40
Crosby, Bing           Film      ROAD TO ZANZIBAR '41
Crosby, Bing           Film      SING YOU SINNERS '38
Crosby, Bing           Film      THAT'S ENTERTAINMENT '74 ****
Crosby, Bing           Film      TOO MUCH HARMONY '33
Crosby, Bing           Film      WAIKIKI WEDDING '37
Crosby, Bing           Film      WE'RE NOT DRESSING '34
Crosby, Bing           Film      WELCOME STRANGER '47
Crosby, Stills, Nash and Young  mr Hit SUITE:JUDY BLUE EYES
Cross, Dennis          Series    THE BLUE ANGELS tv
Cruise, Tom            Film      THE COLOR OF MONEY '86
Cruise, Tom            Film      THE FIRM '93
Cruise, Tom            Film      THE LEGEND '85
Cruise, Tom            Nee       THOMAS MAPOTHER
Crystal, Billy d+      Film      MR. SATURDAY NIGHT '92
Crystal, Billy         Series    SOAP tv
Crystals, The   mr     Hit       DA DOO RON RON
Cullen, Bill           Host      THE PRICE IS RIGHT tv
Culp, Robert           Film      RHINO! '64
Culp, Robert           Film      THE RAIDERS '63
Culp, Robert           Series    I SPY tv
Cummings, Robert       Film      HEAVEN ONLY KNOWS '47
Cummings, Robert       Film      SABOTEUR '42
Curtis, Jamie Lee      Film      A FISH CALLED WANDA '88
Curtis, Jamie Lee      Series    ANYTHING BUT LOVE tv
Curtis, Tony           Film      BALBOA '86
Curtis, Tony           Film      BEACHHEAD '54
Curtis, Tony           Film      FORBIDDEN '53
Curtis, Tony           Film      HOUDINI '53
Curtis, Tony           Film      LEPKE '75
Curtis, Tony           Film      SOME LIKE IT HOT '59 ****
Curtis, Tony           Film      THE DEFIANT ONES '58
Curtis, Tony           Film      THE OUTSIDER '61
Curtis, Tony           Film      THE PERFECT FURLOUGH '58
Curtis, Tony           Film      THE SQUARE JUNGLE '55
Curtis, Tony           Film      WHO WAS THAT LADY? '60
```

Curtis, Tony	Nee	BERNARD SCHWARTZ
Cusack, Cyril	Film	THE HOMECOMING '73
Cusack, Joan	Film	A SMILE LIKE YOURS '97
Cushing, Peter	Film	HORROR OF DRACULA '58
Cushing, Peter	Film	MADHOUSE 74
Cushing, Peter	Film	MANIA '59
Cushing, Peter	Film	NIGHT CREATURES '62
Cushing, Peter	Film	THE BEAST MUST DIE '74
Cushing, Peter	Film	THE GHOUL '75
Cushing, Peter	Film	THE GORGON '64
Cushing, Peter	Film	THE MUMMY '59
Cushing, Peter	Film	THE SKULL '65
Cussler, Clive	Title	INCA GOLD
Cussler, Clive	Title	RAISE THE TITANIC
D'Angelo, Beverly	Film	THE MIRACLE '91
Dahlbeck, Eva	Film	SMILES OF A SUMMER NIGHT'55****
Dailey, Dan	Film	MEET ME AT THE FAIR '53
Dailey, Dan	Film	THE GIRL NEXT DOOR 53
Dali, Salvadore	Painting	THE PERSISTENCE OF MEMORY
Dali, Salvadore	Painting	TUNA-FISHING
Dali, Salvadore	Title	DIARY OF A GENIUS
Dalio, Marcel	Film	RULES OF THE GAME '39 ****
Dallesandro, Joe	Film	HEAT '72
Daltrey, Roger	Film	McVICAR '80
Daltrey, Roger	Film	TOMMY '75
Daly, James	Series	MEDICAL CENTER tv
Daly, John	Host	WHAT'S MY LINE tv
Daly, Timothy	Series	WINGS tv
Daly, Tyne	Series	CAGNEY AND LACEY tv
Damante, Susan	Film	THE STUDENT TEACHERS '73
Damone, Vic	Nee	VITO FARINOLA
Dana, Richard H, Jr.	Title	TWO YEARS BEFORE THE MAST
Dangerfield,Rodney	Nee	JACOB COHEN
Daniel, Yuly	Pen Name	NICOLAY ARZHAK
Daniels, Bebe	Film	DIXIANA '30
Daniels, Jeff	Film	ARACHNOPHOBIA '90
Daniels, Jeff	Film	DISASTER IN TIME '92
Daniels, Phil	Film	MEANTIME '83
Daniels, Phil	Film	QUADROPHENIA '79
Daniels, Phil	Film	SCUM '79
Daniels, William	Film	LADYBUG LADYBUG '63
Dannay, Frederic	Pen Name	ELLERY QUEEN
Danner, Blythe	Film	FUTUREWORLD '76
Danny and the Juniors	mr Hit	AT THE HOP
Danson, Ted	Film	COUSINS '89
Danson, Ted	Series	CHEERS tv
Dante	Poem	INFERNO
Dante	Poem	THE DIVINE COMEDY
Dante	Poem	PARADISO
Danton, Ray	Film	THE GEORGE RAFT STORY '61
Danza, Tony	Series	WHO'S THE BOSS?
Darin, Bobby	Nee	WALDEN ROBERT CASSOTTO
Darin, Bobby s	Hit	SPLASH SPLASH
Darnell, Linda	Film	A LETTER TO THREE WIVES'49****
Darnell, Linda	Film	DAKOTA INCIDENT '56
Darnell, Linda	Film	HANGOVER SQUARE '45
Darnell, Linda	Film	MY DARLING CLEMENTINE '46****
Darnell, Linda	Film	THE LADY PAYS OFF '51
Darnell, Linda	Film	UNFAITHFULLY YOURS '48 ****
Darr, Lisa	Series	FLESH 'N' BLOOD tv
Darrieux, Danielle	Film	LOSS OF INNONENCE '61

Darrieux, Danielle	Film	THE RAGE OF PARIS '38
Darwell, Jane	Film	THE GRAPES OF WRATH '40 ****
Dashwood,Elizabeth	Pen Name	E.M. DELAFIELD
Daste, Jean	Film	ZERO FOR CONDUCT '33 ****
David, Eleanor	Film	SYLVIA '85
Davies, Marion	Film	GOING HOLLYWOOD '33
Davies, Marion	Film	MARIANNE '29
Davis, Bette	Film	ALL ABOUT EVE '50 ****
Davis, Bette	Film	DANGEROUS '35
Davis, Bette	Film	DECEPTION '46
Davis, Bette	Film	EX-LADY '33
Davis, Bette	Film	FASHIONS '34
Davis, Bette	Film	FRONT PAGE WOMAN '35
Davis, Bette	Film	HOUSEWIFE '34
Davis, Bette	Film	IT'S LOVE I'M AFTER '37
Davis, Bette	Film	JEZEBEL '38
Davis, Bette	Film	OLD ACQUAINTANCE '43
Davis, Bette	Film	PAYMENT ON DEMAND '51
Davis, Bette	Film	THE ANNIVERSARY '68
Davis, Bette	Film	THE CORN IS GREEN '45
Davis, Bette	Film	THE GOLDEN ARROW '36
Davis, Bette	Film	THE LETTER '40
Davis, Bette	Film	THE NANNY '65
Davis, Bette	Film	THE SISTERS '38
Davis, Bette	Film	THE STAR '52
Davis, Bette	Film	THE VIRGIN QUEEN '55
Davis, Bette	Film	THE WHALES OF AUGUST '87
Davis, Bette	Film	WATCH ON THE RHINE '43
Davis, Gail	Series	ANNIE OAKLEY tv
Davis, Geena	Film	ANGIE '94
Davis, Geena	Film	HERO '92
Davis, Jim	Cartoon	GARFIELD
Davis, Joan	Series	I MARRIED JOAN tv
Davis, Judy	Film	A PASSAGE TO INDIA '84
Davis, Judy	Film	HEATWAVE '83
Davis, Judy	Film	IMPROMPTU '91
Davis, Judy	Film	THE REF '93
Davis, Ossie	Film	DO THE RIGHT THING '89
Davis, Ossie	Series	EVENING SHADE tv
Davis, Sammi	Film	THE RAINBOW '89
Davis, Sammy Jr	Hit Song	MISTER BOJANGLES
Davis, Sammy Jr	Title	YES, I CAN
Davis, Skeeter	Song	THE END OF THE WORLD
Davis, Spencer Group	mr Hit	GIMME SOME LOVIN
Dawson, Ernest	Poem	CYNARA
Day, Bobby	Comp	ROCKIN ROBBIN
Day, Clarence	Title	LIFE WITH FATHER
Day, Doris	Film	BILLY ROSE'S JUMBO '62
Day, Doris	Film	LOVE ME OR LEAVE ME '55
Day, Doris	Film	MOVE OVER, DARLING '63
Day, Doris	Film	ON MOONLIGHT BAY '51
Day, Doris	Film	THAT TOUCH OF MINK '62
Day, Doris	Film	THE GLASS BOTTOM BOAT '66
Day, Doris	Nee	DORIS VonKAPPELHOFF
Day, Doris	Role	CALAMITY JANE
Day, Laraine	Film	MY DEAR SECRETARY '48
Day-Lewis, Daniel	Film	THE AGE OF INNOCENCE '93
Day-Lewis, Daniel	Film	THE INSURANCE MAN '85
De Carlo, Yvonne	Nee	PEGGY MIDDLETON
de Haviland,Olivia	Films	SEE Haviland, Olivia de
De Lint, Derek	Film	THE ASSAULT '86

De Maupassant, Guy	Title	THE NECKLACE
De Mille, Agnes ba	Musical	OKLAHOMA
De Niro, Robert	Film	AWAKENINGS '90
De Niro, Robert	Film	BRAZIL '85
De Niro, Robert	Film	GOODFELLAS '90
De Niro, Robert	Film	GREETINGS '68
De Niro, Robert	Film	HEAT '95
De Niro, Robert	Film	JACKNIFE '89
De Niro, Robert	Film	MAD DOG AND GLORY '93
De Niro, Robert	Film	MEAN STREETS '73 ****
De Niro, Robert	Film	NIGHT AND THE CITY '92
De Niro, Robert	Film	SLEEPERS '96
De Niro, Robert	Film	THE KING OF COMEDY '83
De Niro, Robert	Film	THE MISSION '86
De Niro, Robert	Film	THE RAGING BULL '80 ****
De Niro, Robert	Film	TRUE CONFESSIONS '81
De Palma, Brian	Film	CARRIE '76
De Sica,Vittorio	Film	THE TAILOR'S MAID '59
De Sica,Vittorio d	Film	BOCCACCIO '70
De Sica,Vittorio d	Film	SHOESHINE '46 ****
De Sica,Vittorio d	Film	THE BICYCLE THIEF '48 ****
De Sica,Vittorio d	Film	UMBERTO D '52 ****
De Silva, Howard	Film	M '51
De Young, Cliff	Film	PULSE '88
Deacon, Brian	Film	JESUS '79
Dean, james	Film	REBEL WITHOUT A CAUSE '55****
Dean, James	Nee	JAMES BYRON
Dean, James	Role	REBEL in R. Without a Cause
Dearden Basil	Film	DEAD OF NIGHT ****
DeBeck, Billy	Cartoon	BARNEY GOOGLE
Debussy, Claude	Comp	IMAGES
Dee, Kiki mr & s	Hit Song	DON'T GO BREAKING MY HEART
Dee, Ruby	Film	A RAISIN IN THE SUN '61 ****
Dee, Sandra	Film	GIDGET '59
Dee, Sandra	Film	I'D RATHER BE RICH '64
Dee, Sandra	Nee	ALEXANDRA ZUCK
Dees, Rick s	Song	DISCO DUCK
Defoe, Daniel	Title	MOLL FLANDERS
Defoe, Daniel	Title	ROBINSON CRUSOE
Dekker, Albert	Film	AMONG THE LIVING '41
Dekker, Albert	Film	THE PRETENDER '47
Del Rio, Delores	Film	FLYING DOWN TO RIO '33
Delany, Dana	Series	CHINA BEACH tv
Delibes(C.P.) Leo	Opera	LAKME
Delon, Alain	Film	ECLIPSE '62
Delon, Alain	Film	THE LEOPARD '63 ****
Delon, Alain	Film	ZORRO '75
Delpy, Julie	Film	BEATRICE '88
DeLuise, Dom	Film	FATSO '80
DeMaupassant, Guy	Title	UNE VIE
Demazis, Orane	Film	HARVEST '37 ****
DeMille, Agnes	Ballet	FALL RIVER LEGEND
DeMille, Agnes	Ballet	RODEO
Demme, Jonathan d	Film	STOP MAKING SENSE '84 ****
Dempsey, Patrick	Film	RUN '90
Deneuve, Catherine	Film	BELLE DE JOUR '67 ****
Deneuve, Catherine	Film	REPULSION '65
Deneuve, Catherine	Film	SCENE OF THE CRIME '86
Deneuve, Catherine	Film	TRISTANA '70
Denner, Charles	Film	BLUEBEARD '62
Denner, Charles	Film	LIFE UPSIDE DOWN '65

Denner, Charles	Film	ROBERT ET ROBERT '78
Dennis, Sandy	Film	THE FOX '68
Denton, Christa	Film	THE GATE '87
Denver, Bob	Series	GILLIGAN'S ISLAND tv
Denver, John	Nee	HENRY JOHN DEUTSCHENDORF Jr.
Denver, John	Song	ROCKY MOUNTAIN HIGH
Depardieu, Gerard	Film	DANTON '82
Depardieu, Gerard	Film	GERMINAL '93
Depardieu, Gerard	Film	LOULOU '80
Depardieu, Gerard	Film	MAITRESSE '76
Depardieu, Gerard	Film	MENAGE '86
Depardieu, Gerard	Film	MY FATHER, THE HERO '94
Depardieu, Gerard	Film	POLICE '84
Depardieu, Gerard	Film	UNDER SATAN'S SUN '87
Depp, Johnny	Film	CRY-BABY '90
Derek, Bo	Nee	MARY CATHLEEN COLLINS
Derek, John	Film	PRINCE OF PIRATES '53
Derek, John	Film	THE FAMILY SECRET '51
Derek, John	Film	THE OUTCAST '54
Derek, John	Film	THUNDERBIRDS '52
Derek, John	Nee	DEREK HARRIS
Dern, Bruce	Film	SMILE '75
Dern, Laura	Film	CITIZEN RUTH '97
Descartes, Rene	Axiom	COGITO ERGO SUM
Descartes, Rene	Axiom	DISCOURS DE LA METHODE
Deuel, Peter	Series	ALIAS SMITH AND JONES tv
Deuel, Peter	Series	LOVE ON A ROOFTOP tv
DeVito, Danny	Film	HOFFA '92
DeVito, Danny	Film	RENAISSANCE MAN '94
DeVito, Danny	Film	RUTHLESS PEOPLE '86
DeVito, Danny	Nee	DANIEL MICHAELI
DeVito, Danny	Series	TAXI tv
DeVito, Danny d+	Film	MATILDA '96
DeWitt, Joyce	Series	THREE'S COMPANY tv
Dey, Susan	Charac	GRACE VAN OWEN in L.A. Law tv
Dey, Susan	Nee	SUSAN SMITH
Dey, Susan	Series	L. A. LAW tv
Diaz de Vivar, Rodrigo Aka		EL CID
Dickens, Charles	Charac	ARTFUL DODGER
Dickens, Charles	Charac	NELL
Dickens, Charles	Charac	TINY TIM
Dickens, Charles	Charac	URIAH HEEP
Dickens, Charles	Title	A TALE OF TWO CITIES
Dickens, Charles	Title	BLEAK HOUSE
Dickey, James	Title	DELIVERANCE
Dickinson, Angie	Film	JESSICA '62
Dickinson, Angie	Nee	ANGELINE BROWN
Dickinson, Angie	Series	POLICE WOMAN tv
Dickinson, Emily	Poem	A VISITOR IN MARL
Diddley, Bo	Nee	ELIAS BATES
Diddley, Bo mr	Hit	WHO DO YOU LOVE?
Didion, Joan	Play	PLAY IT AS IT LAYS
Dietrich, Marlene	Film	DESIRE '36
Dietrich, Marlene	Film	DISHONORED '31
Dietrich, Marlene	Film	GOLDEN EARRINGS '47
Dietrich, Marlene	Film	MOROCCO '30
Dietrich, Marlene	Film	RANCHO NOTORIOUS '52
Dietrich, Marlene	Film	SHANGHAI EXPRESS '32
Dietrich, Marlene	Film	THE SCARLET EMPRESS '34
Dietrich, Marlene	Film	THE SPOILERS '42
Dietrich, Marlene	Film	WITNESS FOR THE PROSECUTION '57****

Diffring, Anton	Film	CIRCUS OF HORRORS '60
Diller, Phyllis	Nee	PHYLLIS DRIVER
Dillman, Bradford	Film	FRANCIS OF ASSISI '61
Dillman, Bradford	Film	PIRANHA '78
Dillon, Matt	Film	BEAUTIFUL GIRLS '96
Dillon, Matt	Film	DRUGSTORE COWBOY '89
Dillon, Matt	Film	TEX '82
Dion and the Belmonts mr	Hit	A TEENAGER IN LOVE
Dire Straits mr	Hit	BROTHERS IN ARMS
Dirks, Rudolph	Cartoon	THE KATZENJAMMER KIDS
Disney Studios	Film	HERCULES(Animated) '97
Ditko, Steve	Cartoon	SPIDER-MAN
Dix, Richard	Film	AMERICAN EMPIRE '42
Dix, Richard	Film	CIMARRON '31
Dix, Richard	Film	THE ARIZONIAN '35
Dix, Richard	Film	THE KANSAN '43
Dix, Richard	Film	THE LOST SQUADRON '32
Dix, Richard	Film	THE WHISTLER MOVIES '44 - '47
Dixon, Ivan	Film	NOTHING BUT A MAN '64
Dixon, Jill	Film	A NIGHT TO REMEMBER '58 ****
Dixon, Mrs. Rumer Haynes	Pen Name	RUMER GODDEN
Doberman,Pvt.Duane	Charac	THE PHIL SILVERS SHOW tv
Doctorow, E.L.	Title	RAGTIME
Dodgson, Charles L.	Pen Name	LEWIS CARROLL
Domergue, Faith	Film	CULT OF THE COBRA '55
Domingo, Placido	Film	LA TRAVIATA '82 ****
Domingo, Placido	Film	OTELLO '86
Domino, Fats mj mr	Hit	BLUEBERRY HILL
Donadieu,Margeurite	Pen Name	MARGUERITE DURAS
Donahue, Troy	Film	A DISTANT TRUMPET '64
Donahue, Troy	Film	MY BLOOD RUNS COLD '65
Donat, Robert	Film	GOODBYE, MR. CHIPS '39
Donat, Robert	Film	THE CITADEL '38
Donat, Robert	Film	THE MAGIC BOX '51 ****
Donat, Robert	Film	THIRTY-NINE(39) STEPS, THE'35****
Donat, Robert	Role	MR. CHIPS
Donizetti, Gaetano	Opera	LUCIA LAMMERMOOR
Donizetti, Gaetano	Opera	LUCIREZIA BORGIA
Donleavy, J.P.	Title	LEILA
Donlevy, Brian	Film	AN AMERICAN ROMANCE '44
Donlevy, Brian	Film	ENEMY FROM SPACE '57
Donlevy, Brian	Film	HANGMEN ALSO DIE '43
Donlevy, Brian	Film	IMPACT '49
Donlevy, Brian	Film	THE CREEPING UNKNOWN '56
Donlevy, Brian	Film	THE GREAT McGINTY '40
Donleavy, J.P.	Title	THE GINGER MAN
Donnadieu,Marguerite	Pen Name	MARGUERITE DURAS
Donne, John	Poem	DEATH BE NOT PROUD
Donner, Richard d	Film	THE OMEN '76
Doobie Bros., The mr	Hit	WHAT A FOOL BELIEVES
Dooley, Paul	Film	A PERFECT COUPLE '79
Doolittle, Hilda	Pen Name	H.D.
Doors, The mr	Hit	LIGHT MY FIRE
Dorff, Stephen	Film	BACKBEAT '93
Dors, Diana	Nee	DIANA FLUCK
Dorsey, Jimmy	JazzHit	ANAPOLA
Dorsey, Tommy	Song	THIS IS IT
Dorsey,Jimmy+Tommy	Hit Song	EVERY LITTLE MOVEMENT
Dos Passos,John R.	Title	U.S.A.
Dostoyevsky,Fyodor	Title	IDIOT, THE
Douglas, Donna	Role	ELLY MAY in tv Dallas

Douglas, Donna	Series	THE BEVERLY HILLBILLIES tv
Douglas, Illeana	Film	GRACE OF MY HEART '96
Douglas, Kirk	Film	A GUNFIGHT '71
Douglas, Kirk	Film	A LOVELY WAY TO DIE '68
Douglas, Kirk	Film	CHAMPION '49
Douglas, Kirk	Film	DETECTIVE STORY '51
Douglas, Kirk	Film	EDDIE MACON'S RUN '83
Douglas, Kirk	Film	FOR LOVE OR MONEY '63
Douglas, Kirk	Film	LUST FOR LIFE '56 ****
Douglas, Kirk	Film	MAN WITHOUT A STAR '55
Douglas, Kirk	Film	MY DEAR SECRETARY '48
Douglas, Kirk	Film	PATHS OF GLORY '57 ****
Douglas, Kirk d+	Film	POSSE '75
Douglas, Kirk	Film	SPARTACUS '60
Douglas, Kirk	Film	THE BIG CARNIVAL '51
Douglas, Kirk	Film	THE BROTHERHOOD '68
Douglas, Kirk	Film	THE DEVIL'S DISCIPLE '59
Douglas, Kirk	Film	THE FINAL COUNTDOWN '80
Douglas, Kirk	Film	THE FURY '78
Douglas, Kirk	Film	THE GLASS MENAGERIE '50
Douglas, Kirk	Film	THE HOOK '63
Douglas, Kirk	Film	THE JUGGLER '53
Douglas, Kirk	Film	THE RACERS '55
Douglas, Kirk	Film	THE VIKINGS '58
Douglas, Kirk	Film	TOWN WITHOUT PITY '61
Douglas, Kirk	Nee	ISSUR DANIELOVITCH
Douglas, Melvyn		RAPTURE '65
Douglas, Melvyn	Film	THE LONE WOLF RETURNS '35
Douglas, Melvyn	Film	THE OLD DARK HOUSE '32
Douglas, Melvyn	Nee	MELVYN HESSELBERG
Douglas, Michael	Film	FATAL ATTRACTION '87
Douglas, Michael	Film	SHINING THROUGH '92
Douglas, Michael	Film	THE GAME '97
Douglas, Michael	Film	THE STAR CHAMBER '83
Douglas, Paul	Film	EVERYBODY DOES IT '49
Douglas, Paul	Film	THE LEATHER SAINT '56
Dourif, Brad	Film	IMPURE THOUGHTS '85
Dow, Tony	Series	LEAVE IT TO BEAVER tv
Downey, Robert Jr.	Film	CHAPLIN '92
Downey, Robert Jr.	Film	RESTORATION '95
Downs, Johnny	Film	CORONADO '35
Dowson, Ernest C.	Pen Name	CYNARA
Dreiser, Theodore	Title	AN AMERICAN TRAGEDY
Dreiser, Theodore	Title	SISTER CARRIE
Drescher, Fran	Role	NANNY tv
Dressler, Marie	Film	DINNER AT EIGHT '33 ****
Dressler, Marie	Film	EMMA '32
Dressler, Marie	Film	TUGBOAT ANNIE '33
Dreyer, Carl T. d	Film	THE PASSION OF JOAN OF ARC '28 ****
Dreyfuss, Richard	Film	ALWAYS '89
Dreyfuss, Richard	Film	ANOTHER STAKEOUT '93
Dreyfuss, Richard	Film	CLOSE ENCOUNTERS OF THE THIRD KIND '77 ****
Dreyfuss, Richard	Film	MOON OVER PARADOR '88
Dreyfuss, Richard	Film	MR. HOLLAND'S OPUS '96
Dreyfuss, Richard	Film	STAKEOUT '87
Dreyfuss, Richard	Film	THE BUDDY SYSTEM '84
Dreyfuss, Richard	Film	THE COMPETITION '801
Dreyfuss, Richard	Film	THE GOODBYE GIRL '77
Drifters, The mr	Hit	SAVE THE LAST DANCE FOR ME
Driscoll, Bobby	Film	THE WINDOW '49

Driscoll, Bobby	Film	TREASURE ISLAND '50
Drury, James	Series	THE VIRGINIAN tv
Dryden, John	Poem	THE HIND AND THE PANTHER
Dryer, Fred	Series	HUNTER tv
Dubois, Marie	Film	SHOOT THE PIANO PLAYER'60****
Duchamp, Marcel	Painting	NUDE DESCENDING A STAIRCASE
Duchaussoy, Michel	Film	THIS MAN MUST DIE '70
Duff, Howard	Film	SHAKEDOWN '50
Duff, Howard	Series	FELONY SQUAD tv
Duffy, Julia	Series	BABY TALK tv
Duggan, Andrew	Series	BOURBON STREET BEAT tv
Dukakis, Olympia	Film	MOONSTRUCK '87
Duke, Patty	Film	BILLIE '65
Dullea, Keir	Film	THE THIN RED LINE '64
Dumas, Alexandre	Title	THE THREE MUSKETEERS
DuMaurier, Daphne	Title	REBECCA
Dunaway, Faye	Film	BONNIE AND CLYDE '67 ****
Dunaway, Faye	Film	CHINATOWN '74 ****
Dunaway, Faye	Film	EYES OF LAURA MARS '78
Dunaway, Faye	Film	LITTLE BIG MAN '70 ****
Dunaway, Faye	Film	THE GAMBLE '88
Dunne, Irene	Film	LIFE WITH FATHER '47 ****
Dunne, Irene	Film	MY FAVORITE WIFE '40
Dunne, Irene	Film	ROBERTA '35
Dunne, Irene	Film	THE MUDLARK '50
Dunning, George d	Film YELLOW SUBMARINE '68 ****(animatd)
Duprez, June	Film	THE THIEF OF BAGDAD '40 ****
Durante, Jimmy	Film	HOLLYWOOD PARTY '34
Durante, Jimmy	Film	PALOOKA '34
Durante, Jimmy	Film	THE GREAT RUPERT '50
Durbin, Deanna	Film	THREE SMART GIRLS '36
Durrell, Lawrence	Title	THE ALEXANDRIA QUARTET
Duryea, Dan	Film	TAGGART '64
Duryea, Dan	Film	THE BAMBOO SAUCER '68
Duryea, Dan	Film	THE BOUNTY KILLER '65
Duryea, Dan	Film	THE UNDERWORLD STORY '50
Duryea, Dan	Film	WORLD FOR RANSOM '54
Duryea, Dan	Series	CHINA SMITH tv
Dusenberry, Ann	Film	LIES '83
Dutton, Charles	Sitcom	ROC tv
Duvall, Robert	Film	CONVICTS '91
Duvall, Robert	Film	IKE '79
Duvall, Robert	Film	THE EAGLE HAS LANDED '77
Duvall, Robert	Film	THE GREAT SANTINI '79
Duvall, Robert	Film	THE OUTFIT '74
Duvall, Robert	Film	TOMORROW '72
Duvall, Shelley	Role	OLIVE OYL in Popeye
Dvorak, Antonin	Comp	NEW WORLD SYMPHONY
Dvorak, Antonin	Comp	SLAVONIC DANCES
Dylan, Bob	Film	THE LAST WALTZ '78 ****
Dylan, Bob	Nee	ROBERT ZIMMERMAN
Dylan, Bob mr	Hit	LIKE A ROLLING STONE
Dyneley, Peter	Film	HOUSE OF MYSTERY '61
Dysart, Richard	Series	L.A, LAW tv
Dzhugshvili, Josef	Visarionovich Aka JOSEPH STALIN
Dzundza, George	Series	LAW & ORDER tv
Eagles, The mr	Hit	HOTEL CALIFORNIA
Earth, Wind and Fire mr Hit	SHINING STAR
Easton, Sheena	Nee	SHEENA SHIRLEY ORR
Eastwood, Clint	Film	HEARTBREAK RIDGE '86
Eastwood, Clint	Film	IN THE LINE OF FIRE '93

Eastwood, Clint	Film	PAINT YOUR WAGON '69
Eastwood, Clint d+	Film	PLAY MISTY FOR ME '71
Eastwood, Clint	Film	THE BEGUILED '71
Eastwood, Clint	Film	THE ENFORCER '76
Eastwood, Clint d+	Film	THE GAUNTLET '77
Eastwood, Clint	Film	TIGHTROPE '84
Eastwood, Clint D+	Film	UNFORGIVEN '92
Eastwood, Clint	Series	RAWHIDE tv
Eastwood, Clint d+	Film	ABSOLUTE POWER '97 ****
Eban, Abba	Title	MY PEOPLE
Eban, Abba	Title	VOICE OF ISRAEL
Ebb, Fred	Lyrics	CABERET
Eberhardt, Richard	Poem	WAYS OF LIGHT
Ebsen, Buddy	Series	THE BEVERLY HILLBILLIES rv
Ebsen, Buddy	tv Role	BARNEY JONES
Eco, Umberto	Title	FOUCAULT'S PENDULUM
Eddy, Nelson	Film	LET FREEDOM RING '39
Eddy, Nelson	Film	MAYTIME '37
Eddy, Nelson	Film	NAUGHTY MARIETTA '35
Eddy, Nelson	Film	SWEETHEARTS '38
Eden, Barbara	Film	HARPER VALLEY P.T.A. '78
Eden, Barbara	Nee	BARBARA HUFFMAN
Eden, Barbara	Series	I DREAM OF JEANNIE tv
Edmonds, Walter D.	Title	DRUMS ALONG THE MOHAWK
Edwards, Anthony	Film	GOTCHA! '85
Edwards, James	Film	HOME OF THE BRAVE '49
Edwards, Vince	Series	BEN CASEY tv
Egan, Richard	Film	CHUBASCO '68
Egan, Richard	Film	DAY OF THE WOLVES '73
Eggar, Samantha	Film	THE WALKING STICK '70
Eichhorn, Lisa	Film	WILDROSE '84
Elgar, Sir Edward	Comp	DREAM OF GERONTIUS
Elgar, Sir Edward	Comp	ENIGMA VARIATIONS
Elgar, Sir Edward	Comp	POMP AND CIRCUMSTANCE
Elgar, Sir Edward	Comp	THE APOSTLES
Eliot, George	Title	ADAM BEDE
Eliot, George	Title	MIDDLEMARCH
Eliot, George	Title	SILAS MARNER
Eliot, George	Title	THE MILL ON THE FLOSS
Eliot, T.S.	Play	MURDER IN THE CATHEDRAL
Eliot, T.S.	Play	THE COCKTAIL PARTY
Eliot, T.S.	Poem	FOUR QUARTERS
Eliot, T.S.	Poem	LOVE SONG OF J. ALFRED PRUFOCK
Eliot, T.S.	Poem	PORTRAIT OF A LADY
Eliot, T.S.	Poem	THE WASTE LAND
Elkin, Stanley	Title	BOSWELL
Eller	Charac	AUNT in Oklahoma
Ellington, Duke	Comp	MOOD INDIGO
Ellington, Duke	Song	SATIN DOLL
Elliott, Chris	Series	GET A LIFE tv
Elliott, Denholm	Film	UNDERWORLD '85
Elliott, George P.	Title	MURIEL
Elliott, Sam	Film	LIFEGUARD '76
Elliott, Sam	Film	PRANCER '89
Elliott, Sam	Series	THE YELLOW ROSE tv
Elliott, William	Film	WYOMING '47
Ellison, James	Film	THE UNDYING MONSTER '42
Ellison, Ralph	Title	INVISIBLE MAN
Elton, John mr & s	Hit Song	DON'T GO BREAKING MY HEART
Elwes, Cary	Film	THE CRUSH '93
Ely, Ron	Nee	RONALD PIERCE

```
Ely, Ron               Series     TARZAN tv
Emerson, Lake and Palmer Hit FROM THE BEGINNING
Emily                  Charac.    OUR TOWN
Ephron, Nola           Screenplay SILKWOOD '83
Erickson, Leif         Series     THE HIGH CHAPARRAL tv
Esposito,Giancarlo Film            FRESH '94
Essex, David           Film       STARDUST '75
Essex, David           Film       THAT'LL BE THE DAY '74
Estes, Rob             Series     SILK STALKINGS tv
Euripides              Heroine    IPHIGENIA
Euripides              TitleRole  MEDEA
Eurythmics, The mr Hit            SWEET DREAMS(ARE MADE OF THIS)
Evans, Barry           Series     DOCTOR IN THE HOUSE tv
Evans, Dale            Nee        FRANCES SMITH
Evans, Gene            Film       DEVIL TIMES FIVE '74
Evans, Gene            Film       THE STEEL HELMET '51
Evans, Gene            Series     MY FRIEND FLICKA tv
Evans, Linda           Role       KRYSTLE in Dynasty tv
Evans, Linda           Series     DYNASTY tv
Evans, Mary Ann        Pen Name   GEORGE ELIOT
Everett, Chad          Nee        RAYMOND CRAMTON
Everett, Rupert        Film       THE RIGHT HAND MAN '87
Everly Bros. mr        Hit        WAKE UP LITTLE SUZY
Evigan, Greg           Series     BJ AND THE BEAR tv
Ewell, Tom             Film       BACK AT THE FRONT '52
Ewell, Tom             Film       FINDERS KEEPERS '51
Ewell, Tom             Nee        S. YEWELL TOMKINS
Eyer, Richard          Film       THE INVISIBLE BOY '57
Eythe, William         Film       THE SONG OF BERNADETTE'43****
Fabian                 Film       RIDE THE WILD SURF '64
Fabricius, Sara Margarethe Pen Name CORA SANDEL
Faes,Peter van der Aka            SIR PETER LELY p
Fairbanks, Douglas Jr. Film CHANCES '31
Fairbanks, Douglas Jr. Film PARACHUTE JUMPER '33
Fairbanks, Douglas Jr. Film RULERS OF THE SEA '39
Fairbanks, Douglas Jr. Film SINBAD THE SAILOR '47
Fairbanks, Douglas Jr. Film THE EXILE '47
Fairbanks, Douglas Jr. Film THE FIGHTING O'FLYNN '49
Fairbanks, Douglas Jr. Film THE GREAT MANHUNT '50
Fairbanks, Douglas Jr. Film THE NARROW CORNER '33
Fairbanks, Douglas Jr. Film THE SUN NEVER SETS '39
Fairbanks, Douglas Sr. Film THE BLACK PIRATE '26
Fairbanks, Douglas Sr. Film THE LAMB '15
Fairbanks, Douglas Sr. Film THE THREE MUSKETEERS '21
Fairbanks, Douglas Sr. Nee DOUGLAS ULLMAN
Fairchild, Morgan      Nee        PATSY McCLENNY
Fairchild, Morgan      Series     FLAMINGO ROAD tv
Faithfull, MarianneFilm           MADHOUSE MANSION '74
Falk, Peter            Film       THE CHEAP DETECTIVE '78
Falk, Peter            Series     COLUMBO tv
Farge, Annie           Series     ANGEL tv
Farigoule, Louis       Pen Name   JULES ROMAINS
Farina, Dennis         Series     CRIME STORY tv
Farmer, Mimsy          Film       MORE '69
Farnum, William        Film       A TALE OF TWO CITIES '17
Farr, Jamie            Nee        JAMEEL FARAH
Farr, Jamie            Series     M*A*S*H tv
Farrar, David          Film       FRIEDA '47
Farrar, David          Film       LOST '55
Farrell, Charles       Film       MOONLIGHT SONATA '38
Farrell, James T.      Title      THE STUDS LONIGAN TRILOGY
```

```
Farrow, Mia          Film      RECKLESS '95
Farrow, Mia          Film      ROSEMARY'S BABY '68 ****
Farrow, Mia          Film      ZELIG '83
Farrow, Mia          Series    PEYTON PLACE tv
Fassbinder,Rainer Werner d Film THE AMERICAN SOLDIER '70
Fassbinder,Rainer Werner d+   Film   FOX AND HIS
                                       FRIENDS '75 ****
Fassbinder,Rainer Werner Film KAMIKAZE '89
Fast, Howard         Title     SPARTACUS
Faulkner, William    Title     ABSALOM, ABSALOM
Faulkner, William    Title     AS I LAY DYING
Faulkner, William    Title     LIGHT IN AUGUST
Faulkner, William    Title     THE SOUND AND THE FURY
Faulkner, William    Title     THE UNVANQUISHED
Faust, Frederick     Pen Name  MAX BRAND
Fawcett-Majors, Farrah Film    SUNBURN '79
Faye, Alice          Film      THAT NIGHT IN RIO '41
Faye, Alice          Film      THE GANG'S ALL HERE '43
Faye, Alice          Nee       ANN LEPPERT
Feldon, Barbara      Series    GET SMART tv
Fender, Freddy       Nee       BALDEMAR G. HUERTA
Fenn, Sherilyn       Film      RUBY '92
Fenn, Sherilyn       Film      TWO-MOON JUNCTION '88
Ferber, Edna         Title     GIANT
Ferber, Edna         Title     SHOW BOAT
Ferber, Edna         Title     SO BIG
Fernandel            Film      FORBIDDEN FRUIT '59
Fernandel            Film      HARVEST '37 ****
Fernandel            Film      PANTALOONS '57
Fernandel            Film      THE LAW IS THE LAW '59
Ferreau, Jon         Film      SWINGERS '96
Ferrer, Jose         Film      THE CAINE MUTINY '54 ****
Ferrer, Mel          Film      A TIME FOR LOVING '71
Ferrer, Mel          Film      LOST BOUNDARIES '49
Ferrigno, Lou  Titl Rol  THE INCREDIBLE HULK,'77(tv pilot)
Fetchit, Stepin      Nee       LINCOLN PERRY
Fiedler, Leslie A. Title       FREAKS
Field, Sally         Film      HEROES '77
Field, Sally         Film      MURPHY'S ROMANCE '85
Field, Sally         Film      NORMA RAE '79
Field, Sally         Film      PUNCHLINE '88
Field, Sally         Film      STEEL MAGNOLIAS '89
Field, Sally         Nee       SALLY MAHONEY
Field, Sally         Series    THE FLYING NUN tv
Fielding, Henry      Play      TOM THUMB
Fields, Shep         Theme     RIPPLING RHYTHYM
Fields, W.C.         Film      DAVID COPPERFIELD '33 ****
Fields, W.C.         Film      IT'S A GIFT '34 ****
Fields, W.C.         Film      POPPY '36
Fields, W.C.         Film      THE BANK DICK '40 ****
Fields, W.C.         Film      THE OLD-FASHIONED WAY '34
Fields, W.C.         Film      YOU'RE TELLING ME '34
Fields, W.C.         Nee       WILLIAM CLAUDE DUKENFIELD
Fiennes, Ralph       Film      THE ENGLISH PATIENT '96
Filipepi,Alessandro Pen Name   SANDRO BOTTICELLI
Finch, Jon           Film      MACBETH '71
Finch, Peter         Film      KIDNAPPED '60
Finch, Peter         Film      MAKE ME AN OFFER '55
Finch, Peter         Film      NETWORK '76
Finch, Peter         Film      THE SHIRALEE '57
Finch, Peter         Nee       WILLIAM MITCHELL
```

Finlay, Frank	Film	OTHELLO '65 ****
Finney, Albert	Film	ANNIE '82
Finney, Albert	Film	LOOPHOLE '80
Finney, Albert	Film	ORPHANS '87
Finney, Albert	Film	SCROOGE '70
Finney, Albert	Film	THE DRESSER '83
Finney, Albert	Film	THE GUMSHOE '72
Finney, Albert	Film	THE PLAYBOYS '92
Finney, Albert	Film	TOM JONES '63 ****
Finney, Albert	Film	UNDER THE VOLCANO '84
Finney, Albert	Film	WOLFEN '81
Finney, Albert	TitleRole	TOM JONES
Firth, Colin	Film	ANOTHER COUNTRY '84
Firth, Colin	Film	VALMONT '89
Firth, Peter	Film	EQUUS '77
Fisher, Bud	Cartoon	MUTT AND JEFF
Fisher, Eddie	Song	WITH THESE HANDS
Fisher, Ham	Cartoon	JOE PALOOKA
Fitzgerald, Barry	Film	AND THEN THERE WERE NONE '45****
Fitzgerald, Barry	Film	EASY COME, EASY GO '47
Fitzgerald, Barry	Nee	WILLIAM JOSEPH SHIELDS
Fitzgerald,F.Scott	Title	TENDER IS THE NIGHT
Fitzgerald,F.Scott	Title	THE CRACK-UP
Fitzgerald,F.Scott	Title	THE GREAT GATSBY
Fitzgerald,F.Scott	Title	THIS SIDE OF PARADISE
Fitzgerald,Geraldine	Film	THE PAWN BROKER '65 ****
Fitzpatrick, Leo	Film	KIDS '95
Five Satins,The mr	Hit	IN THE STILL OF THE NIGHT
Flaherty, Joe	Series	SECOND CITY tv
Flaherty, Robert d	Film	LOUISANA STORY '42***(documentary)
Flaherty, Robert d	Film	MAN OF ARAN '34 ****(documentary)
Flaherty, Robert d	Film	MOANA '25
Flanders, Ed	Series	ST. ELSEWHERE tv
Flanner, Janet	Pen Name	GENET
Fleetwood Mac mr	Hit	RUMOURS
Fleetwoods mr	Hit Song	COME SOFTLY TO ME
Fleming, Eric	Film	CONQUEST OF SPACE '55
Fletcher, Louise	Film	ONE FLEW OVER THE CUKOO'S NEST ' 75 ****
Flynn, Errol	Film	AGAINST ALL FLAGS '52
Flynn, Errol	Film	EDGE OF DARKNESS '43
Flynn, Errol	Film	KIM '50
Flynn, Errol	Film	MONTANA '50
Flynn, Errol	Film	NEVER SAY GOODBYE '46
Flynn, Errol	Film	NORTHERN PURSUIT '43
Flynn, Errol	Film	THE ADVENTURES OF ROBIN HOOD '38****
Flynn, Errol	Film	THE PERFECT SPECIMEN '37
Flynn, Errol	Film	THE SEA HAWK '40 ****
Flynn, Errol	Film	THE SISTERS '38
Flynn, Errol	Film	THE WARRIORS '55
Flynn, Errol	Title	MY WICKED, WICKED WAYS
Follett, Ken	Title	THE EYE OF THE NEEDLE
Folsom, Allan	Title	THE DAY AFTER TOMORROW
Fonda, Bridget	Film	SINGLES '92
Fonda, Henry	Film	FAIL-SAFE '64
Fonda, Henry	Film	GRAPES OF WRATH '40 ****
Fonda, Henry	Film	MISTER ROBERTS '55 ****
Fonda, Henry	Film	MY DARLING CLEMENTINE '46****
Fonda, Henry	Film	MY NAME IS NOBODY '73
Fonda, Henry	Film	SLIM '37
Fonda, Henry	Film	THE MAGNIFICENT DOPE '42

Fonda, Henry	Film	THE OX-BOW INCIDENT '43 ****
Fonda, Henry	Film	TWELVE(12) ANGRY MEN '57 ****
Fonda, Henry	Film	YOUNG MR. LINCOLN '39
Fonda, Henry	Series	THE DEPUTY tv
Fonda, Jane	Film	BARBARELLA '68
Fonda, Jane	Film	CALIFORNIA SUITE '78
Fonda, Jane	Film	CHINA SYNDROME '79 ****
Fonda, Jane	Film	COMES A HORSEMAN '78
Fonda, Jane	Film	JULIA '77 ****
Fonda, Jane	Film	KLUTE '71
Fonda, Jane	Film	STEELYARD BLUES '73
Fonda, Jane	Film	THE CHASE '66
Fonda, Jane	Role	BREE(in Klute)
Fonda, Peter	Film	HIGH-BALLIN' '78
Fontaine, Joan	Film	FRENCHMAN'S CREEK '44
Fontaine, Joan	Film	IVY '47
Fontaine, Joan	Nee	JOAN de HAVILAND
Fonteyn Magot	Film	ROMEO AND JULIET '66
Forbes, Ralph	Film	THE BACHELOR FATHER '31
Ford, Ford Madox	Title	PARADE'S END
Ford, Ford Madox	Title	THE GOOD SOLDIER
Ford, Glenn	Film	CIMARRON '60
Ford, Glenn	Film	CONVICTED '50
Ford, Glenn	Film	COWBOY '58
Ford, Glenn	Film	FATE IS THE HUNTER '64
Ford, Glenn	Film	GALLANT JOURNEY '46
Ford, Glenn	Film	GILDA '46
Ford, Glenn	Film	HEAVEN WITH A GUN '69
Ford, Glenn	Film	JUBAL '56
Ford, Glenn	Film	MEN WITHOUT SOULS '40
Ford, Glenn	Film	PLUNDER OF THE SUN '53
Ford, Glenn	Film	SMITH! '69
Ford, Glenn	Film	TERROR ON A TRAIN '53
Ford, Glenn	Film	TEXAS '41
Ford, Glenn	Film	THE AMERICANO '55
Ford, Glenn	Film	THE FASTEST GUN ALIVE '56
Ford, Glenn	Film	THE GAZEBO '59
Ford, Glenn	Film	THE MAN FROM COLORADO '48
Ford, Glenn	Film	THE MATING OF MILLIE '48
Ford, Glenn	Film	THE ROUNDERS '65
Ford, Glenn	Film	THE SHEEPMAN '58
Ford, Glenn	Film	TRIAL '55
Ford, Glenn	Series	CADE'S COUNTY tv
Ford, Harrison	Charac.	INDIANA JONES in 2
		Indiana Jones Films'84 &'88
Ford, Harrison	Film	AIR FORCE ONE '97 ****
Ford, Harrison	Film	FRANTIC '88
Ford, Harrison	Film	RAIDERS OF THE LOST ARK'81****
Ford, Harrison	Film	SABRINA '95
Ford, Harrison	Film	THE EMPIRE STRIKES BACK'80****
Ford, Harrison	Film	THE FUGITIVE '93
Ford, Harrison	Film	WITNESS '85
Ford, John	Film	THE HURRICANE '37
Ford, John	Nee	SEAN O'FEARNA
Ford, Paul	Series	THE BAILEYS OF BALBOA tv
Ford, Wallace	Film	FREAKS '32
Forrest, Frederic	Film	HAMMETT '83
Forrest, Steve	Film	RASCAL '69
Forrest, Steve	Film	THE WILD COUNTRY '71
Forster, E.M.	Title	A PASSAGE TO INDIA
Forster, E.M.	Title	A ROOM WITH A VIEW

Forster, E.M.	Title	HOWARD'S END
Forster, E.M.	Title	MAURICE
Forster, Robert	Film	ALLIGATOR '80
Forster, Robert	Film	MEDIUM COOL '69 ****
Forster, Robert	Film	STUNTS '77
Forsythe, John	Film	THE CAPTIVE CITY '52
Forsythe, John	Film	TOPAZ '69
Forsythe, John	Nee	JOHN FREUND
Forsythe, John	Series	BACHELOR FATHER tv
Forsythe, John	Series	DYNASTY tv
Forsythe, John	Series	TO ROME WITH LOVE tv
Forsythe, William	Film	PALOOKAVILLE '96
Forsythe,Frederick	Title	DAY OF THE JACKAL
Forsythe,Frederick	Title	THE ODESSA FILE
Fortescue, Gregory	Film	THE CARRIER '88
Fosdick, Charles	Pen Name	HARRY CASTLEMON
Fossey, Brigitte	Film	FORBIDDEN GAMES '51
Foster Stephen	Song	BEAUTIFUL DREAMER
Foster, Hal	Cartoon	PRINCE VALIANT
Foster, Helen	Film	LINDA '29
Foster, Jodie	Film	CARNY '80
Foster, Jodie	Film	FOXES '80
Foster, Jodie	Film	HATE '96
Foster, Jodie	Film	THE ACCUSED '88
Foster, Jodie	Nee	ALICIA CHRISTIAN FOSTER
Foster, Preston	Film	THE HUNTED '48
Foster, Preston	Film	THE MAN WHO DARED '33
Foster, Preston	Series	WATERFRONT tv
Foster, Stephen	Song	I HAD A DREAM THE OTHER NIGHT
Foster, Stephen	Song	MY OLD DOG TRAY
Four Seasons, The	Hit	SHERRY
Four Tops, The mr	Hit	I CAN'T HELP MYSELF
Fournier. Henri	AKA	ALAIN-FOURNIER
Fowles, John	Title	THE MAGUS
Fox, Edward	Film	GALILEO '73
Fox, Edward	Film	THE DAY OF THE JACKAL '73
Fox, Fontaine	Cartoon	TOONERVILLE FOLKS
Fox, Michael J.	Film	BACK TO THE FUTURE '85
Fox, Michael J.	Film	GREEDY '94
Fox, Michael J.	Film	THE FRIGHTENERS '96
Fox, Sidney	Film	MIDNIGHT '34
Foxworth, Robert	Film	THE BLACK MARBLE '80
Foxworth, Robert	Series	FALCON CREST tv
Foxx, Redd	Nee	JOHN SANFORD
Foxx, Redd	Series	SANFORD AND SON tv
Frakes, Jonathan	Series	STAR TREK, THE NEXT GENERATION tv
France, Anatole	Title	PENGUIN ISLAND
Francen, Victor	Film	J'ACCUSE '37
Franciosa, Anthony	Nee	ANTHONY PAPALEO
Francis, Anne	Film	GIRL OF THE NIGHT '60
Francis, Arlene	Film	ONE, TWO, THREE '61 ****
Francis, Arlene	Nee	ARLENE KAZANJIAN
Francis, Connie	Hit Song	MAMA
Francis, Connie	Nee	CONCETTA FRANCONERO
Francis, Connie	Song	STUPID CUPID
Francis, Connie mj	Hit Song	WHO'S SORRY NOW
Francis, Kay	Film	GIRLS ABOUT TOWN '31
Francis, Kay	Film	GIVE ME YOUR HEART '36
Francis, Kay	Film	STORM AT DAYBREAK '33
Francis, Kay	Film	TROUBLE IN PARADISE '32 ****
Franciscus, James	Film	VALLEY OF GWANGI '69

Franciscus, James	Film	YOUNGBLOOD HAWKE '64
Franciscus, James	Series	MR. NOVAK tv
Franklin, Benjamin	Pen Name	RICHARD SAUNDERS
Franklin, Bonnie	Series	ONE DAY AT A TIME tv
Franklin,Aretha mr	Hit	RESPECT
Fredericks, Dean	Series	STEVE CANYON tv
Freeland,Thorton d	Film	FLYING DOWN TO RIO '33
Freeman, Morgan	Film	DEATH OF A PROPHET '81
French, Alice	Pen Name	OCTAVE THANET
French, Victor	Series	CARTER COUNTRY tv
Freud, Sigmund	Title	TOTEM AND TABU
Frewer, Matt	Series	DOCTOR, DOCTOR tv
Frey, Sami	Film	NEA '78
Friels, Colin	Film	DINGO '91
Friml, Rudolf	Operetta	ROSE MARIE
Friml, Rudolf	Operetta	THE FIREFLY
Friml, Rudolf	Operetta	THE VAGABOND KING
Frobe, Gert	Film	THE GREEN ARCHER '61
Frost, Robert	Poem	BIRCHES
Frost, Robert	Poem	NOTHING GOLD CAN STAY
Frost, Robert	Poem	THE ROAD NOT TAKEN
Frost, Robert	Poem	TREE AT MY WINDOW
Frye, Soleil Moon	Series	PUNKY BREWSTER tv
Fugard, Athol	Play	A LESSON FROM A LOES
Fuller, Robert	Series	EMERGENCY tv
Fuller, Robert	Series	LARAMIE tv
Funt, Allen	Series	CANDID CAMERA tv
Furphy, Joseph	Pen Name	TOM COLLINS
Fusco, Paul	Series	ALF tv
Gabin, Jean	Film	GRAND ILLUSION '37 ****
Gabin, Jean	Film	PEPE LE MOKO '37 ****
Gabin, Jean	Film	THE IMPOSTER '44
Gabin, Jean	Film	THE LOWER DEPTHS '36
Gabin, Jean	Film	THE POSSESSORS '58
Gabin, Jean	Film	THE SICILIAN CLAN '69
Gable, Clark	Film	CHAINED '34
Gable, Clark	Film	COMMAND DECISION '48
Gable, Clark	Film	GONE WITH THE WIND '39 ****
Gable, Clark	Film	IT HAPPENED ONE NIGHT'34 ****
Gable, Clark	Film	MOGAMBO '53
Gable, Clark	Film	POSSESSED '31
Gable, Clark	Film	SARATOGA '37
Gable, Clark	Film	THE HUCKSTERS '47
Gable, Clark	Film	THE MISFITS '61
Gable, Clark	Film	THE TALL MEN '55
Gable, Clark	Film	THEY MET IN BOMBAY '41
Gable, Clark	Film	TOO HOT TO HANDLE '38
Gable, Clark	Film	WIFE VS. SECRETARY '36
Gabor, Eva	Series	GREEN ACRES tv
Gage, Nicholas	Title	ELENI
Gallagher, Peter	Film	UNDERNEATH '95
Gallico, Paul	Title	SNOW GOOSE
Galligan, Zach	Film	GREMLINS '84
Galsworthy, John	Pen Name	JOHN SINJOHN
Galsworthy, John	Play	THE SILVER BOX
Galsworthy, John	Title	THE FORSYTE SAGA
Ganz, Bruno	Film	CIRCLE OF DECEIT '81 ****
Ganz, Bruno	Film	IN THE WHITE CITY '83
Ganz, Bruno	Film	KNIFE IN THE HEAD '78
Ganz, Bruno	Film	THE MARQUISE OF O '76
Garbo, Greta	Film	A WOMAN OF AFFAIRS '28

Garbo, Greta	Film	ANNA KARENINA '35 ****
Garbo, Greta	Film	CAMILLE '37
Garbo, Greta	Film	CONQUEST '37
Garbo, Greta	Film	GRAND HOTEL '32 ****
Garbo, Greta	Film	INSPIRATION '31
Garbo, Greta	Film	LOVE '27
Garbo, Greta	Film	MATA HARI '32
Garbo, Greta	Film	NINOTCHKA '39
Garbo, Greta	Film	QUEEN CHRISTINA '33 ****
Garbo, Greta	Film	THE KISS '29
Garbo, Greta	Film	THE PAINTED VEIL '34
Garbo, Greta	Film	THE TEMPTRESS '26
Garbo, Greta	Nee	GRETA GUSTAFSSON
Gardenia, Vincent	Nee	VINCENT SCOGNAMIGLIO
Gardner, Ava	Film	BHOWANI JUNCTION '56
Gardner, Ava	Film	MOGAMBO '53
Gardner, Ava	Film	ON THE BEACH '59 ****
Gardner, Ava	Film	ONE TOUCH OF VENUS '48
Gardner, Ava	Film	THE ANGEL WORE RED '60
Gardner, Ava	Film	THE KILLERS '46 ****
Gardner, Erle Stanley	Charac	PERRY MASON(sleuth)
Garfield, John	Film	BODY AND SOUL '47 ****
Garfield, John	Film	DUST BE MY DESTINY '39
Garfield, John	Film	EAST OF THE RIVER '40
Garfield, John	Film	HE RAN ALL THE WAY '51
Garfield, John	Film	THE POSTMAN ALWAYS RINGS TWICE'46****
Garfield, John	Nee	JULIUS GARFINKLE
Garfolo, Jeanane	Film	MATCHMAKER '97
Gargan, William	Series	MARTIN KANE, PRIVATE EYE tv
Garland, Beverly	Film	THE ALLIGATOR PEOPLE '59
Garland, Judy	Film	A CHILD IS WAITING '63
Garland, Judy	Film	BABES ON BROADWAY '41
Garland, Judy	Film	MEET ME IN ST. LOUIS '44 ****
Garland, Judy	Film	THE CLOCK '45
Garland, Judy	Film	THE HARVEY GIRLS '46
Garland, Judy	Film	THE PIRATE '48
Garland, Judy	Film	THE WIZARD OF OZ '39 ****
Garland, Judy	Nee	FRANCES GUMM
Garland, Richard	Film	THE UNDEAD '57
Garner, Errol mj	Comp	MISTY
Garner, James	Film	MARLOWE '69
Garner, James	Film	ONE LITTLE INDIAN '73
Garner, James	Film	THE GREAT ESCAPE '63 ****
Garner, James	Film	THE WHEELER DEALERS '63
Garner, James	Nee	JAMES BUMGARNER
Garner, James	Series	BRET MAVERICK tv
Garner, James	Series	MAVERICK tv
Garner, James	Series	THE ROCKFORD FILES tv
Garr, Teri	Film	HEAD '68
Garr, Teri	Film	TOOTSIE '82
Garrett, Betty	Film	MY SISTER EILEEN '55
Garson, Greer	Film	JULIA MISBEHAVES '48
Garson, Greer	Film	MRS. MINIVER '42 ****
Garson, Greer	Film	PRIDE AND PREJUDICE '40 ****
Garson, Greer	Film	THE MINIVER STORY '50
Gassman, Vittorio	Film	LOVE AND LARCENY '63
Gassman, Vittorio	Film	THE FAMILY '87
Gassman, Vittorio	Film	THE SLEAZY UNCLE '91
Gassman, Vittorio	Film	THE SUCCESS '63
Gaup, Mikkel	Film	PATHFINDER '88
Gaye, Marvin mr	Hit	CAN I GET A WITNESS?

Gayle, Crystal	Nee	BRENDA GAYLE WEBB
Gaynor, Janet	Film	SUNRISE '27 ****
Gaynor, Janet	Film	THE YOUNG IN HEART '38
Gaynor, Mitzi	Film	FOR LOVE OR MONEY '63
Gaynor, Mitzi	Film	THE JOKER IS WILD '57
Gazzara, Ben	Series	ARREST AND TRIAL tv
Geer, Will	Role	ZEB(Grandpa) in The Waltons tv
Geer, Will	Series	THE WALTONS tv
Geer, Will & Ellen	Film	SILENCE '74
Geeson, Judy	Film	DOOMWATCH '72
Geisel, Theodor	Pen Name	DR. SEUSS
Genet, Jean	Play	THE MAIDS
Genn, Leo	Film	THE WOODEN HORSE '50
George, Anthony	Series	CHECKMATE tv
George,Christopher	Film	DAY OF THE ANIMALS '77
George,Christopher	Series	THE RAT PATROL tv
Gerard, Danny	Series	BROOKLYN BRIDGE tv
Geray, Steve(n)	Film	SO DARK THE NIGHT '46
Gere, Richard	Film	BLOODBROTHERS '78
Gere, Richard	Film	POWER '86
Gere, Richard	Film	SOMMERSBY '93
Gere, Richard	Film	YANKS '79
German, Daniil	Pen Name	DANIIL ALEKSANDROVICH GRANIN
Gershwin, George	Comp	RHAPSODY IN BLUE
Gershwin, George	Opera	PORGY AND BESS
Gershwin, George	Song	'S WONDERFUL
Gershwin, George	Song	BUT NOT FOR ME (Girl Crazy)
Gershwin, George	Song	LET 'EM EAT CAKE
Gershwin, George	Song	LIZA
Gershwin, George	Song	LOVE WALKED IN
Gershwin, George	Song	OF THEE I SING
Gershwin, George	Song	OH LADY BE GOOD
Gershwin, George	Song	THE MAN I LOVE
Getty, Balthazar	Film	LORD OF THE FLIES '90
Giannini,Giancarlo	Film	LOVE AND ANARCHY '73
Giannini,Giancarlo	Film	SEVEN BEAUTIES '76 ****
Giannini,Giancarlo	Film	SWEPT AWAY...BY AN UNUSUAL...
		BLUE SEA OF AUGUST '75 ****
Giannini,Giancarlo	Film	THE INNOCENT '76 ****
Giannini,Giancarlo	Film	THE SEDUCTION OF MIMI '72
Gibbon, Lewis Grassic	Pen Name	JAMES LESLIE MITCHELL
Gibson, Henry	Film	NASHVILLE '75 ****
Gibson, Mel	Film	GALLIPOLI '81
Gibson, Mel	Film	HAMLET '90
Gibson, Mel	Film	MAVERICK '94
Gibson, Mel	Film	RANSOM '96
Gibson, Mel	Film	TEQUILA SUNRISE '88
Gibson, Mel	Film	THE BOUNTY '84
Gibson, Mel	Film	TIM '79
Gibson, Mel d+	Film	BRAVEHEART '95
Gibson,Charles Dana	Art Subs.	THE GIBSON GIRLS
Gide, Andre	Title	THE IMMORALIST
Gielgud, John	Film	PROSPERO'S BOOKS '91
Gifford, Kathy Lee	Nee	KATHIE EPSTEIN
Gilbert, John	Film	DOWNSTAIRS '32
Gilbert, John	Film	QUEEN CHRISTINA '33 ****
Gilbert, John	Film	THE BIG PARADE '25 ****
Gilbert,William S.	Operetta	H.M.S. PINAFORE
Gilmer, Elizabeth	Pen Name	DOROTHY DIX
Gilpin, Peri	Sitcom	FRASIER tv
Gilroy, Frank	Play	SUBJECT WAS ROSES

Giraudoux, Jean	Title	TIGER AT THE GATES
Girotti, Massimo	Film	OSSESSIONE '42
Gish, Lillian	Film	BROKEN BLOSSOMS '19
Gish, Lillian	Film	INTOLERANCE '16 ****
Gish, Lillian	Film	THE BIRTH OF A NATION '15****
Gish, Lillian	Film	THE WHALES OF AUGUST '87
Gish, Lillian	Film	THE WIND '28
Glaser,Paul Michael	Series	STARSKY AND HUTCH tv
Gleason, Jackie	Film	SKIDOO '68
Gleason, Jackie	Film	THE HUSTLER '61 ****
Gleason, Jackie	Series	THE HONEYMOONERS tv
Gleason, Jackie	Series	THE LIFE OF RILEY tv
Gleason, James	Film	THE PLOT THICKENS '36
Glenn, Scott	Film	THE CHALLENGE '82
Gless, Sharon	Role	ROSIE O'NEILL in Trials of R O'N.tv
Gless, Sharon	Series	CAGNEY AND LACEY tv
Glover, Danny	Film	BOPHA! '93
Glover, Danny	Film	THE COLOR PURPLE '85
Glover, John	Film	THE CHOCOLATE WAR '87
Goddard, Paulette	Film	THE CAT AND THE CANARY '39
Goddard, Paulette	Nee	MARION LEVY
Godden, Rumer	Title	BLACK NARCISSUS
Gogol, Nikolay	Title	THE OVERCOAT
Goldberg, Rube	Cartoon	BOOB McNUTT
Goldberg, Whoopi	Film	BOGUS '96
Goldberg, Whoopi	Film	EDDIE '96
Goldberg, Whoopi	Film	SARAFINA! '92
Goldberg, Whoopi	Film	THE ASSOCIATE '96
Goldberg, Whoopi	Film	THE COLOR PURPLE '85
Goldberg, Whoopi	Nee	CARYN JOHNSON
Goldblum, Jeff	Film	BETWEEN THE LINES '77
Goldblum, Jeff	Film	THE FLY '86
Golding, William	Title	LORD OF THE FLIES
Goldman, Gary	Film	THUMBELINA '94
Goldsmith, Oliver	Title	THE VICAR OF WAKEFIELD
Gong Li	Film	RAISE THE RED LANTERN '91****
Gonzales,Jose Vic.	Aka	JUAN GRIS p
Goodman, Benny	Theme	LOVE IN BLOOM
Goodman, Benny(+band)	Film	SWEET AND LOW-DOWN '44
Goodman, John	Film	MATINEE '93
Goodman, John	Film	THE BABE '92
Goodman, John	Film	THE FLINTSTONES '94
Goodman, John	Series	ROSEANNE tv
Goodrich, Samuel	Pen Name	PETER PARLEY
Gorcey and Hall	Film	BOWERY BATTALION '51
Gorcey and Hall	Film	BOWERY BOMBSHELL '46
Gorcey and Hall	Film	CLANCY STREET BOYS '43
Gorcey and Hall	Film	MR. MUGGS STEPS OUT '43
Gorcey, Leo	Films	SEE Gorcey and Hall
Gordon, Bruce	tv Role	FRANK NITTI in THE UNTOUCHABLES tv
Gordon, Glen	Series	THE ADVENTUIRES OF FU MANCHU tv
Gordon, Keith	Film	STATIC '85
Gordon, Ruth	Film	BOARDWALK '79
Gordon, Ruth	Film	HAROLD AND MAUDE '72
Gore, Albert	Title	EARTH IN THE BALANCE
Gorenko, Anna	Pen Name	ANNA AKHMATOVA
Gorman, Cliff	Film	COPS AND ROBBERS '73
Gorme, Eydie	Nee	EDITH GORMEZANO
Gosden, Freeman	RadioSer	AMOS 'N' ANDY radio
Gosfield, Maurice	Series	THE PHIL SILVERS SHOW tv
Gould, Chester	Cartoon	DICK TRACY

```
Gould, Elliott        Film      BUSTING '74
Gould, Elliott        Film      GETTING STRAIGHT '70
Gould, Elliott        Film      MASH '70 ****
Gould, Elliott        Film      THE LONG GOODBYE '73
Gould, Elliott        Film      WHO? '74
Gounod,Chas.Franc.    Comp      MESSE SOLENNELLE
Gounod,Chas.Franc.    Opera     FAUST
Gower, Andre          Film      THE MONSTER SQUAD '87
Gowland, Gibson       Film      GREED '25 ****
Goya, Francisco Jose de Painting DUCHESS OF ALBA
Goya, Francisco Jose de Painting THE NAKED MAJA
Grable, Betty         Film      THE DOLLY SISTERS '45
Graff, Ilene          Series    MR. BELVEDERE tv
Grand Funk Railroad   mr Hit    WE'RE AN AMERICAN BAND
Granger, Farley       Film      AMUCK '72
Granger, Farley       Film      STRANGERS ON A TRAIN '51 ****
Granger, Farley       Film      THEY LIVE BY NIGHT '49
Granger, Stewart      Film      CAPTAIN BOYCOTT '47
Granger, Stewart      Film      COMMANDO '64
Granger, Stewart      Film      FRONTIER HELLCAT '66
Granger, Stewart      Film      MOONFLEET '55
Granger, Stewart      Film      SARABAND '48
Granger, Stewart      Film      SCARAMOUCHE '52
Granger, Stewart      Film      THE PRISONER OF ZENDA'52
Granger, Stewart      Film      THE SECRET INVASION '64
Granger, Stewart      Nee       JAMES STEWART
Grant, Cary           Film      BRINGING UP BABY '38 ****
Grant, Cary           Film      CHARADE '63
Grant, Cary           Film      CRISIS '50
Grant, Cary           Film      GUNGA DIN '39 ****
Grant, Cary           Film      HIS GIRL FRIDAY '40 ****
Grant, Cary           Film      HOLIDAY '38
Grant, Cary           Film      HOUSEBOAT '58
Grant, Cary           Film      INDISCREET '58
Grant, Cary           Film      MONKEY BUSINESS '52
Grant, Cary           Film      MY FAVORITE WIFE '40
Grant, Cary           Film      NORTH BY NORTHWEST '59 ****
Grant, Cary           Film      NOTORIOUS '46
Grant, Cary           Film      PEOPLE WILL TALK '51
Grant, Cary           Film      ROOM FOR ONE MORE '52
Grant, Cary           Film      SHE DONE HIM WRONG '33 ****
Grant, Cary           Film      SUSPICION '41
Grant, Cary           Film      THAT TOUCH OF MINK '62
Grant, Cary           Film      THE BISHOP'S WIFE '47
Grant, Cary           Film      THE GRASS IS GREENER '60
Grant, Cary           Film      THE LAST OUTPOST '35
Grant, Cary           Film      THE PHILADELPHIA STORY'40****
Grant, Cary           Film      THE TOAST OF NEW YORK '37
Grant, Cary           Film      TOPPER '37
Grant, Cary           Film      WINGS IN THE DARK '35
Grant, Cary           Nee       ARCHIBALD LEACH
Grant, Hugh           Film      SIRENS '94
Grant, Lee            Nee       LYOVA ROSENTHAL
Granville, Bonita     Film      THE GUILTY '47
Grass, Gunter         Title     THE TIN DRUM
Grateful Dead, The    mr Hit    TRUCKIN'
Graves, Peter         Series    MISSION IMPOSSIBLE tv
Graves, Robert        Title     I, CLAUDIUS
Gray, Harold          Cartoon   LITTLE ORPHAN ANNIE
Gray, Sally           Film      GREEN FOR DANGER '46 ****
Gray, Sally           Film      LADY IN DISTRESS '39
```

Greaves, R.B. m	Hit Song	TAKE A LETTER, MARIA
Greaza, Walter	Series	TREASURY MEN IN ACTION tv
Green, Graham	Film	LOOKS AND SMILES '81
Green, Henry	Title	LOVING
Greene, Graham	Film	CLEARCUT '91
Greene, Graham	Title	BRIGHTON ROCK
Greene, Graham	Title	OUR MAN IN HAVANA
Greene, Graham	Title	THE HEART OF THE MATTER
Greene, Lorne	Hit Song	RINGO
Greene, Lorne	Series	BATTLESTAR GALACTIA tv
Greene, Lorne	Series	BONANZA tv
Greene, Richard	Film	SUBMARINE PATROL '38
Greene, Richard	Series	THE ADVENTURES OF ROBIN HOOD tv
Greenstreet,Sydney	Film	THREE STRANGERS '46
Greenwood, Joan	Film	THE AMOROUS MR. PRAWN '62
Greenwood, Joan	Film	TIGHT LITTLE ISLAND '49 ****
Greenwood, Joan	Film	YOUNG WIVES' TALE '51
Gregson, John	Film	JACQUELINE '56
Gregson, John	Film	ROONEY '58
Greif, Andreas	Pen Name	ANDREAS GRYPHIUS po & w
Grey, Joel	Nee	JOE KATZ
Grieco, Richard	Series	BOOKER tv
Grier, Pam	Film	COFFY '73
Grier, Pam	Film	THE BIG BIRD CAGE '72
Grieve, Christopher Murray	Pen Name	HUGH MacDIARMID
Grieve,Christopher	Pen Name	HUGH MacDIARMID
Griffith, Andy	Film	A FACE IN THE CROWD '57
Griffith, Andy	Film	ONIONHEAD '58
Griffith, Andy	Series	MATLOCK tv
Griffith, Melanie	Film	A STRANGER AMONG US '92
Griffith, Melanie	Film	PACIFIC HEIGHTS '90
Griffith, Melanie	Film	PARADISE '91
Grindel, Eugene	Pen Name	PAUL ELUARD
Grinevsky, Aleksandr S.	Pen Name	ALEKSANDR GRIN
Grodin, Charles	Film	BEETHOVEN '92
Gronberg, Ake	Film	SAWDUST AND TINSEL '53 ****
Guardino, Harry	Film	JIGSAW '68
Guido di Pietro	Aka	FRA ANGELICO
Guinness, Alec	Film	DAMN THE DEFIANT! '62
Guiness, Alec	Film	LAWRENCE OF ARABIA '62 ****
Guinness, Alec	Film	OLIVER TWIST '48 ****
Guinness, Alec	Film	OUR MAN IN HAVANA '60
Guinness, Alec	Film	THE HORSE'S MOUTH '58
Guinness, Alec	Film	THE LADYKILLERS '55
Guinness, Alec	Film	THE LAVENDER HILL MOB '51
Guinness, Alec	Film	THE PRISONER '55
Guinness, Alec	Film	THE PROMOTER '52
Guinness, Alec	Film	THE SCAPEGOAT '59
Guinness, Alec	Film	TUNES OF GLORY '60 ****
Guiry, Tom	Film	SANDLOT '93
Gulager, Clu	Series	THE VIRGINIAN tv
Gurie, Sigrid	Film	FORGOTTEN WOMAN '39
Guttenberg, Steve	Film	DINER '82
Gwynne, Fred	Series	THE MUNSTERS tv
Hackett, Buddy	Nee	LEONARD HACKER
Hackman, Gene	Film	BITE THE BULLET '75 ****
Hackman, Gene	Film	HOOSIERS '86
Hackman, Gene	Film	MISUNDERSTOOD '84
Hackman, Gene	Film	RIOT '69
Hackman, Gene	Film	SCARECROW '73
Hackman, Gene	Film	THE CONVERSATION '74

Hackman, Gene	Film	THE FRENCH CONNECTION '71****
Hagen, Uta	Film	THE OTHER '72
Hagerty, Julie	Film	GOODBYE, NEW YORK '85
Haggard, Henry(Sir)	Title	SHE
Hagman, Larry	Role	J.R. EWING in Dallas tv
Hagman, Larry	Series	DALLAS tv
Haim, Corey	Film	LUCAS '86
Hale, Alan Jr	Series	GILLIGAN'S ISLAND tv
Hale, Barbara	Role	DELLA STREET IN Perry Mason tv
Hale, Barbara	Series	PERRY MASON tv
Haley, Alex	Title	ROOTS
Haley, Bill & the Comets	mr Hit	ROCK AROUND THE CLOCK
Hall, Arch Jr.	Film	THE SADIST '63
Hall, Huntz	Films	SEE Gorcey and Hall
Hall, Jon	Film	LAST OF THE REDMEN '47
Hall, Monty	Host	LET'S MAKE A DEAL tv
Hall, Peter	Film	THE PEDESTRIAN '74
Hallaren, Jane	Film	LIANNA '83
Halop, Billy	Film	YOU'RE NOT SO TOUGH '40
Hamill, Mark	Film	RETURN OF THE JEDI '83
Hamill, Mark	Film	THE EMPIRE STRIKES BACK'80****
Hamilton, George	Film	A THUNDER OF DRUMS '61
Hamilton, George	Film	LOVE AT FIRST BITE '79
Hamilton, George	Film	THE POWER '68
Hamilton, George	Film	THE VICTORS '63
Hamilton, Linda	Series	BEAUTY AND THE BEAST tv
Hamilton, Neil	Film	AMERICA '24
Hamlin, Harry	Film	BLUE SKIES AGAIN '83
Hammer	Nee	STANLEY KIRK BURRELL
Hammer M.C. mr	Hit	YOU CAN'T TOUCH THIS
Hammerstein, Oscar	Musical	ALLEGRO
Hammett, Dashiell	Title	THE MALTESE FALCON
Hand, David d	Film	BAMBI '42 ****(animated)
Handel, George Frederic	Comp	ACIS AND GALATEA
Handel,George Frideric	Comp	MESSIAH
Handel,George Frideric	Comp	SAUL
Handel,George Frideric	Opera	ALCINA
Handel,George Frideric	Opera	ATALANTA
Handel,George Frideric	Opera	ORLANDO
Handel,George Frideric	Opera	SOSARME
Handy, W.C. mj c	Comp	SAINT LOUIS BLUES
Hanks, Tom	Film	BIG '88
Hanks, Tom	Film	DRAGNET '87
Hanks, Tom	Film	FOREST GUMP '94 ****
Hanks, Tom	Film	JOE VERSUS THE VOLCANO '90
Hanks, Tom	Film	PHILADELPHIA '93
Hanks, Tom d+	Film	THAT THING YOU DO '96
Hannah, Deryl	Film	SPLASH '84
Hanson, Lars	Film	THE WIND '28 ****
Hardenberg,Friedrich	Pen Name	NOVALIS
Hardin, Ty	Series	BRONCO tv
Harding, Ann	Film	ENCHANTED APRIL '35
Harding, Ann	Film	HOLIDAY '30
Harding, Ann	Film	JANIE '44
Harding, Ann	Film	PRESTIGE '32
Harding, Ann	Film	THE FOUNTAIN ,34
Harding, Ann	Film	THE LADY CONSENTS '36
Harding, Ann	Film	WHEN LADIES MEET '33
Hardwicke, Cedric	Film	FOREVER AND A DAY '43
Hardy, Oliver	Film	ZENOBIA '39
Hardy, Oliver	Films	SEE "Laurel & Hardy" for films

```
Hardy, Thomas        Title        JUDE THE UNKNOWN
Hardy, Thomas        Title        UNDER THE GREENWOOD TREE
Hargreaves, John     Film         THE ODD ANGRY SHOT '79
Hari, Mata           Aka          MARGARETHA ZELLE
Harlow, Jean         Film         BOMBSHELL '33
Harlow, Jean         Film         LIBELED LADY '36 ****
Harlow, Jean         Film         PLATINUM BLONDE '31
Harlow, Jean         Film         RED-HEADED WOMAN '32
Harlow, Jean         Film         RIFFRAFF '35
Harlow, Jean         Film         SARATOGA '37
Harlow, Jean         Film         WIFE VS. SECRETARY '36
Harlow, Jean         Nee          HARLEAN CARPENTIER
Harmon, Mark         Film         AFTER THE PROMISE '87
Harper, Jessica      Film         SUSPIRIA '77
Harper, Valerie      Series       RHODA tv
Harper, Valerie      Series       THE HOGAN FAMILY tv
Harrelson, Woody     Film         KINGPIN '96
Harris, Bud          Film         MOON OVER HARLEM '39
Harris, Ed           Film         KNIGHTRIDERS '81
Harris, Ed           Film         THE ABYSS '89
Harris, Joel C. Story Teller      UNCLE REMUS
Harris, John         Pen Name     JOHN WYNDHAM
Harris, Julie        Film         THE HAUNTING '63
Harris, Julie        Film         THE HIDING PLACE '75
Harris, Neil Patrick Series       DOOGIE HOWSER, M.D. tv
Harris, Richard      Film         A MAN CALLED HORSE '70
Harris, Richard      Film         JUGGERNAUT '74
Harris, Richard      Film         THE HERO '72
Harris, Wendell B Jr. d+ Film     CHAMELEON STREET '91
Harrison, Gregory    Series       TRAPPER JOHN, M.D. tv
Harrison, Kathlene   Film         A CHRISTMAS CAROL '51 ****
Harrison, Rex        Film         ESCAPE '48
Harrison, Rex        Film         MAJOR BARBARA '41****
Harrison, Rex        Film         THE CONSTANT HUSBAND '55
Harrison, Rex        Film         THE HAPPY THIEVES '62
Harrison, Rex        Film         THE LONG DARK HALL '51
Harrison, Rex        Film         UNFAITHFULLY YOURS '48 ****
Harrison, Rex        Nee          REGINALD CAREY
Harrold, Kathryn     Film         THE SENDER '82
Harron, Robert       Film         INTOLERANCE '16 ****
Harrow, Lisa         Film         SUNDAY '97 ****
Hart, Delores        Film         LISA '62
Hart, Dolores        Film         WHERE THE BOYS ARE '60
Hart, Ian            Film         LAND AND FREEDOM '96
Hart, Ian            Film         NOTHING PERSONAL '97
Hart, Johnny         Cartoon      WIZARD OF ID
Hart, Lorenz         Hit Song     THERE'S A SMALL HOTEL
Hart, Lorenz lyrics  Song         THOU SWELL
Harte, Bret          Title        THE LUCK OF ROARING CAMP
Hartley, Mariette    Film         M.A.D.D. '83
Harvey, Laurence     Film         ROMEO AND JULIET '54
Harvey, Laurence     Film         ROOM AT THE TOP '59 ****
Harvey, Laurence     Film         THE SILENT ENEMY '58
Harvey, Laurence     Film         THE TRUTH ABOUT WOMEN '58
Harvey, Laurence     Nee          LARUSHKA SKIKNE
Harvey, Laurence d+Film           THE CEREMONY '63
Haskell, David       Film         GODSPELL '73
Hasselhoff, David    Series       BAYWATCH tv
Hasselhoff, David    Series       KNIGHT RIDER tv
Hatcher, Teri        Series       LOIS AND CLARK tv
Hatlo, Jimmy         Cartoon      LITTLE IODINE
```

Hauer, Rutger	Film	SOLDIER OF ORANGE '79
Hauer, Rutger	Film	THE HITCHER '86
Hauer, Rutger	Film	THE OSTERMAN WEEKEND '83
Havens, Richie	Film	WOODSTOCK '70 ****
Havilland, Olivia de	Film	DEVOTION '46
Havilland, Olivia de	Film	LIBEL '59
Havilland, Olivia de	Film	MY COUSIN RACHEL '52
Havilland, Olivia de	Film	MY LOVE CAME BACK '40
Havilland, Olivia de	Film	NOT AS A STRANGER '55
Havilland, Olivia de	Film	PRINCESS O'ROURKE '43
Havilland, Olivia de	Film	THE GREAT GARRICK '37
Havilland, Olivia de	Film	THE HEIRESS '49 ****
Hawke, Ethan	Film	ALIVE '93
Hawke, Ethan	Film	GATTACA '97
Hawkins, Jack	Film	FRONT PAGE STORY '54
Hawkins, Jack	Film	THE INTRUDER '55
Hawkins, Jack	Film	THE SEEKERS '54
Hawkins, Jack	Film	THE TWO-HEADED SPY '58
Hawkins,Coleman mj	Hit	BODY AND SOUL
Hawn, Goldie	Film	BIRD ON A WIRE '90
Hawn, Goldie	Film	OVERBOARD '87
Hawn, Goldie	Film	PRIVATE BENJAMIN '80
Hawn, Goldie	Film	THE FIRST WIVE'S CLUB '96
Hayden, Sterling	Film	FLAMING FEATHER '51
Hayden, Sterling	Film	HELLGATE '52
Hayden, Sterling	Film	SUDDENLY '54
Hayden, Sterling	Film	THE KILLING '56
Hayden, Sterling	Film	THE LAST COMMAND '55
Haydn, Joseph	Comp	ERDODY-String quartets Op.76
Haydn, Joseph	Comp	LONDON-Symphonies Nos. 93,104
Haydn,Franz Joseph	Comp	THE CREATION
Hayes, Helen	Film	A FAREWELL TO ARMS '32
Hayes, Helen	Film	ANOTHER LANGUAGE '33
Hayes, Helen	Film	THE WHITE SISTER '33
Hayes, Helen	Nee	HELEN BROWN
Hayes, Isaac	Film	SAVE THE CHILDREN '73
Hayes, Isaac	Film	WATTSTAX '73
Haynes, Lloyd	Series	ROOM 222 tv
Hays, Robert	Film	AIRPLANE! '80
Hayter, James	Film	TRIO '50
Hayward, Louis	Film	THE HOUSE BY THE RIVER '50
Hayward, Louis	Film	THE SAINT IN NEW YORK '38
Hayward, Susan	Film	ADA '61
Hayward, Susan	Film	DEADLINE AT DAWN '46
Hayward, Susan	Film	I'LL CRY TOMORROW '55
Hayward, Susan	Film	THE STOLEN HOURS '63
Hayward, Susan	Film	THUNDER IN THE SUN '59
Hayward, Susan	Film	TOP SECRET AFFAIR '57
Hayward, Susan	Film	TULSA '49
Hayward, Susan	Nee	EDYTHE MARRINER
Haywood, Chris	Film	STRIKEBOUND '83
Haywood, Chris	Film	THE CLINIC '82
Hayworth, Rita	Film	GILDA '46
Hayworth, Rita	Film	LADY IN QUESTION '40
Hayworth, Rita	Film	SALOME '53
Hayworth, Rita	Film	THE STORY ON PAGE ONE '59
Hayworth, Rita	Nee	MARGARITA CANSINO
Heard, John	Film	BETWEEN THE LINES '77
Hedren, Tippi	Film	THE BIRDS '63
Heflin, Van	Film	KID GLOVE KILLER '42
Heflin, Van	Film	PATTERNS '56

Heflin, Van	Film	POSSESSED '47
Heflin, Van	Film	SATURDAY'S HEROES '37
Heflin, Van	Film	THE PROWLER '51
Heflin, Van	Film	THE RAID '54
Heflin, Van	Film	THE RUTHLESS FOUR 68
Heller, Joseph	Title	CATCH-22
Hellman, Lillian	Play	THE LITTLE FOXES
Hellman, Lillian	Play	TOYS IN THE ATTIC
Hellman, Lillian	Play	WATCH ON THE RHINE
Hemingway, Ernest	Title	A FAREWELL TO ARMS
Hemingway, Ernest	Title	MEN WITHOUT WOMEN
Hemingway, Ernest	Title	OLD MAN AND THE SEA
Hemingway, Ernest	Title	THE SUN ALSO RISES
Hemmings, David	Film	THIRST '79
Hemsley, Sherman	Series	THE JEFFERSONS tv
Hemsley, Sherman	Sitcom	AMEN tv
Henderson, Florence	Series	THE BRADY BUNCH tv
Hendrix, Jimi mr	Hit	ARE YOU EXPERIENCED?
Hendry, Ian	Film	REPULSION '65 ****
Henie, Sonja	Film	ICELAND '42
Henner, Marilu	Series	EVENING SHADE tv
Henreid, Paul	Film	PARDON MY FRENCH '51
Henreid, Paul	Film	THE SCAR '48
Henreid, Paul	Film	THE SPANISH MAIN '45
Henriksen, Lance	Film	PUMPKINHEAD '88
Henschke, Alfred	Pen Name	KLABUND w & po
Henson, Jim	Creator	MUPPETS
Henson, Jim & Creatures Film		BABE '95
Henson, Jim d+ & puppets Film		THE DARK CRYSTAL '83
Hepburn, Audrey	Film	CHARADE '63
Hepburn, Audrey	Film	THEY ALL LAUGHED '81
Hepburn, Audrey	Role	RIMA in Green Mansions
Hepburn, Katharine	Film	ADAM'S RIB '49 ****
Hepburn, Katharine	Film	BRINGING UP BABY '38 ****
Hepburn, Katharine	Film	LITTLE WOMEN '33 ****
Hepburn, Katharine	Film	MARY OF SCOTLAND '36
Hepburn, Katharine	Film	ROOSTER COGBURN '75
Hepburn, Katharine	Film	STAGE DOOR '37 ****
Hepburn, Katharine	Film	SUMMERTIME '55
Hepburn, Katharine	Film	THE AFRICAN QUEEN '51 ****
Hepburn, Katharine	Film	THE LION IN WINTER '68 ****
Hepburn, Katharine	Film	THE LITTLE MINISTER '34
Hepburn, Katharine	Film	THE PHILADELPHIA STORY'40****
Hepburn, Katharine	Film	UNDERCURRENT '46
Hepburn, Katharine	Film	WOMAN OF THE YEAR '42
Hepburn, Katharine	Role	GIGI on Broadway
Herbert, Victor	Comp	BABES IN TOYLAND
Herbert, Victor	Operetta	THE RED MILL
Herman's Hermits mr	Hit	WONDERFUL WORLD
Herman, Jerry	Comp	MAME
Herman, Pee-Wee	Nee	PAUL RUBENFELD
Herriman, George	Cartoon	KRAZY KAT
Hersey, John	Title	INTO THE VALLEY
Hershey, Barbara	Film	DEFENSELESS '91
Hershey, Barbara	Film	TUNE IN TOMORROW . . . '90
Hershey, Barbara	Nee	BARBARA HERZSTINE
Herzog, Emile	Pen Name	ANDRE MAUROIS
Hesse, Herman	Title	SIDDHARTHA
Hesse, Hermann	Title	DEMIAN
Hesse, Hermann	Title	STEPPENWOLF
Hesseman, Howard	Series	HEAD OF THE CLASS tv

Heston, Charlton	Film	ARROWHEAD '53
Heston, Charlton	Film	BAD FOR EACH OTHER '53
Heston, Charlton	Film	BEN-HUR '59
Heston, Charlton	Film	THE HAWAIIANS '70
Heston, Charlton	Film	PLANET OF THE APES '68
Heston, Charlton	Film	SKYJACKED '72
Heston, Charlton	Film	THE SAVAGE '52
Heston, Charlton	Film	THE TEN COMMANDMENTS '56 ****
Heston, Charlton	Film	TOUCH OF EVIL '58 ****
Heston, Charlton	Series	THE COLBYS tv
Hewett,Christopher	Series	MR. BELVEDERE tv
Heywood, Anne	Film	I WANT WHAT I WANT '72
Hibbert, Eleanor	Pen Names	ELEANOR BURFORD, VICTORIA HOLT
Hibbert, Eleanor	Pen Names	JEAN PLAIDY, PHILIPPA CARR
Hickman, Dwayne	Series	THE MANY LOVES OF DOBIE GILLIS tv
Hicks, Sir Seymour	Film	SCROOGE '35
Higgins, Joel	Series	BEST OF THE WEST tv
Hill, Arthur	Film	THE ANDROMEDA STRAIN '71
Hill, Arthur	Series	OWEN MARSHALL,COUNSELOR AT LAW tv
Hill, Bernard	Film	BELLMAN AND TRUE '88
Hiller, Wendy	Film	A MAN FOR ALL SEASONS '66 ****
Hiller, Wendy	Film	MAJOR BARBARA '41 ****
Hiller, Wendy	Film	PYGMALION '38 ****
Hindle, Art	Film	THE SURROGATE '84
Hindman, Earl	Role	WILSON in Home Improvement tv
Hines, Gregory	Film	TAP '89
Hirsch, Judd	Series	DEAR JOHN tv
Hirsch, Judd	Series	TAXI tv
Hirt, Al mj	Tune	JAVA
Hitchcock,Alfred d	Film	CHAMPAGNE '28
Hitchcock,Alfred d	Film	DIAL "M" FOR MURDER '54
Hitchcock,Alfred d	Film	FAMILY PLOT(h's last) '76
Hitchcock,Alfred d	Film	LIFEBOAT '44
Hitchcock,Alfred d	Film	PSYCHO '23
Hitchcock,Alfred d	Film	ROPE '48 + or -
Hitchcock,Alfred d	Film	SABOTAGE '36
Hitchcock,Alfred d	Film	STRANGERS ON A TRAIN '51 ****
Hitchcock,Alfred d	Film	THE LADY VANISHES '38 ****
Hitchcock,Alfred d	Film	THE PARADINE CASE '48
Hitchcock,Alfred d	Film	TOPAZ '69
Hitchcock,Alfred d	Film	VERTIGO '45
Ho, Don	Song	TINY BUBBLES
Hobson, Valerie	Film	BRIDE OF FRANKENSTEIN '35****
Hobson, Valerie	Film	GREAT EXPECTATIONS '46 ****
Hobson, Valerie	Film	THIS MAN IS NEWS '38
Hodge, Stephanie	Series	NURSES tv
Hoffman, Dustin	Film	AMERICAN BUFFALO '96
Hoffman, Dustin	Film	HERO '92
Hoffman, Dustin	Film	KRAMER VS. KRAMER '79 ****
Hoffman, Dustin	Film	LENNY '74 ****
Hoffman, Dustin	Film	LITTLE BIG MAN '70 ****
Hoffman, Dustin	Film	MIDNIGHT COWBOY '69 ****
Hoffman, Dustin	Film	OUTBREAK '95
Hoffman, Dustin	Film	THE GRADUATE '67 ****
Hoffman, Dustin	Film	TOOTSIE '82
Hoffman, Dustin	Role	RATSO in Midnight Cowboy '69
Hogan, Paul	Film	"CROCODILE" DUNDEE '86
Hogarth, Burne	Cartoon	TARZAN
Hogarth, Wm. P.	Title	THE RAKE'S PROGRESS
Hogarth,William P.	Title	MARRIAGE ALA MODE
Holbrook, Hal	Film	THE FOG '78

```
Holden, William         Film        EXECUTIVE SUITE '54
Holden, William         Film        FEDORA '78
Holden, William         Film        MEET THE STEWARTS '42
Holden, William         Film        NETWORK '76 ****
Holden, William         Film        PICNIC '55
Holden, William         Film        S.O.B. '81
Holden, William         Film        STALAG 17 '53 ****
Holden, William         Film        SUNSET BLVD. '50 ****
Holden, William         Film        TEXAS '41
Holden, William         Film        THE BRIDGES AT TOKO-RI '54
Holden, William         Film        THE EARTHLING '80
Holden, William         Film        THE KEY '58
Holden, William         Film        THE PROUD AND PROFANE '56
Holden, William         Film        THE TURNING POINT '52
Holden, William         Film        THE WILD BUNCH '69 ****
Holden, William         Film        YOUNG AND WILLING '43
Holden, William         Nee         WILLIAM BEEDLE
Holiday, Billie         Nee         ELEANORA FAGAN
Holiday, Billie mj      Hit         STRANGE FRUIT
Holiday, Judy           Film        THE MARRYING KIND '52
Holliday, Judy          Film        BELLS ARE RINGING '60
Holliday, Judy          Nee         JUDITH TUVIM
Holliman, Earl          Film        SMOKE '70
Holliman, Earl          Film        THE BISCUIT EATER '72
Holly, Buddy & the Crickets mr Hit THAT'LL BE THE DAY
Holm, Celeste           Film        COME TO THE STABLE '49
Holman, Bill            Cartoon     SMOKEY STOVER
Holt, Jack              Film        DIRIGIBLE '31
Holt, Jack              Film        FLIGHT '29
Holt, Jack              Film        WHIRLPOOL '34
Holt, Patrick           Film        SERENA '62
Holt, Tim               Film        HITLER'S CHILDREN '43
Holt, Tim               Film        THE MAGNIFICENT AMBERSONS '42****
Holt, Victoria          Pen Names   PHILLIPA CARR, JANE PLAIDY
Hope, Bob               Film        ALIAS JESSE JAMES '59
Hope, Bob               Film        MY FAVORITE BLONDE '42
Hope, Bob               Film        ROAD TO SINGAPORE '40
Hope, Bob               Film        ROAD TO ZANZIBAR '41
Hope, Bob               Film        SORROWFUL JONES '49
Hope, Bob               Film        THE CAT AND THE CANARY '39
Hope, Bob               Film        THE LEMON DROP KID '51
Hope, Bob               Film        THE PALEFACE '46
Hope, Bob               Film        THE ROAD TO HONG KONG '62
Hope, Bob               Film        THE SEVEN LITTLE FOYS '55
Hope, Bob               Film        WHERE THERE'S LIFE '47
Hopkins, Anthony        Film        AUGUST '96
Hopkins, Anthony        Film        HOWARDS END '92 ****
Hopkins, Anthony        Film        NIXON '95
Hopkins, Anthony        Film        SHADOWLANDS '93
Hopkins, Anthony        Film        THE DAWNING '88
Hopkins, Anthony        Film        THE EDGE '97
Hopkins, Anthony        Film        THE ELEPHANT MAN '80
Hopkins, Anthony        Film        THE REMAINS OF THE DAY '93
Hopkins, Miriam         Film        OLD ACQUAINTANCE '43
Hopkins, Miriam         Film        SPLENDOR '35
Hopkins, Miriam         Film        THE LADY WITH RED HAIR '40
Hopkins, Miriam         Film        THE STRANGER'S RETURN '33
Hopkins, Miriam         Film        THESE THREE '36 ****
Hopkins, Miriam         Film        TROUBLE IN PARADISE '32 ****
Hopkins, Miriam         Film        WOMAN CHASES MAN '37
Hopper, Dennis          Film        BACKTRACK '89
```

Hopper, Dennis	Film	NAILS '92
Hopper, Dennis	Film	THE AMERICAN FRIEND '77
Hopper, Hedda	Nee	ELDA FURRY
Horne, Lena	Song	ONE FOR MY BABY
Horsley, Lee	Series	MATT HOUSTON tv
Horsley, Lee	Series	PARADISE tv
Horton, Peter	Film	THE BABY-SITTERS CLUB '95
Hoskins, Bob	Film	HEART CONDITION '90
Hoskins, Bob	Film	THE LONG GOOD FRIDAY '81
Houdini, Harry	Nee	EHRICH WEISS
Houlihan, Major	Charac	LORETTA SWIT in M.A.S.H. tv
Houston,Whitney mr	Hit	THE GREATEST LOVE
Howard, Ken	Series	THE WHITE SHADOW tv
Howard, Leslie	Film	BERKELEY SQUARE '33
Howard, Leslie	Film	CAPTURED '33
Howard, Leslie	Film	INTERMEZZO '39
Howard, Leslie	Film	SPITFIRE '42
Howard, Leslie	Film	STAND-IN '37
Howard, Leslie	Nee	LESLIE STAINER
Howard, Leslie d+	Film	PYGMALION '38 ****
Howard, Leslie d+	Film	"PIMPERNEL" SMITH '41
Howard, Moe	Nee	MOSES HOROWITZ
Howard, Ron	Role	OPIE
Howard, Ron	Series	HAPPY DAYS tv
Howard, Ron d	Film	PARENTHOOD '89
Howard, Ron d	Film	THE PAPER '94
Howard, Ronald	Film	FATE TAKES A HAND '61
Howard, Trevor	Film	DUST '85
Howard, Trevor	Film	LIGHT YEARS AWAY '81
Howard, Trevor	Film	MALAGA '60
Howard, Trevor	Film	WINDWALKER '80
Howell, C. Thomas	Film	THE OUTSIDERS '83
Howes, Sally Ann	Film	THURSDAY'S CHILD '43
Hudson, Rochelle	Film	SHOW THEM NO MERCY! '35
Hudson, Rock	Film	A FAREWELL TO ARMS '57
Hudson, Rock	Film	BLINDFOLD '66
Hudson, Rock	Film	GIANT '56 ****
Hudson, Rock	Film	ICE STATION ZEBRA '68
Hudson, Rock	Film	NEVER SAY GOODBYE '56
Hudson, Rock	Film	SECONDS '66
Hudson, Rock	Film	SEMINOLE '53
Hudson, Rock	Film	THE GOLDEN BLADE '53
Hudson, Rock	Film	THE LAWLESS BREED '52
Hudson, Rock	Film	THE TARNISHED ANGELS '58
Hudson, Rock	Film	THIS EARTH IS MINE '59
Hudson, Rock	Film	TOBRUK '67
Hudson, Rock	Nee	ROY SCHERER Jr(later Fitzgerald)
Hudson, Rock	Series	McMILLAN AND WIFE tv.
Hughes, Barnard	Film	DA '88
Hughes, Barnard	Series	THE CAVANAUGHS tv
Hughes, Richard	Title	A HIGH WIND IN JAMAICA
Hugo, Victor	Title	THE TOILERS OF THE SEA
Hulce, Tom	Film	AMADEUS '84
Hulce, Tom	Film	THE INNER CIRCLE '91
Hume, Cronyn	Film	COCOON '85
Humperdink,Engelbert	Nee	ARNOLD DORSEY
Hunt, Helen	Film	TWISTER '96
Hunt, Helen	Series	MAD ABOUT YOU tv
Hunt, Marsha	Film	NONE SHALL ESCAPE '44
Hunter, Bill	Film	BACKROADS '77
Hunter, Evan	Pen Names	ED McBAIN, HUNT COLLINS

Hunter, Henry	Film	YELLOWSTONE '36
Hunter, Holly	Film	MISS FIRECRACKER '89
Hunter, Holly	Film	THE PIANO '93
Hunter, Ian	Film	THE LONG VOYAGE HOME '40
Hunter, Jeffrey	Film	COUNT FIVE AND DIE '58
Hunter, Jeffrey	Film	HELL TO ETERNITY '60
Hunter, Jeffrey	Film	NO MAN IS AN ISLAND '62
Hunter, Jeffrey	Film	SAILOR OF THE KING '53
Hunter, Jeffrey	Series	TEMPLE HOUSTON tv
Hunter, Kim	Nee	JANET COLE
Hunter, Tab	Film	POLYESTER '81
Hunter, Tab	Film	THE AROUSERS '70
Huppert, Isabelle	Film	CACTUS '86
Huppert, Isabelle	Film	PASSION '82
Huppert, Isabelle	Film	THE STORY OF WOMEN '88
Hurd, Hugh	Film	SHADOWS '60
Hurt, John	Film	CHAMPIONS '83
Hurt, John	Film	SCANDAL '89
Hurt, Mary Beth	Film	D.A.R.Y.L. '85
Hurt, Mary Beth	Nee	MARY SUPINGER
Hurt, William	Film	SMOKE '95
Hurt, William	Film	THE DOCTOR '91
Hussey, Olivia	Film	BLACK CHRISTMAS '75
Hussey, Olivia	Film	ROMEO AND JULIET '68
Hussey, Ruth	Film	LOUISA '50
Huston, Anjelica	Film	THE ADDAMS FAMILY '91
Huston, Anjelica	Film	THE DEAD '87
Huston, Anjelica	Film	THE GRIFTERS '90
Huston, Anjelica	Film	THE WITCHES '90
Huston, Walter	Film	ABRAHAM LINCOLN '30
Huston, Walter	Film	DODSWORTH '36 ****
Huston, Walter	Film	MISSION TO MOSCOW '43
Huston, Walter	Film	RAIN '32
Huston, Walter	Film	THE BEAST OF THE CITY '32
Huston, Walter	Film	THE CRIMINAL CODE '31
Huston, Walter	Film	THE RULING VOICE '31
Huston, Walter	Film	THE TREASURE OF THE SIERRA MADRE '48 ****
Hutton Timothy	Film	ICEMAN '84
Hutton, Betty	Film	ANNIE GET YOUR GUN '50
Hutton, Betty	Film	THE PERILS OF PAULINE '47
Hutton, Betty	Nee	BETTY THORNBERG
Hutton, Robert	Film	ALWAYS TOGETHER '48
Hutton, Timothy	Film	DANIEL '83
Hutton, Timothy	Film	TAPS '81
Huxley, Aldous	Title	BRAVE NEW WORLD
Huxley, Aldous	Title	EYELESS IN GAZA
Huxley, Aldous	Title	POINT COUNTER POINT
Hyde-White,Wilfred	Series	THE ASSOCIATES tv
Hyer, Martha	Film	A GIRL NAMED TAMIKO '62
Hylands, Scott	Series	NIGHT HEAT tv
Ibarra, Mertha	Film	GUANTANAMERA '97 ****
Ibsen, Hebrik	Charac	ASE
Ibsen, Henrik	Play	BRAND
Ibsen, Henrik	Play	GHOSTS
Ibsen, Henrik	Play	HEDDA GABLER
Ibsen, Henrik	Play	PEER GYNT
Ibsen, Henrik	Play	THE MASTER BUILDERS
Ibsen, Henrik	Play	THE VIKINGS OF HELGOLAND
Idles, Cinnamon	Film	KIDCO '84
Idol, Billy	Nee	WILLIAM BROAD

Ilsa	Heroine	CASABLANCA '42
Inge, William	Play	BUSSTOP
Inge, William	Play	PICNIC
Inge, William	Title	COME BACK LITTLE SHEBA
Ionesco, Eugene	Play	RHINOCEROS
Ionesco, Eugene	Play	THE BALD SOPRANO
Ireland, Jill	Film	CHINO '75
Ireland, John	Film	I SAW WHAT YOU DID '65
Ireland, John	Film	RAILROADED '47
Ireland, John	Film	THE SCARF '51
Irons, Jeremy	Film	DAMAGE '92
Irons, Jeremy	Film	KAFKA '91
Irons, Jeremy	Film	M. BUTTERFLY '93
Irons, Jeremy	Film	MOONLIGHTING '82 ****
Irons, Jeremy	Film	STEALING BEAUTY '96
Irons, Jeremy	Film	WATERLAND '92
Irving, John	Charac.	GARP
Isley Bros.,The mr	Hit	IT'S YOUR THING
Ito, Robert	Series	QUINCY tv
Ives, Burl	Film	SO DEAR TO MY HEART '49
Ives, Burl	Film	THE McMASTERS '70
Ives, Charles	Comp	THREE PLACES IN NEW ENGLAND
Iwashita, Shima	Film	AN AUTUMN AFTERNOON '62
Jabbar,Kareem Abdul	Nee	LEW ALCINDOR
Jackson 5 mr	Hit	ABC
Jackson, Glenda	Film	BUSINESS AS USUAL '87
Jackson, Glenda	Film	HEDDA '75
Jackson, Glenda	Film	STEVIE '78
Jackson, Glenda	Film	THE MUSIC LOVERS '71
Jackson, Glenda	Film	THE NELSON AFFAIR '73
Jackson, H. H.	Heroine	RAMONA
Jackson, Janet mr	Hit	NASTY
Jackson, Janet mr	Hit	RHYTHM NATION
Jackson, Kate	Series	CHARLIE'S ANGELS tv
Jackson, Shirley	Title	THE LOTTERY
Jackson,Michael mr	Hit	THRILLER
Jacobsson, Ulla	Film	SMILES OF A SUMMER NIGHT'55****
Jaglom, Henry d+	Film	ALWAYS '85
James, Harry	Hit Song	SLEEPY TIME GAL
James, Henry	Title	THE AMBASSADORS
James, Henry	Title	THE GOLDEN BOWL
James, Henry	Title	THE WINGS OF THE DOVE
James, Tommy & the Shandells mr Hit		CRIMSOM AND CLOVER
Jameson, House	Series	THE ALDRICH FAMILY tv
Jannings, Emil	Film	THE LAST COMMAND '28 ****
Janssen, David	Film	THE WORD '78
Janssen, David	Nee	DAVID MEYER
Janssen, David	Series	HARRY-O tv
Janssen, David	Series	THE FUGITIVE tv
Jason, Rick	Series	COMBAT tv
Jay and the Americans mr Hit		THE MAGIC MOMENT
Jazzy Jeff and the Fresh Prince mr Hit		SUMMERTIME
Jeanneret, Chas. Edouard Aka		Le CORBUSIER ac & p
Jeans, Ursula	Film	CAVALCADE '33 ****
Jefferson Airplane mr	Hit	WHITE RABBIT
Jefford, Barbara	Film	ULYSSES '67
Jeffreys, Anne	Series	TOPPER tv
Jeffries, Lionel	Film	THE CRIMSON BLADE '63
Jeffries, Lionel	Film	YOU MUST BE JOKING! '65
Jennings, Claudia	Film	TRUCK STOP WOMEN '74
Jethro Tull mr	Hit	AQUALUNG

Jett, Joan mr	Hit	I LOVE ROCK AND ROLL
Jobim, Antonio Carlos Song		THE GIRL FROM IPANEMA
Joel, Billy mr	Hit	PIANO MAN
Joel, Billy mr	HitSong	WE DIDN'T START THE FIRE
John, Elton	Hit	SAD SONG
John, Elton	Hit Song	CANDLE IN THE WIND
John, Elton	Nee	REGINALD DWIGHT
Johns, Glynis	Film	FRIEDA '47
Johns, Glynis	Film	NUKIE '93
Johns, Glynis	Film	THE BEACHCOMBER '55
Johns, Glynis	Film	THE COURT JESTER '56 ****
Johns, Glynis	Film	THE HALFWAY HOUSE '43
Johns, Glynis	Film	THE SWORD AND THE ROSE '53
Johns, Tracy Camilla Film		SHE'S GOTTA HAVE IT '86
Johnson, Ben	Film	GRAYEAGLE '78
Johnson, Chic	Film	GOLD DUST GERTIE '31
Johnson, Don	Nee	DONALD WAYNE
Johnson, Don	Series	MIAMI VICE tv
Johnson, Kyle	Film	THE LEARNING TREE '69
Johnson, Van	Film	BATTLEGROUND '49
Johnson, Van	Film	INVITATION '52
Johnson, Van	Film	REMAINS TO BE SEEN '53
Johnson, Van	Film	SLANDER '56
Johnson, Van	Film	THE ENEMY GENERAL '60
Johnson, Van	Film	THE SIEGE AT RED RIVER '54
Johnston, Lynn	Cartoon	FOR BETTER OR FOR WORSE
Jolson, Al	Film	GO INTO YOUR DANCE '35
Jolson, Al	Film	THE SINGING FOOL '28
Jolson, Al	Nee	ASA YOELSON
Jones, Barry	Film	SEVEN DAYS TO NOON '50 ****
Jones, Carolyn	Series	THE ADDAMS FAMILY tv
Jones, Charles"Buck" Film		LAZYBONES '25
Jones, Christopher Film		THREE IN THE ATTIC '68
Jones, David	Series	THE MONKEES tv
Jones, Henry	Series	CHANNING tv
Jones, James	Title	FROM HERE TO ETERNITY
Jones, James	Title	SOME CAME RUNNING
Jones, James Earl	Film	THE GREAT WHITE HOPE '70
Jones, Jennifer	Film	CARRIE '52
Jones, Jennifer	Film	THE SONG OF BERNADETTE'43****
Jones, Jennifer	Film	WE WERE STRANGERS '49
Jones, Jennifer	Nee	PHYLLIS ISLEY
Jones, Paul	Film	PRIVILEGE '67
Jones, Shirley	Film	OAKLAHOMA! '55
Jones, Shirley	Series	THE PARTRIDGE FAMILY tv
Jones, Spike mj&c	Hit	COCKTAILS FOR TWO
Jones, Tom	Nee	THOMAS WOODWARD
Jones, Tommy Lee	Film	VOLCANO '97
Jones,Edgar Allan,Jr Series		ACCUSED TV
Jong, Erica	Title	FEAR OF FLYING
Jonson, Ben	Homily	"O RARE"
Joplin, Janice mr	Hit	ME AND BOBBY McGEE
Joplin,Scott mj,c	Comp	MAPLE LEAF RAG
Jordan Neil, d	Film	CRYING GAME '92
Jory, Victor	Film	THE UNKNOWN GUEST '43
Jory, Victor	Series	MANHUNT tv
Josephson, Erland	Film	SCENES FROM A MARRIAGE'73****
Jourdan, Louis	Nee	LOUIS GENDRE
Joyce, James	Title	A PORTRAIT OF THE ARTIST AS A YOUNG MAN
Joyce, James	Title	FINNEGAN'S WAKE

Joyce, James	Title	ULYSSES
Judd, Ashley	Film	RUBY IN PARADISE '93
Judd, Edward	Film	INVASION '66
Judson, Edward Z.C.	Pen Name	NED BUNTLINE
Julia, Raul	Film	ROMERO '89
Julia, Raul	Film	THE PENITENT '88
Jump, Gordon	Series	WKRP IN CINCINNATI tv
Jurgens, Curt	Film	I AIM AT THE STARS '60
Justice Jms. Robertson	Film	RAISING THE WIND '61
Justice, Jms. Robertson	Film	FOXHOLE IN CAIRO '61
Kafka, Franz	Title	AMERIKA
Kafka, Franz	Title	THE TRIAL
Kahn, Chaka mr	Hit	I FEEL FOR YOU
Kane, Carol	Film	NORMAN LOVES ROSE '82
Kant, Immanuel	Title	PERPETUAL PEACE
Kaplan, Gabe	Role	KOTTER tv
Kaplan, Gabriel	Series	WELCOME BACK KOTTER tv
Kapoor, Shashi	Film	SIDDHARTHA '73
Kapoor, Shashi	Film	THE HOUSEHOLDER '63
Karina, Anna	Film	BAND OF OUTSIDERS '64
Karina, Anna	Film	THE NUN '66
Karloff, Boris	Film	BEDLAM '46
Karloff, Boris	Film	BRIDE OF FRANKENSTEIN'35****
Karloff, Boris	Film	FRANKENSTEIN '31
Karloff, Boris	Film	SCARFACE '32
Karloff, Boris	Film	TARGETS '68
Karloff, Boris	Film	THE GHOUL '34
Karloff, Boris	Film	THE BODY SNATCHER '45
Karloff, Boris	Film	THE CLIMAX '44
Karloff, Boris	Film	THE INVISIBLE RAY '36
Karloff, Boris	Film	THE LOST PATROL '34 ****
Karloff, Boris	Film	THE MUMMY '32
Karloff, Boris	Film	THE OLD DARK HOUSE '32
Karloff, Boris	Film	THE RAVEN '35
Karloff, Boris	Film	THE SORCERERS '67
Karloff, Boris	Film	THE WALKING DEAD '36
Karloff, Boris	Nee	WILLIAM HENRY PRATT
Karns, Roscoe	Series	ROCKY KING, INSIDE DETECTIVE tv
Kastner, Peter	Film	YOU'RE A BIG BOY NOW '66
Kaufman, Bel	Title	UP THE DOWN STAIRCASE
Kaufman, Philip	Film	GOLDSTEIN '65
Kaye, Danny	Film	ME AND THE COLONEL '58
Kaye, Danny	Film	THE COURT JESTER '56 ****
Kaye, Danny	Film	THE FIVE PENNIES '59
Kaye, Danny	Film	THE KID FROM BROOKLYN '46
Kaye, Danny	Nee	DAVID KAMINSKY
Kaye, Sammy	Hit Song	UNTIL TOMORROW
Kazan, Elia d	Film	AMERICA, AMERICA '63 ****
Keach, Stacy	Film	DOC '71
Keach, Stacy	Film	LUTHER '74
Keach, Stacy	Film	ROADGAMES '81
Keach, Stacy	Film	THE KILLER INSIDE ME '76
Keach, Stacy	Role	HAMMER in Mike Hammer tv
Keach, Stacy	Series	MICKEY SPILLANE'S MIKE HAMMER tv
Keane, Bill	Cartoon	THE FAMILY CIRCUS
Keaton, Buster	Film	COLLEGE '27
Keaton, Buster	Film	STEAMBOAT BILL, JR. '28
Keaton, Buster	Film	THE CAMERAMAN '28
Keaton, Buster d+	Film	OUR HOSPITALITY '23 ****
Keaton, Buster d+	Film	SHERLOCK, JR. '24 ****
Keaton, Buster d+	Film	THE GENERAL '27 ****

Keaton, Diane	Film	ANNIE HALL '77 ****
Keaton, Diane	Film	CRIMES OF THE HEART '86
Keaton, Diane	Film	INTERIORS '78
Keaton, Diane	Film	REDS '81
Keaton, Diane	Film	SLEEPER '73
Keaton, Diane	Film	THE FIRST WIVE'S CLUB '96
Keaton, Diane	Film	GODFATHER PART II '74 ****
Keaton, Diane	Nee	DIANE HALL
Keaton, Michael	Film	MULTIPLICITY '96
Keaton, Michael	Film	THE PAPER '94
Keaton, Michael	Nee	MICHAEL DOUGLAS
Keel, Howard	Film	DESPERATE SEARCH '52
Keel, Howard	Film	KISMET '55
Keel, Howard	Film	SEVEN BRIDES FOR SEVEN BROTHERS '54 ****
Keel, Howard	Film	THE BIG FISHERMAN '59
Keel, Howard	Film	WACO '66
Keel, Howard	Nee	HAROLD LEEK
Keeler, Ruby	Film	42ND STREET '33 ****
Keeler, Ruby	Film	COLLEEN '36
Keen, Malcolm	Film	THE MANXMAN '29
Keene, Carolyn	Charac	NANCY DREW
Keitel, Harvey	Film	CAMORRA '86
Keitel, Harvey	Film	CLOCKERS '95
Keitel, Harvey	Film	CORRUPT '83
Keitel, Harvey	Film	DEATHWATCH '80
Keitel, Harvey	Film	FINGERS '78
Keitel, Harvey	Film	MEAN STREETS '73 ****
Keith, Brian	Film	SCANDALOUS JOHN '71
Keith, Brian	Film	THOSE CALLOWAYS '65
Keith, Brian	Series	FAMILY AFFAIR tv
Keith, Brian	Series	HARDCASTLE & McCORMICK tv
Keith, David	Film	HEARTBREAK HOTEL '88
Keith, Larry	Series	THE BAXTERS tv
Keith, Penelope	Sitcom	TO THE MANOR BORN tv
Kellerman, Sally	Film	BREWSTER McCLOUD '70
Kellerman, Sally	Film	THE KGB '86
Kelly, Brian	Series	FLIPPER tv
Kelly, Gene	Film	AN AMERICAN IN PARIS '51
Kelly, Gene	Film	BRIGADOON '54
Kelly, Gene	Film	LES GIRLS '57
Kelly, Gene d+	Film	ON THE TOWN '49 ****
Kelly, Gene	Film	SINGIN' IN THE RAIN '52 ****
Kelly, Gene	Film	THE PIRATE '48
Kelly, Gene	Film	THE THREE MUSKETEERS '48
Kelly, Gene	Film	THE TUNNEL OF LOVE '58
Kelly, Grace	Film	REAR WINDOW '54 ****
Kelly, Grace	Film	THE SWAN '56
Kelly, Jim	Film	BLACK BELT JONES '74
Kelly, Paul	Film	FEAR IN THE NIGHT '47
Kelly, Paul	Film	THE PAINTED HILLS '51
Kemp, Gary & Martin	Film	THE KRAYS '90
Kendall, Suzy	Film	FRAULEIN DOKTOR '69
Kendall, Suzy	Film	THE GAMBLERS '69
Kennedy, Adam	Series	THE CALIFORNIANS tv
Kennedy, Arthur	Film	KNOCKOUT '41
Kennedy, George	Film	ZIGZAG '70
Kennedy, George	Series	THE BLUE KNIGHT tv
Kennedy, Sarah	Film	THE WORKING GIRLS '73
Kennedy, William	Title	IRONWEED p-f'84
Kennedy, Leon Isaac	Film	PENITENTIARY '79

Kent, Jean	Film	THE WOMAN IN QUESTION ,50
Kern, Jerome	Comp	ROBERTA
Kern, Jerome	Comp	SHOWBOAT
Kern, Jerome	Song	SMOKE GETS IN YOUR EYES
Kern, Jerome	Song	THE LAST TIME I SAW PARIS
Kern, Jerome	Song	THEY DON'T BELIEVE ME
Kerouac, Jack	Title	ON THE ROAD
Kerr, Bill	Film	DUSTY '82
Kerr, Deborah	Film	BLACK NARCISSUS '46 ****
Kerr, Deborah	Film	PLEASE BELIEVE ME '50
Kerr, Deborah	Film	TEA AND SYMPATHY '56
Kerr, Deborah	Film	THE ADVENTURESS '46
Kerr, Deborah	Film	THE ASSAM GARDEN '85
Kerr, Deborah	Film	THE CHALK GARDEN '64
Kerr, Deborah	Film	THE INNOCENTS '61
Kerr, Deborah	Film	THE JOURNEY '59
Kerr, Deborah	Film	THE PRISONER OF ZENDA '52
Kerr, Deborah	Film	THE SUNDOWNERS '60 ****
Kesey, Ken	Title	ONE FLEW OVER THE CUCKOO'S NEST
Kessel, Maurice	Pen Name	MAURICE DRUON
Ketcham, Hank	Cartoon	DENNIS THE MENACE
Ketchum, Dave	Series	CAMP RUNAMUCK tv
Keyes, Evelyn	Film	HERE COMES MR. jORDAN '41****
Keyes, Evelyn	Film	RENEGADES '46
Keyes, Evelyn	Film	THE MATING OF MILLIE '48
Keyes, Evelyn	Film	THE THRILL OF BRAZIL '46
Khachaturian, Aram	Comp	SABRE DANCE
Khan, Chaka	Nee	YVETTE STEVENS
Kibbee, Guy	Film	BABBITT '34
Kidder, Margot	Film	HEARTACHES '81
Kidder, Margot	Film	SISTERS '73
Kidman, Nicole	Film	THE PEACEMAKER '97
Kiley, Richard	Film	THE LITTLE PRINCE '74
Kilmer, Joyce	Poem	TREES
Kilmer, Val	Film	THE DOORS '91
Kilmer, Val	Film	THE SAINT '97
Kilmer, Val	Film	THUNDERHEART '92
Kilmer, Val	Film	WILLOW '88
Kimitake Hiroaka	Pen Name	YUKIO MISHIMA
King, B.B. mr	Hit	THE THRILL IS GONE
King, Carol	Nee	CAROLE KLEIN
King, Carole mr	Hit	TAPESTRY
King, Frank	Cartoon	GASOLINE ALLEY(early)
King, Larry	Nee	LARRY ZEIGLER
King, Perry	Film	A DIFFERENT STORY '78
King, Perry	Film	THE LORD'S OF FLATBUSH '74
King, Stephan	Title	CHILDREN OF THE CORN
Kingsley, Ben	Film	PASCALI'S ISLAND '88
Kingsley, Ben	Film	SCHINDLER'S LIST '93 ****
Kingsley, Ben	Nee	KRISHNA BANJI
Kinks, The mr	Hit	YOU REALLY GOT ME
Kinski, Klaus	Film	ANDROID '82
Kinski, Klaus	Film	BURDEN OF DREAMS '82
Kinski, Klaus	Film	THE SQUEAKER '65
Kinski, Klaus	Film	WOYZECK '78
Kinski, Nastassia	TitleRole	TESS '80
Kinski, Nastassja	Nee	NASTASSJA NAKSYZNYSKI
Kipling, Rudyard	Title	KIM, JUST SO STORIES
Kipling, Rudyard	Title	RIKKI-TIKKI-TAVI
Kirchenbauer, Bill	Series	JUST THE TEN OF US tv
Kirkland, Sally	Film	ANNA '87

```
Kiss    mr            Hit         ROCK AND ROLL ALL NIGHT
Kissinger, Henry      Title       THE WHITEHOUSE YEARS
Klee, Paul            Painting    FISH MAGIC
Klein, Robert         Film        RIVALS '72
Kline, Kevin          Film        I LOVE YOU TO DEATH '90
Kline, Kevin          Film        SILVERADO '85
Klugman, Jack         Series      QUINCY, M.E. tv
Klugman, Jack         Series      THE ODD COUPLE tv
Knight, Gladys        Hit Song    IF I WERE YOUR WOMAN
Knight, Gladys & the Pips mr Hit MIDNIGHT TRAIN TO GEORGIA
Knight, Shirley       Film        DUTCHMAN '66
Knight, Shirley       Film        THE COUCH '62
Knight, Ted           Nee         TADEUS WLADYSLAW KONOPKA
Knox, Alexander       Film        WILSON '44
Knox, Terence         Series      TOUR OF DUTY tv
Koestler, Arthur      Title       DARKNESS AT NOON
Koppel, Ted           Host        NIGHTLINE tv
Kortner, Fritz        Film        PANDORA'S BOX '28 ****
Koscina, Sylva        Film        LOVE AND MARRIAGE '64
Koteas, Elias         Film        THE ADJUSTER '91
Krause, Brian         Film        SLEEPWALKERS '92
Kristofferson,Kris Film           SONGWRITER '84
Kristofferson,Kris Film           VIGILANTE FORCE '76
Kruger, Otto          Film        THEY WON'T FORGET '37 ****
Kuosawa, Akiro  d     Film        RAN '85
Kurtz, Swoosie        Series      SISTERS tv
Kuznetsov, Anatoly Vasilyevich Pen Name A. ANATOLI
Kwan, Nancy           Film        THE WORLD OF SUZY WONG '60
Kyd, Thomas           Title       SPANISH TRAGEDY, THE
L.L. Cool J  mr       Hit         MAMA SAID KNOCK YOU OUT
La Bahome             Role        MIMI
Ladd, Alan            Film        ALL THE YOUNG MEN '60
Ladd, Alan            Film        AND NOW TOMORROW '44
Ladd, Alan            Film        CAPTAIN CAREY, U.S.A. '50
Ladd, Alan            Film        HELL ON FRISCO BAY '55
Ladd, Alan            Film        SANTIAGO '56
Ladd, Alan            Film        SASKATCHEWAN '54
Ladd, Alan            Film        SHANE '53
Ladd, Alan            Film        THE BADLANDERS '58
Ladd, Alan            Film        THE BLACK KNIGHT '54
Ladd, Alan            Film        THE GREAT GATSBY '49
Ladd, Alan            Film        THE IRON MISTRESS '52
Ladd, Alan            Film        THE MAN IN THE NET '59
Ladd, Alan            Film        THIS GUN FOR HIRE '42
Ladd, Alan            Film        WHISPERING SMITH '48
Ladd, Cheryl          Nee         CHERYL STOPPELMOOR
Ladd, Cheryl          Series      CHARLIE'S ANGELS tv
Lahr, Bert            Film        THE WIZARD OF OZ '39
Lahr, Bert            Role  COWARDLY LION in The Wizard of Oz
Lahti, Christine      Film        HOUSEKEEPING '87
Lahti, Christine      Film        RUNNING ON EMPTY '88
Lai, Francis          Comp        LOVE STORY
Laing, Robert David Title         THE DIVIDED SELF
Lake, Arthur          Film        BLONDIE Films '40's
Lake, Arthur          Series      BLONDIE tv
Lake, Veronica        Film        RAMROD '47
Lake, Veronica        Film        SULLIVAN'S TRAVELS '41 ****
Lake, Veronica        Film        THE SAINTED SISTERS '48
Lake, Veronica        Nee         CONSTANCE OCKLEMAN
Lalo, Edouard         Comp        LE RIO dY's
Lalo, Edouard         Comp        SYMPHONIE ESPAGNOLE
```

Lamarr, Hedy	Film	LET'S LIVE A LITTLE '48
Lamarr, Hedy	Film	THE CONSPIRATORS '44
Lamarr, Hedy	Film	THE FEMALE ANIMAL '58
Lamarr, Hedy	Nee	HEDWIG KIESLER
Lamas, Lorenzo	Series	FALCON CREST tv
Lamb, Charles	Essay	DREAM CHILDREN
Lamb, Charles	Pen Name	ELIA
Lamour, Dorothy	Film	A MEDAL FOR BENNY '45
Lamour, Dorothy	Film	DISPUTED PASSAGE '39
Lamour, Dorothy	Film	DIXIE '43
Lamour, Dorothy	Film	THE HURRICANE '37
Lamour, Dorothy	Film	THE JUNGLE PRINCESS '36
Lamour, Dorothy	Film	TYPHOON '40
Lamour, Dorothy	Nee	MARY KAUMEYER
Lancaster, Burt	Film	A CHILD IS WAITING '63
Lancaster, Burt	Film	AIRPORT '70
Lancaster, Burt	Film	ATLANTIC CITY '80 ****
Lancaster, Burt	Film	FROM HERE TO ETERNITY '53****
Lancaster, Burt	Film	JUDGEMENT AT NUREMBERG'61****
Lancaster, Burt	Film	LAWMAN '71
Lancaster, Burt	Film	ROCKET GIBRALTAR '88
Lancaster, Burt	Film	SCORPIO '73
Lancaster, Burt	Film	SEPARATE TABLES '58 ****
Lancaster, Burt	Film	SEVEN DAYS IN MAY '64
Lancaster, Burt	Film	THE DEVIL'S DISCIPLE '59
Lancaster, Burt	Film	THE HALLELUJAH TRAIL '65
Lancaster, Burt d+	Film	THE KENTUCKIAN '55
Lancaster, Burt	Film	THE KILLERS '46 ****
Lancaster, Burt	Film	THE LEOPARD '63 ****
Lancaster, Burt	Film	THE MIDNIGHT MAN '74
Lancaster, Burt	Film	THE RAINMAKER '56
Lancaster, Burt	Film	THE SCALPHUNTERS '68
Lancaster, Burt	Film	THE SWIMMER '68
Lancaster, Burt	Film	THE TRAIN '64 ****
Lancaster, Burt	Film	THE UNFORGIVEN '60
Lancaster, Burt	Film	THE YOUNG SAVAGES '61
Lancaster, Burt	Film	TRAPEZE '56
Lancaster, Burt	Series	MOSES--THE LAWGIVER tv
Landau, Martin	Series	MISSION IMPOSSIBLE tv
Landers, Judy	Series	MADAME'S PLACE tv
Landis, John d+	Film	SCHLOCK '71
Landon, Michael	Nee	EUGENE OROWITZ
Landon, Michael	Series	BONANZA tv
Landon, Michael	Series	HIGHWAY TO HEAVEN tv
Landon, Michael	Series	LITTLE HOUSE ON THE PRAIRIE tv
Lane, Allan	Film	CONSPIRACY '39
Lane, Charles d+	Film	SIDEWALK STORIES '89
Lane, Priscilla	Film	BLUES IN THE NIGHT '41
Lane, Sara	Film	I SAW WHAT YOU DID '65
Lang, Fritz d	Film	METROPOLIS '26 ****
Lang, Fritz d	Film	SPIES '28
Lange, Hope	Series	THE GHOST AND MRS. MUIR tv
Lange, Jessica	Film	A THOUSAND ACRES '97
Lange, Jessica	Film	COUNTRY '84
Lange, Jessica	Film	FRANCES '82
Lange, Jessica	Film	TOOTSIE '82
Lansbury, Angela	Charac	AUNTIE MAME
Lansbury, Angela	Film	PLEASE MURDER ME '56
Lansbury, Angela	Film	SEASON OF PASSION '59
Lansbury, Angela	Film	THE MIRROR CRACK'D '80
Lansbury, Angela	Series	MURDER, SHE WROTE tv

Lansing, Robert	Series	TWELVE O'CLOCK HIGH tv
Lantz, Walter	Cartoon	WOODY WOODPECKER
Lanza, Mario	Film	FOR THE FIRST TIME '59
Lanza, Mario	Film	SERENADE '56
Lanza, Mario	Film	THE GREAT CARUSO '51
Lanza, Mario	Nee	ALFREDO COCOZZA
Lanzmann, Claude d	Film	SHOAH '85 **** (documentary)
LaPlante, Laura	Film	THE CAT AND THE CANARY '27
Larsen, Capt. Wolf	Charac	in THE SEA WOLF by JACK LONDON
Larsen, Keith	Series	BRAVE EAGLE tv
Larson, Gary	Cartoon	THE FAR SIDE
Lasser, Louise	Film	CRIMEWAVE '85
Lasser, Louise	Series	MARY HARTMAN, MARY HARTMAN tv
Laughton, Charles	Film	MUTINY ON THE BOUNTY '35 ****
Laughton, Charles	Film	PAYMENT DEFERRED '32
Laughton, Charles	Film	REMBRANDT '36
Laughton, Charles	Film	RUGGLES OF RED GAP '35 ****
Laughton, Charles	Film	THE BEACHCOMBER '38
Laughton, Charles	Film	THE PRIVATE LIFE OF HENRY VIII '33 ****
Laughton, Charles	Film	THE SUSPECT '44
Laughton, Charles	Film	THE TUTTLES OF TAHITI '42
Laura	Charac	in THE GLASS MENAGERIE
Laurance, Matthew	Series	DUET tv
Laurel, Stan	Films	SEE Laurel & Hardy -- below
Laurel, Stan	Nee	ARTHUR JEFFERSON
Laurel & Hardy	Film	A CHUMP AT OXFORD '40
Laurel & Hardy	Film	BABES IN TOYLAND '34
Laurel & Hardy	Film	BONNIE SCOTLAND '35
Laurel & Hardy	Film	JITTERBUGS '43
Laurel & Hardy	Film	SONS OF THE DESERT '33
Laurel & Hardy	Film	THE BOHEMIAN GIRL '36
Laurel & Hardy	Film	THE FLYING DEUCES '39
Laurie, Piper	Film	RUBY '77
Lavin, Linda	Series	ALICE tv
Law, John Phillip	Film	DANGER: DIABOLIK '67
Lawford, Peter	Series	THE THIN MAN tv
Lawrence, D.H.	Heroine	MIRIAM
Lawrence, D.H.	Title	LADY CHATTERLY'S LOVER
Lawrence, D.H.	Title	SONS AND LOVERS
Lawrence, D.H.	Title	THE RAINBOW
Lawrence, D.H.	Title	WOMEN IN LOVE
Lawrence, Steve	Nee	SIDNEY LEIBOWITZ
Lawrence, Vicki	Series	MAMA'S FAMILY tv
Le Brock, Kelly	Film	THE WOMAN IN RED '84
Leachman, Cloris	Series	PHYLLIS tv
Learned, Michael	Film	NURSE '80
Learned, Michael	Series	NURSE tv
Learned, Michael	Series	THE WALTONS tv
Lease, Rex	Film	THE MONSTER WALKS '32
Leaud, Jean-Pierre	Film	THE FOUR HUNDRED BLOWS '59****
Leaud, Jean-Pierre	Film	TWO ENGLISH GIRLS '71
LeBlanc, Maurice	Sleuth	ARSENE LUPIN
Led Zeppelin mr	Hit	STAIRWAY TO HEAVEN
Lederer, Francis	Film	PANDORA'S BOX '28 ****
Lederer, Francis	Film	THE GAY DECEPTION '35
Lederer, Francis	Film	VOICE IN THE WIND '44
Lee, Brandon	Film	THE CROW '94
Lee, Brenda	Nee	BRENDA MAE TARPLEY
Lee, Brenda s mr	Song	I'M SORRY
Lee, Bruce	Film	ENTER THE DRAGON '73

```
Lee, Bruce              Nee         LEE YUEN KAM
Lee, Christopher        Film        DIAGNOSIS MURDER '76
Lee, Christopher        Film        JOCKS '87
Lee, Christopher        Film        SCARS OF DRACULA '70
Lee, Christopher        Film        THE DEVIL'S BRIDE '68
Lee, Christopher        Film        THE FACE OF FU MANCHU '65
Lee, Christopher        Film        THEATRE OF DEATH '67
Lee, Gypsy Rose         Nee         ROSE LOUISE HOVICK
Lee, Manfred            Pen Name    ELLERY QUEEN
Lee, Michelle           Nee         MICHELLE DUSIAK
Lee, Peggy              Nee         NORMA EGSTROM
Leger, Alexis Saint-Leger Pen Name  ST. JOHN PERSE
Leger, Marie            Pen Name    ST. JOHN PERSE
Lehar, Franz            Comp        THE MERRY WIDOW
Lehar, Franz            Comp        ZIGEUNERLIEGE
Lehar, Franz            Operetta    EVA
Leigh, Janet            Film        WIVES AND LOVERS '63
Leigh, Janet            Nee         JEANETTE MORRISON
Leigh, Mike   d         Film        SECRETS AND LIES '96
Leigh, Vivien           Film      A STREETCAR NAMED DESIRE'51****
Leigh, Vivien           Film        GONE WITH THE WIND '39 ****
Leigh, Vivien           Film        SHIP OF FOOLS '65 ****
Leigh, Vivien           Film        STORM IN A TEACUP '37
Leigh, Vivien           Film        THE DEEP BLUE SEA '55
Leigh, Vivien           Film        WATERLOO BRIDGE '40
Leigh, Vivien           Nee         VIVIEN HARTLEY
LeMat, Paul             Film        HANDLE WITH CARE '77
LeMat, Paul             Film        MELVIN AND HOWARD '80
LeMat, Paul             Film        STRANGE INVADERS '83
Lemmon, Jack            Film        ALEX AND THE GYPSY '76
Lemmon, Jack            Film        AVANTI '72
Lemmon, Jack            Film        CHINA SYNDROME '79 ****
Lemmon, Jack            Film        GOOD NEIGHBOR SAM '64
Lemmon, Jack            Film        GRUMPIER OLD MEN '95
Lemmon, Jack            Film        LUV '67
Lemmon, Jack            Film        MACARONI '85
Lemmon, Jack            Film        MISSING '82
Lemmon, Jack            Film        PHFFFT! '54
Lemmon, Jack            Film        SOME LIKE IT HOT '59 ****
Lemmon, Jack            Film        THE APARTMENT '60 ****
Lemmon, Jack            Role        ENS. PULVER in Mr. Roberts
Lennon, John   mr       Hit         IMAGINE
Lenya, Lotte            Film        THE THREEPENNY OPERA '31
Lenz, Kay               Film        STRIPPED TO KILL '87
Leonora                 Charac      HEROINE in Il Trovatore
Lerner, Alan Jay        Musical     MY FAIR LADY
Lerner, Michael         Film        ANGUISH '87
LeRoy, Baby             Film        IT'S A GIFT '34 ****
LeRoy, Mervyn           Film        MISTER ROBERTS '55 ****
Leung, Tony             Film        THE LOVER '92
Levin, Ira              Play        NO TIME FOR SARGEANTS
Levinson, Barry d       Film        AVALON '90
Lewis, C. S.            Title       PERELANDRA
Lewis, Emmanuel         Series      WEBSTER tv
Lewis, Huey             Nee         HUGH CREGG
Lewis, Jerry            Film        CINDERFELLA '60
Lewis, Jerry            Film        HOLLYWOOD OR BUST '56
Lewis, Jerry            Film        PARDNERS '56
Lewis, Jerry            Film        THE BELLBOY '60
Lewis, Jerry            Film        THE FAMILY JEWELS '65
Lewis, Jerry            Film        THE STOOGE '53
```

Lewis, Jerry	Nee	JOSEPH LEVITCH
Lewis, Shari	Puppet	LAMB CHOP
Lewis, Sinclair	Title	CASS TIMBERLANE
Lewis, Sinclair	Title	IT CAN'T HAPPEN HERE
Lewis, Sinclair	Title	MAIN STREET
Lewis, Ted	Song	ME AND MY SHADOW
Lewis, Jerry Lee mr	Hit	WHOLE LOTTA SHAKIN' GOING ON
Li Fei-kan	Pen Name	PA CHIN
Light, Judith	Series	WHO'S THE BOSS? tv
Lightfoot, Gordon	Hit Song	CAREFREE HIGHWAY
Lillebakken, Johan	Pen Name	JOHAN FALKBERGET
Lincoln, Elmo	Film	TARZAN OF THE APES '18
		(FIRST TARAZAN FILM)
Lincoln, Elmo	Role	TARZAN
Linden, Hal	Nee	HAROLD LIPSHITZ
Linden, Hal	Series	BARNEY MILLER tv
Linder, Max	Film	MAX '22
Lindsay, Margaret	Film	GARDEN OF THE MOON '38
Lindsey, Joseph	Film	AMONGST FRIENDS '93
Linkletter, Art	Host	HOUSE PARTY tv
Linn-Baker, Mark	Series	PERFECT STRANGERS tv
Liotta, Ray	Film	UNFORGETTABLE '96
Lipinski, Eugene	Film	MOONLIGHTING '82 ****
Liszt, Franz	Comp	LES PRELUDES
Little Anthony & the Imperials mr Hit		TEARS ON MY PILLOW
Little Richard mr	Hit	TUTTI FRUTTI
Little, Cleavon	Film	BLAZING SADDLES '73
Lloyd, Emily	Film	WISH YOU WERE HERE '87
Lloyd, Harold	Film	FOR HEAVEN'S SAKE '26 ****
Lloyd, Harold	Film	PROFESSOR BEWARE '38
Lloyd, Harold	Film	SPEEDY '28
Lloyd, Harold	Film	THE FRESHMAN '25 ****
Lloyd, Harold	Film	THE KID BROTHER '27 ****
LoBianco, Tony	Film	DEMON '77
Lockwood, Margaret	Film	BEDELIA '46
Lockwood, Margaret	Film	JASSY '47
Lockwood, Margaret	Film	THE LADY VANISHES '38 ****
Lockwood, Margaret	Film	THE STARS LOOK DOWN '39 ****
Loden, Barbara d+	Film	WANDA '71
Loder, John	Film	NON-STOP NEW YORK '37
Lola	Role	DAMN YANKEES
Lollobrigida, Gina	Film	FAN-FAN THE TULIP '51
Lollobrigida, Gina	Film	FRISKY '55
Lom, Herbert	Film	THE RINGER '52
Lombard, Carole	Film	FOOLS FOR SCANDAL '38
Lombard, Carole	Film	SUPERNATURAL '33
Lombard, Carole	Film	TWENTIETH CENTURY '34 ****
Lombard, Carole	Film	VIGIL IN THE NIGHT '40
Lombard, Carole	Nee	JANE PETERS
London, Jack	Title	THE CALL OF THE WILD
London, Jack	Title	THE SEA WOLF
London, Julie	HitSong	CRY ME A RIVER
Lone, John	Film	THE LAST EMPEROR '87
Long, Shelly	Film	A VERY BRADY SEQUEL '96
Loos, Anita	Title	GENTLEMEN PREFER BLONDS
Lopez, Jennifer	Film	SELENA '97
Lopez, Vincent mj	Theme	NOLA
Lord, Jack	Film	WALK LIKE A DRAGON '60
Lord, Jack	Nee	JOHN JOSEPH RYAN
Lord, Jack	Series	HAWAII FIVE O tv
Lords, Traci	Film	ICE '93

Loren, Sophia	Film	AIDA '53
Loren, Sophia	Film	ARABESQUE '66
Loren, Sophia	Film	FIREPOWER '79
Loren, Sophia	Film	LADY L '65
Loren, Sophia	Film	LUCKY TO BE A WOMAN '56
Loren, Sophia	Film	MADAME '61
Loren, Sophia	Film	THAT KIND OF WOMAN '59
Loren, Sophia	Film	THE BLACK ORCHID '59
Loren, Sophia	Film	THE GOLD OF NAPLES '54
Loren, Sophia	Film	THE MILLIONAIRESS '60
Loren, Sophia	Film	TWO WOMEN '61 ****
Loren, Sophia	Film	YESTERDAY, TODAY, AND TOMORROW '64 ****
Loren, Sophia	Nee	SOPHIA SCICOLONI
Lorre, Peter	Film	CRACK-UP '37
Lorre, Peter	Film	M '31 ****
Lorre, Peter	Film	THANK YOU, MR. MOTO '38
Lorre, Peter	Film	THE VERDICT '46
Lorre, Peter	Film	THINK FAST, MR. MOTO '37
Lorre, Peter	Films	MR. MOTO MOVIES '37 - '65
Lorre, Peter	Nee	LASZIO LOWENSTEIN
Loti, Pierre	Title	MATELOT
Loudon, Dorothy	Lg. Play	ANNIE
Loughlin, Lori	Series	FULL HOUSE tv
Louis, Pierre	Pen Name	PIERRE LOUYS
Lounsbery, John	Film	THE RESCUERS '77
Love, Bessie	Film	BROADWAY MELODY '29
Love, Suzanna	Film	THE BOOGEYMAN '80
Lovejoy, Frank	Film	THE SOUND OF FURY '51
Lovin Spoonful mr	Hit	DO YOU BELIEVE IN MAGIC ?
Lowe, Edmund	Film	ENCHANTED FOREST '45
Lowe, Edmund	Film	ESPIONAGE '37
Lowe, Edmund	Film	THE SQUEAKER '37
Lowe, Rob	Film	MASQUERADE '88
Lowe, Rob	Film	WAYNE'S WORLD '92
Lowry, Malcolm	Title	UNDER THE VOLCANO
Loy, Myrna	Film	AFTER THE THIN MAN '36
Loy, Myrna	Film	BEST YEARS OF OUR LIVES '46****
Loy, Myrna	Film	EVELYN PRENTICE '34
Loy, Myrna	Film	THE THIN MAN '34 ****
Loy, Myrna	Film	THE THIN MAN GOES HOME '44
Loy, Myrna	Film	TOO HOT TO HANDLE '38
Loy, Myrna	Film	TOPAZE '33
Loy, Myrna	Nee	MYRNA WILLIAMS
Lucas, Craig	Play	PRELUDE TO A KISS
Lucci, Susan	Role	ERICA
Lugosi, Bela	Film	BLACK CAT '34
Lugosi, Bela	Film	DRACULA '31
Lugosi, Bela	Film	THE WOLFMAN '41
Lugosi, Bela	Nee	BELA FERENC BLASKO
Lukas, Paul	Film	DOWNSTAIRS '32
Lukas, Paul	Film	WATCH ON THE RHINE '43
Lumley, Joanna	Film	COLD COMFORT FARM '96
Lundigan, William	Film	FOLLOW ME QUIETLY '49
Lunt/Fontanne	Film	THE GUARDSMAN '31
Lupino, Ida	Film	BEWARE, MY LOVELY '52
Lupino, Ida	Film	HIGH SIERRA '41
Lupino, Ida	Film	JENNIFER '53
Lupino, Ida	Film	MOONTIDE '42
Lupino, Ida	Film	THE GAY DESPERADO '36
LuPone, Patti	Musical	EVITA

Lupton, John	Series	BROKEN ARROW tv
Lymon, Frankie mr	Hit	WHY DO FOOLS FALL IN LOVE?
Lynch, John	Film	NOTHING PERSONAL '97
Lynch, Kelly	Film	OSA '85
Lynch, Ken	Series	THE PLAINCLOTHESMAN tv
Lynch, Peg	Series	ETHEL AND ALBERT tv
Lynn, Diana	Film	PEGGY '50
Lynn, Jeffrey	Film	UNDERGROUND '41
Lynn, Robert	Film	KILLER'S CARNIVAL '65
Lynyrd Skynyrd mr	Hit	FREEBIRD
Lyon, Ben	Film	CRIMSON ROMANCE '34
Lys, Lya	Film	L'AGE d'OR '30 ****
Lytell, Ben	Series	ONE MAN'S FAMILY tv
Lytton, Bulwer	Title	LAST DAYS OF POMPEI
Maas, Peter	Title	SERPICO
MacDonald,Jeanette	Film	LOVE ME TONIGHT '32 ****
MacDonald,Jeanette	Film	MAYTIME '37
MacDowell, Andie	Film	GREEN CARD '90
MacDowell, Andie	Film	MULTIPLICITY '96
MacGraw, Ali	Film	GOODBYE, COLUMBUS '69
Mackay, Mary	Pen Name	MARIE CORELLI
Mackintosh,Elizabeth	Pen Names	JOSEPHINE TEY, GORDON DAVIOT
MacLaine, Shirley	Film	A CHANGE OF SEASONS '80
MacLaine, Shirley	Film	THE TURNING POINT '77
MacLaine, Shirley	Nee	SHIRLEY BEATY
MacLane, Barton	Series	THE OUTLAWS tv
MacLeod, Gavin	Series	THE LOVE BOAT tv
MacMurray, Fred	Film	FAIR WIND IN JAVA '53
MacMurray, Fred	Film	THE FAR HORIZONS '55
MacMurray, Fred	Series	MY THREE SONS tv
Macnee, Patrick	Series	THE AVENGERS tv
MacNicol, Peter	Film	DRAGONSLAYER '81
MacVittie, Bruce	Series	THE STREET tv
Madigan, Amy	Film	FEMALE PERVERSIONS '97
Madonna	Album	EROTICA
Madonna	Film	EVITA '96
Madonna	Nee	MADONNA LOUISE CICCONE
Mahler, Gustav	Comp	DAS LIED VAN DER ERDE
Mahler, Gustav	Symph	RESURRECTION SYMPHONY
Mahoney, Jock	Series	THE RANGE RIDER tv
Mailer, Norman	Title	AN AMERICAN DREAM
Mailer, Norman	Title	THE NAKED AND THE DEAD
Majors, Lee	Nee	HARVEY LEE YEARY 2nd
Majors, Lee	Series	THE FALL GUY tv
Majors, Lee	Series	THE SIX MILLION DOLLAR MAN tv
Malden, Karl	Film	ON THE WATERFRONT '54 ****
Malden, Karl	Film	PATTON '70 ****
Malden, Karl	Nee	MALDEN SEKULOVICH
Malden, Karl	Series	THE STREETS OF SAN FRANCISCO tv
Malle, Louis d	Film	DAMAGE '92
Malone, Dorothy	Film	THE TARNISHED ANGELS '58
Malone, Dorothy	Series	PEYTON PLACE tv
Mandan, Robert	Series	SOAP tv
Manilow, Barry	Hit Song	COPOCABANA
Manilow, Barry	Hit Song	I WRITE THE SONGS
Manilow, Barry	Nee	BARRY ALAN PINCUS
Mansfield, Jayne	Film	THE GIRL CAN'T HELP IT
Mansfield, Jayne	Nee	VERA JANE PALMER
March, Fredric	Film	HOMBRE '67
March, Fredric	Film	THE EAGLE AND THE HAWK '33
March, Fredric	Film	THE SIGN OF THE CROSS '32

March, Fredric	Film	THE YOUNG DOCTORS '61
March, Fredric	Nee	FREDERICK BICKEL
Markey, Enid	Series	BRINGING UP BUDDY tv
Marlowe, Christopher	Play	DOCTOR FAUSTUS
Marlowe, Hugh	Film	TWELVE O'CLOCK HIGH '49 ****
Marlowe, Scott	Film	THE COOL AND THE CRAZY '58
Marsh, Jean	Series	UPSTAIRS DOWNSTAIRS tv
Marshall, E.G.	Series	THE NEW DOCTORS tv
Marshall, E.G.	Series	THE DEFENDERS tv
Marshall, Penny	Series	LAVERNE & sHIRLEY tv
Marshall, Peter	Nee	PIERE LaCOCK
Marshall, William	Film	ABBY '74
Martin, Dean	Film	THE BATTLE OF ALGIERS '65
Martin, Dean	Nee	DINO CROCETTI
Martin, Lori	Series	NATIONAL VELVET tv
Martin, Mary	Musical	SOUTH PACIFIC
Marvin, Lee	Series	M SQUAD tv
Marx, Chico	Nee	LEONARD MARX
Marx, Zeppo	Nee	HERBERT MARX
Mason, Janes	Film	COP-OUT '67
Mason, James	Film	THE RECKLESS MOMENT '49
Massenet,Jules-Emile-F,Opera		LECID
Massenet,Jules-Emile-F,Opera		MANON
Massine, Leonide	Ballet	GAITE PARISIENNE
Mathau, Walter	Nee	WALTER MATUSCHANSKAYASKY
Matlin, Marlee	Series	REASONABLE DOUBTS tv
Matthews, Jessie	Film	THE GOOD COMPANIONS '33
Matthews, Liesel	Film	A LITTLE PRINCESS '95
Maugham,W.Somerset	Title	CAKES AND ALE
Maugham,W.Somerset	Title	OF HUMAN BONDAGE
Mayle, Peter	Title	A YEAR IN PROVENCE
Mayron, Melanie	Film	GIRLFRIENDS '78
McCallum, David	Series	THE MAN FROM U.N.C.L.E. tv
McCann, Chuck	Film	THE PROJECTIONIST '71
McCarthy, Andrew	Film	THE BENIKER GANG '85
McCartney, Paul	Hit	BAND ON THE RUN
McCartney, Paul	Song	THIS ONE
McCloskey, Leigh	Film	INFERNO '80
McClure, Doug	Film	AT THE EARTH'S CORE '76
McClure, Doug	Film	NOBODY'S PERFECT '68
McClure, Doug	Film	THE KING'S PIRATE '67
McClure, Marc	Film	THE PERFECT MATCH '87
McCormack, Mary	Film	PRIVATE PARTS '97
McCrea, Joel	Film	MUSTANG COUNTRY '76
McCrea, Joel	Film	RIDE THE HIGH COUNTRY '62 ****
McCrea, Joel	Film	SOUTH OF ST. LOUIS '49
McCrea, Joel	Film	STARS IN MY CROWN '50
McCrea, Joel	Film	SULLIVAN'S TRAVELS '41 ****
McCrea, Joel	Film	THE OKLAHOMAN '57
McCrea, Joel	Film	THE VIRGINIAN '46
McCrea, Joel	Film	WICHITA '55
McCullers, Carson	Tille	THE HEART IS A LONELY HUNTER
McDaniel, George	Film	LEGACY '75
McDonald, Grace	Film	DANCING ON A DIME '40
McDonnell, Mary	Film	DANCE WITH WOLVES '90 ****
McDormand, Frances	o-a Film	FARGO '96
McDowall, Roddy	Film	ARNOLD '73
McDowall, Roddy	Film	LASSIE COME HOME '43
McDowall, Roddy	Film	MY FRIEND FLICKA '43

McDowell, Malcolm	Film	IF.... '68 ****
McDowell, Malcolm	Film	O LUCKY MAN '73 ****
McDowell, Malcom	Film	A CLOCKWORK ORANGE '77
McElwee, Ross d	Film	SHERMAN'S MARCH '86 ****(doc.)
McGann, Paul	Film	DEALERS '89
McGillis, Kelly	Film	THE ACCUSED '88
McGoohan, Patrick	Film	THE QUARE FELLOW '62
McGoohan, Patrick	Film	WALK IN THE SHADOW '66
McGovern,Elizabeth	Film	SHE'S HAVING A BABY '88
McGraw, Charles	Film	ROADBLOCK '51
McGraw, Charles	Film	THE NARROW MARGIN '52
McGraw, Charles	Film	THE THREAT '49
McGraw, Charles	Series	CASABLANCA tv
McGregor, Ewan	Film	TRAINSPOTTING '96
McGuire, Dorothy	Film	A TREE GROWS IN BROOKLYN'45****
McGuire, Dorothy	Film	CLAUDIA '43
McGuire, Dorothy	Film	CLAUDIA AND DAVID '46
McGuire, Dorothy	Film	FRIENDLY PERSUASION '56 ****
McGuire, Dorothy	Film	MAKE HASTE TO LIVE '54
McIntire, John	Film	THE PHENIX CITY STORY '55
McIntire, John	Series	NAKED CITY tv
McIntire, Tim	Film	AMERICAN HOT WAX '78
McKay, Claude	Title	HOME TO HARLEM
McKay, Gardner	Series	ADVENTURES IN PARADISE tv
McKean, Michael	Film	THIS IS SPINAL TAP '84
McKellan, Ian	Film	ZINA '85
McKenna, Virginia	Film	A TOWN LIKE ALICE '56
McKenney, Ruth	Title	MY SISTER EILEEN
McKinney, Nina Mae	Film	HALLELUJAH '29
McLaglen, Victor	Film	A GIRL IN EVERY PORT '28
McLaglen, Victor	Film	GUNGA DIN '39 ****
McLaglen, Victor	Film	THE LOST PATROL '34 ****
McLaglen, Victor	Film	WHAT PRICE GLORY '26
McManus, George	Cartoon	BRINGING UP FATHER
McMurty, Larry	Title	LONESOME DOVE(p-f'86)
McPhatter,Clyde mr	Hit	MONEY HONEY
McQueen, Steve	Film	BULLITT '68
McQueen, Steve	Film	HELL IS FOR HEROES '62
McQueen, Steve	Film	PAPILLON '73
McQueen, Steve	Film	THE BLOB '58
McQueen, Steve	Film	THE GETAWAY '72
McQueen, Steve	Film	THE GREAT ESCAPE '63 ****
McQueen, Steve	Film	THE REIVERS '69
McQueen, Steve	Film	THE SAND PEBBLES '66
McQueen, Steve	Film	THE TOWERING INFERNO '74
McRaney, Gerald	Series	MAJOR DAD tv
McRaney, Gerald	Series	SIMON & SIMON tv
McVey, Patrick	Series	BIG TOWN tv
Meaney, Colm	Film	THE SNAPPER '93
Meatloaf	Nee	MARVIN LEE ADAY
Meeker, Ralph	Film	PATHS OF GLORY '57 ****
Meeker, Ralph	Film	SHADOW IN THE SKY '51
Meeks, Edith	Film	POISON '91
Megan	Charac	THORN BIRDS
Mellencamp,John mr	Hit	HURT SO GOOD
Melville, Herman	Charac	CAPTAIN AHAB,ISHMAEL
Melville, Herman	Title	OMOO
Menjou, Adolphe	Film	THE SNIPER '52
Menjou, Adolphe	Film	THE SWAN '25
Menotti,Gian Carlo	Opera	AMAHL AND THE NIGHT VISITORS
Menotti,Gian Carlo	Opera	THE CONSUL

Mercer, Marian	Series	IT'S A LIVING tv
Mercouri, Melina	Film	PHAEDRA '62
Mercouri, Melina	Film	TOPKAPI '64
Meredith, Burgess	Film	STREET OF CHANCE '42
Meredith, Burgess	Film	THE GAY ADVENTURE '53
Meredith, Burgess	Film	THE STORY OF G.I. JOE '45
Meredith, George	Title	THE EGOIST
Merkel, Una	Film	THE BANK DICK '40 ****
Merman, Ethel	Musical	ANYTHING GOES
Merman, Ethel	Nee	ETHEL ZIMMERMAN
Merrill, Gary	Film	THE HUMAN JUNGLE '54
Michael, Alex	Series	FAMILY TIES tv
Michael, George	Nee	GEORGIOS PANAYIOTOU
Michael, George	Song	FATHER FIGURE
Michael, George mr	Hit	FAITH
Michener, James B.	Title	IBERIA
Midler, Bette	Film	BEACHES '88
Midler, Bette	Film	STELLA '90
Midler, Bette	Film	THAT OLD FEELING '97
Midler, Bette	Film	THE FIRST WIVE'S CLUB '96
Midler, Bette	Film	THE ROSE '79
Mifune, Toshiro	Film	RASHOMON '50 ****
Mifune, Toshiro	Film	SANJURO '62
Mifune, Toshiro	Film	STRAY DOG '49 ****
Mifune, Toshiro	Film	THE HIDDEN FORTRESS '58
Mifune, Toshiro	Film	THE IDIOT '51
Mifune, Toshiro	Film	THE LIFE OF OHARU '52
Mifune, Toshiro	Film	THE SEVEN SAMURAI '54
Mifune, Toshiro	Film	THRONE OF BLOOD '57 ****
Mifune, Toshiro	Film	YOJIMBO '61
Miles, Sylvia	Film	HEAT '72
Miles, Vera	Film	PSYCHO '60 ****
Miles, Vera	Film	THE SEARCHERS '56 ****
Milland, Ray	Film	CALIFORNIA ,46
Milland, Ray	Film	CIRCLE OF DANGER '51
Milland, Ray	Film	CLOSE TO MY HEART '51
Milland, Ray	Film	DIAL M FOR MURDER '54
Milland, Ray	Film	FROGS '72
Milland, Ray	Film	GOLDEN EARRINGS '47
Milland, Ray	Film	IRENE '40
Milland, Ray	Film	LISBON '56
Milland, Ray	Film	MINISTRY OF FEAR '44
Milland, Ray	Film	PANIC IN YEAR ZERO '62
Milland, Ray	Film	REAP THE WILD WIND '42
Milland, Ray	Film	SAFECRACKER '58
Milland, Ray	Film	THE ATTIC '79
Milland, Ray	Film	THE JUNGLE PRINCESS '36
Milland, Ray	Film	THE LOST WEEKEND '45 ****
Milland, Ray	Film	THE THIEF '52
Milland, Ray	Film	UNINVITED '44
Milland, Ray	Nee	REGINALD TRUSCOTT-JONES
Millar, Kenneth	Pen Names	JOHN, JOHN ROSS, ROSS MacDONALD
Millay,Edna St.Vincent	Title	ARIA DE CAPO
Miller, Ann	Nee	LUCILLE COLLIER
Miller, Cincinnatus Hiner	Pen Name	JOAQUIN MILLER
Miller, Glen	Hit Tune	SUNRISE SERANADE
Miller, Henry	Title	TROPIC OF CANCER
Miller, Mark	Film	SAVANNAH SMILES '82
Mills, Hayley	Film	DEADLY STRANGERS '74
Mills, Hayley	Film	POLLYANNA '60
Mills, Hayley	Film	THE MOON-SPINNERS '64

```
Mills, Hayley & John Film   THE TRUTH ABOUT SPRING '65
Mills, John        Film     ABOVE US THE WAVES '56
Mills, John        Film     IN WHICH WE SERVE '42 ****
Mills, John        Film     DULCIMA '71
Mills, John        Film     DUNKIRK '58
Mills, John        Film     ESCAPADE '55
Mills, John        Film     GREAT EXPECTATIONS '45 ****
Mills, John        Film     THE CIRCLE '59
Mills, John        Film     THE COLDITZ STORY '57
Mills, John        Film     THE WAY TO THE STARS '45 ****
Mills, John        Film     THE YOUNG MR. PITT '42
Mills, John        Film     TUNES OF GLORY '60 ****
Mills, Johnny      Film     THE GARDEN '90
Milne, A.A.        Title    NOW WE ARE SIX
Milne, A.A.        Title    WHEN WE WERE VERY YOUNG
Milner, Martin     Series   ADAM 12 tv
Milner, Martin     Series   ROUTE 66 tv
Mineo, Sal         Film     A PRIVATE'S AFFAIR '59
Mineo, Sal         Film     DINO '57
Mineo, Sal         Film     EXODUS '60
Mineo, Sal         Film     TONKA '58
Minghella, Anthony o-d Film THE ENGLISH PATIENT '96
Minnelli, Liza     Film     CABARET '72
Mira, Brigitte     Film EVERY MAN FOR HIMSELF AND GOD etc.'75****
Mirren, Helen      Film     CAL '84
Mitchell, Cameron  Film     GORILLA AT LARGE '54
Mitchell, Cameron  Film     HAUNTS '77
Mitchell, Cameron  Film     INSIDE THE MAFIA '59
Mitchell, Cameron  Film     MONKEY ON MY BACK '57
Mitchell, Joni     Nee      ROBERTA JOAN ANDERSON
Mitchell, Joni  mr Hit      BIG YELLOW TAXI
Mitchell, Sasha    Series   STEP BY STEP tv
Mitchell, Yvonne   Film     DEMONS OF THE MIND '71
Mitchum, Jim       Film     TRACKDOWN '76
Mitchum, Robert    Film     BANDIDO '56
Mitchum, Robert    Film     CROSSFIRE '47
Mitchum, Robert    Film     FOREIGN INTRIGUE '56
Mitchum, Robert    Film     HIS KIND OF WOMAN '51
Mitchum, Robert    Film     HOME FROM THE HILL '60
Mitchum, Robert    Film     MACAO '52
Mitchum, Robert    Film     MY FORBIDDEN PAST '51
Mitchum, Robert    Film     PURSUED '47
Mitchum, Robert    Film     RAMPAGE '63
Mitchum, Robert    Film     RIVER OF NO RETURN '54
Mitchum, Robert    Film     THE AMBASSADOR '84
Mitchum, Robert    Film     THE RACKET '51
Mitchum, Robert    Film     THE STORY OF G.I. JOE '45
Mitchum, Robert    Film     THE SUNDOWNERS '60 ****
Mitchum, Robert    Film     TWO FOR THE SEESAW 62
Mitchum, Robert    Film     YOUNG BILLY YOUNG '69
Mix, Tom           Film     THE RAINBOW TRAIL '25
Modine, Matthew    Film     BIRDY '84
Modine, Matthew    Film     FULL METAL JACKET '87
Modine, Matthew    Film     STREAMERS '83
Modine, Matthew    Film     THE GAMBLE '88
Modine, Matthew    Film     WIND '92
Modot, Gaston      Film     L'AGE d'OR '30 ****
Mohner, Carl       Film     RIFIFI '54 ****
Mohr, Gerald       Film     THE RING '52
Moliere            Play     L'ECOLE DES FEMMES
Moliere     ---    Pen Name JEAN BAPTISTE POQUELIN
```

Moliere, ---	Play	THE DOCTOR IN SPITE OF HIMSELF
Molina, Alfred	Film	MANIFESTO '88
Monahan, Dan	Film	PORKY'S '81
Monet, Claude	Painting	IMPRESSION: SUNRISE
Monet, Claude	Painting	WATERLILIES
Monet, Claude	Subject	HAYSTACKS
Moniz, Antonio	Aka	ANTONIO EGAS MONIZ
Monkees, The mr	Hit	I'M A BELIEVER
Monroe, Marilyn	Film	BUS STOP '56
Monroe, Marilyn	Film	MISFITS '61
Monroe, Marilyn	Film	NIAGRA '53
Monroe, Marilyn	Film	RIVER OF NO RETURN '54
Monroe, Marilyn	Nee	NORMA JEAN MORTENSON,(later) BAKER
Montalban, Ricardo	Film	BORDER INCIDENT '49
Montalban, Ricardo	Film	SOMBRERO '53
Montalban, Ricardo	Series	FANTASY ISLAND tv
Montand, Yves	Film	CESAR AND ROSALIE '72
Montand, Yves	Film	THE CONFESSION '70
Montand, Yves	Film	THE WAGES OF FEAR '52
Montand, Yves	Film	THE WIDE BLUE ROAD '56
Montand, Yves	Film	VINCENT,FRANCOIS,PAUL AND THE OTHERS '74 ****
Montand, Yves	Nee	IVO LEVI
Monteverdi,Claudio	Opera	ORFEO
Montez, Maria	Film	TANGIER '46
Montgomery, Elizabeth	Series	BEWITCHED tv
Montgomery, George	Film	BADMAN'S COUNTRY '58
Montgomery, Lucy Maud	Title	ANNE OF GREEN GABLES
Montgomery, Robert	Film	HERE COMES MR. JORDAN '41 ****
Montgomery, Robert	Film	HIDE-OUT '34
Montgomery, Robert	Film	THE MYSTERY OF MR. X '34
Montgomery, Robert	Film	THEY WERE EXPENDABLE '45 ****
Moody Blues mr	Hit	NIGHTS IN WHITE SATIN
Moody, Ron	Film	DOGPOUND SHUFFLE '75
Moody, Ron	Film	OLIVER! '68 ****
Moody, Ron	Film	THE TWELVE CHAIRS '70
Moody, Ron	Nee	RONALD MOODNICK
Moore, Clayton	Series	THE LONE RANGER tv
Moore, Demi	Film	GHOST '90
Moore, Demi	Film	MORTAL THOUGHTS '91
Moore, Demi	Nee	DEMETRIA GUYNES
Moore, Dudley	Film	ARTHUR '81
Moore, Dudley	Film	BEDAZZLED '67
Moore, Dudley	Film	LOVESICK '83
Moore, Gar	Film	PAISAN '46
Moore, Gary	Nee	THOMAS GARRISON MORFIT
Moore, Grace	Film	I'LL TAKE ROMANCE '37
Moore, Grace	Film	ONE NIGHT OF LOVE '34
Moore, Grace	Film	WHEN YOU'RE IN LOVE '37
Moore, Julianne	Film	SAFE '95
Moore, Mary Tyler	Film	ORDINARY PEOPLE '80 ****
Moore, Robin	Title	THE GREEN BERETS
Moore, Roger	Film	BED AND BREAKFAST '92
Moore, Roger	Film	ESCAPE TO ATHENA '79
Moore, Roger	Film	FFOLKS '80
Moore, Roger	Film	FOR YOUR EYES ONLY '81
Moore, Roger	Film	GOLD '74
Moore, Roger	Film	OCTOPUSSY '83
Moore, Roger	Series	THE ALASKANS tv
Moore, Terry	Film	MIGHTY JOE YOUNG '49
Moore. Grace	Film	THE KING STEPS OUT '36

Moores, Dick	Cartoon	GASOLINE ALLEY
Moorhead, Agnes	Role	ENDORA in Bewitched tv
Morales, Esai	Film	LA BAMBA '87
More, Kenneth	Film	A NIGHT TO REMEMBER '58 ****
More, Kenneth	Film	REACH FOR THE SKY '56
More, Kenneth	Film	SINK THE BISMARCK! '60
More, Thomas	Title	UTOPIA
Moreau, Jeanne	Film	FRANTIC '57
Moreau, Jeanne	Film	GRISBI '53
Moreau, Jeanne	Film	LUMIERE '76
Moreau, Jeanne	Film	THE BRIDE WORE BLACK '68
Moreau, Jeanne	Film	THE LOVERS '58
Moreau, Jeanne	Film	THE SUMMER HOUSE '93
Moreno, Rita	Film	THE RITZ '76
Moreno, Rita	Nee	ROSITA ALVERIO
Morgan, Dennis	Film	GOD IS MY CO-PILOT '45
Morgan, Harry	Nee	HARRY BRATSBURG
Morgan, Harry	Series	AFTERMASH tv
Morgan, Harry	Series	PETE AND GLADYS tv
Morgan, Helen	Film	APPLAUSE '29
Morgan, Henry	Film	SO THIS IS NEW YORK '48
Morgan, Henry(Harry)	Film	THE WELL '51
Morgan, Michele	Film	FABIOLA '49
Morgan, Michele	Film	HIGHER AND HIGHER '43
Morgan, Michele	Film	MARIE ANTOINETTE '55
Morgan, Michele	Film	MAXIME '58
Morgenstern, Maia	Film	THE OAK '92
Mori, Masayuki	Film	PRINCESS YANG KWEI FEI '55 ****
Moriarty, Cathy	Film	RAGING BULL '80 ****
Moriarty, Michael	Film	THE STUFF '85
Morley, Robert	Film	THE OLD DARK HOUSE '63
Morris, Chester	Film	FLIGHT FROM GLORY '37
Morris, Chester	Film	THE PHANTOM THIEF '46
Morris, Chester	Film	THREE GODFATHERS '36
Morris, Judy	Film	THE PLUMBER '80
Morris, Wayne	Film	THE YOUNGER BROTHERS '49
Morrison, Van	Song	BROWN EYED GIRL
Morrow, Jeff	Film	KRONOS '57
Morrow, Jeff	Film	THIS ISLAND EARTH '54
Morrow, Rob	Series	NORTHERN EXPOSURE tv
Morse, David	Film	THE INDIAN RUNNER '91
Morse, Robert	B'wayRole	TRU
Mortensen, Viggo	Film	THE REFLECTING SKIN '90
Moses, Anna Mary Robertson	Aka	GRANDMA MOSES p
Mosley, Roger E.	Film	LEADBELLY '76
Mostel, Zero	Film	MASTERMIND '76
Mostel, Zero	Film	THE ANGEL LEVINE '70
Mostel, Zero	Film	THE FRONT '76 ****
Mostel, Zero	Film	THE PRODUCERS '68
Mozart, Wolfgang A.	Aria	DOVE SONO
Mozart, Wolfgang A.	Comp	CLEMENZO OI TITO
Mozart, Wolfgang A.	Comp	COSI FAN TUTTE
Mozart, Wolfgang A.	Comp	EINE KLEINE NACHTMUSIK
Mozart, Wolfgang A.	Comp	JUPITER SYMPHONY
Mozart, Wolfgang A.	Comp	THE MAGIC FLUTE
Mozart, Wolfgang A.	Opera	DON GIOVANNI
Mozart,Wolfgang A,	Comp	THE MARRIAGE OF FIGARO
Mr. T	Series	THE A TEAM tv
Muhammad, Shams-ud-din	Pen Name	HAFIZ
Mull, Martin	Film	SERIAL '80
Mulligan, Richard	Series	EMPTY NEST tv

Muni, Paul	Film	BORDERTOWN '35
Muni, Paul	Film	I AM A FUGITIVE FROM A CHAIN GANG '32 ****
Muni, Paul	Film	JUAREZ '39
Muni, Paul	Film	SCARFACE '32
Muni, Paul	Film	THE GOOD EARTH '37 ****
Muni, Paul	Film	THE LAST ANGRY MAN '59
Muni, Paul	Film	THE LIFE OF EMILE ZOLA '37 ****
Muni, Paul	Film	THE WORLD CHANGES '33
Muni, Paul	Nee	MUNI WEISENFREUND
Munro, Hector Hugu	Pen Name	SAKI
Munsel, Patrice	Film	MELBA '53
Murdoch, Iris	Title	UNDER THE NET
Murfree, Mary Noailles	Pen Name	CHARLES EGBERT CRADDOCK
Murphy, Audie	Film	ARIZONA RAIDERS '65
Murphy, Audie	Film	DESTRY '54
Murphy, Audie	Film	GUNSMOKE '53
Murphy, Audie	Film	SIERRA '50
Murphy, Audie	Film	WORLD IN MY CORNER '56
Murphy, Eddie	Film	BEVERLY HILLS COP '84
Murphy, Eddie	Film	COMING TO AMERICA '88
Murphy, Eddie	Film	THE NUTTY PROFESSOR '96
Murphy, Eddy	Film	VAMPIRE IN BROOKLYN '95
Murray, Bill	Film	GHOSTBUSTERS '84
Murray, Bill	Film	STRIPES '81
Murray, Don	Film	COTTER '73
Murray, Don	Film	FROM HELL TO TEXAS '58
Murray, Don	Film	SWEET LOVE, BITTER '67
Murray, James	Film	THE CROWD '28 ****
Musante, Tony	Film	THE INCIDENT '67
Musante, Tony	Film	THE MERCENARY '68
Musante, Tony	Series	TOMA tv
Musharrif-uddin	Pen Name	SA'DI
Mussorgsky, Modest	Comp	PICTURES AT AN EXHIBITION
Myers, Russell	Cartoon	BROOM HILDA
Mynster, Karen-Lise	Film	SOFIE '92
Nabokov, Vladimir	Title	ADA
Nabokov, Vladimir	Title	DAR
Nabokov, Vladimir	Title	LOLITA
Nabokov, Vladimir	Title	PALE FIRE
Nabokov, Vladimir	Title	PNIN
Nabors, Jim	Series	GOMER PYLE, U.S.M.C. tv
Nagel, Conrad	Film	DYNAMITE '29
Naipaul, V.S.	Title	A BEND IN THE RIVER
Naipaul, V.S.	Title	A HOUSE FOR MR. BISWAS
Naish, J. Carrol	Film	KING OF ALCATRAZ '38
Naish, J. Carrol	Role	CHARLIE CHAN tv
Nast, Thomas	Cartoons	HARPER'S WEEKLY
Neagle, Anna	Film	IRENE '40
Neagle, Anna	Film	ODETTE '50
Neagle, Anna	Film	SUNNY '41
Neagle, Anna	Film	THE COURTNEY AFFAIR '47
Neagle, Anna	Film	THE YELLOW CANARY '43
Neagle, Anna	Film	VICTORIA THE GREAT '37
Neal, Patricia	Film	BAXTER '73
Neal, Patricia	Film	HUD '63 ****
Neal, Patricia	Film	THE DAY THE EARTH STOOD STILL '51 ****
Neal, Patricia	Film	THE NIGHT DIGGER '71
Neal, Patricia	Film	THE SUBJECT WAS ROSES '68
Neal, Tom	Film	DETOUR '45
Neeson, Liam	Film	CROSSING THE LINE '91
Neeson, Liam	Film	DARKMAN '90

Neeson, Liam	Film	MICHAEL COLLINS '96
Neeson, Liam	Film	SCHINDLER'S LIST '93 ****
Neff, Hildegarde	Film	SVENGALI '55
Negri, Pola	Film	FORBIDDEN PARADISE '24
Neile, Herman Cyril	Sleuth	BULLDOG DRUMMOND
Nelligan, Kate	TitleRol	ELENI '85
Nelson, Barry	Series	MY FAVORITE HUSBAND tv
Nelson, Craig T.	Film	POLTERGEIST '82
Nelson, Craig T.	Series	COACH tv
Nelson, Jessica	Film	PLAINSONG '82
Nelson, Rick mr+	Hit	HELLO MARY LOU
Nelson, Willie	Film	BARBAROSA '82
Nelson, Willie	Film	HONEYSUCKLE ROSE '80
Nelson, Willie	Film	SONGWRITER '84
Nemec, Corin	Series	PARKER LEWIS CAN'T LOSE tv
Nero, Franco	Film	THE MERCENARY '68
Newman, Barry	Film	AMY '81
Newman, Barry	Film	THE LAWYER '70
Newman, Paul	Film	A NEW KIND OF LOVE '63
Newman, Paul	Film	ABSENCE OF MALICE '81
Newman, Paul	Film	BLAZE '89
Newman, Paul	Film	BUTCH CASSIDY AND THE SUNDANCE KID '69****
Newman, Paul	Film	EXODUS '60
Newman, Paul	Film	FROM THE TERRACE '60
Newman, Paul	Film	HARPER '66
Newman, Paul	Film	HOMBRE '67
Newman, Paul	Film	HUD '63 ****
Newman, Paul	Film	THE COLOR OF MONEY '86
Newman, Paul	Film	THE DROWNING POOL '76
Newman, Paul	Film	THE HUSTLER '61 ****
Newman, Paul	Film	THE OUTRAGE '64
Newman, Paul	Film	THE PRIZE 63
Newman, Paul	Film	THE RACK '56
Newman, Paul	Film	THE STING '73
Newman, Paul	Film	THE VERTDICT '82
Newman, Paul	Film	WINNING '69
Newman, Paul	Film	WUSA '70
Newman, Paul	Role	BUTCH CASSIDY
Newton, Robert	Film	LONG JOHN SILVER '54
Newton, Robert	Film	ODD MAN OUT '47 ****
Newton, Robert	Film	OLIVER TWIST '48 ****
Newton, Robert	Film	THIS HAPPY BREED '44
Ngugi wa Thiong'o	Aka	JAMES NGUGI w
Nicholls, George	Film	FINISHING SCHOOL '34
Nichols, Anne	Play	ABIE'S IRISH ROSE
Nichols, Mike	Nee	MICHAEL IGOR PESCHOWSKY
Nicholson, Jack	Film	BACK DOOR TO HELL '64
Nicholson, Jack	Film	BATMAN '89
Nicholson, Jack	Film	CARNAL KNOWLEDGE '71
Nicholson, Jack	Film	CHINATOWN '74
Nicholson, Jack	Film	FIVE EASY PIECES '70 ****
Nicholson, Jack	TitleRol	FORTUNE '75
Nicholson, Jack	Film	HOFFA '92
Nicholson, Jack	Film	IRONWEED '87
Nicholson, Jack	Film	ONE FLEW OVER THE CUCKOO'S NEST '75****
Nicholson, Jack	Film	THE BORDER '82
Nicholson, Jack	Film	THE PASSENGER '75
Nicholson, Jack	Film	WOLF '94
Nicol, Dr. Davidson	Pen Name	ABIOSEH NICOL
Nielsen, Leslie	Film	HOT SUMMER NIGHT '57
Nielsen, Leslie	Series	POLICE SQUAD tv

```
Niembach, Nicolaus Franz Pen Name NICOLAUS LENAU po
Nierenberg, George T. Film    SAY AMEN, SOMEBODY '82 ****(doc)
Nilsson, Rob d+     Film       HEAT AND SUNLIGHT '88
Nimoy, Leonard      Series     STAR TREK tv
Nin, Anais          Title      A SPY IN THE HOUSE OF LOVE
Nin, Anais          Title      DELTA OF VENUS
Nirvana    mr       Hit        NEVER MIND
Niven, David        Film       CANDLESHOE '77
Niven, David        Film       ENCHANTMENT '48
Niven, David        Film       GUNS OF DARKNESS '62
Niven, David        Film       HAPPY ANNIVERSARY '59
Niven, David        Film       RAFFLES '40
Niven, David        Film       SEPARATE TABLES '58 ****
Niven, David        Film       STAIRWAY TO HEAVEN '46 ****
Niven, David        Film       THE GUNS OF NAVARONE '61
Niven, David        Film       THE PERFECT MARRIAGE '46
Niven, David        Film       THE PINK PANTHER '64
Niven, David        Film       THE SILKEN AFFAIR '57
Niven, David        Role PHINEAS FOGG in Around the World in 80 Days
Niven, David        Title      THE MOON IS A BALLOON
Noiret, Philippe    Film       ALEXANDER '68
Noiret, Philippe    Film       CINEMA PARADISO '88
Noiret, Philippe    Film       THE CLOCKMAKER '73
Noiret, Philippe    Film       THE HOLES '72
Noiret, Philippe    Film       URANUS '91
Noiret, Phillippe   Film       THE POSTMAN '94
Nolan, Kathy        Series     BROADSIDE tv
Nolan, Lloyd        Films      MICHAEL SHAYNE FILMS '40's
Nolan, Tommy        Series     BUCKSKIN tv
Nolte, Nick         Film       NEW YORK STORIES '89
Nolte, Nick         Film       THE DEEP '77
Nolte, Nick         Film       THREE FUGITIVES '89
Nolte, Nick         Film       WEEDS '87
Nora                Charac     in A Doll's House
Norris, Chuch       Film       LONE WOLF McQUADE '83
Norris, Chuck       Nee        CARLOS RAY
Norris, Chuck       Series     WALKER, TEXAS RANGER tv
North, Jay          Series     DENNIS THE MENACE tv
North, Sheree       Nee        DAWN BETHEL
Norway,Nevil Shute  Pen Name   NEVIL SHUTE
Novak, Kim          Film       OF HUMAN BONDAGE '64
Novarro, Ramon      Film       BEN-HUR '26
Novarro, Ramon      Film   THE STUDENT PRINCE IN OLD HEIDELBERG'27***
Novello, Ivor       Film       DOWNHILL '27
Novello, Ivor       Film       THE LODGER '26
Noyes, Alfred       Poem       THE HIGHWAYMAN
O'Brian, Hugh       Film       PROBE '72
O'Brian, Hugh       Nee        HUGH KRAMPKE
O'Brian, Hugh       Series     THE LIFE AND LEGEND OF WYATT EARP tv
O'Brien, Edmond     Film       D.O.A. '50
O'Brien, Edmond     Film       THE BIGAMIST '53
O'Brien, Edmond     Film       THE HITCH-HIKER '53
O'Brien, Edmond     Film       WARPATH '51
O'Brien, Edmond d+  Film       SHIELD FOR MURDER '54
O'Brien, Edna       Title      SOME IRISH LOVING
O'Brien, George     Film       SUNRISE '27
O'Brien, Margaret   Film       GLORY '56
O'Brien, Margaret   Film       MEET ME IN ST. LOUIS '44 ****
O'Brien, Margaret   Film       THE SECRET GARDEN '49
O'Brien, Margaret   Film       THE UNFINISHED DANCE '47
O'Brien, Pat        Film       AMERICAN MADNESS '32
```

O'Brien, Pat	Film	BOMBARDIER '43
O'Brien, Pat	Film	CRACK-UP '46
O'Brien, Pat	Film	GARDEN OF THE MOON '38
O'Brien, Pat	Film	PERILOUS HOLIDAY '46
O'Brien, Pat	Film	RIFFRAFF '47
O'Casey, Sean	Play	JUNO AND THE PAY COCK
O'Casey, Sean	Play	THE PLOUGH AND THE STARS
O'Connell, Jerry	Series	MY SECRET IDENTITY tv
O'Connor, Carroll	Film	LAW AND DISORDER '74
O'Connor, Carroll	Series	ALL IN THE FAMILY tv
O'Connor, Carroll	Series	IN THE HEAT OF THE NIGHT tv
O'Connor, Donald	Film	FRANCIS '49
O'Donnell, Chris	Film	CIRCLE OF FRIENDS '95
O'Donovan, Michael	Pen Name	FRANK O'CONNOR
O'Flaherty, Liam	Title	THE INFORMER
O'Hara, John	Title	APPOINTMENT IN SAMARRA
O'Hara, John	Title	BUTTERFIELD 8
O'Hara, John	Title	TEN NORTH FREDERICK
O'Hara, John	Title	PAL JOEY
O'Hara, Maureen	Film	AGAINST ALL FLAGS '52
O'Hara, Maureen	Film	DANCE, GIRL, DANCE '40
O'Hara, Maureen	Film	HOW GREEN WAS MY VALLEY '41 ****
O'Hara, Maureen	Film	McLINTOCK! '63
O'Hara, Maureen	Film	THE QUIET MAN '52 ****
O'Hara, Maureen	Nee	MAUREEN FITZSIMMONS
O'Keefe, Dennis	Film	T-MEN '47
Q'Keefe, Dennis	Film	THE FAKE '53
O'Keefe, Dennis	Film	UP IN MABEL'S ROOM '44
O'Mara, Kate	Series	DYNASTY tv
O'Morrison, Kevin	Series	CHARLEY WILD, PRIVATE DETECTIVE tv
O'Neal, Ron	Film	SUPERFLY '72
O'Neal, Ryan	Film	LOVE STORY '70
O'Neal, Ryan	Film	NICKELODEON '76
O'Neal, Ryan	Film	THE DRIVER '78
O'Neal, Ryan & Tatum	Film	PAPER MOON '73 ****
O'Neill, Ed	Film	DUTCH '91
O'Neill, Ed	Series	MARRIED .....WITH CHILDREN tv
O'Neill, Eugene	Play	A TOUCH OF THE POET
O'Neill, Eugene	Play	MARCO MILLIONS
O'Neill, Eugene	Play	STRANGE INTERLUDE
O'Neill, Eugene	Play	THE HAIRY APE
O'Neill, Eugene	Play	THE ICEMAN COMETH
O'Neill, Jennifer	Film	SCANNERS '81
O'Neill, Jennifer	Film	THE INNOCENT '76 ****
O'Nolan, Brian	Pen Name	FLANN O'BRIEN
O'Quinn Terry	Film	STEPFATHER '87
O'Toole, Peter	Film	BECKET '64
O'Toole, Peter	Film	LAWRENCE OF ARABIA '62 ****
O'Toole, Peter	Film	MY FAVORITE YEAR '82
O'Toole, Peter	Film	THE LION IN WINTER '68 ****
O'Toole, Peter	Film	THE STUNT MAN '80 ****
Oakie, Jack	Film	ONCE IN A LIFETIME '32
Oates, Joyce Carol	Pen Name	ROSAMOND SMITH
Oates, Joyce Carol	Title	A GARDEN OF EARTHLY DELIGHTS
Oates, Joyce Carol	Title	THE EYE SAGE
Oates, Joyce Carol	Title	THEM
Oates, Warren	Film	COCKFIGHTER '74
Oates, Warren	Film	DILLINGER '73
Oates, Warren	Film	TWO-LANE BLACKTOP '71
Oberon, Merle	Film	'TIL WE MEET AGAIN '40
Oberon, Merle	Film	LYDIA '41

Oberon, Merle	Film	PARDON MY FRENCH '51
Oberon, Merle	Film	TEMPTATION '46
Oberon, Merle	Film	THE DIVORCE OF LADY X '38
Oberon, Merle	Film	THE LODGER '44
Oberon, Merle	Film	THE PRICE OF FEAR '56
Oberon, Merle	Film	THESE THREE '36 ****
Oberon, Merle	Film	WUTHERING HEIGHTS '39 ****
Ochsenknecht, Uwe	Film	MEN ... '85
Odets, Clifford	Play	AWAKE AND SING
Odets, Clifford	Play	GOLDEN BOY
Odets, Clifford	Play	THE COUNTRY GIRL
Odets, Clifford	Play	WAITING FOR LEFTY
Oh, Sandra	Film	DOUBLE HAPPINESS '95
Oland, Warner	Films	CHARLIE CHAN MOVIES
Oldman, Gary	Film	AIR FORCE ONE '97 ****
Oldman, Gary	Film	IMMORTAL BELOVED '94
Oldman, Gary	Film	PRICK UP YOUR EARS '87
Oldman, Gary	Film	ROMEO IS BLEEDING '94
Olin, Ken	Series	THIRTYSOMETHING tv
Olin, Lena	Film	HAVANA '90
Oliver, Edna May	Film	LADIES OF THE JURY '32
Olivier, Laurence	Film	A LITTLE ROMANCE '79
Olivier, Laurence	Film	FIRE OVER ENGLAND '37
Olivier, Laurence	d+ Film	HAMLET '48 ****
Olivier, Laurence	Film	HENRY V '45 ****
Olivier, Laurence	Film	I STAND CONDEMNED '35
Olivier, Laurence	Film	OTHELLO '65 ****
Olivier, Laurence	Film	PRIDE AND PREJUDICE '40 ****
Olivier, Laurence	Film	REBECCA '40 ****
Olivier, Laurence	Film	SLEUTH '72 ****
Olivier, Laurence	Film	THE BEGGAR'S OPERA '53
Olivier, Laurence	Film	THE BETSY '78
Olivier, Laurence	Film	THE BOYS FROM BRAZIL '78
Olivier, Laurence	Film	THE ENTERTAINER ''60
Olivier, Laurence	Film	WUTHERING HEIGHTS '39 ****
Olivier, Laurence	Role	DARCY
Olivier, Laurence	Role	LEAR
Olivier, Laurence	d+ Film	RICHARD III '55
Olivier, Laurence	d+ Film	THREE SISTERS '70 ****
Olmos,Edward James	Film	STAND AND DELIVER '87
Olsen, Ole	Film	GOLD DUST GERTIE '31
Olsen, Ole	Film	HELLZAPOPPIN' '41
Ono, Yoko	Song	DON'T WORRY KYOKO
Ophuls, Marcel	Film	THE SORROW AND THE PITY'70****(doc)
Orbison, Ray mr+	Hit	OH PRETTY WOMAN
Orff, Carl	Comp	CARMINA BURANA
Orton, Joe	Play	LOOT
Orwell, George	Title	1984
Orwell, George	Title	ANIMAL FARM
Osmond, Donny s	Hit Song	GO AWAY LITTLE GIRL
Otto, Miranda	Film	LOVE SERANADE '97 ****
Oursler, Charles F.Aka		ANTHONY ABBOT
Ovid	Poem	AMORES
Ovid	Title	METAMORPHOSES
Owen, Reginald	Film	A CHRISTMAS CAROL '38
Owen, Reginald	Film	A STUDY IN SCARLET '33
Oz, Amos	Title	MY MICHAEL
Pacino, Al	Film	DOG DAY AFTERNOON '75
Pacino, Al	Film	HEAT '95
Pacino, Al	Film	SERPICO '73
Pacino, Al	Film	THE DEVIL'S ADVOCATE '97 ****

Pacino, Al	Film	THE GODFATHER, PART II '74 ****
Pacino, Al	Film	THE GODFATHER, PART III '90
Page, Geraldine	Film	THE TRIP TO BOUNTIFUL '85
Page, Patti	Nee	CLARA ANN FOWLER
Pagliacci	Heroine	NEDDA
Paine, Thomas	Title	COMMON SENSE; THE AMERICAN CRISIS
Pakos, John	Film	FUTZ '69
Palance, Jack	Film	ATTACK! '56
Palance, Jack	Nee	WALTER PALANUIK
Palance, Jack	Series	BRONK tv
Palin, Michael	Film	A PRIVATE FUNCTION '85
Palin, Michael	Film	JABBERWOCKY '77
Palmer, Lilli	Film	BODY AND SOUL '47 ****
Paltrow, Gwyneth	Film	EMMA '96
Pamina fc	Heroine	in THE MAGIC FLUTE by Mozart
Pankin, Stuart	Series	DINOSAURS tv
Papas, Irene	Film	ERENDIRA '83
Papas, Irene	Film	IPHIGENIA '77
Papas, Irene	Film	ISLAND '89
Pare, Michael	Film	INSTANT JUSTICE '87
Parker, Cecil	Film	TONY DRAWS A HORSE '51
Parker, Dorothy	Series	HOT SHOTS tv
Parker, Eleanor	Film	CAGED '50
Parker, Eleanor	Film	LIZZIE '57
Parker, Eleanor	Film	THE NAKED JUNGLE '54
Parker, Eleanor	Film	THE WOMAN IN WHITE '48
Parker, Eleanor	Series	BRACKEN'S WORLD tv
Parker, Fess	Film	THEM ! '54
Parker, Fess	Series	DANIEL BOONE tv
Parker, Jameson	Series	SIMON & SIMON tv
Parker, Jean	Film	BLUEBEARD '44
Parker, Jean	Film	SEQUOIA '34
Parkins, Barbara	Film	THE ASYLUM '72
Parks, Bert	Nee	BERT JACOBSEN
Parks, Larry	Film	THE JOLSON STORY '46
Parton, Dolly	Film	STEEL MAGNOLIAS '89
Pasolini,Pier Paolo d	Film	THE GOSPEL ACCORDING TO ST.MATTHEW'66***
Pastorelli, Robert	Role	ELDIN BERNECKY(in Murphy Brown tv)
Paton, Alan	Title	TOO LATE THE PHALAROPE
Patrick, Nigel	Film	FORBIDDEN CARGO '54
Patrick, Nigel	Film	SAPPHIRE '59
Patrick, Nigel	Film	THE VIRGIN SOLDIERS '69
Patten, Gilbert	Pen Name	BURT L. STANDISH
Patterson, Lorna	Series	PRIVATE BENJAMIN tv
Pavarotti, Luciano	Film	DISTANT HARMONY '87
Paxinou, Katina	Film	ZITA '68
Paxton, Bill	Film	APOLLO THIRTEEN(13) '95
Paxton, Bill	Film	TRAVELER '97
Paxton, Bill	Film	TRESPASS '92
Paxton, Bill	Film	TWISTER '96
Payne, John	Film	EL PASO '49
Payne, John	Film	LARCENY '48
Payne, John	Film	SLIGHTLY SCARLET '56
Payne, John	Film	THE BOSS '56
Payne, John	Film	THE EAGLE AND THE HAWK '50
Payne, John	Film	THE ROAD TO DENVER '55
Payne, John Howard	Song	HOME SWEET HOME
Payton-France, Joe Marie	Series	FAMILY MATTERS tv
Pearl Jam mr	Hit	TEN
Pearl, Minnie	Nee	SARAH OPHELIA CANNON
Peck, Bob	Film	THE KITCHEN TOTO '87

```
Peck, Gregory       Film      ARABESQUE '66
Peck, Gregory       Film      CAPTAIN NEWMAN, M.D. '63
Peck, Gregory       Film      DESIGNING WOMAN '57
Peck, Gregory       Film      MacARTHUR '77
Peck, Gregory       Film      MIRAGE '65
Peck, Gregory       Film      MOBY DICK '56
Peck, Gregory       Film      ON THE BEACH '59 ****
Peck, Gregory       Film      THE BOYS FROM BRAZIL '78
Peck, Gregory       Film      THE BRAVADOS '58
Peck, Gregory       Film      THE CHAIRMAN '69
Peck, Gregory       Film      THE GREAT SINNER '49
Peck, Gregory       Film      THE GUNS OF NAVARONE '61
Peck, Gregory       Film      THE MACOMBER AFFAIR '47
Peck, Gregory       Film      THE OMEN '76
Peck, Gregory       Film      THE PARADINE CASE '48
Peck, Gregory       Film      THE PURPLE PLAIN '54
Peck, Gregory       Film      THE WORLD IN HIS ARMS '52
Peck, Gregory       Film      THE YEARLING '46
Peck, Gregory       Film      TWELVE O'CLOCK HIGH '49 ****
Pederson, Knut      Pen Name  KNUT HAMSUN
Peggoty, Clara      Charac    DAVID COPPERFIELD
Pele                Nee       EDSON ARTANTES de NASCIMENTO
Penn, Sean          Film      COLORS '88
Penn, Sean          Film      DEAD MAN WALKING '95 ****
Penn, Sean          Film      STATE OF GRACE '90
Penn, Sean          Film      THE GAME '97
Penn, Sean          Film      U-TURN '97
Penny, Joe          Series    JAKE AND THE FAT MAN tv
Peppard, George     Film      PENDULUM '69
Peppard, George     Film      THE CARPETBAGGERS '64
Peppard, George     Series    BANACEK tv
Peppard, George     Series    THE A TEAM tv
Percy, Walker       Title     THE MOVIEGOER
Perier, Francois    Film      DEMONIAQUE '58
Perkins, Anthony    Film      FEAR STRIKES OUT '57
Perkins, Anthony    Film      PSYCHO '60 ****
Perkins, Anthony    Film      THE TRIAL '62
Perkins, Carl mr+   Hit       BLUE SUEDE SHOES
Perkins, Elizabeth  Film      ENID IS SLEEPING '90
Perkins, Millie     Film      THE SHOOTING '67
Perlman, Rhea       Film      MATILDA '96
Perlman, Ron        Film      CRONOS '92
Perrault, Charles   Title     PUSS IN BOOTS
Perrino, Valerie    Film      LENNY '74 ****
Pesci, Joe          Film      DEAR MR. WONDERFUL '82
Pescow, Donna       Series    ANGIE tv
Pescow, Donna       Series    OUT OF THIS WORLD tv
Peshkov, Aleksey Maksimovich  Pen Naame MAKSIM GORKY
Peters, Bernadette  Nee       BERNADETTE LAZZARO
Peters, Brock       Film      LOST IN THE STARS '74
Peters, Curtis A.   Aka       PETER ARNO
Peters, Jean        Film      ANNE OF THE INDIES '51
Peters, Jean        Film      VIVA ZAPATA '52 ****
Petersen, William L. Film     MANHUNTER '85
Petrarca,Francesco  Pen Name  PETRARCH po
Petty, Tom & the Heartbreakers  mr Hit REFUGEE
Pfeiffer, Michelle  Film      A THOUSAND ACRES '97
Pfeiffer, Michelle  Film      DANGEROUS MINDS '95
Pfeiffer, Michelle  Film      MARRIED TO THE MOB '88
Pfeiffer, Michelle  Film      TEQUILA SUNRISE '88
Phelps, Peter       Film      STARLIGHT HOTEL '87
```

Phillips, Lou Diamond	Film	LA BAMBA '87
Phillips, Wendy	Series	HOMEFRONT tv
Phoenix, River	Film	DOGFIGHT '91
Phoenix, River	Film	STAND BY ME '86
Phoenix, River	Film	THE THING CALLED LOVE '93
Piaf, Edith	Nee	EDITH GASSION
Picasso, Paolo	Painting	BLUE ROOM
Picasso, Pablo	Painting	CARD PLAYER
Picasso, Pablo	Painting	DORA MAAR SEATED
Piccoli, Michel	Film	BELLE de JOUR '67 ****
Piccoli, Michel	Film	LA BELLE NOISEUSE '91
Piccoli, Michel	Film	LEAP INTO THE VOID '79
Piccoli, Michel	Film	SPOILED CHILDREN 77
Pickens, Slim	Nee	LOUIS LINDLEY
Pickett, Bobby mr	Hit	MONSTER MASH
Pickford, Mary	Film	COQUETTE '29
Pickford, Mary	Film	POLLYANNA '20
Pickford, Mary	Film	SPARROWS '26
Pickford, Mary	Film	SUDS '20
Pickford, Mary	Nee	GLADYS SMITH
Picon, Molly	Film	MAMELE '38
Pidgeon, Walter	Film	FORBIDDEN PLANET '56
Pidgeon, Walter	Film	HOLIDAY IN MEXICO '46
Pidgeon, Walter	Film	HOW GREEN WAS MY VALLEY '41 ****
Pidgeon, Walter	Film	PHANTOM RAIDERS '42
Pidgeon, Walter	Film	THE SELLOUT '52
Pilgrims Progress	Heroine	CHRISTIANA
Pinal, Silvia	Film	SIMON OF THE DESERT '65 ****
Pincherle, Alberto	Pen Name	ALBERTO MORAVIO
Pinchot, Bronson	Series	PERFECT STRANGERS tv
Pink Floyd mr	Hit	THE WALL
Pinsent, Gordon	Film	THE ROWDYMAN '71
Pinter, Harold	Title	THE BIRTHDAY PARTY
Pinza, Ezio	Musical	SOUTH PACIFIC
Pitt, Brad	Film	KALIFORNIA '93
Pitt, Brad	Film	THE DEVIL'S OWN '97
Pitts, ZaSu	Film	GREED '25 ****
Plath, Sylvia	Poems	ARIEL(posthumous)
Platters, The	Hit Song	SMOKE GETS IN YOUR EYES
Pleasence, Donald	Film	CUL-DE-SAC '66
Pleasence, Donald	Film	HALLOWEEN '78
Pleasence, Donald	Film	OUTBACK '71
Pleasence, Donald	Film	THE GUEST '64
Pleasence, Donald	Films	HALLOWEEN MOVIES '78 - '89
Plowright, Joan	Film	THE DRESSMAKER '88
Plowright, Joan	Film	THREE SISTERS '70 ****
Plummer, Christopher	Film	MURDER BY DECREE '79
Plummer, Christopher	Film	OEDIPUS THE KING '68
Plummer, Christopher	Film	THE ASSIGNMENT '77
Plumpe, Friedrich	Pen Name	F.W. MURNAU
Plunkett,Edw.J.M.D.	Pen Name	LORD DUNSANY
Poco mr	Hit	DELIVERIN'
Podesta, Rossana	Film	SEVEN GOLDEN MEN '65
Poe, Edgar Allan	Heroine	IRENE
Poe, Edgar Allan	Poem	FOR ANNIE
Poe, Edgar Allan	Poem	LENORE
Poe, Edgar Allan	Title	LIGEIA
Poitier, Sidney	Film	A RAISIN IN THE SUN '61 ****
Poitier, Sidney	Film	ALL THE YOUNG MEN '60
Poitier, Sidney	Film	EDGE OF THE CITY '57 ****
Poitier, Sidney	Film	IN THE HEAT OF THE NIGHT '67 ****

Poitier, Sidney	Film	THE LOST MAN'69
Poitier, Sidney	Film	THE ORGANIZATION '71
Poitier, Sidney	Film	THE WILBY CONSPIRACY '75
Poitier, Sidney	Film	TO SIR WITH LOVE '67
Polanski, Roman d+	Film	THE TENANT '76
Police, The mr	Hit	EVERY BREATH YOU TAKE
Pollack, Channing	Film	ROCAMBOLE '62
Polo, Teri	Film	QUICK '93
Pons, Lily	Film	HITTING A NEW HIGH '37
Pop, Iggy mr	Hit	LUST FOR LIFE
Pope, Alexander	Poem	THE RAPE OF THE LOCK
Popov, Aleksandr Yakovlevich Pen Name ALEKSANDR YASHIN		
Poquelin, Jean Baptiste Pen Name MOLIERE		
Portaas, Herman	Pen Name	HERMAN WILDENVEY
Porter, Cole	Heroine	KATE
Porter, Cole	Musical	KISS ME KATE
Porter, Cole	Song	I HATE MEN
Porter, Cole	Song	KATIE WENT TO HAITI
Porter, Cole	Song	LET'S DO IT
Porter, Cole	Song	MISS OTIS REGRETS
Porter, Cole	Song	NIGHT AND DAY
Porter, William Sydney Pen Name O. HENRY		
Portman, Eric	Film	MILLIONS LIKE US '43
Portman, Eric	Film	THE GOOD COMPANIONS '56
Portman, Eric	Film	WANTED FOR MURDER '46
Powell, Anthony	Title	A DANCE TO THE MUSIC OF TIME
Powell, Dick	Film	CHRISTMAS IN JULY '40
Powell, Dick	Film	CORNERED '45
Powell, Dick	Film	DAMES '34
Powell, Dick	Film	FLIRTATION WALK '34
Powell, Dick	Film	FOOTLIGHT PARADE '33
Powell, Dick	Film	HAPPINESS AHEAD '34
Powell, Dick	Film	HOLLYWOOD HOTEL '37
Powell, Dick	Film	NAUGHTY BUT NICE'39
Powell, Dick	Film	SUSAN SLEPT HERE '54
Powell, Dick	Film	THANKS A MILLION '35
Powell, Dick	Film	PITFALL '48
Powell, Dick	Film	YOU NEVER CAN TELL '51
Powell, Eleanor	Film	HONOLULU '39
Powell, Eleanor	Film	SENSATIONS '44
Powell, Jane	Film	A DATE WITH JUDY '48
Powell, Jane	Film	ATHENA '54
Powell, Jane	Film	SEVEN BRIDES FOR SEVEN BROTHERS'54****
Powell, Jane	Film	THE GIRL MOST LIKELY '57
Powell, Robert	Film	IMPERATIVE '82
Powell, Robert	Film	MAHLER '74
Powell, Robert	Film	THE THIRTY-NINE STEPS '78
Powell, William	Film	AFTER THE THIN MAN '36
Powell, William	Film	ANOTHER THIN MAN '39
Powell, William	Film	CHARMING SINNERS '29
Powell, William	Film	CROSSROADS '42
Powell, William	Film	FASHIONS '34
Powell, William	Film	LIBELED LADY '36 ****
Powell, William	Film	LIFE WITH FATHER '47 ****
Powell, William	Film	THE KEY '34
Powell, William	Film	THE LAST COMMAND '28 ****
Powell, William	Film	THE THIN MAN '34 ****
Powell, William	Film	THE THIN MAN GOES HOME '44
Powell, William	Film	ZIEGFELD FOLLIES '46
Powell, William	Films	THE THIN MAN '34 + 5 more to ''47
Power, Tyrone	Film	LUCK OF THE IRISH '48

Power, Tyrone	Film	NIGHTMARE ALLEY '47
Power, Tyrone	Film	RAWHIDE '51
Power, Tyrone	Film	SECOND HONEYMOON '37
Power, Tyrone	Film	SUEZ '38
Power, Tyrone	Film	THE LONG GRAY LINE '55
Power, Tyrone	Film	THE MARK OF ZORRO '40
Power, Tyrone	Film	THE RISING OF THE MOON '57
Power, Tyrone	Film	THE SUN ALSO RISES '57
Power, Tyrone	Film	UNTAMED '55
Power, Tyrone	Film	WITNESS FOR THE PROSECUTION '57 ****
Powers, Marie	Film	THE MEDIUM '51
Powers, Stephanie	Nee	STEPHANIA FEDERKIEWICZ
Preminger, Otto d	Film	IN HARM'S WAY '65
Preminger, Otto d	Film	LAURA '44 ****
Prentiss, Paula	Film	M.A.D.D. '83
Prentiss, Paula	Nee	PAULA RAGUSA
Presley, Elvis	Film	FOLLOW THAT DREAM '62
Presley, Elvis	Film	GIRLS! GIRLS! GIRLS! '62
Presley, Elvis	Film	KISSIN COUSINS '64
Presley, Elvis	Film	ROUSTABOUT '64
Presley, Elvis	Film	SPINOUT '66
Presley, Elvis	Hit Song	BLUE SUEDE SHOES
Presley, Elvis	Hit Song	BURNING LOVE
Presley, Elvis	Hit Song	LOVE ME TENDER
Pressburger,Emeric	Film	A CANTERBURY TALE '44
Pressburger,Emeric	Film	BLACK NARCISSUS '46 ****
Pressburger,Emeric	Film	I KNOW WHERE I'M GOING '45 ****
Pressburger,Emeric	Film	STAIRWAY TO HEAVEN '46 ****
Pressburger,Emeric	Film	TALES OF HOFFMAN '51
Pressburger,Emeric	Film THE	LIFE AND DEATH OF COLONEL BLIMP'43****
Pressburger,Emeric	Film	THE RED SHOES '48 ****
Preston, Robert	Film	CLOUDBURST '51
Preston, Robert	Film	S.O.B. '81
Preston, Robert	Film	TULSA '49
Preston, Robert	Hit Song	SEVENTY-SIX TROMBONES in Music Man
Preston, Robert	Musical	MUSIC MAN
Preston, Robert	Nee	ROBERT PRESTON MESERVEY
Preston, Wayde	Series	COLT 45 tv
Pretenders, The mr	Hit	LEARNING TO CRAWL
Prevost, Abbe	Title	MANON LESCAUT
Price, Lloyd mr	Hit	STAGGER LEE
Price, Vincent	Film	ABOMINABLE '71
Price, Vincent	Film	CRY OF THE BANSHEE '70
Price, Vincent	Film	DIARY OF A MADMAN '63
Price, Vincent	Film	MADHOUSE 74
Price, Vincent	Film	THE BAT '59
Price, Vincent	Film	THE COMEDY OF TERRORS '64
Price, Vincent	Film	THE FLY '58
Price, Vincent	Film	THE MAD MAGICIAN '54
Price, Vincent	Film	THE RAVEN '63
Price, Vincent	Film	THE TINGLER '59
Price, Vincent	Film	THEATRE OF BLOOD '73
Price, Vincent	Film	TWICE-TOLD TALES '63
Pridvorov, Yefim	Pen Name	DEMYAN BEDNY
Prince	Nee	PRINCE ROGERS NELSON
Prince mr	Hit	PURPLE RAIN
Procal Harum mr	Hit	A WHITER SHADE OF PALE
Prokofiev, Sergei	Comp	CLASSICAL - Symph. No. 1 in D
Prokofiev, Sergey	Comp	WAR SONATAS
Prokokiev,Sergey	S.Mus.Poem	PETER AND THE WOLF
Prokosch, Frederic	Title	ASIATICS, THE

Proval. David	Film	NUNZIO '78
Prudhomme, Rene Francois Armand	Pen Name	SULLY PRUDHOMME
Pryce, Jonathan	Film	THE PLOUGHMAN'S LUNCH '83
Pryor, Richard	Film	STIR CRAZY '80
Public Enemy mr	Hit	FIGHT FOR POWER
Puccini, Giacomo	Aria	VISSI D'ARTE
Puccini, Giacomo	Heroine	MIMI in La Boheme, TOSCA
Puccini, Giacomo	Opera	LA BOHEME
Puccini, Giacomo	Opera	La TOSCA or Tosca
Puccini, Giacomo	Opera	MANON LESCAUT
Puccini, Giacomo	Opera	TURANDOT(his last)
Pullman, Bill	Film	INDEPENDENCE DAY '96
Pullman, Bill	Film	LOST HIGHWAY '97
Purl, Linda	Series	MATLOCK tv
Puzo, Mario	Title	THE GODFATHER
Quaid, Dennis	Film	DRAGONHEART '96
Quaid, Dennis	Film	DREAMSCAPE '84
Quaid, Dennis	Film	INNERSPACE '87
Quaid, Dennis	Film	SUSPECT '87
Quaid, Randy	Film	KINGPIN '96
Quaid, Randy	Series	DAVIS RULES tv
Queen mr	Hit	BOHEMIAN RHAPSODY
Questal, Mae	Film	A MAJORITY OF ONE '62
Quiller-Couch, Sir Arthur	Pen Name	Q
Quindlin, Anna w	Title	ONE TRUE THING
Quinn, Aidan	Film	AVALON '90
Quinn, Aidan	Film	COMMANDMENTS '97
Quinn, Aidan	Film	CRUSOE '88
Quinn, Aidan	Film	RECKLESS '84
Quinn, Anthony	Film	BARABBAS '62
Quinn, Anthony	Film	CARAVANS '78
Quinn, Anthony	Film	LA STRADA '54 ****
Quinn, Anthony	Film	LION OF THE DESERT '81
Quinn, Anthony	Film	LUST FOR LIFE '56 ****
Quinn, Anthony	Film	THE DESTRUCTORS '74
Quinn, Anthony	Film	THE INHERITANCE '76
Quinn, Anthony	Film	THE SAVAGE INNOCENTS '59
Quinn, Anthony	Role	ZORBA
Quivers, Robin	Film	PRIVATE PARTS '97
Quoirez, Francoise	Pen Name	FRANCOISE SAGAN
R.E.M. mr	Hit	LOSING MY RELIGION
Rabal, Francisco	Film	NAZARIN '58
Racine, Jean	Play	BRITANNICUS
Racine, Jean	Play	LES PLAIDEURS
Racine, Jean	Play	PHEDRE
Radford, Basil	Film	TIGHT LITTLE ISLAND '49 ****
Radner, Gilda	TV Show	SATURDAY NIGHT LIVE tv
Radvanyi, Netty	Pen Name	ANNA SEGHERS
Rae, Charlotte	Series	THE FACTS OF LIFE tv
Rafferty, Chips	Film	THE OVERLANDERS '46
Raft, George	Film	BOLERO '34
Raft, George	Film	BROADWAY '42
Raft, George	Film	NOCTURNE '46
Raft, George	Film	SCARFACE '32
Raft, George	Film	SPAWN OF THE NORTH '38
Ragsdale, William	Series	HERMAN'S HEAD tv
Railsback, Steve	Film	THE STUNT MAN '80 ****
Raimu	Film	MARIUS '31
Rainer, Luise	Film	DRAMATIC SCHOOL '38
Rainer, Luise	Film	THE GOOD EARTH '37 ****
Rains, Claude	Film	THE CLAIRVOYANT '34

Rains, Claude	Film	THE INVISIBLE MAN '33
Rains, Claude	Film	THE PARIS EXPRESS '53
Rains, Claude	Film	THE SEA HAWK '40 ****
Rains, Claude	Film	THE UNSUSPECTED '47
Rains, Claude	Film	THEY WON'T FORGET '37 ****
Raines, Ella	Film	HAIL THE CONQUERING HERO '44 ****
Rains, Ella	Film	THE WEB '47
Ralston, Jobyna	Film	FOR HEAVEN'S SAKE '26 ****
Ralston, Jobyna	Film	KID BROTHER '27 ****
Ralston, Jobyna	Film	THE FRESHMAN '25 ****
Ralston, Vera	Film	SURRENDER '50
Rand, Ayn	Title	THE FOUNTAINHEAD
Randall, Tony	Charac	FELIX UNGER in The Odd Couple tv
Randall, Tony	Film	THE ALPHABET MURDERS '86
Randall, Tony	Nee	LEONARD ROSENBERG
Randall, Tony	Series	THE ODD COUPLE tv
Rapaport, Michael	Film	ZEBRAHEAD '92
Rascals, The mr	Hit	GOOD LOVIN'
Rasche, David	Series	SLEDGE HAMMER tv
Raspighi, Ottorino	Sym, Poem	FOUNTAINS OF ROME
Rathbone, Basil	Film	CONFESSION '37
Rathbone, Basil	Film	THE HOUSE OF FEAR '45
Rathbone, Basil	Film	THE PEARL OF DEATH '44
Rathbone, Basil	Film	THE SPIDER WOMAN '44
Rathbone, Basil	Film	THE WOMAN IN GREEN '45
Rathbone, Basil	Role	SHERLOCK HOLMES
Ratnbone, Basil	Film	THE SCARLET CLAW '44
Ravel, Maurice Jos.	Ballet	DAPHNIS ET CHLOE
Ravel, Maurice Jos.	Comp	BOLERO
Ravel, Maurice Jos.	Comp	PAVANE FOR A DEAD PRINCESS
Ravel, Maurice Jos.	Opera	L'HEURE ESPAGNOLE
Ray, Aldo	Film	BATTLE CRY '55
Ray, Aldo	Film	NIGHTFALL '56
Ray, Aldo	Film	THE NAKED AND THE DEAD '58
Ray, Johnnie	Nee	JOHN ALVIN
Ray, Johnny	Hit Song	CRY
Raye, Martha	Film	WAIKIKI WEDDING '37
Raye, Martha	Nee	MARGARET O'REED
Raymond, Alex	Cartoon	FLASH GORDON
Raymond, Gene	Film	EX-LADY '33
Reade, Charles	Title	THE CLOISTER AND THE HEARTH
Reagan, Ronald	Film	BEDTIME FOR BONZO '51
Reagan, Ronald	Film	LOUISA '50
Reagan, Ronald	Film	THE LAST OUTPOST '51
Reason, Rex	Series	MAN WITHOUT A GUN tv
Reason, Rex	Series	THE ROARING TWENTIES tv
Redding, Otis mr	Hit	THE DOCK OF THE BAY
Reddy, Helen mj,s	Song	I AM WOMAN
Redfield, William	Film	THE CONNECTION '61
Redford, Robert	Film	ALL THE PRESIDENT'S MEN '76 ****
Redford, Robert	Film	BRUBAKER '80
Redford, Robert	Film	HAVANA '90
Redford, Robert	Film	JEREMIAH JOHNSON '72
Redford, Robert	Film	SNEAKERS '92
Redford, Robert	Film	THE CANDIDATE '72
Redford, Robert	Film	THE GREAT GATSBY '74
Redford, Robert	Film	THE NATURAL '84
Redford, Robert	Film	THE STING '73
Redgrave, Michael	Film	JEANNIE '41
Redgrave, Michael	Film	KIPPS '41
Redgrave, Michael	Film	LAW AND DISORDER '58

```
Redgrave, Michael    Film      LONELINESS OF THE LONG DIST.RUNNER'62****
Redgrave, Michael    Film      THE BROWNING VERSION '51
Redgrave, Michael    Film      THE CAPTIVE HEART '46
Redgrave, Michael    Film      THE NIGHT MY NUMBER CAME UP '55 ****
Redgrave, Michael    Film      THE STARS LOOK DOWN '39 ****
Redgrave, Michael    Film      THE WAY TO THE STARS '45 ****
Redgrave, Michael    Film      THE YEARS BETWEEN '43
Redgrave, Michael    Film      TIME WITHOUT PITY '56
Redgrave, Vanessa    Film      A MONTH BY THE LAKE '95
Redgrave, Vanessa    Film      AGATHA '79
Redgrave, Vanessa    Film      BLOWUP '66
Redgrave, Vanessa    Film      HOWARDS END '92
Redgrave, Vanessa    Film      ISADORA '68
Redgrave, Vanessa    Film      JULIA '77 ****
Redgrave, Vanessa    Film      MORGAN! '66
Redgrave, Vanessa    Film      STEAMING '85
Redgrave, Vanessa    Film      WETHERBY '85
Reed, Carol          Film      THE THIRD MAN '49
Reed, Carol d        Film      THE THIRD MAN '49 ****
Reed, Donna          Film      CHICAGO DEADLINE '49
Reed, Donna          Film      RANSOM '56
Reed, Donna          Nee       DONNA BELLE MULLENGER
Reed, Lou  mr        Hit       WALK ON THE WILD SIDE
Reed, Oliver         Film      CASTAWAY '87
Reed, Oliver         Film      HANNIBAL BROOKS '69
Reed, Oliver         Film      OLIVER! '68 ****
Reed, Oliver         Film      RANSOM '77
Reed, Oliver         Film      THE DEVILS '71
Reed, Oliver         Film      THE FOUR MUSKETEERS '75
Reed, Oliver         Film      THE GIRL-GETTERS '66
Reed, Oliver         Film      THE JOKERS '66
Reed, Oliver         Film      THE THREE MUSKETEERS '74
Reed, Robert         Series    THE BRADY BUNCH tv
Reed, Shanna         Series    MAJOR DAD tv
Reed, Walter         Film      BANJO '47
Reese, Della         Nee       DELLOREESE PATRICIA EARLY
Reeve, Christopher   Film      SUPERMAN '78
Reeves, George       Series    THE ADVENTURES OF SUPERMAN tv
Reeves, Keanu        Film      A WALK IN THE CLOUDS '95
Reeves, Keanu        Film      RIVER'S EDGE '86
Reeves, Kenau        Film      SPEED '94
Reeves, Kenau        Film      THE DEVIL'S ADVOCATE '97 ****
Reeves, Steve        Film      HERCULES '59
Reeves, Steve        Film      THE TROJAN HORSE '62
Reid, Britt          Title     THE GREEN HORNET
Reiser, Paul         Series    MY TWO DADS tv
Rekert, Winston      Series    ADDERLY tv
Remick, Lee          Film      LOOT '70
Remick, Lee          Film      THE WHEELER DEALERS '63
Renaldo, Duncan      Series    CISCO KID tv
Renfro, Brad         Film      THE CURE '95
Rennie, Michael      Film      THE DAY THE EARTH STOOD STILL '51 ****
Rennie, Michael      Series    THE THIRD MAN tv
Renoir, Jean d+      Film      RULES OF THE GAME '39 ****
Renoir, Pierre       Film      LA MARSEILLAISE '38
Resin, Dan           Film      HAIL TO THE CHIEF '73
Resonfeld, Samuel    Pen Name  TRISTAN TZARA
Rettig, Tommy        Series    LASSIE tv
Rey, Fernando        Film      THE FRENCH CONNECTION '71 ****
Reyes, Ricardo Neftali Pen Name PABLO NERUDA
Reynolds, Burt       Film      DELIVERANCE '72 ****
```

```
Reynolds, Burt        Film      FUZZ '72
Reynolds, Burt        Film      GATOR '76
Reynolds, Burt        Film      HOOPER '78
Reynolds, Burt        Film      IMPASSE '69
Reynolds, Burt        Film      SEMI-TOUGH '77
Reynolds, Burt        Film      SHAMUS '73
Reynolds, Burt d+     Film      THE END '78
Reynolds, Burt        Film      THE LONGEST YARD '74
Reynolds, Burt        Film      WHITE LIGHTNING '73
Reynolds, Burt        Series    B.L. STRYKER tv
Reynolds, Burt        Series    DAN AUGUST tv
Reynolds, Burt        Series    EVENING SHADE tv
Reynolds, Burt        Series    HAWK tv
Reynolds, Debbie      Film      BUNDLE OF JOY '56
Reynolds, Debbie      Film      THE GAZEBO '59
Reynolds, Debbie      Musical   SINGIN' IN THE RAIN
Reynolds, Joyce       Film      JANIE '44
Reynolds, Joyce       Film      WALLFLOWER '48
Rhyne,Miranda Stewart Film      ANGELA '95
Rhys, Jean            Title     THE WIDE SARGASSO SEA
Rice, Anne            Pen Name  ANNE RAMPLING
Rice, Anne            Title     THE VAMPIRE LESTAT
Rice, Elmer           Play      STREET SCENE
Rice, Tim             Musical   EVITA
Richardson, Ethel     Pen Name  HENRY HANDEL RICHARDSON
Richardson, Joely     Film      HOLLOW REED '97
Richardson, Ralph     Film      SMILEY '56
Richardson, Ralph     Film      THE HEIRESS '49 ****
Richter, Jean Paul Friedrich Pen Name JEAN PAUL
Richter, Paul         Film      DIE NIBELUNGEN '24 ****
Rickles, Don          Series    C.P.O. SHARKEY tv
Riding, Laura Jackson Pen Name LAURA JACKSON
Riefenstahl,Leni d Film        OLYMPIA '36 ****(documentary)
Riefenstahl,Leni d Film        TRIUMPH OF WILL '35 ****(documentary)
Riegert, Peter        Film      THE MASK '94
Righteous Bros. mr Hit         YOU'VE LOST THAT LOVIN' FEELING
Riis, Jacob           Title     THE MAKING OF AN AMERICAN
Rijn, Harmenszoon van Aka      REMBRANDT p
Riley,Jas.Whitcomb Poem        LITTLE ORPHANT ANIE
Rima                  Charac    "BIRD GIRL" of Green Mansions
Rimsky-Korsakov,Nikolai Comp SCHEHERAZADE - Op. 35
Rinehart, Mary Roberts Title THE DOOR
Rinehart, Mary Roberts Title TISH
Ritch, Steven         Film      THE WEREWOLF '56
Ritt, Martin d        Film      SOUNDER '72
Ritter, John          Series    THREE'S COMPANY tv
Rivers, Joan          Nee       JOAN SANDRA MOLINSKY
Rivers, Johnny  mr Hit         POOR SIDE OF TOWN
Robards, Jason        Film      A THOUSAND CLOWNS '65
Robards, Jason        Film      MAX DUGAN RETURNS '83
Robards, Jason        Film      REUNION '89
Robards, Jason Jr.    Film      FOOLS '70
Robards, Jason Jr.    Film      HEIDI '93
Robbins, Jerome       Ballet    WATER MILL
Robbins, Tim          Film      THE PLAYER '92
Robbins, Tom          Title     SKINNY LEGS AND ALL
Rober, Richard        Film      THE WELL '51
Roberts, Julia        Film      THE PELICAN BRIEF '93
Roberts, Pernell      Series    TRAPPER JOHN, M.D. tv
Roberts, Rachel       Rilm      O LUCKY MAN '73 ****
Roberts, Stephen      Film      IF I HAD A MILLION '32
```

Roberts, Theodore	Film	THE TEN COMMANDMENTS '23
Roberts, Xavier id	Toys	CABBAGE PATCH KIDS
Robertson, Cliff	Film	CHARLY '68
Robertson, Cliff	Film	MASQUERADE '65
Robertson, Cliff	Film	OBSESSION '76
Robertson, Dale	Film	LAW OF THE LAWLESS '64
Robertson, James	Film	COMING-OUT PARTY '61
Robeson, May	Film	LADY FOR A DAY '33 ****
Robeson, Paul	Film	SONG OF FREEDOM '36
Robinson, Kathy	Aka	TOTIE FIELDS
Robinson, Smokey & the Miracles mr Hit		OOH BABY BABY
Robinson,Edward G.	Film	A BOY TEN FEET TALL '63
Robinson,Edward G.	Film	BLACKMAIL '39
Robinson,Edward G.	Film	ILLEGAL '55
Robinson,Edward G.	Film	MANPOWER '41
Robinson,Edward G.	Film	NIGHTMARE '56
Robinson,Edward G.	Film	THE LAST GANGSTER '37
Robinson,Edward G.	Film	THE LITTLE GIANT '33
Robinson,Edward G.	Film	THE MAN WITH TWO FACES '34
Robinson,Edward G.	Film	THE PRIZE 63
Robinson,Edward G.	Film	UNHOLY PARTNERS '41
Robinson,Edward G.	Nee	EMMANUEL GOLDENBERG
Roc, Patricia	Film	THE PERFECT WOMAN '49
Rochefort, Jean	Film	LE CRABE TAMBOUR '77
Rodgers, Anton	Film	ROTTEN TO THE CORE '65
Rodgers, Richard	Comp	DO I HEAR A WALTZ?
Rodgers, Richard	Hit Song	THERE'S A SMALL HOTEL
Rodgers, Richard	Musical	ALLEGRO
Rodgers, Richard	Song	THOU SWELL
Roeg, Nicolas	Film	PERFORMANCE '70
Rogers, Ginger	Film	BACHELOR MOTHER '39
Rogers, Ginger	Film	CAREFREE '38
Rogers, Ginger	Film	DREAMBOAT '52
Rogers, Ginger	Film	MONKEY BUSINESS '52
Rogers, Ginger	Film	STAGE DOOR '37 ****
Rogers, Ginger	Film	SWING TIME '36 ****
Rogers, Ginger	Film	THE GAY DIVORCEE '34
Rogers, Ginger	Film	THE THIRTEENTH GUEST '32
Rogers, Ginger	Film	TOM, DICK AND HARRY '41
Rogers, Ginger	Film	TOP HAT '35 ****
Rogers, Ginger	Film	WE'RE NOT MARRIED '52
Rogers, Ginger	Nee	VIRGINIA McMATH
Rogers, Kenny	Song	LADY
Rogers, Mimi	Film	THE RAPTURE '91
Rogers, Roy	Film	IDAHO '43
Rogers, Roy	Nee	LEONARD SLYE
Rogers, Wayne	Film	THE GIG '85
Rogers, Wayne	Sitcom	HOUSE CALLS tv
Rogers, Will	Film	AMBASSADOR BILL '31
Rogers, Will	Film	DOUBTING THOMAS '35
Rogers, Will Jr.	Film	THE BOY FROM OKLAHOMA '54
Rohmer, Eric d	Film	CLAIRE'S KNEE '71
Rolfe, Guy	Film	THE SPIDER AND THE FLY '49
Rolle, Esther	Series	GOOD TIMES tv
Rolling Stones	Film	GIMME SHELTER '70 ****(documentary)
Rolling Stones mr	Hit	ANGIE
Rolling Stones mr	Hit	SATISFACTION
Rolling Stones mr	Hit Song	THE LAST TIME
Rollins, Howard E. Jr	Film	A SOLDIER'S STORY '84
Roman, Lulu	Series	HEE HAW tv
Romberg, Sigmund	Operetta	THE NEW MOON

Rome, Harold	Musical	WISH YOU WERE HERE
Romero, Cesar	Film	THE CASTILLAN '63
Ronettes, The mr	Hit	BE MY BABY
Ronstadt, Linda	Hit Song	OOH BABY BABY
Ronstadt, Linda	Song	BLUE BAYOU
Ronstadt, Linda mr+	Hit	YOU'RE NO GOOD
Rooney, Mickey	Film	BABES ON BROADWAY '41
Rooney, Mickey	Film	HUCKLEBERRY FINN '39
Rooney, Mickey	Film	NATIONAL VELVET '44 ****
Rooney, Mickey	Film	QUICKSAND '50
Rooney, Mickey	Film	STRIKE UP THE BAND '40
Rooney, Mickey	Film	THE FIREBALL
Rooney, Mickey	Film	THE HARDYS RIDE HIGH '39
Rooney, Mickey	Film	THE HUMAN COMEDY '43
Rooney, Mickey	Film	THE SECRET INVASION '64
Rooney, Mickey	Film	THOUSANDS CHEER '43
Rooney, Mickey	Film	YOUNG TOM EDISON '40
Rooney, Mickey	Nee	JOE YULE Jr.
Root, Amanda	Film	PERSUASION '95
Ross, Diana	HitSong	THE BOSS
Ross, Katharine	Film	THE LEGACY '79
Rossini, Giacchino	Opera	LA CENERENTOLA(Cinderella)
Rossini, Giacchino	Opera	LE COMPTE ORY
Rossini, Giacchino	Opera	OTELLO
Rossini, Giacchino	Opera	THE BARBER OF SEVILLE
Rossini, Giacchino	Opera	WILLIAM TELL
Rosten, Leo Calvin	Pen Name	LEONARD Q. ROSS
Roth, Lillian	Title	I'LL CRY TOMORROW
Roth, Philip	Title	GOODBYE, COLUMBUS
Roth, Philip	Title	PORTNOY'S COMPLAINT
Roth, Philip	Title	WHEN SHE WAS GOOD
Roth, Tim	Film	CAPTIVES '95
Roundtree, Richard	Film	EMBASSY '72
Roundtree, Richard	Film	SHAFT '71
Roundtree, Richard	Film	SHAFT'S BIG SCORE '72
Rourke, Mickey	Film	BARFLY '87
Rourke, Mickey	Film	HOMEBOY '88
Rourke, Mickey	Film	YEAR OF THE DRAGON '85
Rowan, Dan	Film	ONCE UPON A HORSE '58
Ruark, Robert	Title	UHURU
Rubin, Jennifer	Film	DELUSION '90
Rubinstein, John	Film	ZACHARIAH '71
Ruggles, Charlie	Film	THIS IS THE NIGHT '32
Ruggles, Charlie	Film	WIVES NEVER KNOW '36
Run D.M.C. mr	Hit	RAISIN' HELL
Rush, Geoffrey o-a	Film	SHINE '96
Rushdie, Salman	Title	MIDNIGHT'S CHILDREN
Russ, William	Film	PASTIME '91
Russell, Jane	Film	FOXFIRE '55
Russell, Jane	Film	THE OUTLAW '43
Russell, John	Series	THE LAWMAN tv
Russell, Kurt	Film	BACKDRAFT '91
Russell, Kurt	Film	BREAKDOWN '97
Russell, Kurt	Film	OVERBOARD '87
Russell, Kurt	Film	TOMBSTONE '93
Russell, Lillian	Nee	HELEN LEONARD
Russell, Rosalind	Film	A MAJORITY OF ONE '62
Russell, Rosalind	Film	AUNTIE MAME '58
Russell, Rosalind	Film	GYPSY '62
Russell, Rosalind	Film	MY SISTER EILEEN '42
Russell, Rosalind	Film	NEVER WAVE AT A WAC '52

Russell, Rosalind	Film	PICNIC '55
Russell, Rosalind	Film	ROSIE! '67
Russell, Rosalind	Film	ROUGHLY SPEAKING '45
Russell, Rosalind	Film	THE VELVET TOUCH '48
Russell, Rosalind	Film	THEY MET IN BOMBAY '41
Russell, Theresa	Film	IMPULSE '90
Russell, Theresa	Nee	THERESA PAUP
Rutherford, Ann	Film	ORCHESTRA WIVES '42
Rutherford, Margaret	Film	MURDER MOST FOUL '65
Rutherford, Margaret	Film	TROUBLE IN STORE '53
Ryan, Meg	Film	PRELUDE TO A KISS '92
Ryan, Mitchell	Film	MY OLD MAN'S PLACE '72
Ryan, Robert	Film	BEST OF THE BADMEN '51
Ryan, Robert	Film	INFERNO '53
Ryan, Robert	Film	THE CROOKED ROAD '65
Ryan, Robert	Film	THE SET-UP '49
Ryan, Tom	Cartoon	TUMBLEWEEDS
Rydell, Christopher	Film	TRAUMA '93
Ryder, Winona	Film	HEATHERS '89
Ryder, Winona	Nee	WINONA HOROWITZ
Ryerson, Ann	Series	PRIVATE SECRETARY tv
Sabu	Film	DRUMS '38
Sade, Donatien Alphonse Francois, comte de Aka MARQUIS DE SADE		
Sagal. Katey	Series	MARRIED .....WITH CHILDREN tv
Sagan, Francoise	Title	BONJOUR TRIESTESSE
Saget, Bob	Series	FULL HOUSE tv
Sahara, Kenji	Film	RODAN '56
Saint, Eva Marie	Film	LOVING '70
Saint, Eva Marie	Film	NORTH BY NORTHWEST '59 ****
Saint-Saens, Camille	Comp	THE CARNIVAL OF THE ANIMALS
Saint-Seans, Camile	Opera	SAMSON AND DELILAH
Sajak, Pat	Host	WHEEL OF FORTUNE tv
Sales, Soupy	Nee	MILTON HINES
Salinger, J.D.	"Girl"	ESME
Salinger, J.D.	Title	NINE STORIES
Salinger, J.D.	Title	THE CATCHER IN THE RYE
Salinger, Matt	Film	BABYFEVER '94
Salten, Felix	Title	BAMBI
Saltykov, Mikhail Yevgrafovich Pen Name SHCHEDRIN		
Salvatori, Renato	Film	OF FLESH AND BLOOD '62
Salzmann, Siegmund Pen Name		FELIX SALTEN
Sam and Dave mr	Hit	SOUL MAN
Samiento, Felix Ruben Garcia Pen Name RUBEN DARIO		
Sanda, Dominique	Film	LE VOYAGE EN DOUCE '80
Sanda, Dominique	Film	THE GARDEN OF THE FINZI-CONTINIS'71****
Sandberg, Carl	Title	SMOKE AND STEEL
Sandburg, Carl	Poem	THE PEOPLE, YES
Sanders, George	Film	ACTION IN ARABIA '44
Sanders, George	Film	CAIRO '63
Sanders, George	Film	LURED '47
Sanders, George	Film	PARIS AFTER DARK '43
Sanders, George	Film	PSYCHOMANIA '71
Sanders, George	Film	THE FALCON TAKES OVER '42
Sanders, George	Film	THE FALCON'S BROTHER '42
Sanders, George	Film	THE MOON AND SIXPENCE '42
Sanders, George	Film	THE SAINT TAKES OVER '40
Sanders, George	Film	THIEVES' HOLIDAY '46
Sands, Diana	Film	GEORGIA, GEORGIA '72
Sands, Julian	Film	WARLOCK '91
Sanford, Isabel	Series	THE JEFFERSONS tv
Sansom, Art	Cartoon	THE BORN LOSER

```
Santana    mr          Hit        BLACK MAGIC WOMAN
Sarandon, Susan        Film       DEAD MAN WALKING '95 ****
Sarandon, Susan        Film       THE CLIENT '94
Sarandon, Susan        Nee        SUSAN TOMALING
Sarmiento, Felix       Pen Name   RUBEN DARIO
Saroyan, William       Hero       ARAM in My Name Is Aram
Saroyan, William       Title      MY NAME IS ARAM
Sarrazin, Michael      Film       THE GUMBALL RALLY '76
Sartre, Jean-Paul      Play       DIRTY HANDS
Sartre, Jean-Paul      Title      L'ETRE ET LE NE ANT
Saunders, Lori         Series     PETTYCOAT JUNCTION tv
Sauser, Frederic       Pen Name   BLAISE CENDRARS
Savage, Ethel Mary Pen Name        ETHEL M. DELL
Savage, Fred           Series     THE WONDER YEARS tv
Savage, John           Film       HAIR '79
Savalas, Telly         Series     KOJAK tv
Saxon, John            Film       MR. KINGSTREET'S WAR '73
Saxton, Anne           Poem       ALL MY PRETTY ONES
Sayers, Dorothy        Title      THE NINE TAILORS
Sayers, Dorothy L.     Charac     LORD PETER WIMSEY(sleuth)
Scardino, Don          Film       SQUIRM '76
Scarlatti, Domenico Comp           KEYBOARD SONATAS
Scheider, Roy          Film       JAWS '75 ****
Scheider, Roy          Film       SORCERER '77
Schell, Maria          Film       GERVAISE '56
Schell, Maria          Film       THE MAJIC BOX '51 ****
Schell, Maximilian     Film       THE CASTLE '68
Schell, Maximilian     Film       THE CHOSEN '81
Schildkraut,Joseph     Film       THE ROAD TO YESTERDAY '25
Schneider, John        Series     DUKES OF HAZARD tv
Schneider, Romy        Film       MADO '76
Schoenberg, Arnold Comp            VERKLARTE NACHT
Schreiner, Olive       Pen Name   RALPH IRON
Schroder, Rick         Film       ACROSS THE TRACKS '91
Schroder, Ricky        Series     SILVER SPOONS tv
Schubert, Franz        Comp       DEATH AND THE MAIDEN
Schubert, Franz        Comp       DIE SCHONE MULLERIN
Schubert, Franz        Comp       QUINTET IN C MAJOR
Schubert, Franz        Comp       UNFINISHED SYMPHONY NO,8 IN B MINOR
Schubert, Franz        Comp       "GREAT" NINTH SYMPHONY
Schubert, Franz        Comp       AVE MARIA
Schulz, Charles        Cartoon    PEANUTS
Schumann, Robert       Comp       CARNAVAL: PRETTY SCENES ON FOUR NOTES
Schwartz,Maurice       d+Film     TEVYE '39
Schwarzeneggar, Arnold Film       ERASER '96
Schwarzenegger, Arnold Film       KINDERGARTEN COP '90
Schwarzenegger, Arnold FIlm       PREDATOR '87
Schwarzenegger, Arnold Film       THE TERMINATOR '84
Schwarzenegger, Arnold Film       TRUE LIES '94
Schwarzenegger, Arnold Film       TWINS '88
Schygulla, Hanna       Film       A LOVE IN GERMANY '84
Schygulla, Hanna       Film       BERLIN ALEXANDERPLATZ '80 ****
Schygulla, Hanna       Film       CIRCLE OF DECEIT '81
Schygulla, Hanna       Film       GODS OF THE PLAGUE '69
Scofield, Paul         Film       A MAN FOR ALL SEASONS '66 ****
Scofield, Paul         Film       BARTLEBY '72
Scofield, Paul         Film       THE TRAIN '64 ****
Scolari, Michael       Role       MIKE in Newhart tv
Scolari, Peter         Series     BOSOM BUDDIES tv
Scott, George C.       Film       HARDCORE '79
Scott, George C.       Film       PATTON '70 ****
```

Scott, George C.	Film	PETULIA '68 ****
Scott, George C.	Film	THE HOSPITAL '71
Scott, Lizabeth	Film	TOO LATE FOR TEARS '49
Scott, Martha	Film	STRANGE BARGAIN '49
Scott, Paul	Title	THE RAJ QUARTET
Scott, Randolph	Film	A LAWLESS STREET '55
Scott, Randolph	Film	BELLE OF THE YUKON '44
Scott, Randolph	Film	CANADIAN PACIFIC '49
Scott, Randolph	Film	COMANCHE STATION '60
Scott, Randolph	Film	GUNFIGHTERS '47
Scott, Randolph	Film	RIDE THE HIGH COUNTRY '62 ****
Scott, Randolph	Film	SEVEN MEN FROM NOW '56
Scott, Randolph	Film	SEVENTH CAVALRY '56
Scott, Randolph	Film	SUGARFOOT '51
Scott, Randolph	Film	THE BOUNTY HUNTER '54
Scott, Randolph	Film	THE DESPERADOES '43
Scott, Randolph	Film	THE SPOILERS '42
Scott, Randolph	Film	THE TEXANS '38
Scott, Randolph	Film	THE WALKING HILLS '49
Scott, Randolph	Film	WESTBOUND '59
Scott, Randolph	Nee	GEORGE RANDOLPH CRANE
Scott, Sir Walter	Title	ROB ROY
Scott, Zachary	Film	GUILTY BYSTANDER '50
Scott, Zachary	Film	RUTHLESS '48
Scott, Zachary	Film	THE SOUTHERNER '45 ****
Scott, Zachary	Film	VIOLENT STRANGER '57
Seaman, Elizabeth Cochrane	Pen Name	NELLY BLY
Seberg, Jean	Film	BREATHLESS '59
Seberg, Jean	Film	MOMENT TO MOMENT '66
Seberg, Jean	Film	TIME OUT FOR LOVE '61
Secada, Jan s	Song	JUST ANOTHER DAY
Sedaka, Neil mr	Hit	BREAKING UP IS HARD TO DO
Sedeka, Neil mr	Hit Song	CALENDER GIRL
Seeger, Pete	Film	THE WEAVERS: WASN'T THAT A TIME!'82 ****
Seeger, Pete s	Hit	TURN! TURN! TURN!
Seferiadis,Georgios	Pen Name	GEORGE SEFERIS
Segal, George	Film	BLUME IN LOVE '73
Segal, George	Film	BYE BYE BRAVERMAN '68
Segal, George	Film	KING RAT '65
Segal, George	Film	LOVING '70
Segal, George	Film	RUSSIAN ROULETTE '75
Segal, George	Film	THE BRIDGE AT REMAGEN '69
Segal, George	Film	THE SOUTHERN STAR '69
Segar, Elzie C.	Cartoon	POPEYE
Segar, Elzie C.	Cartoon	THIMBLE THEATER
Sellecca, Connie	Series	P.S. I LUV U tv
Selleck, Tom	Film	LASSITER '84
Selleck, Tom	Series	MAGNUM, P.I. tv
Sellers, Peter	Film	A SHOT IN THE DARK 64 ****
Sellers, Peter	Film	DR.STRANGELOVE OR: HOW I LEARNED, etc. '64 ****
Sellers, Peter	Film	HOFFMAN '70
Sellers, Peter	Film	ONLY TWO CAN PLAY '62
Sellers, Peter	Film	THE MOUSE THAT ROARED '59
Sellers, Peter	Film	THE OPTIMISTS '73
Sellers, Peter	Film	THE PARTY '68
Sellers, Peter	Film	THE PINK PANTHER '64
Sellers, Peter	Role	CLOUSEAU in Pink Panther movies
Senta	Heroine	THE FLYING DUTCHMAN
Serna, Assumpta	Film	MATADOR '86
Servais, Jean	Film	RIFIFI '54 ****

Seuss, Dr.	Nee	THEODORE SEUSS GEISEL
Seuss, Dr.	Title	GREEN EGGS AND HAM
Seuss, Dr.	Title	HUNCHES IN BUNCHES
Seuss, Dr.	Title	THE CAT IN THE HAT
Sewell, Anna	Title	BLACK BEAUTY
Seymour, Jane	Nee	JOYCE FRANKENBERG
Shackelford, Ted	Series	KNOTS LANDING tv
Shakespeare, Wm.	Charac	SIR TOBY BELCH
Shakespeare, Wm.	Herione	CLEOPATRA
Shannon, Del mr	Hit	RUNAWAY
Sharif, Omar	Film	MAYERLING '68
Sharif, Omar	Film	THE APPOINTMENT '69
Sharif, Omar	Film	THE HORSEMEN '71
Sharif, Omar	Nee	MICHAEL SHALHOUB
Sharif, Omar	TitleRole	DOCTOR ZHIVAGO '65
Sharkey, Ray	Film	THE IDOLMAKER '80
Sharpsteen, Ben d	Film	DUMBO '41 **** (Animated)
Sharpsteen, Ben d	Film	PINOCCHIO '40 ****(animated)
Sharpsteen, Ben d	Film SNOW	WHITE AND THE SEVEN DWARFS'37****
Shatner, William	Film	THE INTRUDER '62
Shatner, William	Series	STAR TREK tv
Shatner, William	Series	T.J. HOOKER tv
Shaver, Helen	Film	INNOCENT VICTIM '89
Shaw, Artie	Hit	FRENESI
Shaw, Geo. Bernard	Play	ARMS AND THE MAN
Shaw, Geo. Bernard	Play	CAESER AND CLEOPATRA
Shaw, Geo. Bernard	Play	CANDIDA
Shaw, Geo. Bernard	Play	MAJOR BARBARA
Shaw, Geo. Bernard	Play	PYGMALION
Shaw, Geo. Bernard	Title THE	SIMPLETON OF THE UNEXPECTED ISLES
Shaw, Henry Whel.	Pen Names	JOSH BILLINGS, UNCLE ESEK
Shaw, Irwin	Title	RICH MAN, POOR MAN
Shaw, Irwin	Title	THE YOUNG LIONS
Shaw, Robert	Film	CUSTER OF THE WEST '68
Shaw, Robert	Film	JAWS '75 ****
Shaw, Robert	Film	THE HIRELING '73
Shaw, Robert	Series	THE BUCCANEERS tv
Shaw, Stan	Film	THE BOYS IN COMPANY C '78
Shearer, Moira	Film	THE RED SHOES '48 ****
Shearer, Norma	Film	ESCAPE '40
Shearer, Norma	Film	MARIE ANTOINETTE '38
Shearer, Norma	Film	RIPTIDE '34
Shearer, Norma	Film	ROMEO AND JULIET '36
Shearer, Norma	Film	THE DIVORCEE '30
Sheedy, Ally	Film	MAN'S BEST FRIEND '93
Sheen, Charlie	Film	THE ARRIVAL '96
Sheen, Charlie	Film	THE BOYS NEXT DOOR '85
Sheen, Charlie	Film	THE THREE MUSKETEERS '93
Sheen, Charlie	Nee	CARLOS ERWIN ESTEVEZ
Sheen, Martin	Film	BADLANDS '73
Sheen, Martin	Film	ENIGMA '82
Sheen, Martin	Film	NO DRUMS, NO BUGLES '71
Sheen, Martin	Film	THE BELIEVERS '87
Sheen, Martin	Nee	RAMON ESTEVEZ
Shelley, Adrienne	Film	TRUST '91
Shelley, Mary w	Title	FRANKIE STEIN
Shelley,Percy Bys.	Poem	TO A SKYLARK
Shepard, Sam	Film	VOYAGER '91
Shepherd, Cybill	Series	THE YELLOW ROSE tv
Shepherd. Cybill	Series	MOONLIGHTING tv
Sheridan, Ann	Film	COME NEXT SPRING '56

Sheridan, Ann	Film	STELLA '50
Sheridan, Ann	Film	THE DOUGHGIRLS '44
Sheridan, Ann	Film	THE UNFAITHFUL '47
Sheridan, Ann	Film	WOMAN ON THE RUN '50
Sheridan, Dinah	Film	GENEVIEVE '53
Sheridan, Dinah	Film	THE RAILWAY CHILDREN '72
Sherwood, Robert E.	Play	ABE LINCOLN IN ILLINOIS
Shire, Talia	Film	ROCKY '76
Shire, Talia	Nee	TALIA COPPOLA
Shirellas, The mr	Hit	SOLDIER BOY
Shirley, Anne	Film	CONDEMMED WOMEN '38
Sholochov, Mikhail A.	Title	QUIET DON
Shroyer, Sonny	Sitcom	ENOS tv
Shu Ching-chun	Pen Name	LAO SHE
Shue, Elizabeth	Film	LEAVING LAS VEGAS '96
Shulz, Charles	Title	HAPPINESS IS A WARM PUPPY
Shum, Mina d	Film	DOUBLE HAPPINESS '95
Shute, Nevil	Title	A TOWN LIKE ALICE
Shute, Nevil	Title	ON THE BEACH
Sibelius, Jean	Comp.	FINLANDIA
Sidney, Sylvia	Film	JENNIE GERHARDT '33
Sidney, Sylvia	Film	PICK-UP '33
Sidney, Sylvia	Film	SABOTAGE '36
Sidney, Sylvia	Film	YOU ONLY LIVE ONCE '37
Siegel, David	Film	SUTURE '93
Siegel, Jerry	Cartoon	SUPERMAN
Signoret, Simone	Film	DIABOLIQUE '55
Signoret, Simone	Film	DIAMOND HUNTERS '56
Signoret, Simone	Film	GAMES '67
Signoret, Simone	Film	L'ADOLESCENTE '79
Signoret, Simone	Film	ROOM AT THE TOP '59 ****
Signoret, Simone	Film	THE CRUCIBLE '57
Sills, Beverly	Nee	BELLE SILVERMAN
Silver, Ron	Film	FELLOW TRAVELER '89
Silverheels, Jay	Role	TONTO in The Lone Ranger tv
Silverheels, Jay	Series	THE LONE RANGER tv
Silvers, Phil	Film	FOLLOW THAT CAMEL '67
Silvers, Phil	Nee	PHILIP SILVERSMITH
Silverstone, Alicia	Film	CLUELESS '95
Sim, Alastair	Film	A CHRISTMAS CAROL '51 ****
Sim, Alastair	Film	GREEN FOR DANGER '46 ****
Simmons, Jean	Film	HOME BEFORE DARK '58
Simmons, Jean	Film	SO LONG AT THE FAIR '50
Simmons, Jean	Film	THE HAPPY ENDING 69
Simmons, Jean	Film	THE INHERITANCE '47
Simmons, Richard	Series	SERGEANT PRESTON OF THE YUKON tv
Simon&Garfunkel mr	Hit	BRIDGE OVER TROUBLED WATERS
Simon, Carly mr	Hit	YOU'RE SO VAIN
Simon, Michel	Film	L'ATALANTE '34 ****
Simon, Michel	Film	LA CHIENNE '31 ****
Simon, Neil	Play	GOD'S FAVORITE
Simon, Neil	Play	LOST IN YONKERS
Simon, Neil	Play	THE GOODBYE GIRL
Simon, Neil	Play	THE ODD COUPLE
Simon, Paul mr	Hit	GRACELAND
Simon. Neil	Play	CHAPTER TWO
Sinatra, Frank	Film	ASSAULT ON A QUEEN '66
Sinatra, Frank	Film	CAN-CAN '60
Sinatra, Frank	Film	DETECTIVE, THE '68
Sinatra, Frank	Film	MEET DANNY WILSON '52
Sinatra, Frank	Film	NONE BUT THE BRAVE '65

Sinatra, Frank	Film	ON THE TOWN '49 ****
Sinatra, Frank	Film	SOME CAME RUNNING '58
Sinatra, Frank	Film	SUDDENLY '54
Sinatra, Frank	Film	THE JOKER IS WILD '57
Sinatra, Frank	Film	THE TENDER TRAP '55
Sinatra, Frank	Hit Song	ALL OR NOTHING AT ALL
Sinatra, Frank	Hit Song	GOOD NIGHT IRENE
Sinatra, Frank	Hit Song	HEY JEALOUS LOVER
Sinatra, Frank	Hit Song	I'LL BE SEEING YOU
Sinatra, Frank	Hit Song	LOVE AND MARRIAGE
Sinclair, Upton	Title	COAL
Sinclair, Upton	Title	OIL
Sinclair, Upton	Title	THE JUNGLE
Sinclair, Upton	Title	WIDE IS THE GATE
Sinclair, Upton	Title	WORLD'S END
Singleton, Penny	Film	BLONDIE '38
Singleton, Penny	Film	BLONDIE Films '40's
Singleton, Penny	Film	LIFE WITH BLONDIE '46
Sinyavsky, Andrey Donatovich	Pen Name	ABRAM TERTZ
Skelton, Red	Film	A SOUTHERN YANKEE '48
Skelton, Red	Film	DuBARRY WAS A LADY '43
Skelton, Red	Film	THE CLOWN '53
Skelton, Red	Film	THE FULLER BRUSH MAN '48
Skelton, Red	Film	THE SHOW-OFF '46
Skelton, Red	Film	THE YELLOW CAB MAN '50
Skelton, Red	Film	WATCH THE BIRDIE '50
Skipworth, Alison	Film	MADAME RACKETEER '32
Skye, Ione	Film	GAS, FOOD LODGING '92
Skye, Ione	Film	RIVER'S EDGE '86
Skye, Ione	Film	THE RACHEL PAPERS '89
Slater, Christian	Film	PUMP UP THE VOLUME '90
Slaughter, Tod	Film	THE FACE AT THE WINDOW '39
Sloan, John French	Printing	BACKYARDS, GREENWICH VILLIAGE
Sloane, Paul d+	Film	THE CLINGING VINE '26
Sly&the Family Stone mr	Hit	EVERYDAY PEOPLE
Smetana, Bed Rich	Opera	THE BARTERED BRIDE
Smith, Adam	Title	SUPERMONEY
Smith, Alexis	Film	THE TURNING POINT '52
Smith, C. Aubrey	Film	THE FOUR FEATHERS '39
Smith, Cheryl	Film	LASERBLAST '78
Smith, Ernest Bramah	Pen Name	ERNEST BRAMAH
Smith, Florence Margaret	Pen Name	STEVIE SMITH
Smith, Jacklyn	Series	CHARLIE'S ANGELS tv
Smith, Jaclyn	Film	NIGHTKILL '80
Smith, John	Series	LARAMIE tv
Smith, Maggie	Film	A ROOM WITH A VIEW '86
Smith, Pam	Film	MISTY '61
Smith, Patti mr	Hit	BECAUSE THE NIGHT
Smith, Sydney	Cartoon	THE GUMPS
Smith, Will	Film	INDEPENDENCE DAY '96
Smith, Will	Series	FRESH PRINCE OF BEL AIR tv
Smith, William	Film	RUNAWAY, RUNAWAY '71
Smitrovich, Bill	Series	LIFE GOES ON tv
Snodgress, Carrie	Film	THE ATTIC '79
Soglow, Otto	Cartoon	LITTLE KING
Solo, Han fc	Charac	in STAR WARS
Solomon J. Rabinowitz AKA		SHALOM ALEICHEM
Somers, Suzanne	Nee	SUZANNE MAHONEY
Somers, Suzanne	Series	THREE'S COMPANY tv
Sommer, Elke	Film	A SHOT IN THE DARK '64 ****
Sommer, Elke	Film	FRONTIER HELLCAT '66

Sommers, Joanie	HitSong	JOHNNY GET ANGRY
Sondergaard, Gale	Film	THE LIFE OF EMILE ZOLA '37 ****
Sondergaard, Gale	Film	THE SPIDER WOMAN '44
Sondheim, Stephan	Comp	INTO THE WOODS
Sondheim, Stephen	Comp	DO I HEAR A WALTZ?
Sondheim, Stephen	Song	LADIES WHO LUNCH
Soo, Jack	Series	BARNEY MILLER tv
Sophocles	Title	ANTIGONE
Sordi, Alberto	Film	I VITELLONI '53 ****
Sorel, Georges	Title	REFLECTIONS ON VIOLENCE
Sorvino, Mira	Film	MIGHTY APHRODITE '95
Sorvino, Mira	Film	MIMIC '97
Sothern, Ann	Film	MAISIE '39
Sothern, Ann	Film	MAISIE WAS A LADY '41
Sothern, Ann	Film	NANCY GOES TO RIO '50
Sothern, Ann	Film	SHADOW ON THE WALL '50
Sothern, Ann	Nee	HARRIETTE LAKE
Sothern, Ann	Sitcom	MY MOTHER THE CAR tv
Soul, David	Film	RAGE '80
Soul, David	Series	STARSKY AND HUTCH tv
Southside Johnny & the Asbury Jukes	mr Hit	THIS TIME
Spacek, Sissy	Film	CARRIE '76
Spacek, Sissy	Film	JFK '91
Spacek, Sissy	Film	MARIE '85
Spacek, Sissy	Film	THE LONG WALK HOME '90
Spacek, Sissy	Film	THE RIVER '84
Spano, Joe	Role	GOLDBLUME (In Hill Street Blues tv)
Spark, Muriel	Title	THE PRIME OF MISS JEAN BRODIE
Speed, Carol	Film	ABBY '74
Spenser, Edmund	Title	THE FAERIE QUEEN
Sperber, Wendie	Series	BABES tv
Spielberg, Stevn d	Film	E.T.: THE EXTRA-TERRESTRIAL '82 ****
Spielberg, Stevn d	Film	SCHINDLER'S LIST '94 ****
Spielberg, Stevn d	Film	THE COLOR PURPLE '85
Spillane, Mickey	Film	THE GIRL HUNTERS '63
Spiner, Brent	Series	STAR TREK, THE NEXT GENERATION tv
Springfield, Dusty	mr Hit	YOU DON'T HAVE TO SAY YOU LOVE ME
Springsteen, Bruce	mr Hit	BORN IN THE U.S.A
Srivastiv, Dhanpat Rai	Pen Name	PREMCHAND
St. James, Susan	Nee	SUSAN MILLER
St. James, Susan	Series	KATE AND ALLIE tv
Stack, Robert	Film	THE CARETAKERS '63
Stack, Robert	Film	THE CORRUPT ONES '66
Stack, Robert	Film	THE SCARFACE MOB '62
Stack, Robert	Nee	ROBERT MODINI
Stack, Robert	Series	THE UNTOUCHABLES tv
Stallone, Sylvester	Film	CLIFFHANGER '93
Stallone, Sylvester	Film	DAYLIGHT '96
Stallone, Sylvester	Film	F.I.S.T. '78
Stallone, Sylvester	Film	NIGHTHAWKS '81
Stallone, Sylvester	Film	OSCAR '91
Stallone, Sylvester	Film	ROCKY '76
Stallone, Sylvester	Role	RAMBO
Stamp, Terence	Film	THE COLLECTOR '65
Stamp, Terence	Film	THE HIT '85
Stamp, Terence	Film	THE MIND OF MR. SOAMES '70
Stanley, Kim	Film	SEANCE ON A WET AFTERNOON '64 ****
Stanley, Kim	Film	THE THREE SISTERS '66
Stanton, Dean	Film	THE HOSTAGE '67
Stanwyck, Barbara	Film	A MESSAGE TO GARCIA '36
Stanwyck, Barbara	Film	CALIFORNIA '46

Stanwyck, Barbara	Film		CRIME OF PASSION '57
Stanwyck, Barbara	Film		DOUBLE INDEMNITY '44 ****
Stanwyck, Barbara	Film		JEOPARDY '53
Stanwyck, Barbara	Film		LADIES OF LEISURE '30
Stanwyck, Barbara	Film		LADY OF BURLESQUE '43
Stanwyck, Barbara	Film		THE FURIES '50
Stanwyck, Barbara	Film		THE MAVERICK QUEEN '56
Stanwyck, Barbara	Film		THE MIRACLE WOMAN '31
Stanwyck, Barbara	Film		THE NIGHT WALKER '64
Stanwyck, Barbara	Film		THE SECRET BRIDE '35
Stanwyck, Barbara	Film		THIS IS MY AFFAIR '37
Stanwyck, Barbara	Film		WITNESS TO MURDER '54
Stanwyck, Barbara	Nee		RUBY STEVENS
Stanwyck, Barbara	Series		THE BIG VALLEY tv
Stapel, Huub	Film		THE LIFT '83
Stapleton, Jean	Nee		JEANNE MURRAY
Stapleton, Jean	Series		ALL IN THE FAMILY tv
Stapleton, Maureen	Film		SWEET LORRAINE '87
Starr, Ringo	Film		CAVEMAN '81
Starr, Ringo	Hit Sing		YOU'RE SIXTEEN
Starr, Ringo	Nee		RICHARD STARKEY
Steele, Barbara	Film		THE GHOST '63
Steely, Dan mr	Hit		RIKKI DON'T LOSE THAT NUMBER
Stegner, Wallace	Title		ANGLE OF REPOSE p-f'72
Steiger, Rod	Film		ACROSS THE BRIDGE '57
Steiger, Rod	Film		GUILTY AS CHARGED '92
Steiger, Rod	Film		IN THE HEAT OF THE NIGHT'67****
Steiger, Rod	Film		THE KINDRED '87
Steiger, Rod	Film		THE LONGEST DAY '62 ****
Steiger, Rod	Film		THE PAWNBROKER '65 ****
Steinbeck, John	Title		THE GRAPES OF WRATH p-f'40
Steinberg, Michael	Film		THE WATERDANCE '92
Sten, Anna	TitleRole		NANA '34
Stenvall, A.	Pen Name		ALEKSIS KIVI w & po
Stephens, Robert	Film		THE ASPHYX '72
Stephenson, James	Film		SHINING VICTORY '41
Steppenwolf mr	Hit		BORN TO BE WILD
Sterling, Jan	Film		RHUBARB '51
Sterling, Robert	Film		ROUGHSHOD '49
Stern, Howard	Title		PRIVATE PARTS
Sterne, Laurence	Title		A SENTIMENTAL JOURNEY
Sterne, Laurence	Title		TRISTRAM SHANDY
Stevens, Connie	Nee		CONCETTA INGOLIA
Stevens, Craig	Series		PETER GUNN tv
Stevens, Onslow	Film		HOUSE OF DRACULA '45
Stevens, Rise	Film		GOING MY WAY '44 ****
Stevenson, Robt. Louie	Title		KIDNAPPED
Stewart, Catherine Mary	Film		NIGHT OF THE COMET '84
Stewart, J.I.M.	Pen Name		MICHAEL INNES
Stewart, James	Film		ANATOMY OF A MURDER '59 ****
Stewart, James	Film		BANDOLERO! '68
Stewart, James	Film		CARBINE WILLIAMS '52
Stewart, James	Film		COME LIVE WITH ME '41
Stewart, James	Film		DESTRY RIDES AGAIN '39 ****
Stewart, James	Film		HARVEY '50
Stewart, James	Film		IT'S A WONDERFUL LIFE '46 ****
Stewart, James	Film		MALAYA '49
Stewart, James	Film	MR.	SMITH GOES TO WASHINGTON'39****
Stewart, James	Film		NO TIME FOR COMEDY '40
Stewart, James	Film		REAR WINDOW '54 ****
Stewart, James	Film		ROPE '48

```
Stewart, James       Film      SHENANDOAH '65
Stewart, James       Film      THE JACKPOT '50
Stewart, James       Film      THE MAN FROM LARAMIE '55
Stewart, James       Film   THE MAN WHO SHOT LIBERTY VALANCE '62 ****
Stewart, James       Film      THE MOUNTAIN ROAD '60
Stewart, James       Film      THE SPIRIT OF ST. LOUIS '57
Stewart, James       Film      TWO RODE TOGETHER '61
Stewart, James       Film      VERTIGO '58
Stewart, Patrick     Series    STAR TREK, THE NEXT GENERATION tv
Stewart, Penelope    Film      VIGIL '84
Stewart, Rob         Series    SWEATING BULLETS tv
Stewart, Rod    mr   Hit       MAGGIE MAE
Sting mr             Hit       IF YOU LOVE SOMEBODY, SET THEM FREE
Sting mr             Nee       GORDON SUMNER
Stokowski, Leopold   Film      FANTASIA '40
Stoltz, Eric         Film      LIONHEART '87
Stoltz, Eric         Film      NAKED IN NEW YORK '94
Stone Lewis          Film      THE MAN WHO CRIED WOLF '37
Stone, Lewis         Film      THE HARDYS RIDE HIGH '39
Stone, Oliver d      Film      JFK '91
Stories, The         Hit Song  BROTHER LOVE
Storm, Gale          Film      THE UNDERWORLD STORY '50
Storm, Gale          Series    MY LITTLE MARGIE tv
Story, Isaac         Pen Name  PETER QUINCE
Stout, Rex           Charac    NERO WOLF
Stowe, Harriet B.    Title     LITTLE EVA
Stowe, Harriet B.    Title     UNCLE TOM'S CABIN
Stowe, Harriet B.    Villian   SIMON LEGREE in Uncle Tom's Cabin
Stowe, Madeleine     Film      BLINK '94
Strand, Robert       Series    BENSON tv
Strasberg, Susan     Film      PSYCH-OUT '68
Strauss, Richard     Opera     ARABELLA
Strauss, Richard     Opera     ELEKTRA
Stravinsky, Igor     Ballet    AGON
Stravinsky, Igor     Comp      THE RITE OF SPRING
Stravinsky, Igor     Opera     OEDIPUS REX
Stravinsky, Igor     Opera     THE NIGHTINGALE
Streep, Meryl        Film      A CRY IN THE DARK '88
Streep, Meryl        Film      HEARTBURN '86
Streep, Meryl        Film      KRAMER VS. KRAMER '79 ****
Streep, Meryl        Film      PLENTY '85
Streep, Meryl        Film      SILKWOOD '83
Streep, Meryl        Ttle Role SOPHIE'S CHOICE '82
Streisand, Barbra    Film      NUTS '87
Streisand, Barbra d+ Film      YENTL '83
Streisand, Barbra    Hit Song  EVERGREEN
Stroheim, Erich von d+ Film    THE WEDDING MARCH '28 ****
Stroheim, Erich von  Film      THE GREAT FLAMARION '45
Stukalov, Nikolay Fyodorovich Pen Name NIKOLAY POGOODIN
Styne, Jule          Comp      FUNNY GIRL
Styron, William      Title     SOPHIE'S CHOICE
Suchet, David        Film      SUNDAY '97 ****
Sue, Marie Joseph    Pen Name  EUGENE SUE
Sukowa, Barbara      Film      LOLA '82
Sukowa, Barbara      Film      ZENTROPA '92
Sullavan, Margaret   Film      NEXT TIME WE LOVE '36
Sullavan, Margaret   Film      NO SAD SONGS FOR ME '50
Sullavan, Margaret   Film      THE MORTAL STORM '40
Sullivan, Barry      Film      PYRO '64
Sullivan, Barry      Film      THE GANGSTER '47
Sullivan, Barry      Film      THIS SAVAGE LAND '68
```

```
Sullivan,Arthur S. Operetta  H.M.S. PINAFORE
Summer, Donna  mr     Hit       SHE WORKS HARD FOR THE MONEY
Summer, Donna  mr     Nee       La DONNA GAINES
Sumner, Gordon Matthew aka      STING
Supremes           Song      I HEARD A SYMPHONY
Supremes, The  mr     Hit       STOP ! IN THE NAME OF LOVE
Supremes, The  mr     Hit Song  WHERE DID OUR LOVE GO
Supremes, The  mr     HitSong   YOU CAN'T HURRY LOVE
Sutherland, Donald Film      A DRY WHITE SEASON '89
Sutherland, Donald Film      BETHUNE '77
Sutherland, Donald Film      BLOOD RELATIVES '78
Sutherland, Donald Film      EYE OF THE NEEDLE '81
Sutherland, Donald Film      GAS '81
Sutherland, Donald Film      MASH '70 ****
Sutherland, Donald Film      ORDINARY PEOPLE '80 ****
Sutherland, Donald Film      THE DAY OF THE LOCUST '75
Sutherland, Donald Film      THRESHOLD '81
Sutherland, Kiefer Film      FLATLINERS '90
Sutton, John       Film      COUNTERFEITERS '48
Svenson, Bo        Film      SPECIAL DELIVERY '76
Sverak, Zdenek     Film      KOLYA '97 ****
Swanson, Gloria    Film      SUNSET BLVD. '50 ****
Swanson, Gloria    Film      THE LOVES OF SUNYA '27
Swayze, Patrick    Film      GHOST '90
Sweeney, D.B.      Film      THE CUTTING EDGE '92
Sweet, Dolph       Series    GIMME A BREAK tv
Swenson, Inga      Series    BENSON tv
Swinburn, Nora     Film      THE RIVER '51 ****
Swit, Loretta      Film      BEER '75
Swit, Loretta      Series    M*A*S*H tv
Sydney, Sylvia     Film      MADAME BUTTERFLY '32
Sydow, Max von     Film      STEPPENWOLF '74
Sydow, Max von     Film      THE REWARD '65
Sydow, Max von     Film      THE SEVENTH SEAL '57
Sydow, Max von     Film      THE SHAME '68 ****
Sydow, Max von     Film      THE VIRGIN SPRING '59
Sykes, Brenda      Film      HONKY '71
Sylvester, William Film      GORGO '61
Talking Heads  mr     Hit       ONCE IN A LIFETIME
Takei, George      Role      SULU -- in STARTREK Movies
Tamerlis, Zoe      Film      SPECIAL EFFECTS '84
Tamiroff, Akim     Film      DANGEROUS TO KNOW '38
Tan, Amy           Title     JOY LUCK CLUB
Tanaka, Kinuyo     Film      SANSHO THE BAILIFF '54 ****
Tandem, Carl Felix Pen Name  CARL SPITTELER
Tandy, Jessica     Film      BUTLEY '74 ****
Tandy, Jessica     Film      THE BIRDS '63
Tandy, Jessica     Play      KING LEAR
Tandy, Jessica     Play      THE FOUR POSTER
Tandy, Jessica     Play      THE GIN GAME
Tarkington, Booth  Title     THE MAGNIFICENT AMBERSONS p-f'19
Tate, Larenz       Film      MENACE II SOCIETY '93
Tati, Jacques d+   Film      MON ONCLE '58 ****
Tati, Jacques d+   Film      MR. HULOT'S HOLIDAY '53
Tati, Jacques d+   Film      PLAY TIME '67 ****
Tatsunosuke, Hasegawa Pen Name SHIMEI FUTABATEI
Taylor, Don        Film      STALAG 17 '53 ****
Taylor, Elizabeth  Film      COURAGE OF LASSIE '46
Taylor, Elizabeth  Film      FATHER OF THE BRIDE '50 ****
Taylor, Elizabeth  Film      GIANT '56 ****
Taylor, Elizabeth  Film      NATIONAL VELVET '44 ****
```

Taylor, Elizabeth	Film	RHAPSODY '54
Taylor, Elizabeth	Film	SANDPIPER '65
Taylor, Elizabeth	Film	SECRET CEREMONY '68
Taylor, Elizabeth	Film	THE COMEDIANS '67
Taylor, Elizabeth	Film	THE ONLY GAME IN TOWN '70
Taylor, Elizabeth	Film	THE V.I.P.'S '63
Taylor, James mr	Hit	YOU'VE GOT A FRIEND
Taylor, James mr	Song	HER TOWN TOO
Taylor, Kent	Series	BOSTON BLACKIE tv
Taylor, Lili	Film	I SHOT ANDY WARHOL '96
Taylor, Noah	Film	FLIRTING '90
Taylor, Rip	Nee	CHARLES ELMER Jr.
Taylor, Robert	Film	AMBUSH '49
Taylor, Robert	Film	BATAAN '43
Taylor, Robert	Film	CONSPIRATOR '49
Taylor, Robert	Film	ESCAPE '40
Taylor, Robert	Film	IVANHOE '52
Taylor, Robert	Film	QUENTIN DURWARD '55
Taylor, Robert	Nee	SPANGLER ARLINGRTON BRUGH
Taylor, Rod	Film	DARKER THAN AMBER '70
Taylor, Rod	Film	THE GLASS BOTTOM BOAT '66
Taylor, Rod	Film	THE LIQUIDATOR '66
Taylor, Rod	Film	THE TIME MACHINE '60
Tchaikovsky, Piotr	Comp	PATHETIQUE - Symph. No. 6 in B Minor
Tchaikovsky, Pyotr	Ballet	SWAN LAKE
Tchaikovsky, Pyotr	Comp	NUTCRACKER SUITE
Tchaikovsky, Pyotr	Comp	PIQUE DAME
Tellez, Fray Gabriel	Pen Name	TIRSO de MOLINA
Temple, Shirley	Film	DIMPLES '36
Temple, Shirley	Film	HEIDI '37
Temple, Shirley	Film	THE LITTLE PRINCESS '39
Temple, Shirley	Film	WEE WILLIE WINKIE '37
Temptations,The mr	Hit	MY GIRL
Tennant, Victoria	Film	THE RAGMAN'S DAUGHTER '72
Tennyson,Alfred L.	Heroine	ENID
Tennyson,Alfred L.	Poem	ENOCH ARDEN
Tennyson,Alfred L.	Poem	LOCKSLEY HALL
Terry-Thomas	Film	MAN IN A COCKED HAT '59
Terzieff, Laurent	Film	THE MILKY WAY '70 ****
Tey, Josephine	Title	BRAT FARRAR
Thackeray, Wm. Makepeace	Title	VANIITY FAIR
Theotocopoulos,Domenikos	Aka	EL GRECO p
Thevenin, Denis	Pen Name	GEORGES DUHAMEL
Thibault, Jacques	Pen Name	ANATOLE FRANCE
Thicke, Alan	Series	GROWING PAINS tv
Thomas, Danny	Nee	MUZYAD YAKHOOB(later AMOS JACOBS)
Thomas, Ernest	Series	WHAT'S HAPPERNING!! tv
Thomas, Jameson	Film	THE FARMER'S WIFE '28
Thomas, Marlo	Series	THAT GIRL tv
Thomas, Philip M.(Michael)	Film	SPARKLE '76
Thomas, Richard	Film	RED SKY AT MORNING '70
Thomas, Scott	Film	SILENT ASSASSINS '88
Thomerson, Tim	Film	TRANCERS '85
Thompson, Emma	Film	HOWARDS END '92 ****
Thompson, Emma	Film	THE REMAINS OF THE DAY '93
Thompson, Jack	Film	THE CLUB '80
Thompson, Marshall	Series	DAKTARI tv
Thompson, Morton	Title	NOT AS A STRANGER
Thompson, R.H.	Film	THE QUARREL '91
Thompson, Sada	Series	FAMILY tv
Thor, Jerome	Series	FOREIGN INTRIGUE tv

Thorpe, Richard	Film	IT'S A BIG COUNTRY '51
Thorton, Billy Bob	d+ Film	SLING BLADE '97 ****
Three Dog Night	mr Hit	JOY TO THE WORLD
Three Stooges, The	Film	THE OUTLAWS IS COMING '65
Thulin, Ingrid	Film	THE SILENCE '63
Thulin, Ingrid	Film	WILD STRAWBERRIES '57 ****
Tibbett, Lawrence	Film	METROPOLITAN '35
Tierney, Gene	Film	DRAGONWYCK '46
Tierney, Gene	Film	LAURA '44 ****
Tierney, Gene	Film	SUNDOWN '41
Tierney, Gene	Film	THE MATING SEASON '51
Tierney, Gene	Film	WHIRLPOOL '49
Tierney, Lawrence	Film	BODYGUARD '48
Tiller, Nadja	Film	ROSEMARY '58
Tilly, Jennifer	Film	BOUND '96
Tobey, Kenneth	Series	THE WHIRLYBIRDS tv
Todd, Ann	Film	MADELEINE '50
Todd, Richard	Film	A MAN CALLED PETER '55
Todd, Richard	Film	BREAKOUT '59
Todd, Richard	Film	THE BOYS '61
Todd, Richard	Film	THE HELLIONS '62
Todd, Richard	Film	THE SWORD AND THE ROSE '53
Todd, Tony	Film	CANDYMAN '92
Tognazzi, Ugo	Film	THE CONJUGAL BED '63
Tognazzi, Ugo	Film	THE HOURS OF LOVE '65
Toler, Sidney	Films	CHARLIE CHAN MOVIES
Tolkien, J.J.R	Charac	BILBO
Tolkien, J.J.R.	Creature	ENT
Tolkien, J.R.R.	Title	THE LAYS OF BELERIAND
Tolkien, J.R.R.	Title	THE LORD OF THE RINGS
Tolstoy, Leo(Count)	Heroine	ANNA
Tolstoy, Leo(Count)	Title	THE DEATH OF IVAN ILYICH
Tomei, Marisa	Film	THE PEREZ FAMILY '95
Tone, Franchot	Film	EXCLUSIVE STORY '36
Tone, Franchot	Film	FAST AND FURIOUS '39
Tone, Franchot	Film	THE KING STEPS OUT '36
Torme, Mel	Nickname	THE VELVET FOG
Torn, Rip	Film	HEARTLAND '79
Torn, Rip	Film	PAYDAY '73
Torn, Rip	Film	TROPIC OF CANCER '70
Torn, Rip	Nee	ELMORE RUAL TORN Jr
Torrent, Ana	Film	CRIA '76
Torrent, Ana	Film	THE NEST '80
Townsend, Robert	d+Film	THE FIVE HEARTBEATS '91
Tracy, Lee	Film	I'LL TELL THE WORLD '45
Tracy, Lee	Series	THE AMAZING MR. MALONE tv
Tracy, Spencer	Film	ADAM'S RIB '49 ****
Tracy, Spencer	Film	CAPTAINS COURAGEOUS '37 ****
Tracy, Spencer	Film	CASS TIMBERLANE '47
Tracy, Spencer	Film	FATHER OF THE BRIDE '50 ****
Tracy, Spencer	Film	FURY '36
Tracy, Spencer	Film	I TAKE THIS WOMAN '40
Tracy, Spencer	Film	INHERIT THE WIND '60
Tracy, Spencer	Film	JUDGMENT AT NUREMBERG '61 ****
Tracy, Spencer	Film	MALAYA '49
Tracy, Spencer	Film	STATE OF THE UNION '48
Tracy, Spencer	Film	THE MOUNTAIN '56
Tracy, Spencer	Film	THE OLD MAN AND THE SEA '58
Tracy, Spencer	Film	THE SEVENTH CROSS '44
Tracy, Spencer	Film	THEY GAVE HIM A GUN '37
Tracy, Spencer	Film	WHIPSAW '35

Traffic mr	Hit	FEELIN' ALRIGHT
Travanti,Daniel J.	Series	HILLSTREET BLUES tv
Travers, Bill	Film	GORGO '61
Travis, Randy	Nee	RANDY TRAYWICK
Travolta, John	Film	GREASE '78
Travolta, John	Film	LOOK WHO'S TALKING '89
Travolta, John	Film	WHITE MAN'S BURDEN '95
Treacher, Arthur	Film	THANK YOU, JEEVES '36
Trevor, Claire	Film	STAGECOACH '39 ****
Trintignant, Jean-Louis	Film	MY NIGHT AT MAUD'S '69
Trintignant, Jean-Louis	Film	THE CROOK '71
Trintignant, Marie	Film	BETTY '92
Troisi, Massimo	Film	THE POSTMAN '94
Trudeau, Garry	Cartoon	DOONESBURY
Tryon, Thomas	Title	THE OTHER
Tryon, Tom	Film	THE CARDINAL '63
Tucker, Forrest	Film	THE CRAWLING EYE '58
Tucker, Sophie	Nee	SOPHIA KALISH
Turner, Big Joe mr	Hit	SHAKE, RATTLE AND ROLL
Turner, Janine	Series	NORTHERN EXPOSURE tv
Turner, Lana	Film	BY LOVE POSSESSED '61
Turner, Lana	Film	CASS TIMBERLANE '47
Turner, Lana	Film	DIANE '55
Turner, Lana	Film	IMITATION OF LIFE '59
Turner, Lana	Film	PORTRAIT IN BLACK '60
Turner, Lana	Film	THE LADY TAKES A FLYER '58
Turner, Lana	Film	THE POSTMAN ALWAYS RINGS TWICE'46****
Turner, Lana	Film	THE PRODIGAL '55
Turner, Tina	Nee	ANNIE MAE BULLOCK
Turner, Tina s	Hit	WHAT'S LOVE GOT TO DO WITH IT
Turow, Scott	Title	ONEL
Turtles, The	HitSong	IT AIN'T ME BABE
Turturro, John	Film	MAC '92
Turturro, John	Film	UNSTRUNG HEROES '95
Tushingham, Rita	Film	THE LEATHER BOYS '63
Tushingham, Rita	Film	THE TRAP '66
Twain, Mark	Title	ROUGHING IT
Twain, Mark	Title	THE INNOCENTS ABROAD
Twain, Mark	Title	THE TRAGEDY OF PUDD'NHEAD WILSON
Twitty, Conway	Nee	HAROLD LLOYD JENKINS
Tyler, Liv	Film	STEALING BEAUTY '96
Tyson, Cicely	Film	SOUNDER '72 ****
U2 mr	Hit	JOSHUA TREE
Uhry, Alfred	Title	DRIVING MISS DAISY
Ullman, Liv	Film	SCENES FROM A MARRIAGE '73 ****
Ullman, Tracey	Film	HOUSEHOLD SAINTS '93
Ullmann, Liv	Film	GABY--A TRUE STORY '87
Ullmann, Liv	Film	THE SHAME '68 ****
Ullmann, Liv	Film	THE WAYWARD GIRL '59
Ulyanov, Vladimir Ilyich	aka	LENIN
Uncas	Charac	THE LAST OF THE MOHICANS - Hero
Underwood, Jay	Film	THE BOY WHO COULD FLY '86
Ure, Mary	Film	WHERE EAGLES DARE '69
Urich, Robert	Series	SPENSER FOR HIRE tv
Urich, Robert	Series	VEGAS tv
Uris, Leon	Hero	ARI
Uris, Leon	Title	BATTLE CRY
Uris, Leon	Title	MITLA PASS
Uris, Leon	Title	QB VII
Uris, Leon	Title	THE HAJ
Uris, Leon	Title	TOPAZ

Uris, Leon	Title	TRINITY
Ustinov, Peter	Film	DEATH ON THE NILE '78
Vaccaro, Brenda	Film	MIDNIGHT COWBOY '45
Valentino, Rudolph	Film	THE SHIEK '21
Valentino, Rudolph	Nee	RUDOLPHO D'ANTONGUOLIA
Valli, Frankie	Nee	FRANK CASTELLUCCIO
Valli, Alida	Film	SENSO '54
Vallone, Raf	Film	TWO WOMEN '61 ****
Van Damme, Jean-Claude d+	Film	THE QUEST '96
Van Dyke, Dick	Film	MARY POPPINS '64 ****
Van Dyke, Dick	Film	THE COMIC '69
Van Eyck, Peter	Film	THE BRAIN '65
Van Eyck, Peter	Film	THE SNORKEL '58
Van Halen mr	Hit	JUMP
Van Patten, Dick	Series	EIGHT IS ENOUGH tv
Vanucci, Andrea	Aka	ANDREA del SARTO p
Varney, Jim	Films	"ERNEST" FILMS '87 - '91
Vaughn, Robert	Series	THE MAN FROM U.N.C.L.E. tv
Vaughn, Robert	Series	THE PROTECTORS tv
Vecelli, Tiziano	Aka	TITIAN
Vee, Bobby mj s	Song	DEVIL OR ANGEL
Veidt, Conrad	Film	CONTRABAND '40
Veidt, Conrad	Film	POWER '34
Veidt, Conrad	Film	UNDER THE RED ROBE '37
Velez, Lupe	Film	MEXICAN SPITFIRE '39
Velez, Lupe	Film	THE GIRL FROM MEXICO '39
Velez, Lupe	Film	THE HALF NAKED TRUTH '32
Ventura, Lino	Film	THE FRENCH DETECTIVE '75
Ventura, Lino	Film	THREE TOUGH GUYS '74
Vera-Ellen	Film	THE BELLE OF NEW YORK '52
Verdi, Giusdeppe	Aria	SEMPRE LIBERA(La Traviata)
Verdi, Giuseppe	Aria	AH FORSVELUI
Verdi, Giuseppe	Aria	CARO NOME
Verdi, Giuseppe	Aria	ERI TU CHE
Verdi, Giuseppe	Comp	REQUIEM
Verdi, Giuseppe	Heroine	AIDA (also an Opera)
Verdi, Giuseppe	Heroine	VIOLETTA in La traviata
Verdi, Giuseppe	Opera	A FORZA DEL DESTINO
Verdi, Giuseppe	Opera	ATILLA
Verdi, Giuseppe	Opera	DON CARLO
Verdi, Giuseppe	Opera	ERNANI
Verdi, Giuseppe	Opera	FALSTAFF v's last
Verdi, Giuseppe	Opera	I VESPRI SICILLANI
Verdi, Giuseppe	Opera	IL TROVATORE
Verdi, Giuseppe	Opera	LA TRAVIATA
Verdi, Giuseppe	Opera	OTELLO
Verdi, Giuseppe	Opera	RIGOLETTO
Verdon, Gwen	Ballet	SWEEET CHARITY
Verdon, Gwen	Film	LEGS '83
Verdugo, Elena	Series	MEET MILLIE tv
Verne, Jules	Charac	NEMO(Captain)
Verne, Jules	Title	MYSTERIOUS ISLAND
Viaud, Louis Marie Julien	Pen Name	PIERRE LOTI
Vidal, Gore	Play	VISIT TO A SMALL PLANET
Vidal, Henri	Film	WHAT PRICE MURDER '58
Villeret, Jacques	Film	ROBERT ET ROBERT '78
Vincent, Jan-Michael	Film	BABY BLUE MARINE '76
Vincent, Jan-Michael	Film	DEFIANCE '80
Vincent, Jan-Michael	Film	WHITE LINE FEVER '75
Vincent, Jan-Michael	Series	AIRWOLF tv
Vint, Alan	Film	MACON COUNTY LINE '74

Virgil	Hero	AENEAS
Voight, Jon	Film	ANACONDA '97
Voight, Jon	Film	CONRACK '74
Voight, Jon	Film	DELIVERANCE '72 ****
Voight, Jon	Film	THE REVOLUTIONARY '70
Volonte,Gian Maria	Film	EBOLI '79
Voltaire	Title	CANDIDE
Von Dohlen, Lenny	Film	ELECTRIC DREAMS ,84
Von Sydow, Max	Film	THE EMIGRANTS '71
Von Sydow, Max	Film	THE MAGICIAN '58
Vonnegut, Kurt w	Title	SLAUGHTERHOUSE FIVE
Waggoner, Lyle	Series	WONDER WOMAN tv
Wagner, Lindsay	Series	THE BIONIC WOMAN tv
Wagner, Richard	Heroine	ELSA, ISOLDE
Wagner, Richard	Heroine	SENTA
Wagner, Richard	Opera	DAS RHEINGOLD
Wagner, Richard	Opera	DIE GOTTERDAMMERUNG
Wagner, Richard	Opera	LOHENGRIN
Wagner, Richard	Opera	SIEGFRIED
Wagner, Richard	Opera	THE FLYING DUTCHMAN
Wagner, Richard	Operas	DER RING DES NIBELUNGEN
Wagner, Robert	Film	BANNING '67
Wagner, Robert	Film	THE MOUNTAIN '56
Wagner, Robert	Series	IT TAKES A THIEF tv
Wagner, Robert	Series	SWITCH tv
Wahl, Ken	Film	THE WANDERERS '79
Wahl, Ken	Series	WISEGUY tv
Waite, Ralph	Series	THE WALTONS tv
Walbrook, Anton	Film	GASLIGHT '40
Walken,Christopher	Film	BRAINSTORM '83
Walken,Christopher	Film	COMMUNION '89
Walken,Christopher	Film	THE FUNERAL '96
Walken,Christopher	Film	THE PROPHECY '95
Walker, Mort	Cartoon	BEETLE BAILEY
Wallace Stone, Dee	Film	E.T. THE EXTRA-TERRESTRIAL'82****
Wallace, Dee	Film	CUJO '83
Wallace, Dee	Film	E.T. THE EXTRA-TERRESTRIAL'82****
Wallace, Jack	Film	THE BEAR '89
Wallace, Lew	Title	BEN-HUR
Waller, Thomas"Fats"	Comp	AIN'T MISBEHAVIN'
Walter, Jessica	Series	AMY PRENTISS tv
Walters, Patricia	Film	THE RIVER '51 ****
Wambaugh, James	Title	THE ONION FIELD
Ward, Mary Augusta	Pen Name	MRS. HUMPHRY WARD
Ward, Sela	Series	SISTERS tv
Warden, Jack	Series	CRAZY LIKE A FOX tv
Warden, Jack	Series	N.Y.P.D. tv
Warner, H.B.	Film	THE KING OF KINGS '27
Warren, Leslie Ann	Film	CLUE '85
Warren,Robert Penn	Title	ALL THE KING'S MEN p-f'47
Warrick, Ruth	Film	DRIFTWOOD '47
Warwick, Dionne mr	Hit	I'LL NEVER FALL IN LOVE AGAIN
Washington, Denzel	Film	GLORY '89 ****
Washington, Denzel	Film	THE MIGHTY QUINN '89
Washington, Denzel	Film	VIRTUOSITY '95
Wass, Ted	Series	BLOSSOM tv
Wasson, Craig	Film	THE OUTSIDER '79
Watanabe, Ken	Film	TAMPOPO '86
Waters, Muddy mr	Hit	ROLLIN' STONE
Waterston, Sam	Film	THE MAN IN THE MOON '91
Watson, John	Pen Name	IAN MACLAREN

Watterson, Bill	Cartoon	CALVIN AND HOBBS
Waugh, Evelyn	Title	A HANDFUL OF DUST
Waugh, Evelyn	Title	BRIDESHEAD REVISITED
Waugh, Evelyn	Title	SCOOP
Wayne, David	Film	THE THREE FACES OF EVE '57
Wayne, David	Nee	WAYNE McMEEKAN
Wayne, John	Film	BRANNIGAN '75
Wayne, John	Film	CHISUM '70
Wayne, John	Film	HATARI! '62
Wayne, John	Film	HONDO '53
Wayne, John	Film	McLINTOCK! '63
Wayne, John	Film	RED RIVER '48 ****
Wayne, John	Film	ROOSTER COGBURN '75
Wayne, John	Film	SANDS OF IWO JIMA '49
Wayne, John	Film	TALL IN THE SADDLE '44
Wayne, John	Film	THE FIGHTING SEABEES '44
Wayne, John	Film	THE LONG VOYAGE HOME '40
Wayne, John	Film	THE LONGEST DAY '62 ****
Wayne, John	Film	THE MAN WHO SHOT LIBERTY VALENCE '62 ****
Wayne, John	Film	THE QUIET MAN '52 ****
Wayne, John	Film	THE SEARCHERS '56 ****
Wayne, John	Film	THE SHOOTIST '76
Wayne, John	Film	STAGECOACH '39 ****
Wayne, John	Film	THE TRAIN ROBBERS '73
Wayne, John	Film	THEY WERE EXPENDABLE '45 ****
Wayne, John	Film	THREE FACES WEST '40
Wayne, John	Film	TYCOON '47
Wayne, John	Nee	MARION MORRISON
Wayne, John d+	Film	ALAMO '60
Weathers, Carl	Role	APOLLO CREED in 4 Rocky Films '72-'85
Weaver, Dennis	Series	GENTLE BEN tv
Weaver, Dennis	Series	McCLOUD tv
Weaver, Sigourney	Film	ALIEN '79
Weaver, Sigourney	Film	ALIENS '86
Weaver, Sigourney	Film	DAVE '93
Weaving, Hugo	Film	PROOF '91
Webb, Clifton	Film	LAURA '44 ****
Webb, Clifton	Film	THE MAN WHO NEVER WAS '56
Webb, Clifton	Film	TITANIC '53
Webb, Clifton	Nee	WEBB PARMALEE HOLLENBECK
Webb, Jack	Film	DRAGNET '54
Webb, Jack d+	Film	PETE KELLY'S BLUES '55
Webb, Jack	Series	DRAGNET tv
Webber, Andrew Lloyd	Musical	PHANTOM OF THE OPERA
Webber, Andrew Lloyd	pr Stg Play	EVITA
Webber, Andrew Lloyd	Song	MUSIC OF THE NIGHT
Webber, Lloyd	Charac	CHE in Evita
Webber, Lloyd	Musical	CATS
Webber, Lloyd	Musical	EVITA
Weill, Kurt mus c	Film	ONE TOUCH OF VENUS '48
Weinstein, Nathan	Pen Name	NATHANAEL WEST
Weissmuller, Johnny	Film	TARZAN FINDS A SON! '39
Weissmuller, Johnny	Film	TARZAN THE APE MAN '32
Weissmuller, Johnny	Film	TARZAN TRIUMPHS '43
Weissmuller, Johnny	Films	TARZAN FILMS '32 - '48
Welch, Raquel	Film	FATHOM '67
Welch, Raquel	Film	FLAREUP '69
Welch, Raquel	Nee	RAQUEL TEJADA
Weld, Tuesday	Film	PLAY IT AS IT LAYS '72
Weller, Peter	Film	ROBOCOP '87

Weller, Peter	Film	SCREAMERS '95
Weller, Peter	Film	SHAKEDOWN '88
Welles, Orson d+	Film	CITIZEN KANE '41 ****
Welles, Orson	Film	COMPULSION '59
Welles, Orson	Film	FERRY TO HONG KONG '61
Welles, Orson	Film	JOURNEY INTO FEAR '42
Welles, Orson	Film	MACBETH '48
Welles, Orson	Film	MAN IN THE SHADOW '57
Welles, Orson d+	Film	OTHELLO '52
Welles, Orson d+	Film	THE STRANGER '46
Welles, Orson	Film	THE THIRD MAN '49 ****
Welles, Orson	Film	TOUCH OF EVIL '58 ****
Welles, Orson	Role	HARRY LIME in Third Man '49
Welles, Orson d+	Film	THE TRIAL '62
Wells, H. G.	Title	TONO BUNGAY
Wells, H.G.	Title	KIPPS
Wells, Mary mr	Hit	MY GUY
Werner, Oskar	Film	INTERLUDE '68
Werner, Oskar	Film	THE LAST TEN DAYS '56
West, Adam	Series	BATMAN tv
West, Mae	Film	GO WEST, YOUNG MAN '36
West, Mae	Film	SHE DONE HIM WRONG '33 ****
West, Nathaniel	Title	THE DAY OF THE LOCUST
Weston, Jack	Film	THE RITZ '76
Westover, Russ	Cartoon	TILLIE THE TOILER
Wharton, Edith	Hero	FROME
Wharton, Edith	Title	A BACKWARD GLANCE
Wharton, Edith	Title	ETHAN FROME
Wharton, Edith	Title	MADAME DeTREYMES
Wharton, Edith	Title	THE AGE OF INNOCENCE p-f'21
Wharton, Edith	Title	THE HOUSE OF MIRTH
Wheeler, Bert	Film	KENTUCKY KERNELS '34
Wheeler, Bert	Film	THE NITWITS '35
Whitaker, Forest	Film	BIRD '88
Whitaker, Forest	Film	DIARY OF A HITMAN '92
White, Barry	Film	COONSKIN '75
White, Michael Jai	Film	SPAWN '97
White, Onna ba	Musical	MUSIC MAN
White, Vanna	Game Show	WHEEL OF FORTUNE tv
White,Phyllis D.J.	Pen Name	P.D. JONES
Whitelaw, Billy	Film	SHADEY '85
Whitman, Stuart	Film	AN AMERICAN DREAM '66
Whitman, Stuart	Film	THE MARK '61
Whitman, Stuart	Film	THE STORY OF RUTH '60
Whitman, Stuart	Series	CIMARRON STRIP tv
Whitman, Walt	Poem	SONG OF MYSELF
Whitman, Walt	Poem Bk	LEAVES OF GRASS
Whitmore, James	Film	THEM! '54
Whitmore, James	Series	TEMPERATURES RISING tv
Who, The mr	Hit	MY GENERATION
Widmark, Richard	Film	BACKLASH '56
Widmark, Richard	Film	CHEYENNE AUTUMN '64
Widmark, Richard	Film	DESTINATION GOBI '53
Widmark, Richard	Film	MADIGAN '68
Widmark, Richard	Film	NIGHT AND THE CITY '50
Widmark, Richard	Film	THE FROGMEN '51
Widmark, Richard	Film	THE TRAP '59
Widmark, Richard	Film	WARLOCK '59
Wight,James Alfred	Pen Name	JAMES HERRIOT
Wilby, James	Film	MAURICE '87
Wilcox, Larry	Series	CHIPS tv

Wild, Jack	Film	MELODY '71
Wild, Jack	Film	PUFNSTUF '70
Wilde, Cornel	Film	A SONG TO REMEMBER '45
Wilde, Cornel d+	Film	MARACAIBO '58
Wilde, Cornel	Film	SHOCKPROOF '49
Wilde, Cornel	Film	THE SCARLET COAT '55
Wilde, Cornel d+	Film	SWORD OF LANCELOT '63
Wilde, Oscar	Play	AN IDEAL HUSBAND
Wilde, Oscar	Play	LADY WINDERMERE'S FAN
Wilde, Oscar	Play	SALOME
Wilde, Oscar	Play	THE IMPORTANCE OF BEING EARNEST
Wilde, Oscar	Title	THE DUCHESS OF PADOA
Wilde, Oscar	Title	THE HAPPY PRINCE
Wilde, Oscar	Title	THE PICTURE OF DORIAN GRAY
Wilder, Gene	Film	STIR CRAZY '80
Wilder, Gene	Nee	JEROME SILBERMAN
Wilder, Thornton	Title	THE BRIDGE OF SAN LUIS REY
Wilding, Michael	Film	TRENT'S LAST CASE '52
Willard, Frank	Cartoon	MOON MULLINS
William, Warren	Film	LADY FOR A DAY '33 ****
William, Warren	Film	PASSPORT TO SUEZ '43
William, Warren	Film	SKYSCRAPER SOULS '32
William, Warren	Film	THE LONE WOLF SPY HUNT '39
William, Warren	Film	THE LONE WOLF STRIKES '40
William, Warren	Film	THE MOUTHPIECE '32
William, Warren	Film	THE OUTCAST '37
William, Warren	Film	UPPERWORLD '34
Williams, Bill	Series	THE ADVENTURES OF KIT CARSON tv
Williams, Esther	Film	DUCHESS OF IDAHO '50
Williams, Esther	Film	JUPITER'S DARLING '55
Williams, Esther	Film	UNGUARDED MOMENT '56
Williams, Guy	Series	LOST IN SPACE tv
Williams, Guy	Series	ZORRO tv
Williams, Hank	Song	HEY GOOD LOOKING
Williams, Hugh	Film	THE DAY WILL DAWN '42
Williams, Paul	Film	FROG '89
Williams, Robin	Film	FATHERS' DAY '97
Williams, Robin	Film	THE BEST OF TIMES '86
Williams, Robin	Film	THE BIRDCAGE '96
Williams, Robin	Film	THE WORLD ACCORDING TO GARP'82 ****
Williams, Robin	Role	MORK
Williams, Robin	Series	MORK & MINDY tv
Williams, Treat	Film	HAIR '79
Williams, Treat	Film	PRINCE OF THE CITY '81
Williams, Van	Series	SURFSIDE SIX tv
Williams, Billy Dee	Film	DEADLY ILLUSION '87
Williams, Billy Dee	Film	HIT! '73
Williams, Spencer Jr	Series	AMOS 'N' ANDY tv
Williams, Tennessee	Heroine	ALMA in Summer and Smoke
Williams, Tennessee	Play	CAMINO REAL
Williams, Tennessee	Play	CAT ON A HOT TIN ROOF
Williams, Tennessee	Play	SUMMER AND SMOKE
Williams, Tennessee	Play	THE GLASS MENAGERIE
Williams, Tennessee	Play	THE NIGHT OF THE IGUANA
Williams, Tennessee	Play	THE ROSE TATOO
Williamson, Nicol	Film	HAMLET '69
Williamson, Nicol	Film	THE RECKONING '69
Williamson, Nicol	Film	EXCALIBUR '81
Willingham, Calder	Title	END AS A MAN
Willis, Bruce	Film	THE FIFTH ELEMENT '97
Willman, Noel	Film	THE REPTILE '66

Willson, Meredith	Musical	THE MUSIC MAN
Wilson, Dooley	Role	SAM in Casablanca
Wilson, Jackie mr	Hit	THAT'S WHY
Wilson, Marie	Series	MY FRIEND IRMA tv
Wilson, Tom	Cartoon	ZIGGY
Wilson. Scott	Film	IN COLD BLOOD '67 ****
Windom, William	Series	MY WORLD AND WELCOME TO IT tv
Winger, Debra	Film	TERMS OF ENDEARMENT '83 ****
Winkler, Henry	Film	HEROES '77
Winninger, Charles	Film	FRIENDLY ENEMIES '42
Winninger, Charles	Film	THE SUN SHINES BRIGHT '53
Winters, Shelley	Film	ALFIE '66
Winters, Shelley	Film	ELLIE '84
Winters, Shelley	Film	LOLITA '62
Winters, Shelley	Film	PLAYGIRL '54
Winters, Shelley	Film	TENNESSEE CHAMP '54
Winters, Shelley	Nee	SHIRLEY SCHRIFT
Wister, Owen	Title	THE VIRGINIAN
Withers, Googie	Film	MIRANDA '48
Witherspoon, Cora	Film	THE BANK DICK '40 ****
Witherspoon, Reese	Film	FREEWAY '96
Wodehouse, P.G.	Charac	JEEVES
Wolf, Howlin'	Nee	CHESTER BURNETT
Wolf, Virginia	Title	A ROOM OF ONE'S OWN
Wolfe, Tom	Title	THE RIGHT STUFF
Wolford, Chloe Anthony	Pen Name	TONI MORRISON
Wonder, Stevie	Nee	STEVLAND MORRIS
Wonder, Stevie mr	Hit	YOU ARE THE SUNSHINE OF MY LIFE
Wonder, Stevie mr	HitSong	MY CHERIE AMOUR
Wong, Anna May	Film	KING OF CHINATOWN '39
Wood Janet	Film	FANGS '75
Wood, Elijah	Film	FLIPPER '96.
Wood, Natalie	Film	GYPSY '62
Wood, Natalie	Film	REBEL WITHOUT A CAUSE '55 ****
Wood, Natalie	Film	WEST SIDE STORY '61 ****
Wood, Natalie	Nee	NATASHA GURDIN
Wood, Peggy	Series	MAMA tv
Woodard, Alfre	Film	CROOKLYN '94
Woodard, Joanne	Film	THE GLASS MENAGERIE '87
Woods, James	Film	COP '87
Woods, James	Film	DIGGSTOWN '92
Woods, James	Film	SALVADOR '86
Woodward, Edward	Film	CALLAN '74
Woodward, Edward	Series	THE EQUALIZER tv
Woodward, Joanne	Film	THE STRIPPER '63
Woodward, Joanne	Film	THE THREE FACES OF EVE '57
Woodward, Joanne	Film	WUSA '70
Woolf, Virginia	Title	ORLANDO
Woolf, Virginia	Title	TO THE LIGHTHOUSE
Woolsey, Robert	Film	DIPLOMANIACS '33
Wopat, Tom	Series	DUKES OF HAZARD tv
Wordsworth,William	Poem	THE DAFFODILS
Wouk, Herman	Title	THE CAINE MUTINY
Wouk, Herman	Title	THE WINDS OF WAR
Wouk, Herman	Title	WAR AND REMEMBRANCE
Wray, Faye	Film	KING KONG '33 ****
Wright, Max	Series	ALF tv
Wright, Richard	Title	NATIVE SON
Wright, Teresa	Film	MRS. MINIVER '42 ****
Wright, Teresa	Film	ROSELAND '77
Wright, Teresa	Film	SHADOW OF A DOUBT '43

Wright, Teresa	Film	THE PRIDE OF THE YANKEES '42 ****
Wright, Willard	Pen Name	S.S. VAN DINE
Wyatt, Jane	Film	BOOMERANG! '47
Wyatt, Jane	Film	CANADIAN PACIFIC '49
Wyler William d	Film	MRS. MINIVER '42 ****
Wyler, William d	Film	BEN-HUR '59
Wylie, Elinor	Poem	VELVET SHOES
Wyman, Jane	Series	FALCON CREST tv
Wyman, Jane	Film	THE GLASS MENAGERIE '50
Wyman, Jane	Film	THE LOST WEEKEND '45 ****
Wyman, Jane	Nee	SARAH JANE FULKS
Wymark, Patrick	Film	THE PSYCHOPATH '66
Wynn, Ed	Film	CINDERFELLA '60
Yanne, Jean	Film	WEEKEND '67
Yardbirds, The mr	Hit	FOR YOUR LOVE
Yates, Peter d	Film	BULLITT '68
Yeats, Wm. Butler	Poem	LAPIS LAZULI
Yes mr	Hit	YOURS IS NO DISGRACE
York, Dick	Series	BEWITCHED tv
York, Michael	Film	ZEPPELIN '71
York, Susannah	Film	IMAGES '72
York, Susannah	Film	TOM JONES '63 ****
Yorke, Henry V.	Pen Name	HENRY GREEN
Young Rascals mr	Hit	HOW CAN I BE SURE?
Young, Alan	Series	MR. ED tv
Young, Chic	Cartoon	BLONDIE
Young, Gig	Film	ARENA '53
Young, Gig	Nee	BYRON BARR
Young, Karen	Film	DEEP IN THE HEART '83
Young, Loretta	Film	A NIGHT TO REMEMBER '43
Young, Loretta	Film	ALONG CAME JONES '45
Young, Loretta	Film	CARAVAN '34
Young, Loretta	Film	ETERNALLY YOURS '39
Young, Loretta	Film	KENTUCKY '38
Young, Loretta	Film	MEN IN HER LIFE '41
Young, Loretta	Film	PAULA '52
Young, Loretta	Film	RAMONA '36
Young, Loretta	Film	THE ACCUSED '48
Young, Loretta	Film	THE BISHOP'S WIFE '47
Young, Loretta	Film	THE CRUSADES '35
Young, Loretta	Film	THE DEVIL'S IN LOVE '33
Young, Loretta	Film	THE FARMER'S DAUGHTER '47
Young, Loretta	Film	THE PERFECT MARRIAGE '46
Young, Loretta	Film	THREE BLIND MICE '38
Young, Neil	Film	YEAR OF THE HORSE '97
Young, Robert	Film	CROSSFIRE '47
Young, Robert	Film	NAVY BLUE AND GOLD '37
Young, Robert	Film	RELENTLESS '48
Young, Robert	Film	STOWAWAY '36
Young, Robert	Film	THE SECOND WOMAN '51
Young, Robert	Series	FATHER KNOWS BEST tv
Young, Robert	Series	MARCUS WELBY, M.D. tv
Youngson, Robert d	Film	THE GOLDEN AGE OF COMEDY '57 ****
Zada, Ramy	Series	DARK JUSTICE tv
Zane, Billy	Film	ORLANDO '93
Zerbe, Anthony	Series	THE YOUNG RIDERS tv
Zetterling, Mai	Film	DANCE LITTLE LADY '55
Zetterling, Mai	Film	NIGHT IS MY FUTURE '48
Zetterling, Mai	Film	TORMENT '44

Zimbalist, Efrem Jr.	Film	A FEVER IN THE BLOOD '61
Zimbalist, Stephanie	Series	REMINGTON STEELE tv
Zimbalist,Efrem Jr	Series	THE F.B.I. tv
Zola, Emile	Title	NANA
Zola, Emile	Title	THE SIN OF FATHER MOURET
Zombies, The mr	HitSong	SHE'S NOT HERE

SECTION II, PART B

Product or PRODUCTS plus	Forename Surname(s)
A NOUS LA LIBERTE '31 ****	Henri Marchand
A TEAM, THE tv	George Peppard, Mr. T.
ABBOT, ANTHONY	Charles F. Oursler
ABBY '74	Carol Speed,William Marshall
ABC	Jackson 5 mr
ABE LINCOLN IN ILLINOIS	Robert E. Sherwood
ABE LINCOLN IN ILLINOIS '40 ****	Raymond Massey
ABIE'S IRISH ROSE	Anne Nichols
ABOMINABLE '71	Vincent Price
ABOUT MRS. LESLIE '54	Shirley Booth
ABOVE SUSPICION '43	Joan Crawford,Fred MacMurray
ABOVE US THE WAVES '56	John Mills
ABRAHAM LINCOLN '30	Walter Huston
ABSALOM, ABSALOM	William Faulkner
ABSENCE OF MALICE '81	Paul Newman
ABSOLUTE POWER '97	Clint Eastwood d+
ABSOLUTION '81	Richard Burton
ABYSS, THE '89	Ed Harris
ACCIDENT '67	Dirk Bogarde
ACCIDENTS '88	Edward Albert
ACCUSED tv	Edgar Allan Jones Jr
ACCUSED, THE '48	Loretta Young
ACCUSED, THE '88	Jodie Foster, Kelly McGillis
ACIS AND GALATEA	George Frederic Handel
ACROSS THE BRIDGE '57	Rod Steiger
ACROSS THE TRACKS '91	Rick Schroder
ACT OF VIOLENCE '49	Van Heflin
ACTION IN ARABIA '44	George Sanders
ADA	Vladimir Nabokov
ADA '61	Susan Hayward, Dean Martin
ADAGIO FOR STRINGS	Samuel Barber
ADAM 12 tv	Martin Milner
ADAM BEDE	George Eliot
ADAM'S RIB '49 ****	Katharine Hepburn,Spencer Tracy
ADAY, MARVIN LEE	Meatloaf
ADDAMS FAMILY, THE '91	Anjelica Huston
ADDAMS FAMILY, THE tv	Carolyn Jones, John Astin
ADDERLY tv	Winston Rekert
ADJUSTER, THE '91	Elias Koteas
ADVENTURES OF AUGIE MARCH, THE	Saul Bellow
ADVENTURES OF FU MANCHU, THE tv	Glen Gordon
ADVENTURES IN PARADISE tv	Gardner McKay
ADVENTURES OF KIT CARSON, THE tv	Bill Williams
ADVENTURES OF RIN TIN TIN, THE tv	Lee Aaker
ADVENTURES OF ROBIN HOOD, THE '38 ****	Errol Flynn
ADVENTURES OF ROBIN HOOD, THE tv	Richard Greene
ADVENTURES OF SUPERMAN, THE tv	George Reeves
ADVENTURESS, THE '46	Deborah Kerr
AENEAS	Virgil
AFRICAN QUEEN, THE '51 ****	Humphrey Bogart,Katharine Hepburn
AFTER THE PROMISE '87	Mark Harmon
AFTER THE THIN MAN '36	Myrna Loy, William Powell

AFTERMASH tv	Harry Morgan
AGAINST ALL FLAGS '52	Errol Flynn, Maureen O'Hara
AGAINST THE WIND '48	Robert Beatty
AGATHA '79	Vanessa Redgrave
AGE OF BRONZE, THE	Augeste Rodin su
AGE OF INNOCENCE, THE	Edith Wharton p-f'21
AGE OF INNOCENCE, THE '93	Daniel Day-Lewis
AGON	Igor Stravinsky
AH FORSVELUI	Giuseppe Verdi
AIDA '53	Sophia Loren
AIDA opera & heroine	Giuseppe Verdi
AIN'T MISBEHAVIN'	Thomas"Fats" Waller mj & c
AIN'T MISBEHAVIN' '55	Rory Calhoun
AIN'T SHE SWEET	Milton Ager
AIR FORCE ONE '97 ****	Gary Oldman, Harrison Ford
AIR ON THE STRING	Johann Sebastian Bach
AIRPLANE! '80	Robert Hays
AIRPORT '70	Burt Lancaster
AIRWOLF tv	Jan-Michael Vincent
AITKEN, LORETTA MARY	Moms Mabley
AKHMATOVA, ANNA	Anna Gorenko
ALAIN	Emile Chartier
ALAIN-FOURNIER	Henri Fournier
ALAMO '60	John Wayne d+
ALASKANS, THE tv	Roger Moore
ALCINA	George Frideric Handel
ALCINDOR, LEW	Kareem Abdul Jabbar
ALDRICH FAMILY, THE tv	House Jameson
ALEICHEM, SHALOM	Solomon J. Rabinowitz
ALEX AND THE GYPSY '76	Jack Lemon
ALEXANDER '68	Philippe Noiret
ALEXANDER NEVSKY '38 ****	Nikolai Cherkassov
ALEXANDRIA QUARTET, THE	Lawrence Durrell
ALF tv	Max Wright, Paul Fusco
ALFIE '66	Michael Caine,Shelley Winters
ALGIERS '38	Charles Boyer
ALIAS JESSE JAMES '59	Bob Hope
ALIAS SMITH AND JONES tv	Peter Deuel
ALICE tv	Linda Lavin
ALICE'S ADVENTURES IN WONDERLAND Lewis Carroll	
ALIEN '79	Sigourney Weaver
ALIENS '86	Sigourney Weaver
ALISON	Elvis Costello mr
ALIVE '93	Ethan Hawke
ALL ABOUT EVE '50 **** Bette Davis,Anne Baxter,George Sanders	
ALL IN THE FAMILY tv	Carroll O'Connor,Jean Stapleton
ALL MY PRETTY ONES	Anne Saxton
ALL OR NOTHING AT ALL	Frank Sinatra
ALL QUIET ON THE WESTERN FRONT '30 ****Lew Ayres, John Wray	
ALL THE KING'S MEN	Robert Penn Warren p-f'47
ALL THE KING'S MEN '49 ****	Broderick Crawford
ALL THE PRESIDENT'S MEN '76 **** Robert Redford	
ALL THE YOUNG MEN '60	Alan Ladd, Sidney Poitier
ALL'S FAIR tv	Richard Crenna
ALLEGRO	Richard Rogers & Oscar Hammerstein
ALLIGATOR '80	Robert Forster
ALLIGATOR PEOPLE '59	Beverly Garland
ALMA	Tennessee Williams
ALMOST PERFECT	Alice Adams
ALONE	Admiral Richard E. Byrd
ALONG CAME JONES '45	Gary Cooper, Loretta Young

ALPHABET MURDERS, THE '66	Tony Randall
ALVERIO, ROSITA	Rita Moreno
ALVIN'S HARMONICA	The Chipmunks
ALVIN, JOHN	Johnnie Ray
ALWAYS '85	Henry Jaglom d+
ALWAYS '89	Richard Dreyfuss
ALWAYS TOGETHER '48	Robert Hutton
AMADEUS '84	F. Murray Abraham, Tom Hulce
AMAHL AND THE NIGHT VISITORS	Gian-Carlo Menotti
AMAZING MR. MALONE, THE tv	Lee Tracy
AMBASSADOR BILL '31	Will Rogers
AMBASSADOR, THE '84	Robert Mitchum
AMBASSADORS, THE	Henry James
AMBUSH '49	Robert Taylor
AMEN	Sherman Hemsley
AMERICA '24	Neil Hamilton
AMERICA, AMERICA '63 ****	Elia Kazan d
AMERICAN BANDSTAND tv	Dick Clark
AMERICAN BUFFALO '96	Dustin Hoffman
AMERICAN DREAM, AN	Norman Mailer
AMERICAN DREAM, AN '66	Stuart Whitman
AMERICAN EMPIRE '42	Richard Dix
AMERICAN FLYERS '85	Kevin Costner
AMERICAN FRIEND, THE '77	Dennis Hopper
AMERICAN HOT WAX '78	Tim McIntire
AMERICAN IN PARIS, AN '51	Gene Kelly, Leslie Caron
AMERICAN MADNESS '32	Pat O'Brien
AMERICAN PRESIDENT, THE '95	Michael Douglas
AMERICAN ROMANCE, AN '44	Brian Donlevy
AMERICAN SOLDIER, THE '70	Rainer Werner Fassbinder d
AMERICANA '81	David Carradine d+
AMERICANO, THE '55	Glenn Ford
AMERIKA	Franz Kafka
AMONG THE LIVING '41	Albert Dekker
AMONGST FRIENDS '93	Joseph Lindsey
AMORES	Ovid
AMOROUS MR. PRAWN, THE '62	Joan Greenwood
AMOS 'N' ANDY radio	Charles Correll,Freeman Gosden
AMOS 'N' ANDY tv	Alan Childress,Spencer Williams Jr
AMUCK '72	Farley Granger
AMY '81	Jenny Agutter, Barry Newman
AMY PRENTISS tv	Jessica Walter
ANAPOLA	Jimmy Dorsey
ANASTASIA '56 ****	Ingrid Bergman, Yul Brynner
ANATOLI, A.	Anatoly Vasilyevich Kuznetsov
ANATOMY OF A MURDER '59 ****	James Stewart, Lee Remick
AMOS 'N' ANDY tv	Alan Childress,Spencer Williams Jr
AMUCK '72	Farley Granger
AMY '81	Jenny Agutter, Barry Newman
AMY PRENTISS tv	Jessica Walter
ANAPOLA	Jimmy Dorsey
ANASTASIA '56 ****	Ingrid Bergman, Yul Brynner
ANATOLI, A.	Anatoly Vasilyevich Kuznetsov
ANATOMY OF A MURDER '59 ****	James Stewart, Lee Remick
AND I LOVE HER	Beatles
AND NOW TOMORROW '44	Alan Ladd
AND THEN THERE WERE NONE '45	**** Barry Fitzgerald,Walt. Huston
ANDERSON, ROBERTA JOAN	Joni Mitchell
ANDROID '82	Klaus Kinski
ANDROMEDA STRAIN, THE '71	Arthur Hill
ANDY '65	Norman Alden

ANGEL AT MY TABLE, AN '90	Jane Campion d
ANGEL FROM TEXAS, AN '40	Eddie Albert
ANGEL LEVINE, THE '70	Zero Mostel
ANGEL tv	Annie Farge
ANGEL WORE RED, THE '60	Ava Gardner
ANGELA '95	Miranda Stewart Rhyne
ANGELICO, FRA	Guido di Pietro
ANGIE	Rolling Stones mr
ANGIE '94	Geena Davis
ANGIE tv	Donna Pescow
ANGLE OF REPOSE	Wallace Stegner p-f'72
ANGRY SILENCE, THE '60	Richard Attenborough
ANGUISH '87	Michael Lerner
ANIMAL CRACKERS '30	Marx Brothers
ANIMAL FARM	George Orwell
ANNA	Count Leo Tolstoy
ANNA '87	Sally Kirkland
ANNA KARENINA '35 ****	Greta Garbo, Fredric March
ANNE OF GREEN GABLES	Lucy Maud Montgomery
ANNE OF THE INDIES '51	Jean Peters
ANNIE	Dorothy Loudon
ANNIE '82	Carol Burnett, Albert Finney
ANNIE GET YOUR GUN '50	Betty Hutton
ANNIE HALL '77 ****	Woody Allen d+, Diane Keaton
ANNIE OAKLEY tv	Gail Davis
ANNIVERSARY, THE '68	Bette Davis
ANOTHER COUNTRY '84	Colin Firth
ANOTHER LANGUAGE '33	Helen Hayes
ANOTHER STAKEOUT '93	Richard Dreyfuss
ANOTHER THIN MAN '39	William Powell
ANTHONY ADVERSE '36	Fredric March
ANTIGONE	Sophocles
ANY TIME AT ALL	Beatles
ANYTHING BUT LOVE tv	Jamie Lee Curtis
ANYTHING GOES	Connie Francis
ANYTHING GOES	Ethel Merman
APARTMENT, THE '60 ****	Jack Lemmon,Shirley MacLaine
APHRODITE	Homer
APOLLO CREED in Rocky	Carl Weathers
APOSTLE, THE	Sholem Asch
APOSTLES, THE	Sir Edward Elgar
APPALACHIAN SPRING	Aaron Copland
APPALOOSA, THE '66	Marlon Brando
APPETITE FOR DESTRUCTION	Guns N' Roses mr
APPLAUSE '29	Helen Morgan
APPLE'S WAY tv	Ronny Cox
APPLESEED, JOHNNY	John Chapman
APPOINTMENT, THE '69	Omar Sharif
APPOINTMENT IN SAMARRA	John O'Hara
AQUALUNG	Jethro Tull mr
ARABESQUE '66	Sophia Loren, Gregory Peck
ARACHNOPHOBIA '90	Jeff Daniels
ARAM	William Saroyan
ARANTES do NASCIMENTO, EDSEN	Pele
ARBLAY, MADAME d'	Fanny Burney
ARE YOU EXPERIENCED?	Jimi Hendrix mr
ARI	Leon Uris
ARIA DE CAPO	Edna St. Vincent Millay
ARIEL(posthumous)	Sylvia Plath
ARIZONA '40	Jean Arthur
ARIZONA RAIDERS '65	Audie Murphy

ARIZONIAN, THE '35	Richard Dix
ARMS AND THE MAN	George Bernard Shaw
ARNIE tv	Herschel Bernardi
ARNO, PETER	Curtis A. Peters
ARNOLD '73	Roddy McDowall
AROUSERS, THE '70	Tab Hunter
ARREST AND TRIAL tv	Ben Gazzara
ARRIVAL, THE '96	Charlie Sheen
ARROWHEAD '53	Charlton Heston
ARROWSMITH '31	Ronald Colman
ARSENE LUPIN	Maurice LeBlanc
ARTFUL DODGER	Charles Dickens
ARTHUR '81	Dudley Moore
ARZHAK, NICOLAY	Yuly Daniel
AS I LAY DYING	William Faulkner
ASE (Charac.)	Hebrik Ibsen
ASIATICS, THE	Frederic Prokosch
ASPHYX, THE '72	Robert Stephens
ASSAM GARDEN, THE '85	Deborah Kerr
ASSASSIN, THE '61	Marcello Mastroianni
ASSAULT ON A QUEEN '66	Frank Sinatra
ASSAULT, THE '86	Derek de Lint
ASSIGNMENT, THE '77	Christopher Plummer
ASSOCIATE, THE '96	Whoopi Goldberg
ASSOCIATES, THE tv	Wilfred Hyde-White
ASTONISHED HEART, THE '50	Noel Coward
ASYLUM, THE '72	Barbara Parkins
AT THE EARTH'S CORE '76	Doug McClure
AT THE HOP	Danny and the Juniors mr
ATALANTA	George Frideric Handel
ATHENA '54	Jane Powell
ATILLA	Giuseppe Verdi
ATLANTIC CITY '80 ****	Burt Lancaster,Susan Sarandon
ATTACK! '56	Jack Palance
ATTIC, THE '79	Ray Milland,Carrie Snodgress
AUGUST '96	Anthony Hopkins
AUNT MARY	Jean Stapleton
AUNTIE MAME	Angela Lansbury
AUSTERLITZ, FREDERICK	Fred Astaire
AUTUMN AFTERNOON, AN '62	Shima Iwashita
AVALON '90	Aidan Quinn,Barry Levinson d
AVANTI! '72	Jack Lemmon
AVE MARIA	Franz Schubert
AVENGERS, THE tv	Patrick Macnee
AWAKE AND SING	Clifford Odets
AWAKENINGS '90	Robert De Niro
B.L. STRYKER tv	Burt Reynolds
BAA BAA BLACKSHEEP tv	Robert Conrad
BABBIT '34	Guy Kibee
BABE '95	Jim Hensen & Creatures
BABE, THE '92	John Goodman
BABES IN TOYLAND	Victor Herbert
BABES IN TOYLAND '34	Stan Laurel, Oliver Hardy
BABES IN TOYLAND '61	Ray Bolger
BABES ON BROADWAY '41	Judy Garland, Mickey Rooney
BABES tv	Wendie Sperber
BABETTEE'S FEAST '87 ****	Stephane Audran, Jean Philippe La Font
BABY BLUE MARINE '76	Jan-Michael Vincent
BABY TALK tv	Julia Duffy
BABY-SITTERS CLUB, THE '95	Ellen Burstyn, Peter Horton

BABYFEVER '94	Matt Salinger
BACHELOR FATHER '31	Ralph Forbes
BACHELOR FATHER tv	John Forsythe
BACHELOR MOTHER '39	Ginger Rogers
BACHELOR, THE '91	Keith Carradine
BACK AT THE FRONT '52	Tom Ewall
BACK DOOR TO HELL '64	Jack Nicholson
BACK TO THE FUTURE '85	Michael J. Fox
BACKBEAT '93	Stephen Dorff
BACKDRAFT '91	Kurt Russell
BACKFIRE '87	Karen Allen
BACKLASH '56	Richard Widmark
BACKLASH '86	David Argue
BACKROADS '77	Bill Hunter
BACKTRACK '89	Dennis Hopper
BACKWARD GLANCE, A	Edith Wharton
BACKYARDS,GREENWICH VILLIAGE	John French Sloan
BAD FOR EACH OTHER '53	Charlton Heston
BAD NEWS BEARS, THE '76	Walter Matthau
BADLANDERS, THE '58	Alan Ladd
BADLANDS '73	Martin Sheen
BADMAN'S COUNTRY '58	George Montgomery
BAILEYS OF BALBOA, THE tv	Paul Ford
BALBOA '86	Tony Curtis
BALD SOPRANO, THE	Eugene Ionesco
BALINE, ISRAEL	Irving Berlin
BALTIMORE BULLET, THE '80	James Coburn
BAMBI	Felix Salten
BAMBI '42 **** (animated)	David Hand d
BAMBOO SAUCER, THE '68	Dan Duryea
BANACEK tv	Robert Blake, George Peppard
BANANA BOAT SONG, THE	Harry Belafonte
BANANAS '71 ****	Woody Allen d+,Jouise Lasser
BAND OF OUTSIDERS '64	Anna Karina
BAND ON THE RUN	Paul McCartney mr
BAND WAGON, THE '53 ****	Fred Astaire, Cyd Charisse
BANDIDO '56	Robert Mitchum
BANDOLERO! '68	James Stewart
BANG-BANG KID, THE '68	Guy Madison
BANJI, KRISHNA	Ben Kingsley
BANJO '47	Walter Reed
BANK DICK, THE '40 ****	W.C. Fields,Cora Witherspoon, Una Merkel
BANNING '67	Robert Wagner
BARABBAS '62	Anthony Quinn
BARBARELLA '68	Jane Fonda
BARBAROSA '82	Willie Nelson
BARBER OF SEVILLE, THE	Giacchino Rossini
BARETTA tv	Robert Blake
BARFLY '87	Mickey Rourke
BARNEY GOOGLE	Billy DeBeck
BARNEY JONES	Buddy Ebsen
BARNEY MILLER tv	Hal Linden, Jack Soo
BARR, BYRON	Gig Young
BARTERED BRIDE, THE	BedRich Smetana
BARTLEBY '72	Paul Scofield
BASSANOVA BABY	Elvis Presley
BAT MASTERSON tv	Gene Barry
BAT, THE '59	Vincent Price
BATAAN '43	Robert Taylor
BATES, ELIAS	Bo Diddley

BATMAN '89	Jack Nicholson
BATMAN tv	Adam West
BATTLE CRY	Leon Uris
BATTLE CRY '75	Aldo Ray
BATTLE OF ALGIERS, THE '65	Jean Martin
BATTLE OF BRITAIN '69	Michael Caine
BATTLEGROUND '49	Van Johnson
BATTLESTAR GALACTIA tv	Lorne Greene
BAXTER '73	Patricia Neal
BAXTERS, THE tv	Larry Keith
BAYWATCH tv	David Hasselhoff
BE MY BABY	The Ronettes mr
BEACHCOMBER, THE '38	Charles Laughton
BEACHCOMBER, THE '55	Glynis Johns
BEACHES '88	Bette Midler
BEACHHEAD '54	Tony Curtis
BEAR, THE '89	Jack Wallace
BEAST MUST DIE, THE '74	Peter Cushing
BEAST OF THE CITY '32	Walter Huston
BEATRICE '88	Julie Delpy
BEATY, SHIRLEY	Shirley MacLaine
BEATY, SHIRLEY	Shirley MacLaine
BEAUTIFUL DREAMER	Stephen Foster
BEAUTIFUL GIRLS '96	Matt Dillon
BEAUTIFUL THING '96	Glen Berry
BEAUTY AND THE BEAST '46****	Jean Morales, Jean Cocteau d
BEAUTY AND THE BEAST tv	Linda Hamilton
BECAUSE THE NIGHT	Patti Smith mr
BECKET '64 ****	Richard Burton,Peter O'Toole
BED AND BREAKFAST '92	Roger Moore
BEDAZZLED '67	Dudley Moore
BEDELIA '46	Margaret Lockwood
BEDLAM '46	Boris Karloff
BEDNY, DEMYAN	Yefim Pridvorov
BEDNYI, DEMYAN	Efim A. Pridvorov
BEDTIME FOR BONZO '51	Ronald Reagan
BEEDLE, WILLIAM	William Holden
BEER BARREL POLKA	Andrew Sisters
BEETHOVEN '92	Charles Grodin
BEETLE BAILEY	Mort Walker
BEGGAR'S OPERA, THE '53	Laurence Olivier
BEGUILED, THE '71	Clint Eastwood
BEHIND THE FRONT '26	Wallace Beery
BELIEVERS, THE '87	Martin Sheen
BELL, ACTON w	Anne Bronte
BELL, CURRER w	Charlotte Bronte
BELL, ELLIS w	Emily Bronte
BELLBOY, THE '60	Jerry Lewis d+
BELLE DE JOUR '67 ****	Catherine Deneuve, Michel Piccoli
BELLE OF NEW YORK, THE '52	Fred Astaire, Vera-Ellen
BELLE OF THE YUKON '44	Randolph Scott
BELLMAN AND TRUE '88	Bernard Hill
BELLS ARE RINGING '60	Judy Holliday
BELOVED ROGUE, THE '27	John Barrymore
BELY, ANDREI po & w	Boris N. Bugayev
BEN CASEY	Vince Edwards
BEN-HUR	Lew Wallace
BEN-HUR '26	Ramon Novarro,Francis X. Bushman
BEN-HUR '59	Charlton Heston,William Wyler d
BEND IN THE RIVER, A	V,.S. Naipaul
BENEDETTO, ANTHONY	Tony Bennett

BENIKER GANG, THE '85	Andrew McCarthy
BENJI '74	Peter Breck
BENSON tv	Robert Strand, Inga Swenson
BEPPO, THE	Geo. Gordon(Lord) Byron
BERLIN ALEXANDERPLATZ'80****	Hanna Schygulla
BERNARD,HENRIETTE ROSINE	Sarah Bernhardt
BERNECKY, ELDIN(in Murphy Brown tv)	Robert Pastorelli
BEST FOOT FORWARD '43	Lucille Ball
BEST OF THE BADMEN '51	Robert Ryan
BEST OF THE WEST tv	Joel Higgins
BEST OF TIMES, THE '86	Robin Williams
BEST YEARS OF OUR LIVES 46 ****	Myrna Loy, Fredric March
BET A LIFE	Chris Elliott
BETHEL, DAWN	Sheree North
BETHUNE '77	Donald Sutherland
BETSY'S WEDDING '90	Alan Alda
BETSY, THE '78	Laurence Olivier
BETTY '92	Marie Trinignant
BETWEEN THE LINES '77	John Heard, Jeff Goldblum
BEVERLY HILLBILLIES, THE tv	Donna Douglas, Buddy Ebsen
BEVERLY HILLS COP '84	Eddie Murphy
BEWARE, MY LOVELY '52	Ida Lupino
BEWITCHED tv	Elizabeth Montgomery,Dick York
BEYOND TOMORROW '40	Richard Carlson
BFS DAUGHTER	John P. Marquand
BHOWANI JUNCTION '56	Ava Gardner
BICKEL, FREDERICK	Fredric March
BICYCLE THIEF, THE '48 ****	Vittorio De Sica d
BIG '88	Tom Hanks
BIG AS LIFE	E.L. Doctorow
BIG BIRD CAGE, THE '72	Pam Grier
BIG CARNIVAL, THE '51	Kirk Douglas
BIG DOLL HOUSE, THE '71	Judy Brown
BIG FISHERMAN, THE '59	Howard Keel
BIG PARADE, THE '25 ****	John Gilbert, Renee Adoree
BIG TOWN tv	Patrick McVey
BIG VALLEY, THE tv	Barbara Stanwyck
BIG YELLOW TAXI	Joni Mitchell mr
BIGAMIST, THE '53	Edmond O'Brien
BIGGER THAN LIFE '56	James Mason
BILBO	J.J.R. Tolkien
BILLIE '65	Patty Duke
BILLINGS, JOSH	Henry Wheeler Shaw
BILLY BATHGATE	E.L. Doctorow
BILLY BUDD	Benjamin Britten
BILLY ROSE'S JUMBO '62	Doris Day
BILLY THE KID	William Bonney
BIONIC WOMAN, THE tv	Lindsay Wagner
BIRCHES	Robert Frost
BIRD '88	Forest Whitaker
BIRD GIRL of Green Mansions	Rima
BIRDCAGE, THE '95	Robin Williams
BIRDS, THE '63	Jessica Tandy, Tippi Hedren
BIRDY '84	Matthew Modine
BIRNBAUM, NATHAN	George Burns
BIRTH OF A NATION, THE '15 ****	Lillian Gish, Mae Marsh
BIRTH OF THE BLUES '41	Bing Crosby
BIRTHDAY PARTY, THE	Harold Pinter
BISCUIT EATER, THE '72	Earl Holliman
BISHOP'S WIFE, THE '47	Cary Grant, Loretta Young
BITE THE BULLET '75 ****	Gene Hackman, Candice Bergen

BITTERSWEET	Noel Coward
BIYIDI, ALEXANDRE	Mongo Beti po & w
BJ AND THE BEAR tv	Greg Evigan
BLACK BEAUTY	Anna Sewell
BLACK BELT JONES '74	Jim Kelly
BLACK CHRISTMAS '75	Olivia Hussey
BLACK KNIGHT, THE '54	Alan Ladd
BLACK MAGIC WOMAN	Santana mr
BLACK MARBLE, THE '80	Robert Foxworth
BLACK NARCISSUS	Rumer Godden
BLACK NARCISSUS '46 ****	Deborah Kerr,Emeric Pressburger
BLACK ORCHID, THE '59	Sophia Loren
BLACK OXEN	Gertrude F. Atherton
BLACK PIRATE, THE '26	Douglas Fairbanks Sr.
BLACK SADDLE tv	Peter Breck
BLACK SHEEP, THE	Honore De Balzac
BLACKMAIL '29	Sara Allgood
BLACKMAIL '39	Edward G. Robinson
BLACULA '72	William Marshall
BLADE '73	Jon Cypher
BLAKE, EUBIE	James Hubert Blake
BLASKO, BELA FERENC	Bela Lugosi
BLAZE '89	Paul Newman
BLAZING SADDLES '74	Mel Brooks d, Cleavon Little
BLEAK HOUSE	Charles Dickens
BLINDFOLD '66	Rock Hudson
BLINK '94	Madeleine Stowe
BLITHE SPIRIT	Noel Coward
BLOB, THE '58	Steve McQueen
BLOCKADE '38	Madeleine Carroll
BLONDIE	Chic Young
BLONDIE '38	Penny Singleton
BLONDIE tv	Pamela Britton, Arthur Lake
BLOOD RELATIVES '78	Donald Sutherland
BLOODBROTHERS '78	Richard Gere
BLOOM COUNTY	Berke Breathed cr
BLOSSOM tv	Mayim Bialik, Ted Wass
BLOWUP '66	Vanessa Redgrave
BLUE '93	Juliette Binoche
BLUE ANGELS, THE tv	Dennis Cross
BLUE BAYOU	Linda Ronstadt
BLUE GARDENIA, THE '53	Anne Baxter
BLUE KNIGHT, THE tv	George Kennedy
BLUE ROOM	Paolo Picasso
BLUE SKIES AGAIN '83	Harry Hamlin
BLUE SUEDE SHOES	Carl Perkins mr
BLUE SUEDE SHOES	Elvis Presley
BLUEBEARD '44	Jean Parker
BLUEBEARD '62	Charles Denner
BLUEBERRY HILL	Fats Domino mj & mr piano
BLUES IN THE NIGHT '41	Priscilla Lane
BLY, NELLY	Elizabeth Cochrane Seaman
BOARDWALK '79	Ruth Gordon
BOCCACCIO '70	Vittorio De Sica d
BODY AND SOUL	Coleman Hawkins mj
BODY AND SOUL '47 ****	John Garfield, Lilli Palmer
BODY SNATCHER, THE '45	Boris Karloff
BODYGUARD '48	Lawrence Tierney
BODYGUARD, THE '92	Kevin Costner
BOGUS '96	Whoopi Goldberg
BOHEMIAN GIRL, THE '36	Stan Laurel, Oliver Hardy

BOHEMIAN RHAPSODY	Queen mr
BOILEAU-DESPREAUX	Nicolas Boileau
BOLD AND THE BRAVE, THE '56	Wendell Corey
BOLERO	Maurice Joseph Ravel
BOLERO '34	George Raft
BOMBARDIER '43	Pat O'Brien
BOMBSHELL '33	Jean Harlow
BONANZA tv	Lorne Greene,Michael Landon,Dan Blocker
BONJOUR TRIESTESSE	Francoise Sagan
BONNIE AND CLYDE '67 ****	Warren Beatty, Faye Dunaway
BONNIE SCOTLAND '35	Stan Laurel, Oliver Hardy
BOOB McNUTT	Rube Goldberg
BOOGEYMAN, THE '80	Suzanna Love
BOOKER tv	Richard Grieco
BOOMERANG! '47	Dana Andrews, Jane Wyatt
BOPHA! '93	Danny Glover
BORACH, FANNY	Fanny Brice
BORDER INCIDENT '49	Ricardo Montalban
BORDER, THE '82	Jack Nicholson
BORDERTOWN '35	Paul Muni
BORN IN THE U.S.A	Bruce Springsteen mr
BORN LOSER, THE	Art Sansom
BORN TO BE WILD	Steppenwolf mr
BORROWER, THE '91	Rae Dawn Chong
BORSALINO '70	Jean-Paul Belmondo
BORSTAL BAY	Brendan Behan
BOSOM BUDDIES tv	Peter Scolari
BOSS, THE	Diana Ross
BOSS, THE '56	John Payne
BOSTON BLACKIE tv	Kent Taylor
BOSWELL	Stanley Elkin
BOTTICELLI, SANDRO	Alessandro Filipepi
BOUND '96	Jennifer Tilly
BOUNTY HUNTER, THE '54	Randolph Scott
BOUNTY KILLER, THE '65	Dan Duryea
BOUNTY, THE '84	Mel Gibson
BOURBON STREET BEAT tv	Andrew Duggan
BOWERY BATTALION '51	Leo Gorcey, Huntz Hall
BOWERY BOMBSHELL '46	Leo Gorcey, Huntz Hall
BOWERY, THE '33	Wallace Beery
BOY FROM OKLAHOMA, THE '54	Will Rogers Jr.
BOY OF THE STREETS '37	Jackie Cooper
BOY TEN FEET TALL, A '63	Edward G. Robinson
BOY WHO COULD FLY, THE '86	Jay Underwood
BOYS FROM BRAZIL, THE '78	Gregory Peck, Laurence Olivier
BOYS IN COMPANY C, THE '78	Stan Shaw
BOYS NEXT DOOR, THE '85	Charlie Sheen
BOYS, THE '61	Richard Todd
BRACKEN'S WORLD tv	Eleanor Parker
BRADY BUNCH, THE tv	Florence Henderson, Robert Reed
BRAIN, THE '65	Peter Van Eyck
BRAINSTORM '83	Christopher Walken
BRAMAH, ERNEST	Ernest Bramah Smith
BRAMBLE BUSH, THE '60	Richard Burton
BRAND	Henrik Ibsen
BRAND, MAX	Frederick Faust
BRANDED tv	Chuck Connors
BRANDENBURG CONCERTOS	Johann Sebastian Bach
BRANNIGAN '75	John Wayne
BRAT FARRAR	Josephine Tey
BRATSBURG, HARRY	Harry Morgan

BRAVADOS, THE '58	Gregory Peck
BRAVE EAGLE tv	Keith Larsen
BRAVE NEW WORLD	Aldous Huxley
BRAVEHEART '95	Mel Gibson d+
BRAZIL '85	Robert De Niro
BREAKDOWN '97	Kurt Russell
BREAKHEART PASS '76	Charles Bronson
BREAKING UP IS HARD TO DO	Neil Sedaka mr
BREAKOUT '59	Richard Todd
BREAKOUT '75	Charles Bronson
BREAKTHROUGH '50	David Brian
BREATHLESS '59	Jean Seberg
BREE in Klute	Jane Fonda
BRENNER tv	Edward Binns
BRET MAVERICK tv	James Garner
BREWSTER McCLOUD '70	Sally Kellerman
BRIDE COMES HOME, THE '35	Claudette Colbert
BRIDE OF FRANKENSTEIN'35****	Boris Karloff, Valerie Hobson
BRIDE WORE BLACK, THE '68	Jeanne Moreau
BRIDE, THE '85	Jennifer Beals
BRIDESHEAD REVISITED	Evelyn Waugh
BRIDGE AT REMAGEN, THE '69	George Segal
BRIDGE OF SAN LUIS REY, THE	Thornton Wilder p-f'28
BRIDGE OVER TROUBLED WATERS	Simon and Garfunkel mr+
BRIDGE TO THE SUN '61	Carroll Baker
BRIDGES AT TOKO-RI, THE '54	William Holden
BRIDGET LOVES BERNIE tv	David Birney
BRIGADOON '54	Gene Kelly, Cyd Charisse
BRIGHTON ROCK	Graham Greene
BRINGING UP BABY '38 ****	Cary Grant, Katharine Hepburn
BRINGING UP BUDDY tv	Enid Markey
BRINGING UP FATHER	George McManus
BRITANNICUS	Jean Racine w
BRITTAIN, VERA w	Mrs. Geo. Edw. Gordon Catlin
BROAD, WILLIAM	Billy Idol
BROADMINDED '31	Joe E. Brown
BROADSIDE tv	Kathy Nolan
BROADWAY '42	George Raft
BROADWAY MELODY '29	Bessie Love
BROKEN ARROW tv	Michael Ansara, John Lupton
BROKEN BLOSSOMS '19	Lillian Gish
BROKEN GLASS	Amy Irving
BRONCO tv	Ty Hardin
BRONK tv	Jack Palance
BRONX ZOO, THE	Ed Asner
BROOKLYN BRIDGE tv	Danny Gerard
BROOM HILDA	Russell Myers
BROTHER LOVE	The Stories
BROTHERHOOD, THE '68	Kirk Douglas
BROTHERS '77	Bernie Casey
BROTHERS IN ARMS	Dire Straits mr
BROTHERS RICO, THE '57	Richard Conte
BROWN EYED GIRL	Van Morrison
BROWN, ANGELINE	Angie Dickinson
BROWN, HELEN	Helen Hayes
BROWNING VERSION, THE '51	Michael Redgrave
BRUBAKER '80	Robert Redford
BRUGH, SPANGLER ARLINGTON	Robert Taylor
BUCCANEER, THE '38	Fredric March
BUCCANEER, THE '58	Yul Brynner
BUCCANEERS, THE tv	Robert Shaw

BUCHINSKI, CHARLES	Charles Bronson
BUCKSKIN tv	Tommy Nolan
BUDDENBROOKS	Thomas Mann
BUDDY HOLLY STORY, THE '78	Gary Busey
BUDDY SYSTEM, THE '84	Richard Dreyfuss
BUGSY '91	Warren Beatty
BULLDOG DRUMMOND	Herman Cyril Neile
BULLDOG DRUMMOND '29	Ronald Colman
BULLITT '68	Steve McQueen, Peter Yates d
BULLOCK, ANNIE MAE	Tina Turner
BULLSHOT '83	Dick Clement
BUMGARNER, JAMES	James Garner
BUNTLINE, NED	Edward Z.C. Judson
BURDEN OF DREAMS '82	Klaus Kinski
BURFORD, ELEANOR	Eleanor Hibbert
BURGLARS, THE '72	Jean-Paul Belmondo
BURKE'S LAW tv	Gene Barry
BURN! '69	Marlon Brando
BURNETT, CHESTER	Howlin' Wolf mr
BURNING GLASS, THE	S.N. Behrman
BURNING LOVE	Elvis Presley
BURR, AARON BIOGRAPHY	Vidal
BURRELL, STANLEY KIRK	Hammer
BURROWS, DALLAS	Orson Bean
BUS STOP	William Inge
BUS STOP '56	Marilyn Monroe
BUSHIDO BLADE, THE '79	Richard Boone
BUSINESS AS USUAL '87	Glenda Jackson
BUSTER '88	Phil Collins
BUSTING '74	Elliott Gould
BUT NOT FOR ME (Girl Crazy)	George Gershwin
BUTCH CASSIDY	Newman, Paul
BUTCH CASSIDY AND THE SUNDANCE KID '69 **** Paul Newman	
BUTLEY '74 ****	Alan Bates, Jessica Tandy
BUTTERFIELD 8	John O'Hara
BY LOVE POSSESSED '61	Lana Turner
BYE BYE BLACKBIRD	Eddie Cantor
BYE BYE BRAVERMAN '68	George Segal
BYRON, JAMES	James Dean
C.P.O. SHARKEY tv	Don Rickles
CABARET '72	Liza Minnelli
CABBAGE PATCH KIDS	Xavier Roberts id
CABERET	Fred Ebb
CACTUS '86	Isabelle Huppert
CADE'S COUNTY tv	Glenn Ford
CAESER AND CLEOPATRA	George Bernard Shaw
CAGED '50	Eleanor Parker
CAGNEY AND LACEY tv	Tyne Daly, Sharon Gless
CAINE MUTINY, THE	Herman Wouk
CAINE MUTINY, THE '54 ****	Humphrey Bogart, Jose Ferrer
CAIRO '63	George Sanders
CAKES AND ALE	W. Sommerset Maugham
CAL '84	Helen Mirren
CALAMITY JANE	Doris Day
CALENDER GIRL	Neil Sedeka
CALIFORNIA '46	Ray Milland, Barbara Stanwyck
CALIFORNIA SUITE '78	Alan Alda, Jane Fonda
CALIFORNIA SUN	Rivieras mr
CALIFORNIANS, THE tv	Adam Kennedy
CALL OF THE WILD, THE	Jack London
CALLAN '74	Edward Woodward

CALVIN AND HOBBS	Bill Watterson
CAMERAMAN, THE '28	Buster Keaton
CAMILLE '37	Greta Garbo
CAMILLE CLAUDEL '88	Isabelle Adjani
CAMINO REAL	Tennessee Williams
CAMORRA '86	Harvey Keitel
CAMP RUNAMUCK tv	Dave Ketchum
CAN I GET A WITNESS?	Marvin Gaye mr
CAN'T FIND MY WAY HOME	Blind Faith mr
CAN-CAN '60	Shirley MacLaine, Frank Sinatra
CANADIAN PACIFIC '49	Randolph Scott, Jane Wyatt
CANDID CAMERA tv	Allen Funt
CANDIDA	George Bernard Shaw
CANDIDATE, THE '72	Robert Redford
CANDIDE	Voltaire
CANDLE IN THE WIND	Elton John
CANDLESHOE '77	David Niven
CANDYMAN '92	Tony Todd
CANNON tv	William Conrad
CANNON, SARAH OPHELIA	Minnie Pearl
CANSINO, MARGARITA	Rita Hayworth
CANTERBURY TALE, A '44	Emeric Pressburger
CAPTAIN AHAB	Herman Melville
CAPTAIN BOYCOTT '47	Stewart Granger
CAPTAIN CAREY, U.S.A. '50	Alan Ladd
CAPTAIN NEWMAN, M.D. '63	Gregory Peck
CAPTAINS COURAGEOUS '37 ****	Freddie Bartholomew, Spencer Tracy
CAPTIVE CITY, THE '52	John Forsythe
CAPTIVE HEART, THE '46	Michael Redgrave
CAPTIVES '95	Bill Pullman, Tim Roth
CAPTURE, THE '50	Lew Ayres
CAPTURED '33	Leslie Howard
CARAVAN '34	Loretta Young
CARAVANS '78	Anthony Quinn
CARBINE WILLIAMS '52	James Stewart
CARD PLAYER	Pablo Picasso
CARDINAL, THE '63	Tom Tryon
CAREER '59	Dean Martin
CAREFREE '38	Fred Astaire, Ginger Rogers
CAREFREE HIGHWAY	Gordon Lightfoot
CARELESS LOVE	Alice Adams
CARETAKERS, THE '63	Robert Stack
CAREY TREATMENT, THE '72	James Coburn
CAREY, REGINALD	Rex Harrison
CARMEN	Alexandre Cesar L. Bizet
CARMINA BURANA	Carl Orff
CARNAL KNOWLEDGE '71	Jack Nicholson
CARNAVAL: PRETTY SCENES ON FOUR NOTES	Robert Schumann
CARNIVAL OF THE ANIMALS, THE	Camille Saint-Saens
CARNY '80	Gary Busey, Jodie Foster
CARO NOME	Giuseppe Verdi
CAROUSEL '56	Gordon MacRae
CARPENTIER, HARLEAN	Jean Harlow
CARPETBAGGERS, THE '64	George Peppard
CARR, PHILIPPA	Eleanor Hibbert
CARR, PHILIPPA	Victoria Holt
CARRE, JOHN le	David John M. Cornwell
CARRIE '52	Jennifer Jones
CARRIE '76	Sissy Spacek, Brian De Palma d
CARRIER, THE '88	Gregory Fortescue
CARROLL, LEWIS	Charles L. Dodgson

CARTER COUNTRY tv	Victor French
CARTOUCHE '64	Jean-Paul Belmondo
CASABLANCA	Ilsa
CASABLANCA '42 ****	Ingrid Bergman, Humphrey Bogart
CASABLANCA tv	Charles McGraw
CASANOVA '70	Marcello Mastroianni
CASBAH '48	Yvonne de Carlo
CASILLAS, FLORENCIA	Vikki Carr
CASS TIMBERLANE	Sinclair Lewis
CASS TIMBERLANE '47	Spencer Tracy, Lana Turner
CASSOTTO, WALDEN ROBERT	Bobby Darin
CAST A DARK SHADOW '55	Dirk Bogarde
CASTAWAY '87	Oliver Reed
CASTELLUCCIO, FRANK	Frankie Valli
CASTILLAN, THE '63	Cesar Romero
CASTLE, THE '68	Maximilian Schell
CASTLEMON, HARRY	Charles Fosdick
CAT AND THE CANARY, THE '27	Laura LaPlante
CAT AND THE CANARY, THE '39	Paulette Goddard, Bob Hope
CAT IN THE HAT, THE	Dr, Seuss
CAT ON A HOT TIN ROOF	Tennessee Williams
CATCH-22	Joseph Heller
CATCHER IN THE RYE, THE	J.D. Salinger
CATHY	Cathy Guisewite
CATLOW '71	Yul Brynner
CATS	Lloyd Webber
CAUGHT '49	Barbara BelGeddes
CAUTIONARY TALES	Hilaire Belloc
CAVALCADE '33 ****	Clive Brook, Ursula Jeans
CAVANAUGHS, THE tv	Barnard Hughes
CAVEMEN '81	Ringo Starr
CEMETARY CLUB, THE '92	Ellen Burstyn
CENDRARS, BLAISE	Frederic Sauser
CENTENNIAL tv	Everett Chad, Robert Conrad
CENTRAL AIRPORT '33	Richard Barthelmess
CEREMONY, THE '63	Laurence Harvey d+
CESAR AND ROSALIE '72	Yves Montand
CHAINED '34	Joan Crawford, Clark Gable
CHAIRMAN, THE '69	Gregory Peck
CHALK GARDEN, THE '64	Deborah Kerr
CHALLENGE, THE '82	Scott Glenn
CHAMELEON STREET '91	Wendell B. Harris Jr. d+
CHAMP, THE '31	Wallace Beery
CHAMPAGNE '28	Alfred Hitchcock d
CHAMPION '49	Kirk Douglas
CHAMPIONS '83	John Hurt
CHANCES '31	Douglas Fairbanks Jr.
CHANGE OF SEASONS, A '80	Shirley MacLaine
CHANNING tv	Henry Jones
CHANTILLY LACE	The Big Bopper mr
CHAPLIN '92	Robert Downey Jr.
CHAPTER TWO	Neil Simon
CHARADE '63	Cary Grant, Audrey Hepburn
CHARLES IN CHARGE tv	Scott Baio
CHARLEY VARRICK '73	Walter Matthau
CHARLEY WILD, PRIVATE DETECTIVE tv Kevin O'Morrison
CHARLIE CHAN MOVIES	Warner Oland
CHARLIE CHAN MYSTERIES	Earl Derr Biggers
CHARLIE CHAN tv	J. Carrol Naish
CHARLIE CHAPLIN CAVALCADE '38 **** Charlie Chaplin
CHARLIE CHAPLIN FESTIVAL '38 **** Charlie Chaplin

CHARLIE'S ANGELS tv	Cheryl Ladd,Kate Jackson,Jacklyn Smith
CHARLY '68	Cliff Robertson
CHARMING SINNERS '29	Ruth Chatterton, William Powell
CHASE, THE '66	Marlon Brando, Jane Fonda
CHASTITY '69	Cher
CHATTERBOX '43	Joe E. Brown
CHAUCHOIN, LILY	Claudette Colbert
CHE in Evita	Lloyd Webber
CHEAP DETECTIVE, THE '78	Peter Falk
CHECKMATE tv	Anthony George
CHEERS tv	Ted Danson, Rhea Perlman
CHEETAH '89	Keith Coogan
CHERISH	The Association mr
CHERRY ORDHARD, THE	Anton P. Chekov
CHEYENNE AUTUMN '64	Richard Widmark
CHICAGO DEADLINE '49	Donna Reed
CHICAGO HOPE tv	E.G. Marshall
CHICHESTER PSALMS	Leonard Bernstein
CHICO AND THE MAN tv	Jack Albertson
CHIEF CRAZY HORSE '55	Victor Mature
CHILD IS WAITING, A '63	Judy Garland, Burt Lancaster
CHILDE HAROLD	Geo. Gordon(Lord) Byron
CHILDREN OF PARADISE'45 ****	Jean-Louis Barrault
CHILDREN OF THE CORN	Stephan King
CHILDREN OF WRATH	Jeppe Aakjaer
CHINA BEACH tv	Dana Delany
CHINA SMITH tv	Dan Duryea
CHINA SYNDROME '79 ****	Jane Fonda, Jack Lemmon
CHINATOWN '74 ****	Jack Nicholson, Faye Dunaway
CHINESE ROULETTE '76	Margit Carstensen
CHINO '73	Jill Ireland
CHIPS tv	Larry Wilcox
CHISUM '70	John Wayne
CHOCOLAT '88	Francois Cluzet
CHOCOLATE WAR, THE '87	John Glover
CHOICES '81	Paul Carafotes
CHOSEN, THE '81	Maximilian Schell
CHRISTIANA	Pilgrim's Progress
CHRISTMAS CAROL, A '38	Reginald Owen
CHRISTMAS CAROL, A '51 ****	Alastair Sim, Kathlene Harrison
CHRISTMAS IN JULY '40	Dick Powell
CHRISTMAS STORY, A '83	Peter Billingsley
CHUBASCO '68	Richard Egan
CHUKA '67	Rod Taylor
CHUMP AT OXFORD, A '40	Stan Laurel, Oliver Hardy
CHURCHILL, LEONARD SPENCER	Sir Winston Chruchill
CHWATT, AARON	Red Buttons
CICCONE, MADONNA LOUISE	Madonna
CIMARRON '31	Richard Dix
CIMARRON '60	Glenn Ford
CIMARRON STRIP tv	Stuart Whitman
CINDERFELLA '60	Jerry Lewis, Ed Wynn
CINEMA PARADISO '88	Philippe Noiret
CIRCLE OF DANGER '51	Ray Milland
CIRCLE OF DECEIT '81 ****	Hanna Schygulla, Bruno Ganz
CIRCLE OF FRIENDS	Maeve Binchy
CIRCLE OF FRIENDS '95	Chris O'Donnell
CIRCLE, THE '59	John Mills
CIRCUS BOY tv	Mickey Braddock
CIRCUS OF HORRORS '60	Anton Diffring
CIRCUS, THE '28	Charlie Chaplin d+

CISCO KID tv	Duncan Renaldo
CITADEL, THE '38	Robert Donat
CITIZEN KANE '41 ****	Orson Welles d+
CITY FOR CONQUEST '40	James Cagney
CITY LIGHTS '31 ****	Charlie Chaplin d+
CLAIRVOYANT, THE '34	Claude Rains
CLAN OF THE CAVE BEARS	Jean M. Auel
CLANCY STREET BOYS '43	Leo Gorcey, Huntz Hall
CLASSICAL- Symph. No. 1 in D	Sergei Prokofiev
CLAUDIA '43	Dorothy McGuire
CLAUDIA AND DAVID '46	Dorothy McGuire
CLAUDINE '74	Diahann Carroll
CLEARCUT '91	Graham Greene
CLEMENZO OI TITO	Wolfgang A. Mozart
CLEOPATRA	William Shakespeare
CLEOPATRA '34	Claudette Colbert
CLIENT, THE '94	Susan Sarandon
CLIFFHANGER '93	Sylvester Stallone
CLIMAX, THE '44	Boris Karloff
CLINGING VINE, THE '26	Leatrice Joy, Paul Sloane
CLINIC, THE '82	Chris Haywood
CLOAK AND DAGGER '46	Gary Cooper
CLOCK, THE '45	Judy Garland
CLOCKERS '95	Harvey Keitel
CLOCKMAKER, THE '73	Philippe Noiret
CLOCKWISE '86	John Cleese
CLOCKWORK ORANGE, A	Anthony Burgess
CLOCKWORK ORANGE, A '77	Malcom McDowdell
CLOISTER AND THE HEARTH, THE	Charles Reade
CLOSE ENCOUNTERS OF THE THIRD KIND '77 **** Richard Dreyfuss	
CLOSE TO MY HEART '51	Ray Milland
CLOUDBURST '51	Robert Preston
CLOUSEAU	Peter Sellers
CLOWN, THE '53	Red Skelton
CLUB, THE '80	Jack Thompson
CLUE '85	Eileen Brennan, Leslie Ann Warren
CLUELESS '95	Alicia Silverstone
COACH tv	Craig T. Nelson
COAL	Upton Sinclair
COCHISE(In Broken Arrow tv)	Michael Ansara
COCKFIGHTER '74	Warren Oates
COCKTAIL MOLOTOV '80	Francois Cluzet
COCKTAIL PARTY, THE	T.S. Eliot
COCKTAILS FOR TWO	Spike Jones
COCOANUTS, THE '29	Marx Brothers
COCOON '85	Hume Cronyn, Don Ameche o-s'86
COCOZZA, ALFREDO	Mario Lanzza
CODY, WILLIAM F.	Buffalo Bill or Buffalo Bill Cody
COFFY '73	Pam Grier
COGITO ERGO SUM	Rene Descartes
COHEN, HOWARD	Howard Cosell
COHEN, JACOB	Rodney Dangerfield
COHON, PETER	Peter Coyote
COLBYS, THE tv	Charlton Heston
COLD COMFORT FARM '96	Eileen Atkins, Joanna Lumley
COLDITZ STORY, THE '57	John Mills
COLE, JANET	Kim Hunter
COLLECTOR '65	Terance Stamp
COLLEEN '36	Ruby Keeler
COLLEGE '27	Buster Keaton
COLLEGE HOLIDAY '36	Jack Benny

COLLIER, LUCILLE	Ann Miller
COLLINS, HUNT	Evan Hunter
COLLINS, MARY CATHLEEN	Bo Derek
COLLINS, TOM	Joseph Furphy
COLOR OF MONEY, THE '86	Tom Cruise & Paul Newman
COLOR PURPLE, THE '85	Danny Glover, Whoopi Goldberg, Steven Spielberg d
COLORS '88	Sean Penn
COLT 45 tv	Wayde Preston
COLUMBO tv	Peter Falk
COMA	Robin Cook
COMA '78	Genevieve Bujold
COMANCHE STATION '60	Randolph Scott
COMBAT tv	Rick Jason
COME BACK, LITTLE SHEBA	William Inge
COME DANCE WITH ME '60	Brigitte Bardot
COME FILL THE CUP '51	James Cagney
COME LIVE WITH ME '41	James Stewart, Hedy Lamarr
COME NEXT SPRING '56	Ann Sheridan
COME SOFTLY TO ME	Fleetwoods mr
COME TO THE STABLE '49	Celeste Holm, Loretta Young
COME-ON, THE '56	Anne Baxter
COMEDIANS, THE '67	Richard Burton, Elizabeth Taylor
COMEDY OF TERRORS, THE '64	Vincent Price
COMES A HORSEMAN '78	Jane Fonda
COMIC, THE '69	Dick Van Dyke
COMING TO AMERICA '88	Eddie Murphy, John Amos
COMING-OUT PARTY '61	James Robertson
COMMAND DECISION '48	Clark Gable
COMMANDMENTS '97	Aidan Quinn
COMMANDO '64	Stewart Granger
COMMISH, THE tv	Michael Chiklis
COMMITMENTS, THE '91	Robert Arkins
COMMON SENSE; THE AMERICAN CRISIS	Thomas Paine
COMMUNION '89	Christopher Walken
COMPETITION, THE '80	Richard Dreyfuss
COMPULSION '59	Orson Welles
COMUS	Thomas A. Arne
CONCRETE JUNGLE, THE '60	Stanley Baker
CONDEMMED WOMEN '38	Anne Shirley
CONEHEADS '93	Dan Aykroyd
CONFESSION '37	Basil Rathbone
CONFESSION, THE '70	Yves Montand
CONFESSIONS OF FELIX KRULL	Thomas Mann
CONFIDENTIAL '35	Donald Cook
CONFLICT '45	Humphrey Bogart
CONGO	Michael Crichton
CONJUGAL BED, THE '63	Ugo Tognazzi
CONNECTION, THE '61	William Redfield
CONQUEST '37	Greta Garbo
CONQUEST OF SPACE '55	Eric Fleming
CONRACK '74	Jon Voight
CONSPIRACY '39	Allan Lane
CONSPIRATOR '49	Robert Taylor
CONSPIRATORS, THE '44	Hedy Lamarr
CONSTANT HUSBAND, THE '55	Rex Harrison
CONSUL, THE	Gian Carlo Menotti
CONTACT '97	Jodie Foster
CONTEMPT '63	Brigitte Bardot
CONTRABAND '40	Conrad Veidt
CONTRACT '80	Leslie Caron

CONVERSATION, THE '74 ****	Gene Hackman, John Cazale
CONVICTED '50	Glenn Ford
CONVICTS '91	Robert Duvall
COOL AND THE CRAZY, THE '58	Scott Marlowe
COONSKIN '75	Barry White
COP '87	James Woods
COP-OUT '67	James Mason
COPOCABANA	Barry Manilow
COPPOLA, NICHOLAS	Nicolas Cage
COPPOLA, TALIA	Talia Shire
COPS AND ROBBERS '73	Cliff Gorman
COQUETTE	George Abbott
COQUETTE '29	Mary Pickford
CORBUSIER, Le ac & p	Chas. Edouard Jeanneret
CORELLI, MARIE	Mary Mackay
CORKY '72	Robert Blake
CORN IS GREEN, THE '45	Bette Davis
CORNERED '45	Dick Powell
CORONADO '35	Johnny Downs
CORRUPT '83	Harvey Keitel
CORRUPT ONES, THE '66	Robert Stack
COSI FAN TUTTE	Wolfgang Amadeus Mozart
COTTER '73	Don Murray
COUCH, THE '62	Shirley Knight
COUNSELLOR-AT-LAW '33 ****	John Barrymore, Bebe Daniels
COUNT FIVE AND DIE '58	Jeffrey Hunter
COUNTDOWN '68	James Caan
COUNTERFEITERS '48	John Sutton
COUNTRY '84	Jessica Lange
COUNTRY GIRL, THE	Clifford Odets
COURAGE OF LASSIE '46	Elizabeth Taylor
COURT JESTER, THE '56 ****	Danny Kaye, Glynis Johns
COURT OF LAST RESORT, THE tv	Lyle Bettger
COURTNEY AFFAIR, THE '47	Anna Neagle
COUSINS '89	Ted Danson
COWARDLY LION	Bert Lahr in The Wizard of Oz
COWBOY '58	Glenn Ford
CRACK IN THE WORLD '65	Dana Andrews
CRACK-UP '37	Peter Lorre
CRACK-UP '46	Pat O'Brien
CRACK-UP, THE	F. Scott Fitzgerald
CRADDOCK, CHARLES EGBERT	Mary Noailles Murfree
CRAMTON, RAYMOND	Chad Everett
CRANE, GEORGE RANDOLPH	Randolph Scott
CRASHOUT '55	William Bendix
CRAWLING EYE, THE '58	Forrest Tucker
CRAZY	Patsy Cline
CRAZY LIKE A FOX tv	Jack Warden
CREATION, THE	Franz Joseph Haydn
CREEPERS '84	Jennifer Connelly
CREEPING UNKNOWN, THE '56	Brian Donlevy
CREGG, HUGH	Huey Lewis
CREST OF THE WAVE '54	Roy Boulting
CRIA '76	Ana Torrent
CRIME OF PASSION '57	Barbara Stanwyck
CRIME STORY tv	Dennis Farina
CRIMEWAVE '85	Louise Lasser
CRIMINAL CODE, THE '31	Walter Huston
CRIMSON AND CLOVER	Tommy James and the Shandells mr
CRIMSON BLADE, THE '63	Lionel Jeffries
CRIMSON ROMANCE '34	Ben Lyon

CRISIS '50	Cary Grant
CRISTILLO, LOUIS	Lou Costello
CROCETTI, DINO	Dean Martin
CROCETTI, DINO	Dean Martin
CROCODILE" DUNDEE '86	Paul Hogan
CRONOS '92	Ron Perlman
CROOK, THE '71	Jean-Louis Trintignant
CROOKED ROAD, THE '65	Robert Ryan
CROOKLYN '94	Alfre Woodard
CROSSFIRE '47	Robert Mitchum, Robert Young
CROSSING THE LINE '91	Liam Neeson
CROSSROADS '42	William Powell
CROSSROADS '86	Ralph Macchio
CROW. THE '94	Brandon Lee
CROWD, THE '28 ****	Eleanor Boardman, James Murray
CRUCIBLE, THE '57	Simone Signoret
CRUSADES, THE '35	Loretta Young
CRUSH, THE '93	Cary Elwes
CRUSOE '88	Aidan Quinn
CRY	Johnny Ray
CRY ME A RIVER	Julie London
CRY OF THE BANSHEE '70	Vincent Price
CRY-BABY '90	Johnny Depp
CUBA '79	Sean Connery
CUJO '83	Dee Wallace
CUL-DE-SAC '66	Donald Pleasence
CULKIN, BONNIE	Bonnie Bedelia
CULT OF THE COBRA '55	Faith Domergue
CURE, THE '17	Charlie Chaplin
CURE, THE '95	Brad Renfro, Joseph Mazzello
CURSE OF THE DEMON '58	Dana Andrews
CURTIS	Ray Billingsley cr
CUSTER OF THE WEST '68	Robert Shaw
CUTTING EDGE, THE '92	D.B. Sweeney
CYNARA	Ernest C. Dowson
D'ABRUZZO, ALPHONSO	Alan Alda
D'ANTONGUOLIA, RUDOLPHO	Rudolph Valentino
D.A.R.Y.L. '85	Mary Beth Hurt
D.O.A. '50	Edmond O'Brien
DA '88	Barnard Hughes
DA DOO RON RON	The Crystals mr
DADDY LONG LEGS	Fred Astaire
DADDY NOSTALGIA '90	Dirk Bogarde
DAFFODILS, THE	William Wordsworth
DAKOTA INCIDENT '56	Linda Darnell
DAKTARI tv	Marshall Thompson
DALLAS '50	Gary Cooper
DALLAS tv	Barbara Bel Geddes, Larry Hagman
DAMAGE '92	Jeremy Irons, Louis Malle d
DAMES '34	Joan Blondell, Dick Powell
DAMN THE DEFIANT! '62	Alec Guinness
DAMN YANKEES	Lola
DAMNED, THE '69	Dirk Bogarde
DAN AUGUST tv	Burt Reynolds
DANCE LITTLE LADY '55	Mai Zetterling
DANCE TO THE MUSIC OF TIME,A	Anthony Powell
DANCE, FOOLS, DANCE '31	Joan Crawford
DANCE, GIRL, DANCE '40	Maureen O'Hara
DANCES WITH WOLVES '90 ****	Kevin Costner, mARY mCdONNELL
DANCIN'IN THE STREET	Martha and the Vandellas mr
DANCING MOTHERS '26	Clara Bow

DANCING ON A DIME '40	Grace McDonald
DANE, CLEMENCE	Winifred Ashton
DANGER: DIABOLIK '67	John Phillip Law
DANGEROUS '35	Bette Davis
DANGEROUS CORNER '34	Virginia Bruce
DANGEROUS MINDS '95	Michelle Pfeiffer
DANGEROUS TO KNOW '38	Akim Tamiroff
DANIEL '83	Timothy Hutton
DANIEL BOONE tv	Fess Parker
DANIELOVITCH, ISSUR	Kirk Douglas
DANTON '82 ****	Gerard Depardieu
DAPHNIS ET CHLOE	Maurice Joseph Ravel
DAR	Vladimir Nabokov
DARCY	Laurence Olivier
DARIO, RUBEN	Felox Sarmiento
DARK CRYSTAL, THE '83	Jim Henson d+ & Puppets
DARK JUSTICE tv	Ramy Zada
DARK LADY	Cher
DARKER THAN AMBER '70	Rod Taylor
DARKMAN '90	Liam Neeson
DARKNESS AT NOON	Arthur Koestler
DARLING '65	Julie Christie
DARWIN ADVENTURE, THE '72	Nicholas Clay
DAS LIED VAN DER ERDE	Gustav Mahler
DAS RHEINGOLD	Richard Wagner
DAVE '93	Sigourney Weaver
DAVID COPPERFIELD	Clara Peggoty
DAVID COPPERFIELD '35 ****	Freddie Bartholomew, W.C. Fields
DAVIOT, GORDON	Elizabeth Mackintosh
DAVIS RULES tv	Randy Quaid
DAWNING, THE '88	Anthony Hopkins
DAY AFTER TOMORROW, THE	Alan Folsom
DAY AT THE RACES, A '37	The Marx Brothers
DAY OF THE ANIMALS '77	Christopher George
DAY OF THE JACKAL	Frederick Forsythe
DAY OF THE JACKAL, THE '73	Edward Fox
DAY OF THE LOCUST, THE	Nathaniel West
DAY OF THE LOCUST, THE '75	Donald Sutherland
DAY OF THE WOLVES '73	Richard Egan
DAY THE EARTH STOOD STILL,THE'51****Michael Rennie,Patricia Neal
DAY TRIPPERS, THE '97	Anne Meara
DAY WILL DAWN, THE '42	Hugh Williams
DAYLIGHT '96	Sylvester Stallone
DAYO	Harry Belefonte
DAYTRIPPERS, THE '97	Anne Meara
de HAVILAND, JOAN	Joan Fontaine
de NASCIMIENTO,EDSON ARANTES	Pele
DE SADE, MARQUIS	Donatien Alphonse Francois, comte de Sade
DEAD MAN WALKING'95 ****	Sean Penn, Susan Sarandon
DEAD OF NIGHT '45 ****	Basil Dearden d
DEAD, THE '87	Angelica Huston
DEADLINE AT DAWN '46	Susan Hayward
DEADLY AFFAIR, THE '67	James Mason
DEADLY ILLUSION '87	Billy Dee Williams
DEADLY STRANGERS '74	Hayley Mills
DEALERS '89	Paul McGann
DEAR JOHN tv	Judd Hirsch
DEAR MR. WONDERFUL '82	Joe Pesci
DEATH AND THE MAIDEN	Franz Schubert
DEATH BE NOT PROUD	John Donne
DEATH COMES TO THE ARCHBISHOP	Willa Cather

DEATH IN THE FAMILY, A	James Agee
DEATH IN VENICE	Thomas Mann
DEATH OF A PROPHET '81	Morgan Freeman
DEATH OF IVAN ILYICH, THE	Count Leo Tolstoy
DEATH OF THE HEART, THE	Elizabeth Bowen
DEATH ON THE NILE '78	Peter Ustinov
DEATH VALLEY DAYS tv	Stanley Andrews
DEATHDREAM '72	John Marley
DEATHWATCH '80	Harvey Keitel
DECAMERON '70	Franco Citti
DECEMBER BRIDE tv	Spring Byington
DECEPTION '46	Bette Davis
DECEPTION '93	Andie McDowell
DECKS RAN RED, THE '58	James Mason
DEDE DINAH	Frankie Avalon
DEEDS	Gary Cooper
DEEP BLUE SEA, THE '55	Vivien Leigh
DEEP IN THE HEART '83	Karen Young
DEEP, THE '77	Nick Nolte, Jacqueline Bisset
DEER PARK, THE	Norman Mailer w
DEF BY TEMPTATION '90	Cynthia Bond
DEFECTOR, THE '66	Montgomery Clift
DEFENDERS, THE tv	E.G. Marshall
DEFENSELESS '91	Barbara Hershey
DEFIANCE '80	Jan-Michael Vincent
DEFIANT ONES, THE '58 ****	Tony Curtis
DELAFIELD, E.M.	Elizabeth Dashwood
DELIVERANCE	James Dickey
DELIVERANCE '72 ****	Burt Reynolds, Jon Voight
DELIVERIN'	Poco mr
DELL, ETHEL M.	Ethel Mary Savage
DELLA STREET in Perry Mason	Barbara Hale
DELTA OF VENUS	Anais Nin
DELUSION '90	Jennifer Rubin
DEMIAN	Hermann Hesse
DEMON '77	Tony LoBianco
DEMONIAQUE '58	Francois Perier
DEMONS OF THE MIND '71	Yvonne Mitchell
DEMYAN BEDNYI po	Alekseyevich
DEMYAN BEDNYI, DENYAN	Efin Al Pridvarov
DENNIS THE MENACE	Hank Ketcham
DENNIS THE MENACE '93	Walter Matthau
DENNIS THE MENACE tv	Jay North
DEPORTED '50	Jeff Chandler
DEPUTY, THE tv	Henry Fonda
DER RING DES NIBELUNGEN	Richard Wagner
DESIGN FOR LIVING '33	Fredric March, Gary Cooper
DESIGNING WOMAN '57	Lauren Bacall, Gregory Peck
DESIGNING WOMEN tv	Delta Burke
DESIRE '36	Marlene Dietrich, Gary Cooper
DESIRE IN THE DUST '60	Raymond Burr
DESIREE '54	Marlon Brando
DESPAIR '79	Dirk Bogarde
DESPERADO '95	Antonio Banderas
DESPERADOES, THE '43	Randolph Scott
DESPERATE '47	Steve Brodie
DESPERATE MOMENT '53	Dirk Bogarde
DESPERATE SEARCH '52	Howard Keel
DESTINATION GOBI '53	Richard Widmark
DESTINATION MOON '50	John Archer
DESTRUCTORS, THE '74	Anthony Quinn

DESTRY '54	Audie Murphy
DESTRY RIDES AGAIN '39 ****	James Stewart, Marlene Dietrich
DETECTIVE, THE '68	Frank Sinatra
DETECTIVE STORY '51	Kirk Douglas
DETOUR '45	Tom Neal
DEUTSCHENDORF,HENRY JOHN Jr.	John Denver
DEVIL AND THE DEEP '32	Tallulah Bankhead
DEVIL OR ANGEL	Bobby Vee
DEVIL TIMES FIVE '74	Gene Evans
DEVIL'S ADVOCATE, THE'97****	Keanu Reeves, Al Pacino
DEVIL'S BRIDE, THE '68	Christopher Lee
DEVIL'S DISCIPLE, THE '59	Kirk Douglas, Burt Lancaster
DEVIL'S IN LOVE, THE '33	Loretta Young
DEVILS, THE '71	Oliver Reed
DEVOTION '46	Olivia de Havilland
DIABOLIQUE '55	Simone Signoret
DIAGNOSIS MURDER '76	Christopher Lee
DIAL "M" FOR MURDER '54	Ray Milland,Alfred Hitchcock d
DIAMOND HUNTERS '56	Simone Signoret
DIANA	Paul Anka mr s
DIANE '56	Lana Turner
DIARY OF A GENIUS	Salvadore Dali
DIARY OF A HITMAN '92	Forest Whitaker
DIARY OF A MADMAN '63	Vincent Price
DICK TRACY	Chester Gould
DIE FLEDERMAUS	Adele
DIE GOTTERDAMMERUNG	Richard Wagner
DIE NIBELUNGEN '24 ****	Paul Richter
DIE SCHONE MULLERIN	Franz Schubert
DIE! DIE! MY DARLING '65	Tallulah Bankhead
DIFF'RENT STROKES tv	Conrad Bain
DIFFERENT STORY, A '78	Perry King
DIFFERENT WORLD, A tv	Lisa Bonet
DIGGSTOWN '92	James Woods
DILLINGER '73	Warren Oates
DIMPLES '36	Shirley Temple
DINER '82	Steve Guttenberg
DINESEN, ISAK	Baroness Karen Dinesen Blixen
DINGAKA '65	Stanley Baker
DINGO '91	Colin Friels
DINKY '35	Jackie Cooper
DINNER AT EIGHT '33 ****	Marie Dressler, John Barrymore
DINNER AT THE RITZ '37	Annabella
DINO '57	Sal Mineo
DINOSAURS tv	Stuart Pankin
DIPLOMANIACS '33	Robert Woolsey
DIRIGIBLE '31	Jack Holt
DIRT BIKE KID, THE '86	Peter Billingsley
DIRTY HANDS	Jean-Paul Sartre
DISASTER IN TIME '92	Jeff Daniels
DISCO DUCK	Rick Dees s
DISCOURS DE LA METHODE	Rene Descartes
DISHONORED '31	Marlene Dietrich
DISPUTED PASSAGE '39	Dorothy Lamour
DISRAELI '29	George Arliss
DISTANCE '75	Paul Benjamin
DISTANT HARMONY '87	Luciano Pavarotti
DISTANT TRUMPET, A '64	Troy Donahue
DIVIDED HEART, THE '54	Cornell Borchers
DIVIDED SELF, THE	Robert David Laing
DIVINE COMEDY, THE	Dante

DIVORCE OF LADY X, THE '38	Merle Oberon
DIVORCEE, THE '30	Norma Shearer
DIX, DOROTHY	Elizabeth Gilmer
DIXIANA '30	Bebe Daniels
DIXIE '43	Bing Crosby, Dorothy Lamour
DO I HEAR A WALTZ?	Richard Rodgers c, Stephen Sondheim c
DO THAT TO ME ONE MORE TIME	The Captain and Tennille m & s
DO THE RIGHT THING '89	Danny Aiello, Ossie Davis
DO YOU BELIEVE IN MAGIC ?	Lovin Spoonful mr
DOBERMAN GANG, THE '72	Byron Mabe
DOC '71	Stacy Keach
DOCK OF THE BAY, THE	Otis Redding mr
DOCKS OF NEW YORK '28 ****	George Bancroft, Betty Compson
DOCTOR FAUSTUS	Christopher Marlowe
DOCTOR IN SPITE OF HIMSELF, THE Moliere	
DOCTOR IN THE HOUSE tv	Barry Evans
DOCTOR MY EYES	Jackson Browne mr
DOCTOR'S DILEMMA '58	Leslie Caron
DOCTOR, DOCTOR tv	Matt Frewer
DOCTOR, THE '91	William Hurt
DODSWORTH '36 ****	Walter Huston, Ruth Chatterton
DOG DAY AFTERNOON '75	Al Pacino
DOGFIGHT '91	River Phoenix
DOGPOUND SHUFFLE '75	Ron Moody
DOLL'S HOUSE	Nora
DOLLY SISTERS, THE '45	Betty Grable
DON CARLO	Giuseppe Verdi
DON GIOVANNI	Wolfgang A. Mozart
DON JUAN	Geo. Gordon(Lord) Byron
DON JUAN deMARCO '95	Marlon Brando
DON'T GO BREAKING MY HEART	Elton John mr & s
DON'T GO BREAKING MY HEART	Kiki Dee mr & s
DON'T WORRY KYOKO	Yoko Ono
DOOGIE HOWSER, M.D. tv	Neil Patrick Harris
DOOMWATCH '72	Judy Geeson
DOONESBURY	Garry Trudeau
DOOR, THE	Mary Roberts Rinehart
DOORS, THE '91	Val Kilmer
DORA MAAR SEATED	Pablo Picasso
DORSEY, ARNOLD	Engelbert Humperdink s
DOUBLE HAPPINESS '95	Sandra Oh, Mina Shum d
DOUBLE INDEMNITY '44 ****	Fred MacMurray, Barbara Stanwyck
DOUBLE OR NOTHING '37	Bing Crosby
DOUBTING THOMAS '35	Will Rogers
DOUGHGIRLS, THE '44	Ann Sheridan
DOUGLAS, MICHAEL	Michael Keaton
DOVE SONO	Wolfgang A. Mozart
DOVE, THE '74	Joseph Bottoms
DOWN MEMORY LANE '49	Steve Allen
DOWNHILL '27	Ivor Novello
DOWNSTAIRS '32	John Gilbert, Paul Lukas
DR. KILDARE tv	Richard Chamberlain
DR. SEUSS	Theodore Seuss Geisel
DR. STRANGELOVE OR: HOW I LEARNED, etc. '78 **** Peter Sellers	
DRACULA '31	Bela Lugosi
DRAGNET '54	Jack Webb
DRAGNET '87	Dan Aykroyd, Tom Hanks
DRAGNET tv	Jack Webb
DRAGON SEED	Pearl Buck
DRAGONHEART '96	Dennis Quaid
DRAGONSLAYER '81	Peter MacNicol

DRAGONWYCK '46	Gene Tierney
DRAMATIC SCHOOL '38	Luise Rainer
DREAM CHILDREN	Charles Lamb
DREAM OF GERONTIUS	Sir Edward Elgar
DREAMBOAT '52	Ginger Rogers
DREAMSCAPE '84	Dennis Quaid
DRED	Harriet Beecher Stowe
DRESSER, THE '83	Albert Finney
DRESSMAKER, THE '88	Joan Plowright
DREXELL'S CLASS tv	Dabney Coleman
DRIFTER, THE '88	Timothy Bottoms
DRIFTWOOD '47	Ruth Warrick
DRIVER, PHYLLIS	Phyllis Diller
DRIVER, THE '78	Ryan O'Neal
DRIVING MISS DAISY	Alfred Uhry p-l'88
DROWNING POOL, THE '76	Paul Newman
DRUGSTORE COWBOY '89	Matt Dillon
DRUMS '38	Sabu
DRUMS ALONG THE MOHAWK	Walter D. Edmonds
DRUON, MAURICE	Maurice Kessel
DRY WHITE SEASON, A '89	Donald Sutherland
DuBARRY WAS A LADY '43	Red Skelton
DUCHESS OF ALBA	Jose de Francisco Goya
DUCHESS OF IDAHO '50	Esther Williams
DUCHESS OF PADOA, THE	Oscar Wilde
DUCK SOUP '33 ****	Marx Brothers
DUEL IN THE JUNGLE '54	Dana Andrews
DUELLISTS, THE '77	Keith Carradine
DUET tv	Matthew Laurance
DUHAMEL, GEORGES	Denis Thevenin
DUKE BLUEBEARD'S CASTLE	Bela Bartok
DUKENFIELD, WILLIAM CLAUDE	W.C. Fields
DUKES OF HAZARD tv	John Schneider, Tom Wopat
DULCIMA '71	John Mills
DULCIMER STREET '48	Richard Attenborough
DUMBLE-SMITH, MICHAEL	Michael Crawford
DUMBO '41 **** (Animated)	Ben Sharpsteen d
DUNKIRK '58	John Mills
DUNSANY, LORD	Edward J.M.D. Plunkett
DURAS, MARGUERITE	Marguerite Donnadieu
DUSIAK, MICHELLE	Michelle Lee
DUST '85	Jane Birkin, Trevor Howard
DUST BE MY DESTINY '39	John Garfield
DUSTY '82	Bill Kerr
DUTCH '91	Ed O'Neill
DUTCHMAN '66	Shirley Knight
DWIGHT, REGINALD	Elton John
DYNAMITE '29	Conrad Nagel
DYNASTY tv	Linda Evans,John Forsythe,Kate O'Mara
E.T. THE EXTRA-TERRESTRIAL'82****Steven Speilberg d,Dee Wallace
EAGLE AND THE HAWK, THE '33	Fredric March
EAGLE AND THE HAWK, THE '50	John Payne
EAGLE HAS LANDED, THE '77	Michael Caine, Robert Duvall
EARLE in High Sierra	Humphrey Bogart
EARLY, DELLOREESE PATRICIA	Della Reese
EARRINGS OF MADAME de ...,THE '53 **** Charles Boyer
EARTH IN THE BALANCE	Albert Gore
EARTHLING, THE '80	William Holden
EAST OF EDEN '55 ****	James Dean, Elia Kazan d
EAST OF THE RIVER '40	John Garfield
EASY COME, EASY GO '47	Barry Fitzgerald

EATING '90	Frances Bergen
EBOLI '79	Gian Maria Volonte
ECLIPSE '62	Alain Delon
EDDIE '96	Whoopi Goldberg
EDDIE MACON'S RUN '83	Kirk Douglas
EDEN '92	Jack Armstrong
EDGE OF DARKNESS '43	Errol Flynn
EDGE OF THE CITY '57 ****	John Casavetes, Sidney Poitier
EDGE, THE '97	Anthony Hopkins
EGOIST, THE	George Meredith
EGSTROM, NORMA	Peggy Lee
EIGHT COUSINS	Louisa May Alcott w
EIGHT IS ENOUGH tv	Dick Van Patten
EIGHT O'CLOCK WALK '52	Richard Attenborough
EINE KLEINE NACHTMUSIK	Wolfgang Amadeus Mozart
EINSTEIN, ALBERT	Albert Brooks
EL CID	Rodrigo Diaz de Vivar
EL GRECO p	Domenikos Theotocopoulos
EL SALON MEXICO	Aaron Copland
ELECTRIC DREAMS '84	Lenny Von Dohlen
ELEKTRA	Richard Strauss
ELENE	Cynewulf
ELENI	Nicholas Gage
ELENI '85	Kate Nelligan
ELEPHANT MAN, THE '80	Anthony Hopkins
ELIA	Charles Lamb
ELIOT, GEORGE	Mary Ann Evans
ELLIE '84	Shelley Winters
ELLY MAY	Donna Douglas
ELMER, CHARLES Jr.	Rip Taylor
ELSA	Richard Wagner
ELUARD, PAUL	Eugene Grindel
ELUSIVE CORPORAL, THE '62	Jean-Pierre Cassel
EMBASSY '72	Richard Roundtree
EMERGENCY tv	Robert Fuller
EMIGRANTS, THE '71	Max Van Sydow
EMMA	Jane Austen
EMMA '32	Marie Dressler
EMMA '96	Gwneth Paltrow
EMPIRE STRIKES BACK, THE '80	**** Mark Hamill, Harrison Ford
EMPTY NEST tv	Richard Muilligan
ENCHANTED APRIL '35	Ann Harding
ENCHANTED FOREST '45	Edmund Lowe
ENCHANTMENT '48	David Niven
END AS A MAN	Calder B. Willingham
END OF THE WORLD THE	Skeeter Davis
END, THE '78	Burt Reynolds d+
ENDORA in Bewitched tv	Agnes Moorhead
ENEMY FROM SPACE '57	Brian Donlevy
ENEMY GENERAL, THE '60	Van Johnson
ENFORCER, THE '51	Humphrey Bogart
ENFORCER, THE '76	Clint Eastwood
ENGLISH PATIENT, THE '96	Anthony Minghella o-d, &
ENGLISH PATIENT, THE '96	Ralph Fiennes,Juliette Binoche o-s
ENID	Alfred Lord Tennyson
ENID IS SLEEPING '90	Elizabeth Perkins
ENIGMA '82	Martin Sheen
ENIGMA VARIATIONS	Sir Edward Elgar
ENKE, ELIZABETH EDITH	Edie Adams
ENOCH ARDEN	Alfred Lord Tennyson
ENOS tv	Sonny Shroyer

ENS. PULVER in Mr. Roberts	Jack Lemmon
ENT	J.J.R. Tolkien
ENTER THE DRAGON '73	Bruce Lee
ENTERTAINER, THE '60	Laurence Olivier
EPSTEIN, KATHIE	Kathy Lee Gifford
EQUALIZER, THE tv	Edward Woodward
EQUUS '77	Richard Burton, Peter Firth
EQUUS b'dway	Richard Burton
ERASER '96	Arnold Schwarzenegger
ERDODY - String quartets Op. 76	Joseph Haydn
ERENDIRA '83	Irene Papas
ERI TU CHE	Giuseppe Verdi
ERICA	Susan Lucci
ERNANI	Giuseppe Verdi
ERNEST" FILMS '87-'91	Jim Varney
EROTICA	Madonna
ESCAPADE '55	John Mills
ESCAPE '40	Norma Shearer, Robert Taylor
ESCAPE '48	Rex Harrison
ESCAPE TO ATHENA '79	Roger Moore
ESEK, UNCLE	Henry Wheeler Shaw
ESME	J.D. Salinger
ESPIONAGE '37	Edmund Lowe
ESTEVEZ, CARLOS ERWIN	Charlie Sheen
ESTEVEZ, RAMON	Martin Sheen
ETERNALLY YOURS '39	Loretta Young
ETHAN FROME	Edith Wharton
ETHEL AND ALBERT tv	Peg Lynch
EVA	Franz Lehar
EVANS, ERNEST	Chubby Checker
EVE OF ST. MARK, THE '44	Anne Baxter
EVELYN PRENTICE '34	Myrna Loy
EVENING SHADE tv	Marilu Henner, Burt Reynolds
EVENING SHADE tv	Ossie Davis
EVERGREEN	Barbra Streisand
EVERY BREATH YOU TAKE	The Police mr
EVERY LITTLE MOVEMENT	Jimmy & Tommy Dorsey
EVERY MAN FOR HIMSELF AND GOD etc '75 ****	Brigitte Mira
EVERYBODY DOES IT '49	Paul Douglas
EVERYBODY'S FINE '90	Marcello Mastroianni
EVERYDAY PEOPLE	Sly and the Family Stone mr
EVIL, THE '78	Richard Crenna
EVITA	Andrew Lloyd Walker, Patti Lupone
EVITA	Lloyd Webber, Tim Rice
EVITA '96	Madonna
EX-LADY '33	Bette Davis, Gene Raymond
EXCALIBUR '81	Nicol Williamson
EXCLUSIVE '37	Fred MacMurray
EXCLUSIVE STORY '36	Franchot Tone
EXECUTIVE SUITE '54	William Holden
EXILE, THE '47	Douglas Fairbanks Jr.
EXODUS '60	Sal Mineo, Paul Newman
EXORCIST, THE '73	Ellen Burstyn
EYE OF THE NEEDLE '81	Donald Sutherland
EYE OF THE NEEDLE, THE	Ken Follett
EYE SAGE, THE	Joyce Carol Oates w
EYELESS IN GAZA	Aldous Huxley
EYES OF LAURA MARS '78	Faye Dunaway
F TROOP tv	Ken Berry
F.B.I., THE tv	Efrem Zimbalist Jr
F.I.S.T. '78	Sylvester Stallone

FABIOLA '49	Michele Morgan
FABLES IN SLANG	George Ade
FACE AT THE WINDOW, THE '39	Tod Slaughter
FACE IN THE CROWD, A '57	Andy Griffith
FACE IN THE RAIN, A '63	Rory Calhoun
FACE OF FU MANCHU, THE '65	Christopher Lee
FACES '68	John Marley, Gena Rowlands
FACES CARVED ON MT. RUSHMORE	Gutzon Borglum su
FACTS OF LIFE, THE tv	Charlotte Rae, Mindy Cohn
FAERIE QUEEN, THE	Edmund Spenser
FAGAN, ELEANORA	Billie Holiday
FAIL-SAFE '64	Henry Fonda
FAIR WIND TO JAVA '53	Fred MacMurray
FAITH	George Michael mr
FAITHFUL '96	Cher
FAITHLESS '32	Tallulah Bankhead
FAKE, THE '53	Dennis O'Keefe
FALCON CREST tv	Ana Alicia, Lorenzo Lamas
FALCON CREST tv	Robert Foxworth, Jane Wyman +
FALCON IN MEXICO, THE '44	Tom Conway
FALCON TAKES OVER, THE '42	George Sanders
FALCON'S BROTHER, THE '42	George Sanders
FALK, CONRAD ROBERT	Robert Conrad
FALKBERGET, JOHAN	Johan Lillebakken
FALL GUY, THE tv	Lee Majors
FALL RIVER LEGEND	Agnes DeMille
FALSTAFF	Giuseppi Verdi (his Last opera)
FAME '80	Irene Cara
FAMILY AFFAIR tv	Brian Keith
FAMILY BUSINESS '86	Fanny Ardant
FAMILY BUSINESS '89	Sean Connery
FAMILY CIRCUS, THE	Bill Keane
FAMILY HONEYMOON '48	Claudette Colbert
FAMILY JEWELS, THE '65	Jerry Lewis
FAMILY MATTERS tv	Joe Marie Payton-France
FAMILY SECRET, THE '51	John Derek
FAMILY TIES tv	Meridith Baxter-Birney, Alex Michael
FAMILY tv	Sada Thompson
FAMILY, THE '70	Charles Bronson
FAMILY, THE '87	Vittorio Gassman
FAN-FAN THE TULIP '51	Gina Lollobrigida
FANDANGO '85	Kevin Costner
FANGS '75	Janet Wood
FANNY '61	Chas.Boyer,Leslie Caron,Maurice Chevalier
FANTASIA '40	Leopold Stokowski
FANTASIST, THE '86	Christopher Cazenove
FANTASTIC VOYAGE '66	Stephen Boyd
FANTASY ISLAND tv	Ricardo Montalban
FAR HORIZONS, THE '55	Fred MacMurray
FAR SIDE, THE	Gary Larson
FARAH, JAMEEL	Jamie Farr
FAREWELL MY LOVELY	Raymond Chandler
FAREWELL TO ARMS, A	Ernest Hemingway
FAREWELL TO ARMS, A '32	Gary Cooper, Helen Hayes
FAREWELL TO ARMS, A '57	Rock Hudson
FARGO '96	Frances McDormand o-a, Joel Coen d
FARINOLA, VITO	Vic Damone
FARMER'S DAUGHTER, THE '47	Loretta Young
FARMER'S WIFE, THE '28	Jameson Thomas
FASHIONS '34	William Powell, Bette Davis
FAST AND FURIOUS '39	Franchot Tone

FAST CAR	Tracy Chapman mr
FASTEST GUN ALIVE, THE '56	Glenn Ford
FATAL ATTRACTION '87	Michael Douglas
FATE IS THE HUNTER '64	Glenn Ford
FATE TAKES A HAND '61	Ronald Howard
FATHER FIGURE	Michael, George s
FATHER KNOWS BEST tv	Robert Young
FATHER OF THE BRIDE '50 ****	Spencer Tracy, Elizabeth Taylor
FATHOM '67	Raquel Welch
FATSO '80	Dom DeLuise
FAUST	Chas. Franc. Gounod
FEAR IN THE NIGHT '47	Paul Kelly
FEAR OF FLYING	Erica Jong
FEAR STRIKES OUT '57	Anthony Perkins
FEARLESS '93	Jeff Bridges
FEARMAKERS '58	Dana Andrews
FEDERKIEWICZ, STEPHANIA	Stephanie Powers
FEDORA '78	William Holden
FEELIN' ALRIGHT	Traffic mr
FELIX UNGER in THE ODD COUPLE tv Tony Randall	
FELLOW TRAVELER '89	Ron Silver
FELONY SQUAD tv	Howard Duff
FEMALE '33	Ruth Chatterton
FEMALE ANIMAL, THE '58	Hedy Lamarr
FERRY TO HONG KONG '61	Orson Welles
FEUD, THE '90	Rene Auberjonois
FEVER IN THE BLOOD, A '61	Efrem Zimbalist Jr.
FEW DAYS WITH ME, A '88	Daniel Auteuil
FFOLKS '80	Roger Moore
FIDELIO(b's only opera)	Ludwig von Beethoven
FIELDS, TOTIE	Kathy Robbinson
FIFTH ELEMENT, THE '97	Bruce Willis
FIFTH MUSKETEER, THE '79	Beau Bridges
FIGHT FOR POWER	Public Ememy mr
FIGHTER, THE '52	Richard Conte
FIGHTING O'FLYNN, THE '49	Douglas Fairbanks Jr.
FIGHTING SEABEES, THE '44	John Wayne
FINAL COUNTDOWN, THE '80	Kirk Douglas
FINDERS KEEPERS '51	Tom Ewell
FINGER POINTS, THE '31	Richard Barthelmess
FINGERS '78	Harvey Keitel, Jim Brown
FINISHING SCHOOL '34	George Nicholls
FINKLEA, TULA	Cyd Charisse
FINLANDIA	Jean Sibelius
FINNEGAN'S WAKE	James Joyce
FIRE OVER ENGLAND '37	Laurence Olivier
FIREBALL, THE '50	Mickey Rooney
FIREFLY, THE	Rudolf Friml
FIREFLY, THE '37	Jeanette MacDonald
FIREPOWER '79	Sophia Loren
FIRM, THE '93	Tom Cruise
FIRST LEGION, THE '51	Charles Boyer
FIRST WIVE'S CLUB,THE'96	Goldie Hawn,Diane Keaton, Bette Midler
FISH CALLED WANDA, A '88	Jamie Lee Curtis
FISH MAGIC	Paul Klee
FITZSIMMONS, MAUREEN	Maureen O'Hara
FIVE EASY PIECES '70 ****	Jack Nicholson, Karen Black
FIVE HEARTBEATS, THE '91	Robert Townsend d+
FIVE PENNIES, THE '59	Danny Kaye
FIXER, THE '68	Alan Bates
FLAME OVER INDIA '59	Lauren Bacall

FLAMING FEATHER '51	Sterling Hayden
FLAMINGO	Earl Bostic mr
FLAMINGO ROAD tv	Morgan Fairchild
FLAREUP '69	Raquel Welch
FLASH GORDON	Alex Raymond
FLASHDANCE '83	Jennifer Beals
FLATLINERS '90	Kiefer Sutherland
FLESH '32	Wallace Beery
FLESH 'N' BLOOD tv	Lisa Darr
FLESH AND FANTASY '43	Charles Boyer
FLETCH '85	Chevy Chase
FLIGHT '29	Jack Holt
FLIGHT FROM GLORY '37	Chester Morris
FLINTSTONES, THE '94	John Goodman
FLIPPER '63	Chuck Connors
FLIPPER '96	Elijah Wood
FLIPPER tv	Brian Kelly
FLIRTATION WALK '34	Dick Powell
FLIRTING '90	Noah Taylor
FLUCK, DIANA	Diana Dors
FLY, THE '58	Vincent Price
FLY, THE '86	Jeff Goldblum
FLYING DEUCES, THE '39	Stan Laurel, Oliver Hardy
FLYING DOWN TO RIO '33	Delores Del Rio, Thornton Freeland d
FLYING DUTCHMAN, THE	Richard Wagner
FLYING DUTCHMAN, THE	Senta
FLYING NUN, THE tv	Sally Field
FOG, THE '78	Adrienne Barbeau, Hal Holbrook
FOLLOW ME QUIETLY '49	William Lundigan
FOLLOW THAT CAMEL '67	Phil Silvers
FOLLOW THAT DREAM '62	Elvis Presley
FOLLOW THE FLEET '36 ****	Fred Astaire, Ginger Rogers
FOOLS '70	Jason Robards Jr.
FOOLS FOR SCANDAL '38	Carole Lombard
FOOTLIGHT PARADE '33	James Cagney, Dick Powell
FOOTLOOSE '84	Kevin Bacon
FOR ANNIE	Edgar Allen Poe
FOR BETTER OR FOR WORSE	Lynn Johnston
FOR HEAVEN'S SAKE '26 ****	Harold Lloyd, Jobyna Ralston
FOR LOVE OR MONEY '63	Kirk Douglas, Mitzi Gaynor
FOR THE FIRST TIME '59	Mario Lanza
FOR WHAT IT'S WORTH	Buffalo Springfield mr
FOR YOUR EYES ONLY '81	Roger Moore
FOR YOUR LOVE	The Yardbirds mr
FORBIDDEN '53	Tony Curtis
FORBIDDEN CARGO '54	Nigel Patrick
FORBIDDEN FRUIT '59	Fernandel
FORBIDDEN GAMES '51	Brigitte Fossey
FORBIDDEN PLANET '56	Walter Pidgeon
FOREIGN AFFAIR, A '48	Jean Arthur
FOREIGN CORRESPONDENT '40****	Joel McCrea
FOREIGN INTRIGUE '56	Robert Mitchum
FOREIGN INTRIGUE tv	Jerome Thor
FOREST GUMP '94 ****	Tom Hanks
FOREVER AND A DAY '43	Cedric Hardwicke
FOREVER DARLING '56	Lucille Ball
FOREVER YOUR GIRL	Paula Abdul mr
FORGIVEN SINNER, THE '61	Jean-Paul Belmondo
FORGOTTEN WOMAN '39	Sigrid Gurie
FORSYTE SAGA, THE	John Galsworthy
FORTUNE '75	Jack Nicholson

FORTY-SECOND (42ND) STREET '33 ****	Ruby Keeler, Warner Baxter
FORZA DEL DESTINO, A	Giuseppe Verdi
FOSTER, ALICIA CHRISTIAN	Jodie Foster
FOUCAULT'S PENDULUM	Umberto Eco
FOUNTAIN, THE '34	Ann Harding
FOUNTAINHEAD, THE	Ayn Rand
FOUNTAINHEAD, THE '49	Gary Cooper
FOUNTAINS OF ROME	Ottorino Raspighi
FUR ELISE	Ludwig von Beethoven
FOUR FEATHERS, THE '39 ****	C. Aubrey Smith, John Clement
FOUR HOURS TO KILL '35	Richard Barthelmess
FOUR HUNDRED BLOWS, THE '59 ****	Jean-Pierre Leaud
FOUR MUSKETEERS, THE '75	Oliver Reed
FOUR POSTER, THE	Jessica Tandy
FOUR QUARTERS	T.S. Eliot po
FOUR SEASONS, THE '81	Alan Alda d+, Carol Burnett
FOURTH PROTOCOL, THE '87	Michael Caine
FOWLER, CLARA ANN	Patti Page
FOX AND HIS FRIENDS '75 ****	Rainer Werner Fassbinder d+
FOX AND THE GRAPES, THE	Aesop
FOX, THE '68	Sandy Dennis
FOXES '80	Jodie Foster
FOXFIRE '55	Jane Russell
FOXHOLE IN CAIRO '61	James Robertson Justice
FRA DIAVALO	Daniel-Franc. E. Auber c
FRAHM, KARL HERBERT	Willy Brandt
FRAMED '75	Joe Don Baker
FRANCE, ANATOLE	Jacques Thibault
FRANCES '82	Jessica Lange
FRANCIS '49	Donald O'Connor
FRANCIS OF ASSISI '61	Bradford Dillman
FRANCONERO, CONCETTA	Connie Francis
FRANK NITTI in THE UNTOUCHABLES tv	Gordon Bruce
FRANKEL, BERNICE	Beatrice Arthur
FRANKENBERG, JOYCE	Jane Seymour
FRANKENSTEIN '31	Colin Clive, Boris Karloff
FRANKIE STEIN	Mary W. Shelley
FRANTIC '57	Jeanne Moreau
FRANTIC '88	Harrison Ford
FRASIER tv	Peri Gilpin
FRAULEIN DOKTOR '69	Suzy Kendall
FREAKS	Leslie A. Fiedler
FREAKS '32	Wallace Ford
FREEBIRD	Lynyrd Skynyrd mr
FREEWAY '96	Reese Witherspoon
FRENCH CONNECTION, THE '71 ****	Gene Hackman, Fernando Rey
FRENCH DETECTIVE, THE '75	Lino Ventura
FRENCHMAN'S CREEK '44	Joan Fontaine
FRENESI	Artie Shaw
FRESH '94	Giancarlo Esposito
FRESH PRINCE OF BEL AIR tv	Will Smith
FRESHMAN, THE '25 ****	Harold Lloyd, Jobyna Ralston
FRESHMAN, THE '90	Marlon Brando
FREUD '62	Montgomery Clift
FREUND, JOHN	John Forsythe
FRIEDA '47	David Farrar, Glynis Johns
FRIENDLY ENEMIES '42	Charles Winninger
FRIENDLY PERSUASION '56 ****	Gary Cooper, Dorothy McGuire
FRIGHTENERS, THE '96	Michael Fox
FRISKY '55	Gina Lollobrigida
FROG '89	Paul Williams

FROGMEN, THE '51	Richard Widmark, Dana Andrews
FROGS '72	Ray Milland
FROM HELL TO TEXAS '58	Don Murray
FROM HERE TO ETERNITY	James Jones
FROM HERE TO ETERNITY'53****	Burt Lancaster,Montgomery Clift,
FROM THE BEGINNING	Emerson, Lake and Palmer mr
FROM THE TERRACE '60	Paul Newman
FROME	Edith Wharton
FRONT PAGE STORY '54	Jack Hawkins
FRONT PAGE WOMAN '35	Bette Davis
FRONT, THE '76 ****	Woody Allen, Danny Aiello, Zero Mostel
FRONTIER HELLCAT '66	Stewart Granger, Elke Sommer
FUGITIVE, THE '93	Harrison Ford
FUGITIVE, THE tv	David Janssen
FULKS, SARAH JANE	Jane Wyman
FULL HOUSE tv	Bob Saget, Lori Loughlin
FULL METAL JACKET '87	Matthew Modine
FULLER BRUSH MAN, THE '48	Red Skelton
FUNERAL, THE '96	Christopher Walken
FUNHOUSE, THE '81	Elizabeth Barridge
FUNNY GIRL	Jule Styne
FUNNYMAN '67	Peter Bonerz
FURIES, THE '50	Barbara Stanwyck
FURNIER, VINCENT	Alice Cooper
FURRY, ELDA	Hedda Hopper
FURY '36	Spencer Tracy
FURY, THE '78	Kirk Douglas
FUTABATEI, SHIMEI	Hasegawa Tatsunosuke
FUTUREWORLD '76	Blythe Danner, Peter Fonda
FUTZ '69	John Pakos
FUZZ '72	Burt Reynolds
GABY '56	Leslie Caron
GABY--A TRUE STORY '87	Liv Ullmann
GAINES, La DONNA	Donna Summer
GAITE PARISIENNE	Leonide Massine
GALILEO '73	Edward Fox
GALLANT HOURS, THE '60	James Cagney
GALLANT JOURNEY '46	Glenn Ford
GALLIPOLI '81	Mel Gibson
GAMBIT '66	Michael Caine
GAMBLE, THE '88	Faye Dunaway, Matthew Modine
GAMBLERS, THE '69	Suzy Kendall
GAME, THE '97	Michael Douglas, Sean Penn
GAMES '67	Simone Signoret
GANDHI '82	Richard Attenborough d
GANG'S ALL HERE, THE '43	Alice Faye
GANGSTER, THE '47	Barry Sullivan
GARDEN OF EARTHLY DELIGHTS,A	Joyce Carol Oates
GARDEN OF THE FINZI-CONTINIS, THE '71 **** Dominique Sanda	
GARDEN OF THE MOON '38	Margaret Lindsay, Pat O'Brien
GARDEN, THE '90	Johnny Mills
GARDENS OF STONE '87	James Caan
GARFIELD	Jim Davis
GARFINKLE, JULIUS	John Garfield
GARP	John Irving
GAS '81	Donald Sutherland
GAS, FOOD LODGING '92	Brooke Adams, Ione Skye
GAS-S-S-S '70	Bud Cort
GASLIGHT '40	Anton Walbrook
GASLIGHT '44	Ingrid Bergman, Charles Boyer
GASOLINE ALLEY--early	Frank King

GASOLINE ALLEY--later	Dick Moores
GASSION, EDITH	Edith Piaf
GATE, THE '87	Christa Denton
GATOR '76	Burt Reynolds
GATTACA '97	Ethan Hawke
GAUNTLET, THE '77	Clint Eastwood d+
GAY ADVENTURE, THE '53	Burgess Meredith
GAY DECEPTION, THE '35	Francis Lederer
GAY DESPERADO, THE '36	Ida Lupino
GAY DIVORCEE, THE '34	Fred Astaire, Ginger Rogers
GAZEBO, THE '59	Glenn Ford, Debbie Reynolds
GEISEL, THEODORE SEUSS	Dr. Seuss
GEISMAN, ELLA	June Allyson
GENDRE, LOUIS	Louis Jourdan
GENERAL, THE '27 ****	Buster Keaton
GENET	Janet Flanner
GENEVIEVE '53	Dinah Sheridan
GENTLE BEN tv	Dennis Weaver
GENTLEMEN PREFER BLONDS	Anita Loos
GEORGE RAFT STORY, THE '61	Ray Danton
GEORGIA ON MY MIND	Ray Charles s
GEORGIA, GEORGIA '72	Diana Sands
GERMINAL '93	Gerard Depardieu
GERONIMO '62	Chuck Connors
GERVAISE '56	Maria Schell
GET A LIFE tv	Chris Elliott
GET SMART tv	Don Adams, Barbara Feldon
GETAWAY, THE '72	Steve McQueen
GETTING IT RIGHT '89	Helena Bonham Carter
GETTING STRAIGHT '70	Elliott Gould
GETTYSBURG '93	Tom Berenger
GHOST '90	Demi Moore, Patrick Swayze
GHOST AND MRS. MUIR, THE tv	Hope Lange
GHOST, THE '63	Barbara Steele
GHOSTBUSTERS '84	Bill Murray
GHOSTS	Henrik Ibsen
GHOUL, THE '34	Boris Karloff
GHOUL, THE '75	Peter Cushing
GIANT	Edna Ferber
GIANT '56 ****	Rock Hudson, Elizabeth Taylor
GIBSON GIRLS, THE	Charles Dana Gibson
GIDGET '59	Sandra Dee
GIG, THE '85	Wayne Rogers
GIGI '58 ****	Leslie Caron, Maurice Chevalier
GIGI on Broadway	Katharine Hepburn
GIGOT '62	Jackie Gleason
GILDA' 46	Rita Hayworth, Glen Ford
GILHOOLEY, EDNA	Ellen Burstyn
GILLIGAN'S ISLAND tv	Bob Denver, Alan Hale Jr
GIMME A BREAK tv	Nell Carter, Dolph Sweet
GIMME SHELTER '70 ****(documentary)	Rolling Stones
GIMME SOME LOVIN'	Spencer Davis Group mr
GIN GAME, THE	Hume Cronyn, Jessica Tandy
GINGER MAN, THE	J.P. Donleavy
GIRL CAN'T HELP IT, THE '56	Jayne Mansfield
GIRL FROM IPANEMA, THE	Antonio Carlos Jobim
GIRL FROM MEXICO, THE '39	Lupe Velez
GIRL HUNTERS, THE '63	Mickey Spillane
GIRL IN EVERY PORT, A '28	Victor McLaglen
GIRL IN HIS POCKET '57	Jean Marais
GIRL MOST LIKELY, THE '57	Jane Powell

GIRL NAMED TAMIKO, A '62	Martha Hyer
GIRL NEXT DOOR, THE '53	Dan Dailey
GIRL OF THE NIGHT '60	Anne Francis
GIRL-GETTERS, THE '66	Oliver Reed
GIRLFRIENDS '78	Melanie Mayron
GIRLS, THE '68	Bibi Andersson
GIRLS ABOUT TOWN '31	Kay Francis
GIRLS! GIRLS! GIRLS! '62	Elvis Presley
GISELLE	Adolphe Chas. Adam
GIVE A GIRL A BREAK '53	Marge Champion
GIVE ME THE NIGHT	George Benson mr & s
GIVE ME YOUR HEART '36	Kay Francis
GLADIATOR, THE '78	Joe E. Brown
GLASS BOTTOM BOAT, THE '66	Doris Day, Rod Taylor
GLASS MENAGERIE, THE	Tennessee Williams
GLASS MENAGERIE, THE '50	Kirk Douglas, Jane Wyman
GLASS MENAGERIE, THE '87	Joanne Woodard
GLASS MENAGERIE, THE '87	Laura
GLASS SLIPPER, THE '55	Leslie Caron
GLORY '89 ****	Matthew Broderick, Denzel Washington
GNOME-MOBILE, THE '67	Walter Brennan
GO AWAY LITTLE GIRL	Donny Osmond s
GO INTO YOUR DANCE '35	Al Jolson
GO TELL IT ON THE MOUNTAIN	James Baldwin
GO WEST, YOUNG MAN '36	Mae West
GOD IS MY CO-PILOT '45	Dennis Morgan
GOD'S FAVORITE	Neil Simon
GODDEN, RUMER	Mrs. Rumer Haynes Dixon
GODFATHER, THE	Mario Puzo
GODFATHER, PART II '74 ****	Al Pacino, Diane Keaton
GODFATHER, THE '72	Marlon Brando, James Caan
GODS OF THE PLAGUE '69	Hanna Schygulla
GODSPELL '73	David Haskell
GOING HOLLYWOOD '33	Bing Crosby, Marion Davies
GOING MY WAY '44 ****	Bing Crosby, Rise Stevens
GOING UP THE COUNTRY	Canned Heat mr
GOLD '74	Roger Moore
GOLD DUST GERTIE '31	Ole Olsen, Chic Johnson
GOLD OF NAPLES, THE '54	Sophia Loren
GOLD RUSH, THE '25 ****	Charlie Chaplin d+
GOLDBERGS, THE '50	Gertrude Berg
GOLDBERGS, THE tv	Gertrude Berg
GOLDBLUME (In Hill Street Blues tv) Joe Spano	
GOLDEN AGE OF COMEDY, THE '57 **** Robert Youngson d	
GOLDEN ARROW, THE '36	George Brent, Bette Davis
GOLDEN BLADE, THE '53	Rock Hudson
GOLDEN BOWL, THE	Henry James
GOLDEN BOY	Clifford Odets
GOLDEN COACH, THE '52	Anna Magnani
GOLDEN EARRINGS '47	Marlene Dietrich, Ray Milland
GOLDEN GIRLS, THE tv	Beatrice Arthur
GOLDENBERG, EMMANUEL	Edward G. Robinson
GOLDENEYE '95	Pierce Brosnan
GOLDFINGER '64	Sean Connery
GOLDSTEIN '65	Philip Kaufman
GOMER PYLE, U.S.M.C. tv	Jim Nabors
GONE WITH THE WIND '39 ****	Clark Gable, Vivien Leigh
GOOD COMPANIONS, THE '33	Jessie Matthews
GOOD COMPANIONS, THE '56	Eric Portman
GOOD EARTH, THE	Pearl Buck
GOOD EARTH, THE '37 ****	Paul Muni, Luise Rainer

GOOD HUMOR MAN, THE '50	Jack Carson
GOOD LOVIN'	The Rascals mr
GOOD NEIGHBOR SAM '64	Jack Lemmon
GOOD NIGHT IRENE	Frank Sinatra
GOOD SOLDIER, THE	Ford Madox Ford
GOOD TIMES tv	Esther Rolle
GOOD VIBRATIONS	The Beach Boys mr
GOODBYE GIRL, THE	Neil Simon
GOODBYE GIRL, THE '77	Richard Dreyfuss, Marsha Mason
GOODBYE PORK PIE '81	Tony Barry
GOODBYE, COLUMBUS	Philip Roth
GOODBYE, COLUMBUS '69	Richard Benjamin, Ali MacGraw
GOODBYE, MR. CHIPS '39	Robert Donat
GOODBYE, MY FANCY '51	Joan Crawford
GOODBYE, NEW YORK '85	Julie Hagerty
GOODFELLAS '90	Robert De Niro
GOONIES, THE '85	Josh Brolin
GORGO '61	William Sylvester, Bill Travers
GORGON, THE '64	Peter Cushing
GORILLA AT LARGE '54	Cameron Mitchell
GORKY, MAKSIM	Aleksey Maksimovich Peshkov
GORMEZANO, EDITH	Eydie Gorme
GOSPEL ACCORDING TO ST.MATTHEW,THE'66**** Pier Paolo Pasolini d
GOTCHA! '85	Anthony Edwards
GOTTLIEB, JOSEPH	Joey Bishop
GRACE OF MY HEART '96	Illeana Douglas
GRACE VAN OWEN in L.A.Law tv Susan Dey
GRACELAND	Paul Simon mr
GRADUATE, THE '67 ****	Anne Bancroft, Dustin Hoffman
GRAND HIGHWAY, THE '87	Richard Bohringer
GRAND HOTEL '32 ****	Greta Garbo, John Barrymore
GRAND ILLUSION '37 ****	Jean Gabin
GRANDE BOUFFE, THE '73	Marcello Mastroianni
GRANDMA MOSES	Mary Anna Moses
GRANIN, DANIIL ALEKSANDROVICH Daniil German
GRAPES OF WRATH, THE	John Steinbeck p-f'40
GRAPES OF WRATH, THE'40 ****	Henry Fonda , Jane Darwell
GRASS HARP, THE	Truman Capote
GRASS IS GREENER, THE '60	Cary Grant
GRASS IS SINGING, THE '81	Karen Black
GRASSHOPPER, THE '70	Jacqueline Bisset
GRAYEAGLE '78	Ben Johnson
GREASE '78	John Travolta
GREASER'S PALACE '72	Allan Arbus
GREAT CARUSO, THE '51	Mario Lanza
GREAT ESCAPE, THE '63 ****	Steve McQueen, James Garner
GREAT EXPECTATIONS '46 ****	John Mills, Valerie Hobson
GREAT FLAMARION, THE '45	Erich von Stroheim
GREAT GARRICK, THE '37	Brian Aherne, Olivia de Haviland
GREAT GATSBY, THE	F. Scott Fitzgerald
GREAT GATSBY, THE '49	Alan Ladd
GREAT GATSBY, THE '74	Robert Redford
GREAT MANHUNT, THE '50	Douglas Fairbanks Jr.
GREAT McGINTY, THE '40	Brian Donlevy
GREAT MEADOW, THE '31	John Mack Brown
GREAT NINTH	Franz Schubert
GREAT PROFILE, THE '40	John Barrymore
GREAT RUPERT, THE '50	Jimmy Durante
GREAT SANTINI, THE '79	Robert Duvall, Blythe Danner
GREAT SINNER, THE '49	Gregory Peck
GREAT WHITE HOPE, THE '70	James Earl Jones

GREATEST LOVE, THE	Whitney Houston mr
GRECO, EL p	Domenikos Theotocopoulos
GREED '25 ****	Gibson Gowland, ZaSu Pitts
GREEDY '94	Michael J. Fox
GREEN ACRES tv	Eddie Albert, Eva Gabor
GREEN ARCHER, THE '61	Gert Frobe
GREEN BERETS, THE	Robin Moore
GREEN EGGS AND HAM	Dr. Seuss
GREEN FOR DANGER '46 ****	Alastair Sim, Sally Gray
GREEN HORNET, THE	Britt Reid
GREEN MANSIONS	Rima
GREEN ONIONS	Booker T. and the MG's mr
GREEN PASTURES, THE	Marc Connelly
GREEN PROMISE, THE '49	Marguerite Chapman
GREEN, HENRY	Henry V. Yorke
GREENE, GLADYS	Jean Arthur
GREENE, GLADYS	Jean Arthur
GREETINGS '68	Robert De Niro
GREYFRIARS BOBBY '61	Donald Crisp
GRIFTERS, THE '90	Anjelica Huston
GRIN, ALEKSANDR	Aleksandr S. Grinevsky
GRIS, JUAN p	Jose Victor Gonzales
GRISBI '53	Jeanne Moreau
GROUP, THE '66	Candice Bergen
GROWING PAINS tv	Alan Thicke
GRUMPIER OLD MEN '95	Jack Lemmon, Walter Matthau
GRYPHIUS, ANDREAS po & w	Andreas Greif
GUANTANAMERA '97	Mertha Ibarra
GUARDSMAN, THE '31	Alfred Lunt, Lynn Fontanne
GUBITOSI, MICHAEL	Robert Blake
GUEST IN THE HOUSE '44	Anne Baxter
GUEST, THE '64	Alan Bates, Donald Pleasence
GUILTY AS CHARGED '92	Rod Steiger
GUILTY BYSTANDER '50	Zachary Scott
GUILTY, THE '47	Bonita Granville
GUMBALL RALLY, THE '76	Michael Sarrazin
GUMM, FRANCES	Judy Garland
GUMPS, THE	Sydney Smith
GUMSHOE, THE '72	Albert Finney
GUNFIGHT, A '71	Kirk Douglas
GUNFIGHTER, THE '50	Gregory Peck
GUNFIGHTERS '47	Randolph Scott
GUNGA DIN '39 ****	Cary Grant, Victor McLaglen
GUNS OF DARKNESS '62	David Niven
GUNS OF NAVARONE, THE '61	Gregory Peck, David Niven
GUNS OF WILL SONNETT, THE tv	Walter Brennan
GUNSMOKE '53	Audie Murphy
GUNSMOKE tv	James Arness(Matt Dillon)
GURDIN, NATASHA	Natalie Wood
GUS '76	Ed Asner
GUSTAFSSON, GRETA	Greta Garbo
GUYNES, DEMETRIA	Demi Moore
GYPSY '62	Rosalind Russell, Natalie Wood
H.D.	Hilda Doolittle
H.E.A.L.T.H. '79	Carol Burnett
H.M.S. PINAFORE	William Gilbert, Arthur Sullivan
HACKER, LEONARD	Buddy Hackett
HAFIZ	Shams-ud-din Muhammad
HAGAR THE HORRIBLE	Dik Browne
HAIL THE CONQUERING HERO '44	**** Eddie Bracken, Ella Raines
HAIL TO THE CHIEF '73	Dan Resin

HAIR '79	John Savage, Treat Williams
HAIRSPRAY '88	Sonny Bono
HAIRY APE, THE	Eugene O'Neill
HAJ,THE	Leon Uris
HALF NAKED TRUTH, THE '32	Lupe Velez
HALFWAY HOUSE, THE '43	Glynis Johns
HALL, DIANE	Diane Keaton
HALLELUJAH '29	Nina Mae McKinney
HALLELUJAH TRAIL, THE '65	Burt Lancaster
HALLOWEEN '78	Donald Pleasence
HALLOWEEN MOVIES '78 - '89	Donald Pleasence
HAMLET '48 ****	Laurence Olivier d+
HAMLET '69	Nicol Williamson
HAMLET '90	Mel Gibson
HAMLET '96	Kenneth Branagh
HAMMER in Mike Hammer tv	Stacy Keach
HAMMETT '83	Frederic Forrest
HAMSUN, KNUT	Knut Pederson
HANDFUL OF DUST, A	Evelyn Waugh
HANDLE WITH CARE '77	Paul LeMat
HANGING TREE, THE '59	Gary Cooper
HANGMEN ALSO DIE '43	Brian Donlevy
HANGOVER SQUARE '45	Linda Darnell
HANNIBAL BROOKS '69	Oliver Reed
HANUSSEN '88	Klaus Maria Brandauer
HAPPINESS AHEAD '34	Dick Powell
HAPPY DAYS tv	Ron Howard
HAPPY ENDING, THE '69	Jean Simmons
HAPPY PRINCE, THE	Oscar Wilde
HAPPY THIEVES, THE '62	Rex Harrison
HARD DAY'S NIGHT	Beatles
HARD DAY'S NIGHT, A '64 ****	The Beatles
HARDCASTLE & McCORMICK tv	Brian Keith
HARDCORE '79	George C. Scott
HARDER THEY FALL, THE '56	Humphrey Bogart
HARDY BOYS MYSTERIES, THE tv	Shaun Cassidy
HARDYS RIDE HIGH, THE '39	Lewis Stone, Mickey Rooney
HARLOW '65	Carroll Baker
HAROLD AND MAUDE '72	Bud Cort & Ruth Gordon
HAROLD IN ITALY	Hector Berlioz
HARPER '66	Lauren Bacall & Paul Newman
HARPER VALLEY P.T.A. '78	Barbara Eden
HARPER'S WEEKLY	Thomas Nast
HARRIS, DEREK	John Derek
HARRY-O tv	David Janssen
HARTLEY, VIVIEN	Vivien Leigh
HARVEST '37 ****	Orane Demazis, Fernandel
HARVEY '50	James Stewart
HARVEY GIRLS, THE '46	Judy Garland
HATARI! '62	John Wayne
HATE '96	Jodie Foster
HAUNTING, THE '63	Julie Harris
HAUNTS '77	Cameron Mitchell
HAVANA '90	Lena Olin
HAVE GUN WILL TRAVEL tv	Richard Boone
HAVILAND, JOAN de	Joan Fontaine
HAWAII '66	Julie Andrews
HAWAII FIVE O tv	Jack Lord
HAWAIIAN EYE tv	Bob Conrad
HAWAIIANS, THE '70	Charlton Heston
HAWK tv	Burt Reynolds

HAYSTACKS	Claude Monet
HAZEL tv	Shirley Booth
HE RAN ALL THE WAY '51	John Garfield
HE WALKED BY NIGHT '48	Richard Basehart
HE'S A RAGPICKER	Irving Berlin
HEAD '68	Teri Garr
HEAD OF THE CLASS tv	Howard Hesseman
HEART CONDITION '90	Bob Hoskins
HEART IS A LONELY HUNTER,THE	Carson McCullers
HEART LIKE A WHEEL '83	Bonnie Bedelia
HEART OF DARKNESS	Joseph Conrad
HEART OF GLASS	Blondie mr
HEART OF THE MATTER, THE	Graham Greene
HEARTACHES '81	Margot Kidder
HEARTBREAK HOTEL '88	David Keith
HEARTBREAK RIDGE '86	Clint Eastwood
HEARTBREAKERS '84	Peter Coyote
HEARTBURN '86	Meryl Streep
HEARTLAND '79	Rip Torn
HEARTS OF THE WEST '75	Jeff Bridges
HEAT '72	Joe Dallesandro, Sylvia Miles
HEAT '95	Robert De Niro, Al Pacino
HEAT AND SUNLIGHT '88	Rob Nilsson d+
HEATHERS '89	Winona Ryder
HEATWAVE '83	Judy Davis
HEAVEN ONLY KNOWS '47	Robert Cummings
HEAVEN WITH A GUN '69	Glenn Ford
HEDDA '75	Glenda Jackson
HEDDA GABLER	Henrik Ibsen
HEE HAW tv	Lulu Roman
HEIDI	Johanna Spyri
HEIDI '37	Shirley Temple
HEIDI '93	Jason Robards Jr.
HEIMBERGER, EDWARD ALBERT	Eddie Albert
HEIRESS, THE '49 ****	Olivia de Havilland, Ralph Richardson
HEIST, THE '79	Charles Aznavour
HELL IS FOR HEROES '62	Steve McQueen
HELL ON FRISCO BAY '55	Alan Ladd
HELL TO ETERNITY '60	Jeffrey Hunter
HELLGATE '52	Sterling Hayden
HELLIONS, THE '62	Richard Todd
HELLO MARY LOU	Rick Nelson mr+
HELLZAPOPPIN' '41	Ole Olsen
HELP! '65	Beatles
HENDERSON THE RAIN KING	Saul Bellow
HENNESEY tv	Jackie Cooper
HENRY V '45 ****	Laurence Olivier, Leslie Banks
HENRY, O.	William Sydney Porter
HENSLEY, VIRGINIA PATTERSON	Patsy Cline
HER PANELLED DOOR '51	Phyllis Calvert
HER TOWN TOO	James Taylor mr s
HERCULES '59	Steve Reeves
HERCULES(Animated) '97	Disney Studios
HERE COME THE BRIDES tv	Robert Brown
HERE COMES MR. JORDAN'41****	Robert Montgomery, Evelyn Keyes
HERE COMES THE SUN	Beatles
HERMAN'S HEAD tv	William Ragsdale
HERO '92	Geena Davis, Dustin Hoffman
HERO, THE '72	Richard Harris
HEROES '77	Sally Field, Henry Winkler
HERRIOT, JAMES	James Alfred Wight

HERZSTINE, BARBARA	Barbara Hershey
HESSELBERG, MELVYN	Melvyn Douglas
HEY GOOD LOOKING	Hank Williams
HEY JEALOUS LOVER	Frank Sinatra
HEY JUDE	The Beatles
HI AND LOIS	Dik Browne
HIDDEN FORTRESS, THE '58	Toshiro Mifune
HIDE-OUT '34	Robert Montgomery
HIDING PLACE, THE '75	Julie Harris
HIGH CHAPARRAL, THE tv	Leif Erickson
HIGH COMMAND, THE '37	Lionel Atwill
HIGH NOON '52 ****	Gary Cooper
HIGH WIND IN JAMAICA, A	Richard Hughes
HIGH-BALLIN' '78	Peter Fonda
HIGHER AND HIGHER '43	Michele Morgan
HIGHLY DANGEROUS '51	Dane Clark
HIGHWAY PATROL tv	Broderick Crawford
HIGHWAY TO HEAVEN tv	Michael Landon
HIGHWAYMAN, THE	Alfred Noyes
HIGHWAYMAN, THE '51	Charles Coburn
HILL STREET BLUES tv Daniel J.Travanti,Veronica Hamel,Joe Spano
HILL, THE '65	Sean Connery
HIND AND THE PANTHER, THE	John Dryden
HINES, MILTON	Soupy Sales
HIRELING, THE '73	Robert Shaw
HIS GIRL FRIDAY '40 ****	Cary Grant, Rosalind Russell
HIS KIND OF WOMAN '51	Robert Mitchum
HIT ME WITH YOUR BEST SHOT	Paul Benetar mr
HIT! '73	Billy Dee Williams
HIT, THE '85	Terence Stamp
HITCH-HIKER, THE '53	Edmond O'Brien
HITCHER, THE '86	Rutger Hauer
HITLER '62	Richard Basehart
HITLER'S CHILDREN '43	Tim Holt
HITTING A NEW HIGH '37	Lily Pons
HOFFA '92	Jack Nicholson, Danny DeVito
HOFFMAN '70	Peter Sellers
HOGAN FAMILY, THE tv	Valerie Harper
HOGAN'S HEROES tv	Bob Crane
HOLD BACK THE DAWN '41	Charles Boyer
HOLES, THE '72	Phillippe Noiret
HOLIDAY '30	Ann Harding
HOLIDAY '38	Cary Grant
HOLIDAY IN MEXICO '46	Walter Pidgeon
HOLLENBECK, WEBB PARMALEE	Clifton Webb
HOLLYWOOD HOTEL '37	Dick Powell
HOLLYWOOD OR BUST '56	Dean Martin, Jerry Lewis
HOLLYWOOD PARTY '34	Jimmy Durante
HOLLYWOOD STORY '51	Richard Conte
HOLT, VICTORIA	Eleanor Hibbert
HOMBRE '67	Fredric March, Paul Newman
HOME BEFORE DARK '58	Jean Simmons
HOME FROM THE HILL '60	Robert Mitchum
HOME IMPROVEMENT tv	Tim Allen
HOME OF THE BRAVE '49	James Edwards
HOME SWEET HOME	John Howard Payne
HOME TO HARLEM	Claude McKay
HOMEBOY '88	Mickey Rourke
HOMECOMING, THE '73	Cyril Cusack
HOMEFRONT tv	Wendy Phillips
HOMICIDAL '61	Patricia Breslin

HOMICIDE '91	Joe Mantegna
HONDO '53	John Wayne
HONEYMOON IN BALI '39	Fred MacMurray
HONEYMOONERS, THE tv	Jackie Gleason, Art Carney
HONEYSUCKLE ROSE '80	Dyan Cannon, Willie Nelson
HONKERS, THE '72	James Coburn
HONKY '71	Brenda Sykes
HONOLULU '39	Eleanor Powell
HOOK, THE '63	Kirk Douglas
HOOPER '78	Burt Reynolds
HOOSIERS '86	Gene Hackman
HOPALONG CASSIDY tv	William Boyd
HOPSCOTCH '80	Walter Matthau
HOROWITZ, MOSES	Moe Howard
HOROWITZ, WINONA	Winona Ryder
HORSE'S MOUTH, THE '58	Alec Guinness
HORSEMEN, THE '71	Omar Sharif
HOSPITAL, THE '71	George C. Scott
HOSTAGE, THE '67	Dean Stanton
HOT SHOTS tv	Dorothy Parker
HOT SUMMER NIGHT '57	Leslie Nielsen
HOTEL tv	James Brolin, Connie Selleca
HOTEL CALIFORNIA	The Eagles mr
HOUDINI '53	Tony Curtis
HOURS OF LOVE, THE '65	Ugo Tognazzi
HOUSE BY THE RIVER, THE '50	Louis Hayward
HOUSE CALLS tv	Wayne Rogers
HOUSE DIVIDED, A	Pearl Buck
HOUSE FOR MR. BISWAS, A	V.S. Naipaul
HOUSE OF DRACULA '45	Onslow Stevens
HOUSE OF FEAR, THE '45	Basil Rathbone
HOUSE OF MIRTH, THE	Edith Wharton
HOUSE OF MYSTERY '61	Peter Dyneley
HOUSE OF THE RISING SUN	The Animals mr
HOUSE PARTY tv	Art Linkletter
HOUSEBOAT '58	Cary Grant
HOUSEHOLD SAINTS '93	Tracey Ullman
HOUSEHOLDER, THE '63	Shashi Kapoor
HOUSEKEEPING '87	Christine Lahti
HOUSEWIFE '34	Bette Davis
HOUSTON STORY, THE '56	Gene Barry
HOVICK, ROSE LOUISE	Gypsy Rose Lee
HOW CAN I BE SURE?	Young Rascals mr
HOW GREEN WAS MY VALLEY '41 ****	Walter Pidgeon, Maureen O'Hara
HOWARD'S END	E.M. Forster
HOWARDS END '92 ****	Anthony Hopkins, Vanessa Redgrave, Emma Thompson
HOWLING, THE '81	Patrick Macnee
HUCKLEBERRY FINN '31	Jackie Coogan
HUCKLEBERRY FINN '39	Mickey Rooney
HUCKSTERS, THE '47	Clark Gable
HUD '63 ****	Patricia Neal, Paul Newman
HUERTA, BALDEMAR	Freddy Fender
HUFFMAN, BARBARA	Barbara Eden
HULA '28	Clara Bow
HUMAN COMEDY, THE '43	Mickey Rooney
HUMAN JUNGLE, THE '54	Gary Merrill
HUMORESQUE '46	Joan Crawford
HUNCHBACK OF NOTRE DAME (Animated) '96****	Disney Studios
HUNCHES IN BUNCHES	Dr. Seuss
HUNTED, THE '48	Preston Foster

HUNTER tv	Fred Dreyer tv+
HURRICANE, THE '37	John Ford, Dorothy Lamour, Mary Astor
HURT SO GOOD	John Mellencamp mr
HURTS SO GOOD	John Cougar s
HUSTLER, THE '61 ****	Paul Newman, Jackie Gleason
I AIM AT THE STARS '60	Curt Jurgens
I AM A FUGITIVE FROM A CHAIN GANG '32 **** Paul Muni
I AM WOMAN	Helen Reddy
I CAN'T HELP MYSELF	The Four Tops mr
I DREAM OF JEANNIE tv	Barbara Eden
I FEEL FOR YOU	Chaka Kahn mr
I GET AROUND	Beach Boys
I HAD A DREAM THE OTHER NIGHT Stephen Foster
I HATE MEN	Cole Porter
I HEARD A SYMPHONY	Supremes, The
I KNOW WHERE I'M GOING '45 **** Emeric Pressburger
I LED THREE LIVES tv	Richard Carlson
I LOVE LUCY tv	Lucille Ball, Desi Arnaz
I LOVE ROCK AND ROLL	Joan Jett mr
I LOVE YOU TO DEATH '90	Kevin Kline
I MARRIED A SHADOW '82	Nathalie Baye
I MARRIED A WITCH '42	Fredric March
I MARRIED JOAN tv	Joan Davis
I MET HIM IN PARIS '37	Claudette Colbert
I MET MY LOVE AGAIN '38	Joan Bennett
I SAW WHAT YOU DID '65	Sara Lane, John Ireland
I SHOT ANDY WARHOL '96	Lili Taylor
I SPY tv	Robert Culp
I STAND CONDEMNED '35	Laurence Olivier
I TAKE THIS WOMAN '40	Spencer Tracy
I VESPRI SICILIANI	Verdi, Giuseppe
I VITELLONI '53 ****	Alberto Sordi
I WALK THE LINE	Johnny Cash
I WANT WHAT I WANT '72	Anne Heywood
I WAS A SHOPLIFTER '50	Scott Brady
I WOULD RATHER BE RIGHT THAN PRESIDENT Henry Clay
I WRITE THE SONGS	Barry Manilow
I, CLAUDIUS	Robert Graves
I'D RATHER BE RICH '64	Sandra Dee
I'LL BE SEEING YOU	Frank Sinatra
I'LL CRY TOMORROW	Lillian Roth
I'LL CRY TOMORROW '55	Susan Hayward
I'LL NEVER FALL IN LOVE AGAIN Dionne Warwick mr
I'LL TAKE ROMANCE '37	Grace Moore
I'LL TELL THE WORLD '45	Lee Tracy
I'M A BELIEVER	The Monkees mr
I'M A POPULAR MAN	George M. Cohan
I'M ALL RIGHT JACK '59	Ian Carmichael
I'M SORRY	Brenda Lee mr
I'VE LIVED BEFORE '56	Jock Mahoney
IBERIA	James B. Michener
ICE '93	Traci Lords
ICE STATION ZEBRA '68	Rock Hudson
ICELAND '42	Sonja Henie
ICEMAN '84	Timothy Hutton
ICEMAN COMETH, THE	Eugene O'Neill
ICEMAN COMETH, THE '73	Lee Marvin
IDAHO '43	Roy Rogers
IDEAL HUSBAND, AN	Oscar Wilde
IDENTITY UNKNOWN '45	Richard Arlen
IDIOT, THE	Fyodor Dosteyevsky

IDIOT, THE '51	Toshiro Mifune
IDOLMAKER, THE '80	Ray Sharkey
IF '68	Malcolm McDowell
IF I HAD A MILLION '32	Stephen Roberts
IF I WERE YOUR WOMAN	Gladys Knight
IF YOU KNEW SUSIE '48	Eddie Cantor
IF YOU LOVE SOMEBODY, SET THEM FREE	Sting mr
IKE '79	Robert Duvall
IL TROVATORE	Girseppe Verdi
IL TROVATORE - Heroine	Leonora
ILLEGAL '55	Edward G. Robinson
ILSA in Casablanca '42	Ingrid Bergman
IMAGES	Claude Debussy
IMAGES '72	Susannah York
IMAGINE	John Lennon mr
IMITATION OF LIFE '34	Claudette Colbert
IMITATION OF LIFE '59	Lana Turner
IMMEDIATE FAMILY '89	Glenn Close
IMMORALIST, THE	Andre Gide
IMMORTAL BELOVED '94	Gary Oldman
IMPACT '49	Brian Donlevy
IMPASSE '69	Burt Reynolds
IMPERATIVE '82	Robert Powell
IMPERSONATOR '61	John Crawford
IMPORTANCE OF BEING EARNEST, THE	Oscar Wilde
IMPOSTER, THE '44	Jean Gabin
IMPRESSION SUNRISE	Claud Monet p
IMPROMPTU '91	Judy Davis
IMPULSE '90	Theresa Russell
IMPURE THOUGHTS '85	Brad Dourif
IN A LONELY PLACE '50	Humphrey Bogart
IN COLD BLOOD '67 ****	Scott Wilson, Robert Blake
IN THE HEAT OF THE NIGHT '67	**** Sidney Poitier, Rod Steiger
IN THE HEAT OF THE NIGHT tv	Carroll O'Connor
IN THE LINE OF FIRE '93	Clint Eastwood
IN THE STILL OF THE NIGHT	The Five Satins
IN THE WHITE CITY '83	Bruno Ganz
IN WHICH WE SERVE '42 ****	Noel Coward, John Mills
INCA GOLD	Clive Cussler
INCIDENT, THE '67	Tony Musante
INCREDIBLE HULK, THE '77	Lou Ferrigno
INCREDIBLE HULK, THE tv	Bill Bixby
INDEPENDENCE DAY '96	Bill Pullman, Will Smith
INDIAN RUNNER, THE '91	David Morse
INDIAN TOMB, THE '59	Debra Paget
INDIANA JONES	Harrison Ford
INDISCREET '58	Ingrid Bergman, Cary Grant
INFERNO	Dante
INFERNO '53	Robert Ryan
INFERNO '80	Leigh McCloskey
INFORMER, THE	Liam O'Flaherty
INGOLIA, CONCETTA	Connie Stevens
INHERIT THE WIND '60	Spencer Tracy
INHERITANCE, THE '47	Jean Simmons
INHERITANCE, THE '76	Anthony Quinn
INN OF THE DAMNED '74	Judith Anderson
INNER CIRCLE, THE '91	Tom Hulce
INNERSPACE '87	Dennis Quaid
INNES, MICHAEL	J.I.M. Stewart
INNOCENT VICTIM '89	Helen Shaver
INNOCENT, THE '76 ****	Giancarlo Giannini, Jennifer O'Neill

INNOCENTS, THE '61	Deborah Kerr
INQUIRY, THE '87	Keith Carradine
INSIDE STRAIGHT '51	David Brian
INSIDE THE MAFIA '59	Cameron Mitchell
INSIGNIFICANCE '85	Gary Busey
INSPIRATION '31	Greta Garbo
INSTANT JUSTICE '87	Michael Pare
INSURANCE MAN, THE '85	Daniel Day-Lewis
INTERIORS '78	Diane Keaton
INTERLUDE '57	June Allyson
INTERLUDE '68	Oskar Werner
INTERMEZZO '39	Leslie Howard, Edna Best
INTERNS, THE '62	Michael Callan
INTO THE VALLEY	John Hersey
INTO THE WOODS	Stephan Sondheim
INTOLERANCE '16 ****	Lilian Gish, Robert Harron
INTRUDER, THE '55	Jack Hawkins
INTRUDER, THE '62	William Shatner
INVASION '66	Edward Judd
INVISIBLE BOY, THE '57	Richard Eyer
INVISIBLE MAN	Ralph Ellison
INVISIBLE MAN, THE '33	Claude Rains
INVISIBLE RAY, THE '36	Boris Karloff
INVISIBLE WOMAN, THE '41	John Barrymore, Virginia Bruce
INVITATION '52	Van Johnson
IPCRESS FILE, THE '65	Michael Caine
IPHIGENIA	Euripides
IPHIGENIA '77	Irene Papas
IRENE	Edgar Allan Poe
IRENE '40	Anna Neagle, Ray Milland
IRISHMAN, THE '78	Michael Craig
IRON CURTAIN, THE '48	Dana Andrews
IRON MISTRESS, THE '52	Alan Ladd
IRON, RALPH	Olive Schreiner
IRONSIDE tv	Raymond Burr
IRONWEED	William Kennedy p-f'84
IRONWEED '87	Jack Nicholson
ISADORA '68	Vanessa Redgrave
ISHMAEL	Herman Melville
ISLAND '89	Irene Papas
ISLAND WITH YOU, AN '48	Esther Williams
ISLEY, PHYLLIS	Jennifer Jones
ISOLDE	Richard Wagner
IT '27	Clara Bow
IT AIN'T ME BABE	The Turtles
IT CAN'T HAPPEN HERE	Sinclair Lewis w
IT DON'T MATTER TO ME	Bread mr
IT HAPPENED ONE NIGHT'34 ****Clark Gable,Claudette Colbert,	
	Frank Capra d
IT TAKES A THIEF tv	Robert Wagner
IT'S A BIG COUNTRY '51	Richard Thorpe
IT'S A GIFT '34 ****	W.C. Fields, Baby LeRoy
IT'S A LIVING tv	Marian Mercer
IT'S A WONDERFUL LIFE'46****	Frank Capra d, James Stewart
IT'S LOVE I'M AFTER '37	Bette Davis
IT'S NEVER TOO LATE '56	Phyllis Calvert
IT'S YOUR THING	The Isley Brothers mr
ITALIANO, ANNA MARIA	Anne Bancroft
IVAN THE TERRIBLE, PART ONE '43 **** Nicolai Cherkassov	
IVANHOE '52	Robert Taylor
IVY '47	Joan Fontaine

J'ACCUSE '37	Victor Francen
J.R. EWING in Dallas tv	Larry Hagman
JABBERWOCKY '77	Michael Palin
JACKNIFE '89	Robert De Niro
JACKPOT, THE '50	James Stewart
JACKSON, LAURA	Laura Jackson Riding
JACOBSEN, BERT	Bert Parks
JACOBY, LEO	Lee J. Cobb
JACQUELINE '56	John Gregson
JAKE AND THE FAT MAN tv	Joe Penny, William Conrad
JAMES, P.D.	Phyllis Dorothy White
JAMMING	Bob Marley mr
JANE EYRE	Emily Bronte
JANIE '44	Joyce Reynolds, Ann Harding
JASSY '47	Margaret Lockwood
JAVA	Al Hirt mj
JAVAL, CAMILLE	Brigitte Bardot
JAWS	Peter Benchley w
JAWS '75 ****	Roy Scheider, Robert Shaw
JAYHAWKERS, THE '59	Jeff Chandler
JEAN BAPTISTE POQUELIN	Moliere
JEANNIE '41	Michael Redgrave
JEEVES	P.G. Wodehouse
JEFFERSON, ARTHUR	Stan Laurel
JEFFERSONS, THE tv	Sherman Hemsley, Isabel Sanford
JENKINS, HAROLD LLOYD	Conway Twitty
JENKINS, RICHARD	Richard Burton
JENNIE GERHARDT '33	Sylvia Sidney
JENNIFER '53	Ida Lupino
JEOPARDY '53	Barbara Stanwyck
JEREMIAH JOHNSON '72	Robert Redford
JEREMY '73	Robby Benson
JERK, THE '79	Steve Martin
JESSICA '62	Angie Dickinson
JESUS '79	Brian Deacon
JESUS OF MONTREAL '89	Lothaire Bluteau
JEZEBEL '38	Bette Davis, George Brent
JFK '91	Kevin Costner,Sissy Spacek,Oliver Stone d
JIGSAW '68	Harry Guardino
JITTERBUGS '43	Stan Laurel, Oliver Hardy
JOCKS '87	Christopher Lee
JOE '70	Peter Boyle
JOE PALOOKA	Ham Fisher
JOHN	Kenneth Millar
JOHN SINJOHN	John Galsworthy
JOHNNY B. GOODE	Chuck Berry mr
JOHNNY GET ANGRY	Joanie Sommers
JOHNSON, CAROL DIAHANN	Diahann Carroll
JOHNSON, CARYN	Whoopi Goldberg
JOKER IS WILD, THE '57	Frank Sinatra, Mitzi Gaynor
JOKERS, THE '66	Oliver Reed
JOLSON STORY, THE '46	Larry Parks
JONES, DAVID ROBERT	David Bowie
JONES, LeROI	Imamu Amiri Baraka
JONES, P.D.	Phyllis White
JOSHUA TREE	U2 mr
JOURNEY INTO FEAR '42	Orson Welles
JOURNEY, THE '59	Deborah Kerr, Yul Brynner
JOY LUCK CLUB	Amy Tan
JOY LUCK CLUB, THE '93	Kieu Chinh
JOY TO THE WORLD	Three Dog Night mr

JUAREZ '39	Paul Muni
JUBAL '56	Glenn Ford
JUDD FOR THE DEFENSE tv	Carl Betz
JUDE THE UNKNOWN	Thomas Hardy
JUDGEMENT AT NUREMBERG '61 ****	Spencer Tracy, Burt Lancaster
JUDITH	Tho. Augustine Arne
JUGGERNAUT '74	Richard Harris
JUGGLER, THE	Marc Chagall
JUGGLER, THE '53	Kirk Douglas
JULIA '77 ****	Jane Fonda, Vanessa Redgrave
JULIA MISBEHAVES '48	Greer Garson
JULIA tv	Diahann Carroll
JUMP	Van Helen mr
JUNGLE PRINCESS, THE '36	Dorothy Lamour, Ray Milland
JUNGLE, THE	Upton Sinclair
JUNO AND THE PAY COCK	Sean O'Casey
JUPITER SYMPHONY	Wolfgang Amadeus Mozart
JUPITER'S DARLING '55	Esther Williams
JUST ABOVE MY HEAD	James Baldwin
JUST ANOTHER DAY	Jan Secada
JUST BEFORE DAWN '46	Warner Baxter
JUST THE TEN OF US tv	Bill Kirchenbauer
JUSTINE '69	Anouk Aimee, Dirk Bogarde
KAFKA '91	Jeremy Irons
KALIFORNIA '93	Brad Pitt
KALISH, SOPHIA	Sophie Tucker
KALOGEROPOULOS, MARIA	Maria Callas
KAM, LEE YUEN	Bruce Lee
KAMIKAZE '89	Rainer Werner Fassbinder
KAMINSKY, DAVID	Danny Kaye
KAMINSKY, MELVIN	Mel Brooks
KANSAN, THE '43	Richard Dix
KATE	Cole Porter
KATE AND ALLIE tv	Susan St, James
KATIE WENT TO HAITI	Cole Porter
KATZ, JOE	Joel Grey
KATZENJAMMER KIDS, THE	Rudolph Dirks
KAUMEYER, MARY	Dorothy Lamour
KAZANJIAN, ARLENE	Arlene Francis
KELL, JOSEPH	Anthony Burgess
KENNER '69	Jim Brown
KENTUCKIAN, THE '55	Burt Lancaster d+
KENTUCKY '38	Loretta Young
KENTUCKY KERNELS '34	Bert Wheeler
KEY LARGO '48	Humphrey Bogart
KEY, THE '34	William Powell
KEY, THE '58	William Holden
KEYBOARD SONATAS	Domenico Scarlatti
KID BROTHER, THE '27 ****	Harold Lloyd, Jobyna Ralston
KID FROM BROOKLYN, THE '46	Danny Kaye
KID FROM SPAIN, THE '32	Eddie Cantor
KID GLOVE KILLER '42	Van Heflin
KID, THE '21	Charlie Chaplin d+
KIDCO '84	Cinnamon Idles
KIDNAPPED	Robert Louie Stevenson
KIDNAPPED '38	Warner Baxter
KIDNAPPED '60	Peter Finch
KIDS '95	Leo Fitzpatrick
KIESLER, HEDWIG	Hedy Lamarr
KIKA '93	Peter Coyote
KILLER INSIDE ME, THE '76	Stacy Keach

KILLER SHREWS, THE '59	James Best
KILLER'S CARNIVAL '65	Robert Lynn
KILLERS, THE '46 ****	Burt Lancaster, Ava Gardner
KILLERS, THE '64	Lee Marvin, John Cassavetes
KILLING, THE '56	Sterling Hayden
KIM '50	Errol Flynn
KIM, JUST SO STORIES	Rudyard Kipling
KINDERGARTEN COP '90	Arnold Schwarznegger
KINDRED, THE '87	Rod Steiger
KING '78	Cicely Tyson, Paul Winfield
KING AND COUNTRY '64	Dirk Bogarde
KING IN NEW YORK, A '57	Charles Chaplin d+
KING KONG '33 ****	Robert Armstrong,Fay Wray,Bruce Cabot
KING LEAR	Jessica Tandy
KING OF ALCATRAZ '38	J. Carrol Naish
KING OF BAD TASTE	Chuck Barrie
KING OF BURLESQUE '35	Warner Baxter
KING OF CHINATOWN '39	Anna May Wong
KING OF COMEDY, THE '83	Robert De Niro
KING OF KINGS, THE '27	H.B. Warner
KING OF THE JUNGLE '33	Buster Crabbe
KING STEPS OUT, THE '36	Grace Moore, Franchot Tone
KING TUT	Steve Martin
KING'S PIRATE, THE '67	Doug McClure
KINGPIN '96	Woody Harrelson, Randy Quaid
KIPPS	H.G. Welles
KIPPS '41	Michael Redgrave
KISMET '44	Ronald Colman
KISMET '55	Ann Blyth, Howard Keel
KISS ME KATE	Cole Porter
KISS, THE '29	Greta Garbo
KITCHEN TOTO, THE '87	Bob Peck
KITTEN WITH A WHIP '64	Ann-Margret
KIVI, ALEKSIS w & po	A. Stenvall
KLABUND w & po	Alfred Henschke
KLASS, EUGENE	Gene Barry
KLEIN, CAROLE	Carol King
KLUTE '71	Jane Fonda
KNIFE IN THE HEAD '78	Bruno Ganz
KNIGHT RIDER tv	David Hasselhoff
KNIGHTRIDERS '81	Ed Harris
KNOCK ON ANY DOOR '49	Humphrey Bogart
KNOCKOUT '41	Arthur Kennedy
KNOTS LANDING tv	Teri Austin, Ted Shackelford
KOJAK tv	Telly Savalas
KOLYA '97 ****	Zdenek Sverek
KONIGSBERG, ALLEN	Woody Allen
KONOPKA, TADEUS WLADYSLAW	Ted Knight
KOTCH '71	Walter Matthau
KOTTER tv	Gabe Kaplan
KRAMER VS. KRAMER '79 ****	Dustin Hoffman, Meryl Streep
KRAMPKE, HUGH	Hugh O'Brian
KRAYS, THE '90	Gary Kemp, Martin Kemp
KRAZY KAT	George Herriman
KRONOS '57	Jeff Morrow
KRYSTLE in Dynasty tv	Linda Evans
KUBELSKY, BENJAMIN	Jack Benny
KUNG FU tv	David Carradine
L'ADOLESCENTE '79	Simone Signoret
L'AGE D'OR '30 ****	Gaston Modot, Lya Lys
L'ARLESIANA	Francesco Cilea

L'ARLESIENNE	Alexandre C.C.L. Bizet
L'ATALANTE '34 ****	Michel Simon
L'ECOLE DES FEMMES	Moliere
L'ETRE ET LE NE ANT	Jean-Paul Sartre
L'HEURE ESPAGNOLE	Maurice J. Ravel
L-SHAPED ROOM, THE '63	Leslie Caron
L.A. LAW tv	Richard Dysart, Susan Dey
LA BAMBA '87	Esai Morales, Lou Diamond Phillips
LA BELLE NOISEUSE '91	Michel Piccoli
LA BOHEME	Giacoma Puccini
LA CENERENTOLA(Cinderella)	Giacchino Rossini
LA CHIENNE '31 ****	Michel Simon
LA FEMME INFIDELE '69	Stephane Audran
LA MARSEILLAISE '38	Pierre Renoir
LA STRADA '54 ****	Anthony Quinn, Giulietta Masina
La TOSCA or Tosca	Giacomo Puccini
LA TRAVIATA	Giuseppe Verdi
LA TRAVIATA '62 ****	Placido Domingo
LaCOCK, PIERRE	Peter Marshall
LACOMBE, LUCIEN '74 ****	Aurore Clement
LADIES OF LEISURE '30	Barbara Stanwyck
LADIES OF THE JURY '32	Edna May Oliver
LADIES WHO LUNCH	Stephen Sondheim
LADY	Kenny Rogers
LADY CHATTERLY'S LOVER	D.H. Lawrence
LADY CONSENTS, THE '36	Ann Harding
LADY FOR A DAY '33 ****	May Robeson, Warren William
LADY IN DISTRESS '39	Sally Gray
LADY IN QUESTION '40	Rita Hayworth
LADY L '65	Sophia Loren
LADY OF BURLESQUE '43	Barbara Stanwyck
LADY PAYS OFF, THE '51	Linda Darnell
LADY VANISHES, THE'38 ****	Alfred Hitchcock d,Margaret Lockwood
LADY WINDERMERE'S FAN	Oscar Wilde
LADY WITH RED HAIR, THE '40	Miriam Hopkins
LADYBUG LADYBUG '63	William Daniels
LADYKILLERS, THE '55	Alec Guinness
LAKE, HARRIETTE	Ann Sothern
LAKME	Leo(C.P.) Delibes c
LAMB CHOP	Shari Lewis
LAMB, THE '15	Douglas Fairbanks Sr.
LAND AND FREEDOM '96	Ian Hart
LAND OF THE GIANTS tv	Gary Conway
LANDLORD, THE '70	Beau Bridges
LAO SHE	Shu Ching-chun
LAPIS LAZULI	Wm. Butler Yeats
LARA in Dr. Zhivago	Julie Christie
LARAMIE tv	Robert Fuller, John Smith
LARCENY '48	John Payne
LAREDO tv	Neville Brand
LASERBLAST '78	Cheryl Smith
LASSIE COME HOME '43	Roddy McDowall
LASSIE tv	Tommy Rettig
LASSITER '84	Tom Selleck
LAST ANGRY MAN, THE '59	Paul Muni
LAST COMMAND, THE '28 ****	Emil Jannings, William Powell
LAST COMMAND, THE '55	Sterling Hayden
LAST DAYS OF POMPEI	Lytton, Bulwer
LAST EMPEROR, THE '87	John Lone
LAST FRONTIER, THE '56	Victor Mature
LAST GANGSTER, THE '37	Edward G. Robinson

LAST GRENADE, THE '70	Stanley Baker
LAST OF SHEILA, THE '73	James Coburn, James Mason
LAST OF THE MOHICANS	James Fenimore Cooper
LAST OF THE MOHICANS,THE-Hero Uncas	
LAST OF THE REDMEN '47	Jon Hall
LAST OUTPOST, THE '35	Cary Grant
LAST OUTPOST, THE '51	Ronald Reagan
LAST PICTURE SHOW,THE'71****	Timothy Bottoms, Jeff Bridges
LAST TEN DAYS, THE '56	Oskar Werner
LAST TIME I SAW PARIS,THE	Jerome Kern
LAST TIME, THE	Rolling Stones mr
LAST WALTZ, THE '78 ****	Bob Dylan
LATE GEORGE APLEY, THE '47	Ronald Colman
LATINO '85	Robert Beltran
LAUGHTER '30	Nancy Carroll
LAURA'44 ****	Clifton Webb,Gene Tierney,O.Preminger d
LAVENDER HILL MOB, THE '51	Alec Guinness
LAVERNE & SHIRLEY tv	Penny Marshall
LAW & ORDER tv	George Dzundza
LAW AND DISORDER '58	Michael Redgrave
LAW AND DISORDER '74	Carroll O'Connor
LAW IS THE LAW, THE '59	Fernandel
LAW OF THE LAWLESS '64	Dale Robertson
LAW OF THE TROPICS '41	Constance Bennett
LAWD in The Green Pastures	Marc Connelly
LAWLESS BREED, THE '52	Rock Hudson
LAWLESS STREET, A '55	Randolph Scott
LAWMAN '71	Burt Lancaster
LAWMAN. THE tv	John Russell
LAWRENCE OF ARABIA '62 ****	Peter O'Toole, Alec Guiness
LAWYER, THE '70	Barry Newman
LAYLA	Eric Clapton mr
LAYS OF BELERIAND	J.J.R. Tolkien
LAZYBONES '25	Charles "Buck" Jones
LAZZARO, BERNADETTE	Bernadette Peters
Le BAL '82	John Lennon, Paul McCartney
LE COMPTE ORY	Giacchino Rossini
LE CRABE TAMBOUR '77	Jean Rochefort
LE RIO dY's	Edouard Lalo
LE VOYAGE EN DOUCE '80	Dominique Sanda
LEACH, ARCHIBALD	Cary Grant
LEADBELLY '76	Roger E. Mosley
LEAP INTO THE VOID '79	Michel Piccoli
LEAR	Laurence Olivier
LEARNING TO CRAWL	The Pretenders mr
LEARNING TREE, THE '69	Kyle Johnson
LEATHER BOYS, THE '63	Rita Tushingham
LEATHER SAINT, THE '56	Paul Douglas
LEAVE IT TO BEAVER tv	Barbara Billingsley,Jerry Mathers, Tony Dow
LEAVES OF GRASS	Walt Whitman
LEAVING LAS VEGAS '95	Nicolas Cage, Elizabeth Shue
LeCARRE, JOHN	David Conrwell
LECID	Jules-Emile Massenet
LeCOCK, PIERRE	Peter Marshall
LEEK, HAROLD	Howard Keel
LEGACY '75	George McDaniel
LEGACY, THE '79	Katharine Ross
LEGEND, THE '85	Tom Cruise
LEGS '83	Gwen Verdon
LEIBOWITZ, SIDNEY	Steve Lawrence

LEILA	J.P. Donleavy
LELY, SIR PETER p	Peter van der Faes
LEMON DROP KID, THE '51	Bob Hope
LENAU, NICOLAUS po	Nicolaus Franz Niembach
LENIN, NIKOLAY st	Vladimir Ilyich Ulyanov
LENNY '74 ****	Dustin Hoffman, Valerie Perrino
LENORE	Edgar Allan Poe
LEONARD, HELEN	Lillian Russell
LEOPARD, THE 63 ****	Burt Lancaster, Alain Delon
LEPKE '75	Tony Curtis
LEPPERT, ANN	Alice Faye
LeROI JONES	Imamu Imiri Baraka
LES PLAIDEURS	Jean Racine
LES PRELUDES	Franz Liszt
LES SYLPHIDES	Frederic Chopin c
LESSON FROM A LOES, A	Athol Fugard
LeSUEUR, LUCILLE	Joan Crawford
LET 'EM EAT CAKE	George Gershwin
LET FREEDOM RING '39	Nelson Eddy
LET ME WHISPER IN YOUR EAR	Beatles
LET'S DANCE	David Bowie mr
LET'S DO IT	Cole Porter
LET'S LIVE A LITTLE '48	Hedy Lamarr
LET'S MAKE A DEAL tv	Monty Hall
LETTER TO THREE WIVES, A '49 **** Jeanne Crain, Linda Darnell
LETTER, THE '40	Bette Davis
LEVI, IVO	Yves Montand
LEVITCH, JOSEPH	Jerry Lewis
LEVY, MARION	Paulette Goddard
LI'L ABNER	Al Capp
LIANNA '83	Jane Hallaren
LIBEL '59	Dirk Bogarde, Olivia de Havilland
LIBELED LADY '36 ****	Jean Harlow, William Powell
LIES '83	Ann Dusenberry
LIFE AND DEATH OF COLONEL BLIMP '43 **** Emeric Pressburger
LIFE AND LEGEND OF WYATT EARP, THE tv Hugh O'Brian
LIFE GOES ON tv	Bill Smitrovich
LIFE OF EMILE ZOLA, THE '37 **** Paul Muni, Gale Sondergaard
LIFE OF OHARU, THE '52	Toshiro Mifune
LIFE OF RILEY, THE '48	William Bendix
LIFE OF RILEY, THE tv	Jackie Gleason
LIFE OF SAMUEL JOHNSON LL.D.,THE James Boswell w
LIFE UPSIDE DOWN '65	Charles Denner
LIFE WITH BLONDIE '46	Penny Singleton
LIFE WITH FATHER	Clarence Day
LIFE WITH FATHER '47 ****	Irene Dunne, William Powell
LIFE WITH FATHER tv	Leon Ames
LIFEBOAT '44	Tallulah Bankhead, Alfred Hitchcock d
LIFEGUARD '76	Sam Elliott
LIFT, THE '83	Huub Stapel
LIGEIA	Edgar Allan Poe
LIGHT IN AUGUST	William Faulkner
LIGHT MY FIRE	The Doors mr
LIGHT THAT FAILED, THE '39	Ronald Colman, Ida Lupino
LIGHT YEARS AWAY '81	Trevor Howard
LIGHTHORSEMEN '87	Jon Blake
LIKE A ROLLING STONE	Bob Dylan mr
LILI '53 ****	Leslie Caron, Jean-Pierre Aumont
LILIES '97	Brent Carver
LILITH '64	Warren Beatty
LIME, HARRY fc in Third Man '49 Orson Welles

```
LIMELIGHT '52                      Charlie Chaplin d+
LINDA '29                          Helen Foster
LINDLEY, LOUIS                     Slim Pickens
LINEUP, THE '58                    Warner Anderson
LINEUP, THE tv                     Warner Anderson
LION IN WINTER, THE '68 **** Katharine Hepburn, Peter O'Toole
LION OF THE DESERT '81             Anthony Quinn
LIONHEART '87                      Eric Stoltz
LIPSHITZ, HAROLD                   Hal Linden
LIQUIDATOR, THE '66                Rod Taylor
LISA '62                           Delores Hart
LISBON '56                         Ray Milland
LITTLE BIG MAN '70 ****            Dustin Hoffman, Faye Dunaway
LITTLE EVA                         Harriett Beecher Stowe
LITTLE FOXES, THE                  Lillian Hellman
LITTLE GIANT, THE '33              Edward G. Robinson
LITTLE HOUSE ON THE PRAIRIE tv Michael Landon
LITTLE IODINE                      Jimmy Hatlo
LITTLE KING                        Otto Soglow
LITTLE LULU                        Marjorie Buell
LITTLE MINISTER, THE '34           Katharine Hepburn
LITTLE ORPHAN ANNIE                Harold Gray
LITTLE ORPHANT ANIE                James Whitcomb Riley
LITTLE PRINCE, THE '74             Richard Kiley
LITTLE PRINCESS, A '95             Liesel Matthews
LITTLE PRINCESS, THE '39           Shirley Temple
LITTLE ROMANCE, A '79              Laurence Olivier
LITTLE WOMEN                       Louisa May Alcott
LITTLE WOMEN '33 ****        Katharine Hepburn, Joan Bennett d+
LITTLEST OUTLAW, THE '55           Pedro Armendariz
LIVES OF A BENGAL LANCER, THE '35 **** Gary Cooper
LIVING REED, THE                   Pearl Buck
LIZA                               George Gershwin
LIZZIE '57                         Eleanor Parker
LLOYD'S OF LONDON '36              Freddie Bartholomew
LOBO tv                            Claude Akins
LOCKSLEY HALL                      Alfred Lord Tennyson
LODGER, THE '26                    Ivor Novello
LODGER, THE '44                    Merle Oberon
LOHENGRIN                          Richard Wagner
LOIS AND CLARK tv                  Teri Hatcher
LOLA '61                           Anouk Aimee
LOLA '82                           Barbara Sukowa
LOLITA                             Vladimir Nabokov
LOLITA '62              James Mason,Shelley Winters,Sue Lyon
LONDON - Symphonies  Nos. 93-104 Joseph Haydn
LONE RANGER, THE tv                Clayton Moore, Jay Silverheels
LONE WOLF McQUADE '83              Chuck Norris
LONE WOLF RETURNS, THE '35         Melvyn Douglas
LONE WOLF SPY HUNT, THE '39        Warren William
LONE WOLF STRIKES, THE '40         Warren William
LONELINESS OF THE LONG DISTANCE RUNNER'62****Michael Redgrave
LONELY BOY                         Paul Anka mr s
LONESOME DOVE(p-f'86)              Larry McMurty
LONG DARK HALL, THE '51            Rex Harrison
LONG GOOD FRIDAY, THE '81          Bob Hoskins
LONG GOODBYE, THE '73              Elliott Gould
LONG GRAY LINE, THE '55            Tyrone Power
LONG JOHN SILVER '54               Robert Newton
LONG LOST FATHER '34               John Barrymore
LONG VOYAGE HOME, THE '40          Ian Hunter, John Wayne
```

LONG WALK HOME, THE '90	Sissy Spacek
LONG, LONG TRAILER, THE '54	Lucille Ball, Desi Arnaz
LONGEST DAY, THE '62 ****	John Wayne, Rod Steiger
LONGEST YARD, THE '74	Burt Reynolds
LOOK BACK IN ANGER '58	Richard Burton
LOOK WHO'S TALKING '89	John Travolta, Kirstie Alley
LOOKING BACKWARD	Edward Bellamy
LOOKING FORWARD '33	Lionel Barrymore
LOOKS AND SMILES '81	Graham Green
LOON LAKE	E.L. Doctorow
LOOPHOLE '80	Albert Finney
LOOT	Orton, Joe
LOOT '70	Lee Remick
LOOTERS, THE '55	Rory Calhoun
LORD JIM	Joseph Conrad
LORD OF THE FLIES	William Golding
LORD OF THE FLIES '63	James Aubrey
LORD OF THE FLIES '90	Balthazar Getty
LORD OF THE RINGS, THE	J.J.R. Tolkein
LORD PETER WIMSEY(sleuth)	Dorothy L Sayers
LORD'S OF FLATBUSH, THE '74	Perry King
LORNA DOONE	Richard D. Blackmore
LOSING MY RELIGION	R.E.M. mr
LOSS OF INNOCENCE '61	Danielle Darrieux
LOST '55	David Farrar
LOST BOUNDARIES '49	Mel Ferrer
LOST HORIZON '37 ****	Frank Capra d, Ronald Colman
LOST IN SPACE tv	Guy Williams
LOST IN THE STARS '74	Brock Peters
LOST IN YONKERS	Neil Simon
LOST PATROL, THE '34 ****	Victor McLaglen, Boris Karloff
LOST SQUADRON, THE '32	Richard Dix
LOST WEEKEND, THE '45 ****	Ray Milland, Jane Wyman
LOTI, PIERRE	Louis Marie Julien Viaud
LOTTERY BRIDE, THE '30	Jeanette MacDonald
LOTTERY, THE	Shirley Jackson
LOU GRANT tv	Edward(Ed) Asner
LOUISA '50	Ruth Hussey, Ronald Reagan
LOUISANA STORY '42 ****(documentary)	Robert Flaherty d
LOULOU '80	Gerard Depardieu
LOUYS, PIERRE	Pierre Louis
LOVE '27	Greta Garbo
LOVE AND ANARCHY '73	Giancarlo Giannini
LOVE AND LARCENY '63	Vittorio Gassman
LOVE AND MARRIAGE	Frank Sinatra
LOVE AND MARRIAGE '64	Sylva Koscina
LOVE AT FIRST BITE '79	George Hamilton
LOVE BOAT, THE tv	Gavin MacLeod
LOVE IN BLOOM	Benny Goodman
LOVE IN BLOOM	Jack Benny
LOVE IN GERMANY, A '84	Hanna Schygulla
LOVE ME OR LEAVE ME '55	Doris Day
LOVE ME TENDER	Elvis Presley mr+
LOVE ME TONIGHT '32 ****Maurice Chevalier, Jeanette MacDonald	
LOVE ON A ROOFTOP tv	Peter Deuel
LOVE SERANADE '97 ****	Miranda Otto
LOVE SONG OF J. ALF.PRUFOCK	T.S. Eliot
LOVE STORY	Francis Lai
LOVE THY NEIGHBOR '40	Jack Benny
LOVE WALKED IN(The Goldwyn Follies) George Gershwin	
LOVELY TO LOOK AT '52	Kathryn Grayson

LOVELY WAY TO DIE, A '68	Kirk Douglas
LOVER, THE '92	Tony Leung
LOVERS, THE '58	Jeanne Moreau
LOVES OF SUNYA, THE '27	Gloria Swanson
LOVESICK '83	Dudley Moore
LOVING	Henry Green
LOVING '70	Eva Marie Saint, George Segal
LOWENSTEIN, LASZIO	Peter Lorre
LOWER DEPTHS, THE '36	Jean Gabin
LUCAS '86	Corey Haim
LUCIA LAMMERMOOR	Gaetano Donizetti
LUCK AND PLUCK	Horatio Alger
LUCK OF ROARING CAMP, THE	Bret Harte
LUCK OF THE IRISH '48	Tyrone Power
LUCKY JIM	Kingsley Amis
LUCKY TO BE A WOMAN '56	Charles Boyer, Sophia Loren
LUCREZIA BORGIA	Gaetano Donizewtti
LUCY SHOW, THE tv	Lucille Ball
LULU	Alan Berg
LUMIERE '76	Jeanne Moreau
LUNA '79	Jill Clayburgh
LURED '47	George Sanders
LUST FOR LIFE	Iggy Pop mr
LUST FOR LIFE '56 ****	Kirk Douglas, Anthony Quinn
LUTHER '74	Stacy Keach
LUV '67	Jack Lemmon
LYDIA '41	Merle Oberon
M '31 ****	Peter Lorre
M '51	Howard da Silva
M SQUAD tv	Lee Marvin
M*A*S*H tv	Alan Alda,Jamie Farr,Loretta Swit
M. BUTTERFLY '93	Jeremy Irons
M.A.D.D.'83	Mariette Hartley, Paula Prentiss
MAC '92	John Turturro
MACAO '52	Robert Mitchum
MACARONI '85	Jack Lemmon
MacARTHUR '77	Gregory Peck
MACBETH '48	Orson Welles d+
MACBETH '71	Jon Finch
MacDIARMID, HUGH	Christopher Grieve
MacDONALD, ROSS	Kenneth Millar
MACGYVER tv	Richard Dean Anderson
MACHINE-GUN KELLY '58	Charles Bronson
MACKENZIE, SEAFORTH	Kenneth Mackenzie
MACLAREN, IAN	John Watson
MACMANUS, DECLAN	Elvis Costello
MACOMBER AFFAIR, THE '47	Gregory Peck, Joan Bennett
MACON COUNTY LINE '74	Alan Vint
MAD ABOUT YOU tv	Helen Hunt
MAD DOG AND GLORY '93	Robert De Niro
MAD LITTLE ISLAND '57	Jeannie Carson
MAD MAGICIAN, THE '54	Vincent Price
MADAME '61	Sophia Loren
MADAME BUTTERFLY '32	Sylvia Sidney
MADAME DeTREYMES	Edith Wharton
MADAME RACKETEER '32	Alison Skipworth
MADAME SOUSATZKA '88	Shirley MacLaine
MADAME'S PLACE tv	Judy Landers
MADELEINE '50	Ann Todd
MADHOUSE '74	Vincent Price, Peter Cushing
MADHOUSE MANSION '74	Marianne Faithfull

MADIGAN '68	Richard Widmark
MADO '76	Romy Schneider
MAGGIE MAE	Rod Stewart mr
MAGIC '78	Anthony Hopkins
MAGIC BOX, THE '51 ****	Robert Donat, Maria Schell
MAGIC FLUTE, THE	Wolfgang A. Mozart
MAGIC FLUTE, THE by Mozart	Pamina fc
MAGIC MOMENT, THE	Jay and the Americans mr
MAGIC MOUNTAIN	Thomas Mann
MAGICIAN, THE '58	Max von Sydow
MAGNETIC MONSTER, The '53	Richard Carlson
MAGNIFICENT AMBERSONS, THE	Booth Tarkington p-f'19
MAGNIFICENT AMBERSONS, THE '42 **** Joseph Cotten, Tim Holt
MAGNIFICENT DOPE, THE '42	Henry Fonda
MAGNUM, P.I. tv	Tom Selleck
MAGUS, THE	John Fowles
MAHLER '74	Robert Powell
MAHONEY, SALLY	Sally Field
MAHONEY, SUZANNE	Suzanne Somers
MAIDS, THE	Jean Genet
MAIN STREET	Sinclair Lewis
MAISIE '39	Ann Sothern
MAISIE WAS A LADY '41	Ann Sothern
MAITRESSE '76	Gerard Depardieu
MAJOR BARBARA	Geo. Bernard Shaw
MAJOR BARBARA '41 ****	Wendy Hiller, Rex Harrison
MAJOR DAD tv	Gerald McRaney, Shanna Reed
MAJOR HOULIHAN in M*A*S*H	Loretta Swit
MAJORITY OF ONE, A '62	Rosalind Russell, Mae Questal
MAKE HASTE TO LIVE '54	Dorothy McGuire
MAKING OF AN AMERICAN, THE	Jacob Riis
MALAGA '60	Trevor Howard
MALAYA '49	Spencer Tracy, James Stewart
MALICE '93	Alec Baldwin
MALICIOUS '73	Laura Antonelli
MALTESE FALCON, THE	Dashiell Hammett
MALTESE FALCON, THE '41 **** Humphrey Bogart,Mary Astor, Peter Lorre
MAMA	Connie Francis
MAMA SAID KNOCK YOU OUT	L.L. Cool J mr
MAMA tv	Peggy Wood
MAMA'S FAMILY tv	Vicki Lawrence
MAMBO '54	Silvana Mangano
MAME	Jerry Herman
MAMELE '38	Molly Picon
MAMMOTH HUNTERS, THE	Jean Auel
MAN AGAINST CRIME tv	Ralph Bellamy
MAN CALLED HORSE, A '70	Richard Harris
MAN CALLED PETER, A '55	Richard Todd
MAN FOR ALL SEASONS, A	Robert Bolt
MAN FOR ALL SEASONS, A '66 **** Paul Scofield, Wendy Hiller
MAN FROM COLORADO, THE '48	Glenn Ford
MAN FROM LARAMIE, THE '55	James Stewart
MAN FROM PLANET X, THE '51	Robert Clarke
MAN FROM U.N.C.L.E, THE tv	Robert Vaughn, David McCallum
MAN I LOVE, THE(Rhapsody in Blue) George Gershwin
MAN I MARRIED, THE '40	Joan Bennett
MAN IN A COCKED HAT, '59	Terry-Thomas
MAN IN THE MOON, THE '91	Sam Waterston
MAN IN THE NET, THE '59	Alan Ladd
MAN IN THE SHADOW '57	Orson Welles

```
MAN OF ARAN '34 ****(documentary) Robert Flaherty
MAN ON A TIGHTROPE '53        Fredric March
MAN UPSTAIRS, THE '58         Richard Attenborough
MAN WHO CRIED WOLF, THE '37   Lewis Stone
MAN WHO DARED, THE '33        Preston Foster
MAN WHO NEVER WAS, THE '56    Clifton Webb
MAN WHO PLAYED GOD, THE '32   George Arliss
MAN WHO SHOT LIBERTY VALANCE,THE'62**** James Stewart,
                                          John Wayne

MAN WITH TWO FACES, THE '34   Edward G. Robinson
MAN WITHOUT A GUN tv          Rex Reason
MAN WITHOUT A STAR '55        Kirk Douglas
MAN'S BEST FRIEND '93         Ally Sheedy
MANHATTAN '79                 Woody Allen d+
MANHUNT tv                    Victor Jory
MANHUNTER '86                 William L. Petersen
MANIA '59                     Peter Cushing
MANIAC '62                    Kerwin Mathews
MANIFESTO '88                 Alfred Molina
MANNEQUIN '37                 Joan Crawford
MANNIX tv                     Mike Connors
MANON                         Jules-Emile-F. Massenet
MANON LESCAUT                 Abbe Prevost
MANON LESCAUT                 Giacomo Puccini
MANPOWER '41                  Edward G. Robinson
MANXMAN, THE   '29            Malcolm Keen
MANY LOVES OF DOBIE GILLIS, THE tv Dwayne Hickman
MAPLE LEAF RAG                Scott Joplin mj
MAPOTHER, THOMAS              Tom Cruise
MARA OF THE WILDERNESS '65    Adam West
MARACAIBO '58                 Cornel Wilde d+
MARCO MILLIONS                Eugene O'Neill
MARCUS WELBY, M.D. tv         Robert Young
MARGARITAVILLE                Jimmy Buffet
MARGIE '46                    Jeanne Crain
MARIANNE '29                  Marion Davies
MARIE '85                     Sissy Spacek
MARIE ANTOINETTE '38          Norma Shearer
MARIE ANTOINETTE '55          Michele Morgan
MARIUS '31                    Raimu
MARK OF ZORRO, THE '40        Tyrone Power
MARK SABER tv                 Tom Conway
MARK TWAIN                    Samuel Clemens
MARK, THE '61                 Stuart Whitman
MARLOWE '69                   James Garner
MARNIE '64                    Sean Connery
MARQUISE OF O, THE '76        Bruno Ganz
MARRIAGE ALA MODE             William P. Hogarth
MARRIED ....WITH CHILDREN tv  Ed O'Neill. Katey Sagal
MARRIED TO THE MOB '88        Michelle Pfeiffer
MARRINER, EDYTHE              Susan Hayward
MARRYING KIND, THE '52        Judy Holiday
MARRYING MAN, THE '91         Kim Basinger
MARTIN KANE, PRIVATE EYE tv   William Gargan
MARTY '55                     Ernest Borgnine, Betsy Blair
MARX, HERBERT                 Zeppo Marx
MARX, LEONARD                 Chico Marx
MARY                          Sholem Asch
MARY HARTMAN,MARY HARTMAN tv Louise Lasser
MARY OF SCOTLAND '36          Katharine Hepburn
MARY POPPINS '64 ****         Julie Andrews, Dick Van Dyke
```

MARYLAND '40	Fay Bainter
MASH '70 ****	Donald Sutherland, Elliott Gould
MASK '85	Cher
MASK, THE '94	Jim Carrey, Peter Riegert
MASQUERADE '65	Cliff Robertson
MASQUERADE '88	Rob Lowe
MASSACRE '34	Richard Barthelmess
MASSACRE IN ROME '73	Richard Burton
MASTER BUILDERS, THE	Henrik Ibsen
MASTERMIND '76	Zero Mostel
MATADOR '86	Assumpta Serna
MATCHMAKER '97	Janeane Garfolo
MATCHMAKER, THE '58	Shirley Booth
MATELOT	Pierre Loti
MATERIAL GIRL	Madonna mr+
MATEWAN '87	Chris Cooper
MATILDA '96	Danny DeVito d+, Rhea Perlman
MATINEE '93	John Goodman
MATING OF MILLIE, THE '48	Glenn Ford, Evelyn Keyes
MATING SEASON, THE '51	Gene Tierney
MATLOCK tv	Andy Griffith, Linda Purl
MATT HOUSTON tv	Lee Horsley
MATUSCHANSKAYASKY, WALTER	Walter Mathau
MAUDE tv	Beatrice Arthur-title role-heroine
MAURICE	E.M. Forster
MAURICE '87	James Wilby
MAUROIS, ANDRE	Emile Herzog
MAVERICK '94	Mel Gibson
MAVERICK tv	James Garner
MAX '22	Max Linder
MAX DUGAN RETURNS '83	Jason Robards
MAXIME '58	Michele Morgan
MAYBERRY R.F.D. tv	Ken Berry
MAYERLING '36	Charles Boyer
MAYERLING '68	Omar Sharif
MAYOR OF HELL, THE '33	James Cagney
MAYTIME '37	Nelson Eddy, Jeanette MacDonald
McBAIN, ED	Evan Hunter
McCLENNY, PATSY	Morgan Fairchild
McCLOUD tv	Dennis Weaver
McHALES NAVY tv	Ernest Borgnine
McLINTOCK! '63	Maureem O'Hara, John Wayne
McMASTERS, THE '70	Burl Ives
McMATH, VIRGINIA	Ginger Rogers
McMEEKAN, WAYNE	David Wayne
McMILLAN AND WIFE tv	Rock Hudson
McVICAR '80	Roger Daltrey
ME AND BOBBY McGEE	Janice Joplin mr
ME AND MY SHADOW	Ted Lewis
ME AND THE COLONEL '58	Danny Kaye
MEAN STREETS '73 ****	Robert De Niro, Harvey Keitel
MEANTIME '83	Phil Daniels
MECHANIC, THE '72	Charles Bronson
MEDAL FOR BENNY, A '45	Dorothy Lamour
MEDEA	Euripides(Title & Heroine)
MEDICAL CENTER tv	James Daly
MEDIUM COOL '69 ****	Robert Forster, Verna Bloom
MEDIUM, THE '51	Marie Powers
MEET DANNY WILSON '52	Frank Sinatra
MEET ME AT THE FAIR '53	Dan Dailey
MEET ME IN ST. LOUIS'44 ****	Judy Garland, Margaret O'Brien

MEET MILLIE tv	Elena Verdugo
MEET THE STEWARTS '42	William Holden
MEIR in A Woman Called Golda '82	Ingrid Bergman
MELBA '53	Patrice Munsel
MELODY '71	Jack Wild
MELVIN AND HOWARD '80	Paul LeMat
MEN ... '85	Uwe Ochsenknecht
MEN WITHOUT SOULS '40	Glenn Ford
MEN WITHOUT WOMEN	Ernest Hemingway
MEN, THE '50	Marlon Brando
MENACE II SOCIETY '93	Larenz Tate
MENAGE '86	Gerard Depardieu
MEPHISTO '81	Klaus Maria Brandauer
MERCENARY, THE '68	Tony Musante, Franco Nero
MERMAIDS '90	Cher
MERRY WIDOW, THE	Franz Lehar
MESERVEY, ROBERT PRESTON	Robert Preston
MESSAGE TO GARCIA, A '36	Wallace Beery, Barbara Stanwyck
MESSE SOLENNELLE	Charles-Francois Gounod
MESSIAH	George Frideric Handel
METAMORPHOSES	Ovid
METROPOLIS '26 ****	Fritz Lang d
METROPOLITAN '35	Lawrence Tibbett
MEUN(G), JEAN de	Jean Clopinel
MEXICAN SPITFIRE '39	Lupe Velez
MEYER, DAVID	David Janssen
MEYERBEER, GIACOMO c	Jakob Liebmann Beer
MIAMI VICE tv	Don Johnson
MICHAEL COLLINS '96	Liam Neeson
MICHAEL SHAYNE FILMS 40's	Lloyd Nolan
MICHAELI, DANIEL	Danny DeVito
MICKEY SPILLANE'S MIKE HAMMER tv	Stacy Keach
MICKLEWHITE, MAURICE	Michael Caine
MIDDLEMARCH	George Eliot
MIDDLETON, PEGGY	Yvonne De Carlo
MIDNIGHT '34	Sidney Fox
MIDNIGHT CALLER tv	Gary Cole
MIDNIGHT CLEAR, A '92	Peter Berg
MIDNIGHT COWBOY '69 ****	Dustin Hoffman, Brenda Vaccaro
MIDNIGHT MAN, THE '74	Burt Lancaster
MIDNIGHT TRAIN TO GEORGIA	Gladys Knight and the Pips mr
MIDNIGHT'S CHILDREN	Solomon Rushdie
MIGHTY APHRODITE '95	Woody Allen d+, Mira Sorvina
MIGHTY BARNUM, THE '34	Wallace Beery
MIGHTY JOE YOUNG '49	Terry Moore
MIGHTY QUINN, THE '89	Denzel Washington
MIKADO '39	Kenny Baker
MIKE in Newhart tv	Michael Scolari
MIKROKOSMOS	Bela Bartok
MILDRED PIERCE	James M. Cain
MILL ON THE FLOSS, THE	George Eliot
MILLER'S CROSSING '90	Gabriel Byrne
MILLER, AGATHA MARY CLARISSA	Agatha Christie
MILLER, JOAQUIN	Cincinnatus Hiner Miller
MILLER, SUSAN	Susan St. James
MILLIONAIRE, THE '31	George Arliss
MILLIONAIRESS, THE '60	Sophia Loren
MILLIONS LIKE US '43	Eric Portman
MIMI	Giacomo Puccini
MIMI in La Boheme	Giacomo Puccini
MIMIC '97	Mira Sorvino

MIND BENDERS, THE '62	Dirk Bogarde
MIND OF MR. SOAMES, THE '70	Terence Stamp
MINISTRY OF FEAR '44	Ray Milland
MINIVER STORY, THE '50	Greer Garson
MIRACLE OF MORGAN'S CREEK, THE '44 **** Eddie Bracken	
MIRACLE WOMAN, THE '31	Barbara Stanwyck
MIRACLE, THE '59	Carroll Baker
MIRACLE, THE '91	Beverly D'Angelo
MIRAGE '65	Gregory Peck
MIRANDA '48	Googie Withers
MIRIAM	D.H. Lawrence
MIRROR CRACK'D, THE '80	Angela Lansbury
MISERY '90	Kathy Bates, James Caan
MISFITS, THE '61	Clark Gable, Marilyn Monroe
MISHIMA, YUKIO	Kimitake Hiroaka
MISS FIRECRACKER '89	Holly Hunter
MISS OTIS REGRETS	Cole Porter c
MISSA SOLEMNIS	Ludwig van Beethoven
MISSING '82	Jack Lemmon
MISSING JUROR, THE '44	Janis Carter
MISSION IMPOSSIBLE tv	Cinnamon Carter, Peter Graves,
	Martin Landau
MISSION TO MOSCOW '43	Walter Huston
MISSION, THE '86	Robert De Niro
MISSISSIPPI '35	Bing Crosby
MISTER BOJANGLES	Sammy Davis Jr
MISTER ROBERTS '55 **** Henry Fonda,Jack Lemmon,Mervyn LeRoy	
MISTER SANDMAN	The Chordettes
MISTRAL, GABRIELA po	Lucila Godoy Alcayaga
MISTY	Errol Garner mj & c
MISTY '61	Pam Smith
MISUNDERSTOOD '84	Gene Hackman
MITCHELL '75	Joe Don Baker
MITCHELL, JAMES LESLIE	Lewis Grassic Gibbon
MITCHELL, WILLIAM	Peter Finch
MITLA PASS	Leon Uris
MOANA '25	Robert Flaherty d
MOD SQUAD, THE tv	Michael Cole
MODERN TIMES '36 ****	Charlie Chaplin d+
MODERNS, THE '88	Keith Carradine
MODINI, ROBERT	Robert Stack
MOGAMBO '53	Clark Gable, Ava Gardner
MOHAWK '56	Scott Brady
MOLIERE	Jean Baptiste Poquelin
MOLINA, TIRSO de	Fray Gabriel Tellez
MOLINSKY, JOAN SANDRA	Joan Rivers
MOLL FLANDERS	Daniel Defoe
MOMENT TO MOMENT '66	Jean Seberg
MOMMIE DEAREST	Christina Crawford w
MON ONCLE '58 ****	Jacques Tati d+
MONDAY, MONDAY	Momas and the Papas mr
MONEY HONEY	Clyde McPhatter mr
MONIZ, ANTONIO EGAS	Antonio Moniz
MONKEES, THE tv	David Jones
MONKEY BUSINESS '31	Groucho,Harpo,Chico & Zeppo Marx
MONKEY BUSINESS '52	Ginger Rogers, Cary Grant
MONKEY ON MY BACK '57	Cameron Mitchell
MONSTER MASH	Bobby Pickett
MONSTER SQUAD, THE '87	Andre Gower
MONSTER WALKS, THE '32	Rex Lease
MONSTER, THE '94	Roberto Benigni d+

MONTANA '50	Errol Flynn
MONTENEGRO '81	Susan Anspach
MONTH BY THE LAKE, A '95	Vanessa Redgrave
MOOD INDIGO	Duke Ellington
MOODNICK, RONALD	Ron Moody
MOON AND SIXPENCE, THE	W. Sommerset Maugham
MOON AND SIXPENCE, THE '42	George Sanders
MOON IS A BALLOON, THE	David Niven
MOON MULLINS	Frank Willard
MOON OVER HARLEM '39	Bud Harris
MOON OVER PARADOR '88	Richard Dreyfuss
MOON-SPINNERS, THE '64	Hayley Mills
MOONFLEET '55	Stewart Granger
MOONLIGHT SONATA	Ludwig van Beethoven
MOONLIGHT SONATA '38	Charles Farrell
MOONLIGHTING '82 ****	Jeremy Irons, Eugene Lipinski
MOONLIGHTING tv	Cybill Shepherd
MOONRAKER, THE '58	George Baker
MOONRISE '48	Dane Clark
MOONSTRUCK '87 ****	Cher, Olympia Dukakis, Nicolas Cage
MOONTIDE '42	Ida Lupino
MORAVIO, ALBERTO	Alberto Pincherle
MORE '69	Mimsy Farmer
MORFIT, THOMAS GARRISON	Gary Moore
MORGAN! '66	Vanessa Redgrave
MORK	Robin Williams
MORK & MINDY tv	Robin Williams
MORO, CESAR po	Alfredo Quispez Asin
MOROCCO '30	Gary Cooper, Marlene Dietrich
MORRIS, STEVLAND	Stevie Wonder
MORRISON, JEANETTE	Janet Leigh
MORRISON, MARION	John Wayne
MORRISON, TONI	Chloe Anthony Wolford
MORTAL STORM, THE '40	Margaret Sullavan
MORTAL THOUGHTS '91	Demi Moore
MORTENSON,(later BAKER), NORMA JEAN	Marilyn Monroe
MOSES	Sholem Asch
MOSES, GRANDMA p	Anna Mary Robertson Moses
MOSES--THE LAWGIVER tv	Burt Lancaster
MOTHERS-IN-LAW tv	Eve Arden
MOUNTAIN ROAD, THE '60	James Stewart
MOUNTAIN, THE '56	Spercer Tracy, Robert Wagner
MOUSE THAT ROARED, THE '59	Peter Sellers
MOUTHPIECE, THE '32	Warren William
MOVE OVER, DARLING '63	Doris Day
MOVIEGOER, THE	Walker Percy
MOVIN' ON tv	Claude Akins
MR. BELVEDERE tv	Christopher Hewett, Ilene Graff
MR. CHIPS	Robert Donat
MR. DEEDS GOES TO TOWN '36 ****	Gary Cooper, Jean Arthur
MR. ED tv	Alan Young
MR. HOLLAND'S OPUS '96	Richard Dreyfuss
MR. HULOT'S HOLIDAY '53	Jacques Tati d+
MR. MOM '83	Teri Garr
MR. MOTO MOVIES '37 - '65	Peter Lorre
MR. MUGGS STEPS OUT '43	Leo Gorcey & Huntz Hall
MR. NOVAK tv	James Franciscus
MR. PEEPERS tv	Wally Cox
MR. SATURDAY NIGHT '92	Billy Crystal d+
MR. SMITH GOES TO WASHINGTON '39 ****	James Stewart, Jean Arthur

MRS. MINIVER '42 ****	Greer Garson, Teresa Wright,
	William Wyler d
MUDLARK, THE '50	Irene Dunne
MULLENGER, DONNA BELLE	Donna Reed
MULTIPLICITY '96	Michael Keaton, Andie MacDowell
MUMMY'S CURSE, THE '44	Lon Chaney Jr.
MUMMY, THE '32	Boris Karloff
MUMMY, THE '59	Peter Cushing
MUNSTERS, THE tv	Fred Gwynne
MUPPETS	Jim Henson
MURDER BY DECREE '79	Christopher Plummer
MURDER IN THE CATHEDRAL	T.S. Eliot
MURDER MOST FOUL '65	Margaret Rutherford
MURDER! '30	Herbert Marshall
MURDER, SHE WROTE tv	Angela Lansbury
MURDERS IN THE ZOO '33	Lionel Atwill
MURIEL	George P. Elliott
MURNAU, F.W.	Friedrich Plumpe
MURPHY BROWN tv	Candice Bergen
MURPHY'S ROMANCE '85	Sally Field
MURRAY, JEANNE	Jean Stapleton
MUSIC LOVERS, THE '71	Glenda Jackson
MUSIC MAN	Robert Preston, Onna White ba
MUSIC MAN, THE	Meredith Willson
MUSIC OF THE NIGHT	Andrew Lloyd Webber
MUSTANG COUNTRY '76	Joel McCrea
MUTINY ON THE BOUNTY '35 ****	Charles Laughton, Clark Gable
MUTT AND JEFF	Bud Fisher
MY BLOOD RUNS COLD '65	Troy Donahue
MY CHERIE AMOUR	Stevie Wonder
MY COUSIN RACHEL '52	Olivia de Havilland
MY DARLING CLEMENTINE '46 ****	Henry Fonda, Linda Darnell
MY DEAR SECRETARY '48	Laraine Day, Kirk Douglas
MY DREAM IS YOURS '49	Jack Carson
MY FAIR LADY	Alan Jay Lerner
MY FATHER, THE HERO '94	Gerard Depardieu
MY FAVORITE HUSBAND tv	Barry Nelson
MY FAVORITE WIFE '40	Cary Grant, Irene Dunne
MY FAVORITE YEAR '82	Peter O'Toole
MY FOOLISH HEART '49	Dana Andrews
MY FORBIDDEN PAST '51	Robert Mitchum
MY FRIEND FLICKA '43	Roddy McDowall
MY FRIEND FLICKA tv	Gene Evans
MY FRIEND IRMA tv	Marie Wilson
MY GENERATION	The Who mr
MY GIRL	The Temptations mr
MY GUY	Mary Wells mr
MY LITTLE MARGIE tv	Gale Storm
MY LOVE CAME BACK '40	Olivia de Havilland
MY MICHAEL	Amos Oz
MY MOTHER THE CAR tv	Ann Sothern
MY NAME IS ARAM	William Saroyan
MY NAME IS NOBODY '73	Henry Fonda
MY NIGHT AT MAUD'S '69	Jean-Louis Trintignant
MY OLD DOG TRAY	Stephen Foster
MY OLD MAN'S PLACE '72	Mitchell Ryan
MY PEOPLE	Abba Eban
MY SECRET IDENTITY tv	Jerry O'Connell
MY SISTER EILEEN	Ruth McKenney
MY SISTER EILEEN '42	Rosalind Russell
MY SISTER EILEEN '55	Betty Garrett

MY THREE SONS tv	Fred MacMurray
MY TWO DADS tv	Paul Reiser
MY WICKED, WICKED WAYS	Errol Flynn
MY WORLD AND WELCOME TO IT tv	William Windom
MYSTERIOUS ISLAND	Jules Verne
MYSTERY OF MR. X, THE '34	Robert Montgomery
N.Y.P.D. tv	Jack Warden
NADINE '87	Kim Basinger
NAILS '92	Dennis Hopper
NAKED AND THE DEAD, THE	Norman Mailer
NAKED AND THE DEAD, THE '58	Aldo Ray
NAKED CITY tv	John McIntire
NAKED IN NEW YORK '94	Eric Stoltz
NAKED JUNGLE, THE '54	Eleanor Parker
NAKED MAJA, THE	Francisco Jose de Goya
NAKSYZNYSKI, NASTASSJA	Nastassja Kinski
NANA	Emile Zola
NANA '34	Anna Sten
NANA '55	Charles Boyer
NANCY DREW	Carolyn Keene
NANCY GOES TO RIO '50	Ann Sothern
NANNY tv	Fran Drescher
NANNY, THE '65	Bette Davis
NAPOLEAN '27 ****	Antonin Artaud
NARROW CORNER, THE '33	Douglas Fairbanks, Jr.
NARROW MARGIN, THE '52	Charles McGraw
NASHVILLE '75 ****	Henry Gibson, Karen Black
NASTY	Janet Jackson
NATIONAL VELVET	Enid Bagnold
NATIONAL VELVET '44 ****	Mickey Rooney, Elizabeth Taylor
NATIONAL VELVET tv	Lori Martin
NATIVE SON	Richard Wright
NATURAL, THE '84	Robert Redford
NAUGHTY BUT NICE '39	Dick Powell
NAUGHTY MARIETTA '35	Nelson Eddy, Jeanette MacDonald
NAVY BLUE AND GOLD '37	Robert Young
NAZARENE, THE	Sholem Asch
NAZARIN '58	Francisco Rabal
NEA '78	Sami Frey
NECKLACE, THE	Guy De Maupassant
NEDDA	Pagliacci
NELL	Charles Dickebs
NELSON AFFAIR, THE '73	Glenda Jackson
NELSON, PRINCE ROGERS	Prince
NEMO	James Mason
NEMO(Captain)	Jules Verne
NERO WOLFE	Rex Stout
NERUDA, PABLO	Ricardo Neftali Reyes
NESS in the Untouchables tv	Kevin Costner
NEST, THE '80	Ana Torrent
NETWORK '76 ****	Wm. Holden, Peter Finch, Sidney Lumet d
NEVER MIND	Nirvana mr
NEVER NEVER LAND '80	Petula Clark
NEVER SAY GOODBYE '46	Errol Flynn
NEVER SAY GOODBYE '56	Rock Hudson
NEVER WAVE AT A WAC '52	Rosalind Russell
NEW DOCTORS, THE tv	E.G. Marshall
NEW KIND OF LOVE, A '63	Paul Newman
NEW MOON, THE	Sigmund Romberg
NEW WORLD SYMPHONY	Antonin Dvorak
NEW YORK STORIES '89	Woody Allen d, Nick Nolte

NEXT TIME WE LOVE '36	Margaret Sullavan
NGUGI, JAMES w	Ngugi wa Thiong'o
NIAGRA '53	Marilyn Monroe
NICKEL MOUNTAIN '85	Michael Cole
NICKELODEON '76	Ryan O'Neal
NICOL, ABIOSEH	Dr. Davidson Nicol
NIGHT AND DAY	Cole Porter
NIGHT AND THE CITY '50	Richard Widmark
NIGHT AND THE CITY '92	Robert De Niro
NIGHT AT THE OPERA , A '35 ****	Marx Brothers
NIGHT COURT tv	Harry Anderson
NIGHT CREATURES '62	Peter Cushing
NIGHT DIGGER, THE '71	Patricia Neal
NIGHT HAS EYES, THE '42	James Mason
NIGHT HEAT tv	Scott Hylands
NIGHT HEAVEN FELL, THE '58	Brigitte Bardot
NIGHT IS MY FUTURE '48	Mai Zetterling
NIGHT MY NUMBER CAME UP, THE '55 ****	Michael Redgrave
NIGHT OF THE COMET '84	Catherine Mary Stewart
NIGHT OF THE IGUANA, THE	Tennessee Williams
NIGHT TO REMEMBER, A '43	Loretta Young
NIGHT TO REMEMBER, A'58 ****	Kenneth More, Jill Dixon
NIGHT WALKER, THE '64	Barbara Stanwyck
NIGHTFALL '56	Aldo Ray
NIGHTHAWKS '81	Sylvester Stallone
NIGHTINGALE, THE	Igor Stravinsky
NIGHTKILL '80	Jaclyn Smith
NIGHTLINE tv	Ted Koppel
NIGHTMARE '42	Diana Barrymore
NIGHTMARE '56	Edward G. Robinson
NIGHTMARE ALLEY '47	Tyrone Power
NIGHTS IN WHITE SATIN	Moody Blues mr
NIGHTS OF CABIRIA '57 ****	Giuletta Masina
NIJINSKY '80	Alan Bates
NINE HOURS TO RAMA '63	Horst Buchholz
NINE STORIES	J.D. Salinger w
NINE TAILORS, THE	Dorothy Sayers w
NINETEEN EIGHTY-FIVE (1985)	Anthony Burgess
NINETEEN EIGHTY-FOUR (1984)	George Orwell
NINOTCHKA '39	Greta Garbo
NITWITS, THE '35	Burt Wheeler
NIXON '95	Anthony Hopkins
NO DRUMS, NO BUGLES '71	Martin Sheen
NO MAN IS AN ISLAND '62	Jeffrey Hunter
NO SAD SONGS FOR ME '50	Margaret Sullavan
NO TIME FOR COMEDY	S.N.Behrman
NO TIME FOR COMEDY '40	James Stewart
NO TIME FOR SARGEANTS	Ira Levin
NOBLE HOUSE	James Clavell
NOBODY'S PERFECT '68	Doug McClure
NOCTURNE '46	George Raft
NOLA	Vincent Lopez
NON-STOP NEW YORK '37	John Loder
NONE BUT THE BRAVE '65	Frank Sinatra
NONE SHALL ESCAPE '44	Marsha Hunt
NOOSE HANGS HIGH, THE '48	Bud Abbott & Lou Costello
NORMA	Vincenzo Bellini
NORMAN LOVES ROSE '82	Carol Kane
NORTH BY NORTHWEST '59 ****	Cary Grant, Eva Marie Saint, Alfred Hitchcock d
NORTHERN EXPOSURE tv	Rob Morrow, Janine Turner, Barry Corbin

NORTHERN PURSUIT '43	Errol Flynn
NOSTROMO	Joseph Conrad
NOT AS A STRANGER	Morton Thompson
NOT AS A STRANGER '55	Olivia de Havilland
NOT OF THIS EARTH '57	Paul Birch
NOTHING BUT A MAN '64	Ivan Dixon
NOTHING GOLD CAN STAY	Robert Frost
NOTHING PERSONAL '97	Ian Hart, John Lynch
NOTORIOUS '46	Cary Grant
NOVALIS	Friedrich Hardenberg
NOW WE ARE SIX	A.A. Milne w
NUDE DESCENDING A STAIRCASE	Marcel Duchamp
NUKIE '93	Glynis Johns
NUN, THE '66	Anna Karina
NUNZIO '78	David Proval
NURSE '80	Michael Learned
NURSE tv	Michael Learned
NURSES tv	Stephanie Hodge
NURSES, THE tv	Shirl Conway
NUTCRACKER SUITE	Pyotr Tchaikovsky
NUTS '87	Barbra Streisand
NUTTY PROFESSOR, THE '63	Jerry Lewis
NUTTY PROFESSOR, THE '96	Eddie murphy
NYPD BLUE tv	Amy Brenneman
O LUCKY MAN '73 ****	Malcolm McDowell,Rachel Roberts
O RARE	Johnson, Ben
O'BRIEN, FLANN	Brian O'Nolan
O'CONNOR, FRANK	Michael O'Donovan
O'FEARNA, SEAN	John Ford
O'REED, MARGARET	Martha Raye
OAK, THE '92	Maia Morgenstern
OASIS, THE '84	Chris Makepeace
OBSESSION '76	Cliff Robertson
OCKLEMAN, CONSTANCE	Veronica Lake
OCTOPUSSY '83	Roger Moore
ODD ANGRY SHOT, THE '79	John Hargreaves
ODD COUPLE, THE	Neil Simon
ODD COUPLE, THE tv	Tony Randall, Jack Klugman
ODD MAN OUT '47 ****	James Mason, Robert Newton
ODESSA	Bee Gees mr
ODESSA FILE, THE	Frederick Forsythe
ODETTE '50	Anna Neagle
OEDIPUS REX	Igor Stravinsky
OEDIPUS THE KING '68	Christopher Plummer
OF FLESH AND BLOOD '62	Renato Salvatori
OF HUMAN BONDAGE	W. Somerset Maughan
OF HUMAN BONDAGE '64	Kim Novak
OF MICE AND MEN '39 ****	Lon Chaney Jr.,Burgess Meredith
OF THEE I SING	George Gershwin
OFF THE COURT	Arthur Ashe
OFFICIAL STORY, THE '85 ****	Hector Alterio
OH LADY BE GOOD	George Gershwin
OH PRETTY WOMAN	Ray Orbison mr
OHANIAN, KREKER	Michael Connors
OIL	Upton Sinclair
OKLAHOMA	Agnes De Mille ba
OKLAHOMA '55	Shirley Jones, Gordon McRae
OKLAHOMA KID, THE '39	James Cagney
OKLAHOMA, Aunt in	Eller
OKLAHOMAN, THE '57	Joel McCrae
OLAN	Pearl Buck

```
OLD ACQUAINTANCE '43           Bette Davis, Miriam Hopkins
OLD DARK HOUSE, THE '32        Melvyn Douglas, Boris Karloff
OLD DARK HOUSE, THE '63        Robert Morley
OLD MAN AND THE SEA            Ernest Hemingway
OLD MAN AND THE SEA, THE '58   Spencer Tracy
OLD WIVES' TALE, THE           Arnold Bennett
OLD-FASHIONED WAY, THE '34     W.C. Fields
OLE BUTTERMILK SKY             Hoagy Carmichael
OLIVE OYL in Popeye            Shelley Duvall
OLIVER TWIST '48 ****          Alec Guinness, Robert Newton
OLIVER! '68 ****              Ron Moody, Oliver Reed
OLIVIER OLIVIER '92            Francois Cluzet
OLYMPIA                        Edouard Manet
OLYMPIA '36 ****(documentary) Leni Riefenstahl d
OMEN, THE '76                  Gregory Peck, Richard Donner d
OMOO                           Herman Melville
ON BORROWED TIME '39           Lionel Barrymore
ON GOLDEN POND '81             Henry Fonda
ON MOONLIGHT BAY '51           Doris Day
ON THE BEACH                   Nevil Shute
ON THE BEACH '59 ****          Gregory Peck, Ava Gardner
ON THE RIGHT TRACK '81         Gary Coleman
ON THE ROAD                    Jack Kerouac
ON THE TOWN '49 ****           Gene Kelly d+, Frank Sinatra
ON THE WATERFRONT '54 ****     Marlon Brando, Karl Malden
ON VALENTINE'S DAY '86         William Converse-Roberts
ONCE IN A LIFETIME             Talking Heads mr
ONCE IN A LIFETIME '32         Jack Oakie
ONCE UPON A HORSE '58          Dan Rowan, Dick Martin
ONE DAY AT A TIME tv           Bonnie Franklin
ONE DEADLY SUMMER '83          Isabelle Adjani
ONE FLEW OVER THE CUCKOO'S NEST '75 **** Jack Nicholson,
                                             Louise Fletcher
ONE FLEW OVER THE CUCKOO'S NEST Ken Kesey
ONE FOOT IN HEAVEN '41         Fredric March
ONE FOR MY BABY                Lena Horne
ONE HOUR WITH YOU '32     Maurice Chevalier,Jeanette MacDonald
ONE LITTLE INDIAN '73          James Garner
ONE MAN'S FAMILY tv            Ben Lytell
ONE NIGHT OF LOVE '34          Grace Moore
ONE TOUCH OF VENUS '48         Ava Gardner, Kurt Weill c(Music)
ONE TRUE THING                 Anna Quindlin w
ONE, TWO, THREE '61 ****       James Cagney, Arlene Francis
ONEL                           Scott Turow
ONION FIELD, THE               James Wambaugh
ONIONHEAD '58                  Andy Griffith
ONLY GAME IN TOWN, THE '70     Elizabeth Taylor
ONLY TWO CAN PLAY '62          Peter Sellers
ONLY WHEN I LAUGH '81          Marsha Mason
OOH BABY BABY                  Linda Ronstadt
OOH BABY BABY                  Smokey Robinson & the Miracles mr
OPEN CITY '45 ****             Anna Magnani
OPERATION PETTICOAT tv         John Astin
OPERATION SNAFU '61            Sean Connery
OPIE                           Ron Howard
OPPOSITE SEX, THE '56          June Allyson
OPTIC, OLIVER                  William T. Adams
OPTIMISTS, THE '73             Peter Sellers
ORCHESTRA WIVES '42            Ann Rutherford
ORDINARY PEOPLE '80 ****    Donald Sutherland, Mary Tyler Moore
ORFEO                          Claudio Monteverdi
```

ORGANIZATION, THE '71	Sidney Poitier
ORGANIZER, THE '63	Marcello Mastroianni
ORLANDO	George Frideric Handel
ORLANDO	Virginia Woolf
ORLANDO '93	Billy Zane
OROWITZ, EUGENE	Michael Landon
ORPHANS '87	Albert Finney
ORPHEUS '49	Jean Marais
ORR, SHEENA SHIRLEY	Sheena Easton
ORWELL, GEORGE	Eric Blair
OSA '85	Kelly Lynch
OSCAR '91	Don Ameche, Sylvester Stallone
OSSESSIONE '42	Massimo Girotti
OSTERMAN WEEKEND, THE '83	Rutger Hauer
OTELLO	Giacchino Rossini
OTELLO	Giuseppi Verdi
OTELLO '86	Placido Domingo
OTHELLO '52	Orson Welles d+
OTHELLO '65 ****	Laurence Olivier, Frank Finlay
OTHER MEN'S WOMEN '31	Mary Astor
OTHER, THE	Thomas Tryon
OTHER, THE '72	Uta Hagen
OUR HOSPITALITY '23 ****	Buster Keaton d+
OUR HOUSE tv	Wilford Brimley
OUR MAN IN HAVANA	Graham Greene
OUR MAN IN HAVANA '60	Alec Guinness
OUR MISS BROOKS tv	Eve Arden
OUR MOTHER'S HOUSE '67	Dirk Bogarde
OUR TOWN	Emily
OUT '88	Peter Coyote
OUT OF THIS WORLD '45	Eddie Bracken
OUT OF THIS WORLD tv	Donna Pescow
OUTBACK '71	Gary Bond, Donald Pleasence
OUTBREAK '95	Dustin Hoffman
OUTCAST, THE '37	Warren William
OUTCAST, THE '54	John Derek
OUTFIT, THE '74	Robert Duvall
OUTLAND '81	Sean Connery
OUTLAW TERRITORY '53	Macdonald Carey
OUTLAW, THE '43	Jane Russell
OUTLAWS, THE tv	Barton MacLane
OUTPOST IN MALAYA '52	Claudette Colbert
OUTRAGE, THE '64	Paul Newman
OUTSIDE THE WALL '50	Richard Basehart
OUTSIDER, THE '61	Tony Curtis
OUTSIDER, THE '79	Craig Wasson
OUTSIDERS, THE '83	C. Thomas Howell
OVER MY DEAD BODY '42	Milton Berle
OVER THERE	George M. Cohan
OVERBOARD '87	Goldie Hawn, Kurt Russell
OVERCOAT, THE	Nikolai Gogol
OVERLANDERS, THE '46	Chips Rafferty
OWEN in L.A. Law tv	Susan Dey
OWEN MARSHALL, COUNSELOR AT LAW tv	Arthur Hill
OX-BOW INCIDENT, THE'43****	Henry Fonda, Dana Andrews
P.S. I LOVE YOU	Beatles
P.S. I LUV U tv	Connie Sellecca
PA CHIN	Li Fei-kan
PACIFIC HEIGHTS '90	Melanie Griffith
PACK, THE '77	Joe Don Baker
PAID '31	Joan Crawford

PAINT YOUR WAGON '69	Lee Marvin, Clint Eastwood
PAINTED HILLS, THE '51	Paul Kelly
PAINTED VEIL, THE '34	Greta Garbo
PAISAN '46	Gar Moore
PAL JOEY	John O'Hara
PALANUIK, WALTER	Jack Palance
PALE FIRE	Vladimir Nabokov
PALEFACE, THE '48	Bob Hope
PALM BEACH STORY, THE '42	Claudette Colbert
PALMER, VERA JANE	Jayne Mansfield
PALOOKA '34	Jimmy Durante
PALOOKAVILLE '96	William Forsythe
PALS '87	Don Ameche
PANAYIOTOU, GEORGIOUS	George Michael
PANDORA'S BOX '28 ****	Louise Brooks, Fritz Kortner, Francis Lederer
PANIC IN YEAR ZERO '62	Ray Milland
PANTALOONS '57	Fernandel
PAPA LOVES MAMBO	Perry Como
PAPA'S GOT A BRAND NEW BAG	James Brown mr
PAPALEO, ANTHONY	Anthony Franciosa
PAPER MOON '73 ****	Ryan & Tatum O'Neal
PAPER, THE '94	Ron Howard d, Michael Keaton
PAPERHOUSE '88	Charlotte Burke
PAPILLON '73	Steve McQueen
PARACHUTE JUMPER '33	Douglas Fairbanks Jr.
PARADE'S END	Ford Madox Ford
PARADINE CASE, THE '48	Alfred Hitchcock d, Gregory Peck
PARADISE '91	Melanie Griffith
PARADISE tv	Lee Horsley
PARADISO	Dante
PARALLAX VIEW, THE '74	Warren Beatty
PARANOID	Black Sabbath mr
PARDNERS '56	Dean Martin, Jerry Lewis
PARDON MY FRENCH '51	Paul Henreid, Merle Oberon
PARDON MY SARONG '42	Bud Abbott, Lou Costello
PARENTHOOD '89	Steve Martin, Ron Howard d
PARIS AFTER DARK '43	George Sanders
PARIS EXPRESS, THE '53	Claude Rains
PARIS HONEYMOON '39	Bing Crosby
PARIZADO	Arabian Nights
PARKER LEWIS CAN'T LOSE tv	Corin Nemec
PARLEY, PETER	Samuel Goodrich
PARTRIDGE FAMILY, THE tv	Shirley Jones
PARTY, THE '68	Peter Sellers
PASCALI'S ISLAND '88	Ben Kingsley
PASSAGE TO INDIA	Adela
PASSAGE TO INDIA, A	E.M. Forster
PASSAGE TO INDIA, A '84	Judy Davis
PASSENGER, THE '75	Jack Nicholson
PASSION '82	Isabelle Huppert
PASSION OF JOAN OF ARC, THE '28 **** Carl Theodor Dreyer d	
PASSPORT TO SUEZ '43	Warren William
PASTIME '91	William Russ
PATHETIQUE - Symph. No. 6 in B Minor Piotr Ilyich Tchaikovsky	
PATHETIQUE-Piano Sonata in C Minor Ludwig von Beethoven	
PATHFINDER	Jms. Fennimore Cooper
PATHFINDER '88	Mikkel Gaup
PATHS OF GLORY '57 ****	Kirk Douglas, Ralph Meeker
PATRIOT GAMES	Tom Clancy w
PATTERNS '56	Van Heflin

PATTON '70 ****	George C. Scott , Karl Malden
PAUL, JEAN	Jean Paul Friedrich Richter
PAULA '52	Loretta Young
PAUP, THERESA	Theresa Russell
PAVANE FOR A DEAD PRINCESS	Maurice Joseph Ravel
PAWNBROKER, THE '65 ****	Rod Steiger, Geraldine Fitzgerald
PAYDAY '73	Rip Torn
PAYMENT DEFERRED '32	Charles Laughton
PAYMENT ON DEMAND '51	Bette Davis
PAYROLL '61	Michael Craig
PEACEMAKER, THE '97	Nicole Kidman
PEANUTS	Charles Shulz
PEARL OF DEATH, THE '44	Basil Rathbone
PEARL, THE '48	Pedro Armendariz
PEDESTRIAN, THE '74	Peter Hall
PEER GYNT	Henrik Ibsen
PEGGY '50	Charles Coburn, Diana Lynn
PELICAN BRIEF, THE '93	Julia Roberts
PENDULUM '69	George Peppard
PENGUIN ISLAND	Anatole France w
PENITENT, THE '88	Raul Julia
PENITENTIARY '79	Leon Isaac Kennedy
PENTHOUSE '33	Warner Baxter
PEOPLE VS.LARRY FLYNT,THE'96	**** Woody Harrelson,
	Courtney Love
PEOPLE WILL TALK '35	Mary Boland
PEOPLE WILL TALK '51	Cary Grant
PEOPLE'S CHOICE, THE tv	Jackie Cooper
PEOPLE, YES, THE	Carl Sandburg
PEPE LE MOKO '37 ****	Jean Gabin
PERE GORIOT, Le	Honore de Balzac
PERELANDRA	C.S. Lewis
PEREZ FAMILY, THE '95	Marisa Tomei
PERFECT COUPLE, A '79	Paul Dooley
PERFECT FURLOUGH, THE '58	Tony Curtis
PERFECT MARRIAGE, THE '46	David Niven, Loretta Young
PERFECT MATCH, THE '87	Marc McClure
PERFECT SPECIMEN, THE '37	Errol Flynn
PERFECT STRANGERS tv	Mark Linn-Baker, Bronson Pinchot
PERFECT WOMAN, THE '49	Patricia Roc
PERFORMANCE '70	Nicolas Roeg
PERILOUS HOLIDAY '46	Pat O'Brien
PERILS OF PAULINE, THE '47	Betty Hutton
PERMANENT RECORD '88	Alan Boyce
PERMIT ME VOYAGE	James Agee
PERPETUAL PEACE	Immanuel Kant
PERRY MASON tv	Raymond Burr, Barbara Hale
PERRY MASON tv Role	Barbara Hale as Della Street
PERRY MASON(sleuth)	Erle Stanley Gardner
PERRY, LINCOLN	Stepin Fetchit
PERSE, ST. JOHN	Alexis Saint-Leger
PERSE, ST. JOHN	Marie Leger
PERSISTENCE OF MEMORY, THE	Salvadore Dali
PERSKE, BETTY JOAN	Lauren Bacall
PERSONA '66	Bibi Andersson
PERSUASION '95	Amanda Root
PESCHOWSKY, MICHAEL IGOR	Mike Nichols
PETE AND GLADYS tv	Harry Morgan
PETE KELLY'S BLUES '55	Jack Webb d+
PETER AND THE WOLF	Sergey S. Prokokiev
PETER GUNN tv	Craig Stevens

PETER PAN	James M. Barrie(Sir)
PETERS, JANE	Carole Lombard
PETRARCH po	Francesco Petrarca
PETTICOAT JUNCTION tv	Bea Benaderet, Lori Saunders
PETULIA '68 ****	Julie Christie, George C. Scott
PEYTON PLACE tv	Dorothy Malone, Mia Farrow
PHAEDRA '62	Melina Mercouri
PHANTOM OF THE OPERA	Andrew Lloyd Webber
PHANTOM RAIDERS '42	Walter Pidgeon
PHANTOM THIEF, THE '46	Chester Morris
PHEDRE	Jean Racine
PHENIX CITY STORY, THE '55	John McIntire
PHFFFT! '54	Jack Lemmon
PHIL SILVERS SHOW, THE tv	Maurice Gosfield
PHIL SILVERS SHOW, THE tv	Pvt. Duane Doberman
PHILADELPHIA '93	Tom Hanks
PHILADELPHIA STORY, THE '40 ****	Cary Grant,Katharine Hepburn
PHINEAS FOGG in Around the World in 80 Days'56	David Niven
PHYLLIS tv	Cloris Leachman
PIANO MAN	Billy Joel mr
PIANO, THE '93	Jane Campion d, Holly Hunter
PICK-UP '33	Sylvia Sidney
PICNIC	William Inge
PICNIC '55	William Holden, Rosalind Russell
PICTURE OF DORIAN GRAY, THE	Oscar Wilde
PICTURE SNATCHER '33	James Cagney
PICTURES AT AN EXHIBITION	Modest Mussorgsky
PIERCE, RONALD	Ron Ely
PILGRIM'S PROGRESS	John Bunyan
PILGRIMAGE '33	Heather Angel
PILLOW TALK '59	Doris Day, Rock Hudson
PIMPERNEL" SMITH '41	Leslie Howard d+
PINCUS, BARRY ALAN	Barry Manilow
PINK PANTHER, THE '64	David Niven, Peter Sellers
PINKY '49	Ethel Barrymore, Jeanne Crain
PINOCCHIO '40 ****(animated)	Ben Sharpsteen d
PIQUE DAME	Pyotr Tchaikovsky
PIRANHA '78	Bradford Dillman
PIRATE, THE '48	Judy Garland & Gene Kelly
PIRATES '86	Walter Matthau
PITFALL '48	Dick Powell
PLACE IN THE SUN, A '51	Montgomery Clift
PLACE OF ONE'S OWN, A '45	James Mason
PLAGUE, THE	Albert Camus w
PLAIDY, JEAN	Eleanor Hibbert, Victoria Holt
PLAINCLOTHESMAN, THE tv	Ken Lynch
PLAINSMAN, THE '36	Gary Cooper
PLAINSONG '82	Jessica Nelson
PLANET OF THE APES '68	Charlton Heston
PLATINUM BLONDE '31	Jean Harlow
PLATOON '86	Tom Berenger
PLAY IT AGAIN, SAM '72	Woody Allen
PLAY IT AS IT LAYS	Joan Didion
PLAY IT AS IT LAYS '72	Tuesday Weld
PLAY MISTY FOR ME '71	Clint Eastwood d+
PLAY TIME '67 ****	Jacques Tati d+
PLAYBOYS, THE '92	Albert Finney
PLAYER, THE '92	Tim Robbins, Robert Altman d
PLAYGIRL '54	Shelley Winters
PLEASE BELIEVE ME '50	Deborah Kerr
PLEASE MR. POSTMAN	Marvelettes mr

PLEASE MURDER ME '56   Angela Lansbury
PLEASURE SEEKERS, THE '64   Ann-Margret
PLENTY '85   Meryl Streep
PLOT THICKENS, THE '36   James Gleason
PLOUGH AND THE STARS, THE   Sean O'Casey
PLOUGHMAN'S LUNCH, THE '83   Jonathan Pryce
PLUMBER, THE '80   Judy Morris
PLUNDER OF THE SUN '53   Glenn Ford
PLUNDERERS, THE '60   Jeff Chandler
PNIN   Vladimir Nabokov
POGOODIN, NIKOLAY   Nikolay Fyodorovich Stukalov
POINT COUNTER POINT   Aldous Huxley
POISON '91   Edith Meeks
POLICE '84   Gerard Depardieu
POLICE SQUAD tv   Leslie Nielsen
POLICE WOMAN tv   Angie Dickinson
POLLYANNA '20   Mary Pickford
POLLYANNA '60   Hayley Mills
POLTERGEIST '82   Craig T. Nelson
POLYESTER '81   Tab Hunter
POMP AND CIRCUMSTANCE   Sir Edward Elgar
POOR SIDE OF TOWN   Johnny Rivers mr
POPEYE   Elzie C. Segar
POPI '69   Alan Arkin
POPPY '36   W.C. Fields
POQUELIN, JEAN BAPTISTA   Moliere
PORCUPINE, PETER   William Cobbett
PORGY AND BESS   George Gershwin
PORKY'S '81   Dan Monahan
PORTNOY'S COMPLAINT   Philip Roth
PORTRAIT IN BLACK '60   Lana Turner
PORTRAIT OF A LADY   T.S. Eliot
PORTRAIT OF THE ARTIST AS A YOUNG MAN, A   James Joyce
POSSE '75   Kirk Douglas d+
POSSESSED '31   Joan Crawford, Clark Gable
POSSESSED '47   Joan Crawford, Van Heflin
POSSESSORS, THE '58   Jean Gabin
POSTMAN ALWAYS RINGS TWICE, THE James M. Cain
POSTMAN ALWAYS RINGS TWICE, THE '46 **** Lana Turner,
                                           John Garfield
POSTMAN, THE '94   Massimo Troisi, Phillippe Noiret
POWER '28   William Boyd
POWER '34   Conrad Veidt
POWER '86   Richard Gere
POWER, THE '68   George Hamilton
PRANCER '89   Sam Elliott
PRATT, WILLIAM HENRY   Boris Karloff
PREDATOR '87   Arnold Schwarzenegger
PRELUDE TO A KISS   Craig Lucas
PRELUDE TO A KISS '92   Alec Baldwin, Meg Ryan
PREMCHAND   Dhanpat Rai Srivastiv
PRESIDENT'S ANALYST, THE '67 **** James Coburn,
                                        Godfrey Cambridge
PRESIDIO, THE '88   Sean Connery
PRESTIGE '32   Ann Harding
PRESUMED INNOCENT '90   Bonnie Bedalia, Harrison Ford
PRETENDER, THE '47   Albert Dekker
PRICE IS RIGHT, THE tv   Bill Cullen
PRICE OF FEAR, THE '56   Merle Oberon
PRICK UP YOUR EARS '87   Gary Oldman
PRIDE AND PREJUDICE '40 **** Greer Garson, Laurence Olivier

PRIDE OF THE YANKEES '42 **** Gary Cooper, Teresa Wright
PRIME OF MISS JEAN BRODIE, THE Muriel Spark
PRINCE IGOR   Aleksandr P. Borodin
PRINCE OF PIRATES '53   John Derek
PRINCE OF PLAYERS '55   Richard Burton
PRINCE OF THE CITY '81   Treat Williams
PRINCE VALIANT   Hal Foster
PRINCESS O'ROURKE '43   Olivia DeHavilland
PRINCESS YANG KWEI FEI '55 **** Masayuki Mori
PRINCESSE TAM TAM '35   Josephine Baker
PRISONER OF ZENDA, THE '37 **** Ronald Colman,
                                  Madeleine Carroll
PRISONER OF ZENDA, THE '52   Stewart Granger, Deborah Kerr
PRISONER, THE '55   Alec Guinness
PRIVATE BENJAMIN '80   Goldie Hawn
PRIVATE BENJAMIN tv   Lorna Patterson, Ann Ryerson
PRIVATE EYES, THE '80   Tim Conway
PRIVATE FUNCTION, A '85   Michael Palin
PRIVATE LIFE OF HENRY VIII,THE'33 **** Charles Laughton
PRIVATE PARTS   Howard Stern
PRIVATE SECRETARY tv   Ann Ryerson
PRIVATE'S AFFAIR, A '59   Sal Mineo
PRIVILEGE '67   Paul Jones
PRIZE, THE '63   Paul Newman, Edward G. Robinson
PROBE '72   Hugh O'Brian
PRODIGAL, THE '55   Lana Turner
PRODUCERS, THE '68   Zero Mostel
PROFESSIONALS, THE '66   Lee Marvin
PROFESSOR BEWARE '38   Harold Lloyd
PROJECTIONIST, THE '71   Chuck McCann
PROMOTER, THE '52   Alec Guinness
PROOF '91   Hugo Weaving
PROPHECY, THE '95   Christopher Walken
PROPHET, THE   Sholem Asch
PROSPERO'S BOOKS '91   John Gielgud
PROTECTORS, THE tv   Robert Vaughn
PROUD AND PROFANE, THE '56   William Holden
PROUD MARY   Creedence Clearwater Revival mr
PROWLER, THE '51   Van Heflin
PRUDHOMME, SULLY   Rene Francois Armand Prudhomme
PSYCH-OUT '68   Susan Strasberg
PSYCHO '60 **** Anthony Perkins,Vera Miles,Alfred Hitchcock d,
PSYCHOMANIA '71   George Sanders
PSYCHOPATH, THE '66   Patrick Wymark
PUBLIC ENEMY, THE '31   James Cagney
PUFNSTUF '70   Jack Wild
PULP '72   Michael Caine
PULSE '88   Cliff DeYoung
PUMP UP THE VOLUME '90   Christian Slater
PUMPKIN EATER, THE '64   Anne Bancroft
PUMPKINHEAD '88   Lance Henriksen
PUNCHLINE '88   Sally Field
PUNKY BREWSTER tv   Soleil Moon Frye
PUPPET ON A CHAIN   Allstair MacLean
PUPPY LOVE   Paul Anka
PURPLE HEART, THE '44   Dana Andrews
PURPLE PLAIN, THE '54   Gregory Peck
PURPLE RAIN   Prince mr
PURSUED '47   Robert Mitchum
PUSHOVER '54   Fred MacMurray
PUSS IN BOOTS   Charles Perrault

PYGMALION	George Bernard Shaw
PYGMALION '38 ****	Leslie Howard d+, Wendy Hiller
PYRO '64	Barry Sullivan
PYX '73	Karen Black
Q '82	David Carradine
QB VII	Leon Uris
QUADROPHENIA '79	Phil Daniels
QUANTEZ '57	Fred MacMurray
QUANTUM LEAP tv	Scott Bakula
QUARE FELLOW, THE '62	Patrick McGoohan
QUARREL, THE '91	R.H. Thompson
QUARTER TO THREE	"U.S." Gary Bonds mr
QUARTET '49 ****	Arthur Crabtree
QUARTET '81	Alan Bates
QUATORZE JUILLET '32	Annabella
QUEDENS, EUNICE	Eve Arden
QUEEG in Mutiny On The Bounty '54	Humphrey Bogart
QUEEN CHRISTINA '33 ****	Greta Garbo, John Gilbert
QUEEN, ELLERY	Frederic Dannay or Manfred Lee
QUENTIN DURWARD '55	Robert Taylor
QUEST, THE '96	Jean-Claude Van Damme d+
QUICK '93	Teri Polo
QUICKSAND '50	Mickey Rooney
QUIET DON	Mikhail A. Sholochov
QUIET MAN, THE '52 ****	John Wayne, Maureen O'Hara
QUIGLEY, JANE	Jane Alexander
QUINCE, PETER	Isaac Story
QUINCY tv	Robert Ito
QUINCY, M.E. tv	Jack Klugman
QUINTET IN C MAJOR	Franz Schubert
R.U.R.	Karel Capek
RABBI BEN EZRA	Robert Browning
RABID '77	Marilyn Chambers
RACERS, THE '55	Kirk Douglas
RACHEL PAPERS, THE '89	Ione Skye
RACK, THE '56	Paul Newman
RACKET, THE '51	Robert Mitchum
RADAR in MASH '70	Gary Burghoff
RAFFLES '30	Ronald Colman
RAFFLES '40	David Niven
RAGE '80	David Soul
RAGE OF PARIS, THE '38	Danielle Darrieux
RAGGED DICK	Horatio Alger
RAGING BULL '80 ****	Robert De Niro, Cathy Moriarty
RAGMAN'S DAUGHTER, THE '72	Victoria Tennant
RAGTIME	E.L. Doctorow
RAGTIME '81	James Cagney
RAGUSA, PAULA	Paula Prentiss
RAID, THE '54	Van Heflin
RAIDERS OF THE LOST ARK '81 ****	Harrison Ford, Karen Allen
RAIDERS, THE '52	Richard Conte
RAIDERS, THE '63	Robert Culp
RAILROADED '47	John Ireland
RAILWAY CHILDREN, THE '72	Dinah Sheridan
RAIN '32	Joan Crawford, Walter Huston
RAINBOW TRAIL, THE '25	Tom Mix
RAINBOW, THE	D.H. Lawrence
RAINBOW, THE '89	Sammi Davis
RAINMAKER, THE '56	Burt Lancaster
RAINTREE COUNTY '57	Elizabeth Taylor
RAISE THE RED LANTERN '91 ****	Gong Li

```
RAISE THE TITANIC              Clive Cussler
RAISIN IN THE SUN, A '61****   Sidney Poitier, Ruby Dee
RAISIN' HELL                   D.M.C Run mr
RAISING ARIZONA '87            Nicolas Cage
RAISING THE WIND '61           James Robertson Justice
RAJ QUARTET, THE               Paul Scott
RAKE'S PROGRESS, THE           William P. Hogarth
RAMBLIN' MAN                   Alman Brothers mr
RAMBO                          Sylvester Stallone
RAMONA                         Helen Hunt Jackson
RAMONA '36                     Loretta Young
RAMPAGE '63                    Robert Mitchum
RAMPLING, ANNE                 Anne Rice
RAMROD '47                     Veronica Lake
RAN '85                        Akiro Kurosawa d
RANCHO NOTORIOUS '52           Marlene Dietrich
RANGE RIDER, THE tv            Jock Mahoney
RANSOM '56                     Donna Reed
RANSOM '77                     Oliver Reed
RANSOM '96                     Mel Gibson
RAPE OF THE LOCK, THE          Alezander Pope
RAPTURE '65                    Melvyn Douglas
RAPTURE, THE '91               Mimi Rogers
RASCAL '69                     Steve Forrest
RASHOMON '50 ****              Toshiro Mifune
RAT PATROL, THE tv             Christopher George
RATIONING '44                  Wallace Beery
RATSO                          Dustin Hoffman
RAVEN, THE '35                 Boris Karloff
RAVEN, THE '63                 Vincent Price
RAWHIDE '51                    Tyrone Power
RAWHIDE tv                     Clint Eastwood
RAY, CARLOS                    Chuck Norris
RAZOR'S EDGE, THE              W. Somerset Maugham
REACH FOR THE SKY '56          Kenneth More
REAL MCCOYS, THE tv            Walter Brennan, Richard Crenna
REAP THE WILD WIND '42         Ray Milland
REAR WINDOW '54 ****           Grace Kelly, James Stewart
REASONABLE DOUBTS tv           Marlee Matlin
REBECCA                        Daphne du Maurier
REBECCA '40 ****               Laurence Olivier
REBEL                          James Dean
REBEL WITHOUT A CAUSE'55****   James Dean, Natalie Wood
REBEL, THE tv                  Nick Adams
RECKLESS '84                   Aidan Quinn
RECKLESS '95                   Mia Farrow
RECKLESS MOMENT, THE '49       Joan Bennett, James Mason
RECKONING, THE '69            Nicol Williamson
RED BALL EXPRESS '52           Jeff Chandler
RED MILL, THE                  Victor Herbert
RED RIVER '48 ****             John Wayne, Montgomery Clift
RED RUBBER BALL                Cyrkle
RED SHOES, THE '48 ****        Moira Shearer,Emeric Pressburger
RED SKY AT MORNING '70         Richard Thomas
RED STORM RISING               Tom Clancy
RED-HEADED WOMAN '32           Jean Harlow
REDS '81                       Diane Keaton, Warren Beatty
REF, THE '93                   Judy Davis
REFLECTING SKIN, THE '90       Viggo Mortensen
REFLECTIONS ON VIOLENCE        Georges Sorel
REFUGEE                        Tom Petty & the Heartbreakers mr
```

REIVERS, THE '69	Steve McQueen
RELENTLESS '48	Robert Young
RELUCTANT SAINT, THE '62	Maxmilian Schell
RELUCTANT SPY, THE '63	Jean Marais
REMAINS OF THE DAY, THE '93	Anthony Hopkins, Emma Thompson
REMAINS TO BE SEEN '53	June Allyson, Van Johnson
REMBRANDT '36	Charles Laughton
REMBRANDT p	Harmenszoon van Rijn
REMEMBER MY NAME '78	Geraldine Chaplin
REMEMBER THE DAY '41	Claudette Colbert
REMINGTON STEELE tv	Pierce Brosnan, Stephanie Zimbalist
RENAISSANCE MAN '94	Danny DeVito
RENAULT, MARY	Mary Challans
RENDEZ-VOUS '85	Juliette Binoche
RENEGADES '46	Evelyn Keyes
REPRISAL! '56	Guy Madison
REPTILE, THE '66	Noel Willman
REPULSION '65 ****	Catherine Deneuve, Ian Hendry
REQUIEM	Giuseppe Verdi
RESCUERS, THE '77	John Lounsbery
RESPECT	Aretha Franklin mr
RESTORATION '95	Robert Downey Jr.
RESURRECTION SYMPH.	Gustav Mahler
RESURRECTION '80	Ellen Burstyn
RETURN OF THE JEDI '83	Mark Hamill
REUNION '89	Jason Robards
REUNION IN VIENNA '33	John Barrymore
REVOLUTIONARY, THE '70	Jon Voight
REWARD, THE '65	Max von Sydow
RHAPSODY '54	Elizabeth Taylor
RHAPSODY IN BLUE	George Gershwin
RHAPSODY IN BLUE '45	Robert Alda
RHINO! '64	Robert Culp
RHINOCEROS	Eugene Ionesco
RHODA tv	Valerie Harper
RHUBARB '51	Jan Sterling
RHYTHM NATION	Janet Jackson mr
RICH MAN, POOR MAN	Irwin Shaw
RICHARDSON, HENRY HANDEL	Ethel Richardson
RICOCHET ROMANCE '54	Marjorie Main
RIDE THE HIGH COUNTRY '62 ****	Randolph Scott, Joel McCrea
RIDE THE WILD SURF '64	Fabian
RIDER ON THE RAIN '70	Charles Bronson
RIDICULE '96	Charles Berling
RIFFRAFF '35	Jean Harlow
RIFFRAFF '47	Pat O'Brien
RIFIFI '54 ****	Jean Servais, Carl Mohner
RIGHT HAND MAN, THE '87	Rupert Everett
RIGHT STUFF, THE	Tom Wolfe
RIGOLETTO	Giuseppe Verdi
RIKKI DON'T LOSE THAT NUMBER	Dan Steely mr
RIKKI-TIKKI-TAVI	Rudyard Kipling
RIMA	Audrey Hepburn
RING, THE '27	Carl Brisson
RING, THE '52	Gerald Mohr
RINGER, THE '52	Herbert Lom
RINGO	Lorne Greene
RIOT '69	Gene Hackman
RIPPLING RHYTHYM	Shep Fields c
RIPTIDE '34	Norma Shearer
RISK, THE '60	Tony Britton

RITE OF SPRING, THE	Igor Stravinsky
RITZ, THE '76	Rita Moreno, Jack Weston
RIVALS '72	Robert Klein
RIVER OF NO RETURN '54	Robert Mitchum, Marilyn Monroe
RIVER, THE '51 ****	Patricia Walters, Nora Swinburn
RIVER, THE '84	Sissy Spacek
ROAD NOT TAKEN, THE	Robert Frost
ROAD TO DENVER, THE '55	John Payne
ROAD TO GLORY, THE '36	Fredric March
ROAD TO HONG KONG, THE '62	Bob Hope
ROAD TO SINGAPORE '40	Bing Crosby, Bob Hope
ROAD TO YESTERDAY, THE '25	Joseph Schildkraut
ROAD TO ZANZIBAR '41	Bing Crosby, Bob Hope
ROADBLOCK '51	Charles McGraw
ROADGAMES '81	Stacy Keach
ROARING TWENTIES, THE '39	James Cagney
ROARING TWENTIES, THE tv	Rex Reason
ROB ROY	Sir Walter Scott
ROBBERY '67	Stanley Baker
ROBE, THE '53	Richard Burton
ROBERT ET ROBERT '78	Charles Denner, Jacques Villeret
ROBERTA	Jerome Kern
ROBERTA '35	Irene Dunne
ROBIN AND MARIAN '76	Sean Connery
ROBINSON CRUSOE	Daniel Defoe
ROBINSON, RAY CHARLES	Ray Charles
ROBOCOP '87	Peter Weller
ROC	Charles Dutton
ROCAMBOLE '62	Channing Pollock
ROCK AND ROLL ALL NIGHT	Kiss mr
ROCK AROUND THE CLOCK	Bill Haley and the Comets mr
ROCK, THE '96	Sean Connery
ROCKET GIBRALTAR '88	Burt Lancaster
ROCKETEER, THE '91	Bill Campbell
ROCKFORD FILES, THE tv	James Garner
ROCKIN' ROBBIN	Bobby Day
ROCKY '76	Sylvester Stallone, Talia Shire
ROCKY KING, INSIDE DETECTIVE tv	Roscoe Karns
ROCKY MOUNTAIN HIGH	John Denver
RODAN '56	Kenji Sahara
RODEO	Agnes DeMille ba
ROLLERBALL '75	James Caan
ROLLIN' STONE	Muddy Waters mr
ROMAINS, JULES	Louis Farigoule
ROMEO AND JULIET '36	Norma Shearer
ROMEO AND JULIET '54	Laurence Harvey
ROMEO AND JULIET '66	Margot Fonteyn
ROMEO AND JULIET '68	Olivia Hussey
ROMEO IS BLEEDING '94	Guy Oldman, Lena Olin
ROMERO '89	Raul Julia
ROOKIE OF THE YEAR '93	Gary Busey
ROOKIES, THE tv	Georg Stanford Brown
ROOM 222 tv	Lloyd Haynes
ROOM AT THE TOP	John Braine
ROOM AT THE TOP '59 ****	Laurence Harvey, Simone Signoret
ROOM FOR ONE MORE '52	Cary Grant
ROOM OF ONE'S OWN	Virginia Woolf
ROOM WITH A VIEW, A	E.M. Forster
ROOM WITH A VIEW, A '86	Maggie Smith
ROONEY '58	John Gregson
ROOSTER COGBURN '75	Katharine Hepburn, John Wayne

ROOTS	Alex Haley w
ROOTS tv	Ed Asner, Lloyd Bridges & others
ROOTS tv	LeVar Burton, John Amos
ROPE '48	Alfred Hitchcock d,James Stewart
ROSE MARIE	Rudolf Friml
ROSE TATOO, THE	Tennessee Williams
ROSE, THE '79	Bette Midler, Alan Bates
ROSEANNE tv	Roseanne Arnold, John Goodman
ROSELAND '77	Teresa Wright
ROSEMARY '58	Nadja Tiller
ROSEMARY'S BABY '68 ****	Mia Farrow, John Cassavetes
ROSENBAUM, BORGE	Victor Borge
ROSENBERG, LEONARD	Tony Randall
ROSENBERG, LEV SAMOYLOVICH	Leon Bakst
ROSENTHAL, LYOVA	Lee Grant
ROSIE O'NEILL	Sharon Gless
ROSIE! '67	Rosalind Russell
ROSS, JOHN	Kenneth Millar
ROSS, LEONARD Q.	Leo Calvin Rosten
ROTTEN TO THE CORE '65	Anton Rodgers
ROUGHING IT	Mark Twain
ROUGHLY SPEAKING '45	Rosalind Russell
ROUGHSHOD '49	Robert Sterling
ROUNDERS, THE '65	Glenn Ford
ROUSTABOUT '64	Elvis Presley
ROUTE 66 tv	Martin Milner
ROWDYMAN, THE '71	Gordon Pinsent
ROXANNE '87	Steve Martin
ROY "MAD DOG" EARLE	Humphrey Bogart
RUBENFELD, PAUL	Pee-Wee Herman
RUBY '77	Piper Laurie
RUBY '92	Danny Aiello, Sherilyn Fenn
RUBY IN PARADISE '93	Ashley Judd
RUDY '93	Sean Astin
RUGGLES OF RED GAP '35 ****	Charles Laughton, Mary Boland
RULE BRITANNIA	Thomas A. Arne
RULERS OF THE SEA '39	Douglas Fairbanks Jr.
RULES OF THE GAME '39 ****	Marcel Dalio, Jean Renoir d+
RULING VOICE, THE '31	Walter Huston
RUMOURS	Fleetwood Mac mr
RUN '90	Patrick Dempsey
RUNAWAY	Del Shannon mr
RUNAWAY, RUNAWAY '71	William Smith
RUNNING ON EMPTY '88	Christine Lahti
RUSSIAN ROULETTE '75	George Segal
RUTHLESS '48	Zachary Scott
RUTHLESS FOUR, THE '68	Van Heflin
RUTHLESS PEOPLE '86	Danny DeVito
RYAN, JOHN JOSEPH	Jack Lord
RYTHM NATION	Janet Jackson mr
'S WONDERFUL	George Gershwin
S.O.B. '81	Willaim Holden, Robert Prestonm
SA'DI	Musharrif-uddin
SABOTAGE '36	Sylvia Sidney,Alfred Hitchcock d
SABOTEUR '42	Robert Cummings
SABRE DANCE	Aram Khachaturian
SABRINA '54	Humphrey Bogart
SABRINA '95	Harrison Ford
SAD SACK, THE	George Baker
SAD SONG	Elton John mr

SADE, MARQUIS de	Donatien Alphonse Francois, comte de Sade
SADIST, THE '63	Arch Hall Jr.
SAFARI '56	Victor Mature
SAFE '95	Julianne Moore
SAFECRACKER, THE '58	Ray Milland
SAGAN, FRANCOISE	Francoise Quoirez
SAHARA	Clive Cussler
SAHARA '43	Humphrey Bogart
SAILOR OF THE KING '53	Jeffrey Hunter
SAINT IN NEW YORK, THE '38	Louis Hayward
SAINT LOUIS BLUES	W.C. Handy mj & c
SAINT TAKES OVER, THE '40	George Sanders
SAINT, THE '97	Val Kilmer
SAINTED SISTERS, THE '48	Veronica Lake
SAKI	Hector Hugu Munro
SALOME	Oscar Wilde
SALOME '53	Rita Hayworth
SALTEN, FELIX	Siegmund Salzmann
SALVADOR '86	James Woods
SAM in Casablanca	Dooley Wilson
SAMSON AND DELILAH	Camile Saint-Seans
SAND PEBBLES, THE '66	Steve McQueen
SANDEL, CORA	Sara Margarethe Fabricius
SANDFORD, JOHN	John Camp
SANDLOT, THE '93	Tom Guiry
SANDPIPER '65	Eliizabeth Taylor
SANDS OF IWO JIMA '49	John Wayne
SANFORD AND SON tv	Redd Foxx
SANFORD, JOHN	Redd Foxx
SANJURO '62	Toshiro Mifune
SANSHO THE BAILIFF '54 ****	Kinuyo Tanaka
SANTIAGO 56	Alan Ladd
SAPPHIRE '59	Nigel Patrick
SARABAND '48	Stewart Granger
SARAFINA! '92	Whoopi Goldberg
SARATOGA '37	Clark Gable, Jean Harlow
SARGEANT PEPPER'S LONELY HEART CLUB BAND	Beatles mr
SARKISIAN, CHERILYN	Cher
SARTO, ANDREA del p	Andrea Vanucci
SASKATCHEWAN '54	Alan Ladd
SATIN DOLL	Duke Ellington
SATISFACTION	The Rolling Stones mr
SATURDAY IN THE PARK	Chicago mr
SATURDAY NIGHT LIVE tv	Gilda Radner
SATURDAY'S HEROES '37	Van Heflin
SAUL	George Frideric Handel
SAUNDERS, RICHARD	Benjamin Franklin
SAVAGE INNOCENTS, THE '59	Anthony Quinn
SAVAGE, THE '52,	Charlton Heston
SAVANNAH SMILES '82	Mark Miller
SAVE THE CHILDREN '73	Isaac Hayes
SAVE THE LAST DANCE FOR ME	The Drifters mr
SAWDUST AND TINSEL '53 ****	Ake Gronberg
SAY AMEN, SOMEBODY '82 **** (documentary)	George T.Nierenberg d
SAYONARA '57	Marlon Brando, Red Buttons
SCALPHUNTERS, THE '68	Burt Lancaster
SCANDAL '89	John Hurt
SCANDALOUS JOHN '71	Brian Keith
SCANNERS '81	Jennifer O'Neill
SCAPEGOAT, THE '59	Alec Guinness

SCAR, THE '48	Joan Bennett, Paul Henreid
SCARAMOUCHE '52	Stewart Granger
SCARECROW AND MRS. KING tv	Bruce Boxleitner
SCARECROW '73	Gene Hackman
SCARECROW, THE '82	John Carradine
SCARF, THE '51	John Ireland
SCARFACE '32	Paul Muni, Boris Karloff, George Raft
SCARFACE MOB, THE '62	Robert Stack
SCARLET CLAW, THE '44	Basil Rathbone
SCARLET COAT, THE '55	Cornel Wilde
SCARLET EMPRESS, THE '34	Marlene Dietrich
SCARS OF DRACULA '70	Christopher Lee
SCENE OF THE CRIME '86	Catherine Deneuve
SCENES FROM A MALL '91	Woody Allen
SCENES FROM A MARRIAGE '73 ****	Liv Ullmann, Erland Josephson
SCHEHERAZADA	Arabian Nights
SCHEHERAZADE - Op. 35	Nikolai Rimsky-Korsakov
SCHERER, ROY Jr. (later Fitzgerald)	Rock Hudson
SCHINDLER'S LIST '93 ****	Liam Neeson, Ben Kingsley, Steven Spielberg d
SCHLOCK '71	John Landis d+
SCHOOL'S OUT	Alice Cooper mr
SCHRIFT, SHIRLEY	Shelley Winters
SCHWARTZ, BERNARD	Tony Curtis
SCICOLONI, SOPHIA	Sophia Loren
SCOGNAMIGLIO, VINCENT	Vincent Gardenis
SCOOP	Evelyn Waugh
SCORPIO '73	Burt Lancaster
SCOUNDREL, THE '35	Charles MacArthur
SCREAM '96	Neve Campbell
SCREAMERS '95	Peter Weller
SCROOGE '35	Sir Seymour Hicks
SCROOGE '70	Albert Finney
SCUM '79	Phil Daniels
SEA AROUND US, THE	Rachel L. Carson
SEA HAWK, THE '40 ****	Errol Flynn, Claude Rains
SEA WOLF, THE	Jack London
SEA WOLF, THE by Jack London	Capt. Wolf Larsen
SEANCE ON A WET AFTERNOON '64 ****	Richard Attenborough, Kim Stanley
SEARCH, THE '48 ****	Montgomery Clift
SEARCHERS, THE '56 ****	John Wayne, Vera Miles
SEASON OF PASSION '59	Angela Lansbury
SEBASTIAN '68	Dirk Bogarde
SECOND CITY tv	Joe Flaherty
SECOND HONEYMOON '37	Tyrone Power
SECOND WOMAN, THE '51	Robert Young
SECONDS '66	Rock Hudson
SECRET AGENT, THE	Joseph Conrad
SECRET BRIDE, THE '35	Barbara Stanwyck
SECRET CEREMONY '68	Elizabeth Taylor
SECRET GARDEN, THE '49	Margaret O'Brien
SECRET HEART, THE '46	Claudette Colbert
SECRET INVASION, THE '64	Stewart Granger, Mickey Rooney
SECRETS OF WOMEN '52	Ingmar Bergman d
SEDUCTION OF MIMI, THE '72	Giancarlo Giannini
SEEKERS, THE '54	Jack Hawkins
SEFERIS, GEORGE	Georgios Seferiadis
SEGAL, ROBERT	Robby Benson
SEGHERS, ANNA	Netty Radvanyi
SEINFELD tv	Jason Alexander

SEKULOVICH, MALDEN	Karl Malden
SELENA '97	Jennifer Lopez
SELLOUT, THE '52	Walter Pidgeon
SEMI-TOUGH '77	Burt Reynolds
SEMINOLE '53	Rock Hudson
SEMPRE LIBERA(La Traviata)	Giuseppe Verdi
SENDER, THE '82	Kathryn Harrold
SENSATIONS '44	Eleanor Powell
SENSO '54	Alida Valli
SENTA	Richard Wagner
SENTIMENTAL JOURNEY, A	Laurence Sterne
SEPARATE TABLES '58 ****	Burt Lancaster, David Niven
SEPTEMBER AFFAIR '50	Joseph Cotten
SEQUOIA '34	Jean Parker
SERENA '62	Patrick Holt
SERENADE '56	Mario Lanza
SERGEANT PRESTON OF THE YUKON tv Richard Simmons	
SERIAL '80	Martin Mull
SERPICO	Peter Maas
SERPICO '73	Al Pacino
SERVANT, THE '63	Dirk Bogarde
SET-UP, THE '49	Robert Ryan
SEUSS, DR.	Theodor Geisel
SEVEN AGAINST THEBES	Aeschylus w
SEVEN BEAUTIES '76 ****	Giancarlo Giannini
SEVEN BRIDES FOR SEVEN BROTHERS '54 **** Howard Keel, Jane Powell	
SEVEN DAYS IN MAY '64	Burt Lancaster
SEVEN DAYS LEAVE '42	Lucille Ball
SEVEN DAYS TO NOON '50 ****	Barry Jones
SEVEN GOLDEN MEN '65	Rossana Podesta
SEVEN KEYS TO BALDPATE	George M. Cohan
SEVEN LITTLE FOYS, THE '55	Bob Hope
SEVEN MEN FROM NOW '56	Randolph Scott
SEVEN SAMURAI, THE '54 ****	Toshiro Mifune
SEVEN-UPS, THE '73	Roy Scheider
SEVENTEEN '40	Jackie Cooper
SEVENTH CAVALRY '56	Randolph Scott
SEVENTH CROSS, THE '44	Spencer Tracy
SEVENTH SEAL, THE '57 ****	Max von Sydow, Ingmar Bergman d
SEVENTH VEIL, THE '45	James Mason
SEVENTY-SIX TROMBONES in The Music Man Robert Preston	
SHADEY '85	Billy Whitelaw
SHADOW IN THE SKY '51	Ralph Meeker
SHADOW OF A DOUBT '43	Joseph Cotten, Teresa Wright
SHADOW ON THE WALL '50	Ann Sothern
SHADOWLANDS '85	Joss Ackland, Claire Bloom
SHADOWLANDS '93	Anthony Hopkins
SHADOWS '60	Hugh Hurd
SHAFT '71	Richard Roundtree
SHAFT'S BIG SCORE '72	Richard Roundtree
SHAG '89	Phoebe Cates
SHAKE IT UP	The Cars mr
SHAKE, RATTLE AND ROLL	Big Joe Turner mr
SHAKEDOWN '50	Howard Duff
SHAKEDOWN '88	Peter Weller
SHALHOUB, MICHAEL	Omar Sharif
SHALOM ALEICHEM	Solomon J. Rafinowitz
SHAME, THE '68 ****	Liv Ullmann, Max von Sydow
SHAMPOO '75	Warren Beatty, Julie Christie
SHAMUS '73	Burt Reynolds

SHANE '53 ****	Alan Ladd, Jean Arthur
SHANGHAI EXPRESS '32	Marlene Dietrich
SHANKS '74	Marcel Marceau
SHATTERED '91	Tom Berenger
SHAW, HENRY WHEELER	Josh Billings w
SHCHEDRIN	Mikhail Yegrafovich Saltykov
SHE	Henry Haggard(Sir)
SHE	Ursula Andress
SHE '21	Betty Blythe
SHE DONE HIM WRONG '33 ****	Mae West, Cary Grant
SHE WORKS HARD FOR THE MONEY	Donna Summer mr
SHE'S A WOMAN	Beatles
SHE'S GOTTA HAVE IT '86	Tracy Camilla Johns
SHE'S HAVING A BABY '88	Elizabeth McGovern
SHE'S NOT HERE	The Zombies mr
SHEEPMAN, THE '58	Glenn Ford
SHELTERING SKY, THE	Paul Bowles
SHENANDOAH '65	James Stewart
SHERIFF OF COCHISE, THE tv	John Bromfield
SHERLOCK HOLMES	Basil Rathbone
SHERLOCK HOLMES '32	Clive Brook
SHERLOCK, JR. '24 ****	Buster Keaton d+
SHERMAN'S MARCH '86 ****(documentary)	Ross McElwee d
SHERRY	The Four Seasons mr
SHIEK, THE '21	Rudolph Valentino
SHIELD FOR MURDER '54	Edmond O'Brien d+
SHIELDS, WILLIAM JOSEPH	Barry Fitzgerald
SHINE '96	Geoffrey Rush o-a
SHINING HOUR, THE '38	Joan Crawford
SHINING STAR	Earth, Wind and Fire mr
SHINING THROUGH '92	Michael Douglas
SHINING VICTORY '41	James Stephenson
SHIP OF FOOLS '65 ****	Vivien Leigh, Oskar Werner
SHIPS WITH WINGS '42	John Clements
SHIPWRECKED '90	Gabriel Byrne
SHIRALEE, THE '57	Peter Finch
SHOAH '85 ****(documentary)	Claude Lanzmann d
SHOCK, THE '23	Lon Chaney Sr.
SHOCKPROOF '49	Cornel Wilde
SHOE	Jeff MacNelly cr
SHOESHINE '46 ****	Vittorio De Sica d
SHOGUN	James Clavell
SHOOT THE PIANO PLAYER '60****	Charles Aznavour,Marie Dubois
SHOOTING, THE '67	Millie Perkins
SHOOTIST, THE '76	John Wayne, Lauren Bacall
SHORT CUT TO HELL '57	James Cagney d
SHOT IN THE DARK, A '64 ****	Peter Sellers, Elke Sommer
SHOT, THE '96	Dan Bell
SHOTGUN SLADE tv	Scott Brady
SHOUT AT THE DEVIL '76	Lee Marvin
SHOUT, THE '78	Alan Bates
SHOW BOAT	Edna Ferber
SHOW THEM NO MERCY! '35	Rochelle Hudson
SHOW-OFF, THE '46	Red Skelton
SHOWBOAT	Jerome Kern
SHRIKE, THE '55	June Allyson
SHUTE, NEVIL	Nevil Shute Norway
SICILIAN CLAN, THE '69	Jean Gabin
SIDDHARTHA	Herman Hesse
SIDDHARTHA '73	Shashi Kapoor
SIDEWALK STORIES '89	Charles Lane d+

SIEGE AT RED RIVER, THE '54	Van Johnson
SIEGFRIED	Richard Wagner
SIERRA '50	Audie Murphy
SIGN OF THE CROSS, THE '32	Fredric March
SIGN OF THE PAGAN '54	Jeff Chandler
SILAS MARNER	George Eliot
SILBERMAN, JEROME	Gene Wilder
SILENCE '74	Will & Ellen Geer
SILENCE, THE '63	Ingrid Thulin
SILENCERS, THE '66	Dean Martin
SILENT ASSASSINS '88	Scott Thomas
SILENT ENEMY, THE '58	Laurence Harvey
SILENT WORLD, THE '56	Jacques-Yves Cousteau d+
SILK STALKINGS tv	Rob Estes
SILKEN AFFAIR, THE '57	David Niven
SILKWOOD '83	Meryl Streep, Nola Ephron w
SILVER BOX, THE	John Galsworthy
SILVER SPOONS tv	Ricky Schroder
SILVERADO '85	Kevin Kline
SILVERMAN, BELLE	Beverly Sills
SILVERSMITH, PHILIP	Phil Silvers
SIMBA '55	Dirk Bogarde
SIMON & SIMON tv	Jameson Parker, Gerald McRaney
SIMON '80	Alan Arkin
SIMON LEGREE in Uncle Tom's Cabin	Harriet B. Stowe
SIMON OF THE DESERT '65 ****	Claudio Brook, Silvia Pinal
SIMPLETON OF THE UNEXPECTED ISLES, THE	Geo. Bernard Shaw
SIMPSONS, THE	Matt Groening
SIN OF FATHER MOURET, THE	Emile Zola
SINBAD THE SAILOR '47	Douglas Fairbanks, Jr.
SING YOU SINNERS '38	Bing Crosby
SINGIN' IN THE RAIN '52 ****	Gene Kelly, Debbie Reynolds
SINGING FOOL, THE '28	Al Jolson
SINGLES '92	Bridget Fonda
SINK THE BISMARCK ! '60	Kenneth More
SIR TOBY BELCH	William Shakespeare
SIRENS '94	Hugh Grant
SIROCCO '51	Humphrey Bogart
SISTER CARRIE	Theodore Dreiser
SISTERS '73	Margot Kidder
SISTERS tv	Swoosie Kurtz, Sela Ward
SISTERS, THE '38	Bette Davis, Errol Flynn
SIX DAY BIKE RIDER '34	Joe E. Brown
SIX MILLION DOLLAR MAN, THE tv Lee Majors,	
	"Colonel Steve Austin"
SKAG '79	Karl Malden
SKIDOO '68	Jackie Gleason
SKIKNE, LARUSHKA	Laurence Harvey
SKINNY LEGS AND ALL	Tom Robbins
SKULL, THE '65	Peter Cushing
SKY'S THE LIMIT, THE '43	Fred Astaire
SKYJACKED '72	Charlton Heston
SKYLARK '41	Claudette Colbert
SKYSCRAPER SOULS '32	Warren William
SLANDER '56	Van Johnson
SLAUGHTERHOUSE FIVE	Kurt Vonnegut w
SLAVONIC DANCES	Antonin Dvorak
SLEAZY UNCLE, THE '91	Vittorio Gassman
SLEDGE HAMMER tv	David Rasche
SLEEPER '73	Woody Allen d+, Diane Keaton
SLEEPERS '96	Kevin Bacon, Robert De Niro

SLEEPING CITY, THE '50	Richard Conte
SLEEPWALKERS '92	Brian Krause
SLEEPY TIME GAL	Harry James
SLEUTH '72 ****	Laurence Olivier, Michael Caine
SLIGHTLY SCARLET '56	John Payne
SLIM '37	Henry Fonda
SLIPPERY WHEN WET	Bon Jovi mr
SLITHER '73	James Caan
SLYE , LEONARD	Roy Rogers
SMALL WONDER tv	Dick Christie, Ione Skye
SMILE '75	Bruce Dern
SMILE LIKE YOURS, A '97	Joan Cusack
SMILES OF A SUMMER NIGHT'55 **** Ulla Jacobsson,Eva Dahlbeck	
SMILEY '56	Ralph Richardson
SMILEY'S PEOPLE	John Le Carre
SMITH! '69	Glenn Ford
SMITH, FRANCES	Dale Evans
SMITH, GLADYS	Mary Pickford
SMITH, ROSAMOND	Joyce Carol Oates
SMITH, STEVIE	Florence Margaret Smith
SMITH, SUSAN	Susan Dey
SMITHEREENS '82	Susan Berman
SMOKE '70	Earl Holliman
SMOKE '95	William Hurt
SMOKE AND STEEL	Carl Sandberg
SMOKE GETS IN YOUR EYES	Jerome Kern
SMOKE GETS IN YOUR EYES	The Platters mj s
SMOKEY STOVER	Bill Holman
SMOKY '46	Anne Baxter, Fred MacMurray
SNAPPER, THE '93	Colm Meaney
SNEAKERS '92	Robert Redford
SNIPER, THE '52	Adolphe Menjou
SNORKEL, THE '58	Peter Van Eyck
SNOW GOOSE	Paul Gallico
SNOW WHITE AND THE SEVEN DWARFS'37**** Ben Sharpsteen d	
SO BIG	Edna Ferber
SO DARK THE NIGHT '46	Steve(n) Geray
SO DEAR TO MY HEART '49	Burl Ives
SO ENDS OUR NIGHT '41	Fredric March
SO LONG AT THE FAIR '50	Jean Simmons
SO PROUDLY WE HAIL! '43	Claudette Colbert
SO THIS IS NEW YORK '48	Henry Morgan
SOAP tv	Billy Crystal, Robert Mandan
SOFIE '92	Karen-Lise Mynster
SOLDIER BOY	The Shirellas mr
SOLDIER OF ORANGE '79	Rutger Hauer
SOLDIER'S STORY, A '84	Howard E. Rollins Jr.
SOLOMON AND SHEBA '59	Yul Brynner
SOMBRERO '53	Ricardo Montalban
SOME CAME RUNNING	James Jones
SOME CAME RUNNING '58	Frank Sinatra
SOME IRISH LOVING	Edna O'Brien
SOME LIKE IT HOT '59 ****	Jack Lemmon, Tony Curtis
SOMMERSBY '93	Richard Gere
SONG OF BERNADETTE, THE '43 **** Jennifer Jones,William Eythe	
SONG OF MYSELF	Walt Whitman
SONG TO REMEMBER, A '45	Cornel Wilde
SONGWRITER '84	Willie Nelson,Kris Kristofferson
SONS	Pearl Buck
SONS AND LOVERS	D.H. Lawrence
SONS OF THE DESERT '33	Stan Laurel, Oliver Hardy

SOOKY '31	Jackie Cooper
SOPHIE'S CHOICE	William Styron
SORCERER '77	Roy Scheider
SORCERERS, THE '67	Boris Karloff
SORROW AND THE PITY, THE '70****(documentary) Marcel Ophuls d	
SORROWFUL JONES '49	Bob Hope
SOSARME	George Frideric Handel
SOUL MAN	Sam and Dave mr
SOUND AND THE FURY, THE	William Faulkner
SOUND AND THE FURY, THE '59	Yul Brynner
SOUND OF FURY, THE '51	Frank Lovejoy
SOUND OF MUSIC, THE '65	Julie Andrews
SOUNDER '72 ****	Cicely Tyson, Martin Ritt d
SOUTH OF ST. LOUIS '49	Joel McCrea
SOUTH PACIFIC	Mary Martin, Ezio Pinza
SOUTHERN STAR, THE '69	George Segal
SOUTHERN YANKEE, A '48	Red Skelton
SOUTHERNER, THE '45 ****	Zachary Scott
SPACEBALLS '87	Mel Brooks d+
SPADE in Maltese Falcon '41	Humphrey Bogart
SPANISH GARDENER, THE '56	Dirk Bogarde
SPANISH MAIN, THE '45	Paul Henreid
SPANISH TRAGEDY, THE	Thomas Kyd
SPARKLE '76	Philip M.(Michael) Thomas
SPARROWS '26	Mary Pickford
SPARTACUS	Howard Fast
SPARTACUS '60	Kirk Douglas
SPAWN '97	Michael Jai White
SPAWN OF THE NORTH '38	George Raft
SPECIAL DELIVERY '76	Bo Svenson
SPECIAL EFFECTS '84	Zoe Tamerlis
SPEED '94	Kenau Reeves
SPEEDY '28	Harold Lloyd
SPELLBOUND '45	Ingrid Bergman
SPENSER FOR HIRE tv	Robert Urich
SPIDER AND THE FLY, THE '49	Guy Rolfe
SPIDER WOMAN, THE '44	Basil Rathbone, Gale Sondergaard
SPIDER-MAN	Steve Ditko
SPIES '28	Fritz Lang d
SPINNING MULE	Samuel Crompton
SPINNING WHEEL	Blood, Sweat and Tears mr
SPINOUT '66	Elvis Presley
SPIRIT OF ST. LOUIS, THE '57	James Stewart
SPITFIRE '42	Leslie Howard
SPITTELER, CARL	Carl Felis Tandem
SPLASH '84	Daryl Hannah
SPLASH SPLASH	Bobby Darin mr s
SPLENDOR '35	Miriam Hopkins
SPOILED CHILDREN '77	Michel Piccoli
SPOILERS, THE '42	Marlene Dietrich, Randolph Scott
SPOILERS, THE '55	Anne Baxter, Jeff Chandler
SPY IN THE HOUSE OF LOVE, A	Anais Nin
SQUARE JUNGLE, THE '55	Tony Curtis
SQUEAKER, THE '37	Edmund Lowe
SQUEAKER, THE '65	Klaus Kinski
SQUIRM '76	Don Scardino
SSSSSSS '73	Strother Martin
ST. ELSEWHERE tv	Ed Flanders
STAGE DOOR '37 ****	Katharine Hepburn, Ginger Rogers
STAGECOACH '39 ****	Claire Trevor, John Wayne
STAGECOACH '66	Ann-Margaret

STAGGER LEE	Lloyd Price mr
STAINER, LESLIE	Leslie Howard
STAIRWAY TO HEAVEN	Led Zeppelin mr
STAIRWAY TO HEAVEN '46 ****	Emeric Pressburger, David Niven
STAKEOUT '87	Richard Dreyfuss
STALAG 17 '53 ****	William Holden, Don Taylor
STALIN, JOSEPH	Josef Visarionovich Dzhugshvili
STAMPEDE '49	Rod Cameron
STAND AND DELIVER '87	Edward James Olmos
STAND BY ME '86	River Phoenix
STAND-IN '37	Leslie Howard
STANDISH, BURT L.	Gilbert Patten
STAR CHAMBER, THE '83	Michael Douglas
STAR TREK tv	William Shatner, Leonard Nimoy
STAR TREK, THE NEXT GENERATION tv	Brent Spiner, Patrick Stewart, Jonathan Frakes
STAR WARS	Han Solo fc
STAR! '68	Julie Andrews
STAR, THE '52	Bette Davis
STARDUST	Hoagy Carmichael
STARDUST '75	David Essex
STARKEY, RICHARD	Ringo Starr
STARLIGHT HOTEL '87	Peter Phelps
STARMAN '84	Jeff Bridges
STARS IN MY CROWN '50	Joel McCrea
STARS LOOK DOWN, THE '39 ****	Michael Redgrave, Margaret Lockwood
STARSKY AND HUTCH tv	Paul Michael Glaser, David Soul
STATE OF THE UNION '48	Spencer Tracy
STATE'S ATTORNEY '32	John Barrymore
STATIC '85	Keith Gordon
STAVISKY '74	Jean-Paul Belmondo
STAYING ALIVE	The Bee Gees mr
STAYING TOGETHER '89	Sean Astin
STEALING BEAUTY '96	Jeremy Irons, Liv Tyler
STEAMBOAT BILL, JR. '28	Buster Keaton
STEAMING '85	Vanessa Redgrave
STEEL '80	Lee Majors
STEEL HELMET, THE '51	Gene Evans
STEEL MAGNOLIAS '89	Sally Field & Dolly Parton
STEELYARD BLUES '73	Jane Fonda
STELLA '50	Ann Sheridan
STENDHAL	Marie Henri Boyle
STEP BY STEP tv	Sasha Mitchell
STEPFATHER '87	Terry O'Quinn
STEPPENWOLF	Hermann Heese
STEPPENWOLF '74	Max von Sydow
STERN, DANIEL	Marie-C. Agoult
STEVE CANYON tv	Dean Fredericks
STEVENS, RUBY	Barbara Stanwyck
STEVENS, YVETTE	Chaka Khan
STEVIE '78	Glenda Jackson
STEWART, JAMES	Stewart Granger
STING	Gordon Matthew Sumner
STING, THE '73	Paul Newman, Robert Redford
STIR '80	Bryan Brown
STIR CRAZY '80	Richard Pryor, Gene Wilder
STOLEN HOURS, THE '63	Susan Hayward
STONE KILLER, THE '73	Charles Bronson
STOOGE, THE '53	Dean Martin, Jerry Lewis
STOOLIE, THE '74	Jackie Mason

STOP MAKING SENSE '84 ****		Jonathan Demme d, David Byrne
STOP! IN THE NAME OF LOVE		The Supremes mr
STOPPELMOOR, CHERYL			Cheryl Ladd
STORM AT DAYBREAK '33		Kay Francis
STORM IN A TEACUP '37			Vivien Leigh
STORM, THE '38				Charles Bickford
STORMY WEATHER				Howard Arlen
STORY OF G.I. JOE, THE '45		Burgess Meredith, Robert Mitchum
STORY OF RUTH, THE '60		Stuart Whitman
STORY OF WOMEN, THE '88		Isabelle Huppert
STORY ON PAGE ONE, THE '59		Rita Hayworth
STOWAWAY '36				Robert Young
STRAIGHT DOPE, THE			Cecil Adams
STRAIT-JACKET '64			Joan Crawford
STRANGE BARGAIN '49			Martha Scott
STRANGE FRUIT				Billie Holiday mj
STRANGE INTERLUDE			Eugene O'Neill
STRANGE INVADERS '83			Paul LeMat
STRANGER AMONG US, A '92		Melanie Griffith
STRANGER, THE				Albert Camus
STRANGER, THE '46			Orson Welles d+
STRANGER, THE '67			Marcello Mastroianni
STRANGER, THE '87			Bonnie Bedelia
STRANGERS '53				Ingrid Bergman
STRANGERS ON A TRAIN '51****	Farley Granger,Alfred Hitchcock d
STRANGLER, THE '64			Victor Buono
STRAPLESS '89				Blair Brown
STRAY DOG '49 ****			Toshiro Mifune
STREAMERS '83				Matthew Modine
STREET OF CHANCE '42			Burgess Meredith
STREET SCENE				Elmer Rice
STREET, THE tv				Bruce McVittie
STREETCAR NAMED DESIRE, A '51 **** Marlon Brando,Vivien Leigh
STREETS '90				Christina Applegate
STREETS OF SAN FRANCISCO, THE tv Karl Malden
STRIKE UP THE BAND '40		Mickey Rooney
STRIKEBOUND '83				Chris Haywood
STRIPES '81				Bill Murray
STRIPPED TO KILL '87			Kay Lenz
STRIPPER, THE '63			Joanne Woodward
STUDENT PRINCE IN OLD HEIDELBERG, THE '27**** Ramon Novarro
STUDENT TEACHERS, THE '73		Susan Damante
STUDS LONIGAN TRILOGY, THE		James T. Farrel
STUDY IN SCARLET, A '33		Reginald Owen
STUFF, THE '85				Danny Aiello, Michael Moriarty
STUNT MAN, THE '80 ****		Peter O'Toole, Steve Railsback
STUNTS '77				Robert Forster
STUPID CUPID				Connie Francis
SUBJECT WAS ROSES			Frank Gilroy
SUBJECT WAS ROSES, THE '68		Patricia Neal
SUBMARINE PATROL '38			Richard Greene
SUBTERRANEANS, THE '60		Leslie Caron
SUCCESS, THE '63			Vittorio Gassman
SUCH GOOD FRIENDS '71			Dyan Cannon
SUDDENLY '54				Sterling Hayden & Frank Sinatra
SUDS '20				Mary Pickford
SUE, EUGENE				Marie Joseph Sue
SUEZ '38				Tyrone Power
SUGARFOOT '51				Randolph Scott
SUITE: JUDY BLUE EYES			Crosby,Stills,Nash and Young mr
SULLIVAN'S EMPIRE '67			Thomas Carr

SULLIVAN'S TRAVELS '41 ****	Joel McCrea, Veronica Lake
SULLIVAN, JOHN	Fred Allen
SULLIVANS, THE '44	Anne Baxter
SULLY PRUDHOMME	Rene Francois Armand Prudhomme
SUMMER AND SMOKE	Tennessee Williams
SUMMER HOUSE, THE '93	Jeanne Moreau
SUMMERTIME	Jazzy Jeff & The Fresh Prince mr
SUMMERTIME '55	Katharine Hepburn
SUMMERTIME BLUES	Eddie Cochran mr
SUMNER, GORDON	Sting
SUN ALSO RISES, THE	Ernest Hemingway
SUN ALSO RISES, THE '57	Tyrone Power
SUN NEVER SETS, THE '39	Douglas Fairbanks Jr.
SUN SHINES BRIGHT, THE '53	Charles Winninger
SUNBURN '79	Farrah Fawcett-Majors
SUNDAY '97 ****	David Suchet, Lisa Harrow
SUNDAY WOMAN, THE '76	Jacqueline Bisset
SUNDOWN '41	Gene Tierney
SUNDOWNERS, THE '60 ****	Deborah Kerr, Robert Mitchum
SUNNY '41	Anna Neagle
SUNRISE '27 ****	George O'Brien, Janet Gaynor
SUNRISE SERANADE	Frankie Carle, Glan Miller
SUNSET BLVD. '50 ****	William Holden, Gloria Swanson
SUNSHINE BOYS, THE '75	Walter Matthau
SUNSHINE OF YOUR LOVE	Cream mr
SUPERCOP '96	Jackie Chan
SUPERFLY '72	Ron O'Neal
SUPERMAN	Jerry Siegel
SUPERMAN '78	Christopher Reeve
SUPERMONEY	Adam Smith
SUPERNATURAL '33	Carole Lombard
SUPINGER, MARY	Mary Beth Hurt
SURFSIDE SIX tv	Van Williams
SURPRISE PACKAGE '60	Yul Brynner
SURRENDER '50	Vera Ralston
SURROGATE, THE '84	Art Hindle
SUSAN SLEPT HERE '54	Dick Powell
SUSPECT '87	Dennis Quaid
SUSPECT, THE '44	Charles Laughton
SUSPICION '41	Cary Grant
SUSPIRIA '77	Jessica Harper
SUTURE '93	David Siegel
SVENGALI '31	John Barrymore
SVENGALI '55	Hildegarde Neff
SWAN LAKE	Pyotr Tchaikovsky
SWAN, THE '25	Adolphe Menjou
SWAN, THE '56	Grace Kelly
SWEATING BULLETS tv	Rob Stewart
SWEEET CHARITY	Gwen Verdon
SWEEPINGS '33	Lionel Barrymore
SWEET AND LOW-DOWN '44	Benny Goodman & band
SWEET DREAMS(ARE MADE OF THIS)	The Eurythmics mr
SWEET EMOTION	Aerosmith mr
SWEET LOVE, BITTER '67	Don Murray
SWEETHEARTS '38	Nelson Eddy, Jeanette MacDonald
SWEPT AWAY---BY AN UNUSUAL--- ETC.'75 ****	Giancarlo Giannini
SWIMMER, THE '68	Burt Lancaster
SWING TIME '36 ****	Fred Astaire, Ginger Rogers
SWINGERS '96	Jon Ferreau
SWITCH tv	Robert Wagner
SWOON '92	Craig Chester

SWORD AND THE ROSE, THE '53	Richard Todd, Glynis Johns
SWORD OF LANCELOT '63	Cornel Wilde d+
SYDENSTRICKER, PEARL	Pearl Buck
SYLVIA '65	Carroll Baker
SYLVIA '85	Eleanor David
SYMPHONIE ESPAGNOLE	Edouard Lalo
SYMPHONIE FANTASTIQUE	Hector Berlioz
SYNANON '65	Chuck Connors
T-MEN '47	Dennis O'Keefe
T.J. HOOKER tv	William Shatner
TABU '31	Anna Chevalier
TAGGART '64	Dan Duryea
TAI-PAN	James Clavell
TAILOR'S MAID, THE '59	Vittorio De Sica
TAKE A LETTER, MARIA	R.B. Greaves m
TALE OF TWO CITIES, A	Charles Dickens w
TALE OF TWO CITIES, A '17	William Farnum
TALE OF TWO CITIES, A '58	Dirk Bogarde
TALE OF TWO CITIES, A'35****	Ronald Colman, Elizabeth Allen
TALES OF HOFFMAN '51	Emeric Pressburger
TALK OF THE TOWN,THE'42 ****	Jean Arthur, Ronald Colman
TALL IN THE SADDLE '44	John Wayne
TALL MAN, THE tv	Clu Gulager
TAMARIND SEED, THE '74	Julie Andrews
TAMPOPO '86	Ken Watanabe
TANGIER '46	Maria Montez
TAP '89	Gregory Hines
TAPESTRY	Carole King mr
TAPS '81	Timothy Hutton
TARANTULA '55	John Agar
TARAWA BEACHHEAD '58	Julie Adams
TARGETS '68	Boris Karloff
TARNISHED ANGELS, THE '58	Rock Hudson, Dorothy Malone
TARPLEY, BRENDA MAE	Brenda Lee
TARZAN	Burne Hogarth
TARZAN FILMS '32 - '48	Johnny Weissmuller
TARZAN FILMS '49 - '53	Lex Barker
TARZAN FINDS A SON! '39	Johnny Weissmuller
TARZAN OF THE APES '18	Elmo Lincoln (1st Tarzan Film)
TARZAN THE APE MAN '32	Johnny Weissmuller
TARZAN TRIUMPHS '43	Johnny Weissmuller
TARZAN tv	Ron Ely
TAXI tv	Danny DeVito, Judd Hirsch
TEA AND SYMPATHY	Robert Anderson
TEA AND SYMPATHY '56	Deborah Kerr
TEARS ON MY PILLOW	Little Anthony & the Imperials mr
TEENAGER IN LOVE, A	Dion and the Belmonts mr
TEJADA, RAQUEL	Raquel Welch
TELEFON '77	Charles Bronson
TEMPERATURES RISING tv	James Whitmore
TEMPEST '28	John Barrymore
TEMPEST '59	Silvana Mangano
TEMPLE HOUSTON tv	Jeffrey Hunter
TEMPTATION '46	Merle Oberon
TEMPTRESS, THE '26	Greta Garbo
TEN	Pearl Jam mr
TEN COMMANDMENTS, THE '23	Theodore Roberts
TEN COMMANDMENTS, THE '56 ****	Charlton Heston, Yul Brynner
TEN FROM YOUR SHOW OF SHOWS '73 ****	Sid Caesar, Imogene Coca
TEN LITTLE INDIANS	Agatha Christie w
TEN NORTH FREDERICK	John O'Hara

TENANT, THE '76	Roman Polanski d+
TENDER IS THE NIGHT	F. Scott Fitzgerald
TENDERFOOT, THE '32	Joe E. Brown
TENNESSEE CHAMP '54	Shelley Winters
TENSION '49	Richard Basehart
TENTH VICTIM, THE '65	Marcello Mastroianni
TEQUILA SUNRISE '88	Mel Gibson, Michelle Pfeiffer
TERMINATOR, THE '84	Arnold Schwarzenegger
TERMS OF ENDEARMENT '83 ****	Shirley MacLaine, Debra Winger
TERROR ON A TRAIN '53	Glenn Ford
TERTZ, ABRAM	Andrey Donatovich Sinyavsky
TESS '80	Nastassia Kinski
TESTAMENT '83	Jane Alexander
TEVYE '39	Maurice Schwartz d+
TEX '82	Matt Dillon
TEXANS, THE '38	Randolph Scott
TEXAS '41	Glenn Ford, William Holden
TEXAS RANGERS, THE '36	Fred MacMurray
TEXASVILLE '90	Jeff Bridges
TEY, JOSEPHINE	Elizabeth Mackintosh
THANET, OCTAVE	Alice French
THANK YOU, JEEVES '36	Arthur Treacher
THANK YOU, MR. MOTO '38	Peter Lorre
THANKS A MILLION '35	Dick Powell
THAT GIRL tv	Marlo Thomas
THAT KIND OF WOMAN '59	Sophia Loren
THAT MAN FROM RIO '64	Jean-Paul Belmondo
THAT NIGHT IN RIO '41	Alice Faye
THAT OLD FEELING '97	Bette Midler
THAT THING YOU DO '96	Tom Hanks d+
THAT TOUCH OF MINK '62	Cary Grant, Doris Day
THAT'LL BE THE DAY	Buddy Holly and the Crickets mr
THAT'LL BE THE DAY '74	David Essex
THAT'S ENTERTAINMENT'74 ****	Fred Astaire, Bing Crosby
THAT'S WHY	Jackie Wilson mr
THEATRE OF BLOOD '73	Vincent Price
THEATRE OF DEATH '67	Christopher Lee
THEE I LOVE	Pat Boone
THEM	Joyce Carol Oates
THEM! '54	Jms. Whitmore,Jms. Arness,Fess Parker
THERE'S A SMALL HOTEL	Richard Rodgers & Lorenz Hart
THESE THREE '36 ****	Miriam Hopkins, Merle Oberon
THEY ALL LAUGHED '81	Audrey Hepburn
THEY DON'T BELIEVE ME	Jerome Kern
THEY GAVE HIM A GUN '37	Spencer Tracy
THEY LIVE BY NIGHT '49	Farley Granger
THEY MET IN BOMBAY '41	Clark Gable, Rosalind Russell
THEY WERE EXPENDABLE'45 ****	Robert Montgomery, John Wayne
THEY WERE SISTERS '45	Phyllis Calvert
THEY WON'T FORGET '37 ****	Claude Rains, Otto Kruger
THIEF '81	James Caan
THIEF OF BAGHDAD,THE'40****	Sabu, June Duprez
THIEF OF PARIS, THE '67	Jean-Paul Belmondo
THIEF, THE '52	Ray Milland
THIEVES' HIGHWAY '49	Richard Conte
THIEVES' HOLIDAY '46	George Sanders
THIMBLE THEATER	Elzie C. Segar
THIN MAN GOES HOME, THE '44	William Powell, Myrna Loy
THIN MAN, THE '34 ****	William Powell, Myrna Loy
THIN MAN, THE '34 + 5 more to'47	William Powell
THIN MAN, THE tv	Peter Lawford

THIN RED LINE, THE '64	Keir Dullea
THING CALLED LOVE, THE '93	River Phoenix
THING, THE '51	James Arness
THINK FAST, MR. MOTO '37	Peter Lorre
THIRD GENERATION, THE '79	Eddie Constantine
THIRD MAN, THE '49 ****	Orson Welles, Carol Reed
THIRD MAN, THE tv	Michaek Rennie
THIRD SECRET, THE '64	Stephen Boyd
THIRST '79	David Hemmings
THIRTEENTH GUEST, THE '32	Ginger Rogers
THIRTY-NINE STEPS, THE '78	Robert Powell
THIRTY-NINE(39) STEPS,THE'35 ****	Robert Donat,
	Madeleine Carroll
THIRTYSOMETHING tv	Ken Olin
THIS EARTH IS MINE '59	Rock Hudson
THIS GUN FOR HIRE '42	Alan Ladd
THIS HAPPY BREED '44	Robert Newton
THIS IS IT	Tommy Dorsey
THIS IS MY AFFAIR '37	Barbara Stanwyck
THIS IS SPINAL TAP '84	Michael McKean
THIS IS THE NIGHT '32	Charlie Ruggles
THIS ISLAND EARTH '54	Jeff Morrow
THIS MAN AND MUSIC	Burgess, Anthony
THIS MAN MUST DIE '70	Michel Duchaussoy
THIS ONE	Paul McCartney
THIS SAVAGE LAND '68	Barry Sullivan
THIS SIDE OF PARADISE	F. Scott Fitzgerald
THIS TIME	Southside Johnny and the Asbury Jukes mr
THORN BIRDS	Megan
THORNBERG, BETTY	Betty Hutton
THOSE CALLOWAYS '65	Brian Keith
THOU SWELL	Richard Rodgers c,
	Lorenz Hart -- lyrics
THOUSAND ACRES, A '97	Jessica Lange, Michelle Pfeiffer
THOUSAND CLOWNS, A '65	Jason Robards
THOUSANDS CHEER '43	Mickey Rooney
THREAT, THE '49	Charles McGraw
THREE BLIND MICE '38	Loretta Young
THREE FACES OF EVE, THE '57	Joanne Woodward, David Wayne
THREE FACES WEST '40	John Wayne
THREE FUGITIVES '89	Nick Nolte
THREE GODFATHERS '36	Chester Morris
THREE IN THE ATTIC '68	Christopher Jones
THREE IS A FAMILY '44	Fay Bainter
THREE MUSKETEERS, THE	Alexandre Dumas
THREE MUSKETEERS, THE '21	Douglas Fairbanks Sr
THREE MUSKETEERS, THE '48	Gene Kelly
THREE MUSKETEERS, THE '74	Oliver Reed, Richard Chamberlain
THREE MUSKETEERS, THE '93	Charlie Sheen
THREE PLACES IN NEW ENGLAND	Charles Ives
THREE SISTERS '70 ****	Laurence Olivier d+, Joan Plowright
THREE SISTERS, THE	Anton P. Chekov
THREE SISTERS, THE '66	Kim Stanley
THREE SMART GIRLS '36	Deanna Durbin
THREE STRANGERS '46	Sydney Greenstreet
THREE TALL WOMEN	Edward Albee
THREE THE HARD WAY '74	Jim Brown
THREE TOUGH GUYS '74	Lino Ventura
THREE'S COMPANY tv	Joyce DeWitt,John Ritter,Suzanne Somers
THREEPENNY OPERA, THE '31	Lotte Lenya
THREESOME '94	Lara Flynn Boyle

THRESHOLD '81	Donald Sutherland
THRILL IS GONE, THE	B.B. King mr
THRILL OF BRAZIL, THE '46	Evelyn Keyes
THRILLER	Michael Jackson mr
THRONE OF BLOOD '57 ****	Toshiro Mifune
THUMBELINA '94	Gary Goldman
THUNDER IN THE SUN '59	Susan Hayward
THUNDER OF DRUMS, A '61	George Hamilton
THUNDERBALL '65	Sean Connery
THUNDERBIRDS '52	John Derek
THUNDERHEART '92	Val Kilmer
THURSDAY'S CHILD '43	Sally Ann Howes
TIC TAC DOUGH tv	Jack Barry
TICKET TO HEAVEN '81	Nick Mancuso
TIGER AT THE GATES	Jean Giraudoux
TIGHT LITTLE ISLAND '49 ****	Basil Radford, Joan Greenwood
TIGHTROPE '84	Clint Eastwood
'TIL WE MEET AGAIN '40	Merle Oberon
TILLIE THE TOILER	Russ Westover
TIM '79	Mel Gibson
TIME FOR GREATNESS, A	Herbert Agar
TIME FOR LOVING, A '71	Mel Ferrer
TIME MACHINE, THE '60	Rod Taylor
TIME OUT FOR LOVE '61	Jean Seberg
TIME WITHOUT PITY '56	Michael Redgrave
TIMEBOMB '91	Michael Biehn
TIN CUP '96	Kevin Costner
TIN DRUM, THE	Gunter Grass
TINGLER, THE '59	Vincent Price
TINY ALICE	Edward Albee
TINY BUBBLES	Don Ho
TINY TIM	Charles Dickens
TISH	Mary Roberts Rinehart
TITANIC '53	Clifton Webb
TITIAN	Tiziano Vecelli
TO A LOUSE	Robert Burns
TO A SKYLARK	Percy Bysshe Shelley
TO A WATERFOWL	William Cullen Bryant
TO MARY---WITH LOVE '36	Warner Baxter
TO ROME WITH LOVE tv	John Forsythe
TO TELL THE TRUTH tv	Bud Collyer
TO THE LIGHTHOUSE	Virginia Woolf
TO THE MANOR BORN	Penelope Keith
TOAST OF NEW YORK, THE '37	Edward Arnold, Cary Grant
TOBACCO ROAD	Erskine Caldwell
TOBRUK '67	Rock Hudson
TODAY SHOW	Katie Couric, Bryant Gumbel
TOILERS OF THE SEA	Victor Hugo
TOM JONES	Albert Finney
TOM JONES '63 ****	Albert Finney, Susannah York
TOM THUMB	Henry Fielding
TOM, DICK AND HARRY '41	Ginger Rogers
TOMA tv	Tony Musante
TOMAHAWK '51	Yvonne de Carlo
TOMALING, SUSAN	Susan Sarandon
TOMBSTONE '93	Kurt Russell
TOMKINS, S. YEWELL	Tom Ewell
TOMMY '75	Roger Daltrey
TOMORROW '72.	Robert Duvall
TONKA '58	Sal Mineo
TONO BUNGAY	H. G. Wells

TONTO in The Lone Ranger tv   Jay Silverheels
TONY DRAWS A HORSE '51   Cecil Parker
TOO HOT TO HANDLE '38   Clark Gable, Myrna Loy
TOO LATE FOR TEARS '49   Lizabeth Scott
TOO LATE THE HERO '70   Michael Caine
TOO LATE THE PHALAROPE   Alan Paton
TOO MANY HUSBANDS '40   Jean Arthur
TOO MUCH HARMONY '33   Bing Crosby
TOO YOUNG TO KISS '51   June Allyson
TOONERVILLE FOLKS   Fontaine FoX
TOOTSIE '82 **** Dustin Hoffman, Jessica Lange, Teri Garr
TOP HAT '35 ****   Fred Astaire, Ginger Rogers
TOP SECRET AFFAIR '57   Susan Hayward
TOPKAPI '64   Melina Mercouri
TOPAZ   Leon Uris
TOPAZ '69   John Forsythe, Alfred Hitchcock d
TOPAZE '33   John Barrymore, Myrna Loy
TOPPER '37   Constance Bennett, Cary Grant
TOPPER tv   Anne Jeffreys
TORA! TORA! TORA! '70   Martin Balsam
TORMENT '44   Mai Zetterling
TORN. ELMORE RUAL Jr   Rip Torn
TORRENT, THE '26   Ricardo Cortez
TOTEM AND TABU   Sigmund Freud
TOUCH OF EVIL '58 ****   Charlton Heston, Orson Welles
TOUCH OF LARCENY, A '59   James Mason
TOUCH OF THE POET, A   Eugene O'Neill
TOUR OF DUTY tv   Terence Knox
TOVARICH '37   Charles Boyer, Claudette Colbert
TOWERING INFERNO, THE '74   Steve McQueen
TOWN LIKE ALICE, A   Nevil Shute
TOWN LIKE ALICE, A '56   Virginia McKenna
TOWN WITHOUT PITY '61   Kirk Douglas
TOYS IN THE ATTIC   Lillian Hellman
TOYS IN THE ATTIC '63   Dean Martin
TRACKDOWN '76   Jim Mitchum
TRAGEDY OF PUDD'NHEAD WILSON, THE Mark Twain
TRAIN ROBBERS, THE '73   Ann-Margaret, John Wayne
TRAIN, THE '64 ****   Burt Lancaster, Paul Scofield
TRAINSPOTTING '96   Ewan McGregor
TRAITORS, THE '63   Patrick Allen
TRANCERS '85   Tim Thomerson
TRAP, THE '59   Richard Widmark
TRAP, THE '66   Rita Tushingham
TRAPEZE '56   Burt Lancaster
TRAPPED '49   Lloyd Bridges
TRAPPER JOHN, M.D. tv   Pernell Roberts, Gregory Harrison
TRAUMA '93   Christopher Rydell
TRAVELER '97   Bill Paxton
TRAVELLING NORTH '87   Julia Blake
TRAYWICK, RANDY   Randy Travis
TREASURE ISLAND '34   Wallace Beery
TREASURE ISLAND '50   Bobby Driscoll
TREASURE OF THE SIERRA MADRE,THE'48**** Humphrey Bogart,
                                              Walter Huston
TREASURY MEN IN ACTION tv   Walter Greaza
TREE AT MY WINDOW   Robert Frost
TREE GROWS IN BROOKLYN, A '45 **** Dorothy McGuire,
                                              Joan Blondell
TREES   Joyce Kilmer
TRENT'S LAST CASE '52   Michael Wilding

TRESPASS '92	Bill Paxton
TREVOR, WILLIAM	William Cox
TRIAL '55	Glenn Ford
TRIAL, THE	Franz Kafka
TRIAL, THE '62	Anthony Perkins, Orson Welles d+
TRINITY	Leon Uris
TRIO '50	James Hayter
TRIP TO BOUNTIFUL, THE '85	Geraldine Page
TRISTANA '70	Catherine Deneuve
TRISTRAM SHANDY	Laurence Sterne
TRIUMPH OF THE WILL '35 ****(documentary) Leni Riefenstahl d
TROJAN HORSE, THE '62	Steve Reeves
TROPIC OF CANCER	Henry Miller
TROPIC OF CANCER '70	Rip Torn
TROTSKY, LEON	Lev Davidovich Bronstein
TROUBLE IN PARADISE '32 ****	Miriam Hopkins, Kay Francis
TROUBLE IN STORE '53	Margaret Rutherford
TRU	Robert Morse
TRUCK STOP WOMEN '74	Claudia Jennings
TRUCKIN'	The Grateful Dead mr
TRUE CONFESSIONS '81	Robert De Niro
TRUSCOTT-JONES, REGINALD	Ray Milland
TRUST '91	Adrienne Shelley
TRUTH ABOUT WOMEN, THE '58	Laurence Harvey
TUCK EVERLASTING '80	Margaret Chamberlain
TUGBOAT ANNIE '33	Marie Dressler
TULSA '49	Susan Hayward, Robert Preston
TUMBLEWEEDS	Tom Ryan cr
TUNA-FISHING	Salvadore Dali
TUNE IN TOMORROW . . . '90	Barbara Hershey
TUNES OF GLORY '60 ****	Alec Guinness, John Mills
TUNNEL OF LOVE, THE '58	Gene Kelly
TURANDOT(his last)	Giacomo Puccini
TURN! TURN! TURN!	The Byrds mr Pete Seeger mr
TURNING POINT, THE '52	William Holden, Alexis Smith
TURNING POINT, THE '77	Anne Bancroft, Shirley MacLaine
TUTTI FRUTTI	Little Richard mr
TUTTLES OF TAHITI, THE '42	Charles Laughton
TUVIM, JUDITH	Judy Holliday
TWELVE CHAIRS, THE '70	Ron Moody
TWELVE O'CLOCK HIGH '49 ****	Gregory Peck, Hugh Marllowe
TWELVE O'CLOCK HIGH tv	Robert Lansing
TWELVE(12) ANGRY MEN '57 ****	Henry Fonda, Lee J. Cobb
TWEN. THOU.(20,000) LEAGUES UNDER THE SEA '54**** Kirk Douglas
TWENTIETH CENTURY '34 ****	John Barrymore, Carole Lombard
TWICE-TOLD TALES '63	Vincent Price
TWILIGHT OF HONOR '63	Richard Chamberlain
TWINS '88	Arnold Schwarzenegger
TWIST, THE	Chubby Checker
TWISTER '96	Helen Hunt, Bill Paxton
TWO ENGLISH GIRLS '71	Jean-Pierre Leaud
TWO FOR THE SEESAW 62	Robert Mitchum
TWO RODE TOGETHER '61	James Stewart
TWO WOMEN '61 ****	Sophia Loren, Raf Vallone
TWO YEARS BEFORE THE MAST	Richard H. Dana, Jr.
TWO-LANE BLACKTOP '71	Warren Oates
TWO-MOON JUNCTION '88	Sherilyn Fenn
TYCOON '47	John Wayne
TYPHOON '40	Dorothy Lamour
TZARA, TRISTAN	Samuel Resonfeld
U.S.A.	John Roderigo Dos Passos

U-TURN '97	Sean Penn
UGLY AMERICAN, THE '63	Marlon Brando
UHURU	Robert Ruark
ULLMAN, DOUGLAS	Douglas Fairbanks Sr
ULTIMATE WARRIOR, THE '75	Yul Brynner
ULYSSES	James Joyce
ULYSSES '67	Barbara Jefford
UMBERTO D '52 ****	Vittorio De Sica
UMBRELLAS, THE	Christo at
UN COEUR EN HIVER '92	Daniel Auteuil
UNBORN, THE '91	Brooke Adams
UNCLE REMUS	Joe D. Harris
UNCLE TOM'S CABIN	Harriet Beecher Stowe
UNCLE VANYA	Anton Pavlovich Chekov
UNCONQUERED '47	Gary Cooper
UNDEAD, THE '57	Richard Garland
UNDER SATAN'S SUN '87	Gerard Depardieu
UNDER THE GREENWOOD TREE	Thomas Hardy
UNDER THE NET	Iris Murdoch
UNDER THE RED ROBE '37	Conrad Veidt
UNDER THE VOLCANO	Malcolm Lowry
UNDER THE VOLCANO '84	Albert Finney
UNDERCURRENT '46	Katharine Hepburn
UNDERGROUND '41	Jeffrey Lynn
UNDERNEATH '95	Peter Gallagher
UNDERTOW '49	Scott Brady
UNDERWORLD '85	Denholm Elliott
UNDERWORLD STORY, THE '50	Dan Duryea, Gale Storm
UNDYING MONSTER, THE '42	James Ellison
UNE VIE	Guy DeMaupassant
UNFAITHFUL, THE '47	Ann Sheridan
UNFAITHFULLY YOURS '48 ****	Rex Harrison, Linda Darnell
UNFAITHFULS, THE '60	Mai Britt
UNFINISHED DANCE, THE '47	Margaret O'Brien
UNFINISHED SYMPHONY NO, 8 IN B MINOR	Franz Schubert
UNFORGETTABLE	Nat King Cole
UNFORGETTABLE '96	Ray Liotta
UNFORGIVEN '92	Clint Eastwood d+
UNFORGIVEN, THE '60	Burt Lancaster
UNGUARDED MOMENT '56	Esther Williams
UNHOLY GARDEN, THE '31	Ronald Colman
UNHOLY PARTNERS '41	Edward G. Robinson,Edward Arnold
UNHOLY THREE, THE '25	Lon Chaney
UNHOLY THREE, THE '30	Lon Chaney
UNINVITED '44	Ray Milland
UNKNOWN GUEST, THE '43	Victor Jory
UNMARRIED WOMAN, AN '78 ****	Jill Clayburgh, Alan Bates
UNSTRUNG HEROES '95	John Turturro
UNSUSPECTED, THE '47	Claude Rains
UNTAMED '55	Tyrone Power
UNTAMED FRONTIER '52	Joseph Cotten
UNTIL TOMORROW	Sammy Kaye
UNTOUCHABLES, THE '87 ****	Kevin Costner, Sean Connery
UNTOUCHABLES, THE tv	Robert Stack
UNVANQUISHED, THE	William Faulkner
UP IN MABEL'S ROOM '44	Dennis O'Keefe
UP THE DOWN STAIRCASE	Bel Kaufman
UPPERWORLD '34	Warren William
UPSTAIRS DOWNSTAIRS tv	Jean Marsh
URANUS '91	Philippe Noiret
URIAH HEEP	Charles Dickens

UTOPIA	Thoras More
V.I.P.'S, THE '63	Richard Burton, Elizabeth Taylor
VAGABOND '85	Sandrine Bonnaire
VAGABOND KING, THE	Rudolf Friml
VALDEZ IS COMING '71	Burt Lancaster
VALLEY OF GWANGI '69	James Franciscus
VALLEY OF THE SUN '42	Lucille Ball
VALMONT '89	Colin Firth
VAMPIRE LESTAT, THE	Anne Rice
VAN DINE, S.S.	Willard Wright
VANESSA	Samuel Barber
VANIITY FAIR	William Makepeace Thackeray
VEGAS tv	Robert Urich
VELVET FOG, THE	Mel Torme
VELVET SHOES	Elinor Wylie po
VELVET TOUCH, THE '48	Rosalind Russell
VENUS	Frankie Avalon mr s
VERBOTEN! '59	James Best
VERCORS	Jean Bruller
VERDICT, THE '46	Peter Lorre
VERDICT, THE '82	Paul Newman
VERKLARTE NACHT	Arnold Schoenberg
VERTIGO '58 ****	James Stewart, Alfred Hitchcock d
VERY BRADY SEQUEL, A '96	Shelly Long
VICAR OF WAKEFIELD, THE	Oliver Goldsmith
VICTIM '61	Dirk Bogarde
VICTORS, THE '63	George Hamilton
VICTORY '40	Fredric March
VIGIL '84	Penelope Stewart
VIGIL IN THE NIGHT '40	Carole Lombard
VIGILANTE FORCE '76	Kris Kristofferson
VIKINGS OF HELGOLAND, THE	Henrik Ibsen
VIKINGS, THE '58	Kirk Douglas
VINCENT,FRANCOIS,PAUL AND THE OTHERS'74**** Yves Montand	
VIOLENT ENEMY, THE '68	Tom Bell
VIOLENT SATURDAY '55	Victor Mature
VIOLENT STRANGER '57	Zachary Scott
VIOLETTA in La traviata	Giuseppi Verdi
VIRGIN QUEEN, THE '55	Bette Davis
VIRGIN SOLDIERS, THE '69	Nigel Patrick
VIRGIN SPRING, THE '59	Max von Sydow
VIRGINIAN, THE	Owen Wister
VIRGINIAN, THE '29	Gary Cooper
VIRGINIAN, THE '46	Joel McCrea
VIRGINIAN. THE tv	Lee J. Cobb, James Drury, Clu Gulager
VIRTUOSITY '95	Denzel Washington
VIRUS '80	Sonny Chiba
VISIT TO A SMALL PLANET	Gore Vidal
VISIT, THE '64	Ingrid Bergman
VISITOR IN MARL, A	Emily Dickinson
VISSI D'ARTE	Giacomo Puccini
VIVA ZAPATA! '52 ****	Marlon Brando, Jean Peters
VOICE IN THE WIND '44	Francis Lederer
VOICE OF ISRAEL	Abba Eban
VOLCANO '97	Tommy Lee Jones
VOLPONE '39	Harry Baur
VOLTAIRE	Francois Marie Arouet
VOLTAIRE '33	George Arliss
von KAPPELHOFF, DORIS	Doris Day
VOYAGE TO THE BOTTOM OF THE SEA tv Richard Basehart	
VOYAGER '91	Sam Shepard

WACO '66	Howard Keel
WAGES OF FEAR, THE '52	Yves Montand
WAIKIKI WEDDING '37	Bing Crosby, Martha Raye
WAITING FOR GODOT	Samuel Beckett
WAITING FOR LEFTY	Clifford Odets
WAKE UP LITTLE SUZY	Everly Brothers mr
WALK IN THE CLOUDS, A '95	Keanu Reeves
WALK IN THE SHADOW '66	Patrick McGoohan
WALK LIKE A DRAGON '60	Jack Lord
WALK ON THE WILD SIDE	Lou Reed mr
WALKABOUT '71	Jenny Agutter
WALKER, TEXAS RANGER tv	Chuck Norris
WALKING DEAD, THE '36	Boris Karloff
WALKING HILLS, THE '49	Randolph Scott
WALKING STICK, THE '70	Samantha Eggar
WALL, THE	Pink Floyd mr
WALLFLOWER '48	Joyce Reynolds
WALTONS, THE tv	Will Geer,Michael Learned,Ralph Waite
WANDA '71	Barbara Loden d+
WANDERERS, THE '79	Ken Wahl
WANTED FOR MURDER '46	Eric Portman
WAPSHOT CHRONICLES, THE	John Cheever
WAR AND REMEMBRANCE	Herman Wouk
WAR OF THE WORLDS, THE '53	Gene Barry
WAR REQUIEM, opus 66	Benjamin Britten
WAR SONATAS	Sergey Prokofiev
WARD, ARTEMUS	Charles F. Browne
WARD, MRS. HUMPHRY	Mary Augusta Ward
WARGAMES '83	Matthew Broderick
WARLOCK '59	Richard Widmark
WARLOCK '91	Julian Sands
WARPATH '51	Edmond O'Brien
WARRIORS, THE '55	Errol Flynn
WARRIORS, THE '79	Michael Beck
WASH, THE '88	Mako
WASTE LAND, THE	T.S. Eliot
WATCH ON THE RHINE	Lillian Hellman
WATCH ON THE RHINE '43	Bette Davis, Paul Lukas
WATCH THE BIRDIE '50	Red Skelton
WATER MILL	Jerome Robbins
WATERDANCE, THE '92	Michael Steinberg
WATERFRONT tv	Preston Foster
WATERLAND '92	Jeremy Irons
WATERLILIES	Claude Monet
WATERLOO BRIDGE '40	Vivien Leigh
WATERWORLD '95	Kevin Costner
WATTSTAX '73	Isaac Hayes
WAY OF ALL FLESH, THE	Samuel Butler
WAY OF THE WORLD, THE	William Congreve
WAY TO THE STARS, THE '45 ****	John Mills, Michael Redgrave
WAYNE, DONALD	Don Johnson
WAYS OF LIGHT	Richard Eberhardt
WAYWARD GIRL, THE '59	Liv Ullmann
WE DIDN'T START THE FIRE	Billy Joel mr
WE WERE STRANGERS '49	Jennifer Jones
WE'RE AN AMERICAN BAND	Grand Funk Railroad mr
WE'RE NOT DRESSING '34	Bing Crosby
WE'RE NOT MARRIED '52	Ginger Rogers, Fred Allen
WEAPON, THE '56	Steve Cochran
WEAVERS: WASN'T THAT A TIME!, THE '82 ****	Pete Seeger s+
WEB, THE '47	Ella Rains

WEBB, BRENDA GAYLE	Crystal Gayle
WEBSTER tv	Emmanuel Lewis
WEDDING IN BLOOD '73	Stephane Audran
WEDDING MARCH, THE '28 ****	Erich von Stroheim d+
WEDDING NIGHT, THE '35	Gary Cooper
WEDDING, A '78	Carol Burnett
WEE WILLIE WINKIE '37	Shirley Temple
WEEDS '87	Nick Nolte
WEEK'S VACATION, A '80	Nathalie Baye
WEEKEND '67	Jean Yanne
WEIGHT, THE	The Band mr
WEISENFREUND, MUNI	Paul Muni
WEISS, EHRICH	Harry Houdini
WELCOME BACK KOTTER tv	Gabriel Kaplan
WELCOME STRANGER '47	Bing Crosby
WELCOME TO HARD TIMES	E.L. Doctorow
WELL, THE '51	Harry Morgan, Richard Rober
WELL-TEMPERED CLAVIER, THE	Johann Sebastian Bach
WELLS, JULIA	Julie Andrews
WEREWOLF, THE '56	Steven Ritch
WEST OF ZANZIBAR '28	Lon Chaney Sr.
WEST POINT STORY '50	James Cagney
WEST SIDE STORY '61 ****	Natalie Wood, Rita Moreno
WEST, NATHANAEL	Nathan Weinstein
WESTBOUND '59	Randolph Scott
WESTERNER, THE '40	Gary Cooper
WESTWORLD '73	Richard Benjamin
WETHERBY '85	Vanessa Redgrave
WHALES OF AUGUST, THE '87	Bette Davis, Lillian Gish
WHAT A FOOL BELIEVES	The Doobie Brothers mr
WHAT PRICE GLORY '26	Victor McLaglen
WHAT PRICE GLORY '52	James Cagney
WHAT PRICE MURDER '58	Henri Vidal
WHAT'S HAPPERNING!! tv	Ernest Thomas
WHAT'S LOVE GOT TO DO WITH IT?	Tina Turner
WHAT'S MY LINE tv	John Daly
WHAT? '73	Marcello Mastroianni
WHEEL OF FORTUNE tv	Pat Sajak, Vanna White
WHEELER DEALERS, THE '63	Lee Remick, James Garner
WHEN COMEDY WAS KING '60 ****	Charlie Chaplin plus several
WHEN LADIES MEET '33	Ann Harding
WHEN SHE WAS GOOD	Philip Roth
WHEN WE WERE VERY YOUNG	A. A. Milne
WHERE DID OUR LOVE GO?	The Supremes mr
WHERE EAGLES DARE '69	Richard Burton, Mary Ure
WHERE THE BOYS ARE '60	Dolores Hart
WHERE THERE'S LIFE '47	Bob Hope
WHIPSAW '35	Spencer Tracy
WHIRLPOOL '34	Jack Holt
WHIRLPOOL '49	Gene Tierney
WHIRLYBIRDS, THE tv	Ken Tobey
WHISPERING SMITH '48	Alan Ladd
WHISTLER MOVIES '44 - '47	Richard Dix
WHITE LIGHTNING '73	Burt Reynolds
WHITE LINE FEVER '75	Jan-Michael Vincent
WHITE MAN'S BURDEN '95	John Travolta
WHITE RABBIT	Jefferson Airplane mr
WHITE SHADOW, THE tv	Ken Howard
WHITE SISTER, THE '33	Helen Hayes
WHITEHOUSE YEARS, THE	Henry Kissenger
WHITER SHADE OF PALE, A	Procal Harum mr

```
WHO DO YOU LOVE?                  Bo Diddley mr
WHO WAS THAT LADY? '60           Tony Curtis
WHO'S SORRY NOW                  Connie Francis mj  s
WHO'S THE BOSS? tv              Tony Danza, Judith Light
WHO? '74                         Elliott Gould
WHOLE LOTTA SHAKIN' GOING ON Jerry Lee Lewis mr
WHOOPEE! '30                     Eddie Cantor
WHY DO FOOLS FALL IN LOVE?       Frankie Lymon mr
WICHITA '55                      Joel McCrea
WIDE BLUE ROAD, THE '56         Yves Montand
WIDE IS THE GATE                 Upton Sinclair
WIDE SARGASSO SEA                Jean Rhys
WIFE VS. SECRETARY '36          Clark Gable, Jean Harlow
WIFEMISTRESS '77                 Marcello Mastroianni
WILBY CONSPIRACY, THE '75       Sidney Poitier
WILD BLUE YONDER, THE '51       Wendell Corey
WILD BUNCH, THE '69 ****        William Holden, Ernest Borgnine
WILD COUNTRY, THE '71           Steve Forrest
WILD STRAWBERRIES '57 ****      Ingrid Thulin, Bibi Andersson
WILD WILD WEST, THE tv          Robert Conrad
WILDENVEY, HERMAN                Herman Portaas
WILDROSE '84                     Lisa Eichhorn
WILLIAM TELL                     Giacchino Rossini
WILLIAMS, MYRNA                  Myrna Loy
WILLIAMS, ROBERT                 Robert Guillaume
WILLOW '88                       Val Kilmer
WILSON '44                       Alexander Knox
WILSON in Home Improvement tv Earl Hindman
WIND '92                         Matthew Modine
WIND AND THE LION, THE '75      Sean Connery
WIND, THE '28 ****              Lilian Gish, Lars Hanson
WINDOW, THE '49                  Bobby Driscoll
WINDRIDER '86                    Tom Burlinson
WINDS OF WAR, THE                Herman Wouk
WINDWALKER '80                   Trevor Howard
WINESBURG, OHIO                  Sherwood Anderson
WING AND A PRAYER '44           Don Ameche
WINGS                            Tim Daly
WINGS '27                        Clara Bow
WINGS tv                         Crystal Bernard, Timothy Daly
WINGS OF THE DOVE, THE          Henry James
WINNING '69                      Paul Newman
WINTER CARNIVAL '39             Richard Carlson
WISEGUY tv                       Ken Wahl
WISH YOU WERE HERE               Harold Rome c
WISH YOU WERE HERE '87          Emily Lloyd
WITCHES, THE '90                 Anjelica Huston
WITH THESE HANDS                 Eddie Fisher
WITNESS '85                      Harrison Ford
WITNESS FOR THE PROSECUTION '57 **** Marlene Dietrich,
                                              Tyrone Power
WITNESS TO MURDER '54           Barbara Stanwyck
WIVES AND LOVERS '63            Janet Leigh
WIVES NEVER KNOW '36            Charlie Ruggles
WIZARD OF ID                     Johnny Hart
WIZARD OF OZ, THE '39 ****      Judy Garland, Bert Lahr
WKRP IN CINCINNATI  tv          Loni Anderson, Gordon Jump
WOLF '94                         Jack Nicholson
WOLFEN '81                       Albert Finney
WOLFMAN, THE '41                Lon Chaney, Jr., Bela Lugosi
WOMAN CHASES MAN '37            Miriam Hopkins
```

WOMAN IN FLAMES, A '82	Mathieu Carriere
WOMAN IN GREEN, THE '45	Basil Rathbone
WOMAN IN QUESTION, THE '50	Jean Kent
WOMAN IN WHITE, THE '48	Eleanor Parker
WOMAN IS A WOMAN, A '60	Jean-Paul Belmondo
WOMAN OF AFFAIRS, A '28	Greta Garbo
WOMAN OF THE YEAR '42	Katherine Hepburn
WOMAN TIMES SEVEN '67	Shirley MacLaine
WOMAN'S VENGEANCE, A '47	Ann Blyth, Charles Boyer
WOMEN, THE '39	Joan Crawford
WOMEN IN LOVE	D.H. Lawrence
WONDER WOMAN tv	Lynda Carter, Lyle Waggoner
WONDER YEARS, THE tv	Fred Savage
WONDERFUL WORLD	Herman's Hermits mr
WOODEN HORSE, THE '50	Leo Genn
WOODSTOCK '70 ****	Joan Baez, Richie Havens
WOODWARD, THOMAS	Tom Jones
WOODY WOODPECKER	Walter Lantz
WORD, THE '78	David Janssen
WORKING GIRLS, THE '73	Sarah Kennedy
WORLD ACCORDING TO GARP, THE '82 **** Robin Williams	
WORLD CHANGES, THE '33	Paul Muni
WORLD FOR RANSOM '54	Dan Duryea
WORLD IN HIS ARMS, THE '52	Gregory Peck
WORLD IN MY CORNER '56	Audie Murphy
WORLD MOVES ON, THE '34	Madeleine Carroll
WORLD WITHOUT END '56	Hugh Marlowe
WORLD WITHOUT SUN '64 **** (documentary) Jacques Cousteau d	
WORLD'S END	Upton Sinclair
WOYZECK '78	Klaus Kinski
WUSA '70	Paul Newman, Joanne Woodward
WUTHERING HEIGHTS	Emily Bronte
WUTHERING HEIGHTS '39 ****	Merle Oberon, Laurence Olivier
WYNDHAM, JOHN	John Harris
WYOMING '47	William Elliott
YAKETY YAK	The Coasters mr
YAKHOOB, MUAYAD (later JACOBS, AMOS) Danny Thomas	
YANKEE BUCCANEER '52	Jeff Chandler
YANKS '79	Richard Gere
YASHIN, ALEKSANDR	Aleksandr Yakovlevich Popov
YEAR IN PROVENCE, A	Peter Mayle
YEAR OF THE DRAGON '85	Mickey Rourke
YEAR OF THE HORSE '97	Neil Young
YEARLING, THE '46	Gregory Peck, Clem Bevan
YEARS BETWEEN, THE '46	Michael Redgrave
YEARY, HARVEY LEE 2nd	Lee Majors
YELLOW CAB MAN, THE '50	Red Skelton
YELLOW CANARY, THE '43	Anna Neagle
YELLOW ROSE, THE tv	Sam Elliott, Cybill Shepherd
YELLOW SUBMARINE	Beatles
YELLOW SUBMARINE '68 **** (animated) George Dunning d	
YELLOWSTONE '36	Henry Hunter
YENTL '83	Barbra Streisand d+
YES IT IS	Beatles
YES, I CAN	Sammy Davis
YESTERDAY, TODAY, AND TOMORROW '64 **** Sophia Loren	
YOELSON, ASA	Al Jolson
YOJIMBO '61 ****	Toshiro Mifune
YOU ARE THE SUNSHINE OF MY LIFE Stevie Wonder mr	
YOU CAN'T HURRY LOVE	The Supremes mr

YOU CAN'T TOUCH THIS	M.C. Hammer mr
YOU DON'T HAVE TO SAY YOU LOVE ME	Dusty Springfield mr
YOU MUST BE JOKING! '65	Lionel Jeffries
YOU NEVER CAN TELL '51	Dick Powell
YOU ONLY LIVE ONCE '37	Sylvia Sidney
YOU REALLY GOT ME	The Kinks mr
YOU SEND ME	Sam Cooke mr
YOU'RE A BIG BOY NOW '66	Peter Kastner
YOU'RE NO GOOD	Linda Ronstadt mr+
YOU'RE NOT SO TOUGH '40	Billy Halop
YOU'RE SIXTEEN	Ringo Starr
YOU'RE SO VAIN	Carly Simon mr
YOU'RE TELLING ME '34	W.C. Fields
YOU'VE GOT A FRIEND	James Taylor mr
YOU'VE LOST THAT LOVIN' FEELING	Rightous Brothers mr
YOUNG AND WILLING '43	William Holden
YOUNG BILLY YOUNG '69	Robert Mitchum
YOUNG DILLINGER '65	Nick Adams
YOUNG DOCTORS, THE '61	Fredric March
YOUNG DR. KILDARE '38	Lew Ayres
YOUNG IN HEART, THE '38	Janet Gaynor
YOUNG LIONS, THE	Irwin Shaw
YOUNG MR. LINCOLN '39	Henry Fonda
YOUNG MR. PITT, THE '42	John Mills
YOUNG RIDERS, THE tv	Anthony Zerbe
YOUNG SAVAGES, THE '61	Burt Lancaster
YOUNG TOM EDISON '40	Mickey Rooney
YOUNG WIVES' TALE '51	Joan Greenwood
YOUNGBLOOD HAWKE '64	James Franciscus
YOUNGER BROTHERS, THE '49	Wayne Morris
YOURCENAR, MARGUERITE	Marguerite de Crayencour
YOURS IS NO DISGRACE	Yes mr
YULE, JOE Jr.	Mickey Rooney
ZACHARIAH '71	John Rubinstein
ZARAK '57	Victor Mature
ZARDOZ '74	Sean Connery
ZEB(Grandpa)in The Waltons tv	Will Geer
ZEBRAHEAD '92	Michael Rapaport
ZEIGLER, LARRY	Larry King
ZELIG '83	Woody Allen, Mia Farrow
ZELLE, MARGARETHA	Mara Hari
ZENOBIA '39	Oliver Hardy
ZENTROPA '92	Barbara Sukowa
ZEPPELIN '71	Michael York
ZERO FOR CONDUCT '33 ****	Jean Daste
ZIEGFELD FOLLIES '46	William Powell
ZIGEUNERLIEGE	Franz Lehar
ZIGGY	Tom Wilson
ZIGZAG '70	George Kennedy
ZIMMERMAN, ETHEL	Ethel Merman
ZIMMERMAN, ROBERT	Bob Dylan
ZINA '85	Ian McKellen
ZITA '68	Katina Paxinou
ZORBA	Anthony Quinn
ZORRO '75	Alain Delon
ZORRO tv	Guy Williams
ZUCK, ALEXANDRA	Sandra Dee
ZULEIKA DOBSON	Max Beerbohm
ZULU '64	Michael Caine

UPDATE PAGES

If you find Proper Names not included in this PROPER NAME FINDER and would like to keep the new names for future reference, here is a simple way to record them.

Enter the new Name, Title, Award information, or River information on a numbered line. In the last space on the numbered line, the "WHERE?" column, indicate where in the CROSSWORD PROPER NAME FINDER this entry belongs. Here abbreviations do very well, "MD" may indicate the MAIN DICTIONARY, "PP" the PERSON-PRODUCT and PRODUCT-PERSON sections. "AWD" may signify AWARDS, and "R" mean RIVERS. Note: a new person winning an Award will belong in the AWARD section and MAIN DICTIONARY.

Now in the section where the entry belongs, pencil in the line number between the two printed entries where the new name fits alphabetically.

		WHERE?
1.	*Leer, Leander*	*MD*
2.		
3.		
4.		
5.		
6.		
7.		
8.		
9.		
10.		
11.		
12.		
13.		
14.		
15.		
16.		
17.		

Here is how the entry above will appear in the Main Dictionary:

Leeds,	PETER tv		Leal,	ANTONIO po Port
Leeds,	PHIL tv+		Leaming,	BARBARA bio,w Am
Leek,	TIIU tv	_1_	Lean,	DAVID (Sir) o-d '57
_1_ Leemans,	TUFFY fb hf		Leandro	ALEM st Arg
Leese,	HOWARD mr-kbds,guit Am		Leandro de	MORATIN w Sp
Leeser,	ISAAC r-rabbi Am		Leann	HUNLEY tv
Leeuw,	GERARDUS van der e Dut		LeAnn	RIMES s-cnt Am

WHERE?

18. _____

19. _____

20. _____

21. _____

22. _____

23. _____

24. _____

25. _____

26. _____

27. _____

28. _____

29. _____

30. _____

31. _____

32. _____

33. _____

34. _____

35. _____

36. _____

37. _____

38. _____

39. _____

40. _____

41. _____

42. _____

43. _____

44. _____

45. _____

46. _____

47. _____

48. _____

49. _____

50. _____

51. _____

52. _____

53. _____

54. _____

55. _____

56. _____

57. _____

58. _____

59. _____

60. _____

61._____

62._____

63._____

64._____

65._____

66._____

67._____

68._____

69._____

70._____

71._____

72._____

73._____

74._____

75._____

76._____

77._____

78._____

79._____

80._____

81._____

82._____

83._____

84._____

85._____

86._____

87._____

88._____

89._____

90._____

91._____

92._____

93._____

94._____

95._____

96._____

97._____

98._____

99._____

100._____

101._____

102._____

103._____

-- ----- WHERE?

104._____ | _____
105._____ | _____
106._____ | _____
107. _____ | _____
108._____ | _____
109._____ | _____
110._____ | _____
111._____ | _____
112._____ | _____
113._____ | _____
114._____ | _____
115._____ | _____
116._____ | _____
117._____ | _____
118._____ | _____
119._____ | _____
120._____ | _____
121._____ | _____
122._____ | _____
123._____ | _____
124._____ | _____
125._____ | _____
126._____ | _____
127._____ | _____
128._____ | _____
129._____ | _____
130._____ | _____
131._____ | _____
132._____ | _____
133._____ | _____
134._____ | _____

After filling these four pages with new names, a bound, lined notebook provides an excellent place in which to continue entering new names.

Anticipating revisions of the *Crossword Proper Name Finder* probably at three year intervals, the Publisher, CREATIVE ARTS BOOK COMPANY would greatly appreciate receiving copies of the words you have added. Mail to:

        CREATIVE ARTS BOOK COMPANY

        833 Bancroft Way,

        Berkeley, CA 94710

     Or FAX to: (510) 848 - 4844

CROSSWORD PROPER NAME FINDER

OPERATING INSTRUCTIONS - SECTION III - AWARDS

The AWARD SECTION is a chronological listing of all awards selected to be included in this book.. These begin with the first British Poet Laureate in the year 1619. Until 1900, only Poets Laureate are listed.

Olympic Games Gold Medal Awards began in 1896, although the first one included in our book is for a 1900 Award. Olympic Gold Medal Award winners are included based on their being sought in crossword puzzle clues, or that they have been awarded multiple gold medals

Beginning in 1901, Nobel Prizes were awarded annually in their several categories. All NOBEL PRIZE WINNERS are included.

Pulitzer Prizes began in 1917. All PULITZER PRIZE WINNERS for Fiction, Drama, Music, and Poetry are included plus selected winners for awards in other categories. Most of the "other categories" selections are again based on appearances in puzzles.

OSCAR Awards began in 1928, for 1927 Movies. All BEST ACTOR and ACTRESS(o-a) AWARDS, all BEST SUPPORTING ACTOR and ACTRESS (o-s) AWARDS, and All BEST DIRECTOR(o-d) AWARDS are included. The BEST PICTURE AWARD(o-p) is listed ONLY when one of that picture's actors, actresses or director has also won an OSCAR...

Within each year of this chronological listing, all TITLES, MOVIE NAMES, SPORTS AWARDS, and Nobel Prize Winners (where no title is listed with the award) are listed alphabetically, with the TITLES and MOVIE NAMES, or SPORT CATEGORY in CAPS, and the Nobel winners(and Poets Laureate) in lower case as Surname, First Name. Pulitzer, Oscar, Grammy, and Sports Award winners are entered after their respective activity or title with the First Name Surname, in Capitalized lower case. Nationalities are indicated for all NOBEL and OLYMPIC GAMES GOLD

MEDAL winners. Nationalities are NOT indicated for
PULITZER winners--who are all American, Oscar winners,
Poets Laureate(who are all British), and major sports annual
award winners.

Listed award winners in major sports include annual Most
Valuable Player Awards in Hockey, beginning in 1927, in
Baseball beginning in 1931, and in Basketball beginning in
1956. Included also are Annual Cy Young Awards for the
outstanding pitchers in baseball, which began in 1956.
Football Most Valuable Player Awards began in 1955.

Nobel Prize Winners and Poets Laureate are listed 10 spaces
to the right of the year of their award. This facilitates the
alphabetizing within each year of these names with the
TITLES, MOVIE NAMES., and SPORTS AWARDS, which all are
listed immediately following the respective award year. This
spacing also makes it easier to search for a particular Nobel
winner.

All Award Winners in Section IV are also in the Main
Dictionary, with the code and year of his or her award
following the "Surname,   FIRST NAME" listing.

CROSSWORD PROPER NAME FINDER
Section III
THE AWARDS SECTION

DESIGNATION CODES FOR AWARDS

NOBEL PRIZES

n-c	Nobel Prize Chemistry	n-m	Nobel Prize Medicine,
n-e	Nobel Prize Economics		Bio-chem, Physiology
n-l	Nobel Prize Literature	n-p	Nobel Prize Physics
		n-x	Nobel Prize Peace

PULITZER PRIZES

p-b	Pulitzer Prize Biography	p-m	Pulitzer Prize Music
p-c	Pulitzer Prize Criticism	p-n	Pulitzer Prize NonFiction
p-d	Pulitzer Prize Drama	p-p	Pulitzer Prize Photography
p-e	Pulitzer Prize Editorial	p-q	Pulitzer Prize Poetry
p-f	Pulitzer Prize Fiction	p-r	Pulitzer Prize Reporting
p-h	Pulitzer Prize History	p-x	Pulitzer Prize Cartooning

OSCAR AWARDS

o-a	Oscar-Best Actor(Actress)
o-d	Oscar-Best Director
o-s	Oscar-Best Supporting Actor(Actress)
o-p	Oscar-Best Picture

GRAMMY AWARD

g-r	Grammy Award

POET LAUREATE--GR. BRITAIN

pol	Poet Laureate

SPORTS AWARDS

o-g	Olympic Gold Medal
hf	Sports Hall of Fame

HOCKEY AWARDS

ho-m HO Most Valuable Player

BASEBALL AWARDS

b-mv B Most Valuable Player
b-cy B Cy Young Award-Pitching

BASKETBALL AWARDS

bb-m BB Most Valuable Player

FOOTBALL AWARDS

fb-d	FB Most Valuable Player--Defense
fb-m	FB Most Valuable Player--Offense

Remember:

All pol's are British. All Pulitzer Winners are American. No
Nationalities are indicated for Oscar Winners, or for Winners
of Awards in Professional Sports.

1619	Jonson, Ben pol to 1637
1638	Davenant, Sir William pol to 1668
1688	Dryden, John pol to 1688
1688	Shadwell, Thomas pol to 1692
1692	Tate, Nahum pol to 1715
1715	Rowe, Nicholas pol to 1718
1718	Eusden, Laurence pol to 1730
1730	Cibber, Colley pol to 1757
1757	Whitehead, William pol to 1785
1785	Warton, Thomas pol to 1790
1790	Pye, Henry James pol to 1813
1813	Southey, Robert pol to 1843
1843	Wordsworth, William pol to 1850
1850	Tennyson, Alfred pol to 1892
1892	Austin, Alfred pol to 1913
1900 OL.GMS:	HAMMER THROW--John Flanagan(Am) o-g
1900 OL.GMS:	STANDING BROAD JUMP, STANDNG HIGH JUMP,
	STANDNG HOP,STEP & JUMP--Ray C. Ewry(Am) 3 o-g's
1901	Behring, Emil A. von (German) n-m
1901	Dunant, Jean H. (Swiss) n-x
1901	Hoff, Jacobus H van't(Dutch) n-c
1901	Passy, Frederic(Fr.) n-x
1901	Sully Prudhomme, Rene F.A. (Fr) n-l
1901	Roentgen, Wilhelm C.(Ger) n-p
1902	Ducommun, Elie(Swiss) n-x
1902	Fischer, Emil(Ger) n-c
1902	Gobat, Charles A.(Swiss) n-x
1902	Lorentz, Hendrik A.(Dutch) n-p
1902	Mommsen, Theodor(Ger) n-l
1902	Ross, Ronald(Sir)(Br) n-m
1902	Zeeman, Pieter(Dutch) n-p
1903	Arrhenius, Svante A.(Swe) n-c
1903	Bjornson, Bjornsterne(Nor) n-l
1903	Cremer, Sir William R.(Brit) n-x
1903	Curie, Marie & Pierre(Fr) n-p
1903	Finsen, Niels R.(Dane) n-m
1904	Echegaray, Jose(Span) n-l
1904	Mistral, Frederic(Span) n-l
1904 OL.GMS:	HAMMER THROW--John Flanagan(Am) o-g
1904 OL.GMS:	SHOT PUT-16 LB.--Ralph Rose(Am) o-g
1904 OL.GMS:	STANDING BROAD JUMP, STANDING HIGH JUMP,
	STANDING HOP,STEP & JUMP--Ray C.Ewry(Am)3 o-g's
1904	Pavlov, Ivan P.(Russ) n-m
1904	Rayleigh, Lord John W.(Brit) n-p
1904	Ramsay, Sir William(Brit) n-c
1904	Strutt, John W.(Brit) n-p
1905	Baeyer, Adolf von(Ger) n-c
1905	Koch, Robert(Ger) n-m
1905	Lenard, Philipp E.A. von(Ger) n-p
1905	Sienkiewicz, Henryk(Pol) n-l
1905	Suttner, Baroness Bertha von(Austr) n-x
1906	Carducci, Giosue(Italy) n-l
1906	Golgi, Camillo(Italy) n-m
1906	Ramon y Cajal, Santiago(Span) n-m
1906	Roosevelt, Theodore(Amer) n-x
1906	Thomson, Sir Joseph J.(Brit) n-p
1906	Moissan, Henri (Fr)n-c
1907	Buchner, Eduard(Ger) n-c
1907	Kipling, Rudyard(Brit) n-l
1907	Laveran, Charles L.A.(Fr) n-m
1907	Michelson, Albert A.(Amer) n-p

1907	Moneta, Ernesto T.(Ital) n-x
1907	Renault, Louis(Fr) n-x
1908	Arnoldson, Klas P.(Swed) n-x
1908	Bajer, Fredrik(Dane) n-x
1908	Ehrlich, Paul(Ger) n-m
1908	Eucken, Rudolf C.(Ger) n-l
1908	Lippmann, Gabriel(Fr) n-p
1908	Metchnikoff, Elie(Fr) n-m

1908 OL.GMS: HAMMER THROW--John Flanagan(Am) o-g

1908 OL.GMS: SHOT PUT-16 LB.--Ralph Rose(Am) o-g

1908 OL.GMS: STANDING BROAD JUMP, STANDING HIGH JUMP---
                    Ray C. Ewry(Am)2 o-g's

1908 OL.GMS: POLE VAULT -- Alfred C. Gilbert(Am)   o-g

1908	Rutherford, Ernest(Br) n-c
1909	Beernaert, Auguste M.F.(Belg) n-x
1909	Braun, Carl F.(Ger) n-p
1909	Constant,Paul H.B.B. d'Estournelles de(Fr)n-x
1909	Kocher, Emil T.(Swis) n-m
1909	Lagerlof, Selma(Swe) n-l
1909	Marconi, Guglielmo(iT) n-p
1909	Ostwald, Wilhelm(Ger) n-c
1910	Heyse, Paul J.L.(Ger) n-l
1910	Kossel, Albrecht(Ger) n-m
1910	Waals, Johannes D van der(Dut) n-p
1910	Wallach, Otto(Ger) n-c
1911	Asser, Tobias M. C.(Dutch) n-x
1911	Curie, Marie(Fr) n-c
1911	Fried, Alfred H.(Aust) n-x
1911	Gullstrand, Allvar(Swe) n-m
1911	Maeterlinck, Maurice(Belg) n-l
1911	Wien, Wilhelm(Ger) n-p
1912	Carrel, Alexis(Fr) n-m
1912	Dalen, Nils G.(Swe) n-p
1912	Grignard, Victor(Fr) n-c
1912	Hauptmann, Gerhart n-l

1912 OL.GMS: DECATHALON-Jim Thorpe(Am) o-g(disqualified
                    in 1912--earlier pro ball--restored
                                        posthumously)

1912	Sabatier, Paul(Fr) n-c
1912	Root, Elihu(Am) n-x
1913	Bridges, Robert(Br) pol to 1930
1913	Kamerlingh-Onnes, Heike(Dut) n-p
1913	Lafontaine, Henri(Belg) n-x
1913	Richet, Charles R.(Fr) n-m
1913	Tagore, Rabindranath(India) n-l
1913	Werner, Alfred(Swiss) n-c
1914	Barany, Robert(Aus) n-m
1914	Laue, Max von(Ger) n-p
1914	Richards, Theodore W.(Am) n-c
1915	Bragg, Sir William H.(Br) n-p
1915	Bragg, Sir William L.(Br) n-p
1915	Rolland, Romain(Fr) n-l
1915	Willstatter, Richard M.(Ger) n-c
1916	Heidenstam, Verner von(Swe) n-l
1917	Barkla, Charles G.(Br) n-p
1917	Gjellerup, Karl A.(Dan) n-l
1917	Pontoppidan, Henrik(Dan) n-l
1918	Haber, Fritz(Ger) n-c

1918 HIS FAMILY--Ernest Poole p-f Am(All Pulitzers)

1918	Planck, Max K.E.L.(Ger) n-p

1918 WHY MARRY?--Jesse Lynch Williams p-d

```
1919            Bordet, Jules (Belg)  n-m
1919            Spitteler, Carl F. G. (Swi)  n-l
1919            Stark, Johannes (Ger)  n-p
1919 THE MAGNIFICENT AMBERSONS--Booth Tarkington p-f
1919            Wilson, Woodrow (Am)  n-x
1920 BEYOND THE HORIZON--Eugene O'Neill p-d
1920            Bourgeois, Leon V.A. (Fr)  n-x
1920            Guillaume, Charles E. (Fr)  n-p
1920            Hamsun, Knut (Nor)  n-l
1920            Krogh, Schack A.S. (Dan)  n-m
1920            Nernst, Walther H. (Ger)  n-c
1920 OL.GMS: JAVELIN THROW--Jonni Myyra (Finn) o-g
1920 OL.GMS: 10,000 METER RUN--Paavo Nurmi (Finn) o-g
1921 AGE OF INNOCENCE--Edith Wharton p-f
1921            Branting, Karl H. (Swe)  n-x
1921            Einstein, AlbertZ (Ger-Am)  n-p
1921            France, Anatole (Fr)  n-l
1921            Lange, Christian L. (Nor)  n-x
1921 MISS LULU BETT--Zona Gale p-d
1921            Soddy, Frederick (Br)  n-c
1921 THE AMERICANIZATION OF EDWARD BOK--Edward Bok p-b
1922 A DAUGHTER OF THE MIDDLE BORDER-Hamlin Garland p-b
1922 ALICE ADAMS--Booth Tarkington p-f
1922 ANNA CHRISTIE--Eugene O'Neill p-d
1922            Aston, Francis W. (Br)  n-c
1922            Benavente, Jacinto (Sp)  n-l
1922            Bohr, Niels (Dan)  n-p
1922 COLLECTED POEMS--Edwin Arlington Robinson p-q
1922            Hill, Archibald V. (Br)  n-m
1922            Meyerhof, Otto F. (Ger)  n-m
1922            Nansen, Fridtjof (Nor)  n-x
1922 THE FOUNDING OF NEW ENGLAND-James Truslow Adams p-h
1923 BALLAD OF THE HARP-WEAVER - Edna St.Vincent Millay p-q
1923            Banting, Frederick G. (Can)  n-m
1923 ICEBOUND--Owen Davis (Am) p-d
1923            Macleod, John J.R. (Scot)  n-m
1923            Millikan, Robert A. (Am)  n-p
1923 ONE OF OURS--Willa Cather p-f
1923 --- POETRY, 1922: A MISCELLANY--
                         Edna St. Vincent Millay p-q
1923            Pregl, Fritz (Aus)  n-c
1923            Yeats, William Butler (Irish)  n-l
1924            Einthoven, Willem (Dut)  n-m
1924 HELL-BENT FOR HEAVEN--Hatcher Hughes p-d
1924 NEW HAMPSHIRE: A POEM WITH NOTES AND GRACE NOTES--
                         Robert Friost p-q
1924 OL.GMS: 800 METER RUN--Douglas Lowe (Br) o-g
1924 OL.GMS: 5,000 METER RUN-Paavo Murmi (Finn) o-g
1924 OL.GMS: DISCUS THROW--Clarence Howser (Am) o-g
1924 OL.GMS: JAVELIN THROW--Jonni Myyra (Finn) o-g
1924            Reymont, Wladyslaw (Pol)  n-l
1924            Siegbahn, Karl M.G. (Swe)  n-p
1924 THE ABLE McLAUGHLINS--Margaret Wilson p-f
1925            Dawes, Charles G. (Am)  n-x
1925            Chamberlain, Sir J. Austen (Brit)  n-x
1925            Franck, James (Ger)  n-p
1925            Hertz, Gustav (Ger)  n-p
1925            Shaw, George Bernard (Irish-Br)  n-l
1925 SO BIG--Edna Ferber p-f
1925 THE MAN WHO DIED TWICE-Edwin Arlington Robinson p-q
```

1925 THEY KNEW WHAT THEY WANTED--Sidney Howard p-d
1925   Zsigmondy, Richard A.(Ger) n-c
1926 ARROWSMITH--Sinclair Lewis p-f (refused prize)
1926   Briand, Aristide(Fr) n-x
1926   Deledda, Grazia(It) n-l
1926 CRAIG'S WIFE--George Kelly p-d
1926   Fibiger, Johannes A.G.(Dan) n-m
1926   Perrin, Jean-B.(Fr) n-p
1926   Stresemann, Gustav(Ger) n-x
1926   Svedberg, Theodor(Swe) n-c
1926 WHAT'S O'CLOCK--Amy Lowell p-q
1927   Bergson, Henri(Fr) n-l
1927   Buisson, Ferdinand E.(Fr) n-x
1927   Compton, Arthur H.(Am) n-p
1927 EARLY AUTUMN--Louis Bromfield p-f
1927 FIDDLER'S FAREWELL--Leonora Speyer p-q
1927 HOCKEY: Herb Gardiner Montreal ho-m
1927 IN ABRAHAM'S BOSOM--Paul Green p-d
1927   Quidde, Ludwig(Ger) n-x
1927   Wagner-Jauregg, Julius(Aus) n-m
1927   Wieland, Heinrich O.(Ger) n-c
1927   Wilson, Charles T.R.(Br) n-p
1928 BRIDGE OF SAN LUIS REY--Thornton Wilder p-f
1928 HOCKEY: Howie Morenz Monttreal ho-m
1928 MAIN CURRENTS IN AMERICAN THOUGHT--
                         Vernon Louis Parrington p-h
1928   Nicolle, Charles J.H.(Fr) n-m
1928 OL.GMS: 800 METER RUN--Douglas Lowe(Br) o-g
1928 OL.GMS: 10,000 METER RUN--Paavo Nurmi(Finn) o-g
1928 OL.GMS: FIGURE SKATING SINGLES-Sonja Henie(Nor)o-g
1928   Richardson, Sir Owen W.(Br) n-p
1928 SEVENTH HEAVEN--Janet Gaynor o-a,Frank Borzage o-d
1928 STRANGE INTERLUDE--Eugene O'Neill p-d
1928 THE WAY OF ALL FLESH--Emil Jannings o-a
1928 TRISTRAM--Edwin Arlington Robinson p-q
1928   Undset, Sigrid(Nor) n-l
1928   Windaus, Adolf Otto R.(Ger) n-c
1929   Broglie, Prince Louis-Victor de(Fr) n-p
1929 COQUETTE--Mary Pickford o-a
1929   Eijkman, Christiaan(Dut) n-m
1929   Euler-Chelpin, Hans von(Swe) n-c
1929   Harden, Sir Arthur(Br) n-c
1929 HOCKEY: Roy Worters NY ho-m
1929   Hopkins, Sir Frederick G.(Br) n-m
1929 IN OLD ARIZONA--Warner Baxter o-a
1929 JOHN BROWN'S BODY--Stephen Vincent Benet p-q
1929   Kellogg, Frank B.(Am) n-x
1929   Mann, Thomas(Ger) n-l
1929 SCARLET SISTER MARY--Julia M. Peterkin p-f
1929 STREET SCENE--Elmer Rice p-d
1930 ALL QUIET ON THE WESTERN FRONT o-p --
                         Lewis Milestone o-d
1930 DISRAELI--George Arliss o-a
1930   Fischer, Hans(Ger) n-c
1930 HOCKEY: Nels Stewart Mont ho-m
1930   Landsteiner, Karl(Am) n-m
1930 LAUGHING BOY--Oliver LaFarge p-f
1930   Lewis, Sinclair(Am) n-l
1930   Masefield, John(Br) pol to 1967
1930   Raman, Sir Chandrasekhara V.(India) n-p

1930 SELECTED POEMS--Conrad Aiken p-q
1930   Soderblom, Nathan(Swed) n-x
1930 THE DIVORCEE--Norma Shearer o-a
1930 THE GREEN PASTURES--Marc Connelly p-d
1931   Addams, Jane(Am) n-x
1931 BASEBALL:Frank Frisch StL b-mv,Lefty Grove Phil b-mv
1931   Bergius, Friedrich(Ger) n-c
1931   Bosch, Karl(Ger) n-c
1931   Butler, Nicholas Murray(Am) n-x
1931 CHARLES W. ELIOT--Henry James p-b
1931 COLLECTED POEMS-Robert Frost p-q
1931 FREE SOUL--Lionel Barrymore o-a
1931 HOCKEY: Howie Morenz Montho ho-m
1931   Karlfeldt, Erik A.(Swe) n-l
1931 MIN AND BILL--Marie Dressler o-a
1931   Warburg, Otto H.(Ger) n-m
1931 YEARS OF GRACE--Margaret Ayer Barnes p-f
1932   Adrian, Edgar D.(Br) n-m
1932 BASEBALL: Charles Klein Phil b-mv,
                              Jimmie Foxx Phil(AL) b-mv
1932 DR. JEKYLL AND MR. HYDE--Fredric March o-a
1932   Galsworthy, John(Br) n-l
1932   Heisenberg, Werner(Ger) n-p
1932 HOCKEY: Howie Morenz Mont ho-m
1932   Langmuir, Irving(Am) n-c
1932 MY EXPERIENCES IN THE WORLD WAR--
                          Gen. John J. Pershing p-h
1932 OF THE I SING--Ira Gershwin, George S. Kaufman &
                              Morrie Ryskind
1932 OL.GMS: FIGURE SKATING SINGLES--Sonja Henie(Nor)o-g
1932   Sherrington, Sir Charles S.(Br) n-m
1932 SIN OF MADELON CLAUDET--Helen Hayes o-a
1932 THE FLOWERING STONE--George Dillon p-q
1932 THE GOOD EARTH--Pearl S. Buck p-f
1933   Angell, Sir Norman(Br) n-x
1933 BASEBALL: Carl Hubbell NY b-mv,
                  Jimmie Foxx Phil(AL) b-mv
1933 BOTH YOUR HOUSES--Maxwell Anderson p-d
1933   Bunin, Ivan A.(USSR) n-l
1933 CAVALCADE o-p --Frank Lloyd o-d
1933 CONQUISTADOR--Archibald MacLeish p-q
1933   Dirac, Paul A. M.(Br) n-p
1933 GROVER CLEVELAND--Allan Nevins p-b
1933 HOCKEY   Eddie Shore Bos ho-m
1933   Morgan, Thomas H.(Am) n-m
1933 MORNING GLORY--Katherine Hepburn o-a
1933 PRIVATE LIFE OF HENRY VIII--Charles Laughton o-a
1933   Schrodinger, Erwin(Aus) n-p
1933 THE SIGNIFICANCE OF SECTIONS IN AMERICAN HISTORY--
                          Frederick J. Turner p-h
1933 THE STORE--T.S. Stribling p-f
1934 BASEBALL: Dizzy Dean StL b-mv,
                  Mickey Cochran Det b-mv
1934 COLLECTED VERSE--Robert Hillyer p-q
1934   Henderson, Arthur(Br) n-x
1934 HOCKEY   Aurel Joliet Mont
1934 IT HAPPENED ONE NIGHT o-p --Clark Gable o-a,
                  Claudette Colbert o-a, Frank Capra o-d
1934 LAMB IN HIS BOSOM--Caroline Miller p-f
1934 MEN IN WHITE--Sidney Kingsley p-d

```
1934          Minot, George R.(Am)  n-m
1934          Murphy, William P.(Am)  n-m
1934          Pirandello, Luigi(It)  n-l
1934 S.F. CHRONICLE--Royce Brier p-r
1934          Urey, Harold C.(Am)  n-c
1934          Whipple, G.H.(Am)  n-m
1935 BASEBALL: Gabby Hartnett Chi b-mv,
              Hank Greenberg Det b-mv
1935 BRIGHT AMBUSH--Audrey Wurdemann p-q
1935          Chadwick, Sir James(Br)  n-p
1935 DANGEROUS--Bette Davis o-a
1935 HOCKEY: Eddie Shore Bos ho-m
1935          Joliot-Curie, Frederic(Fr)  n-c
1935          Joliot-Curie, Irene(Fr)  n-c
1935 NOW IN NOVEMBER--Josephine W. Johnson p-f
1935          Ossietzky, Carl von(Ger)  n-x
1935 R. E. LEE--Douglas Southall Freeman p-b
1935          Spemann, Hans(Ger)  n-m
1935 THE INFORMER--Victor McLaglen o-a & John Ford o-d
1935 THE OLD MAID--Zoe Akins p-d
1936          Anderson, Carl D.(Am)  n-p
1936 ANTHONY ADVERSE--Gale Sondergaard o-s
1936 BASEBALL: Carl Hubbell NY b-mv, Lou Gehrig NY(AL)b-mv
1936 COME AND GET IT--Walter Brennan o-s
1936          Dale, Sir Henry H.(Br)  n-m
1936          Debye, Peter J.W.(Dut)  n-m
1936          Hess, Victor F.(Aus)  n-p
1936 HOCKEY:  Eddie Shopre Bos ho-m
1936 HONEY IN THE HORN--Harold L. Davis p-f
1936 IDIOT'S DELIGHT--Robert E. Sherwood p-d
1936          Loewi, Otto(Am)  n-m
1936 OL.GMS: FIGURE SKATING SINGLES--Sonja Henie(Nor)o-g
1936 OL.CMS: 100,200 METER,LONGJUMP+--Jesse Owens(Am)4 o-g's
1936          O'Neill, Eugene(Am)  n-l
1936          Saavedra Lamas, Carlos de(Arg)  n-x
1936 STORY OF LOUIS PASTEUR--Paul Muni o-a
1936 STRANGE HOLINESS--Robert P. Tristram Coffin p-q
1936 THE GREAT ZIEGFELD o-p --Luise Rainer o-a
1936 THE THOUGHT AND CHARACTER OF WILLIAM JAMES--
                       Ralph Barton Perry p-b
1937 A FURTHER RANGE--Robert Frost p-q
1937 BASEBALL:   Joe Medwick Stl b-mv,
              Charley Gehringer Det b-mv
1937 CAPTAINS COURAGEOUS--Spencer Tracy o-a
1937          Cecil of Chelwood, Viscount(Brit)  n-x
1937          Davisson, Clinton J.(Am)  n-p
1937          Gard, Roger Martin du(Fr)  n-l
1937 GONE WITH THE WIND--Margaret Mitchell p-f
1937 HAMILTON FISH: THE INNER HISTORY OF THE GRANT
                 ADMINISTRATION--Allan Nevins p-b
1937          Haworth, Walter N.(Br)  n-c
1937 HOCKEY:  Babe Siebert Mont ho-m
1937 IN OLD CHICAGO--Alice Brady o-s
1937          Karrer, Paul(Swi)  n-c
1937 LIFE OF EMILE ZOLA--Joseph Schildkraut o-s
1937          Szent-Gyorgyi, Albert(Hung-Am)  n-m
1937 THE FLOWERING OF NEW ENGLAND--Van Wyck Brooks p-h
1937 THE GOOD EARTH--Luise Rainer o-a
1937          Thomson, George P.(Br)  n-p
```

1937 YOU CAN'T TAKE IT WITH YOU--George S. Kaufman &
                                    Moss Hart p-d
1938 BASEBALL: Ernie Lombardi Cin b-mv, Jimmie Foxx Bos b-mv
1938 BOYS TOWN--Spencer Tracy o-a
1938   Buck, Pearl S.(Am) n-l
1938 COLD MORNING SKY--Marya Zaturenska p-q
1938   Fermi, Enrico(It-Am) n-p
1938   Heymans, Corneille J.F.(Belg) n-m
1938 HOCKEY: Eddie Shore Bos ho-m
1938 JEZEBEL--Bette Davis o-a & Fay Bainter o-s
1938 KENTUCKY--Walter Brennan o-s
1938   Kuhn, Richard(Ger) n-c
1938 OUR TOWN--Thornton Wilder p-d
1938 THE LATE GEORGE APLEY--John P. Marquand p-f
1938 YOU CAN'T TAKE IT WITH YOU o-p--Framk Capra o-d
1939 ABE LINCOLN IN ILLINOIS--Robert E. Sherwood p-d
1939 BASEBALL: Bucky Walters Cin b-mv,
                  Joe DiMaggio NY(AL) b-mv
1939   Butenandt, Adolf F.J.(Ger) n-c
1939   Domagk, Gerhard(Ger) n-m
1939 GONE WITH THE WIND o-p--Vivien Leigh o-a,
              Hattie McDaniel o-s & Victor Fleming o-d
1939 GOODBYE MR. CHIPS--Robert Donat o-a
1939 HOCKEY: Toe Blake Mont ho-m
1939   Lawrence, Ernest O.(Am) n-p
1939   Ruzicka, Leopold(Swi) n-c
1939 SELECTED POEMS--John Gould Fletcher p-q
1939   Sillanpaa, Frans E.(Fin) n-l
1939 STAGECOACH--Thomas Mitchell o-s
1939 THE YEARLING--Marjorie K. Rawlings p-f
1940 ABRAHAM LINCOLN: THE WAR YEARS--Carl Sandburg p-h
1940 BASEBALL: Frank McCormick Cin b-mv,
              Hank Greenberg Det b-mv
1940 COLLECTED POEMS--Mark Van Doren p-q
1940 HOCKEY: Ebbie Goodfellow Detroit ho-m
1940 KITTY FOYLE--Ginger Rogers o-a
1940 THE GRAPES OF WRATH--John Steinbeck p-f
1940 THE GRAPES OF WRATH --Jane Darwell o-s, John Ford o-d
1940 THE PHILADELPHIA STORY--James Stewart o-a
1940 THE TIME OF YOUR LIFE--William Saroyan p-d
1940 THE WESTERNER--Walter Brennan o-s
1940 WOODROW WILSON, LIFE & LETTERS--Ray Stannard Baker p-b
1941 BASEBALL: Dolph Camilli Br b-mv, Joe DiMaggio NY b-mv
1941 HOCKEY: Bill Cowley Bos ho-m
1941 HOW GREEN WAS MY VALLEY o-p--Donald Crisp o-s,
                                    John Ford o-d
1941 SERGEANT YORK-- Gary Cooper o-a
1941 SUNDERLAND CAPTURE--Leonard Bacon p-q
1941 SUSPICION--Joan Fontaine o-a
1941 THE GREAT LIE--Mary Astor o-s
1941 THERE SHALL BE NO NIGHT--Robert E. Sherwood p-d
1942 BASEBALL: Mort Cooper StL b-mv, Joe Gordon NY b-mv
1942 HOCKEY:Tom Anderson NY ho-m
1942 IN THIS OUR LIFE--Ellen Glasgow p-f
1942 JOHNNY EAGER--Van Heflin o-s
1942 MRS. MINIVER o-p --Greer Garson o-a,
              Teresa Wright o-s & William Wyler o-d
1942 NEWSPAPER ENTERPRISE ASSN.--Herbert L. Block p-x
1942 THE DUST WHICH IS GOD--William Rose Benet p-q
1942 YANKEE DOODLE DANDY--James Cagney o-a

1943 ADMIRAL OF THE OCEAN SEA (COLUMBUS)--
                    Samuel Eliot Morison p-b
1943 A WITNESS TREE--Robert Frost p-q
1943 BASEBALL: Stan Musial StL b-mv,
                    Spurgeon Chandler NY b-mv
1943 CASABLANCA o-p --Michael Curtiz o-d
1943   Dam, Henrik C. P.(Dan) n-m
1943   Doisy, Edward A.(Am) n-m
1943 DRAGON'S TEETH--Upton Sinclair p-f
1943 FOR WHOM THE BELL TOLLS--Katina Paxinou o-s
1943   Hevesy, Georg de(Hung) n-c
1943 HOCKEY: Bill Cowley Bos ho-m
1943 SECULAR CANATA NO. 2--William Schuman p-m
1943   Stern, Otto(Am) n-p
1943 THE MORE THE MERRIER--Charles Coburn o-s
1943 THE SKIN OF OUR TEETH--Thornton Wilder p-d
1943 THE SONG OF BERNADETTE--Jennifer Jones o-a
1943 WATCH ON THE RHINE--Paul Lukas o-a
1944 BASEBALL: Martin Marion StL b-mv,Hal Newhouser Det b-mv
1944   Erlanger, Joseph(Am) n-m
1944 GASLIGHT--Ingrid Bergman o-a
1944   Gasser, Herbert S.(Am) n-m
1944 GOING MY WAY o-p --Bing Crosby o-a,
                    Barry Fitzgerald o-s & Leo McCarey d
1944   Hahn, Otto(Ger) n-c
1944 HOCKEY: Babe Pratt Toronto ho-m
1944   Jensen, Johannes V.(Dan) n-l
1944 JOURNEY IN THE DARK--Martin Flavin p-f
1944 NONE BUT THE LONELY HEART--Ethel Barrymore o-s
1944   Pyle, Ernest Taylor p-r
1944   Rabi, Isidor Isaac(Am) n-p
1944 SYMPHONY NO. 4, OP. 34--Howard Hanson p-m
1944 WESTERN STAR--Stephen Vincent Benet p-q
1945 A BELL FOR ADANO--John Hersey p-f
1945 APPALACHIAN SPRING--Aaron Copland p-m
1945 A TREE GROWS IN BROOKLYN--James Dunn o-s
1945 BASEBALL: Phil Cavarretta Chi b-mv,
                    Hal Newhouser Det b-mv
1945   Chain, Ernst B.(Br) n-m
1945   Fleming, Sir Alexander(Br) n-m
1945   Florey, Sir Howard W.(Br) n-m
1945 GEORGE BANCROFT: BRAHMIN REBEL--Russell Nye p-b
1945 HARVEY--Mary Chase p-d
1945 HOCKEY   Elmer Lach Mont ho-m
1945   Hull, Cordell(Am) n-x
1945 MILDRED PIERCE--Joan Crawford o-a
1945   Mistral, Gabriela(Chile) n-l
1945 NATIONAL VELVET--Anne Revere o-s
1945 THE LOST WEEKEND o-p--Ray Milland o-a,Billy Wilder o-d
1945   Vertanen, Artturi I.(Fin) n-c
1945 V-LETTER AND OTHER POEMS--Karl Shapiro p-q
1945   Wolfgang, Pauli(Am) n-p
1946   Balch, Emily G.(Am) n-x
1946 BASEBALL: Stan Musial StL b-mv, Ted Williams Bos b-mv
1946 BEST YEARS OF OUR LIVES o-p --Fredric March o-a,
                    Harold Russell o-s & William Wyler o-d
1946   Bridgman, Percy Williams(Am) n-p
1946   Hesse, Hermann(Ger-Swi) n-l
1946 HOCKEY: Max Bentley Chicagi ho-m
1946   Mott, John R.(Am) n-x

1946	Muller, Hermann J.(Am) n-m
1946	Northrop, John H.(Am) n-c
1946	Stanley, Wendell M.(Am) n-c
1946	STATE OF THE UNION-Russel Crouse&Howard Lindsay p-d
1946	Sumner, James B.(Am) n-c
1946	THE AGE OF JACKSON--Arthur M. Schlesinger, Jr. p-h
1946	THE CANTICLE OF THE SUN--Leo Sowerby p-m
1946	THE RAZOR'S EDGE--Anne Baxter o-s
1946	TO EACH HIS OWN--Olivia de Havilland o-a
1947	A DOUBLE LIFE--Ronald Colman o-a
1947	ALL THE KING'S MEN--Robert Penn Warren p-f
1947	BASEBALL: Bob Elliott Bos(NL) b-mv,Joe DiMaggio NY b-mv
1947	Cori, Carl F. & Gerty T.(Am) n-m
1947	Appleton, Sir Edward V.(Br) n-p
1947	GENTLEMAN'S AGREEMENT o-p --Celeste Holm o-s &
	Elia Kazan o-d
1947	Gide, Andre(Fr) n-l
1947	HOCKEY: Maurice Richard Mont ho-m
1947	LORD WEARY'S CASTLE--Robert Lowell p-q
1947	MIRACLE ON 34TH STREET--Edmund Gwenn o-s
1947	Robinson, Sir Robert(Br) n-c
1947	SYMPHONY NO. 3--Charles E. Ives p-m
1947	THE AUTOBIOGRAPHY OF WILLIAM ALLEN WHITE--
	William Allen White p-b
1947	THE FARMER'S DAUGHTER--Loretta Young o-a
1948	ACROSS THE WIDE MISSOURI--Bernard De Voto p-h
1948	A STREETCAR NAMED DESIRE--Tennessee Williams p-d
1948	BASEBALL: Stan Musial Stl b-mv, Lou Boudreau Clev B-mv
1948	Blackett, PATRICK M.S.(Br) n-p
1948	Eliot, T. S.(Br) n-l
1948	HAMLET o-p--Laurence Olivier o-a,
1948	HOCKEY: Buddy O'Connor NY Rangers ho-m
1948	JOHNNY BELINDA--Jane Wyman o-a
1948	KEY LARGO--Claire Trevor o-s
1948	Muller, Paul H.(Swi) n-m
1948	OL. GMS: 10,000 METER RUN--Emil Zatopek(Czech) o-g
1948	OL. GMS: DECATHLON--Bob Mathais(Am) o-g
1948	OL. GMS: FIGURE SKAT.-SINGLES--Dick Button(Am) o-g
1948	SYMPHONY NO. 3--Walter Piston p-m
1948	TALES OF THE SOUTH PACIFIC--James A. Michener p-f
1948	THE AGE OF ANXIETY--W.H. Auden p-q
1948	TREASURE OF SIERRA MADRE--Walter Huston o-s
1948	Tiselius, Arne W.K.(Swe) n-c
1949	ALL THE KING'S MEN o-p --Broderick Crawford o-a &
	Mercedes McCambridge o-s
1949	BASEBALL:Jackie Robinson Br b-mv,Ted Williams Bos b-mv
1949	DEATH OF A SALESMAN--Arthur Miller p-d
1949	Faulkner, William(Am) n-l
1949	Giauque, William F.(Am) n-c
1949	GUARD OF HONOR--James Gould Cozzens p-f
1949	Hess, Walter R.(Swi) n-m
1949	HOCKEY: Sid Abel Det ho-m
1949	LOUISIANA STORY--Virgil Thomson p-m
1949	Moniz, Antonio(Port) n-m
1949	Orr,Lord John Boyd of Brechin Mearms(Br)n-x
1949	TERROR AND DECORUM--Peter Viereck p-q
1949	THE HEIRESS--Olivia de Havilland o-a
1949	TWELVE O'CLOCK HIGH--Dean Jagger o-s
1949	Yukawa, Hideki(Japan) n-p
1950	Alder, Kurt(Ger) n-c

1950 ALL ABOUT EVE o-p --Geo. Sanders o-s,
                          Jos. L. Mankiewicz o-d
1950 ANNIE ALLEN--Gwendolyn Brooks p-q
1950 BASEBALL:Jim Konstanty Phil b-mv, Phil Rizzuto NY b-mv
1950 BORN YESTERDAY--Judy Holliday o-a
1950   Bunche, Ralph J.(Am) n-x
1950 CYRANO DE BERGERAC--Jose Ferrer o-a
1950   Diels, Otto P. H.(Ger) n-c
1950 HARVEY--Josephine Hull o-s
1950   Hench, Philip S.(Am) n-m
1950 HOCKEY: Chuck Rayner NYR ho-m
1950   Kendall, Edward C.(Am) n-m
1950   Powell, Cecil F.(Br) n-p
1950   Reichstein, Tadeus(Swi) n-m
1950   Russell, Bertrand(Br) n-l
1950 SOUTH PACIFIC--R. Rodgers, O. Hammerstein &
                          Joshua Logan p-d
1950 THE CONSUL--Gian-Carlo Menotti p-m
1950 THE WAY WEST--Guthrie, A. B. Jr. p-f
1951 A STREETCAR NAMED DESIRE--Vivien Leigh o-a,
                Kim Hunter o-s, Karl Malden o-s
1951 BASEBALL: Roy Campanella Br b-mv, Yogi Berra NY b-mv
1951   Cockroft, Sir John D.(Br) n-p
1951 COMPLETE POEMS--Carl Sandberg p-q
1951 GIANTS IN THE EARTH--Douglas Moore p-m
1951 HOCKEY: Milt Schmidt Bos ho-m
1951   Jouhaux, Leon(Fr) n-x
1951   Lagerkvist, Par F.(Swe) n-l
1951   McMillan, Edwin M.(Am) n-c
1951   Seaborg, Glenn T.(Am) n-c
1951 THE AFRICAN QUEEN--Humphrey Bogart o-a
1951   Theiler, Max(Am) n-m
1951 THE TOWN--Conrad Richter p-f
1951   Walton, Ernest T.S,(Irish) n-p
1952 BASEBALL: Hank Sauer Chi b-mv, Bobby Shantz Phil b-mv
1952   Bloch, Felix(Am) n-p
1952 COLLECTED POEMS--Marianne Moore p-q
1952 COME BACK LITTLE SHEBA--Shirley Booth o-a
1952 HIGH NOON--Gary Cooper o-a
1952 HOCKEY: Gordie Howe Det ho-m
1952   Martin, Archer J.P.(Br) n-c
1952   Mauriac, Francois(Fr) n-l
1952   Purcell, Edward M.(Am) n-p
1952   Schweitzer, Albert(Fr) n-x
1952 OL. GMS: 200 METER RUN-WOMEN--Marjorie Jackson(Aust)o-g
1952 OL. GMS: 5,000 METER RUN--Emil Zatopek(Czech) o-g
1952 OL. GMS: 10,000 METER RUN--Emil Zatopek(Czech) o-g
1952 OL. GMS: DECATHLON--Bob Mathais(Am) o-g
1952 OL. GMS: FIG. SKTG--SINGLES--Dick Button(Am) o-g
1952 OL. GMS: MARATHON--Emil Zatopek(Czech) o-g
1952 OL. GMS: POLE VAULT--Robert Richards(Am) o-g
1952 OL. GMS: SHOT PUT-16 LB.--Parry O'Brien Am o-g
1952 OL. GMS: TRIPLE JUMP--Adhemar de Silva Braz o-g
1952 SYMPHONY CONCERTANTE--Gail Kubik p-m
1952   Synge, Richard L.M.(Br) n-c
1952 THE BAD AND THE BEAUTIFUL Gloria Grahame o-s
1952 THE CAINE MUTINY--Herman Wouk p-f
1952 THE SHRIKE--Joseph Kramm p-d
1952 VIVA ZAPATA--Anthony Quinn o-s
1952   Waksman, Selman A.(Am) n-m

1953 BASEBALL: Roy Campanella Br b-mv, Al Rosen Clev b-mv
1953   Churchill, Sir Winston(Br) n-l
1953 COLLECTED POEMS--Archibald MacLeish p-q
1953 FROM HERE TO ETERNITY o-p --Frank Sinatra o-s,
               Donna Reed o-s & Fred Zinnemann o-d
1953 HOCKEY: Gordie Howe Det ho-m
1953   Krebs, Hans A.(Br) n-m
1953   Lipmann, Fritz A.(Am) n-m
1953   Marshall, George C.(Am) n-x
1953 PICNIC--William Inge p-d
1953 ROMAN HOLIDAY--Audrey Hepburn o-a
1953 STALAG 17--William Holden o-a
1953   Staudinger, Hermann(Ger) n-c
1953 THE OLD MAN AND THE SEA--Ernest Hemingway p-f
1953   Zernike, Frits(Dut) n-p
1954 A STILLNESS AT APPOMATTOX--Bruce Catton p-h
1954 BASEBALL: Willie Mays NY b-mv, Yogi Berra NY(AL) b-mv
1954   Born, Max(Br) n-p
1954   Bothe, Walter(Ger) n-p
1954 CONCERTO FOR TWO PIANOS AND ORCHESTRA-Quincy Porter p-m
1954   Enders, John F.(Am) n-m
1954   Hemingway, Ernest(Am) n-l
1954 HOCKEY: Al Rollins Chi ho-m
1954 ON THE WATERFRONT o-p --Marlon Brando o-a,
               Eva Marie Saint o-s & Elia Kazan o-d
1954   Pauling, Linus C.(Am) n-c
1954   Robbins, Frederick C.(Am) n-m
1954 TEAHOUSE OF THE AUGUST MOON--John Patrick p-d
1954 THE BAREFOOT CONTESSA--Edmond O'Brien o-s
1954 THE COUNTRY GIRL--Grace Kelly o-a
1954 THE SPIRIT OF ST. LOUIS--Charles A. Lindbergh p-b
1954 THE WAKING--Theodore Roethke p-q
1954 WASHINGTON POST--Herbert L. Block p-x
1954   Weller, Thomas H.(Am) n-m
1955 A FABLE--William Faulkner p-f
1955 BASEBALL: Roy Campanella Br b-mv, Yogi Berra NY b-mv
1955 CAT ON A HOT TIN ROOF--Tennessee Williams p-d
1955 COLLECTED POEMS--Wallace Stevens p-q
1955 EAST OF EDEN--Jo Van Fleet o-s
1955 FOOTBALL: Harlon Hill Chi fb-m
1955 HOCKEY: Ted Kennedy CHI ho-m
1955   Kusch, Polykarp(Am) n-p
1955   Lamb, Willis E.(Am) n-p
1955   Laxness, Halldor K.(Iceland) n-l
1955 MARTY o-p --Ernest Borgnine o-a & Delbert Mann o-d
1955 MISTER ROBERTS--Jack Lemmon o-s
1955   Theorell, Alex H.T.(Swe) n-m
1955 THE ROSE TATOO--Anna Magnani o-a
1955 THE SAINT OF BLEECKER STREET-Gian-Carlo Menotti p-m
1955   Vigneaud, Vincent du(Am) n-c
1956 ANASTASIA--Ingrid Bergman o-a
1956 ANDERSONVILLE--MacKinlay Kantor p-f
1956   Bardeen, John(Am) n-p
1956 BASEBALL: Don Newcomb Br b-mv, Mickey Mantle NY b-mv
               Don Newcomb Br b-cy,
1956 BASKETBALL: Bob Pettit StL bb-m
1956   Bratain, Walter H.(Am) n-p
1956   Cournand, Andre F.(Am) n-m
1956 FOOTBALL: Frank Gifford NY fb-m
1956   Forssmann, Werner(Ger) n-m

1956   Hinshelwood, Sir Cyril N.(Br)   n-c
1956 HOCKEY: Jean Belifeau Mont ho-m
1956   Jimenez, Juan Ramon(Sp)   n-l
1956 LUST FOR LIFE--Anthony Quinn o-s
1956 OL. GMS: 200 METER RUN--Bobby Morrow(Am) o-g
1956 OL. GMS: 200 METER RUN-WOMEN--Betty Cuthbert(Aust) o-g
1956 OL. GMS: 400 METER HURDLES--Glenn Davis(Am) o-g
1956 OL. GMS: DISCUS--Al Oerter(Am) o-g
1956 OL. GMS: POLE VAULT--Robert Richards(Am) o-g
1956 OL. GMS: SHOT PUT-16 LB.--Parry O'Brien(Am) o-g
1956 OL. GMS: TRIPLE JUMP--Adhemar de Silva(Braz) o-g
1956 OL. WNT. GMS: DOWNHILL, SLALOM & GIANT SLALOM
                SKIING--Anton(Toni) Sailer(Aus) 3 o-g's
                WOMEN SINGLES FIG.SKATING-Tenley Albright o-g
1956 POEMS, NORTH AND SOUTH--Elizabeth Bishop p-q
1956   Richards, Dickinson W. Jr.(Am)   n-m
1956   Semenov, Nikolai N.(USSR)   n-c
1956   Shockley, William(Am)   n-p
1956 SYMPHONY NO. 3--Ernest Tch p-m
1956 THE AGE OF REFORM--Richard Hofstadter p-h
1956 THE DIARY OF ANNE FRANK--Frances Goodrich &
                Albert Hackett p-d
1956 THE KING AND I--Yul Brynner o-a
1956 WRITTEN ON THE WIND--Dorthy Malone o-s
1957 BASEBALL: Hank Aaron Mil b-mv, Mickey Mantle NY b-mv
                Warren Spahn Mil b-cy
1957 BASKETBALL: Bob Cousy Bos bb-m
1957   Bovet, Daniel(It)   n-m
1957   Camus, Albert(Fr)   n-l
1957 FOOTBALL: John Unitas Balt fb-m
1957 HOCKEY: Gordie Howe Det ho-m
1957   Lee, Tsung-dao(Am)   n-p
1957 LONG DAY'S JOURNEY INTO NIGHT--Eugene O'Neill p-d
1957 MEDITATIONS ON ECCLESIASTES--Norman Dello Joio p-m
1957   Pearson, Lester B.(Can)   n-x
1957 PROFILES IN COURAGE--John F. Kennedy p-b'57
1957 SAYONARA--Red Buttons o-s
1957 THE BRIDGE ON THE RIVER KWAI o-p --Alec Guinness o-a,
                & David Lean o-d
1957 THE THREE FACES OF EVE--Joanne Woodward o-a
1957 THINGS OF THIS WORLD--Richard Wilbur p-q
1957   Todd, Sir Alexander R.(Br)   n-c
1957   Yang, Chen Ning(Am)   n-p
1958 A DEATH IN THE FAMILY--James Agee p-f
1958 BASEBALL: Ernie Banks Chi b-mv, Jackie Jensen Bos b-mv
                Bob Turley NY(AL) b-cy
1958 BASKETBALL: Bill Russell Bos bb-m
1958   Beadle, George W.(Am)   n-m
1958   Cherenkov, Pavel(Rus)   n-p
1958 FOOTBALL: Jim Brown Cle fb-m
1958   Frank, Ilya(USSR)   n-p
1958 GEORGE WASHINGTON, Vols. I - VI--
                Douglas Southall Freeman p-b
1958 HOCKEY: Gordie Howe Det ho-m
1958 I WANT TO LIVE--Susan Hayward o-a
1958   Lederberg, Joshua(Am)   n-m
1958 LOOK HOMEWARD, ANGEL--Ketti Frings p-d
1958   Pasternak, Boris L.(Rus)   n-l(declined)
1958   Pire, Georges(Belg)   n-x
1958 PROMISES: POEMS 1954-1956--Robert Penn Warren p-q

```
1958          Sanger, Frederick(Br)  n-c
1958 SEPARATE TABLES--David Niven o-a & Wendy Hiller o-s
1958          Tamm, Igor Y.(Rus)  n-p
1958          Tatum, Edward L.(Am)  n-m
1958 THE BIG COUNTRY--Burl Ives o-s
1958 THE MUSIC FROM PETER GUN(album)--Henry Mancini g-r
1958 VANESSA--Samuel Barber p-m
1958 VOLARE--Domenico Modugno g-r
1959 BASEBALL: Ernie Banks Chi b-mv, Nellie Fox Chi(AL) b-mv
                     Early Wynn Chi(AL) b-cy
1959 BASKETBALL: Bob Pettit StL bb-m
1959 BEN-HUR o-p MGM--Charlton Heston o-a, Hugh Griffith o-s
                            & William Wyler o-d
1959          Chamberlain, Owen(Am)  n-p
1959 COME DANCE WITH ME(album)--Frank Sinatra g-r
1959 CONCERTO FOR PIANO AND ORCHESTRA--John La Montaine p-m
1959 DIARY OF ANNE FRANK--Shelley Winters o-s
1959 FOOTBALL: Charlie Conerly NY fb-m
1959          Heyrovsky, Jaroslav(Czech)  n-c
1959 HOCKEY: Andy Bathgate NYR ho-m
1959 J. B. --Archilbald MacLeish p-d
1959          Kornberg, Arthur(Am)  n-m
1959 MACK THE KNIFE--Bobby Darin g-r
1959          Noel-Baker, PHILIP J.(Br)  n-x
1959          Ochoa, Severo(Am)  n-m
1959          Quasimodo, Salvatore(It)  n-l
1959 ROOM AT THE TOP--Simone Signoret o-a
1959          Segre, Emilio G.(Am)  n-p
1959 SELECTED POEMS 1928-1958--Stanley Kunitz p-q
1959 THE TRAVELS OF JAIMIE McPHEETERS--Robert L. Taylor p-f
1960 ADVISE AND CONSENT--Allen Drury p-f
1960 BASEBALL: Dick Groat Pitt b-mv,  Roger Maris NY b-mv
                     Vernon Law Pitt b-cy
1960 BASKETBALL: Wilt Chamberlain StL bb-m
1960          Bumet, Sir F. MacFarlane(Austral)  n-m
1960 BUTTERFIELD 8--Elizabeth Taylor o-a
1960 BUTTON DOWN MIND(album)--Bob Newhart g-r
1960 ELMER GANTRY--Burt Lancaster o-a & Shirley Jones o-s
1960 FIORELLO--George Abbott, Jerry  Bock, Sheldon Harnick and
                            Jerome Weidman p-d
1960 FOOTBALL: Norm Van Brocklin Phil fb-m
1960          Glaser, Donald A.(Am)  n-p
1960 HEART'S NEEDLE--W.D. Snodgrass p-q
1960 HOCKEY: Gordie Howe Det ho-m
1960 JOHN PAUL JONES--Samuel Eliot Morison p-b
1960          Libby, Willard F.(Am)  n-c
1960          Luthuli, Albert J.(S.Afr)  n-x
1960          Medawar, Peter B.(Br)  n-m
1960 OL. GMS:100,200 MTRS.& RELAY--Wilma Rudolph(Am)3 o-g's
1960 OL. GMS: 110 METER HURDLES--Lee Calhoun(Am) o-g
1960 OL. GMS: 400 METER HURDLES--Glenn Davis(Am) o-g
1960 OL. GMS: 800 METER RUN--Peter Snell(N.Zea) o-g
1960 OL. GMS: BOXING-LT. HEAVYWT--Cassius Clay(Am) o-g
1960 OL. GMS: DISCUS THROW--Al Oerter(Am) o-g
1960 OL. GMS: TRIPLE JUMP--Jozef Schmidt(Pol) o-g
1960          Perse, Saint-John(Fr)  n-l
1960 SECOND STRING QUARTET--Elliott Carter p-m
1960 SPARTACUS--Peter Ustinov o-s
1960 THE APARTMENT o-p --Billy Wilder o-d
1960 THEME FROM A SUMMER PLACE--Percy Faith g-r
```

```
1961 ALL THE WAY HOME--Tad Mosel p-d
1961      Andric, Ivo(Yugo) n-l
1961 BASEBALL: Frank Robinson Cinn b-mv, Roger Maris NY b-mv
                Whitey Ford NY b-cy
1961 BASKETBALL: Bill Russell Bos bb-m
1961      Bekesy, Georg von(Am) n-m
1961      Calvin, Melvin(Am) n-c
1961 CHICAGO TRIBUNE--Carey Orr p-x
1961 FOOTBALL: Y.A. Tittle NY fb-m
1961      Hammarskjold, Dag(Swed) n-x
1961 HOCKEY: Bernie Geoffrion Mont ho-m
1961      Hofstadter, Robert(Am) n-p
1961 JUDGMENT AT NUREMBERG--Maximilian Schell o-a
1961 JUDY AT CARNEGIE HALL(album)--Judy Garland g-r
1961 MOON RIVER--Henry Mancini g-r
1961      Mossbauer, Rudolf L.(Ger) n-p
1961 SYMPHONY NO. 7--Walter Piston p-m
1961 TIMES THREE: SELECTED VERSE FROM THREE DECADES--
                     Phyllis McGinley p-q
1961 TO KILL A MOCKINGBIRD--Harper Lee p-f
1961 TWO WOMEN--Sophia Loren o-a
1961 WEST SIDE STORY o-p --George Chakiris o-s,
          Rita Moreno o-s,Jerome Robbins + Robert Wise o-d
1962 BASEBALL:  Maury Wills LA b-mv, Mickey Mantle NY b-mv
                Don Drysdale LA b-cy
1962 BASKETBALL: Bill Russell Bos bb-m
1962      Crick, Francis H. C.(Br) n-m
1962 FOOTBALL: Jim Taylor GB fb-m
1962 HOCKEY: Jacques Plante Mont ho-m
1962 HOW TO SUCCEED IN BUSINESS WITHOUT REALLY
                TRYING--Abe Burrows & Frank Loesser p-d
1962 I LEFT MY HEART IN SAN FRANCISCO--Tony Bennett g-r
1962      Kendrew, John C.(Br) n-c
1962      Landau, Lev. D.(USSR) n-p
1962      Pauling, Linus C.(Am) n-x
1962      Perutz, Max F.(Br) n-c
1962 POEMS--Alan Dugan p-q
1962      Steinbeck, John(Am) n-l
1962 SWEET BIRD OF YOUTH--Ed Begley o-s
1962 THE CRUCIBLE--Robert Ward p-m
1962 THE EDGE OF SADNESS--Edwin O'Connor p-f
1962 THE FIRST FAMILY(album)--Vaughn Meader g-r
1962 THE MAKING OF THE PRESIDENT 1960--Theodore H, White p-n
1962 THE MIRACLE WORKER--Anne Bancroft o-a & Patty Duke o-s
1962 TO KILL A MOCKINGBIRD--Gregory Peck o-a
1962      Watson, James D.(Am) n-m
1962      Wilkins, Maurice H.F.(Br) n-m
1963 BASEBALL:  Sandy Koufax LA b-mv,  Elston Howard NY b-mv
                Sandy Koufax LA b-cy
1963 BASKETBALL: Bill Russell Bos bb-m
1963 DAYS OF WINE AND ROSES--Henry Mancini g-r
1963      Eccles, Sir John C.(Austral) n-m
1963 FOOTBALL: Jim Brown Cle fb-m, Y,A, Tittle NY fb-m
1963      Goeppert-Mayer, Maria(Am) n-p
1963 HENRY JAMES(biog.), Vols. II --Leon Edel p-b
1963 HOCKEY:   Gordie Howe Det ho-m
1963      Hodgkin, Alan L.(Br) n-m
1963 HUD--Patricia Neal o-a &  Melvyn Douglas o-s
1963      Huxley, Andrew F.(Br) n-m
1963      Jensen, J. Hans D.(Ger) n-p
```

1963 LILIES OF THE FIELD--Sidney Poitier o-a
1963   Natta, Giulio(It) n-c
1963 PIANO CONCERTO NO. 1--Samuel Barber p-m
1963 PICTURES FROM BREUGHEL--William Carlos Williams p-q
1963   Seferis, Giorgos(Greek) n-l
1963 THE BARBARA STREISAND ALBUM--Barbara Streisand g-r
1963 THE GUNS OF AUGUST--Barbara W. Tuchman p-n
1963 THE REIVERS--William Faulkner p-f
1963 THE V.I.P.s--Margaret Rutherford o-s
1963   Wigner, Eugene P.(Am) n-p
1963   Ziegler, Karl(Ger) n-c
1964 ANTI-INTELLECTUALISM IN AMERICAN LIFE--
                              Richard Hofstadter p-n
1964 AT THE END OF THE OPEN ROAD--Louis Simpson p-q
1964 BASEBALL: Ken Boyer StL b-mv, Brooks Robinson Bal b-mv
               Dean Chance LA(AL) b-cy
1964 BASKETBALL: Oscar Robertson, Cin bb-m
1964   Basov, Nikolai G.(Rus) n-p
1964   Bloch, Konrad E.(Am) n-m
1964 FOOTBALL: Lenny Moore Bal fb-m
1964 HOCKEY: Jean Geliveau Mont ho-m
1964   Hodgkin, Dorothy C.(Br) n-c
1964 JOHN KEATS--Walter Jackson Bate p-b
1964   King, Martin Luther Jr.(Am) n-x
1964   Lynen, Feodor(Ger) n-m
1964 MARY POPPINS--Julie Andrews o-a
1964 MY FAIR LADY o-p,--Rex Harrison o-a & George Cukor o-d
1964 OL. GMS: 100 METER RUN-WOMEN--Wynona Tyus(Am) o-g
1964 OL. GMS: 400 METER RUN-WOMEN--Betty Cuthbert(Aust) o-g
1964 OL. GMS: 800 METER RUN--Peter Snell(N.Zea) o-g
1964 OL. GMS: 1500 METER RUN--Peter Snell(N.Zea)o-g
1964 OL. GMS: DISCUS--Al Oerter(Am) o-g
1964   Prochorov, Aleksander M.(Rus) n-p
1964   Sartre, Jean Paul(Fr) n-l(declined)
1964 STAN GETZ, ASTRUD GILBERTO(Album)--Getz/Gilberto g-r
1964 THE GIRL FROM IPANEMA--Stan Getz, Astrud Gilberto g-r
1964 TOKAPI--Peter Ustinov o-s
1964   Townes, Charles H.(Am) n-p
1964 ZORBA THE GREEK--Lila Kedrova o-s
1965 A PATCH OF BLUE--Shelley Winters o-s
1965 A TASTE OF HONEY--Herb Alpert g-r
1965 A THOUSAND CLOWNS--Martin Balsam o-s
1965 BASEBALL: Willie Mays SF b-mv,Zoilo Versalles Minn b-mv
               Sandy Koufax LA b-cy
1965 BASKETBALL: Bill Russell Bos bb-m
1965 CAT BALLOU--Lee Marvin o-a
1965 DARLING--Julie Christie o-a
1965   Feynman, Richard P.(Am) n-p
1965 FOOTBALL: Jin Brown Cle fb-m
1965 HOCKEY: Bobby Hull Chi ho-m
1965   Jacob, Francois(Fr) n-m
1965   Lwoff, Andre(Fr) n-m
1965   Monod, Jacques(Fr) n-m
1965 O STRANGE NEW WORLD--Howard Mumford Jones p-n
1965   Schwinger, Julian S.(Am) n-p
1965 SEPTEMBER OF MY YEARS(album)--Frank Sinatra g-r
1965 77 DREAM SONGS--John Berryman p-q
1965   Sholokhov, Mikhail(Rus) n-l
1965 THE KEEPERS OF THE HOUSE--Shirley Ann Grau p-f
1965 THE SUBJECT WAS ROSES--Frank D. Gilroy p-d

```
1965        Tomonaga, Shin'ichiro(Japan)  n-p
1965        UNICEF  n-x
1965        Woodward, Robert B.(Am)   n-c
1966        Agnon, Samuel Joseph(Israel)  n-l
1966 A MAN AND HIS MUSIC(album)--Frank Sinatra g-r
1966 A MAN FOR ALL SEASONS o-p--Paul Scofield o-a &
                        Fred Zinnemann o-d
1966 A THOUSAND DAYS--Arthur M. Schlesinger Jr. p-b
1966 BASEBALL:Roberto Clemente Pitt b-mv,
             Frank Robinson Bal b-mv, Sandy Koufax LA b-cy
1966 BASKETBALL: Wilt Chamberlain bb-m
1966 COLLECTED STORIES OF KATHERINE ANNE PORTER--
                        Katherine Anne Porter p-f
1966 FOOTBALL: Larry Wilson StL   fb-d, Bart Starr GB fb-m
1966 HOCKEY: Bobby Hull Chi ho-m
1966        Huggins, Charles B.(Am)   n-m
1966        Kastler, Alfred(Fr)  n-p
1966 LIFE OF THE MIND IN AMERICA--Perry Miller p-h
1966        Mulliken, Robert S.(Am)  n-c
1966        Rous, Francis Peyton(Am)   n-m
1966        Sachs, Nelly(Swe)  n-l
1966 SELECTED POEMS--Richard Eberhart p-q
1966 STRANGERS IN THE NIGHT--Frank Sinatra g-r
1966 THE FORTUNE COOKIE--Walter Matthau o-s
1966 VARIATIONS FOR ORCHESTRA--Leslie Bassett p-m
1966 WANDERING THROUGH WINTER--Edwin Way Teale p-n
1966 WHO'S AFRAID OF VIRGINIA WOOLF?--Elizabeth Taylor o-a &
                        Sandy Dennis o-s
1967 A DELICATE BALANCE--Edward Albee p-d
1967        Asturias, Miguel Angel(Guatemala)   n-l
1967 BASEBALL:  Orlando Cepeda StL b-mv,
                        Carl Yastrzemski Bos b-mv
                Mike McCormick SF b-cy,Jim Lonberg Bos b-cy
1967 BASKETBALL: Wilt Chamberlain Phil bb-m
1967        Bethe, Hans A.(Am)   n-p
1967 BONNIE AND CLYDE--Estelle Parsons o-s
1967 COOL HAND LUKE--George Kennedy o-s
1967        Eigen, Manfred(Ger)  n-c
1967 FOOTBALL: Deacon Jones LA fb-d, John Unitas Bal fb-m
1967        Granit, Ragnar(Swe)  n-m
1967 GUESS WHO'S COMING TO DINNER--KATHARINE HEPBURN o-a
1967        Hartline, Haldan Keffer(Am)   n-m
1967 HOCKEY: Stan Mikita Chi ho-m
1967 IN THE HEAT OF THE NIGHT o-p--Rod Steiger o-a
1967 LIVE OR DIE--Anne Sexton p-q
1967        Norrish, Ronald G.W.(Br)   n-c
1967        Oliphant, Patrick B.(Am-Denver Post)p-x
1967        Porter, Sir George(Br)   n-c
1967 QUARTET NO. 3--Leon Kirchner p-m
1967 SGT, PEPPER'S LONELY HEART CLUB BAND(album)--
                        The Beatles g-r
1967 THE FIXER--Bernard Malamud p-f
1967 THE PROBLEM OF SLAVERY IN WESTERN CULTURE--
                        David Brion Davis p-n
1967 UP, UP AND AWAY--5th Dimension g-r
1967        Wald, George(Am)  n-m
1968        Alvarez, Luis W.(Am)  n-p
1968 BASEBALL: Bob Gibson StL b-mv, Dennis McLain Det b-mv
             Bob Gibsin StL b-cy,  Dennis McLain Det b-cy
1968 BASKETBALL: Wilt Chamberlain Phil bb-m
```

1968 BY THE TIME I GET TO PHOENIX(album)--Glen Campbell g-r
1968   Cassin, Rene(Fr)   n-x
1968 CHARLY--Cliff Robertson o-a
1968   Day-Lewis, Cecil(Br) pol to 1972
1968 ECHOES OF TIME AND THE RIVER--George Crumb p-m
1968 FOOTBALL: Deacon Jones LA fb-d, Earl Morall Bal fb-m
1968 FUNNY GIRL--Barbra Streisand o-a(tie)
1968 HOCKEY: Stan Mikita Chi ho-m
1968   Holley, Robert W.(Am) n-m
1968   Kawabata, Yasunari(Japan) n-l
1968   Khorana, H. Gobind(Am) n-m
1968 MRS. ROBINSON--Simon & Garfunkel g-r
1968   Nirenberg, Marshall W.(Am) n-m
1968 OL. GMS: 100 METER RUN-WOMEN--Wynona Tyus(Am) o-g
1968 OL. GMS: DISCUS--Al Oerter(Am) o-g
1968 OL. GMS: FIGURE SKATING-- Peggy Fleming(Am) o-
1968 OL. GMS: HIGH JUMP--Dick Fosbury(Am) o-g
1968 OL. GMS: SKIING--Jean Claude Killy(Fr) 3 o-g's
1968 OL. GMS: TRIPLE JUMP--Viktor Saneev(Rus) o-g
1968   Onsager, Lars(Am) n-c
1968 ROSEMARY'S BABY--Ruth Gordon o-s
1968 ROUSSEAU AND REVOLUTION--Will and Ariel Durant p-n
1968 THE CONFESSIONS OF NAT TURNER--William Styron p-f
1968 THE HARD HOURS--Anthony Hecht p-q
1968 THE LION IN WINTER--Katharine Hepburn o-a(tie)
1968 THE SUBJECT WAS ROSES--Jack Albertson o-s
1969   Barton, Sir Derek H.R.(Br) n-c
1969 BASEBALL: Willie McCovey SF b-mv,
                          Harmon Killebrew Mil b-mv
            Tom Seaver Mets b-cy, Dennis McLain Det b-cy
                    Tied with Mike Cuellar Balt b-cy
1969 BASKETBALL: Wes Unseld Bal bb-m
1969   Beckett, Samuel(Irish) n-l
1969 BLOOD, SWEAT AND TEARS(album) g-r
1969 CACTUS FLOWER--Goldie Hawn o-s
1969   Delbruk, Max(Am) n-m
1969 FOOTBALL: Dick Butkas Chi fb-d, Roman Gabriel LA fb-m
1969   Frisch, Ragnar(Norw) n-e
1969   Hassel, Odd(Nor) n-c
1969   Hershey, Alfred Day(Am) n-m
1969 HOCKEY: Phil Esposito Bos ho-m
1969 HOUSE MADE OF DAWN--N. Scott Momaday p-f
1969 LET THE SUNSHINE IN--5th Dimension, Aquarius g-r
1969   Luria, Salvador(Am) n-m
1969 MIDNIGHT COWBOY o-p--John Schlesinger o-d
1969   Gell-Mann Murray(Am) n-p
1969 OF BEING NUMEROUS--Geirge Oppen p-q
1969 SO HUMAN AN ANIMAL: HOW WE ARE SHAPED BY
            SURROUNDINGS AND EVENTS--Rene Jules Dubos p-n
1969 STRING QUARTET NO. 3--Karel Husa p-m
1969 THE ARMIES OF THE NIGHT--Norman Mailer p-n
1969 THE GREAT WHITE HOPE--Howard Sackler p-d
1969 THE PRIME OF MISS JEAN BRODIE--Maggie Smith o-a
1969 THEY SHOOT HORSES, DON'T THEY--Gig Young o-s
1969   Tinbergen, Jan(Dutch) n-e
1969 TRUE GRIT--John Wayne o-a
1970 AIRPORT--Helen Hayes o-s
1970   Alfven, Hannes(Swe) n-p
1970   Axelrod, Julius(Am) n-m

1970 BASEBALL: Johnny Bench Cinn b-mv,
                          John(Boog) Powell Balt b-mv
              Bob Gibson StL b-cy, Jim Perry Minn b-cy
1970 BASKETBALL: Willis Reed NY bb-m
1970   Borlaug, Norman E.(Am) n-x
1970 BRIDGE OVER TROUBLED WATERS(both single & album)--
                          Simon & Garfunkel g-r's
1970 COLLECTED STORIES--Jean Stafford p-f
1970 FOOTBALL: Dick Butkus Chi fb-d, John Brodie SF fb-m
1970 GANDHI'S TRUTH--Eric H. Erikson p-n
1970 HOCKEY: Bobby Orr Bos ho-m
1970 HUEY LONG--T. Harry Williams p-b
1970   Katz, Sir Bernard(Br) n-m
1970   Leloir, Luis F.(Arg) n-c
1970   Neel, Louis(Fr) n-p
1970 NO PLACE TO BE SOMEBODY--Charles Gordone p-d'70
1970 PATTON o-p --George C. Scott o-a(refused) &
                          Franklin Schaffner o-d
1970 PRESENT AT THE CREATION: MY YEARS IN THE STATE
                          DEPARTMENT--Dean Acheson p-h
1970 RYAN'S DAUGHTER--John Mills o-s
1970   Samuelson, Paul A.(Am) n-e
1970   Solzhenitsyn, Aleksandr I.(Rus)   n-l
1970 TIME'S ENCOMIUM--Charles W. Wuorinen p-m
1970 UNTITLED SUBJECTS--Richard Howard p-q
1970   VonEuler, Ulf(Swe) n-m
1970 WOMEN IN LOVE--Glenda Jackson o-a
1971 BASEBALL: Joe Torre StL b-mv, Vida Blue Oak b-mv,
                  Ferguson Jenkins Chi b-cy, Vida Blue Oak b-cy
1971 BASKETBALL: Lew Alcindor Mil bb-m
1971   Brandt, Willy(W. Ger) n-x
1971 FOOTBALL: Carl Eller Min fb-d, Bob Griese Mia fb-m
1971   Gabor, Dennis(Br) n-p
1971   Herzberg, Gerhard(Can) n-c
1971 HOCKEY: Bobby Orr Bos ho-m
1971 IT'S TOO LATE--Carole King g-r
1971 KLUTE--Jane Fonda o-a
1971   Kuznets, Simon(Am) n-e
1971   Neruda, Pablo(Chili) n-l
1971   Sutherland, Earl W. Jr(Am) n-m
1971 SYNCHRONISMS NO. 6--Mario Davidovsky p-m
1971 TAPESTRY(album)--Carole King g-r
1971 THE CARRIER OF LADDERS--William S. Merwin p-q
1971 THE EFFECT OF GAMMA RAYS ON MAN-IN-THE-MOON-
                          MARIGOLDS--Paul Zindel p-d
1971 THE FRENCH CONNECTION o-p --Gene Hackman o-a &
                          William Friedkin o-d
1971 THE LAST PICTURE SHOW--Ben Johnson o-s,
                          Cloris Leachman o-s
1971 THE RISING SUN--John Toland p-n
1972   Anfinsen, Christian B.(Am) n-c
1972 ANGLE OF REPOSE--Wallace Stegner p-f
1972   Arrow, Kenneth J.(Am) n-e
1972 BASEBALL: Johnny Bench Cin b-mv, Dick Allen Chi b-mv
              Steve Carlton Phil b-cy, Gaylord Perry Clev b-cy
1973 BASKETBALL: Kareem Abdul-Jabbar Mil bb-m
1972   Betjeman, John(Sir)(Br) pol to 1984
1972   Boll, Heinrich(W.Ger) n-l
1972   Bardeen, John(Am) n-p
1972 BUTTERFLIES ARE FREE--Eileen Heckart o-s

1972 CABARET--Liza Minnelli o-a, Joel Grey o-s &
                                    Bob Fosse o-d
1972 COLLECTED POEMS--James Wright p-q
1972   Cooper, Leon N.(Am) n-p
1972   Edelman, Gerald M.(Am) n-m
1972 ELEANOR AND FRANKLIN--Joseph P. Lash p-b
1972 FOOTBALL: Joe Greene Pit fb-d, Larry Brown Wash fb-m
1972   Hicks, Sir John R.(Br) n-e
1972 HOCKEY: Bobby Orr Bos ho-m
1972   Moore, Stanford(Am) n-c
1972 OL, GMS: 5K&10K METER RUNS--Lasse Viren(Finn) 2X o-g's
1972 OL. GMS: GYMNASTICS--Olga Korrbut(Rus) 3X o-g's
1972 OL. GMS: SWIMMING--Mark Spitz(Am) 7X o-g's
1972 OL. GMS: TRIPLE JUMP--Viktor Saneev(Rus) o-g
1972   Porter, Rodney R.(Br) n-m
1972   Schrieffer, John R.(Am) n-p
1972 STILWELL AND THE AMERICAN EXPERIENCE IN CHINA,
                    1911-1945--Barbara W.Tuchman p-n
1972   Stein, William H.(Am) n-c
1972 THE CONCERT FOR BANGLA DESH g-r
1972 THE FIRST TIME EVER I SAW YOUR FACE--Roberta Flack g-r
1972 THE GODFATHER o-p --Marlon Brando o-a(refused)
1972 WINDOWS--Jacob Druckman p-m
1973 A TOUCH OF CLASS--Glenda Jackson o-a
1973 BASEBALL: Pete Rose Cin b-mv, Reggie Jackson Oak b-mv
                  Tom Seaver NY b-cy, Jim Palmer Bal b-cy
1973 BASKETBALL: Dave Cowens Bos bb-m
1973 CHILDREN OF CRISIS,VOLUMES II & III--Robert Coles p-n
1973   Esaki, Leo(Japan) n-p
1973   Fischer, Ernst Otto(W.Ger) n-c
1973 FIRE IN THE LAKE: THE VIETNAMESE AND THE AMERICANS
                  IN VIETNAM--Frances FitzGerald p-n
1973 FOOTBALL: Alan Paige Min fb-d, O.J. Simpson Buf fb-m
1973   Frisch, Karl von(Ger) n-m
1973   Giaever, Ivar(Am) n-p
1973 HOCKEY: Bobby Clarke Phil ho-m
1973 INNERVISIONS(album)--Stevie Wonder g-r
1973   Josephson, Brian D.(Br) n-p
1973 KILLING ME SOFTLY WITH HIS SONG--Roberta Flack g-r
1973   Kissinger, Henry(Am) n-x
1973   Le Duc Tho(N.Vietnam) n-x (refused)
1973   Lorenz, Konrad(Ger-Aus) n-m
1973 PAPER MOON--Tatum O'Neal o-s
1973 SAVE THE TIGER--Jack Lemmon o-a
1973 STRING QUARTET NO. 3--Elliott Carter p-m
1973 THAT CHAMPIONSHIP SEASON--Jason Miller p-d
1973 THE OPTIMIST'S DAUGHTER--Eudora Welty p-f
1973 THE PAPER CHASE--John Houseman o-s
1973   Tinbergen, Nikolaas(Br) n-m
1973 UP COUNTRY--Maxine Winokur Kumin p-q
1973   Wassily, Leontief(Am) n-e
1973   White, Patrick(Austral) n-l
1973   Wilkinson, Sir Geoffrey(Br) n-c
1974 ALICE DOESN'T LIVE HERE ANYMORE--Ellen Burstyn o-a
1974 BASEBALL: Steve Garvey LA b-mv, Jeff Burroughs Tex b-mv
          Mike Marshall LA b-cy, Jim(Catfish) Hunter Oak b-cy
1974 BASKETBALL: Kareem Abdul-Jabbar bb-m
1974 BOSTON GLOBE--Paul Szep p-x
1974   Claude, Albert(Am) n-m
1974   Duve, Christian Rene de(Belg) n-m

```
1974          Flory, Paul J.(Am)   n-c
1974 FOOTBALL: Jeo Greene Pit fb-d,  Ken Stabler Oak fb-m
1974 FULFILLIGNESS' FIRST FINALE(album)--Stevie Wonder g-r
1974 HARRY AND TONTO--Art Carney o-a
1974          Hayek, Friedrich A. von(Aus)   n-e
1974          Hewish, Antony(Br)   n-p
1974 HOCKEY: Phil Esposito Bos ho-m
1974 I HONESTLY LOVE YOU--Olivia Newton-John g-r
1974          Johnson, Eyvind(Swe)   n-l
1974          MacBride, Sean(Irish)   n-x
1974          Martinson, Harry Edmund(Swe)   n-l
1974 MURDER ON THE ORIENT EXPRESS--Ingrid Bergman o-s
1974          Myrdal, Gunnar(Swed)   n-e
1974 NOTTURNO--Donald Martino p-m
1974          Palade, George Emil(Rom-Am)   n-m
1974          Ryle, Martin(Br)    n-p
1974          Sato, Eisaku(Jap)   n-x
1974 THE DENIAL OF DEATH--Ernest Becker p-n
1974 THE GODFATHER, PART II o-p --Robert DeNiro o-s &
                         Francis Ford Coppola o-d
1975          Baltimore, David(Am)   n-m
1975 BASEBALL:  Joe Morgan Cin b-mv,  Fred Lynn Bos b-mv
                  Tom Seaver NY b-cy,  Jim Palmer Bal b-cy
1975 BASKETBALL: Bob McAdoo Buf bb-m
1975          Bohr, Aage(Dan)   n-p
1975          Cornforth, John(Austral-Br)   n-c
1975          Dulbecco, Renato(It-Am)   n-m
1975 FOOTBALL:Curley Culp Hou fb-d,Fran Tarkenton Min fb-m
1975 FROM THE DIARY OF VIRGINIA WOOLF--Dominick Argento p-m
1975 HOCKEY: Bobby Clartke Phil ho-m
1975          Kantorovich, Leonid(Rus)   n-e
1975          Koopmans, Tjalling(Dut)   n-e
1975 LOVE WILL KEEP US TOGETHER--Captain & Tennille g-r
1975          Montale, Eugenio(It)   n-l
1975          Mottelson, Ben(US-Dan)   n-p
1975 ONE FLEW OVER THE CUCKOO'S NEST o-p-Jack Nicholson o-a,
                  Louise Fletcher o-a & Milos Forman o-d
1975 PILGRIM AT TINKER CREEK--Annie Dillard p-n
1975          Prelog, Vladimir(Yugo-Swiss)   n-c
1975          Rainwater, James(Am)   n-p
1975          Sakharov, Andrei(Rus)   n-x
1975 SEASCAPE--Edward Albee p-d
1975 SHAMPOO--Lee Grant o-s
1975 STILL CRAZY AFTER ALL THESE YEARS(album)-Paul Simon g-r
1975          Temin, Howard(Am)   n-m
1975 THE KILLER ANGELS--Michael Shaara p-f
1975 THE SUNSHINE BOYS--George Burns o-s
1975 TURTLE ISLAND--Gary Snyder p-q
1976 A CHORUS LINE--Michael Bennett, Nicholas Dante,
     James Kirkwoo, Edward Kleban & Marvin Hamlisch p-d
1976 AIR MUSIC--Ned Rorem p-m
1976 ALL THE PRESIDENT'S MEN--Jason Robards o-s
1976 BASEBALL:  Joe Morgan Cin b-mv, Thurman Munson NY b-mv
                  Randy Jones San Diego b-cy, Jim Palmer Bal b-cy
1976 BASKETBALL: Kareem Abdul-Jabbar bb-m
1976          Bellow, Saul(Am)   n-l
1976          Blumberg, Baruch S.(Am)   n-m
1976          Corrigan, Mairead(N.Ireland)   n-x
1976 FOOTBALL: Jerry Shark Cle fb-d,  Bert Jones Bal fb-m
1976          Friedman, Milton(Am)   n-e
```

1976   Gajdusek, Daniel Carleton(Am)   n-m
1976 HOCKEY: Bobby Clarke Phil ho-m
1976 HUMBOLDT'S GIFT--Saul Bellow p-f
1976 LAMY OF SANTA FE--Paul Horgan p-h
1976   Lipscomb, William N.(Am)   n-c
1976 NETWORK--Peter Finch o-a, Faye Dunaway o-a   &
                              Beatrice Straight o-s
1976 OL. GMS: 1500 METER RUN-WOMEN-Tatyana Kazankina(Rus)o-g
1976 OL. GMS: 5K& 10K METER RUNS--Lasse Viren(Finn)2X o-g's
1976 OL, GMS: BOXING--Michael Spinks(Am)   o-g
1976 OL. GMS: DECATHALON--Bruce Jenner(Am)   o-g
1976 OL. GMS: FIGURE SKATING--Dorothy Hamill(Am)   o-g
1976 OL. GMS: GYMNASTICS--Nadia Comaneci(Rom)3 o-g's
1976 OL. GMS: TRIPLE JUMP--Viktor Saneev(Rus) o-g
1976 PHILADELPHIA INQUIRER--Tony Auth p-x
1976   Richter, Burton(Am) n-p
1976 SELF-PORTRAIT IN A CONVEX MIRROR--John Ashbery p-q
1976 SONGS IN THE KEY OF LIFE(album)--Stevie Wonder g-r
1976 THIS MASQUERADE--George Benson g-r
1976   Ting, Samuel C. C.(Am)   n-p
1976 WHY SURVIVE? BEING OLD IN AMERICA--Robert N. Butler p-n
1976   Williams, Betty(N.Ireland)   n-x
1977   Aleixandre, Vicente(Sp)   n-l
1977   Anderson, Philip W.(Am)   n-p
1977 ANNIE HALL o-p --Diane Keaton o-a & Woody Allen o-d
1977 BASEBALL: George Foster Cin b-mv, Rod Carew Min b-mv
               Steve Carlton Phi b-cy, Sparky Lyle NY b-cy
1977 BASKETBALL: Kareem Abdul-Jabbar bb-m
1977 BEAUTIFUL SWIMMERS--William W. Warner p-n
1977 BOSTON GLOBE--Paul Szep p-x
1977 DEVINE COMEDIES--James Merrill p-q
1977   Guillemin, Roger C.L.(Am)   n-m
1977 HOCKEY: Guy Lafleur Mont ho-m
1977 HOTEL CALIFORNIA--Eagles g-r
1977 JULIA--Jason Robards o-s   & Vanessa Redgrave o-s
1977   Meade, James E,(Br)   n-e
1977   Mott, Sir Nevill F.(Br)   n-p
1977   Ohlin, Bertil(Swe)   n-e
1977   Prigogine, Ilya(Belg)   n-c
1977 RUMOURS(album)--Fleetwood Mac g-r
1977   Schally, Andrew V.(Am)   n-m
1977 THE GOODBYE GIRL--Richard Dreyfuss o-a
1977 THE SHADOW BOX--Michael Cristofer p-d
1977   Van Vleck, John H.(Am)   n-p
1977 VISIONS OF TERROR AND WONDER--Richard Wenick p-m
1977   Yalow, Rosalyn S.(Am)   n-m
1978   Arber, Werner(Swi)   n-m
1978 BASEBALL: Dave Parker Pitt b-mv, Jim Rice Bos b-mv
               Gaylord Perry SD b-cy, Ron Guidry NY b-cy
1978 BASKETBALL: Bill Walton Port bb-m
1978   Begin, Menachem(Israel)   n-x
1978 CALIFORNIA SUITE--Maggie Smith o-s
1978 COLLECTED POEMS--Howard Nemerov p-q
1978 COMING HOME--Jon Voight o-a & Jane Fonda o-a
1978 DEJA VU FOR PERCUSSION AND ORCHESTRA--
                              Michael Colgrass p-m
1978 ELBOW ROOM--James Alan McPherson p-f
1978 FOOTBALL: Randy Gradishar Den fb-d,
               Earl Campbell Hou fb-m
1978 HOCKEY: Guy Lafleur Mont ho-m

1978 JUST THE WAY YOU ARE--Billy Joel g-r
1978   Kapitsa, Pyotr(Rus) n-p
1978   Mitchell, Peter(Br) n-c
1978   Nathans, Daniel(Am) n-m
1978 NEW YORK TIMES--William Safire p-c
1978   Penzias, Arno(Am) n-p
1978   Sadat, Anwar(Egypt) n-x
1978 SAMUEL JOHNSON--Walter Jackson Bate p-b
1978 SATURDAY NIGHT FEVER(album)--Bee Gees g-r
1978   Simon, Herbert A.(Am) n-e
1978   Singer, Isaac Bashevis(Am) n-l
1978   Smith, Hamilton O.(Am) n-m
1978 THE DEER HUNTER o-p-Christopher Walken o-s &
                                Michael Cimino o-d
1978 THE DRAGONS OF EDEN--Carl Sagan p-n
1978 THE GIN GAME--Donald L. Coburn p-d
1978   Wilson, Robert(Am) n-p
1979 AFTERTONES OF INFINITY--Joseph Schwantner p-m
1979 BASEBALL:Willie Stargell Pitt b-mv,Don Baylor Cal b-mv
        Keith Hernandez StL b-mv(Tie with Willie St.,above)
                Bruce Sutter Chi b-cy, Mike Flanagab Bal b-cy
1979 BASKETBALL: Moses Malone Hous bb-m
1979 BEING THERE--Melvyn Douglas o-s
1979   Brown, Herbert C.(Am) n-c
1979 BURIED CHILD--Sam Shepard p-d
1979   Cormack, Alian M.(Am) n-m
1979   Elytis, Odysseus(Greek) n-l
1979 52ND STREET(album)--Billy Joel g-r
1979 FOOTBALL: Lee Roy Selmon Tam fb-d,
                                Earl Campbell Hou fb-m
1979   Glashow, Sheldon L.(Am) n-p
1979 HOCKEY: Bryan Trottier NY Islanders ho-m
1979   Hounsfield, Geoffrey N.(Br) n-m
1979 KRAMER VS. KRAMER o-p --Dustin Hoffman o-a,
                Meryl Streep o-s, Robert Benton o-d
1979   Lewis, Sir Arthur(Br) n-e
1979 NORMA RAE --Sally Field o-a
1979 NOW AND THEN: POEMS 1976-1978--Robert Penn Warren p-q
1979 ON HUMAN NATURE--Edward O. Wilson p-n
1979   Salam, Abdus(Pakistan) n-p
1979   Schultz, Theodore W.(Am) n-e
1979   Teresa, Mother (Alban.-India) n-x
1979 THE STORIES OF JOHN CHEEVER--John Cheever p-f
1979 WASHINGTON POST--Herbert L. Block p-x
1979   Weinberg, Steven(Am) n-p
1979 WHAT A FOOL BELIEVES--The Doobie Brothers g-r
1979   Wittig, George(Ger) n-c
1980 BACH: AN ETERNAL GOLDEN BRAID--Donald R. Hofstadter &
                                Escher Godel p-n
1980 BASEBALL: Mike Schmidt Phi B-mv, George Brett KC b-mv
                Steve Carlton Phi b-cy, Steve Stone Bal b-cy
1980 BASKETBALL: Kareem Abdul-Jabbar bb-m
1980   Benacerraf, Baruj(Am) n-m
1980   Berg, Paul(Am) n-c
1980 CHRISTOPHER CROSS(album)--Christopher Cross g-r
1980 COAL MINER'S DAUGHTER--Sissy Spacek o-a
1980   Cronin, James W.(Am) n-p
1980   Dausset, Jean(Fr) n-m
1980   Esquivel, Adolfo Perez((Arg) n-x
1980   Fitch, Val L.(Am) n-p

1980 FOOTBALL:Lester Hayes Oak fb-d, Earl Campbell Hou fb-m
1980   Gilbert, Walter(Am) n-c
1980 HOCKEY: Wayne Gretzky Edmonton ho-m
1980 IN MEMORY OF A SUMMER DAY--David Del Tredici p-m
1980   Klein, Lawrence R.(Am) n-e
1980 MELVIN AND HOWARD--Mary Steenburgen o-s
1980   Milosz, Czeslaw(Pol-Am) n-l
1980 OL. GMS: 0.5K,1K,1.5k,5k and 10k METER SPEED SKATING--
                        Eric Heiden(Am) 5X o-g's
1980 OL. GMS: WOMEN - 500M SKATING--Karin Enke Ger o-g
1980 OL, GMS: 1500M TRACK--Sebastian Coe(Br) o-g
1980 OL. GMS: 1.5k MTR RUN-WOMEN--Tatyana Kazankina(Rus)o-g
1980 ORDINARY PEOPLE o-p --Timothy Hutton o-s &
                        Robert Redford o-d
1980 RAGING BULL--Robert DeNiro o-a
1980 SAILING--Christopher Cross g-r
1980   Sanger Frederick(Br) n-c
1980 SELECTED POEMS--Donald Justice p-q
1980   Snell, George(Am) n-m
1980 TALLEY'S FOLLY--Lanford Wilson p-d
1980 THE EXECUTIONER'S SONG--Norman Mailer p-f
1980 THE RISE OF THEODORE ROOSEVELT--Edmund Morris p-b
1981 A CONFEDERACY OF DUNCES--John Kennedy Toole p-f
1981 ARTHUR--John Gielgud o-s
1981 BASEBALL:Mike Schmidt Phl b-mv,Rollie Fingers Mil b-mv
        Fernando Valenzuela LA b-cy, Rollie Fingers Mil b-cy
1981 BASKETBALL: Julius Irving Phil
1981 BETTE DAVIS EYES--Kim Carnes g-r
1981   Bloembergen, Nicolaas(Am) n-p
1981   Canetti, Elias(Bulg-Br) n-l
1981 CHARIOTS OF FIRE o-p
1981 CRIMES OF THE HEART--Beth Henley p-d
1981 DOUBLE FANTASY(album) John Lennon, Yoko Ono g-r
1981 FIN-DE-SIECLE VIENNA: POLITICS AND CULTURE--
                        Carl E. Schorske p-n
1981 FOOTBALL:Joe Klecko NYJets fb-d, Ken Anderson Cin fb-m
1981   Fukui, Kenichi(Japan) n-c
1981 HOCKEY: Wayne Gretzky Edm ho-m
1981   Hoffmann, Roald n-c
1981   Hubel, David H.(Am) n-m
1981 ON GOLDEN POND--Henry Fonda o-a, Katharine Hepburn o-a
1981 REDS--Maureen Stapleton o-s
1981   Schaalow, Arthur(Am) n-p
1981   Siegbahn, Kai Manne(Swe) n-p
1981   Sperry, Roger Wolcott(Am) n-m
1981 THE MORNING OF THE POEM--James Schuyler p-q
1981   Tobin, James(Am) n-e
1981   Wiesel, Tosten N.(Am) n-m
1982 AN OFFICER AND A GENTLEMAN--Louis Gossett Jr. o-s
1982 A SOLDIER'S PLAY--Charles Fuller p-d
1982 BASEBALL: Dale Murphy Atl b-mv, Robin Yount Mil b-mv
        Steve Carlton Phi b-cy, Pete Vuckovich Mil b-cy
1982 BASKETBALL   Moses Malone Hous bb-m
1982   Bergstrom, Sune(Swe) n-m
1982 CONCERTO FOR ORCHESTRA--Roger Sessions p-m
1982 FOOTBALL: Mark Gastineau NYJ fb-d, Dan Fouts SD fb-m
1982 GANDHI o-p--Ben Kingsley o-a, Richard Attenborough o-d
1982 GRANT: A BIOGRAPHY--William S. McFeely p-b
1982 HOCKEY   Wayne Gretzky Edm ho-m
1982   Klug, Aaron(S.Afr) n-c

```
1982        Marquez, Gabriel Garcia(Colom-Mex)  n-l
1982        Myrdal, Alva(Swe)  n-x
1982 RABBIT IS RICH--Updike, John p-f
1982        Robles, Garcia(Mex)  n-x
1982 ROSANNA--Toto g-r
1982        Samuelsson, Bengt(Swe)  n-m
1982 SOPHIE'S CHOICE--Meryl Streep o-a
1982        Stigler, George J.(Am)  n-e
1982 THE COLLECTED POEMS--Sylvia Plath p-q
1982 THE SOUL OF A NEW MACHINE--Tracy Kidder p-n
1982 TOOTSIE--Jessica Lange o-s
1982 TOTO IV(album)--Toto g-r
1982        Vane, John R.(Br)  n-m
1982        Wilson, Kenneth G.(Am)  n-p
1983 BASEBALL: Dale Murphy Atl b-mv, Cal Ripken Jr Bal b-mv
                 John Denny Phil b-cy,  LaMar Hoyt Chi b-cy
1983 BASKETBALL   Moses Malone Phil bb-m
1983 BEAT IT--Michael Jackson g-r
1983        Hughes, Ted(Br) pol to date('95)
1983 FOOTBALL: Jack Lambert Pit fb-d,
                          Joe Theisman Wash fb-m
1983        Fowler, William A.(Am)  n-p
1983        Golding, William(Br)  n-l
1983 HOCKEY   Wayne Gretzky Edm ho-m
1983 IS THERE NO PLACE ON EARTH FOR ME?--Susan Sheehan p-n
1983        McClintock, Barbara(Am)  n-m
1983 'NIGHT, MOTHER--Marsha Norman p-d
1983 SELECTED POEMS--Galway Kinnell p-q
1983        Surbrahmanyan, Chandrasekhar(Am)  n-p
1983        Taube, Henry(Can)  n-c
1983 TENDER MERCIES--Robert Duvall o-a
1983 TERMS OF ENDEARMENT o-p --Shirley MacLaine o-a,
              Jack Nicholson o-s, James L. Brooks o-d
1983 THE COLOR PURPLE--Alice Walker p-f
1983 THE YEAR OF LIVING DANGEROUSLY--Linda Hunt o-s
1983 THREE MOVEMENTS FOR ORCHESTRA--Ellen T. Zwilich p-m
1983 THRILLER(album)--Michael Jackson g-r
1983        Walesa, Lech(Pol)  n-x
1984 AMADEUS o-p --F. Murray Abraham o-a & Milos Forman o-d
1984 AMERICAN PRIMITIVE--Mary Oliver p-q
1984 A PASSAGE TO INDIA--Peggy Ashcroft o-s
1984 BASEBALL:  Ryne Sandberg Chi b-mv,
                        Willie Hernandez Det b-mv & b-cy
              Rick Sutcliffe Chi b-cy,
1984 BASKETBALL   Larry Bird Bos bb-m
1984 CANTI del SOLE--Bernard Rands p-m
1984 CAN'T SLOW DOWN(album)--Lionel Richie g-r
1984 FOOTBALL   Mike Haines LARaiders fb-d,
                          Dan marino Mia fb-m
1984 GLENGARRY GLEN ROSS--David Mamet p-d
1984 HOCKEY   Wayne Gretzky Edm ho-m
1984        Hughes, Ted(Br)   pol to  --- 1996+
1984 IRONWEED--William Kennedy p-f
1984        Jerne, Niels K.(Br-Dan) n-m
1984        Koehler, Georges J.F.(Ger)  n-m
1984        Meer, Simon van der(Dut)  n-p
1984        Merrifield, Bruce(Am)  n-c
1984        Milstein, Cesar(Br-Arg) n-m
1984 OL. GMS: DIVING -- Greg Louganis(Am)   2X  o-g's
1984 OL. GMS: 100,200 METER DASHES--Carl Lewis(Am) 2X  o-g's
```

1984 OL. GMS: 110 METER HURDLES--Roger Kingdom(Am) o-g
1984 OL. GMS: 1500 METER RUN--Sebastian Coe(Br) o-g
1984 OL. GMS: DECATHALON--Daley Thompson(Br) o-g
1884 OL. GMS: FIGURE SKATING--Scott Hamilton(Am) o-g
1984 OL. GMS: FIGURE SKATING--Katarina Witt(Ger) o-g
1984 OL. GMS: SKIING-SLALOM--Phil Mahre(Am) o-g
1984 OL. GMS: SPEED SKATING(Women)--1000 m and 1500 m --
                          Karin Enke(E.Ger) 2 o-g's
1984 PLACES IN THE HEART--Sally Field o-a
1984   Rubbia, Carlo(It) n-p
1984   Siefert, Jaroslav(Czech) n-l
1984 SOCIAL TRANSFORMATION OF AMERICAN MEDICINE--
                          Paul Starr p-n
1984   Stone, Sir Richard(Br) n-e
1984 THE KILLING FIELDS--Haing S. Ngor o-s
1984   Tutu, Bishop Desmond(S.Afr) n-x
1984 WHAT'S LOVE GOT TO DO WITH IT--Tina Turner g-r
1985 BASEBALL: Willie McGee StL b-mv, Don Mattingly NY b-mv
             Dwight Gooden NY b-cy, Bret Saberhagen KC b-cy
1985 BASKETBALL: Larry Bird Bos bb-m
1985   Brown, Michael S.(Am) n-m
1985 COCOON--Don Ameche o-s
1985 FOOTBALL: Howie Long LAR & Andre Trippett NE fb-d(Tie)
             Walter Payton Chi fb-m
1985   Goldstein,Joseph L.(Am) n-m
1985   Hauptman, Herbert A.(Am) n-c
1986 HOCKEY: Wayne Gretzky Edm ho-m
1985   Karle, Jerome(Am) n-c
1985 KISS OF THE SPIDER WOMAN--William Hurt o-a
1985   Klitzing, Klaus von(W.Ger) n-p
1985 FOREIGN AFFAIRS--Alison Lurie p-f
1985   Modigliani, Franco(Ital-Am) n-e
1985 NO JACKET REQUIRED(album)--Phil Collins g-r
1985 PRIZZI'S HONOR--Angelica Huston o-s
1985 RIVER RUN(Symph)--Stephen Albert p-m
1985   Simon, Claude(Fr) n-l
1985 SUNDAY IN THE PARK WITH GEORGE--Stephen Sondheim &
                          James Lapine p-d
1985 THE GOOD WAR--Studs Terkel p-n
1985 THE TRIP TO BOUNTIFUL--Geraldine Page o-a
1985 WE ARE THE WORLD--USA for Africa g-r
1985 YIN--Carolyn Kizer--p-q
1986 BASEBALL:Mike Schmidt Phi b-mv,Roger Clemens Bos b-mv
             Mike Scott Tex b-cy, Roger Clemens Bos b-cy
1986 BASKETBALL: Larry Bird Bos bb-m
1986   Binnig, Gerd(W.Ger) n-p
1986   Buchanan, James M.(Am) n-e
1986 CHILDREN OF A LESSER GOD--Marlee Matlin o-a
1986   Cohen, Stanley(Am) n-m
1986 COMMON GROUND--J. Anthony Lukas p-n
1986 FOOTBALL:Lawrence Taylor NYG fb-d,Phill Simms NYG fb-m
1986 GRACELAND(album)--Paul Simon g-r
1986 HANNAH AND HER SISTERS--Dianne Wiest o-s &
                          Michael Cane o-s
1986   Herschbach, Dudley(Am) n-c
1986 HIGHER LOVE--Steve Winwood g-r
1986 HOCKEY: Wayne Gretzky Edm ho-m
1986   Lee, Yuan T.(Am) n-c
1986   Levi-Momtalcini, Rita(It-Am) n-m
1986 LONESOME DOVE--Larry McMurtry p-f

```
1986 MOVE YOUR SHADOW--Joseph Lelyveld p-n
1986        Polanyi, John C.(Can)  n-c
1986        Rohrer, Heinrich(Swi)  n-p
1986        Ruska, Ernest(Ger)  n-p
1986        Soyinka, Wole(Nigeria)  n-l
1986 THE COLOR OF MONEY--Paul Newman o-a
1986 THE FLYING CHANGE--Henry Taylor p-q
1986        Wiesel, Elie(Romanian-US) n-x
1986 WIND QUINTET IV--George Perle p-m
1987 ARAB AND JEW--David K. Shipler p-n
1987 BASEBALL: Andre Dawson Chi b-mv, George Bell Tor b-mv
             Steve Bedrosian Phi B-cy, Roger Clemens Bos b-cy
1987 BASKETBALL: Magic Johnson LA Lakers bb-m
1987        Bednorz, J. Georg(W.Ger)  n-p
1987        Brodsky, Joseph(Rus-Am)  n-l
1987        Cram, Donald J.(Am)  n-c
1987 FENCES--August Wilson p-d
1987 FOOTBALL: Reggie White Phi fb-d,  Jerry Rice SF fb-m
1987 GRACELAND--Paul Simon g-r
1987 HOCKEY: Wayne Gretzky Edm ho-m
1987        Lehn, Jean-Marie(Fr)  n-c
1987 MOONSTRUCK--Cher o-a & Olympia Dukakis o-s
1987        Muller, K. Alex(Swi)  n-p
1987        Pedersen, Charles J.(Am)  n-c
1987        Sanchez, Oscar Arias(Costa Ric)  n-x
1987        Solow, Robert M.(Am)  n-e
1987        Tonegawa, Susumu(Japan)  n-m
1987 THE FLIGHT INTO EGYPT--John Harbison p-m
1987 THE JOSHUA TREE(album)-- U2 g-r
1987 THE UNTOUCHABLES--Sean Connery o-s
1987 THOMAS AND BEULAH--Rita Dove p-q
1987 WALL STREET--Michael Douglas o-a
1987 WASHINGTON POST--Berke Breathed
1988 A FISH CALLED WANDA--Kevin Kline o-s
1988        Allais, Maurice(Fr) n-e
1988 BASEBALL: Kirk Gibson LA b-mv,  Jose Canesco Oak b-mv
             Orel Hershiser LA b-cy,  Frank Viola Minn b-cy
1988 BASKETBALL: Michael Jordan Chi bb-m
1988 BELOVED--Toni Morrison p-f
1988        Black, Sir James(Br)  n-m
1988        Deisenhofer, Johann(W.Ger)  n-c
1988 DON'T WORRY, BE HAPPY--Bobby McFerrin g-r
1988 DRIVING MISS DAISY--Alfred Uhry p-d
1988        Elion, Gertrude B.(Am)  n-m
1988 FAITH(album)--George Michael g-r
1988 FOOTBALL:Mike Singletary Chi fb-d, Roger Craig SF fb-m
1988        Hitchings, George H.(Am)  n-m
1988 HOCKEY: Mario Lemieux Pittsburg ho-m
1988        Huber, Robert(W.Ger)  n-c
1988        Lederman, Leon M.(Am)  n-p
1988        Mahfouz, Naguib(Egypt)  n-l
1988        Michel, Hartmut(W.Ger)  n-c
1988 OL. GMS: 100,200 METER,RELAY-Florence Joyner(Am)3 o-g's
1988 OL. GMS: 100 METER DASH--Carl Lewis(Am) o-g
1988 OL. GMS: 110 METER HURDLES--Roger Kingdom(Am) o-g
1988 OL. GMS: DIVING--Greg Louganis(Am)  2 o-g's
1988 OL. GMS: FIGURE SKATING--Katarina Witt(Ger)  o-g
1988 OL. GMS: HEPTHALON--Jackie Joyner-Kersee(Am)  o-g
1988 OL. GMS: POLE VAULT--Sergei Bubka(Ukraine) o-g
1988 OL. GMS: SWIM 400,800 M.,MEDLEY--Janet Evans(Am)3X o-g's
```

```
1988 OL. GMS: SWIMMING--Matt Biondi(Am)5X o-g's
1988 PARTIAL ACCOUNTS: NEW AND SELECTED POEMS--
                      William Meredith p-q
1988 RAIN MAN o-p --Dustin Hoffman o-a & Barry Levinson o-d
1988        Schwartz, Melvin(Am)  n-p
1988        Steinberger, Jack(Am)  n-p
1988 THE ACCIDENTAL TOURIST--Geena Davis o-s
1988 THE ACCUSED--Jodie Foster o-a
1988 THE MAKING OF THE ATOMIC BOMB--Richard Rhodes p-n
1988 12 NEW ETUDES FOR PIANO--William Bolcom p-m
1989 A BRIGHT SHINING LIE: JOHN PAUL VANN AND AMERICA
                IN VIETNAM--Neil Sheehan p-n
1989        Altman, Sidney(Am)  n-c
1989 BASEBALL: Kevin Mitchell SF b-mv, Robin Yount Mil b-mv
              Mark Davis SanD b-cy, Bret Saberhagen KC b-cy
1989 BASKETBALL: Magic Johnson LA Lakers bb-m
1989        Bishop, J. Michael(Am)  n-m
1989 BREATHING LESSONS--Anne Tyler p-f
1989        Cech, Thomas R.(Am)   n-c
1989        Cela, Camilo Jose(Sp)  n-l
1989        Dehmelt, Hans G.(Ger-Am)  n-p
1989 DRIVING MISS DAISY o-p --Jessica Tandy o-a
1989 FOOTBALL: Tim Harris GB fb-d,  Joe Montana SF fb-m
1989 GLORY--Denzel Washington o-s
1989        Haavelmo, Trygve(Nor)  n-e
1989 HOCKEY: Wayne Gretzky Los Angeles ho-m
1989        Lama, Dalai(Tibet)  n-x
1989 MY LEFT FOOT--Daniel Day-Lewis o-a, Brenda Fricker o-s
1989 NEW AND COLLECTED POEMS--Richard Wilbur p-q
1989 NICK OF TIME(album)--Bonnie Raitt g-r
1989 OSCAR WILDE--Richard Ellmann p-b
1989        Paul, Wolfgang(Ger)  n-p
1989        Ramsey, Norman F.(Am)  n-p
1989 THE HEIDI CHRONICLES--Wendy Wasserstein p-d
1989        Varmus, Harold E.(Am)  n-m
1989 WHISPERS OUT OF TIME--Roger Reynolds p-m
1989 WIND BENEATH MY WINGS--Bette Midler g-r
1990 AND THEIR CHILDREN AFTER THEM--Dale Maharidge
                      and Michael Williamson p-n
1990 ANOTHER DAY IN PARADISE--Phil Collins g-r
1990 BACK ON THE BLOCK(album)--Quincy Jones g-r
1990 BASEBALL:  Barry Bonds Pitt b-mv,
                          Rickey Henderson Oak b-mv
              Doug Drabek Pitt b-cy,  Bob Welch Oak b-cy
1990 BASKETBALL: Magic Johnson LA Lakers bb-m
1990 BUFFALO NEWS--Tom Toles p-x
1990        Corey, Elias James(Am)  n-c
1990 DUPLICATES; A CONCERTO FOR TWO PIANOS AND
                ORCHESTRA--Mel Powell
1990 FOOTBALL: Bruce Smith Buf fb-d,  Warren Moon Hou fb-m
1990        Friedman, Jerome I.(Am)  n-p
1990 GHOST--Whoopi Goldberg o-s
1990 GOODFELLAS--Joe Pesci o-s
1990        Gorbachev, Mikhail S.(USSR)  n-x
1990 HOCKEY: Mark Messier Edm ho-m
1990        Kendall, Henry W.(Am)  n-p
1990        Markowitz, Harry M.(Am)  n-e
1990        Miller, Merton H.(Am)  n-e
1990 MISERY--Kathy Bates o-a
1990        Murray, Joseph E.(Am)  n-m
```

```
1990        Paz, Octavio(Mex)  n-l
1990 REVERSAL OF FORTUNE--Jeremy Irons o-a
1990        Sharpe, William F.(Am)  n-e
1990        Taylor, Richard E.(Can)  n-p
1990 THE MAMBO KINGS PLAY SONGS OF LOVE--Oscar Hijuelos p-f
1990 THE PIANO LESSON--August Wilson p-d
1990 THE WORLD DOESN'T END--Charles Simic p-q
1990        Thomas, E. Donnall(Am)  n-m
1991        Aung San Suu Kyi((Myanmarese)  n-x
1991 BASEBALL:  Terry Pendleton Atl b-mv,
                                    Cal Ripken Jr Bal b-mv
                Tom Glavine Atl b-cy, Roger Clemens Bos b-cy
1991 BASKETBALL: Michael Jordan Chi bb-m
1991 CITY SLICKERS--Jack Palance o-s
1991        Coase, Ronald H.(Br-Am)  n-e
1991 DOWN AT THE TWIST AND SHOUT--Mary Chapin Carpenter g-r
1991        Ernst, Richard R.(Swi)  n-c
1991 FOOTBALL:Pat Swilling NO fb-d, Thurman Thomas Buf fb-m
1991        Gennes, Pierre-Giles de(Fr)  n-p
1991        Gordimer, Nadine(S.Afr)  n-l
1991 HOCKEY: Brett Hull StL ho-m
1991        Neher, Edwin(Ger)  n-m
1991 LOST IN YONKERS--Neil Simon p-d
1991 NEAR CHANGES--Mona Van Duyn p-q
1991 RABBIT AT REST--John Updike p-f
1991        Sakmann, Bert(Ger)  n-m
1991 SYMPHONY--Shulamit Ran p-m
1991 THE ANTS--Bert Holldobler and Edward O. Wilson p-n
1991 THE FISHER KING--Mercedes Ruehl o-s
1991 THE SILENCE OF THE LAMBS o-p --Anthony Hopkins o-a,
                Jody Foster o-a & Jonathon Demme o-d
1991 UNFORGETTABLE( both single and album)--
                Natalie Cole with Nat "King" Cole g-r's
1992 A THOUSAND ACRES--Jane Smiley p-f
1992 BASEBALL:  Barry Bonds Pitt b-mv, Greg Maddus Chi b-cy
                        Dennis Eckersley Oak b-mv & b-cy
1992 BASKETBALL: Michael Jordan Chi bb-m
1992        Becker, Gary S.(Am)  n-e
1992        Charpak, Georges(Pol-Fr)  n-p
1992        Fisher, Edmond H.(Am)  n-m
1992 FOOTBALL: Junior Seau SD fb-d,  Steve Young SF fb-m
1992 HOCKEY: Mark Messier NYR ho-m
1992 HOWARDS END--Emma Thompson o-a
1992        Krebs, Edwin G.(Am)  n-m
1992        Marcus, Rudolph A.(Can-Am)  n-c
1992        Menchu, Rigoberta(Guatem)  n-x
1992 MY COUSIN VINNY--Marisa Tomei o-s
1992 OL, GMS: 100 METER DASH--Gail Devers(Am) o-g
1992 OL. GMS: 400 METER RUN-WOMEN--Marie-Jose Perec(Fr)o-g
1992 OL. GMS: FIGURE SKATING Kristi Yamaguchi(Am)  o-g
1992 OL. GMS: HEPTHALON--Jackie Joyner-Kersee(Am)  o-g
1992 OL. GMS: JAVELIN THROW--Jan Zelezny(Czech) o-g
1992 OL. GMS: SWIMMING 800 METER--Janet Evans(Am) o-g
1992 PHILADELPHIA DAILY NEWS--Signe Wilkinson p-x
1992 SCENT OF A WOMAN--Al Pacino o-a
1992 SELECTED POEMS--James Tate p-q
1992 TEARS IN HEAVEN--Eric Clapton g-r
1992 THE FACE OF THE NIGHT, THE HEART OF THE DARK--
                                    Wayne Peterson p-m
1992 THE KENTUCKY CYCLE--Robert Schenkkan p-d
```

1992 THE PRIZE: THE EPIC QUEST FOR OIL--Daniel Yergin p-n
1992 UNFORGIVEN o-p --Gene Hackman o-s, Clint Eastwood o-d
1992 UNPLUGGED(album)--Eric Clapton g-r
1992   Walcott, Derek(W.Indies) n-l
1993 A GOOD SCENT FROM A STRANGE MOUNTAIN--
                    Robert Olen Butler p-f
1993 ANGELS IN AMERICA: MILLENNIUM APPROACHES--
                         Tony Kushner p-d
1993 BASEBALL: Barry Bonds SF b-mv, Frank Thomas Chi b-mv
                Greg Maddux Atl b-cy, Jack McDowell Chi b-cy
1993 BASKETBALL: Charles Barkley Phoe bb-m
1993   Fogel, Robert W.(Am) n-e
1993 FOOTBALL: Bruce Smith Buf fb-d, Emmit Smith Dal fb-m
1993 HOCKEY: Mario Lemieaux Pitt ho-m
1993   Hulse, Russell A.(Am) n-p
1993 I WILL ALWAYS LOVE YOU--Whitney Houston g-r
1993   Klerk, Frederik W. de(S.Afr) n-x
1993 LINCOLN AT GETTYSBURG--Garry Wills p-n
1993   Mandela, Nelson(S.Afr) n-x
1993   Morrison, Toni(Am) n-l
1993   Mullis, Kary B.(Am) n-c
1993   North, Douglass C.(Am) n-e
1993 PHILADELPHIA--Tom Hanks o-a
1993 SCHINDLER'S LIST op & Steven Spielberg o-d
1993   Smith, Michael(Br-Can) n-c
1993   Sharp, Phillip A.(Am) n-m
1993   Roberts, Richard J.(Br) n-m
1993   Taylor, Joseph H.(Am) n-p
1993 THE BODYGUARD(album)--Whitney Houston g-r
1993 THE FUGITIVE--Tommy Lee Jones o-s
1993 THE PIANO--Holly Hunter o-a & Anna Paquin o-s
1993 THE WILD IRIS--Louise Gluck p-q
1993 TROMBONE CONCERTO--Christopher Rouse p-m
1993 TRUMAN--David McCulloogh p-b
1994 ALL I WANNA DO -- Sheryl Crow g-r(best rec.)
1994 BASEBALL: Jeff Bagwell Hou b-mv, Frank Thomas Chi b-mv
                Greg Maddux Atl b-cy, David Cone KC b-cy
1994 BASKETBALL: Hakeem Olajuwon Hou bb-m
1994   Brockhouse, Bertram N.(Can)n-p'94
1994 BLUE SKY--Jessica Lange o-a
1994 BULLETS OVER BROADWAY--Dianne Wiest o-s
1994 ED WOOD--Martin Landau o-s
1994 FOOTBALL: Deion Sanders SF fb-d, Steve Young SF fb-m
1994 FOREST GUMP o-p --Tom Hanks o-a & Robert Zemeckis o-d
1994   Gilman, Alfred G.(Am)n-m'94
1994   Harsanyl, John C.(Am)n-e'94
1994 HOCKEY: Sergel Fedorov Det ho-m
1994   Nash, John F.(Am)n-e'94
1994 NEON VERNACULAR--Yusef Komunyakaa p-q
1994   Oe, Kenzaburo(Japan) n-l
1994   Olah, George A.(Am)n-c'94
1994 OLYMPIC GAMES: DOWNHILL SKIING--Tommy Moe(Am) og
1994   Pares, Shimon(Isr)n-x'94
1994 LENIN'S TOMB: THE LAST DAYS OF THE SOVIET EMPIRE--
                         David Remnick p-n
1994   Rabin, Yitzhak(Isr)n-x'94
1994   Rodbell, Martin(Am)n-m'94
1994 THE SHIPPING NEWS--E. Annie Prouix p-f
1994 THREE TALL WOMEN--Edward Albee p-d

1995 BASEBALL: Barry Larkin Cin b-mv, Mo Vaughn Bos b-mv
                Garry Maddux Atl b-cy, Randy Johnson Sea b-cy
1995 BASKETBALL: Shaquille O'Neal Orlando bb-m
1995 BRAVEHEART o-p -- Mel Gibson o-d
1995   Crutzen, Paul,(Dut) n-c
1995 DEAD MAN WALKING--Susan Sarandon o-a
1995 FOOTBALL: Bryce Paup BUF fb-d, Brett Favre GB fb-m
1995 HARRIET BEECHER STOWE: A LIFE--John D. Hedrick p-b
1995   Heaney, Seamus(Irish) · n-l
1995 HOCKEY: Eric Lindros Phil ho-m
1995 LEAVING LAS VEGAS--Nicolas Cage o-a
1995   Lewis, Edward B.(Am) n-m
1995   Lucas, Robert E. Jr(Am) n-e
1995 MIGHTY APHRODITE--Mira Sorvino o-s
1995   Molina, Mario(Am) n-c
1995   Nusslein-Volhard, Christiane(Ger) m-m
1995   Perl, Martin(Am) n-p
1995   Reines, Frederick(Am) n-p
1995   Rotblat, Joseph(Br) n-x
1995   Rowland, F. Sherwood(Am) n-c
1995 STRINGMUSIC--Martin Gould p-m
1995 THE BEAK OF THE FINCH: A STORY OF EVOLUTION IN OUR
                            TIME--Jonathan Weiner p-n
1995 THE HOMEFRONT IN WORLD WAR II--
                            Doris Kearns Goodwin p-h
1995 THE SIMPLE TRUTH--Phillip Levine p-q
1995 THE STONE DIARIES--Carol Shields p-f
1995 THE UNUSUAL SUSPECTS--Kevin Spacey o-s
1995   Weihaus, Eric F.(Am) n-m
1995 THE YOUNG MAN FROM ATLANTA--Horton Foote p-d

1996 BASEBALL: Ken Caminiti SD b-mv,Juan Gonzales TX b-mv
1996   John Smoltz Atl b-cy'96, Pat Hentgen Tor b-cy
1996 BASKETBALL: Michael Jordan CHI bb-m
1996 FARGO--Frances McDormand o-a
1996 FOOTBALL:Bruce Smith BUFF fb-d,Terrell Davis DEN fb-m
1996 GOD, A BIOGRAPHY--Jack Miles p-b
1996 HOCKEY: Mario Lemieyx PITT ho-m
1996 INDEPENDENCE DAY--Richard Ford p-f
1996 JERRY MAGUIRE--Cuba Gooding jr o-s
1996 LILACS FOR VOICE AND ORCHESTRA--George Walker p-m
1996 OL. GMS: 100 METER DASH--Gail Devers(Am) o-g
1996 OL. GMS:200,400 METER RUNS-Michael Johnson(Am)2 o-g's
1996 OL. GMS: JAVELIN THROW--Jan Zelezny(Czech) o-g
1996 RENT--Jonathan Larsen p-d
1996 SHINE--Geoffrey Rush o-a
1996 THE DREAM OF THE UNIFIED FIELD--Jorie Graham p-q
1996 THE ENGLISH PATIENT o-p--Juliette Binoche o-s,
                            Anthony Minghella o-d
1996 THE HAUNTED LAND FACING EUROPE'S GHOSTS AFTER
                    COMMUNISM--Tina Rosenberg p-n
1997 ALIVE TOGETHER: NEW AND SELECTED POEMS--
                            Lisel Mujeller p-q
1997 ANGELA'S ASHES: A MEMOIR--Frank McCourt p-b
1997 ASHES TO ASHES: AMERICA'S HUNDRED YEAR CIGARETTE WAR.
            THE PUBLIC HEALTH, AND THE UNABASHED TRIMUPH
                OF PHILIP MORRIS---Richard Kluger p-n
1997 BASEBALL: Ken Griffey Jr Seat b-mv
          Pedro Martinez Mont b-cy Roger Clemens Tor b-cy
1997 BASKETBALL: Karl Malone bb-m
1997 BLOOD ON THE FIELDS--Wynton Marsalis p-m

1997	Boyer, Paul(Am) n-c
1997	Chu, Steven(Am) n-p
1997	Cohen-Tannoudji(Fr) n-p
1997	Fo, Dario(It) n-l
1997	Merton, ROBERT(Am) n-e
1997	Phillips, William D.(Am) n-p
1997	Prusiner, Stanley(Am) n-m
1997	Scholes, Myron(Am) n-e
1997	Skou, Jens(Den) n-c

1997 THE TALE OF AN AMERICAN DREAMER--Steven Milhauser p-f

1997	Walker, John(Am) n-c
1997	Williams, Jody(Am) n-x

1998 AMERICAN PASTORAL--Philip Roth p-n

1998 AS GOOD AS IT GETS--Helen Hunt o-a,Jack Nicholson o-a

1998 BLACK ZODIAC--Charles Wright p-q

1998   Furchgott, Robert(Am) n-m

1998 GOOD WILL HUNTING--Robin Williams o-s

1998 GUNS,GERMS, AND STEEL: THE FATES OF HUMAN SOCIETIES--
                         Jared Diamond p-n

1998 HOW I LEARNED TO DRIVE--Paula Vogel p-d

1998	Hume, John(Irish) n-x
1998	Ignarro, Louis(Am) n-m
1998	Kohn, Walter(Am) n-c

1998 L.A. CONFIDENTIAL--Kim Basinger o-s

1998	Laughlin, Robert(Am) n-p
1998	Murad, Ferid(Am) n-m

1998 PERSONAL HISTORY--Katharine Graham p-b

1998	Pople, John(Am) n-c
1998	Saramago, Jose(Port) n-l
1998	Stormer, Horst(Am) n-p

1998 STRING QUARTET NO. 2, MUSICA INSTRUMENTALIS--
                         Aaron Jay Kernis p-m

1998 SUMMER FOR THE GODS: THE SCOPES TRIAL AND AMERICA'S
        CONTINUING DEBATE OVER SCIENCE AND RELIGION--
                         Edward J. Larson p-h

1998 TITANIC o-p -- James Cameron o-d
1998	Trimble, David(Irish) n-x
1998	Tsui, Jens(Den) n-p

1999 AFFLICTION -- James Coburn o-s

1999 LIFE IS BEAUTIFUL -- Roberto Benigni o-a

1999 SAVING PRIVATE RYAN-- Steven Speilberg o-d

1999 SHAKESPEARE IN LOVE o-p -- Gwyneth Paltrow o-a,
                         Judi Dench o-s

SECTION IV -- The B O N U S Section
RIVERS

All River Names are in Bold Face Italics
RIVER <--, LAKE <-- ,OCEAN <-- *are WATER BODIES into*
the accompanying River(s) flow(s).
River --> flows into the accompanying RIVER or WATER BODY
SPECIFIC PLACE NAMES, CITIES OR BORDERS ARE IN CAPITALS
General locations: Countries or Continents are in Capitalized Lower Case
CHINA/RUS = the LOCATION of a *BORDER RIVER*

Note these abbreviations: B=BAY, G=GULF, S=SEA, O=OCEAN

Aa	Latvia	*Adige -->*	*ADRIATIC SEA*
Aar(e)	BERNE,INTERLAK.,	*Adour*	France
Aar(e)	Switzerland	*Adour -->*	*BAY OF BISCAY*
AAR(E) <--	*Reuss*	*ADRIATIC S <--*	*Adige, Bosna,*
Aar(e) -->	*RHINE*	*ADRIATIC S <--*	*Drin(i), Kerka*
Abacaxis	Brazil	*ADRIATIC S <--*	*Krka,Devoll*
Abacaxis -->	*PARANA URARIA*	*ADRIATIC S <--*	*Piave,Pescara,*
Abaete	Brazil	*ADRIATIC S <--*	*Po, Reno,Seman,*
Abaete -->	*SAO FRANCISCO*	*ADRIATIC S <--*	*Vijose*
Abakan	Russia	*AEGEAN SEA <--*	*Axios, Marica,*
Abakan -->	*JENISEJ*	*AEGEAN SEA <--*	*Marista,Nestos*
Aberdeen,Scot.	*DEE*	*AEGEAN SEA <--*	*Pinios, Strimon,*
Abiseo	Peru	*AEGEAN SEA <--*	*Varda*
Abiseo -->	*HUALLAYABAMBA*	Afghanistan	*CABUL, FARAH,*
Abitau	*N.W.T., Canada*	Afghanistan	*HARI RUD,*
Abitau -->	*LK TAZIN*	Afghanistan	*HELMAND*
Abiti	Ont., Canada	Afghanistan	*MURGAB, OXUS,*
Abiti -->	*JAMES BAY*	Afghanistan	*QONDUZ,*
Abra	Philippines	AFGHAN./TAJIKI.	*P'ANDZ*
Abuna	Bolivia, Brazil	*Afram*	Ghana
Abuna -->	*MADEIRA*	*Agan*	Russia
Acaray	Paraguay	*Agan -->*	*OB*
Acaray -->	*PARANA*	*Agno*	Philippines
Acari	Brazil	*Agra*	*YAMUNA*
Acari(Braz)-->	*CANUMA*	*Agri*	Italy
Acari	Peru	*Agri -->*	*G OF TARANTO*
Acari(Peru)-->	*PACIFIC*	*Agrio*	Argentina
Achtuba	Russia	*Agrio -->*	*NEUGUEN*
Achtuba -->	*CASPIAN SEA*	*Aguan*	Honduras
Acoyapa	Nicaragua	*Aguan -->*	*CARIBBEAN*
Acoyapa -->	*LK NICARAGUA*	*Aguanus*	Que., Canada
Acre	Brazil	*Aguanus -->*	*GofST LAWRENCE*
Acre -->	*PURUS*	*Aguapei*	Brazil
Acua	Brazil	*Aguapei -->*	*PARANA*
Acua -->	*MUCUIM*	*Aguarico*	Ecuador
Acuraua	Brazil	*Aguarico -->*	*NAPO*
Acuraua -->	*TARAUCA*	*Agueda*	PORT./SPAIN, Sp
Adaja	Spain	*Agueda -->*	*DOURO*
Adams	Br.Columbia,Can.	*Aguirre*	Venezuela
Adams -->	*THOMPSON*	*Aguirre -->*	*ORINOCO*
Adda	Lombardy. Italy	*Agusan*	Philippines
Adda -->	*PO*	*Ai*	India
Adige	VERONA, Italy	*Ain*	France
ADIGE <--	*Lk Garda*	*Ain -->*	*RHONE*

Aire	England, LEEDS	Alaska	*YUKON*
Aire	YORKSHIRE	*Alazeja*	Siberia
Aire -->	*OUSE*	*Alazeja* -->	*EAST SIBERIAN S*
Aisch	Germany	Albania	*ARTA, BOJANA,*
Aisch -->	*REGNITZ*	Albania	*DEVOLL, DRIN,*
Aisne	France	Albania	*ERZENI, MATIA,*
Aisne -->	*OISE*	Albania	*LK SCUTARI, MAT,*
Ajaju	Colombia	Albania	*OSUM, SEMAN*
Ajaju -->	*APAPORIS*	Albania	*SHKUMBI, VIJOSE,*
Ajan	Russia	*Albany*	Ontario
Ajan -->	*CHETA*	*ALBANY* <--	*Ogoki*
Ajarani	Brazil	*Albany* -->	*HUDSON BAY*
Ajarani -->	*BRANCO*	ALBANY, NY	*HUDSON*
Akanyuru	Burundi, Rwanda	ALBANY, GA	*FLINT*
Akobo (Akubu)	ETHIOPIA/SUDAN	*Albemarle Snd*	N. Carolina
Akobo -->	*PIBOR*	*Albemarle Snd->*	*ATLANTIC*
Alabama	*BEAR, CAHABA,*	Alberta	*ATHABASCA, BOW,*
Alabama	*CONECUH, COOSA,*	Alberta	*BEAVER, HAY,*
Alabama	*LK MARTIN,*	Alberta	*MIKKWA, PEACE*
Alabama	*MOBILE, PEA,*	Alberta	*LK ATHABASCA,*
Alabama	*PERDIDO, SIPSEY,*	Alberta	*PEMBINA,*
Alabama	*SEPULGA, TOWN,*	Alberta	*RED DEER, SAND,*
Alabama	*TALLAPOOSA,*	Alberta	*SIMONETTE,*
Alabama	*TENSAW,*	Alberta	*WABASCA,*
Alabama	*TENNESSEE,*	Alberta	*WANDERING,*
Alabama	*TOMBIGBEE,*	Alberta	*WASCANA,*
Alabama	GADSDEN, Georgia,	Alberta	*WILD HAY*
Alabama	MONTGOMERY,	ALBUQUERQUE	*RIO GRANDE*
Alabama	ROME, SELMA	*Alcovy*	Georgia
ALABAMA <--	*Coosa, Tallapoosa,*	*Alcovy* -->	*JACKSON LAKE*
ALABAMA <--	*Tombigbee,*	*Aldan*	Siberia
Alabama -->	*MOBILE*	*ALDAN* <--	*Amga, Maja,*
Alagon	Spain	*ALDAN* <--	*Timpton, Ucur*
Alagon -->	*TAGUS*	*Aldan* -->	*LENA*
Alalau	Brazil	*Alde*	England
Alalau -->	*JAUAPERI*	*Alde* -->	*NORTH SEA*
Alamo	California	*Alegre*	Brazil
Alamo -->	*SALTON SEA*	*Alegre* -->	*ITENES*
Alamos	Mexico	*Alexandra*	Australia
Alamos -->	*SABINAS*	*Alexandra* -->	*LEICHHARDT*
ALAMOSA, CO	*RIO GRANDE*	ALEXANDRIA, VA	*POTOMAC*
Aland	Germany	*Alfios*	Greece
Aland -->	*ELBE*	*Alfios* -->	*MEDITERRANEAN*
Alaska	*BLACK, CHENA,*	Algeria	*CHELIFF (Shelif),*
Alaska	*CHULITNA, COPPER*	Algeria	*MEDJERDA,*
Alaska	*COLVILLE, DELTA*	Algeria	*SEYBOUSE,*
Alaska	*EAGLE, KOBUK,*	Alhue	Chile
Alaska	*KOYUKUK,*	*Aliakmon*	Greece
Alaska	*KUSKOWIN,*	*Alibori* -->	*NIGER*
Alaska	*LK NAKNEK,*	*Alima* -->	*CONGO*
Alaska	*NENANA, NOATAK,*	*Alle*	Germany, Poland
Alaska	*OLD CROW,*	*Alleghany*	NY , OLEAN,
Alaska	*PORCUPINE,*	*Alleghany*	PITTSBURGH, PA
Alaska	*SALCHA, STONY,*	*Alleghany* -->	*OHIO*
Alaska	*SHEENJEK,*	ALLENTOWN, PA	*LEHIGH*
Alaska	*STEWART, SWIFT,*	*Aller*	Germany
Alaska	*SUSTINA, TANANA,*	*ALLER* <--	*Fuhse, Leine*
Alaska	*WHITE, WOOD,*	*Aller* -->	*WESER*

Allier	France	Amo -->	*JAMUNA*
Allier -->	*LOIRE*	Amu Darya	AFGHAN./TAJIKIST.
Alligator	N. Carolina	Amu Darya -->	*ARAL SEA*
Alligator -->	*ALBEMARLE SND*	Amur(Heilong)	RUS./MANCHURIA
Almeria	Spain	AMUR <--	*Hailar, Huma,*
Almonte	Spain	AMUR <--	*Silka, Songhua,*
Almonte -->	*TAGUS*	AMUR <--	*Zeja*
Aln	England,	Amur -->	*S OF OKHOTSK*
Aln	England,	Anabar	Russia
Aln	NORTHUMBERLAND	Anabar -->	*LAPTEV S*
Aln -->	*NORTH SEA*	Anadyr	Russia
Alpheus	Greece	Anadyr -->	*BERING S*
Alsea	Oregon	Anamu	Brazil
Alsea -->	*PACIFIC*	Anamu -->	*TROMBETAS*
Alsek	BC,Yukon, Can.	Anaua	Brazil
Alsek -->	*GULF OF ALASKA*	Anaua -->	*BRANCO*
Alstead	Sask., Canada	ANDAMAN S <--	*Salween,Sittoung*
Alstead -->	*KNEE LK*	Andorra	*VALERA*
Alt	Romania	Angara	Russia
Alta	Norway	ANGARA <--	*Cuna*
Altamaha	Georgia	Angara -->	*JENISEJ*
ALTAMAHA <--	*Ocmulgee,Oconee*	Angling	Manitoba, Can.
Altamaha -->	*ATLANTIC*	Angling -->	*NELSON*
Altmuhl	Germany	Angola	*CHOBE, EONGO,*
Altmuhl -->	*DANUBE*	Angola	*CUANDO, CUANZA,*
ALTON, IL	*MISSISSIPPI*	Angola	*CUBANGO, CUITO*
Aluta	Romania	Angola	*CUNENE, KASAI,*
Alz	Germany	Angola	*KUNENE, KWANDO*
Alz -->	*INN*	Angola	*KWANZA, LUENA*
Alzette -->	*SAUER*	ANGO./NAMIBIA	*CUBANGO*
Amajac	Mexico	ANGO./NAMIBIA	*OKAVANGO*
Amajac -->	*MOCTEZUMA*	ANGOLA/ZAIRE	*KASAI*
Amaka	Nicaragua	ANGOLA/ZAMBIA	*KWANDO*
Amaka -->	*COCO*	Angrapa	Lithuania, Pol.
Amana	*Brazil*	Angrapa -->	*PREGOL'A*
Amana -->	*MEUES*	ANN ARBOR, MI	*HURON*
AMAZON <--	*Apa, Ica, Japura,*	Animas	CO, NM
AMAZON <--	*Javari, Javary,*	Animas -->	*SAN JUAN*
AMAZON <--	*Jurua, Madeira,*	Antler	Sask., Canada
AMAZON <--	*Maicuru, Maranon,*	Antler -->	*SOURIS*
AMAZON <--	*Nanay,Napo,Negro,*	Apiaca	Brazil
AMAZON <--	*Paru,Porini,Purus*	Apiaca -->	*SAO MANUEL*
AMAZON <--	*Solimoes,Tapajos,*	Apiau	Brazil
AMAZON <--	*Tefe,Trombetas,*	Apiau -->	*MUCAJEL*
AMAZON <--	*Uatama, Xingu,*	Apon	Venezuela
AMAZON <--	*Xineu*	Apon -->	*LK MARACAIBO*
Amazon -->	*PARA*	Apore	Brazil
Ameca	Mexico	Apore -->	*PARANAIBA*
Ameca -->	*PACIFIC*	APPLETON, WI	*FOX*
AMES, IA	*SKUNK*	Apure	Venezuela
Amga	Russia	Apure -->	*ORINOCO*
Amga -->	*ALDAN*	Aquio	Colombia
Amgun	Siberia	Aquio -->	*NEGRO*
Amgun -->	*AMUR*	Araca	Brazil
AMIENS, Fr.	*SOMME*	Araca -->	*DEMINI*
Amite	Louisiana	Aragon	Spain
Amite -->	*LK MAUREPAS*	Aragon -->	*ARGA*
Amo	Bhutan, India	Araguaia	Brazil

ARAGUAIA <--	Claro	Arkansas	OUACHITA,SALINE,
Araguaia -->	TOCANTINS	Arkansas	ST. FRANCIS,
Araks(Aras)	AZERB./IRAN	Arkansas	SULPHUR,
Araks -->	CASPIAN SEA	Arkansas	VERDIGRIS
Aral Sea	Uzbekistan	Arkansas	WASHITA, WHITE,
ARAL SEA <--	Amu Darya,	AR/MS	MISSISSIPPI
ARAL SEA <--	Syrdarja	AR/TN	MISSISSIPPI
ARARAT, MT.	ARAS(nearby)	Arkansas Riv.	CO, FORT SMITH,KS
Araua	Brazil	Arkansas	LAMAR, PUEBLO,
Araua	MATAURA	Arkansas	LITTLE ROCK, OK,
Arauca	Venezuela	Arkansas	PINE BLUFF,TULSA,
Arauca -->	ORINOCO	Arkansas	WICHITA
Arda	Bulgaria	ARKANSAS <--	Neosho,
Arda -->	MARICA	ARKANSAS <--	Purgatoire,
Ardila	Portugal,Spain	ARKANSAS <--	Verdigris
Ardila -->	GUADIANA	Arkansas -->	MISSISSIPPI
Argentina	BERMEJO, CHICO,	Arlanza	Spain
Argentina	COLORADO,	ARLES	RHONE
Argentina	DESEADO, DULCE,	ARLINGTON, VA	POTOMAC
Argentina	GRANDE, NEGRO	Arly -->	RHONE
Argentina	NEUQUEN,PARANA	Arm	Sask., Canada
Argentina	PILCOMAYO,	Arm -->	LAST MTN. LK
Argentina	RIO de la PLATA,	Armenia	ARAS, ARAKS,
Argentina	SALADO #1 & S.#2	Armenia	ARAXES, CYRUS,
Argentina	SAN JAVIER,	Armenia	EUPHRATES,
Argentina	SEGUNDO,TEUCO	Armenia	HALYS,KUR,KURA
ARGEN./BRAZIL	URUGUAY Riv.	Armenia	RAZDAN, TIGRIS,
ARGEN./PARAG.	PARANA,	Armenia	ZANGA
ARGEN./PARAG.	PILCOMAYO	ARMEN./TURK.	ARAS
ARGEN./URUG.	URUGUAY Riv.	ARNHEM	RHINE
Arges	Romania	Arno	FLORENCE, Italy,
Arges -->	DANUBE	Arno	PISA, TUSCANY
Argesul	Romania	Arno -->	LIGURIAN SEA
Argesul -->	DANUBE	Aro	Venezuela
Ariari	Colombia	Aro -->	ORINOCO
Ariari -->	GUAVARIE	Aroostook	Maine
Ariege	France	ARTESIA	PECOS
Ariege -->	GARRONE	Artibonite	Haiti
Arikaree	Colorado	Artic Red	N.W.Territ.,Can.
Arikaree -->	N.FK. REPUBLICAN	Artic Red -->	MACKENZIE
Arinos	Brazil	ARTIC OCEAN<--	Horton
Arinos -->	JURUENA	Atrato -->	CARIBBEAN SEA
Ariporo	Colombia	Arun	Nepal
Ariporo -->	CASANARE	Arut	Borneo
Aripuana	Brazil	Aruwimi	Zaire
ARIPUANA <--	Roosevelt	Aruwimi -->	CONGO
Aripuana -->	MADEIRA	Arve -->	RHONE
Arizona	COLORADO,GILA,	Ashepoo	S. Carolina
Arizona	RIO PUERCO,SALT	Ashepoo -->	ATLANTIC
Arizona	LITTLE COLORADO,	Asia	AMU, AMUR
Arizona	RIO SAN JOSE,	Ashley	CHARLESTON, SC
Arizona	VERDE, VIRGIN,	Assiniboine	Manitoba, Can.
Arizona	ZUNI,	ASSINIBOINE<--	Souris
AZ/CA Border	COLORADO	Assiniboine-->	RED
AZ/NV Border	LK MEAD	ASTORIA, OR	COLUMBIA
Arkansas	BUFFALO,	ASUNCION	PILCOMAYO
Arkansas	COSSATOT, RED,	ASWAN	NILE
Arkansas	CURRENT,	ATBARA, Sud.	NILE

Atbara(h)	Sudan	Atuel -->	SALADO
Atbara(h) -->	NILE	Aube	France
Athabasca	Alberta, Can.	Aube -->	SEINE
ATHABASCA <--	Pembina,	Auburn	Australia
ATHABASCA <--	Wandering,	Auburn -->	BURNETT
ATHABASCA <--	Wild Hay	Aucilla	Florida
Athabasca -->	LK ATHABASCA	Aucilla -->	GULF OF MEXICO
ATLANTA, GA	CHATTAHOOCHEE	Aude	France
ATLANTIC <--	Albermarle Snd,	Aude -->	MEDITERRANEAN
ATLANTIC <--	Altamaha,Amazon,	Aue	Germany
ATLANTIC <--	Bandama,Bandon,	Aue -->	FUHSE
ATLANTIC <--	Bann, Barrows,	AUGUSTA, GA	SAVANNAH
ATLANTIC <--	Berbice,Cacheu,	AUGUSTA, ME	KENNEBEC
ATLANTIC <--	Blackwater,Chicco	Aulne	France
ATLANTIC <--	Casamance,	Auob	Namibia, S. Afr.
ATLANTIC <--	Colorado(Arg),	Auob -->	MOLOPO
ATLANTIC <--	Contas,Corantyne,	Auro	Greece
ATLANTIC <--	Corubal, Cuanza,	AUSBERG	LECH
ATLANTIC <--	Cunene, Deseado,	Australia	BARWON, BOGAN,
ATLANTIC <--	Davo, Doce, Erne,	Australia	BULLOO, DARLING
ATLANTIC <--	Edisto,Essquibo,	Australia	BURDEKIN, DALY
ATLANTIC <--	Foyle, Gaba,	Australia	DAWSON, DeGREY,
ATLANTIC <--	Gambia, Grajua,	Australia	DRYSDALE,
ATLANTIC <--	Guadiana, Gurupi,	Australia	FITZROY, HERBERT
ATLANTIC <--	Great Pee Dee,	Australia	FLINDERS,
ATLANTIC <--	James, Komoe,	Australia	LACHLAN,
ATLANTIC <--	Konkoure, LaHave,	Australia	LK ARGYLE,
ATLANTIC <--	Lee, Lima, Lofa,	Australia	LK BULLOO,
ATLANTIC <--	Machias,Maine(Ir)	Australia	MACQUARIE,
ATLANTIC <--	Mana,Maro,Maroni,	Australia	MURRAY, PAROO,
ATLANTIC <--	Merrimack, Minho,	Australia	MITCHELL, ROPER,
ATLANTIC <--	Mino, Mono, Moy,	Australia	TALBRAGAR, TAY,
ATLANTIC <--	Mucuri, Mullica,	Australia	VICTORIA,
ATLANTIC <--	Negro, Neuse,	Australia	WARWICK
ATLANTIC <--	Ogeechee, Ogooue,	Austria	DANUBE(DONAU),
ATLANTIC <--	Oeipoque, Orange,	Austria	DRAU,DRAVE,INN,
ATLANTIC <--	Orinoco,Oueme,	Austria	ENNS,ISER, KAMP,
ATLANTIC <--	Oum er Rbia, Pra,	Austria	LECH, MUR,
ATLANTIC <--	Oyapock, Para,	Austria	LK BODENSEE,
ATLANTIC <--	Parnaiba,	Austria	LK CONSTANCE,
ATLANTIC <--	Rio de la Plata,	Austria	MARCH, MURZ,
ATLANTIC <--	St. Marys, Tano,	Austria	NAMOI,RAAB,RABA
ATLANTIC <--	St. Paul, Saloum,	Austria	SALZA, SALZACH,
ATLANTIC <--	Sao Francisco,	Austria	THAYA, YBBS
ATLANTIC <--	Santee,Sassandra,	AVIGNON	TRAUN, RHONE
ATLANTIC <--	Sebou, Savannah,	Avon	BATH,BRISTOL,Eng,
ATLANTIC <--	Senegal, Shannon,	Avon	STRATFORD on AV.
ATLANTIC <--	Suir,Swakop,Taw,	Avon -->	SEVERN
ATLANTIC <--	Tamar,Tensift,	Awash	Ethiopia
ATLANTIC <--	Ugab, Tocantinas	Awash -->	LK ZIWAY
ATLANTIC <--	Tocantinas, Tywi,	Axios	Greece
ATLANTIC <--	Torridge,Volta,	Axios -->	AEGEAN SEA
ATLANTIC <--	Waini	Azerbaijan	ARAS, KURA
Atrato	Colombia	AZER/IRAN	ARAS
ATRATO <--	Sucio	AZER/TURKEY	ARAS
Atrato -->	CARIBBEAN		

Babai	Nepal	*Baoule* -->	*BAKOY*
Babine	Br.Columbia,Can.	*Baraboo,WI* -->	*Wisconsin*
Babine -->	*SKEENA*	*Barada*	Syria
Back	N.W. Terr., Can.	*Baram*	Maylasia
Back -->	*CHANTREY INLET,*	*Baram* -->	*SOUTH CHINA S*
Back -->	*ARTIC*	*Barama*	Guyana
Bad	S. Dakota	*Barama* -->	*WAINI*
Bad -->	*MISSOURI*	*Barcau*	Romania
Bado	Pakistan	*Barcau* -->	*KOROS*
Bafing	Guinea	*Barcoo*	Australia
Bafing#1 -->	*SENEGAL*	*Barcoo* -->	*THOMSON*
Bafing#2 -->	*BANI*	*BARENTS S* <--	*Pechora,Tuloma,*
Bagoe	Mali	*BARENTS S* <--	*Severnaja Dvina,*
Bagoe -->	*BANI*	*Barge Canal*	UTICA, NY
Bahr al-Gazal	Sudan	*Barito*	Borneo,Indonesia,
Bahr al-Gazal->	*WHITE NILE*	*Barito* -->	*JAVA SEA*
Bahr Salamat	*See Salamat,Bahr*	*Baro*	Ethiopia
Bailong(Jialing	China	*Baro* -->	*PIBOR*
Bailong(Jialing	*YANGTZE*	*Barren*	Kentucky
Baja, Hung.	*DANUBE*	*Barren* -->	*GREEN*
BAJAdeMARAJO<--	*Capim*	*Barrow*	Ireland
BAKERSFIELD,CA	*KERN*	*BARROW* <--	*Nore*
Bakoy	Mali	*Barrow* -->	*ATLANTIC*
BAKOY <--	*Baoule*	*Barwon*	Australia
Bakoy -->	*SENEGAL*	*BARWON* <--	*Namoi*
Balkh	Afghanastan	*Barwon* -->	*DARLING*
BALLINA,Ire.	*MOY*	*Barycz*	Poland
Balsas(Rio das)	Brazil	*Barycz* -->	*ODRA(Oder)*
Balsas(Rio das)	*PARNAIBA*	BASEL	*RHINE*
Balsas	Mexico	*Bateau*	Canada
Balsas -->	*PACIFIC*	BATH, Eng	*AVON*
BALTIC SEA <--	*Dvina,Lava,Neman,*	*Battle*	Alber.,Sask.,Can,
BALTIC SEA <--	*Oder(Odra),Peene,*	*Battle* -->	*N. SASKATCHEWAN*
BALTIC SEA <--	*Parseta,Slupia,*	*Baudo*	Colombia
BALTIC SEA <--	*Wista*	*Baudo* -->	*PACIFIC*
Baluchistan	*BOLAN, MOOLA*	*Baures*	Bolivia
Banas -->	*CHAMBAL*	*BAURES* <--	*San Martin*
Bandama	*Ivory Coast*	*Baures* -->	*ITENES*
BANDAMA <--	*Lk Kossou, Nzi,*	Bavaria	*EGER, ILLER,*
BANDAMA <--	*Red Bandama*	Bavaria	*ISAR, MAIN*
Bandama -->	*ATLANTIC*	*Bavispe*	Mexico
Bandon	Ireland	*B OF BENGAL*<---	*Brahmani, Ganges,*
Bandon -->	*ATLANTIC*	*B OF BENGAL*<---	*Hugli,Godavari,*
BANGKOK	*CHAO PHYARA*	*B OF BENGAL*<---	*Irrawaddy,Kaladan*
Bangladesh	*GANGES, JAMUNA*	*B OF BENGAL*<---	*Krishna,Manahadi*
BANGOR, ME	*PENOBSCOT*	*B OF BISCAY*<--	*Gironde, Loire*
BANGUI	*UBANGI*	*B OF FUNDY* <--	*St. John*
Bani	Mali	*Bear*	Alabama
BANI <--	*Bagoe, Bafing#2,*	*Bear* -->	*TENNESSEE*
BANI <--	*Banifing, Kani*	*Bear Lk*	Canada,
Bani -->	*NIGER*	*Bear Lk*	ID/NV Border
Banifing -->	*BANI*	*BEAUFORT S* <--	*Firth*
BANJUL	*GAMBIA*	BEAUMONT, TX	*NECHES*
Bann	COLERAINE, Ir	*Beaver*	Alberta,Sask.,Can
Bann -->	*ATLANTIC*		

BEAVER <--	Sand	BERLIN	HAVEL, SPREE
Beaver -->	CHURCHILL	Bermejo(Teuco)	Argentina
BEDFORD, Eng.	GREAT OUSE	Bermejo -->	PARAGUAY River
Beech	Tennessee	BERNE	AAR(E)
Beech -->	TENNESSEE Riv.	Berounka	Czechoslovakia
Bega(Bagej)	Romania, Yugo.	Berounka -->	VLATAVA
Bega(Bagej)-->	TISZA	Berretyo	Hungary
Begna	Norway	Betwa	India
Bei	China	Bheri	Nepal
Bei -->	XI	Bhima	India
BEIJING	TONGHUI	Bhima -->	KRISHNA
Belaja	Russia	Bhutan	KURU, MANAS
Belaja -->	KAMA	Bia	Ghana, IvoryCst.
Belarus	DVINA, NEMAN,	Bia -->	GULF OF GUINEA
Belarus	PRIPET	Biabo	Peru
BELARUS/POLAND	BUG	Biabo -->	HUALLAGA
Belgium	AMBLEVE, BOUCO,	BIDEFORD, Eng.	TORRIDGE
Belgium	DEMER, DENDER,	Biferno	Italy
Belgium	ESCAUT,LEIE,LYS	Big	Sask., Canada
Belgium	LESSE, MAAS,	Big -->	BEAVER
Belgium	MANJEL.MARK,	Big Black	Mississippi
Belgium	METHE, MEUSE,	Big Sandy	Kentucky
Belgium	OISE, OURTHE,	BIG SANDY <--	Tug Fork
Belgium	RUPEL, SAMBRE,	Big Sandy --->	OHIO
Belgium	SCHELDT, SEMOIS	Big Sioux	IA/SD Border,IO,
Belgium	SCHELDE(Escuat),	Big Sioux	MN/WI Border
Belgium	SENNE, VESDRE,	Big Sioux -->	MISSOURI
Belgium	WARCHE, YSER	Bighorn	Montana, Wyoming
BELG./NETH.	MAAS	BIGHORN <--	Shoshone
BELGRADE	DANUBE	Bighorn -->	YELLOWSTONE
Belice	Italy	BIHAC, Bosnia	UNA
Belize	SAN LUIS, Guat	Bija	Russia
Belize -->	CARIBBEAN	Bija -->	OB
Bellamy	New Hampshire	Bikin	Russia
Belle	Michigan	Bikin -->	USSURI
Belle -->	ST. CLAIR	BILLINGS, MT	YELLOWSTONE
Belly	Alberta, Can.	Biloxi	Mississippi
Belly -->	OLD MAN	Biloxi -->	GULF OF MEXICO
BENARES,India	GANGES	Biobio	Chile
BEND, OR	DESCHUTES	BIOBIO <--	Laja
Beni	Bolivia	Biobio -->	PACIFIC
BENI <--	Madidi,	Birch	Alberta, Canada
BENI <--	Santa Elena	Birch -->	LK CLAIRE
Beni -->	MADRE DE DIOS	Bir'usa	Russia
Benin	MEKROU,	Bir'usa -->	TASEJEVA
Benin	OKAPAJA, OUEME	Birzava	Romania, Yugo.
BENIN/NIGERIA	OKAPAJA	Birzava -->	TAMIS
Benue(Benoue)	Nigeria	Biscayne Bay	MIAMI
BENUE <--	Faro, Gongola	BISMARK, ND	MISSOURI
Benue -->	NIGER	Bistrita	Romania
Berau	Borneo	Bistrita -->	SIRET
Berbice -->	ATLANTIC	Bitter Lks	Egypt
Berens	Manitoba,Ont,Can.	Black	Alaska
BERENS <--	Throat	Black -->	PORCUPINE
Berens -->	LK WINNIPEG	Black	Wisconsin
Berezina -->	DNEPR	Black -->	MISSISSIPPI
BERING SEA <--	Kamkatka,	BLACK SEA <--	Bug, Danube, Don
BERING SEA <--	Kuskowin, Yukon	BLACK SEA <--	Dnepr, Dnestr,

Blackwater-->	ATLANTIC	Bomu	Cent. Afr. Rep.
Blanco	Argentina	BONDO,Zaire	UELE
Blanco -->	ESMERALDAS	BONN	RHINE
Blanco	Bolivia	Boopi	Bolivia
Blanco -->	BAURES	Boopi -->	BENI
Blitzen	Oregon	BORDEAUX	GARONNE
Blue	Colorado	Borneo	ARUT, BARITO,
Blue -->	COLORADO	Borneo	BERAU, IWAN,
Blue	Oklahoma	Borneo	KAHAYAN, KAYAN,
Blue -->	RED	Borneo	KAPUAS, PADAS,
Blue Nile	Ethiopia	Borneo	PAWAN, SEBUKU
BLUE NILE <--	Lk Tana	Bosna	Yugoslavia
Blue Nile -->	NILE	Bosna -->	ADRIATIC SEA
Bobonaza	Ecuador	Bosnia-Herceg.	DRINA, SAVA,
Bobonaza -->	PASTAZA	Bosnia-Herceg.	VRBAS
Bobr	Poland	BOS.-H./CROA.	SAVA, UNA
Bobr -->	ODRA	BOS.-H./JUGO.	DRINA
Bode	Germany	BOSTON	CHARLES
Bode -->	SAALE	Botswana	LIMPOPO,LINYANTI
Bodrog	Hungary	Botswana	LK DOW,LK NGAMI,
BODROG <--	Uh	Botswana	MOLOPO, NGUGHA,
Bodrog -->	TISZA	Botswana	OKAVANGO,
Boeuf	Louisiana	Botswana	SHASHE, THAOGE,
Boeuf -->	OUACHITA	BOT./NAMIBIA	LINYANTI
Bogan	Australia	BOT./S. AFR.	LIMPOPO, MOLOPO
Bogan -->	DARLING	BOT./ZIMBAB.	SHASHE
Boise	BOISE, Idaho	Bou Regreg	RABAT
Boise -->	SNAKE	Boulder	Montana
Bojaya	Colombia	Boulder -->	JEFFERSON
Bojaya -->	ATRATO	Bow	Alberta, CALGARY
Bojana	Albania	Bow -->	OLDMAN
Bol'saja Cuja->	LENA	Bowron	Br.Columbia, Can
Bolan	Baluchistan,	Bowron -->	FRASER
Bolan	Pakistan,QUETTA	Boyer	Iowa
Bolanos	Mexico	Boyer -->	MISSOURI
Bolanos -->	GRANDE de	Boyne	DROGHEDA, Ir
Bolivia	SANTIAGO,ABUNA,	Boyne -->	IRISH SEA
Bolivia	APERE, BAURES,	Brahamani	India
Bolivia	BENI, BOOPI,	Brahamani -->	BAY OF BENGAL
Bolivia	GRANDE, ICHILO,	Branco	Brazil
Bolivia	ITENEZ, IVARI	BRANCO <--	Mucajai, Surumu
Bolivia	LAUCA, LK POOPO,	Branco -->	NEGRO
Bolivia	MADERIA, MADIDI	Brazil	ABUNA, AMAZON,
Bolivia	MADRE de DIOS,	Brazil	ARACA, BALSAS,
Bolivia	MAMORE, MIZQUE,	Brazil	ARAGUAIA,
Bolivia	ORTHON,PILAYA,	Brazil	ARPUANA,
Bolivia	PARAGUAY,	Brazil	BRANCO, CAPIM
Bolivia	PILCOMAYO,	Brazil	CONTAS, CORUA,
Bolivia	SAN MARTIN,	Brazil	CURUA, DOCE,
Bolivia	SAN PABLO, YATA	Brazil	ENVIRA, FORMOSO,
Bolivia	SANTA ELENA,	Brazil	FRESCO, GRANDE,
Bolivia	SECURE, ARLIA,	Brazil	GUAPORE, GURUPI,
Bolivia	YACUMA,	Brazil	IACO,ICA,ICANA
BOLIV./BRAZ.	ABUNA, MAMORE,	Brazil	IGUACU, IJUI,
BOLIV./BRAZ.	ITENIS(Guapore)	Brazil	IRIRI, ITENIS,
BOLIV./PERU	HEATH,	Brazil	ITUXI, IVAI,
BOLIV./PERU	LK TITICACA	Brazil	JAMARI, JAPURA,
Bolsaja Cuja	Russia	Brazil	JAVARI, JURENA,

Brazil	JURUA, LK AIMA,	Br. Columbia	NECHAKO, NICOLA,
Brazil	LK FEIA,LK MIRIM	Br. Columbia	OKANOGAN
Brazil	MACHADO,	Br. Columbia	PARSNIP, PEACE,
Brazil	MADEIRA,	Br. Columbia	PETITOT,SAN JOSE,
Brazil	MAICURU,	Br. Columbia	SKAGIT, SKEENA,
Brazil	MAMORE,	Br. Columbia	STIKINE, STUART,
Brazil	MAPUERA, NEGRO,	Br. Columbia	WEST ROAD
Brazil	MAU(IRENG),	Broad	SC, COLUMBIA
Brazil	MIRANDA,	Broad -->	CONGAREE
Brazil	MUCAJAI,	BROWNSVILLE,TX	RIO GRANDE
Brazil	MUCUIM, NORTES,	Brule	Michigan
Brazil	PARANA, PAUINI,	Brule -->	MENOMINEE
Brazil	PARACATU,PURUS	Bruneau	Idaho
Brazil	PARAGUAY, PARU,	Bruneau -->	SNAKE
Brazil	PARANAIBA,	BUDAPEST	DANUBE
Brazil	PIORINI, POTI,	BUENOS AIRES	MATANZA
Brazil	PUTUMAYO,,	Buffalo	Arkansas
Brazil	ROOSEVELT	Buffalo -->	WHITE
Brazil	SANGUE,	BUFFALO, NY	NIAGRA
Brazil	RIO DA VARZEA,	Bug	Poland,POL/BELOR
Brazil	RIO DAS VELHAS,	Bug	POL/UKR,Ukraine
Brazil	RIOS DOS BOIS,	BUG <--	Narew
Brazil	SANTA TERESA,	Bug -->	WISTA
Brazil	SAO FRANCISCO,	Bulgaria	ARDA, DANUBE,
Brazil	SAO MANUEL,	Bulgaria	ISKAR,LOM,
Brazil	SAUERUINA,	Bulgaria	MARICA,MARITSA,
Brazil	SUCUNDURI,	Bulgaria	MESTA, OGOSTA,
Brazil	SURUMU,SUCURIO	Bulgaria	OSMA, SKUT
Brazil	TAPAJOS,TATAUA,	Bulgaria	STRUMA, VIT,
Brazil	SUIA-MICU, TEA,	Bulgaria	YANTRA
Brazil	TARAUACA, TEFE,	BUL./RUMANIA Bo	DANUBE
Brazil	TIBAJI, TIETE,	Bulkley	Br.Columbia,Can.
Brazil	TOCANTINAS	Bulkley -->	SKEENA
Brazil	UATUMA, UAUPES,	Buller	New Zealand
Brazil	URUDUIA, XERUA,	Buller -->	TASMAN SEA
Brazil	XINGU	Bulloo	Australia
BRAZ./GUYANA	MAU(Irena),	Bulloo -->	LK BULLOO
BRAZ./GUYANA	TACUTU(Takutu)	Burdekin	Australia
BRAZ./PARAG.	APA, PARANA	Burdekin -->	CORAL SEA
BRAZ./PERU	JAVARI(Yavari)	Bureja	Russia
BRAZ./URUGYAY	JAGUARAO,	Bureja -->	AMUR
BRAZ./URUGYAY	YAGUARON	Burkima Faso	BLACK VOLTA,
Brazos	Texas, WACO	Burkima Faso	KOMOE,LERABA,
Brazos -->	RIO GRANDE	Burkima Faso	OUALE,RED VOLTA
BRAZZAVILLA	CONGO	Burkima Faso	WHITE VOLTA
Brda	Poland	B.FASO/GHANA	BLACK VOLTA
Brda -->	WISTA	BURLINGTON, VT	WINOOSKI
BREMEN, Ger.	WESER	Burma	CHINDWIN, HKA,
BRESLAW, Pol.	ODER	Burma	HKOK,INDAWGYI,
BRIA,CentAfrRep	KOTTO	Burma	IRRAWADDY, LOI,
BRIDGWATER,Eng.	PARRETT	Burma	KALADAN,
BRISTOL CHAN<--	Parrett, Severn,	Burma	MALIKHA,MEKONG,
BRISTOL CHAN<--	Usk	Burma	MYITNGE, NAM,
BRISTOL, Eng.	AVON	Burma	NMAI, PEGU,
Br. Columbia	FRASER, ISKUT,	Burma	SALWEEN, SALWIN,
Br. Columbia	KISPIOX,	Burma	SHWELI,SITTOUNG,
Br. Columbia	KOOTENAY	Burma	TAPING
Br. Columbia	MOBERLY, NASS,	BURMA/THAILAND	THAUNGYIN

Burnett	Australia	California	*MERCED,MONO LK,*
Burnett -->	*PACIFIC*	California	*OWENS,PIT,PUTAH,*
Burnt	Oregon	California	*RUBICON,RUSSIAN,*
Burnt -->	*SNAKE*	California	*STONY, TULE LK,*
Burro Burro	Guyana	California	*SACRAMENTO*
Burro Burro-->	*ESSEQUIBO*	California	*SALINAS,*
Burundi	*AKANYARU,*	California	*SAN JOAQUIN,*
Burundi	*KAGERA,*	California	*TUOLUMNE,*
Burundi	*LK TANGANYIKI,*	California	*TRINITY*
Burundi	*MALAGARAZI,*	CA/NV	*LK TAHOE*
Caiapo -->	*RUZIZI, RUVUBU*	*Cam*	CAMBRIDGE, Eng.
BURUNDI/ZAIRE	*RUZIZI*	*Cam* -->	*GREAT OUSE*
Bush	S.Carolina	*Camana*	Peru
Bush -->	*SALUDA*	*Camana* -->	*PACIFIC*
BUTTE, MT	*CLARK FORK*	*Camaqua*	Brazil
Ca	Vietnam	*Camaqua* -->	*PACIFIC*
Ca -->	*S.CHINA SEA*	Cambodia	*BASSAC, KANG,*
Cabixi	Brazil	Cambodia	*LK TONLESAP*
Cabixi -->	*Itenes*	Cambodia	*MEKONG, PORONG,*
Cabrera	Colombia	Cambodia	*SAB, SAN,*
Cabrera -->	*MAGDALENA*	Cambodia	*SEKHONG,*
Cache	Illinois	Cambodia	*SEN, SREPOK,*
Cache -->	*MISSISSIPPI*	Cambodia	*TONLESAP*
Caddo	Arkansas	CAMBRIDGE	*CAM*
Caddo -->	*OUACHITA*	Cameroon	*DJA,FARO,NGOKO,*
CAEN, Fr.	*ORNE*	Cameroon	*NYONG, SANAGA,*
Caete	Brazil	Cameroon	*VINA*
Caete -->	*PURUS*	Camer./Chad	*LOGONE*
Cagayan	Philippines	Camer./Congo	*NGOKO*
Cagayan -->	*LUZON STRAIT*	*Camina*	Chile
Caguan	Colombia	*Camu*	Brazil
Caguan -->	*CAQUETA*	*Camu* -->	*POANA*
Cahaba	Alabama	*Camuy*	Puerto Rico
Cahaba -->	*ALABAMA*	*Canaan*	New Brunswck,Can
Cai	Brazil	*Canaan* -->	*ST. JOHN*
Cai -->	*GUAIBA*	Canada	*BACK, BATEAU,*
Caia	Portugal	Canada	*BEAR LK, FRASER,*
Caia -->	*GUADIANA*	Canada	*HAY, KOKOSAK,*
Caiapo	Brazil	Canada	*LAIRD,LK ABITIBI*
Caiapo -->	*ARAGUAIA*	Canada	*LK CREE,*
Caine	Bolivia	Canada	*LK GARRY*
Caine -->	*GRANDE*	Canada	*LK KOOTENAY,*
CAIRO, Egypt	*NILE*	Canada	*LK LOUISE*
CAIRO, IL	*MISSISSIPPI, OH*	Canada	*LK NIPIGON*
Calamus	Nebraska	Canada	*LK SIMCOE*
Calamus -->	*NORTH LOUP*	Canada	*LK OKANAGAN*
CALCUTTA	*HUGLI*	Canada	*MACKENZIE,PEEL,*
Caldwell	Pennsylvania	Canada	*NELSON,OTTAWA,*
Caledon	Lesotho	Canada	*PEMBINA,*
Caledon	LESOTHO/S.AFR	Canada	*PETAWAWA*
Caledon -->	*ORANGE*	Canada	*RAINY LK, RED,*
Calgary	*BOW*	Canada	*RICHELIEU*
CALI, Colum.	*CAUCA*	Canada	*SAGUENAY,*
California	*CLEAR LK, EEL,*	Canada	*SKEENA,SLAVE,*
California	*EAGLE LK, KERN,*	Canada	*SLAVE LK,THELON,*
California	*FEATHER,*	Canada	*YUKON*
California	*KLAMATH,*	Canada/USA	*ST. LAWRENCE*
California	*LK TAHOE, MAD,*	*Canadian*	NORMAN, OK

Canadian -->	ARKANSAS RIV.	Casiguiare-->	ORINOCO
Canama	Brazil	CASPER, WY	NORTH PLATTE
Canama	ARIPUANA	Caspian Sea	Kzahstan,
Canas	Puerto Rico	Caspian Sea	KZAHSTAN/IRAN
Canuma	Brazil	CASPIAN S <--	Emba,Kuma,Kura,
CANUMA <--	Sucunduri	CASPIAN S <--	Qezel Owzan,
Canuma -->	MADEIRA	CASPIAN S <--	Terek,Ural,Volga
Cane	Louisiana	Cass	Michigan
Cane -->	RED	Cass -->	SAGINAW
Caney	Kansas, Oklahoma	Cassai	See Kasai
Caney -->	VERDIGRIS	Catalonia	EBRO
Cannon	Minnesota	Catawba	N. & S. Carolina
Cannon -->	MISSISSIPPI	Catawba -->	WATEREE
Canoe	Br.Columbia,Can.	Cauca	CALI, Columbia
Canoe -->	COLUMBIA	Cauca -->	MAGDALENA
Capanaparo -->	ORINOCO	Caura	Venezuela
Cape Fear	N. Carolina	Caura -->	ORINOCO
Cape Fear -->	ATLANTIC	Caures	Brazil
Capim	Brazil	Caures -->	NEGRO
Capim -->	BAJA DE MARAJO	Cauto	Cuba
Caqueta	Colombia	Cauto -->	SALADO
CAQUETA <--	Apaporis, Yari	Cavally	IVRY CST/LIBERIA
Caqueta(Japura)	AMAZON	Cavally(Cavalla	Liberia
Cara	Russia, Siberia	Cavally -->	ATLANTIC
Cara -->	LENA	Cebollati	Uruguay
Caraiva	Brazil	Cebollati -->	LK MIRIM
Caraiva -->	ATLANTIC	Cebu	NAGA, Phil
Carapa	Paraguay	Cedar	Iowa, ND,
Carapa -->	PARANA	Cedar	WATERLOO
Carapo	Venezuela	Cedar -->	IOWA RIV.
Carapo -->	ARO	CELEBES S <--	Kayan
Carare	Colombia	CentAfrRep	BAHR AOUK,BOMU,
Carare -->	MAGDALENA	CentAfrRep	CHARI, CHINKO,
CARDIGAN, Ire.	TEIFI	CentAfrRep	KOTTO, LOBAYE,
CARIBBEAN <--	Atrato, Belize,	CentAfrRep	MAMBERE, MBARI,
CARIBBEAN <--	Escondido,Hondo,	CentAfrRep	OUAKA, OUHAM,
CARIBBEAN <--	Kurinwas,Patuca,	CentAfrRep	SANGHA, UBANGI
CARIBBEAN <--	Magdalena, Sinu,	C.A.REP/CHAD	BAHR AOUK,
CARIBBEAN <--	Punta Gorda,	C.A.R./ZAIRE	UBANGI
CARIBBEAN <--	San Juan, Unare	Cere	France
CARIBBEAN <--	Sico Tinto	Cere -->	DORDOGNE
CARIBBEAN <--	Tocuyo,	Cesar	Colombia
Cariboo	Br.Columbia, Can.	Cesar -->	ARIGUANI
Cariboo -->	QUESNEL	CESIS, Latvia	GAUJA
CARLISLE, Eng.	EDEN	Cess	Liberia
Caroni	Venezuela	Cestos	Liberia
CARONI <--	Paragua	CESTOS <--	Nuon
Caroni -->	ORINOCO	Cestos -->	ATLANTIC
Carrao	Venezuela	Chad	BAHR AOUK,CHARI,
Carrao -->	CARONI	Chad	BAHR SALAMAT,
Carrot	Saskatchewan,Can	Chad	LK CHAD, LOGONE,
Carrot -->	SASKATCHEWAN R	Chad	OUHAM, SHARI,
Carson	Nevada	Chad	VINA
CARSON <--	Truckee	Chama	Venezuela
Casamance	Senegal	Chama -->	LAG. D MARACAIBO
Casamance -->	ATLANTIC	Chamaya	Peru
Casanare	Colombia	Chamaya -->	MARANON
Casanare -->	META	Chambal	India

CHAMBAL <--	Banas, Parbati	Chicapa -->	KASAI
Chambal -->	YAMUNA	Chico	Argentina
Chanca	Portugal	Chico, Arg -->	ATLANTIC
Chang	See Yangtze	Chicopee	Massachusetts
Changane	Mozambique	Chicopee -->	CONNECTICUT RIV.
Changane -->	LIMPOPO	Chiers	France
Chao Phyara	BANGKOK	Chiers -->	MEUSE
Chao Phyara-->	G OF THAILAND	Chile	BIOBIO, CHOAPA,
Chapare	Peru	Chile	COPIAPO, ELQUI,
Chapare -->	ICHILO	Chile	GRANDE, HUASCO,
CHARBAROVSK,Rus	AMUR	Chile	HURTADO, ITATA,
Charente	France, SAINTES	Chile	LAJA, LK TORO
Charente -->	ATLANTIC	Chile	LK LLANQUIHUE,
Chari	Cent.Afr.Rep.,	Chile	LIMARI,LLUTA,LOA
Chari	Chad	Chile	MAIPO,MATAQUITO
CHARI <--	Bahr Aouk,	Chile	MAULE, NUBLE,
CHARI <--	Bahr Salamat,	Chile	RAPEL
CHARI <--	Logone, Ouham	Chilko	Br.Columbia,Can.
Chari -->	LK CHAD	Chilko -->	CHILKOTIN
Charles	BOSTON, Mass.	China	AMUR, ARGUN,
Charles -->	ATLANTIC	China	CHANG, CHUMAR,
CHARLESTON, SC	ASHLEY, COOPER,	China	DATONG, DRECHO,
CHARLESTON, SC	WANDO	China	DZACHU, FEN,
CHARLESTON, WV	KANAWAHA	China	FENHO, FUCHUN,
Charon	STYX	China	GAN,HAILAR,
Chattahoochee	ATLANTA, GA/AL	China	HAN, HUAI, HUMA ,
Chattahoochee->	LK SEMINOLE	China	HANKIANG,
CHATTANOOGA,TN	TENNESSEE Riv.	China	HOANGHO
Chay	Vietnam	China	HONGSHUI, ILI,
Cheat	W. Virginia	China	HUANGHWANGHO
Cheat -->	MONONGAHELA	China	JIALING,KERULEN,
Cheliff	Algeria	China	KHOTAN, KIALING,
Cheliff -->	MEDITERRANEAN	China	KUMARA,LAOHA
Chemung	ELMIRA, NY	China	LIAO,LITANG,LOHO
Chenab	India, Pakistan	China	LK BAMTSO, LUAN
CHENAB <--	Jhelum, Ravi	China	LK BORNOR,LK TAI
Chenab -->	SUTLEJ	China	LK CHAO,LK TELLI,
Chepo	Panama	China	LK EBINOR, LUO,
Cher	France	China	MACHU, MANASS,
Cher -->	LOIRE	China	MEKONG, MIN,
Cherlen	See Kerulen	China	MINKIANG,
CHESAPEAKE B<--	Delaware,	China	NANDING
CHESAPEAKE B<--	Patuxent,Potomac	China	NEN,OCHINA,PEI,
CHESAPEAKE B<--	Susquehanna	China	PEIHO,RUO,SI,TAO
CHESTER, Eng.	DEE	China	SALWEEN,SIKIANG
Cheta	Russia	China	SUNGARI, TARIM,
Cheta -->	LAPTEV SEA	China	TSANGPO, TUMEN,
CHETA <--	Kotuj, Popigaj	China	TUNG,TUO,URUNGU
Chetco	BROOKINGS, OR	China	WEI, WEIHO, XI,
Chetco -->	PACIFIC	China	WU, WUKIANG,XUN,
CHEYENNE, WY	CROW	China	YALU, YANGTZE,
Cheyenne	South Dakota	China	YARKAND,YELLOW
Cheyenne -->	MISSOURI	China	YING, YONGDING,
Chi	Thailand	China	YUAN, YUEN,
Chi -->	MUN	China	YUKIANG
CHICAGO	DES PLAINES,	CHINA/N.KOREA	TUMEN
CHICAGO	LK MICHIGAN	Chindwin	Burma
Chicapa	Angola, Zaire	Chindwin -->	IRAWADDY

Chinko	Cent.Afr.Rep.	Claro -->	*ARAGUAIA*
Chinko -->	*MBOMOU(UBANGI)*	Clear Lk	California
Chippewa	EAU CLAIRE, WI	Clear Lk	Iowa
CHIPPEWA <--	*Red Cedar*	Clearwater	Idaho, LEWISTON
Chippewa -->	*MISSISSIPPI*	Clearwater-->	*SNAKE*
Chixoy	Guatemala	CLEVELAND, OH	*CUYAHOGA,*
CHNANG,Cambo.	*SAB*	CLEVELAND, OH	*LK ERIE*
Chinko -->	*UBANGI*	Clinch	TN, VA
Chitina	Alaska	Clinch -->	*NORRIS LAKE*
Chitina -->	*COPPER*	CLINTON, IL	*MISSISSIPPI*
Chiumbe	Angola, Zaire	Clutha	New Zealand
Chiumbe -->	*KASAI*	Clutha -->	*PACIFIC*
Choapa	Chile	Clyde	GLASGOW,Scotland
Choapa -->	*PACIFIC*	Clyde -->	*SOLWAY FIRTH*
Chobe	BOTSWA/NAMIBIA	Cna	Russia
Chobe -->	*ZAMBEZI*	Cna -->	*MOSKA*
Chopim	Brazil	Coal	Yukon, Can.
Chopim -->	*IGUACU*	Coal -->	*LIARD*
Chop'or	Russia	Coari	Brazil
Chop'or -->	*DON*	Coari -->	*AMAZON*
Choptank	Maryland	Cobre	Panama
Choptank -->	*CHESAPEAKE B*	Cobre -->	*SAN PABLO*
Chor	Russia	Coca	Ecuador
Chor -->	*USSURI*	Coca -->	*NAPO*
Chowan	N. Carolina	Coco	Honduras, Nicar.
Chowan -->	*ALBEMARLE SND*	Coco	HOND./NICA.
Chu(Xarn)	Vietnam, Laos	COCO <--	*Waspuk*
Chu -->	*G OF TONKIN*	Coco -->	*CARIBBEAN*
Chubut	Argentina	Cohansey	New Jersey
Chubut -->	*ATLANTIC*	Coig	Argentina
Chulitna	Alaska	Coig -->	*PACIFIC*
Chumar	China	COLCHESTER,Eng.	*COLNE*
Churchill	Manitoba,Saskat.	COLERAINE, Ire.	*BANN*
CHURCHILL <--	*Mudjatik,*	Collins	Tennessee
CHURCHILL <--	*Reindeer*	Collins -->	*CUMBERLAND*
Churchill -->	*HUDSON B*	Colne	COLCHESTER, Eng.
CHUTAG,Mongol.	*SELENGE*	Colne -->	*NORTH SEA*
Cikoj	Russia	COLOGNE, Ger.	*RHINE*
Cikoj -->	*SELENGE*	Colombia	*APAPORIS,ARIARI,*
Cimarron	New Mexico, OK	Colombia	*ATRATO, CAQUETA*
Cimarron -->	*RIO GRANDE*	Colombia	*CASANARE,*
CINCINNATI	*LICKING, OHIO*	Colombia	*CAUCA, GUAINIA,*
Cipa	Russia	Colombia	*GUAVIARE, MAYO*
Cipa -->	*VITIM*	Colombia	*INIRIDA, META,*
Cipo	Brazil	Colombia	*MAGDALENA,*
Cipo -->	*RIO DAS VELHAS*	Colombia	*MIRA,MURRI,*
Cisnes	Chile	Colombia	*NECHI,OKANOGAN,*
Clam	Michigan	Colombia	*PATIA,PUTUMAYO,*
Clam -->	*MUSKEGAN*	Colombia	*SALDANA, SINU,*
Clare	GALWAY, Ireland	Colombia	*SAN JORGE, TOMO,*
Clare -->	*GALWAY BAY*	Colombia	*SAN JUAN, UVA,*
Clarence	Australia	Colombia	*YARI, VICHADA,*
Clarence -->	*PACIFIC*	Colombia	*VAUPES(UAUPES),*
Clarion	Pennsylvania	COLOM./ECUADOR	*PUTUMAYO,*
Clarion -->	*ALLEGHENY*	COLOM./ECUADOR	*SAN MIGUEL*
Clark Fork	BUTTE, MISSOULA,	COLOM./PERU	*AMAZON,*
Clark Fork-->	*LK PEND OREILLE*	COLOM./PERU	*PUTUMAYO,*
Claro	Brazil	COLOM./VENEZ.	*META, NEGRO,*

COLOM./VENEZ.	*ORINOCO*	*Congo(Zaire)*	BRAZZAVILLA,
Colorado	*APISHAPA,*	*Congo(Zaire)*	CONGO/ZAIRE
Colorado	*ARIKAREE, BLUE,*	*Congo(Zaire)*	KASAI, LUALABA,
Colorado	*COLORADO Riv.,*	*Congo(Zaire)*	LEOPOLDVILLE
Colorado	*DOLORES, GILA,*	*Congo(Zaire)*	Zaire
Colorado	*GREEN, GUNNISON,*	*CONGO(Zaire)<--Alima, Aruwimi,*
Colorado	*LA PLATA, WHITE,*	*CONGO(Zaire)<--Kasai,Likouala,*
Colorado	*PURGATOIRE,*	*CONGO(Zaire)<--Lindi, Lomani,*
Colorado	*S.PLATTE, YAMPA*	*CONGO(Zaire)<--Lualaba, Sangha*
COLORADO,Arg<--Grande, Salado#2	*CONGO(Zaire)<--Tshuapa. Ubangi,*
Colorado,Arg->	*ATLANTIC*	*Congo -->*	*ATLANTIC*
COLORADO,TX<--	*Llano, San Saba*	Conneticut	HARTFORD, MA, NH
Colorado, US	AZ/CA, AZ, CO,	Conneticut	NH/VT
Colorado, US	GRAND JUNCTION.	Conneticut-->	*LONG ISLAND SND*
Colorado, US	UT, YUMA	Cononaco	Ecuador
COLORADO,US<--	*Blue,Dirty Devils*	Cononaco -->	*CURARAY*
COLORADO,US<--	*Gila,Green,White,*	Contas	Brazil
COLORADO,US<--	*Gunnison, Yampa,*	Contas -->	*ATLANTIC*
COLORADO,US<--	*Little Colorado,*	Conwy	Wales
Colorado,US-->	*G. OF CALIFORNIA*	Conwy -->	*IRISH SEA*
COLORADO R.Dam	*LK MEAD*	*COOK INLET,AK <* *Sustina*
Columbia	ASTORIA, Oregon,	*COOK STRAIT<--* *Wairau*
Columbia	OR/WA, WA	Coosa	Alabama
COLUMBIA <--	*Cowlitz,*	Coosa -->	*ALABAMA Riv.*
COLUMBIA <--	*Deschutes,Lewis,*	Copiapo	Chile
COLUMBIA <--	*John Day,Kalama,*	Copiapo -->	*PACIFIC*
COLUMBIA <--	*Kootenay, Snake,*	Copper	Alaska
COLUMBIA <--	*Pend Oreille,*	Copper -->	*GULF OF ALASKA*
COLUMBIA <--	*Sandy, Spokane,*	Coquille	BANDON, Oregon
COLUMBIA <--	*Umatilla, Yakima*	Coquille -->	*PACIFIC*
COLUMBIA <--	*Willamette,*	*CORAL S <--*	*Burdekin, Fly,*
Columbia -->	*PACIFIC*	*CORAL S <--*	*Herbert*
COLUMBUS, OH	*SCIOTO*	*Corantijn*	GUYANA/SURINAME
Colville	Alaska	*CORANTIJN <--*	*Lucie, New*
Colville -->	*ARCTIC OCEAN*	*Corantijn -->*	*ATLANTIC*
Comet	Australia	*Corentyne*	*see Corantijn*
COMPIEGNA, Fr.	*OISE*	*CORK, Ire.*	*LEE*
Cona	Russia	*Corubal*	Guinea Bissau
Cona -->	*VIL'UJ*	*Corubal -->*	*ATLANTIC*
Concho	Texas	*Corumba*	Brazil
Concho -->	*COLORADO(Texas}*	*Corumba -->*	*PARANAIBA*
Conchos	Mexico	CORVALLIS, OR	*WILLAMETTE*
CONCHOS <--	*Florido*	*Corrientes-->*	*TIGRE*
Conchos -->	*RIO GRANDE=Bravo*	*Cossatot*	Arkansas
Concord	Massachusetts	*Cossatot -->*	*MILLWOOD LAKE*
CONCORD, NH	*MERRIMACK*	Costa Rica	*IRAZU,LK ARENAL,*
Conecuh	Alabama	Costa Rica	*MATINA, POAS,*
Conecuh -->	*ESCAMBIA*	Costa Rica	*SAN CARLOS,*
Conejos	Colorado	Costa Rica	*TARCOLES,*
Conejos -->	*RIO GRANDE*	Costa Rica	*TENORIA*
Confuso	Paraguay	COSTA R,/NICA.	*SAN JUAN*
Confuso -->	*PARAGUAY Riv.*	COSTA R./PANA.	*SIXAOLA*
Congaree	COLUMBIA, SC	COUNCIL BLUFFS	*MISSOURI*
Congaree -->	*LK MARION*	*Cowlitz*	Washington
Congo	*ALIMA, LIKOUALA,*	*COWLITZ <--*	*Toutle*
Congo	*SANGHA, UELE*	*Cowlitz -->*	*COLUMBIA*
CONGO/ZAIRE	*CONGO, UBANGI*	*Coyle*	Argentina
Congo(Zaire)	Angola,	CRACOW, Pol.	*WISTA*

CRAIG, CO	*WHITE*	Cuyuni -->	*ESSQUIBO*
Crasna(Kraszna)	Romania, Hung	Cyprus	*PEDIAS, PEDIEOS*
Crasna(Kraszna)	*TISZA*	Czechoslovakia	*BECVA, DANUBE,*
Crater Lk	Oregon	Czechoslovakia	*BEROUNKA, DYJE,*
Crazy Woman Cr.	Wyoming	Czechoslovakia	*EGER, ELBE,GRAU*
Crazy Woman Cr.	*POWDER*	Czechoslovakia	*HORNAD, HRON,*
Croatia	*VUKA*	Czechoslovakia	*IPEL, ISAR, ISER,*
CROATIA/HUNG.	*DRAVA*	Czechoslovakia	*LABE, MZE,*
Crow Wing	Minnesota	Czechoslovakia	*LABOREC,LUZNICE,*
Crow Wing -->	*MISSISSIPPI*	Czechoslovakia	*MARCH, MOLDAU,*
Cuando(Kwando)	ANGOLA/ZAMBIA	Czechoslovakia	*NISA, MORAVA,*
Cuango(Kwango)	Angola,	Czechoslovakia	*NITRA,ODER,OHRE,*
Cuango(Kwango)	ANGOLA/ZAIRE	Czechoslovakia	*OLSE, ONDAVA*
Cuango(Kwango)	*KASAI*	Czechoslovakia	*OPPA, OTAVA,*
Cuanza	Angola	Czechoslovakia	*SAZAVA,SLANA,*
Cuanza -->	*ATLANTIC*	Czechoslovakia	*TISZA,VAG*
Cuao	Venezuela	Czechoslovakia	*TORYSA, UH, VAH,*
Cuao -->	*ORINOCO*	Czechoslovakia	*VLTAVA, WAAG*
Cuarto	Argentina	*Da*	Vietnam
Cuba	*CAUTO, ZAZA*	*Dadu*	China
Cubango	Angola,Botswana	*Dadu* -->	*MIN(G)*
Cuiaba	Brazil	*Daka*	Ghana
CUIABA <--	*Manso*	*Daka* -->	*LK VOLTA*
Cuiaba -->	*PARAGUAI*	*Dal*	Sweden
Cuito	Angola	DALLAS, TX	*TRINITY*
Cuito -->	*CUBANGO*	*Daly*	Australia
Cuiuni	Brazil	*Daly* -->	*TIMOR SEA*
Cuiuni -->	*NEGRO*	*Damoh*	India
CUJA, Rus.	*LENA*	*Damour*	Lebanon
Culuene	Brazil	*Dan*	Virginia
Culuene -->	*TAMITATOLA*	*Dan* -->	*JOHN H.KERR Res.*
Culym	Russia	*Danube*	Austria, BAJA,
Culym -->	*OB*	*Danube*	BELGRADE, Bulg.,
Cumberland	NASHVILLE, TN	*Danube*	Cz, BUDAPEST,
Cumberland -->	*TENNESSEE Riv.*	*Danube*	BULG./ROM., Ger
Cun'a	Russia	*Danube*	LINZ, NOVI SAD,
Cun'a -->	*PODKAMENNAJA*	*Danube*	Romania, RUSE,
Cuna	Russia	*Danube*	ULM,VIENNA,Yugo,
CUNA <--	*Uda*	DANUBE <--	*Altmuhl, Arges,*
Cuna -->	*ANGARA*	DANUBE <--	*Argesul,Drava*
Cunene(Kunene)	Angola	DANUBE <--	*Drave, Drau*
Cunene -->	*ATLANTIC*	DANUBE <--	*Enns,Gunz,Hron,*
Curaray	Ecuador	DANUBE <--	*Iller,Ilz,Inn,*
Curaray -->	*NAPO*	DANUBE <--	*Ipel(Ipoly),Isar*
Current	Missouri	DANUBE <--	*Iskar,Iskur,Jiu,*
Current -->	*BLACK*	DANUBE <--	*Lech.Lom, Naab,*
Curua	Brazil	DANUBE <--	*Nab, Ogosta,Olt,*
Curua -->	*IRIRI*	DANUBE <--	*Oltol,Osma,Osum,*
Curuca	Brazil	DANUBE <--	*Prut(h), Raab,*
Curuca -->	*JAVARI*	DANUBE <--	*Raba,Saalach,Sau*
CUSCO, Peru	*URUBAMBA*	DANUBE <--	*Skhyl,Sava(Save)*
Cuvo	Angola	DANUBE <--	*Sio,Siret,Skut,*
Cuvo -->	*ATLANTIC*	DANUBE <--	*Tamis,Tisza,Ulm,*
Cuyahoga	CLEVELAND, Ohio	DANUBE <--	*Traun, Vag, Vah,*
Cuyahoga -->	*LAKE ERIE*	DANUBE <--	*Vedea,Vils,Vuka,*
Cuyuni	Venezuela	DANUBE <--	*Waag,Wornitz,Vit*
CUYUNI <--	*Aponguao,*	DANUBE <--	*Velika Morava,*
CUYUNI <--	*Mazaruni, Supamo*	DANUBE <--	*Yantra, Ybbs*

Danube -->	BLACK SEA	Denmark	HOLM, LILLEAA,
Darling	Australia	Denmark	LONBORG, OMME,
DARLING <--	Bogan, Barwon,	Denmark	SKIVE, STOR,
DARLING <--	Macquarie, Paroo	Denmark	STORAA, SUSAA,
Darling -->	MURRAY	Denmark	VARDE, VORGOD
Dasht	Pakistan	DENVER, CO	SOUTH PLATTE
Dasht -->	GULF OF OMAN	Derwent	England
Datong	China	Derwent,Eng-->	OUSE
Datong -->	YELLOW	Derwent	Tasmania
Daugava	RIGA, Latvia	Derwent -->	TASMAN SEA
Daugava -->	GULF OF RIGA	DES MOINES,IA	DES MOINES River
Daule	Ecuador	Des Moines	DES MOINES, Iowa
Daule -->	PACIFIC	Des Moines -->	MISSISSIPPE
DAUPHIN LK <--	Valley	Des Plaines	CHICAGO
DAVENPORT, IA	MISSISSIPPI	Deschutes	BEND, Oregon
Davo -->	ATLANTIC	Deschutes -->	COLUMBIA
Dawa(Daua)	Ethiopia,	Deseado	Argentina
Dawa(Daua)	ETHIOPIA/KENYA	Deseado -->	ATLANTIC
Dawa(Daua) -->	JUBBA	Desna	Ukraine, Russia
DAWSON, AK	KLONDIKE, YUKON	Desna -->	DNEPR
Dawson	Australia	Des Plaines-->	LK MICHIGAN
Dawson -->	PACIFIC	DETROIT,MI	DETROIT Riv.
Daying	see Taping	DETROIT,MI	LK ST. CLAIR
DAYTON, OH	GREAT MIAMI,MAD	Detroit Riv.	DETROIT, MI
DEAD SEA <--	Arnon, Jordan	Detroit Riv-->	LK ST. CLAIR
Dean	Br.Columbia,Can.	Deveron	Scotland
Dean -->	DEAN CHANNEL	Deveron -->	NORTH SEA
Dease	Br.Columbia,Can.	Devils	Texas
Dease -->	LIARD	Devils -->	RIO GRANDE
Deben	England	Devoll	Albania, FIER
Dee	CHESTER, Eng.	Devoll -->	ADRIATIC
Dee(Eng.) -->	IRISH SEA	DEVON, Eng.	EXE
Dee	ABERDEEN, Scot	Digul	New Guinea,
Dee(Scot.) -->	NORTH SEA	Digul	Indonesia
Deel	Ireland	Digul -->	ARAFURA SEA
Deel -->	SHANNON	Dirty Devil	Utah
Deerfield	Massachusetts	Dirty Devil-->	COLORADO
De Grey	Australia	Dismal	Nebraska
De Grey -->	INDIAN OCEAN	Dismal -->	MIDDLE LOUP
Delaware	NJ/PA, NY/PA	Dix	Kentucky
Delaware	PA,PHILADELPHIA,	Dix -->	KENTUCKY Riv.
Delaware	TRENTON	Dja	Cameroon
DELAWARE <--	Lehigh,	Dja -->	NGOKO
DELAWARE <--	Schuylkill	Dnestr	MOLDAV./UKRAINE
Delaware -->	CHESAPEAKE B	Dnestr -->	BLACK SEA
DELHI, India	YAMUNA	Dnepr	KIEV,Ukraine,Rus
Delta	Alaska	DNEPR <--	Berezina, Desna,
Delta -->	TANANA	DNEPR <--	Pripet,
Demer	Belgium	Dnepr -->	BLACK SEA
Demini	Brazil	Dnieper	See Dnepr
Demini -->	NEGRO	Dniester	See Dnestr
Demjanka	Russia	Doce	Brazil
Demjanka -->	IRTYSH	Doce -->	ATLANTIC
Dender	Belgium	Dolores	Colorado
Dender -->	SCHELDE	Dominican Rep.	OZAMA, YUNA
Denmark	ASA, GELSAA,	Don	ABERDEEN, Scot
Denmark	GUDEM, GUDENAA,	Don -->	NORTH SEA

Don	ROSTOV, Russia	Dvina -->	*BALTIC SEA*
DON <--	*Manyc, Sal*	Dwina	Poland
Don -->	*SEA OF AZOV*	Dye	Congo
Donau	See Danube	Dyje(Thaya)	Czechoslovakia
Dor	India	Dyje -->	*MORAVA*
Dordogne	France	Eagle	Yukon, Can.
Dordogne -->	*GIRONDE*	Eagle -->	*PORCUPINE*
Doubs	France, Switz	Eagle Lk	California
Doubs -->	*SAONE*	E.SIBER. S <---*Alazeja, Kolyma*
Douro	OPORTO, Port.	EAU CLAIRE,WI	*CHIPPEWA*
Draa(Qued Draa)Morocco		Ebro	CATALONIA,Iberia
Draa -->	*ATLANTIC*	Ebro	Spain, ZARAGOZA
Drau(Drava)	Austria,VILLACH	EBRO <--	*Aragon,Arba,Ega,*
Drava	CROATIA/HUNGARY	EBRO <--	*Gallego, Huerva,*
Drava	Hungary,MARIBOR,	EBRO <--	*Jalon, Segre,*
Drava	Slovenia, Yugo.	Ebro -->	*MEDITERRANEAN*
Drava -->	*DANUBE*	Echoing	Manitoba,Ontario
DRESDEN Ger.	*ELBE*	Echoing -->	*GODS*
Drim	Yugoslavia	Ecuador	*AGUARICO,*
Drin	Albania	Ecuador	*BLANCO, COCA,*
Drin -->	*ADRIATIC SEA*	Ecuador	*BOBONAZA,*
Drin -->	*DRIN GULF*	Ecuador	*CONAMBO,*
DRIN GULF <--	*Drin*	Ecuador	*CONONACO*
Drina	BOSN.-HERC./YUGO	Ecuador	*CURARY, DAULE,*
Drina	Montenegro, Yugo	Ecuador	*ESMERALDAS,*
Drina -->	*SAVA*	Ecuador	*MARONA,PASTAZA*
Drome	France	Ecuador	*NAPO, PINTOYACU,*
Drome -->	*RHONE*	Ecuador	*PUTUMAYO,UPANO*
Drweca	Poland	Ecuador	*SAN MIGUEL,*
Drweca -->	*WISTA*	Ecuador	*ZAMORA*
Drysdale	Australia	Eden	CARLISLE, Eng.
Drysdale -->	*TIMOR SEA*	Eden -->	*SOLWAY FIRTH*
DUBLIN, Ire.	*LIFFEY*	Eder	Germany
DUBUQUE, IA	*MISSISSIPPI*	Eder -->	*FULDA*
Dubysa	Lithuania	EDIRNE, Turk.	*EVROS*
Duck	Tennessee	Edisto	S. Carolina
Duck -->	*TENNESSEE Riv.*	Edisto -->	*ATLANTIC*
Duero	Portugal, Spain	Eel	California
DUERO <--	*Elsa, Eresma,*	Eel -->	*PACIFIC*
DUERO <--	*Riaza*	Ega	Spain
Duero(Douro)->	*ATLANTIC*	Ega -->	*EBRO*
Dulce	Argentina	Egypt	*BITTER LKS,*
Dulce -->	*LG. MAI CHIQUITA*	Egypt	*LK EDKU,LK IDKU,*
DULUTH, MN	*LK. SUPERIOR*	Egypt	*LK MARYUT, NILE*
DUMFRIES,Scot.	*NITH*	Eider	Germany
Duna	See Danube	Eider -->	*NORTH SEA*
Dunau	See Danube	Eigun	*See Amur*
Dunav	See Danube	Ekwan	Ontario, Can.
Dunajec	Poland	Ekwan -->	*JAMES BAY*
DUNAJEC <--	*Poprad*	EL PASO, TX	*RIO GRANDE*
Dunajec -->	*WISTA*	El Salvador	*JIBOA, LAPAZ,*
Dundrea	See Danube	El Salvador	*LEMPA*
Durance	France	Elbe(Labe)	Cz.,DRESDEN,Ger.
Durance -->	*RHONE*	Elbe	HAMBURG,Hungary,
DURHAM Eng.	*WEAR*	Elbe	MEISSEN, PRAGUE
Dvina	Belarus, Latvia,	ELBE <--	*Aland, Berounka,*
Dvina	Russia	ELBE <--	*Elde,Havel,Iser,*
DVINA <--	*Suchona*	ELBE <--	*Jeetze, Moldau,*

ELBE <--	*Mulde, Ohre,*	Eresma	Spain
ELBE <--	*Saale, Vltava,*	Eresma -->	*DUERO*
Elbe -->	*NORTH SEA*	Erft	Germany
Elde	Germany	Erft -->	*RHINE*
Elde -->	*ELBE*	Erges(Erjas)	PORTUGAL/SPAIN
Elk	Tennessee, WV	Erges(Erjas)->	*TAGUS*
Elk -->	*TENNESSEE Riv.*	Erie Canal	UTICA, NY
Elkhorn	Nebraska	Erne	ENNISKILLEN, Ire
Elkhorn -->	*PLATTE*	Erne -->	*ATLANTIC*
ELKO, NV	*HUMBOLDT*	Ertix	*See Irtysh*
ELMIRA, NY	*CHEMUNG*	Erzeni	Albania
Elqui	Chile	Escanaba	Wisconsin
Elqui -->	*PACIFIC*	Escanaba -->	*GREEN BAY*
Elster	Germany	Escaut	see Schelde
Ema	Estonia	Escondido	Nicaragua
Emba	Kazakhstan	ESCONDIDO <--	Rama
Emba -->	*CASPIAN SEA*	Escondido -->	*CARIBBEAN*
EMPORIA, KS	*NEOSHO*	Esla	Spain
Ems	Germany	ESLA <--	Tera
Ems -->	*NORTH SEA*	Esla -->	*DUERO*
En	*See Inn*	ESMERALDAS	Ecuador
Ena	Norway	ESMERALDAS <--	Blanco
England	*AIRE, ALDE, ALN,*	Esmeraldas -->	*PACIFIC*
England	*AVON,CAM,COLNE,*	ESSEN, Ger.	*RUHR*
England	*DEBEN, DEE, DON,*	ESSEX, Eng.	*CAM*
England	*DERWENT, EDEN,*	ESSEQUIBO	Guyana
England	*EXE,GREAT OUSE,*	ESSEQUIBO <--	Cuyuni, Rewa
England	*HUMBER, KENNET,*	Essequibo -->	*ATLANTIC*
England	*LEA,LK CONISTON,*	Estonia	*EMA, KASARI,*
England	*LUNE, MEDWAY,*	Estonia	*LK PEIPUS,NARVA,*
England	*MERSEY, OUSE,*	Estonia	*PARNU*
England	*PARRETT, PENK,*	Ethiopia	*ABAY, AKOBO,*
England	*RIBBLE, ROTHER,*	Ethiopia	*AWASH, BARO,*
England	*SEVERN, STOUR,*	Ethiopia	*BLUE NILE,*
England	*SWALE, TAME*	Ethiopia	*DAWA,FAFAN,GILA,*
England	*TAMAR, TAW, TEE,*	Ethiopia	*LK ABAYA,LK ABE,*
England	*TEES,THAMES,TILL*	Ethiopia	*LK SHOLA, MAREB,*
England	*TORRIDGE, TRENT,*	Ethiopia	*LK TANA, NOFER,*
England	*TWEED,TYNE,URE,*	Ethiopia	*LK ZEWAY, OMO,*
England	*USK, WAVENY,*	Ethiopia	*TAKAZE, TEKEZE ,*
England	*WEAR,WEAVER,*	Ethiopia	*WEB*
England	*WELLAND,*	ETON, Eng.	*THAMES*
England	*WENSUM,WHARFE,*	Etowah	Georgia
England	*WITHAM,WYE,YARE*	Etowah -->	*WEISS LAKE*
English	Iowa	EUGENE, OR	*WILLAMETTE*
English -->	*IOWA Riv.*	Euphrates	Armenia, Iran,
English Chan	POOLE	Euphrates	Iraq, Syria
ENGLISH CHAN<--	Avon, Exe, Orne,	Euphrates -->	*SHATT al-ARAB*
ENGLISH CHAN<--	Rance, Rother,	Eure	France
ENGLISH CHAN<--	Seine, Somme	Eure -->	*SEINE*
ENNISKILLEN,Ire	*ERNE*	EVANSVILLE,IN	*OHIO*
Enns	Austria	Evros(Marica)	Bulgaria,EDIRNE
Enns -->	*DANUBE*	Evros(Merica)	GREECE/TURKEY
Envira	Brazil	EVROS <--	Arda
ENVIRA <--	Tarauaca	Evros -->	*AEGEAN SEA*
Envira -->	*JURUA*	Evrotas	Greece
Equitor.Guinea	*BENITO, CAMPO,*	Exe	DEVON, England,
Equitor.Guinea	*MUNI*	Exe	EXETER,TIVERTON

Exe -->	*ENGLISH CHAN.*	*Flat* -->	*RED*
Exploits	Newfoundland	*Flathead Lk*	Montana
Exploits -->	*LABRADOR SEA*	*Flesk*	Ireland
Fafan	Ethiopia	*Flinders*	Australia
FAIRBANKS, AK	*TANANA*	*Flinders* -->	*GofCARPERTERIA*
Fajardo	Puerto Rico	*Flint*	ALBANY, Georgia
Faleme	Guinea, Senegal	*Flint* -->	*LK SEMINOLE*
Faleme -->	*SENEGAL*	FLORENCE, It	*ARNO*
Fane	Ireland	*Flores*	Argentina
Fane -->	*IRISH SEA*	Florida	*KISSIMMEE,*
Farah	Afghanistan	Florida	*LK DORA,*
FARGO, ND	*RED of the North*	Florida	*LK OKEECHOBEE*
Faria	Israel	Florida	*SUWANEE*
Faro	Cameroon	*Florido*	Mexico
Faro -->	*BENUE*	*Florido* -->	*CONCHOS*
Feale	Ireland	*Floyd*	Iowa, SIOUX CITY
Feather	California	*Floyd* -->	*MISSOURI*
FEATHER <--	*Yuba*	*Flumendosa*	Sardinia
Feather -->	*SACRAMENTO*	*Fly*	New Guinea
Fen	China	*Fly* -->	*CORAL SEA*
Fen -->	*YELLOW(HUANG)*	*Formoso*	Brazil
Fenho	China	*Formoso* -->	*CORRENTE*
FERRARA, It	*PO*	FORT SMITH,AR	*ARKANSAS*
FIER, Alb.	*DEVOLL*	FORT WAYNE,IN	*MAUMEE,*
Fimi	Zaire	FORT WAYNE,IN	*ST.JOSEPH*
Fimi -->	*KASAI*	*Forth*	Scot., STIRLING
Finke	Australia	*Forth* -->	*FIRTH OF FORTH*
Finland	*II,IIJOKI,IVALO,*	*Foyle*	Ireland,
Finland	*KALA, KITINEN,*	*Foyle*	LONDONDERRY
Finland	*KOKEMAKI,*	*FOYLE* <--	*Finn*
Finland	*LAPUAN, LK JUO,*	*Foyle* -->	*ATLANTIC*
Finland	*LK KEMI, LK KIVI,*	Fox	APPLETON,
Finland	*LK MUO,LK NASI,L*	Fox	GREEN BAY, WI
Finland	*LK OULO, LK PURO,*	Fox -->	*GREEN BAY*
Finland	*LK PYHA, LK SIMO,*	France	*ADOUR,AIN,AIRE,*
Finland	*LOTTA, MUONIO,*	France	*AISNE, ALLIER,*
Finland	*OULU, OUNAS,*	France	*ARIEGE, AUBE,*
Finland	*PASVIK, SIIKA,*	France	*AUDE, AULNE,*
Finland	*SIMO, TENO,*	France	*CHARENTE, EURE,*
Finland	*TORINO*	France	*GARD,GERS,INDRE*
FINLAND/NORWAY	*Teno(Tana)*	France	*GARONNE,*
Finn	Ireland	France	*GIRONDE, ISERE*
Finn -->	*FOYLE*	France	*LK ANNECY, LOIR,*
Firat	Turkey	France	*LKCAZAUX, LOIRE,*
Firth	Yukon, Can.	France	*LOT, LUY, LYS,*
Firth -->	*BEAUFORT S*	France	*MARNE, MAYENE,*
FIRTHofCLYDE <--	*Clyde*	France	*MEUSE, MOSELLE,*
FirthofClyde ->	*IRISH SEA*	France	*OISE,ORNE,RHONE,*
FirthofForth	EDINBURGH, Scot.	France	*RISLE, SAAR,*
FirthofForth ->	*NORTH SEA*	France	*SAMBRE, SAONE,*
Fish	Namibia	France	*SCARPE,SEINE,*
Fish -->	*ORANGE*	France	*SOMME,TARN,VAR,*
Fisher	Montana	France	*VESLE, VEZERE,*
Fisher -->	*KOOTENAI*	France	*VIAUR, VIENNE,*
Fitzroy	Australia	France	*VIRE,YONNE, YSER*
Fitzroy -->	*INDIAN OCEAN*	FRANCE/GERMAN	*RHINE*
Flanders	*YSER*	FRANCE/SWITZ	*LK GENEVA*
Flat	Michigan	FRANKFORT, Ger.	*ODER*

Fraser	Can,Br.Columbia,	*Garonne* -->	*GIRONDE*
Fraser	VANCOUVER	*Garry*	Scotland
FRASER <--	*Nechako,San Jose*	GARY, IN	*LK. MICHIGAN*
FRASER <--	*Thompson,*	*Gauja*	CESIS, Latvia
FRASER <--	*West Road,Willow*	*Geba*	Guinea-Bissau
Fraser -->	*STR. OF GEORGIA*	*Geba* -->	*ATLANTIC*
Fr. Guiana	*MANA*	*Gediz*	Turkey
FR.GUIA./SURIN	*MARONI*	*Gelsaa*	Denmark
Fresco	Brazil	*Genale*	*see Jubba*
Fresco -->	*XINGU*	*Genesee*	NY, ROCHESTER
Frio	Texas	*Genil*	Spain
Frio -->	*CHOKE CANYON LK*	GENT, Belg.	*ESCAUT,SCHELDE*
Fuchun	China, HANGCHOW	*George*	Quebec
Fuchun	*HANGCHOW B*	*George* -->	*UNGAVA BAY*
Fuerte	Mexico	Georgia	*ALABAMA,*
Fuerte -->	*GULF OF CALIF.*	Georgia	*ALTAMAH,*
Fuhse	Germany	Georgia	*CONECUH,ETOWAH*
FUHSE <--	*Aue*	Georgia	*FLINT, LK MARTIN,*
Fuhse -->	*ALLER*	Georgia	*OCMULGEE,*
Fulda	Germany, KASSEL	Georgia	*OCONEE,PIGEON,*
FULDA <--	*Eder*	Georgia	*GEECHEE, PEA,*
Fulda -->	*WESER*	Georgia	*SATILLA,*
Gabon	*IVINDA, NGOUNIE,*	Georgia	*SAVANNAH*
Gabon	*OGOOUE*	GA/SC	*SAVANNAH*
GADSDEN, AL	*ALABAMA*	*Georgina*	Australia
Gallego	Spain	Germany	*AISCH,ALLE,ALZ,*
Gallego -->	*EBRO*	Germany	*ALLER, ALTMUHL,*
GALWAY Ire.	*CLARE*	Germany	*AUE, BODE, EDER,*
Gam(Jin)	Vietnam, China	Germany	*DANUBE(DONAU),*
Gam(Jin) -->	*RED HONG*	Germany	*EIDER,ELBE,ELDE,*
Gambia	*GAMBIA*	Germany	*ELSTER,EMS,ERFT,*
Gambia	BANJUL, Guinea,	Germany	*FULDA, FUHSE,*
Gambia	Senegal	Germany	*GUNZ, HAVEL*
Gambia -->	*ATLANTIC*	Germany	*HELME, HUNTE,*
Gambie	*See Gambia*	Germany	*ILLER,ILZ,INN,ISAR*
Gan	China, NANCHANG	Germany	*ISER, JAGSL,*
Gan -->	*POYANG HU*	Germany	*JEETZE, KOCHER,*
Gana	Nigeria	Germany	*LAHN,LECH,LEINE,*
Gandak	Nepal	Germany	*LIPPE,NAAB,NAHE,*
Gandak -->	*GANGES*	Germany	*LK BODENSEE*
Gander	Newfoundland	Germany	*LK CONSTANCE,*
Gander -->	*LABRADOR SEA*	Germany	*MAIN,LK MURITZEE*
Ganges	BENARES, India,	Germany	*MOSEL, MULDE,*
Ganges	Bangladesh,	Germany	*NECKAR, NEISSE,*
Ganges	Pakistan, PABNA	Germany	*ODER,OKER,OSTE,*
GANGES <--	*Gandak,Ghaghara,*	Germany	*PEENE,PEGNITZ,*
GANGES <--	*Gomati,Jamuna,*	Germany	*RANDOW,REGEN,*
GANGES <--	*Karnali,Meglina,*	Germany	*REAZAT,REMAS,*
GANGES <--	*Rapti,Son,Yamuna*	Germany	*RHEIN, RHINE,*
Ganges -->	*BAY OF BENGAL*	Germany	*RUHR, SAALE*
GAO, Mali	*NIGER*	Germany	*SAAR, SALZACH,*
Gard	France	Germany	*SAUER,SIEG,*
Gard -->	*RHONE*	Germany	*SPREE, TAUBER,*
GARISSA,Kenya	*TANA*	Germany	*UCKER, UNSTRUT,*
Garonne	BORDEAUX,France,	Germany	*VECHT, VILS*
Garonne	TOULOUSE	Germany	*WARNOW,WERRA,*
GARONNE <--	*Ariege,Gers,Lot,*	Germany	*WESER, WORNITZ*
GARONNE <--	*Tarn*	GER/LUXEMB.	*MOSEL,OUR,SAUER*

GER/POL	ODER(ODRA),	Grand -->	MISSOURI
GER/POL	NEISSE(NYSA)	Grand	S. Dakota
GER/SWITZ	LK BODENESEE	Grand -->	LK OAHE
Gers	France	GRAND FORKS,ND	RED LAKE(river)
Gers -->	Garrone	GRAND JUNCTION	COLORADO Riv.
Ghana	BLACK VOLTA,	Grande	Arg. Boliv.,Braz
Ghana	DAKA,KULPAWN,	Grande(Arg)-->	COLORADO
Ghana	LK VOLTA,OTI,PRA,	GRANDE(BOL)<--	Mizque
Ghana	RED VOLTA,	Grande(Bol)-->	ICHILO
Ghana	TANO, VOLTA,	Grande(Braz)->	SAO FRANCISCO
Ghana	WHITE VOLTA	Grande(Chil)->	LIMARE
GHANA/IVORY CST	BLACK VOLTA	Grande	Mexico, Nica.
Ghaghari	India	Grande(Urug)-->	URUGUAY Riv.
Ghaghari -->	GANGES	Grande d Mat.	Nicarauga
Gila	AZ., CO., NM,	GRANDEdMAT.<--	Tuma
Gila	TEMPE, AZ	Grande dMat.->	CARIBBEAN
GILA <--	Salt	Grn.deSantiago	Mexico
Gila -->	COLORADO	GR.dSANTIAGO<--	Bolanos
Gila	Ethiopia	Gr.dSantiago->	PACIFIC
Gironde	France	Grass	New York
GIRONDE <--	Dordogne,Garrone	Grass -->	ST. LAWRENCE
GIZA, Egypt	NILE	Grau	Czechoslovakia
Glama	Norway	GRAZ, Austria	MUR
GLAMA <--	Lagen	Great Bear Lk	N.W. Terr., Can.
Glama -->	NORTH SEA	Great Bear Riv.	N.W. Terr,, Can.
GLASCOW, Scot	CLYDE	Great Bear R.->	MACKENZIE
GLASCOW, ND	MILK	Great Falls,MT	MISSOURI
Glen	Scotland	Great Miami	DAYTON, OH
Glomma	Norway	GREAT MIAMI<--	Mad
Glommen	Norway	Great Miami-->	OHIO
Godovari	India	Great Ouse	BEDFORD, England
GODAVARI <--	Indravati,	GREAT OUSE<--	Cam, Wissey
GODAVARI <--	Inirida,Manjra,	Great Ouse-->	NORTH SEA
GODAVARI <--	Uva, Wainganga,	Great Pee Dee	N.& S. Carolina
GODAVARI <--	Wardha	GRT.PEE DEE<--	Lynches,Pee Dee
Godavari -->	BENGAL	Grt.Pee Dee-->	ATLANTIC
Gods	Manitoba, Can.	Great Ruaha	See Ruaha
GODS <--	Red Sucker	Great Salt Lk	Utah
Gods -->	HAYES	GREAT SALT LK	Jordan, Weber
Gogra	India	GR.SLAVE LK<--	Hay, Slave,
Gomati	India	GR.SLAVE LK<--	Talston
Gomati -->	GANGES	Greece	ALFIOS,ALIAKMON,
GON,Georgia,	KURU	Greece	ALPHEUS, ARDA,
Gonam	Siberia	Greece	ARTA,AURO,AXIOS,
Gonam -->	UCUR	Greece	EVROS, EVROTAS,
Gongola	Nigeria	Greece	ILISSOS, IRI,
Gongola -->	BENUE	Greece	LK COPAIS,LERNA,
Goose	N. Dakota	Greece	LK KARLA,NESTOS,
Goose -->	RED	Greece	LK VOLVE,PENEUS,
Gorgan	Iran	Greece	PENEIOS, PINIOS,
GORKY, Rus	OKA, VOLGA	Greece	RHOUPHIA,
Gota	Sweden	Greece	ROUFIAS,SARANTA
Grajua	Brazil	Greece	STRIMON,
Grajua -->	ATLANTIC	Greece	STRUMA, VARDAR
Grand	GRAND RAPIDS, MI	GREECE/TURKEY	MARICA(Meric),
Grand -->	LK MICHIGAN	GREECE/TURKEY	EVROS
Grand	Iowa, Missouri	Green	Kentucky
GRAND <--	Thompson	GREEN <--	Pond,San Rafael,

Green -->	OHIO	G OF MEXICO<--	Perdido, Suwanee
Green	Utah, Wyoming	G OF MEXICO<--	Rio Grande=Bravo
GREEN <--	Price, Yampa	G OF MEXICO<--	Sabine, Trinity,
Green -->	COLORADO	G OF MEXICO<--	San Antonio Riv.
GREEN BAY, WI	FOX	G ofRHAMBHAT<--	Narmada, Tapi
GREEN BAY <--	Escanaba, Fox	G OF RIGA<--	Daugava
GRENOBLE, Fr	ISERE	G.ofST LAWR.<--	Olomane, Moisie,
Guadiana	Portugal, Spain	G.ofST LAWR.<--	St. Lawrence
Guadiana -->	ATLANTIC	G OF THAIL.<--	Chao Phyara=Ping
Guainia(Negro)	Colombia, Venez.	G OF VENICE<--	Piave
Guanare	Venezuela	Gumal(Kundar)	Pakistan
Guanare -->	APURE	Gumal -->	INDUS
Guapore	See Itenes	Gumti	India
Guarico	Venezuela	Gunnison	Colorado
GUARICO <--	Orituco	Gunnison -->	COLORADO
Guarico -->	APURE	Gunz	Germany
Guatemala	AZUL, BELIZE,	Gunz -->	DANUBE
Guatemala	BRAVO, CHIAPAS,	Gurara	Nigeria
Guatemala	CHIXOY, IXCAN	Gurara -->	NIGER
Guatemala	LAPAZ, LK DULCE,	Gurupi	Brazil
Guatemala	LK GUIJA,NEGINO,	Gurupi -->	ATLANTIC
Guatemala	LK PETEN,	Guyana	BERBICE, NEW,
Guatemala	MOTAGUA,	Guyana	CORANTYNE,
Guatemala	PASION,POLOCHIC,	Guyana	CUYUNI
Guatemala	SAMALA, SARSTUN	Guyana	ESSQUIBO,
GUATA/SAN SALV	PAZ	Guyana	IRENG, MAZARUNI,
Guaviare	Colombia	Guyana	REWA, WAINI
Guaviare -->	ORINOCO	GUYANA/BRAZIL	IRENG(MAU)
Guayamouc	Haiti	GUYANA/SURINA.	CORANTYNE
Guayape	Honduras	GUYANA/VENZ.	APONGUAO,
GUAYAPE <--	Jalan	GUYANA/VENZ.	CUYUNI
Guayape -->	PATUCA	Guyandot	WV
Guayas	Ecuad.,GUAYAQUIL	Gwda(Gwaa)	Poland
Guayàs -->	PACIFIC	Gwda -->	NOTEC
Guden	Denmark	Gwaii	Zimbabwe
Gudenaa	Denmark	GYOR, Hung.	RABA
Guinea	BAFING, FALEME,	Hadejia	Nigeria
Guinea	KONKOURE,	Hadejia -->	LK CHAD
Guinea	KOULOUNTOU,	Hailar	China
Guinea	NIGER, SENEGAL,	Hailar -->	AMUR
Guinea	TINKISSO	Haiti	ARTIBONITE,
Guinea-Bissau	CACHEU,CORUBAL	Haiti	GUAYAMOUC
Guinea-Bissau	GEBA,	Haliri	Iran
G OF AK <--	Copper,	Halys	Armenia, Turkey
G OF CA <--,	Colorado,Fuerte,	HAMBURG, Ger.	ELBE
G OF CA <--,	Sinaloa, Sonora,	HAMELN, Ger.	WESER
G OF CA <--,	INALOA, Yaqui	Hamu	New Guinea
G.ofCARPENTR<	Mitchell, Roper,	Han	China, SEOUL,
G.ofCARPENTR<	Staaten	Han	S.Korea
G of FINL.<--	Neva	HAN <--	Yongding
G of GUINEA<--	Niger, Nyong,	Han -->	YANGTZE
G of GUINEA<--	Sanaga	Han-Gang	SEOUL, S.Korea
G.ofHONDURAS<--	Ulua	Han-Gang -->	YELLOW SEA
G of MAINE<--	Kennebec,Saco	Hang Pu	SHANGHAI
G of MAINE<--	Penobscot,	Hang Pu -->	YANGTZE
G OF MEXICO<--	Lavaca, Mobile,	HANGCHOW,CHINA	FUCHUN
G OF MEXICO<--	Nueces, Panuco,	HANGCHOW B <--	Fuchun
G OF MEXICO<--	Pascagoula,Pearl	Hankiang	China

HANOI, Vietn.	*RED*	*Hondo* -->	*CARIBBEAN*
HARBIN, China	*SONGHUA*	Honduras	*AGUAN, COCO,*
Hari	Indonesia	Honduras	*GUAYAPE, JALAN,*
Hari -->	*SOUTH CHINA S*	Honduras	*LEMPA, LK CRIBA,*
Harirud	Afghanist.,HERAT	Honduras	*LK YOJOA, MOCAL,*
Harirud	IRAN/AFGHAN.	Honduras	*NEGRO, OLANCHO,*
Harirud	Turkmenistan	Honduras	*PATUCA, PAULAYA*
Harlem	New York	Honduras	*SEGOVIA,,*
HARRISBURG, PA	*SUSQUEHANNA*	Honduras	*SICO TINTO,*
Hart	Yukon, Can	Honduras	*SULACO, ULUA,*
Hart -->	*PEEL*	Honduras	*WAMPU, WANKS,*
HARTFORD, CN	*CONNECTICUT*	HOND./NICAR.	*COCO*
Hasbani	Lebanon	*Hongshui*	China
Hatchie	Tennessee	*Hongshui* -->	*XUN*
Hatchie -->	*MISSISSIPPI*	HONOLULU, HI	*MANOA, NUUANU,*
Havel	BERLIN, Germany	*Hoosic*	New York
HAVEL <--	*Spree*	*Horn*	N.W. Territ.,Can
Havel -->	*ELBE*	*Horn* -->	*MACKENZIE*
HAVRE, MT	*MILK*	*Hornad*	Czechoslovakia
Haw	N. Carolina	*Horton*	N.W. Territ.,Can
Haw -->	*CAPE FEAR*	*Horton* -->	*ARCTIC OCEAN*
Haw -->	*Jordan Lk*	*Hron*	Czechoslovakia
Hay	Alberta, Can.	*Hron* -->	*DANUBE*
Hay -->	*GREAT SLAVE LK*	*Huai*	China
Hayes	Manitoba, Can.	*HUAI* <--	*Ying*
HAYES <--	*Gods, Stupart*	*Huai* -->	*LK HONGZE*
Hayes -->	*HUDSON BAY*	*Huallaga*	Peru
Haynes	New Jersey	*HUALLAGA* <--	*Mayo*
Heart	N. Dakota	*Huallaga* -->	*MARANON*
Heart -->	*MISSOURI*	*Huang(Yellow)*	China
Heath	BOLIVIA/PERU	*Huasco*	Chile
Heath -->	*MADRE DE DIOS*	*Huasco* -->	*PACIFIC*
Heilong	See Amur	*Hudson*	ALBANY,NEWARK,NY
Helmand	Afghanistan	*Hudson*	NEW YORK CITY,
Helme	Germany	*Hudson*	TROY,NJ\NY,NYACK
Helme -->	*UNSTRUT*	*Hudson*	YONKERS
Hemavati	India	*HUDSON* <--	*Mohawk*
Henares	Spain	*Hudson* -->	*ATLANTIC*
Henrad	Hungary	*HUDSON B* <--	*Albany, Kogaluc,*
HERAT,Afghan.	*HARIRUD*	*HUDSON B* <--	*Nelson, Quoich,*
Herbert	Australia	*HUDSON B* <--	*Seal, Severn,*
Herbert -->	*CORAL SEA*	*HUDSON B* <--	*Tha-anne,Thelon,*
HERMOSILLO,Mex.	*SONORA*	*HUDSON B* <--	*Winisk*
Hernad	Hungary,Slovakia	*Huerva*	Spain
Hernad -->	*TISZA*	*Huerva* -->	*EBRO*
HILO, HI	*WAILUKU*	*Hugli*	CALCUTTA, India
Himalaya	*INDUS*	*Hugli* -->	*BAY OF BENGAL*
Hiwassee	TN, GA	*Huang*	See Yellow
Hiwassee -->	*TENNESSEE*	*Huma*	China
Hka	Burma	*Huma* -->	*AMUR*
Hkok(Kok)	Burma, Thailand	*Humber*	England
Hkok(Kok) -->	*MEKONG*	*HUMBER* <--	*Ouse, Trent*
HO CHI MINH	*SAIGON*	*Humber* -->	*NORTH SEA*
Hoangho	China	*Humber*	TORONTO
Holm	Denmark	*Humber* -->	*LK ONTARIO*
Holston	KNOXVILLE, TN	*Humboldt*	ELKO, Nevada
Holston -->	*LITTLE TENNESSEE*	*HUMBOLDT* <--	*Reese*
Hondo	MEXICO/BELIZE	*Humboldt* -->	*HUMBOLT SINK*

Hungary	*BERRETYO, BODVA,*	*Ii*	Finland
Hungary	*DANUBE, DRAVA,*	*Iijoki*	Finland
Hungary	*DUNA, HENRAD,*	*Iijoki* -->	*GULF OF BOTHNIA*
Hungary	*IPOLY, KAPOS,*	*Ijssel*	Netherlands
Hungary	*KOROS, MAROS,*	*IJSSEL* <--	*Vecht*
Hungary	*LK BALATON,MURA*	*Ijssel* -->	*IJSSELMEER*
Hungary	*LK FERTO, PECS,*	*Ijui*	Brazil
Hungary	*POPRAD, RAAB,*	*IJUI* <--	*Rio da Varzea*
Hungary	*RABA,RABCA,SAJO*	*Ijui* -->	*URUGUAY Riv.*
Hungary	*SARVIS, SIO, ZALA*	*Ik*	Russia
Hungary	*SZAMOS, TARNA,*	*Ikopa*	Madagascar
Hungary	*THEISS, TISZA*	*Ikopa* -->	*MOZAMBIQUE CHA.*
Hungary	*VISTULA,WISTA,,*	*Ilek*	Kazakhstan
Hungshui	China	*Ilek* -->	*URAL*
Hunse	Netherlands	*Ili*	China, Russia
Hunte	Germany	*Ili* -->	*LAKE BALKHASH*
HURON, SD	*JAMES*	*Ilissos*	Greece
Huron	ANN ARBOR, MI	*Iller*	Bavaria, Ger
Huron -->	*LK ERIE*	*Iller* -->	*DANUBE*
Hurtado	Chile	Illinois	*ELKHORN,*
Hurtado -->	*LIMARI*	Illinois	*KANKAKEE*
Hvita	Iceland	Illinois	*LA MOINE, OHIO,*
Hwangho	China	Illinois	*MACKINAW, ROCK,*
Hydaspes	India	Illinois	*SANGAMON,*
HYDERABAD,Pak.	*INDUS*	Illinois	*SKILLET FORK,*
Hyland	Yukon, Can.	Illinois	*SPOON, WABASH*
Hyland -->	*LIARD*	IL/KY	*OHIO*
Iaco(Yaco)	Brazil	IL/MO	*MISSISSIPPI*
Iaco -->	*PURUS*	*Illinois Riv.*	PEORIA
Ialomita	Romania	*ILLINOIS Riv.*	Kankakee, Spoon,
Ibar	Montenegro,Yugo.	*ILLINOIS Riv.*	La Moine,
Iberia, Sp	*EBRO*	*ILLINOIS Riv.*	Mackinaw,
Ibicui	Brazil	*ILLINOIS Riv.*	Sangamon
Ibicui -->	*URUGUAY Riv.*	*Illinois* -->	*MISSISSIPPI*
Ibina	Zaire	*Ilz*	Germany
Ica(Putumayo)	Brazil, Colombia	*Ilz* -->	*DANUBE*
Ica -->	*AMAZON*	*Imjin-gang*	N. Korea
Icana(Isana)	Brazil	*Imjin-gang*-->	*HAN-GANG*
Icana -->	*NEGRO*	India	*AI, BANAS,*
Iceland	*HVITA,LK MYVATH*	India	*BRAHMANI,*
Iceland	*JOKULSA,*	India	*BRAHMAPUTRA,*
Iceland	*THJORSA*	India	*CAUVERY, DOR,*
Ichilo(Mamore)	Bolivia	India	*CHAMBRAL,*
Ichilo -->	*MADRE de DIOS*	India	*CHENAB,*
Idaho	*BOISE, LOCHSA,*	India	*DAMOH, GANDAK,*
Idaho	*LK COEUR d'ALENE*	India	*GANGES,*
Idaho	*LK PEND OREILLE,*	India	*GHAGHARA,*
Idaho	*PAYETTE, PRIEST,*	India	*GODOVARI,GOGRA,*
Idaho	*PEND OREILLE,*	India	*GOMATI, GUMTI,*
Idaho	*PRIEST LK,RAFT,*	India	*HEMAVATI, HUGL,*
Idaho	*SALMON, SNAKE*	India	*INDUS, HYDASPES,*
ID/NV	*BEAR LK*	India	*INDRAVATI,JAWAI,*
ID/OR	*SNAKE*	India	*IRAWADI,JAMUNA,*
Iguacu	Brazil	India	*KARNALI, KAVERI,*
Iguacu -->	*PARANA*	India	*KISTNA, KOSI,*
Iguassu	Brazil	India	*KRISHNA, KUSI,*
Iguassu -->	*PARANA*	India	*LK CHILKA,MANAS,*
Iguazu -->	*PARANA*	India	*LK COLAIR, NIRA,*

India	*LK WULAR,*	Iowa	*MISSOURI,*
India	*MAHANADI,*	Iowa	*NODAWAY,*
India	*MANJRA, NARMADA*	Iowa	*SPIRIT LK, TURKEY*
India	*NARMEDA, PENN,*	Iowa	*SKUNK, STORM LK,*
India	*PARBATI, PENNER*	Iowa	*THOMPSON*
India	*REHR, RAPTI,*	Iowa	*WAPSIPINICON*
India	*SANKH, SARDA,*	IA/IL	*MISSISSIPPI*
India	*SIND, SON, SONAR,*	IA/NE	*MISSOURI*
India	*SUTLEJ, TAPI,*	IA/SD	*BIG SIOUX*
India	*TAPTI, TEL,*	IA/WI	*MISSISSIPPI*
India	*TUNGA, VINDHYAS,*	*IOWA* <--	*English*
India	*WARDHA, YAMUNA,*	*Iowa* -->	*MISSISSIPPI*
India	*WAINGANGA,*	*Ipel*	Czechoslovakia
INDIAN O <--	*De Grey, Fitzroy,*	*Ipel(Ipoly)* -->	*DANUBE*
INDIAN O <--	*Kaveri, Mangoro,*	*Ipoly*	Hungary
INDIAN O <--	*Murray, Pangani,*	IQUITOS, Peru	*AMAZONAS*
INDIAN O <--	*Penner, Rueha,*	Iran	*ARAKS, BAMPUR,*
INDIAN O <--	*Ruvuma, Tana, Tay,*	Iran	*CASPIAN SEA,*
INDIAN O <--	*Wami, Zambezi*	Iran	*EUPHRATES,*
Indiana	*LK MONROE,*	Iran	*GORGAN, HALIRI,*
Indiana	*MAUMEE, OHIO,*	Iran	*JAGIN, KARKHEH,*
Indiana	*ST. JOSEPH,*	Iran	*KARUN, LK NIRIS,*
Indiana	*TIPPECANOE,*	Iran	*LK NIRIZ, MAND,*
Indiana	*WABASH, WHITE*	Iran	*LK TASHT, MUND,*
IN/KY	*OHIO*	Iran	*LK TUZLU, RABCH,*
INDIANAPOLIS, I	*WHITE*	Iran	*LK URMIA, NAHANG*
Indigirka	Siberia	Iran	*MASHKEL, RUD,*
INDIGIRKA <--	*Moma*	Iran	*QEZEL OWZAN, RUD*
Indigirka -->	*SIBERIAN S*	Iran	*SAFIDRUD, SEFID,*
Indonesia	*BARITO, HARI,*	Iran	*SHUR, TAB, ZAB*
Indonesia	*KAJAN, KAMPAR,*	Iran	*TIGRIS, ZEYENDEH*
Indonesia	*KAPUAS,*	IRAN/AFGHAN.	*HARIRUD*
Indonesia	*LK RANAU,*	IRAN/PAKISTAN	*NAHANG*
Indonesia	*LK TOWUTI, MUSI,*	Iraq	*EUPHRATES,*
Indonesia	*MAHAKAM, PAWAN,*	Iraq	*TIGRIS, ZAB*
Indravati	India	Ireland	*BANDON, BANN,*
Indravati -->	*GODAVARI*	Ireland	*BARROW, BOYNE,*
Indre	France	Ireland	*BLACKWATER,*
Indre -->	*LOIRE*	Ireland	*BRIDE, CAVAN,*
Indus	Himalaya,	Ireland	*CLARE, DEEL*
Indus	HYDERAHAD,	Ireland	*ERNE, FANE, FEALE,*
Indus	India, Pakistan,	Ireland	*FINN, FOYLE, LEE,*
Indus	SUKKUR, Tibet	Ireland	*LIFFEY, LK CARRA,*
INDUS <--	*Gumal, Kabol,*	Ireland	*LK CONN, LK DERG,*
INDUS <--	*Sutlej, Zhab*	Ireland	*LK CORRIB,*
Indus -->	*ARABIAN SEA*	Ireland	*LK DOO, LK ERNE,*
Ingur -->	*BLACK SEA*	Ireland	*LK GOWNA, LK KEY,*
Inirida	Colombia	Ireland	*LK LOUGH,*
Inirida -->	*GUAVIARE*	Ireland	*LK MASK,*
Inn(En)	AUS./GER., Ger.,	Ireland	*LK NEOGH, LK REE,*
Inn(En)	Switz.	Ireland	*LK TAY, MAIGUE,*
INN <--	*Alz, Sallach*	Ireland	*MAINE, MUNSTER,*
Inn -->	*DANUBE*	Ireland	*MOY, NORE,*
INTERLAKEN, Swi	*AAR(E)*	Ireland	*SHANNON, SUCK,*
Iowa	*BIG SIOUX, CEDAR,*	Ireland	*SLANEY, SUIR*
Iowa	*CLEAR LK, FLOYD,*	*Ireng(Mau)*	GUYANA/BRAZIL
Iowa	*DES MOINES,*	*Ireng(Mau)* -->	*TACUTU*
Iowa	*GRAND, MAPLE,*	*Iri*	Greece

Iriri	Brazil	Italy	OGLIO, OMBRONE,
IRIRI <--	Curua	Italy	ORCO, PANARO
Iriri -->	XINGU	Italy	PARMA, PESCARA,
IRISH S <--	Dee(Eng.),Boyne,	Italy	PIAVE,PO,RAPIDO,
IRISH S <--	Conwy,Fane,Lune,	Italy	RENO,SALSO,SELE,
IRISH S <--	Liffey,Mersey	Italy	RUBICON, SANGRO,
IRISH S <--	Ribble, Slaney,	Italy	SECCHIA, SIMETO,
IRISH S <--	Teifi	Italy	STURA, TANARO,
IRKUTSK,Rus.	ANGARA	Italy	TARO, TEVERE,
Irrawaddy	Burma, PROME,	Italy	TIBER, TICINO,
Irrawaddy	MANDALAY	Italy	TIRSO, TREBBIA,
IRRAWADDY <--	Chindwin, Nmai,	Italy	VOLTURNO
IRRAWADDY <--	Shweli, Taping	Itata	Chile
Irrawaddy -->	BAY OF BENGAL	ITATA <--	Nuble
Irtys(Irtysh)	OMSK,Rus,Siberia	Itata -->	PACIFIC
IRTYS <--	Demjanka, Isim,	Itenes(Guapore)	Bolivia
IRTYS <--	Konsa,Lk Zajsan,	Itenes(Guapore)	BOLIVIA/BRAZIL
IRTYS <--	Om', Tobol	Itenes -->	MAMORE
Irtys -->	OB	Ituxi	Brazil
Isaac	Australia	Ituxi -->	PURUS
Isaac -->	MACKENZIE	Ivai	Brazil
Isana	See Icana	Ivai -->	PARANA
Isar	Bavaria, Czech.,	Ivory Coast	BAGOE, BANDAMA,
Isar	Germany. MUNICH	Ivory Coast	DAVO, KOMOE, NZI,
Isar -->	DANUBE	Ivory Coast	LOBO,LK KOSSOU,
Iser	Aus.,Czech.,Ger.	Ivory Coast	RED BANDANA,
Iser -->	ELBE	Ivory Coast	SASSANDRA,
Isere	GRENOBLE, France	Ivory Coast	WHITE BANDAMA
Isere -->	RHONE	IV.CST/LIBERIA	NUON
Iset	Russia	Ixcan	Guatemala
Iset -->	TOBOL	Ixcan -->	LACANTUN
Isim	Russia	Izma	Russia, UCHTA
ISIM <--	Nura, Turgaj	Izma -->	PECORA
Isim -->	IRTYSH	JACKSON, MS	PEARL
Iskar(Iskur)	Bulgaria, SOFIA	JACKSON, WY	SNAKE
Iskar -->	DANUBE	JACKSONVILLE,FL	ST. JOHNS
Iskut	Br. Columbia,Can.	Jagin	Iran
Iskut -->	STIKINE	Jagsl	Germany
Israel	ARNON, FARIA,	Jagsl -->	NECKAR
Israel	JORDAN, LAKHISH,	Jaguarao	See Yaguaron
Israel	ISHON, LK HULEH,	Jailing	China
Israel	MALIK, SARIDA,	Jailing -->	YANGTZE
Israel	SOREO, YARKON	JAJCE, Bosnia	VRBAS
Israel	New Hampshire	JAKUTSK, Rus.	LENA
Israel -->	CONNECTICUT	Jalan	Honduras
Italy	ADDA,ADIGE,AGRI,	Jalan -->	Guayapa
Italy	ANIENE, ANIO,	Jalon	Spain
Italy	ARNO, BELICE,	Jalon -->	EBRO
Italy	BIFERNO,	Jamari	Brazil
Italy	BRADANO,CHIENTI,	Jamari -->	MADEIRA
Italy	CRATI, LIRI,	James(East)	RICHMOND, VA
Italy	LIVENSA,LK COMO,	James(East)<--	Rivanna
Italy	LK ISEO,MANNU,	James(East)-->	ATLANTIC
Italy	LK LUGANO, NERA,	James(West)	ND, HURON,
Italy	LK MAGGIORE,	James(West)	MITCHELL,SD
Italy	LK NEMI-GARDA,	James(West)-->	MISSOURI
Italy	METAURO, MINCIO,	James B	ONTARIO/QUEBEC
Italy	MONTONE,OFANTO,	JAMES B <--	Ekwan

Jamuna	Bangladesh,India	*Jucar* -->	*MEDITERRANEAN*
JAMUNA <--	*Manas*	*Judith*	Montana
Jamuna -->	*GANGES*	*Judith* -->	*MISSOURI*
Jana	Siberia	*Judoma*	Rus., Siberia
JANA <--	*Sartang*	*Judoma* -->	*MAJA*
Jana -->	*LAPTEV SEA*	*Juniata*	Pennsylvania
Japan	*LK BIWA,LK TOYA,*	*Juniata* -->	*SUSQUEHANNA*
Japan	*LK TOWADA, YODO*	*Jur*	Sudan
Japura	Brazil	*Jur* -->	*BAHR al GAZHAL*
Japura -->	*AMAZON*	*Jurua*	Brazil
Jarama	Spain	*JURUA* <--	*Envira, Xerua*
JARAMA <--	*Manzanares*	*Jurua* -->	*AMAZON*
Jarama -->	*TAGUS*	*Juruena*	Brazil
Jauma	India	*JURUENA* <--	*Rio de Sangue,*
Jauma -->	*GANGES*	*JURUENA* <--	*Saueruina*
Java	*BRANTAS, LIWUNG,*	*Juruena* -->	*TAPAJOS*
Java	*SOLO*	*Jutai*	Brazil
Javari	*See Yavari*	*Jutai* -->	*AMAZON*
Javari -->	*AMAZON*	*Juznyi Bug*	Ukraine
Jawai	India	*Juznyi Bug*-->	*BLACK SEA*
Jeetze	Germany	*Kabol*	Afghan.,Pakistan
Jeetze -->	*ELBE*	*Kabol* -->	*INDUS*
Jenisej	Siberia	*Kabompo*	Zambia
JENISEJ <--	*Angara, Kazyr,*	*Kabompo* -->	*ZAMBEZI*
JENISEJ <--	*Kurejka,*	KABONGO,Zaire	*ZAMBEZI*
JENISEJ <--	*Nizn'ajaTunguska*	*Kaduna*	Nigeria
JENISEJ <--	*Podkamennaja*	*KADUNA* <--	*Mariga*
	Tunguska	*Kaduna* -->	*NIGER*
Jenisej -->	*KARA SEA*	*Kafu*	Uganda
JERUSALEM	*KEDRON*	*Kafue*	Zambia
Jhelum	Kashmir,Pakistan	*KAFUE* <--	*Lunga*
Jhelum -->	*CHENAB*	*Kafue* -->	*ZAMBEZI*
Jialing	China	*Kagera*	Burundi, Rwanda,
Jialing -->	*YANGTZE*	*Kagera*	Tanzania
Jiboa	El Salvador	*Kagera* -->	*LK VICTORIA*
Jiboa -->	*PACIFIC*	*Kahayan*	Borneo
Jin(China)	*See Gam(Vietnam)*	*Kahayan* -->	*JAVA SEA*
Jinsha	*See Yangtze*	*Kala*	Finland
Jiu(Jiul)	Romania	*Kaladan*	Burma, India
JIU <--	*Motrul*	*Kaladan* -->	*BAY OF BENGAL*
Jiu -->	*DANUBE*	*Kalama*	Washington
John Day	Oregon	*Kalama* -->	*COLUMBIA*
John Day -->	*COLUMBIA*	*Kalix*	Sweden
Jokulsa	Iceland	*Kama*	PERM, Russia
JOLIET, IL	*JORDAN, YARMUK*	*KAMA* <--	*V'atka*
Jong	Sierra Leone	*Kama* -->	*VOLGA*
Jordan	*JORDAN, YARMUK*	*Kamcatka*	Russia
Jordan	Isr,Jordan,Syria	*Kamcatka* -->	*BERING SEA*
JORDAN <--	*Yarmuk*	*Kamp*	Austria
Jordan -->	*DEAD SEA*	*Kampar*	Indonesia
Jordan	Utah	*Kampar* -->	*STRT. of MALACCA*
Jordan -->	*GREAT SALT LK*	*Kan*	KANSK, Siberia
J.BONAPRTE G<--	*Ord*	*Kan* -->	*YANGTZE*
Joz	Lebanon	*Kanawha*	CHARLESTON, WV
Jubba(Genale)	Somalia,Ethiopia	*Kanawha* -->	*OHIO*
JUBBA <--	*Dawa(Daua)*	*Kang(Kong)*	Cambodia, Laos
Jubba -->	*INDIAN OCEAN*	*Kang* -->	*MEKONG*
Jucar	Spain	*Kankakee*	Illinois, JOLIET

Kankakee -->	*ILLINOIS Riv.*	Kazakhstan	*ARAL SEA, EMBA,*
KANKAN,Guinea	*MILO*	Kazakhstan	*CASPIAN SEA,*
KANPUR,India	*GANGES*	Kazakhstan	*ILEK,ISIM,NURA,*
Kansas	*ARKANSAS,*	Kazakhtsan	*LK BALKHASH,*
Kansas	*KANSAS, KAW,*	Kazakhstan	*LK ZAJSAN,TOBOL,*
Kansas	*MISSOURI,*	Kazakhstan	*LK ZAJSAN,*
Kansas	*NEOSHO, OSAGE,*	Kazakhstan	*TURGAJ,*
Kansas	*REPUBLICAN,*	Kazakhstan	*SYRDARJA, UIL,*
Kansas	*LK CHENEY,*	Kazakhstan	*URAL*
Kansas	*LK KIRWIN,*	KAZAK./IRAN	*CASPIAN SEA*
Kansas	*LK MILFORD,*	*Kazym*	*Russia*
Kansas	*SALINE, SOLOMON,*	*Kazym* -->	*OB*
Kansas	*SMOKEY HILL,*	*Kazyr*	Russia
Kansas	*VERDIGRIS*	*Kazyr* -->	*YENISEY*
KS/MO Bor.	*MISSOURI*	KEARNY, NE	*PLATTE*
KANSAS CITY,MO	*KANSAS(Kaw),*	*Kedron*	JERUSALEM
KANSAS CITY,MO	*MISSOURI*	*Keele*	N.W. Terr., Can.
Kansas(Kaw)	KANSAS CITY,KS	*Keele* -->	*MACKENZIE*
Kansas(Kaw)	TOPEKA	*Keiro*	Kenya
KANSAS <--	*Republican,*	KENEMA,S.Leone.	*MOA*
KANSAS <--	*Smoky Hill,*	*Kennebago*	Maine
KANSAS <--	*Solomon*	*Kennebec*	AGUSTA, Maine
Kansas(Kaw)-->	*MISSOURI*	*Kennebec* -->	*GULF OF MAINE*
KANSK, Rus.	*KAN*	*Kennet*	England
Kapos	Hungary	KENOSHA, WI	*LK MICHIGAN*
Kapuas	Borneo,Indonesia	Kentucky	*BARREN,*
KAPUAS -->	*S. CHINA SEA*	Kentucky	*BIG SANDY, SALT,*
Kara	Togo	Kentucky	*DIX,GREEN, OHIO,*
Kara -->	*OTI*	Kentucky	*KENTUCKY Riv.,*
Kara Sea	Russia	Kentucky	*POND,POWELL,*
KARA SEA <--	*Ob,P'asina,Pur,*	KY/MO Bor.	*MISSISSIPPI*
KARA SEA <--	*Tajmyra,Taz,*	KY/OH Bor.	*KY/OH, OHIO*
KARA SEA <--	*Yenisey(Jenisej)*	KY/WV Bor.	*TUG FORK*
Karakoro	MALI/MAURATANIA	*Kentucky Riv.*	FRANKFORT, KY
Karakoro -->	*SENEGAL*	*KENTUCKY Riv*<--*Dix*	
KARDZAHLI,Bulg.	*ARDA*	*Kentucky Riv*->	*OHIO*
Karkheh	Iran	Kenya	*GALANA,*
Karnali	Nepal, India	Kenya	*LK RUDOLF*
KARNALI <--	*Sarda*	Kenya	*LK TURKANA,TANA,*
Karnali -->	*GANGES*	Kenya	*LK VICTORIA,*
Karun	Iran	Kenya	*TURKWELL*
Kasai(Cassai)	Angola, Zaire	KEOKUK, IA	*MISSISSIPPI*
KASAI <--	*Fimi, Loange,*	*Kern*	BAKERSFIELD, CA
KASAI <--	*Lukenie, Wamba*	*Kerulen(Cherlen*	China, Mongolia
Kasai -->	*CONGO*	*Kerulen* -->	*HAILAR*
Kasari	Estonia	*Ket*	Russia
Kasemieh	Lebanon	*Ket* -->	*OB*
Kashmir,India	*JHELUM* Indus	KHANEH, Iran	*LK URMIA*
KASSEL, Ger	*FULDA*	*Khong*	Laos
Katonga	Uganda	*Khotan*	China
Kaveri	India	*Kialing*	China
Kaveri -->	*INDIAN OCEAN*	*Kickapoo*	Wisconsin
Kaw(Kansas)	KANSAS CITY,KS	*Kickapoo* -->	*WISCONSIN Riv.*
Kaw(Kansas)	TOPEKA	KIEV, Ukraine	*DNIEPER*
Kayakuk	Alaska	*Kikori*	New Guinea
Kayan	Borneo	KILKENNY, Ire.	*NORE*
Kayan -->	*CELEBES SEA*	*Kirenga*	Russia
KAYES, Mali	*SENEGAL*	*Kirenga* -->	*LENA*

Kispiox	Br.Columbia, Can.	*Kotto*	Cent. Afr. Rep
Kispiox -->	*SKEENA*	*Kotto -->*	*UBANGI*
Kissimmee	Florida	*Kotuj*	Russia
Kissimmee -->	*LK OKEECHOBEE*	*KOTUJ <--*	*Mojjero*
Kistna	India	*Kotuj -->*	*CHETA*
KISUMU,Kenya	*LK VICTORIA*	*Koulountou*	Guinea, Senegal
Kitinen	Finland	*Koulountou-->*	*GAMBIE(Gambia)*
Kizil	Turkey	*Koyukuk*	Alaska
Kizil -->	*BLACK SEA*	*Koyukuk -->*	*YUKON*
Klamath	CA, OR	KRAKOW	*WISTA*
KLAMATH <--	*Trinity*	*Kraszna*	*see Crasna*
Klamath -->	*PACIFIC*	*Krishna*	India
Klar	Norway, Sweden	*Krishna -->*	*B OF BENGAL*
Kl'az'ma	Russia	KRSKO,Slovenia	*SAVA*
KL'AZ'MA <--	*Nerl'*	*Kuban*	Russia
Kl'az'ma -->	*OKA*	*Kuban -->*	*BLACK SEA*
Klondike	DAWSON,Yukon,Can.	*Kubango*	South Africa
Klondike -->	*YUKON*	*Kulpawn*	Ghana
Knabur	Syria	*Kulpawn -->*	*WHITE VOLTA*
Knife	N.Dakota	*Kum*	S.Korea
Knife -->	*MISSOURI*	*Kuma*	Russia
KNOXVILLE,TN	*HOLSTON*	*Kuma -->*	*CASPIAN S*
Kobuk	Alaska	*Kumara*	China
Kobuk -->	*KOTZEBUE SOUND*	*Kundar*	*See Gumal*
Kocher	Germany	*Kunene*	*See Cunene*
Kocher -->	Neckar	*Kur*	Armenia
Kogaluc	Quebec	*Kura*	Armenia, Georgia
Kogaluc -->	*HUDSON BAY*	*Kura*	Azerbaijan,
Koi	Vietnam	*Kura*	SALYAN
Kok	*See Hkok*	*Kura -->*	*CASPIAN S*
Kokemaki	Finland	*Kurejka*	Russia
Koksoak	Quebec, Can.	*Kurejka -->*	*YENISEY*
Koksoak -->	*UNGAVA BAY*	*Kurinwas*	Nicaragua
Kolima	Siberia	*Kurinwas -->*	*CARIBBEAN*
KOLN(Cologne)	*RHINE*	*Kuruman*	South Africa
Kolyma	Russia, Siberia	*Kuruman -->*	*MOLOPO*
KOLYMA <--	Omolon, Sugoj	*Kusi*	India
Kolyma -->	*EAST SIBERIAN S*	*Kuskowin*	Alaska
Komadugu	Nigeria	*Kuskowin -->*	*BERING SEA*
Komadugu	*LK CHAD*	*Kutai*	Malaysia
Komoe	Ivory Coast	*Kwando*	*See Cuando*
KOMOE <--	*Leraba*	*Kwango*	*see Cuango*
Komoe -->	*ATLANTIC*	*Kwanza*	Angola
Konda	Russia	*Kwenge*	Congo
Konda -->	*IRTYSH*	*Kwenge -->*	*KWILU*
Kong	*See Kang*	*Kwilu*	Congo
Konkoure	Guinea	*KWILU <--*	*Kwenge*
Konkoure -->	*ATLANTIC*	*Kwilu -->*	*WAMBA*
Kootenai	*See Kootenay*	*Kostroma*	Russia
Kootenay	Br.Columbia, MT	*Kostroma -->*	*VOLGA*
KOOTENAY <--	*Fisher*	*L'amin*	Russia
Kootenay -->	*COLUMBIA*	*L'amin -->*	*OB*
Korea	*HAN, YALU*	*La Moine*	Illinois
Koros(Koro)	Hungary	*La Moine -->*	*ILLINOIS Riv.*
Koros -->	*TISZA*	*La Plata*	CO, NM
Kosi	India, Nepal	*La Plata -->*	*SAN JUAN*
Kostroma	Russia	*Labe*	*See Elbe*
Kostroma -->	*VOLGA*	*Laborec*	Czech

LABRADOR S <--	Exploits,Gander	Lebanon	JOZ, KASEMIEH,
Lachlan	Australia	Lebanon	LEONTES, LITANI
Lachlan -->	MURRAY	Lebanon	LYCOS, ORONTES
LAFAYETTE, IN	WABASH	Lech	AUSBERG,Aus,Ger,
Lagen	Norway	Lech -->	DANUBE
Lagen -->	GLAMA	Lee	CORK, Ireland
L.MAI CHIQUI<--	Dulce	Lee -->	ATLANTIC
LaHave	Nova Scotia, Can.	Leech Lk	Minnesota
LaHave -->	ATLANTIC	LEEDS, Eng.	AIRE
Lahn	Germany	Lehigh	ALLENTOWN, PA
Lahn -->	RHINE	Lehigh -->	DELAWARE
Lainio	Sweden	Leie	See Lys
Laja	Chile	LEIGE, Belg.	OURTHE, MEUSE
Laja -->	BIOBI	Leine	HANNOVER, Ger
Lak	Kenya	Leine -->	ALLER
Lake	Lk as abbreviat.	Leitha	Austria, Hungary
Lakish	Israel	Leitha -->	RABA
LkErie-Ontario	NIAGRA	Lek	Netherlands
Lk Sup.-Huron	ST. MARYS	Lek -->	MAAS
LAMAR, CO	ARKANSAS	LeMANS, Fr.	SARTHE
Lamin	Russia	LENNINGRAD,Rus.	NEVA
Lamin -->	OB	LEOBEN, Aus.	MUR
Lamoille	Vermont	Leontes	Lebanon
Lamoille -->	LK CHAMPLAIN	Lempa	El Salv., Hondur
LA/MS Bor.	MISSISSIPPI	LEMPA <--	Mocal
LANCASTER,Eng.	LUNE	Lempa -->	PACIFIC
Laoang	Philippines	Lena	CUJA, JAKUTSK,
Laoha	China	Lena	LENSK,Rus,SANGAR
Laoha -->	LIAO	Lena	Siberia,SINSKOJE
Laos	KHONG, KONG,NOI,	Lena	YAKUTSK, ZIGANSK
Laos	MEKONG, NAMHOU,	LENA <--	Aldan, Cara,
Laos	OU, SEBANG, XARN	LENA <--	Bol'saja Cuja,
LAOS/THAILAND	MEKONG	LENA <--	Kirenga, Linde,
Lapaz	El Salvador,Guat	LENA <--	Mina, Nuja,
Laptev Sea	Russia, Siberia	LENA <--	Ol'okma, Sinaja,
LAPTEV S <--	Anabar, Cheta,	LENA <--	Vil'uj, Vitim
LAPTEV S <--	Jana,Lena,Olenok	Lena -->	LAPTEV SEA
Lapuan	Finland	LENSK, Rus.	LENA
Laramie	Wyoming	Leon	Texas
Laramie -->	MORTH PLATTE	Leon -->	TROY BELTON LK
LAREDO, TX	RIO GRANDE	LEOPOLDVILLE	CONGO(Zaire)
LAS CRUCES,NM	RIO GRANDE	Leraba	BURK./IVORY CST
Lascia	Sardinia	Leraba -->	KOMOE
Latvia	AA,DAUGAVA,	Lerma	Mexico
Latvia	DVINA(West),	Lerna	Greece
Latvia	GAUJA, OGRE	Lesotho, Afr.	CALEDON, ORANGE
Latvia	LIELUPE, VENTA	LESOTHO/S.AFR.	CALEDON
Lauca	Bolivia. Chile	Lesse	Belgium
LAUSANNE,Swi	LK GENEVA	Lewis	Washington
Lava	Poland	Lewis -->	COLUMBIA
LAVA <--	Lyna	LEWISTON, ID	SNAKE
Lava -->	BALTIC SEA	Liao(Xiliao)	N.E. China
Lavaca	Texas	Liao -->	YELLOW SEA
Lavaca -->	GULF OF MEXICO	Liard	Canada,Yukon,
Lea	England	LIARD <--	Dease, Hyland,
Leaf	Mississipppi	LIARD <--	Petitot
Leaf -->	PASCAGOULA	Liard -->	MACKENZIE
Lebanon	DAMOUR, HASBANI	Licking	CINCINNATI, Ohio

Licking -->	*OHIO*	*Little* -->	*RED*
Liberia	*CAVALLY, CESS,*	*Litt. Colorado*	AZ, CO
Liberia	*CESTOS, LOFA,*	*LITTLE ROCK,AR*	*ARKANSAS*
Liberia	*MANNA,MANO,*	*Livenza*	Italy
Liberia	*MORRO, NUON,*	LIVERPOOL,Eng.	*MERSEY*
Liberia	*SAN PEDRO,*	LIVINGSTONE	*ZAMBEZI*
Liberia	*ST.JOHN, ST.PAUL*	*Liwung*	Java
LIBER/IVRY CST.	*CAVALLY*	*Ljusne*	Sweden
LIBER/MONROVIA	*ST.PAUL*	*Lk Abaya*	Ethiopia
LIBER/SIER LEO	*MARO*	*Lk Abe*	Ethiopia
Liechtenstein	*RHINE, SAMINA*	*Lk Abert*	Oregon
LIECHTEN/SWI	*RHINE*	*Lk Abitibi*	Canada
LIEGE, Belg.	*MEUSE*	*Lk Achkel*	Tunisia
Lielupe	Latvia, Lithunia	*Lk Ageri*	Switzerland
Liffey	DUBLIN, Ireland	*Lk Aima*	Brazil
Liffey -->	*IRISH SEA*	*Lk Albert*	Ugandi, Zaire
LIGURIAN S <--	*Arno*	*Lk Alte*	Norway
Likati	Zaire	*Lk Annecy*	France
Likouala	Congo	*Lk Aral*	*See Aral Sea*
Likouala -->	*CONGO*	*Lk Arenal*	Costa Rica
Lilleaa	Denmark	*Lk Argyle*	Australia
Lima	Portugal, Spain	*Lk Argyle* -->	*ORD*
Lima -->	*ATLANTIC*	*Lk Aru*	Tibet
Limari	Chile	*Lk Athabasca*	Alberta
LIMARE <--	*Grande, Hurtado*	*Lk Awe*	Scotland
Limari -->	*PACIFIC*	*Lk Baikal*	Russia, Siberia
Limay	Argentina	*LK BAIKAL* <--	*Selenge*
Limay -->	*NEGRO*	*Lk Baikal* -->	*ANGARA*
LIMERICK,Ire.	*SHANNON*	*Lk Bala*	Wales
Limia	*See Lima*	*Lk Balaton*	Hungary
Limpopo	Botswana,Mozamb.	*Lk Balkhash*	Kazahstan
Limpopo	S.Africa,XAI-XAI,	*LK BALKHASH* <--	*Ili*
Limpopo	Zimbabwe	*Lk Bam*	Tibet
LIMPOPO <--	*Changane,*	*Lk Bamtso*	China
LIMPOPO <--	*Olifants, Shashe*	*Lk Barlee*	Australia
Limpopo -->	*MOZAMBIQUE CHN.*	*Lk Bemidji*	Minnesota
LINCOLN, Eng.	*WITHAM*	*Lk Bitter*	*See Bitter Lks*
Linde	Siberia	*Lk Biwa*	Japan
Linde -->	*LENA*	*Lk Bodensee*	Austria, Germany
Lindi	Zaire	*Lk Bodensee*	GER/SWITZ
Lindi -->	*CONGO*	*LK BODENSEE* <--	*Thur*
Linth	Switzerland	*Lk Bodensee* -->	*RHINE*
Linyanti	Botswana	*Lk Bornor*	China
LINYANTI <--	*Kwando, Okavango*	*Lk Buloo*	Australia
Linyanti -->	*ZAMBEZI*	*LK BULLOO* <--	*Bulloo*
LINZ, Aus.	*DANUBE*	*Lk Bum*	Tibet
Lippe	Germany	*Lk Burt*	Michigan
Lippe -->	*RHINE*	*Lk Carite*	Puerto Rico
Liri	Italy	*Lk Carra*	Ireland
LISBON, Port.	*TAGUS*	*Lk Cayuga*	New York
Litang	China	*Lk Cazaux*	France
Litang -->	*YANGTZE*	*Lk Chad*	Chad
Litani	Lebanon	*LK CHAD* <--	*Chari, Komadugu*
Lithuania	*DUBYSA, LIELUPE,*	*Lk Champlain*	NY/VT Bor.
Lithuania	*NEMAN, NEMUNAS,*	*LK CHAMPLAIN* <--	*Lamoille,*
Lithuania	*NERIAS,PREGOLYA,*	*LK CHAMPLAIN* <--	*Winooski*
Lithuania	*RUSNE, VENTA*	*Lk Chany*	Russia
Little	Texas	*Lk Chao*	China

Lk Chapala	Mexico	*LK HOPNGZE <--*	*Huai*
Lk Chelan	Washington	*Lk Huleh*	Israel
Lk Cheney	Kansas	*LK HURON <--*	*Saginaw,St.Marys*
Lk Chilka	India	*Lk Iatt*	Louisiana
Lk Clear	*See Clear Lk*	*Lk Idku*	Egypt
Lk Colair	India	*Lk Ilmen*	Russia
Lk Como	Italy	*Lk Iseo*	Italy
Lk Coniston	England	*Lk Ister*	Norway
Lk Conn	Ireland	*Lk It'men'*	Russia
Lk Constance	*See Lk Bodensee*	*LK IT'MEN' <--*	*Msta*
Lk Copais	Greece	*Lk Itasca*	Minnesota
Lk Corrib	Ireland	*Lk Jackson*	Wyoming
Lk Cowan	Australia	*Lk Jagok*	Tibet
Lk Crater	*See Crater Lake*	*Lk Jouy*	Switzerland
Lk Cree	Canada	*Lk Juo*	Finland
Lk Criba	Honduras	*Lk Kariba*	Zambia, Zinbabwe
L Couer d'Alene	Idaho	*Lk Karla*	Greece
Lk Debo	Mali	*Lk Kemi*	Finland
Lk Derg	Ireland	*Lk Key*	Ireland
Lk Djerid	Tunisia	*Lk Kerr*	Virginia
Lk Doo	Ireland	*Lk Kirwin*	Kansas
Lk Dora	Florida	*Lk Kivi*	Finland
Lk Dow	Botswana	*Lk Kivu*	Rwanda, Zaire
Lk du Guiers	Senegal	*Lk Kootenay*	Canada
Lk du Guiers->	*SENEGAL*	*Lk Kossou*	Ivory Coast
Lk Dulce	Guatemala	*Lk Kossou -->*	*BANDAMA*
Lk Eagle	*See Eagle Lk*	*Lk Kyoga*	Uganda
Lk Ebmor	China	*Lk Ladoga*	Russia
Lk Edku	Egypt	*LK LADOGA <--*	*Ojat', Volchov*
Lk Elton	Russia	*Lk Ladoga -->*	*NEVA*
Lk Enid	Mississippi	*Lk Lanao*	Philippines
Lk Erie	CLEVELAND,ERIE,	*Lk Larto*	Louisiana
Lk Erie	PA, TOLEDO, OH	*Lk Leech*	*See Leech Lake*
LK ERIE <--	*Cuyahoga, Huron,*	*Lk Leman*	*See Lk Geneva*
LK ERIE <--	*Maumee,Sandusky*	*Lk Llanquihue*	Chile
Lk Erne	Ireland	*Lk Loiza*	Puerto Rico
Lk Eyre	Australia	*Lk Lomand*	Scotland
Lk Falcon	Texas	*Lk Lough*	Ireland
Lk Feia	Brazil	*Lk Louise*	Canada
Lk Ferto	Hungary	*Lk Lugano*	Italy, Switz
Lk Flathead	*See Flathead Lk*	*Lk Lynn*	W. Virginia
Lk Frome	Australia	*Lk Maggiore*	Italy, LOCARNO
*Lk Garda=Lago d*Italy		*Lk Malaren*	Sweden
Lk Garda -->	*ADIGE*	*Lk Malawai*	*See Lk Nyasa*
Lk Garou	Mali	*Lk Mamry*	Poland
Lk Garry	Canada	*Lk Managua*	Nicaragua
Lk Goplo	Poland	*Lk Marion*	S. Carolina
Lk Gowna	Ireland	*LK MARION <--*	*Wateree*
Lk Geneva	LUASANNE, Switz.	*Lk Martin*	Alabama, Georgia
Lk Geneva	FRANCE/SWITZ	*Lk Maryut*	Egypt
LK GENEVA<-->	*Rhone thru Lk G.*	*Lk Mask*	Ireland
Lk Grand	Maine	*Lk Mead*	AZ/NV Bor.
Lk Great Bear	*See Grt Bear Lk*	*Lk Mead*	COL. RIVER DAM
Lk Great Salt	*See Grt Salt Lk*	*LK MEAD <--*	*Virgin, Colorado*
Lk Guija	Guatemala	*Lk Mena*	Tibet
Lk Hawea	New Zealand	*Lk Merin*	Uruguay
Lk Hebgen	Montana	*Lk Michigan*	CHICAGO,GARY,IN
Lk Hongze	China	*Lk Michigan*	KENOSHA, WI

Lk Michigan	MILWAUKEE	*Lk Placid*	New York
LK MICHIGAN<--	*Des Plaines,*	*Lk Poopo*	Bolivia
LK MICHIGAN<--	*Grand, Muskegon*	*LK POWELL,UT*	*< San Juan*
Lk Milford	Kansas	*Lk Poygan*	Wisconsin
Lk Mirim	Brazil, Uruguay	*lk Prettyboy*	Maryland
LK MIRIM <--	*Cebollati,*	*Lk Priest*	*See Priest Lake*
LK MIRIM <--	*Tacauri,Yaguaron*	*Lk Puru*	Finland
Lk Mjosa	Norway	*Lk Pyha*	Finland
Lk Mono	*See Mono Lk*	*Lk Pyramid*	*See Pyramid Lk*
Lk Monroe	Indiana	*Lk Rainy*	*See Rainy Lake*
Lk Moosehead	Maine	*Lk Ranau*	Indonesia
Lk Muo	Finland	*Lk Ranco*	Chile
Lk Muritzee	Germany	*Lk Ree*	Ireland
Lk Murray	S. Carolina	*Lk Reindeer*	*See Reindeer Lk*
LK MURRAY <--	*Saluda*	*Lk Rivu*	Zaire
Lk Mweru	Zaire	*Lk Rudolf*	Kenya,
LK MWERA <--	*Luapula*	*Lk Rudolf*	*See Lk Turkana*
Lk Mwera -->	*LUVUA*	*LK RUDOLF <--*	*Omo*
Lk Myvatn	Iceland	*Lk Rukwa*	Tanzania
Lk Naknek	Alaska	*LK RUKWA <--*	*Rungwa*
Lk Nam	Tibet	*Lk Sakami*	*Quebec*
Lk Nasi	Finland	*LK SAKAMI <--*	*Sakami*
Lk Nemi-Garda	Italy	*Lk Scutari*	Albania, Yugoslavi
Lk Neogh	Ireland	*Lk Sebec*	Maine
Lk Ness	Scotland	*Lk Sego*	Russia
Lk Neuchatel	Switz	*Lk Seneca*	New York
Lk Neva	Russia	*Lk Shin*	Scotland
Lk Ngami	Botswana	*Lk Shola*	Ethiopia
Lk Nipigon	Canada, Ontario	*Lk Silja*	Sweden
Lk Niris	Iran	*Lk Simcoe*	Canada
Lk Niriz	Iran	*Lk Simo*	Finland
Lk Norris	Kentucky	*Lk Sinoe*	Romania
LK NORRIS <--	*Powell*	*Lk Slave*	*See Slave Lk*
Lk Nyasa	Malawai, Mozamb,	*Lk Smith*	Virginia
Lk Nyasa	Tanzania	*Lk Snasa*	Norway
Lk Nyasa -->	*RUVUMA*	*Lk Spirit*	*See Spirit Lk*
Lk Oahe	S. Dakota	*Lk Squam*	New Hampshire
LK OAHE <--	*Grand*	*Lk St. Clair*	DETROIT, MI
Lk Oahe -->	*MISSOURI*	*LK ST.CLAIR<--*	*Detroit River*
LkOfThe Ozarks	Missouri	*Lk St.-Jean*	Quebec, Can.
LKo't'OZARKS<--	Sac	*LK ST.-JEAN<--*	*Peribonca*
Lk Ohau	New Zealand	*Lk Storm*	*See Storm Lk*
Lk Ohrid	Yugoslavia	*Lk Superior*	DULUTH, MN
Lk Okanagan	Canada	*LK SUPERIOR<--*	*St. Louis*
Lk Okeechobee	Florida	*Lk Swan*	Utah
LK OKEECHOBEE	*Kissimmee*	*Lk Taal*	Philippines
Lk Onega	Rusia	*Lk Tahoe*	CA/NV, RENO, NV
Lk Oneida	New York	*Lk Tai*	China
Lk Onota	Massachusetts	*Lk Tablerock*	*See Tablerock Lk*
Lk Ontario	ROCHESTER, NY	*Lk Tana*	Ethiopia
Lk Ontario	TORONTO,	*Lk Tana -->*	*BLUE NILE*
LK ONTARIO <--	*Humber, Niagra,*	*Lk Tanganyiki*	Burundi
LK ONTARIO <--	*Oswego*	*LK TANGANYIKI*	*<--Igombe,Rusizi*
Lk Ontario -->	*ST. LAWRENCE*	*Lk Tasht*	Iran
Lk Oulo	Finland	*Lk Taupo*	New Zealand
Lk Peipus	Estonia	*Lk Taupo -->*	*WAIKATO*
Lk Pend Oreille	Idaho	*Lk Tay*	Ireland
Lk Peten	Guatemala	*Lk Tay*	Scotland

Lk Telli	China	Lobo -->	*SASSANDRA*	
Lk Texoma	TX/AR Bor., AR	LOCARNO, Italy	*LK MAGGIORE*	
LK TEXOMA <--	*Washita*	Lochsa	Idaho	
Lk Thun	Switzerland	Lofa	Liberia	
Lk Thun	Utah	Lofa -->	*ATLANTIC*	
LK THUN <--	*Utah River*	Logone	Chad	
Lk Titicaca	BOLIVIA/PERU	LOGONE <--	*Vina*	
Lk Tonlesap	Cambodia	Logone -->	*CHARI*	
Lk Torch	Michigan	Loho	China	
Lk Toro	Chile	Loi	Burma	
Lk Tosu	Tibet	Loi -->	*MEKONG*	
Lk Towada	Japan	Loir	France	
Lk Towuti	Indonesia	Loir -->	*LOIRE*	
Lk Toya	Japan	Loire	France, NANTES,	
Lk Tule	*See Tule Lk*	Loire	ORLEANS, TOURS	
Lk Tumba	Congo	LOIRE <--	*Allier, Cher,*	
Lk Turkana	Kenya	LOIRE <--	*Indre, Loir,*	
Lk Tuz	Turkey	LOIRE <--	*Sarthe, Vienne*	
Lk Tuzlu	Iran	Loire -->	*BAY OF BISCAY*	
Lk Uri	Switzerland	Lom	Bulgaria	
Lk Urmia	Iran, KHANEH	Lom -->	*DANUBE*	
Lk Van	Turkey	Lomami .	Zaire	
Lk Vanern	Sweden	Lomani -->	*CONGO*	
Lk Vattern	Sweden	LOMBARDIA, It	*ADDA*	
Lk Vera	Paraguay	Lonborg	Denmark	
Lk Victoria	Kenya, Ugandi	LONDON, Eng.	*THAMES*	
LK VICTORIA <--	*Kagera*	LODONDERRY, Ire.	*FOYLE*	
Lk Volta	Ghana	Lot	France	
LK VOLTA <--	*Black Volta, Daka,*	Lot -->	*GARONNE*	
LK VOLTA <--	*Oti, White Volta*	Lotta	Finland	
Lk Volve	Greece	Lougen	Norway	
Lk Vyrnwy	Wales	Louisiana	*AMITE, BOEUF,*	
Lk Waldo	Oregon	Louisiana	*BAYOU TECHE*	
Lk Winnebago	Wisconsin	Louisiana	*LK IATT, LK LARTO*	
LK WINNEBAGO<--	*Wolf*	Louisiana	*OUACHITA, PEARL,*	
LK WINNIPEG<--	*Red River North,*	Louisiana	*RED, SABINE,*	
LK WINNIPEG<--	*Saskatchewan Riv*	Louisiana	*TENSAS,*	
LK WINNIPEG<--	*Winnipeg Riv.*	LOUISVILLE, KY	*OHIO*	
Lk Wular	India	Loup	Nebraska	
Lk Yojoa	Honduras	LOUP <--	*North Loup*	
Lk Ypoa	Paraguay	Loup -->	*PLATTE*	
Lk Zajsan	Kazakhstan	Lovat'	Russia	
Lk Zajsan -->	*IRTYS*	Lovat' -->	*LK IT'MEN'*	
Lk Zeway	Ethiopia	LOWELL, MA	*MERRIMACK*	
Lk Zug	Switzerland	Lualaba	Zaire	
Llano	Texas	Lualaba -->	*CONGO*	
Llano -->	*COLORADO(TX)*	Luan	China	
Lluta	Chile	Luan -->	*YELLOW SEA*	
Lluta -->	*PACIFIC*	Luangwa	Zambia	
Lo(Panlong)	Vietnam, China	Luangwa -->	*ZAMBEZI*	
Lo -->	*RED HONG*	Luapula	Zambia	
Loa	Chile	Luapula -->	*LK MWERA*	
Loa -->	*PACIFIC*	Lubilash	Congo	
Loange	Congo	Lucie	Suriname	
Loange -->	*KASAI*	Lucie -->	*CORANTIJN*	
Lobaye	Cent. Afr. Rep.	Luena	Angola	
Loboye -->	*UBANGI*	Luena -->	*ZAMBEZIE*	
Lobo	Ivory Coast	Lugenda	Mozambique	

Lugende -->	RUVUMA	Mana		Fr. Guiana
Lukenie	Zaire	Mana -->		ATLANTIC
Lukenie -->	FIMI	Manas		Bhutan, India
Lukuga	Zaire	Manas -->		JAMUNA
Lule	Sweden	Manass		China
Lulonga	Zaire	MANAUS, Braz.		AMAZON, NEGRO
Lulua	Congo	Manawatu		New Zealand
Lumber	N. Carolina	Manchuria		SUNGARI
Lumber -->	LITTLE PEE DEE	MANCHU./N.KOREA		YALU
Lundi	Zimbabwe	MANCHUR./SIBER.E		AMUR, USSURI
Lundi -->	SAVE	Mand		Iran
Lune	Eng., LANCASTER	MANDALAY, Burma		IRRAWADDY
Lune -->	IRISH SEA	Mangoky		Madagascar
Lunga	Zambia	Mangoky -->		MOZAMBIQUE CHAN.
Lunga -->	KAFUE	Mangoro		Madagascar
Luo	China	Mangoro -->		INDIAN OCEAN
Luo -->	YELLOW	Mania		Madagascar
Lurio	Tanzania	Mania -->		MOZAMBIQUE CHAN.
Lurio -->	MOZAMBIQUE CHN.	MANILA		MARIKINA
Luvironza	Rwanda	Manitoba		ASSINIBOINE,
Luvua	Zaire	Manitoba		BERENS, HAYES,
LUVUA <--	Lk Mwera	Manitoba		CHURCHILL, ODEI
Luwego	Tanzania	Manitoba		LK WINNIPEG,
Luwego -->	GREAT RUAHA	Manitoba		NELSON, SEAL,
Luxembourg	ALZETTE,	Manitoba		RED of the North
Luxembourg	MOSELLE,	Manitoba		RED SUCKER,STULL
Luxembourg	SAUER, SURE	Manitoba		ROSEAU,STUPART,
LUXOR, Egypt	NILE	Manitoba		SWAN, THROAT,
Luy	France	Manitoba		VALLEY, WINNIPEG
Luznice	Czechoslovakia	MANIT./SASKAT.		REINDEER LK
Lycos	Lebanon	Manjel		Belgium
Lyna	Poland	Manjra		India
Lyna -->	LAVA	Manjra -->		GODAVARI
Lynches	N.& S. Carolina	Manna		Liberia
Lynches -->	GREAT PEE DEE	MANNHEIM, Ger.		RHINE
LYON, Fr.	RHONE, SAONE	Mannu		Italy, Sardinia
Lys	Belgium, France	Mano		Liberia
Lys -->	SCHELDT	Mano -->		MARO
Malheur -->	SNAKE	Manoa		HONOLULU
Mali	BAFING#1, BAGOE,	Manso		Brazil
Mali	BAFING#2, BAKOY,	Manso -->		CUIABA
Mali	BANI, BANIFING,	Mantaura		New Zealand
Mali	BAOULE, FALEME,	Mantua		New Jersey
Mali	KANI, LK DEBO,	Manu		Peru
Mali	LK GAROU,	Manu -->		MADRE DE DIOS
Mali	SENEGAL	Manyc		Russia
MALI/MAURITAN.	KARAKORO	Manyc -->		DON
MALI/SENEGAL	FALEME	Manzanares		MADRID, Sp.
Malik	Israel	Manzanares -->		JARAMA
Malikha	Burma	Maple		Iowa
Malo	Uruguay	Maple -->		MISSOURI
Mambere	Cent. Afr. Rep.	Mapuera		Brazil
Mambere -->	UBANGI	Mapuera -->		TROMBETAS
Mamore	Bolivia	MARABA, Braz.		TOCANTINAS
MAMORE <--	Itenes, Guapore,	Maranon		Peru
MAMORE <--	Secure, Yacuma,	MARANON <--		Huallaga,Pastaza
MAMORE <--	Yata	MARANON <--		Tigre, Ucayali,
Mamore -->	MADEIRA	Maranon -->		AMAZON(AS)

March	Austria	Mbari	Cent. Afr. Rep.
March	Czech., Morava	Mbari -->	*UBANGI*
Mareb	Ethiopia	Mbenkuru	Tanzania
Marias	Montana	Mearin	Brazil
MARIAS <--	*Teton*	Meause	Netherlands
Marias -->	*MISSOURI*	Medina	Texas
MARIBOR,Sloven.	*DRAVA*	Medina -->	*SAN ANTONIO Riv.*
Marica	*See Evros*	MEDITERRANEAN<--	*Aude, Cheliff,*
Marico	*See Limpopo*	MEDITERRANEAN<--	*Ebro, Jucar,*
Maries	Missouri	MEDITERRANEAN<--	*Mejerda, Nile,*
Maries -->	*OSAGE*	MEDITERRANEAN<--	*Mijares,Moulouya*
Mariga	Nigeria	MEDITERRANEAN<--	*Orontes, Qishon,*
Mariga -->	*KADUNA*	MEDITERRANEAN<--	*Rhone, Seybouse,*
Marikina	MANILA, Phil.	MEDITERRANEAN<--	*Segura,Ter,Tiber*
Marista	Bulgaria,Turkey	MEDITERRANEAN<--	*Tevere,Turia,Var*
Marista -->	*AEGEAN SEA*	Medjerda	Algeria, Tunisia
Mark	Belgium	Medway	Eng, MAIDSTONE
Marne	France	Medway -->	*NORTH SEA*
Marne -->	*SEINE*	MEISSEN, Ger.	*ELBE*
Maro	LIBER/SIER LEONE	Meghna	Bangladesh
Maro -->	*ATLANTIC*	Meghna -->	*GANGES*
Maroni	FR.GUIANA/SURIN.	Mejerda	Algeria, Tunisia
Maroni -->	*ATLANTIC*	Mejerda -->	*MEDITERRANEAN*
Maros(Mures)	Hungary, Romania	Mekong	Burma, Cambodia,
Maros -->	TISZA	Mekong	China, Laos,
Maryland	*CHESTER,CHOPTANK*	Mekong	LAOS/THAIL.
Maryland	*LK PRETTYBOY,*	Mekong	PHNOM PENN, Camb.
Maryland	*PATUXENT,POTOMAC*	Mekong	Thailand,Vietnam
Mashkel	Iran	MEKONG <--	*Hkok, Lang, Loi,*
Massachusetts	*CHARLES,CHICOPEE*	MEKONG <--	*Mun,Sab,San,Sar,*
Massachusetts	*CONCORD,LK ONOTA*	Mekong -->	*S CHINA SEA*
Massachusetts	*CONNECTICUT,*	Mekrou	Benin, Niger
Massachusetts	*DEERFIELD,*	Mekrou -->	*NIGER Riv.*
Massachusetts	*MERRIMACK,NASHUA*	MELBOURNE	*PT. PHILLIPE BAY*
Massachusetts	*QUABOAG, TAUNTO*	MEMPHIS, Egypt	*NILE*
Matanza	BUENOS AIRES	MEMPHIS, TN	*MISSISSIPPI*
Mat	Albania	Menam	Thailand
Mataquito	Chile	Menominee	MI, WI
Mataquito -->	*PACIFIC*	Merced	California
Matia	Albania	Merced -->	*SAN JOAQUIN*
Matina	Costa Rica	Meric	*See Evros*
Mato	Venezuela	Merrimack	CONCORD, LOWELL.
Mato -->	*ORINOCO*	Merrimack	MA, NASHUA, NH
Matsang	Tibet	MERRIMACK <--	*Souhegan*
Mau(Ireng)	BRAZIL/GUYANA	Merrimack -->	*ATLANTIC*
Mau(Ireng) -->	*TACUTU*	Mersey	England
Maule	Chile	MERSEY <--	*Weaver*
Maule -->	*PACIFIC*	Mersey -->	*IRISH SEA*
Maumee	FORT WAYNE,	Mesai	Colombia
Maumee	TOLEDO, IN, OH	Messalo	Mozambique
Maumee -->	*LAKE ERIE*	Messalo -->	*MOZAMBIQUE CHAN.*
MAUN, Botswana	*OKARANGO*	Mesta	*See Nestos*
MAURIT./SENEGA	*SENEGAL*	Meta	Colom,.Venezuela
Mayenne	France	META <--	*Casanare, Pauto,*
Mayo	Colombia	META <--	*Upia*
Mayo -->	*HUALLAGA*	Meta -->	*ORINOCO*
Mazaruni	Guyana	Metauro	Italy
Mazaruni -->	*CUYUNI*	Meuse	Belg., Fr.,LIEGE

Meuse	NAMUR, SEDAN,	MN/WI Bor.	*ST. CROIX*
Meuse	VERDUN	*Mino*	*See Minho*
MEUSE <--	*Ourthe, Sambre,*	MINOT, ND	*SOURIS*
MEUSE <--	*Semois*	*Mira*	Colombia,Ecuador
Meuse(Maas) -->	*NORTH SEA*	*Mira* -->	*PACIFIC*
Mexico	*BALSAS, BRAVO,*	*Mira*	Portugal
Mexico	*CONCHOS,FLORIDO,*	*Miranda*	Brazil
Mexico	*FUERTE, GRANDE*	*Miranda* -->	*PARAGUAY Riv.*
Mexico	*LERMA,LK CHAPALA*	Mississippi	*BIG BLACK,LEAF,*
Mexico	*PANUCO,RIO BRAVO*	Mississippi	*LK ENID, PEARL,*
Mexico	*SALADO, SINALOA*	Mississippi	*PASCAGOULA,PEARL,*
Mexico	*SONORA, TABASCO,*	Mississippi	*SKUNA, YAZOO*
Mexico	*YAQUI*	Mississippi	*TALLAHATCHIE,*
MEXICO/BELIZE	*HONDO*	*Mississippi*	ALTON, CAIRO, IL
MEXICO/TX Bor.	*RIO GRANDE*	*Mississippi*	CLINTON,DUBUQUE,
Meyping	Thailand	*Mississippi*	DAVENPORT,KEOKUK
Mezen	Russia	*Mississippi*	MEMPHIS, MOLINE,
Mezen -->	*ARTIC OCEAN*	*Mississippi*	NEW ORLEANS,
Miami	Ohio	*Mississippi*	QUINCY,ST LOUIS,
MIAMI, FL	*BISCAYNE BAY*	*Mississippi*	ST. PAUL,AR/MS,
Michigan	*BRULE,CASS,FLAT,*	*Mississippi*	AR/TN, IA/IL,
Michigan	*DETROIT, GRAND,*	*Mississippi*	IA/WI, IL/MO,
Michigan	*LK BURT, HURON,*	*Mississippi*	KY/MO,LA/MS,
Michigan	*LK ST.CLAIR*	*Mississippi*	MN/WI, MO/TN
Michigan	*LK TORCH, ROCK,*	*MISSISSIPPI* <--	*Arkansas, Iowa,*
Michigan	*MENOMINEE,*	*MISSISSIPPI* <--	*Des Moines,Ohio,*
Michigan	*MUSKEGON,SAGINAW*	*MISSISSIPPI* <--	*Des Moines,*
Michigan	*ST. CLAIR,*	*MISSISSIPPI* <--	*Hatchie,Illinois*
Michigan	*ST. JOSEPH*	*MISSISSIPPI* <--	*Missouri, Rock,*
Mijares	Spain	*MISSISSIPPI* <--	*Rum, St. Croix,*
Mijares -->	*MEDITERREAN SEA*	*MISSISSIPPI* <--	*Skunk,St.Francis*
Mikkwa	Alberta, Can.	*MISSISSIPPI* <--	*Turkey, White,*
Mikkwa -->	*PEACE*	*MISSISSIPPI* <--	*Wapsipinicon,*
MILAN, Italy	*ADDA*	*MISSISSIPPI* <--	*Wisconsin*
MILES CITY, MT	*YELLOWSTONE*	Missouri	*GRAND, MARIES,*
Milk	GLASCOW, ND,	Missouri	*LK OF THE OZARKS*
Milk	HAVRE, MT	Missouri	*NODAWAY, OSAGE,*
Milk -->	*MISSOURI*	Missouri	*PLATTE, SAC,*
Milo	KANKAN, Guinea	Missouri	*THOMPSON,*
Milo -->	*NIGER*	Missouri	*TABLEROCK LK,*
MILWAUKEE, WI	*LK MICHIGAN*	*Missouri*	BISMARK,ND,
Min(g)	China	*Missouri*	COUNCIL BLUFFS,
MIN(G) <--	*Dadu*	*Missouri*	GREAT FALLS, MT,
Min(g) -->	*YANGTZE*	*Missouri*	KANSAS CITY, MO,
Mincio	Italy	*Missouri*	OMAHA,NE, PIERRE,
Mindanao	Philippines	*Missouri*	ST.JOSEPH,MO,SD,
Miner	Yukon, Can.	*Missouri*	IA/NE,KS/MO,IA
Miner -->	*PORCUPINE*	*MISSOURI* <--	*Floyd, Grand,*
Minho(Mino)	Portugal, Spain	*MISSOURI* <--	*James, Judith,*
Minho(Mino) -->	*ATLANTIC*	*MISSOURI* <--	*Kansas, Knife,*
Minkiang	China	*MISSOURI* <--	*Maple, Madison,*
Minnesota	*LEECH LK,*	*MISSOURI* <--	*Marias, Milk,*
Minnesota	*LK BEMIDJI,*	*MISSOURI* <--	*Moreau, Nodaway,*
Minnesota	*LK ITASCA,RAINY,*	*MISSOURI* <--	*Osage,Platte,Sun*
Minnesota	*RAINY LK, RUM,*	*MISSOURI* <--	*Redwater,Smith,*
Minnesota	*ST. CROIX,*	*Missouri* -->	*MISSISSIPPI*
Minnesota	*ST. LOUIS*	MITCHELL, SD	*JAMES*
MN/WI Bor.	*MISSISSIPPI,*	*Mitchell*	Australia

Mitchell -->	G.OF CARPENTERIA	Montana	LK HEBGEN,MARIAS
Mizque	Bolivia	Montana	MILK, MISSOURI,
Mizque -->	GRANDE	Montana	POWDER,RED ROCK,
Moa	KENEMA,	Montana	REDWATER, SMITH,
Moa	Sierra Leonne	Montana	SUN,TETON,TONGUE
Moa -->	PACIFIC	Montana	YELLOWSTONE
Moberly	Br.Columbia,Can.	Montenegro	DRINA, IBAR,
Moberly -->	PEACE	Montenegro	MORACA, ZETA
MOBILE, AL	TOMBIGBEE	MONTGOMERY, AL	ALABAMA Riv.
Mobile	Alabama	Montone	Italy
MOBILE <--	Alabama Riv.	MONTPELIER, VT	WINOOSKI
Mobile -->	GULF OF MEXICO	MONTREAL, Ont.	ST. LAWRENCE
Mocal	Honduras	Moola	Baluchistan,Paki.
Mocal -->	LEMPA	MOPTI, Mali	NIGER
Modder	South Africa	Moraca	Montenegro
Modder -->	VAAL	Morado	Chile
Mofer	Ethiopia	Morava, Czech.	MARCH
Mohawk	NY,ROME,UTICA,	Morava	AUS./SLOVAK.,Cz.
Mohawk	ILION	MORAVA <--	Dyje
Mohawk -->	HUDSON	Morava -->	DANUBE
Moisie	Quebec, Can.	MORAY FIRTH <--	Ness
MOISIE <--	Wacouno	Moray Firth -->	NORTH SEA
Moisie -->	G.OF ST.LAWRENCE	Moreau	S. Dakota
Mojjero	Russia	Moreau -->	MISSOURI
Mojjero -->	KOTUJ	Morghab	See Murgab
Mokau	New Zealand	Morona	Ecuador, Peru
Mokau -->	TASMAN SEA	Morona -->	MARANON
Moksa	Russia	Moros	Romania
Moksa -->	OKA	Morro	Liberia
Moldau	Czechoslovakia	Morocco	MOULOUYA, SEBOU,
Moldau -->	ELBE	Morocco	SOUS,OUM er RBIA,
Moldavia	DNIESTER	Morocco	TENSIFT, WADI,ZA
MOLDAV/RUMANIA	PRUT	Mortes, Rio das	Brazil
MOLINE, IL	MISSISSIPPI,ROCK	Mortes -->	ARAGUAIA
Mologa	Russia	MOSCOW	MOSCOW River
Molopo	Botswana, S.Afr	Moscow River	MOSCOW
MOLOPO <--	Auob, Kuruman,	Mosel	Ger., KOBLENZ,
MOLOPO <--	Nosop	Mosel	TRIER,LUXEM./GER
Moma	Siberia, Rus.	MOSEL <--	Saar, Sauer
Moma -->	INDIGIRKA	Mosel -->	RHINE
Monaco	VESUBIE	Moselle	Fr.,Luxembourg
Mondego	Portugal	Moskva	Russia
Mongo	Sierra Leone	Moskva -->	OKA
Mongo -->	LITTLE SCARCIES	Mossy	Saskatchewan,Can
Mongolia	KERULEN, ONON,	Mossy -->	SASKATCHEWAN Riv.
Mongolia	ORCHON, SELENGE	Motagua	Guatemala
Mono	Togo	Motagua -->	GULF OF HONDURAS
Mono -->	ATLANTIC	MO/TN Bor.	MISSISSIPPI
Mono Lk	California	Motrul	Romanua
Mono	Togo	Motrul -->	JIU
MONO <--	Ogou	Moulouya	Morocco
Mono -->	ATLANTIC	MOULOUYA <--	Za
Monongahela	PITTSBURGH, PA	Moulouya -->	MEDITERRANEAN
Monongahela-->	OHIO	Moy	BALLINA, Ireland
MONROE, LA	OUACHITA	Moy -->	ATLANTIC
Montana	FISHER, JUDITH,	Mozambique	CHANGANE,LIMPOPO
Montana	FLATHEAD LAKE,	Mozambique	LK NYASA, LURIO,
Montana	KOOTENAI,MADISON	Mozambique	LUGENDE,MESSALO,

Mozambique	*PUNGOE, ROVUMA,*	N.E. China	*LIAO*
Mozambique	*SABIE, SAVE,*	*N'uja*	Siberia
Mozambique	*ZAMBEZI*	Naab	Germany
MOZAMB./TANZAN.	*RUVUMA*	*Nab (Naab)* -->	*DANUBE*
MOZAMB.CHAN.<--	Ikopa, Limpopo,	*Nadym*	Russia
MOZAMB.CHAN.<--	Lurio, Mangoky,	*Nadym* -->	*OB GULF*
MOZAMB.CHAN.<--	Mania, Messalo,	*NAGA, Phil.*	*CEBU*
MOZAMB.CHAN.<--	Onilahy, Pungoe,	*Nahang*	*See Nihing*
MOZAMB.CHAN.<--	Save, Sofia,	*Nahe*	Germany
MOZAMB.CHAN.<--	*Zambezi*	*Nahe* -->	*RHINE*
Mpoko	Cent. Afr. Rep.	*Nahr az-Zarga*	*See Zarga*
Msta	Russia	*Nak*	Tibet
Msta -->	*LK IT'MEN'*	*Naktong*	S. Korea
Mucajai	Brazil	*Nal*	Pakistan
Mucajai -->	*BRANCO*	*Nam*	N. Korea
Muco	Colombia	*Nam*	Burma
Mucuim	Brazil	*Nam* -->	*SALWEEN*
Mucuim -->	*Purus*	Namibia	*AUOB,FISH,NOSOP,*
Mucuri	Brazil	Namibia	*OKAVANGO,SWAKOP,*
Mucuri -->	*ATLANTIC*	Namibia	*UGAB*
Mudjatik	Saskatchewan,Can	NAMIBIA/S.AFR.	*ORANGE*
Mudjatik -->	*CHURCHILL*	*Namhou*	Laos
Mugu	Nepal	*Namoi*	Australia
Mulde	Germany	*Namoi* -->	*BARWON*
Mulde -->	*ELBE*	*Namsen*	Norway
Mullica	New Jersey	NAMUR, Belg.	*MEUSE*
Mullica -->	*ATLANTIC*	*Nan*	Thailand
Mun	Thailand	*Nan* -->	*YOM*
Mun -->	*MEKONG*	*Nana*	Cent. Afr. Rep.
Muna	Siberia	*Nanay*	Peru
Muna -->	*LENA*	*Nanay* -->	*AMAZON*
MUNCIE, IN	*WHITE*	NANCHANG,CHINA	*GAN*
Mund	Iran	*Nanding*	China
MUNICH, Ger.	*ISAR*	*Nanding* -->	*SALWEEN*
Muonio	Finland	NANKING(Nanying)	*YANGTZE*
Mur (Mura)	GRAZ, Aus, Hung	NANTES, Fr.	*LOIRE*
Mur -->	*DRAU (Drava)*	*Napo*	Ecuador
Mura	*See Mur*	*NAPO* <--	*Aguarico, Coca,*
Mures	*See Maros*	*NAPO* <--	*Curaray*
Muresul	Romania	*Napo* -->	*AMAZON (AS)*
Muresul -->	*TISZA*	*Narayani*	Nepal
Murgab (Morghab)	Afghanistan,	*Narenta*	Yugoslavia
Murgab (Morghab)	Turkmenistan	*Narew*	Poland
MURMANSK, Rus.	*TULOMA*	*Narew* -->	*BUG*
Murray	Australia	*Narmada*	India
MURRAY <--	*Darling, Lachlan*	*Narmada*	India
Murray -->	*SOUTHERN OCEAN*	*Narmada* -->	*GULF OF KHAMBHAT*
Murri	Colombia	*Narva*	Estonia
Murri -->	*PACIFIC*	NASHUA, NH	*MERRIMACK*
Murz	Austria	*Nashua*	Massachusetts
Musi	Indonesia	NASHVILLE, TN	*CUMBERLAND*
Muskegon Riv.	MI, MUSKEGON	*Nass*	Br.Columbia,Can.
Muskegon -->	*LK MICHIGAN*	*Nass* -->	*PORLAND INLET*
Muskingum	Ohio	*Nata*	Botswana
Muskingum -->	*OHIO Riv.*	*Nau*	Tibet
MWANZA,Tanzania	*LK VICTORIA*	*Navia*	Spain
Myitnge	Burma	Nebraska,	*DISMAL, ELKHORN,*
Mze	Czechoslovakia	Nebraska	*LOUP, NEMAHA,*

Nebraska	NORTH LOUP	Neris	Lithuania
Nebraska	NIOBRARA,PLATTE,	Neris -->	NEMUNUS
Nebraska	REPUBLICAN	Nerl'	Russia
Nechako	Br.Columbia, Can	Nerl' -->	KL'AZ'MA
Nechako -->	FRASER	Ness	Scotland
Neches	BEAUMONT, TX	NESS <--	Lk Ness
Neches -->	SABINE	Ness -->	MORAY FIRTH
Nechi	Colombia	Nestos(Mesta)	Greece, Bulgaria
Nechi -->	MAGDALENA	Nestos -->	AEGEAN SEA
Neckar	Ger, STUTTGART	Nethe	Belgium
NECKAR <--	Jagsl, Kocher	Netherlands	DOMMEL,
Neckar -->	RHINE	Netherlands	HUNSE, IJSSEL,
Negino	Guatemala	Netherlands	KROMME,LEK,MAAS,
Negro	Argentina,	Netherlands	MEUSE,RHINE,WAAL
NEGRO(Arg) <--	Limay, Neuquen	Netherlands	SCJELDT, VECHT,
Negro(Arg) -->	ATLANTIC	Netherlands	YSEL, YSSEL
Negro	Brazil, MANAUS	Neuquen	Argentina
NEGRO(Braz)<--	Araca, Branco,	Neuquen -->	NEGRO
NEGRO(Braz)<--	Demini,Icana,	Neuse	NEW BERN, SC, NC
NEGRO(Braz)<--	Siapa,Tea,Uaupes	Neuse -->	ATLANTIC
Negro(Braz)-->	AMAZON	Neva	Russia, URK,
Negro	Uruguay	Neva	ST. PETERSBURG,
NEGRO(Urug)<--	Yi	Neva -->	GULF OF FINLAND
Negro(Urug)-->	URUGUAY Riv.	Nevada	HUMBOLDT,REESE,
Negro	Honduras	Nevada	PYRAMID LK,
Neisse(Nysa)	Germany, Poland	Nevada	TRUCKEE, VIRGIN,
Niesse	·GERMAN/POLAND	Nevada	WALKER
Niesse -->	ODER	New	Guyana
Nelson	Manitoba, Can	New -->	CORANTIJN
NELSON <--	Odei	New	CHARLESTON,WV,VA
Nelson -->	HUDSON BAY	NEW BERN, NC	NEUSE
Nemaha	Nebraska	New Brunswick	ST. JOHN,TOBIQUE
Neman(Nemunas)	Belarus, Lith.	New Guinea	AMBERNO,FLY,HAMU
Neman(Nemunas)	RUSSIA/LITHUANIA	New Guinea	KIKORI, PURARI,
NEMAN <--	Neris	New Guinea	SEPIK,
Neman -->	BALTIC SEA	New Hampshire	BELLAMY, ISRAEL
Nemunas	see Neman	New Hampshire	CONNECTICUT,
Nen	China,	New Hampshire	LK SQUAM, SACO
Nen -->	SONGHUA	New Hampshire	MERRIMACK,
Nen	England	New Hampshire	SOUHEGAN,
Nenana	Alaska	New Hampshire	PISCATAQUA,
Nenana -->	TANANA	NH/VT	CONNECTICUT
Nene	England	New Jersey	COHANSEY,
Nene -->	NORTH SEA	New Jersey	HAYNES, MANTUA,
Neosho	EMPORIA, Kansas	New Jersey	MULLICA,PASSAIC,
Neosho -->	ARKANSAS Riv.	New Jersey	RAMAPO, RARITAN,
Nepal	ARUN,BABAI,BHERI	New Jersey	TUCKAHOE
Nepal	GANDAK,KARNALI,	NJ/NY	HUDSON
Nepal	KOSI,MUGU,RAPTI,	NJ/PA	DELAWARE
Nepal	NARAYANI, SARDA,	New Mexico	CIMARRON, GILA,
Nepal	SETI	New Mexico	LA PLATA, PECOS,
Ner	Russia	New Mexico	RIO PUERTO, UTE
Nera	Italy	New Mexico	SAN JOSE,
Nera -->	TIBER	New Mexico	SAN JUAN,
Nerbudda	India	NM/UT	SAN JUAN
Nerca	Russia	NEW ORLEANS	MISSISSIPPI
Nerca -->	SILKA	New York	ALLEGHENY, GRASS
Neretva	Yugoslavia	New York	GENESEE, HARLEM,

New York	*HOOSIC, HUDSON,*	Nigeria
New York	*LK CUYAGA,*	Nigeria
New York	*LK ONEIDA,*	Nigeria
New York	*LK PLACID,MOHAWK*	Nihing(Nahang)
New York	*LK SENECA,TIOGA,*	Nihing(Nahang)
New York	*NIAGRA,OSWEGO*	Nihing -->
NY/PA	*DELAWARE*	*Nile*
NY/VT	*LK CHAMPLAIN*	*Nile*
NEW YORK CITY	*HUDSON*	*Nile*
New Zealand	*BULLER, CLUTHA,*	*Nile*
New Zealand	*HURUNUI,LK TAUPO*	NILE <--
New Zealand	*MOKAU,RANGITAIKI*	*Nile* -->
New Zealand	*RANGITIKEI,*	*Niobrara*
New Zealand	*TAIERI, TAMAKI,*	*Nira*
New Zealand	*WAIKATO,'WAIPE,*	*Nisa*
New Zealand	*WAIRAU, WAITAKI,*	*Nith*
New Zealand	*WAIROA,WANGANUI*	*Nitra*
NEWARK, NJ	*HUDSON*	*Nizn'ajaTungusk.*
NEWCAST-on-TYNE	*TYNE*	*NIZN'AJA TNG.*<--
Newfoundland	*EXPLOITS, GANDER*	*NIZN'AJA TNG.*<--
Ngoko	*See Sangha*	*Nizn'ajaTng.*-->
Nhiha	Vietnam	*Nmai*
Niagra	BUFFALO, NY,	*Nmai* -->
Niagra	LKS ERIE,ONTARIO	*Noatak*
Niagra	Ontario	*Noatak* -->
Niagra -->	*LAKE ONTARIO*	*Nodaway*
Niari	Congo	*Nodaway* -->
Nicaragua	*COCO, ESCONDIDO,*	*Noi*
Nicaragua	*GRANDE,KURINWAS,*	*Nore*
Nicaragua	*LK NAMAGUA,RAMA,*	*Nore* -->
Nicaragua	*PUNTA GORDA,TUMA*	NORMAN, OK
Nicaragua	*TIPTIAPA, WANKS,*	Normandy
Nicaragua	*WASPUK*	*Norn*
NICAR./HOND.	*COCO*	*N Canadian*
Nicola	Br.Columbia, Can	North Carolina
Nicola -->	*THOMPSON*	North Carolina
Nidd	England	North Carolina
Nidd -->	*OUSE*	North Carolina
Niemen	Poland	North Carolina
NIEUPORT, Belg.	*YSER*	North Dakota
Niger	*MEKROU, NIGER,*	North Dakota
Niger	*SIRBA*	North Dakota
NIGER/NIGERIA	*KAMADUGU YOBE*	North Dakota
Niger	GAO, MOPTI,Mali,	North Dakota
Niger	Nigeria, SIGUIRI	North Dakota
Niger	Guinea	North Dakota
NIGER <--	*Alibori, Bani,*	North Korea
NIGER <--	*Benue, Gurura,*	North Korea
NIGER <--	*Kaduna, Mariga,*	*North Loup*
NIGER <--	*Mekrou, Milo,*	*North Loup* -->
NIGER <--	*Oli, Sirba,*	*North Platte*
NIGER <--	*Sokoto, Sota,*	*NORTH PLATTE*<--
NIGER <--	*Tinkisso*	*NORTH PLATTE*<--
Niger -->	*GULF OF GUINEA*	*NORTH SEA* <--
Nigeria	*BENUE, GONGOLA,*	*NORTH SEA* <--
Nigeria	*GURARA, HADEJIA,*	*NORTH SEA* <--
Nigeria	*KADUNA, MARIGA,*	*NORTH SEA* <--
Nigeria	*KOMADUGU GANA,*	*NORTH SEA* <--

KOMADUGU YOBE,	
NIGER, RIMA,	
SOKOTO, ZAMFARA	
Pakistan, Iran	
IRAN/PAKISTAN	
ARABIAN SEA	
ALTBANA, ASWAN,	
CAIRO,GIZA,Egypt	
LUXOR,MEMPHIS,	
Sudan	
Blue&White Niles	
MEDITERRANEAN	
Nebraska, SD, WY	
India	
See Neisse	
DUMFRIES, Scot.	
Czechoslovakia	
Russia	
Taimura, Turu,	
Vivi	
JENESEJ	
Burma	
IRRWADDY	
Alaska	
KOTZEBUE SOUND	
Iowa, Missouri	
MISSOURI	
Laos	
Ireland,KILKENNY	
BARROW	
CANADIAN	
ORNE	
Scotland	
OKLAHOMA CITY,OK.	
CAPE FEAR,CHOWAN,	
GREAT PEE DEE,	
HAW,LUMBER,NEUSE,	
ROANOKE, TAR,	
YADKIN,	
CEDAR, HEART,	
JAMES, KNIFE	
MILK, MISSOURI,	
RED LAKE,ROSEAU,	
RED of the NORTH	
RUSH, SHEYENNE	
SOURIS,	
IMJIN,NAM,YALU,	
TAEDONG,TUMEN,	
Nebraska	
LOUP	
CASPER, Wyoming	
Laramie,	
Sweetwater	
Alde,Aller,Aln,	
Colne,Dee,Deben,	
Deveron,Don,Ems,	
Eider,Elbe,Glama	
Firth of Forth,	

NORTH SEA <--	Great Ouse,Maas, Nzi		Ivory Coast
NORTH SEA <--	Medway, Meuse, Nzi -->		BANDAMA
NORTH SEA <--	Moray Firth,	Ob	Russia, Siberia
NORTH SEA <--	Nene,Orwell,Oste	OB <--	Agan,Culym,Irtys
NORTH SEA <--	Rhine,Schelde,	OB <--	Kazym,Ket,Lamin,
NORTH SEA <--	Spey,Stour,Tay,	OB <--	Pim, Poluj, Tom,
NORTH SEA <--	Tees,Thames,Tyne	OB <--	Tym, Vach,
NORTH SEA <--	Wear, Welland,	OB <--	Vas'ugan
NORTH SEA <--	Weser, Witham,	Ob -->	ARTIC OCEAN
NORTH SEA <--	Yare,Yser,Ythan	OB GULF <--	Pur, Taz
Northumberland	AWN, TYNE	Ochina	China
Norway	ALTA,BARDU,ENA,	Ochota	Russia
Norway	BEGNA,GLAMA,KLAR	Ochota -->	SEA OF OKHOTSK
Norway	GLOMMA, GLOMMEN,	Ocmulgee	MACON, Georgia
Norway	LAGEN, LK ALTE,	Ocmulgee -->	ALTAMAHA
Norway	LK ISTER,LOUGEN,	Oconee	Georgia
Norway	LK MJOSA,NAMSEN,	Oconee -->	ALTAMAHA
Norway	LK SNASA, ORKLA,	Odei	Manitoba, Can
Norway	OI,OTRA, OTTER,	Odei -->	NELSON
Norway	PASVIK, RANA,	Oder(Odra)	BRESLAW,Czech.,
Norway	RAUMA,REISA,TANA	Oder(Odra)	FRANKFORT, Ger.
N.W.T.(N.WestTe)	ARTIC RED, BACK,	Oder(Odra)	GER./POL.,Poland
N.W.T.	HORN, HORTON,	Oder(Odra)	STETTIN,
N.W.T.	LIARD, KEELE,	ODER(ODRA) <--	Neisse, Warta
N.W.T.	GREAT BEAR LK&RV	ODER(ODRA) <--	Nysa Luzycka
N.W.T.	MACKENZIE,QUOICH	Oder(Odra) -->	ODERHOFF->BALTIC
N.W.T.	RAMPARTS, SLAVE,	Oderhoff	Germany
N.W.T.	TALSTON, TESLIN,	ODERHOFF <--	Oder,Oeene,Ucker
N.W.T.	THA-ANNE,THELON,	Odiel	Spain
N.W.T.	TROUT	Odra	See
NORWICH, Eng.	WENSUM, YARE	Ofanto	Italy
Nosop(Nossob)	BOTSWANA/S.AFR.	OGDEN, UT	WEBER
Nosop(Nossob)	Namabia	Ogeechee	Georgia
Nosop -->	MOLOPO	Ogeechee -->	ATLANTIC
Notec	Poland	Oglio	Italy
NOTEC <--	Gwda	Oglio -->	PO
Notec -->	WARTA	Ogoki	Ontario, Can.
NOTTINGHAM,Eng.	TRENT	Ogoki -->	ALBANY
Nova Scotia,Can.	LaHAVE,ST. MARYS	Ogooue	Gabon
NOVI SAD, Yugo.	DANUBE	OGOOUE <--	Ivinda, Ngounie
Nuble	Chile	Ogooue -->	ATLANTIC
Nuble -->	ITATA	Ogosta	Bulgaria
Nueces	Texas	Ogosta -->	DANUBE
Nueces -->	GULF OF MEXICO	Ogre	Latvia
Nuja	VITIM, Rus.	Ohio	CUYAHOGA, MIAMI,
Nuja -->	LENA	Ohio	MAUMEE,MUSKINGUM
Nulhegan	Vermont	Ohio	SANDUSKY,SCIOTO,
Nuon	IVORY CST./LIBER	Ohio	ST.JOSEPH,WABASH
Nuon	Liberia	OH/WV Bor.	OHIO
Nuon -->	CESTOS	Ohio	CAIRO,CINCINNATI
Nura	Kazakhstan	Ohio	EVANSVILLE,IL,IN
Nura -->	ISIM	Ohio	KY, LOUISVILLE,
NURNBERG, Ger.	REGNITZ	Ohio	IL/KY,IN/KY,PA,
Nuuanu	HONOLULU	Ohio	KY/OH,OH/WV,WV
NYACK, NY	HUDSON	Ohio	PITTSBURG,
Nyong	Cameroon	Ohio	WHEELING
Nyong -->	GULF OF GUINEA	OHIO <--	Alleghany,
Nysa	See Neisse	OHIO <--	Big Sandy, Green

OHIO	<--	Great Miami,	*Olt* -->	*DANUBE*
OHIO	<--	Kanawha,Licking	Oltul	Romania
OHIO	<--	Kentucky Riv.,	*Oltul* -->	*DANUBE*
OHIO	<--	Monongahela,	Om'	Russia
OHIO	<--	Muskingum,Salt,	*Om'* -->	*IRTYS*
OHIO	<--	Scioto,Tenessee,	OMAHA, NE	*MISSOURI*
OHIO	<--	Wabash	Ombrone	Italy
Ohio -->		*MISSISSIPPI*	Omme	Denmark
Ohre		Czechoslovakia	Omo	Ethiopia
Ohre -->		*ELBE*	*Omo* -->	*LK RUDOLF*
Oi		Norway	Omoloj	Siberia
Oiapoque		Brazil	*Omoloj* -->	*LAPTEV SEA*
Oiapoque -->		*ATLANTIC*	Omolon	Russia
Oise		Belgium, France,	*Omolon* -->	*KOLYMA*
Oise		CAMPIEGNA,	OMSK, Rus.	*IRTYS(Irtish)*
Oise		PICARDY	Ondava	Czechoslovakia
OISE	<--	Aisne	Onega	Russia
Oise -->		*SEINE*	*Onega* -->	*WHITE SEA(Artic)*
Ojat'		Russia	Onilahy	Madagascar
OJAT'	<--	Svir	*Onilahy* -->	*MOZAMBIQUE CHAN.*
Ojat' -->		*LK LADOGA*	Onon	Mongolia, Russia
Oka		GORKY,OREL,Rus.	*Onon* -->	*SILKA*
OKA	<--	Klazma, Moksa,	Ontario	*ALBANY, BERENS,*
OKA	<--	Prona, Tosa	Ontario	*EKWAN,LK NIPIGON*
Oka -->		*VOLGA*	Ontario	*OGOKI, SEVERN*
Okanogan		Br.Columbia, WA,	Ontario	*SACHIGO, THROAT,*
Okanogan -->		*COLUMBIA*	Ontario	*WINISK*
Okarango		MAUN, Botswana	ONT./QUEBEC	*OTTOWA*
Okavango		South Africa	*Onylahy*	Madagascar
OKAVANGO	<--	Ngugha, Thaoge	OPORTO, Port.	*DOURO*
Okavango -->		*LINYANTI*	Oppa	Czechoslovakia
Oker		Germany	Orange	Lesotho, S. Afr.
Oklahoma		*ARKANSAS,*	*ORANGE* <--	*Brak, Fish, Vaal*
Oklahoma		*CANADIAN, GRAND,*	*Orange* -->	*ATLANTIC*
Oklahoma		*CIMARRON, RED,*	Orantes	Syria
Oklahoma		*NORTH CANADIAN,*	Orbigo	Spain
Oklahoma		*WASHITA*	Orchon	Mongolia
OKLAHOMA CITY		*NORTH CANADIAN*	*Orchon* -->	*SELENGE*
OK/TX		*RED*	Orcia	Tuscany
Okpara		BENIN/NIGERIA	Orco	Italy
Okpara -->		*OUEME*	Ord	Australia
Okwa		Botswana	ORD <--	*Lk Argyle*
Olancho		Honduras	Oregon	*BLITZEN,COLUMBIA*
Old Crow		N.W. Territories	Oregon	*CRATER LK,IMNAHA,*
Old Crow -->		*PORCUPINE*	Oregon	*DESCHUTES,*
OLEAN, NY		*ALLEGHANY*	Oregon	*JOHN DAY,KLAMATH*
Olen'ok		Siberia	Oregon	*LK ABERT,MALHEUR*
Olen'ok -->		*LAPTEV SEA*	Oregon	*OWYHEE, POWDER,*
Oli		Nigeria	Oregon	*ROGUE, SANDY,*
Oli -->		*NIGER*	Oregon	*SNAKE, SILVIES,*
Olifants		South Africa	Oregon	*UMPQUA, UMATILLA*
Olifants -->		*LIMPOPO*	Oregon	*WILLAMETTE*
Ol'okma		Russia	OR/WA	*COLUMBIA*
Ol'okma -->		*LENA*	OREL, Rus.	*OKA*
Olomane		Quebec, Can.	*Orel*	Russia
Olomane -->		*G OF ST.LAWRENCE*	ORENBURG, Rus.	*URAL*
Olse		Czechoslovakia	*Oreti*	New Zealand
Olt		Romania	*Orinoco*	S. America,Venez.

ORINOCO	<--	Apure,Arauca,Aro	
ORINOCO	<--	Capanaparo,Caura	
ORINOCO	<--	Caroni,Guaviare,	
ORINOCO	<--	Casiquiare,	
ORINOCO	<--	Mata, Meta, Pao,	
ORINOCO	<--	Suaprue, Tigre,	
ORINOCO	<--	Tomo, Ventauri,	
ORINOCO	<--	Vichada, Zuata	
Orinoco	-->	*ATLANTIC*	
Orituco		Venezuela	
Orituco	-->	*GUARICO*	
Orkla		Norway	
ORLEANS, Fr.		*LOIRE*	
Orne		CAEN, France,	
Orne		NORMANDY	
Orne	-->	*ENGLISH CHANNEL*	
ORONO, ME		*PENOBSCOT*	
Orontes		Lebanon, Syria	
Orontes	-->	*MEDITERRANEAN*	
ORSK		*URAL*	
Orthon		Bolivia	
Orthon	-->	*MADRE DE DIOS*	
Orwell		IPSWICH, England	
Orwell	-->	*NORTH SEA*	
Osage		Kansas, Missouri	
OSAGE	<--	*Maries*	
Osage	-->	*MISSOURI.*	
OSAKA, Jap.		*YODO*	
Oshion		Israel	
Osma		Bulgaria	
Osma	-->	*DANUBE*	
Osum		Albania	
Osum, Alb.	-->	*SEMAN*	
Osum		Bulgaria	
Osum,(Bulg.)->		*DANUBE*	
Oste		Germany	
Oste -->		*North Sea*	
Oswego		New York	
Oswego	-->	*LK ONTARIO*	
Otava		Czech.	
Otava	-->	*VLTAVA*	
Oti		Ghana	
OTI	<--	*Kara, Ouale*	
Oti	-->	*LK VOLTA*	
Otra		Norway	
Ottawa		Canada,	
Ottawa		ONTARIO/QUEBEC	
Ottawa	-->	*ST. LAWRENCE*	
Otter		Norway	
Ou		Laos	
Ou	-->	*JAILING*	
Ouachita		AR, LA, MONROE,	
OUACHITA	<--	*Saline, Tensas*	
Ouachita	-->	*RED*	
Ouaka		Cent. Afr. Rep.	
Ouaka	-->	*UBANGI*	
Ouale		Burkina Faso	
Ouale	-->	*OTI*	
Oubangi			See Ubangi
Oueme			Benin
OUEME	<--		*Okapara*
Oueme	-->		*ATLANTIC*
OUESSO, Congo			*SANGHA*
Ouham			Cent. Afr. Rep.
Ouham	-->		*CHARI*
Oulu			Finland
Oum er Rbia			Morocco
Oum er Rbia-->			*ATLANTIC*
Ounas			Finland
Our			GER/LUX., Luxemb.
Our	-->		*SAUER*
Ouse			England, SUSSEX,
Ouse			YORKSHIRE
OUSE	<--		*Aire, Derwent,*
OUSE	<--		*Nidd,Ure,Wharfe*
Ouse	-->		*HUMBER*
Outhre			Belgium, LIEGE
Ourthe	-->		*MEUSE*
Owens			California
Owyhee			Oregon
Owyhee	-->		*SNAKE*
Oxus			Afghanistan
Ozama			Dominican Rep.
P'andz(Panj)			AFGHAN./TAJIK.
P'asina			Russia
P'asina	-->		*KARA SEA*
Pa Sak			Thailand
Pa Sak	-->		*CHAO PARAYA*
PABNA, Bangl.			*GANGES*
Pachitea			Peru
Pachitea	-->		*UCAYLI*
PACIFIC	<--		*Biobio, Clutha,*
PACIFIC	<--		*Columbia,Copiapo*
PACIFIC	<--		*Choapa, Daule,*
PACIFIC	<--		*Dawson, Elqui,*
PACIFIC	<--		*Esmeraldas,*
PACIFIC	<--		*Guayas, Huasco,*
PACIFIC	<--		*Itata,Jiboa,Loa,*
PACIFIC	<--		*Klamath, Lempa,*
PACIFIC	<--		*Limare,Lluta,Mad*
PACIFIC	<--		*Maipo,Mala,Maule*
PACIFIC	<--		*Mataquito, Mira,*
PACIFIC	<--		*Moa,Murri,Patia,*
PACIFIC	<--		*Paz,Quinault,*
PACIFIC	<--		*Rangitaiki,Rapel*
PACIFIC	<--		*Rimac, Rogue,*
PACIFIC	<--		*Russian,Salinas,*
PACIFIC	<--		*Samala,San Juan,*
PACIFIC	<--		*Santa, Soleduck,*
PACIFIC	<--		*Sepik, Tambo,*
PACIFIC	<--		*Taieri, Tumbes,*
PACIFIC	<--		*Umpqua, Vitor,*
PACIFIC	<--		*Wairoa, Waitiki,*
PACIFIC	<--		*Warwick*
Padas			Borneo
Pager			Uganda

Pahang	Malaysia	PARANAIBA <--	Rio dos Bois
Pahang -->	S CHINA SEA	Paranaiba -->	ATLANTIC
Pakistan	BADO, BOLAN,	Parbati	India
Pakistan	CHENAB, DASHT,	Parbati -->	CHAMBAL
Pakistan	GUMAL,INDUS,NAL	Pardo	Brazil
Pakistan	JHELUM, KUNDAR,	Pardo -->	PARANA
Pakistan	MOOLA, NIHING,	Parma	Italy
Pakistan	PORALI, RAVI,	PARIS	SEINE
Pakistan	SUTLEJ, ZHOB	Parnaiba	Brazil
Palena	Chile	PARNAIBA <--	Poti
Palouse	ID, WA	Parnaiba -->	ATLANTIC
Palouse -->	SNAKE	Parnu	Estonia
PAMLICO SOUND	·Tar	Paroo	Australia
Pampanga	Philippines	Paroo -->	DARLING
Panama	BAYANO, CHAGRES,	Parrett	BRIDGWATER, Eng.
Panama	CHEPO, PANUGO,	Parrett -->	BRISTOL CHANNEL
Panama	SAMBU, TURIA,	Parseta	Poland
Panaro	Italy	Parseta -->	BALTIC SEA
Pangani	Tanzania	Parsnip	Br.Columbia,Can.
Pangani -->	INDIAN OCEAN	Parsnip -->	WILLISTON LK
Panj	See P'andz	Paru	Brazil
Panlong	See Lo	Paru -->	AMAZON
Panuco	Mexico, TAMPICO	Pascagoula	Mississippi
Panuco -->	GULF OF MEXICO	PASCAGOULA <--	Leaf
Panugo	Panama	Pascagoula -->	GULF OF MEXICO
Pao	Venezuela	Pasig	Philippines
Pao -->	ORINOCO	Pasion	Guatemala
Para	Brazil	Passaic	New Jersey
Para -->	ATLANTIC	Pastaza	Ecuador
Paracatu	Brazil	PASTAZA <--	Bobonaza
PARACATU <--	Preto	Pastaza -->	MARANON
Paracatu -->	SAO FRANCISCO	Pasvik	Finland, Norway
Paragua	Venezuela	Patia	Colombia
Paragua -->	CARONI	Patia -->	PACIFIC
Paraguai	See Paraguay	PATNA, India	GANGES
Paraguay	ACARAY, APA,	Patuca	Honduras
Paraguay	LK VERA,LK YPOA,	PATUCA <--	Guayape, Wampu
Paraguay	PARAGUAY Rv.,	Patuca -->	CARIBBEAN
Paraguay	PARANA,PILCOMAYO	Patuxent	Maryland
Paraguay	TAQUARI, YPANE	Patuxent -->	CHESAPEAKE BAY
Paraguay	TEBICUARY,	Pauini	Brazil
Paraguay Riv.	Bolivia	Pauini -->	PURUS
PARAGUAY Rv<--	Apa, Bermejo,	Paulaya	Honduras
PARAGUAY Rv<--	Miranda,	Paulaya -->	SICO TINTO
PARAGUAY Rv<--	Pilcomayo, Ypane	Pauto	Colombia
Paraguay Rv-->	PARANA	Pauto -->	META
Paraiba	Brazil	Pawan	Borneo,Indonesia
Parana	Arg.,Braz.,Parag	Pawcatuck	Rhode Island
Parana	SANTA FE	Pawtuxet	Rhode island
PARANA <--	Acaray, Iguacu,	Payette	Idaho
PARANA <--	Ivai	Payette -->	SNAKE
PARANA <--	Paraguay Riv.,	Paz	GUAT./SAN SALV.
PARANA <--	Pardo,Salado#1,	Paz -->	PACIFIC
PARANA <--	Sucuriu, Tiete,	Pea	Alabama, Georgia
PARANA <--	Tebicuary,Verde,	Peace	Alberta, B.C.
PARANA <--	Tercero,	PEACE <--	Mikkwa,Moberly,
Parana -->	RIO de la PLATA	PEACE <--	Wabasca
Paranaiba	Brazil	Peace -->	SLAVE

Pearl	JACKSON,MI,LA	Perene -->	*UCAYALI*
Pearl -->	*GULF OF MEXICO*	Peribonca	Quebec, Can.
Pecora(Pechora)	Russia	*PERIBONCA* <--	*Savane*
PECORA <--	*Izma, Usa*	Peribonca -->	*LK ST.-JEAN*
Pecora -->	*BARENTS SEA*	PERM, Russia	*KAMA*
Pecos	ARTESIA,NM,TX	PERTH, Austra.	*TAY*
Pecos -->	*RIO GRANDE*	Peru	*APURIMAC,*
Pecs	Hungary	Peru	*CURARAY,*
Pedias	Cyprus	Peru	*CORRIENTES,*
Pedieos	Cyprus	Peru	*HUALLAGA,*
Pee Dee	N.Carolina	Peru	*LK TITICACA,*
PEE DEE <--	*Yadkin*	Peru	*MADRE DE DIOS,*
Pee Dee -->	*GREAT PEE DEE*	Peru	*MALA, MARANON,*
PEEBLES, OH	*TWEED*	Peru	*MANU,MARONA,NAPO*
Peel	Yukon, Can.	Peru	*NANAY, PACHITEA,*
PEEL <--	*Hart, Wind*	Peru	*PASTAZA, PERENE,*
Peel -->	*MACKENZIE*	Peru	*SANTA, TAMBO,*
Peene	Germany	Peru	*TAPICHE, TIGRE*
Peene -->	*ODERHOFF-->BALTIC*	Peru	*UCAYLI,URUBAMBA,*
Pegnitz	Germany	Peru	*VITOR, YACO,*
Pegnitz -->	*MAIN*	Peru	*YAVARI*
Pegu	Burma	*Pescara*	Italy
Pei	China	*Pescara* -->	*ADRIATIC SEA*
Peiho	China	*Petawawa*	Canada
Pelly	Yukon, Can.	*Petiotot*	Alberta, B.C.,
Pelly -->	*YUKON*	*Petiotot*	N.W.T., Can.
Pembina	Alberta, Can.	*Petitot* -->	*LIARD*
Pembina -->	*ATHABASCA*	PHEONIX, AZ	*SALT*
Pend Oreille	Idaho	PHILADELPHIA,	*DELAWARE,*
Pend Oreille->	*COLUMBIA*	PHILADELPHIA,	*SCHUYLKILL*
Peneios	Greece	Philippines	*ABRA,AGNO,AGUSAN*
Peneus	Greece	Philippines	*CAGAYAN, CHICO,*
Penganga	India	Philippines	*LOANG, LK LANAO,*
Penganga -->	*WAINGANGA*	Philippines	*LK TAAL, MAGAT,*
Penk	England,STAFFORD	Philippines	*MINDANAO,*
Penk -->	*TRENT*	Philippines	*PAMPANGA, PASIG*
Penner	India	PHNOM PENN,Camb.	*MEKONG*
Penner -->	*INDIAN OCEAN*	*Phyara*	BANGKOK, Thail.
Pennsylvania	*ALLEGHENY,*	*Piave*	Italy
Pennsylvania	*CALDWELL,CLARION*	*Piave* -->	*GULF OF VENICE*
Pennsylvania	*DELAWARE,LEHIGH,*	Picardie, Fr.	*OISE*
Pennsylvania	*JUNIATA,LICKING,*	PIERRE, SD	*MISSOURI*
Pennsylvania	*MONONGAHELA,*	*Pigeon*	Georgia
Pennsylvania	*OHIO, SCHRADER,*	*Pilaya*	Bolivia
Pennsylvania	*SUSQUEHANNA,*	*Pilaya* -->	*PILCOMAYO*
Pennsylvania	*TOWANDA,*	*Pilcomayo*	ARG/PARAG.
Pennsylvania	*SCHUYLKILL,*	*Pilcomayo*	ASUNCION,
Penobscot	BANGOR,ME,ORONO	*Pilcomayo*	Bol.,Para.,PILAR
Penobscot -->	*GULF OF MAINE*	*PILCOMAYO* <--	*Pilaya*
Penzina	Russia	*Pilcomayo* -->	*PARAGUAY River*
Penzina -->	*SEA OF OKHOTSK*	*Pilica*	Poland
PEORIA, IL	*ILLINOIS*	*Pilica* -->	*WISTA*
Perak	Malaysia	*Pim*	Russia
Perak -->	*STRAITof MALACCA*	*Pim* -->	*OB*
Perales	Spain	*Pindo*	Ecuador
Perdido	Alabama	PINE BLUFF, AR	*ARKANSAS*
Perdido -->	*GULF OF MEXICO*	*Ping*	Thailand
Perene	Peru	*PING* <--	*Yom*

Ping -->	G OF THAILAND	Poscua	Chile
Pinios	Greece	PORTLAND, OR	WILLAMETTE
Pinios -->	AEGEAN SEA	Port Phillipe B	MELBOURNE
Piorini	Brazil	Portneuf	Quebec
Piorini -->	AMAZON	Portneuf -->	ST.LAWRENCE
PISA, Italy	ARNO	Portugal	CAVADO,CHANCA,
Piscataqua	New Hampshire	Portugal	DOURO, DUERO,
Pit	California	Portugal	GUADIANA, LIMA,
Pit -->	LK SHASTA	Portugal	MINHO,MIRA,MINO,
Pitea	Sweden	Portugal	MIRA, MONDEGO,
PITTSBURGH	OH, ALLEGHENY,	Portugal	SABAR, SABOR,
PITTSBURGH	MONONGAHELA	Portugal	SADO, SEDA, SOR,
Plata	Argentina	Portugal	TAGO,TAGUS,TEJO,
Platte	KEARNY, NE, MO	Portugal	TAMEGA,TUA,VOUGA
PLATTE <--	Elkhorn, Loup	Portugal	ZATAS, ZEZERE
Platte -->	MISSOURI	Poti	Brazil
PLYMOUTH, Eng.	TAMAR	Poti -->	PARNAIBA
Po	Italy,TURIN(O)	Potomac	ARLINGTON,
PO <--	Adda, Oglio,	Potomac	ALEXANDRIA, MA,
PO <--	Tanaro, Tessin,	Potomac	ROANOKE,VA, WV
PO <--	Ticino,Trebbia,	Potomac	WASHINGTON, DC
Po -->	ADRIATIC SEA	Potomac -->	CHESAPEAKE BAY
Poas	Costa Rica	Poultney	Vermont
Podkamennaja T.	Russia	Powder	Montana, Wyoming
PODKAMANNAJA T.	<-- Cun'a	POWDER <--	Crazy Woman Cr.
Podkamennaja T.	--> JENISEJ	Powder	Oregon
Poland	ALLE,BIALA,BRDA,	Powder -->	SNAKE
Poland	BUG,BZURA,EWINA,	Powell	Kentucky
Poland	DNIESTER, GWDA,	Powell -->	LK NORRIS
Poland	LAVA, LK GOPLO,	Pra	Ghana
Poland	LK MAMRY, LYNA,	Pra -->	ATLANTIC
Poland	NAREW, NEISSE,	PRAGUE, Czech.	ELBE
Poland	NIEMAN, NOTEC,	Pratigau	Switzerland
Poland	NYSA, PARSETA,	Pregol'a	Lithuania
Poland	PILICA, PRIPET,	PREGOL'A <--	Anagrapa
Poland	PROSNA,SAN,SERET	Pregol'a -->	BALTIC SEA
Poland	SLUPIA, STYR,	Preto	Brazil
Poland	STYRPA, WARTA,	Preto -->	PARACATU
Poland	WIEPRZ, WISTA,	Price	Utah
Poland	WISTOKA	Price -->	GREEN
POLAND/BELARUS	BUG	Priest	Idaho
POLAND/GER.	ODRA(Oder)	Priest -->	PEND OREILLE
POLAND/UKR.	BUG	Priest Lk	Idaho
Polochic	Guatemala	Prip'at	Belarus, Poland
Polochic -->	LAGO DE IZABAL	Prip'at -->	DNEPR
POOLE, Eng.	ENGLISH CHANNEL	PROME, Burma	IRRAWADDY
Pond	Kentucky	Prosna	Poland
Pond -->	GREEN	Provo	Utah
Popigaj	Russia	Provo -->	UTAH LK
Popigaj -->	CHETA	Prussia	RUHR
Poprad	Slovenske	Prut	MOLDOVA/ROMANIA
Poprad -->	DUNAJEC	Prut	Romania
Porali	Pakistan	Prut(h) -->	DANUBE
Porcupine	Alaska	PUEBLO, CO	ARKANSAS
PORCUPINE <--	Black, Eagle,	Puelo	Chile
PORCUPINE <--	Miner, Old Crow	Puerco, Rio	Arizona
Porcupine -->	YUKON	PUERCO, RIO<--	Rio San Jose
Porong	Cambodia	Puerco, Rio-->	RIO GRANDE

Puerto Rico	*ANASCO, CAMUY,*	*Raft*	Idaho, Utah
Puerto Rico	*CANAS, FAJARDO,*	*Raft -->*	*SNAKE*
Puerto Rico	*LK CARITE, TANAMA*	Rahue	Chile
Puerto Rico	*LK LOIZA, YAUCO*	Rainy	Minnesota
Puget Sound	Washington	*Rainy Lk*	Canada, MN/ONT.
Puget Sound<--	*Skagit*	*Rajang*	Malaysia
Pukhan-gang	S. Korea	*Rajang -->*	*SOUTH CHINA SEA*
Pukhan-gang-->	*NAMNAN-GANG*	*Rama*	*Nicaragua*
Pungoe	Mozambique	*Rama -->*	*ESCONDIDO*
Pungoe -->	*MOZANBIQUE CHAN.*	*Ramapo*	New Jersey
Punta Gorda	Nicaragua	*Ramparts*	N.W. Terr., Can.
Punta Gorda-->	*CARIBBEAN*	*Ramparts -->*	*MACKENZIE*
Pur	Russia	*Rana*	Norway
Pur -->	*OB GULF*	*Randow*	Germany
Purari	New Guinea	*Randow -->*	*UCKER*
Purus	Brazil, Peru	*Rance*	France
PURUS <--	*Iaco, Ituxi,*	*Rance -->*	*ENGLISH CHANNEL*
PURUS <--	*Mucuim, Pauini,*	*Randow*	Germany
PURUS <--	*Tapaua*	*Ranea*	Sweden
Purus -->	*AMAZON*	*Rangitikei*	New Zealand
Putah	California	*Rangitikei -->*	*TASMAN SEA*
Putumayo	Brazil, Columbia,	*Rapel*	Chile
Putumayo	COLOMBIA/ECUADOR	*Rapel -->*	*PACIFIC*
Putumayo	COLOMBIA/PERU	*Rapidan*	Virginia
Putumayo	Ecuador	*Rapidan -->*	*RAPPAHANNOCK*
PUTUMAYO <--	*San Miguel*	*Rapido*	Italy
Putumayo -->	*AMAZON*	*Rapti*	India, Nepal
Pyramid Lk	Nevada	*Rapti -->*	*GANGES*
Qezel Owzan	Iran	*Raritan*	NJ, RUTGER
Qezel Owzan-->	*CASPIAN SEA*	*Raska*	Yugoslavia
Qishon	Israel	*Rauma*	Norway
Qishon -->	*MEDITERRANEAN*	*Ravi*	Pakistan
Qonduz	Afghanestan	*Ravi -->*	*CHENAB*
Qonduz -->	*AMU DARYA*	*Razdan*	Armenia
Qu'Appelle	Saskatchewan, Can	READING, PA	*SCHUYLKILL*
Qu'Appelle -->	*ASSINIBOINE*	Red	Michigan
Quaboag	Massachusetts	*RED <--*	*Flat*
Quebec	*GEORGE, KOKSOAK,*	*Red -->*	*LK MICHIGAN*
Quebec	*MOISIE, OLOMANE,*	Red	AR, LA, OK,
Quebec	*PERIBONCA,*	Red	OK/TX Bor., TX
Quebec	*PORTNEUF,*	*RED <--*	*Little, Ouachita,*
Quebec	*SAGUENAY, SAKAMI*	*RED <--*	*Sulphur, Wichita*
Quebec	*ST. MAURICE,*	*Red -->*	*ATCHAFALAYA*
Quebec	*ST. LAWRENCE,*	*Red(Asia)*	HANOI, Vietnam
Quebec	*SAVANE, WACOUNO*	Red Bandama	Ivory Coast
QUETTA, Pakis.	*BOLAN*	*Red Bandama-->*	*BANDAMA*
Quinault	Washington	RED BLUFF, CA	*SACRAMENTO*
Quinault -->	*PACIFIC*	*Red Cedar*	Wisconsin
QUINCY, IL	*MISSISSIPPI*	*Red Cedar -->*	*CHIPPEWA*
Quinto	Argentina	*Red Deer*	Alberta, Can.
Quoich	N.W. Terr., Can.	*Red Deer -->*	*S. SASKATCHEWAN*
Quoich -->	*HUDSON BAY*	*Red Hong*	HANOI, Vietname
Raba(Raab)	Aus., GYOR, Hung.	*RED HONG <--*	*Lo*
RABA <--	*Leitha*	*Red Hong -->*	*GULF OF TONKIN*
Raba(Raab) -->	*DANUBE*	*Red Lake(riv.)*	GRAND FORKS, ND
RABAT, Mor.	*BOU REGREG*	*Red Lake -->*	*RED -- NORTH*
Rabca	Hungary	*Red Rv of North*	Canada, FARGO, ND,
Rabch	Iran	*Red Rv of North*	WINNIPEG

RED--NORTH <--	Assiniboine,	Rhode Island	BLACKSTONE,
RED--NORTH <--	Goose,Red Lake,	Rhode Island	PAWCATUCK,
RED--NORTH <--	Roseau,Sheyenne,	Rhode Island	PAWTUXET
RED--NORTH <--	Wild Rice	Rhone	ARLES,AVIGNON,Fr.
Red--North -->	LAKE WINNIPEG	Rhone	LYON,SION,Switz.
Red River	Manit.,Winnepeg	Rhone	VALENCE
Red Rock	Montana	RHONE <--	Ain, Arly, Arve,
Red Rock -->	BEAVERHEAD	RHONE <--	Drome, Durance,
Red Sucker	Manitoba, Can.	RHONE <--	Gard,Isere,Saone
RED SUCKER <--	Stull	Rhone -->	MEDITERREAN SEA
Red Sucker -->	GODS	Rhouphia	Greece
Red Volta	KAYA, Burkina,	Riaza	Spain
Red Volta	Ghana	Riaza -->	DUERO
Red Volta -->	WHITE VOLTA	Ribble	England, PRESTON
REDDING, CA	SACRAMENTO	Ribble -->	IRISH SEA
Redwater	Montana	Richelieu	Canada
Redwater -->	MISSOURI	RICHMOND, VA	JAMES
Reese	Nevada	RIGA, Latv.	DAUGAVA
Reese -->	HUMBOLDT	Rima	Nigeria
Regen	Germany	Rima -->	SOKOTO
REGINA, Sask.	WASCANA	Rimac	Peru
Regnitz	Ger., NURNBERG	Rimac -->	PACIFIC
REGNITZ <--	Aisch, Rezat	Rio da Varzea	Brazil
Regnitz -->	MAIN	Rio da Varzea	-IJUI
Rehr	India	Rio das Velhas	Brazil
Reindeer	Saskatchewan, Ca	Rio das Velhas	-->SAO FRANCISCO
Reindeer -->	CHURCHILL	RIO de laPLATA	<-- Parana,Urug.R.
Reindeer Lk	SASKATCH./MANIT.	Rio de laPlata	--> ATLANTIC
Reisa	Norway	Rio de Sangue	SeeSangue,Rio de
Rems	Germany	Rio dos Bois	Brazil
RENNES, Fr.	ILLE	Rio dos Bois->	PARANAIBA
Reno	Italy	Rio Bravo	Mexico
Reno -->	ADRIATIC	Rio Grande	ALBUQUERQUE, CO
RENO, NV	TRUCKEE	Rio Grande	ALAMOSA, EL PASO
Republican	KS,NE	Rio Grande	BROWNSVILLE,
Republican -->	KANSAS Riv.	Rio Grande	LAS CRUCES,TX
Reuss	Switzerland	Rio Grande	LAREDO,MEXICO/TX
Reuss -->	AAR(E)	RIO GRANDE <--	Brazos, Devils,
Rewa	Guyana	RIO GRANDE <--	Pecos,Rio Puerto
Rewa -->	ESSEQUIBO	RIO GRANDE <--	Salado
Rezat	Germany	Rio Grande -->	GULF OF MEXICO
Rezat -->	REGNITZ	Rio Puerto	New Mexico
Rhein	Germany	Rio Puerto -->	RIO GRANDE
Rhine	ARNHEM, BASEL,	Rio Salado	New Mexico
Rhine	BONN, COLOGNE,	Rio Salado -->	COLORADO
Rhine	FRANCE/GER.,Ger.	Rio San Jose	See San Jose,Rio
Rhine	Liechtenstein,	Risle	France
Rhine	KOBLENZ, KOLN,	Rivanna	Virginia
Rhine	LIECHTEN./SWITZ	Rivanna -->	JAMES
Rhine	MAINZ, MANNHEIM,	ROANOKE, VA	POTOMAC
Rhine	Netherlands,	Roanoke	NC, VA
Rhine	ROMAGEN, SWITZ.	Roanoke -->	ALBERMARLE SOUND
RHINE <--	Aar(e),Erft,Ill,	ROCHESTER, NY	GENESEE,
RHINE <--	Lahn,Lk Bodensee	ROCHESTER, NY	LK ONTARIO
RHINE <--	Lippe,Main,Mosel	Rock	IL, MI, MOLINE,
RHINE <--	Nahe,Neckar,Ruhr	Rock	ROCKFORD
RHINE <--	Waal	Rock -->	MISSISSIPPI
Rhine -->	NORTH SEA	ROCKFORD, IL	ROCK

Roer	See Rur	Russia	ANGARA,CARA,DON
Rogue	Oregon	Russia	BOL'SAJA CUJA,
Rogue -->	PACIFIC	Russia	CUNA, DESNA, IK,
Rokel	Sierra Leone	Russia	CHOP'OR,DEMJANKA
ROMA, Italia	TEVERE	Russia	DNIEPER. DVINA,
Romania	ALT,ALUTA,ARGES,	Russia	ILI,ISET, IRTYS,
Romania	ARGESUL,BISTRITA	Russia	ISIM, IZMA, KAMA
Romania	BUZDU,CRASNA,JIU	Russia	JENISEJ,KAMCATKA
Romania	DANUBE,IALOMITA	Russia	KAN,KARA,KIRENGA,
Romania	LK SINOE,MAROS,	Russia	KOLYMA,KAZYM,KET
Romania	MORESUL,OLT,PRUT	Russia	KLAZMA, KOLIMA,
Romania	OLTUL, SIRET	Russia	KONDA,LAMIN,LENA
Romania	SOMESUL,TIMIS,	Russia	KOSTROMA, KOTUJ,
Romania	TISZA, VEDEA	Russia	LK CHANY,LK NEVE,
ROME, GA	ALABAMA	Russia	LK ELTON,LK SEGO,
ROME, Italy	TIBER	Russia	LK ILMEN, MANYC,
ROME, NY	MOHAWK	Russia	LK LADOGA,MAJA,
Ronuro	Brazil	Russia	LK ONEGA,LOVAT',
Ronuro -->	XINGU	Russia	MEZAN', MOJJERO
Roosevelt	Brazil	Russia	MOKSA, MOLOGA,
Roosevelt -->	ARIPUANA	Russia	MOSKVA,MSTA,NER,
Roper	Australia	Russia	NADYM, NERCA,OB,
Roper -->	G.of CARPENTERIA	Russia	NERL',NEVA,OKA,
Ros	Russia	Russia	NIZN'AJA,OB GULF
Roseau	Manitoba,Can.,ND	Russia	OCHOTA, OJAT',
Roseau -->	RED -- NORTH	Russia	OL'OKMA,OM,OREL,
ROSTOV, Rus.	DON	Russia	OMOLON. ONEGA,
Rother	England, RYE	Russia	P'ASINA, PECORA,
Rother -->	ENGLISH CHANNEL	Russia	PODKAMENNAJA T.
ROTTERDAM,Neth.	MAAS	Russia	PENZINA,PIM,PUR,
ROUEN, Fr.	SEINE	Russia	POLOJ, POPIGAJ,
Roufias	Greece	Russia	PRONA, ROS, SAL,
Rovuma	See Ruvuma	Russia	SAMARA, SELMGS,
Ruaha(Great)	Tanzania	Russia	SEVERNAJA DVINA,
Ruaha -->	INDIAN OCEAN	Russia	SILKA, SUCHONA,
Rubicon	California	Russia	SUGOJ,SURA,SVIR,
Rubicon	Italy	Russia	TAVDA,TAZ,TEREK,
Rud	Iran	Russia	TOBOL, TULOMA,
Rufiji	Tanzania	Russia	TUMCA,TURA,TURU,
Ruhr	ESSEN, Ger.,	Russia	TYM,UCUR,UDA,UFA
Ruhr	Prussia	Russia	UNZA, URAL, USA,
Ruhr -->	RHINE	Russia	UZOLA, V'ATKA,
Ruki	Zaire	Russia	VACH,VALKA,VAGA,
Rum	Minnesota	Russia	VAS'UGAN, VITIM,
Rum -->	MISSISSIPPI	Russia	VOLCHOV, VOLGA,
Rungwa	Tanzania	Russia	VYCEGDA, ZEJA
Rungwa -->	LK RUKWA	RUS./KAZAKHST.	UJ
Runnymede,Eng.	THAMES	Russian	California
Ruo	China	Russian -->	PACIFIC
Rupel	Belgium	Ruvu	Tanzania
Rur(Roer)	Germany, Neth.	Ruvubu	Burundi
Rur -->	MAAS	Ruvuma	MOZAMB./TANZANIA
RUSE, Bulg.	DANUBE	RUVUMA <--	Lugende
Rush	N. Dakota	Ruvuma -->	INDIAN OCEAN
Rush -->	SHEYENNE	Ruzizi	Burundi
Rusne	Lithuania	Ruzizi	BURUNDI/ZAIRE
Russia	ABAKAN, AMUR,	Rusizi -->	LK TANGANYIKI
Russia	AANABAR,ANADYR,	Rwanda	AKANYARU, KAGERA

Rwanda	*LK KIVU,*	St. JOSEPH,MO	*MISSOURI*
Rwanda	*LUVIRONZA*	St.Lawrence	CANADA/USA
RYE, Eng.	*ROTHER*	St.Lawrence	MONTREAL,Quebec,
Saalach	Aus.,GER./AUS.	St.Lawrence	TROIS RIVIERS
Saalach	SALZBURG	ST.LAWRENCE<--	*Grass, Ottawa,*
Saalach -->	*INN*	ST.LAWRENCE<--	*Saguenay,*
Saale	Germany	ST.LAWRENCE<--	*St. Maurice*
SAALE <--	*Bode, Unstrut*	St.Lawrence-->	*G OF ST.LAWRENCE*
Saale -->	*ELBE*	ST.LO, France	*VIRE*
Saar	France, Germany	St.Louis	Minnesota
Saar -->	*MOSEL*	St.Louis -->	*LK SUPERIOR*
Sab	CHHNANG,Cambodia	St.LOUIS, MO	*MISSISSIPPI*
Sab -->	*MEKONG*	St.Marys	LKS SUPER.-HURON
Sabi	*See Save*	St.Marys -->	*LAKE HURON*
Sabie	Mozambique,S.Afr	St.Marys	Nova Scotia,Can.
Sabie -->	*KOMATI*	St.Marys -->	*ATLANTIC*
Sabine	LA, TX	St.-Maurice	Quebec
SABINE <--	*Neches*	St.-Maurice-->	*ST. LAWRENCE*
Sabine -->	*GULF OF MEXICO*	St.PAUL, MN	*MISSISSIPPI*
Sabar	Portugal	*St.Paul*	LIB./MONROVIA
Sabor	Portugal	*St.Paul*	Liberia,
Sabor -->	*DOURO*	*St.Paul -->	*ATLANTIC*
Sac	Missouri	ST.PETERSBURG	*NEVA*
Sac -->	*LK OF THE OZARKS*	Sajo(Slana)	Hungary,Slovakia
Sachigo	Ontario, Can.	*Sajo -->	*TISZA*
Sachigo -->	*SEVERN*	Sak	Tibet
Saco	Maine, New Hamp.	Sakami	Quebec, Can.
Saco -->	*GULF OF MAINE*	Sakami -->	*LK SAKAMI*
Sacramento	CA, RED BLUFF,	Sakarya	Turkey
Sacramento	REDDING	Sakarya -->	*SEA OF MARMARA*
SACRAMENTO <--	*American,Feather*	Sal	Russia
SACRAMENTO <--	*San Joaquin,*	Sal -->	*DON*
Sacramento -->	*SanFRANCISCO BAY*	Salach	*See Saalach*
Sado	Portugal	Salado	Argentina
Safidrud	Iran	SALADO <--	*San Javier,*
Saginaw	Michigan	SALADO <--	*Tunuyan*
Saginaw -->	*LK HURON*	Salado -->	*PARANA*
Saguenay	Canada, Quebec	Salado	Mexico
Saguenay -->	*ST. LAWRENCE*	Salado -->	*RIO GRANDE=BRAVO*
Saigon	HO CHI MINH	Salamat,Bahr	Chad
Saint	use ST. as abbr.	Salamat,Bahr->	*CHARI*
St. Clair	Michigan	Salambria	Thessaly
St. Clair <-->	*LK HURON*	Salcha	Arkansas
St. Croix#1	ME/NEW BRUNS.	Salcha -->	*TANANA*
St. Croix#1-->	*BAY OF FUNDY*	Saldana	Colombia
St. Croix#2	MN, MN/WI, WI	Saldana -->	*MAGDALENA*
St. Croix#2-->	*MISSISSIPPI*	SALEM, OR	*WILLAMETTE*
St. Francis	Arkansas	Salinas	California
St. Francis-->	*MISSISSIPPI*	Salinas -->	*PACIFIC*
St. John	Liberia	Saline	Arkansas, Kansas
St. John	ME,ME/NEW BRUN.	Saline -->	*OUACHITA*
St, John	New Brunswick	Salmon	Idaho
ST. JOHN <--	*Tobique*	Salmon -->	*SNAKE*
St. John -->	*BAY OF FUNDY*	Saloum	Senegal
St. Johns	JACKSONVILLE	Saloum -->	*ATLANTIC*
St. Joseph	FORT WAYNE, IN,	Salso	Italy
St. Joseph	OH, MI	Salt	Arizona, PHOENIX
St. Joseph -->	*MAUMEE*	SALT, AZ <--	*Verde*

Salt, AZ -->	GILA	San Miguel -->	PUTUMAYO
Salt	Kentucky	San Narev	Poland
Salt, KY -->	OHIO	San Pablo	Bolivia
Saluda	S. Carolina	San Pedro	Liberia
Saluda -->	LK MURRAY	San Rafael	Utah
Salween	Burma, China,	San Rafael -->	GREEN
Salween	Tibet	San Saba	Texas
SALWEEN <--	Nam, Nanding,	San Saba -->	COLORADO, TX
SALWEEN <--	Thaungyin	Sanaga	Camreoon
Salween -->	ANDAMAN SEA	Sanaga -->	GULF OF GUINEA
SALYAN, Nepal	KURA	Sand	Alberta, Can.
Salza	Austria	Sand -->	BEAVER
Salzach	AUS/GER	Sandusky	Ohio
Salzach -->	INN	Sandusky -->	LK ERIE
Samala	Guatemala	Sandy	Oregon
Samala -->	PACIFIC	Sandy -->	COLUMBIA
Samara	Russia	Sanga	Congo
Samara -->	VOLGA	Sangamon	Illinois
Samassi	Sardinia	Sangamon -->	ILLINOIS Riv.
Sambre	Belgium,France	SANGAR, Rus.	LENA
Sambre -->	MEUSE	Sangha (Ngoko)	Cameroon,Congo,
Sambu	Panama	Sangha (Ngoko)	OUESSO
Sambu -->	G OF PANAMA	SANGHA <--	Dja
Samina	Liechtenstein	Sangha -->	CONGO (ZAIRE)
San	Cambodia	Sangro	Italy
San	Poland	Sangue,Rio de	Brazil
San -->	WISTA	Sangue,Rio de	--> JURUÉNA
San (Xan)	Cambodia,	Sankh	India
San (Xan)	Vietnam	Santa	Peru
San -->	MEKONG	Santa -->	PACIFIC
San Antonio Rv.	SAN ANTONIO,TX	Santa Elena	Bolivia
SAN ANTONIO<--	Medina	Santa Elena-->	BENI
San Antonio-->	G OF MEXICO	SANTA FE,Braz.	PARANA
San Carlos	Costa Rica	Santa Teresa	Brazil
San Carlos -->	SAN JUAN	Santa Teresa->	TOCANTINS
SAN FRANCISCO B <--	Sacramento	Santee	S. Carolina
San Javier	Argentina	Santee -->	ATLANTIC
San Javier -->	SALADO	Sanyati	Zimbabwe
San Joaquin	CA, STOCKTON	Sao Francisco	Brazil
SAN JOAQUIN<--	Merced	SaoFRANCISCO<--	Grande,Paracatu
San Joaquin-->	SACRAMENTO	SaoFRANCISCO<--	Urucuia
San Jorge	Colombia	SaoFrancisco->	ATLANTIC
San Jorge -->	MAGDALENA	Sao Manuel	Brazil
San Jose	Br.Columbia,Can.	Sao Manuel -->	TAPAJOS
San Jose -->	FRASER	Saone	LYON, France
San Jose,Rio	New Mexico	SAONE <--	Doubs
San Jose,Rio->	RIO PUERCO	Saone -->	RHONE
San Juan	Colombia	Saranta	Greece
San Juan -->	PACIFIC	Sarda (Mahakali)	India, Nepal
San Juan	COSTA RICA/NICA	Sarda -->	KARNALI
SAN JUAN <--	San Carlos	Sardinia	COGHINAS,MANNU,
San Juan -->	CARIBBEAN	Sardinia	FLUMENDOSA,
San Juan	New Mexico, UT	Sardinia	LASCIA
SAN JUAN <--	La Plata	Sardinia	TIRSO, SAMASSI,
San Juan -->	COLORADO	SARH, Chad	SHARI
San Martin	Bolivia	Sarida	Israel
San Martin -->	BAURES	Sarine	Switzerland
San Miguel	ECUADOR/COLOMB.	Sarstun	Guatemala

Sartang	Siberia	Scotland	*DEVERON,DON,ESK,*
Sartang -->	*JANA*	Scotland	*FINDHORN, FORTH,*
Sarthe	LeMANS	Scotland	*GARRY, GLEN,*
Sarthe -->	*LOIRE*	Scotland	*LK AWE,LK LOMAND*
Sarus	Turkey	Scotland	*LK NESS,LK SHIN,*
Sarvis	Hungary	Scotland	*LK TAY,NESS,NITH*
Sarvis -->	*SIO*	Scotland	*NORN, SPEY, TAY,*
Saskatchewan	*BEAVER, CARROT,*	Scotland	*TEVIOT, TUMMEL,*
Saskatchewan	*CHURCHILL,MOSSY,*	Scotland	*TWEED,TYNE,YTHAN*
Saskatchewan	*MUDJATIK, SWAN,*	S of Azov	*Russia, Ukraine*
Saskatchewan	*QU'APPELLE,*	S OF AZOV <--	*Don*
Saskatchewan	*REINDEER,*	S OF JAPAN <--	*Tumen*
Saskatchewan	*SASKATCHEWAN Rv*	S of MARMARA<--	*Sakarya*
Saskatchewan	*WHITE FOX*	S of OKHOTSK<--	*Ochota, Penzina*
SASKATCHEWAN<--	Carrot, Mossy	Seal	Manitoba, Can.
Saskatchewan->	*LAKE WINNIPEG*	Seal -->	*HUDSON BAY*
Sassandra	Ivory Coast	Sebang	Laos
SASSANDRA <--	*Lobo*	Sebou	Morocco
Sassandra -->	*ATLANTIC*	Sebou -->	*ATLANTIC*
Satilla	Georgia	Sebuku	Borneo
Sau -->	*DANUBE*	Secchia	Italy
Sauer(Sure)	Ger.,Luxembourg,	Secure	Bolivia
Sauer	GER./LUXEMBOURG	Secure -->	*MAMORE*
SAUER <--	*Our*	Seda	Portugal
Sauer -->	*MOSEL*	SEDAN, Fr.	*MEUSE*
Saueruina	Brazil	*Sefid*	Iran
Saueruina -->	*JURUENA*	Segovia	Honduiras
Sava	BOSNIA-H./CRO.,	*Segre*	Spain
Sava	Croatia, KRANJ,	*Segre* -->	*EBRO*
Sava	KRSKO, SISAK,	*Segundo*	Argentina
Sava	SLOVENIA, ZAGREB	*Segundo* -->	*LAGU.MarCHIQUITA*
Sava	Yugoslavia	*Segura*	Spain
SAVA <--	*Drina,Una,Vrbas,*	*Segura* -->	*MEDITERRANEAN*
Sava -->	*DANUBE*	*Seihun*	Turkey
Savane	Quebec, Can	*Seine*	Fr.,PARIS,ROUEN
Savane -->	PERIBONCA	*SEINE* <--	*Aube,Eure,Marne,*
Save	Zimbabwe	*SEINE* <--	*Oise, Yonne*
SAVE <--	*Lundi*	*Seine* -->	*ENGLISH CHANNEL*
Save -->	*MOZAMBIQUE CHAN.*	Sekhong	Cambodia
Savannah	AUGUSTA,GA/SC,SC	*Sele*	Italy
Savannah -->	*ATLANTIC*	*Selenge,(-nga)*	CHUTAG, Mongolia
Saxtons	Vermont	*Selenge,(-nga)*	Russia
Sazava	Czechoslovakia	*SELENGE* <--	*Orchon*
Sazava -->	*VLTAVA*	*Selenge* -->	*LK BAIKAL*
Scarcy	Sierra Leone	*Seman*	Albania
Scarpe	France	*Seman* -->	*ADRIATIC*
Schelde(Escaut)	ANTWERP, Belg.,	*Semois*	Belgium
Schelde(Escaut)	Fr.,GENT,	*Semois* -->	*MEUSE*
SCHELDE <--	*Dender*	*Sen*	Cambodia
Schelde -->	*NORTH SEA*	SELMA, AL	*ALABAMA Riv.*
Schrader	Pennsylvania	Senegal	*CASAMANCE,FALEME*
Schuylkill	PA, PHILADELPHIA	Senegal	*GAMBIE(Gambia),*
Schuylkill	READING	Senegal	*KOULOUNTOU,*
Schuylkill -->	*DELAWARE*	Senegal	*LK du GUIERS,*
Scioto	COLUMBUS, Ohio	Senegal	*SENEGAL, SALOUM,*
Scioto -->	*OHIO Riv.*	Senegal	*VALL.duLOUGGUERE*
Scotland	*AFFRIC,AFTON,AYR*	Senegal Riv.	Guinea, KAYES,
Scotland	*ANNAN,CLYDE,DEE,*	Senegal Riv.	Mali,

Senegal Riv.	MAURIT./SENEGAL	Siberia	*MOMA,MUNA,N'UJA,*
SENEGAL <--	*Bafing#1, Bakoy,*	Siberia	*OLEN'OK, OMOLOJ,*
SENEGAL <--	*Faleme,Karakoro,*	Siberia	*POPIGAJ,SARTANG,*
SENEGAL <--	*Lk du Guiers,*	Siberia	*SIN'AJA,TAJMYRA,*
Senegal -->	*ATLANTIC*	Siberia	*TIMPTON, T'UNG,*
Sengu	*See Orange*	Siberia	*UCUR, VIL'UJ,*
Senne	Belgium	*Sico Tinto*	Honduras
SEOUL,S.Korea	*HAN, HAN-GANG*	*Sico Tinto* -->	*CARIBBEAN*
Sepik	New Guinea	*Sieg*	Germany
Sepik -->	*PACIFIC*	Sierra Leone	*JONG,MOA,MONGO,*
Sepulga	Alabama	Sierra Leone	*ROKEL,ROKKEL*
Seret	Poland	Sierra Leone	*SCARCY, WAANJE*
Seti	Nepal	SIGUIRI,Guinea	*NIGER*
Severn	England, Wales	*Siika*	Finland
SEVERN <--	*Avon, Wye*	*Sikiang*	China
Severn -->	*BRISTOL CHANNEL*	*Sil*	Spain
Severn(Canada)	Ontario	*Silka*	Russia
SEVERN <--	*Sachigo*	*Silka* -->	*AMUR*
Severn -->	*HUDSON BAY*	*Silvies*	Oregon
Severnaja *Dvina*	Russia	*Simeto*	Italy
SEVERNAJA DVINA	<-- *Vaga, Vycegd*	*Simo*	Finland
Severnaja *Dvina*	--> *BARENTS SEA*	*Simonette*	Alberta, Can.
Sevier	Utah	*Simonette* -->	*SMOKY*
Seybouse -->	*MEDITERRANEAN*	*Sin'aja*	Siberia
Seyhan	Turkey	*Sin'aja* -->	*LENA*
Seylan	Turkey	*Sinaloa*	Mexico
SHANGHAI	*HANG PU*	*Sinaloa* -->	*G. OF CALIFORNIA*
Shannon	Ireland,LIMERICK	*Sind*	India
SHANNON <--	*Deel,Maigue,Suck*	SINSKOJE, Sib.	*LENA*
Shannon -->	*ATLANTIC*	*Sinu*	Colombia
Shari	Angola,SARH,Chad	*Sinu* -->	*CARIBBEAN SEA*
Shari -->	*LAKE CHAD*	*Sio*	Hungary
Shashe	BOTSWA./ZIMBABWE	*SIO* <--	*Kapos,Sarviz*
Shashe -->	*LIMPOPO*	*Sio* -->	*DANUBE*
SHASTA LK,CA	<-- Pit	SION, Switz.	*RHONE*
SHATTal-ARAB	<-- Euphrates, *igris*	*Sioux*	S. Dakota
Sheenjek	Alaska	SIOUX CITY, IA	*FLOYD*
Sheenjek -->	*YUKON*	*Sipsey*	Alabama
Shelif	Algeria	*Sipsey* -->	*TOMBIGBEE*
Sheyenne	N. Dakota	*Sirba*	Niger
SHEYENNE <--	*Rush*	*Sirba* -->	*NIGER Riv.*
Sheyenne -->	*RED -- NORTH*	*Siret*	Romania
Shire	Malawi	*Siret* -->	*DANUBE*
Shire -->	*ZAMBEZI*	SISAK,Croatia	*SAVA*
Shkumbi	Albania	*Sittoung*	Burma
Shoshone	Wyoming	*Sittoung* -->	*ANDAMAN SEA*
Shoshone -->	*BIGHORN*	*Sixaola*	COSTA R./PANAMA
Shur	Iran	*Sixaola* -->	*CARIBBEAN*
Shweli	Burma	*Skagit*	Br.Colum.Can.,WA
Shweli -->	*IRRAWADDY*	*Skagit* -->	*PUGET SOUND*
Si	China	*Skeena*	Br.Columbia,Can.
SIAN(Xi'an),Chi	*WEI*	*SKEENA* <--	*Kispiox*
Siapa	Venezuela	*Skeena* -->	*HECATE STRAIT*
Siapa -->	*NEGRO*	*Skillet Fork*	Illinois
Siberia	*ALAZEJA, ALDAN,*	*Skillet Fork* ->	*WABASH*
Siberia	*AMGA,CARA,GONAN,*	*Skive*	Denmark
Siberia	*INDIGIRKA,KOLYMA*	SKOPJE,Macedon.	*VARDAR*
Siberia	*LENA,LINDE,MAJA,*	*Skuna*	Mississippi

Skunk	AMES, Iowa	*Song*	Vietnam
Skunk -->	MISSISSIPPI	*Songhua*	China, HARBIN
Skut	Bulgaria	*SONGJUA* <--	*Nen*
Skut -->	DANUBE	*Songhua* -->	*AMUR*
Slana	*See Sajo*	*Sor*	Portugal
Slaney	Ireland, WEXFORD	*Soreo*	Israel
Slaney -->	*IRISH SEA*	*Souhegan*	New Hampshire
Slave	Alb.,N.W.T.,Can.	*Souhegan* -->	*MERRIMACK*
SLAVE <--	*Peace*	*Souris*	MINOT, ND,
Slave -->	*GREAT SLAVE LK*	*Souris*	Manitoba, Can.
Slave Lk	Canada	*Souris* -->	*ASSINIBOINE*
Slovokia	*SAJO(SLANA)*	*Sous*	Morocco
Slupia	Poland	*Sous* -->	*ATLANTIC*
Slupia -->	*BALTIC SEA*	South	use S. as abbr,
Smith	Montana	S. Africa	*AUOB, BRAK,*
Smith -->	*MISSOURI*	S. Africa	*KUBANGO,KURUMAN,*
Smoky	Alberta, Can.	S. Africa	*LIMPOPO, MODDER,*
SMOKY <--	*Simonette*	S. Africa	*MOLOPO,OLIFANTS,*
Smoky -->	*PEACE*	S. Africa	*ORANGE, SABIE,*
Smoky Hill	Kansas	S. Africa	*TUGELA, VAAL*
Smoky Hill -->	*KANSAS Riv.*	S. AFR/ZIMBAB.	*LIMPOPO*
Snake	ID, ID/OR	S. Carolina	*ASHEPOO, BROAD,*
Snake	JACKSON,LEWISTON	S. Carolina	*CONGAREE,EDISTO,*
Snake	ID,OR,WA,WY	S. Carolina	*GREAT PEE DEE,*
SNAKE <--	*Owyhee, Palouse,*	S. Carolina	*LK MARION,SALUDA*
SNAKE <--	*Payette,Powder,*	S. Carolina	*LK MURRAY,SANTEE*
SNAKE <--	*Raft, Salmon*	S. Carolina	*LYNCHES, SAVANNAH*
Snake -->	*COLUMBIA*	S. Carolina	*TUGULOS, WATEREE*
Snowy	Australia	*S. CHINA S* <--	*Kapuas, Hari,*
Snowy -->	*TASMAN SEA*	*S. CHINA S* <--	*Mekong, Pahang,*
Sobat	Sudan	*S. CHINA S* <--	*Rajang, Xia*
Sobat -->	*WHITE NILE*	S. Dakota	*CHEYENNE, JAMES,*
SOFIA, Bulg.	*ISKER*	S. Dakota	*LK OAHE,MISSOURI,*
Sofia	Madagascar	S. Dakota	*MOREAU,NIOBRARA,*
Sofia -->	*MOZAMBIQUE CHAN.*	S. Dakota	*SIOUX*
Sokoto	Nigeria	S. Korea	*HAN-GANG,*
Sokoto -->	*NIGER*	S. Korea	*PUKHAN-GANG*
Soleduck	Washington	*South Platte*	DENVER, CO, NE
Soleduck -->	*PACIFIC*	*SOUTHERN O* <--	*Murray*
Solimoes	Brazil	Spain	*ADAJA, ALAGON,*
Solimoes -->	*AMAZON*	Spain	*ALMERIA,ALMONTE,*
Solo	Java	Spain	*ARAGON, ARBA*
Solomon	Kansas	Spain	*ARLANZA,BARBATE,*
Solomon -->	*KANSAS Riv.*	Spain	*CABRIEL, CEGA,*
SOLWAY FIRTH <--	*Eden*	Spain	*CINCA, DOURO,*
Somalia	*JUBBA*	Spain	*DUERO,EBRO,EGA,*
Somersetshire,	*EXE*	Spain	*ERESMA, ERGES,*
Somesul	Romania	Spain	*GENILGALLEGO,*
Somjin	S. Korea	Spain	*ESLA, GUADIANA,*
Somme	AMIENS, France	Spain	*HENARES,HUERVA,*
SOMME <--	*Ancre*	Spain	*JALON, JARAMA,*
Somme -->	*ENGLISH CHANNEL*	Spain	*JUCAR,LIMA,MINO,*
Son	India	Spain	*MIJARES, MINHU,*
Son -->	*GANGES*	Spain	*NAVIA, ODIEL,*
Sonar	India	Spain	*ORBIGO, PERALES*
Sonora	HERMOSILLO, Mex.	Spain	*RIAZA,SIL,SEGRE,*
Sonora -->	*G OF CALIFORNIA*	Spain	*SEGURA,TER,TERA,*
Song	Tibet	Spain	*TAGUS,TAJO,TINTO*

Spain	*TOROTE, TURIA,*	Sucuriu	Brazil
Spain	*ULLA*	Sucuriu -->	*PARANA*
Spey	Scotland	Sudan	*ATBARA,JUR,NILE,*
Spey -->	*NORTH SEA*	Sudan	*BAHR al GAZAL,*
Spirit Lk	IO, WA	Sudan	*SOBAT, SUE*
Spokane	Washington	Sudan	*WHITE NILE,*
Spokane -->	*COLUMBIA*	Sue	Sudan
Spoon	Illinois	Sue -->	*JUR*
Spoon -->	*ILLINOIS Riv.*	Sugoj	Russia
Spree	BERLIN, Germany	Sugoj -->	*KOLYMA*
Spree -->	*HAVEL*	Suia-Micu	Brazil
Squamish	Br.Columbia,Can.	Suia-Micu -->	*XINGU*
Squamish -->	*STR.OF GEORGIA*	Suir	Ire., WATERFORD
St. Lo	*VIRE*	Suir -->	*ATLANTIC*
Staaten	Australia	SUKKUR, Pakis.	*INDUS*
Staaten -->	*G.OF CARPENTERIA*	Sulaco	Honduras
STAFFORE Eng.	*PENK*	*Sulphur*	Texas, Arkansas
STETTIN, Pol.	*ODER*	*Sulphur* -->	*RED*
Stewart	N.W. Terr., Can.	*Sumida*	TOKYO
Stewart -->	*YUKON*	*Sumida* -->	*TOKYO BAY*
Stikine	Br.Columbia, Can	Sun	Montana
STIKINE <--	*Iskut*	Sun -->	*MISSOURI*
Stikine -->	*FREDERICK SOUND*	Sungari	China, Manchuria
STOCKTON, CA	*SAN JOAQUIN*	Supamo	Venezuela
Stony	Alaska	SUPAMO <--	*Yuruari*
Stony -->	*KUSKOWIN*	Supamo -->	*CUYUNI*
Stony	California	Sura	Russia
Stor	Denmark	Sura -->	*VOLGA*
Storaa	Denmark	SURAT, India	*TAPTI*
Storm Lk	Iowa	Sure	See Sauer
Stour	England	Suriname	*COPPENAME,*
Stour -->	*NORTH SEA*	Suriname	*CORANTIJN, ITANY*
ST.ofGEORGIA<--	Fraser, Squamish	Suriname	*LUCIE, MORONI*
ST.ofMALACCA<--	Kampar, Perak	Surumu	Brazil
Strimon(Struma)	Greece, Bulgaria	Surumu -->	*BRANCO*
Strimon -->	*AEGEAN SEA*	Sustina	Alaska
Struma	See Strimon	Sustina -->	*COOK INLET*
Stuart	Br.Columbia, Can	Susquehanna	HARRISBURG, PA
Stuart -->	*NECHAKO*	Susquehanna	WILKES-BARRE
Stull	Manitoba, Can.	SUSQUEHANNA<--	*Juniata*
Stull -->	*RED SUCKER*	Susquehanna-->	*CHESAPEAKE BAY*
Stupart	Manitoba, Can.	Sussex, Eng.	*OUSE*
Stupart -->	*HAYES*	Sutlej	India,Pak.,Tibet
Stura	Italy	SUTLEJ <--	*Chenab*
STUTTGART,Ger.	*NECKAR*	Sutlej -->	*INDUS*
Strypa	Poland	Suwanee	Florida
Styr	Poland	Suwanee -->	*GULF OF MEXICO*
Styx	CHARON	Svir	Russia
Suapure	Venezuela	Svir -->	*OJAT'*
Suapure -->	*ORINOCO*	Swakop	Namibia
Suchona	Russia	Swakop -->	*ATLANTIC*
Suchona -->	*DVINA*	Swale	England
Sucio	Colombia	Swan	Manitoba,Saskat.
Sucio -->	*ATRATO*	Swan -->	*LK WINNIPEGOSIS*
Suck	Ireland	Swanee	See Suwanee
Suck -->	*SHANNON*	Sweden	*ANGERMAN, DAL,*
Sucunduri	Brazil	Sweden	*GOTA,KALIX,KLAR,*
Sucunduri -->	*CANUMA*	Sweden	*LAINIO, LJUSNE,*

Sweden	*LK MALAREN,*	*Tallahatchie*	Mississippi
Sweden	*LK SILJA, LULE,*	*Tallahatchie->*	*YAZOO*
Sweden	*LK VANERN,PITEA*	*Tallapoosa*	Alabama
Sweden	*LK VATTERN,*	*Tallapoosa -->*	*ALABAMA Riv.*
Sweden	*RANEA,TORNEA*	*Talston*	N.W. Terr., Can.
Sweden	*UME,*	*Talston -->*	*GREAT SLAVE LK*
Sweden	*WINDEL*	*Tama*	Japan,TOKYO
Sweetwater	Wyoming	*Tama -->*	*TOKYO BAY*
Sweetwater -->	*NORTH PLATTE*	*Tamaki*	New Zealand
Swift	Alaska	*Tamar*	Eng., PLYMOUTH
Swift -->	*KUSKOWIN*	*Tamar(Eng.)-->*	*ATLANTIC*
Switzerland	*AAR,AARE,BROYE,*	*Tamar*	Tazmania
Switzerland	*DOUBS,INN,LINTH,*	*Tamar -->*	*BASS STRAIT*
Switzerland	*LK AGERI,LK JOUY*	*Tambo*	Australia
Switzerland	*LK GENEVA,*	*Tambo -->*	*PACIFIC*
Switzerland	*LK LUGANO,LK URI*	*Tambo*	Peru
Switzerland	*LK NEUCHATEL,*	*Tambo -->*	*UCAYALI*
Switzerland	*LK THUN, LK ZUG*	*Tamega*	Portugal
Switzerland	*MAGGIA,PRATIGAU,*	*Tamega -->*	*DOURO*
Switzerland	*REUSS,RHINE,THUR*	*Tamis(Timis)*	Yugo., Romania
Switzerland	*RHONE,SARINE,*	*Tamis -->*	*DANUBE*
Switzerland	*TICINO*	*Tana*	GARISSA,Kenya
Syrdarja	Kazakhstan	*Tana -->*	*INDIAN OCEAN*
Syrdarja -->	*ARAL SEA*	*Tana*	Nor.,FINLND/NOR.
Syria	*ASI, BALIKH,*	*Tana(Teno) -->*	*ARTIC OCEAN*
Syria	*BARADA,EUPHRATES*	*Tanama*	Puerto Rico
Syria	*JORDAN, KNABUR,*	*Tanana*	Alaska,FAIRBANKS
Syria	*ORONTES*	*TANANA <--*	*Delta, Nenana,*
Szamos	Hungary	*TANANA <--*	*Salcha, Wood*
Tab	Iran	*Tanama -->*	*YUKON*
Tabasco	Mexico	*Tanaro*	Italy
Tablerock Lk	Missouri	*Tanaro -->*	*PO*
Tachia	Taiwan	TANGA,Tanzania	*PANGANI*
Tacuari	Uruguay	*Tano*	Ghana
Tacuari -->	*LK MIRIM*	*Tano -->*	*ATLANTIC*
Tacutu	Brazil	*Tanshui*	Taiwan
TACUTU <--	*Mau(Ireng)*	Tanzania	*IGOMBE, KAGERA,*
Tacutu -->	*BRANCO*	Tanzania	*LK EYASI,*
Taedong	N. Korea	Tanzania	*LK RUKWA,*
Tago	Portugal	Tanzania	*LK NYASSA*
Tagus(Tajo,-jo)	LISBON,Portugal,	Tanzania	*LK VICTORIA,*
Tagus	Spain, TOLEDO	Tanzania	*LUWEGU, NIOMBE,*
TAGUS <--	*Alagon, Almonte,*	Tanzania	*PANGANI, RUEHA,*
TAGUS <--	*Erges, Jarama,*	Tanzania	*RUNGWA, WAMI*
TAGUS <--	*Zezere*	TANZAN./UGAND.	*LK VICTORIA*
Tagus -->	*ATLANTIC*	TANZAN./ZAIRE	*LK TANGANYIKA*
Taieri	New Zealand	*Tao*	China
Taieri -->	*PACIFIC*	*Tao -->*	*YELLOW*
Taiwan	*TACHIA, TANSHUI,*	*Tapajos*	Brazil
Taiwan	*WUCHI*	*TAPAJOS <--*	*Juruena,*
TAJ MAHAL	*YAMUNA*	*TAPAJOS <--*	*Sao Manuel*
Tajmyra	Siberia	*Tapajos -->*	*AMAZON*
Tajmyra -->	*KARA SEA*	*Tapaua*	Brazil
Tajo	*See Tagus*	*Tapaua -->*	*PURUS*
Takaze	Ethiopia	*Tapi*	India
Takutu	*See Tacutu*	*Tapi -->*	*GULF OF KHAMBHAT*
Talbragar	Australia	*Tapiche*	Peru
Talbragar -->	*MACQUARIE*	*Tapiche -->*	*UCAYALI*

Taping (Daying)	Burma, China	Tennessee	*CUMBERLAND, DUCK,*
Taping -->	*IRRAWADDY*	Tennessee	*HATCHIE, HIWASSEE,*
Tapti	India, SURAT	Tennessee	*HOLSTON,*
Taquari	Brazil	Tennessee	*TENNESSEE Riv.*
Taquari -->	*PARAQUAY Riv.*	*Tennessee Riv.*	AL, CHATTANOOGA,
Tar	N. Carolina	*Tennessee Riv.*	TN
Tar -->	*PAMLICO SOUND*	*TENESSEE* <--	*Bear, Beeck,*
Taraira	*See Traira*	*TENESSEE* <--	*Duck, Elk*
Tarauaca	Brazil	*Tennessee* -->	*OHIO*
Tarauaca -->	*ENVIRA*	Teno	*See Tana*
Tarcoles	Costa Rica	Tenoria	Costa Rica
Tarim	China	Tensas	Louisiana
Tarlia	Bolivia	Tensas -->	*OUACHITA*
Tarn	France	Tensaw	Alabama
Tarn -->	*GARRONE*	Tensift	Morocco
Tarna	Hungary	Tensift -->	*ATLANTIC*
Tarna -->	*ZAGYVA*	Teodoro	Brazil
Taro	Italy	Ter	Spain
TARTAR STR. <--	*Amur*	Ter -->	*MEDITERRANEAN*
TASMAN S <--	*Buller, Derwent,*	Tera	Spain
TASMAN S <--	*Mokau, Snowy,*	Tera -->	*ESLA*
TASMAN S <--	*Rangitikei,*	Tercero	Argentina
TASMAN S <--	*Waikato,*	Tercero -->	*PARANA*
TASMAN S <--	*Wanganui,*	Terek	Russia
Tauber	Germany	Terek -->	*CASPIAN SEA*
Tauber -->	*MAIN*	TERESINA, Braz.	*PARANAIBA*
Taunton	Massachusetts	TERRE HAUTE, IN	*WABASH*
Tavda	Russia	Teslin	N.W. Terr., Can.
Tavda -->	*TOBOL*	Teslin -->	*YUKON*
Taw	BARNSTAPLE, Eng.	Tessin	Italy
Taw -->	*ATLANTIC*	Tessin -->	*PO*
Tay	PERTH, Aust	TETE, Mozam.	*ZAMBEZI*
Tay -->	*INDIAN OCEAN*	Teton	Montana
Tay	PERTH, Scotland	Teton -->	*MARIAS*
Tay -->	*NORTH SEA*	Teuco	*See Bermejo*
Taz	Russia	Tevere (Tiber)	ROMA, Italia
Taz -->	*OB GULF*	TEVERE <--	*Nera*
Tazmania	*DERWENT, TAMAR*	Tevere -->	*MEDITERRANEAN*
Tea	Brazil	Teviot	Scotland
Tea -->	*NEGRO*	Texas	*BRAZOS, FRIO, LEON*
Tea	Congo	Texas	*LAVZACA, LITTLE,*
Tebicuary	Paraguay	Texas	*LK FALCON, LLANO,*
Tebicuary -->	*PARANA*	Texas	*LK TEXOMA, MEDINA*
Teche, Bayou	Louisiana	Texas	*NECHES, NEUCUS,*
Tedzen	*See Harirud*	Texas	*PECOS, RED, SABINE*
Tee	England	Texas	*RIO GRANDE,*
Tees	England	Texas	*SAN ANTONIO Riv,*
Tees -->	*NORTH SEA*	Texas	*SAN SABA, SULPHUR*
Tefe	Brazil	Texas	*TRINITY, WICHITA*
Tefe -->	*AMAZON*	Thailand	*CHAUPAYA, CHI,*
Teifi	CARDIGAN, Wales	Thailand	*HKOK (KOK), MEKONG*
Teifi -->	*IRISH SEA*	Thailand	*MENAM, MUN, NAM*
Tejo	*See Tagus*	Thailand	*MEYPING, PA SAK,*
Tekeze	Ethiopia	Thailand	*PING, YOM*
Tel	India	*Thames*	Eng., ETON, LONDON
Telico	Argentina	*Thames*	RUNNYMEDE
TEMPE, AZ	*GILA*	*Thames* -->	*NORTH SEA*
Tennessee	*BEECH, CANEY, ELK,*	*Thaungyin*	BURMA/THAILAND

Thaungyin -->	SALWEEN	TISZA <--	Sajo, Zagyva
Thaya	See Dyje	Tisza -->	DANUBE
Tha-anne	N.W. Terr., Can.	TIVERTON, Eng.	EXE
Tha-anne -->	HUDSON BAY	Tobique	New Brunswick,
Theiss	Hungary	Tobique -->	ST. JOHN
Thelon	N.W. Terr., Can.	Tobol	Russia,Kazakhst.
Thelon -->	HUDSON BAY	TOBOL <--	Tavda, Tura, Uj
Thessaly,Greece	SALAMBRIA	Tobol -->	IRTYSH
Thjorsa	Iceland	Tocantins	Brazil
Thompson	Br.Columbia,Can.	TOCANTINS <--	Araguaia,
THOMPSON <--	Nicola	TOCANTINS <--	Santa Teresa
Thompson -->	FRASER	Tocantins -->	ATLANTIC
Thompson	Iowa, Missouri	Tocuyo	Venezuela
Thompson -->	GRAND	Tocuyo -->	CARIBBEAN SEA
Throat	Ontario, Can.	Togo	KARA,MONO,OGOU,
Throat -->	BERENS	Togo	OTI
Thur	Switzerland	TOKYO, Jap.	ARA,SUMIDA,TAMA
Thur -->	LK BODENSEE	TOKYO BAY <--	Ara,Sumida,Tama
Tibaji	Brazil	TOLEDO, OH	MAUMEE, LK ERIE
Tibaji -->	PARANAPANEMA	TOLEDO, Sp.	TAGUS
Tiber	See Tevere	Tolten	Chile
Tibet	INDUS, LK ARU,	Tom'	TOMSK, Siberia
Tibet	LK BAM, LK BUM,	Tom' -->	OB
Tibet	LK JAGOK,LK NAM,	Tombigbee	Alabama, MOBILE
Tibet	LK MENA,LK TOSU,	TOMBIGBEE <--	Sipsey
Tibet	MATSANG,NAK,NAU,	Tombigbee -->	ALABAMA
Tibet	SAK,SALWEEN,SONG	Tomo	Colombia
Ticino	Italy, Switz.	Tomo -->	ORINOCO
Ticino -->	PO	TOMSK, Russia	TOM
Tiete	Brazil,SAO PAULO	Tonghui	BEIJING, China
Tiete -->	PARANA	Tongue	Montana
Tigre	Ecuador, Peru	Tongue -->	YELLOWSTONE
TIGRE <--	Corrientes	TOPEKA, KS	KANSAS(Kaw)
Tigre -->	MARANON	Torch	Saskatchewan
Tigre	Venezuela	TORCH <--	White Fox
Tigre -->	ORINOCO	Torch -->	SASKATCHEWAN Rv.
Tigris	Armenia, Iran,	TORINO, Italy	PO
Tigris	Iraq, Turkey	Torino	Finland
Tigris -->	SHATT al-ARAB	Tornea	Sweden
Till	England	TORONTO, Ont.	HUMBER,
Timis	See Tamis	TORONTO, Ont.	LK ONTARIO
TIMOR SEA <--	Daly, Drysdale,	Torote	Spain
TIMOR SEA <--	Victoria	Torridge	BIDEFORD, Eng.
Timpton	Siberia	Torridge -->	ATLANTIC
Timpton -->	ALDAN	TORUN, Pol.	WISTA
Tinkisso	Guinea	Torysa	Czechoslovakia
Tinkisso -->	NIGER	TOULOUSE, Fr.	GARONNE
Tinto	Honduras	TOURS, Fr.	LOIRE
Tinto	Spain	Toutle	Washington
Tioga	New York	Toutle -->	COWLITZ
Tippecanoe	Indiana	Towanda	Pennsylvania
Tippecanoe -->	WABASH	Town	Alabama
Tiptiapa	Nicaragua	Town -->	TENNESSEE
Tirso	Italy, Sardinia	Traira	See Taraira
Tisza(Tisa)	Czech., Hungary,	Traun	Austria
Tisza	Romania, Yugo.	Traun -->	DANUBE
TISZA <--	Hernad, Koros,	Trebbia	Italy
TISZA <--	Maros, Muresul	Trebbia -->	PO

Trent	NOTTINGHAM,Eng.	*Tura*	Russia
TRENT <--	*Penk*	*Tura* -->	*TOBOL*
Trent -->	*HUMBER*	*Turgaj*	Kazakhstan
TRENTON, NJ	*DELAWARE*	*Turgaj* -->	*ISIM*
TRIER, Ger.	*MOSEL*	*Turia*	Spain, VALENCIA
Triete	Braz.,SAO PAULO	*Turia* -->	*MEDITERRANEAN*
Trinity	California	TURIN, Italy	*PO*
Trinity -->	*KLAMATH*	Turkey	*ARAS, EUPHRATES,*
Trinity	DALLAS, Texas	Turkey	*FIRAT, GEDIZ,*
Trinity -->	*GULF OF MEXICO*	Turkey	*HALYS, IRMAK,*
TROIS-RIVIERES	*ST. LAWRENCE*	Turkey	*KIZIL, SEIHUN,*
Trombetas	Brazil	Turkey	*SEYHAN, SEYLAN,*
TROMBETAS <--	*Mapuera*	Turkey	*TIGRIS, ZAB*
Trombetas -->	*AMAZON*	*Turkey*	Iowa
Trout	N.W. Terr.,Can.	*Turkey* -->	*MISSISSIPPI*
Trout -->	*MACKENZIE*	Turkmenistan	*HARIRUD(TEDZEN)*
TROY, NY	*HUDSON*	*Turkwell*	Kenya
Truando	Colombia	*Turu*	Russia
Truckee	Nevada, RENO	*Turu* -->	*NIZN'AJA T.*
Truckee -->	*CARSON*	*Turvo*	Brazil
Tsangpo	China	*Turvo* -->	*RIO DOS BOIS*
TSAVO, Kenya	*GALANA*	Tuscany,Italy	*ARNO, ORCIA*
T'ung	Siberia	*Tweed*	England,PEEBLES,
T'ung -->	*VIL'UJ*	*Tweed*	Scotland
Tua	Portugal	*Tym*	Russia
Tua -->	*DOURO*	*Tym* -->	*OB*
Tuckahoe	New Jersey	*Tyne*	England, HEXHAM,
Tueco(Bermejo)	Argentina	*Tyne*	JARROW, Scotland
Tueco -->	*PARANA*	*Tyne*	NEWCASTLE-Upon-
Tug Fork	KY/WV		TYNE
Tug Fork -->	*BIG SANDY*	*Tyne*	Northumberland
Tugalos	S. Carolina	*Tyne* -->	*NORTH SEA*
Tuira	Panama	*Tywi*	Wales
Tule Lk	California	*Tywi* -->	*ATLANTIC*
Tuloma	MURMANSK, Rus.	*Uatuma*	Brazil
Tuloma -->	*BARENTS SEA*	UATUMA <--	*Urubu*
TULSA, OK	*ARKANSAS*	*Uatuma* -->	*AMAZON*
Tuma	Nicaragua	*Uaupes(Vaupes)*	Brazil, Colombia
Tuma -->	*GRANDE MATAGALPA*	*Uaupes* -->	*NEGRO*
Tumca	Russia	*Ubangi*	BANGUIU, Congo,
Tumen	N. Korea	*Ubangi*	Cent.Afr.Rep.,
Tumbes	Ecuador	*Ubangi*	Zaire
Tumbes -->	*PACIFIC*	UBANGI <--	*Chinko, Kotto,*
Tumen	CHINA/N.KOREA	UBANGI <--	*Lobaye, Mambere,*
Tumen -->	*SEA OF JAPAN*	UBANGI <--	*Mbari,Ouaka,Uele*
Tummel	Scotland	*Ubangi* -->	*CONGO*
Tundza	Bulgaria	Ubekistan,Rus.	*ARAL SEA*
Tundza -->	*MARICA*	*Ucayali*	Peru
Tunga	India	UCAYALI <--	*Apurimac,Perene,*
Tunisia	*LK ACHKEL,*	UCAYALI <--	*Pachitea, Tambo,*
Tunisia	*LK DJERID,*	UCAYALI <--	*Tapiche,*
Tunisia	*MEDJERDA*	UCAYALI <--	*Urubamba*
Tunuyan	Argentina	*Ucayali* -->	*MARANON*
Tunuyan -->	*SALADO*	UCHTA, Rus.	*IZMA*
Tuo	China	*Ucker(Uecker)*	Germany
Tuo -->	*YANGTZE*	UCKER <--	*Randow*
Tuolumne	YOSEMITE NAT.PK.	*Ucker* -->	*ODERHOFF->BALTIC*
Tuolumne -->	*SAN JOAQUIN*	*Ucur*	Russia, Siberia

UCUR <--	*Gonam*	*Urucuia*	Brazil
Ucur -->	*ALDAN*	*Urucuia* -->	*SAO FRANCISCO*
Uda	Russia	*Uruguay*	*CEBOLLATI,GRANDE*
Uda -->	*CUNA*	*Uruguay*	*MALO, NEGRO,*
Uele	BONDO, Congo,	*Uruguay*	*TACAURI, YI*
Uele	WELLE, Zaire	*URUGUAY Rv.* <--	*Grande, Ibicui,*
Uele -->	*UBANGI*	*URUGUAY Rv.* <--	*Ijui, Negro*
Ufa	Russia	*Uruguay* -->	*RIO de la PLATA*
Ugab	Namibia	*Urungo*	China
Ugab -->	*ATLANTIC*	*Usa*	Russia
Uganda	*ASWA, KATONGA,*	*Usa* -->	*PECORA*
Uganda	*KAFU,LK ALBERT,*	*Usk*	Eng., NEWPORT,
Uganda	*LK KYOGA,PAGER,*	*Usk*	Wales
Uganda	*LK VICTORIA,*	*Usk* -->	BRISTOL CHANNEL
UGANDA/ZAIRE	*LK ALBERT*	*Ussuri*	MANCHU./SIBERIA
Uh(Uz)	Czech.,Ukraine	*Ussuri* -->	*AMUR*
Uh -->	*BODROG*	Utah	*COLORADO,*
Uil	Russia	Utah	*GREAT SALT LAKE,*
Uil -->	*URAL*	Utah	*GREEN, JORDAN,*
Uj	RUS./KAZAKHSTAN	Utah	*LK SWAN, LK THUN*
Uj ->	*TOBOL*	Utah	*PRICE,PROVO,RAFT*
Ukraine	*BUG,DNEPR,DNESTR*	Utah	*SAN JUAN, VIRGIN,*
Ukraine	*JUZNYI BUG, UH*	Utah	*SAN RAFAEL,*
Ulimar	Uruguay	*UTAH LK* <--	*Provo*
Ulla	Spain	*Utah River*	thru LK THUN
ULM, Ger.	*DANUBE*	*Utah* -->	*LAKE THUN*
Ulm -->	*DANUBE*	*Ute*	New Mexico
Ulua	Honduras	UTICA, NY	*ERIE(Barge)CANAL*
Ulua -->	*G OF HONDURAS*	UTICA, NY	*MOHAWK*
Ume	Sweden	*Uva*	Colombia
Umatilla	Oregon	*Uva* -->	*GUAVIARE*
Umatilla -->	*COLUMBIA*	*Uz*	See Uh
Umpqua	Oregon	*Uzbek*	OSH
Umpqua -->	*PACIFIC*	*Uzola*	Russia
Una	BOS.-H./CROAT.	*Uzola* -->	*VOLGA*
Una	Yugoslavia	*V'atka*	Russia
Una -->	*SAVA*	*V'atka* -->	*KAMA*
Unare	Venezuela	*Vaal*	S. Africa
Unare -->	*CARIBBEAN*	*VAAL* <--	*Modder*
UNGAVA BAY <--	*George,Koksoak*	*Vaal* -->	*ORANGE*
Unstrut	Germany	*Vach*	Russia
UNSTRUT <--	*Helme*	*Vach* -->	*OB*
Unstrut -->	*SAALE*	*Vag*	Czechoslovakia
Unza	Russia	*Vaga*	Russia
Unza -->	*VOLGA*	*Vaga* -->	*SEVERNAJA DVINA*
Upia	Colombia	*Vah*	ZILINA,Slovakia,
Upia -->	*META*	*Vah*	Czechoslovakia
Ural	ORAL, ORENBERG,	*Vah(Vag,Waag)*	--> *DANUBE*
Ural	ORSK, Russia	*Valdiva*	Chile
URAL <--	*Ilek,Uil*	VALENCE, Fr.	*RHONE*
Ural -->	*CASPIAN SEA*	VALENCIA,Spain	*TURIA*
Ure	YORKSHIRE, Eng.	*Valera*	Andorra
URE <--	*Swale*	*Valley*	Manitoba, Can.
Ure -->	*OUSE*	*Valley* -->	*DAUPHIN LK*
Urubamba	Peru	*Var*	France
Urubamba -->	*UCAYALI*	*Var(o)* -->	*MEDITERRANEAN*
Urubu	Brazil	*Vardar(Axios)*	Greece, SKOPJE,
Urubu -->	*UATUMA*	*Vardar*	Macedonia, Yugo.

Vardar -->	AEGEAN SEA	Vietnam	BO,CA,CHAY,CHU,
Varde	Denmark	Vietnam	DA, DONGNAI, GAM
Varzea, Rio da	SeeRio da Varzea	Vietnam	KOI,LO,MA,MEKONG
Vas'ugan	Russia	Vietnam	NHIHA,RED HONG,
Vas'ugan -->	OB	Vietnam	SONG, XAN(SAN)
Vatka	See V'atka	Vijose	Albania
Vaupes	See Uaupes	Vijose -->	ADRIATIC
Vecht	Germany, Nether.	Vil'uj	Siberia
Vecht -->	IJSSEL	VIL'UJ <--	Cona, T'ung
Vedea	Romania	Vil'uj -->	LENA
Vedea -->	DANUBE	VILLACH, Aus.	DRAU
Velhas,Rio das	=Rio das Velhas	Vils	Germany
Velika Morava	Yugoslavia	Vils -->	DANUBE
Velika Morava	·DANUBE	Vina	Cameroon, Chad
Venezuela	APONGUAO, APURE,	Vina -->	LOGONE
Venezuela	ARAUCA, CARAPOP,	Vindhyas	India
Venezuela	CAPANAPARO,	Vire,	France, ST. LO
Venezuela	CARONI,CARRAO,	Virgin	NV, AZ, UT
Venezuela	CASEQUIARE,CAURA	Virgin -->	LK MEAD
Venezuela	CUYUNI, GUANARE,	Virginia	DAN, JAMES,
Venezuela	GUARICO, MATO,	Virginia	LK KERR,LK SMITH
Venezuela	ORINOCO, PAO,	Virginia	NEW, POTOMAC,
Venezuela	ORITUCO,PARAGUA,	Virginia	RAPIDAN,RIVANNA,
Venezuela	SIAPA, SUAPURE,	Virginia	ROANOKE,
Venezuela	SUPAMO, TIGRE,	Vistula	See Wista
Venezuela	TOCUYO, UNARE,	Vit	Bulgaria
Venezuela	VANTAURI,YURUARI	Vit -->	DANUBE
Venezuela	ZUATA	Vitim	Russia
VENZ/COLOMBIA	META, ORINOCO	Vitim -->	LENA
VENZ/GUYANA	CUYUNI	Vitor	Peru
Venta	Latvia, Lithu.	Vitor -->	PACIFIC
Ventauri	Venezuela	Vivi	Russia
Ventauri -->	ORINOCO	Vivi -->	NIZN'AJA TUNGUSKA
Verde	Arizona	Vltava	Czechoslovakia
Verde, AZ -->	SALT	VLTAVA <--	Berounka, Otava,
Verde	Brazil	VLTAVA <--	Sazava
Verde -->	PARANA	Vltava -->	ELBE
Verdigris	Arkansas, Kansas	Volchov	Russia
Verdigris -->	ARKANSAS Riv.	Volchov -->	LK LADOGA
VERDUN, Fr.	MEUSE	Volga	GORKY, Russia
Vermont	LAMOILLE,	VOLGA <--	Kama, Kostroma,
Vermont	NULHEGAN,	VOLGA <--	Oka,Samara,Sura,
Vermont	POULTNEY,SAXTONS	VOLGA <--	Unza, Uzola
Vermont	WINOOSKI	Volga -->	CASPIAN SEA
VERONA, It.	ADIGE	Volta	Ghana
Vesdre	Belgium	VOLTA <--	Lk Volta
Vesle	France	Volta -->	ATLANTIC
Vesubie	Monaco	Volta Blanche	See White Volta
Vezere	France	Volta Noire	See Black Volta
Viaur	France	Volta Rouge	See Red Volta
Vichada	Colombia, Venez.	Volturno	Italy
Vichada -->	ORINOCO	Vorgod	Denmark
Victoria	Australia	Vouga	Portugal
Victoria -->	TIMOR SEA	Vrbas	Bosnia-Hercegov.
VICTORIA FALLS	ZAMBEZI	Vrbas	JAJCE, Yugo.
VIENNA(WEIN)Aus	DANUBE	Vrbas -->	SAVA
Vienne	France	Vuka	Croatia
Vienne -->	LOIRE	Vuka -->	DANUBE

Vycegda	Russia	*Warnow*	Germany
Vycegda -->	*SEVERNAJA DVINA*	*Warrego*	Australia
Waag	Czechoslovakia	WARSAW, Pol.	*WISTA*
Waal	Netherlands	*Warta(Warthe)*	Poland
Waal -->	*RHINE*	*WARTA* <--	*Notec*
Waanje	Sierra Leone	*Warta* -->	*ODRA*
Wabasca	Alberta, Can.	Washington	*COLUMBIA,COWLITZ*
Wabasca -->	*PEACE*	Washington	*KALAMA, LEWIS,*
Wabash	IL/IN, IL, IN,	Washington	*LK CHELAN,*
Wabash	LAFAYETTE, Ohio,	Washington	*OKANOGAN,PALOUSE*
Wabash	TERRE HAUTE	Washington	*PUGET SOUND,*
WABASH <--	*Skillet Fork,*	Washington	*SKAGIT, SNAKE,*
WABASH <--	*Tippecanoe*	Washington	*SOLEDUCK,SPOKANE*
Wabash -->	*OHIO*	Washington	*TOUTLE, YAKIMA*
WACO, TX	*BRAZOS*	WASHINGTON, DC	*POTOMAC*
Wacouno	Quebec, Can.	*Washita*	Oklahoma
Wacouno -->	*MOISIE*	*Washita* -->	*LK TEXOMA-->RED*
Wadi	Morocco	*Waskana*	REGINA, Alberta
Waihou	New Zealand	*Waspuk*	Nicaragua
Waikato	New Zealand	*Waspuk* -->	*COCO*
WAIKATO <--	*Lk Taupo*	*Wateree*	S. Carolina
Waikato -->	*TASMAN SEA*	*Wateree* -->	*LK MARION*
Wailuku	HILO, HI	WATERFORD,Ire.	*SUIR*
Wainganga	India	WATERLOO, IA	*CEDAR*
WAINGANGA <--	*Penganga*	WAUSAU, WI	*WISCONSIN*
Wainganga -->	*GODAVARI*	*Waveny*	England
Waini	Guyana	*Wear*	England
Waini	*ATLANTIC*	*Wear* -->	*NORTH SEA*
Wairau	New Zealand	*Weaver*	England
Wairau -->	*COOK STRAIT*	*Weaver* -->	*MERSEY*
Wairi	New Zealand	*Web*	Ethiopia
Wairoa	New Zealand	*Weber*	OGDEN, Utah
Wairoa -->	*PACIFIC*	*Weber* -->	*GREAT SALT LAKE*
Waitaki	New Zealand	*Wei*	China,SIAN
Waitaki -->	*PACIFIC*	*Wei* -->	*YELLOW*
Wales	*CONWY, DEE,*	*Weiho*	China
Wales	*LK BALA, SEVERN,*	*Welland*	England
Wales	*LK VYRNWY,TEIFI,*	*Welland* -->	*NORTH SEA*
Wales	*TYWI, USK, WYE*	*Wensum*	England
Walker	Nevada	*Wensum* -->	*YARE*
Walker -->	*WALKER LK, NV*	*Werra*	Germany
Wamba	Congo	*Werra* -->	*FULDA-WESER*
WAMBA <--	*Kwango, Kwilu*	*Weser*	BREMAN,, Ger.,
Wamba -->	*KASAI*	*Weser*	HAMELIN,
Wami	Tanzania	*WESER* <--	*Aller, Fulda,*
Wami -->	*INDIAN OCEAN*	*WESER* <--	*Hunte*
Wampu	Honduras	*Weser* -->	*NORTH SEA*
Wampu -->	*PATUCA*	*West Road*	Br.Columbia,Can,
Wandering	Alberta, Can.	*West Road* -->	*FRASER*
Wandering -->	*ATHABASCA*	W. Virginia	*ELK, GUYANDOT,*
Wanganui	New Zealand	W. Virginia	*KANAWHA,LK LYNN,*
Wanganui -->	*TASMAN SEA*	W. Virginia	*NEW,OHIO,POTOMAC*
Wanks	Hondur., Nicar.	WEXFORD, Ire.	*SLANEY*
Wapsipinicon	Iowa	*Wharfe*	England
Wapsipinicon->	*MISSISSIPPI*	*Wharfe* -->	*OUSE*
Warche	Belgium	WHEELING, WV	*OHIO*
Wardha	India	*White*	Yukon
Wardha -->	*GODAVARI*	*White* -->	*YUKON*

White	Arkansas	Wisconsin Riv.	WAUSAU
WHITE <--	Black	WISCONSIN Riv.	<Kickapoo
White -->	MISSISSIPPI	Wisconsin -->	MISSISSIPPI
White(East)	IN,INDIANAPOLIS,	Wissey	England
White(East)	MUNCIE	Wissey -->	GREAT OUSE
White -->	WABASH	Wista(Vistula)	Hungary, KRAKOW,
White(West)	Colorado, Utah	Wista	Poland, TORUN,
White -->	GREEN	Wista	WARSAW
White Bandama	Ivory Coast	WISTA <--	Brda,Bug,Bzora,
White Bandama	--> LK KOSSOU	WISTA <--	Drweca, Dunajec,
White Fox	Saskatchewan,Can	WISTA <--	Pilica, San,
White Fox -->	TORCH	WISTA <--	Wieprz, Wkra
White Mouth	Manitoba	Wista -->	BALTIC SEA
White Mouth-->	WINNIPEG Riv.	Wistoka	Poland
White Nile	Sudan	Witham	England, LINCOLN
WHITE NILE <--	Blue Nile, Sobat	Witham -->	NORTH SEA
White Nile -->	NILE	Wolf	Wisconsin
WHITE SEA <--	Dvina, Onega	Wolf -->	LK WINNEBAGO
White Volta	Ghana	Wood	Alaska
WHITE VOLTA<--	Kulpawn,	Wood -->	TANANA
WHITE VOLTA<--	Red Volta	Wornitz	Germany
White Volta-->	LK VOLTA	Wornitz -->	DANUBE
Wichada	Venezuela	Wu	China
Wichita	Texas	Wu -->	YANGTZE
Wichita -->	RED	Wuchi	Taiwan
WICHITA, KS	ARKANSAS	Wukiang	China
Wieprz	Poland	Wye	England, Wales,
Wieprz -->	WISTA	Wye -->	SEVERN
Wild Hay	Alberta, Can.	Wyoming	BIGHORN, CROW,
Wild Hay -->	ATHABASCA	Wyoming	GREEN, LARAMIE,
Wild Rice	N. Dakota	Wyoming	LK JACKSON,
WILKES-BARRE,PA	SUSQUEHANNA	Wyoming	POWDER,NIOBRARA,
Willamette	CORVALLIS,EUGENE	Wyoming	N.PLATTE, SNAKE,
Willamette	OR.,PORTLAND,	Wyoming	SHOSHONE,
Willamette	SALEM	Wyoming	YELLOWSTONE
Willamette -->	COLUMBIA	XAI-XAI, Mozam.	LIMPOPO
Willow	Br.Columbia,Can,	Xan	See San
Willow -->	FRASER	Xarn	See Chu
Wind	Yukon, Can.	Xerua	Brazil
Wind -->	PEEL	Xerua -->	JURUA
Windel	Sweden	Xi	China
Winisk	Ontario, Can.	XI <--	Xun
Winisk -->	HUDSON BAY	Xi -->	SOUTH CHINA S
WINNIPEG	ASSINIBOINE,	Xiliao	See Liao
WINNIPEG	RED of the NORTH	Xingu	Brazil
Winnipeg Riv.	Manitoba	XINGU <--	Fresco, Iriri,
WINNIPEG Rv.<--	White Mouth	XINGU <--	Ronuro,Suia-Micu
Winnipeg Rv-->	LK WINNIPEG	Xingu -->	AMAZON
Winooski	BURLINGTON,	Xun	China
Winooski	MONTPELIER, VT	Xun -->	XI
Winooski -->	LAKE CHAMPLAIN	Yaco	See Iaco
Wisconsin	BLACK, CHIPPEWA,	Yacuma	Bolivia
Wisconsin	ESCANABA, FOX,	Yacuma -->	MAMORE
Wisconsin	KICKAPOO,	Yadkin	N. Carolina
Wisconsin	LK POYGAN,	Yadkin -->	PEE DEE
Wisconsin	MENOMINEE,	Yaguaron(Jaguara	BRAZIL/URUGUAY
Wisconsin	RED CEDAR,	Yaguaron -->	LK MIRIM
Wisconsin	ST. CROIX, WOLF	Yakima	Washington

Yakima -->	COLUMBIA	Yongding	China
YAKUTSK,Russia	LENA	Yongding -->	HAN
Yalu	ANTUNG,China,	Yongsan	S. Korea
Yalu	MANCHURIA/N.KOR.	YONKERS, NY	HUDSON
Yalu	N. Korea	Yonne	France
Yalu -->	YELLOW SEA	Yonne -->	SEINE
Yampa	Colorado	Yorkshire,Eng.	AIRE, URE, OUSE
Yampa -->	GREEN	YOSEMITE NAT.PK.	TOULOMNE
Yamuna (Jumna)	AGRA, India	Ypane	Paraguay
YAMUNA <--	Chambal	Ypane -->	PARAGUAY River
Yangtze (Chang)	NANKING, China	Ysel	Netherlands
YANGTZE <--	Han, Litang, Pu,	Yser	Belgium,Flanders
YANGTZE <--	Hang Jialing,Wu,	Yser	France,NIEUPOORT
YANGTZE <--	Kan,Min,Tuo,Yuan	Yser -->	NORTH SEA
Yantra	Bulgaria	Yssel	Netherlands
Yantra -->	DANUBE	Ythan	Scotland
Yapura	Colombia	Ythan -->	NORTH SEA
Yaqui	Mexico	Yuan	China
Yaqui -->	G. OF CALIFORNIA	Yuan -->	YANGTZE
Yare	England, NORWICH	Yuba	California
YARE <--	Wensum	Yuba -->	FEATHER
Yare -->	NORTH SEA	Yuen	China
Yari	Colombia	Yugoslavia	BOSNA, CAZMA,
Yari -->	CAQUETA	Yugoslavia	DANUBE, DRAVA,
Yarkand (Yarkant,	China	Yugoslavia	DRIM, DRINA,
Yarkon	Israel	Yugoslavia	IBAR, KRKA,
Yarmuk	JORDAN/SYRIA	Yugoslavia	LK OHRID,NARENTA
Yarmuk -->	JORDAN Riv.	Yugoslavia	NERETVA, RASKA,
Yarra	Australia	Yugoslavia	SAVA, TAMIS, UNA
Yata	Bolivia	Yugoslavia	VARDAR, VRBAS,
Yata -->	MAMORE	Yugoslavia	VELIKA MORAVA,
Yauco	Puerto Rico	Yukiang	China
Yavari (Javari)	PERU/BRAZIL	Yukon	FIRTH, HART,
Yavari -->	AMAZON (AS)	Yukon	HYLAND,KLONDIKE,
Yazoo	Mississippi	Yukon	LIARD,MACKENZIE,
YAZOO <--	Tallahatchie	Yukon	MACMILLAN,MINER,
Yazoo -->	MISSISSIPPI	Yukon	PEEL,PELLY,WIND
Ybbs	Austria	Yukon Riv.	AK,Canada, DAWSON
Ybbs -->	DANUBE	YUKON RIV. <--	Klondike,Koyukuk
Yellow (Huang)	China	YUKON RIV. <--	Pelly,Macmillan,
YELLOW (Huang<--	Datong,Fen,Luo,	YUKON RIV. <--	Porcupine,Tanama
YELLOW (Huang<--	Tao, Wei	YUKON RIV. <--	Sheenjek,Teslin,
Yellow (Huang->	YELLOW SEA	YUKON RIV. <--	White
YELLOW S <--	Han Gang, Liao,	Yukon Riv. -->	BERING SEA
YELLOW S <--	Luan,Yalu,Yellow	YUMA, AZ	COLORADO
Yellowstone	BILLINGS, MT,	Yuna	Dominican Repub.
Yellowstone	MILES CITY	Yuruari	Venezuela
YELLOWSTONE<--	Tongue	Yuruari -->	SUPAMO
Yellowstone-->	MISSOURI	Za	Morocco
Yenisey	See Jenisej	Za -->	MOULOUYA
Yi	Uruguay	Zab	Iran,Iraq,Turkey
Yi -->	NEGRO	ZAGREB,Croatia	SAVA
Ying	China	Zagyva	Hungary
Ying -->	HUAI	ZAGYVA <--	Tarna
Yobe	Nigeria	Zagyva -->	TISZA
Yodo	Japan, OSAKA	Zaire	ARUWIMI, CONGO,
Yom	Thailand	Zaire	FIMI, KASAI
Yom -->	PING	Zaire	KWANGO, KWENGE,

Zaire	*KWILU,LK ALBERT,*
Zaire	*LK KIVU,LK MWERU*
Zaire	*LK EDWARD,LINDI,*
Zaire	*TANGANYIKA,*
Zaire	*LK TUMBA,LOMAMI,*
Zaire	*LUAPULA,LUKENIE,*
Zaire	*LUVUA, UBANGI,*
Zaire	*UELE,WAMBA,ZAIRE*
ZAIRE/ZAMBIA	*LUAPULA*
Zaire	*See Congo*
Zala	Hungary
Zambesi	Angola, TETE,
Zambesi	LIVINGSTONE,
Zambesi	Mozambique,
Zambesi	VICTORIA FALLS,
Zambesi	Zambia
Zambesi	ZAMBIA/ZIMBABWE
ZANBEZI <--	*Kabompo, Kafue,*
ZANBEZI <--	*Laungwa,Linyanti*
ZANBEZI <--	*Luena, Shire*
Zambesi -->	*MOZAMBIQUE CHAN.*
Zambia	*KABOMPO, KAFUE,*
Zambia	*LK KARIBA,*
Zambia	*LUANGWA, LUNGA,*
Zambia	*LUAPULA,ZAMBEZI*
ZAMBIA/ZIMBAB.	*ZAMBEZI*
Zamfara	Nigeria
Zamfara -->	*SOKOTO*
Zamora	Ecuador
ZAMORA <--	*Upano*
Zanga	Armenia
ZARAGOZA, Sp.	*EBRO*
Zarga,Nahr az-	Jordan
Zarga -->	*Jordan Riv.*
Zatas	Portugal
Zaza	Cuba
Zeja	Russia
Zeja -->	*AMUR*
Zeta	Montenegro
Zeyendeh	Iran
Zezere	Portugal
Zezere -->	*TAGUS*
Zhob	Pakistan
Zhob -->	*INDUS*
ZIGANSK,Siberia	*LENA*
ZILINA,Slovakia	*VAH*
Zimbabwe	*GWAII,LIMPOPO,*
Zimbabwe	*LK KARIBA,LUNDI,*
Zimbabwe	*SABI, SANYATI,*
Zimbabwe	*SAVE, SHASHE,*
Zuata	Venezuela
Zuata -->	*ORINOCO*
Zuni	Arizona
Zuni -->	*LITTLE COLORADO*